2017 TAX LEGISLATION

Tax Cuts and Jobs Act

Law, Explanation and Analysis

This publication is designed to provide accurate and authoritative information in regard to the subject matter covered. It is sold with the understanding that the publisher is not engaged in rendering legal, accounting, or other professional service. If legal advice or other expert assistance is required, the services of a competent professional person should be sought.

ISBN 978-0-8080-4677-6

2700 Lake Cook Road
Riverwoods, IL 60015
800 344 3734
CCHGroup.com

Printed in the United States of America

SUSTAINABLE FORESTRY INITIATIVE

Certified Chain of Custody
Promoting Sustainable Forestry
www.sfiprogram.org
SFI-01028

Tax Cuts and Jobs Act

On December 20, 2017, Congress passed the Tax Cuts and Jobs Act (P.L. 115-97) after a 51-48 vote in the Senate and a 224-201 vote in the House of Representatives. The bill was originally presented in the House after months of work putting policy proposals by House committees and the President into legislative language. After initial passage in the House, the Senate then passed its own version of the law, and a Conference Committee was established to reconcile the two very different pieces of legislation. The Tax Cuts and Jobs Act Conference Committee presented final bill text on December 15, 2017.

Final passage of the Conference bill by both houses of Congress was not without drama, as after a vote in the House, the Senate Parliamentarian determined that two provisions of the conference bill, and the name of the bill itself, failed to comply with the strict requirements of the Byrd rule, which allowed for passage by a simple majority in the Senate using budget reconciliation rules. The two offending provisions were removed, and the official name of the bill was changed to "An Act to provide for reconciliation pursuant to titles II and V of the concurrent resolution on the budget for fiscal year 2018," and the vote in the Senate was held. A vote in the House followed, and President Trump signed the bill into law on December 22, 2017.

The Tax Cuts and Jobs Act represents the most significant overhaul of the Internal Revenue Code in more than 30 years. It provides significant reductions in tax rates for individuals, corporations, and small businesses, reforms the U.S. taxation of international transactions and businesses, eliminates dozens of individual and business tax deductions, enhances many tax credits and deductions, as well as many other changes. Every U.S. taxpayer, foreign or domestic, individual or business, high-income or low-income, is impacted by the provisions of the act.

About This Work and Wolters Kluwer

Since 1913, Wolters Kluwer has provided tax professionals with the most comprehensive, ongoing, practical and timely analysis of the federal tax law. In the spirit of this tradition, Wolters Kluwer is providing practitioners with a single integrated law and explanation of the tax provisions of the Tax Cuts and Jobs Act (P.L. 115-97) As always, Wolters Kluwer remains dedicated to responding to the needs of tax professionals in helping them quickly understand and work with these new laws as they take effect.

December 2017

Contributors

Alan K. Davis, J.D., CPA
Meadows, Collier, Reed,
Cousins, Crouch & Ungerman, LLP
Dallas, Texas

Elizabeth Dold, J.D., LL.M.
Groom Law Group, Chartered
Washington, D.C.

William D. Elliott, J.D., LL.M.
Elliott, Thomason & Gibson, LLP
Dallas, Texas

Charles R. Goulding, J.D., CPA, MBA
Energy Tax Savers Inc./
R&D Tax Savers, Inc.
Syosset, New York

J. Leigh Griffith, J.D., LL.M.
Waller Lansden Dortch & Davis, LLP
Nashville, Tennessee

James R. Hamill, Ph.D., CPA
Reynolds Hix & Co., P.C.
Albuquerque, New Mexico

Ethan S. Kroll, J.D., Ph.D.
Baker & McKenzie LLP
Palo Alto, California

Mark Leeds, J.D., LL.M.
Mayer Brown LLP
New York, New York

Stewart R. Lipeles, J.D.
Baker & McKenzie LLP
Palo Alto, California

Robert J. Misey, Jr., J.D., LL.M.
Reinhart Boerner Van Deuren
Chicago, IL and Milwaukee, WI

Vincent O'Brien, CPA
Vincent J. O'Brien, CPA, PC/M+O=CPE,
Inc.
Lynbrook, New York

Lewis J. Saret, J.D., CPA
Law Office of Lewis J. Saret
Washington, DC

Michael Schlesinger, J.D., LL.M.
Schlesinger & Sussman
Clifton, New Jersey

Josh O. Ungerman, J.D., CPA
Meadows, Collier, Reed, Cousins,
Crouch & Ungerman, LLP
Dallas, Texas

Brian T. Whitlock, CPA, J.D., LL.M.
Gies College of Business
University of Illinois
Chicago, Illinois

Brigen Winters, J.D., LL.M.
Groom Law Group, Chartered
Washington, D.C.

Wolters Kluwer, Tax and Accounting
EDITORIAL STAFF

¶1 Features of This Publication

This publication is your complete guide to the tax provisions of the Tax Cuts and Jobs Act (P.L. 115-97) (officially known as "An Act to provide for reconciliation pursuant to titles II and V of the concurrent resolution on the budget for fiscal year 2018").

The core portion of this publication contains the Explanations of this Act. The explanations outline all of the impending tax law changes and what they mean for you and your clients. The explanations also feature practical guidance, examples, planning opportunities and strategies, as well as pitfalls to be avoided.

The publication also contains numerous other features designed to help you locate and understand the changes made by this Act. A more detailed description of these features appears below.

TAXPAYERS AFFECTED

Taxpayers Affected contains a detailed look at how the various pieces of tax legislation affect specific categories of taxpayers. This chapter provides a quick reference for readers who want to know the impact that the laws will have on their clients. *Taxpayers Affected begins at ¶6.*

EXPLANATIONS

Explanations are designed to give you a complete, accessible understanding of the new law. Explanations are arranged by subject for ease of use. There are two main finding devices you can use to locate explanations on a given topic. These are:

- A detailed table of contents at the beginning of the publication listing all of the Explanations of the provisions;
- A table of contents preceding each chapter.

Each Explanation contains special features to aid in your complete understanding of the tax law. These include:

- A summary at the beginning of each explanation providing a brief overview of the impacted provisions;
- A background or prior law discussion that puts the law changes into perspective;
- Editorial aids, including examples, cautions, planning notes, elections, comments, compliance tips, and key rates and figures, that highlight the impact of the sunset provisions;
- Charts and examples illustrating the ramifications of specific law changes;
- Captions at the end of each explanation identifying the Code sections added, amended or repealed, as well as the Act sections containing the changes;
- Cross references to the law and committee report paragraphs related to the explanation;
- A line highlighting the effective date of each law change, marked by an arrow symbol; and

The Explanations begin at ¶105.

AMENDED CODE PROVISIONS

Changes to the Internal Revenue Code made by the legislation appear under the heading "Code Sections Added, Amended or Repealed." Deleted Code material or the text of the Code Section prior to amendment appears in the amendment notes following each amended Code provision. *The text of the Code begins at ¶5001.*

Sections of the acts that do not amend the Internal Revenue Code, appear in full text following "Code Sections Added, Amended or Repealed." *The text of these provisions appears in Act Section order beginning at ¶7005.*

COMMITTEE REPORTS

The Tax Cuts and Jobs Act Conference Committee produced a Joint Explanatory Statement on the Tax Cuts and Jobs Act (P.L. 115-97) on December 15, 2017 (H. REPT. 115-466). This explanation explains the intent of Congress regarding the provisions of the Act. *The pertinent sections of the Joint Explanatory Statement on the Tax Cuts and Jobs Act (P.L. 115-97 appear in Act Section order beginning at ¶10,001.*

SPECIAL FINDING DEVICES

Other special tables and finding devices in this book include:

- A table cross-referencing Code Sections to the Explanations (*see ¶25,001*);
- A table showing all Code Sections added, amended or repealed (*see ¶25,005*);
- A table of Act Sections not amending the Internal Revenue Code (*see ¶25,015*); and
- An Act Section table amending Code Section table (*see ¶25,020*).

CLIENT LETTERS

Sample client letters allow you to quickly communicate to clients and customers the changes made by the Tax Cuts and Jobs Act (P.L. 115-97) (*see ¶27,001*).

¶2 Table of Contents

¶3 Detailed Table of Contents

CHAPTER 1. INDIVIDUAL TAXES (INCOME, AMT, ESTATE AND GIFT)

TAXES AND RETURNS

CAPITAL GAINS AND OTHER PROVISIONS

CHAPTER 2. DEDUCTIONS, EXCLUSIONS, AND CREDITS FOR INDIVIDUALS

STANDARD DEDUCTION AND PERSONAL

ITEMIZED DEDUCTIONS

CHAPTER 4. DEPRECIATION AND EXPENSE DEDUCTIONS

CHAPTER 5. BUSINESS INCOME, DEDUCTIONS AND CREDITS

INCOME, EXCLUSIONS, ETC.
BUSINESS DEDUCTIONS
ORDINARY AND NECESSARY EXPENSES
ACCOUNTING FOR BUSINESSES
BUSINESS TAX CREDITS

CHAPTER 6. COMPENSATION, RETIREMENT, EDUCATION AND DISABILITY BENEFITS

CHAPTER 7. INTERNATIONAL TAX PROVISIONS

CHAPTER 8. EXEMPT ORGANIZATIONS, EXCISE TAXES, BONDS, AND OTHER PROVISIONS

CHAPTER 9. TAXATION OF INSURANCE COMPANIES

Taxpayers Affected

TAX CUTS AND JOBS ACT

Tax Cuts and Jobs Act

¶6 Overview

The Tax Cuts and Jobs Act (P.L. 115-97) was approved by the House of Representatives and the Senate on December 20, 2017, and President Trump signed the bill into law December 22, 2017.

The act is the largest overhaul of the Internal Revenue Code in over 30 years, affecting every taxpayer type both within and without the United States. It includes reductions in tax rates for both individuals and businesses, the elimination or reduction of many deductions, exclusions, and credits with the enhancement of other deductions and credits. The corporate AMT is eliminated, the taxation of pass-through entities is reformed, and international taxation laws are changed to move the United States from a worldwide system to a territorial system.

¶10 Effect on Individuals, Generally

Individual income tax rates.—The individual income tax rates and bracket amounts are modified for tax years 2018 through 2025. The temporary tax rates are 10, 12, 22, 24, 32, 35, and 37 percent (¶105)

Alternative minimum tax (AMT).—The AMT exemption amounts are temporarily increased for individuals after 2017 and before 2026. Beginning in 2018, the exemption amounts are $109,400 for married individuals filing separately or surviving spouses, $70,300 for single or head of household filers, and $54,700 for married filing separately. The phaseout thresholds are also temporarily increased after 2017 to $1 million if married filing jointly or surviving spouse and $500,000 for all other individuals (¶110).

Individual health insurance mandate.—Effective for months beginning after December 31, 2018, the amount owed by any taxpayer under the individual health insurance mandate "shared responsibility payment" for lack of minimum essential health insurance for themselves and their dependents is zero (¶140).

Standard deduction.—The basic standard deduction amounts are increased to: $12,000 for single individuals and married individuals filing separately; $18,000 for heads of household; and $24,000 for married individuals filing jointly (including surviving spouses). The increased amounts, which are adjusted annually for inflation, are effective for tax years 2018 through 2025 (¶205).

Personal and dependency exemptions.—The deduction for personal and dependency exemptions is temporarily repealed for tax years 2018 through 2025 (¶210).

State and local tax deduction.—The itemized deduction by individuals for state, local, and foreign property taxes, and state and local income taxes and general sales taxes paid or accrued during the tax year is limited for tax years 2018 through 2025. An individual cannot deduct foreign real property taxes, but may still claim an itemized deduction of up to $10,000 ($5,000 for married taxpayer filing a separate return) for state and local property taxes, income taxes, and general sales taxes paid or accrued in the tax year (¶215).

Personal casualty and theft losses.—The itemized deduction for personal casualty and theft losses is limited to those attributable to a federally declared disaster (¶235).

Moving expenses.—The deduction for moving expenses is temporarily repealed for tax years 2018 through 2025. The exclusion for qualified moving expense reimbursements is suspended for tax years 2018 through 2025 (¶260, ¶610).

¶12 Effect on Homeowners

State and local tax deduction.—The itemized deduction of individuals for state, local, and foreign property taxes, and state and local income taxes and general sales taxes paid or accrued during the tax year is limited for tax years 2018 through 2025. An individual cannot deduct foreign real property taxes, but may still claim an itemized deduction of up to $10,000 ($5,000 for married taxpayer filing a separate return) for state and local property taxes, income taxes, and general sales taxes paid or accrued in the tax year (¶215).

Home mortgage interest.—The itemized deduction for home mortgage interest is subject to new limitations for tax years 2018 through 2025. A taxpayer is limited to claiming the home mortgage interest deduction only for interest paid or accrued on acquisition debt during those years; the deduction of interest on home equity debt is suspended. The maximum amount that may be treated as acquisition debt is also reduced to $750,000 ($375,000 if married filing separately) for any acquisition debt incurred after December 15, 2017 (¶220).

Personal casualty and theft losses.—The itemized deduction for personal casualty and theft losses is limited to those attributable to a federally declared disaster (¶235).

Mortgage information on Form 1098.—Form 1098 is required to include the amount of the outstanding mortgage, the address of the property, and the loan origination date (¶606).

¶14 Effect on High-Income Taxpayers

Alternative minimum tax (AMT).—The AMT exemption amounts are temporarily increased for individuals after 2017 and before 2026. Beginning in 2018, the exemption amounts are $109,400 for married individuals filing separately or surviving spouses, $70,300 for single or head of household filers, and $54,700 for married filing separately. The phaseout thresholds are also temporarily increased after 2017 to $1 million if married filing jointly or surviving spouse and $500,000 for all other individuals (¶110).

Itemized deduction.—The overall limitation on itemized deductions is suspended, applicable to tax years beginning after 2017 and before 2026 (¶250).

Employee compensation.—For purposes of the limitation on the deduction for employee compensation paid by publicly held corporations, the definition of covered employee is expanded to include both the principal executive officer and the principal financial officer, as well as the other three most highly compensated employees. Employees who are covered employees after December 31, 2016, remain as covered employees for all future tax years. The exclusions from the limitation for commission-based and performance based compensation have been repealed (¶540).

Executive compensation.—A new excise tax has been established, payable by exempt organizations on remuneration in excess of $1 million and any excess parachute payments made to certain highly-compensated current and former employees in the tax year (¶810).

¶15 Effect on Seniors

Estate, gift, and generation-skipping transfer tax.—The basic exclusion amount for purposes of federal estate and gift taxes and the exemption amount for purposes of the generation-skipping transfer (GST) tax is doubled from $5 million to $10 million, before adjustment for inflation, for the estates of decedents dying and gifts and generation-skipping transfers made after 2017 and before 2026 (¶ 115).

Medical expenses.—The adjusted gross income (AGI) threshold to claim itemized deduction for unreimbursed expenses paid for the medical care of the taxpayer or the taxpayer's spouse or dependents is temporarily reduced to 7.5 percent of AGI (¶ 225).

¶ 17 Effect on Investors

Rollover of capital gain.—The election to defer recognition of capital gain realized on the sale of publicly traded securities if the taxpayer used the sale proceeds to purchase common stock or a partnership interest in a specialized small business investment company (SSBIC) is repealed (¶ 270).

¶ 18 Effect on Disabled Persons

ABLE accounts.—Individuals are allowed to roll over amounts from qualified tuition plans (also known as section 529 plans) to an ABLE account if the ABLE account is owned by the same designated beneficiary of the 529 plan or a member of the designated beneficiary's family before January 1, 2026. Under certain circumstances, the contribution limitation to ABLE accounts is increased for contributions made by the designated beneficiary before January 1, 2026 (¶ 645).

¶ 19 Effect on Bond Investors

Advanced refunding bonds.—Interest paid on advance refunding bonds issued after 2017 is not excludable from gross income as interest paid on state and local government bonds (¶ 870).

Tax credit bonds.—New tax credit bonds cannot be issued after December 31, 2017 (¶ 875).

¶ 21 Effect on Parents

Personal and dependency exemptions.—The deduction for personal and dependency exemptions is temporarily repealed for tax years 2018 through 2025 (¶ 210).

Child tax credit.—The child tax credit is temporarily expanded after 2017 by increasing the credit amount for each qualifying child to $2,000, increasing the phaseout threshold to $400,000 if married filing jointly ($200,000 for other taxpayers), and providing a $500 nonrefundable credit for each dependent who is not a qualifying child. The refundable portion of the credit (additional child tax credit) is limited to $1,400 per qualifying child, but is indexed for inflation and the earned income threshold is reduced to $2,500. A taxpayer must include a qualifying child's Social

Security number on his or her return to receive the nonrefundable or refundable portion of the credit with respect to the child (¶280).

Qualified tuition programs.—Section 529 qualified tuition plans are modified to allow the plans to distribute no more than $10,000 in tuition expenses incurred during the tax year for designated beneficiaries enrolled at a public, private, or religious elementary or secondary school (¶640).

ABLE accounts.—Individuals are allowed to roll over amounts from qualified tuition plans (also known as section 529 plans) to an ABLE account if the ABLE account is owned by the same designated beneficiary of the 529 plan or a member of the designated beneficiary's family before January 1, 2026. Under certain circumstances, the contribution limitation to ABLE accounts is increased for contributions made by the designated beneficiary before January 1, 2026 (¶645).

¶23 Effect on Students

Student loans.—Eligibility to exclude discharge of student loan debt from gross income is temporarily expanded to include discharges of eligible student loans before 2026 due to the student's death or total and permanent disability (¶265).

Qualified tuition programs.—Section 529 qualified tuition plans are modified to allow the plans to distribute no more than $10,000 in tuition expenses incurred during the tax year for designated beneficiaries enrolled at a public, private, or religious elementary or secondary school (¶640).

¶24 Effect on Military Personnel

Hazardous duty area.—The Sinai Peninsula of Egypt is a qualified hazardous duty area for the applicable period and is treated the same as a combat zone for purposes of certain tax benefits for members of the U.S. Armed Forces. The applicable period is generally the portion of the first tax year beginning after June 9, 2015, and any subsequent tax year beginning before January 1, 2026 (¶135).

Moving expenses.—The deduction for moving expenses is temporarily repealed for tax years 2018 through 2025. The exclusion for qualified moving expense reimbursements is suspended for tax years 2018 through 2025. However, the special rules for a member of the Armed Forces to deduct moving expenses and exclude in-kind moving expenses, and reimbursements or allowances, continues to apply during these tax years (¶260, ¶610).

¶25 Effect on Employees

Miscellaneous itemized deductions.—The deductibility of miscellaneous itemized deductions is temporarily repealed for tax years 2018 through 2025 (¶245).

Employee stock options.—Employees who are granted stock options are able to elect to defer recognition of income for up to five years. The election is not available to certain executives, highly compensated officers, and "one-percent owners" of the corporation. The corporation must maintain a written plan under which at least 80 percent of all employees providing services to the corporation are granted stock options with the same rights and privileges (¶605).

Moving expenses.—The exclusion for qualified moving expense reimbursements is suspended for tax years 2018 through 2025 (¶610).

Bicycle commuting expenses.—After December 31, 2017, and before January 1, 2026, taxpayers are not permitted to exclude any amount from their income for qualified bicycle commuting reimbursements (¶615).

¶26 Effect on Inventors

Self-created property.—A patent, invention, model or design (patented or not), or secret formula or process is excluded the definition of a capital asset for dispositions after December 31, 2017, if it is held by the taxpayer who created the property or a taxpayer with a substituted or transferred basis from the taxpayer who created the property (¶130).

¶27 Effect on Professional Gamblers

Gambling losses.—The rule that a deduction for wagering losses is limited to the amount of wagering winnings, applies not only to the actual costs of wagers, but to other expenses incurred by the individual in connection with that individual's gambling activities (¶240).

¶28 Effect on Corporations

Corporate tax rate.—For tax years beginning after December 31, 2017, the graduated corporate rate structure is eliminated and corporate taxable income is taxed at a 21-percent flat rate (¶305).

Alternative minimum tax (AMT).—The alternative minimum tax (AMT) for corporations has been repealed beginning after 2017 (¶310).

Dividends-received deduction.—For tax years beginning after December 31, 2017, the 70-percent dividends-received deduction is reduced to 50 percent and the 80-percent dividends-received deduction is reduced to 65 percent (¶315).

Contributions to capital.—The definition of contribution to capital for purposes of Code Sec. 118(a) is modified to exclude contributions by any governmental entity or civic group that are not made by a shareholder in its capacity as a shareholder (¶320).

¶29 Effect on S Corporations

Qualified business income deduction (passthrough deduction).—Noncorporate taxpayers may deduct up to 20 percent of domestic qualified business income from a partnership, S corporation, or sole proprietorship. A similar deduction is allowed for specified agricultural or horticultural cooperatives. A limitation based on wages paid, or on wages paid plus a capital element, is phased in for taxpayers with taxable income above a threshold amount. The deduction is not allowed for certain service trades or businesses, but this disallowance is phased in for lower income taxpayers. The deduction applies to tax years 2018 through 2025 (¶330).

Qualified beneficiary of electing small business trust.—A nonresident alien individual may be a potential current beneficiary of an ESBT. The new law is effective on January 1, 2018 (¶360).

Charitable contribution deduction for electing small business trust.—The charitable contribution deduction of an ESBT is generally to be determined by the rules applicable to individuals, not to the rules generally applicable to trusts. This change applies to tax years beginning after December 31, 2017 (¶365).

S corporation conversions to C corporations.—S corporations that convert to C corporations should take any resulting Code Sec. 481(a) adjustments into account over a six-year period. In addition, if an eligible terminated S corporation distributes money after the post-termination transition period, the accumulated adjustments account will be allocated to such distribution (¶370).

¶30 Effect on Public Safety Officers and Their Survivors

Length of service award exclusion for bona fide public safety volunteers.—The dollar limit on the length of service award exclusion from Code Sec. 457 for bona fide public safety volunteers is doubled from $3,000 to $6,000 effective for tax years beginning after December 31, 2017 (¶635).

¶32 Effect on Charitable Donors

Charitable contribution deductions.—The percentage limitation on the charitable deduction contribution base is increased to 60 percent of an individual's adjusted gross income for cash donations to public charities in 2018 through 2025. The deduction for amounts paid for college athletic seating rights is repealed. The exception to contemporaneous written acknowledgment requirement for contributions of $250 or more is repealed (¶230).

Charitable contribution deduction for electing small business trust.—The charitable contribution deduction of an ESBT is generally to be determined by the rules applicable to individuals, not to the rules generally applicable to trusts. This change applies to tax years beginning after December 31, 2017 (¶365).

¶33 Effect on International Business

Treatment of sale or exchange of partnership interests by foreign persons.—Gain or loss from the sale or exchange of a partnership interest is effectively connected with a U.S. trade or business to the extent that the transferor would have had effectively connected gain or loss had the partnership sold all of its assets at fair market value as of the disposition date. The transferee of a partnership interest must withhold 10 percent of the amount realized on the sale or exchange unless the transferor certifies that it is not a nonresident alien or foreign corporation (¶350).

¶36 Effect on Retirement Plan Participants

Recharacterization of IRA contributions.—The special rule that allows a contribution to one type of an IRA to be recharacterized as a contribution to the other type of IRA will no longer apply to a conversion contribution to a Roth IRA after 2017. Recharacterization is still permitted with respect to other contributions. For example, an individual may make a contribution for a year to a Roth IRA and, before the due date for the individual's income tax return for that year, recharacterize it as a contribution to a traditional IRA (¶620).

Rollovers of plan loan offset amounts.—For plan loan offset amounts that are treated as distributed after 2017, a participant whose plan terminates or who is severed from employment while having a plan loan outstanding will have until the due date for filing their tax return for that year to contribute the loan balance to an IRA in order to avoid the loan being taxed as a distribution IRA (¶625).

Qualified 2016 disaster distributions from retirement plans.—The 10 percent additional tax under Code Sec. 72(t) is waived for any qualified 2016 disaster distribution. Eligible individuals who take such distributions can spread their taxable income over three years, and have three years to repay the amount (¶630).

¶38 Effect on Businesses Generally

Section 179 expensing.—The section 179 dollar limitation is increased to $1 million and the investment limitation is increased to $2.5 million for tax years beginning after 2017. The definition of qualified real property eligible for expensing is redefined to include improvements to the interior of any nonresidential real property ("qualified improvement property"), as well as roofs, heating, ventilation, and air-conditioning property, fire protection and alarm systems, and security systems installed on such property. The exclusion from expensing for property used in connecting with lodging facilities, such as residential rental property, is eliminated. The $25,000 section 179 expensing limit on certain heavy vehicles is inflation-adjusted after 2018 (¶405).

Bonus depreciation-generally—The bonus depreciation rate is increased to 100 percent for property acquired and placed in service after September 27, 2017 and before January 1, 2023. The rate phases down thereafter. Used property and films, television shows, and theatrical productions are eligible for bonus depreciation.

Property used by rate-regulated utilities and property of certain motor vehicle, boat, and farm machinery retail and lease businesses that use floor financing indebtedness is excluded from bonus depreciation (¶410).

Depreciation of luxury cars.—The annual limits on depreciation deductions for "luxury cars" are almost quadrupled for property placed in service after 2017. The IRS will need to issue a safe harbor in order to allow taxpayers to claim depreciation after the first year a vehicle is placed in service if the 100 percent bonus depreciation deduction is claimed (¶415).

Computers as listed property.—Computers and related peripheral equipment are no longer "listed property" subject to strict substantiation and depreciation requirements, effective for property placed in service after December 31, 2017 (¶420).

Recovery periods for MACRS real property.—Assuming a technical correction is enacted, qualified improvement property is assigned a 15-year recovery period as intended by Congress. The property classes for 15-year leasehold improvement property, retail improvement property, and restaurant property are eliminated. The MACRS alternative depreciation system (ADS) must be used by an electing real property trade or business to depreciate residential rental property, nonresidential real property, and qualified improvement property (¶425).

Limitation on deduction of business interest.—The deduction of business interest is limited for any tax year beginning after 2017 to the sum of the taxpayer's business interest income, floor plan financing, and 30 percent of adjusted taxable income. The limitation generally applies to all taxpayers, but does not apply for small businesses with average gross receipts of $25 million or less (adjusted for inflation). Any disallowed interest generally may be carried forward indefinitely. In the case of a partnership or S corporation, the deduction limitation applies at the entity level, except that disallowed interest of the entity is allocated to each partner or shareholder as excess business interest (¶510).

Net operating losses.—Net operating losses (NOLs) may no longer be carried back but may be carried forward indefinitely. However, the five-year carryback period for farming losses is reduced to two years and a two-year carryback and 20-year carryforward period is retained for insurance companies other than life insurance companies. A net operating loss may only reduce 80 percent of taxable income in a carryback or carryforward tax year. The taxable income limitation does not apply to non-life insurance companies (¶515).

Excess business losses for noncorporate taxpayers.—Excess business losses of noncorporate taxpayers are not allowed for tax years beginning in 2018 through 2025. Any disallowed excess business loss is treated as a net operating loss (NOL) carryover to the following tax year. However, the passive activity loss rules apply before application of the excess business loss rules (¶520).

Research and experimental expenditures.—Research and experimental expenditures paid or accrued after 2021 generally must be amortized ratably over five years. Any amount paid or incurred in connection with the development of any software is treated as a research or experimental expenditure for this purposes of this amortization provision. A 15-year amortization period applies to research or experimental expenditures attributable to foreign research (¶525).

¶38

Domestic production activities deduction.—The domestic production activities deduction (DPAD) under Code Sec. 199 is repealed for tax years beginning after 2017 (¶530).

Employer's deduction for entertainment, commuting benefits, and meals.—Business expense deductions are eliminated for some entertainment costs and commuting benefits after 2017 and for some employer-provided meal expenses after 2025 (¶535).

Non-tangible personal property as employee achievement awards.—For purposes of employee achievement awards, employers are prohibited from deducting awards that are given in cash, cash equivalents, gift cards, gift coupons, gift certificates, vacations, meals, lodging, tickets to theater or sporting events, stocks, bonds, other securities or similar items (¶537).

Employee compensation.—For purposes of the limitation on the deduction for employee compensation paid by publicly held corporations, the definition of covered employee is expanded to include both the principal executive officer and the principal financial officer, as well as the other three most highly compensated employees. Employees who are covered employees after December 31, 2016, remain as covered employees for all future tax years. The exclusions from the limitation for commission-based and performance based compensation have been repealed (¶540).

Fines and penalties.—Businesses may not deduct fines and penalties incurred due to the violation of a law (or the investigation of a violation) if a government (or similar entity) is a complainant or investigator. Exceptions to this rule are available in certain cases where the payment was compensation for damages, compliance with the law, paid to satisfy a court order where the government is not a party, or paid for taxes due (¶545).

Local lobbying expenses.—The deduction for local lobbying expenses by a taxpayer as an ordinary and necessary business is repealed for expenses paid after December 22, 2017 (¶555).

Paid family and medical leave.—Eligible employers are entitled to claim a credit for paid family and medical leave equal to 12.5 percent of wages paid to qualifying employees during any period in which such employees are on family and medical leave (FML) provided that the rate of payment is 50 percent of the wages normally paid to the employee. The credit is part of the general business credit and only available for wages paid in tax years beginning after December 31, 2017, and before January 1, 2020 (¶585).

¶39 Effect on Passthrough Entities

Qualified business income deduction (passthrough deduction).—Noncorporate taxpayers may deduct up to 20 percent of domestic qualified business income from a partnership, S corporation, or sole proprietorship. A similar deduction is allowed for specified agricultural or horticultural cooperatives. A limitation based on wages paid, or on wages paid plus a capital element, is phased in for taxpayers with taxable income above a threshold amount. The deduction is not allowed for certain service trades or businesses, but this disallowance is phased in for lower income taxpayers. The deduction applies to tax years 2018 through 2025 (¶330).

Basis limitation on partner losses.—The basis limitation on partner losses applies to a partner's distributive share of charitable contributions and foreign taxes (¶340).

Substantial built-in loss upon transfer of partnership interest.—The Code Sec. 743 definition of a "substantial built-in loss" is modified so that a substantial built-in loss also exists if the transferee would be allocated a net loss in excess of $250,000 upon a hypothetical disposition at fair market value by the partnership of all partnership assets immediately after the transfer of the partnership interest (¶345).

Treatment of sale or exchange of partnership interests by foreign persons.—Gain or loss from the sale or exchange of a partnership interest is effectively connected with a U.S. trade or business to the extent that the transferor would have had effectively connected gain or loss had the partnership sold all of its assets at fair market value as of the disposition date. The transferee of a partnership interest must withhold 10 percent of the amount realized on the sale or exchange unless the transferor certifies that it is not a nonresident alien or foreign corporation (¶350).

Technical termination of partnerships.—The rule providing for technical termination of partnerships is repealed for partnership tax years beginning after December 31, 2017 (¶355).

¶41 Effect on Foreign Entities and Activities

Foreign-source portion of dividends.—Effective generally for distributions after December 31, 2017, a 100-percent participation exemption deduction is allowed for the foreign-source portion of dividends received from specified 10-percent owned foreign corporations by U.S. corporate shareholders, subject to a one-year holding period (a participation dividends-received deduction (DRD)). No foreign tax credit or deduction is allowed for any taxes paid or accrued with respect to a dividend that qualifies for the deduction. The participation DRD is not available for hybrid dividends received from CFCs (¶705).

Specified 10-percent owned foreign corporations.—Amounts received by a domestic corporation upon the sale or exchange of stock in a foreign corporation held for at least one year that are treated as Section 1248 dividends are also treated as dividends for purposes of the participation dividends-received deduction (DRD) (¶707).

Deferred foreign income upon transition to participation exemption system of taxation.—A transition tax is generally imposed on accumulated foreign earnings, without requiring an actual distribution, upon the transition to the new participation exemption system. Under the transition rule, for the last tax year beginning before January 1, 2018, any U.S. shareholder of any CFC or other foreign corporation (other than a PFIC that is not a CFC) that is at least 10-percent owned by a domestic corporation must include in income its pro rata share of the accumulated post-1986 foreign earnings of the corporation as of November 2, 2017, or December 31, 2017, whichever amount is greater (mandatory inclusion) (¶710).

Recapture of overall domestic losses.—A taxpayer may elect to recapture pre-2018 unused overall domestic losses (ODLs) by recharacterizing up to 100 percent of the taxpayer's U.S. source taxable income as foreign source taxable income, from 2018 through 2027 (¶715).

Foreign Tax Credit.—The Code Sec. 902 deemed-paid foreign tax credit is repealed and the Code Sec. 960 deemed-paid foreign tax credit is modified so that it is determined on a current year basis. A new foreign tax credit limitation basket is added for foreign branch income (¶720 and ¶725).

Cross-border inventory sales.—Income from cross-border sales of inventory is sourced on the basis of the production activities (¶730).

U.S. shareholders of controlled foreign corporations.—A current year inclusion of global intangible low-taxed income (GILTI) by a person who is a U.S. shareholder of a controlled foreign corporation (CFC). Domestic corporations are provided with reduced rates of U.S. tax on their foreign-derived intangible income (FDII) and global intangible low-taxed income (GILTI) (¶735).

Foreign base company oil related income.—Foreign base company oil related income is eliminated as a category of foreign base company income and so is no longer subpart F income (¶737).

Withdrawal of qualified investments.—The subpart F inclusion for a CFC's previously excluded subpart F income withdrawn from foreign base company shipping operations is repealed. Also repealed is the subpart F inclusion for amounts withdrawn from qualified investment in less developed countries and decreases in export trade assets (¶741).

CFC stock attribution rules.—Stock ownership may be attributed downward from a foreign person to a related U.S. person for purposes of determining whether a U.S. person is a U.S. shareholder of a corporation, such that the foreign corporation is a CFC (¶743).

Definition of U.S. shareholder.—The definition of a U.S. shareholder is expanded to include a shareholder who owns 10 percent or more of a foreign corporation's stock by value. The definition of a U.S. shareholder now applies for purposes of Title 26 (¶745).

Period of CFC status.—The requirement that a foreign corporation must be a CFC for an uninterrupted period of 30 days or more before a U.S. shareholder is required to include amounts in gross income under Subpart F is eliminated (¶747).

Base erosion and anti-abuse tax.—Applicable taxpayers are required to pay tax equal to the base erosion minimum tax amount for the tax year. The base erosion minimum tax amount is generally derived by comparing 10 percent (five percent for tax years beginning in calendar year 2018) of the taxpayer's modified taxable income (determined by disregarding certain deductions with respect to base erosion payments made to foreign related persons) to the taxpayer's regular tax liability (reduced for certain credit amounts). For tax years beginning after December 31, 2025, the 10-percent rate is increased to 12.5 percent and the taxpayer's regular tax liability is reduced by the aggregate amount of allowable credits. Applicable taxpayers include corporations (except RICs, REITs, or S corporations) with average annual gross receipts of at least $500 million over the past three tax years and a base erosion percentage of three percent (determined by dividing the aggregate deductions with respect to base erosion payments by the aggregate amount of allowed deductions with some exceptions). An 11-percent rate and two percent base erosion percentage apply to taxpayers that are members of an affiliated group that includes a bank or registered securities dealer. In addition, new reporting requirements will require the collection of information regarding a taxpayer's base erosion payments and the applicable penalty for failure to report is increased (¶750).

Income shifting through intangible property transfers.—The Code Sec. 936(h)(3)(B) definition of intangible property is modified to include goodwill, going concern value, and workforce in place as well as any other item the value of which is not attributable to tangible property or services of any individual. The new law also clarifies the authority of the Secretary of the Treasury to require the use of certain valuation methods in determining the value of intangible property in the context of Code Sec. 367(d) transfers and Code Sec. 482 intercompany pricing allocationse (¶755).

Related party payments involving hybrid entities or hybrid transactions.—A deduction is not allowed for any disqualified related party amount paid or accrued in a hybrid transaction or by, or to, a hybrid entity (¶760).

Surrogate foreign corporation dividends.—Dividends received from surrogate foreign corporations are not eligible for lower tax rate treatment as qualified dividend income (¶765).

Insiders in expatriated corporations.—The excise tax rate on stock compensation received by insiders in an expatriated corporation increases from 15 percent to 20 percent (¶770).

Passive foreign investment company rules.—The rule for determining what is not considered passive income for a passive foreign investment company (PFIC) has been modified. The test for nonpassive income that is based on whether a corporation is predominantly engaged in an insurance business has been replaced with a test based on the amount of the corporation's insurance liabilities (¶775).

Interest expense.—The fair market value method for allocating and apportioning interest expense may no longer be used (¶780).

¶42 Effect on Small Businesses

Miscellaneous itemized deductions.—The deductibility of miscellaneous itemized deductions is temporarily repealed for tax years 2018 through 2025 (¶245).

Methods of accounting.—The cash method of accounting and other simpler accounting methods have been made available to more taxpayers. Most taxpayers who meet a $25 million average annual gross receipts test will be able to use the cash method, will not be required to apply the inventory or uniform capitalization (UNICAP) rules, and will not be required to use the percentage of completion method for small construction contracts (¶570).

¶45 Effect on Airline Industry

Aircraft management services.—Payments made by aircraft owners for aircraft management services related to maintenance and support of, or flights on, the owner's aircraft are not subject to the excise tax imposed on the taxable transportation of persons or property by air (¶820).

¶42

¶46 Effect on Banking and Finance Industry

Carried interests.—Capital gain passed through to fund managers via a partnership profits interest (carried interest) in exchange for investment management services must meet an extended three-year holding period to qualify for long-term capital gain treatment (¶335).

FDIC premiums.—Rule changes limit the deduction for the applicable percentage of Federal Deposit Insurance Corporation (FDIC) premiums paid by banks and other financial institutions with consolidated assets of over $10 billion. Banks and other financial institutions with more than $50 billion in assets may not deduct the applicable percentage of any FDIC premium paid. The changes apply for tax years beginning after December 31, 2017 (¶565).

¶49 Effect on Liquor Industry

Production period for beer, wine and distilled spirits.—The aging period for beer, wine, and distilled spirits is excluded from the production period for purposes of the UNICAP interest capitalization rules for interest paid or accrued during the 2018 and 2019 calendar years. Accordingly, producers of beer, wine and distilled spirits are able to deduct interest expenses attributable to a shorter production period for two years (¶825).

Beer excise tax.—The excise tax on beer is lowered to $16 per barrel on the first six million barrels brewed by the brewer or imported by the importer during a calendar year. Beer brewed or imported in excess of the six million barrel limit continues to be taxed at $18 per barrel. In the case of small brewers, such brewers would be taxed at a rate of $3.50 per barrel on the first 60,000 barrels domestically produced during a calendar year, and $16 per barrel on any further barrels produced. The provision applies to beer removed after December 31, 2017 and before January 1, 2020 (¶830).

Transfer of beer between bonded facilities.—Beer may be removed from one bonded brewery to another bonded brewery without payment of tax if the transfer is between independent proprietors and the transferee accepts responsibility for the tax (¶835).

Wine excise tax credit.—For wine removed after December 31, 2017 and before January 1, 2020, the credit against the wine excise tax for small domestic producers is made available to all wine producers and importers regardless of the number of gallons of wine produced. Foreign producers, however, must elect to assign the credit to importers (¶840).

Alcohol content level of wine.—Alcohol-by-volume levels of the first two tiers of the excise tax on wine are modified by changing 14 percent to 16 percent, effective for wine removed after 2017 and before 2020 (¶845).

Taxation of mead and certain low-alcohol by volume wines.—Mead and certain low-alcohol by volume wines are taxed at the lowest rate applicable to "still wine"—$1.07 per wine gallon of wine, effective for wine removed after December 31, 2017 and before January 1, 2020 (¶850).

¶49

Distilled spirits excise tax.—A tiered tax rate is created for distilled spirits removed in 2018 and 2019 (¶855).

Transfer of bulk distilled spirits.—Distillers are allowed to transfer distilled spirits in bond in containers other than bulk containers without payment of tax for spirits transferred after 2017 and before 2020 (¶860).

¶50 Effect on Health Industry

Individual health insurance mandate.—Effective for months beginning after December 31, 2018, the amount owed by any taxpayer under the individual health insurance mandate "shared responsibility payment" for lack of minimum essential health insurance for themselves and their dependents is zero (¶140).

Medical expenses.—The adjusted gross income (AGI) threshold to claim itemized deduction for unreimbursed expenses paid for the medical care of the taxpayer or the taxpayer's spouse or dependents is temporarily reduced to 7.5 percent of AGI (¶225).

¶52 Effect on Housing and Mortgage Industry

Home mortgage interest.—The itemized deduction for home mortgage interest is limited for tax years 2018 through 2025. A taxpayer is limited to claiming the home mortgage interest deduction only for interest paid or accrued on acquisition debt during those years; the deduction of interest on home equity debt is suspended. The maximum amount that may be treated as acquisition debt is also reduced to $750,000 ($375,000 if married filing separately) for any acquisition debt incurred after December 15, 2017 (¶220).

¶53 Effect on Estates Generally

Estate income tax rates.—The income tax rates and bracket amounts for estates and trusts are modified for tax years 2018 through 2025. The temporary tax rates are 10, 24, 35, and 37 percent (¶105)

Estate, gift, and generation-skipping transfer tax.—The basic exclusion amount for purposes of federal estate and gift taxes and the exemption amount for purposes of the generation-skipping transfer (GST) tax is doubled from $5 million to $10 million, before adjustment for inflation, for the estates of decedents dying and gifts and generation-skipping transfers made after 2017 and before 2026 (¶115).

¶54 Effect on Insurance Industry

Passive foreign investment company rules.—The rule for determining what is not considered passive income for a passive foreign investment company (PFIC) has been modified. The test for nonpassive income that is based on whether a corporation is predominantly engaged in an insurance business has been replaced with a test based on the amount of the corporation's insurance liabilities (¶775).

Net operating losses.—The operations loss deduction (OLD) for life insurance companies is repealed for losses arising in tax years beginning after December 31, 2017. Instead, life insurance companies are allowed a net operating loss (NOL) deduction (¶905).

Small life insurance company deduction.—The small life insurance company deduction is repealed for tax years beginning after 2017 (¶910).

Life insurance company reserves.—For tax years beginning after 2017, life insurance reserves for a contract are determined as the greater of the net surrender value or 92.81-percent of the statutory reserve. For existing contracts, the difference in reserve amounts under the old and new methods is taken into account as a deduction or income over an eight-year period. Income or loss resulting from a change in the basis for determining life insurance reserves is treated as adjustments attributable to a change in the method of accounting (¶915).

Dividends received deduction.—For purposes of the life insurance company proration rules for reducing dividends received deductions and reserve deductions with respect to untaxed income, a company's share is 70 percent and a policyholder's share is 30 percent (¶920).

Property and casualty insurance companies.—For tax years beginning after 2017, the proration rule for reduction of losses incurred by property and casualty insurance companies is modified to replace the 15 percent reduction with a reduction equal to 5.25 percent divided by the top corporate income tax rate. The rate of interest used to discount unpaid losses is changed to a rate based on the corporate bond yield curve using a 60-month period. In addition, the period for determining loss payment patterns is extended for certain lines of business. Lastly, the election to use a taxpayer's own historical loss payment pattern for all lines of business is repealed and all taxpayers will now use an aggregate industry-experience based loss payment pattern (¶925 and ¶930).

Policy acquisition expenses.—The required time period for capitalization and amortization of specified policy acquisition expenses for insurance companies is increased from a 120-month period to a 180-month period. In addition, the percentage of net premiums used for determining general deductions treated as specified premium costs for a tax year after 2017 are increased to: (i) 2.09 percent for annuity contracts; (ii) 2.45 percent for group life insurance contracts; and (iii) 9.2 percent for all other specified insurance contracts (¶935).

Pre-1984 policyholder surplus accounts.—Life insurance companies with pre-1984 operating income held in policyholder surplus accounts may no longer defer tax on this income until it is distributed to shareholders. For each of the eight tax years beginning after December 31, 2017, 1/8th of the remaining balance in a pre-1984 policyholder surplus account is treated as distributed and must be added to the life insurance company's taxable income for the year. The life insurance company's taxable income may not be less than zero (¶940).

Reporting requirements and other rules.—Reporting requirements are imposed with respect to the purchase of an existing life insurance contract in a reportable policy sale and on the payor in the case of a death benefit payment from that contract. The

¶54

exceptions to the transfer for value rules do apply to reportable policy sales. The method of determining the tax basis in a life insurance contract is clarified (¶945).

Additional deduction and estimated tax.—The additional deduction and special estimated tax payment rules for insurance companies required to discount unpaid losses are repealed after 2017 (¶950).

¶56 Effect on Securities Dealer Industry

Carried interests.—Capital gain passed through to fund managers via a partnership profits interest (carried interest) in exchange for investment management services must meet an extended three-year holding period to qualify for long-term capital gain treatment (¶335).

¶57 Effect on Surface Transportation and Road Building Industry

Methods of accounting.—The cash method of accounting and other simpler accounting methods have been made available to more taxpayers. Most taxpayers who meet a $25 million average annual gross receipts test will be able to use the cash method, will not be required to apply the inventory or uniform capitalization (UNICAP) rules, and will not be required to use the percentage of completion method for small construction contracts (¶570).

¶60 Effect on Commuters

Bicycle commuting expenses.—After December 31, 2017, and before January 1, 2026, taxpayers are not permitted to exclude any amount from their income for qualified bicycle commuting reimbursements (¶615).

¶61 Effect on Tax Return Preparers

Due diligence tax return preparer requirement.—The due diligence tax return preparer penalty is expanded to apply to a taxpayer's eligibility to file as head of household (¶120).

¶66 Effect on Tax-Exempt Entities

Unrelated business taxable income.—Exempt organizations with more than one unrelated business will be required to calculate unrelated business taxable income separately for each unrelated trade or business. Unrelated business taxable income will be increased by the nondeductible amount of certain fringe benefit expenses paid or incurred by an exempt organization after December 31, 2017 (¶805 and ¶807).

Executive compensation.—A new excise tax has been established, payable by exempt organizations on remuneration in excess of $1 million and any excess parachute payments made to certain highly-compensated current and former employees in the tax year (¶810).

Investment income of private colleges and universities.—A new 1.4 percent excise tax applies to the net investment income of certain private colleges and universities (¶815).

¶68 Effect on Educational Institutions

Investment income of private colleges and universities.—A new 1.4 percent excise tax applies to the net investment income of certain private colleges and universities (¶815).

¶71 Effect on Empowerment Zones, Enterprise Communities, Renewal Communities, and Community Development Entities

Qualified opportunity zones.—A population census tract that is a low-income community may be designated as a qualified opportunity zone by a State. A taxpayer may elect to exclude from gross income, gain on the sale or exchange of any property to an unrelated party in the tax year of the sale or exchange if the gain is reinvested in a qualified opportunity zone within 180 days of the sale or exchange. The deferred gain is recognized on the earlier of the date on which the qualified opportunity zone investment is disposed of or December 31, 2026 (¶145).

¶75 Effect on Native Americans

Alaska Native settlement trusts.—New rules have been enacted to establish the tax treatment of payments received by Alaska Native Corporations and transfers made to Alaska Native Settlement Trusts (¶325).

¶76 Effect on IRS Administration

Inflation adjustments.—Generally, for tax years beginning after December 31, 2017, the Chained Consumer Price Index for All Urban Consumers (C-CPI-U) is to be used in making annual adjustments for inflation. Exceptions apply to some amounts reset for 2018 (¶125).

Levies.—The time limit that the IRS has to return monetary proceeds from a wrongfully levied sale of property has been extended to two years from the date of levy.

Additionally, the time limit for a taxpayer to bring a civil action for wrongful levy has been extended to two years from the date of the notice of seizure (¶880).

¶78 Effect on Divorced Persons

Alimony and separate maintenance payments.—The deduction for alimony and separate maintenance payments, as well as the inclusion of the payments in gross income, are repealed. The repeal, however, is only effective for divorce or separation instruments executed or modified after 2018 (¶255).

¶80 Effect on Farmers

Depreciation.—New farming machinery and equipment placed in service after December 31, 2017 are classified as 5-year MACRS property rather than 7-year MACRS property. The 7-year property classification, however, continues to apply to grain bins, cotton ginning assets, and fences (¶435).

Citrus plants.—The special rule for deducting the costs incurred in connection with replanting citrus plants lost by reason of casualty is modified. The modified rule allows for a deduction in certain instances when the cost is incurred by a person other than the taxpayer (¶440).

¶82 Effect on Virtual Currency

Like-kind exchanges.—Like-kind exchanges are allowed only for real property after 2017. Thus, as under current law, no gain or loss is recognized on the exchange of real property held for productive use in a trade or business or for investment if that real property is exchanged solely for real property of like kind that will be held either for productive use in a trade or business or for investment. Like-kind exchanges are not allowed for depreciable tangible personal property, and intangible and nondepreciable personal property after 2017 (¶505).

¶84 Effect on Legislators

Living expenses.—The special provision allowing Members of Congress a deduction of up to $3,000 per year of living expenses incurred while on official business in the District of Columbia is stricken (¶560).

¶88 Effect on Construction Industry

Methods of accounting.—The cash method of accounting and other simpler accounting methods have been made available to more taxpayers. Most taxpayers who meet a $25 million average annual gross receipts test will be able to use the cash method, will not be required to apply the inventory or uniform capitalization (UNICAP) rules, and will not be required to use the percentage of completion method for small construction contracts (¶570).

¶90 Effect on Historic Preservation

Rehabilitation credit.—The 20 percent credit for qualified rehabilitation expenditures with respect to certified historic structures is now claimed ratably over a five-year period. In addition, the 10 percent credit for qualified rehabilitation expenditures with respect to non-historic structures first placed in service before 1936 is eliminated (¶590).

¶92 Effect on Pharmaceutical Industry

Orphan drug credit.—The amount of the elective tax credit for qualified clinical testing expenses that are paid or incurred with respect to low or unprofitable drugs for rare diseases and conditions (i.e., the orphan drug credit) is reduced to 25 percent. In addition, taxpayers may elect a reduced credit in lieu of reducing otherwise allowable deductions (¶595).

Individual Taxes (Income, AMT, Estate & Gift)

TAXES AND RETURNS

CAPITAL GAINS AND OTHER PROVISIONS

TAXES AND RETURNS

¶105 Individual Income Tax Rates

SUMMARY OF NEW LAW

The individual income tax rates and bracket amounts are modified for tax years 2018 through 2025. The temporary tax rates are 10, 12, 22, 24, 32, 35, and 37 percent. In addition, the "kiddie tax" is simplified for tax years beginning before 2026 by applying ordinary and capital gains rates applicable to trusts and estates to the net unearned income of a child. The tax treatment of capital gains and qualified dividends remains unchanged.

BACKGROUND

Individuals generally determine their income tax liability by applying the appropriate tax rate schedule (or the tax tables) to their taxable income based on their filing status. There are seven applicable income tax rates: a 10-percent rate; a 15-percent rate; a 25-percent rate; a 28-percent rate; a 33-percent rate; a 35-percent rate; and a 39.6-percent rate (Code Sec. 1(i)). The rate schedules are divided into several ranges of income, referred to as income brackets. The bracket amounts are annually adjusted for inflation.

Kiddie tax. A "kiddie tax" is imposed on the net unearned income of a child meeting certain statutory requirements. (Code Sec. 1(g)). Generally, these rules apply to a child if:

- the child is required to file a tax return;
- the child does not file a joint return for the tax year;
- the child's investment income is more than $2,100 (for 2018);
- either of the child's parents is alive at the end of the year; and
- at the end of the tax year, the child is either: (a) under the age of 18; (b) under the age of 19 and does not provide more than half of his or her own support with earned income; or (c) under the age of 24, a full-time student, and does not provide more than half of his or her own support with earned income.

Under these rules, the net unearned income of a child (for 2018, over $2,100) is taxed at the parents' tax rates if the parents' tax rates are higher than those of the child. The remainder of a child's taxable income, i.e., earned income plus unearned income up to $2,100 (for 2018), less the child's standard deduction, is taxed at the child's rates, whether or not the kiddie tax applies to the child. Generally, a child is permitted to use the preferential tax rates for qualified dividends and capital gains (Code Sec. 1(h)).

The kiddie tax is calculated by computing the "allocable parental tax." The "allocable parental tax" is the amount of tax that results from subtracting the tax that would be imposed on a parent without regard to the special rules relating to a child's net unearned income from the tax that would be imposed on the parent's taxable income if such income included the net unearned income of all children of the parent (Code Sec. 1(g)(3)(A)). A child's net unearned income is the child's unearned income less the sum of (1) the minimum standard deduction allowed to dependents ($1,050 for 2018), and (2) the greater of (a) such minimum standard deduction amount or (b) the amount of allowable itemized deductions that are directly connected with the production of the unearned income (Code Sec. 1(g)(4)). A child's share of any allocable parental tax of his or her parent is equal to an amount that bears the same ratio to the total allocable parental tax as the child's net unearned income bears to the aggregate net unearned income of all children of such parent to whom the special rules on net unearned income apply (Code Sec. 1(g)(3)(B)).

A child usually must file a separate return to report his or her income (Code Sec. 1(g)(6)). In this case, items on the parents' return are not affected by the child's income, and the total tax due from the child is the greater of:

BACKGROUND

- the tax on all of the child's income, calculated at the rates applicable to single individuals; or

- the sum of (a) the tax that would be imposed on a single individual if the child's taxable income were reduced by net unearned income, plus (b) the child's share of the allocable parental tax (Code Sec. 1(g)(1)).

In some instances, a parent may elect to report a child's unearned income on the parent's return (Code Sec. 1(g)(7)).

Capital gains rates. In the case of an individual, estate, or trust, any adjusted net capital gain that would otherwise be taxed at the 10- or 15-percent rate is taxed at zero percent. Any adjusted net capital gain that would otherwise be taxed at rates over 15-percent but below 39.6 percent is taxed at a 15-percent rate. A 20-percent rate applies to any adjusted net capital gain received by taxpayers in the top 39.6-percent income tax bracket.

Unrecaptured section 1250 gain is taxed at a maximum rate of 25 percent, and 28-percent rate gain is taxed at a maximum rate of 28 percent. Any amount of unrecaptured section 1250 gain or 28-percent rate gain otherwise taxed at a 10- or 15-percent rate is taxed at the otherwise applicable rate.

In addition, a tax is imposed on net investment income in the case of an individual, estate, or trust. In the case of an individual, the tax is 3.8 percent of the lesser of (1) net investment income, which includes gains and dividends, or (2) the excess of modified adjusted gross income over the threshold amount of $200,000 ($250,000 for married taxpayers filing jointly and surviving spouses), and $125,000 for a married taxpayer filing separately (Code Sec. 1411).

NEW LAW EXPLAINED

Temporary modification of income tax rates.—The individual income tax rate structure is temporarily replaced with a new rate structure for tax years beginning after December 31, 2017, and before January 1, 2026, as follows (Code Sec. 1(j)(1) and (2), as added by the Tax Cuts and Jobs Act (P.L. 115-97)):

SINGLE TAXPAYERS
FOR TAX YEARS BEGINNING IN 2018

If taxable income is:		The tax is:	of the amount
Over—	but not over—		over—
$0	$9,525	10%	$0
9,525	38,700	$952.50 + 12%	9,525
38,700	82,500	4,453.50 + 22%	38,700
82,500	157,500	14,089.50 + 24%	82,500
157,500	200,000	32,089.50 + 32%	157,500

¶105

NEW LAW EXPLAINED

If taxable income is:		The tax is:	of the amount
Over—	but not over—		over—
200,000	500,000	45,689.50 + 35%	200,000
500,000	. . . . .	150,689.50 + 37%	500,000

**MARRIED INDIVIDUALS FILING SEPARATE RETURNS
FOR TAX YEARS BEGINNING IN 2018**

If taxable income is:		The tax is:	of the amount
Over—	but not over—		over—
$ 0	$9,525	10%	$0
9,525	38,700	$952.50 + 12%	9,525
38,700	82,500	4,453.50 + 22%	38,700
82,500	157,500	14,089.50 + 24%	82,500
157,500	200,000	32,089.50 + 32%	157,500
200,000	300,000	45,689.50 + 35%	200,000
300,000	. . . . .	80,689.50 + 37%	300,000

**MARRIED INDIVIDUALS FILING JOINT RETURNS AND SURVIVING SPOUSES
FOR TAX YEARS BEGINNING IN 2018**

If taxable income is:		The tax is:	of the amount
Over—	but not over—		over—
$ 0	$19,050	10%	$0
19,050	77,400	$1,905 + 12%	19,050
77,400	165,000	8,907 + 22%	77,400
165,000	315,000	28,179 + 24%	165,000
315,000	400,000	64,179 + 32%	315,000
400,000	600,000	91,379 + 35%	400,000
600,000	. . . . .	161,379 + 37%	600,000

**HEADS OF HOUSEHOLD
FOR TAX YEARS BEGINNING IN 2018**

If taxable income is:		The tax is:	of the amount
Over—	but not over—		over—
$ 0	$13,600	10%	$0
13,600	51,800	$1,360.00 + 12%	13,600

NEW LAW EXPLAINED

If taxable income is:		The tax is:	
Over—	but not over—		of the amount over—
51,800	82,500	5,944 + 22%	51,800
82,500	157,500	12,698 + 24%	82,500
157,500	200,000	30,698 + 32%	157,500
200,000	500,000	44,298 + 35%	200,000
500,000	. . . . .	149,298 + 37%	500,000

ESTATES AND TRUSTS
FOR TAX YEARS BEGINNING IN 2018

If taxable income is:		The tax is:	
Over—	but not over—		of the amount over—
$ 0	2,550	10%	$0
2,550	9,150	$255 + 24%	2,550
9,150	12,500	1,839 + 35%	9,150
12,500	. . . . .	3,011.50 + 37%	12,500

For tax years beginning after December 31, 2018, the bracket thresholds are to be annually adjusted for inflation using the Chained Consumer Price Index for All Urban Consumers (C-CPI-U) (see ¶ 125) (Code Sec. 1(j)(3), as added by the 2017 Tax Cuts Act).

> **Comment:** The filing thresholds for an individual to file an income tax return for 2018 are modified (see ¶ 120) as a result of the increase in the standard deduction (see ¶ 205) and repeal of the personal and dependency exemption (¶ 210).

Kiddie tax. Effective for tax years beginning after December 31, 2017, and before January 1, 2026, the "kiddie tax" is simplified by effectively applying ordinary and capital gains rates applicable to trusts and estates to the net unearned income of a child (Code Sec. 1(j)(4), as added by the 2017 Tax Cuts Act). As a result, taxable income attributable to earned income is taxed according to a single individual's tax brackets and rates. Taxable income attributable to net unearned income is taxed according to the brackets applicable to trusts and estates, with respect to both ordinary income and income taxed at preferential rates.

> **Comment:** A child's "kiddie tax" is no longer affected by the tax situation of his or her parent or the unearned income of any siblings.

Maximum rates on capital gains. The maximum rates on net capital gain and qualified dividends are generally retained after 2017 and are 0 percent, 15 percent, and 20 percent. The breakpoints between the zero- and 15-percent rates ("15-percent breakpoint") and the 15- and 20-percent rates ("20-percent breakpoint") are the same amounts as the breakpoints under prior law, except the breakpoints are indexed

¶105

NEW LAW EXPLAINED

using the C-CPI-U (see ¶125) in tax years beginning after 2018 (Code Sec. 1(j)(5)(A) and (C), as added by the 2017 Tax Cuts Act).

For 2018, the 15-percent breakpoint is $77,200 for joint returns and surviving spouses (one-half of this amount ($38,600) for married taxpayers filing separately), $51,700 for heads of household, $2,600 for estates and trusts, and $38,600 for other unmarried individuals. The 20-percent breakpoint is $479,000 for joint returns and surviving spouses (one-half of this amount for married taxpayers filing separately), $452,400 for heads of household, $12,700 for estates and trusts, and $425,800 for other unmarried individuals (Code Sec. 1(j)(5)(B), as added by the 2017 Tax Cuts Act). Therefore, in the case of an individual (including an estate or trust) with adjusted net capital gain, to the extent the gain would not result in taxable income exceeding the 15-percent breakpoint, such gain is not taxed. Any adjusted net capital gain that would result in taxable income exceeding the 15-percent breakpoint but not exceeding the 20-percent breakpoint is taxed at 15 percent. The remaining adjusted net capital gain is taxed at 20 percent.

> **Comment:** As under prior law, unrecaptured section 1250 gain generally is taxed at a maximum rate of 25 percent, and 28-percent rate gain is taxed at a maximum rate of 28 percent. In addition, an individual, estate, or trust also remains subject to the 3.8 percent tax on net investment income (NII tax).

Practical Analysis: William D. Elliott, Partner at Elliott, Thomason & Gibson, LLP in Dallas, Texas, notes that seven tax brackets are adopted. Further, the kiddie tax for unearned income of children is now taxed at the tax rates of trusts and estates and no longer the parents' tax bracket. The changes in the tax brackets end in 2025.

▶ **Effective date.** The amendments made by this section apply to tax years beginning after December 31, 2017 (Act Sec. 11001(c) of the Tax Cuts and Jobs Act (P.L. 115-97)).

Law source: Law at ¶5005. Committee Report at ¶10,010.

— Act Sec. 11001(a) of the Tax Cuts and Jobs Act (P.L. 115-97), adding Code Sec. 1(j);

— Act Sec. 11001(c), providing the effective date.

¶105

¶110 Alternative Minimum Tax (AMT) for Individuals

SUMMARY OF NEW LAW

The AMT exemption amounts are temporarily increased for individuals after 2017 and before 2026. Beginning in 2018, the exemption amounts are $109,400 if married filing jointly or surviving spouse, $70,300 if single or head of household, and $54,700 if married filing separately. The phaseout thresholds are also temporarily increased after 2017 to $1 million if married filing jointly or surviving spouse and $500,000 for all other individuals. The temporary dollars amounts are indexed for inflation after 2018.

BACKGROUND

An alternative minimum tax (AMT) is imposed on an individual, estate, or trust. A taxpayer's AMT for a tax year is the excess of the taxpayer's tentative minimum tax over regular tax liability (Code Sec. 55). For an individual, estate, or trust, the tentative minimum tax is equal to: 26 percent of the taxpayer's alternative minimum taxable income (AMTI) up to a certain threshold amount adjusted annually for inflation, plus 28 percent of any AMTI in excess of the threshold amount. For 2017, the threshold amount is $187,800 ($93,900 for married filing separately) (Rev. Proc. 2016-55).

AMTI is the taxpayer's regular taxable income increased by AMT tax preference items and modified by AMT adjustments (Code Secs. 56 and 57). A tax preference item is a deduction or exclusion not allowed in computing AMTI including the exclusion of gain from qualified small business stock, depletion deductions, and tax-exempt interest earned on private activity bonds. AMT adjustments are items of income or deductions that are computed differently in determining AMTI including certain itemized deductions, personal exemptions, the standard deduction, incentive stock options, depreciation, and net operating losses (NOLs).

A certain amount of a taxpayer's AMTI is exempt from the AMT. For individuals, the AMT exemption amount for 2017 is $84,500 for married filing jointly or surviving spouse, $54,300 for single or head of household, and $42,250 for married filing separately. For estates and trusts, the AMT exemption amount is $24,100, but is zero for the portion of an electing small business trust. The exemption amount is phased out 25 percent for each $1 that AMTI exceeds certain threshold amounts. For individuals, the threshold amount for 2017 is $160,900 for married filing jointly, $120,700 for single or head of household, and $80,450 for married filing separately. For estates or trusts, the threshold amount for 2017 is $80,450.

A noncorporate taxpayer may claim the AMT foreign tax credit in computing their tentative minimum tax. Subject to limits, AMT liability may also be reduced by nonrefundable personal credits and general business credits.

NEW LAW EXPLAINED

Exemption amount and phaseout thresholds for individuals temporarily increased.—The AMT exemption amounts and phaseout thresholds are temporarily

NEW LAW EXPLAINED

increased for individuals for tax years beginning after December 31, 2017, and before January 1, 2026 (Code Sec. 55(d)(4), as added by the Tax Cuts and Jobs Act (P.L. 115-97)). Beginning in 2018, the AMT exemption amounts are:

* $109,400 for married individuals filing jointly or surviving spouses;

* $70,300 for single or head of household filers; and

* $54,700 for married individuals filing separately (i.e., 50 percent of the amount for married individuals filing jointly) (Code Sec. 55(d)(4)(A)(i), as added by the 2017 Tax Cuts Act).

The threshold amounts for phaseout or reduction of the AMT exemption amount are also temporarily increased after 2017. The phaseout threshold is $1 million for married individuals filing jointly or surviving spouses, and 50 percent of this amount for all other individuals. Thus, the phaseout threshold is $500,000 for an individual filing as single, head of household, or married filing separately (Code Sec. 55(d)(4)(A)(ii), as added by the 2017 Tax Cuts Act).

> **Comment:** The exemption amount continues to phase out 25 percent for each $1 that AMTI exceeds certain threshold amounts. Thus, the AMT exemption amount is completely phased out for an individual for 2018 when AMTI reaches $1,437,600 if married individual filing jointly or surviving spouse, $781,200 if filing as single or head of household, and $718,800 if married filing separately.

> **Comment:** The AMT exemption amount and phaseout threshold for an estate or trust are not impacted by these changes. Any of the temporary increases in the exemption amount and phaseout threshold for an individual are inapplicable to a trust or estate. The corporate AMT is repealed effective for tax years beginning after December 31, 2017 (see ¶310).

In the case of any tax year beginning after 2018, the temporary increases in the AMT exemption amounts and phaseout thresholds are adjusted annually for inflation using the Chained Consumer Price Index for All Urban Consumers (C-CPI-U) in the cost-of-living adjustment (see ¶125) (Code Sec. 55(d)(4)(B), as added by the 2017 Tax Cuts Act). These adjustments are temporary increases only and no additional adjustment of the temporary increases will apply.

Net disaster losses. An individual may claim an additional standard deduction amount for his or her net disaster loss in tax years beginning in 2016 and 2017 (Act Sec. 11028(c) of the 2017 Tax Cuts Act). The additional standard deduction is allowed in computing alternative minimum tax liability (AMT). For this purpose, a net disaster loss is the qualified disaster-related personal casualty losses, over any personal casualty gains. A qualified disaster-related personal loss means a personal casualty loss arising in a disaster area after on or after January 1, 2016, that is attributable to a federally declared disaster. See also ¶235 for a discussion of additional relief for claiming casualty loss deductions related to net disaster losses in 2016 and 2017.

¶105

NEW LAW EXPLAINED

▶ **Effective date.** The amendments made by this section apply to tax years beginning after December 31, 2017 (Act Sec. 12003(b) of the Tax Cuts and Jobs Act (P.L. 115-97)). The special rules related to personal casualty losses related to net disaster losses for 2016 and 2017 are effective on December 22, 2017, the date of enactment.

Law source: Law at ¶5135 and ¶7015. Committee Report at ¶10,300.

— Act Sec. 12003(a) of the Tax Cuts and Jobs Act (P.L. 115-97), adding Code Sec. 55(d)(4);

— Act Sec. 11028(a) and (c);

— Act Sec. 12003(b), providing the effective date.

¶115 Estate, Gift, and Generation-Skipping Transfer Tax Exclusions

SUMMARY OF NEW LAW

The basic exclusion amount for purposes of federal estate and gift taxes and the exemption amount for purposes of the generation-skipping transfer (GST) tax is doubled from $5 million to $10 million, before adjustment for inflation, for the estates of decedents dying and gifts and generation-skipping transfers made after 2017 and before 2026.

BACKGROUND

The Internal Revenue Code imposes a federal estate tax, a gift tax, and a generation skipping transfer (GST) tax, commonly referred to as the federal "transfer taxes." The estate and gift taxes comprise a unified form of transfer taxes (i.e., a tax levied upon the transfer of a person's property at death and during life). Estate and gift taxes are progressive and are based on cumulative transfers during life and at death. As set forth in Code Sec. 2001, the unified transfer tax rates range from 18 percent on cumulative transfers of $10,000 or less to a maximum rate of 40 percent, applicable to cumulative transfers over $1,000,000. However, due to the operation of the unified credit, the effective minimum rate is also 40 percent. The unified credit, also referred to as the "applicable credit amount" (Code Sec. 2010), is a one-time credit to be used against taxable estate or gift taxes payable.

The amount of the unified credit is based on the amount of tentative tax that would be determined under Code Sec. 2001(c) using the applicable exclusion amount as the taxable estate. The applicable exclusion amount is effectively the amount of property that can be excluded from estate or gift taxes during an individual's lifetime. And, under the concept of "portability," the unused portion of a decedent's applicable exclusion amount may be utilized by the estate of the decedent's surviving spouse at his or her later death. To take advantage of this provision, a special election must be made by the predeceased spouse's estate on its estate tax return, Form 706. This election is often referred to as the portability, or the deceased spousal unused

BACKGROUND

exclusion (DSUE), election. With the U.S. Supreme Court's decision in *E. Windsor*, SCt., 2013-2 USTC ¶ 60,667, the portability of a deceased spouse's unused exclusion amount is available to a surviving same-sex spouse so long as the couple was legally married.

The applicable exclusion amount for a surviving spouse who dies after December 31, 2010, is the sum of:

• the basic exclusion amount ($5.49 million for 2017); and

• the aggregate DSUE amount.

Any portion of the predeceased spouse's applicable exclusion amount that was used to reduce his or her estate tax liability may not be used to reduce the surviving spouse's estate tax liability. The term "deceased spousal unused exclusion amount" (DSUE amount) is the lesser of:

• the basic exclusion amount, or

• the last deceased spouse's applicable exclusion amount, minus

• the amount with respect to which the tentative tax is determined under Code Sec. 2001(b)(1) on the estate of such deceased spouse.

The third federal transfer tax, the GST tax (Code Secs. 2601 through 2663), exists primarily to keep wealthy individuals from avoiding the estate tax by using "generation-skipping transfers," that is, passing their property at death (or during lifetime) to their grandchildren (or great-grandchildren), rather than to their children. The lifetime exemption amount for purposes of the GST tax is based on the basic exclusion amount used for the estate and gift taxes. Consequently, the exemption on generation-skipping transfers occurring in 2017 is $5.49 million. Unlike the estate or gift tax, the concept of portability does not apply to the GST tax exemption.

NEW LAW EXPLAINED

Estate and gift tax exclusion doubled.—The basic exclusion amount for purposes of federal estate and gift taxes will be doubled from $5 million to $10 million, before adjustment for inflation, for the estates of decedents dying and gifts made after 2017 and before 2026 (Code Sec. 2010(c)(3)(C), as amended by the Tax Cuts and Jobs Act of 2017 (P.L. 115-97)). The $10 million amount is adjusted annually for inflation in the case of any decedent dying in a calendar year after 2017 using the using the Chained Consumer Price Index for All Urban Consumers (C-CPI-U) in the cost-of-living adjustment (see ¶ 125) (Code Sec. 2010(c)(3)(B)(ii), as amended by the 2017 Tax Cuts Act).

Caution: The change in methodology for making inflation adjustments using chained-CPI rather than average CPI may result in smaller adjustments after 2017, particularly higher dollar amounts such as the estate and gift tax exclusion amount. For example, the basic exclusion amount would be $11.2 million applicable to decedents dying and gifts made in 2018 ($22.4 million for married couple using portability) based on the inflation-adjusted amount of $5.6 million provided in Rev. Proc. 2017-58 using average CPI. However, the IRS may issue a revised inflation adjustment for the basic exclusion amount applicable for 2018

¶115

NEW LAW EXPLAINED

using chained CPI that results in a lower basic exclusion amount. For decedents dying and gifts made after 2025, the basic exclusion amount will revert to $5 million, as adjusted for inflation using chained CPI.

Example 1: Bruce Payne, a wealthy single individual dies in 2018 leaving a taxable estate of $10 million. His estate will owe no federal estate taxes. Instead, if he had died in 2017, the estate tax payable would have been $1,804,000.

Example 2: Carol Cologne, a wealthy widow dies in 2018 leaving a taxable estate of $20 million. Her late husband died earlier in 2018 having used only $2 million of his available estate tax exclusion amount. Her estate will owe no federal estate tax. However, if the couple had died under the same circumstances in 2017, the estate tax payable would have been $4,408,000.

Comment: Because the doubling of the estate and gift tax exclusion amount will expire for decedents dying and gifts made after December 31, 2025, the next several years present a tremendous opportunity for wealthy individuals and married couples to make large gifts, including those that leverage the amount of the available exclusion, such as those to grantor retained annuity trusts (GRATs).

Comment: According to the IRS Statistics of Income tables presenting data on estate tax return data for Filing Year 2016 (https://www.irs.gov/statistics/soi-tax-stats-estate-tax-filing-year-tables, see Table 1 showing data from estate tax returns filed in 2016, by tax status and size of gross estate), a total of 5,219 taxable returns were filed contrasted with 7,192 nontaxable returns. Of the taxable returns, 2,402 fell within the $5 to $10 million gross estate range, 1,293 in the $10 to $20 million range. Only 300 returns were filed with gross estates in excess of $50 million. These statistics primarily reflect data from the estates of decedents who died in 2015, when the basic exclusion amount was $5.43 million, but also include some returns for decedents who died in years prior to 2015, as well as a small number of estates with respect to deaths that occurred in 2016. The large increase in the basic exclusion amount after 2017 will no doubt lead to further decreases in the number of taxable estates.

GST tax exemption amount. Because the exemption from the GST tax is computed by reference to the basic exclusion amount used for estate and gift tax purposes (Code Sec. 2631), the GST exemption amount for GSTs occurring in 2018 will be $10 million, before adjustment for inflation. Portability does not apply for purposes of the GST tax.

Corresponding adjustments with respect to prior gifts. In addition to the increase in the basic exclusion amount, the 2017 Tax Cuts Act modifies the computation of gift tax payable and estate tax payable in cases where gifts have been made in prior years. (Code Sec. 2001(g), as amended by the 2017 Tax Cuts Act). With respect to the computation of gift tax payable, the tax rates in effect at the time of the decedent's death are to be used rather than the rates that were in effect at the time the gifts were

NEW LAW EXPLAINED

made (Code Sec. 2001(g)(1), as amended by the 2017 Tax Cuts Act). And, the Secretary of the Treasury is directed to prescribe regulations clarifying the computation of estate tax payable in situations where the basic exclusion amount was different in the year of the decedent's death as opposed to the year when the prior gifts were made (Code Sec. 2001(g)(2), as amended by the 2017 Tax Cuts Act).

> **Practical Analysis:** Josh O. Ungerman, JD CPA, and Alan K. Davis, JD, CPA, Partners at Meadows, Collier, Reed, Cousins, Crouch and Ungerman, LLP, comment that the only transfer tax change in the Act consists of the doubling of the Code Sec. 2010(c) basic exclusion amount from $5 million to $10 million for transfers made and decedents dying after December 31, 2017, and before January 1, 2026. The exclusion remains subject to an annual inflation adjustment which results in an exclusion for 2018 of $11.2 million. This change applies for estate and gift tax and causes the GST exemption to increase by the same amount. According to the estimates of the Urban-Brookings Tax Policy Center, this change is expected to initially reduce the number of taxable estates from 5,500 estates to only 1,700 taxable estates per year and reduce revenue from the federal estate tax from $20.4 billion in 2017 to $12.6 billion in 2018.
>
> The change opens the door to a new round of planning for those taxpayers who have fully utilized their pre-2017 Tax Cuts Act existing exclusion amounts especially because the current increase sunsets in eight years. These planning opportunities are enhanced by the absence of any Act sections aimed at reducing discounts for family controlled business interests that were included in the proposed Code Sec. 2704 regulations withdrawn by the IRS in late 2017. Finally, it is important to note that although the dollar amount of assets per couple that can now pass without estate tax is increased, there was no change to the application of Code Sec. 1014 which allows assets in the gross estate to receive a new basis for income tax purposes equal to fair market value.

> **Practical Analysis:** Lewis J. Saret, Founder, Law Office of Lewis J. Saret, in Washington, DC, observes that doubling the estate tax exclusion from $5 to $10 million, indexed for inflation, but lapsing after 2025, will only impact a small segment of the population, roughly one out of 500 taxpayers based on 2017 data. However, this change will create a strong incentive for such taxpayers to make gifts to take advantage of the increased estate tax exclusion before it lapses on December 31, 2025, or possibly sooner if the composition of the legislative and executive branches changes before 2025.

▶ **Effective date.** The amendments made by this section are effective for decedents dying and for gifts and generation-skipping transfers made after December 31, 2017 (Act Sec. 11061(c) of the Tax Cuts and Jobs Act (P.L. 115-97)).

Law source: Law at ¶6070 and ¶6075. Committee Report at ¶10,270.

— Act Sec. 11061(a) of the Tax Cuts and Jobs Act of 2017 (P.L. 115-97), adding Code Sec. 2010(c)(3)(C);

¶115

NEW LAW EXPLAINED

— Act Sec. 11061(b), amending Code Sec. 2001(g);

— Act Sec. 11061(c), providing the effective date.

¶120 Individual Income Tax Returns, Filing Threshold, and Tax Preparer Due Diligence

SUMMARY OF NEW LAW

The filing thresholds for an individual to file an income tax return are modified after 2017 as a result of the increase in the standard deduction and repeal of the personal and dependency exemption. In addition, the due diligence tax return preparer penalty is expanded to apply to a taxpayer's eligibility to file as head of household.

BACKGROUND

For each tax year, an income tax return must be filed by a U.S. citizen or a resident alien who has at least a specified minimum amount of gross income (Code Sec. 6012). The filing threshold for most individuals depends on the taxpayer's filing status and the sum of personal exemptions deduction and the standard deduction, including the additional standard deduction for the aged and/or blind, adjusted annually for inflation. A taxpayer is generally not required to file a federal income tax return for 2017 if his or her gross income is below the following thresholds (Rev. Proc. 2016-55):

Single individual	$10,400
Single individual, 65 or older or blind	11,950
Single individual, 65 or older and blind	13,500
Married individual, separate return	4,050
Married couple, joint return	20,800
Married couple, joint return, one spouse 65 or older or blind	22,050
Married couple, joint return, one spouse 65 or older and blind	23,300
Married couple, joint return, both spouses 65 or older or blind	23,300
Married couple, joint return, both spouses 65 or older and blind	25,800
Head of household	13,400
Head of household, 65 or older or blind	14,950
Head of household, 65 or older and blind	16,500
Qualifying widow(er) (surviving spouse)	16,750
Qualifying widow(er) (surviving spouse), 65 or older or blind	18,000
Qualifying widow(er) (surviving spouse), 65 or older and blind	19,250

Filing status. The tax rates applicable to an individual, as well as filing requirements and standard deduction amounts, for a tax year are determined by reference to the taxpayer's filing status. There are four tax rate schedules for individuals: married persons filing joint returns and surviving spouses; head of household; single; and

¶120

BACKGROUND

married persons filing separate returns. Whether a taxpayer can file as single or either married filing separately or a joint return is generally governed by the taxpayer's marital status on the last day of the year (Code Sec. 7703(a)). Married taxpayers can either file separate returns, or elect to file a joint return (Code Sec. 6013).

In order for a taxpayer to file a return using head of household status, a number of requirements must be satisfied. A U.S. citizen or resident alien who is unmarried or considered unmarried at the end of the tax year and who maintains as his or her home as a household that is the principal place of abode for certain qualifying individuals for more than half the year may use the filing status of head of household (Code Sec. 2(b)). The taxpayer must occupy the household as his or her home for the entire tax year. However, temporary absences due to illness, education, business, vacation, or military service do not affect head of household status, as long as it is reasonable to assume that the taxpayer will return, and the taxpayer continues to maintain the household in anticipation of his or her return. The taxpayer may change the location of the household during the year without affecting his or her filing status. The taxpayer must actually occupy the home; it is not sufficient to simply pay the maintenance costs. A qualifying individual must be either a qualifying child of the taxpayer or another individual for whom the taxpayer is entitled to a dependency exemption including the taxpayer's parents (Code Sec. 2(b)).

Due diligence requirement. A taxpayer must also meet specific requirements to qualify for the child tax credit (Code Sec. 24), the American Opportunity and lifetime learning credits (Code Sec. 25A), and the earned income credit (Code Sec. 32). Tax return preparers are required to meet due diligence requirements in ensuring that their clients meet the qualifications for these credits on returns or refund claims on which the credits are claimed (Code Sec. 6695(g)). Tax return preparers comply with this due diligence requirement by completing a Form 8867, Paid Preparer's Due Diligence Checklist, document the calculation of the credit(s) using either the appropriate IRS worksheet or other means of calculation, retaining these items in records, and must not know, or have reason to know, that the client does not qualify for the credit(s) (Reg. § 1.6695-2; Temp. Reg. § 1.6695-2T). Each failure to exercise such due diligence results in a $500 penalty (Code Sec. 6695(g)).

NEW LAW EXPLAINED

Filing thresholds increased; preparer due diligence requirements added for head of household status.—The rules for determining the filing threshold for an individual to file a federal income tax return are modified for tax years beginning after December 31, 2017, and before January 1, 2026, as a result of the temporary repeal of the personal exemption deduction (see ¶ 210) and the temporary increase in the standard deduction amount (see ¶ 205).

With respect to an individual who is not married (single or head of household), an individual is required to file a tax return if his or her gross income for the tax year exceeds the applicable standard deduction (Code Sec. 6012(f), as added by the 2017 Tax Cuts Act). A married individual reaches the filing threshold if his or her gross income,

NEW LAW EXPLAINED

when combined with the individual's spouse's gross income for the tax year, is more than the standard deduction applicable to a joint return, and provided that:

- the individual and his or her spouse, at the close of the tax year, had the same household as their home;

- the individual's spouse does not file a separate return; and

- neither the individual nor his or her spouse is a dependent of another taxpayer who has income (other than earned income) in excess of the standard deduction for dependents provided under Code Sec. 63(c)(5)(A).

> **Comment:** The standard deduction amounts are adjusted annually for inflation for tax years beginning after 2018 and before 2026 using the Chained Consumer Price Index for All Urban Consumers (C-CPI-U) in the cost-of-living adjustment (see ¶125) (Code Sec. 63(c)(7)(B), as added by the 2017 Tax Cuts Act). The standard deduction amount for a dependent, as well as the additional standard deduction amounts for the aged and/or blind are also adjusted for inflation. However, these amounts are adjusted for inflation after 2017 using chained chained-CPI rather than averaged CPI (Code Sec. 63(c)(4), as amended by the 2017 Tax Cuts Act). As a result, the IRS may issue revised inflation adjustments for 2018 for the standard deduction for a dependent, as well as the standard deduction amounts for the aged and/or blind.

Assuming the is no revised inflation adjustment in the amount of the additional standard deduction for taxpayers over age 65 or who are blind, the filing thresholds for 2018 are as follows:

Single individual	$12,000
Single individual, 65 or older or blind	13,600
Single individual, 65 or older and blind	15,200
Married individual, separate return	12,000
Married couple, joint return	24,000
Married couple, joint return, one spouse 65 or older or blind	25,300
Married couple, joint return, one spouse 65 or older and blind	26,600
Married couple, joint return, both spouses 65 or older or blind	26,600
Married couple, joint return, both spouses 65 or older and blind	29,200
Head of household	18,000
Head of household, 65 or older or blind	19,600
Head of household, 65 or older and blind	21,200
Qualifying widow(er) (surviving spouse)	24,000
Qualifying widow(er) (surviving spouse), 65 or older or blind	25,300
Qualifying widow(er) (surviving spouse), 65 or older and blind	26,600

Tax return preparer due diligence. Effective for tax years beginning after December 31, 2017, the requirement that tax return preparers must satisfy due diligence in ensuring that clients qualify for the child, American Opportunity, lifetime learning, and earned income tax credits is extended to apply to head of household status. Each failure to exercise such due diligence in ensuring that a client meets the requirements of head of household status, and thus qualifies for the filing threshold for head of

NEW LAW EXPLAINED

household status, will result in a $500 penalty (Code Sec. 6695(g), as amended by the Tax Cuts and Jobs Act (P.L. 115-97)).

▶ **Effective date.** The amendments made by this section apply to tax years beginning after December 31, 2017 (Act Secs. 11001(c) and 11041(f) of the Tax Cuts and Jobs Act (P.L. 115-97)).

Law source: Law at ¶6170 and ¶6290. Committee Report at ¶10,010 and ¶10,160.

— Act Sec. 11001(b) of the Tax Cuts and Jobs Act (P.L. 115-97), amending Code Sec. 6695(g);

— Act Sec. 11041(e) adding Code Sec. 6012(f);

— Act Secs. 11001(c) and 11041(f), providing the effective date.

¶125 Inflation Adjustments Using Chained Consumer Price Index (C-CPI-U)

SUMMARY OF NEW LAW

Generally, for tax years beginning after December 31, 2017, the Chained Consumer Price Index for All Urban Consumers (C-CPI-U) is to be used in making annual adjustments for inflation.

BACKGROUND

Throughout the Internal Revenue Code, there are many instances where a codified amount, whether it is a tax-bracket range, deduction amount, the amount of income at which a deduction is no longer available, retirement plan contribution limit, or even the dollar amount of a penalty, is adjusted annually for inflation. This is generally done to avoid a diminishment in the value of a tax benefit due to the relative decline in the value of the dollar over time. For example, income amounts for an individual working in the same position every year generally tend to increase annually in order to, at least in part, account for inflation through the application of cost-of-living increases. If the income ranges for a tax bracket were not also annually adjusted for inflation, those annual cost-of-living increases would eventually cause the individual to move up to a higher tax bracket, while the purchasing power of his income has remained unchanged (a phenomenon known as "bracket creep").

Inflation adjustments for any particular year for most amounts under the Internal Revenue Code are generally calculated by taking the average Consumer Price Index (CPI) for the 12-month period ending August 31 of the *previous* year, dividing that amount by the average CPI for the 12-month period ending on August 31 of the prescribed base year for that amount, then multiplying that quotient by the statutory amount, and rounding as required by the statute (Code Sec. 1(f)(3), (4), and (6)). So, for example, the statutory amount for the standard deduction for an unmarried person is $3,000, with a base year of 1987 (Code Sec. 63(c)(2)(C) and (4)(B)(i)). So, to calculate what that amount was for 2017, the IRS took the average CPI for the

BACKGROUND

12-month period ending August 31, 2016, divided by the average CPI for the 12-month period ending August 31, 1987, multiplied by $3,000 (714.886/335.5 × $3,000 = $6,392.42). The amount is then rounded down to the next lowest multiple of $50 to arrive at $6,350, which is the amount of the standard deduction for an unmarried individual in 2017 (Rev. Proc. 2016-55).

The Consumer Price Index is one of several indices calculated by the Bureau of Labor Statistics (BLS) (part of the Department of Labor) to determine inflation and adjustments to amounts provided in the Internal Revenue Code are required to use the Consumer Price Index for All-Urban Consumers (Code Sec. 1(f)(5)). The Consumer Price Index for All-Urban Consumers is abbreviated as CPI-U by the BLS, but, for tax purposes, the Internal Revenue Code, Treasury regulations, and the IRS all shorten this to simply "CPI." "CPI-U" and "CPI" tend to be used interchangeably.

The general methodology of calculating the CPI is to undertake a survey of monthly prices for a "basket" of goods in urban areas, which captures about 88 percent of the population of the United States, and calculate an index for the monthly change in prices from a base year (in the case of the CPI, the base year is 1967, and the base index amount is 100). Over time, this basket of goods has been adjusted to incorporate technological advances and modern consumption choices (e.g., replacing purchases of typewriters with purchases of computers). Those amounts are then normalized in order to create a consistent index (*BLS Handbook of Methods*, Chapter 17 (6/2015)).

The IRS will typically announce the inflation-adjusted amounts applicable to a particular tax year in two major releases in the prior October. A Revenue Procedure will include inflation adjustments to amounts applicable to income taxes, estate and gift taxes, and excise taxes (for example, Rev. Proc. 2016-55 for 2017 amounts). An IRS Notice will include adjustments applicable to retirement plans (for example, Notice 2017-64 for 2018 amounts), only a limited number of which use the CPI as of August 31 as a standard of adjustment; most use the same methodology used by the Social Security Administration to make annual Social Security adjustments (Reg. § 1.415(d)-1). A handful of other adjustments are made annually outside of these two major IRS releases (for example, depreciation caps for luxury vehicles in Rev. Proc. 2017-29). In total, the CPI is used to adjust more than 200 statutory amounts across more than 60 provisions of the Internal Revenue Code.

NEW LAW EXPLAINED

Chained consumer price index to be used in calculating annual inflation adjustments.—For tax years beginning after December 31, 2017 (December 31, 2018, for individual tax brackets and the standard deduction), the calculation of annual inflation adjustments will be made by using the Chained Consumer Price Index for All Urban Consumers (C-CPI-U) (Code Sec. 1(f)(3) and (6), as amended by the Tax Cuts and Jobs Act (P.L. 115-97)). The C-CPI-U is calculated in much the same way as the CPI, but rather than simply accounting for the impact of inflation on the price of goods, it also accounts for consumers' diminished capacity to achieve the same standard of living due

NEW LAW EXPLAINED

to the increase in the price of consumer goods (*BLS Handbook of Methods*, Chapter 17 (6/2015)). The effect is that adjustments for inflation will be smaller.

> **Comment:** The difference between the two methods of calculating inflation is not insignificant. Between October 2007 and October 2017, the rate of inflation using CPI has been around 18 percent, while the rate of inflation using C-CPI-U has been around 16 percent. Although this difference may appear small, it can have a much larger impact on higher amounts, such as tax bracket income thresholds or the applicable exclusion amount (unified credit) for estate and gift taxes and the exemption amount for the generation-skipping transfer tax.

Just as with CPI, the adjustment for a calendar year is based upon the average monthly C-CPI-U for the 12-month period ending on August 31 of the *prior* year. However, because the method of calculating C-CPI-U requires the additional step of making a determination of the impact of inflation on purchasing decisions, the C-CPI-U for any given month is actually the result of an iterative release by the Bureau of Labor Statistics (BLS). An initial value is calculated and announced during the month following the month at issue, which is then reassessed and re-released (with any changes) as an interim amount. Within one year, the interim amount is announced as final. However, for purposes of calculating inflation adjustments, the interim amount is to be used (Code Sec. 1(f)(6), as added by the 2017 Tax Cuts Act).

Many of the changes contained in the 2017 Tax Cuts Act are temporary. For example, the reduced tax rates, increased standard deduction, and elimination of the personal exemption are all temporary, applying to tax years beginning before 2026. However, the replacement of CPI-U with C-CPI-U in calculating annual inflation adjustments is *not* temporary and applies to all amounts that are adjusted for inflation, including the permanent brackets applicable after 2025, even if the temporary changes are allowed to expire (Code Sec. 1(f)(2)(A), as amended by the 2017 Tax Cuts Act and Act Sec. 11002(d) of the 2017 Tax Cuts Act). This is accomplished by adjusting the CPI-U for the base year by an amount that is adjusted to reset the index using C-CPI-U for that base year (Code Sec. 1(f)(3), as amended by the 2017 Tax Cuts Act).

> **Caution:** The amounts that apply to retirement plans that are annually adjusted using Social Security methodology per Reg. § 1.415(d)-1 are not affected by these changes. Unless the regulations are reissued and amended to mandate the use of C-CPI-U or the Social Security methodology is changed to mandate such use, these amounts will continue to be annually adjusted using CPI-U.

> **Comment:** Some annual inflation adjustments that use the August 31 CPI amount are required under regulation or IRS administrative guidance (see, for example, annual inflation adjustments made to certain rules under the arbitrage bond rules under Code Sec. 148). Presumably, these items will have to be amended and reissued in order to make the switch over to C-CPI-U.

Practical Analysis: William D. Elliott, Partner at Elliott, Thomason & Gibson, LLP in Dallas, Texas, observes that the measurement of cost of living expense changes is now based on the Chained Consumer Price Index for All Urban Consumers (C-CPI-

NEW LAW EXPLAINED

U) instead of prior CPI-U. The difference pertains to allowing for consumer substitution between item categories in the market basket of consumer goods and services that make up the index.

▶ **Effective date.** The amendments made by this section apply to tax years beginning after December 31, 2017 (Act Sec. 11002(e) of the Tax Cuts and Jobs Act (P.L. 115-97)).

Law source: Law at ¶5005, ¶5020, ¶5030, ¶5035, ¶5045, ¶5050, ¶5060, ¶5065, ¶5075, ¶5135, ¶5150, ¶5165, ¶5170, ¶5180, ¶5235, ¶5240, ¶5245, ¶5250, ¶5265, ¶5270, ¶5285, ¶5295, ¶5335, ¶5350, ¶5365, ¶5370, ¶5375, ¶5385, ¶5445, ¶5475, ¶5495, ¶5565, ¶5570, ¶5715, ¶5795, ¶5850, ¶5990, ¶6075, ¶6080, ¶6085, ¶6105, ¶6110, ¶6125, ¶6135, ¶6190, ¶6225, ¶6230, ¶6265, ¶6270, ¶6275, ¶6290, ¶6295, ¶6300, ¶6305, ¶6310, ¶6320, ¶6325, ¶6350, and ¶6360. Committee Report at ¶10,020.

— Act Sec. 11002(a) of the Tax Cuts and Jobs Act (P.L. 115-97), amending Code Sec. 1(f)(3);

— Act Sec. 11002(b), striking Code Sec. 1(f)(7), redesignating Code Sec. 1(f)(6) as Code Sec. 1(f)(7) and adding new Code Sec. 1(f)(6);

— Act Sec. 11002(c)(1), amending Code Sec. 1(f)(2)(A);

— Act Sec. 11002(c)(2), amending Code Sec. 1(i);

— Act Sec. 11002(d), amending Code Secs. 23(h)(2), 25A(h)(1)(A)(ii) and (2)(A)(ii), 25B(b)(3)(B), 32(b)(2)(B)(ii)(II) and (j)(1)(B), Code Sec. 36B(f)(2)(B)(ii)(II), 41(e)(5)(C)(i) and (ii), 42(e)(3)(D)(ii), (h)(3)(H)(i)(II) and (h)(6)(G), 45R(d)(3)(B)(ii), 55(d)(4)(A)(ii), 59(j)(2)(B), 62(d)(3)(B), 63(c)(4)(B), 68(b)(2)(B), 125(i)(2)(B), 132(f)(6)(A)(ii), 135(b)(2)(B)(ii), 137(f)(2), 146(d)(2)(B), 147(c)(2)(H)(ii), 151(d)(4)(B), 162(o)(3), 179(b)(6)(A)(ii), 213(d)(10)(B), 219(b)(5)(C)(i)(II) and (g)(8)(B), 220(g)(2), 221(f)(1)(B), 223(g)(1)(B), 280F(d)(7)(B), 408A(c)(3)(D)(ii), 430(c)(7)(D)(vii)(II), 512(d)(2)(B), 513(h)(2)(C)(ii), 831(b)(2)(D)(ii), 877A(a)(3)(B)(i)(II), 911(b)(2)(D)(ii)(II), 1274A(d)(2), 2010(c)(3)(B)(ii), 2032A(a)(3)(B), 2503(b)(2)(B), 4161(b)(2)(C)(i)(II), 4261(e)(4)(A)(ii), 4980I(b)(3)(C)(v)(II), 5000A(c)(3)(D)(ii), 6039F(d), 6323(i)(4)(B), 6334(g)(1)(B), 6601(j)(3)(B), 6651(i)(1), 6652(c)(7)(A), 6695(h)(1), 6698(e)(1), 6699(e)(1), 6721(f)(1), 6722(f)(1), 7345(f)(2), 7430(c)(1), 7872(g)(5), and 9831(d)(2)(D)(ii)(II);

— Act Sec. 11002(e), providing the effective date.

CAPITAL GAINS AND OTHER PROVISIONS

¶130 Self-Created Property as Capital Asset

SUMMARY OF NEW LAW

A patent, invention, model or design (patented or not), or secret formula or process is excluded from the definition of a capital asset for dispositions after December 31, 2017, if it is held by the taxpayer who created the property or a taxpayer with a substituted or transferred basis from the taxpayer who created the property.

BACKGROUND

Some self-created intangibles cannot be capital assets for certain taxpayers. Copyrights and literary, musical, or artistic compositions cannot be capital assets in the hands of the taxpayer who created them, or in the hands of a taxpayer whose basis is determined in whole or part by reference to the basis of the taxpayer who created them (Code Sec. 1221(a)(3)). However, a taxpayer in either of these categories may elect to treat musical compositions and copyrights in musical works as capital assets (Code Sec. 1221(b)(3); Reg. § 1.1221-3).

Letters or memoranda and similar property cannot be capital assets in the hands of the taxpayer who created them, the taxpayer for whom they were prepared or created, or a taxpayer with substitute or carryover basis from the person who created them or for whom they were created (Code Sec. 1221(a)(3)).

NEW LAW EXPLAINED

Patents, inventions, designs, and secret formulas are not capital assets.—In the case of dispositions after December 31, 2017, a patent, invention, model or design (patented or not), or secret formula or process is not a capital asset in the hands of (1) the taxpayer whose personal efforts created the property, or (2) a taxpayer with a substituted or transferred basis from the taxpayer whose personal efforts created the property (Code Sec. 1221(a)(3), as amended by the Tax Cuts and Jobs Act (P.L. 115-97)). Thus, gains or losses from the sale or exchange of a patent, invention, model or design, or a secret formula or process that is held either by the taxpayer who created the property or a taxpayer with a substituted or transferred basis from the taxpayer who created the property will not be capital gains or losses.

These types of self-created property also do not qualify for the capital gain/ordinary loss rule for dispositions after December 31, 2017 (Code Sec. 1231(b)(1)(C), as amended by the 2017 Tax Cuts Act).

> **Caution:** According to the Conference Committee Report, the exclusion of these self-created works from capital assets also applies when the taxpayer's basis is determined by reference to the basis of a person for whom the property was created (Conference Report on H.R. 1, Tax Cuts and Jobs Act (H. Rept. 115-466)). However, the amended statutory language apparently still limits this "for whom created" rule to letters, memoranda and similar property.

> **Comment:** Although patents will be excluded from the definition of capital asset after 2017, a qualified holder's gain on the disposition of a patent to an unrelated person may still be taxed at the lowest capital gain tax rate. Qualified holders include the creator of the patent and persons who provided financial backing to the creator (Code Sec. 1235).

▶ **Effective date.** The amendment made by this section applies to dispositions after December 31, 2017 (Act Sec. 13314(c) of the Tax Cuts and Jobs Act (P.L. 115-97).

Law source: Law at ¶5975 and ¶5980. Committee Report at ¶10,540.

— Act Sec. 13314(a) of the Tax Cuts and Jobs Act (P.L. 115-97), amending Code Sec. 1221(a)(3);

NEW LAW EXPLAINED

— Act Sec. 13314(b), amending Code Sec. 1231(b)(1)(C);

— Act Sec. 13314(c), providing the effective date.

¶135 Sinai Peninsula of Egypt a Qualified Hazardous Duty Area

SUMMARY OF NEW LAW

The Sinai Peninsula of Egypt is a qualified hazardous duty area for the applicable period and is treated the same as a combat zone for purposes of certain tax benefits for members of the U.S. Armed Forces. The applicable period is generally the portion of the first tax year beginning after June 9, 2015, and any subsequent tax year beginning before January 1, 2026.

BACKGROUND

Members of the U.S. Armed Forces serving in a combat zone, as designated by Executive Order of the President of the United States, are entitled to numerous tax benefits. Military personnel may exclude from gross income all pay received for any month, even a part of which, was spent in a combat zone or in a hospital due to wounds, disease, or injury incurred while serving in a combat zone (Code Sec. 112). However, it does not apply to time spent in a hospital for any month beginning more than two years after the date of the end of the combatant activities that zone. Such pay is also not subject to withholding (Code Sec. 3401(a)(1)).

The gross income exclusion also applies to commissioned officers, but it is limited to the maximum enlisted amount, which is the sum of:

- the highest rate of basic pay at the highest pay grade that enlisted personnel may receive, and

- the amount of hostile fire/imminent danger pay that the officer receives (Reg. § 1.112-1).

While excluded from gross income, combat pay is included in earned income for purposes of computing the earned income tax credit and calculating the refundable portion of the child tax credit (Code Secs. 24(d)(1) and 32(c)(2)(B)(vi)). Similarly, combat pay may be treated as compensation in determining the amount members of the military can contribute to their individual retirement accounts (IRAs).

The tax liability of a member of the U.S. Armed Forces is forgiven in the year the individual dies:

- while in active service in a combat zone, or

- from wounds, disease, or injury incurred while serving in a combat zone.

¶135

BACKGROUND

Any unpaid taxes that relate to tax years prior to service in a combat zone may also be abated. If the decedent filed a joint return, only the decedent's portion of joint tax liability is forgiven. This tax forgiveness rule also applies to U.S. military and civilian employees killed in terrorist or military actions, including specific domestic terrorist attacks (Code Sec. 692).

For purposes of determining surviving spouse status (and joint filing status) for a spouse of a military member who is missing in a combat zone, the military member is considered to have died on the date his or her status changed from missing to dead rather than the actual date of death (Code Secs. 2(a)(3) and 6013(f)(1)). The surviving spouse may use surviving spouse status for the two years following the year in which his or her spouse is deemed to have died.

An estate tax reduction is available for members of the Armed Forces who are killed while serving in a combat zone (Code Sec. 2201). The tax forgiveness discussed above extends to tax on income received by another after the decedent's death as income in respect of a decedent (Reg. § 1.692-1(a)(2)(ii)).

Administrative relief may be provided to members of the military in a combat zone or who are continuously hospitalized as a result of injuries received in a combat zone by suspending tax examination and collection actions during this time (Code Secs. 7508 and 7508A). Examination and collection actions that can be precluded or suspended include tax return audits, mailings of notices, and other actions involving the collection of overdue taxes. The collection period for taxpayers hospitalized for combat zone injuries may not be suspended by reason of any period of continuous hospitalization or the 180 days thereafter (Code Sec. 7508(e)(3)). As a result, the collection period expires 10 years after assessment, plus the actual time spent in a combat zone, regardless of the length of the postponement period available for hospitalized individuals to comply with their tax obligations.

Members of the military are also exempt from the telephone excise tax for toll telephone service that originates in a combat zone (Code Sec. 4253(d)).

NEW LAW EXPLAINED

Egypt's Sinai Peninsula is a qualified hazardous duty area; treated as combat zone.—The Sinai Peninsula of Egypt is a qualified hazardous duty area and members of the U.S. Armed Forces members serving there are considered to be serving in a combat zone (Sec. 11026(b) of the Tax Cuts and Jobs Act (P.L. 115-97)). As a result, such members of the military are entitled to combat zone tax benefits.

A qualified hazardous duty area is treated in the same manner as if it were a combat zone for purposes of the following provisions of the Code:

- exclusions from income for combat zone compensation (Code Sec. 112);

- special rule for determining surviving spouse status where the deceased spouse was in missing status as a result of service in a combat zone (Code Sec. 2(a)(3));

- forgiveness of income taxes of members of the military dying in the combat zone or by reason of combat zone incurred wounds (Code Sec. 692);

NEW LAW EXPLAINED

- reduction in estate taxes for members of the military dying in the combat zone or by reason of combat-zone incurred wounds (Code Sec. 2201);

- exemption from income tax withholding for military pay for any month in which an employee is entitled to the exclusion from income (Code Sec. 3401(a)(1));

- exemption from the telephone excise tax for toll telephone service that originates in a combat zone (Code Sec. 4253(d));

- special rule permitting filing of a joint return where a spouse is in missing status as a result of service in a combat zone (Code Sec. 6013(f)(1));

- suspension of time provisions (Code Sec. 7508) (Sec. 11026(a) of the 2017 Tax Cuts Act).

> **Comment:** Although this designation impacts a relatively small number of members of the military (454 troops, as reported by the Multinational Force & Observers website http://mfo.org/en/contingents, visited 12/8/2017), Sen. John Cornyn, R-Texas and Sen. Amy Klobuchar, D-Minn., introduced the measure to provide combat pay and tax benefits in light of the heightened volatility in the area and increased threat to their lives from regional and Islamic State groups (https://homeland.house.gov/press/homeland-security-bipartisan-delegation-examines-spread-islamist-terror-threats-u-s-allies/, visited 12/8/2017).

Members of the military serving in the Sinai Peninsula of Egypt are granted combat zone tax benefits if, as of December 22, 2017, they are entitled to special pay under section 310 of Title 37 of the United States Code (Sec. 11026(b) of the 2017 Tax Cuts Act). Combat zone tax benefits begin June 9, 2015, and apply to every subsequent tax year through December 31, 2025 (Sec. 11026(c) of the 2017 Tax Cuts Act). The Sinai Peninsula of Egypt is considered a qualified hazardous duty zone for the same period (Sec. 11026(b) of the 2017 Tax Cuts Act).

The exemption from income tax withholding under Code Sec. 3401(a)(1) for members of the military serving in the Sinai Peninsula of Egypt is applicable from December 22, 2017, through December 31, 2025.

▶ **Effective date.** The amendments made by this section generally apply to members of the U.S. Armed Forces serving in Sinai Peninsula of Egypt beginning on June 9, 2015 (Act Sec. 11026(d)(1) of the Tax Cuts and Jobs Act (P.L. 115-97)). The amendment for wage withholding applies to remuneration paid after December 22, 2017, the date of enactment (Act Sec. 11026(d)(2) of the 2017 Tax Cuts Act).

Law source: Law at ¶7010. Committee Report at ¶10,110.

— Act Sec. 11026(a) of the Tax Cuts and Jobs Act (P.L. 115-97), applying Code Secs. 2(a)(3), 112, 692, 2201, 3401(a)(1), 4253(d), 6013(f)(10), and 7508;

— Act Sec. 11026(b), designating qualified hazardous duty area;

— Act Sec. 11026(c), determining applicable periods;

— Act Sec. 11026(d), providing the effective date.

¶140 Individual Health Insurance Mandate under the Affordable Care Act

SUMMARY OF NEW LAW

Effective for months beginning after December 31, 2018, the amount owed by any taxpayer under the individual health insurance mandate "shared responsibility payment" for lack of minimum essential health insurance for themselves and their dependents is zero.

BACKGROUND

Beginning in 2014, a penalty was imposed on applicable individuals for each month they failed to maintain "minimum essential coverage" for themselves and their dependents (Code Sec. 5000A). This penalty is also referred to as a "shared responsibility payment," and the requirement to maintain minimum essential coverage is known as the "individual mandate."

The monthly penalty amount for a taxpayer is equal to $1/12$ of the greater of:

- a flat dollar amount equal to the applicable dollar amount for each of the individuals who were not properly insured by the taxpayer, up to a maximum of 300 percent of the applicable dollar amount, or

- an applicable percentage of income (Code Sec. 5000A(c)(2)).

The flat dollar amount is the sum of the applicable dollar amounts for each individual lacking minimum essential coverage that the taxpayer is required to insure (Code Sec. 5000A(c)(2)(A)). The applicable dollar amount is: $95 for 2014, $325 for 2015, $695 for 2016, $695 for 2017, and $695, adjusted for inflation in later years (Code Sec. 5000A(c)(3); Rev. Proc. 2016-55). Due to the 300 percent limitation, the maximum penalty for purposes of the flat dollar amount is: $285 in 2014, $975 in 2015, and $2,085 in 2016 and 2017.

The applicable percentage of income is an amount equal to a percentage of the excess of the taxpayer's household income over the taxpayer's filing threshold for the tax year. The percentages are: one percent for tax years beginning in 2014, two percent for tax years beginning in 2015, and 2.5 percent for tax years beginning after 2015 (Code Sec. 5000A(c)(2)(B)). For purposes of this calculation, household income has the same meaning as used in determining the filing threshold exemption from the penalty (Code Sec. 5000A(c)(4)(B)).

NEW LAW EXPLAINED

The amount of the penalty imposed on individuals without health insurance is zero.—For months beginning after December 31, 2018, the amount a taxpayer would otherwise owe for each month they fail to have "minimum essential coverage" for themselves and their dependents is zero (Code Sec. 5000A(c), as amended by the Tax

NEW LAW EXPLAINED

Cuts and Jobs Act (P.L. 115-97)). No other Affordable Care Act tax or provision is affected.

> **Compliance Tip:** Individuals with coverage during the year should receive a reporting form. Marketplace Exchanges are to provide Form 1095-A, Health Insurance Marketplace Statement, if the Marketplace provided coverage. An individual with employer or other health coverage ought to receive Form 1095-B, Health Coverage (indicating coverage provided), or Form 1095-C, Employer-Provided Health Insurance Offer and Coverage (indicating coverage offered or not offered, and coverage provided). These forms can be useful in applying the shared responsibility rules primarily by showing which months (if any) the individual maintained coverage during the year. Presumably, Exchanges will continue to issue Form 1095-A after 2018 since these are necessary for premium tax credit purposes.

> **Comment:** Though the tax imposed under Code Sec. 5000A is zeroed out, Code Sec. 5000A(f) and Reg. § 1.5000A-2 will still be relevant because they outline the key concept of minimum essential coverage (MEC). Employers that do not offer their employees MEC under an eligible employer sponsored plan may still be liable for large employer shared responsibility payments (Code Sec. 4980H). Individuals who are eligible for MEC for any month do not qualify for the premium tax credit for that month (Code Sec. 36B(c)(2)). Reimbursements under a qualified small employer health reimbursement arrangement are included in an employee's income unless the employee had MEC (Code Sec. 9831(d)(4)(B)(iii)).

▶ **Effective date.** The amendments made by this section apply to months beginning after December 31, 2018 (Act Sec. 11081(b) of the Tax Cuts and Jobs Act (P.L. 115-97)).

Law source: Law at ¶6135. Committee Report at ¶10,290.

— Act Sec. 11081(a) of the Tax Cuts and Jobs Act (P.L. 115-97), amending Code Sec. 5000A(c);

— Act Sec. 11081(b), providing the effective date.

¶145 Capital Gains Reinvested in Qualified Opportunity Zones

SUMMARY OF NEW LAW

A population census tract that is a low-income community may be designated as a qualified opportunity zone by a State. A taxpayer may elect to exclude from gross income, gain on the sale or exchange of any property to an unrelated party in the tax year of the sale or exchange if the gain is reinvested in a qualified opportunity zone within 180 days of the sale or exchange. The deferred gain is recognized on the earlier of the date on which the qualified opportunity zone investment is disposed of or December 31, 2026.

BACKGROUND

Temporary tax incentives have been used for many years to encourage economic growth and development in low-income communities and disaster areas. Empowerment and enterprise zones (Code Secs. 1391—1397F), renewal communities (Code Secs. 1400E—14000U-3), and new markets tax credit (Code Sec. 45D), for example, were created to benefit economically disadvantaged areas. The Gulf Opportunity Zone (Code Sec. 1400N) and New York Liberty Zone (Code Sec. 1400L) were created to provide incentives to revive areas devastated by disasters. Tax incentives could include increased depreciation and expense allowances, increased credit limits, treatment of certain losses as net operating losses, and special rules for tax exempt bonds.

Taxpayers may qualify for the new markets tax credit for equity investments made in low-income communities through a qualified community development entity (CDE) (Code Sec. 45D). The equity investment must be made within five years after the CDE receives an allocation of the national credit limitation amount for the calendar year ($3.5 billion for each of the calendar years through 2019). The credit is equal to five percent of the equity investment for the first three allowance dates and six percent of the equity investment for the next four allowance dates. The total credit available is equal to 39 percent of the investment over seven years. Active involvement of the low-income communities is required with strict penalties if the investment is terminated before seven years. The allocation of credit amounts and CDE certification is the responsibility of the Department of Treasury's Community Development Financial Institutions Fund (CDFI).

Low-income communities, as defined for purposes of the new markets tax credit, are population census tracts that have a poverty rate of at least 20 percent, or

- if outside a metropolitan area, have a median family income of 80 percent or less of the statewide median family income, or

- if within a metropolitan area, have a median family income of 80 percent or less of the greater of statewide median family income or the metropolitan area median family income (Code Sec. 45D(e)(1)), or

- if within a high migration rural county, have a median family income of 85 percent or less of the statewide median family income (Code Sec. 45D(e)(5)(a)).

Certain census tracts with low populations, less than 2,000, that are located within a designated empowerment zone can be treated as a low-income community. The tract must be contiguous to one or more low-income communities that do not qualify as low income through the low-population provision (Code Sec. 45D(e)(4)).

The IRS may designate "targeted populations" that qualify as low-income communities, and provide rules to determine which entities are qualified active low-income community businesses with respect to such populations (Code Sec. 45D(e)(2)). A targeted population is defined as: individuals or an identifiable group of individuals who (1) are "low-income persons" or (2) otherwise lack adequate access to loans or equity investments (Reg. § 1.45D-1(d)(9); Notice 2006-60). A targeted population is not required to be within a single census tract.

> **Comment:** As of the end of 2016, the new markets tax credit generated $8 of private investment for every $1 of federal funding, created 178 million square

BACKGROUND

feet of manufacturing, office and retail space and financed over 5,400 businesses (New Markets Tax Credit Program Fact Sheet, https://www.cdfifund.gov/Documents/NMTC%20Fact%20Sheet_Mar2017.pdf).

NEW LAW EXPLAINED

Qualified opportunity zones created.—A population census tract that is a low-income community, as defined for purposes of the new markets tax credit under Code Sec. 45D may be designated as a qualified opportunity zone (Code Sec. 1400Z-1(a) and (c)(1), as added by the Tax Cuts and Jobs Act (P.L. 115-97)). The chief executive officer of a state may nominate a low-income community for this designation by notifying the Secretary of Treasury in writing by March 22, 2018 (i.e., the end of the determination period). The Secretary must certify the nomination within 30 days of receiving the nomination (i.e., the consideration period) (Code Sec. 1400Z-1(b)(1), as added by the 2017 Tax Cuts Act). The chief executive officer may request a 30-day extension of either the determination period or the consideration period, or both (Code Sec. 1400Z-1(b)(2), as added by the 2017 Tax Cuts Act). For purposes of this provision, a "state" includes any U.S. possession and a "chief executive officer" generally refers to a state's governor, but also includes the mayor of the District of Columbia (Code Sec. 1400Z-1(c)(3), as added by the 2017 Tax Cuts Act; Conference Report on H.R. 1, Tax Cuts and Jobs Act (H. Rept. 115-466)).

Number of designations. The number of population census tracts designated as qualified opportunity zones in a state may not exceed 25 percent of the low-income communities in that state (Code Sec. 1400Z-1(d)(1), as added by the 2017 Tax Cuts Act). However, if there are less than 100 low-income communities in a state, 25 population census tracts may be designated (Code Sec. 1400Z-1(d)(2), as added by the 2017 Tax Cuts Act).

Contiguous tract designation. A population census tract that is not a low-income community may still be designated as qualified opportunity zones if the tract is contiguous to a low-income community that is designated as a qualified opportunity zone and the median family income of the tract does not exceed 125 percent of the contiguous qualified opportunity zone (Code Sec. 1400Z-1(e), as added by the 2017 Tax Cuts Act). This contiguous tract designation is limited to no more than five percent of the qualified opportunity zones in the state (Code Sec. 1400Z-1(e)(2), as added by the 2017 Tax Cuts Act).

Period of designation. The designation as a qualified opportunity zone remains in effect through the end of the 10th calendar year beginning on or after the date of designation (Code Sec. 1400Z-1(f), as added by the 2017 Tax Cuts Act).

Exclusion of gain reinvested in qualified opportunity fund. A taxpayer may elect to exclude from gross income gain on the sale or exchange of any property to an unrelated party in the tax year of the sale or exchange if the gain is reinvested in a qualified opportunity zone within 180 days of the sale or exchange (Code Sec. 1400Z-2(a)(1)(A), as added by the 2017 Tax Cuts Act). The amount of gain that can be excluded is equal to the amount of gain invested in the qualified opportunity fund (Code Sec.

NEW LAW EXPLAINED

1400Z-2(a)(1)(B), as added by the 2017 Tax Cuts Act). Only one election may be made with respect to a sale or exchange (Code Sec. 1400Z-2(a)(2), as added by the 2017 Tax Cuts Act).

> **Caution:** No election may be made for any sale or exchange after December 31, 2026.

Deferral of gain. The election allows the taxpayer to defer including the gain in the taxpayer's gross income until the tax year in which:

- the investment is sold or exchanged, or
- December 31, 2026, whichever is earlier (Code Sec. 1400Z-2(b)(1), as added by the 2017 Tax Cuts Act).

If deferred gain is recognized on December 31, 2026, before the fund investment is sold, the recognized gain increases the basis in the fund for purposes of determining any gain that will be recognized on a subsequent sale (Code Sec. 1400Z-2(b)(2)(B)(ii), as added by the 2017 Tax Cuts Act).

> **Caution:** The reference in Code Sec. 1400Z-2(b)(2)(B)(ii) to increasing basis by the gain recognized by reason of Code Sec. 1400Z-2(a)(1)(B) was apparently intended to be to Code Sec. 1400Z-2(b)(1)(B), relating to the mandatory December 31, 2026, recognition date.

The amount of gain the taxpayer must include is the excess of:

- the amount of gain excluded or the fair market value of the property on the date of the sale or exchange, whichever is less, over
- the taxpayer's basis in the investment (Code Sec. 1400Z-2(b)(2)(A), as added by the 2017 Tax Cuts Act).

Determination of basis. For purposes of determining the amount of deferred gain that is recognized, the taxpayer's basis in the investment is treated as zero (Code Sec. 1400Z-2(b)(2)(B)(i), as added by the 2017 Tax Cuts Act). However, the longer the taxpayer holds the investment, the more his or her basis in the investment is increased. If an investment is held:

- for at least five years, the zero basis is increased by 10 percent of the gain originally deferred (Code Sec. 1400Z-2(b)(2)(B)(iii), as added by the 2017 Tax Cuts Act), and
- for at least seven years, basis is increased by five percent of the gain originally deferred, in addition to the amount of basis increase for investments held for at least 5 years (Code Sec. 1400Z-2(b)(2)(B)(iv), as added by the 2017 Tax Cuts Act).

> **Comment:** If the qualified opportunity fund is sold before five years, the basis is $0 for purpose of determining the recognized deferred gain and the entire deferred gain is recognized. If the fund is held at least five years but less than seven years, the $0 dollar basis is increased by 10 percent of the deferred gain and 90 percent of the deferred gain is recognized if the fund is sold. If the fund is held at least seven years but less than 10 years before it is sold the $0 basis is increased by 15 percent of the investment and 85 percent of the deferred gain is recognized. The deferred gain will be recognized as income on December 31, 2026, if the fund has not been sold by that date, determined by increasing the $0

NEW LAW EXPLAINED

basis by five percent if the fund was held at least five years but less than seven years and by 15 percent if the fund was held at least seven years.

If the value of the fund investment has decreased on the date it is sold or, if earlier, on the mandatory December 31, 2026, recognition date, a taxpayer determines the amount of deferred gain that is recognized by reference to the fair market value on the date of sale or the earlier December 31, 2026, recognition date (Code Sec. 1400Z-2(b)(2)(A), as added by the 2017 Tax Cuts Act). For this purpose, basis is also considered $0 and is increased as described above if the fund investment as been held at least five years.

Finally, if the investment in the qualified opportunity fund is held for at least 10 years, a taxpayer may elect to treat the basis on the date of sale as the fair market value of the qualified opportunity fund on the date of its sale or exchange (Code Sec. 1400Z-2(c), as added by the Tax Cuts Act). Consequently, if the value of the fund has increased beyond the initial amount of invested deferred gain and the election is made, gain on the appreciation in the fund is not recognized.

Example: On January 2, 2018, ABC Corp. sells property to an unrelated party and has a resulting gain of $1 million, which ABC Corp then reinvests in InvestFund, a qualified opportunity fund, on March 30, 2018. ABC Corp sells its investment in InvestFund on April 2, 2021, for $1.5 million. Since ABC Corp held its investment in InvestFund for under five years, its basis in the investment is $0. In its 2021 tax year, ABC Corp must recognize the deferred gain of $1 million as well as the $500,000 in appreciation.

Example: Assume same facts as Example above, except that ABC Corp sells the investment in 2025. Since the investment is held for more than seven years, ABC Corp's basis increases from $0 to $150,000, thus reducing the amount of deferred gain it must include to $850,000 ($1,000,000 – $150,000). The additional $500,000 in appreciation must also be recognized.

10% of deferred gain—	$100,000
5% of deferred gain—	$50,000
	$150,000

At the election of a taxpayer, a taxpayer's basis in an investment held for at least 10 years is equal to the fair market value of the property on the date of sale or exchange (Code Sec. 1400Z-2(c), as added by the 2017 Tax Cuts Act).

Example: ABC invests $1 million of deferred gain in a qualified opportunity fund on January 1, 2025. On December 31, 2026, ABC must recognize the entire $1 million deferred gain ($1 million deferred gain less $0 basis) even though the investment in the fund has not been sold. The $0 basis in the investment is not

---

NEW LAW EXPLAINED

increased because ABC has not owned the fund for at least five years. On January 1, 2037, ABC sells its interest in the fund for $1.5 million. Since ABC has held the investment for 10 or more years, it may elect to treat the basis as $1.5 million and no additional gain is recognized. If ABC does not make the election, its basis is considered to be $1 million (under the provision deferred gain that was previously recognized on December 31, 2026, increases basis) and $500,000 gain is recognized.

Example: Assume the same facts as in the Example above except that the value of the fund has decreased to $400,000. ABC will not make the fair market value election, and recognizes a $600,000 loss ($400,000 less $1 million previously recognized gain).

Mixed investment. If a taxpayer pays more for a qualified fund than the gain from a sale or exchange that it wishes to defer under this provision, the investment in the qualified opportunity fund is treated as two separate investments. The deferral rules would only apply to the investment with respect to the gain which is deferred (Code Sec. 1400Z-2(e)(1), as added by the Tax Cuts Act).

> **Comment:** The creation of qualified opportunity zones is intended to spur investment in low-income communities by allowing taxpayers to defer gain from the sale of any asset by reinvesting that gain in a qualified opportunity fund. To encourage long-term investment, taxpayers may exclude appreciation (post-acquisition gain) in the fund if they retain the investment for at least 10 years. The maximum amount of initially deferred gain (i.e., the original investment in the fund) that can totally escape taxation is 15 percent if the fund is held at least seven years.

Qualified opportunity fund. A qualified opportunity fund is a corporation or partnership organized for the purpose of investing in qualified opportunity zone property that holds at least 90 percent of its assets in such property (Code Sec. 1400Z-2(d)(1), as added by the 2017 Tax Cuts Act). The determination of the 90-percent requirement is the average of the percentage of qualified zone property held by the fund on the last day of the first six-month period of the fund's tax year and on the last day of the fund's tax year.

Qualified opportunity zone property is:

- qualified opportunity zone stock,
- qualified opportunity zone partnership interest, or
- qualified opportunity zone business property (Code Sec. 1400Z-2(d)(2), as added by the 2017 Tax Cuts Act).

Qualified opportunity zone stock is original issue stock in a domestic corporation acquired after December 31, 2017, solely in exchange for cash (Code Sec. 1400Z-2(d)(2)(B), as added by the 2017 Tax Cuts Act). The corporation must be a qualified opportunity zone business at the time of issue (or was being organized as

¶145

NEW LAW EXPLAINED

such if a new corporation) and for substantially all the fund's holding period. The qualified small business stock redemption rules of Code Sec. 1202(c)(3) apply to qualified opportunity zone stock (Code Sec. 1400Z-2(d)(2)(B)(ii), as added by the 2017 Tax Cuts Act).

A qualified opportunity zone partnership interest is any capital or profits interest in a domestic partnership acquired after December 31, 2017, from the partnership solely in exchange for cash (Code Sec. 1400Z-2(d)(2)(C), as added by the 2017 Tax Cuts Act). The partnership must be a qualified opportunity zone business at the time of acquisition (or was being organized as such if a new partnership) and for substantially all of the fund's holding period.

Qualified opportunity zone business property is tangible property used in a trade or business of the qualified opportunity fund, if:

- purchased, as defined in Code Sec. 179(d)(2), by the qualified opportunity fund after December 31, 2017,

- originally used or substantially improved by the qualified opportunity find, and

- used in a qualified opportunity zone during substantially all of the qualified opportunity fund's holding period (Code Sec. 1400Z-2(d)(2)(D)(i), as added by the 2017 Tax Cuts Act).

The related party rules of Code Sec. 179(d)(8) apply (Code Sec. 1400Z-2(d)(2)(D)(iii), as added by the 2017 Tax Cuts Act).

> **Caution:** The reference in Code Sec. 1400Z-2(d)(2)(D)(iii) to the related party rules applying to qualified opportunity zone stock Code Sec. 1400Z-2(d)(2)(A)(i) was apparently intended to be to Code Sec. 1400Z-2(d)(2)(D)(i)(I), relating to the definition of purchase for the purposes of qualified opportunity zone business property.

Property is considered to be substantially improved if, during the 30-month period beginning after the date of acquisition, additions to basis with respect to the property in the hands of the qualified opportunity fund exceed its adjusted basis at the beginning of the 30-month period (Code Sec. 1400Z-2(d)(2)(D)(ii), as added by the 2017 Tax Cuts Act).

> **Caution:** The reference in Code Sec. 1400Z-2(d)(2)(D)(ii) to determining substantial improvement for purposes of a qualified opportunity zone partnership interest Code Sec. 1400Z-2(d)(2)(A)(ii) was apparently intended to be to Code Sec. 1400Z-2(d)(2)(D)(i)(II), relating to substantial improvement of the qualified opportunity zone business property by the qualified opportunity fund.

A qualified opportunity zone business is a trade or business in which substantially all of the tangible property owned or leased by the taxpayer is qualified opportunity zone business property (Code Sec. 1400Z-2(d)(3)(A), as added by the Tax Cuts and Jobs Act of 2017). For this purpose, qualified opportunity zone business property is determined in the same manner as under Code Sec. 1400Z-2(d)(2)(D), except that the term "qualified opportunity business" is substituted for "qualified opportunity fund." The business must also satisfy the requirements as an enterprise zone business under Code Sec. 1397C(b)(2), (4) and (8), but not as a qualified redevelopment bond

NEW LAW EXPLAINED

under Code Sec. 144(c)(6)(B) (Code Sec. 1400Z-2(d)(3)(A)(ii) and (iii), as added by the 2017 Tax Cuts Act).

If tangible property ceases to be qualified opportunity zone business property, it will continue to be treated as such for the lesser of (a) five years after the date it ceases to be qualified opportunity zone business property or (b) the date it is no longer held by a qualified opportunity zone business (Code Sec. 1400Z-2(d)(3)(B), as added by the 2017 Tax Cuts Act).

Failure to maintain 90-percent Investment Standard. A qualified opportunity fund must pay a penalty for each month it fails to hold at least 90 percent of its assets in qualified opportunity zone property (Code Sec. 1400Z-2(f)(1), as added by the 2017 Tax Cuts Act), unless the failure is due to reasonable cause (Code Sec. 1400Z-2(f)(3), as added by the 2017 Tax Cuts Act). The amount of the penalty is the:

- excess of 90 percent of its aggregated assets over the aggregate amount of qualified opportunity property held,
- multiplied by the underpayment rate under Code Sec. 6621(a)(2) for that month.

A qualified opportunity fund that is organized as a partnership must proportionally take the penalty into account as part of each partners' distributive share (Code Sec. 1400Z-2(f)(2), as added by the 2017 Tax Cuts Act).

> **Example:** Ninety percent of all assets of BuildFund Partnership, a qualified opportunity zone fund, is qualified opportunity property. The assets cease to be qualified opportunity property as of May 15, 2020. BuildFund must pay a penalty for each month that more than 10 percent of the total amount of its assets are not qualified opportunity fund property. For example, assume BuildFund had total assets worth $1 million, 80 percent of which were qualified opportunity property for a six-month period before once again meeting the 90 percent threshold. Assuming an underpayment penalty for those months of 4 percent, BuildFund must pay a penalty of $4,000 ($900,000 − $800,000 x 4 percent) each month for 6 months.

Applicable rules. For purposes of Code Sec. 1400Z-2, persons are treated as related if they meet the definition under Code Sec. 267(b) or Code Sec. 707(b)(1), except that direct or indirect ownership limitation in the outstanding stock of the corporation or capital interest or profit interest in the partnership is "20 percent" rather than "50 percent" (Code Sec. 1400Z-2(e)(2), as added by the 2017 Tax Cuts Act).

If the taxpayer is a decedent and the inclusion of the deferred gain is not properly included in his or her gross income, the amount is to be included in the gross income of the estate under Code Sec. 691 (Code Sec. 1400Z-2(e)(3), as added by the 2017 Tax Cuts Act).

The IRS is authorized to issue regulations to carry out the purposes of Code Sec. 1400Z-2, including rules:

NEW LAW EXPLAINED

- for certification of qualified opportunity funds,
- to ensure qualified opportunity funds have reasonable time to reinvest the return of capital from investments in qualified opportunity zone stock and qualified opportunity zone partnership interests, and reinvest proceeds from the disposition of qualified opportunity zone property, and
- to prevent abuse (Code Sec. 1400Z-2(e)(4), as added by the 2017 Tax Cuts Act).

    Comment: The certification process for a qualified opportunity fund will be done by the Community Development Financial Institutions Fund (CDFI Fund) in a similar manner to the process in place for allocating the new markets tax credit (Conference Report on H.R. 1, Tax Cuts and Jobs Act (H. Rept. 115-466)).

    Comment: Beginning December 22, 2022, the IRS, or its delegate, must submit an annual report to Congress on the opportunity zone incentives. The report is to include: (a) an assessment of investments held by the qualified opportunity fund at both the national and state levels; (b) the number of qualified opportunity funds; (c) the amount of assets held by class; (d) the percentage of qualified opportunity zone census tracts designated that received qualified opportunity fund investments; and (e) an assessment of impact of the investments on economic indicators such as job creation, poverty reduction and new businesses (Conference Report on H.R. 1, Tax Cuts and Jobs Act (H. Rept. 115-466)).

▶ **Effective date.** The amendments made by this section apply on December 22, 2017, the date of enactment (Act Sec. 13823(d) of the Tax Cuts and Jobs Act (P.L. 115-97)).

Law source: Law at ¶6040 and ¶6045. Committee Report at ¶10,990.

— Act Sec. 13823(a) and (c) of the Tax Cuts and Jobs Act (P.L. 115-97), adding Code Secs. 1400Z-1 and 1400Z-2;

— Act Sec. 13823(b), adding Code Sec. 1016(a)(38);

— Act Sec. 13823(d), providing the effective date.

Deductions, Exclusions, and Credits for Individuals

2

STANDARD DEDUCTION AND PERSONAL EXEMPTIONS

ITEMIZED DEDUCTIONS

ADJUSTMENTS TO GROSS INCOME

EXCLUSION FROM GROSS INCOME

PERSONAL TAX CREDITS

STANDARD DEDUCTION AND PERSONAL EXEMPTIONS

¶205 Standard Deduction for Individuals

SUMMARY OF NEW LAW

The basic standard deduction amounts for individuals are temporarily increased for tax years 2018 through 2025. The standard deductions amounts for 2018 are: $24,000 for married individuals filing jointly (including surviving spouses), $18,000 for heads of household, and $12,000 for single individuals and married individuals filing separately. The increased amounts are adjusted annually for inflation for tax years beginning after 2018 and before 2026.

BACKGROUND

An individual taxpayer who does not elect to itemize deductions computes taxable income by subtracting from adjusted gross income (AGI) the standard deduction, as well as the deduction for personal exemptions. Taxpayers have a choice of itemizing deductions or claiming the standard deduction, whichever will result in a higher deduction. The standard deduction amount is the sum of the basic standard deduction, plus an additional standard deduction amounts for aged (at least 65) and/or blind taxpayers, if applicable (Code Sec. 63(c)).

The basic standard deduction amount varies according to the taxpayer's filing status and is adjusted annually for inflation. For 2018, the amount of the basic standard deduction is $13,000 for married individuals filing joint returns and surviving spouses, $6,500 for single individuals and married individuals filing separate returns, and $9,550 for heads of households (Rev. Proc. 2017-58). In the case of a dependent for whom a deduction for a personal exemption is allowed to another taxpayer, the standard deduction for 2018 may not exceed the greater of $1,050 or the sum of $350 plus the individual's earned income, up to the applicable standard deduction amount for single taxpayers ($6,500 for 2018).

The additional standard deduction amounts for 2018 for the aged and/or blind is $1,300 for married individuals, whether filing jointly or separately, and surviving spouses, and $1,600 for unmarried individuals, whether filing as single or as head of household. (Code Sec. 63(f); Rev. Proc. 2017-58). The additional standard deduction amount are also adjusted annually for inflation.

NEW LAW EXPLAINED

Basic standard deduction temporarily increased.—Effective for tax years beginning after December 31, 2017, and before January 1, 2026, the basic standard deduction amounts are increased to:

- $24,000 for married individuals filing jointly (including surviving spouses);
- $18,000 for heads of household;

NEW LAW EXPLAINED

- $12,000 for single individuals and married individuals filing separately (Code Sec. 63(c)(7)(A), as added by the Tax Cuts and Jobs Act (P.L. 115-97)).

These dollar amounts are adjusted annually for inflation for tax years beginning after 2018 and before 2026 using the Chained Consumer Price Index for All Urban Consumers (C-CPI-U) in the cost-of-living adjustment (see ¶ 125) (Code Sec. 63(c)(7)(B), as added by the 2017 Tax Cuts Act). The standard deduction amount for a dependent, as well as the additional standard deduction amounts for the aged and/or blind, not affected by the law and are not temporarily increased.

> **Comment:** The standard deduction amount for a dependent, as well as the additional standard deduction amounts for the aged and/or blind are adjusted for inflation. However, these amounts are adjusted for inflation after 2017 using chained chained-CPI rather than averaged CPI (Code Sec. 63(c)(4), as amended by the 2017 Tax Cuts Act). As a result, the IRS may issue revised inflation adjustments for 2018 for the standard deduction for a dependent, as well as the standard deduction amounts for the aged and/or blind.

> **Practical Analysis:** William D. Elliott, Partner at Elliott, Thomason & Gibson, LLP in Dallas, Texas, comments that the standard deduction is increased materially to $24,000 for married individuals filing a joint return, $18,000 for head of-household filers and $12,000 for all other individuals effective for 2018. The standard deduction is indexed for inflation using the C-CPI-U tables, starting in 2019.

Net disaster losses. An individual may claim an additional standard deduction amount for his or her net disaster loss in tax years beginning in 2016 and 2017 (Act Sec. 11028(c) of the 2017 Tax Cuts Act). The additional standard deduction is also allowed in computing alternative minimum tax liability (AMT). For this purpose, a net disaster loss is the qualified disaster-related personal casualty losses, over any personal casualty gains. A qualified disaster-related personal loss means a personal casualty loss arising in a disaster area after on or after January 1, 2016, that is attributable to a federally declared disaster. See also ¶ 235 for a discussion of additional relief for claiming casualty loss deductions related to net disaster losses in 2016 and 2017.

▶ **Effective date.** The amendment made by this section applies to tax years beginning after December 31, 2017 (Act Sec. 11021(b) of the Tax Cuts and Jobs Act (P.L. 115-97)). The special rules related to personal casualty losses related to net disaster losses for 2016 and 2017 are effective on December 22, 2017, the date of enactment.

Law source: Law at ¶5170 and ¶7015. Committee Report at ¶10,050.

— Act Sec. 11021(a) of the Tax Cuts and Jobs Act (P.L. 115-97), adding Code Sec. 63(c)(7);

— Act Sec. 11028(a) and (c);

— Act Sec. 11021(b), providing the effective date.

¶210 Personal and Dependency Exemptions

SUMMARY OF NEW LAW

The deduction for personal and dependency exemptions is temporarily repealed for tax years 2018 through 2025.

BACKGROUND

An individual, in determining taxable income, may reduce adjusted gross income (AGI) by claiming a personal exemption deduction and an exemption deduction for each person he or she claims as a dependent on his or her tax return (Code Sec. 151). A dependent is defined as an individual that is a qualifying child or qualifying relative of the taxpayer for the year (Code Secs. 151(c) and 152; Prop. Reg. § 1.152-1(a)). However, anyone claimed as a dependent by another taxpayer is barred from claiming another individual as a dependent. Thus, a married individual cannot be claimed as a dependent if he or she files a joint return with his or her spouse for the same tax year, unless the return was solely filed as a claim for refund of estimated or withheld taxes.

The amount of a personal exemption (for the taxpayer and spouse) and of a dependency exemption (for each of the taxpayer's dependents) is adjusted annually for inflation. The exemption amount is $4,150 for 2018 (Code Sec. 151(d); Rev. Proc. 2017-58). An individual whose AGI exceeds an applicable threshold amount based on filing status must reduce the amount of their otherwise allowable exemption deduction (Code Sec. 151(d)(3)). The applicable threshold amounts for 2018 are: $320,000 for married individuals filing a joint return and surviving spouses; $293,350 for heads of households; $266,700 for single individuals and $160,000 for married individuals filing a separate return.

Estates and trusts. In lieu of the deduction for personal exemptions, an estate is allowed a deduction of $600, and a trust is generally allowed a deduction of either $100 or, if required to distribute all its income currently, $300 (Code Sec. 642(b)(1) and (2)). An amount equal to the personal exemption of an individual is allowed in the case of a qualified disability trust (Code Sec. 642(b)(2)(C)).

Withholding requirements. The amount of tax required to be withheld by an employer from an employee's wages is partly based on the number of withholding exemptions or allowance the employee claims on his or her Form W-4. The amount of each withholding exemption is equal to the amount of one personal exemption prorated to the payroll period. An employee is entitled to the following withholding exemptions: (1) an exemption for the individual, unless he or she is allowed to be claimed as a dependent by another person; (2) an exemption to which the employee's spouse would be entitled, unless that spouse files a Form W-4 for that tax year claiming an exemption for his or her self; (3) an exemption for each dependent, so long as the employee's spouse does not also claim a withholding exemption for the same dependent on a Form W-4; (4) additional withholding allowances (taking into account estimated itemized deductions, estimated tax credits, and any additional

BACKGROUND

deductions provided by the IRS); and (5) a standard deduction allowance (Code Sec. 3402(f)).

Levies. An exemption from an IRS levy is provided for the amount of an individual's wages or salary for personal services that is equal to the sum of the standard deduction and the total value of the personal exemptions allowed to the individual, divided by the number of times the taxpayer is paid, except for the first 15 percent (Code Sec. 6334(d)).

NEW LAW EXPLAINED

Temporary repeal of the personal and dependency exemption deduction.—The deduction for personal and dependency exemptions by an individual taxpayer is temporarily repealed for tax years beginning after December 31, 2017, and before January 1, 2026 (Code Sec. 151(d)(5), as added by the Tax Cuts and Jobs Act (P.L. 115-97)).

> **Comment:** The rules for determining the filing threshold for an individual to file a federal income tax return are modified for tax years beginning in 2018 through 2025 as a result of the temporary repeal of the personal exemption deduction and the increase in the standard deduction (see ¶ 205). See ¶ 120 for discussion of filing thresholds for tax years beginning after 2017.

Qualified disability trusts. The annual amount a qualified disability trust is allowed to deduct for tax years beginning after December 31, 2017, and before January 1, 2026, is modified (Code Sec. 642(b)(2)(C)(iii), as added by the 2017 Tax Cuts Act). For those tax years, when the personal exemption is repealed and effectively zero, the annual deduction is $4,150, indexed for inflation after 2018.

Withholding requirements. The deduction for personal exemptions, as applied for withholding purposes, is temporarily repealed for tax years beginning after December 31, 2017, and before January 1, 2026 (Code Sec. 3402(a)(2), as amended by the 2017 Tax Cuts Act; Act Sec. 11041(f)(2) of the 2017 Tax Cuts Act). The IRS is authorized to administer the withholding rules under Code Sec. 3402 for tax years beginning before January 1, 2019, without regard to the repeal of the personal exemptions (now referred to as "allowances"). In other words, at the IRS's discretion, wage withholding rules might remain the same as under present law for 2018. The 2018 annual personal exemption amount, under prior law, was scheduled to increase to $4,150, and the IRS has stated that it will issue withholding tables to be implemented by February 2018. The withholding provision will apply to tax years beginning before 2019, and its implementation is authorized pursuant to Code Sec. 3402 (Act Sec. 11041(f)(2) of the 2017 Tax Cuts Act).

Levies. The amount exempted from an IRS levy on an individual's wages or salary for personal services for tax years beginning after December 31, 2017, and before January 1, 2026, is modified (Code Sec. 6334(d)(4), as added by the 2017 Tax Cuts Act). For those years, when the personal exemption is temporarily repealed and effectively zero, the levy exemption is equal to the sum of the standard deduction and the total of $4,150 multiplied by the number of the individual's dependents for the tax year in which the levy occurs, divided by the number of times the taxpayer is

¶210

NEW LAW EXPLAINED

paid, except for the first 15 percent. The $4,150 amount is indexed annually for inflation after 2018 using the Chained Consumer Price Index for All Urban Consumers (C-CPI-U) in the cost-of-living adjustment (see ¶ 125).

Practical Analysis: Vincent O'Brien, President of Vincent J. O'Brien, CPA, PC, and M+O=CPE, Inc, Lynbrook, NY, observes that in the past, higher-income individuals already had the benefit of personal and dependent exemptions reduced or eliminated by the phaseout that applied to such exemptions. In addition, taxpayers who were subject to the alternative minimum tax (AMT) also had some or all of the benefit of these exemptions eliminated. As a result, this new Act Section will generally have no significant effect for such taxpayers. In addition, many taxpayers that used to benefit from exemptions, especially those who claimed exemptions for dependent children, the expanded child credit (see ¶280) should generally offset the loss of this deduction.

Practical Analysis: William D. Elliott, Partner at Elliott, Thomason & Gibson, LLP in Dallas, Texas, notes that the personal exemption is repealed for the years 2018 through 2025. Corresponding relief is provided for tax return filing obligations for those whose gross income does not exceed the applicable standard deduction. As an acknowledgment to the lateness of these amendments to the filing season, the IRS is given discretion to continue with the 2017 wage withholding rules for 2018.

▶ **Effective date.** The amendments made by this section apply to tax years beginning after December 31, 2017 (Act Sec. 11041(f) of the Tax Cuts and Jobs Act (P.L. 115-97)).

Law source: Law at ¶5285, ¶5625, ¶6090, ¶6095, ¶6100, and ¶6230. Committee Report at ¶10,160.

— Act Sec. 11041(a) of the Tax Cuts and Jobs Act (P.L. 115-97), amending Code Sec. 151(d) and adding Code Sec. 151(d)(5);

— Act Sec. 11041(b), adding Code Sec. 642(b)(2)(C)(iii);

— Act Sec. 11041(c), striking Code Sec. 3401(e) and amending Code Sec. 3402(a), (b), (f), (g), (l), (m), (n), and 3405(a);

— Act Sec. 11041(d) adding Code Sec. 6334(d)(4);

— Act Sec. 11041(f), providing the effective dates.

¶210

ITEMIZED DEDUCTIONS

¶215 Deduction of State and Local Taxes by Individuals

SUMMARY OF NEW LAW

The itemized deduction by individuals for state, local, and foreign property taxes, and state and local income taxes and general sales taxes paid or accrued during the tax year is limited for tax years 2018 through 2025. An individual cannot deduct foreign real property taxes, but may still claim an itemized deduction of up to $10,000 ($5,000 for married taxpayer filing a separate return) for state and local property taxes, income taxes, and general sales taxes paid or accrued in the tax year. An individual may also still claim a deduction for state and local real or personal property taxes paid or accrued in carrying on a trade or business or income-producing activity.

BACKGROUND

Taxes paid or accrued by an individual during the tax year that are not directly connected with a trade or business, or with property held for the production of income, may be deducted only as an itemized deduction on Schedule A of Form 1040 for federal income tax purposes. This includes: (1) state, local, and foreign income taxes; (2) state and local sales taxes in lieu of deducting state and local income taxes; (3) state, local, and foreign real property taxes; (4) state and local personal property taxes; and (5) federal and state generation-skipping transfer (GST) taxes imposed on income distributions (Code Sec. 164). A self-employed individual may deduct 50 percent of his or her federal self-employment taxes as an above-the-line deduction in computing adjusted gross income (AGI).

State, local, and foreign taxes directly attributable to a trade or business, or imposed on property held for the production of income are deductible either as ordinary and necessary business expenses or investment expenses. This includes income taxes, property taxes, sales taxes, and employment taxes, but deductions are expressly not allowed for most types of federal taxes, estate and inheritance taxes, and real estate taxes imposed on another taxpayer. Taxes that are otherwise deductible as business or income-producing expenses cannot be deducted but must be capitalized if paid or accrued in connection with the acquisition or disposition of property.

NEW LAW EXPLAINED

Limitation of itemized deduction for certain income, property, and sales taxes.—
The deduction for taxes paid or accrued by an individual during the tax year that are not directly connected with a trade or business, or with property held for the production of income, is limited for tax years beginning after December 31, 2017, and before January

NEW LAW EXPLAINED

1, 2026. Specifically, for tax years 2018 through 2025, an individual may claim an itemized deduction on Schedule A of up to only $10,000 ($5,000 for married taxpayer filing a separate return) for: (1) state and local real property taxes; (2) state and local personal property taxes; and (3) state and local income taxes, as well as state and local sales taxes deducted in lieu of state and local income taxes (Code Sec. 164(b)(6), as added by the Tax Cuts and Jobs Act (P.L. 115-97)).

For purposes of applying the dollar limit above, if an individual prepays before 2018 a state or local income tax imposed for a tax year beginning after 2017, the payment is treated as paid on the last day of the tax year for which the tax is imposed (Code Sec. 164(b)(6), as amended by the 2017 Tax Cuts Act). Thus, an individual cannot claim an itemized deduction in 2017 on a prepayment of income tax for a future tax year in order to avoid the dollar limit for tax years 2018 through 2025 (Conference Report on H.R. 1, Tax Cuts and Jobs Act (H. Rept. 115-466)).

> **Comment:** The prepayment restriction specifically applies to state or local income taxes; it does not refer to state and local property taxes. The IRS has issued guidance that a deduction for the prepayment of state and local real property taxes in 2017 depends on whether the taxes are assessed under state and local law prior to 2018 (IRS News Release IR-2017-210). If the taxes are assessed and prepaid in 2017, then the taxpayer may deduct the prepayments in 2017. On the other hand, prepayments of property taxes in 2017 that are not assessed until 2018, may not be deducted in 2017.

> **Example:** County A assesses property tax on July 1, 2017, for the period July 1, 2017, through June 30, 2018. On July 31, 2017, it sends notices of assessment to residents and bills the tax in two installments due September 30, 2017, and January 31, 2018. If a taxpayer elects to pay the second installment by December 31, 2017, then he or she claim a deduction for the prepayment of the taxes on his or her 2017 return.

> **Example:** County A intends to make the usual assessment of property taxes in July 2018 for the property tax year July 1, 2018, through June 30, 2019. The county will also accept prepayments of property taxes for the 2018-2019 property tax year. A taxpayer that prepays 2018-2019 property taxes in 2017 may not claim a deduction for prepayments on his or her 2017 income tax return because the taxes are not assessed in 2017.

A taxpayer may still claim an itemized deduction for foreign income taxes subject to the $10,000/$5,000 limit. However, no deduction is available for foreign real property taxes for tax years 2018 through 2025 (Code Sec. 164(b)(6), as amended by the 2017 Tax Cuts Act).

> **Comment:** A taxpayer whose adjusted gross income (AGI) exceeds a threshold normally must reduce the amount of itemize deductions claimed on his or her federal income tax return. However, the phaseout for itemized deductions is

¶215

NEW LAW EXPLAINED

temporarily repealed for tax years beginning after 2017 and before 2026 (sees ¶250).

In the case of state and local real property and personal property taxes, a deduction is still allowed with no dollar limit if the taxes are paid or accrued in carrying on a trade or business, or on property held for the production of income. Thus, state and local property taxes may be deducted in computing an individual's Schedule C, Schedule E, or Schedule F of Form 1040. For example, an individual may deduct property taxes if the taxes are imposed on business or income producing assets such as residential rental property.

Caution: A deduction is still allowed for state and local income taxes if the taxpayer are paid or accrued in carrying on a trade or business, or on property held for the production of income. However, as written, the language of Code Sec. 164(b)(6) is that state and local income taxes are subject to the $10,000/$5,000 limit regardless of whether or not they are paid or accrued in a business or for the production of income.

Comment: The deduction for federal and state generation-skipping transfer (GST) taxes imposed on income distributions is not affected. An individual who received a income distribution from a GST trust and paid GST taxes on the distribution may continue to claim an itemized deduction for the taxes.

Practical Analysis: Vincent O'Brien, President of Vincent J. O'Brien, CPA, PC, and M+O=CPE, Inc, Lynbrook, NY, observes that some taxpayers who are residents of high-tax states used to have a portion of the benefit of their deduction for state and local taxes eliminated by the alternative minimum tax (AMT). Nevertheless, the elimination of all but $10,000 of this deduction will typically result in a substantial tax increase for such taxpayers.

Possible benefit for taxes paid in December 2017. To the extent that a taxpayer was able to pay the fourth quarter 2017 installment of estimated income taxes due to a state in December of 2017, the taxpayer might benefit from deducting the payment on the taxpayer's 2017 federal income tax return, since the new limitation becomes effective for the 2018 tax year. Similarly, a taxpayer may also benefit from a payment that occurred in December 2017 for real estate taxes that were assessed and billed in 2017. Such assessments often provide the taxpayer with the option of waiting until 2018 to pay some portion of the tax, but having paid it in December 2017 might provide a benefit. The benefit of any such December 2017 payments may be reduced or eliminated, if a taxpayer is subject to the AMT in 2017, since deductions for these taxes are added back to the taxpayer's income for the purpose of computing the AMT.

Real estate taxes related to a business (or similar) activity. The new itemized deduction limits apply to real estate taxes paid for a taxpayer's home. If the real estate taxes are paid for rental property or property used in a trade or business, those real estate taxes can be separately deducted elsewhere on a taxpayer's income tax return, and they are not counted against the $10,000 limit on state and local taxes.

NEW LAW EXPLAINED

> **Real estate tax related to home office.** A self-employed taxpayer who reports his or her trade or business on Schedule C and who uses a portion of his or her residence as a qualified home office will be able to deduct the share of real estate taxes related to the home office, and this deduction will remain separate from the limitation imposed on Schedule A. However, the home office deduction is subject to limitation, based on the income earned by the taxpayer in the related activity.
>
> The home office deduction for a self-employed individual is reported on Form 8829. To the extent that a trade or business is conducted through a business entity, such as an S corporation, deductions for a qualified home office are generally deducted on the separate tax return for the entity.
>
> **Caution.** A taxpayer who received a home office deduction as part of employee business expenses that used to be deductible as a miscellaneous itemized deduction on Schedule A will no longer be permitted to deduct the home office or any other employee business expenses, beginning in 2018 (see ¶245).

▶ **Effective date.** The amendment made by this section applies to tax years beginning after December 31, 2016 (Act Sec. 11042(b) of the Tax Cuts and Jobs Act (P.L. 115-97)).

Law source: Law at ¶5350. Committee Report at ¶10,170.

— Act Sec. 11042(a) of the Tax Cuts and Jobs Act (P.L. 115-97), adding Code Sec. 164(b)(6);

— Act Sec. 11042(b), providing the effective date.

¶220 Home Mortgage Interest Deduction

SUMMARY OF NEW LAW

The itemized deduction for home mortgage interest is limited for tax years 2018 through 2025. A taxpayer is limited to claiming the home mortgage interest deduction only for interest paid or accrued on acquisition debt during those years; the deduction of interest on home equity debt is suspended. The maximum amount that may be treated as acquisition debt is also reduced to $750,000 ($375,000 if married filing separately) for any acquisition debt incurred after December 15, 2017.

BACKGROUND

Personal interest generally is not deductible. However, interest paid on a home mortgage (i.e., qualified residence interest) may be claimed by an individual as an itemized deduction on Schedule A of Form 1040 (Code Sec. 163(h)(2)(D)). Qualified residence interest is interest that paid or accrued during the tax year on either acquisition indebtedness or home equity indebtedness secured by the taxpayer's qualified residence by a mortgage, deed of trust, or land contract (Code Sec. 163(h)(3) and (4)). A qualified residence for this purpose includes the taxpayer's principal

BACKGROUND

residence and one other residence such as a vacation home that is not rented out at any time during the tax year or that is used by the taxpayer for a minimum number of days. A qualified residence can be a house, condominium, cooperative, mobile home, house trailer, or boat.

Acquisition indebtedness is debt incurred in acquiring, constructing or substantially improving a qualified residence of the taxpayer and which secures the residence. Refinanced debt remains acquisition indebtedness to the extent that it does not exceed the principal amount of acquisition indebtedness immediately before refinancing. The maximum amount treated as acquisition indebtedness is $1 million ($500,000 if married filing separately).

Home equity indebtedness is any debt other than acquisition indebtedness that is secured by a qualified residence. Interest on such debt is deductible even if the proceeds are used for personal expenditures. The aggregate amount of home equity indebtedness may not exceed $100,000 ($50,000 if married filing separately) and may not exceed the fair market value of the qualified residence reduced by the acquisition indebtedness.

Acquisition indebtedness may constitute home equity indebtedness to the extent the debt exceeds the dollar limits for acquisition indebtedness, but subject to the dollar and fair market value limits for home equity indebtedness (Rev. Rul. 2010-25). Thus, an individual can deduct interest paid on up to $1.1 million of such debt ($550,000 if married filing separately) as qualified residence interest. Interest attributable to debt over these limits is nondeductible personal interest.

Qualified principal residence debt. An individual may exclude from gross income a limited amount of qualified principal residence debt discharged before January 1, 2017, or subject to an arrangement that is entered into and evidenced in writing before January 1, 2017 (Code Sec. 108(a)(1)(E) and (h)). The debt generally must be incurred in the acquisition, construction, or substantial improvement of the individual's principle residence and secured by the residence. The exclusion is limited to $2 million ($1 million for married taxpayers filing separately).

NEW LAW EXPLAINED

Deduction for home equity interest suspended and acquisition debt limits reduced for 2018 through 2025.—The itemized deduction for home mortgage interest (i.e., qualified residence interest) is temporarily limited to interest on acquisition debt for tax years beginning after December 31, 2017, and before January 1, 2026 (Code Sec. 163(h)(3)(F)(i)(I), as added by the Tax Cuts and Jobs Act (P.L. 115-97)). A taxpayer may not claim an itemized deduction for mortgage interest paid or accrued on any home equity debt of any qualified residence of the taxpayer for tax years beginning in 2018 through 2025.

> **Comment:** The temporary suspension of the deduction for interest on home equity debt ends after 2025. Thus, a taxpayer may claim the deduction for tax years beginning in 2026.

¶220

NEW LAW EXPLAINED

Limitation on acquisition indebtedness. The maximum amount that may be treated as acquisition debt is also reduced to $750,000 ($375,000 if married filing separately) for tax years beginning after December 31, 2017, and before January 1, 2026 (Code Sec. 163(h)(3)(F)(i)(II), as added by the 2017 Tax Cuts Act). The reduction generally applies to any acquisition debt incurred after December 15, 2017. The maximum amount that may be treated as acquisition debt remains $1 million ($500,000 if married filing separately) for any acquisition debt incurred with respect to the taxpayer's principal residence on or before December 15, 2017 (Code Sec. 163(h)(3)(F)(i)(III), as added by the 2017 Tax Cuts Act). The acquisition debt incurred on or before December 15, 2017, reduces the $750,000/$375,000 limit to any acquisition debt incurred after December 15, 2017.

The $1 million ($500,000 if married filing separately) dollar limit will also continue to apply to a taxpayer who enters a binding written contract before December 15, 2017, to close on the purchase of a principal residence before January 1, 2018, so long as the residence is purchased before April 1, 2018 (Code Sec. 163(h)(3)(F)(i)(IV), as added by the 2017 Tax Cuts Act). Similarly, the higher limit continues to apply to any debt incurred after December 15, 2017, to refinance existing acquisition debt on the taxpayer's principal residence to the extent the amount of the debt resulting from the refinancing does not exceed the amount of the refinanced debt (Code Sec. 163(h)(3)(F)(iii), as added by the 2017 Tax Cuts Act). Thus, the maximum dollar amount that may be treated as acquisition debt on the taxpayer's principal residence will not decrease by reason of a refinancing. The exception for refinancing existing acquisition will not apply after: (1) the expiration of the term of the original debt; or (2) the earlier of the expiration of the first refinancing of the debt or 30 years after the date of the first refinancing.

> **Comment:** A taxpayer whose adjusted gross income (AGI) exceeds a threshold normally must reduce the amount of itemize deductions claimed on his or her federal income tax return. However, the phaseout for itemized deductions is temporarily repealed for tax years beginning after 2017 and before 2026 (sees ¶ 250).

Qualified principal residence debt. The $2 million ($1 million) limit on the exclusion of discharged qualified principal residence debt is not affected by the temporary reduction the limit of acquisition debt for home mortgage interest deduction (Code Sec. 163(h)(3)(F)(iv), as added by the 2017 Tax Cuts Act).

Practical Analysis: Vincent O'Brien, President of Vincent J. O'Brien, CPA, PC, and M+O=CPE, Inc, Lynbrook, NY, observes that the new mortgage deduction rules take on added importance, since the mortgage deduction will become one of the more important itemized deductions for taxpayers, now that many other itemized deductions will be eliminated by the new law.

Deduction for second homes is still in place. Earlier proposals would have eliminated the deduction for mortgage acquisition debt for a second home. The final version of the law preserves the mortgage interest deduction for a second home. Despite the new lower limit on mortgage loan for a newly-acquired home, interest remains

---

NEW LAW EXPLAINED

deductible for loans that are used to buy, build, or substantially improve a taxpayer's principal residence and one other residence of the taxpayer, which is selected for the tax year. If a taxpayer owns more than two residences, the taxpayer must continue to select only one second home each year for the purpose of the mortgage interest deduction.

Mortgage proceeds used for a business (or similar) activity. The new mortgage deduction limits apply if the taxpayer uses mortgage loan proceeds to buy, build or substantially improve the taxpayer's home. If a mortgage is secured by the home of the taxpayer, but the proceeds are used to purchase rental property, property used in a trade or business or investment property, then the interest on such a loan can be separately deducted elsewhere on a taxpayer's income tax return. Such interest is not subject to the new mortgage interest deduction limitation, and such loan balances are not counted against the limit.

For example, if the mortgage proceeds were used to purchase rental property owned in the taxpayer's own name, the interest would be deducted on Schedule E of Form 1040. If, instead, the proceeds were used to purchase trade or business property used in a taxpayer's sole proprietorship, the interest would be deducted on Schedule C of Form 1040. If proceeds are used to purchase investments, the interest would be deductible on Form 4952. To the extent that such an activity is conducted through a separate entity, the interest deduction would be deductible on the tax return for the separate entity for which the loan proceeds were used.

Mortgage interest related to home office. A self-employed taxpayer who reports his or her trade or business on Schedule C of Form 1040, and who uses a portion of his or her residence as a qualified home office will continue to be able to deduct the share of mortgage interest related to the home office, without regard to the mortgage limitation. (Note: The home office deduction is subject to limitation, based on the income earned by the taxpayer in the related activity.)

To the extent that a taxpayer's mortgage balance exceeds the applicable dollar limit on loans ($750,000 for loans for newly-acquired property or $1 million for qualified grandfathered loans), the portion of the mortgage interest that is allocable to the home office is not subject to this dollar limitation and remains deductible in full.

Example. In 2018, a taxpayer's mortgage balance on his or her principal residence is $1.5 million for the entire year, and the taxpayer incurs interest of $75,000. The mortgage is grandfathered and the applicable balance limit on the mortgage loan deduction is $1 million. If the taxpayer has no home office use, the deduction on Schedule A for mortgage interest will be $50,000 ($1 million limit divided by $1.5 million loan balance multiplied by $75,000 of interest incurred), and the remaining $25,000 ($75,000 minus $50,000) represents excess interest, which is nondeductible on Schedule A.

If the same taxpayer uses 10 percent of his or her residence as a qualified home office, $5,000 of the interest that is otherwise deductible on Schedule A is allocable to the home office (computed as $50,000 allowable interest multiplied by 10 percent home office percentage). In addition, the taxpayer is permitted to deduct the portion of the excess mortgage interest that is allocable to the home office. This results in an additional $2,500 of interest being

NEW LAW EXPLAINED

deductible as part of the home office deduction (computed as $25,000 excess interest multiplied by 10 percent).

The home office deduction for a self-employed individual is reported on Form 8829. To the extent that a trade or business is conducted through a business entity, such as an S corporation, deductions for a qualified home office are generally deducted on the separate tax return for the entity.

Caution. A taxpayer who received a home office deduction as part of employee business expenses that used to be deductible as a miscellaneous itemized deduction on Schedule A will no longer be permitted to deduct the home office or any other employee business expenses, beginning in 2018 (see ¶245).

▶ **Effective date.** The amendments made by this section apply to tax years beginning after December 31, 2017 (Act Sec. 11043(b) of the Tax Cuts and Jobs Act (P.L. 115-97)).

Law source: Law at ¶5300. Committee Report at ¶10,180.

— Act Sec. 11043(a) of the Tax Cuts and Jobs Act (P.L. 115-97), adding Code Sec. 163(h)(3)(F);

— Act Sec. 11043(b), providing the effective date.

¶225 Medical Expense Deduction

SUMMARY OF NEW LAW

The adjusted gross income (AGI) threshold to claim itemized deduction for unreimbursed expenses paid for the medical care of the taxpayer or the taxpayer's spouse or dependents is temporarily reduced to 7.5 percent of AGI for tax years 2017 and 2018.

BACKGROUND

An itemized deduction is allowed to an individual on Schedule A of Form 1040 for expenses paid during the tax year for the medical care of the taxpayer, the taxpayer's spouse, or the taxpayer's dependent to the extent that the expenses exceed 10 percent of the taxpayer's adjusted gross income (AGI) (Code Sec. 213). For individuals who attain age 65 before the close of the year, the threshold to claim an itemized deduction for medical expenses is 7.5 percent of AGI for tax years beginning before January 1, 2017. On a joint return, the percentage limitation is based on the total AGI of both spouses.

Expenses paid for medical care include amounts paid for the diagnosis, cure, mitigation, treatment, or prevention of disease, and for treatments affecting any part or function of the body (Code Sec. 213(d)). Only payments for legal medical services

BACKGROUND

rendered by physicians, surgeons, dentists, and other medical practitioners qualify as medical expenses. Amounts paid for equipment, supplies, and diagnostic devices may be deductible if needed for medical care. Medical care expenses must be incurred primarily to alleviate or prevent a physical or mental defect or illness and do not include expenses that are merely beneficial to general health, such as vitamins or a vacation.

Medical expenses also include premiums paid for insurance that covers the expenses of medical care and amounts paid for transportation to get medical care, to the extent that the premiums have not been excluded from taxable income through the employer exclusion or self-insured deduction. Amounts paid for long-term care services and limited amounts paid for qualified long-term care insurance contract are medical expenses. The cost of medicine and drugs is deductible only for medicine and drugs that require a prescription, except for insulin.

NEW LAW EXPLAINED

Medical expense deduction AGI threshold temporarily reduced.—The threshold to claim an itemized deduction for unreimbursed expenses paid for the medical care of the taxpayer or the taxpayer's spouse or dependents is reduced to 7.5 percent of adjusted gross income (AGI) for all taxpayers for tax years beginning after December 31, 2016, and before January 1, 2019 (Code Sec. 213(f) as amended by the Tax Cuts and Jobs Act (P.L. 115-97)). The reduced threshold applies for both regular tax and alternative minimum tax purposes (Code Sec. 56(b)(1)(B) as amended by the Tax Cuts and Jobs Act).

> **Comment:** As a result of this change, the reduced AGI threshold for the medical expense deduction is available for expenses incurred in 2017 and 2018.

> **Comment:** A taxpayer whose AGI exceeds a threshold normally must reduce the amount of itemize deductions claimed on his or her federal income tax return. However, the phaseout for itemized deductions is temporarily repealed for tax years beginning after 2017 and before 2026 (sees ¶250).

▶ **Effective date.** The amendments made by this section applies to tax years beginning after December 31, 2016 (Act Sec. 11027(c) of the Tax Cuts and Jobs Act (P.L. 115-97)).

Law source: Law at ¶5140 and ¶5350. Committee Report at ¶10,120.

— Act Sec. 11027(a) of the Tax Cuts and Jobs Act (P.L. 115-97), amending Code Sec. 213(f);

— Act Sec. 11027(b), amending Code Sec. 56(b)(1)(B);

— Act Sec. 11027(c), providing the effective date.

¶230 Charitable Contribution Deductions

SUMMARY OF NEW LAW

The percentage limitation on the charitable deduction contribution base is increased to 60 percent of an individual's adjusted gross income for cash donations to public charities in 2018 through 2025. The deduction for amounts paid for college athletic seating rights is repealed. The exception to contemporaneous written acknowledgment requirement for contributions of $250 or more is repealed.

BACKGROUND

Taxpayers may deduct certain charitable contributions made during the tax year to charities, governments, and other qualified organizations (Code Sec. 170). Individuals can claim an allowable charitable deduction if they elect to itemize their deductions for the tax year (Code Sec. 63(e)).

An individual's deductible charitable donations for a tax year are limited to a specified percentage of the contribution base, which is the individual's adjusted gross income (AGI) computed without regard to any net operating loss carryback (Code Sec. 170(b)(1)(G)). In general, an individual's deductible donations are limited to—

- 50 percent of the contribution base, for donations of cash or nonappreciated (ordinary income) property to public charities, private foundations other than nonoperating private foundations, and certain governmental units and other organizations (collectively, "50 percent organizations") (Code Sec. 170(b)(1)(A));

- the lesser of (i) 30 percent of the contribution base or (ii) the excess of 50 percent of the contribution base over the amount of contributions subject to the 50-percent limit, for donations of cash or nonappreciated property to nonoperating private foundations or "for the use of" 50 percent organizations (Code Sec. 170(b)(1)(B));

- 30 percent of the contribution base (after taking into account donations other than capital gain property donations), for donations of appreciated capital gain property to 50 percent organizations; an individual may elect to bring all appreciated capital gain property donations for a tax year within the 50-percent limit (Code Sec. 170(b)(1)(C));

- the lesser of (i) 20 percent of the contribution base or (ii) the excess of 30 percent of the contribution base over the amount of contributions subject to the 30-percent limit, for donations of appreciated capital gain property to nonoperating private foundations (Code Sec. 170(b)(1)(D)); and

- 20 percent of the contribution base, for donations of capital gain property "for the use of" 50 percent organizations and nonoperating private foundations (Code Sec. 170(b)(1)(D)).

Donors can generally carry forward for five years their charitable contributions that exceed the deductible limit for the year of the donation (Code Sec. 170(d)).

Charitable donations connected with college athletic events. If a donor receives or expects to receive a substantial benefit in return for a payment to charity, the

BACKGROUND

payment is generally not a deductible charitable contribution (see *American Bar Endowment,* SCt, 86-1 USTC ¶9482). However, the donor may be able to deduct the portion of the donation that is more than the value of the return benefit received (see Rev. Rul. 67-246). A donor who makes a charitable donation to, or for, a college or university and receives back in return the right to purchase tickets to athletic events in the institution's athletic stadium can deduct 80 percent of the payment as a charitable contribution. This special treatment does not apply if the donor receives tickets instead of the *right to purchase* tickets. Any part of the payment that is for the actual cost of tickets is not deductible (Code Sec. 170(l)).

Substantiation for donations of $250 or more. A donor who claims a charitable deduction must maintain reliable written records on the contribution, regardless of its value or amount (Reg. § 1.170A-13). Further, no deduction is allowed for any charitable contribution of $250 or more—for both cash and noncash donations—unless the donor substantiates the donation with a contemporaneous written acknowledgment by the donee organization (Code Sec. 170(f)(8)(A); Reg. § 1.170A-13(f)). A donor is not required to obtain the acknowledgment if the donee files a return with the IRS reporting the information required to be included in a valid acknowledgment (Code Sec. 170(f)(8)(D)). Until final regulations are issued, however, donors must obtain the required substantiation from the donee.

NEW LAW EXPLAINED

Percentage limit for cash charitable contributions by individuals temporarily increased.—The income-based percentage limit is temporarily increased from 50 percent to 60 percent for an individual taxpayer's cash charitable contributions to public charities, private foundations other than nonoperating private foundations, and certain governmental units (i.e., "50 percent organizations"). The 60-percent contribution base limit applies to qualifying cash contributions made in any tax year beginning after December 31, 2017, and before January 1, 2026 (Code Sec. 170(b)(1)(G)(i), as added by the Tax Cuts and Jobs Act (P.L. 115-97)). The individual may carry forward for five years any qualifying cash contributions that exceed the 60-percent ceiling for the tax year of the contribution (Code Sec. 170(b)(1)(G)(ii), as added by the 2017 Tax Cuts Act).

Cash contributions that qualify for the 60-percent limit are not taken into account in determining contributions that are allowed under the 50-percent limit of Code Sec. 170(b)(1)(A) (Code Sec. 170(b)(1)(G)(iii)(I), as added by the 2017 Tax Cuts Act). For each tax year beginning after December 31, 2017, and before January 1, 2026, and for each tax year to which any 60-percent cash contribution is carried over, the aggregate contribution limitation allowed under Code Sec. 170(b)(1)(A) must be reduced (but not below zero) by the total contributions allowed under the 60-percent limit provision. Further, in determining allowable contributions under Code Sec. 170(b)(1)(B) for donations of cash or nonappreciated property to nonoperating private foundations or "for the use of" 50 percent organizations, any references to the 50-percent limit determination under Code Sec. 170(b)(1)(A) must also include the 60-percent limit

¶230

NEW LAW EXPLAINED

determination under Code Sec. 170(b)(1)(G) (Code Sec. 170(b)(1)(G)(iii)(II), as added by the 2017 Tax Cuts Act)

> **Comment:** The 60-percent limit for cash contributions to public charities is intended to "encourage taxpayers to provide essential monetary support to front-line charities," because "a robust charitable sector is vital to our economy" and "charitable giving is critical to ensuring that the sector thrives" (Report of the House Ways and Means Committee on H.R. 1, Tax Cuts and Jobs Act, H. Rept. 115-409, p. 177). However, the Urban-Brookings Tax Policy Center believes that the increased standard deduction amount (see ¶205) and the scaling back of many individual itemized deductions will substantially reduce the number of taxpayers who elect to itemize, and significantly reduce the tax incentive to donate. The Tax Policy Center estimates that individual giving will decline by between $12 billion and $20 billion in 2018 (i.e., between four and five percent), with similar effects in the long run (see "The House Tax Bill Is Not Very Charitable to Nonprofits," at http://www.taxpolicycenter.org/taxvox/house-tax-bill-not-very-charitable-nonprofits).

> **Comment:** A taxpayer whose adjusted gross income (AGI) exceeds a threshold normally must reduce the amount of itemize deductions claimed on his or her federal income tax return. However, the phaseout for itemized deductions is temporarily repealed for tax years beginning after 2017 and before 2026 (sees ¶250).

Charitable deduction for college athletic seating rights payments repealed. A charitable deduction is not allowed for any payment to a college or university in exchange for which the payer receives the right to purchase tickets or seating at an athletic event (Code Sec. 170(l), as amended by the 2017 Tax Cuts Act). Thus, the charitable deduction for amounts paid for college athletic seating rights has been effectively repealed.

> **Comment:** This charitable deduction has been eliminated because "taxpayers should only be permitted a charitable deduction commensurate with the value of assets given to charity" (Report of the House Ways and Means Committee on H.R. 1, Tax Cuts and Jobs Act, H. Rept. 115-409).

Substantiation exception for donee-reported contributions repealed. The provision relieving a donor from the requirement to obtain a contemporaneous written acknowledgment for any charitable contribution of $250 or more if the donee organization reports the required information to the IRS has been repealed (Code Sec. 170(f)(8)(D), as stricken by the 2017 Tax Cuts Act). A donor who makes a contribution of $250 or more in the 2017 tax year and later is not allowed a charitable deduction unless the donor substantiates the donation with a contemporaneous written acknowledgment by the donee (Code Sec. 170(f)(8); Reg. § 1.170A-13(f)).

> **Practical Analysis:** William D. Elliott, Partner at Elliott, Thomason & Gibson, LLP in Dallas, Texas, comments that the limit for cash contributions to charities is increased from 50 percent of AGI to 60 percent of AGI, effective for 2018. Deductions are

NEW LAW EXPLAINED

> denied for those made for college athletic event seating rights, effective for 2018. Substantiation of charitable contributions is repealed for certain contributions reported by donee organizations, effective for 2017, which is an unusual effective date.

> **Practical Analysis:** Brian T. Whitlock, Adjunct Professor in the Gies College of Business at the University of Illinois at Urbana-Champaign, observes that Act Section 13704 disallows any charitable contribution deduction paid in exchange for college athletic event seating rights. Previously, taxpayers could deduct 80 percent of amounts paid for such seat licenses as a charitable contribution deduction. This change provides consistency with the disallowance under Code Sec. 274 of entertainment expenses as a business expense (see ¶535). In addition, Act Section 13705 effectively repeals the ability of taxpayers to use the Schedule B of Form 990 filed by an exempt organization to satisfy the charitable contribution substantiation requirement imposed on taxpayers who are seeking to claim a charitable contribution deduction under Code Sec. 170.

▶ **Effective date.** The amendments made by this section generally apply to contributions made in tax years beginning after December 31, 2017 (Act Secs. 11023(b) and 13704(b) of the Tax Cuts and Jobs Act (P.L. 115-97)). The repeal of the exception to the contemporaneous written acknowledgment requirements applies to contributions made in tax years beginning after December 31, 2016 (Act Sec. 13705(b) of the 2017 Tax Cuts Act).

Law source: Law at ¶5320. Committee Report at ¶10,080.

— Act Sec. 11023(a) of the Tax Cuts and Jobs Act (P.L. 115-97), redesignating Code Sec. 170(b)(1)(G) as (H) and adding Code Sec. 170(b)(1)(G);

— Act Sec. 13704(a), amending Code Sec. 170(l);

— Act Sec. 13705(a), striking Code Sec. 170(f)(8)(D) and redesignating Code Sec. 170(f)(8)(E) as (D);

— Act Secs. 11023(b), 13704(b), and 13705(b), providing the effective dates.

¶235 Personal Casualty and Theft Loss Deduction

SUMMARY OF NEW LAW

The itemized deduction for personal casualty losses is temporarily limited in tax years 2018 through 2025 to losses attributable to federally declared disasters. Temporary relief from the casualty loss rules is provided for net disaster losses occurring in 2016 and 2017.

BACKGROUND

A taxpayer may generally deduct losses sustained during the tax year and not compensated for by insurance or otherwise (Code Sec. 165). For an individual, losses are deductible only if incurred in a trade or business, transaction entered into for profit, or arising from a fire, storm, shipwreck, or other casualty, or from theft (Code Sec. 165(c)). Personal casualty or theft losses are deductible only to the extent to which they exceed $100 per casualty or theft (Code Sec. 165(h)(1)). Further, personal casualty or theft losses for a tax year are deductible only if they exceed personal casualty gains, and only to the extent of the sum of the amount of personal casualty gains plus the amount by which the excess of personal casualty losses over gains is greater than 10 percent of the taxpayer's adjusted gross income (AGI) (Code Sec. 165(h)(2)). The deduction for casualty losses is an itemized deduction. Individuals who elect the standard deduction may not claim a deduction for casualty losses incurred during the tax year.

If a taxpayer has a casualty loss from a disaster that occurred in a federally declared disaster area, the taxpayer can elect to deduct the loss on his or her return for the tax year in which the disaster occurred or for the tax year immediately preceding the tax year in which the disaster occurred (Code Sec. 165(i)). For example, a calendar-year taxpayer who suffers a disaster loss any time during 2017 may elect to deduct it on his or her 2016 return, or the taxpayer could wait and deduct it on his or her 2017 return in the regular manner. In either case, the taxpayer is still subject to the $100 and 10 percent of AGI limits. A federally declared disaster is any disaster subsequently determined by the President of the United States to warrant assistance by the Federal Government under the Robert T. Stafford Disaster Relief and Emergency Assistance Act.

Special rules also apply to net disaster losses as a result of Hurricanes Harvey, Irma, or Maria in 2017 (Act Sec. 504 of the Disaster Tax Relief and Airport and Airway Extension Act of 2017 (P.L. 115-63)). The dollar limitation applicable to each casualty or theft is increased to $500 and the 10-percent AGI limitation is waived for net disaster losses for the tax year from the hurricanes. A net disaster loss is the excess of qualified disaster-related personal casualty losses, over any personal casualty gains.

NEW LAW EXPLAINED

Personal casualty and theft loss deduction limited in 2018 through 2025; special rules apply for net disaster losses in 2016 and 2017.—The itemized deduction for personal casualty losses is limited in tax years beginning after December 31, 2017, and before January 1, 2026, to losses attributable to federally declared disasters (Code Sec. 165(h)(5)(A), as added by the Tax Cuts and Jobs Act (P.L. 115-97)). A taxpayer may still claim personal casualty losses not attributable federally declared disasters to offset any personal casualty gains during 2018 through 2025. However, any such personal casualty gains used to offset personal casualty losses attributable to a federally declared disaster are not taken into account in determining the taxpayer's 10 percent of AGI limitation (Code Sec. 165(h)(5)(B), as added by the 2017 Tax Cuts Act).

¶235

NEW LAW EXPLAINED

Comment: A taxpayer whose adjusted gross income (AGI) exceeds a threshold normally must reduce the amount of itemize deductions claimed on his or her federal income tax return. However, the phaseout for itemized deductions is temporarily repealed for tax years beginning after 2017 and before 2026 (sees ¶ 250).

Additional relief for 2016 and 2017 disasters. If an individual has a net disaster loss for tax years beginning in 2016 or 2017, the $100 limitation applicable to each casualty related to the disaster is increased to $500 and the 10 percent AGI limitation is waived (Act Sec. 11028(c) of the 2017 Tax Cuts Act). For this purpose, a net disaster loss is the qualified disaster-related personal casualty losses, over any personal casualty gains. A qualified disaster-related personal loss means a personal casualty loss arising in a disaster area after on or after January 1, 2016, that is attributable to a federally declared disaster. For an individual who does not itemize deductions, his or her standard deduction is increased by the amount of the casualty loss attributable to the disaster (see ¶ 205).

> **Practical Analysis:** William D. Elliott, Partner at Elliott, Thomason & Gibson, LLP in Dallas, Texas, comments that personal casualty loss deductions are changes to be permitted if the loss was attributable to a disaster declared as such by the President under the governing authority, effective 2018.

▶ **Effective date.** The amendment made by this section limiting personal casualty losses to federal disaster areas declared disaster areas applies to losses incurred in tax years beginning after December 31, 2017 (Act Sec. 11044(b) of the Tax Cuts and Jobs Act (P.L. 115-97)). The special rules related to personal casualty losses related to net disaster losses for 2016 and 2017 are effective on December 22, 2017, the date of enactment.

Law source: Law at ¶5310 and ¶7015. Committee Report at ¶10,190.

— Act Sec. 11044(a) of the Tax Cuts and Jobs Act (P.L. 115-97), adding Code Sec. 165(h)(5);

— Act Sec. 11028(a) and (c)

— Act Sec. 11044(b) providing the effective date

¶240 Gambling Losses

SUMMARY OF NEW LAW

Losses from gambling or wagering transactions for purposes of deducting winnings is clarified to include any deduction otherwise allowed to the taxpayer for federal income tax purposes in carrying on any wagering transaction, and not just the actual costs of wagers. The change is effective for tax years 2018 through 2025.

BACKGROUND

An individual can deduct gambling losses only to the extent of the amount of gambling winnings included in his or her gross income (Code Sec. 165(d)). This limitation applies to taxpayers who are in the trade or business of gambling as well. For most individuals, deductible gambling losses are miscellaneous itemized deductions not subject to the two-percent-of-adjusted-gross-income (AGI) floor (Code Sec. 67(b)(3)). Professional gamblers, however, can deduct losses as an adjustment to gross income (AGI) (i.e., an above-the-line deduction).

Individuals in the trade or business of gambling are also allowed to deduct reasonable business expenses (Mayo v. Commissioner, Dec. 58,524, 136 TC 81). The business expenses are not subject to the gambling loss limitation since they are not related to wagering transactions (AOD 2011-06 (Dec. 20, 2011)).

The combined losses of both spouses on a joint return are allowed to the extent of their combined gains (Reg. §1.165-10). Furthermore, the losses need not be incurred in the same type of gambling to offset winnings. For example, lottery winnings can offset casino losses (Herman Drews v. Commissioner, Dec. 21,658, 25 TC 1354).

Documentation is required to support the deduction. A taxpayer's diary or other regularly maintained record supplemented by verifiable documentation will usually be accepted for proof of winnings or losses if it contains the date, amount, type of bet, name and address of the gambling establishment, and the names of any persons present with the taxpayer. Verifiable documentation includes wagering tickets, cancelled checks, and credit records (Rev. Proc. 77-29, 1977-2 CB 538).

NEW LAW EXPLAINED

Losses from wagering transactions clarified.—The term "losses from wagering transactions" is clarified to include any deduction otherwise allowable in calculating federal income tax incurred in carrying on any wagering transaction (Code Sec. 165(d) as amended by the Tax Cuts and Jobs Act (P.L. 115-97)). The provision is effective for tax years beginning after December 31, 2017, and before January 1, 2026.

> **Comment:** The change is intended to clarify that the limitation on losses from wagering transactions applies not only to the actual costs of wagers incurred by an individual, but to other expenses incurred by the individual in connection with the conduct of that individual's gambling activities. Thus, for example, expenses incurred in travelling to and from a casino fall within the scope of the gambling loss limitation, and these expenses may only be deducted to the extent of gambling winnings (Conference Report on H.R. 1, Tax Cuts and Jobs Act (H. Rept. 115-466)).

> **Practical Analysis:** Charles R. Goulding, President, Energy Tax Savers and R&D Tax Savers in Syosset, New York, comments that this Act Section leaves the deduction for gambling losses relatively intact. The main revision overturns court rulings which permitted a deduction for expenses incurred in connection with the wagering. The new rules permit a deduction only for the actual wager. Other than this

NEW LAW EXPLAINED

provision, taxpayers should keep some basic principles in mind to avoid common misconceptions associated with the deduction. First, the deduction is available only to taxpayers whom itemize deductions. Second, internet gambling based activities do not qualify for the deduction, even if the source originates overseas. This distinction will become increasingly relevant as gamblers continue to flock toward electronic gambling alternatives. Finally, and perhaps most important, gambling losses are only deductible to the extent of claimed gambling winnings. Thus, if the taxpayer is in a net gambling loss position the deduction will be of no benefit.

Comment: A taxpayer whose adjusted gross income (AGI) exceeds a threshold normally must reduce the amount of itemize deductions claimed on his or her federal income tax return. However, the phaseout for itemized deductions is temporarily repealed for tax years beginning after 2017 and before 2026 (sees ¶250).

▶ **Effective date.** The amendment made by this section applies to tax years beginning after December 31, 2017 (Act Sec. 11050(b) of the Tax Cuts and Jobs Act (P.L. 115-97)).

Law source: Law at ¶5310. Committee Report at ¶10,250.

— Act Sec. 11050(a) of the Tax Cuts and Jobs Act (P.L. 115-97), amending Code Sec. 165(d);

— Act Sec. 11050(b), providing the effective date.

¶245 Miscellaneous Itemized Deductions

SUMMARY OF NEW LAW

The deductibility of miscellaneous itemized deductions is temporarily repealed for tax years 2018 through 2025.

BACKGROUND

Certain itemized deductions of an individual are treated as miscellaneous itemized deductions and are only allowed to the extent that their total exceeds two percent of the individual's adjusted gross income (AGI) (Code Sec. 67(a); Temp. Reg. § 1.67-1T). The deductions are reported on Schedule A of Form 1040. The two-percent-of-AGI limit is applied after other deduction limits, such as the 50-percent limit on meals and entertainment, are applied.

In general, the deductions affected by the two-percent floor include, but are not limited to, the following:

* unreimbursed employee expenses (including expenses for travel, lodging, meals, entertainment, continuing education, subscriptions to professional journals, union or professional dues, professional uniforms, job hunting, and business use of an employee's home);

BACKGROUND

- expenses paid or incurred for the production or collection of income (including investment advisory fees, subscriptions to investment advisory publications, certain attorneys' fees, and safety deposit box rental), or for the determination, collection, or refund of tax (including tax counsel fees and appraisal fees) that are deductible under Code Sec. 212; and
- "hobby" expenses that are deductible under Code Sec. 183.

Miscellaneous itemized deductions subject to the two-percent-of-AGI limit may not be claimed by an individual in calculating his or her alternative minimum tax (AMT) liability (Code Sec. 56(b)(1)(A)).

NEW LAW EXPLAINED

Temporary suspension of miscellaneous itemized deductions.—All miscellaneous itemized deductions that are subject to the two-percent-of-AGI limit are temporarily repealed for tax years beginning after December 31, 2017, and before January 1, 2026 (Code Sec. 67(g), as added by the Tax Cuts and Jobs Act (P.L. 115-97)). Thus, no miscellaneous itemized deduction subject to the two-percent-of-AGI limit may be claimed by an individual on Schedule A of Form 1040 for tax years 2018 through 2025. An individual also remains unable to claim such deductions in calculating his or her AMT liability, regardless of tax year.

> **Practical Analysis:** William D. Elliott, Partner at Elliott, Thomason & Gibson, LLP in Dallas, Texas, comments that the new law repeals all itemized deductions subject to the two-percent-of-AGI floor, effective for the period 2018 through 2025. This Act Section will surprise a large number of taxpayers.

> **Practical Analysis:** Brian T. Whitlock, Adjunct Professor in the Gies College of Business at the University of Illinois at Urbana-Champaign, observes that this Act Section suspends all miscellaneous itemized deductions that were previously subject to the two percent floor under prior law Code Secs. 62, 67, and 212 for any taxable year after December 31, 2017, and before January 1, 2026. This Act Section would not affect individuals claiming similar expenses to the extent that they were related to an individual's sole proprietorship or rental real estate activity. It is curious that this Act Section was not accompanied by a repeal of the alternative minimum tax (AMT) on individuals.

▶   **Effective date.** The amendment made by this section applies to tax years beginning after December 31, 2017 (Act Sec. 11045(b) of the Tax Cuts and Jobs Act (P.L. 115-97)).

Law source: Law at ¶5175. Committee Report at ¶10,200.

— Act Sec. 11045(a) of the Tax Cuts and Jobs Act (P.L. 115-97), adding Code Sec. 67(g);

— Act Sec. 11045(b), providing the effective date.

¶245

¶250 Phaseout or Overall Limitation on Itemized Deductions (Pease Limitation)

SUMMARY OF NEW LAW

The phaseout or overall limitation on itemized deductions is temporarily repealed for tax years 2018 through 2025.

BACKGROUND

Once an individual determines adjusted gross income (AGI), he or she may claim certain itemized deductions of personal expenses specifically authorized by the Code in determining taxable income. Alternatively, he or she can simplify their deductions by claiming a standard deduction based on their filing status rather than itemizing deductions. Itemized deductions include deductions for medical and dental expenses, certain taxes, interest, charitable contributions, casualty and theft losses, and certain miscellaneous expenses. An individual whose AGI exceeds an applicable threshold amount based on filing status must reduce the total amount of otherwise allowable itemized deductions. The threshold amounts are adjusted annually for inflation (Code Sec. 68). For 2017, the AGI thresholds are: $313,800 for married individuals filing jointly or surviving spouses; $287,650 for heads of households; $261,500 for unmarried individuals filing as single; and $156,900 for married individuals filing separately (Rev. Proc. 2016-55).

If an individual's AGI exceeds the applicable threshold amount, he or she must reduce the amount of allowable itemized deductions by the lesser of: (1) three percent of the excess of the taxpayer's AGI over the applicable threshold amount, or (2) 80 percent of allowable itemized deductions, reduced by the deductions for medical expenses, investment interest, casualty and theft losses, and wagering losses. The reduction is applied after all other limitations on itemized deductions are applied, including the limit on charitable contributions, the limit on certain meal and entertainment expenses, and the two-percent-of-AGI limitation on miscellaneous itemized deductions (see ¶245).

NEW LAW EXPLAINED

Phaseout of itemized deductions temporarily repealed.—The phaseout or overall limitation on itemized deductions is temporarily repealed applicable to tax years beginning after December 31, 2017, and before January 1, 2026 (Code Sec. 68(f), as added by the Tax Cuts and Jobs Act (P.L. 115-97)).

▶ **Effective date.** The amendments made by this section apply to tax years beginning after December 31, 2017 (Act Sec. 11046(b) of the Tax Cuts and Jobs Act (P.L. 115-97)).

Law source: Law at ¶5180. Committee Report at ¶10,210.

— Act Sec. 11046(a) of the Tax Cuts and Jobs Act (P.L. 115-97), adding Code Sec. 68(f);

— Act Sec. 11046(b), providing the effective date.

¶250

ADJUSTMENTS TO GROSS INCOME

¶255 Alimony and Separate Maintenance Payments

SUMMARY OF NEW LAW

The deduction for alimony and separate maintenance payments, as well as the inclusion of the payments in gross income, are repealed. The repeal, however, is only effective for divorce or separation instruments executed or modified after 2018.

BACKGROUND

Alimony and separate maintenance payments may be claimed as a deduction in calculating adjusted gross income (AGI) (an above-the-line deduction) of the payor (Code Secs. 62(a)(10) and 215). The payments must be included in the gross income of the payee or recipient (Code Secs. 61(a)(8) and 71). These rules apply only if the payments are made in cash under a divorce or separation agreement that does not require continuation or substitution of payments after the payee's death. The spouses must be legally separated, must not file a joint return, and must not be members of the same household. Payments that a divorce or separation instrument fixes as payable to support the payor's child or noncash property settlements are not considered qualified alimony or separate maintenance payments.

The payee spouse of an alimony trust is treated as a beneficiary of the trust and subject to the same tax treatment as the beneficiary of a regular trust, regardless of whether the trust already existed or was created at the time of divorce or separation (Code Sec. 682). As a result, the income the payee spouse is entitled to receive from the trust is taxable to him or her and excludable from the gross income of the payor spouse. However, because income from the trust is taxable to the payee spouse as a beneficiary rather than as alimony, the payor spouse may not claim a deduction for any trust distribution to the payee spouse.

NEW LAW EXPLAINED

Alimony deduction and exclusion repealed for instruments executed or modified after 2018.—The deduction of qualified alimony and separate maintenance payments by a payor, the inclusion of the payments in gross income by the payee, and the special rules for alimony trusts are generally repealed after 2018 (Code Sec. 71, 215, and 682 stricken by the Tax Cuts and Jobs Act (P.L. 115-97)). However, the repeal is only effective for any divorce or separation instruments:

- executed after December 31, 2018; and

- executed before January 1, 2019, and modified after 2018 provided that the modification expressly provides that the repeal of the qualified alimony and separate maintenance rules of the Internal Revenue Code apply (Act Sec. 11051(c) of the 2017 Tax Cuts Act).

NEW LAW EXPLAINED

Comment: A taxpayer may continue to deduct qualified alimony and separate maintenance payments made, or exclude such payments received from gross income, after 2018 if his or her divorce or separation instrument is: (1) executed before 2019; or (2) is modified after 2018 so long as it does not expressly provide that the that the repeal of the qualified alimony and separate maintenance rules of the Internal Revenue Code apply. The special rules applicable to alimony trusts will also continue to apply after 2018 under the same conditions as for the deduction and the exclusion.

Caution: Since the rules applicable to alimony or separate maintenance payments still apply to certain divorce or separation instruments after 2018, other rules which are amended or repealed by the 2017 Tax Cuts Act will also continue to apply. Examples include rules related to additional withholding allowances, requirements to include taxpayer identification numbers (TIN), and the definition of compensation for the purpose of IRA contributions deductions.

Practical Analysis: Charles R. Goulding, President, Energy Tax Savers and R&D Tax Savers in Syosset, New York, comments that one of the major tax surprises is the elimination of the long standing alimony tax deduction. Previously alimony payers could deduct alimony payments and recipients had to report them as income. Almost 600,000 alimony payers used this deduction. Typically the after tax economic benefit is more valuable to the alimony payer who is normally in the higher tax bracket. Alimony is normally the result of intense negotiations between the parties and their divorce attorneys, and the after tax economics are often considered. One concern is that the loss of the deduction will cause alimony payers to negotiate lower payments. As this Act Section kicks in for settlements in 2019 and beyond it is clear parties will be given additional time to consider their options.

Practical Analysis: William D. Elliott, Partner at Elliott, Thomason & Gibson, LLP in Dallas, Texas, notes that deduction for alimony payments arising in a divorce are repealed. The effective dates are specifically tailored. Generally, the repeal is effective after December 31, 2018, but for agreements executed before December 31, 2018, but modified after that date, then the new rules apply to modifications, if the agreement so provides. Thus, the parties can control whether the new rules apply to post-2018 amendments to a divorce agreement. This repeal of alimony will be disruptive to taxation of divorces and especially disadvantage payors of alimony. Previously, the parties could control who bears the burden of taxation.

▶ **Effective date.** The amendments made by this section apply to: (1) any divorce or separation instrument (as defined in Code Sec. (b)(2) as in effect before December 22, 2017, the date of the enactment) and executed after December 31, 2018; (2) any divorce or separation instrument executed on or before December 31, 2018, and modified after that date if the modification expressly provides that the amendments made by this section apply to the modification (Act Sec. 11015(c) of the Tax Cuts and Jobs Act (P.L. 115-97)).

¶255

NEW LAW EXPLAINED

Law source: Law at ¶5160, ¶5165, ¶5185, ¶5230, ¶5290, ¶5355, ¶5365, ¶5370, ¶5385, ¶5460, ¶5470, ¶5630, ¶6095, ¶6315, and ¶6340. Committee Report at ¶10,260.

— Act Sec. 11051(a) of the Tax Cuts and Jobs Act (P.L. 115-97), striking Code Sec. 215;

— Act Sec. 11051(b)(1), amending Code Sec. 61(a), striking Code Secs. 71 and 682;

— Act Sec. 11051(b)(2), (3), and (4), amending Code Secs. 121(d)(3), 152(d)(5), 219(f)(1), 220(f)(7), 223(f)(7), 382(l)(3)(B)(iii), 408(d)(6), 3402(m)(1), 6742(d)(3), 7701(a)(17), and striking Code Sec. 62(a)(10);

— Act Sec. 11051(c), providing the effective date.

¶260 Moving Expense Deduction

SUMMARY OF NEW LAW

The deduction for moving expenses is temporarily repealed for tax years 2018 through 2025. However, the special rules for a member of the Armed Forces to deduct moving expenses and exclude in-kind moving expenses, and reimbursements or allowances, continues to apply during these tax years.

BACKGROUND

An employee or self-employed individual may claim a deduction in calculating adjusted gross income (AGI) (an above-the-line deduction) for reasonable expenses of moving himself or herself, as well as family members, if the move is related to starting work in a new location (Code Secs. 62(a)(15) and 217). The taxpayer must satisfy certain conditions related to distance from the previous residence and minimum period of employment in the new location to deduct moving expenses. Deductible moving expenses are limited to the cost of transportation of household goods and personal effects, and travel to the new residence, including lodging but not meals.

Special rules apply to moving expenses paid or incurred by a member of the Armed Forces of the United States who is on active duty and moves pursuant to a military order and incident to a permanent change of station (Code Sec. 217(g)). First, the individual is exempt from the minimum distance and minimum period of employment conditions for claiming the moving expense deduction. Second, the individual may exclude from gross income the value of any moving and storage expenses furnished in-kind by the United States government to the individual, his or her spouse, and dependents, as well as any reimbursements or allowance for those expenses. An exclusion is also provided for moving and storage expenses incurred by the spouse or dependents of an Armed Forces member, even if they do not reside with the member either before or after the move.

NEW LAW EXPLAINED

Moving expense deduction temporarily repealed; special rules for Armed Forces members retained.—The deduction for moving expenses is generally repealed for tax years beginning after December 31, 2017, and before January 1, 2026 (Code Sec. 217(k), as added by the Tax Cuts and Jobs Act (P.L. 115-97)). Thus, an employee or self-employed individual may not claim an above-the-line deduction in calculating adjusted gross income for moving expenses in 2018 through 2025.

The special rules applicable to a member of the Armed Forces of the United States will continue to apply after 2017. Thus, the Armed Forces member may still claim a deduction for moving expenses and exclude from income in-kind moving and storage expenses, as well as reimbursement or allowance for those expenses, in 2018 through 2025 if he or she is on active duty and moves pursuant to a military order and incident to a permanent change of station (Code Sec. 217(g)).

Practical Analysis: William D. Elliott, Partner at Elliott, Thomason & Gibson, LLP in Dallas, Texas, comments that the deduction for moving expenses in Code Sec. 217(a) is repealed, except for exclusions of amounts attributable to in-kind moving and storage expenses (and reimbursements or allowances for these expenses) for members of the Armed Forces (or their spouse or dependents) on active duty that move pursuant to a military order and incident to a permanent change of station, with the changes applicable for the years 2018 through 2025.

Practical Analysis: Brian T. Whitlock, Adjunct Professor in the Gies College of Business at the University of Illinois at Urbana-Champaign, observes that this Act Section effectively suspends Code Sec. 217 deductible employee moving expenses for any individual other than members of the Armed Forces effective for tax years beginning after December 31, 2017, and before January 1, 2026. See ¶610 for the companion provision that requires employers to include reimbursements and payments for employee moving expenses in the gross wages of employees and thus makes all such payment subject to income and employment tax.

▶ **Effective date.** The amendment made by this section applies to tax years beginning after December 31, 2017 (Act Sec. 11049(b) of the Tax Cuts and Jobs Act (P.L. 115-97)).

Law source: Law at ¶5360. Committee Report at ¶10,240.

— Act Sec. 11049(a) of the Tax Cuts and Jobs Act (P.L. 115-97), adding Code Sec. 217(k);

— Act Sec. 11049(b), providing the effective date.

¶260

EXCLUSION FROM GROSS INCOME

¶265 Discharge of Debt Income from Student Loans

SUMMARY OF NEW LAW

Eligibility to exclude discharge of student loan debt from gross income is temporarily expanded to include discharges of eligible student loans before 2026 due to the student's death or total and permanent disability.

BACKGROUND

A taxpayer's gross income generally includes discharge of debt income if a taxpayer is released from a debt for less than the full amount of the obligation (Code Sec. 108). An exception to this rules is that the discharge of a student loan does not give rise to discharge of debt income if the discharge is pursuant to a provision in the loan agreement under which all or a part of the student loan is forgiven, provided the student works for a certain period of time in certain professions for any of a broad class of employers (Code Sec. 108(f)). In addition, an individual's gross income does not include forgiveness of loans made by tax-exempt charitable organizations (e.g., educational organizations or private foundations) if the proceeds of such loans are used to pay costs of attendance at an educational institution or to refinance outstanding student loans and the student is not employed by the lender organization.

> **Caution:** This exclusion does not apply to the extent the taxpayer is insolvent or is involved in a bankruptcy case (Code Sec. 108(a)(2)).

The exclusion applies if the proceeds are used to refinance any loan made to assist an individual in attending an educational institution, not just loans made by educational organizations. The refinancing loan must be made under a program that requires the student to fulfill a public-service work requirement. A student loan is any loan to an individual to assist him or her in attending an educational organization described in Code Sec. 170(b)(1)(A)(ii), if the lender is: (1) the United States or an instrumentality or agency thereof; (2) a U.S. state, territory, or possession or the District of Columbia or any political subdivision thereof; (3) certain tax-exempt public benefit corporations that control a State, county, or municipal hospital and whose employees have been deemed to be public employees under State law; or (4) an educational organization that originally received the funds from which the loan was made from the United States, a State, or a tax-exempt public benefit corporation.

NEW LAW EXPLAINED

Student loan debt discharge exclusion expanded before 2025 due to death or disability.—The exclusion of discharge of debt income for student loans is expanded to include discharges because of the student's death or total and permanent disability. The exclusion applies to discharge of debt income due to the discharge of an eligible loan

NEW LAW EXPLAINED

after December 31, 2017, and before January 1, 2026 (Code Sec. 108(f)(5)(A), as added by the Tax Cuts and Jobs Act (P.L. 115-97)). Loans eligible for this exclusion are loans made by:

- the United States (or an instrumentality or agency of the United States);

- a state (or political subdivision of a state);

- certain tax-exempt public benefit corporations that control a state, county, or municipal hospital and whose employees have been deemed to be public employees under state law;

- an educational organization that originally received the funds from which the loan was made from the United States, a state, or a tax-exempt public benefit corporation; or

- private education loans (for this purpose, private education loan is defined in section 140(7) of the Consumer Protection Act) (Code Sec. 108(f)(5)(B), as added by the 2017 Tax Cuts Act).

> **Example:** Bridgett becomes totally and permanently disabled in 2018 as the result of an accident. She has an outstanding student loan that was made by the State of New York, which is cancelled by the state due to her disability. Because the discharge is due to Bridgett's total and permanent disability, it does not give rise to discharge of debt income in the tax year.

Comment: The legislative text provides a broad catch-all exclusion for discharge of debt income of an eligible loan on account of the death or total and permanent disability of the student. It also provides specific references to provisions in the Higher Education Act of 1965 of loan forgiveness in the case of death and total and permanent disability.

> **Practical Analysis:** Brian T. Whitlock, Adjunct Professor in the Gies College of Business at the University of Illinois at Urbana-Champaign, observes that this Act Section expands the current exclusion of income available due to the discharge of student debt occurring after December 31, 2017, and before January 1, 2026, to include a discharge occurs on account of the death or "total and permanent disability" of the student and also include "private education loans" as defined under Section 140(7) of the Consumer Protection Act. The Act Section makes the Code Sec. 108 exclusion consistent with the Higher Education of 1965 which had permitted the discharge of student debt in the event of death or total and permanent disability.

▶ **Effective date.** The amendment made by this section applies to discharges of debt after December 31, 2017 (Act Sec. 11301(b) of the Tax Cuts and Jobs Act (P.L. 115-97)).

Law source: Law at ¶5220. Committee Report at ¶10,140.

— Act. Sec. 11031(a) of the Tax Cuts and Jobs Act (P.L. 115-97), adding Code Sec. 108(f)(5);

— Act Sec. 11031(b), providing the effective date.

¶265

¶270 Rollover of Capital Gain from Publicly Traded Securities

SUMMARY OF NEW LAW

The election to defer recognition of capital gain realized on the sale of publicly traded securities if the taxpayer used the sale proceeds to purchase common stock or a partnership interest in a specialized small business investment company (SSBIC) is repealed for sales after 2017.

BACKGROUND

C corporations and individuals may elect to defer recognition of capital gain realized on the sale of publicly traded securities if the taxpayer uses the sales proceeds within 60 days to purchase common stock or a partnership interest in a specialized small business investment company (SSBIC). Sales proceeds that exceed the cost of the SSBIC common stock or partnership interest must be recognized as gain. Ordinary gain cannot be deferred (Code Sec. 1044(a)). The election is not available to estates, trusts, subchapter S corporations and partnerships. The taxpayer's basis in the SSBIC stock or partnership interest is reduced, in the order acquired, by the amount of any unrecognized gain on the sale of the securities.

The amount of capital gain that an individual may elect to roll over by purchasing an interest in an SSBIC for a tax year is limited to the lesser of $50,000 or $500,000, reduced by any gain previously excluded. These limits are $25,000 and $250,000, respectively, for married individuals filing separate returns; and $250,000 and $1 million, respectively, for C corporations (Code Sec. 1044(b)).

NEW LAW EXPLAINED

Rollover of capital gain from publicly traded securities into specialized small business investment companies is repealed.—The election to rollover gain from the sale of publicly traded securities if the sale proceeds are used to purchase common stock or a partnership interest in a specialized small business investment company is repealed for sales after 2017 (Code Sec. 1044, prior to being stricken by the Tax Cuts and Jobs Act (P.L. 115-97)).

▶ **Effective date.** The amendments made by this section apply to sales after December 31, 2017 (Act Sec. 13313(c) of the Tax Cuts and Jobs Act (P.L. 115-97).

Law source: Law at ¶5940 and ¶5950. Committee Report at ¶10,530.

— Act Sec. 13313(a) of the Tax Cuts and Jobs Act (P.L. 115-97), striking Code Sec. 1044;

— Act Sec. 13313(b), amending Code Sec. 1016(a)(23);

— Act Sec. 13313(c), providing the effective date.

¶270

PERSONAL TAX CREDITS

¶280 Child Tax Credit

SUMMARY OF NEW LAW

The child tax credit is temporarily expanded after 2017 by increasing the credit amount for each qualifying child to $2,000, increasing the phaseout threshold to $400,000 if married filing jointly ($200,000 for other taxpayers), and providing a $500 nonrefundable credit for each dependent who is not a qualifying child. The refundable portion of the credit (additional child tax credit) is limited to $1,400 per qualifying child, but is indexed for inflation and the earned income threshold is reduced to $2,500. A taxpayer must include a qualifying child's Social Security number on his or her return to receive the nonrefundable or refundable portion of the credit with respect to the child.

BACKGROUND

An individual may claim the child tax credit of up to $1,000 for each qualifying child he or she supports during the tax year (Code Sec. 24). The definition of qualifying child for this purpose is the same as that for claiming a dependency exemption, except that the child must not have attained the age of 17 by the end of the year and must be a U.S. citizen, national, or resident. The taxpayer's return must include the name and taxpayer identification number (TIN) of each qualifying child claimed for the credit. The TIN of a qualifying child must be issued prior to the filing of the return for the tax year.

The child tax credit is $1,000 per qualifying child but phases out once the taxpayer's modified adjusted gross income (MAGI) exceeds $110,000 if married filing jointly, $75,000 if filing as single, and $55,000 if married filing separately (Code Sec. 24(b)). The credit is reduced by $50 for each $1,000, or fraction thereof, of MAGI above the threshold amount. MAGI is defined as AGI determined without regard to the exclusions from gross income for foreign earned income, foreign housing expenses, and U.S. possession income. The credit is allowed only for tax years consisting of 12 months except in cases where the tax year closes due to the death of the taxpayer.

The child tax credit is generally a nonrefundable personal credit and allowed against both the taxpayer's regular tax liability and alternative minimum tax (AMT) liability (Code Sec. 26). A portion of the credit is refundable to the extent it exceeds the taxpayer's tax liability. This is referred to as the additional child tax credit (ACTC) and is equal to the lesser of the unclaimed portion of the nonrefundable credit amount (i.e., up to $1,000 per child) or 15 percent of the taxpayer's earned income in excess of $3,000 (Code Sec. 24(d)). For a taxpayer with three or more qualifying children, the ACTC is either the unclaimed portion of the nonrefundable credit amount or the excess of the taxpayer's share of Social Security taxes, including one-half of any self-employment taxes, over his or her earned income credit for the tax year. Military families may elect to include otherwise excludable combat zone pay in

BACKGROUND

their earned income when calculating the ACTC. Schedule 8812 is used to calculate the ACTC. The ACTC is disallowed for any taxpayer electing to exclude from gross income any foreign earned income and foreign housing expenses.

NEW LAW EXPLAINED

Modification of child tax credit and new credit for qualifying dependents after 2017.—The child tax credit is temporarily expanded effective for tax years beginning after 2017 (Code Sec. 24(h)(1), as added by the Tax Cuts and Jobs Act (P.L. 115-97)). Specifically, the following modifications to the credit are effective for tax years beginning after December 31, 2017, and before January 1, 2026:

- The credit amount is increased to $2,000 per qualifying child (Code Sec. 24(h)(2), as added by the 2017 Tax Cuts Act).

- The threshold amount when the credit begins to phase out is increased to $400,000 if married filing jointly and $200,000 for any other filing status (Code Sec. 24(h)(3), as added by the 2017 Tax Cuts Act). The credit is reduced by $50 for $1,000 (or fraction thereof) that a taxpayer's modified adjusted gross income (MAGI) exceeds the threshold amount. The threshold amounts are not indexed for inflation.

- A taxpayer may claim a $500 credit for each dependent who is not a qualifying child for purposes of the child tax credit (Code Sec. 24(h)(4), as added by the 2017 Tax Cuts Act). A dependent for this purpose is a qualifying relative (and not a qualifying child) for purposes of claiming a dependency exemption under Code Sec. 152(b). In addition, the dependent must be a U.S. citizen, national, or resident of the United States. The $500 credit may not be claimed for a dependent who is resident of contiguous country to the United States (i.e., Mexico and Canada).

  Comment: The deduction for personal and dependency exemptions is temporarily repealed for tax years 2018 through 2025 (see ¶210), but the definition of a dependent is still applicable for the child tax credit and other tax benefits.

  Compliance Note: A taxpayer must file either Form 1040 or Form 1040A to claim the child tax credit. The child tax credit cannot be claimed by a taxpayer filing Form 1040-EZ.

Refundable child tax credit. A portion of the child tax credit remains refundable after 2017 and before 2026, referred to as the additional child tax credit (ACTC), except that the earned income threshold is temporarily decreased by $500. For tax years beginning in 2018 through 2025, a taxpayer is eligible for a refund equal to 15 percent of his or her earned income in excess of $2,500 (as opposed to $3,000) to the extent the child tax credit exceeds the taxpayer's tax liability (Code Sec. 24(h)(6), as added by the 2017 Tax Cuts Act).

The refundable amount for 2018 through 2025 is limited to $1,400 per qualifying child regardless that the credit is $2,000 per qualifying child (Code Sec. 24(h)(5), as added by the 2017 Tax Cuts Act). In addition, the $500 credit for each dependent who is not a qualifying child is disregarded in calculating the ACTC (i.e., the refundable portion is only for qualifying children claimed by the taxpayer for the credit). The $1,400

¶280

NEW LAW EXPLAINED

refund limitation per qualifying child for the ACTC is indexed annually for inflation after 2018 using the Chained Consumer Price Index for All Urban Consumers (C-CPI-U) in the cost-of-living adjustment (see ¶125).

Compliance Note: A taxpayer claiming the ACTC must complete Schedule 8812.

Taxpayer identification number required. A taxpayer must include on his or her return a qualifying child's Social Security number (SSN) to receive either the refundable or nonrefundable portion of the credit with respect to that child (Code Sec. 24(h)(7), as added by the 2017 Tax Cuts Act). A SSN issued by the Social Security Administration (SSA) to the qualifying child is valid for purpose of the ACTC only if the child is a U.S. citizen or the SSN authorizes the individual to work in the United States under Section 205(c)(2)(B)(i) of the Social Security Act. In addition, the SSN must be issued to the qualifying child on or before the due date of the taxpayer's return.

Comment: A Social security card labeled "not valid for employment" merely allows the holder to receive federal benefits (e.g., Medicaid) and it does not give the holder a valid SSN to work in the United States. A Social Security card that reads "Valid for work only with DHS authorization" or "Valid for work only with INS authorization" is valid for work in the United States if the authorization is still valid.

A taxpayer who cannot claim the child tax credit because a qualifying child does not have a Social Security number may nonetheless qualify for the nonrefundable $500 credit for the child (Code Sec. 24(h)(4)(C), as added by the 2017 Tax Cuts Act).

Comment: A taxpayer can claim the nonrefundable $500 credit for any person claimed who could be claimed as a dependent. In order to claim a dependency exemption for any person, the taxpayer must include a taxpayer identification number (TIN) of the dependent on his or her return (Code Sec. 151(e)). This may be satisfied by including the dependent's SSN, TIN, or adoption taxpayer identification number (ATIN) (Reg. § 301.6109-1). Thus, a SSN is only required for a qualifying child in claiming the child tax credit. A SSN is not required to claim the nonrefundable $500 credit for a child or nonchild dependent.

Practical Analysis: William D. Elliott, Partner at Elliott, Thomason & Gibson, LLP in Dallas, Texas, comments that the tax credit for children (qualifying children) is modified in several respects. increased temporarily to $2,000 per child, and an additional $500 nonrefundable credit is provided for qualifying dependents other than children. The maximum refundable amount may not exceed $1,400 per child, with some features to avoid abuse, such as requiring Social Security numbers for each qualifying child for whom credit is claim (but this confirmation requirement does not apply to the $500 nonrefundable credit for nonchild dependents). The income phaseout is rather large, starting at $400,000 for joint returns and $200,000 for all other taxpayers, neither of which is indexed. This provision was the subject of last minute political negotiations. The changes are effective in 2018.

Practical Analysis: Vincent O'Brien, President of Vincent J. O'Brien, CPA, PC, and M+O=CPE, Inc, Lynbrook, NY, observes that practitioners who are preparing income tax projections for individual clients for the 2018 tax year should note that the higher phaseout threshold for the child credit will allow more taxpayers to benefit from the child credit, whereas the benefit has been phased out in prior years.

The new phaseout threshold is more than double the old phaseout threshold ($400,000 for married taxpayers filling a joint return and $200,000 for all other taxpayers, up from $110,000 for married taxpayers filling a joint return and $75,000 for single and heads of household).

▶ **Effective date.** The amendment made by this section applies to tax years beginning after December 31, 2017 (Act Sec. 11022(b) of the Tax Cuts and Jobs Act (P.L. 115-97)).

Law source: Law at ¶5025. Committee Report at ¶10,070.

— Act Sec. 11022(a) of the Tax Cuts and Jobs Act (P.L. 115-97), adding Code Sec. 24(h);

— Act Sec. 11022(b), providing the effective date.

Corporations and Passthrough Entities

3

CORPORATIONS

PASSTHROUGH ENTITIES

CORPORATIONS

¶305 Corporate Income Tax Rate

SUMMARY OF NEW LAW

For tax years beginning after December 31, 2017, the graduated corporate tax rate structure is eliminated and corporate taxable income is taxed at a 21-percent flat rate. No special rate is provided for personal service corporations (PSCs); therefore, PSCs

SUMMARY OF NEW LAW

are also taxed at a 21-percent rate. The alternative tax for net capital gains and the rules disallowing the graduated corporate tax rates or the accumulated earnings credit to transferee corporations upon certain transfers are repealed. The new law further modifies the rules limiting the use of multiple tax benefits of controlled corporate groups to leave only the limitation on the use of the accumulated earnings credit as a result of the repeal of the corporate alternative minimum tax and the elimination of the graduated corporate tax rate structure. In addition, for taxpayers subject to the normalization method of accounting (e.g., regulated public utilities), the new law provides for the normalization of excess deferred tax reserves resulting from the reduction of corporate income tax rates (with respect to prior depreciation or recovery allowances taken on assets placed in service before the corporate rate reduction takes effect).

BACKGROUND

Corporations determine their annual income tax liability by applying a graduated rate of tax to their taxable income. The corporate income tax rates consist of four brackets. The top corporate tax rate is 35 percent on taxable income in excess of $10 million (Code Sec. 11(a) and (b)(1)). The corporate taxable income brackets and tax rates are set forth in the table below.

Taxable Income	Tax Rate
First $50,000	15%
$50,001-$75,000	25%
$75,001-$10 million	34%
over $10 million	35%

A corporation with taxable income over $100,000 must pay an additional tax equal to five percent of the amount in excess of $100,000, up to a maximum additional tax of $11,750. Corporations with taxable income in excess of $15 million must pay an additional tax equal to three percent of the amount in excess of $15 million, up to a maximum additional tax of $100,000 (Code Sec. 11(b)(1)). The extra five percent tax operates to phase out the benefits of graduated tax rates for corporations with taxable incomes between $100,000 and $335,000. A corporation having taxable income of $335,000 or more gets no benefit from the lower graduated tax rates and pays, in effect, a flat tax at a 34-percent rate. Similarly, the extra three-percent tax recaptures the benefits of the 34-percent rate in a manner analogous to the recapture of the 15 percent and 25-percent rates.

> **Comment:** Presently, the United States has one of the highest statutory corporate tax rates among developed countries. The average corporate income tax rate among nations in the Organization for Economic Co-operation and Development (OECD) is 22.5 percent. The high statutory rates create a competitive disadvantage for U.S. businesses and force U.S. businesses to move overseas. The high tax rates also encourage U.S. companies to keep their foreign earnings abroad instead of investing them into expansion and employment in the United States. In addition, according to OECD reports, counties with high corporate

BACKGROUND

rates, such as the United States, lose revenue in foreign direct investment as compared to countries with lower corporate tax rates.

The benefits of the graduated corporate tax rates do not apply to the taxable income of a qualified personal service corporation (PSC). Instead, a qualified PSC is subject to a flat 35-percent tax rate (Code Sec. 11(b)(2)).

Alternative tax for net capital gains. If a corporation has a net capital gain for any tax year, the corporation will pay an alternative tax if it is less than the tax computed in the regular manner. Under the alternative tax, the portion of the corporation's taxable income that is net capital gain is subject to a maximum tax rate of 35 percent. The alternative tax rate is applied to the lesser of a corporation's net capital gain or its taxable income (Code Sec. 1201(a)).

> **Comment:** In other words, the current alternative tax rate for net capital gains of corporations is 35 percent for years in which a corporation's ordinary income tax rate exceeds 35 percent. In effect, this alternative tax does not currently apply because the maximum corporate income tax rate is 35 percent.

An alternative maximum tax rate of 23.8 percent applies to the qualified timber gain of a C corporation for the tax year beginning in 2016. Qualified timber gain is the net gain from the sale or exchange of timber described in Code Sec. 631(a) (cutting of standing timber) and Code Sec. 631(b) (disposal of timber with a retained economic interest or outright sale). The special rate applies only to timber that had been held for more than 15 years (Code Sec. 1201(b)).

Taxation of REITs on net capital gain. Generally, real estate investment trusts (REITs) are subject to a tax on net capital gain. However, a REIT can pay capital gain dividends to its shareholders in order to reduce its capital gains tax liability. A REIT may elect to retain, rather than distribute, its net long-term capital gains and pay the tax on such gains, while its shareholders include their proportionate share of the undistributed long-term capital gains in income and receive a credit for their share of the tax paid by the REIT. Specifically, the REIT may designate amounts as undistributed capital gains in respect of its shareholders' shares or its holders' beneficial interests. The REIT must then pay tax on the net capital gain within 30 days after the close of its tax year (Code Sec. 857(b)(3)).

Foreign tax credit limitation - capital gains. Special rules apply to capital gains and losses that require certain adjustments when calculating the foreign tax credit limitation (Code Sec. 904(b)(2) and (3)). Specifically, foreign source capital gains and losses are subject to (1) a capital gain net income limitation adjustment (i.e., U.S. capital loss adjustment), and (2) a capital gain rate differential adjustment.

If there is a capital gains rate differential (e.g., capital gains are taxed at lower rates than ordinary income), adjustments must be made to capital gains and foreign source losses when calculating the numerator of the foreign tax credit limitation fraction. Capital gains, but not losses, are also adjusted in the denominator of the fraction. The adjustment is needed to take into account the difference between the maximum U.S. tax rate and the more favorable capital gains rates. For individuals, the capital gain tax rate differential exists for any tax year in which the taxpayer is subject to Code Sec. 1(h), relating to the maximum capital gains tax rate. For corporations, a differen-

BACKGROUND

tial exists if the corporate rate under Code Secs. 11, 511, 831(a) or 831(b) exceeds the alternative rate of Code Sec. 1201(a) (Code Sec. 904(b)(3)(D)). A reduction of capital gain net income is required by the rate differential portion of the income. The rate differential portion is the excess of the highest applicable rate over the alternative rate over the highest applicable rate (Code Sec. 904(b)(3)(D)).

Disallowance of graduated corporate tax rates or accumulated earnings credit to transferee corporations. Under Code Sec. 1551, the graduated corporate tax rates or the accumulated earnings credit may be disallowed to a transferee corporation that is controlled by the transferor or its stockholders. This provision may be utilized by the IRS when a corporation transfers all or part of its property, other than money, to a controlled corporation and the transferee corporation was either (i) created for the purpose of acquiring the property, or (ii) not actively engaged in business at the time of the transfer.

If the IRS utilizes the disallowance provision, it is up to the transferee corporation to prove that the major purpose of the transfer was not to secure the benefits of the graduated tax rates or the accumulated earnings credit. The IRS may disallow application of the graduated corporate tax rates or accumulated earnings credits for indirect, as well as direct transfers (Code Sec. 1551(a)).

Control means ownership of at least 80 percent of the voting power or value of the stock of each corporation. For a transfer by five or fewer persons, control means ownership of at least 80 percent of the value or voting power of each corporation's stock and more than 50 percent of the value or voting power of each corporation's stock (taking into account the ownership of each individual only to the extent their stock ownership is identical with respect to each corporation) after the transfer (Code Sec. 1551(b)). In determining whether control exists, special constructive stock ownership rules apply.

Limitation on multiple tax benefits of controlled groups of corporations. Corporations that are component members of controlled groups on a December 31 are required to share specific tax benefits for their tax years including that December 31 (Code Sec. 1561). These benefits include: (1) use of the Code Sec. 11(b) graduated bracket amounts; (2) use of the $250,000 ($150,000 if any component member is a personal service corporation) amount for purposes of computing the Code Sec. 535(c) accumulated earnings credit; and (3) use of the $40,000 exemption amount for purposes of computing the amount of minimum tax (Code Sec. 1561(a)).

The tax benefit amounts are generally divided equally among the group members, unless all of the members consent to an apportionment plan providing for an unequal allocation of these amounts (Reg. § 1.1561-3(b)).

A controlled group of corporation consists of corporations related through certain stock ownership. Controlled corporate groups generally include (i) a parent-subsidiary controlled group, (ii) a brother-sister controlled group, and (iii) a combined group (Code Sec. 1563(a)).

Tax withholding on disposition of U.S. real property. Generally, the disposition of a U.S. real property interest by a foreign person is subject to income tax withholding. The withholding obligation falls on the transferee. Generally, the transferee is re-

¶305

BACKGROUND

quired to deduct and withhold a tax equal to 15 percent of the total amount realized on the disposition (10 percent for dispositions on or before February 16, 2016) (Code Sec. 1445(a)). A higher rate of withholding applies to certain dispositions by domestic partnerships, estates and trusts, and distributions by foreign corporations, real estate investment trusts (REITs), and regulated investment companies (RICs) (generally 35 percent of the gain realized) (Code Sec. 1445(e)).

NEW LAW EXPLAINED

21-percent flat corporate income tax rate established; normalization requirements provided.—Reduction in corporate tax rate. For tax years beginning after December 31, 2017, the graduated corporate tax rate structure is eliminated and corporate taxable income is taxed at a 21-percent flat rate (Code Sec. 11(b), as amended by the Tax Cuts and Jobs Act (P.L. 115-97)).

> **Comment:** The new law does not provide a special rate for personal service corporations (PSCs); therefore, PSCs are also taxed at a 21-percent rate.

> **Comment:** The lower corporate tax rate will allow domestic corporations to remain globally competitive and will increase international investments in the United States. Also, it is expected that the lower corporate tax rate will lead to economic growth and jobs creation because U.S. corporations will have more money to invest. In addition, the lower corporate tax rate will provide less incentives for U.S. companies to shift operations and employees abroad and will encourage investment of their foreign earnings into business expansion and employment in the United States.

> **Comment:** Presumably, the Code Sec. 15 tax proration rules apply to the corporate tax rate change. There is nothing in the text of the 2017 Tax Cuts Act or the final Conference Committee Report that specifically indicates that Code Sec. 15 does not apply to the corporate rate change under Code Sec. 11(b). Also, it does not appear that any of the existing exceptions in Code Sec. 15 apply. However, caution is required since there is no specific mention of the Code Sec. 15 proration rules in any of the Committee Reports, summaries, etc. produced by the Joint Committee on Taxation and Congress leading up to final passage of the law. On the other hand, the legislative text does specifically state that Code Sec. 15 does not apply to the individual rate changes in Code Sec. 1(j). In addition, a number of other changes in the legislation could be considered a "rate change"—for example, the repeal of the alternative minimum tax (AMT) for corporations. It is not clear whether the Code Sec. 15 proration rules will apply for AMT changes or not, and how this will interact with the corporate rate change under Code Sec. 11(b) in prorating tax liability. It will be helpful if the Treasury Department issues some guidance on this issue.

The alternative tax for net capital gains is repealed (Act Sec. 13001(b)(2) of the 2017 Tax Cuts Act, striking Code Sec. 1201).

> **Comment:** The alternative tax is obsolete in light of the new 21-percent corporate tax rate.

NEW LAW EXPLAINED

Other changes. A definition of undistributed capital gain is provided for purposes of the rules related to the taxation of REITs on net capital gains. Specifically, undistributed capital gain is the excess of the net capital gain over the deduction for dividends paid (as defined in Code Sec. 561) determined with reference to capital gain dividends only (Code Sec. 857(b)(3)(F), as amended by the 2017 Tax Cuts Act).

The new law also clarifies that, for purposes of the capital gain rate differential adjustment in determining the foreign tax credit limitation, there is a capital gain rate differential for any year if Code Sec. 1(h) applies to the tax year. In addition, the rate differential portion of foreign source net capital gain, net capital gain, or the excess of net capital gain from sources within the United States over net capital gain, as the case may be, is the same proportion of such amount as (1) the excess of (i) the highest rate of tax set forth in Code Sec. 1(a), (b), (c), (d), or (e) (whichever applies), over (ii) the alternative rate of tax determined under Code Sec. 1(h), bears to (2) the rate referred to in item (i) (Code Sec. 904(b)(3)(D) and (E), as added by the 2017 Tax Cuts Act).

Moreover, the rules for withholding of tax on dispositions of U.S. real property are modified to replace the 35-percent tax required to be withheld on certain dispositions by domestic partnerships, estates and trusts, and distributions by foreign corporations, REITs, and RICs with the highest rate of tax in effect for the tax year under Code Sec. 11(b) (Code Sec. 1445(e), as amended by the 2017 Tax Cuts Act).

In addition, the provision disallowing the graduated corporate tax rates or the accumulated earnings credit to transferee corporations upon certain transfers is repealed (Act Sec. 13001(b)(5)(A) of the 2017 Tax Cuts Act, striking Code Sec. 1551).

The new law further modifies the former rules limiting the use of multiple tax benefits of controlled group of corporations to leave only the limitation on the use of the accumulated earnings credit. Specifically, the component members of a controlled group of corporations on a December 31 are limited, for purposes of Subtitle A of the Code, for their tax years which include that December 31, to one $250,000 ($150,000 if any component member is a personal service corporation) accumulated earnings credit under Code Sec. 535(c). This amount must be divided equally among the component members of the group on that December 31, unless an unequal allocation is allowed by regulations (Code Sec. 1561(a), as amended by the 2017 Tax Cuts Act).

> **Comment:** This change reflects the repeal of the corporate alternative minimum tax and the elimination of the graduated corporate tax rate structure by the 2017 Tax Cuts Act.

If a corporation has a short tax year that does not include a December 31 and is a component member of a controlled group of corporations with respect to that tax year, then for purposes of Subtitle A of the Code, the amount used in computing the accumulated earnings credit of the corporation for that tax year is determined by dividing $250,000 (or $150,000) by the number of corporations that are component members of the group on the last day of that tax year. For this purpose, the definition of component member in Code Sec. 1563(b) is applied as if the last day were substituted for December 31 (Code Sec. 1561(b), as amended by the 2017 Tax Cuts Act).

NEW LAW EXPLAINED

Comment: The effective date provided for the amendment to Code Sec. 1561 is for transfers made after December 31, 2017 (Act Sec. 13001(c)(3) of the 2017 Tax Cuts Act). However, this effective date does not appear to be correct given the subject and application of Code Sec. 1561. More likely, the amendment to Code Sec. 1561 should apply to tax years beginning after December 31, 2017. Also, it is likely that the effective date for transfers made after December 31, 2017, is intended to apply to the repeal of Code Sec. 1551, which concerns transfers to corporations.

Normalization requirements. For taxpayers subject to the normalization method of accounting (e.g., regulated public utilities), the new law provides for the normalization of excess deferred tax reserves resulting from the reduction of corporate income tax rates (with respect to prior depreciation or recovery allowances taken on assets placed in service before the corporate rate reduction takes effect).

Specifically, a taxpayer is not treated as using a normalization method of accounting with respect to any public utility property for purposes of Code Sec. 167 or 168, if the taxpayer, in computing its cost of service for ratemaking purposes and reflecting operating results in its regulated books of account, reduces the excess tax reserve more rapidly or to a greater extent than such reserve would be reduced under the average rate assumption method (Act Sec. 13001(d)(1) of the 2017 Tax Cuts Act).

For this purpose, the excess tax reserve is the excess of:

(1) the reserve for deferred taxes (described in Code Sec. 168(i)(9)(A)(ii)) as of the day before the corporate rate reductions (provided in the amendments made by Act Sec. 13001 of the 2017 Tax Cuts Act) take effect, over

(2) the amount which would be the balance in the reserve if the amount of the reserve were determined by assuming that the corporate rate reductions were in effect for all prior periods (Act Sec. 13001(d)(3)(A) of the 2017 Tax Cuts Act).

The average rate assumption method is the method under which the excess in the reserve for deferred taxes is reduced over the remaining lives of the property as used in the taxpayer's regulated books of account that gave rise to the reserve for deferred taxes. Under this method, during the time period in which timing differences for the property (i.e., differences between tax depreciation and regulatory depreciation with respect to the property) reverse, the amount of the adjustment to the reserve for the deferred taxes is calculated by multiplying:

(1) the ratio of the aggregate deferred taxes for the property to the aggregate timing differences for the property as of the beginning of the period in question, by

(2) the amount of the timing differences that reverse during that period (Act Sec. 13001(d)(3)(B) of the 2017 Tax Cuts Act).

Comment: In other words, under this method, the excess tax reserve is reduced as the timing differences reverse over the remaining life of the asset. To ensure that the deferred tax reserve, including the excess tax reserve, is reduced to zero at the end of the regulatory life of the asset that generated the reserve, the amount of the timing difference that reverses during a tax year is multiplied by the ratio of (1) the aggregate deferred taxes as of the beginning of the period in

NEW LAW EXPLAINED

question to (2) the aggregate timing differences for the property as of the beginning of the period in question.

Comment: The reversal of timing differences generally occurs when the amount of the tax depreciation taken with respect to an asset is less than the amount of the regulatory depreciation taken with respect to the asset.

Example: A calendar year regulated utility placed property costing $100 million in service in 2016. For regulatory (book) purposes, the property is depreciated over 10 years on a straight line basis with a full year's allowance in the first year. For tax purposes, the property is depreciated over 5 years using the 200 percent declining balance method and a half-year placed in service convention.

Normalization calculation for corporate rate reduction
(Millions of dollars)

	2016	2017	2018	2019	2020	2021	2022	2023	2024	2025	Total
Tax expense	20	32	19.2	11.52	11.52	5.76	0	0	0	0	100
Book depreciation	10	10	10	10	10	10	10	10	10	10	100
Timing difference	10	22	9.2	1.52	1.52	(4.24)	(10)	(10)	(10)	(10)	0
Tax rate	35%	35%	21%	21%	21%	31.1%	31.1%	31.1%	31.1%	31.1%	
Annual adjustment to reserve	3.5	7.7	1.9	0.3	0.3	(1.3)	(3.1)	(3.1)	(3.1)	(3.1)	0
Cumulative deferred tax reserve	3.5	11.2	13.1	13.5	13.8	12.5	9.3	6.2	3.1	(0.0)	0
Annual adjustment at 21%						(0.9)	(2.1)	(2.1)	(2.1)	(2.1)	(9.3)
Annual adjustment at average rate						(1.3)	(3.1)	(3.1)	(3.1)	(3.1)	(13.8)
Excess tax reserve						0.4	1.0	1.0	1.0	1.0	4.5

The excess tax reserve as of December 31, 2017, the day before the corporate rate reduction takes effect, is $4.5 million (the cumulative deferred tax reserve as of December 31, 2017 ($11.2 million), minus the cumulative timing difference as of December 31, 2017 ($32 million), multiplied by 21 percent). The taxpayer will begin taking the excess tax reserve into account in the 2021 tax year, which is the first year in which the tax depreciation taken with respect to the property is less than the depreciation reflected in the regulated books of account. The annual adjustment to the deferred tax reserve for the 2021 through 2025 tax years is multiplied by 31.1 percent, which is the ratio of the aggregate deferred

---

¶305

NEW LAW EXPLAINED

> taxes as of the beginning of 2021 ($13.8 million) to the aggregate timing differences for the property as of the beginning of 2021 ($44.2 million) (Conference Report on H.R. 1, Tax Cuts and Jobs Act (H. Rept. 115-466)).

Alternative method for certain taxpayers. If, as of the first day of the tax year that includes December 22, 2017:

(1) the taxpayer was required by a regulatory agency to compute depreciation for public utility property on the basis of an average life or composite rate method, and

(2) the taxpayer's books and underlying records did not contain the vintage account data necessary to apply the average rate assumption method, then

(3) the taxpayer is treated as using a normalization method of accounting if, with respect to such jurisdiction, the taxpayer uses the alternative method for public utility property that is subject to the regulatory authority of that jurisdiction (Act Sec. 13001(d)(2) of the 2017 Tax Cuts Act).

For this purpose, the alternative method is the method in which the taxpayer:

(1) computes the excess tax reserve on all public utility property included in the plant account on the basis of the weighted average life or composite rate used to compute depreciation for regulatory purposes, and

(2) reduces the excess tax reserve ratably over the remaining regulatory life of the property (Act Sec. 13001(d)(3)(C) of the 2017 Tax Cuts Act).

Tax increase for normalization violation. If, for any tax year ending after December 22, 2017, the taxpayer does not use a normalization method of accounting for the corporate rate reductions provided in the amendments made by Act Sec. 13001 of the 2017 Tax Cuts Act:

(1) the taxpayer's tax for the tax year is increased by the amount by which it reduces its excess tax reserve more rapidly than permitted under a normalization method of accounting, and

(2) the taxpayer is not treated as using a normalization method of accounting for purposes of Code Sec. 168(f)(2) and (i)(9)(C) (Act Sec. 13001(d)(4) of the 2017 Tax Cuts Act).

Practical Analysis: Michael Schlesinger, Partner at Schlesinger & Sussman, Clifton, NJ and author of PRACTICAL GUIDE TO S CORPORATIONS (7th Ed.), notes that here are only three ways to remove money from a C corporation: salary, loans to shareholders or dividends. Congress has kept the provision prescribing that dividends are taxed at capital gain rates. This dividend capital gain tax provision applied to a small closely held C corporate business could yield adverse taxation for the shareholders especially for those taxpayers taxed at the 15 percent rate on their dividends. To illustrate, assume that a C corporation is owned by one individual

NEW LAW EXPLAINED

shareholder and it earns $1,000; and pays the 21 percent corporate tax leaving it with $790 (1,000 – [21% × 1,000]). Assume the shareholder pays a tax of 15 percent on the dividend and the corporation declares a dividend of $790 with the sole shareholder paying a tax of $118.50 (15% × 790 = 118.50) on the dividend. The effective tax rate on $1,000 of income is 32.85% (210 [corporate tax] + 118.50 [tax on dividends] = 328.50; 328.50 divided by $1,000 = 32.85%). If only $190 is declared as a dividend leaving $600 in the corporation, then the tax on the dividend is $28.50 (190 × 15% = 28.50) and the effective tax rate is now 23.85% (210 + 28.50 = 238.50; 238.50 divided by 1,000 = 23.85%). But this means that $600 stays entirely in the corporation under this scenario (1,000 – [210 tax + 190 dividend] = 600), and there is the possibility of accumulated earnings tax under Code Sec. 531 if the corporation cannot justify accumulating earnings. Additionally, when this $600 is distributed to the shareholder as a dividend or the corporation pays the $600 to the shareholder as a salary, the $600 will be taxed again.

In contrast, if the small family business was incorporated as an S corporation and could not qualify for Code Sec. 199A's special taxation for passthrough entities, the shareholder will be taxed at the individual tax rates. Assume that the taxpayer in the above example is in the 24-percent tax bracket (single taxpayers whose taxable income is less than $157,500; married filing jointly, taxable income less than $315,000); thus leaving the shareholder with $760 after taxes (1,000 – 240 = 760). If the S corporation can qualify for Code Sec. 199A treatment for its taxable income, then there will be more than $760 of after tax income.

Practical Analysis: Jim Hamill, Director of Tax Practice at Reynolds, Hix & Co., P.A. in Albuquerque, NM, observes that the lower corporate tax rate will be accompanied by two existing benefits for shareholders. First, there continues to be a preferential rate for qualified dividends. Second, the Code Sec. 1202 exclusion continues and may offer a zero tax rate for gains from qualified small business stock. These three factors will change the choice-of-entity decision for clients with the right fact pattern. For example, if a dollar of corporate income is taxed at 21 cents, the after-tax profit of 79 cents may then be distributed and taxed again at a rate not exceeding 23.8 percent, which is an additional 18.8 cents of tax. In this "worst case" scenario—two levels of tax at the highest rates—the total tax burden is 39.8 percent. If profits are retained and recognized through a later stock or asset sale, shareholder-level gains may be entirely tax free if the requirements of Code Sec. 1202 are satisfied. This does not mean that the slide in corporate tax filings will be entirely reversed, particularly with the new deduction for certain types of passthrough entity income, but the mathematics of entity choice have been altered by the new legislation.

▶ **Effective date.** The amendments made by this section generally apply to tax years beginning after December 31, 2017 (Act Sec. 13001(c) of the Tax Cuts and Jobs Act (P.L. 115-97)). The amendment relating to the withholding rules on disposition of U.S. real property interests applies to distributions made after December 31, 2017. The amendment relating to the Code Sec. 1561 limitation on the use of the accumulated earnings credit by

NEW LAW EXPLAINED

controlled corporate groups applies to transfers made after December 31, 2017 [applies to tax years beginning after December 31, 2017].

Law source: Law at ¶5440, ¶5515, ¶5575, ¶5590, ¶5605, ¶5635, ¶5655, ¶5715, ¶5720, ¶5725, ¶5760, ¶5765, ¶5770, ¶5800, ¶5820, ¶5970, ¶6025, ¶6030, ¶6050, ¶6055, ¶6060, ¶6065, ¶6245, ¶6280, ¶6330, and ¶6335. Committee Report at ¶10,310.

— Act Sec. 13001(a) of the Tax Cuts and Jobs Act (P.L. 115-97), amending Code Sec. 11(b);

— Act Sec. 13001(b)(1), amending Code Secs. 280C(c)(3)(B)(ii)(II), 860E(e)(2)(B), 860E(e)(6)(A)(ii), and 7874(c)(1)(B);

— Act Sec. 13001(b)(2), striking Code Sec. 1201 and Code Sec. 1374(b)(4), and amending Code Secs. 12, 453A(c)(3), 527(b), 594(a), 691(c)(4) , 801(a), 831(e), 832(c)(5), 834(b)(1)(D), 852(b)(3)(A), 857(b)(3), 882(a)(1), 904(b), 1381(b), 6425(c)(1)(A), 6655(g)(1)(A)(i), and 7518(g)(6)(A);

— Act Sec. 13001(b)(3) through (7), amending Code Secs. 535(c)(5), 852(b)(1), 1445(e), 1446(b)(2)(B), 1561, as amended by Act Sec. 12001, and 7518(g)(6)(A), and striking Code Sec. 1551;

— Act Sec. 13001(c), providing the effective date;

— Act Sec. 13001(d).

¶310 Alternative Minimum Tax (AMT) for Corporations

SUMMARY OF NEW LAW

The alternative minimum tax (AMT) for corporations has been repealed, for tax years beginning after 2017. Any unused minimum tax credit of a corporation may be used to offset regular tax liability for any tax year. In addition, a portion of unused minimum tax credit is refundable in 2018 through 2021. The refundable portion is 50 percent (100 percent in 2021) of any excess minimum tax for the year over any credit allowable against regular tax for that year.

BACKGROUND

An alternative minimum tax (AMT) is imposed on a corporation equal to the excess of the taxpayer's tentative minimum tax for the year, over regular tax liability (Code Sec. 55). For a corporation, tentative minimum tax is 20 percent of the taxpayer's alternative minimum taxable income (AMTI). A small corporation is exempt from AMT if its average annual gross receipts do not exceed $7.5 million for the previous three tax years. The dollar threshold is reduced to $5 million for a corporation in its first three years of existence.

AMTI is the taxpayer's regular taxable income increased by AMT tax preference items and modified by AMT adjustment (Code Secs. 56 and 57). Corporate tax preference items not allowed in computing AMTI include deductions for depletion and intangible drilling costs, as well the exclusion of tax-exempt interest on private

BACKGROUND

activity bonds. Corporate AMT adjustments include net operating losses (NOLs), depreciation, gains and losses, as well as adjusted current earnings (ACE). A corporation generally must also reduce or cut back certain tax preference items before calculation of its AMTI. A corporation may avoid having an AMT preference or adjustment by electing to capitalize certain expenses and deduct them ratably for regular tax purposes beginning with the tax year (or month) in which the expenses were made (Code Sec. 59(e)). The amortization period is three years for circulation expenses, 60 months for intangible drilling costs (IDC), and 10 years for mineral exploration and development expenses.

If a corporation is subject to AMT in any tax year, it may claim a tax credit against its regular income tax liability for AMT paid in previous tax years (Code Sec. 53(c)). The minimum tax credit is equal to the corporation's AMT liability for the current year, less any minimum tax credit claimed in previous years. If the taxpayer was a small corporation exempt from AMT, its minimum credit is limited to the extent the corporation's regular tax liability (reduced by other credits) exceeds 25 percent of the excess (if any) of the corporation's regular tax (reduced by other credits) over $25,000 (Code Sec. 55(e)(5)).

The minimum credit is limited to the extent that the regular tax liability, reduced by other nonrefundable credits, exceeds the taxpayer's tentative minimum tax for the tax year. Any unused minimum credit may be carried forward indefinitely as a credit against regular tax liability to the extent that the regular tax liability reduced by all other nonrefundable credits exceeds the tentative AMT liability for the tax year. The credit may not be used to offset any future AMT liability. However, a corporation may elect to claim a portion of its unused minimum tax credits outstanding, instead of claiming the bonus depreciation deduction on the property it placed in service during the tax year that qualifies for bonus depreciation (Code Sec. 168(k)(4)). In addition, any minimum tax credit carryover from a C corporation tax year may offset the built-in gains tax of a corporation in an S corporation year (Code Sec. 1374(b)(3)(B)).

NEW LAW EXPLAINED

Corporate AMT repealed; minimum tax credit refundable in 2018 through 2021.—The alternative minimum tax (AMT) is repealed for corporations for tax years beginning after December 31, 2017 (Code Sec. 55(a), as amended by the Tax Cuts and Jobs Act (P.L. 115-97)). Thus, the AMT is only applicable to individuals, estates, and trusts after 2017.

> **Comment:** The AMT exemption amounts and phaseout thresholds for individuals (but not estates and trusts) are temporarily increased beginning in 2018 (see ¶110). Partnership or S corporations are not subject to AMT, but instead a partner or S corporation shareholder computes AMT liability separately by taking into account their share of partnership or S corporation items.

A corporation's tentative minimum tax is zero ($0) for purposes of the minimum tax credit (AMT credit) beginning in 2018 (Code Sec. 53(d)(2), as amended by the 2017 Tax Cuts Act). As a result, a minimum tax credit claimed by a corporation beginning

¶310

NEW LAW EXPLAINED

after 2017 is generally limited to the taxpayer's regular tax liability, reduced by other nonrefundable credits. The minimum tax credit is the corporation's AMT liability from tax years prior to its repeal and carried over to tax years after 2017 (Code Sec. 53(e), as added by the 2017 Tax Cuts Act). Any minimum tax credit carryover from a C corporation tax year may continue to offset the built-in gain tax of an S corporation until tax years beginning after December 31, 2021 (Code Sec. 1374(b)(3)(B), as amended by the 2017 Tax Cuts Act).

Any unused minimum tax credit is refundable for tax years beginning in 2018, 2019, 2020, and 2021 (Code Sec. 53(e), as added by the 2017 Tax Cuts Act). The refundable credit amount is equal to 50 percent (100 percent for tax years beginning in 2021) of the excess of the minimum tax credit for the tax year, over the amount allowable for the year against regular tax liability. Thus, the full amount of the minimum tax credit is allowed in tax years beginning before 2022. If a corporation has a short tax year, then the refundable credit amount for that year is prorated based on the number of days in the short year compared to 365 days.

Election to claim unused AMT credits in lieu of bonus depreciation. The annual election provided to corporations to claim unused minimum tax credits in place of bonus depreciation on property placed in service during the tax year of the election is repealed, effective for tax years beginning after December 31, 2017 (Code Sec. 168(k)(4), stricken by the 2017 Tax Cuts Act).

General business credit and effect on other rules. Since corporate AMT is repealed, a corporation's tentative minimum tax is zero ($0) after 2017 for purposes of the tax liability limitation of the general business credit (Code Sec. 38(c)(6)(E), as added by the 2017 Tax Cuts Act). This means that a corporation may claim the credit to the extent it does not exceed 25 percent of its net regular tax liability above $25,000.

> **Comment:** Since the corporate AMT is repealed, a corporation may forgo the election to amortize certain expenses to avoid any AMT adjustment or preference with regard to the expenses (circulation expenses, intangible drilling costs, and mineral exploration and development expenses) (Code Sec. 59(e)).

> **Comment:** A net operating loss (NOL) deduction of a corporation from tax years beginning after 2017 is determined without regard to any AMT adjustments or preferences due to the repeal of the corporate AMT. Thus, an NOL carried back to determine the corporation's alternative minimum taxable income (AMTI) in tax years before 2018 is calculated the same as for regular tax liability.

▶ **Effective date.** The amendments made by this section generally apply to tax years beginning after December 31, 2017 (Act Secs. 12001(c) and 12002(d)(1) of the Tax Cuts and Jobs Act (P.L. 115-97)). The amendment striking the minimum tax credit carryover of an S corporation arising in a tax year in which the corporation was a C corporation to offset the built-in gains tax of the S corporation applies to tax years beginning after December 31, 2021 (Act. Sec. 12002(d)(2) of the 2017 Tax Cuts Act).

Law source: Law at ¶5010, ¶5015, ¶5055, ¶5090, ¶5135, ¶5140, ¶5145, ¶5150, ¶5315, ¶5745, ¶5750, ¶5800, ¶5805, ¶5850, ¶5920, ¶6025, ¶6245, and ¶6280. Committee Report at ¶10,300.

NEW LAW EXPLAINED

— Act Sec. 12001(a) of the Tax Cuts and Jobs Act (P.L. 115-97), amending Code Sec. 55(a);

— Act Sec. 12002(a) and (b), adding Code Sec. 53(e) and amending Code Sec. 53(d)(3);

— Act Secs. 12001(b) and 12002(c), amending Code Secs. 11(d), 38(c)(6), 53(d)(2), 55(b)(1), 55(b)(3), 55(c)(1), 55(d), 56(b)(2), 58(a), 59(a), 847(9), 882(a)(1), 897(a)(2)(A), 911(f), 962(a)(1), 1374(b)(3)(B), 1561(a), 6425(c)(1)(A), 6655(e)(2), 6655(g)(1)(A), and striking Code Secs. 12(7), 55(e), 56(c), 56(g), 59(b), 59(f), 168(k)(4), and 848(i);

— Act Secs. 12001(c) and 12002(d), providing the effective dates.

¶315 Dividends-Received Deduction

SUMMARY OF NEW LAW

For tax years beginning after December 31, 2017, the 70-percent dividends-received deduction is reduced to 50 percent and the 80-percent dividends-received deduction is reduced to 65 percent.

BACKGROUND

Generally, a corporation is allowed a deduction for dividends received from other taxable domestic corporations (Code Sec. 243(a)). The amount of the deduction is generally equal to 70 percent of the dividend received.

In the case of any dividend received from a 20-percent owned corporation, the amount of the deduction is equal to 80 percent of the dividend received (Code Sec. 243(c)). A 20-percent owned corporation is any corporation if 20 percent or more of the stock of such corporation (by vote and value) is owned by the taxpayer. For this purpose, certain preferred stock is excluded.

> **Key Rates and Figures:** Dividends subject to the 70-percent dividends-received deduction are taxed at a maximum rate of 10.5 percent (30 percent of the 35 percent top corporate tax rate). Dividends subject to the 80-percent dividends-received deduction are taxed at a maximum rate of 7 percent (20 percent of the 35 percent top corporate tax rate).

In the case of a dividend received from a corporation that is a member of the same affiliated group, the deduction is equal to 100 percent of the dividend received (Code Sec. 243(a)(3) and (b)(1)). For this purpose, an affiliated group is defined in Code Sec. 1504(a) (Code Sec. 243(b)(2)).

A domestic corporation is entitled to a 70-percent deduction for the U.S.-source portion of dividends received from a foreign corporation (other than a passive foreign investment company (PFIC)) that is at least 10-percent owned, by vote and value, by the domestic corporation (Code Sec. 245(a)(1)). The deduction is 80 percent in the case of dividends received from a 20-percent owned corporation. A 100-percent deduction is allowed for eligible dividends received from a wholly owned foreign subsidiary all of whose income is effectively connected with a U.S. business (Code Sec. 245(b)).

BACKGROUND

A U.S. corporation is allowed a 100-percent deduction for any dividends received from a corporation that are distributed from earnings and profits attributable to foreign trade income for a period during which such corporation was a foreign sales corporation (FSC) (Code Sec. 245(c)(1)). A 70-percent dividends-received deduction (80 percent in the case of dividends received from a 20-percent-owned corporation) is provided for any dividend received by a U.S. corporation from another corporation that is distributed out of earnings and profits attributable to "effectively connected income" received or accrued by such other corporation while it was an FSC (Code Sec. 245(c)(1)(B)). Effectively connected income includes all income that is actually effectively connected with a U.S. trade or business and is subject to U.S. income tax, and all income that is deemed to be effectively connected and is subject to U.S. tax (e.g., by the FSC rules on investment income) (Code Sec. 245(c)(4)).

The aggregate dividends-received deduction under Code Secs. 243 and 245 is limited to 70 percent of the receiving corporation's taxable income if it owns less than 20 percent of the distributing corporation, and to 80 percent of its taxable income if it owns 20 percent or more of the distributing corporation (Code Sec. 246(b)).

The 70-percent corporate dividends-received deduction (80 percent in the case of dividends received from a 20-percent owned corporation) is reduced in the case of dividends received with respect to debt-financed portfolio stock by a percentage related to the amount of debt incurred to purchase the stock (Code Sec. 246A(a)).

For purposes of the foreign tax credit limitation, dividends from a foreign corporation are treated as income from foreign sources to the extent the amount of the dividend exceeds the amount that is 100/70th (100/80th in the case of a 20-percent owned corporation) of the amount of the deduction allowable under Code Sec. 245 (Code Sec. 861(a)(2)).

NEW LAW EXPLAINED

Dividends-received deduction reduced.—For tax years beginning after December 31, 2017, the 70-percent dividends-received deduction is reduced to 50 percent and the 80-percent dividends-received deduction is reduced to 65 percent (Code Sec. 243(a)(1) and (c)(1), as amended by the Tax Cuts and Jobs Act (P.L. 115-97)).

> **Comment:** The dividends-received deduction is reduced to reflect the new lower corporate tax rate of 21 percent.

> **Key Rates and Figures:** Dividends subject to the new 50-percent dividends-received deduction will be taxed at a maximum rate of 10.5 percent (50 percent of the 21 percent new corporate tax rate). Dividends subject to the new 65-per-cent dividends-received deduction will be taxed at a maximum rate of 7.35 percent (35 percent of the 21 percent new corporate tax rate).

A 50-percent dividends-received deduction (65 percent in the case of dividends received from a 20-percent-owned corporation) is provided for any dividend received by a U.S. corporation from another corporation that is distributed out of earnings and profits attributable to effectively connected income received or accrued by such other

¶315

NEW LAW EXPLAINED

corporation while it was an FSC (Code Sec. 245(c)(1)(B), as amended by the 2017 Tax Cuts Act).

In addition, the aggregate amount of deductions allowed under Code Secs. 243 and 245, and Code Sec. 250, is limited to 50 percent of the receiving corporation's taxable income if it owns less than 20 percent of the distributing corporation, and to 65 percent of its taxable income if it owns 20 percent or more of the distributing corporation (Code Sec. 246(b)(3), as amended by the 2017 Tax Cuts Act). Also, the 50-percent dividends-received deduction (65 percent in the case of dividends received from a 20-percent owned corporation) is reduced in the case of dividends received with respect to debt-financed portfolio stock by a percentage related to the amount of debt incurred to purchase the stock (Code Sec. 246A(a)(1), as amended by the 2017 Tax Cuts Act).

Finally, for purposes of the foreign tax credit limitation, dividends from a foreign corporation are treated as income from foreign sources to the extent the amount of the dividend exceeds the amount that is 100/50th (100/65th in the case of a 20-percent owned corporation) of the amount of the deduction allowable under Code Sec. 245 (Code Sec. 861(a)(2), as amended by the 2017 Tax Cuts Act).

> **Practical Analysis:** William D. Elliott, Partner at Elliott, Thomason & Gibson, LLP in Dallas, Texas, comments that changes were made to the dividends received deduction in Code Sec. 243 for domestic corporations. The dividends received deduction, formally 70 percent is reduced to 50 percent and the former 80-percent dividends received deduction for 20-percent owned corporations has been changed to 65 percent, effective for 2018.

▶ **Effective date.** The amendments made by this section apply to tax years beginning after December 31, 2017 (Act Sec. 13002(f) of the Tax Cuts and Jobs Act (P.L. 115-97)).

Law source: Law at ¶5390, ¶5395, ¶5405, ¶5410, and ¶5775. Committee Report at ¶10,310.

— Act Sec. 13002(a) of the Tax Cuts and Jobs Act (P.L. 115-97), amending Code Sec. 243(a)(1) and (c);

— Act Sec. 13002(b), amending Code Sec. 245(c)(1)(B);

— Act Sec. 13002(c), amending Code Sec. 246(b)(3);

— Act Sec. 13002(d), amending Code Sec. 246A(a)(1);

— Act Sec. 13002(e), amending Code Sec. 861(a)(2);

— Act Sec. 13002(f), providing the effective date.

¶315

¶320 Contribution of Capital to Corporations

SUMMARY OF NEW LAW

The definition of contribution to capital is modified to exclude contributions by any governmental entity or civic group that are not made by a shareholder in its capacity as a shareholder. The special rules for contributions to water and sewage disposal utilities are eliminated.

BACKGROUND

Contributions to the capital of a corporation are excluded from the corporation's gross income. A contribution is exempt whether it is made by shareholders or by persons other than shareholders (Code Sec. 118(a), Reg. § 1.118-1).

However, the exemption does not apply to any contribution in aid of construction or any other contribution as either a customer or potential customer. Thus, most corporate regulated utilities cannot treat contributions received in aid of construction or any other contributions by a customer or potential customer as a nontaxable contribution. Contributions that a utility receives to provide or encourage the provision of services to or for the benefit of the contributor must be reported as income by the utility (Code Sec. 118(b)).

There is an exception to this rule for water and sewage disposal utilities, under which money or property received by such utilities qualifies as a tax-free contribution to the capital if: (1) the amount is a contribution in aid of construction; (2) in the case of contribution of property other than water or sewerage disposal facilities, the amount meets the requirements of the expenditure rule; (3) the amount (or property acquired or constructed with such amount) is excluded from the utility's rate base for rate-making purposes. Water and sewage disposal utilities are not allowed any deductions or credits for expenditures that constitute a contribution in aid of construction. Also, the adjusted basis of any property acquired by water and sewage disposal utilities with contributions in aid of construction is zero (Code Sec. 118(c)).

An extended statute of limitations period is provided for the assessment of deficiencies attributable to a contribution of property other than water or sewage disposal facilities that is treated as a contribution to capital of a water or sewage disposal utility (Code Sec. 118(d)).

NEW LAW EXPLAINED

Definition of contribution to capital modified.—For purposes of applying the general rule under Code Sec. 118(a) that excludes from a corporation's gross income any contributions to capital, contribution to capital does not include:

- any contribution in aid of construction or any other contribution as a customer or potential customer, and

NEW LAW EXPLAINED

- any contribution by any governmental entity or civic group (other than a contribution made by a shareholder as such) (Code Sec. 118(b), as added by the Tax Cuts and Jobs Act (P.L. 115-97)).

  Comment: The new law eliminates the special rules for contributions to water and sewage disposal utilities and the extended statute of limitations period for the assessment of deficiencies attributable to such contributions.

The IRS is authorized to issue regulations or other guidance as may be necessary or appropriate to carry out this provision, including regulations or other guidance for determining whether any contribution constitutes a contribution in aid of construction (Code Sec. 118(c), as added by the 2017 Tax Cuts Act).

Practical Analysis: William D. Elliott, Partner at Elliott, Thomason & Gibson, LLP in Dallas, Texas, observes that the provisions of Code Sec. 118 pertaining to contributions to capital were amended to exclude from the definition of contribution to capital (1) any contribution in aid of construction or any other contribution as a customer or potential customer, and (2) any contribution by any governmental entity or civic group (other than a contribution made by a shareholder as such), all of which is intended to be applicable only to corporations, effective on the date of enactment, with an exception for master development plans approved by a governmental entity prior to date of enactment.

▶ **Effective date.** The provision generally applies to contributions made after December 22, 2017, the date of the enactment (Act Sec. 13312(b)(1) of the Tax Cuts and Jobs Act (P.L. 115-97)). The provision will not apply to any contributions made after December 22, 2017, the date of enactment, by a governmental entity, which is made pursuant to a master development plan that has been approved prior to such date by a governmental entity (Act Sec. 13312(b)(2) of the Tax Cuts Act).

Law source: Law at ¶320. Committee Report at ¶10,520.

— Act Sec. 13312(a) of the Tax Cuts and Jobs Act (P.L. 115-97), striking Code Sec. 118(b), (c), and (d), redesignating Code Sec. 118(e) as (d), and adding new Code Sec. 118(b) and (c);

— Act Sec. 13312(b), providing the effective date.

¶325 Alaska Native Corporations and Settlement Trusts

SUMMARY OF NEW LAW

New rules have been enacted to establish the tax treatment of payments received by Alaska Native Corporations and transfers made to Alaska Native Settlement Trusts. Native Corporations are not required to recognize income for certain payments assigned to Settlement Trusts and can also deduct contributions to Settlement Trusts.

¶325

BACKGROUND

In 1971 the Alaska Native Claims Settlement Act (ANCSA) was enacted to settle claims between Alaskan natives, the State of Alaska, and the federal government. Under ANCSA (43 U.S.C. §1601 et seq.), the Alaskan native tribes gave up their territorial claims to land in exchange for title to 44 million acres of land that they had historically used, and $962.5 million. The compensation was to be transferred to 12 regional Alaska Native Corporations (Native Corporations). A thirteenth Native Corporation was later established for the benefit of Alaska natives living outside of Alaska.

Under the ANCSA, the Native Corporations could create Alaska Native Settlement Trusts (Settlement Trusts) to "promote the health, education and welfare of its beneficiaries and preserve the heritage and culture of Natives" (43 U.S.C. §1601 et seq.; 43 U.S.C. §1629e). A Settlement Trust generally permits the separation of portfolio assets from the business assets of a Native Corporation, and allows these portfolio assets to be invested to provide income to Alaska Natives and their future generations free of business risks of the Native Corporations.

Before enactment of Code Sec. 646, the IRS took the position that a Native Corporation's transfer of property to a Settlement Trust constituted a distribution of assets to the Settlement Trust's individual beneficiaries, who were then currently taxed on the assets to the extent of the Native Corporation's current or accumulated earnings and profits under Code Sec. 301. Thus, beneficiaries could be taxed on Native Corporation's transfer to a Settlement Trust, even though they had received only an illiquid beneficial interest in the Trust (S. Rep. No. 107-30, Restoring Earnings to Lift Individuals and Empower Families (RELIEF) Act of 2001 (S. 896)). This tax treatment of individual beneficiaries was considered to inhibit the formation of Settlement Trusts.

A Settlement Trust established by a Native Corporation may elect to have special rules apply to the trust and its beneficiaries with respect to the trust (Code Sec. 646(c), as enacted by the Economic Growth and Tax Relief Reconciliation Act of 2001 (P.L. 2001-17)). The electing Settlement Trust will pay tax on its income at the lowest rate specified in Code Sec. 1(c) for ordinary income and capital gains of an individual (Code Sec. 646(b)(1) and (2)). No amount will be included in the gross income of the beneficiaries by reason of a contribution to the electing Settlement Trust (Code Sec. 646(d)(1)). The law also provides rules governing the treatment of distributions to beneficiaries by an electing Settlement Trust, the reporting requirements associated with the election (Code Sec. 6039H), and the consequences of the trust's disqualification due to the allowance of certain impermissible dispositions of trust interests or Native Corporation stock (Code Sec. 646(e)). The Code Sec. 646 provisions regarding the income tax treatment of an electing Settlement Trust and its beneficiaries, and the reporting requirements under Code Sec. 6039H of a fiduciary of an electing Settlement Trust, were made permanent for tax years beginning after December 31, 2012, by the American Taxpayer Relief Act of 2012 (P.L. 112-240).

NEW LAW EXPLAINED

Tax treatment of payments made to Alaska Native Corporations and Alaska Native Settlement Trusts clarified.—The tax treatment of transactions between

NEW LAW EXPLAINED

Alaska Native Corporations (Native Corporations) and Alaska Native Settlement Trusts (Settlement Trusts) is clarified by the following new provisions:

- Native Corporations are not required to recognize income for certain payments assigned to Settlement Trusts (Code Sec. 139G, as added by the Tax Cuts and Jobs Act (P.L. 115-97)), and

- Native Corporations can deduct contributions to Settlement Trusts (other than those made pursuant to Code Sec. 139G) (Code Sec. 247, as added by the 2017 Tax Cuts Act).

Settlement Trusts may also elect to defer recognition of income for payments received from Native Corporations (Code Sec. 247(g), as added by the 2017 Tax Cuts Act).

Additionally, information reporting is required for deductible contributions made by Native Corporations to Settlement Trusts (Code Sec. 6039H(e), as added by the 2017 Tax Cuts Act).

Native Corporations assignment of payments under ANCSA to Settlement Trusts. The value of payments that would otherwise be made or treated as made to any one of the 13 Native Corporations under the Alaska Native Claims Settlement Act (ANCSA), (43 U.S.C. 1601 et seq.) will not be included in the gross income of the Native Corporation provided that the payments:

- are assigned in writing to a Settlement Trust, and

- were not received by the Native Corporation before it made the assignment to the Settlement Trust (Code Sec. 139G(a), as added by the 2017 Tax Cuts Act).

This nonrecognition rule also applies to payments that would otherwise have been made to a Village Corporation pursuant to 7(j) of the ANSCA (43 U.S.C. 1606(j)) (Code Sec. 139G(a), as added by the 2017 Tax Cuts Act).

A Settlement Trust that receives assigned payments from a Native Corporation must include the payments in its gross income when the payments are received pursuant to assignment. The assigned payments will have the same character as if they were received by the Native Corporation. The amount of any assignment made by a Native Corporation to a Settlement Trust must be described with reasonable particularity. It may either be described as a percentage of one or more payments, or as a fixed dollar amount (Code Sec. 139G(b) and (c), as added by the 2017 Tax Cuts Act).

An assignment to a Settlement Trust must specify whether it is made in perpetuity or for a period of time, and whether the assignment may be revoked (Code Sec. 139G(d), as added by the 20017 Tax Cuts Act).

A Native Corporation cannot take a deduction for any amounts received under the ANCSA that were excluded from income under Code Sec. 139G(a) (Code Sec. 139G(e), as added by the 2017 Tax Cuts Act).

The terms "Native Corporation" and "Settlement Trust" are defined under Code Sec. 646(h) (Code Sec. 139G(f), as added by the 2017 Tax Cuts Act).

¶325

NEW LAW EXPLAINED

Deductions for contributions by Native Corporations. A Native Corporation may elect annually to deduct contributions made to a Settlement Trust (Code Sec. 247(a) and (e), as added by the 2017 Tax Cuts Act).

> **Comment:** No deduction will be allowed to a Native Corporation for amounts that were made nontaxable underCode Sec. 139G, as added by the Tax Cuts Act.

If otherwise allowable, the Native Corporation's deduction will be available regardless of whether or not it has made an election under Code Sec. 646 (Code Sec. 247(a), as added by the 2017 Tax Cuts Act).

The deduction will be equal to the amount of payment in the case of cash contributions, regardless of the method of payment (including currency, coins, money order, or check). In the case of all other forms of payment, the deduction will be equal to *the lesser of* the Native Corporation's adjusted basis in the property contributed, or the fair market value of the property contributed (Code Sec. 247(b), as added by the 2017 Tax Cuts Act).

A Native Corporation's deduction under Code Sec. 247(a) cannot exceed its taxable income (as determined without regard to such deduction), for the tax year in which the contribution was made. If the aggregate amount of the contributions exceeds the Native Corporation's taxable income for the tax year, the amount of the excess may be carried over in each of the 15 succeeding years (Code Sec. 247(c), as added by the 2017 Tax Cuts Act).

The terms "Native Corporation" and "Settlement Trust" are defined under Code Sec. 646(h) (Code Sec. 247(d), as added by the 2017 Tax Cuts Act).

Election to claim deductions. A Native Corporation may elect to claim deductions under Code Sec. 247 on its income tax return or an amendment or supplement to the return. Each election will only be effective for the tax year. The Native Corporation's election may be revoked by a timely filed amendment or supplement to its income tax return (Code Sec. 247(e), as added by the 2017 Tax Cuts Act).

If a Native Corporation claims a deduction under Code Sec. 247, the earnings and profits of the Native Corporation for the tax year will be reduced by the amount of the deduction. This rule is contrary to the rule in Code Sec. 646(d)(2), which precludes such reductions. No gain or loss will be recognized by a Native Corporation with respect to deductible contributions (Code Sec. 247(f)(1), (f)(2), as added by the 2017 Tax Cuts Act).

Unless a Settlement Trust elects to defer income under Code Sec. 247(g) (discussed below), it must include in income the amount of any deduction allowed with respect to a contribution received, in the tax year in which the contribution was received (Code Sec. 247(f)(3), as added by the 2017 Tax Cuts Act).

Holding period and basis rules. The holding period under Code Sec. 1223 of a Settlement Trust will include the period that the property was held by the transferring Native Corporation. A Settlement Trust's basis in contributed property for which the Native Corporation claimed a deduction is the lesser of:

- the adjusted basis that the Native Corporation has in the property immediately before the contribution, or

NEW LAW EXPLAINED

- the fair market value of the property immediately before its contribution (Code Sec. 247(f)(5), as added by the 2017 Tax Cuts Act).

Prohibited transfers. No deduction under Code Sec. 247 is allowed with respect to any contribution to a Settlement Trust of subsurface property rights (estates) or timber resources (43 U.S.C. 1629(e)(a)(2) and 1629(e)(c)(2)) (Code Sec. 247(f)(6), as added by the 2017 Tax Cuts Act).

Deferral of income recognition by Settlement Trusts. Except for cash contributions received, a Settlement Trust may elect to defer recognition of income for contributed properties (on a property-by-property basis, if desired) until the sale or exchange of a property (Code Sec. 247(g)(1), as added by the 2017 Tax Cuts Act). In the case of such a property, income or gain realized on the sale or exchange of the property will be treated as:

- ordinary income for the income or gain realized on the sale or exchange of the property that is an amount that is less than or equal to the amount of income that would be included in income at the time of contribution under Code Sec. 247(g)(2)(A), but for the Settlement Trust's election to defer gain, and

- having the same tax character as if the deferral election did not apply for the amounts of income or gain that are in excess of the amount of income that would be included at the time of contribution under Code Sec. 247(g)(2)(B), but for the Settlement Trust's election to defer gain.

Election procedure. A Settlement Trust may make an yearly election to defer gain on any property (other than cash) that it received as a contribution during the tax year. Any property for which this election is made must be identified and described with reasonable particularity on the Settlement Trust's income tax return or amendment or supplement to the return. The election will be effective only for that tax year. Such an election can be revoked on a timely filed amendment or supplement to the Settlement Trust's income tax return (Code Sec. 267(g)(3)(A) and (B)).

If a Settlement Trust disposes of a property for which an income deferral election was made, within the first tax year after the property was contributed to the Settlement Trust:

- the deferral election would be treated as if it had not been made;

- any income or gain that would have been included in the year of contribution under Code Sec. 247(f)(3) but for the Settlement Trust's income deferral election, is include in income for the tax year of the contribution; and

- the Settlement Trust must pay any increase in tax relating to the inclusion, plus applicable interest, as well as an additional 10 percent on the increase amount, plus interest (Code Sec. 247(g)(3)(C)(i), as added by the 2017 Tax Cuts Act).

The increase in tax applicable with respect to a disposition of property within the first tax year after contribution to a Settlement Trust may be assessed, or a court proceeding may be initiated without assessment, within four years after the date on which the return making the election for such property was filed, despite the three-year limitations period on assessment and collection in Code Sec. 6501(a) (Code Sec. 247(g)(3)(C)(ii), as added by the 2017 Tax Cuts Act).

¶325

NEW LAW EXPLAINED

Information reporting of Native Corporation's deductible contributions to Settlement Trusts. A Native Corporation that makes an election to deduct a contribution to a Settlement Trust under Code Sec. 247(e) must provide the Settlement Trust with a statement regarding the election no later than the January 31 of the calendar year after the calendar year in which the contribution was made. This statement must include:

- the total contributions to which the election under Code Sec. 247(e) applies;

- for each contribution, whether it was in cash;

- for each contribution that was not in cash, the date that the Native Corporation acquired the property, and the adjusted basis and fair market value of the property on the date it was contributed to the Settlement Trust;

- the date on which each contribution was made to the Settlement Trust; and

- such additional information that the IRS determines is needed or appropriate for identifying each contribution and to the Settlement Trust's accurate inclusion of the income relating to such contributions (Code Sec. 6039H(e), as added by the 2017 Tax Cuts Act).

▶ **Effective date.** The provisions of Code Sec. 139G, prescribing the tax treatment of assignments to Settlement Trusts, apply to tax years beginning after December 31, 2016 (Act Sec. 13821(a)(3) of the Tax Cuts and Jobs Act (P.L. 115-97)). The provisions of Code Sec. 247, allowing a deduction for contributions to Settlement Trusts, apply to tax years for which the period of limitation on refund or credit under Code Sec. 6511 has not expired (Act Sec. 13821(b)(3)(A) of the 2017 Tax Cuts Act). If the period of limitation on a credit or refund from the deduction expires before the end of the one-year period beginning on December 22, 2017, the date of enactment, the refund or credit of the overpayment may be allowed if the claim is filed before the close of the one-year period (Act Sec. 13821(b)(3)(B) of the 2017 Tax Cuts Act). The provisions of Code Sec. 6039H(e), requiring information reporting, apply to tax years beginning after December 31, 2016 (Act Sec. 13821(c)(3) of the 2017 Tax Cuts Act).

Law source: Law at ¶5255, ¶5415, and ¶6195. Committee Report at ¶10,970.

— Act Sec. 13821(a) of the Tax Cuts and Jobs Act of 2017 (P.L. 115-97), adding Code Sec. 139G;

— Act Sec. 13821(b), adding Code Sec. 247;

— Act Sec. 13821(c), adding Code Sec. 6039H(e);

— Act Sec. 13821(a)(3), 13821(b)(3), and 13821(c)(3), providing the effective dates.

¶325

PASSTHROUGH ENTITIES

¶330 Qualified Business Income Deduction (Passthrough Deduction)

SUMMARY OF NEW LAW

Noncorporate taxpayers may deduct up to 20 percent of domestic qualified business income from a partnership, S corporation, or sole proprietorship. A similar deduction is allowed for specified agricultural or horticultural cooperatives. A limitation based on wages paid, or on wages paid plus a capital element, is phased in for taxpayers with taxable income above a threshold amount. The deduction is not allowed for certain service trades or businesses, but this disallowance is phased in for lower income taxpayers. The deduction applies to tax years 2018 through 2025.

BACKGROUND

Individuals compute their federal income tax liability for a tax year by multiplying their taxable income by the applicable tax rate, subtracting allowable credits, and adding other taxes if warranted (e.g., self-employment tax, household employment tax, etc.). There are four schedules of tax rates based on an individual's filing status: single, married filing jointly and surviving spouses, married filing separately, and head of household. The tax rates are graduated, so income is taxed at higher rates as the individual earns more. For 2017, the regular individual income tax rates are 10, 15, 25, 28, 33, 35, and 39.6 percent (Code Sec. 1).

Passthrough business income. An individual who receives business income from a passthrough entity—such as a partnership, an S corporation, or a sole proprietorship—is taxed on that income at the regular individual income tax rates. A partner takes into account the partnership's items of income, gain, loss, deduction, and credit based on the partnership's accounting method, and regardless of whether the income is distributed to the partners (Code Secs. 701 and 702). Similarly, an S corporation shareholder takes into account the S corporation's items of income, gain, loss, deduction, and credit based on the S corporation's accounting method, and regardless of whether the income is distributed to the shareholders (Code Sec. 1366). An unincorporated sole proprietorship is not treated as separate from its owner for federal income tax purposes, so the owner is taxed directly on the income from the business (Reg. § 301.7701-3(b)(1)(ii)).

An individual partner or S corporation shareholder must report his or her share of partnership or S corporation income or loss on Part II of Schedule E (Form 1040), Supplemental Income and Loss. An individual who owns and operates a business as a sole proprietor must figure the business income or loss on Schedule C (Form 1040), Profit or Loss From Business, or Schedule C-EZ (Form 1040), Net Profit From Business. The individual reports the Schedule C, Schedule C-EZ, and Schedule E income or loss on his or her individual tax return.

¶330

BACKGROUND

Cooperatives. A cooperative is basically a corporation that is owned and controlled by those with or for whom it does business. The cooperative operates at cost, and its profits are shared based on patronage, not on equity ownership. A cooperative deals with or for its members (patrons) under an arrangement by which the patrons obtain patronage dividends or per-unit retain allocations measured by their dealings with the cooperative. Taxable corporations operating on a cooperative basis, and farmers' cooperatives that are otherwise exempt from federal income tax under Code Sec. 521, are taxed at regular corporate rates, but certain special deductions are allowed (Code Secs. 1381 and 1382).

Penalty for substantial understatement of income tax. A taxpayer may be subject to a 20-percent accuracy-related penalty for a substantial understatement of income tax for the tax year (Code Sec. 6662(a)). In general, a substantial understatement exists when the tax understatement is more than the greater of 10 percent of the tax required to be shown on the return, or $5,000 (Code Sec. 6662(d)(1)(A)).

NEW LAW EXPLAINED

New deduction provided for portion of passthrough business income.—An individual taxpayer may deduct up to 20 percent of certain domestic qualified business income from a partnership, S corporation, or sole proprietorship for a tax year (Code Sec. 199A, as added by the Tax Cuts and Jobs Act (P.L. 115-97)). The deduction is generally limited to the greater of (1) 50 percent of W-2 wages paid by the business, or (2) the sum of 25 percent of the W-2 wages paid plus 2.5 percent of the unadjusted basis of certain property the business uses to produce qualified business income. This limit may be phased-in or eliminated if the taxpayer's taxable income meets certain threshold requirements (Code Sec. 199A(b)(2) and (3), as added by the 2017 Tax Cuts Act). The deduction is generally not allowed for certain service trades or businesses, but this disallowance is phased-in for taxpayers whose taxable income meets certain threshold requirements (Code Sec. 199A(d), as added by the 2017 Tax Cuts Act).

For individual taxpayers, the Code Sec. 199A deduction is not allowed in determining adjusted gross income (Code Sec. 62(a), as amended by the 2017 Tax Cuts Act). Further, it is not an itemized deduction, but it is available to individuals who itemize deductions and to those who claim the standard deduction (Code Sec. 63(b) and (d), as amended by the 2017 Tax Cuts Act; Conference Report on H.R. 1, Tax Cuts and Jobs Act (H. Rept. 115-466), p. 39).

A similar 20-percent deduction is available for agricultural or horticultural cooperatives (Code Sec. 199A(g), as added by the 2017 Tax Cuts Act).

The Code Sec. 199A deduction applies to tax years beginning after December 31, 2017, and before January 1, 2026 (Code Sec. 199A(i), as added by the 2017 Tax Cuts Act; Act Sec. 11011(e) of the 2017 Tax Cuts Act).

Deduction amount. A noncorporate taxpayer can claim a Code Sec. 199A deduction for a tax year for the sum of—

NEW LAW EXPLAINED

(1) the *lesser* of—

    (a) the taxpayer's "combined qualified business income amount"; or

    (b) 20 percent of the excess of the taxpayer's taxable income over the sum of (i) the taxpayer's net capital gain under Code Sec. 1(h) and (ii) the taxpayer's aggregate qualified cooperative dividends; *plus*

(2) the *lesser* of—

    (a) 20 percent of the taxpayer's aggregate qualified cooperative dividends; or

    (b) the taxpayer's taxable income minus the taxpayer's net capital gain (Code Sec. 199A(a), as added by the 2017 Tax Cuts Act).

The Code Sec. 199A deduction cannot be more than the taxpayer's taxable income (reduced by net capital gain) for the tax year (Code Sec. 199A(a), as added by the 2017 Tax Cuts Act). Further, in determining the deduction amount, the taxpayer's taxable income is computed without regard to the Code Sec. 199A deduction (Code Sec. 199A(e)(1), as added by the 2017 Tax Cuts Act).

> **Comment:** The Code Sec. 199A deduction is similar to the domestic production activities deduction under Code Sec. 199, which the 2017 Tax Cuts Act has repealed (see ¶530). Both deductions allow taxpayers to deduct a portion of their "taxable income" if it is less than a portion of their relevant business income. Neither deduction can be claimed if the taxpayer has no relevant business income. It is anticipated that the IRS will provide a new worksheet or form for calculating the Code Sec. 199A deduction, similar to Form 8903, Domestic Production Activities Deduction.

Combined qualified business income amount. A taxpayer's combined qualified business income amount for a tax year equals—

(1) the sum of the deductible amounts determined for each qualified trade or business carried on by the taxpayer; plus

(2) 20 percent of the taxpayer's aggregate qualified REIT dividends and qualified publicly traded partnership income (Code Sec. 199A(b)(1), as added by the 2017 Tax Cuts Act).

A qualified trade or business's "deductible amount" is generally the *lesser* of—

(1) 20 percent of the taxpayer's qualified business income from the trade or business; or

(2) a "W-2 wages/qualified property limit," which is the *greater* of—

    (a) 50 percent of the W-2 wages of the trade or business; or

    (b) the sum of 25 percent of the W-2 wages of the trade or business, plus 2.5 percent of the unadjusted basis immediately after acquisition of all qualified property of the trade or business (Code Sec. 199A(b)(2), as added by the 2017 Tax Cuts Act).

> **Comment:** The qualified property component means that a taxpayer might be able to claim the Code Sec. 199A deduction if the taxpayer carries on a qualified trade or business that has few or no employees but generates income using its depreciable tangible assets.

NEW LAW EXPLAINED

> **Example 1:** Thomas operates a sole proprietorship that makes personalized protective covers for smartphones. The business buys a machine for $100,000 that can quickly produce the covers, and places the machine in service in 2020. In that year, the business has no employees. The W-2 wages/qualified property limit on the business's deductible amount for 2020 is $2,500, which is the greater of (1) 50% of W-2 wages ($0 × 50% = $0), or (2) the sum of 25% of W-2 wages ($0) plus 2.5% of the unadjusted basis of the machine immediately after its acquisition ($100,000 × 0.025 = $2,500).

The Treasury is instructed to provide guidance on how the combined qualified business income amount rules apply when the taxpayer has a short tax year, or acquires or disposes of the major portion of a trade or business or a separate unit of a trade or business (Code Sec. 199A(b)(5), as added by the 2017 Tax Cuts Act).

> **Comment:** The Conference Committee Report states that if a taxpayer has a short tax year that does not contain a calendar year ending during the short year, only wages paid, elective deferrals made under Code Sec. 402(g)(3), and compensation actually deferred under Code Sec. 457 during the short tax year should be treated as the taxpayer's W-2 wages for the short year. The Report further states that amounts treated as W-2 wages for a tax year should not be treated as W-2 wages for any other tax year (Conference Report on H.R. 1, Tax Cuts and Jobs Act (H. Rept. 115-466), p. 32, fn 51).

Modifications to W-2 wages/qualified property limit. The W-2 wages/qualified property limit described above does not apply if the taxpayer's taxable income for the tax year is equal to or less than a $157,500 threshold amount ($315,000 for taxpayers filing a joint return) (Code Sec. 199A(b)(3)(A) and (e)(2)(A), as added by the 2017 Tax Cuts Act).

For other taxpayers, the W-2 wages/qualified property limit may be phased in. If the taxpayer's taxable income for the tax year is more than the $157,500 threshold amount ($315,000 for a joint return) but not more than $207,500 ($415,000 for a joint return), and if the W-2 wages/qualified property limit amount for the qualified trade or business is less than 20 percent of the taxpayer's qualified business income for that trade or business, then—

(1) the W-2 wages/qualified property limit does not apply for the qualified trade or business; and

(2) the amount that is 20 percent of the taxpayer's qualified business income from the qualified trade or business is reduced by a reduction amount (Code Sec. 199A(b)(3)(B)(i) and (e)(2)(A), as added by the 2017 Tax Cuts Act).

The reduction amount is calculated by—

(1) subtracting the qualified trade or business's W-2 wages/qualified property limit amount from the amount that is 20 percent of the taxpayer's qualified business income from the trade or business; then

(2) multiplying the difference determined in (1) above by a fraction: the numerator is the amount by which the taxpayer's taxable income for the tax year exceeds

NEW LAW EXPLAINED

the $157,500 threshold amount ($315,000 for a joint return), and the denominator is $50,000 ($100,000 for a joint return) (Code Sec. 199A(b)(3)(B)(ii) and (iii), as added by the 2017 Tax Cuts Act).

Example 2: Hans and Wendy are married. Wendy has a qualified business that is not a specified service business. For the 2018 tax year, they file a joint return reporting taxable income of $345,000. In that tax year, 20% of the qualified business income from Wendy's business is $15,000. Wendy's share of wages paid by the business in the tax year is $20,000, so 50% of the W-2 wages from the business is $10,000. (For purposes of this example, assume that no qualified property factors into the calculation.) The $15,000 amount is reduced by 30% (($345,000 taxable income - $315,000 threshold amount) / $100,000) of $5,000 ($15,000 - $10,000), which equals $1,500 (0.3 × $5,000). Hans and Wendy take a Code Sec. 199A deduction of $13,500 ($15,000 - $1,500).

Comment: The threshold amounts are adjusted for inflation for tax years beginning after 2018 (Code Sec. 199A(e)(2)(B), as added by the 2017 Tax Cuts Act).

Qualified trade or business. A taxpayer can claim the Code Sec. 199A deduction for income from many types of trades or businesses carried on by the taxpayer, but not for certain specified service trades or businesses (with exceptions). Also, performing services as an employee is not a qualified trade or business (Code Sec. 199A(d)(1), as added by the 2017 Tax Cuts Act).

A specified service trade or business is any trade or business—

- that involves the performance of services in the fields of accounting, actuarial science, athletics, brokerage services, consulting, financial services, health, law, or the performing arts; or

- that involves the performance of services consisting of investing and investment management, trading, or dealing in securities, partnership interests, or commodities; or

- whose principal asset is the reputation or skill of one or more of its employees or owners (Code Sec. 199A(d)(2), as added by the 2017 Tax Cuts Act).

  Comment: Note that architecture and engineering are *not* specified service trades or businesses, and so can be qualified trades or businesses for Code Sec. 199A purposes if they otherwise qualify. Further, for guidance on the types of activities that qualify as services in the fields of health, the performing arts, and consulting, the Conference Committee referred to guidance in the rules for determining whether a qualified personal service corporation may use the cash method of accounting (see Temporary Reg. § 1.448-1T(e)(4); Conference Report on H.R. 1, Tax Cuts and Jobs Act (H. Rept. 115-466), pp. 30-31, fns. 44-46).

A taxpayer carrying on a specified service trade or business can claim a modified qualified business deduction, however, if his or her taxable income for the tax year is less than—

¶330

NEW LAW EXPLAINED

- $415,000 for taxpayers filing a joint return ($315,000 threshold amount + $100,000); or

- $207,500 for all other taxpayers ($157,500 threshold amount + $50,000) (Code Sec. 199A(d)(3)(A) and (e)(2), as added by the 2017 Tax Cuts Act).

If this income requirement is met, the taxpayer takes into account only a percentage of his or her qualified items of income, gain, deduction, or loss, and W-2 wages and unadjusted basis of qualified property, that are allocable to the specified service in computing qualified business income, W-2 wages, and unadjusted basis of qualified property for the tax year (Code Sec. 199A(d)(3)(A)(ii), as added by the 2017 Tax Cuts Act). The applicable percentage equals 100 percent reduced (not below zero) by the ratio of (1) the taxpayer's taxable income for the tax year in excess of the $157,500 threshold amount ($315,000 for a joint return), over (2) $50,000 ($100,000 in the case of a joint return) (Code Sec. 199A(d)(3)(B), as added by the 2017 Tax Cuts Act).

Example 3: Theo has taxable income of $187,500, of which $134,000 is attributable to an accounting sole proprietorship (i.e., a specified service business) after paying wages of $67,000 to employees. Because his taxable income is less than the $207,500 threshold for specified service businesses, Theo can claim the Code Sec. 199A deduction, but only for an applicable percentage of his qualified items of income, gain, deduction, or loss, and the W-2 wages, from the accounting business. (For purposes of this example, assume that no qualified property factors into the calculation.) Theo has a 40% applicable percentage (1 - ($187,500 - $157,500)/$50,000 = 1 - 30,000/50,000 = 1 - 0.6 = 0.4). In determining includible qualified business income, Theo takes into account 40% of $134,000, or $53,600. In determining the includible W-2 wages, Theo takes into account 40% of $67,000, or $26,800. Theo calculates the deduction by taking the lesser of: 20% of $53,600 ($10,720), or 50% of $26,800 ($13,400). Theo can take a Code Sec. 199A deduction for $10,720.

Example 4: Harold and Winona are married. They file a joint return on which they report taxable income of $345,000 (determined without regard to the Code Sec. 199A deduction). Harold is a partner in the XYZ Partnership, a qualified trade or business that is not a specified service business. Winona operates Winnie's Web Consulting, a sole proprietorship qualified trade or business that is a specified service business. They also received $10,000 in qualified REIT dividends during the tax year. Harold and Winona determine their Code Sec. 199A deduction for the tax year as follows (for purposes of this example, assume that no qualified property factors into the calculation):

Harold's allocable share of qualified business income from the XYZ Partnership is $300,000, so 20% of the qualified business income from XYZ is $60,000 ($300,000 × 0.20). Harold's allocable share of wages paid by XYZ is $100,000, so 50% of the W-2 wages from the business is $50,000 ($100,000 × 0.5). Harold and Winona's taxable income is above the $315,000 threshold amount for a joint

---

NEW LAW EXPLAINED

return, so the wage limit for XYZ is phased in. Accordingly, the $60,000 amount is reduced by 30% (($345,000 - $315,000)/$100,000) of the difference between $60,000 and $50,000, or $3,000 (($60,000 - $50,000) × 0.3). Harold's deductible amount for the XYZ Partnership is $57,000 ($60,000 - $3,000).

Winona's qualified business income and W-2 wages from Winnie's Web Consulting are $325,000 and $150,000, respectively. Because their taxable income is less than the $415,000 joint-return threshold for specified service businesses, Harold and Winona can claim the Code Sec. 199A deduction for Winona's consulting business, but only for an applicable percentage of the qualified items of income, gain, deduction, or loss, and the W-2 wages from that business. Further, because their taxable income is above the $315,000 threshold amount for a joint return, the exclusion of qualified business income and W-2 wages from Winona's consulting business are phased in.

Winona has an applicable percentage of 70% (1 - ($345,000 -$315,000)/$100,000 = 1 - $30,000/$100,000 = 1 - 0.3 = 0.7). In determining includible qualified business income, Winona takes into account $227,500 ($325,000 × 0.7). In determining includible W-2 wages, Winona takes into account $105,000 ($150,000 × 0.7). Winona calculates the deductible amount for her consulting business by taking the lesser of 20% of her $227,500 of includible qualified business income ($45,500) or 50% of her $105,000 of includible W-2 wages ($52,500). Although Harold and Winona's taxable income is above the threshold amount for a joint return, the wage limit is not binding because the 20% of includible qualified business income of the consulting business ($45,500) is less than 50% of its includible W-2 wages ($52,500). Winona's deductible amount for Winnie's Web Consulting is $45,500.

Harold and Winona's combined qualified business income amount of $104,500, which consists of the $57,000 deductible amount for the XYZ Partnership, plus the $45,500 deductible amount for Winnie's Web Consulting, plus 20% of the $10,000 qualified REIT dividends ($2,000). However, their Code Sec. 199A deduction for the tax year is limited to $69,000, which is 20% of their $345,000 taxable income, because that amount is less than their qualified business income amount for the year.

Qualified business income. The qualified business income of a qualified trade or business carried on by a taxpayer for a tax year is the net amount of the business's qualified items of income, gain, deduction, and loss (Code Sec. 199A(c) (1), as added by the 2017 Tax Cuts Act). Items of income, gain, deduction, and loss are qualified to the extent they are effectively connected with the conduct of a trade or business within the United States, and are included or allowed in determining taxable income for the tax year (Code Sec. 199A(c) (3) (A), as added by the 2017 Tax Cuts Act).

Example 5: ABC Company is a qualified business for Code Sec. 199A purposes. For the tax year, ABC has $100,000 of ordinary income from inventory sales,

NEW LAW EXPLAINED

> and makes a $25,000 expenditure that must be capitalized and amortized over five years under applicable tax rules. ABC's net business income is $95,000 ($100,000 minus the $5,000 current-year ordinary amortization deduction). ABC's qualified business income is not reduced by the entire amount of the capital expenditure, only by the amount deductible in determining taxable income for the year.

Code Sec. 864(c) applies to determine if items of income, deduction, etc., are "effectively connected," but by substituting "qualified trade or business (within the meaning of section 199A)" for "nonresident alien individual or a foreign corporation" or "a foreign corporation" (Code Sec. 199A(c)(3)(A)(i), as added by the 2017 Tax Cuts Act).

A taxpayer includes his or her qualified business income from sources within Puerto Rico if all such income is taxable under Code Sec. 1 for the tax year (Code Sec. 199A(f)(1)(C)(i), as added by the 2017 Tax Cuts Act).

If the net amount of qualified income, gain, deduction, and loss is less than zero, the loss is carried over to the next tax year (Code Sec. 199A(c)(2), as added by the 2017 Tax Cuts Act). Any deduction allowed in the next tax year is reduced (but not below zero) by 20 percent of any carryover qualified business loss (Conference Report on H.R. 1, Tax Cuts and Jobs Act (H. Rept. 115-466), p. 29).

> **Example 6:** Richard carries on two qualified businesses, Business A and Business B. In 2018, Richard has qualified business income of $20,000 from Business A and a qualified business loss of $50,000 from Business B. Richard cannot claim the Code Sec. 199A deduction for 2018, but has a carryover qualified business loss of $30,000 to 2019. In 2019, Richard has qualified business income of $20,000 from Business A and $50,000 from Business B. To determine his Code Sec. 199A deduction for 2019, Richard reduces the 20% deductible amount determined for the $70,000 qualified business income from Businesses A and B by 20% of the $30,000 carryover qualified business loss.

> **Example 7:** Herbert and Whitney are married. They file a joint return for the tax year, on which they report taxable income of $200,000 (determined without regard to the Code Sec. 199A deduction). Herbert has a sole proprietorship qualified trade or business, and Whitney is a partner in the LMO Partnership, a qualified trade or business. Neither qualified business is a specified service business. They have a carryover qualified business loss of $50,000. Herbert and Whitney determine their Code Sec. 199A deduction for the tax year as follows (for purposes of this example, assume that no qualified property factors into the calculation):
>
> Herbert's qualified business income from his business is $150,000, so 20% of the qualified business income is $30,000. Herbert and Whitney's taxable income is

NEW LAW EXPLAINED

below the $315,000 threshold amount for a joint return, so the wage limit does not apply to Herbert's business. Herbert's deductible amount for his business is $30,000.

Whitney's allocable share of qualified business loss from the LMO Partnership is $40,000, so 20% of the qualified business loss is $8,000. Because their taxable income is below the $315,000 threshold amount for a joint return, the wage limit does not apply to Whitney's partnership. Whitney's deductible amount for the LMO Partnership is an $8,000 reduction to the deduction amount.

Herbert and Whitney's combined qualified business income amount is $12,000, which consists of the $30,000 deductible amount for Herbert's business, the $8,000 reduction for the LMO Partnership, and a $10,000 reduction attributable to the carryover qualified business loss (20% × $50,000). Their deduction is limited to 20% of their $200,000 taxable income, or $40,000. Since their combined qualified business income amount is less than 20% of their taxable income, Herbert and Whitney's Code Sec. 199A deduction amount for the tax year is $12,000.

Qualified items of income, gain, deduction, or loss do not include—

(1) items of short-term capital gain or loss, or long-term capital gain or loss;

(2) dividends, income equivalent to a dividend, or payments in lieu of dividends;

(3) interest income which is not properly allocable to a trade or business;

(4) the excess of gain over loss from commodities transactions, other than those entered into in the normal course of the trade or business or with respect to stock in trade or property held primarily for sale to customers in the ordinary course of the trade or business, property used in the trade or business, or supplies regularly used or consumed in the trade or business;

(5) the excess of foreign currency gains over foreign currency losses from Code Sec. 988 transactions, other than transactions directly related to the business needs of the business activity;

(6) net income from notional principal contracts, other than clearly identified hedging transactions that are treated as ordinary (i.e., not treated as capital assets);

(7) amounts from an annuity not received in connection with the trade or business; or

(8) items of deduction or loss properly allocable to an amount described in (1)-(7) (Code Sec. 199A(c)(3)(B), as added by the 2017 Tax Cuts Act).

Qualified business income does not include—

• reasonable compensation paid to the taxpayer by the business for services rendered;

• guaranteed payments to a partner for services rendered;

• payments described in Code Sec. 707(a) to a partner for services rendered (to the extent provided in regulations);

• qualified REIT dividends;

¶330

NEW LAW EXPLAINED

- qualified cooperative dividends; or
- qualified publicly traded partnership income (Code Sec. 199A(c)(1) and (4), as added by the 2017 Tax Cuts Act).

In determining alternative minimum taxable income under Code Sec. 55, qualified business income is determined without regard to the minimum tax preferences and adjustments under Code Secs. 56–59 (Code Sec. 199A(f)(2), as added by the 2017 Tax Cuts Act).

W-2 wages. W-2 wages are wages that the taxpayer's qualified trade or business paid to its employees during the calendar year that ends in the business's tax year. They also include annual deferrals under Code Sec. 401(k) plans, simplified employee pensions, Code Sec. 403(b) annuities, amounts deferred under Code Sec. 457 deferred compensation plans, and designated Roth contributions (Code Sec. 199A(b)(4)(A), as added by the 2017 Tax Cuts Act).

For Code Sec. 199A deduction purposes, W-2 wages must be properly allocable to qualified business income (Code Sec. 199A(b)(4)(B), as added by the 2017 Tax Cuts Act). They also must be properly included in a return—e.g., Form W-2, Wage and Tax Statement—filed with the Social Security Administration on or before the 60th day after the filing due date (including extensions) (Code Sec. 199A(b)(4)(C), as added by the 2017 Tax Cuts Act).

If a taxpayer has qualified business income from sources within Puerto Rico, all of which is subject to federal income tax under Code Sec. 1 for the tax year, the taxpayer's W-2 wages for the qualified trade or business conducted there are determined without regard to the withholding exclusion under Code Sec. 3401(a)(8) for wages paid to certain U.S. citizens for services in Puerto Rico (Code Sec. 199A(f)(1)(C)(ii), as added by the 2017 Tax Cuts Act).

Qualified property. Qualified property is depreciable tangible property held by and available for use in the qualified trade or business at the close of the tax year, and is used during the tax year to produce qualified business income. To be qualified, the property's depreciable period cannot end before the close of the tax year (Code Sec. 199A(b)(6)(A), as added by the 2017 Tax Cuts Act). The depreciable period begins on the date the taxpayer first places the property in service. The period ends on the later of (1) the date 10 years after the placed-in-service date, or (2) the last day of the last full year in the applicable recovery period that would apply under Modified Accelerated Cost Recovery System (MACRS) depreciation without regard to the alternative depreciation system (ADS) (Code Sec. 199A(b)(6)(B), as added by the 2017 Tax Cuts Act).

Property that is sold is no longer available for use in the trade or business, and is not taken into account in determining the qualified property limitation (Conference Report on H.R. 1, Tax Cuts and Jobs Act (H. Rept. 115-466), p. 38).

The Treasury is instructed to provide guidance for determining the unadjusted basis immediately after acquisition of qualified property acquired in like-kind exchanges or involuntary conversions. Further, the Treasury must apply anti-abuse rules similar to those under Code Sec. 179(d)(2) to prevent taxpayers from manipulating the deprecia-

NEW LAW EXPLAINED

ble period of qualified property by using related party transactions (Code Sec. 199A(h), as added by the 2017 Tax Cuts Act).

Partnerships and S corporations. For partnerships and S corporations, the Code Sec. 199A deduction is applied at the partner or shareholder level. Each partner must take into account his or her allocable share, and each shareholder must take into account his or her pro rata share, of each qualified item of income, gain, deduction, and loss. Further, each partner or shareholder is treated as having W-2 wages and unadjusted basis immediately after acquisition of qualified property for the tax year, in an amount equal to his or her allocable or pro rata share of the partnership's or S corporation's W-2 wages and unadjusted basis for the tax year as determined in the regulations. The share of W-2 wages is determined in the same manner as the partner's or shareholder's share of wage expenses. The share of the unadjusted basis of qualified property is determined in the same manner as the partner's or shareholder's allocable share of depreciation (Code Sec. 199A(f)(1)(A), as added by the 2017 Tax Cuts Act).

> **Example 8:** Pete is a partner in the PDQ Partnership. If Pete is allocated a deductible amount of 10% of wages paid by the partnership to employees for the tax year, he must be allocated 10% of the W-2 wages of the partnership for purposes of calculating the wage limit for the Code Sec. 199A deduction.

Trusts and estates. Trusts and estates are eligible for the Code Sec. 199A deduction (Conference Report on H.R. 1, Tax Cuts and Jobs Act (H. Rept. 115-466), p. 40). Rules similar to those under Code Sec. 199(d)(1)(B)(i) (as in effect on December 1, 2017) for the domestic production activities deduction apply for apportioning any W-2 wages and unadjusted basis of qualified property between fiduciaries and beneficiaries (Code Sec. 199A(f)(1)(B), as added by the 2017 Tax Cuts Act).

Agricultural or horticultural cooperatives. A specified agricultural or horticultural cooperative may claim a Code Sec. 199A deduction for a tax year, equal to the *lesser* of—

(1) 20 percent of the excess of the cooperative's gross income over any qualified cooperative dividends paid during the tax year for the tax year; or

(2) a "W-2 wages/qualified property limit," which is the *greater* of—

    (a) 50 percent of the cooperative's W-2 wages from its trade or business; or

    (b) the sum of 25 percent of the cooperative's W-2 wages from its trade or business, plus 2.5 percent of the unadjusted basis immediately after acquisition of all of the cooperative's qualified property (Code Sec. 199A(g)(1), as added by the 2017 Tax Cuts Act).

The deduction amount cannot be more than the cooperative's taxable income for the tax year (Code Sec. 199A(g)(2), as added by the 2017 Tax Cuts Act).

A specified agricultural or horticultural cooperative is an organization subject to the cooperative income tax rules at Code Secs. 1381-1383, and engaged in—

¶330

NEW LAW EXPLAINED

(1) manufacturing, producing, growing, or extracting an agricultural or horticultural product;

(2) marketing agricultural or horticultural products that the cooperative's patrons manufactured, produced, grew, or extracted; or

(3) providing supplies, equipment, or services to farmers or to organizations engaged in the activities described in (1) or (2) (Code Sec. 199A(g)(3), as added by the 2017 Tax Cuts Act).

Other definitions. A qualified REIT dividend is a dividend received from a real estate investment trust that is not a capital gain dividend under Code Sec. 857(b)(3) or a qualified dividend income under Code Sec. 1(h)(11) (Code Sec. 199A(e)(3), as added by the 2017 Tax Cuts Act).

A qualified cooperative dividend is a patronage dividend under Code Sec. 1388(a), a per-unit retain allocation under Code Sec. 1388(f), a qualified written notice of allocation under Code Sec. 1388(c), or similar amounts that are includible in gross income and received from certain local benevolent life insurance associations, mutual ditch or irrigation companies, mutual or cooperative telephone companies, cooperative organizations, or an organization governed by the federal tax rules that applied to cooperatives and their patrons before enactment of Code Secs. 1381–1388 (Code Sec. 199A(e)(4), as added by the 2017 Tax Cuts Act).

Qualified publicly traded partnership income is the sum of (1) the net amount of the taxpayer's allocable share of each qualified item of income, gain, deduction, and loss from a publicly traded partnership under Code Sec. 7704(a) that is not treated as a corporation under Code Sec. 7704(c) (without regard to reasonable compensation, guaranteed payments, or other payments to the taxpayer or partner for services rendered); plus (2) any gain recognized by the taxpayer from disposing his or her partnership interest, to the extent the gain is treated as realized from the sale or exchange of property other than a capital asset under Code Sec. 751(a) (Code Sec. 199A(e)(5), as added by the 2017 Tax Cuts Act).

Substantial understatement penalty. A taxpayer who claims the Code Sec. 199A deduction may be subject to the 20-percent accuracy-related penalty for a substantial understatement of income tax if the understatement is more than the greater of five percent (not 10 percent) of the tax required to be shown on the return for the tax year, or $5,000 (Code Sec. 6662(d)(1)(C), as added by the 2017 Tax Cuts Act).

Additional Treasury guidance. The Treasury must prescribe regulations to carry out the purposes of Code Sec. 199A, including rules on appropriate reporting requirements, allocating items and wages, and applying the Code Sec. 199A deduction to tiered entities (Code Sec. 199A(f)(4), as added by the 2017 Tax Cuts Act).

Practical Analysis: Jim Hamill, Director of Tax Practice at Reynolds, Hix & Co., P.A. in Albuquerque, NM, observes that while the deduction applies at the partner or shareholder level, the complexity of partnership and S corporation tax filings will

NEW LAW EXPLAINED

increase. Increasing tax complexity is often seen with more separately-stated items in required reporting by passthrough entities. K-1 reporting will now need to include information for each qualified trade or business conducted by a passthrough entity, with identification of that business as being a specified service activity or not being a specified service activity, the W-2 wages of the entity and the unadjusted basis of depreciable assets, all tied to the statutory definitions applicable to the limitations and computation of the deduction.

Additionally, for taxpayers above the income threshold, the expanded Code Sec. 179 deduction or bonus depreciation allowance will not affect the ability to use depreciable assets to increase the deduction limitation. The unadjusted basis of tangible recovery property is included in the limitation for the entire recovery period that would apply to such property, even if the taxpayer has claimed a full deduction under Code Sec. 179 or bonus depreciation. Treasury is also directed to determine how substituted basis transactions such as like-kind exchanges and involuntary conversions will affect the capital calculation. Guidance should also be provided with respect to Code Sec. 743 adjustments (partner level) and Code Sec. 734 adjustments (partnership level) that are allocable to depreciable assets.

Furthermore, the deduction limitation applicable to partners with income above the threshold requires the partnership to determine the unadjusted basis of depreciable partnership property. Uncertain tax positions of a partnership now subject to the centralized audit rules may include a land-building allocation that will affect the qualified business income limitation of a partner with taxable income above the threshold.

Lastly, because the final legislation followed the Senate provision, the House's use of the activity definitions of the passive loss rules was avoided. This was a welcome change, but tax advisors should be cautioned that Congress seems increasingly willing to use passive-loss determinations in new legislation (*e.g.*, the net investment income tax and the Code Sec. 761(f) qualified joint venture definition) and it may be increasingly important to understand the Code Sec. 469 passive-loss provisions for reasons apart from Code Sec. 469.

Practical Analysis: J. Leigh Griffith, Partner at Waller Lansden Dortch & Davis, LLP in Nashville Tennessee observes that the new special deduction for qualified business income of a passthrough (particularly passthroughs that are not service businesses) is a structural change in historic tax law and a major savings/incentive for such businesses. The deduction for non-professional service business owners is (i) the lesser of the combined qualified U.S. business income of the taxpayer (partner or member) reduced by net capital gains or (ii) 20 percent of the taxpayer's taxable income less capital gains. However, the deduction is limited to the taxpayer's allocable share of 50 percent of the W-2 wages paid by the passthrough or 25 percent of the W-2 wages plus 2.5 percent of the original unadjusted basis of the tangible property used in the business. There is also a 20 percent deduction for qualified REIT dividends and for certain cooperative dividends. If the owner's taxable income is below a threshold ($315,000 if filing a joint return or $157,000 for others)

NEW LAW EXPLAINED

the W-2 limit above does not apply. The deduction for a professional service business is only available for owners with taxable income below the threshold.

Additionally, the 20 percent deduction for "qualified business income" derived from business activities in the United States of passthrough entities (partnerships and S corporations) will not be applicable to the owners of many passthrough service businesses because of their taxable income exceeding the threshold described below. However, for some partners of such businesses and S corporation shareholders, the benefit may be very meaningful. The deduction is only available to taxpayers whose taxable income is $315,000 or less if married and filing a joint return or $157,500 for other taxpayers. While $315,000 is a substantial joint income, if the qualified business income from the service business(es) is reduced by the reasonable compensation for services that the taxpayer provides for the passthrough entity(s) with respect to any qualified business, the benefit will be substantially reduced if not eliminated. It appears the reduction for an owner of an S corporation is for reasonable compensation paid and for partnerships the amount of guaranteed payment and/or payments for services rendered other than in the capacity of a partner. Specifically the statute excludes (i) reasonable compensation paid for the taxpayer's services, (ii) guaranteed payments to a partner, and (iii) to the extent provided in regulations, payments to a partner for services to the passthrough for services rendered to the trade or business in a capacity other than that of a partner. The Senate report supports this construction. If an S corporation does not provide reasonable compensation to a shareholder employee, is there audit risk that the reduction in the qualified business income will include not only the nominal compensation paid but also recharacterization of all or a portion of the income as reasonable compensation? The statute uses the term "paid" and the Senate Report uses the term "treated as reasonable compensation."

Lastly, many professional service limited liability companies and partnerships have two tiers of partners. A capital partner who significantly participates in the net profits of the entity at the end of the year and has rather modest guaranteed payments and non-capital partners whose compensation is largely guaranteed payments. The requirement that the qualified business income is reduced by guaranteed payments may change this common structure of professional service limited liability companies and partnerships.

Practical Analysis: Charles R. Goulding, President, Energy Tax Savers and R&D Tax Savers in Syosset, New York, comments that due to the specified service trade or business exclusion, most accountants, consultants, healthcare providers and attorney service providers cannot avail themselves of this deduction, but architects and engineers have been spared and will have access to this deduction.

▶ **Effective date.** The amendments made by this section apply to tax years beginning after December 31, 2017 (Act Sec. 11011(e) of the Tax Cuts and Jobs Act (P.L. 115-97)).

Expiration date. The Code Sec. 199A deduction will not apply to tax years beginning after December 31, 2025 (Code Sec. 199A(i), as added by the 2017 Tax Cuts Act).

¶330

NEW LAW EXPLAINED

Law source: Law at ¶5165, ¶5170, ¶5320, ¶5325, ¶5345, ¶5405, ¶5610, ¶5615, ¶6095, and ¶6285. Committee Report at ¶10,030.

— Act Sec. 11011(a) of the Tax Cuts and Jobs Act (P.L. 115-97), adding new Code Sec. 199A;

— Act Sec. 11011(b), amending Code Secs. 62(a), 63(b) and (d), and 3402(m)(1);

— Act Sec. 11011(c), adding Code Sec. 6662(d)(1)(C);

— Act Sec. 11011(d), amending Code Secs. 170(b)(2)(D), 172(d), 246(b)(1), 613(a), and 613A(d)(1);

— Act Sec. 11011(e), providing the effective date.

¶335 Holding Period for Capital Gain Passed Through to Partners with Carried Interests

SUMMARY OF NEW LAW

Capital gain passed through to fund managers via a partnership profits interest (carried interest) in exchange for investment management services must meet an extended three-year holding period to qualify for long-term capital gain treatment.

BACKGROUND

A "carried interest" in a partnership is an interest that consists of the right to receive future partnership profits, and is given to a partner in exchange for performing services for the partnership. Carried interests are often used by partnerships in the investment management business. Such a partnership interest is not taxed when a fund-manager partner receives it. The IRS generally treats the receipt of a partnership profits interest for services as a nontaxable event (Rev. Proc. 93-27, 1993-2 CB 343). This treatment applies only to substantially nonvested profits interests (Rev. Proc. 2001-43, 2001-1 CB 191).

If *property*, instead of cash, is transferred in exchange for performing services, the service provider generally has to recognize income for the tax year in which the property is first substantially vested (Code Sec. 83). On the other hand, property that is subject to a substantial risk of forfeiture—including when the right to the property depends on the future performance of substantial services—is considered "nonvested" property. A service provider may elect to recognize income for the tax year of the transfer even if the property is substantially nonvested (Code Sec. 83(b)).

Under proposed regulations, a partnership interest is "property" for purposes of Code Sec. 83 (Proposed Reg. § 1.83-3(e); NPRM REG-105346-03, 5/24/2005). The transfer of a profits interest to a service provider would be included in gross income when it becomes substantially vested, or, for a substantially nonvested interest, at the time of the grant if a Code Sec. 83(b) election is in place. Further, a partnership and a partner would be allowed to elect a safe harbor that treats the fair market value of a

BACKGROUND

compensatory partnership interest as being equal to the liquidation value of the interest (Proposed Reg. § 1.83-3(l)). However, the grant of a true profits interest in a partnership would result in no income inclusion under Code Sec. 83, because the fair market value of the property received by the service provider would be zero (House Committee Report for the Tax Cuts and Jobs Act (P.L. 115-97) (H.R. Rep. No. 115-409, p. 275, fn. 572)).

In recent years, the tax treatment of income from a carried interest given in exchange for asset management services—such as services for private equity funds, venture capital funds, and hedge funds—has been a hotly contested issue. Investment funds are usually partnerships, with the fund manager as the general partner and the investors as limited partners. The fund manager itself is generally a partnership whose members have investment management expertise. The fund manager receives management fees and a carried interest. Income from the carried interest, which tends to be in the range of 20 to 25 percent of profits, passes through from the fund manager partnership to its member partners whose professional skill generates capital income for the fund's investors. The income may be short-term or long-term capital gain realized by the underlying investment fund as it sells off investment assets. The bone of contention has been that long-term capital gain allocated to the individual partners may represent compensation for services as fund managers. Some who view this income as compensation for services have called for it to be taxed at ordinary income rates.

The holding period for a capital asset is the length of time that the taxpayer owns the property before disposing of it. The tax treatment of recognized gain or loss depends, in part, on whether the taxpayer's holding period is short-term or long-term. Long-term gain or loss arises from assets held for more than one year; anything else is short-term gain or loss (Code Secs. 1222 and 1223).

"Net capital gain" is the excess of net long-term capital gain for the tax year over net short-term capital loss for the tax year (Code Sec. 1222(11)). For an individual taxpayer, an estate, or a trust, any adjusted net capital gain that otherwise would be taxed at the ordinary 10- or 15-percent rate is not taxed. Any adjusted net capital gain that otherwise would be taxed at the ordinary rates over 15 percent and below 39.6 percent is taxed at a 15-percent rate. Any adjusted net capital gain that otherwise would be taxed at the ordinary 39.6-percent rate is taxed at a 20-percent rate (Code Sec. 1(h)(1)).

NEW LAW EXPLAINED

Holding period increased for long-term capital gains from "carried interest" in investment partnership.—A three-year holding period applies to certain net long-term capital gain with respect to any applicable partnership interest held by the taxpayer. This rule applies notwithstanding Code Sec. 83 and any Code Sec. 83(b) election in effect (Code Sec. 1061(a), as added by the Tax Cuts and Jobs Act (P.L. 115-97)).

If a taxpayer holds an applicable partnership interest at any time during the tax year, this rule treats as short-term capital gain—taxed at ordinary income rates—the amount

NEW LAW EXPLAINED

of the taxpayer's net long-term capital gain from the applicable interest that exceeds the amount of such gain calculated as if a three-year holding period applies instead of a one-year period. In making this calculation, long-term capital losses also are taken into account as if a three-year holding period applies (Code Sec. 1061(a), as added by the 2017 Tax Cuts Act).

An "applicable partnership interest" is any interest in a partnership that is transferred to or held by the taxpayer in connection with the performance of services by the taxpayer or a related person in any applicable trade of business, even if the taxpayer made contributions to the partnership (Code Sec. 1061(c)(1), as added by the 2017 Tax Cuts Act). An applicable partnership interest does not include (1) any interest in a partnership held by a corporation, or (2) any capital interest in the partnership that provides the taxpayer with a right to share in partnership capital based on the amount of capital contributed or on the value of the interest subject to tax under Code Sec. 83 when the interest is received or vested (Code Sec. 1061(c)(4), as added by the 2017 Tax Cuts Act).

The three-year holding period applies notwithstanding the rules of Code Sec. 83 or a Code Sec. 83(b) election. As a result, the fact that an individual may have included an amount in income upon acquiring the applicable partnership interest, or may have made a Code Sec. 83(b) election with respect to the applicable partnership interest, does not change the required three-year holding period for long-term capital gain treatment (Joint Explanatory Statement of the Conference Committee, Conference Report on H.R. 1, Tax Cuts and Jobs Act (H. Rept. 115-466), p. 269).

An "applicable trade or business" is one whose regular business activity consists of (1) raising or returning capital, and (2) either investing in or disposing of specified assets, or developing specified assets (Code Sec. 1061(c)(2), as added by the 2017 Tax Cuts Act). "Specified assets" are securities, commodities, real estate held for rental or investment, cash or cash equivalents, or options or derivative contracts with respect to these assets. An interest in a partnership to the extent of the partnership's proportionate interest in these assets is also a specified asset (Code Sec. 1061(c)(3), as added by the 2017 Tax Cuts Act).

If a taxpayer transfers an applicable partnership interest to a related person, the taxpayer must include in gross income as short-term capital gain so much of the taxpayer's net long-term capital gain attributable to the sale or exchange of an asset held for not more than three years as is allocable to the interest. The amount included as short-term capital gain on the transfer is reduced by the amount treated as short-term capital gain on the transfer for the tax year under Code Sec. 1061(a) (Code Sec. 1061(d)(1), as added by the 2017 Tax Cuts Act). A "related person" is a family member under the Code Sec. 318(a)(1) attribution rules, or a colleague who performed a service within the current calendar year or the preceding three calendar years in an applicable trade or business in which or for which the taxpayer performed a service (Code Sec. 1061(d)(2), as added by the 2017 Tax Cuts Act).

To the extent provided by the Treasury, the short-term capital gain treatment for carried interest gain under Code Sec. 1061(a) will not apply to income or gain attributable to an

¶335

NEW LAW EXPLAINED

asset not held for portfolio investment on behalf of third party investors (Code Sec. 1061(b) and (c)(5), as added by the 2017 Tax Cuts Act).

The Treasury may require reporting or issue regulations or other guidance, as is necessary to carry out the purpose of Code Sec. 1061 (Code Sec. 1061(e) and (f), as added by the 2017 Tax Cuts Act).

Practical Analysis: Mark Leeds, Partner at Mayer Brown, LLP in New York, comments that the three-year holding rules for carried interest are intended to capture interests held by the sponsors of flow-through entities such as private equity, hedge and other investment funds. According to this provision, a partner (other than a corporation) will not be entitled to report gains as long-term capital gains with respect to an "applicable partnership interest" unless the property being disposed of has been held for more than three years. An applicable partnership interest is a partnership interest that is transferred to, or held by, a taxpayer in connection with the taxpayer's performance of services in an "applicable trade or business." Applicable trade or business includes raising capital and investing and developing specified assets such as securities, commodities, options, derivatives or real estate for rent or investment. The applicable partnership interest rule does not apply to the extent the return to the partner is commensurate with either the amount of capital contributed or the amount that was included as compensation income by the taxpayer at the time of grant or vesting of the relevant partnership interest. Importantly, if a holder of an applicable partnership interest makes a gift of the partnership interest, the holder will be required to include unrecognized short-term capital gains (determined using the three-year holding period) in income at the time of the transfer.

Practical Analysis: J. Leigh Griffith, Partner at Waller Lansden Dortch & Davis, LLP in Nashville Tennessee, observes that a potential exception to the three-year holding period requirement for partnership interests received in connection with services is perhaps more narrow than one may initially think. An "applicable business" is a partnership involved on a regular, continuous and substantial basis in (i) raising or returning capital and (ii) investing in certain securities or the development of rental or investment real estate, with respect to which the taxpayer or any related person provided substantial services. This would indicate that receipt of a profits interest by a taxpayer will be exempt from the three-year rule unless the activity is a serial activity in which the taxpayer or a related person is engaged. A related person for these purposes, however, is not only a family member but also a person who performed services within the current or preceding three calendar years in an applicable trade or business in which or for which the taxpayer performed a service. Thus, even if the taxpayer's activities are not themselves regular, continuous, and substantial, the activities of others performing services in the same activity (whether conducted in one or more entities) are potentially considered as well.

Furthermore, the three-year holding period for an interest in a partnership involved on a regular, continuous and substantial basis in raising or returning capital and investing in certain securities or the development of rental or investment real estate

NEW LAW EXPLAINED

applies to capital interests as well as profits interests. The statute provides that the three-year holding requirement applies notwithstanding the rules of Code Sec. 83 or any election in effect under Code Sec. 83. However, there is an exception for capital interests wherein the participation of such interest in capital is commensurate with either (i) the amount of capital contributed at the receipt of such interest or (ii) the value that was subject to tax under Code Sec. 83 upon receipt or vesting of such interest. Presumably the exception applies if the capital account associated with the interest equals the value used in the Code Sec. 83(b) election with the result only a one year holding period is required. For profits interests, the value and the capital account will be different and the three-year holding period will apply.

▶ **Effective date.** The amendments made by this section apply to tax years beginning after December 31, 2017 (Act Sec. 13309(c) of the Tax Cuts and Jobs Act (P.L. 115-97)).

Law source: Law at ¶5960 and ¶5965. Committee Report at ¶10,500.

— Act Sec. 13309(a) of the Tax Cuts and Jobs Act (P.L. 115-97), redesignating Code Sec. 1061 as Code Sec. 1062, and adding new Code Sec. 1061.

— Act Sec. 13309(c), providing the effective date.

¶340 Scope of Basis Limitation on Partner Losses

SUMMARY OF NEW LAW

The basis limitation on partner losses applies to a partner's distributive share of charitable contributions and foreign taxes.

BACKGROUND

A partner's distributive share of partnership loss is not allowed to the extent that it exceeds the adjusted basis of the partner's partnership interest. Disallowed loss is allowed as a deduction at the end of the next partnership tax year to the extent that the partner's adjusted basis at that point exceeds zero (Code Sec. 704(d); Reg. § 1.704-1(d)(1)).

A partner's basis in its partnership interest is increased by its distributive share of income, and decreased by distributions by the partnership. A partner's basis is also decreased by its distributive share of partnership losses and expenditures not deductible in computing partnership taxable income and not properly chargeable to capital account (Code Sec. 705).

When a partnership makes a charitable contribution of appreciated property, a partner generally can claim as a deduction his or her distributive share of the property's fair market value (Code Sec. 702(a)(4)). In turn, the partner's basis is reduced, but only by the partner's distributive share of the adjusted basis of the contributed property (and not its fair market value) (Rev. Rul. 96-11, 1996-1 CB 140).

¶340

BACKGROUND

A partnership is not allowed to claim deductions for charitable contributions or foreign taxes (Code Sec. 703(a)(2)(B) and (C)). With respect to foreign taxes, as with charitable contributions made by the partnership, the partners take into account their distributive share of the foreign taxes paid by the partnership (Code Sec. 702(a)(6)).

Under current regulations, the basis limitation on partner losses does not take into account the partner's share of partnership charitable contributions or foreign taxes (Reg. § 1.704-1(d)(2)). Moreover, in a private letter ruling, the IRS took the position that a partner's deduction for its share of the partnership's charitable contributions is not limited by the basis limitation on partner losses (IRS Letter Ruling 8405084).

NEW LAW EXPLAINED

Basis limitation on partner losses takes into account charitable contributions and foreign taxes.—The basis limitation on partner losses is modified to take into account a partner's distributive share of (1) partnership charitable contributions, and (2) taxes paid or accrued to foreign countries and U.S. possessions. For a charitable contribution by the partnership, the amount of the basis limitation on partner losses is decreased by the partner's distributive share of the adjusted basis of the contributed property. A special rule provides that if the partnership makes a charitable contribution of property whose fair market value is greater than its adjusted basis, the basis limitation on partner losses does not account for the partner's distributive share of the excess (Code Sec. 704(d), as amended by the Tax Cuts and Jobs Act (P.L. 115-97)).

▶ **Effective date.** The amendment made by this section applies to partnership tax years beginning after December 31, 2017 (Act Sec. 13503(b) of the Tax Cuts and Jobs Act (P.L. 115-97)).

Law source: Law at ¶5640. Committee Report at ¶10,610.

— Act Sec. 13503(a) of the Tax Cuts and Jobs Act (P.L. 115-97), amending Code Sec. 704(d);

— Act Sec. 13503(b), providing the effective date.

¶345 Definition of Substantial Built-In Loss Upon Transfer of Partnership Interest

SUMMARY OF NEW LAW

The Code Sec. 743 definition of a "substantial built-in loss" is modified so that a substantial built-in loss also exists *if the transferee would be allocated* a net loss in excess of $250,000 upon a hypothetical disposition at fair market value by the partnership of all partnership assets immediately after the transfer of the partnership interest.

BACKGROUND

Upon the transfer of a partnership interest, a partnership generally does not adjust the basis of partnership property unless (1) the partnership has made a one-time Code Sec. 754 election to adjust basis, or (2) the partnership has a substantial built-in loss immediately after the transfer (Code Sec. 743(a)). If the partnership does have substantial built-in loss immediately after the transfer, adjustments are made with respect to the transferee partner.

The purpose of the adjustments is to account for differences between the transferee partner's proportionate share of the adjusted basis of the partnership property and the transferee's basis in its partnership interest (Code Sec. 743(b)). The adjustments essentially approximate the result of a direct purchase by the transferee partner of its share of the partnership property.

For example, if the basis of T's (a transferee's) interest in a partnership is substantially less than T's share of the adjusted basis to the partnership of the partnership's property, the adjusted basis of partnership property will be decreased by that difference with respect to T. That is, the adjusted basis of partnership property with respect to T will be adjusted downward to its fair market value, thereby preventing T from taking advantage of any built-in loss.

A substantial built-in loss exists if *the partnership's adjusted basis* in the property exceeds by more that $250,000 the fair market value of that property (Code Sec. 743(d)(1)).

NEW LAW EXPLAINED

Test for substantial built-in loss modified to apply at transferee partner level.— The definition of a "substantial built-in loss" is modified so that a substantial built-in loss also exists *if the transferee would be allocated* a net loss in excess of $250,000 upon a hypothetical disposition at fair market value by the partnership of all partnership assets immediately after the transfer of the partnership interest (Code Sec. 743(d)(1), as amended by the Tax Cuts and Jobs Act (P.L. 115-97)). In other words, even if the partnership itself does not have an overall built-in loss, depending on allocations of gain under the partnership agreement, a basis adjustment may be mandated with respect to a transferee.

> **Example:** Partnership ABC has not made a Code Sec. 754 election. The partnership has two assets, X and Y. Asset X has a built-in gain of $1 million; Asset Y has a built-in loss of $900,000. Under the partnership agreement, any gain on the sale of Asset X is specially allocated to Partner A. Partners A, B and C share equally in all other partnership items, including the built-in loss in Asset Y. Each of Partner B and C has a net built-in loss of $300,000 (one third of $900,000) allocable to her partnership interest. But the partnership itself does not have an overall built-in loss. Rather, it has a net built-in gain of $100,000 ($1 million minus $900,000). Partner C sells her partnership interest to D for $33,333. The test for a substantial built-in loss applies both at the partnership

NEW LAW EXPLAINED

level and at the transferee partner level. If the partnership were to sell all of its assets for cash at their fair market value immediately after the transfer to D, D would be allocated a loss of $300,000 (one third of the built-in loss of $900,000 in Asset Y). A substantial built-in loss exists under the partner-level test, and the partnership adjusts the basis of its assets accordingly with respect to D (Joint Committee on Taxation, Description of the Chairman's Mark of the "Tax Cuts and Jobs Act" (JCX-51-17), November 9, 2017).

▶ **Effective date.** The amendment made by this section applies to transfers of partnership interests after December 31, 2017 (Act Sec. 13502(b) of the Tax Cuts and Jobs Act (P.L. 115-97)).

Law source: Law at ¶5650. Committee Report at ¶10,600.

— Act Sec. 13502(a) of the Tax Cuts and Jobs Act (P.L. 115-97), amending Code Sec. 743(d);

— Act Sec. 13502(b), providing the effective date.

¶350 Treatment of Sale or Exchange of Partnership Interests by Foreign Persons

SUMMARY OF NEW LAW

Gain or loss from the sale or exchange of a partnership interest is effectively connected with a U.S. trade or business to the extent that the transferor would have had effectively connected gain or loss had the partnership sold all of its assets at fair market value as of the disposition date. The transferee of a partnership interest must withhold 10 percent of the amount realized on the sale or exchange unless the transferor certifies that it is not a nonresident alien or foreign corporation.

BACKGROUND

A foreign person that is engaged in a trade or business in the United States is taxed on income or gain that is "effectively connected" with the conduct of that trade or business (Code Secs. 871(b) and 882(a)). The effectively connected test considers (1) the extent to which income or gain is derived from assets used in the conduct of the U.S. trade or business (the "asset use" test), and (2) whether the activities of the trade or business were a material factor in realizing the income or gain (the "business activities" test) (Code Sec. 864(c)(2)).

A foreign partner in a partnership is treated as engaged in the conduct of a trade or business within the United States if the partnership is so engaged (Code Sec. 875). Even though the source of gain or loss from the sale or exchange of personal property is generally determined based on where the seller resides (Code Sec. 865(a)), a foreign

BACKGROUND

partner may have effectively connected income due to the "asset use" or "business activities" of the partnership in which he is an investor.

Special rules treat gain or loss on the sale of U.S. real property interests as effectively connected with the conduct of a U.S. trade or business (Code Sec. 897(a)). If consideration received by a nonresident alien or foreign corporation for its interest in a partnership is attributable to a U.S. real property interest, that consideration is treated as received from the sale or exchange in the United States of the real property (Code Sec. 897(g)).

The IRS and the courts have clashed over the treatment of sales of partnership interests by foreign persons. A key piece of guidance is a 1991 revenue ruling that dealt with the sale of an interest in a foreign partnership (Rev. Rul. 91-32, 1991 CB 107). There, the IRS said that if there is unrealized gain or loss in partnership assets that would be treated as effectively connected with the conduct of a U.S. trade or business if those assets were sold by the partnership, some or all of a foreign person's gain or loss from the sale of a partnership interest may be treated as effectively connected.

In 2017, the Tax Court rejected the IRS's reasoning and held that, in general, a foreign person's gain or loss on the sale of an interest in a partnership engaged in a U.S. trade or business is foreign-source (*Grecian Magnesite Mining*, Dec. 60,968, 149 TC No. 3 (July 13, 2017)).

Gain from sales of U.S. real property interests may be subject to a 15-percent withholding tax on the amount realized on the transfer (Code Sec. 1445(e)(5)).

NEW LAW EXPLAINED

Foreign person's gain or loss on sale of partnership interest treated as effectively connected.—Gain or loss from any sale, exchange, or other disposition of a partnership interest is effectively connected with a U.S. trade or business, to the extent that the transferor would have had effectively connected gain or loss had the partnership sold all of its assets at fair market value as of the date of the sale or exchange. Any gain or loss from the hypothetical asset sale must be allocated to interests in the partnership in the same manner as nonseparately stated income and loss (Code Sec. 864(c)(8)(A), (B), and (D), as added by the Tax Cuts and Jobs Act (P.L. 115-97)).

Gain or loss treated as effectively connected income under this provision is reduced by the amount treated as effectively connected income under Code Sec. 897, which relates to gain or loss of a nonresident alien or foreign corporation from the disposition of a U.S. real property interest (Code Sec. 864(c)(8)(C), as added by the 2017 Tax Cuts Act).

In addition, the transferee of a partnership interest must withhold 10 percent of the amount realized on the sale or exchange, unless the transferor certifies that it is not a nonresident alien or foreign corporation. The amount withheld may be reduced, at the transferor's or transferee's request, if the IRS determines that the reduced amount will not jeopardize income tax collection on the gain realized. If the transferee fails to withhold the correct amount, the partnership must deduct and withhold from distribu-

NEW LAW EXPLAINED

tions to the transferee partner an amount equal to the amount the transferee failed to withhold (Code Sec. 1446(f), as added by the 2017 Tax Cuts Act).

The Treasury is instructed to prescribe regulations and other appropriate guidance to apply these provisions and carry out the withholding requirements (Code Secs. 864(c)(8)(E) and 1446(f)(6), as added by the 2017 Tax Cuts Act). It is anticipated that the Treasury will provide regulations allowing a broker, as agent of the transferee, to fulfill the obligation to deduct and withhold (Conference Report on H.R. 1, Tax Cuts and Jobs Act (H. Rept. 115-466), p. 369).

▶ **Effective date.** The amendment made by this section treating gain or loss on the sale or exchange of a partnership interest as effectively connected with the conduct of a trade or business in the United States applies to sales, exchanges, and dispositions on or after November 27, 2017 (Act Sec. 13501(c)(1) of the Tax Cuts and Jobs Act (P.L. 115-97)). The amendment requiring withholding on sales or exchanges of partnership interests applies to sales, exchanges, and dispositions after December 31, 2017 (Act Sec. 13501(c)(2) of the 2017 Tax Cuts Act).

Law source: Law at ¶5785 and ¶6055. Committee Report at ¶10,590.

— Act Sec. 13501(a) of the Tax Cuts and Jobs Act (P.L. 115-97), amending Code Sec. 864(c)(1) and adding Code Sec. 864(c)(8);

— Act Sec. 13501(b), redesignating Code Sec. 1446(f) as (g), and adding Code Sec. 1446(f);

— Act Sec. 13501(c), providing the effective date.

¶355 Technical Termination of Partnerships

SUMMARY OF NEW LAW

The rule providing for technical termination of partnerships is repealed for partnership tax years beginning after December 31, 2017.

BACKGROUND

A partnership is considered terminated if (1) no part of any business, financial operation, or venture of the partnership continues to be carried on by any of its partners, or (2) within a 12-month period, there is a sale or exchange of 50 percent of more of the total interest in partnership capital and profits (Code Sec. 708(b)). The second type of termination—sale or exchange of 50 percent of total partnership interest—is termed a "technical termination."

A technical termination causes two deemed transfers:

(1) The terminated partnership is deemed to contribute all of its assets and liabilities to a new partnership in exchange for an interest in the new partnership; and

BACKGROUND

(2) Immediately afterwards, in a liquidating distribution, the terminated partnership is deemed to distribute its interests in the new partnership to the purchasing partner and the remaining partners (Reg. § 1.708-1(b)(4)).

Neither the remaining partners nor the partnership generally recognize gain or loss on the deemed contribution to the new partnership and the subsequent deemed liquidating distribution.

A technical termination causes the following tax consequences:

- The terminated partnership's tax year closes on the date of the sale or exchange that triggers the termination. The resulting short tax year may cause a bunching of the partnership income for the remaining partners (Reg. § 1.708-1(b)(3)).

- The new partnership must file new tax elections regarding accounting methods, depreciation methods, installment sales, and amortizations and depletions.

- Generally, partnership depreciation recovery periods restart.

- The new partnership must file a new Code Sec. 754 optional basis adjustment election (Reg. § 1.708-1(b)(5)).

Thus, a technical termination does not necessarily end the partnership's existence, but only terminates some of the "old" partnership's tax attributes.

NEW LAW EXPLAINED

Technical termination of partnerships repealed.—The rule providing for the technical termination of partnerships is repealed (Code Sec. 708(b)(1), as amended by the Tax Cuts and Jobs Act (P.L. 115-97)).

Practical Analysis: J. Leigh Griffith, Partner at Waller Lansden Dortch & Davis, LLP in Nashville Tennessee, notes the advantage of no technical termination will often be the continued use of the prior depreciation method and remaining lives for the historic asset basis. The disadvantage is the new owners will be required to live with the existing partnership elections and accounting methods. A closing of the books method may be used to allocate income and loss between the "old partners" and the "new partners" with the same effect on the determination of pre-closing income and loss as the closing of the tax year a technical termination would have produced.

Practical Analysis: Jim Hamill, Director of Tax Practice at Reynolds, Hix & Co., P.A. in Albuquerque, NM, observes that the repeal of the "technical termination" provisions will avoid several common tax filing problems with partnerships. First, many final returns for the terminated partnership are filed late because the tax advisor was unaware that a termination had occurred until the due date had passed. Second, terminations created often surprising results for depreciation computations, including bonus depreciation, in the year of the termination. Compliance issues often led to the selection of a form of owner change just to avoid the termination. For example,

NEW LAW EXPLAINED

> redemptions of partner interests rather than a cross purchase by continuing owners could avoid a termination. Now the form selected will be driven by economic (and perhaps legal) considerations rather than the need to avoid an artificial termination of the partnership.

▶ **Effective date.** The amendment made by this section applies to partnership tax years beginning after December 31, 2017 (Act Sec. 13504(c) of the Tax Cuts and Jobs Act (P.L. 115-97)).

Law source: Law at ¶5315, ¶5645, and ¶5650. Committee Report at ¶10,620.

— Act Sec. 13504(a) of the Tax Cuts and Jobs Act (P.L. 115-97), amending Code Sec. 708(b)(1);

— Act Sec. 13504(b), amending Code Sec. 168(i)(7)(B) and Code Sec. 743(e); and

— Act Sec. 13504(c), providing the effective date.

¶360   Qualified Beneficiary of Electing Small Business Trust (ESBT)

SUMMARY OF NEW LAW

A nonresident alien individual may be a potential current beneficiary of an ESBT, effective on January 1, 2018.

BACKGROUND

All shareholders of an S corporation must be individuals, estates, certain specified trusts or certain tax-exempt organizations (Code Sec. 1361(b)(1)(B)). An electing small business trust ("ESBT") may be a shareholder of an S corporation. Generally, the eligible beneficiaries of an ESBT include individuals, estates, and certain charitable organizations eligible to hold S corporation stock directly

Each potential current beneficiary of an ESBT is treated as a shareholder, except that for any period in which there is no potential current beneficiary of the trust, the trust itself is treated as the shareholder. A potential current beneficiary is a person who is entitled to a distribution from the trust or who may receive a distribution at the discretion of any person. Any person who may benefit from a power of appointment is not a potential current beneficiary if the power has not been exercised. A nonresident alien individual may not be a shareholder of an S corporation and may not be a potential current beneficiary of an ESBT without causing disqualification of the S corporation election. If the potential current beneficiaries of an ESBT would disqualify an entity from S corporation status, the ESBT has a grace period of one year to dispose of its stock in the S corporation, thereby avoiding disqualification.

BACKGROUND

The portion of an ESBT which consists of the stock of an S corporation is treated as a separate trust and generally is taxed on its share of the S corporation's income at the highest rate of tax imposed on individual taxpayers. This income is not taxed to the beneficiaries of the ESBT. This is the case whether or not the income is distributed be the ESBT (Code Sec. 641(a) and (c)).

NEW LAW EXPLAINED

Expansion of qualifying beneficiaries of electing small business trust (ESBT) to include nonresident aliens.—A nonresident alien individual may be a potential current beneficiary of an electing small business trust (ESBT) without causing the loss of the S corporation election (Code Sec. 1361(c)(2)(B)(v), as amended by the Tax Cuts and Jobs Act (P.L. 115-97). Thus, an ESBT's nonresident alien potential current beneficiaries would not be considered to be disqualifying shareholders under Code Sec. 1361(b)(1)(C). Accordingly, the ESBT's share of S corporation income is taxed to the ESBT (whether or not distributed) , not to its nonresident alien potential current beneficiaries.

> **Comment:** Although the new law permits a nonresidential alien individual to be a potential current beneficiary of an ESBT, it does not allow a nonresidential alien to be an S corporation shareholder.

Practical Analysis: William D. Elliott, Partner at Elliott, Thomason & Gibson, LLP in Dallas, Texas, comments that the requirements of beneficiaries of an electing small business trust (ESBT) was expanded to include non-resident aliens, effective on January 1, 2018. This change contributes to greater flexibility on designing S Corporations.

Practical Analysis: Michael Schlesinger, Partner at Schlesinger & Sussman, Clifton, NJ and author of PRACTICAL GUIDE TO S CORPORATIONS (7th Ed.), notes that Code Sec. 641(c) prescribes that ESBT income is taxed at the highest individual tax rate which is now 37 percent. Further, the general rules of Subchapter J for computation of income do not apply; thus, the ESBT cannot deduct Subchapter S items passed through to it by distributing the income to the beneficiaries. While income received by the beneficiaries of the ESBT is not taxable to them, a 37-percent income tax is a very steep price to pay for the pass through of income.

An alternative means to pass income to a non-resident alien would be for the non-resident alien to form a partnership with the S corporation providing that the partnership has a substantial business purpose. The partnership would allow the non-resident alien to have income taxed at regular rates, not at the highest individual income tax rate as required by an ESBT.

▶ **Effective date.** The amendment made by this section is effective on January 1, 2018 (Act Sec. 13541(b) of the Tax Cuts and Jobs Act (P.L. 115-97)).

¶360

NEW LAW EXPLAINED

Law source: Law at ¶6015. Committee Report at ¶10,760.

— Act Sec. 13541(a) of the Tax Cuts and Jobs Act (P.L. 115-97), amending Code Sec. 1361(c)(2)(B)(v);

— Act Sec. 13541(b), providing the effective date.

¶365 Charitable Contribution Deduction for Electing Small Business Trust (ESBT)

SUMMARY OF NEW LAW

The charitable contribution deduction of an ESBT is generally to be determined by the rules applicable to individuals, not to the rules generally applicable to trusts. This change applies to tax years beginning after December 31, 2017.

BACKGROUND

An electing small business trust (ESBT) can be an S corporation shareholder so long as the trust does not have as a beneficiary any person other than an individual, estate, or organization eligible to accept charitable contributions under Code Sec. 170 (other than a political entity) (Code Sec. 1361(e)(1)(A)(i). The portion of an ESBT that consists of the stock of an S corporation is treated as a separate trust and generally is taxed on its share of the S corporation's income at the highest rate of tax imposed on individual taxpayers. This income is not taxed to the beneficiaries of the ESBT. This is the case whether or not the income is distributed by the ESBT.

The deduction for charitable contributions by an ESBT is determined by the rules applicable to trusts, rather than the rules applicable to individuals. Generally, a trust is allowed a charitable contribution deduction for amounts of gross income, without limitation, which pursuant to the terms of the governing instrument are paid for a charitable purpose. No carryover of excess contributions is allowed. An individual is allowed a charitable contribution deduction limited to certain percentages of adjusted gross income generally with a five-year carryforward of amounts in excess of this limitation.

NEW LAW EXPLAINED

Charitable deduction of ESBT determined by rules for individuals.—The charitable contribution deduction of an electing small business trust (ESBT) is not determined by the rules generally applicable to trusts under Code Sec. 642(c) (Code Sec. 641(c)(2)(E)(i), as added by the Tax Cuts and Jobs Act (P.L. 115-97)). The deduction, instead is determined by rules applicable to individuals (Code Sec. 641(c)(2)(E)(ii), as added by the 2017 Tax Cuts Act). Thus, the percentage limitations and carryforward

NEW LAW EXPLAINED

provisions applicable to individuals apply to charitable contributions made by the portion of an ESBT holding S corporation stock.

Specifically for purposes of the contribution base for percentage limitations under Code Sec. 170(b)(1)(G), adjusted gross income is computed in the same manner as in the case of an individual. However, the deductions for costs which are paid or incurred in connection with the administration of the trust and which would not have been incurred if the property were not held in such trust are to be treated as allowable in arriving at adjusted gross income (Code Sec. 641(c)(2)(E)(ii), as added by the 2017 Tax Cuts Act).

Practical Analysis: William D. Elliott, Partner at Elliott, Thomason & Gibson, LLP in Dallas, Texas, comments that the rules governing charitable contributions by an electing small business trust (ESBT) are changed to those rules applicable to individuals, effective after December 31, 2017. This is a taxpayer favorable change inasmuch as the prior rule tied the rules for charitable contribution of ESBT to those of trusts and estate.

Practical Analysis: Michael Schlesinger, Partner at Schlesinger & Sussman, Clifton, NJ and author of PRACTICAL GUIDE TO S CORPORATIONS (7th Ed.), notes that Congress has increased the Code Sec. 170 deduction to 60 percent of an individual taxpayer's contribution base. Unless taxpayers have itemized deductions in excess of the new standard deduction, there is no tax incentive for individuals to make tax deductible contributions. Consequently, many tax exempt entities such as religious institutions, educational organizations, Planned Parenthood, *etc.*, will suffer.

▶ **Effective date.** The amendment made by this section applies to tax years beginning after December 31, 2017 (Act Sec. 13542(b) of the Tax Cuts and Jobs Act (P.L. 115-97)).

Law source: Law at ¶5620. Committee Report at ¶10,770.

— Act Sec. 13542(a) of the Tax Cuts and Jobs Act (P.L. 115-97), adding Code Sec. 641(c)(2)(E);

— Act Sec. 13542(b), providing the effective date.

¶370 S Corporation Conversions to C Corporations

SUMMARY OF NEW LAW

S corporations that convert to C corporations should take any resulting Code Sec. 481(a) adjustments into account over a six-year period. In addition, if an eligible terminated S corporation distributes money after the post-termination transition period, the accumulated adjustments account will be allocated to such distribution.

¶370

BACKGROUND

Generally, once S corporation status ends, C corporation rules apply. There are, however, special rules for distributions during the post-termination transition period (Code Sec. 1371(e)). Distributions made by a former S corporation during its post-termination transition period are treated in the same manner as if the distributions were made by an S corporation. The post-termination transition period is:

(1) the period beginning on the day after termination of S corporation status and ending on the later of (i) the day that is one year after the termination, or (ii) the due date for filing the return for the last year as an S corporation (including extensions);

(2) the 120-day period beginning on the date of any determination pursuant to an audit following the termination of the corporation's S election and which adjusts a Subchapter S item of income, loss, or deduction of the corporation arising during the S period (as defined in Code Sec. 1368(e)(2)); and

(3) the 120-day period beginning on the date of a determination that the corporation's election under Code Sec. 1362(a) had terminated for a previous tax year (Code Sec. 1377(b)).

An S corporation's accumulated adjustment account determines the tax effect of distributions when the corporation has accumulated earnings and profits. Additionally, if the corporation's S election is terminated, the accumulated adjustment account balance will be necessary to determine the amount of money that can be distributed tax-free during the post-termination period (Code Sec. 1371(e)). Distributions from a terminated S corporation are treated as paid from its accumulated adjustment account if made during the post-termination transition period.

When the taxable income of a taxpayer is computed under a different accounting method than the prior year (e.g., when changing from the cash method to the accrual method), Code Sec. 481(a) adjustments need to be made. In computing taxable income for the year of change, the taxpayer must take into account those adjustments which are necessary to prevent items of income or expense from being duplicated or omitted (Code Sec. 481(a)(2)). The year of change is the tax year for which the taxable income of the taxpayer is computed under a different method than the prior year (Reg. § 1.481-1(a)). Net adjustments that decrease taxable income generally are taken into account entirely in the year of change, and net adjustments that increase taxable income generally are taken into account ratably during the four-tax-year period beginning with the year of change (Rev. Proc. 2015-13, I.R.B. 2015-5, 419).

NEW LAW EXPLAINED

Period relating to adjustments attributable to S corporation conversions to C corporation extended.—Any Code Sec. 481(a) adjustment resulting from an accounting method change that is attributable to an eligible S corporation's revocation of its S corporation election during the two-year period beginning on December 22, 2017, will be taken into account ratably over a six-year period beginning with the year of change (Code Sec. 481(d), as added by the Tax Cuts and Jobs Act (P.L. 115-97)). An eligible terminated S corporation is any C corporation:

NEW LAW EXPLAINED

- which was an S corporation on the day before December 22, 2017;
- which during the two-year period beginning on December 22, 2017, makes a revocation of its election under Code Sec. 1362(a); and
- the owners of the stock of which, determined on the date of revocation, are the same owners (and in identical proportions) as on December 22, 2017 (Code Sec. 481(d)(2), as added by the 2017 Tax Cuts Act).

If an eligible terminated S corporation distributes money after the post-termination transition period, the accumulated adjustments account will be allocated to such distribution. Further, the distribution will be chargeable to accumulated earnings and profits in the same ratio as the amount of such accumulated adjustments account bears to the amount of such earnings and profits (Code Sec. 1371(f), as added by the 2017 Tax Cuts Act).

> **Practical Analysis:** William D. Elliott, Partner at Elliott, Thomason & Gibson, LLP in Dallas, Texas, comments that two changes were made to a conversion from a S Corporation to a C Corporation. First, the Code Sec. 481(a) adjustments from such a conversion is taken into account over six years beginning with the year of change, and second, distributions of money by the S Corporation during the post-termination period is now chargeable to the accumulated adjustments account.

▶ **Effective date.** No specific effective date is provided by the Act. The provision is, therefore, considered effective on December 22, 2017, the date of enactment.

Law source: Law at ¶5555 and ¶6020. Committee Report at ¶10,780.

— Act Sec. 13543(a) of the Tax Cuts and Jobs Act (P.L. 115-97), adding Code Sec. 481(d);

— Act Sec. 13543(b), adding Code Sec. 1371(f).

Depreciation and Expense Deductions

¶405 Section 179 Expensing of Depreciable Assets

SUMMARY OF NEW LAW

The Code Sec. 179 dollar limitation is increased to $1 million and the investment limitation is increased to $2.5 million for tax years beginning after 2017. The definition of qualified real property eligible for expensing is redefined to include improvements to the interior of any nonresidential real property ("qualified improvement property"), as well as roofs, heating, ventilation, and air-conditioning property, fire protection and alarm systems, and security systems installed on such property. The exclusion from expensing for tangible personal property used in connection with lodging facilities (such as residential rental property) is eliminated. The $25,000 Code Sec. 179 expensing limit on certain heavy vehicles is inflation-adjusted after 2018.

BACKGROUND

Taxpayers (other than estates, trusts, and certain noncorporate lessors) may elect to treat the cost of qualifying property, called "section 179 property," as a deductible expense rather than a capital expenditure (Code Sec. 179). Section 179 property is generally defined as new or used depreciable tangible section 1245 property that is purchased for use in the active conduct of a trade or business (Code Sec. 179(d)(1)).

Dollar limitation. For tax years beginning in 2017, the inflation-adjusted dollar limit on the cost of section 179 property that the taxpayer can elect to deduct is $510,000 (Code Sec. 179(b)(1); Rev. Proc. 2017-58).

BACKGROUND

Investment limitation. The annual dollar limit is reduced dollar for dollar by the portion of the cost of section 179 property placed in service during the tax year that exceeds an investment limitation (Code Sec. 179(b)(2)). The inflation-adjusted investment limitation is $2,030,000 for tax years beginning in 2017 (Rev. Proc. 2017-58).

$25,000 SUV limitation. The maximum amount of the cost of a sport utility vehicle (SUV) that may be expensed under Code Sec. 179 if the SUV is exempt from the luxury car caps (e.g., has a gross vehicle weight rating in excess of 6,000 pounds) is limited to $25,000. The $25,000 limitation also applies to exempt trucks with an interior cargo bed length of less than six feet and exempt passenger vans that seat fewer than ten persons behind the driver's seat. To qualify, the vehicle must be rated at not more than 14,000 pounds gross vehicle weight. Exempt cargo vans are generally not subject to the $25,000 limitation (Code Sec. 179(b)(5)). This limitation is not inflation-adjusted.

Qualified real property. A taxpayer may elect to treat qualified real property as section 179 property (Code Sec. 179(f)(1)). Qualified real property generally consists of qualified leasehold improvements as defined in Code Sec. 168(e)(6), qualified restaurant property as defined in Code Sec. 168(e)(7), and qualified retail improvement property as defined in Code Sec. 168(e)(8) (Code Sec. 179(f)(2)). These types of property are depreciable under MACRS over 15-years using the straight-line method.

Property used in connection with lodging. Property that is used predominantly to furnish lodging or in connection with the furnishing of lodging does not qualify for expensing (Code Sec. 179(d)(1)). The term "lodging facility" includes an apartment house (e.g., MACRS residential rental property), hotel, motel, dormitory, or (subject to certain exceptions) any other facility or part of a facility where sleeping accommodations are provided and let. However, property used by a hotel, motel, inn, or other similar establishment is not considered used in connection with the furnishing of lodging if more than half of the living quarters are used to accommodate tenants on a transient basis (rental periods of 30 days or less) (Code Sec. 50(b)(2)(B); Reg. § 1.48-1(h)(1)(i) and (2)(ii)). Property used in the living quarters of a lodging facility, including beds and other furniture, refrigerators, ranges, and other equipment is used predominantly to furnish lodging (Reg. § 1.48-1(h)(1)(i)). Property that is used predominantly in the operation of a lodging facility or in serving tenants is used in connection with the furnishing of lodging, whether furnished by the owner of the lodging facility or another person. Examples of property used in connection with the furnishing of lodging include lobby furniture, office equipment, and laundry and swimming pool equipment. Property used in furnishing electrical energy, water, sewage disposal services, gas, telephone service or similar services are not used in connection with the furnishing of lodging (Reg. § 1.48-1(h)(1)(ii)).

NEW LAW EXPLAINED

Code Sec. 179 deduction limitations increased, qualified real property expensing expanded, lodging facility property made eligible, $25,000 limit on SUVs inflation-adjusted—The overall Code Sec. 179 expensing dollar limitation is increased from $500,000 (inflation-adjusted to $510,000 for 2017) to $1 million, and the investment

¶405

NEW LAW EXPLAINED

limitation is increased from $2 million (inflation-adjusted to $2,030,000 in 2017) to $2.5 million, effective for property placed in service in tax years beginning after December 31, 2017 (Code Sec. 179(b)(1) and (2), as amended by the Tax Cuts and Jobs Act (P.L. 115-97)).

These increases are permanent and will be inflation-adjusted for tax years beginning after 2018 (Code Sec. 179(b)(6), as amended by the 2017 Tax Cuts Act). The amount of the inflation adjustment is based on the cost-of-living adjustment determined under Code Sec. 1(f)(3) for the calendar year in which the tax year begins, by substituting calendar year 2017 for calendar year 2016. When adjusting the dollar limitation or the investment limitation for inflation, the resulting amount must be rounded to the nearest multiple of $10,000.

Qualified real property definition expanded. The definition of qualified real property that taxpayers may elect to treat as section 179 property is significantly expanded. Effective for tax years beginning after 2017, qualified real property is defined as:

(1) Qualified improvement property; and

(2) Any of the following improvements to nonresidential real property that are placed in service after the nonresidential real property was first placed in service:

- roofs;

- heating, ventilation, and air-conditioning property;

- fire protection and alarm systems; and

- security systems (Code Sec. 179(f), as amended by the 2017 Tax Cuts Act).

Comment: As under prior law, a taxpayer must elect to treat qualified real property as section 179 property (Code Sec. 179(d)(1)(B)(ii), as amended by the 2017 Tax Cuts Act). If the election is made and the total cost of all section 179 property, including qualified real property, exceeds the investment limitation ($2.5 million in 2018), the dollar limitation ($1 million in 2018) is subject to reduction.

Qualified improvement property is an improvement to *an interior portion* of a building that is nonresidential real property provided the improvement is placed in service after the date that the building was first placed in service. However, improvements related to the enlargement of the building, an elevator or escalator, or the internal structural framework of the building are not qualified improvement property (Code Sec. 168(e)(6), as amended by the 2017 Tax Cuts Act).

Comment: Previously, qualified real property eligible for expensing consisted of qualified leasehold improvement property, qualified retail improvement property, and qualified restaurant improvements and buildings that are eligible for an MACRS 15-year recovery period. Qualified leasehold improvement property is any improvement to the interior portion of a building that is not residential rental property and is made under or pursuant to the terms of a lease by the lessor or lessee. Qualified retail improvement property is any improvement to the interior portion of a building that is not residential rental property, which is open to the general public, and is used in the retail trade or business of selling

NEW LAW EXPLAINED

tangible personal property to the general public. The improvement to leasehold or retail improvement property must be placed in service more than three years after the date the building was first placed in service by any person, and improvements related to the enlargement of the building, any elevator or escalator, any structural component benefitting a common area, or the internal structural framework of the building do not qualify. Qualified restaurant property is a restaurant building or any improvement to a restaurant building. No additional restrictions apply to restaurant property.

Comment: Qualified improvement property became a category of property eligible for bonus depreciation for property placed in service after 2015 (Code Sec. 168(k)(3), as added by Division Q of P.L. 114-113 (PATH Act), December 18, 2015). See ¶410. The new law does not change the definition of qualified improvement property but now includes it as a category of property eligible for expensing under Code Sec. 179 as "qualified real property." Under the new law, qualified real property also includes roofs, HVAC property, fire protection or alarm systems, and security systems placed in service in or on a commercial building after the building is placed in service. Under prior law, qualified real property included only 15-year leasehold improvement property, 15-year retail improvement, and 15-year restaurant improvements and buildings.

Comment: A separate provision eliminates the 15-year recovery period for 15-year leasehold improvement property, 15-year retail improvement, and 15-year restaurant improvements and buildings effective for property placed in service after 2017 (Code Sec. 168(e)(3)(E), as amended by the 2017 Tax Cuts Act). In its place, Congress intended to assign a 15-year recovery period for qualified improvement property (Conference Report on H.R. 1, Tax Cuts and Jobs Act (H. Rept. 115-466)). However, the final bill text, while eliminating the 15-year classifications for leasehold improvement property, etc., inadvertently failed to assign a 15-year recovery period to qualified improvement property. A technical correction will be necessary. See ¶425 for a detailed discussion of qualified improvement property.

Comment: The new Code Sec. 179 provision is unfavorable to restaurant owners. Previously, restaurant buildings and improvements to the exterior as well as the interior of a restaurant building qualified for expensing under the qualified real property category. Under the new law, a restaurant improvement (or improvement to any other type of building) must meet the definition of "qualified improvement property." This means that only internal improvements to a restaurant building (and also roofs, HVAC property, fire protection and alarm systems, and security systems) will qualify for expensing. Furthermore, because restaurant buildings are not "qualified improvement property," they cannot be depreciated over the intended 15-year recovery period for qualified improvement property or expensed under Code Sec. 179 as qualified improvement property.

Exclusion for property used in connection with lodging repealed. Effective for property placed in service in tax years beginning after December 31, 2017, property that is used predominantly to furnish lodging or in connection with the furnishing of

¶405

NEW LAW EXPLAINED

lodging qualifies for Code Sec. 179 expensing (Code Sec. 179(d)(1), as amended by the 2017 Tax Cuts Act).

> **Comment:** The primary impact of this provision is to allow expensing of section 1245 property purchased for use in connection with a residential rental building. See *"Background"* section above for examples of types of property that are used in connection with the furnishing of lodging and are now eligible for expensing.

$25,000 limit on certain vehicles adjusted for inflation. The $25,000 maximum Code Sec. 179 deduction that may be claimed on specified vehicles that are exempt from the luxury car caps will be adjusted for inflation in tax years beginning after 2018 (Code Sec. 179(b)(6), as amended by the 2017 Tax Cuts Act).

> **Comment:** The $25,000 limit applies to a sport utility vehicle, a truck with an interior cargo bed length less than six feet, or a van that seats fewer than 10 persons behind the driver's seat, if the vehicle is exempt from the Code Sec. 280F annual depreciation caps because it has a gross vehicle weight rating in excess of 6,000 pounds or is otherwise exempt, and is rated at not more than 14,000 pounds gross vehicle weight (Code Sec. 179(b)(5)).

The amount of the inflation adjustment is based on the cost-of-living adjustment determined under Code Sec. 1(f)(3) for the calendar year in which the tax year begins, but substituting calendar year 2017 for calendar year 2016. When adjusting the $25,000 limit for inflation, the resulting amount must be rounded to the nearest multiple of $100.

Practical Analysis: Charles R. Goulding, President, Energy Tax Savers and R&D Tax Savers in Syosset, New York, comments that Code Sec. 179 is a longstanding favorable treatment of purchased property that allows businesses to expense eligible assets. To further incentivize and increase business spending, the Act increased both the annual cap and the phaseout limits. The annual limit has been raised from $500,000 to $1,000,000, and the phaseout limitation has been increased from $2 million to $2.5 million. This means that if a company's eligible expenditures are below $2.5 million, they can utilize up to $1 million in Code Sec. 179 expensing, and if their expenditures exceed $2.5 million, they can utilize up to the difference between their expenditures and $3.5 million. This increase will benefit many medium to large sized firms, since these companies were constrained by the previous annual and phaseout caps.

Property eligible for Code Sec. 179 expensing has also been expanded to include items related to buildings and structures. This would include roofs, heating, ventilation and air-conditioning property, fire protection and alarm systems, and security systems. Traditionally, there have been arguments that HVAC and other building improvements have been able to be claimed for Code Sec. 179 expensing if the client is making a lease-hold improvement since that can be treated as a business expense. However, by expanding the definition of Code Sec. 179 to include building equipment, owner-operators are now incentivized to make investments into their properties and no preferential treatment is given to tenants on an operating lease. In

---

NEW LAW EXPLAINED

some cases, many of these items are ineligible for bonus depreciation treatment and therefore this is their only path for accelerated expensing.

Practical Analysis: Michael Schlesinger, Partner at Schlesinger & Sussman, Clifton, NJ and author of PRACTICAL GUIDE TO S CORPORATIONS (7th Ed.), notes that with the change made to Code Sec. 179 to stimulate the economy by allowing additional first-year depreciation deduction for new and used property plus increasing Code Sec. 179's expensing to $1,000,000 should produce greater taxpayer investment.

Unfortunately, Congress still has not put parity into the law for utilization of Code Sec. 179's expense provisions. A classic example of disparity is Code Sec. 179(d)(4)'s provision which prevents estates and trusts from utilizing Code Sec. 179.

Where this prohibition is painfully illustrated is with S corporations. If an S corporation has an estate and/or a trust for a shareholder, Reg. § 1.179-1(f)(3) provides that the trust or estate may not deduct its allocable share of the Code Sec. 179 expense elected by the S corporation and the S corporation's basis in Code Sec. 179 property shall not be reduced to reflect any portion of the Code Sec. 179 expense that is allocable to the trust or estate. However, the S corporation may claim a depreciation deduction under Code Sec. 168 or a Code Sec. 38 credit (if available) with respect to any depreciable basis resulting from the trust or estate's inability to claim its allocable portion of the Code Sec. 179 expense.

Other examples which require planning due to Congress' restrictions include the following:

> If an S corporate shareholder plans to dispose of his or her stock where gain or loss is not recognized in whole or in part (including transfers of an S corporate interest at death) and the shareholder has not been able to fully utilize his or her Code Sec. 179 deduction due to Code Sec. 179's income limitation, Reg. § 1.179-3(h)(2) states that immediately before the transfer of the shareholder's stock in the S corporation, the shareholder's basis is increased by the amount of the shareholder's outstanding carryover of disallowed deduction with respect to his or her S corporate interest.

Code Sec. 179(d)(6) prescribes that members of a controlled group cannot expense totally more than $1,000,000 in a taxable year. Code Sec. 179(d)(7) states that for purposes of determining a control group for Code Sec. 179 purposes, the group is determined using a "more than 50 percent" ownership test rather than "at least an 80 percent" one. So, if an S corporation owns more than 50 percent of the stock of another corporation, then care must be practiced so as not to run afoul of Code Sec. 179(b)(1)'s dollar limitation.

For a taxpayer to utilize Code Sec. 179's expensing, the taxpayer must have taxable income. If a taxpayer does not have sufficient taxable income to utilize Code Sec. 179's immediate write off, then they are trapped by Code Sec. 179(b)(3)'s carryforward provisions which in a nutshell provide that any unused deductions can be carried forward but the amount to be expensed in a carried forward year is limited to

NEW LAW EXPLAINED

> the maximum annual dollar cost ceiling, investment limitation, or, if lesser, Code Sec. 179(b)(3)'s income limitation.

▶ **Effective date.** The provisions apply to property placed in service in tax years beginning after December 31, 2017 (Act Sec. 13101(d) of the Tax Cuts and Jobs Act (P.L. 115-97)).

Law source: Law at ¶5335. Committee Report at ¶10,320.

— Act Sec. 13101(a) of the Tax Cuts and Jobs Act (P.L. 115-97), amending Code Sec. 179(b);

— Act Sec. 13101(b)(1), amending Code Sec. 179(d)(1)(B);

— Act Sec. 13101(b)(2), amending Code Sec. 179(f);

— Act Sec. 13101(c), amending last sentence of Code Sec. 179(d)(1);

— Act Sec. 13101(d), providing the effective date.

¶410 Additional Depreciation Allowance (Bonus Depreciation)

SUMMARY OF NEW LAW

The bonus depreciation rate is increased to 100 percent for property acquired and placed in service after September 27, 2017, and before January 1, 2023. The rate phases down thereafter. Used property, films, television shows, and theatrical productions are eligible for bonus depreciation. Property used by rate-regulated utilities, and property of certain motor vehicle, boat, and farm machinery retail and lease businesses that use floor financing indebtedness, is excluded from bonus depreciation.

BACKGROUND

A 50-percent bonus depreciation deduction is allowed for the first tax year qualifying MACRS property is placed in service. The property's original use must begin with the taxpayer (so the property must be new) and it must be placed in service after December 31, 2007, and before January 1, 2020 (or before January 1, 2021, for longer production period property (LPP) and certain noncommercial aircraft (NCA)) (Code Sec. 168(k)). The bonus depreciation allowance rate was temporarily increased from 50 percent to 100 percent for qualified property acquired after September 8, 2010, and before January 1, 2012, and placed in service before January 1, 2012 (before January 1, 2013, for LPP and NCA).

The bonus depreciation rate is 50 percent for qualified property placed in service in 2017. It drops to 40 percent for 2018, and to 30 percent for 2019. These deadlines are extended for one year for NCA and LPP (so the rate is 50 percent for property placed in service in 2017 or 2018, 40 percent for 2019, and 30 percent for 2020 (Code Sec. 168(k)(6)).

BACKGROUND

There is no limit on the total amount of bonus depreciation that may be claimed in any given tax year. The amount of the bonus depreciation deduction is not affected by a short tax year. The bonus depreciation deduction is allowed in full for alternative minimum tax (AMT) purposes. In addition, the regular depreciation deductions claimed on property that qualifies for bonus depreciation are also allowed in full for AMT purposes even if an election out of bonus depreciation is made (Code Sec. 168(k)(2)(G)).

Qualifying property. The bonus depreciation allowance is available only for new property (i.e., property the original use of which begins with the taxpayer after December 31, 2007) that is:

- depreciable under MACRS and has a recovery period of 20 years or less;
- MACRS water utility property;
- computer software depreciable over three years under Code Sec. 167(f); or
- qualified improvement property (Code Sec. 168(k)(2)(A)).

Qualified improvement property is any improvement to an interior portion of a building that is nonresidential real property if the improvement is placed in service after the date the building was first placed in service by any person. Qualified improvement property, however, does not include improvements attributable to the enlargement of a building, any elevator or escalator, or the internal structural framework of the building (Code Sec. 168(k)(3)). No specific MACRS recovery period is assigned to qualified improvement property. Unless qualified improvement property meets the separate definitions for 15-year qualified leasehold improvement property, 15-year retail improvement property, or 15-year restaurant property, it is depreciated as MACRS 39-year nonresidential real property.

Longer production period property and noncommercial aircraft. In the case of LPP and NCA:

- The original use of the property must begin with the taxpayer;
- The property must be acquired by the taxpayer before 2020 or acquired pursuant to a binding contract entered into before 2020; and
- The property must be placed in service before 2021 (Code Sec. 168(k)(2)(B)(i) and (k)(2)(C)(i)).

If the NCA or LPP is constructed, the acquisition deadline is satisfied if the taxpayer begins manufacturing, constructing, or producing the NCA or LPP before January 1, 2020 (Code Sec. 168(k)(2)(E)(i)). Progress expenditures in 2020 can qualify for bonus depreciation only for NCA, but not for LPP (Code Sec. 168(k)(2)(B)(ii) and (iv)).

LPP is property that:

- meets the general requirements for qualifying property;
- is subject to the Code Sec. 263A uniform capitalization rules;
- has a production period greater than one year and a cost exceeding $1 million; and

¶410

BACKGROUND

- has a MACRS recovery period of at least 10 years or is used in the trade or business of transporting persons or property for hire, such as commercial aircraft (i.e., "transportation property") (Code Sec. 168(k)(2)(B)(i)).

Election out. A taxpayer may elect out of the bonus depreciation allowance for any class of property for the tax year (Code Sec. 168(k)(7)).

Luxury car depreciation caps. Unless the taxpayer elects out of bonus depreciation, the first-year Code Sec. 280F depreciation cap for passenger automobiles that qualify for bonus depreciation is increased by $8,000 for vehicles placed in service during 2017, $6,400 for 2018, and $4,800 for 2019 (Code Sec. 168(k)(2)(F)).

Coordination with long-term contract method of accounting. Solely for purposes of determining the percentage of completion under the Code Sec. 460(b)(1)(A) long-term contract accounting method, the cost of property with a MACRS recovery period of seven years or less that qualifies for bonus depreciation is taken into account as a cost allocated to the contract as if bonus depreciation had not been enacted. This rule applies to property placed in service in 2010 (2010 or 2011 for LPP), and property placed in service after December 31, 2012, and before January 1, 2020 (before January 1, 2021, for LPP) (Code Sec. 460(c)(6)(B)).

NEW LAW EXPLAINED

Bonus depreciation extended and increased to 100 percent; additional modifications made.—The 50-percent bonus depreciation rate is increased to 100 percent for qualified property acquired and placed in service after September 27, 2017, and before January 1, 2023 (Code Scc. 168(k)(1)(A) and (6)(A), as amended by the Tax Cuts and Jobs Act (P.L. 115-97)). The 100-percent allowance is phased down by 20 percent per calendar year for property placed in service after 2022. In general, the bonus depreciation percentage rates are as follows:

- 100 percent for property placed in service after September 27, 2017, and before January 1, 2023;
- 80 percent for property placed in service after December 31, 2022, and before January 1, 2024;
- 60 percent for property placed in service after December 31, 2023, and before January 1, 2025;
- 40 percent for property placed in service after December 31, 2024, and before January 1, 2026;
- 20 percent for property placed in service after December 31, 2025, and before January 1, 2027;
- 0 percent (bonus expires) for property placed in service after December 31, 2026 (Code Sec. 168(k)(6)(A), as amended by the 2017 Tax Cuts Act).

Property acquired before September 28, 2017. Property acquired before September 28, 2017, is subject to the 50-percent rate if placed in service in 2017, a 40-percent rate if placed in service in 2018, and a 30-percent rate if placed in service in 2019. Property

¶410

NEW LAW EXPLAINED

acquired before September 28, 2017, and placed in service after 2019 is not eligible for bonus depreciation. However, In the case of longer production property (LPP) and noncommercial aircraft (NCA), each of these placed-in-service dates is extended one year. Thus, a 50 percent rate applies to LPP and NCA acquired before September 28, 2017 and placed in service in 2017 or 2018, a 40 percent rate applies if such property is placed in service in 2019, and a 30 percent rate applies if such property is placed in service in 2020 (Code Sec. 168(k)(8), as added by the 2017 Tax Cuts Act)). These are the phase-down ratesa that applied before enactment of the 2017 Tax Cuts Act. They continue to apply to property acquired before the September 28, 2017, cut-off date set by Congress.

> **Caution:** Since the amendments made by the 2017 Tax Cuts Act apply to property acquired after September 27, 2017 (Act Sec. 13201(h) of P.L. 115-97) it is unclear how newCode Sec. 168(k)(8) can apply to the very property it is addressing (i.e., property acquired before September 28, 2017). In the case of property other than LPP and NCA acquired before September 28, 2017 and placed in service after September 27, 2017, the issue is of no apparent importance because the same phase-out rule applied prior to enactment of the 2017 Tax Cuts Act. However, in the case of LPP, the pre-2017 Tax Cuts Act rules prevented a taxpayer from claiming bonus depreciation on progress expenditures paid or incurred in the 2020 tax year (Code Sec. 168(k)(2)(B)(ii), prior to amendment by P.L. 115-97). Code Sec. 168(k)(9) provides no such restriction. Presumably, the rule contained in Code Sec. 168(k)(2)(B)(ii), prior to amendment by P.L. 115-97, will continue to apply to LPP acquired before September 28, 2017 by reason of the effective date of the 2017 Tax Cuts Act.

If a written binding contract for the acquisition of property is in effect prior to September 28, 2017, the property is not considered acquired after the date the contract is entered into (Act Sec. 13201(h)(1) of the 2017 Tax Cuts Act). Consequently, property subject to a binding written contract entered into before September 28, 2017, is not eligible for the 100-percent rate, and is subject to a 40-percent rate if placed in service in 2018 (2019 in the case of LPP and NCA) and a 30-percent rate if placed in service in 2019 (2020 in the case of LPP and NCA). The 50-percent rate applies if such property is placed in service in 2017 (2017 or 2018 in the case of LPP and NCA).

> **Comment:** Prior to the enactment of the Protecting Americans from Tax Hikes Act of 2015 (PATH Act) on December 18, 2015, property acquired before January 1, 2008 (or pursuant to a written binding contract entered into before January 1, 2008) was not eligible for bonus depreciation, and property acquired before September 8, 2010 (or pursuant to a written binding contract entered into before September 8, 2010) was not eligible for the 100-percent bonus depreciation rate that applied to property placed in service after September 7, 2010, and before January 1, 2012 (before January 1, 2013 for LLP and NCA). With the passage of time, the acquisition date and binding contract requirements became irrelevant and were stricken by the PATH Act, effective for property placed in service after December 31, 2015. Now that an acquisition date requirement is reinstated for purposes of determining whether a 50-percent or 100-percent rate will apply, various issues revolving around the definition of an "acquisition" are back in

NEW LAW EXPLAINED

play. The acquisition date requirements in the context of the 100-percent bonus depreciation rate for property acquired after September 7, 2010, were specifically addressed in Rev. Proc. 2011-26. The IRS will presumably issue similar guidance in the future for purposes of determining whether property is considered acquired after September 27, 2017, and eligible for the 100-percent rate. See also Reg. § 1.168(k)-1(b)(4) for rules regarding the determination of acquisition dates.

Specified plants. The applicable rates above also apply to specified plants acquired after September 27, 2017, except that the date the specified plant was planted or grafted replaces the placed in service date (Code Sec. 168(k)(5)(A) and (6)(C), as amended by the 2017 Tax Cuts Act). In general, a specified plant is any tree or vine which bears fruits or nuts, and any other plant which will have more than one yield of fruits or nuts and which generally has a pre-productive period of more than two years from the time of planting or grafting to the time at which such plant begins bearing fruits or nuts (Code Sec. 168(k)(5)).

Property with longer production period and noncommercial aircraft. In the case of property with a longer production period (LPP) and noncommercial aircraft (NCA), the placed-in-service deadlines for property acquired after September 27, 2017, are extended for one year. The applicable rates are as follows:

- 100 percent for property placed in service after September 27, 2017, and before January 1, 2024;

- 80 percent for property placed in service after December 31, 2023, and before January 1, 2025;

- 60 percent for property placed in service after December 31, 2024, and before January 1, 2026;

- 40 percent for property placed in service after December 31, 2025, and before January 1, 2027;

- 20 percent for property placed in service after December 31, 2026, and before January 1, 2028;

- 0 percent (bonus expires) for property placed in service after December 31, 2027 (Code Sec. 168(k)(6)(B), as amended by the 2017 Tax Cuts Act).

2027 production expenditures for LPP do not qualify for bonus depreciation (Code Sec. 168(k)(2)(B)(ii), as amended by the 2017 Tax Cuts Act). This rule does not apply to noncommercial aircraft (NCA).

Election to apply 50-percent rate. A taxpayer may elect to apply the 50-percent rate instead of the 100-percent rate for qualified property placed in service during the taxpayer's first tax year ending after September 27, 2017. The time and manner of making the election will be provided by the IRS (Code Sec. 168(k)(10), as added by the 2017 Tax Cuts Act). For example, a calendar year taxpayer making this election can apply the 50-percent rate to all qualified property placed in service in 2017 and ignore the 100-percent rate that would otherwise apply to qualified property acquired and placed in service after September 27, 2017, and before January 1, 2018.

Comment: When Congress last increased the bonus rate from 50 percent to 100 percent, the IRS provided a similar election to use the 50-percent rate on a

NEW LAW EXPLAINED

property class basis (Rev. Proc. 2011-26). For example, the election could be made to apply to all 5-year property only. Presumably, the IRS will again provide a similar rule.

Caution: The explanation below for qualified improvement property assumes that qualified improvement property placed in service after December 31, 2017, will have a 15-year recovery period as intended by Congress.

The original Senate bill would have provided a 10-year recovery period for qualified improvement property. The House bill contained no provision. The final bill, according to the Conference Report on H.R. 1, Tax Cuts and Jobs Act (H. Rept. 115-466) sets a 15-year recovery period for qualified improvement property. However, the text of the final bill omits the provision which would have given a 15-year recovery period for qualified improvement property. A technical correction will be needed to create a 15-year recovery period for qualified improvement property; in the absence of such a correction, all such property will be treated as 39-year nonresidential real property, effective for property placed in service after December 31, 2017 (no acquisition date requirement applies). See ¶425 for a detailed discussion of qualified improvement property.

An unintended consequence of failing to provide a 15-year recovery period for qualified improvement property placed in service after December 31, 2017, is that such property will not qualify for bonus depreciation if placed in service after that date. As explained below, qualified improvement property was removed as a specific category of bonus depreciation property, effective for property placed in service after December 31, 2017 (Code Sec. 168(k)(3), as stricken by the 2017 Tax Cuts Act) on the assumption that all qualified improvement property would have a 15-year recovery period and, therefore, qualify for bonus depreciation under the general rule that allows MACRS property with a recovery period of 20 years or less qualify for bonus depreciation.

Qualified improvement property. Qualified improvement property is removed as a specifically named category of property eligible for bonus depreciation, effective for property placed in service after December 31, 2017 (this provision applies without regard to the acquisition date) (Code Sec. 168(k)(2)(A)(i)(IV) and (k)(3), stricken by the 2017 Tax Cuts Act). However, all qualified improvement property remains eligible for bonus depreciation (assuming the correction described in the "*Caution*" above is made).

It was previously necessary to list qualified improvement property as a separate category of property eligible for bonus depreciation because some types of improvements which met the definition of qualified improvement property had a recovery period of 39 years. Therefore, this 39-year qualified improvement property would not have been eligible for bonus depreciation without the separate category for qualified improvement property because bonus depreciation generally otherwise only applies to property with an MACRS recovery period of 20 years or less (Code Sec. 168(k)(2)(A)(i)). The 2017 Tax Cuts Act, however, provides a standard 15-year recovery period for all qualified improvement property (assuming the correction discussed above is made) placed in service after December 31, 2017. This means qualified

¶410

NEW LAW EXPLAINED

improvement will qualify for bonus depreciation because it has a recovery period of 20 years or less.

Comment: The new law does not change the definition of qualified improvement property. It simply assigns a 15-year recovery period and straight-line method to such property (assuming the correction discussion above is made). Qualified improvement property is defined as an improvement to the interior of nonresidential real property, but does not include improvements for expenditures attributable to the enlargement of a building, any elevator or escalator, or the internal structural framework of a building (Code Sec. 168(e)(6), as added by the 2017 Tax Cuts Act). The new law eliminates the categories of 15-year qualified leasehold improvement property, 15-year qualified retail improvement property, and 15-year restaurant property, effective for property placed in service after December 31, 2017. A 15-year recovery period (and bonus depreciation) will apply to this type of property when placed in service after December 31, 2017, only if the definitional requirements of 15-year qualified improvement property are satisfied. See ¶425 for a detailed discussion.

Example: A calendar-year taxpayer makes an improvement to the interior of an office building in June 2016. Assume the improvement is depreciable over 39 years as nonresidential real property because it does not satisfy the definition of 15-year qualified leasehold improvement, 15-year retail improvement, or 15-year restaurant property. Even though the improvement has a 39-year recovery period, it may qualify for bonus depreciation because, for property placed in service in 2017, qualified improvement property is listed as a separate category of property eligible for bonus depreciation. If the same improvement is made in 2018, the recovery period of the improvement is 15 years and the improvement may qualify as bonus depreciation under the bonus depreciation category for MACRS property with a recovery period of 20 years or less.

Exclusion for property of rate-regulated utility. Under a new provision, rate-regulated utilities are prevented from claiming bonus depreciation, effective for property acquired and placed in service after September 27, 2017 (Code Secs. 168(k)(9) and 163(j)(7)(A)(iv), as added by the 2017 Tax Cuts Act). Specifically, property does not qualify for bonus depreciation if it is primarily used in a trade or business of furnishing or selling for regulated rates:

- electrical energy or water;
- sewage disposal services;
- gas or steam through a local distribution system; or
- transportation of gas or steam by pipeline.

Rates are regulated if established or approved by a state or political subdivision thereof, by any agency or instrumentality of the United States, by a public service or public utility commission or other similar body of any state or political subdivision thereof, or by the governing or ratemaking body of an electric cooperative.

NEW LAW EXPLAINED

Exclusion for property used by certain motor vehicle, boat, farm machinery businesses that used floor financing indebtedness. Property used in a trade or business that has had floor plan financing indebtedness does not qualify for bonus depreciation if the floor plan financing interest on the indebtedness was taken into account under the new rules that limit the business interest deduction to 30 percent of adjusted taxable income plus floor plan financing interest and interest income (Code Secs. 168(k)(9) and 163(j)(9), as added by the 2017 Tax Cuts Act). Floor plan financing indebtedness means indebtedness:

- used to finance the acquisition of motor vehicles held for sale or lease; and
- secured by the inventory acquired (Code Sec. 163(j)(9), as added by the 2017 Tax Cuts Act).

A motor vehicle means:

- any self-propelled vehicle designed for transporting persons or property on a public street, highway, or road;
- a boat; or
- farm machinery or equipment.

   Comment: The interest deduction limitation does not apply in any tax year that a taxpayer meets the gross receipts test of Code Sec. 448(c) by having average annual gross receipts for the three-tax-year period ending with the prior tax year that do not exceed $25 million (Code Sec. 163(j)(3), as added by the 2017 Tax Cuts Act). However, if a taxpayer has had floor financing interest in any tax year that it is not exempt from the 30-percent deduction limitation by reason of the gross receipts test or otherwise, the exclusion from bonus depreciation continues to apply in tax years that it is exempt.

   The 30 percent of taxable business limitation on deductible interest is discussed at ¶510.

Used property qualifies for bonus depreciation. Effective for property acquired and placed in service after September 27, 2017, property previously used by an unrelated person may qualify for bonus depreciation if it meets "acquisition requirements" (Code Sec. 168(k)(2)(A)(ii), as amended by the 2017 Tax Cuts Act). The acquisition requirements are met if:

- the taxpayer did not use the property at any time before acquiring it; and
- the taxpayer acquired the property by "purchase" within the meaning of Code Sec. 179(d)(2) (Code Sec. 168(k)(2)(E)(ii), as amended by the 2017 Tax Cuts Act).

Under Code Sec. 179(d)(2), any acquisition is considered a purchase unless the property:

- is acquired from a person whose relationship to the taxpayer would bar recognition of a loss in any transaction between them under Code Sec. 267 (with the taxpayer's family limited to spouse, ancestors and lineal descendants) or Code Sec. 707(b);

¶410

NEW LAW EXPLAINED

- is acquired by one member of a controlled group of corporations from another member (substituting 50 percent for the 80 percent that would otherwise apply with respect to stock ownership requirements);

- has a basis in the hands of the acquiring taxpayer determined in whole or in part by reference to the adjusted basis of the person from who the property was acquired (e.g., a gift or section 1022 basis property); or

- has a basis determined under Code Sec. 1014(a) relating to inherited or bequeathed property (Reg. § 1.179-4(c)).

Used property received in carryover basis transactions. The acquisition is also subject to the cost requirements of Code Sec. 179(d)(3) (Code Sec. 168(k)(2)(E)(ii)(II), as added by the 2017 Tax Cuts Act). Code Sec. 179(d)(3) (see also Reg. § 1.179-4(d)) provides that the cost of property eligible for Code Sec. 179 expensing does not include the portion of the basis of property that is determined by reference to the basis of other property held at any time by the person acquiring the property (e.g., the carryover basis in a like-kind exchange does not qualify for expensing but any additional cash paid does) (Conference Report on H.R. 1, Tax Cuts and Jobs Act (H. Rept. 115-466)).

> **Comment:** According to the Conference Report on H.R. 1, Tax Cuts and Jobs Act (H. Rept. 115-466), the reference to Code Sec. 179(d)(3) means that in the case of trade-ins, like-kind exchanges, or involuntary conversions, bonus depreciation only applies to any money paid in addition to the trade-in property or in excess of the adjusted basis of the replaced property. This limitation should only apply when the replacement property is used property. Bonus depreciation regulations currently in effect provide that bonus depreciation may be claimed on the carryover and excess basis of property acquired in a like-kind exchange if the property received in the exchange meets all other qualification requirements, including the original use requirement (Reg. § 1.168(k)-1(f)(5)).

Rule for sale-leasebacks eliminated. Since the original use requirement is now supplemented with the rule above allowing used property to qualify for bonus depreciation, a special rule for sale-leasebacks in Code Sec. 168(k)(2)(E)(ii), prior to amendment by the 2017 Tax Cuts Act, has been stricken.

> **Comment:** The eliminated rule provides an exception to the requirement that original use must begin with the taxpayer in a sale-leaseback. The rule applies to new property that was originally placed in service after December 31, 2007, by a person who sells it to the taxpayer and then leases it from the taxpayer within three months after the date that the property was originally placed in service. In this situation, the property is treated as originally placed in service by the taxpayer-lessor, and the taxpayer-lessor's placed-in-service date is deemed to occur no earlier than the date that the property is used by the lessee under the leaseback.

Bonus allowed for film and television productions and live theatrical productions. Bonus depreciation is allowed for a qualified film, television show, or theatrical production placed in service after September 27, 2017, if it would have qualified for the Code Sec. 181 expense election without regard to the $15 million expensing limit or the December 31, 2016, expiration date (Code Sec. 168(k)(2)(A)(i), as amended by

NEW LAW EXPLAINED

the 2017 Tax Cuts Act). A qualified film or television production is placed in service at the time of its initial release or broadcast. A qualified live theatrical production is placed in service at the time of its initial live staged performance (Code Sec. 168(k)(2)(H), as added by the 2017 Tax Cuts Act).

> **Comment:** Property acquired before September 28, 2017, does not qualify for bonus depreciation at the 100-percent rate (Act Sec. 13201(h)(1) of the 2017 Tax Cuts Act). If a film, television show, or theatrical production is deemed acquired before that date, bonus depreciation may not be claimed because it would not be qualified property. A 50-percent rate, however, would apply to other types of qualified property acquired before September 28, 2017. The IRS may need to provide guidance on how the acquisition requirement applies to films, television shows, and theatrical productions. One possibility is that the acquisition date for this purpose may be deemed to occur, at least in the case of a film or television show, when the production "commences," as defined below. Another possibility is to adapt the generally applicable rule for tangible property produced by or for a taxpayer that treats acquisition as occurring when physical work of a significant nature begins (Reg. § 1.168(k)-1(b)(4)(iii)(B)).

> **Comment:** The Code Sec. 181 deduction expired effective for productions commencing after December 31, 2016 (Code Sec. 181(g)) and was not extended by the new law. In the case of a film or television show, a production commences on the date of first principal photography. A theatrical production commences on the date of the first public performance before a paying audience. If a Code Sec. 181 election is made, production costs are expensed in the tax year paid or incurred. If the production does not commence until after the December 31, 2016, expiration date, costs expensed under Code Sec. 181 are subject to recapture. Under the bonus depreciation rule, production costs will now be expensed in the tax year the production is placed in service and without regard to the $15 million limit.

> **Comment:** A taxpayer generally makes an election under Code Sec. 181 on the income tax return for the tax year in which production costs are first paid or incurred (Reg. § 1.181-2(b)) and not at the later time when the production is placed in service, as defined above for bonus depreciation purposes. A taxpayer that made a Code Sec. 181 election at the time a production commenced is prohibited from claiming bonus depreciation on the same production if it is placed in service after September 27, 2017, unless the IRS grants permission to revoke the election (Code Sec. 181(b) and (c)). Automatic consent, however, will be granted without filing a letter ruling request if the taxpayer recaptures previously claimed deductions under Code Sec. 181 (Reg. § 181-2(d)(2)).

Coordination with passenger automobile depreciation caps. The first-year depreciation cap on a passenger vehicle that is subject to the annual depreciation limitations of Code Sec. 280F because its gross vehicle rate rating does not exceed 6,000 pounds is increased by $8,000 if 100-percent bonus depreciation is claimed. This is the same increase that applies when bonus depreciation is claimed at a 50-percent rate. The scheduled decrease in the $8,000 bump-up to $6,400 in 2018 and $4,800 in 2019 to reflect the formerly-scheduled decreases in the bonus rate from 50 percent to 40

NEW LAW EXPLAINED

percent in 2018 and to 30 percent in 2019 will only apply to vehicles acquired before September 28, 2017, and placed in service after September 27, 2017 (Code Sec. 168(k)(2)(F)(iii), as amended by the 2017 Tax Cuts Act).

> **Comment:** The annual depreciation caps are substantially increased by the new law (Code Sec. 280F(a), as amended by the 2017 Tax Cuts Act). In addition, for taxpayers that claim 100-percent bonus depreciation on a vehicle subject to the caps, the IRS will likely need to issue a safe harbor similar to one that was previously issued when a 100-percent bonus rate applied, that will allow such taxpayers to claim depreciation deductions after the first-year a vehicle is placed in service. See ¶415.

Long-term accounting method relief. In determining the percentage of completion under Code Sec. 460(b)(1)(A) for purposes of the long-term contract method of accounting, the cost of property with a MACRS recovery period of 7 years or less that qualifies for bonus depreciation is taken into account as a cost allocated to the contract as if the bonus depreciation had not been enacted. The provision applies only to property placed in service (1) after December 31, 2009, and before January 1, 2011 (before January 1, 2012, in the case of property with a longer production period) and (2) after December 31, 2012, and before January 1, 2027 (before January 1, 2028, in the case of long production property) (Code Sec. 460(c)(6)(B), as amended by the 2017 Tax Cuts Act).

> **Comment:** With the exception of transportation property, property with a longer production period must have a recovery period of 10 years or greater. Thus, longer production property that is not transportation property does not qualify for the special treatment provided by this provision. Transportation property is tangible personal property used in the trade or business of transporting persons or property, such as an airliner, and is not subject to the rule that requires a MACRS depreciation period of 10 years or greater in order to constitute long-production property (Code Sec. 168(k)(2)(B)(iii)).

Corporate election to claim unused AMT credits in lieu of bonus depreciation. The annual election provided to corporations to claim unused alternative minimum tax (AMT) credits in place of bonus depreciation on property placed in service during the tax year of the election is stricken effective for tax years beginning after December 31, 2017 (Code Sec. 168(k)(4), stricken by the 2017 Tax Cuts Act).

> **Comment:** The corporate AMT is repealed, effective for tax years beginning after December 31, 2017. See ¶310.

Practical Analysis: Charles R. Goulding, President, Energy Tax Savers and R&D Tax Savers in Syosset, New York, comments that the extension and expansion of Bonus Depreciation was likely included to incentivize companies to increase capital investment. Unlike much of the Act, the 100 percent bonus depreciation starts retroactively on September 28, 2017, and continues for five years (six years for long production period property) and then phases down 20 percent per year thereafter. Capital investments made since September 28 through the end of the year will get

---

¶410

NEW LAW EXPLAINED

> 100 percent bonus treatment on their 2017 tax returns. In addition, for the first time the purchase of used items will also qualify for bonus. In the case of used items the transaction of purchase must be arms length.

▶ **Effective date.** The amendments generally apply to property which is acquired after September 27, 2017, and is placed in service after September 27, 2017. For this purpose, property shall not be treated as acquired after the date on which a written binding contract is entered into for such acquisition (Act Sec. 13201(h)(1) of the Tax Cuts and Jobs Act (P.L. 115-97)). The amendments related to specified plants apply to specified plants planted or grafted after September 27, 2017 (Act. Sec. 13201(h)(2) of the 2017 Tax Cuts Act).

Law source: Law at ¶5315 and ¶5530. Committee Report at ¶10,340.

— Act Sec. 13201(a) of the Tax Cuts and Jobs Act (P.L. 115-97), amending Code Sec. 168(k)(1), (5), and (6), and adding Code Sec. 168(k)(8);

— Act Sec. 13201(b), amending Code Sec. 168(k)(2) and (5), and Code Sec. 460(c)(6)(B);

— Act Sec. 13201(c), amending Code Sec. 168(k)(2);

— Act Sec. 13201(d), adding Code Sec. 168(k)(9);

— Act Sec. 13201(e), adding Code Sec. 168(k)(10);

— Act Sec. 13201(f), amending Code Sec. 168(k)(2)(F);

— Act Sec. 13201(g), amending Code Sec. 168(k)(2)(A), and adding Code Sec. 168(k)(2)(A)(i)(IV) and (V), and 168(k)(2)(H);

— Act Sec. 13201(h), providing the effective dates.

¶415 Depreciation Caps on Luxury Cars

SUMMARY OF NEW LAW

The annual limits on depreciation deductions for "luxury cars" are nearly quadrupled for property placed in service after 2017. The IRS will need to issue a safe harbor in order to allow taxpayers to claim depreciation after the first year a vehicle is placed in service if the 100-percent bonus depreciation deduction is claimed.

BACKGROUND

Annual depreciation deductions that may be claimed for "passenger automobiles" are limited to specific dollar amounts (Code Sec. 280F(a)). These caps are often referred to as the "luxury car caps" even though they generally affect vehicles in the $18,000 purchase price range and above. The caps are adjusted each year for inflation (Code Sec. 280F(d)(7)); however, the caps in effect for the year the vehicle is placed in service continue to apply throughout its recovery period (Rev. Proc. 2003-75). The limits are reduced to reflect any personal (as opposed to business) use of the vehicle (Code Sec. 280F(a)(2)).

¶415

BACKGROUND

If bonus depreciation is claimed on a vehicle, the first-year depreciation cap that is otherwise applicable is increased by $8,000. The $8,000 bump-up is scheduled to decrease to $6,400 in 2018 and to $4,800 in 2019 (Code Sec. 168(k)(2)(F)(iii)).

The Code Sec. 179 expense deduction and the bonus depreciation allowance are treated as a depreciation deduction for the tax year in which a car is placed in service (Code Sec. 280F(a)(1)(B) and (d)(1)). Thus, the combined Code Sec. 179 deduction, bonus deduction, and regular first-year depreciation deduction is limited to the applicable first-year depreciation cap. Depreciation deductions in subsequent years of the vehicle's recovery period are limited to the applicable cap for the applicable year in the recovery period.

Separate caps apply to (a) passenger automobiles other than trucks (including SUVs) and vans, and to (b) trucks (including SUVs) and vans.

Deductions that are disallowed by the depreciation cap are deferred until after the end of the vehicle's recovery period, when the taxpayer may begin to deduct the unrecovered basis of the vehicle at a specified annual rate.

For Cars Placed in Service		Depreciation Allowable in—				
After	Before	Year 1	Year 2	Year 3	Year 4, etc.	Authority
12/31/10	1/01/12	$11,060 * $3,060	$4,900	$2,950	$1,775	Rev. Proc. 2011-21
12/31/11	1/01/13	$11,160 * $3,160	$5,100	$3,050	$1,875	Rev. Proc. 2012-23
12/31/12	1/01/14	$11,160 * $3,160	$5,100	$3,050	$1,875	Rev. Proc. 2013-21
12/31/13	1/01/15	$11,160 * $3,160	$5,100	$3,050	$1,875	Rev. Proc. 2014-21, modified by Rev. Proc. 2015-19
12/31/14	1/01/16	$11,160 * $3,160	$5,100	$3,050	$1,875	Rev. Proc. 2015-19, modified by Rev. Proc. 2016-23
12/31/15	1/01/17	$11,160 * $3,160	$5,100	$3,050	$1,875	Rev. Proc. 2016-23
12/31/16	1/01/18	$11,160 * $3,160	$5,100	$3,050	$1,875	Rev. Proc. 2017-29

* The higher first-year limit applies if the vehicle qualifies for, and the taxpayer does not elect out of, bonus depreciation.

Assuming that the 200-percent declining balance method and half-year convention apply, a car placed in service in 2017 on which bonus depreciation is claimed at the 50-percent rate is subject to the first-year cap if the cost of the vehicle exceeds $18,600 ($9,300 bonus + (9,300 remaining basis × 20 percent first-year table percentage) = $11,160).

Trucks (including SUVs treated as trucks) and vans are subject to their own set of depreciation caps that reflect the higher costs associated with such vehicles. However, the caps do not apply to trucks and vans that have a gross vehicle weight rating (GVWR) greater than 6,000 pounds, or to certain trucks and vans that, because of their design, are not likely to be used for personal purposes. Although the deprecia-

BACKGROUND

tion caps do not apply, the cost that can be taken into account for purposes of the Code Sec. 179 expense election cannot exceed $25,000 for an SUV with a GVWR in excess of 6,000 pounds, a pickup truck with a GVWR in excess of 6,000 pounds and a bed length of less than six feet, or a passenger van that seats fewer than 10 persons behind the driver's seat (Code Sec. 179(b)(5)).

For Trucks and Vans Placed in Service		Depreciation Allowable in—				
After	Before	Year 1	Year 2	Year 3	Year 4, etc.	Authority
12/31/10	1/01/12	$11,260 * $3,260	$5,200	$3,150	$1,875	Rev. Proc. 2011-21
12/31/11	1/01/13	$11,360 * $3,360	$5,300	$3,150	$1,875	Rev. Proc. 2012-23
12/31/12	1/01/14	$11,360 * $3,360	$5,400	$3,250	$1,975	Rev. Proc. 2013-21
12/31/13	1/01/15	$11,460 * $3,460	$5,500	$3,350	$1,975	Rev. Proc. 2014-21, modified by Rev. Proc. 2015-19
12/31/14	1/01/16	$11,460 * $3,460	$5,600	$3,350	$1,975	Rev. Proc. 2015-19 modified by Rev. Proc. 2016-23
12/31/15	1/01/17	$11,560 * $3,560	$5,700	$3,350	$2,075	Rev. Proc. 2016-23
12/31/16	1/01/18	$11,560 * $3,560	$5,700	$3,450	$2,075	Rev. Proc. 2017-29

* The higher first-year limit applies if the vehicle qualifies for bonus depreciation and no election out is made.

Assuming that the 200-percent declining balance method and half-year convention apply and that 50-percent bonus depreciation is claimed, a truck or van placed in service in 2017 is subject to the first-year cap if the cost of the vehicle exceeds $19,266 ($9,633 bonus + ($9,633 remaining basis × 20 percent) = $11,560).

NEW LAW EXPLAINED

Depreciation caps for passenger automobiles increased.—The annual depreciation caps are increased, effective for vehicles placed in service after December 31, 2017 (Code Sec. 280AF(a)(1)(A), as amended by the Tax Cuts and Jobs Act (P.L. 115-97)). The increased caps that apply to vehicles placed in service in 2018 are:

- Tax Year 1...............$10,000 ($18,000 if bonus depreciation claimed)

- Tax Year 2...............$16,000

- Tax Year 3...............$ 9,600

- Tax Years 4-6.........$ 5,760

Any unrecovered basis remaining at the end of the regular recovery period of a vehicle is recovered at the rate of $5,760 per tax year (Code Sec. 280F(a)(1)(B), as amended by the 2017 Tax Cuts Act).

¶415

NEW LAW EXPLAINED

> **Comment:** The recovery period of a vehicle is five years. However, the 5-year recovery period covers six tax years because, under the MACRS half-year or mid-quarter convention, a full year's depreciation is not allowed in the tax year that the vehicle is placed in service.

These caps are adjusted annually for inflation effective for vehicles placed in service after 2018 (Code Sec. 280F(d)(7), as amended by the 2017 Tax Cuts Act). The $8,000 bump-up to the first-year cap if bonus depreciation is claimed is not adjusted for inflation.

> **Comment:** For vehicles placed in service in 2018, the preceding caps will apply to all types of vehicles. However, the IRS figures inflation adjustments differently for (1) trucks (including SUVs treated as trucks) and vans and (2) regular passenger cars. Thus, beginning in 2019 when these figures are first adjusted for inflation, separate inflation adjusted caps will be provided for trucks (including SUVs) and vans, and for regular passenger cars.

$8,000 increase in first-year cap if bonus depreciation claimed. The first-year depreciation cap on a passenger vehicle that is subject to the annual depreciation limitations of Code Sec. 280F is increased by $8,000 if 100-percent bonus depreciation is claimed. This is the same increase that applies when bonus depreciation is claimed at a 50-percent rate. However, the scheduled decrease in the $8,000 bump-up to $6,400 in 2018 and $4,800 in 2019 is eliminated (Code Sec. 168(k)(2)(F)(iii), as amended by the 2017 Tax Cuts Act). Thus, the $8,000 increase will continue to apply. However, the scheduled decrease in the $8,000 bump-up to $6,400 in 2018 and $4,800 in 2019 will only apply in the rare situation where a vehicles was acquired before September 28, 2017, and placed in service after September 27, 2017.

No depreciation deductions after first recovery year if 100-percent bonus claimed unless IRS provides safe harbor. When Congress last enacted a 100-percent bonus rate in the Tax Relief, Unemployment Insurance Reauthorization, and Job Creation Act of 2010 (P.L. 111-312), for property acquired after September 8, 2010, and placed in service before January 1, 2012, an unforeseen consequence was that taxpayers claiming the 100-percent bonus deduction on a vehicle were limited to a deduction equal to the first-year cap amount and could not claim any further depreciation deductions until after the end of the vehicle's regular recovery period. This is because (1) the basis of qualified property is reduced by the full amount of depreciation, including the bonus and Code Sec. 179 allowance, without regard to the caps, and (2) depreciation deductions that are disallowed by the depreciation caps (including bonus depreciation) are deferred until after the end of the vehicle's recovery period (Code Sec. 280F(a)(1)(B)).

The IRS, however, provided a safe harbor method that allowed a taxpayer to compute depreciation as if a 50-percent bonus rate applied, so that depreciation deductions could be claimed during the entire recovery period of the vehicle (Rev. Proc. 2011-26, § 3.03(5)(c), 2011-16 I.R.B. 664).

> **Comment:** According to the General Explanation of Tax Legislation Enacted in the 111th Congress (JCS-2-11) (the "Blue Book" explanation), Congress intended that a 50-percent bonus depreciation rate apply to vehicles placed in service after September 8, 2010, that were eligible for the 100-percent rate and subject to the

NEW LAW EXPLAINED

Code Sec. 280F depreciation limitations. The report further states that a technical correction might be necessary to accomplish this result (see JCS-2-11, footnote 1597). The IRS safe harbor in effect accomplished this result and no technical correction was enacted.

The following example illustrates why the safe harbor will once again be needed.

Example: A car (5-year MACRS property) costing $35,000 that is subject to the luxury car limitations is placed in service in November 2017 by a calendar-year taxpayer. The taxpayer claims 100-percent bonus depreciation on its 5-year property, including the vehicle. The 100-percent rate applies to property acquired and placed in service after September 27, 2017 (see ¶410). However, because the first-year depreciation cap for the vehicle is $11,160, the bonus deduction that may be deducted is limited to $11,160. If the IRS does not reinstate the safe harbor method of accounting, the $23,840 excess ($35,000 - $11,160) may only be recovered at the rate of $1,875 per year beginning in 2023, which is the first year after the end of the vehicle's recovery period. No regular depreciation deductions are allowed after the first year of the vehicle's regular recovery period because the vehicle's basis for computing depreciation deductions is reduced to $0 by the entire amount of the bonus depreciation allowable without regard to the first-year depreciation cap. The table percentages when applied to a depreciable basis of $0 are equal to $0 in each year of the vehicle's regular 5-year recovery period. The same problem applies to vehicles placed in service in 2018 and later years in which 100-percent bonus depreciation applies.

Year	Regular Deduction	Luxury Car Cap	Allowable Depreciation
2017	$35,000	$11,160	$11,160
2018	$0	$5,100	$0
2019	$0	$3,050	$0
2020	$0	$1,875	$0
2021	$0	$1,875	$0
2022	$0	$1,875	$0
		TOTAL	$11,160

Comment: A taxpayer may elect to apply the 50-percent rate instead of the 100-percent rate for property placed in service during the taxpayer's first tax year ending after September 27, 2017 (Code Sec. 168(k)(8), as added by the 2017 Tax Cuts Act). See ¶410. Thus, for the 2017 tax year only, the taxpayer in the preceding example could avoid the adverse result by electing the 50-percent rate. The election, however, would apply to all 5-year property placed in service during the 2017 tax year and not just vehicles with a 5-year recovery period. As previously mentioned, however, the IRS is likely to issue a safe harbor to resolve this unintended situation.

$25,000 limit on certain vehicles adjusted for inflation. The $25,000 maximum Code Sec. 179 deduction that may be claimed on specified vehicles that are exempt from

¶415

NEW LAW EXPLAINED

the luxury car caps will be adjusted for inflation in tax years beginning after 2018 (Code Sec. 179(b)(6), as amended by the 2017 Tax Cuts Act).

> **Comment:** The $25,000 limit applies to a sport utility vehicle, truck with an interior cargo bed length less than six feet, and a van that seats fewer than 10 persons behind the driver's seat if the vehicle is exempt from the annual depreciation caps because it has a gross vehicle weight rating in excess of 6,000 pounds, or if it is otherwise exempt, and is rated at not more than 14,000 pounds gross vehicle weight (Code Sec. 179(b)(5)).

The amount of the inflation adjustment is based on the cost-of-living adjustment determined under Code Sec. 1(f)(3) for the calendar year in which the tax year begins, by substituting calendar year 2017 for calendar year 2016. When adjusting the $25,000 limit for inflation, the resulting amount must be rounded to the nearest multiple of $100.

▶ **Effective date.** The provisions apply to property placed in service after December 31, 2017, in tax years ending after such date (Act Sec. 13202(c) of the Tax Cuts and Jobs Act (P.L. 115-97)).

Law source: Law at ¶5445. Committee Report at ¶10,350.

— Act Sec. 13202(a) of the Tax Cuts and Jobs Act (P.L. 115-97), amending Code Sec. 280F(a)(1) and (d)(7);

— Act Sec. 13202(c), providing the effective date.

¶420 Computers as Listed Property

SUMMARY OF NEW LAW

Computers and related peripheral equipment are no longer "listed property" subject to strict substantiation and depreciation requirements, effective for property placed in service after December 31, 2017.

BACKGROUND

To deduct an expense for "listed property," a high level of substantiation is required. No deduction (or credit) is allowed for listed property unless the taxpayer can substantiate each expenditure or use by adequate records or sufficient evidence corroborating the taxpayer's own statement, and the *Cohan* rule (2 USTC ¶489) cannot be applied (Code Sec. 274(d)(4); Temporary Reg. §1.274-5T(a)(4) and (c)). Listed property is defined as:

• passenger automobiles and other property used as a means of transportation;

• entertainment, recreational, and amusement property;

• computers and peripheral equipment; and

• any other property specified by regulation (Code Sec. 280F(d)(4)(A)).

BACKGROUND

The elements of each expenditure or use for listed property that must be substantiated are—

(1) the amount of each separate expenditure;

(2) the amount of each business/investment use based on the appropriate measure (i.e., mileage for vehicles, time for other listed property) and the total use of the listed property for the tax year;

(3) the date of the expenditure or use; and

(4) the business purpose of the expenditure or use (Code Sec. 274(d); Temporary Reg. § 1.274-5T(b)(6)).

Fringe benefits. Generally, an employee can exclude from gross income a working condition fringe benefit, which is any property or service provided to an employee, to the extent the employee would have been allowed a business expense deduction under Code Sec. 162 or a depreciation deduction under Code Sec. 167 had the employee paid for the property or services without reimbursement (Code Sec. 132(a) and (d)). However, an employee cannot exclude the value of the use of listed property as a working condition fringe unless the employee substantiates the exclusion amount as required by Code Sec. 274(d) (Reg. § 1.132-5(c)(1); Temporary Reg. § 1.274-5T(e)(1)(i)).

Depreciation of listed property. If listed property, such as a computer, is not used more than 50 percent for business in the tax year that it is placed in service, depreciation must be computed using the straight-line method under the MACRS alternative depreciation system (ADS), and no first-year bonus depreciation deduction or Code Sec. 179 expense allowance may be claimed (Code Sec. 280F(b)(1), (b)(3) and (d)(1); Reg. § 1.280F-6(d)). If the listed property satisfies the more-than-50-percent business use requirement in the tax year that it is placed in service but fails to meet that test in a later tax year that occurs during any year of the property's ADS recovery period, previous depreciation deductions (including any bonus depreciation deduction and any amount expensed under Code Sec. 179) claimed in tax years before business use drops to 50 percent or less are subject to recapture in such later year (Code Secs. 280F(b)(2) and 168(k)(2)(D)(ii); Temporary Reg. § 1.280F-3T(c) and (d)).

> **Comment:** Computers and peripheral equipment are 5-year MACRS property (Code Sec. 168(e)(3)(B)(iv) and (i)(2)). A 5-year recovery period also applies under the ADS system (Code Sec. 168(g)(3)(C)).

Under a generally applicable rule, any amount expensed under Code Sec. 179 is recaptured if business use of the expensed asset falls to 50 percent or less during any year of the expensed asset's recovery period (Code Sec. 179(d)(10); Reg. § 1.179-1(e)). If a property is not a listed property and business use falls to 50 percent or less, the Code Sec. 179 deduction is subject to recapture but bonus depreciation and regular depreciation deductions are not recaptured.

For purposes of determining the depreciation deduction allowed to an employee (including first-year bonus depreciation allowance and Code Sec. 179 expense allowance), or the amount of any deduction allowable to the employee for rentals or other payments under a lease of listed property, employee use of listed property can be

BACKGROUND

treated as use in a trade or business only if the use is for the convenience of the employer and required as a condition of employment (Code Sec. 280F(d)(1) and (3)).

> **Comment:** An employee may not depreciate or expense under Code Sec. 179 the cost of a computer or other listed property unless its use is for the convenience of the employer and required as a condition of employment. If these two requirements are not satisfied, none of the use of the computer is considered business use (Rev. Rul. 86-129, 1986-2 CB 48).

NEW LAW EXPLAINED

Computers and peripheral equipment removed from listed property treatment.—Effective for property placed in service after December 31, 2017, computers and peripheral equipment are removed from the definition of listed property (Code Sec. 280F(d)(4)(A), as amended by the Tax Cuts and Jobs Act (P.L. 115-97)). As a result, the cost of computers and peripheral equipment can be deducted or depreciated like other business property and are no longer subject to the strict substantiation requirements of Code Sec. 274(d).

> **Comment:** The removal of computers from listed property status will allow more employees to depreciate or expense the cost of computers because the convenience of the employer and condition of employment requirements of Code Sec. 280F(d)(3) will no longer apply.

A conforming amendment strikes a provision which excludes a computer or peripheral equipment from the definition of listed property if it is used exclusively at a regular business establishment and owned or leased by the person operating the establishment (Code Sec. 280F(d)(4)(B), stricken by the 2017 Tax Cuts Act).

Impact on depreciation. The declassification of computers as listed property means that a computer used 50 percent or less for business purposes in the year that it is placed in service is no longer required to be depreciated under the MACRS alternative depreciation system (ADS) using the straight-line method and a five-year ADS recovery period. Instead, the five-year recovery period and the 200-percent declining balance method under the MACRS general depreciation system (GDS) will apply. Furthermore, if the computer is placed in service after 2017, bonus depreciation may be claimed even if business use is 50 percent or less, because the rule under Code Sec. 168(k)(2)(D)(ii) that bonus depreciation may not be claimed on a listed property used 50 percent or less for business in the year it is placed in service will no longer apply.

Removal of computers from listed property status also means that if business use drops to 50 percent or less in a tax year after the computer is placed in service, the listed property recapture rules will not apply. Consequently, regular depreciation deductions (including any bonus deduction) will not be recaptured upon such a business use decline. However, as explained below, Code Sec. 179 recapture is still required.

Impact on section 179 expensing. Under current law, property may not be expensed under Code Sec. 179 if it is not used more than 50 percent for trade or business purposes in the tax year that it is placed in service (Code Sec. 179(d)(10); Reg.

NEW LAW EXPLAINED

§ 1.179-1(d)(1)). This rule applies to listed and nonlisted property (Temporary Reg. § 1.280F-3T(c)(1)). Thus, although computers are no longer considered listed property if placed in service after December 31, 2017, the failure to use the computer more than 50 percent in a trade or business in the tax year that the computer is placed in service will continue to prevent a taxpayer from expensing the portion of the cost of the computer that is not attributable to business use.

The amount expensed under Code Sec. 179 is recaptured if business use falls to 50 percent or less during any year of the expensed asset's recovery period (Code Sec. 179(d)(10); Reg. § 1.179-1(e)). However, if the Code Sec. 179 deduction is claimed on a listed property, the amount recaptured is determined by applying the listed property recapture rules when business use drops to 50 percent or less (Code Sec. 280F(d)(1)). That is, the listed property recapture rules take precedence in determining the recapture amount. As a result of the removal of computers from listed property classification, the Code Sec. 179 recapture rules will now be used to determined the amount of Code Sec. 179 allowance that is recaptured. The recapture amount included in ordinary income under these recapture rules is the difference between the Code Sec. 179 expense allowance claimed and the depreciation (including bonus depreciation, if applicable) that would have been allowed on the amount expensed for prior tax years and the tax year of recapture (Reg. § 1.179-1(e)(1)).

> **Caution:** Since the provision declassifying computers as listed property applies to property placed in service after December 31, 2017, the listed property recapture rules continue to apply to computers placed in service before January 1, 2018.

Impact on fringe benefits. The declassification of computers as listed property means that employees no longer must meet the substantiation requirements under Code Sec. 274(d) in order to exclude the value of the availability of the computer from income as a working condition fringe benefit (Temporary Reg. § 1.274-5T(e)). The new law does not affect the IRS's authority to determine the appropriate characterization of computers as a working condition fringe benefit under Code Sec. 132(d), or that the personal use of computers that are provided primarily for business purposes may constitute a *de minimis* fringe benefit under Code Sec. 132(e), the value of which is so small as to make accounting for it administratively impracticable.

▶ **Effective date.** The provisions apply to property placed in service after December 31, 2017, in tax years ending after such date (Act Sec. 13202(c) of the Tax Cuts and Jobs Act (P.L. 115-97).

Law source: Law at ¶5445. Committee Report at ¶10,350.

— Act Sec. 13202(b) of the Tax Cuts and Jobs Act (P.L. 115-97), amending Code Sec. 280F(d)(4);

— Act Sec. 13202(c), providing the effective date.

¶420

¶425 Recovery Periods for MACRS Real Property

SUMMARY OF NEW LAW

Assuming a technical correction is enacted, qualified improvement property is assigned a 15-year recovery period as intended by Congress. The property classes for 15-year leasehold improvement property, retail improvement property, and restaurant property are eliminated. The MACRS alternative depreciation system (ADS) must be used by an electing real property trade or business to depreciate residential rental property, nonresidential real property, and qualified improvement property.

BACKGROUND

"Qualified improvement property" is a category of property which is eligible for the 50-percent MACRS bonus depreciation deduction (Code Sec. 168(k)(2)(A)(i)(IV)). In general, qualified improvement property is defined as an improvement to the interior of a nonresidential building but does not include improvements related to the enlargement of the building or to the internal structural framework of the building. In addition, improvements related to elevators and escalators are not qualified improvement property (Code Sec. 168(k)(3)).

The depreciation period for qualified improvement property is either 15 years or 39 years. A 15-year recovery period applies if the qualified improvement property meets the definitions provided for 15-year qualified leasehold improvement property, 15-year qualified restaurant property, or 15-year qualified retail improvement property (Code Sec. 168(e)(3)(E)(iv), (v), and (ix)). In all other cases, the default recovery period for qualified improvement property is 39 years under the rule that treats an addition or improvement to nonresidential real property (whether or not depreciated under MACRS) as MACRS 39-year nonresidential real property (Code Sec. 168(i)(6)).

15-year qualified leasehold improvement property and 15-year qualified retail improvement property are defined similarly to qualified improvement property, except that 15-year qualified leasehold improvements must be made to the interior of the building pursuant to a lease more than three years after the leased building was first placed in service (Code Sec. 168(e)(6)), and 15-year retail improvements must be made to the interior of a building open to the general public and used in the retail trade or business of selling tangible personal property to the general public more than three years after the building was first placed in service (Code Sec. 168(e)(8)). 15-year restaurant property is broadly defined to mean any improvement to a restaurant building (interior or exterior) regardless of when the building was placed in service. Moreover, 15-year restaurant property also includes a restaurant building (Code Sec. 168(e)(7)).

Certain categories of property, such as property used predominantly outside of the United States, must be depreciated using the MACRS alternative depreciation system (ADS) (Code Sec. 168(g)). Under ADS, property is depreciated using the straight-line method over recovery periods generally equal to the class life of the property. Usually, the ADS recovery period is longer than the regular recovery period that

BACKGROUND

would otherwise apply under MACRS. For example, the ADS recovery period for 39-year nonresidential real property and 27.5-year residential rental property is 40 years (Code Sec. 168(g)(2)(C)).

NEW LAW EXPLAINED

Depreciation of real property.—The Tax Cuts and Jobs Act (P.L. 115-97) makes the following changes related to MACRS recovery periods for real property, effective for property placed in service after December 31, 2017:

- qualified improvement property is assigned a 15-year recovery period (however, see "*Caution*," below);

- the property classes for 15-year leasehold improvement property, retail improvement property, and restaurant improvements and buildings are eliminated;

- the MACRS alternative depreciation system (ADS) must be used by an electing real property trade or business to depreciate residential rental property, nonresidential real property, and qualified improvement property (effective for tax years beginning after December 31, 2017); and

- the ADS recovery period for residential rental property is reduced from 40 years to 30 years

   Caution: The explanations in this section assume that qualified improvement property placed in service after December 31, 2017, will have a 15-year recovery period as intended by Congress.

   The original Senate bill would have provided a 10-year recovery period for qualified improvement property. The House bill contained no provision. The final bill, according to the Conference Report on H.R. 1, Tax Cuts and Jobs Act (H. Rept. 115-466) sets a 15-year recovery period for qualified improvement property effective for property placed in service after December 31, 2017. However, the text of the final bill inadvertently omits the provision which would have given a 15-year recovery period for qualified improvement property. A technical correction will be needed to create a 15-year recovery period for qualified improvement property. In the absence of such a correction, all such property will be treated as 39-year nonresidential real property, effective for property placed in service after December 31, 2017.

   An unintended consequence of failing to provide a 15-year recovery period for qualified improvement property placed in service after December 31, 2017, is that such property will not qualify for bonus depreciation. As explained at ¶410, qualified improvement property was removed as a specific category of bonus depreciation property, effective for property placed in service after December 31, 2017 (Code Sec. 168(k)(3), as stricken by the 2017 Tax Cuts Act) on the assumption that all qualified improvement property would have a 15-year recovery period and, therefore, qualify for bonus depreciation under the general rule that allows MACRS property with a recovery period of 20 years or less to qualify for bonus depreciation.

¶425

NEW LAW EXPLAINED

Qualified improvement property assigned 15-year recovery period. Assuming a technical correction is made, qualified improvement property is assigned a recovery period of 15 years, effective for property placed in service after December 31, 2017. Qualified improvement property is depreciated using the straight-line method and half-year convention or, if applicable, the mid-quarter convention (Code Sec. 168(b)(3)(G), as added by the 2017 Tax Cuts Act)). The alternative depreciation system (ADS) recovery period for qualified improvement property is 20 years assuming a technical correction is made (Code Sec. 168(g)(3)(B), as amended by the 2017 Tax Cuts Act).

> **Comment:** The amended table in Code Sec. 168(g)(3)(B), makes an erroneous reference to subparagraph (D)(iv) of Code Sec. 168(e)(3) in establishing the intended 20-year ADS period for qualified improvement property. In the original Senate Bill, subparagraph (D)(iv) of Code Sec. 168(e)(3) added qualified improvement property to the list of property with a 10-year recovery period. Subparagraph (D)(iv) was not included in the text of the final bill because the final bill intended to change the recovery period of qualified improvement property to 15-years instead. See *"Caution,"* above.

The definition of qualified improvement property for purposes of the new 15-year recovery period is the same as the definition that has applied for bonus depreciation purposes. Specifically, qualified improvement property is defined as any improvement to an interior portion of a building which is nonresidential real property if the improvement is placed in service after the date the building was first placed in service by any taxpayer (Code Sec. 168(e)(6)(A), as added by the 2017 Tax Cuts Act). However, qualified improvement property does not include expenditures attributable to:

- the enlargement of a building;
- any elevator or escalator; or
- the internal structural framework of a building (Code Sec. 168(e)(6)(B), as added by the 2017 Tax Cuts Act).

> **Comment:** Qualified improvement property has been a category of property eligible for bonus depreciation since the enactment of the Protecting Americans from Tax Hikes Act of 2015 (December 18, 2015) (P.L. 114-113) (PATH Act), effective for property placed in service after December 31, 2015. However, the depreciation period for property which met the definition of qualified improvement property for bonus depreciation purposes was 15 years if the improvement also met the definition of a qualified leasehold improvement, a qualified retail improvement, or a qualified restaurant improvement. If the 15-year recovery period did not apply, then the qualified improvement property was depreciated over 39 years as MACRS nonresidential real property. Under the new law, all qualified improvement property is assigned a 15-year recovery period. The 15-year recovery periods previously provided for a qualified leasehold, retail, and restaurant improvements are repealed.

> **Comment:** The definition of qualified improvement property for bonus depreciation purposes was formerly located in Code Sec. 168(k)(3), relating to bonus

NEW LAW EXPLAINED

depreciation. The new law moves the definition of qualified improvement property to Code Sec. 168(e)(6), and assigns a 15-year recovery period (assuming a correction is made; see "*Caution*," above). Qualified improvement property, however, still remains eligible for bonus depreciation even though it has been removed as a separate category of bonus depreciation property. Now that all qualified improvement property is assigned a 15-year recovery period, it will qualify for bonus depreciation under the generally applicable rule requiring that bonus depreciation property must have a recovery period of 20 years of less. Previously, some qualified improvement property had a 39-year recovery period and could not have qualified for bonus depreciation unless qualified improvement property was treated as a separate category of bonus depreciation property without regard to its recovery period. This special treatment is no longer necessary.

Section 179 deduction on qualified improvement property. Effective for tax years beginning after 2017, the definition of qualified real property eligible for expensing under Code Sec. 179 is changed to include qualified improvement property (Code Sec. 179(f), as amended by the 2017 Tax Cuts Act). See ¶405.

15-year qualified leasehold, retail, and restaurant improvement property classes eliminated. The property classifications for 15-year qualified leasehold improvement property, qualified retail improvement property, and qualified restaurant property are removed (Code Sec. 168(e)(3)(E), as amended by the 2017 Tax Cuts Act; Code Sec. 168(e)(6), (7), and (8), stricken by the 2017 Tax Cuts Act). See "*Background*" section, above, for the definition of these categories of property. All improvements which previously qualified for a 15-year recovery period as qualified leasehold improvement property or qualified retail improvement property fall within the definition of qualified improvement property and have a 15-year recovery period, effective for property placed in service after December 31, 2017 (assuming a correction is made; see "*Caution*," above). Improvements to a restaurant will only qualify for the 15-year recovery period for qualified improvement property if the improvement to is to the interior of the restaurant and does not relate to an enlargement or the internal structural framework of the building, or to an elevator or escalator. External improvements to a restaurant and restaurant buildings which currently qualify as 15-year qualified restaurant property do not meet the definitional requirements of qualified improvement property and are not eligible for the 15-year recovery period. Such property will be depreciated over 39 years, effective for property placed in service after December 31, 2017.

> **Comment:** If any property meets the definition of 15-year qualified leasehold improvement property or 15-year qualified retail property, it will necessarily meet the definitional requirements of qualified improvement property and be eligible for the new 15-year recovery period that applies to such property when a technical correction is enacted. Consequently, the elimination of these two property classifications has no negative impact. Not all 15-year restaurant property, however, will meet the definitional requirements of 15-year qualified improvement property. Most significantly, 15-year qualified restaurant property is defined to include restaurant buildings. Qualified improvement property only

¶425

NEW LAW EXPLAINED

includes internal improvements to a building. This means that a restaurant building will not qualify for a 15-year recovery period as qualified improvement property. Instead, effective for restaurants placed in service after December 31, 2017, restaurant buildings will once again be treated as nonresidential real property and the 39-year recovery period for nonresidential real property applies. 15-year restaurant property is also defined to include external as well as internal improvements. Since external improvements to a building are excluded from the definition of qualified improvement property, external improvements to a restaurant will also be treated as 39-year nonresidential real property, effective for improvements placed in service after December 31, 2017.

Real property trade or business electing out of interest deduction limits must use ADS for residential rental property, nonresidential real property, and qualified improvement property. An electing real property trade or business must use the MACRS alternative depreciation system (ADS) to depreciate any nonresidential real property, residential rental property, or qualified improvement property it holds (Code Sec. 168(g)(1), as amended by the 2017 Tax Cuts Act; Code Sec. 168(g)(8), as added by the 2017 Tax Cuts Act). The provision is effective for tax years beginning after December 31, 2017 (Act Sec. 13204(b)(2) of the 2017 Tax Cuts Act).

An electing real property trade or business is a real property trade or business that elects out of new rules which disallow deduction for net interest expense in excess of 30 percent of a business' adjusted taxable income (Code Sec. 163(j)(7)(B), as added by the 2017 Tax Cuts Act). "Real property trade or business" means any real property development, redevelopment, construction, reconstruction, acquisition, conversion, rental, operation, management, leasing, or brokerage trade or business (Code Sec. 469(c)(7)(C)). See ¶510 for a discussion of the net interest deduction limitation and the election out for a real property trade or business.

> **Comment:** The ADS period for nonresidential real property is 40 years. The ADS period for residential rental property is reduced from 40 years to 30 years, effective for property placed in service after December 31, 2017 (Code Sec. 168(g)(2)(C), as amended by the 2017 Tax Cuts Act). The ADS period for qualified improvement property is intended to be 20 years, although a technical correction is necessary to create the intended 15-year regular depreciation period for such property. See "*Caution*," above.

Regular and ADS recovery periods for MACRS residential rental and MACRS nonresidential real property. The MACRS alternative depreciation system (ADS) recovery period for residential rental property is reduced from 40 years to 30 years (Code Sec. 168(g)(2)(C), as amended by the 2017 Tax Cuts Act).

> **Comment:** A provision in the original Senate bill would have reduced the recovery period for MACRS residential rental property from 27.5 years to 25 years, and would have reduced the recovery period for nonresidential real property from 39 years to 25 years, effective for property placed in service after December 31, 2017. This provision was dropped from the final bill. Consequently, the recovery period remains 27.5 years for residential rental property and 39 years for nonresidential real property. The ADS recovery period for nonresidential real property remains 40 years.

NEW LAW EXPLAINED

> **Practical Analysis:** Charles R. Goulding, President, Energy Tax Savers and R&D Tax Savers in Syosset, New York, comments that while the elimination of the Qualified Leasehold, Restaurant and Retail Improvement categories are eliminated, nearly all of the items included in these eliminated categories will be available in the Qualified Improvement Property (QIP) category. During the five years of 100 percent bonus items that Qualify as QIP will be fully expensed and thereafter the portions not expensed will require 15 year straight line depreciation.

▶ **Effective date.** The amendments in this section apply to property placed in service after December 31, 2017 (Act Sec. 13204(b)(1) of the Tax Cuts and Jobs Act (P.L. 115-97). The amendment requiring an electing real property trade or business to use ADS to depreciate its real property is effective for tax years beginning after December 31, 2017 (Act Sec. 13204(b)(2) of the 2017 Tax Cuts Act).

Law source: Law at ¶5315. Committee Report at ¶10,370.

— Act Sec. 13204(a)(1)(A), of the Tax Cuts and Jobs Act (P.L. 115-97) amending Code Sec. 168(e)(3)(E);

— Act Sec. 13204(a)(1)(B), striking Code Secs. 168(e)(6), (7), and (8);

— Act Sec. 13204(a)(2), adding Code Sec. 168(b)(3)(G);

— Act Sec. 13204(a)(3)(A), adding Code Secs. 168(g)(1)(F) and Code Sec. 168(g)(8);

— Act Sec. 13204(a)(3)(B), amending Code Sec. 168(g)(3)(B);

— Act Sec. 13204(a)(3)(C), amending Code Sec. 168(g)(2)(C);

— Act Sec. 13204(a)(4), adding Code Sec. 168(e)(6) and striking Code Sec. 168(k)(2)(A)(iv) and (k)(3);

— Act Sec. 13204(b), providing the effective date.

¶435 Depreciation of Farm Property

SUMMARY OF NEW LAW

New farming machinery and equipment placed in service after December 31, 2017, are classified as 5-year MACRS property rather than 7-year MACRS property. The 7-year property classification, however, continues to apply to grain bins, cotton ginning assets, and fences.

BACKGROUND

Machinery and equipment, grain bins, and fences used in agriculture are classified as 7-year MACRS property (Rev. Proc. 87-56, Asset Class 01.1). Agriculture is defined as the production of crops or plants, vines, and trees; livestock; the operation of farm dairies, nurseries, greenhouses, sod farms, mushroom cellars, cranberry bogs, apiaries (i.e., bee production activities), and fur farms; and the performance of agricul-

BACKGROUND

tural, animal husbandry, and horticultural services (Asset Class 01.1). A 10-year alternative depreciation system (ADS) recovery period applies.

Under an expired provision, a five-year recovery period applies to any machinery or equipment (other than a grain bin, cotton ginning asset, fence, or other land improvement) if the original use began with the taxpayer after 2008, and the property was used by the taxpayer in a farming business and placed in service in 2009 (Code Sec. 168(e)(3)(B)(vii), as added by the Emergency Economic Stabilization Act of 2008 (P.L. 110-343)). Such property has a recovery period of 10 years under ADS (Code Sec. 168(g)(3)(B), as amended by P.L. 110-343). This provision was not extended.

3-, 5-, 7-, and 10-year MACRS property placed in service after 1988 and used in a farming business may not be depreciated using the 200-percent declining balance (DB) method which normally applies to these property classes (the 150-percent DB method has always applied to 15- and 20-year property whether or not used in farming). Instead, farming property in these classes is depreciated using the 150-percent DB method (unless the ADS or straight-line method is required or elected) (Code Sec. 168(b)(2)(B)).

NEW LAW EXPLAINED

Farming machinery depreciated over five years; 200-percent DB method allowed; ADS required if farming business elects out of interest deduction limits.—Modifications to the treatment of certain farm equipment include:

- a decrease in the 7-year recovery period for new farming machinery and equipment to 5-year recovery period, and

- elimination of the rule requiring use of the 150-percent declining balance method on property used in a farming business.

Five-year recovery period for new farming machinery and equipment. Effective for property placed in service after December 31, 2017, a 5-year recovery period applies to any machinery or equipment (other than any grain bin, cotton ginning asset, fence, or other land improvement) used in a farming business if the original use commences with the taxpayer after December 31, 2017 (Code Sec. 168(e)(3)(B)(vii), as amended by the Tax Cuts and Jobs Act (P.L. 115-97). Generally, a 7-year recovery period previously applied to this property (Rev. Proc. 87-56, Asset Class 01.1).

A 10-year alternative depreciation system (ADS) recovery period applies to farming machinery and equipment with a 5- or 7-year recovery period. Code Sec. 168(g)(3)(B), referencing Code Sec. 168(e)(3)(B)(vii) and Asset Class 01.1 of Rev. Proc. 87-56, both provide a 10-year ADS period.

> **Caution:** The provision only applies to new machinery and equipment used in a farming business. A 7-year recovery period continues to apply to used farming machinery and equipment.

200-percent declining method allowed for farming property. The provision that requires MACRS 3-, 5-, 7-, and 10-year property placed in service after 1988 and used in a farming business to be depreciated using the 150-percent declining balance (DB)

NEW LAW EXPLAINED

method instead of the normally applicable 200-percent DB method is repealed, effective for property placed in service after December 31, 2017 (Code Sec. 168(b)(2)(B), as stricken by the 2017 Tax Cuts Act).

> **Comment:** A taxpayer may now elect to depreciate any class of 3-, 5-, 7-, or 10-year farming property using the 150-percent declining balance method (Code Sec. 168(b)(2)(C), as redesignated by the 2017 Tax Cuts Act). The election was not previously available because such property had to be depreciated using the 150-percent declining balance method unless an election to use the MACRS straight-line method or the MACRS alternative depreciation system (ADS) was made.

Farming business defined. As defined in Code Sec. 263A(e)(4) and Reg. § 1.263A-4(a)(4), the term "farming business" means a trade or business involving the cultivation of land or the raising or harvesting of any agricultural or horticultural commodity (e.g., the trade or business of operating a nursery or sod farm; the raising or harvesting of trees bearing fruit, nuts, or other crops; the raising of ornamental trees (other than evergreen trees that are more than six years old at the time they are severed from their roots); and the raising, shearing, feeding, caring for, training, and management of animals). A farming business includes processing activities that are normally incident to the growing, raising, or harvesting of agricultural or horticultural products. A farming business does not include contract harvesting of an agricultural or horticultural commodity grown or raised by another taxpayer, or merely buying and reselling plants or animals grown or raised by another taxpayer.

Farming business electing out of interest deduction limitation must use ADS for property with recovery period of 10 years or greater. Any property with a recovery period of 10 years or greater which is held by an "electing farming business" that makes an election out of the new rules which disallow the deduction for net interest expense in excess of 30 percent of the business' adjusted taxable income must be depreciated using the MACRS alternative depreciation system (ADS) (Code Sec. 168(g)(1)(G), as added by the 2017 Tax Cuts Act). See ¶510 for discussion of 30-percent limitation on business interest expense deductions.

> **Comment:** Under ADS, the straight-line method applies using a recovery period that is usually longer than the regular recovery period. The ADS recovery period is the asset's class life, usually as shown in Rev. Proc. 87-56.

An electing farming business is a farming business (as defined above) that elects out of the interest deduction limitation, or any trade or business of a "specified agricultural or horticultural cooperative" (as defined in new Code Sec. 199A(g)(2)) with respect to which the cooperative makes an election out of the interest deduction limitation (Code Sec. 167(j)(7)(C), as added by the 2017 Tax Cuts Act).

A specified agricultural or horticultural cooperative is an organization to which part I of subchapter T applies, and which is engaged in—

(1) the manufacturing, production, growth, or extraction in whole or significant part of any agricultural or horticultural product;

(2) the marketing of agricultural or horticultural products which its patrons have so manufactured, produced, grown, or extracted; or

¶435

NEW LAW EXPLAINED

(3) the provision of supplies, equipment, or services to farmers or to organizations in items (1) or (2) (Code Sec. 199A(g), as added by the 2017 Tax Cuts Act).

▶ **Effective date.** The amendments reducing the recovery period of farm machinery and allowing use of the 200-percent declining method apply to property placed in service after December 31, 2017, in tax years ending after such date (Act Sec. 13203(c) of the Tax Cuts and Jobs Act (P.L. 115-97)). The amendment requiring an electing farming business to use ADS to depreciate property with a recovery period of 10 years or greater applies to tax years beginning after December 31, 2017 (Act Sec. 13205(b) of the 2017 Tax Cuts Act).

Law source: Law at ¶5315. Committee Report at ¶10,360 and ¶10,380.

— Act Sec. 13203(a) of the Tax Cuts and Jobs Act (P.L. 115-97), amending Code Sec. 168(e)(3)(B);

— Act Sec. 13203(b), striking Code Sec. 168(b)(2)(B), and redesignating Code Sec. 168(b)(2)(C) and (D) as Code Sec. 168(b)(2)(B) and (C);

— Act Sec. 13205(a), adding Code Sec. 168(g)(1)(G);

— Act Secs. 13203(c) and 13205(b), providing the effective dates.

¶440 Expensing of Certain Costs of Replanting Citrus Plants

SUMMARY OF NEW LAW

The special rule for deducting the costs incurred in connection with replanting citrus plants lost by reason of casualty is modified. The modified rule allows for a deduction in certain instances when the cost is incurred by a person other than the taxpayer.

BACKGROUND

A taxpayer that is subject to the uniform capitalization (UNICAP) rules must capitalize all direct costs and an allocable portion of most indirect costs that are associated with certain production or resale activities. The UNICAP rules generally apply to: (1) real or tangible personal property produced by the taxpayer for use in a trade or business or in an activity engaged in for profit; (2) real or tangible personal property produced by the taxpayer for sale to customers; and (3) real or personal property, both tangible and intangible, acquired by the taxpayer for resale (Code Sec. 263A).

The UNICAP rules apply to plants and animals produced by certain farming businesses (corporations, partnerships, and tax shelters) that are required to use the accrual method of accounting. For other farming businesses, the UNICAP rules apply only to plants produced in the farming business that have a preproductive period of more than two years (Code Sec. 263A(d)(1)).

BACKGROUND

The UNICAP rules do not apply to costs that are attributable to the replanting, cultivation, maintenance, and development of any plants (of the same type of crop) bearing an edible crop for human consumption (normally eaten or drunk by humans) that were lost or damaged while in the hands of the taxpayer as the result of freezing temperatures, disease, drought, pests, or casualty. Replanting or maintenance costs may be incurred on domestic property other than the damaged property if the acreage does not exceed that of the damaged property (Code Sec. 263A(d)(2)(A)).

This casualty exception can also apply to amounts paid by a person other than the taxpayer holding the crops if:

- the taxpayer has an equity interest of more than 50 percent in the damaged plants at all times during the tax year in which the replanting costs were paid or incurred; and

- the other person holds any part of the remaining equity interest and materially participates in the planting, maintenance, cultivation, or development of the damaged plants during the tax year in which these amounts were paid or incurred (Code Sec. 263A(d)(2)(B)).

Whether an individual materially participates is determined in a manner similar to that for determining whether there is material participation for net earnings from self-employment income purposes (Code Sec. 263A(d)(2)(B); see Code Secs. 2032A(e)(6) and 1402(a)(1)).

NEW LAW EXPLAINED

Certain costs of replanting citrus plants lost to casualty deductible by a person other than the taxpayer.—A temporary exception to the UNICAP rules applies to certain costs incurred by persons other than the taxpayer in connection with replanting citrus plants following loss or damage while in the taxpayer's hands due to freezing temperatures, disease, drought, pests, or casualty (Code Sec. 263A(d)(2)(C)(i), as added by the Tax Cuts and Jobs Act (P.L. 115-97)). A person other than the taxpayer may deduct the replanting costs if:

- the taxpayer has an equity interest of at least 50 percent in the replanted citrus plants at all times during tax year that the replanting costs were paid or incurred, and the person who incurred the costs holds any part of the remaining equity interest; or

- the person who incurred the replanting costs acquires all of the taxpayer's equity interest in the land on which the lost or damaged citrus plants were located at the time of the loss or damage, and the replanting is on that land.

This rule does not apply to costs paid or incurred after December 22, 2027 (i.e., 10 years after the date of enactment) (Code Sec. 263A(d)(2)(C)(ii), as added by the 2017 Tax Cuts Act).

¶440

NEW LAW EXPLAINED

Practical Analysis: Charles R. Goulding, President, Energy Tax Savers and R&D Tax Savers in Syosset, New York, comments that under current tax law, U.S. citrus growers are permitted to fully expense the cost of replacing Citrus trees but only if they bear 100 percent of the cost. This Act Section enables growers to still qualify for expensing if they bring in outside investors as long as they retain a majority interest. Citrus growers in California and in particular Florida post Hurricane Irma have been suffering from extensive citrus crop loss. This Act Section enjoyed the full support from all 29 members of the Florida Congressional delegation including all Senators and Congressman. U.S. citrus growers also face increasing competition from South American and South African growers that are stronger and are positioned to fill in any U.S. void.

▶ **Effective date.** The amendment made by this section applies to costs paid or incurred after December 22, 2017, the date of enactment (Act Sec. 13207(b) of the Tax Cuts and Jobs Act (P.L. 115-97)).

Law source: Law at ¶5425. Committee Report at ¶10,400.

— Act Sec. 13207(a) of the Tax Cuts and Jobs Act (P.L. 115-97), adding new Code Sec. 263A(d)(2)(C);

— Act Sec. 13207(b), providing the effective date.

Business Income, Deductions and Credits

5

INCOME EXCLUSIONS, ETC.

¶505 Like-Kind Exchanges of Real Property

SUMMARY OF NEW LAW

Like-kind exchanges are allowed only for real property after 2017. Thus, as under current law, no gain or loss is recognized on the exchange of real property held for productive use in a trade or business or for investment if that real property is exchanged solely for real property of like kind that will be held either for productive use in a trade or business or for investment. Like-kind exchanges are not allowed for depreciable tangible personal property, and intangible and nondepreciable personal property after 2017.

BACKGROUND

Gain or loss on the disposition of property can be deferred if the taxpayer receives like-kind property in exchange (Code Sec. 1031). Specifically, no gain or loss is recognized on a transfer of property held for productive use in a trade or business or for investment, to the extent the property is exchanged for property of like kind that will be held for productive use in a trade or business or for investment (Code Sec. 1031(a)(1)). Like-kind property is property of the same nature or character. There are three categories of like-kind property: (1) depreciable tangible personal property, (2) intangible and nondepreciable personal property, and (3) real property (Reg. §§ 1.1031(a)-1 and 1.1031(a)-2).

Virtually any real property is like-kind to other real property, regardless of how dissimilar the properties are. For instance, improved real estate is like-kind to unimproved real estate, urban lots are like-kind to rural tracts, commercial property is like-kind to residential rental or investment property, etc. A leasehold or similar property interest with at least 30 years left to run is like-kind to a fee title (Reg. § 1.1031(a)-1(c)). However, real property in the United States is not like-kind to real property outside the United States (Code Sec. 1031(h)(1)).

Ineligible property. Property that is not eligible for a like-kind exchange includes: (1) stock in trade or inventory property held primarily for sale; (2) stocks, bonds or notes, other than stock in a mutual ditch, reservoir or irrigation company described in Code Sec. 501(c)(12)(A) that is treated as real property under applicable state law; (3) other securities or evidences of indebtedness or interest; (4) partnership interests; (5) certificates of trust or beneficial interests; and (6) chooses in action (Code Sec.

BACKGROUND

1031(a)(2) and (j)). Thus, for instance, real property held primarily for sale is not eligible for a like-kind exchange. Although partnership interests are not eligible, if the partnership has elected out of subchapter K (that is, if it has elected to not be treated as a partnership for tax purposes), an interest in the partnership is treated as an interest in each of the partnership's assets, rather than a partnership interest (Code Sec. 1031(a)(2)).

Timing. Dispositions in a like-kind exchange do not have to be simultaneous. In a deferred exchange, a taxpayer may relinquish property before receiving the replacement property. Conversely, in a reverse-Starker exchange, the taxpayer may receive the replacement property before relinquishing the surrendered property. In a deferred exchange, once one property has been transferred, the taxpayer must identify the property for the second transfer within 45 days; and the second transfer must actually occur within 180 days or, if earlier, before the due date (including extensions) for the taxpayer's return for the tax year the property is relinquished (Code Sec. 1031(a)(3)). The IRS has provided a safe harbor for reverse-Starker exchanges (also known as parking transactions) that incorporates similar deadlines (Rev. Proc. 2000-37).

NEW LAW EXPLAINED

Like-kind exchanges limited to real property.—Like-kind exchanges are allowed only for real property after 2017. Thus, as under current law, no gain or loss is recognized on the exchange of real property held for productive use in a trade or business or for investment if that real property is exchanged solely for real property of like kind that will be held either for productive use in a trade or business or for investment. Like-kind exchanges are not allowed for depreciable tangible personal property, and intangible and nondepreciable personal property after 2017 (Code Sec. 1031(a)(1), as amended by the Tax Cuts and Jobs Act (P.L. 115-97)).

> **Comment:** Although most real property is like-kind to other real property, disputes as to whether properties are genuinely like-kind are still likely to arise when an exchange involves limited or partial property interests, such as life estates, remainder interests, and tenancies-in-common.

As under current law: (1) real property is not eligible for a like-kind exchange if it is held primarily for sale (Code Sec. 1031(a)(2), as amended by the 2017 Tax Cuts Act); (2) real property in the United States and foreign real property are not like-kind (Code Sec. 1031(h), as amended by the 2017 Tax Cuts Act); and (3) an interest in a partnership that has elected out of subchapter K is treated as an interest in each of the partnership's assets, rather than a partnership interest (Code Sec. 1031(e), as amended by the 2017 Tax Cuts Act).

> **Caution:** The Code no longer expressly provides that stock in a mutual ditch, reservoir or irrigation company described in Code Sec. 501(c)(12)(A) is eligible for a like-kind exchange if it is treated as real property under applicable state law (Code Sec. 1031(i), as stricken by the 2017 Tax Cuts Act). The Report by the House Ways and Means Committee provides that real property eligible for like-

¶505

NEW LAW EXPLAINED

kind exchange treatment under present law should continue to be eligible for like-kind exchange treatment. Specifically, stock in a mutual ditch, reservoir, or irrigation company should still be eligible for a like-kind exchange if the shares are treated as real property or as an interest in real property under applicable state law at the time of the exchange (Report of the Committee on Ways and Means on H.R. 1, Rep. 115-409). However, the Conference Committee Report does not contain similar language.

Transition rule. The restriction of like-kind exchanges to real property does not apply to an exchange if the relinquished property is disposed of or the replacement property is received on or before December 31, 2017 (Act Sec. 13303(c)(2) of the 2017 Tax Cuts Act).

> **Comment:** This transition rule allows taxpayers to complete a deferred or reverse-Starker exchange that involves depreciable tangible personal property or intangible and nondepreciable personal property. However, the 45-day identification deadline and the 180-day exchange deadline still apply.

Practical Analysis: Jim Hamill, Director of Tax Practice at Reynolds, Hix & Co., P.A. in Albuquerque, NM, observes that this is a win for the real estate industry. The JCT (and Representative Camp's 2014 reform proposals) had previously proposed eliminating Code Sec. 1031 in its entirety, or limiting the annual deferral to one million dollars. Personal property exchanges will no longer be available, but real property exchanges survive intact. Most exchanges do involve real property, both in number and total dollar amount, but it is also common to see exchanges of planes, fleet vehicles, highway construction equipment, and so on, and those personal property exchanges will now be taxable.

▶ **Effective date.** The amendments made by this section generally apply to exchanges completed after December 31, 2017 (Act Sec. 13303(c)(1) of the Tax Cuts and Jobs Act (P.L. 115-97). However, the amendments do not apply to an exchange if (1) the property disposed of by the taxpayer in the exchange is disposed of on or before December 31, 2017; or (2) the property received by the taxpayer in the exchange is received on or before December 31, 2017 (Act Sec. 13303(c)(2) of the 2017 Tax Cuts Act).

Law source: Law at ¶5945. Committee Report at ¶10,440.

— Act Sec. 13303(a) of the Tax Cuts and Jobs Act (P.L. 115-97), amending Code Sec. 1031(a)(1);

— Act Sec. 13303(b), amending Code Sec. 1031(a)(2), (e) and (h), and striking Code Sec. 1031(i);

— Act Sec. 13303(c), providing the effective date.

¶505

BUSINESS DEDUCTIONS

¶510 Limitation on Deduction of Business Interest

SUMMARY OF NEW LAW

The deduction of business interest is limited for any tax year beginning after 2017 to the sum of the taxpayer's business interest income, floor plan financing, and 30 percent of adjusted taxable income. The limitation generally applies to all taxpayers, but does not apply for small businesses with average gross receipts of $25 million or less (adjusted for inflation). Any disallowed interest generally may be carried forward indefinitely. In the case of a partnership or S corporation, the deduction limitation applies at the entity level, except that disallowed interest of the entity is allocated to each partner or shareholder as excess business interest.

BACKGROUND

Interest and other borrowing expenses incurred in a trade or business are generally deductible from gross income in the year paid or accrued depending on the taxpayer's method of accounting (Code Sec. 163). If a debt instrument is issued with original issue discount (OID), the OID is deducted as interest by the issuer of the debt over the life of the obligation on a yield to maturity basis. There are several limitations on the deduction of interest including tax-exempt interest, interest from obligations not in registered form, interest paid in connection with insurance contracts, and interest paid on original issue discount (OID) high-yield obligation. Interest may also be required to be capitalized if allocable to the production of certain property.

In the case of a taxpayer other than a corporation, the amount of investment interest they may deduct in a given tax year may not exceed net investment income (Code Sec. 163(d)). Any excess investment interest expense is carried forward indefinitely until net investment income is recognized. Investment interest is interest paid or accrued by the taxpayer on debt allocable to property held for investment that is otherwise deductible. However, investment expenses are determined after application of the two-percent-over adjusted gross income (AGI) limitation on miscellaneous itemized deductions. Investment income is the gross income derived from property held for investment or from its disposition including interest received, annuities, dividends, royalties, and short-term gain on the disposition of property. However, investment income includes capital gain and qualified dividend income only to the extent that the taxpayer elects to treat it as investment income.

A corporation is not allowed to deduct disqualified interest paid or accrued during the tax year if: (1) the debt-to-equity ratio of the corporation exceeds 1.5 to 1.0 as of the close of the tax year; and (2) the corporation has net interest expenses for the tax year that exceed 50 percent of its adjusted taxable income (Code Sec. 163(j)). Interest disallowed may be carried forward and treated as disqualified interest in succeeding tax years. In addition, any excess limitation (i.e., the excess of 50 percent of the

BACKGROUND

adjusted taxable income of the payor over the payor's net interest expense) can be carried forward three years. Disqualified interest is generally interest paid or accrued by the taxpayer: (1) to a related person not subject to U.S. income tax on the interest; (2) on debt held by an unrelated person in which there is a disqualified guarantee by a related person; and (3) to a taxable real estate investment trust (REIT) by a subsidiary of the trust. This limitation is often referred to as the "earnings stripping" rule.

NEW LAW EXPLAINED

Limitation on deduction of business interest for all taxpayers.—The deduction of interest paid or accrued on a debt incurred in a trade or business is limited regardless of the form the taxpayer's business is organized (i.e., corporation, partnership, sole proprietorship, etc.) effective for tax years beginning after December 31, 2017 (Code Sec. 163(j), as amended by the Tax Cuts and Jobs Act (P.L. 115-97)). An exception to the limitation is provided for a small business with average gross receipts of $25 million or less. Any interest not deductible generally may be carried forward indefinitely to succeeding tax years, subject to certain restrictions for partnerships and S corporations.

> **Comment:** The limitation on the deduction of business interest, along with the reduction of income tax rates for corporation (¶305) and the business income deduction for passthrough entities (¶330), helps to reduce the differences in marginal tax rates based on different sources of financing and in the choice of business entities.

Limitation on business interest. The deduction for business interest for any taxpayer is limited in any tax year to the sum of:

- business interest income of the taxpayer for the tax year;
- 30 percent of the taxpayer's adjusted taxable income for the year, including any increases in adjusted taxable income as a result of a distributive share in a partnership or S corporation (discussed below), but not below zero; and
- floor plan financing interest of the taxpayer for the tax year (Code Sec. 163(j)(1), as added by the 2017 Tax Cuts Act).

> **Comment:** The practical effect of the rule is to limit the deduction of net interest expenses to 30 percent of the taxpayer's adjusted taxable income. The deduction for business interest and floor plan financing interest is permitted to full extent of business interest income and floor plan financing interest. If the taxpayer has any interest expenses that exceed these amounts, then the deduction is limited to 30 percent of adjusted taxable income.

Business interest. Business interest for purposes of the limitation means any interest paid or accrued on debt properly allocable to a trade or business of the taxpayer (Code Sec. 163(j)(5), as added by the 2017 Tax Cuts Act). It does not include any investment interest. Business interest income is the amount of interest includible in the taxpayer's gross income for the tax year that is properly allocable to a trade or business (Code Sec. 163(j)(6), as added by the 2017 Tax Cuts Act). It does not include

¶510

NEW LAW EXPLAINED

any investment income. Investment interest and investment income in this context has the same meaning as for the limitation on the deduction of interest by taxpayers other than corporations.

> **Comment:** Investment interest is interest allocable to property that produces interest, dividends, annuities, royalties, gains, or losses not derived in the ordinary course of a trade or business. It also includes interest in a trade or business activity that is not a passive activity and in which the taxpayer does not materially participate. Investment income is the gross income derived from property held for investment purposes or from its disposition (Code Sec. 163(d)).

Adjusted taxable income. The adjusted taxable income of a taxpayer for purposes of the limitation is the taxpayer's regular taxable income computed without regard to:

- any item of income, gain, deduction, or loss that is not properly allocable to a trade or business;
- any business interest or business interest income;
- the amount of any net operating loss (NOL) deduction;
- the 20-percent deduction for qualified business income of a passthrough entity under Code Sec. 199A (see ¶330); and
- in tax years beginning before January 1, 2022, and allowable deduction for depreciation, amortization, or depletion (Code Sec. 163(j)(8), as added by the 2017 Tax Cuts Act).

> **Comment:** The IRS is authorized to provide other adjustments to the computation of adjusted taxable income as it deems necessary.

Floor plan financing indebtedness. Floor plan financing interest is interest paid or accrued on debt use to finance the acquisition of motor vehicles held for sale or lease to retail customers and secured by the inventory (Code Sec. 163(j)(9), as added by the 2017 Tax Cuts Act). A motor vehicle for this purpose includes any self-propelled vehicle designed for transporting people or property on a public street, highway, or road, as well as a boat, and farm machinery or equipment

> **Comment:** Any property used in a trade or business that has had floor plan financing indebtedness is not qualified property (¶410) eligible for the additional first-year depreciation deduction (bonus depreciation) if the floor plan financing interest to the debt is taken into account for purposes of the business interest deduction limitation (Code Sec. 168(k)(9), as added by the 2017 Tax Cuts Act).

Trade or business. A trade or business for purposes of calculating the business interest deduction limitation does not include the performance of services as an employee (Code Sec. 163(j)(7)(A)(i), as added by the 2017 Tax Cuts Act). Thus, wages of an employee are not included as part of the taxpayer's adjusted taxable income.

A taxpayer may also elect to exclude from the limitation any real property trade or business as defined under the passive activity rules (Code Sec. 163(j)(7)(A)(ii) and (B), as added by the 2017 Tax Cuts Act). An electing real property trade or business is any real estate development, redevelopment, construction, reconstruction, acquisition, conversion, rental, operation, management, leasing, or brokerage trade or business.

NEW LAW EXPLAINED

Thus, interest expenses paid or accrued in the electing real property trade or business is not business interest subject to the limitation. The election is made at a time and manner as provided by the IRS. Once made, the election is irrevocable.

> **Comment:** Under the passive activity rules, the way in which a taxpayer otherwise groups activities does not control the determination of the taxpayer's real property trades or businesses (Reg. § 1.469-9(d)).

> **Comment:** If a taxpayer elects to exclude a real property trade or business from the business interest limitation, then the business must use the alternative depreciation system (ADS) for certain property (Code Secs. 163(j)(10)(A) and 168(g)(1)(F), as added by the 2017 Tax Cuts Act). This includes any nonresidential real property, residential rental property, and qualified improvement property (¶ 405) held by the electing real property trade or business (Code Sec. 168(g)(8), as added by the 2017 Tax Cuts Act).

Similarly, a taxpayer may elect to exclude from the limitation any farming business as defined under the uniform capitalization rules, as well as any trade or business of a specified agricultural or horticultural cooperative that makes the election (Code Sec. 163(j)(7)(A)(iii) and (C), as added by the 2017 Tax Cuts Act). An electing farming business is any trade or business involving the cultivation of land or the raising or harvesting of any agricultural or horticultural commodity. It also includes a trade or business of operating a nursery or sod farm, or the raising or harvesting of trees bearing fruit, nuts, or other crops, or ornamental trees (an evergreen tree that is more than six years old at the time it is severed from the roots is not an ornamental tree). Interest expenses paid or accrued in a an electing farming business is not business interest subject to the limitation. The election is made at a time and manner as provided by the IRS. Once made, the election is irrevocable.

> **Comment:** If a taxpayer elects to exclude a farming business from the business interest limitation, then the business must use the alternative depreciation system (ADS) for any property with a recovery period of 10 years or more (Code Secs. 163(j)(10)(B) and 168(g)(1)(G), as added by the 2017 Tax Cuts Act).

A trade or business for purposes of the limitation does not include the furnishing or sale of a public utility if the rates for the utility are established or approved by a State, political subdivision of a State, agency or instrumentality of the United States, public service or public utility commission, or governing or ratemaking body of an elective cooperative (Code Sec. 163(j)(7)(A)(iv), as added by the 2017 Tax Cuts Act). A regulated public utility includes the trade or business of furnishing or sale of: (1) electrical energy, water, or sewage disposal services, (2) gas or steam through a local distribution system, or (3) transportation of gas or steam by pipeline.

> **Comment:** Any property primarily used the trade or business of a regulated utility and electric cooperative as described above is not qualified property (¶ 410) eligible for the additional first-year depreciation deduction (bonus depreciation) (Code Sec. 168(k)(9), as added the 2017 Tax Cuts Act).

> **Comment:** The limitation on the deduction of business interest is intended to apply after the application of other limitations on interest. For example, the Code Sec. 163(j) limitation applies to interest that is required to be deferred if paid on

NEW LAW EXPLAINED

an original issue discount (OID) high-yield obligation. The business interest limitation also applies after application of the capitalization rules (House Committee Report for the Tax Cuts and Jobs Act (P.L. 115-97) (H.R. Rep. No. 115-409).

Small business exception. The limitation on the deduction of business interest does not apply to any taxpayer that meets the $25 million gross receipts test for a corporation or partnership under Code Sec. 448(c) to use the cash method of accounting after 2017 (Code Sec. 163(j)(3), as added by the 2017 Tax Cuts Act). A taxpayer meets the small business test for the tax year if its average annual gross receipts for the three tax years ending with the prior tax year do not exceed $25 million, adjusted for inflation after 2018 (¶570). In the case of a taxpayer that is not a corporation or partnership, the gross receipts test is applied in the same manner as if the taxpayer were a corporation or partner. The small business exception is not available to tax shelter.

Carryforward of disallowed business interest. Any business interest not allowed as a deduction for the tax year under these rules may be carried forward and treated as business interest paid or accrued in the succeeding tax year (Code Sec. 163(j)(2), as added by the 2017 Tax Cuts Act). The interest may be carried forward indefinitely, subject to certain restrictions for partnerships and S corporations (discussed below).

In the case of a nontaxable acquisition or liquidation of a corporation under Code Sec. 381, the acquiring corporation generally succeeds to any carryover of disallowed business interest to tax years ending after the date of distribution or transfer (Code Sec. 381(c)(20), as added by the 2017 Tax Cuts Act). Similarly, the amount of any pre-change loss of a loss corporation (i.e., target corporation) that may be used to offset post-change taxable income of an acquiring corporation includes the carryover of disallowed business interest to the tax year ending with the ownership change or in which the change date occurs (Code Sec. 382(d)(3), as added by the 2017 Tax Cuts Act). A loss corporation for this purpose includes any corporation with carryforwards of disallowed business interest deductions (Code Sec. 382(k)(1), as amended by the 2017 Tax Cuts Act).

Application to partnerships and S corporations. In the case of a partnership or S corporation, the limitation on the deduction of business interest is applied at the entity level. Any deduction for business interest is taken into account in determining the non-separately stated taxable income or loss of the partnership or S corporation (Code Sec. 163(j)(4)(A)(i) and (D), as added by the 2017 Tax Cuts Act). While any business interest not deductible generally may be carried forward indefinitely to succeeding tax years, restrictions apply for partnerships and S corporations (discussed below).

The adjusted taxable income of each partner or shareholder is determined without regard to the partner's or shareholder's distributive share of any item of income, gain, deduction, or loss of the partnership or S corporation (Code Sec. 163(j)(4)(A)(ii)(I) and (D), as added by the 2017 Tax Cuts Act). This prevents doubled counting of the same dollars used in the adjusted taxable income of the entity generating addition interest deductions passed through to the partners or shareholders.

¶510

NEW LAW EXPLAINED

Example 1: The ABC partnership is owned equally by XYZ, Inc. and an individual. ABC generates $200 of noninterest during the tax year, but its only expense is $60 of business interest. Its deduction for business interest is limited to $60 (30 percent of its adjusted taxable income of $200). ABC deducts $60 of business interest and reports ordinary business income of $140.

XYZ's distributive share of ordinary business income of ABC is $70. It has no taxable income from its other operations and $25 of business interest expenses. XYZ's adjusted taxable income for the year is computed without regard to the $70 distributive share of the non-separately stated income of ABC. As a result, XYZ has adjusted taxable income of $0 and its deduction for business interest is limited to $0 (30 percent of adjusted taxable income of $0). The $25 of business interest expenses may not be deducted for the tax year, but may be carried forward for up to five years.

In the absence of the double counting rule, XYZ's adjusted taxable income for the year would include the $70 distributive share of the non-separately stated income of ABC. Its deduction for business interest would be limited to $21 (30 percent of adjusted taxable income of $70), resulting in a disallowance of only $4. Thus, XYZ's share of ABC's adjusted taxable income ($100) would generate $51 of interest deduction ($21 deduction for XYZ, plus $30 from distributive share of ABCs' deduction). If XYZ were a passthrough entity rather than a C corporation, additional deductions could be available at each tier.

If a partnership or S corporation has an excess taxable income for purposes of the deduction limit, then the excess is passed through to the partners or shareholders. Specifically, the adjusted taxable income of each partner or shareholder is increased by the partner's or shareholder's distributive share of the entity's excess taxable income (Code Sec. 163(j)(4)(A)(ii)(II) and (D), as added by the 2017 Tax Cuts Act). A partner's or shareholder's distributive share of partnership excess taxable income is determined in the same manner as the partner's or shareholder's distributive share of non-separately stated taxable income or loss of the entity.

The excess taxable income of a partnership or S corporation is a percentage of the entity's adjusted taxable income for the year (Code Sec. 163(j)(4)(C) and (D), as added by the 2017 Tax Cuts Act). The percentage is:

- 30 percent of the entity's adjusted taxable income, over its net excess business interest (the excess of business interest of the entity, reduced by floor plan financing interest, over business interest income; over

- 30 percent of the entity's adjusted taxable income.

This addition to a partner's or shareholder's adjusted taxable income, allows them to deduct more interest than they may have paid or incurred during the year, to the extent the entity could have deducted more business interest.

¶510

NEW LAW EXPLAINED

> **Example 2:** Assume the same facts as in Example 1 above, except that the ABC partnership has only $40 of business interest for the tax year. Its limit on its interest deduction is $60 for the year. Thus, the excess amount for ABC is $20 ($60 - $40). The excess taxable income for ABC is $66.67 (($20/$60) × $200) and XYZ's distributive share is $33.33. XYZ's deduction for business interest is limited to 30 percent of the sum of its adjusted taxable income plus its distributive share of the excess taxable income from ABC partnership is $10 (30 percent × ($0 + $33.33). As a result of the rule, XYZ may deduct $10 of business interest and has an interest deduction disallowance of $15.

Carryforwards for partnerships and S corporations. Unlike other taxpayers, any disallowed interest of a partnership or S corporation is not carried forward to the succeeding tax year. Instead, the disallowed interest of the entity is treated as excess business interest that is allocated to each partner or shareholder in the same manner as any non-separately state taxable income or loss (Code Sec. 163(j)(4)(B)(i) and (D), as added by the 2017 Tax Cuts Act).

The allocated excess business interest for the current tax year is treated by the partner or shareholder as business interest paid or accrued by the partner or shareholder in the next succeeding year. In other words, the allocated excess business interest is carried forward to next succeeding tax year by the partner or shareholder but only to the extent the partner or shareholder is allocated excess taxable income from the entity in the succeeding year (Code Sec. 163(j)(4)(B)(ii)(I) and (D), as added by the 2017 Tax Cuts Act). Excess taxable income allocated to a partner or shareholder for any tax year must be used against excess business interest from the entity from all tax years before it may be used against any other business interest.

If the partner or shareholder does not have enough excess taxable income from the entity to offset the carried forward excess business interest, then the interest must continue to be carried forward to succeeding tax years (Code Sec. 163(j)(4)(B)(ii)(II) and (D), as added by the 2017 Tax Cuts Act). In all subsequent tax years, the excess business interest carried forward by the partner or shareholder is treated as paid or accrued in the next subsequent tax year that may only be used against excess taxable income allocated by the entity to the partner or shareholder for that tax year.

The adjusted basis of a partner's or shareholder's interest in the entity is reduced (but not below zero) by the amount of excess business interest allocated by the entity to the partner or shareholder (Code Sec. 163(j)(4)(B)(iii)(I) and (D), as added by the 2017 Tax Cuts Act). However, if the partner or shareholder sells or otherwise disposes of the interest in the partnership or S corporation, then their adjusted basis is increased immediately before the disposition by the excess (if any) of:

- the amount of the basis reduction due to the excess business interest allocated by the entity to the partner or shareholder, over

NEW LAW EXPLAINED

- any portion of the excess business interest allocated to the partner or shareholder which has previously been treated as interest paid or accrued by the partner (Code Sec. 163(j)(4)(B)(iii)(II) and (D), as added by the 2017 Tax Cuts Act).

A disposition for purposes of an increase in the adjusted basis of a partnership or S corporation interest includes any transactions in which gain is not recognized in whole or part (including the death of the partner of shareholder). Also, no deduction is allowed to the transferor or transferee for any excess business interest that increases the adjusted basis in the entity.

▶ **Effective date.** The amendments made by this section apply to tax years beginning after December 31, 2017 (Act Sec. 13301(c) of the Tax Cuts and Jobs Act (P.L. 115-97)).

Law source: Law at ¶5300, ¶5455, and ¶5460. Committee Report at ¶10,420.

— Act Sec. 13301(a) of the Tax Cuts and Jobs Act (P.L. 115-97), amending Code Sec. 163(j);

— Act Sec. 13301(b), adding Code Sec. 381(c)(20), adding Code Sec. 382(d)(3), and amending Code Sec. 382(k)(1);

— Act Sec. 13301(c), providing the effective date.

¶515 Net Operating Losses (NOLs)

SUMMARY OF NEW LAW

Net operating losses (NOLs) arising in a tax year ending after 2017 are generally not allowed to be carried back but may only be carried forward indefinitely. However, the five-year carryback period for farming losses is retained but is reduced to two years and a two-year carryback and 20-year carryforward period is retained for insurance companies other than life insurance companies. An NOL arising in a tax year beginning after 2017 may only reduce 80 percent of taxable income in a carryback or carryforward tax year. The taxable income limitation does not apply to non-life insurance companies.

BACKGROUND

A net operating loss ("NOL") generally means the amount by which a taxpayer's business deductions exceed its gross income. In general, an NOL is carried back two years and then carried forward 20 years to offset taxable income in the carryback and carryforward years. Extended carryback periods apply to the following types of losses:

- three years for an NOL of an individual arising from a fire, storm, shipwreck, other casualty, or theft (Code Sec. 172(b)(1)(E)(ii)(I));
- three years for an NOL of a small business or taxpayer engaged in farming if the loss is attributable to a federally declared disaster (Code Sec. 172(b)(1)(E)(ii)(II) and (III));

BACKGROUND

- five years in the case of a farming loss (Code Sec. 172(b)(1)(F) and (h)); and
- 10-years in the case of a specified liability loss (Code Sec. 172(b)(1)(C) and (f)).

Farming loss. A farming loss is the smaller of (1) the amount that would be the NOL for the tax year if only income and deductions attributable to farming businesses were taken into account, or (2) the NOL for the tax year. A taxpayer may elect to waive the five-year carryback for a farming loss. In this case, the two-year carryback period generally applies. For ordering purposes, the farming loss is treated as a separate NOL to be taken into account after the remaining portion of the NOL for the tax year (Code Sec. 172(h)(1).

Specified liability loss. A specified liability loss is the portion of an NOL that is attributable to product liability or arises out of satisfaction of a liability under federal or state law requiring land reclamation, nuclear power plant decommissioning, drilling platform dismantling, environmental remediation, or a payment under any workers' compensation act (Code Sec. 172(f)(1)(B)(i)).

REITS. Real estate investment trust NOLs may not be carried back but may be carried forward 20 years (Code Sec. 172(b)(1)(B)).

Corporate equity reduction interest loss (CERT). A C corporation may not carry back a portion of its NOL if $1 million or more of interest expense is incurred in a "major stock acquisition" of another corporation or in an "excess distribution" by the corporation (Code Sec. 172(b)(1)(D) and (g)). The amount subject to the limitation is the lesser of: (1) the corporation's deductible interest expense allocable to the CERT, or (2) the amount by which the corporation's interest expense for the current tax year exceeds the average interest expense for the three tax years preceding the tax year in which the CERT occurs.

Computation of NOL. Code Sec. 172(d) lists various modifications that corporate and non-corporate taxpayers must make in computing taxable income for purposes of determining the NOL for a tax year. For this purpose, the domestic production activities deduction is not allowed (Code Sec. 172(d)(7)).

NEW LAW EXPLAINED

NOL deduction limited; carryback eliminated and unlimited carryforwward period provided.—Net operating losses (NOLs) arising in tax years beginning after 2017 may only reduce 80 percent of a taxpayer's taxable income in carryback and carryforward years. The generally applicable two-year carryback period, as well as the longer carryback periods for special types of losses, are eliminated, effective for NOLs arising in tax years ending after 2017. NOLs, however, may be carried forward indefinitely. Exceptions described below apply to farming losses and losses of casualty and property insurance companies (Code Sec. 172, as amended by the Tax Cuts and Jobs Act (P.L. 115-97).

> **Caution:** The effective date provides that the provision limiting an NOL deduction to 80 percent of taxable income is effective for NOLs arising in tax years *beginning* after 2017 (Act Sec. 13302(e)(1) of P.L. 115-97). On the other hand, the effective date eliminating the two-year carryback period is effective for NOLs

NEW LAW EXPLAINED

arising in tax years *ending* after 2017 (Act Sec. 13302(e)(2) of P.L. 115-97). The difference is important to a 2017/2018 fiscal year filer. An NOL arising in the 2017/2018 fiscal-year may not be carried back two years since it arose in a tax year ending after 2017. However, the same NOL is not subject to the 80 percent of taxable income limitation because the NOL did not arise in a tax year beginning after 2017.

The committee report states that the effective date for both the 80 percent taxable income limitation and the elimination of the two-year carryback and twenty-year carryforward period is for NOLs arising in tax years beginning after 2017 (Conference Report on H.R. 1, Tax Cuts and Jobs Act (H. Rept. 115-466)).

NOL deduction limited to 80 percent of taxable income. Effective for net operating losses that arise in tax years beginning after December 31, 2017, the NOL deduction for a tax year is limited to the lesser of:

- the aggregate of net operating loss carryovers (i.e., carryforwards) to the tax year, plus NOL carrybacks to the tax year; or

- 80 percent of taxable income computed for the tax year without regard to the NOL deduction allowed for the tax year (Code Sec. 172(a), as amended by the 2017 Tax Cuts Act (P.L. 115-97)).

   Comment: Since the 80 percent taxable income limit applies to losses arising in tax years beginning after December 31, 2017, NOL carrybacks and carryforwards attributable to losses that arose in tax years beginning before January 1, 2018, are not subject to the 80 percent limitation (Act Sec. 13302(e)(1) of the 2017 Tax Cuts Act).

In determining the amount of a NOL that remains available for carryback or carryforward, the taxable income for any prior tax year to which the NOL was carried is not treated as exceeding 80 percent (Code Sec. 172(b)(2), as amended by the 2017 Tax Cuts Act).

Taxable income of REIT. In the case of a real estate investment trust (REIT), the 80 percent taxable income limitation is determined by reference to "real estate investment trust taxable income" as defined in Code Sec. 857(b)(2) but without regard to the dividends paid deduction (Code Sec. 172(d)(6)(C), as added by 2017 Tax Cuts Act).

NOL carrybacks generally eliminated and carryforwards allowed indefinitely. The carryback of NOLs is generally eliminated, except for NOLs attributable to farm losses and certain insurance companies as described below. The 20-year limitation on carryforwards is also eliminated and NOLs may be carried forward indefinitely (Code Sec. 172(b)(1)(A), as amended by 2017 Tax Cuts Act). This change is effective for NOLs arising in tax years ending after December 31, 2017 (Act Sec. 13302(e)(2) of the 2017 Tax Cuts Act). As a result of the elimination of NOL carrybacks except for NOLs attributable to farm losses and certain insurance companies, the special carryback rules that apply to the following have also been eliminated:

- real estate investment trusts (Code Sec. 172(b)(1)(B), stricken by the 2017 Tax Cuts Act);

- specified liability losses (Code Sec. 172(b)(1)(C), stricken by the 2017 Tax Cuts Act);

NEW LAW EXPLAINED

- limitation on carryback of excess interest loss in a corporate equity reduction transaction (CERT) (Code Sec. 179(b)(1)(D), stricken by the 2017 Tax Cuts Act);

- certain casualty and disaster losses of individuals, small businesses, and farmers (Code Sec. 172(b)(1)(E), stricken by the 2017 Tax Cuts Act);

- farming losses (Code Sec. 172(b)(1)(F), stricken by the 2017 Tax Cuts Act).

Two-year carryback for farming losses. The five-year carryback period for farming losses is replaced with a two-year carryback period (Code Sec. 172(b)(1)(B), as added by the 2017 Tax Cuts Act). This provision is effective for NOLs arising in tax years ending after December 31, 2017 (Act Sec. 13302(e)(2) of the 2017 Tax Cuts Act).

> **Comment:** The definition of a farming loss remains unchanged and taxpayers may continue to waive the carryback period (Code Sec. 172(b)(1)(B)(ii) and (iv), as added by the 2017 Tax Cuts Act). Also, as under prior law, where a NOL for a tax year consists of both a farming loss and a non-farming loss, the two losses are treated separately and the farming loss is taken into account in carryback and carryforward years after the non-farming loss (Code Sec. 172(b)(1)(B)(iii), as added by the 2017 Tax Cuts Act). This rule was previously provided by a cross-reference to a similar rule for specified liability losses (Code Sec. 172(f)(5), stricken by the 2017 Tax Cuts Act).

Two-year carryback and 20-year carryforward for casualty and property insurance company losses. The NOL of an insurance company other than a life insurance company (e.g., a property and casualty insurance company) may continue to be carried back two years and forward twenty years (Code Sec. 172(b)(1)(C), as added by the 2017 Tax Cuts Act). In addition, the 80 percent taxable income limitation does not apply to a non-life insurance company. Thus, the deductible amount of a non-life insurance company's NOL for a tax year is the sum of the NOL carryovers to the tax year, plus the NOL carrybacks to the tax year (Code Sec. 172(f), as added by the 2017 Tax Cuts Act).

> **Comment:** The two-carryback and 20-year carryforward period are retained for insurance companies other then life insurance companies. In addition, the 80 percent of taxable income limitation does not apply to these companies. The operations loss deduction for life insurance companies is repealed and life insurance companies will claim NOLs in a manner similar to other corporations under Code Sec. 172 (i.e., no carryback, indefinite carryforward, and 80 percent taxable income limitation on deduction). The NOL deduction of a life insurance company is determined by treating the NOL for any tax year generally as the excess of the life insurance deductions for such tax year, over the life insurance gross income for such tax year. See ¶905 for the treatment of life insurance companies.

Determination of remaining carryback or carryforward. In determining the portion of a NOL that arose in a tax year beginning after 2017 that remains for carryback or carryforward, the new 80 percent taxable income limitation applies. Consequently, the portion of such a NOL that remains available for carryback or carryforward to another tax year is the excess, if any, of the amount of the loss over the sum of 80

¶515

NEW LAW EXPLAINED

percent of the taxable income (computed with certain of the modifications described in Code Sec. 172(d)) for each of the tax years to which the loss was previously carried (Code Sec. 172(b)(2), as amended by 2017 Tax Cuts Act).

Modifications to taxable income in computing NOL for loss year. A taxpayer's NOL for the tax year is computed in the same manner as taxable income or loss with certain modifications. Effective for tax years beginning after December 31, 2017, the 20-percent deduction for qualified business income of a passthrough entity under Code Sec. 199A (see ¶330) and the deduction for foreign-derived intangible income (FDII) under Code Sec. 250 (¶735) are not taken into account for this purpose (Code Sec. 172(d)(8) and (d)(9), as added by the 2017 Tax Cuts Act). The domestic production activities deduction under Code Sec. 199 is removed from the list of deductions that may not be claimed in computing the NOL for a loss year as the deduction has been repealed effective for tax years beginning after 2017 (see ¶530) (Code Sec. 172(d)(7), stricken by the 2017 Tax Cuts Act).

Practical Analysis: Mark Leeds, Partner at Mayer Brown, LLP in New York, notes that the modified rules for a NOL for corporations and REITs generally limit the NOL deduction to 80 percent of taxable income for losses arising in taxable years beginning in 2018 and after. This Act also eliminates any ability to carryback NOL (other than for farming losses) and provides for an indefinite carryforward (instead of the current maximum of 20 years). The existing rules are preserved for insurance companies, other than life insurance companies. These rules would apply to losses arising in taxable years arising after 2017. The sale of companies such as private equity or portfolio company with a lot of associated deductions will be impacted by these changes. This Act will negatively affect the valuation of deferred tax assets held by reporting companies.

▶ **Effective date.** The amendments made by this section limiting net operating losses (NOLs) to 80 percent of taxable income, determining the amount of remaining carryback or carryforward, and exempting life insurance companies from the 80 percent of taxable income limitation apply to losses arising in tax years beginning after December 31, 2017 (Act Sec. 13302(e)(1) of the Tax Cuts and Jobs Act (P.L. 115-97)).

The amendments eliminating the carryback periods, making the carryforward period indefinite, reducing the farming loss carryback period from five years to two years, and allowing a two-year carryback and twenty-year carryforward for the NOL of an insurance company apply to NOLs arising in tax years ending after December 31, 2017 (Act Sec. 13302(e)(2) of the 2017 Tax Cuts Act).

The amendments removing the Code Sec. 199 manufacturing deduction from and adding the 20 percent deduction for qualified business income (Code Sec. 199A) and the deduction for foreign-derived intangible income (Code Sec. 250) to the list of deductions not taken into account in computing an NOL are effective for tax years beginning after 2017.

Law source: Law at ¶5325 and ¶5595. Committee Report at ¶10,430.

— Act Sec. 13302(a) of the Tax Cuts and Jobs Act (P.L. 115-97), amending Code Sec. 172(a), (b)(2), and (d)(6);

NEW LAW EXPLAINED

— Act Sec. 13302(b), amending Code Sec. 172(b)(1)(A) and striking Code Sec. 172(b)(1)(B) through (F)

— Act Sec. 13302(c), adding Code Sec. 172(b)(1)(B) and striking Code Sec. 172(f), (g), and (h);

— Act Sec. 13302(d), adding Code Sec. 172(b)(1)(C) and (f);

— Act Sec. 13302(e), providing the effective date for the preceding provisions;

— Act Sec. 13305(b)(3), striking Code Sec. 172(d)(7);

— Act 13305(c), providing the effective date for the preceding provision;

— Act Sec. 11011(d)(1) adding Code Sec. 172(d)(8)

— Act Sec. 11011(e), providing the effective date of the preceding provision.

— Act Sec. 14202(b)(1), adding Code Sec. 172(d)(9)

— Act Sec. 14202(c), providing the effective date of the preceding provision.

¶520 Excess Business Losses for Noncorporate Taxpayers

SUMMARY OF NEW LAW

Excess business losses of noncorporate taxpayers are not allowed for tax years beginning in 2018 through 2025. Any disallowed excess business loss is treated as a net operating loss (NOL) carryover to the following tax year. However, the passive activity loss rules apply before application of the excess business loss rules.

BACKGROUND

A taxpayer's method of accounting determines when deductions and credits can be taken (Code Sec. 461(a)). Ordinarily, taxpayers on the cash method take deductions and credits in the year in which they are paid. Accrual-method taxpayers take deductions or credits in the year in which the items are accrued or incurred. Items accrue when: (1) all events have occurred that fix the fact of liability and the liability can be determined with reasonable accuracy (the "all-events test"), and (2) economic performance has occurred (Code Sec. 461(h)). A number of special timing rules and exceptions may also apply to taxes for accrual-method taxpayers, contested liabilities, prepaid interest for cash-method taxpayers, amounts accrued by reason of death of an accrual-method taxpayer, tax shelters, excess farm losses, and dividends or interest paid by mutual savings banks.

Passive activity losses (PALs). Under the passive activity rules, losses and expenses attributable to passive activities may be deducted only from income attributable to passive activities (Code Sec. 469). The effect of this treatment is to prohibit the use of passive losses to offset nonpassive income. A passive activity is any trade or business activity in which the taxpayer owns an interest but does not materially participate. Passive activities generally include rental activities, regardless of whether the tax-

BACKGROUND

payer materially participates in the activity. The passive activity rules apply to individuals, trusts, estates, closely held C corporations, and personal service corporations. The passive activity rules do not apply to S corporations and partnerships, but do apply to losses and credits that these entities pass through to their respective shareholders and partners.

A passive activity loss is the amount by which passive activity deductions from all passive activities exceed passive activity gross income from all passive activities for the tax year (Code Sec. 469(d)(1)). A taxpayer's passive activity loss for the tax year is disallowed and may not be deducted against other income. The disallowed passive activity loss is carried forward until the taxpayer has available passive activity income to offset (Code Sec. 469(b)).

Excess farm losses. Taxpayers other than C corporations that receive applicable subsidies, such as Commodity Credit Corporation (CCC) loans and agricultural program payments, cannot deduct their excess farm losses (Code Sec. 461(j)). Disallowed losses can be carried forward to the next tax year. The disallowance of excess farm losses is applied before the rules that limit passive activity losses.

An "excess farm loss" is the excess of the taxpayer's aggregate deductions for the tax year that are attributable to farming businesses, over the applicable threshold amount for the tax year in which the farming business receives applicable subsidies. The threshold amount is the greater of: $300,000 ($150,000 for a married taxpayer filing a separate return) or the taxpayer's aggregate net farm income for the five preceding tax years.

Net operating losses. A net operating loss (NOL) for the tax year is the excess of allowable deductions over gross income, with certain modifications (Code Sec. 172). If a taxpayer has an NOL for the current tax year, no deduction is allowed in the year the loss is incurred. Instead, the taxpayer carries the NOL to other tax years as a deduction against taxable income in those years. The NOL deduction amount may not exceed the amount of taxable income for the year of the deduction.

NEW LAW EXPLAINED

Excess business losses of noncorporate taxpayers disallowed.—Excess business losses of noncorporate taxpayers are not allowed for tax years beginning after December 31, 2017, and before January 1, 2026 (Code Sec. 461(l)(1)(B), as added by the Tax Cuts and Jobs Act (P.L. 115-97)). Any excess business loss that is disallowed is treated as a net operating loss (NOL) carryover to the following tax year (Code Sec. 461(l)(2), as added by the 2017 Tax Cuts Act). However, noncorporate taxpayers must apply the passive activity loss rules before application of the rules for excess business losses (Code Sec. 461(l)(6), as added by the 2017 Tax Cuts Act).

> **Comment:** For losses arising in tax years beginning after December 31, 2017, an NOL may only reduce 80 percent of taxable income in a carryback or carryforward tax year. See ¶515 for further details on the modified NOL rules.

NEW LAW EXPLAINED

An "excess business loss" is the excess, if any, of:

- the taxpayer's aggregate deductions for the tax year from the taxpayer's trades or businesses, determined without regard to whether or not such deductions are disallowed for such tax year under the excess business loss limitation; over

- the sum of:

  — the taxpayer's aggregate gross income or gain for the tax year from such trades or businesses, plus

  — $250,000, adjusted annually for inflation (200 percent of the $250,000 amount in the case of a joint return) (Code Sec. 461(l)(3)(A), as added by the 2017 Tax Cuts Act).

The $250,000 amount above is adjusted annually for inflation for tax years beginning after December 31, 2018, using the Chained Consumer Price Index for All Urban Consumers (C-CPI-U) in the cost-of-living adjustment (see ¶ 125) (Code Sec. 461(l)(3)(B), as added by the 2017 Tax Cuts Act).

Example: For 2018, Ned Brown has $1 million of gross income and $1.4 million of deductions from a retail business that is not a passive activity. His excess business loss is $150,000 ($1,400,000 − ($1,000,000 + $250,000)). Brown must treat his excess business loss of $150,000 as an NOL carryover to 2019.

Comment: During the period that excess business losses are disallowed (tax years beginning after December 31, 2017, and before January 1, 2026), the limit on excess farm losses of noncorporate taxpayers will not apply (Code Sec. 461(l)(1)(A), as added by the 2017 Tax Cuts Act).

Partnerships and S corporations. For partnerships and S corporations, the limit on excess business losses is applied at the partner or shareholder level (Code Sec. 461(l)(4), as added by the 2017 Tax Cuts Act; Conference Report on H.R. 1, Tax Cuts and Jobs Act (H. Rept. 115-466)). Each partner's distributive share or each S corporation shareholder's pro rata share of items of income, gain, deduction, or loss of the partnership or S corporation is taken into account by the partner or shareholder in applying the excess business loss rules to the partner's or shareholder's tax year with or within which the partnership's or S corporation's tax year ends.

Reporting requirements. The IRS is authorized to issue additional reporting requirements that it determines are necessary to carry out the purposes of the excess business loss rules (Code Sec. 461(l)(5), as added by the 2017 Tax Cuts Act)).

▶ **Effective date.** The amendments made by this section apply to tax years beginning after December 31, 2017 (Act Sec. 11012(b) of the Tax Cuts and Jobs Act (P.L. 115-97)).

Law source: Law at ¶ 5535. Committee Report at ¶ 10,040.

— Act Sec. 11012(a) of the Tax Cuts and Jobs Act (P.L. 115-97), adding Code Sec. 461(l);

— Act Sec. 11012(b), providing the effective date.

¶525 Research and Experimental Expenditures

SUMMARY OF NEW LAW

Research and experimental expenditures paid or accrued after 2021 generally must be amortized ratably over five years. Any amount paid or incurred in connection with the development of any software is treated as a research or experimental expenditure for this purposes of this amortization provision. A 15-year amortization period applies to research or experimental expenditures attributable to foreign research.

BACKGROUND

A taxpayer may use one of three alternative methods to account for research and experimental expenditures: (1) currently deduct the expenditures in the year in which they are paid or incurred; (2) elect to treat the expenditures as deferred expenses, amortizable over a period of at least 60 months beginning in the month that benefits are first realized from the expenditures; or (3) elect to amortize the expenditures over 10 years beginning in the tax year in which they are paid or incurred (Code Secs. 174 and 59(e)). A taxpayer that fails to account for its research and experimental expenditures using one of these three methods is generally required to capitalize the expenditures (Reg. § 1.174-1).

If the 10-year amortization election is made by a taxpayer other than a corporation, the amortization deduction is claimed in full for alternative minimum tax (AMT) purposes and is not subject to adjustment (Code Sec. 59(e)). In the case of a taxpayer other than a corporation, the Code Sec. 174 deduction is allowed in full for AMT purposes if a taxpayer materially participates in the activity (Code Sec. 56(b)(2)(D)). In the case of a corporation, the research deduction is allowed in full for AMT purposes even if the 10-year amortization election is not made.

No deduction is generally allowable for expenditures for the acquisition or improvement of land or of depreciable or depletable property used in connection with any research or experimentation (Code Sec. 174(f)). In addition, no deduction is allowed for research expenses incurred for the purpose of ascertaining the existence, location, extent, or quality of any deposit of ore or other mineral, including oil and gas (Code Sec. 174(d)).

A credit is also allowed for increased research and experimental expenses (Code Sec. 41).

NEW LAW EXPLAINED

Five-year amortization of research expenditures; 15-years for foreign research expenditures.—Amounts paid or incurred for specified research or experimental expenditures after December 31, 2021, generally must be amortized ratably over five years (Code Sec. 174(a), as amended by Tax Cuts and Jobs Act (P.L. 115-97)). The amortization period begins at the mid-point of the tax year in which the expenditures are paid or incurred.

NEW LAW EXPLAINED

Comment: The rule that allows taxpayers to currently deduct research and experimental expenditures is eliminated after 2021. Similarly, the rule that taxpayers may elect an amortization period 60 months or greater beginning when benefits are first realized is eliminated after 2021. The rule in Code Sec. 59(e) which allows a taxpayer to elect 10-year amortization of research and experimental expenditures beginning in the year the expenditures are paid or incurred remains available after 2021, but the specific reference in Code Sec. 174 has been removed.

Planning Note: Taxpayers with significant losses have often elected 10-year amortization to reduce amounts that could be subject to expiration under the 20-year net operating loss (NOL) carryfoward limitation even if they had no alternative minimum tax (AMT) liability. However, NOLs arising in tax years ending after December 31, 2017, may be carried forward indefinitely (see ¶515). Thus, taxpayers are less likely to elect 10-year amortization.

Amounts paid or incurred for specified research or experimental expenditures after December 31, 2021, attributable to foreign research must be amortized ratably over 15 years (Code Sec. 174(a)(2), as amended by the 2017 Tax Cuts Act). Foreign research for this purpose is defined by reference to Code Sec. 41(d)(4)(F) to mean any research conducted outside the United States, the Commonwealth of Puerto Rico, or any possession of the United States. Similar to the general five-year amortization period, the 15-year amortization period for foreign research begins at the mid-point of the tax year in which the expenditures are paid or incurred.

Comment: There is no restriction on the deduction of research or experimental expenditures attributable to foreign research if paid or accrued before 2022.

Specified research or experimental expenditures. The five-year amortization period (15-year period for foreign research) applies to specified research or experimental expenditures which are simply research or experimental expenditures paid or incurred by the taxpayer during a tax year in connection with the taxpayer's trade or business (Code Sec. 174(b), as amended by the 2017 Tax Cuts Act).

Comment: Research and experimental expenditures are defined in Reg. § 1.174-2.

Any amount paid or incurred in connection with the development of any software is treated as a research or experimental expenditure for purposes of this amortization provision (Code Sec. 174(c)(3), as added by the 2017 Tax Cuts Act).

Comment: Under current law, the IRS allows a taxpayer to treat all software development expenses as currently deductible even if such expenses do not otherwise meet the requirements of Code Sec. 174 (Rev. Proc. 2000-50). However, no portion of software development costs paid or incurred after 2021 are currently deductible and all such expenses must be amortized as research expenditures over five years (15-years for foreign research).

Expenditures for acquiring land, acquiring or improving depreciable property, or acquiring property subject to a depletion allowance continue to not be treated as research expenditures for this purpose even if used in connection with research and experimentation and depreciation and depletion allowances on such property are considered research expenditures (Code Sec. 174(c)(1), as amended by the 2017 Tax

¶525

NEW LAW EXPLAINED

Cuts Act). Also, amounts paid or incurred for the purpose of determining the existence, location, extent, or quality of an ore, mineral, or oil and gas deposit continue to not be treated as research expenditures (Code Sec. 174(c)(2), as amended the 2017 Tax Cuts Act).

Amortization after disposition. Taxpayers must continue to amortize research or experimental expenditures under these rules even if the property with respect to which the expenditures were paid or incurred is disposed, retired, or abandoned during the five-year amortization period (15-year period for foreign research) (Code Sec. 174(d), as amended by the 2017 Tax Cuts Act). No deduction of the unamortized portion of the expenditures is allowed.

Change in method of accounting. The switch to a five-year amortization period (15-year period for foreign research) and other changes is a change in accounting method (Act Sec. 13206(b) of the 2017 Tax Cuts Act). However, it is not be necessary taxpayers to file an accounting method change and no Code Sec. 481(a) adjustment is required or allowed. Instead, the changes only apply on a cut-off basis to research or experimental expenditures paid or incurred in tax years beginning after December 31, 2021. The change is treated as initiated by taxpayers and as made with the consent with the IRS.

Coordination with research credit. The amount capitalized and otherwise eligible for amortization over five-years (15-years for foreign research) after 2021 is reduced by the excess (if any) of the research credit allowed for the tax year and the amount allowable as a deduction for the tax year as qualified research expenses or basic research expenses (Code Sec. 280C(d)(1), as amended by the 2017 Tax Cuts Act)).

> **Comment:** For amounts paid or accrued before 2022, the deduction otherwise allowed for the portion of qualified research expenses (as defined in Code Sec. 41(b)) or basic research expenses (as defined in Code Sec. 41(e)(2)) is reduced by the amount of the research credit (Code Sec. 280C(d)(1), prior to amendment by the 2017 Tax Cuts Act). The same rule applies for amounts paid or accrued after 2021 except that only the amount otherwise allowed as an amortization deduction during the tax year that the credit is claimed reduces the research credit.

In a conforming amendment, the definition of qualified research for purposes of the research credit (Code Sec. 41) is adjusted to mean research with respect to which expenditures paid or incurred after 2021 are treated as specified research or experimental expenditures under Code Sec. 174. In other words, qualified research relates to research costs which must be amortized over five-years (15-years for foreign research (Code Sec. 41(d)(1)(A), as amended by the 2017 Tax Cuts Act). For amounts paid or incurred before 2022, qualified research is defined by reference to expenditures which may be currently deducted under Code Sec. 174. No change is made to the additional requirements for the research credit, such as the requirement that the research be undertaken for the purpose of discovering information which technological in nature and intended to be useful in the development of a new or improved business component of the taxpayer.

NEW LAW EXPLAINED

> **Practical Analysis:** Charles R. Goulding, President, Energy Tax Savers and R&D Tax Savers in Syosset, New York, comments that the requirement that all R&D expenditures must be amortized starting in 2022 is likely more about meeting the revenue goals of the Act than expected permanent legislation, but only time will tell. The addition that all software, the fast growing segment of R&D, is also now included is likewise of interest. Lastly, the removal of the "only reasonable research expenditures" clause of Code Sec. 174 is likely more related to the difficulty in proving reasonableness than any major policy change.

▶ **Effective date.** The amendments made by this section apply to amounts paid or incurred in tax years beginning after December 31, 2021 (Act Sec. 13206(e) of the Tax Cuts and Jobs Act (P.L. 115-97)).

Law source: Law at ¶5060, ¶5330, and ¶5440. Committee Report at ¶10,390.

— Act Sec. 13206(a) of the Tax Cuts and Jobs Act (P.L. 115-97), amending Code Sec. 174;

— Act Sec. 13206(b) providing change of accounting method rules;

— Act Sec. 13206(d) amending Code Sec. 41(d)(1)(A) and Code Sec. 280C(c);

— Act Sec. 13206(e), providing the effective date.

¶530 Domestic Production Activities Deduction (DPAD)

SUMMARY OF NEW LAW

The domestic production activities deduction (DPAD) under Code Sec. 199 is repealed for tax years beginning after 2017.

BACKGROUND

The domestic production activities deduction (DPAD) is generally equal to nine percent of the lesser of qualified production activities income or taxable income (adjusted gross income for individuals, estates, and trusts) (Code Sec. 199). A taxpayer's qualified production activities income (QPAI) is its domestic production gross receipts (DPGR), reduced by allocable cost of goods sold and other deductions, expenses, and losses.

DPGR are generally gross receipts of the taxpayer that are derived from: (1) any sale, exchange, or other disposition, or any lease, rental, or license, of qualifying production property that was manufactured, produced, grown or extracted by the taxpayer in whole or in significant part within the United States; (2) any sale, exchange, or other disposition, or any lease, rental, or license, of qualified film produced by the taxpayer; (3) any sale, exchange, or other disposition, or any lease, rental, or license, of electricity, natural gas, or potable water produced by the taxpayer in the United

BACKGROUND

States; (4) construction of real property performed in the United States by a taxpayer in the ordinary course of a construction trade or business; or (5) engineering or architectural services performed in the United States for the construction of real property located in the United States.

The DPAD for a tax year is limited to 50 percent of the W-2 wages paid by the taxpayer to its employees for the calendar year ending during the tax year that are properly allocable to the taxpayer's DPGR (the wages that the taxpayer deducts in calculating its QPAI).

NEW LAW EXPLAINED

Domestic production activities deduction repealed.—The domestic production activities deduction (DPAD) is repealed for tax years beginning after December 31, 2017 (Code Sec. 199, as stricken by the Tax Cuts and Jobs Act (P.L. 115-97)).

▶ **Effective date.** The amendment made by this section applies to tax years beginning after December 31, 2017 (Act 13305(c) of the Tax Cuts and Jobs Act (P.L. 115-97)).

Law source: Law at ¶5190, ¶5205, ¶5245, ¶5250, ¶5320, ¶5325, ¶5340, ¶5365, ¶5375, ¶5380, ¶5405, ¶5545, ¶5610, and ¶5615. Committee Report at ¶10,460.

— Act Sec. 13305(a) of the Tax Cuts and Jobs Act (P.L. 115-97), striking Code Sec. 199;

— Act Sec. 13305(b), amending Code Secs. 74(d)(2)(B), 86(b)(2)(A), 135(c)(4)(A), 137(b)(3)(A), 170(b)(2)(D), 219(g)(3)(A)(ii), 221(b)(2)(C), 222(b)(2)(C), 246(b)(1), 469(i)(3)(F)(iii), 613(a), and 613A(d)(1), and striking Code Sec. 172(d)(7);

— Act Sec. 13305(c), providing the effective date.

ORDINARY AND NECESSARY EXPENSES

¶535 Employer's Deduction for Entertainment, Commuting Benefits, and Meals

SUMMARY OF NEW LAW

Business expense deductions are eliminated for most entertainment costs and commuting benefits after 2017, as well as certain employer-provided meal expenses after 2025.

BACKGROUND

Employers and other taxpayers generally may deduct ordinary and necessary business expenses, including cash and noncash compensation (fringe benefits) paid for services rendered (Code Sec. 162(a)(1)). Special requirements and limits apply to several types of business expense deductions, including entertainment expenses,

BACKGROUND

traveling and commuting benefits, and expenses for employer-provided meals for employees (Code 274).

Entertainment expenses. Expenses for entertainment, or for a facility used in connection with entertainment, are generally deductible only to the extent: (1) they are directly related to the active conduct of the taxpayer's trade or business, or (2) they are associated with the active conduct of the taxpayer's trade or business, and the expense item directly precedes or follows a substantial and bone fide business discussion (Code Sec. 274(a)(1)).

Entertainment includes any activity of a type that is generally considered to constitute entertainment, amusement, or recreation, such as entertaining at night clubs, cocktail lounges, theaters, country clubs, golf and athletic clubs and sporting events, and on hunting, fishing, vacation, and similar trips. Entertainment may include expenses that satisfy personal or family needs, such as food and beverages, a hotel room, or a car (Reg. § 1.274-2(b)). When entertainment expense deductions are disallowed for any portion of a facility, that portion is treated as used for personal, living and family purposes rather than as an asset used in a trade or business (Code Sec. 274(g)). A club is an entertainment facility unless it is used primarily to further the taxpayer's trade or business and the expense item is directly related to the active conduct of that trade or business (Code Sec. 274(a)(2)(C)). Club dues are not deductible (Code Sec. 274(a)(3)).

Deductions for tickets to entertainment and sporting events are subject to two additional rules. First, an expense for seats in a skybox or other luxury box that is leased for more than one event is limited to the sum of the face value of non-luxury box seat tickets for the events. Second, the expense that is taken into account for a ticket to an entertainment event or facility cannot exceed the face value of the ticket (so, for instance, additional payments to scalpers or other resellers are not taken into account). However, this limit does not apply to tickets to a charitable sporting event. A charitable sporting event is one that benefits a Section 501(c)(3) tax-exempt organization, and for which volunteers perform substantially all of the work (Code Sec. 274(l)).

The deduction for entertainment is generally limited to 50 percent of the expense, but there are several exceptions, including: (a) certain entertainment expenses for goods, services, and facilities that are treated as compensation to an employee-recipient; (b) expenses for recreational, social, or similar activities and related facilities primarily for the benefit of employees who are not highly compensated employees; (c) expenses for entertainment available to the general publicers; and (d) entertainment expenses for goods, services, and facilities that are includible in the gross income of a non-employee recipient as compensation for services rendered or as a prize or award (Code Sec. 274(e) and (n)).

Entertainment expense deductions must satisfy strict substantiation requirements. The taxpayer must show (a) the amount of the expense; (b) the time and place of the entertainment; (c) the business purpose of the expense, and (d) the business relationship with the persons entertained (Code Sec. 274(d)).

Transportation and commuting benefits. The cost of traveling between an individual's residence and work location is almost always a nondeductible personal com-

BACKGROUND

muting expense rather than a deductible business expense (Reg. §§1.162-2(e) and 1.262-1(b)(5)). However, an employer may deduct qualified transportation fringe benefits that are excludable from the employee's income (Code Sec. 132(a)(5)).

A qualified transportation fringe is (a) transportation in a commuter highway vehicle (most commonly a van pool) between the employee's residence and workplace; (b) a transit pass; (c) qualified parking; or (d) a qualified bicycle commuting reimbursement. For 2017, the employee's exclusion is limited to $255 per month for aggregated highway vehicle transport and transit passes, or for qualified parking benefits ($260 per month for 2018) (Rev. Proc. 2016-55 and Rev. Proc. 2017-58). The maximum exclusion for bicycle commuting reimbursements is $20 per month (Code Sec. 132(f)). Thus, these transportation fringes can defray a significant amount of an employee's commuting expenses and increase the employer's deductible business expenses, all without increasing the employee's income.

Employer-provided meals. In certain situations, an employer may deduct expenses for meals it provides to employees, and the employees may exclude the value of the meals from gross income. For instance, if an employer provides meals to employees and their spouses and dependents for the employer's convenience and on the employer's business premises, the value of the meals is excludable from the employee's income (Code Sec. 119(a)). The employer can claim a business expense deduction, but it is subject to the general rule that limits deductions for food and beverages to 50 percent of the expense (Code Sec. 274(n); IRS Chief Counsel Advice 201151020).

In contrast, employer-provided meals are fully deductible if they are de minimis fringe benefits. De minimis fringes are benefits that are so small as to make accounting for them unreasonable or impractical. An employer's operation of an eating facility for employees is a de minimis fringe benefit if (a) the facility is located at or near the employer's business premises, and (b) revenue derived from the facility normally equals or exceeds its direct operating costs. De minimis fringe benefits are excludable from the employee's income (Code Sec. 132(e)). The employer may deduct the full cost of de minimis fringe meals because they are exempt from the 50-percent limit that applies to most meal expenses (Code Sec. 274(n)(2)(B)).

NEW LAW EXPLAINED

Deductions eliminated for some entertainment, meal and transportation expenses.—Business expense deductions are eliminated or reduced as follows:

- deductions are eliminated for most entertainment expenses after 2017 (Code Sec. 274(a)(1), as amended by the Tax Cuts and Jobs Act (P.L. 115-97));

- deductions are eliminated for transportation and commuting benefits after 2017 (Code Sec. 274(a)(4), as added by the 2017 Tax Cuts Act, and Code Sec. 274(l), as amended by the 2017 Tax Cuts Act); and

- deductions are eliminated after 2025 for employer-provided meals that are excludable from an employee's income or are *de minimis* fringes (Code Sec. 274(o), as added by the 2017 Tax Cuts Act).

NEW LAW EXPLAINED

Entertainment expenses. Entertainment expenses, including expenses for a facility used in connection with entertainment, that are paid or incurred after 2017 generally are not deductible. The exception that allowed deductions for entertainment expenses that were directly related to, or associated with, the active conduct of the taxpayer's trade or business is eliminated (Code Sec. 274(a)(1), as amended by the 2017 Tax Cuts Act).

Since directly-related and associated-with entertainment expenses are not deductible, the following related provisions are also removed: (1) the rules that treated a club as an entertainment facility unless it was used primarily to further, and was directly related to the active conduct of, the taxpayer's trade or business (Code Sec. 274(a)(2)(C), as stricken by the 2017 Tax Cuts Act); (2) the limit on deductions for tickets to entertainment and sporting events, including the special rules for seats in skyboxes and the special exception for charitable sporting events (Code Sec. 274(l)(1)(B), as stricken by the 2017 Tax Cuts Act); and (3) the 50-percent limit on entertainment expense deductions (Code Sec. 274(n)(1)(B), as stricken by the 2017 Tax Cuts Act).

> **Comment:** Some entertainment-related rules do no change. As under current law, club dues and membership costs are not deductible (Code Sec. 274(a)(3)) and when entertainment deductions are disallowed with respect to any portion of a facility, that portion is treated as a personal, rather than a business asset (Code Sec. 274(g)).
>
> Some entertainment expenses also remain fully deductible, including: (1) certain entertainment expenses for goods, services, and facilities that are treated as compensation to an employee-recipient; (2) expenses for recreational, social, or similar activities and related facilities primarily for the benefit of employees who are not highly compensated employees; (3) expenses for entertainment sold to customers; and (4) entertainment expenses for goods, services, and facilities that are includible in the gross income of a non-employee recipient as compensation for services rendered or as a prize or award (Code Sec. 274(e) and (n)(2)(A)). As under current law, these deductions must satisfy strict substantiation requirements; however, the taxpayer will not have to substantiate the time and place of the entertainment (Code Sec. 274(d), as amended by the 2017 Tax Cuts Act).

Transportation and commuting benefits. An employer cannot deduct expenses paid or incurred after December 31, 2017, for any qualified transportation fringe as defined under Code Sec. 132(f) (van pools, transit passes, qualified parking, and bicycle commuting) (Code Sec. 274(a)(4), as added by the 2017 Tax Cuts Act).

An employer also cannot deduct expenses paid or incurred after 2017 for providing any transportation, or any payment or reimbursement, to an employee in connection with travel between the employee's residence and place of employment, except as necessary to ensure the employee's safety. This prohibition does not apply to a qualified bicycle commuting reimbursement (as described in Code Sec. 132(f)(5)(F)) that is paid or incurred after December 31, 2017, and before January 1, 2026 (Code Sec. 274(l), as added by the 2017 Tax Cuts Act).

> **Comment:** Qualified bicycle commuting benefits are includible in the employee's income for tax years beginning after 2017 and before 2026 (see ¶ 615).

¶535

NEW LAW EXPLAINED

Caution: It is not clear how this exception for qualified bicycle commuting benefits will coordinate with the blanket prohibition on deductions for qualified transportation fringes.

Employer-provided meals. No deduction is allowed for amounts that an employer pays or incurs after December 31, 2025, for:

- meals that are excludable from an employee's income under Code Sec. 119(a) because they are provided to employees and their spouses and dependents for the employer's convenience and on the employer's business premises; or

- food, beverage, and facility expenses for meals that are *de minimis* fringe benefit under Code Sec. 132(e) (Code Sec. 274(o), as added by the 2017 Tax Cuts Act).

Comment: The employer's deduction for meal expenses is eliminated only for expenses described in Code Secs. 119(a) or 132(e). Thus, an employer may continue to deduct 50 percent of its expenses for food, beverages, and related facilities that are furnished on its business premises primarily for its employees, such as in a typical company cafeteria or executive dining room (Code Sec. 274(e)(1); Reg. § 1.274-2(f)(2)(ii)).

Practical Analysis: William D. Elliott, Partner at Elliott, Thomason & Gibson, LLP in Dallas, Texas, comments that the Act substantially affects Code Sec. 274 entertainment expenses. Expenses for entertainment activities, membership dues, and expenses for a facility pertaining to entertainment activities are no longer deductible, effective 2018. Also repealed are expenses for qualified transportation fringe expenses and commuting expenses, except for providing safety for employees, effective 2018. Expenses for food and beverage expenses associated with operating a trade or business (meals consumed by employees on work travel) remain deductible.

▶ **Effective date.** The amendments made by this section generally apply to amounts incurred or paid after December 31, 2017 (Act Sec. 13304(e)(1) of the Tax Cuts and Jobs Act (P.L. 115-97)). The amendment related to the elimination of the deduction for employer-provided meals that are excludable by employees or are *de minimis* fringe benefits applies to amounts incurred or paid after December 31, 2025 (Act Sec. 13304(e)(2) of the 2017 Tax Cuts Act).

Law source: Law at ¶5435 and ¶6340. Committee Report at ¶10,450.

— Act Sec. 13304(a) of the Tax Cuts and Jobs Act (P.L. 115-97), amending Code Secs. 274(a), (d), (n), and 7701(b)(5)(A)(iv), and striking Code Sec. 274(l);

— Act Sec. 13304(b), amending Code Sec. 274(n);

— Act Sec. 13304(c), amending Code Sec. 274(a), and adding Code Sec. 274(a)(4) and (l);

— Act Sec. 13304(d), redesignating Code Sec. 274(o) as 274(p) and adding new Code Sec. 274(o);

— Act Sec. 13304(e), providing the effective date.

¶535

¶537   Prohibition on Non-Tangible Personal Property as Employee Achievement Awards

SUMMARY OF NEW LAW

For purposes of employee achievement awards, employers are prohibited from deducting awards that are given in cash, cash equivalents, gift cards, gift coupons, gift certificates, vacations, meals, lodging, tickets to theater or sporting events, stocks, bonds, other securities or similar items.

BACKGROUND

In general, employers may deduct under Code Sec. 162 or 212 the cost of achievement awards given to employees for length of service or for safety achievement, subject to certain limitations (Code Sec. 274(j)). A maximum $400 deduction limit applies on the amount an employer may deduct with respect to all nonqualified employee achievement plan awards (safety and length of service) provided to the same employee. In the case of one or more qualified plan awards (safety and length of service) made to a single employee, the employer's deduction limitation for all such qualified plan awards may not exceed $1,600. All qualified and nonqualified employee achievement awards must meet the following requirements:

- the award must be an item of tangible personal property, other than gift certificates, entitling an employee to choose between receiving merchandise, cash, or a reduction in the balance on an account with the issuer of a gift certificate; and

- the award must be by reason of an employee's length of service achievement or safety achievement.

Work-related prizes and awards are excludable from the recipient's gross income only if they qualify as employee achievement awards (Code Sec. 74(c)(1)). An employee achievement award is an item of tangible personal property that is transferred by an employer to an employee for length of service achievement or safety achievement, awarded as part of a meaningful presentation, and awarded under conditions and circumstances that indicate the payment is not disguised compensation. The exclusion does not apply to awards of cash, gift certificates, or equivalent items (Senate Committee Report for the Tax Reform Act of 1986 (P.L. 99-514)).

NEW LAW EXPLAINED

Non-tangible personal property prohibited as employee achievement award.— The definition of "tangible personal property," for purposes of what is a deductible as an employee achievement award is amended to exclude cash, cash equivalents, gift cards, gift coupons, and gift certificates (except an arrangement giving an employee the limited right to select and receive tangible personal property from a limited number of pre-selected or pre-approved items) (Code Sec. 274(j)(3)(A)(ii), as added by the Tax Cuts and Jobs Act (P.L. 115-97)). The term also excludes vacations, meal, lodging,

NEW LAW EXPLAINED

tickets to theater or sporting events, stocks, bonds, other securities, and other similar items. This amendment is not intended to be an inference that present law and guidance is changed (Conference Report on H.R. 1, Tax Cuts and Jobs Act (H. Rept. 115-466)).

> **Practical Analysis:** Brian T. Whitlock, Adjunct Professor in the Gies College of Business at the University of Illinois at Urbana-Champaign, observes that this Act Section attempts to clarify that the deduction limitations under Code Sec. 274(j) relate only to awards of "tangible personal property." Congress was apparently concerned that the term "tangible personal property" was being liberally interpreted. Under this Act Section, cash, gift cards, gift coupons and gift certificates and other similar cash equivalents are specifically excluded. Similarly, the Act Section specifically excludes in-kind gifts such as vacations, meals, lodging, tickets to entertainment events and marketable securities. Awards of tangible personal property continue to be excludable from wages and employment taxes under Code Sec. 74(c), as no change was made in the companion provision.

▶ **Effective date.** The amendments made by this section apply to amounts paid or incurred after December 31, 2017 (Act Sec. 13310(b) of the Tax Cuts and Jobs Act (P.L. 115-97)).

Law source: Law at ¶5435. Committee Report at ¶10,510.

— Act Sec. 13310(a) of the Tax Cuts and Jobs Act (P.L. 115-97), amending Code Sec. 274(j)(3)(A)(i) and adding Code Sec. 274(j)(3)(A)(ii);

— Act Sec. 13310(b), providing the effective date.

¶540 Limitation on Excessive Employee Compensation

SUMMARY OF NEW LAW

For purposes of the limitation on the deduction for employee compensation paid by publicly held corporations, the definition of covered employee is expanded to include both the principal executive officer and the principal financial officer, as well as the other three most highly compensated employees. Employees who are covered employees after December 31, 2016, remain as covered employees for all future tax years. The exclusions from the limitation for commission-based and performance based compensation have been repealed.

BACKGROUND

A publicly held corporation may not deduct applicable employee compensation (remuneration) in excess of $1 million paid to any covered employee for a tax year (Code Sec. 162(m)(1)). The $1 million cap is reduced by excess parachute payments that are not deductible by the corporation (Code Sec. 162(m)(4)(F)).

BACKGROUND

Generally, "covered employees" include the chief operating officer (CEO) of the corporation and the four most highly compensated employees of the corporation other than the CEO, whose compensation is required to be reported to the shareholders by the Securities and Exchange Commission (SEC) under the Securities Exchange Act of 1934 (Code Sec. 162(m)(3); Notice 2007-49). This includes the principal executive officer (PEO), the principal financial officer (PFO), and the three most highly compensated officers other than the PEO or PFO must disclose their compensation.

Compensation subject to the deduction limit generally includes the taxable wages paid to the employee for services performed (Code Sec. 162(m)(4); Reg. § 1.162-27). Types of compensation that are not taken into account in determining whether compensation exceeds the $1 million limit include: specified commissions, compensation based on performance goals, income payable under a written binding contract that was in effect on February 17, 1993, and compensation paid before a corporation became publicly held. Payments excluded from the definition of compensation include: (1) payments to a tax-favored retirement plan (including salary reduction contributions), and (2) amounts that are excludable from the executive's gross income (such as employer-provided health benefits and miscellaneous fringe benefits).

NEW LAW EXPLAINED

Requirements for the limitations on employee remuneration amended.—Effective for tax years beginning after December 31, 2017, the definitions of "covered employee," "compensation," and "publicly held corporation" have been modified for purposes of the limitation on the deduction for excessive employee compensation paid by publicly held corporations.

Covered employee. A covered employee is any employee of the corporation who:

- is the principal executive officer (PEO) of the corporation (or an individual acting in such capacity) at any time during the tax year;

- is the principal financial officer (PFO) of the corporation (or an individual acting in such capacity) at any time during the tax year;

- is among the three highest compensated officers for the tax year (other than the PEO or the PFO); or

- was a covered employee of the corporation (or any predecessor) for any prior tax year beginning on or after January 1, 2017 (Code Sec. 162(m)(3), as amended by the Tax Cuts and Jobs Act (P.L. 115-97)).

> **Comment:** Amendments to Code Sec. 162(m) reflect changes made by to the definition of covered employees made by Notice 2007-49.

Compensation. The exceptions for commissions and performance-based compensation are repealed (Code Sec. 162(m)(4), as amended by the 2017 Tax Cuts Act). Applicable employee compensation (remuneration) for tax years beginning after 2017, includes any cash and noncash benefits paid for services, including commissions and performance-based compensation, but does not include:

NEW LAW EXPLAINED

- income from specified employee trusts, annuity plans, or pensions;

- any benefit that is reasonably anticipated to be tax free under the Code;

- income payable under a written binding contract which was in effect on February 17, 1993; and

- compensation paid before a corporation became publicly held (Code Sec. 162(m)(4), as amended by the 2017 Tax Cuts Act).

A covered employee's compensation is still subject to the deduction limit even if it is paid to or includible in the income of another person. This includes compensation paid to a covered employee's estate, a beneficiary of the employee's estate, or to a former spouse (Code Sec. 162(m)(4)(F), as added by the 2017 Tax Cuts Act; Conference Report on H.R. 1, Tax Cuts and Jobs Act (H. Rept. 115-466)).

A transition rule applies to compensation provided pursuant to a written binding contract which was in effect on November 2, 2017, and that is not modified in any material respect on or after such date (Act Sec. 13601(e)(2) of the 2017 Tax Cuts Act). Compensation paid pursuant to a plan qualifies for this exception provided that the right to participate in the plan is part of a written binding contract with the covered employee in effect on November 2, 2017. The fact that a plan was in existence on November 2, 2017 is not by itself sufficient to qualify the plan for the exception for binding written contracts (Conference Report on H.R. 1, Tax Cuts and Jobs Act (H. Rept. 115-466)).

Example: A covered employee is hired by XYZ Corporation on October 2, 2017. One of the terms of her written employment contract is that she is eligible to participate in the company's deferred compensation plan. The written plan provides for participation after six months of employment, amounts payable under the plan are not subject to discretion, and the corporation does not have the right to amend materially the plan or terminate the plan except on a prospective basis. Payments to the executive under the plan meet the binding contract exception even though she was not actually a participant in the plan on November 2, 2017.

The binding written contract exception ceases to apply to amounts paid after there has been a material modification to the terms of the contract. The exception also does not apply to new contracts entered into or renewed after November 2, 2017. For this purpose, any contract entered into on or before November 2, 2017, that is renewed after such date is treated as a new contract. A contract that may be terminated or cancelled unconditionally by either party to the contract is treated as a new contract. However, a contract that can be terminated or cancelled only by terminating the employment relationship of the covered employee is not covered by this rule (Conference Report on H.R. 1, Tax Cuts and Jobs Act (H. Rept. 115-466)).

¶540

NEW LAW EXPLAINED

Practical Analysis: Brigen Winters, Principal at Groom Law Group, Chartered in Washington, D.C., observes that public companies subject to the expanded compensation deduction limit will need to examine whether their outstanding performance awards will satisfy the transition rule for compensation pursuant to a written binding contract in effect on November 2, 2017. Companies will need to pay particular attention to whether performance awards under which the company reserves discretion over payment will qualify for the transition rule.

Publicly held corporations. The $1 million deduction cap for covered employees only applies to publicly held corporations. Effective for tax years beginning after 2017, publicly held corporations include all domestic publicly traded corporations and all foreign companies publicly traded through American depository receipts (ADRs) (Code Sec. 162(m)(2) as amended by the 2017 Tax Cuts Act). According to the Conference Committee Report, publicly held corporations may also include large private C corporation and S corporations that are not publicly traded (Conference Report on H.R. 1, Tax Cuts and Jobs Act (H. Rept. 115-466)).

▶ **Effective date.** The amendments made by this section generally apply to tax years beginning after December 31, 2017 (Act Sec. 13601(e) of the Tax Cuts and Jobs Act (P.L. 115-97)). The amendments do not apply to remuneration which is provided pursuant to a written binding contract which was in effect on November 2, 2017, and which was not modified in any material respect on or after November 2, 2017.

Law source: Law at ¶5295. Committee Report at ¶10,790.

— Act Sec. 13601(a) of the 2017 Tax Cuts Act (P.L. 115-97), amending Code Sec. 162(m)(4), (m)(5), and (m)(6);

— Act Sec. 13601(b), amending Code Sec. 162(m)(3)(A) and (3)(B) and adding Code Sec. 162(m)(3)(C);

— Act Sec. 13601(c) amending Code Sec. 162(m)(2) and (m)(3);

— Act Sec. 13601(d), adding Code Sec. 162(m)(4)(F);

— Act Sec. 13601(e), providing the effective date.

¶545 Deduction for Fines, Penalties, and Other Amounts

SUMMARY OF NEW LAW

Businesses generally may not deduct fines and penalties paid or incurred after December 21, 2017, due to the violation of a law (or the investigation of a violation) if a government (or similar entity) is a complainant or investigator. Exceptions to this rule are available in certain cases where the payment was compensation for damages, compliance with the law, paid to satisfy a court order where the government is not a party, or paid for taxes due.

¶545

BACKGROUND

Fines and penalties paid to a government entity for the violation of any law (including settlement payments) are not deductible business expenses (Code Sec. 162(f)). This includes fines and penalties imposed by federal, state, local, and foreign governments (Reg. § 1.162-21(a)).

The amount of a fine or penalty does not include (1) legal fees and related expenses paid or incurred in the defense of an action in which the nondeductible fine or penalty may be imposed, or (2) court costs assessed against the taxpayer (Reg. § 1.162-21(b)(2)). Compensatory damages, including damages under Section 4A of the Clayton Antitrust Act, which are intended to return the parties to the status quo, do not constitute fines or penalties. Where the payments serve both purposes, the court will decide what purpose the payment is designated to serve (Reg. § 1.162-21(b)).

NEW LAW EXPLAINED

Prohibition of deduction for fines and penalties amended; reporting requirement added.—Fines and penalties paid or incurred after December 21, 2017, except under any binding order agreement entered into before December 22, 2017, are not deductible as business expenses if paid or incurred to, or at the direction of, any federal, state or foreign government or governmental entity due to the violation of a law (or the investigation or inquiry into the potential violation of a law) (Code Sec. 162(f)(1), as amended by the Tax Cuts and Jobs Act (P.L. 115-97). There are certain exceptions to this rule, including:

- amounts paid that constitute restitution (including the remediation of property) for damages due or may be due to the violation (or potential violation) of a law (Code Sec. 162(f)(2)(A)(i)(I), as amended by the 2017 Tax Cuts Act);

- amounts paid to come into compliance with a violated law, or the investigation or inquiry into the violation or potential violation of a law (Code Sec. 162(f)(2)(A)(i)(II), as amended by the 2017 Tax Cuts Act);

- amounts paid to satisfy a court order where the government is not a party (Code Sec. 162(f)(3), as amended by the 2017 Tax Cuts Act); and

- amounts paid for taxes due (Code Sec. 162(f)(4), as amended by the 2017 Tax Cuts Act).

In order for the restitution or compliance exceptions to apply, the payment must be identified as restitution or compliance in a court order or settlement agreement. In addition, restitution for the failure to pay a tax imposed under the Internal Revenue Code, would be deductible only to the extent that deduction for the tax would have been allowable if it had been timely paid (Code Sec. 162(f)(2)(A)(ii) and (iii), as amended by the 2017 Tax Cuts Act.

Nongovernment entities. The following nongovernment entities are treated as governmental entities for purposes of Code Sec. 162(f):

- any nongovernmental entity which exercises self-regulatory powers (including the authority to impose sanctions) in connection with a qualified board or exchange ,

¶545

NEW LAW EXPLAINED

defined in Code Sec. 1256(g)(7) (Code Sec. 162(f)(5)(A), as amended by the 2017 Tax Cuts Act), and

- any nongovernmental entity with self-regulatory powers (including the authority to impose sanctions) that was established by governmental regulations in order to perform an essential governmental function (Code Sec. 162(f)(5)(B), as amended by the 2017 Tax Cuts Act.

Reporting requirements. The officer or employee that has control over the suit or agreement, or the individual designated by the government or entity must file a return with the IRS (Code Sec. 6050X(a) and (c), as amended by the 2017 Tax Cuts Act. This return must state:

- the total amount to be paid as a result of the suit or agreement,
- any amount to be paid for restitution or remediation of property, and
- any amount to be paid for compliance (Code Sec. 6050X(a)(1), as added by the 2017 Tax Cuts Act).

The return must be filed at the time the agreement is entered into Code Sec. 6050X(a)(3), as added by the 2017 Tax Cuts Act)

In addition, the individual filing the return must also simultaneously provide a statement to each person or entity that is a party to the suit or agreement. The statement must provide: the name of the government or entity, and the information included in the return that the individual filed with the IRS (Code Sec. 6050X(b), as added by the 2017 Tax Cuts Act).

For the purposes of the reporting requirements, a suit or agreement is defined as:

- a suit that results in a court order in which a government or entity has authority or
- an agreement that is entered into with respect to a violation or potential violation of the law, over which a government or entity has authority.

The amount of the suit or agreement must exceed $600. The IRS may change that amount as necessary to ensure efficient administration (Code Sec. 6050X(a)(2), as added by the 2017 Tax Cuts Act)

Practical Analysis: William D. Elliott, Partner at Elliott, Thomason & Gibson, LLP in Dallas, Texas, comments that the deduction for fines, penalties, and other amounts in Code Sec. 162(f) was amended to provide some exceptions to the general rule of nondeductibility. Payments for restitution or to come into compliance with any law that is identified as restitution, remediation, or compliance oriented are deductible. Several conditions and restrictions apply to the new rules to limit their use. The effective date is date of enactment, but subject to several exceptions.

▶ **Effective date.** The amendments by this section generally apply to amounts paid or incurred on or after December 22, 2017, the date of enactment, except that they will not apply to amounts paid or incurred under any binding order or agreement entered into before December 22, 2017 (Act Sec. 13306(a)(2) and Act Sec. 13306(b)(3) of the Tax Cuts and

NEW LAW EXPLAINED

Jobs Act (P.L. 115-97)). The exception will not apply to an order or agreement requiring court approval unless the approval was obtained before December 22, 2017.

Law source: Law at ¶5295 and ¶6205. Committee Report at ¶10,470.

— Act Sec. 13306(a) of the 2017 Tax Cuts Act (P.L. 115-97), amending Code Sec. 162(f);

— Act Sec. 13306(b)(1), adding Code Sec. 6050X;

— Act Sec. 13306(a)(2) and (b)(3), providing the effective date.

¶550 Deduction for Settlements Paid for Sexual Harassment or Abuse Subject to Nondisclosure Agreements

SUMMARY OF NEW LAW

A taxpayer may not claim a deduction as an ordinary and necessary business expense any settlement or payment made after December 22, 2017, for sexual harassment or sexual abuse if subject to a nondisclosure agreement.

BACKGROUND

Settlement payments made to avoid litigation, including any related attorneys's fees and court costs, are generally deductible as ordinary and necessary business expenses provided the origin and character of the litigation indicates that the cause of action arose from a business activity under the origin of the claim doctrine (*D. Gilmore, SCt.,* 63-1 USTC ¶9285). Accordingly, if the acts that gave rise to the litigation were performed in the ordinary conduct of the taxpayer's business, payments made in settlement of lawsuits are deductible.

NEW LAW EXPLAINED

Elimination of deduction for settlements paid for sexual harassment or abuse subject to nondisclosure agreements.—No deduction may be claimed for any settlement or payment paid or incurred after December 22, 2017, related to sexual harassment or sexual abuse if the settlement is subject to a nondisclosure agreement. Attorney's fees related to such payments or agreements are also not deductible (Code Sec. 162(q), as added by the Tax Cuts and Jobs Act (P.L. 115-97)).

> **Practical Analysis:** William D. Elliott, Partner at Elliott, Thomason & Gibson, LLP in Dallas, Texas, comments that a new Code Sec. 162(q) is added denying deductions for settlement or payments related to sexual harassment or sexual abuse if subject to nondisclosure agreement, effective at date of enactment.

NEW LAW EXPLAINED

▶ **Effective date.** The amendments made by this section apply to amounts paid or incurred after December 22, 2017 (Act Sec. 13307(b) of the Tax Cuts and Jobs Act (P.L. 115-97)).

Law source: Law at ¶5295. Committee Report at ¶10,480.

— Act Sec. 13307(a) of the 2017 Tax Cuts Act (P.L. 115-97), redesignating subsection Code Sec. 162(q) as subsection (r) and inserting the new subsection (q);

— Act Sec. 13307(b), providing the effective date.

¶555 Deduction of Local Lobbying Expenses

SUMMARY OF NEW LAW

The deduction for local lobbying expenses by a taxpayer as an ordinary and necessary business is repealed for expenses paid after December 22, 2017.

BACKGROUND

A taxpayer may claim business deductions for certain types of expenses incurred with respect to legislation of any local council or similar governing body (local legislation) (Code Sec. 162(e)(2)). The deductible expenses relate to:

(1) appearances before, submission of statements to, or sending of communications to, committees or individual members of local legislative bodies with respect to legislation or proposed legislation of direct interest to the taxpayer;

(2) communication of information between the taxpayer and an organization of which he is a member with respect to legislation or proposed legislation of direct interest to the taxpayer or to such organization; and

(3) the portion of membership dues in such an organization which is attributable to the activities described in (1) and (2).

Legislation or proposed legislation is of direct interest to a taxpayer if it is of such a nature that it will, or may reasonably be expected to, affect the taxpayer's trade or business, whether the effect be beneficial or detrimental or immediate. It is not of direct interest to the taxpayer merely because it may affect business in general; however, if it affects the taxpayer's trade or business, it is of direct interest to him even though it also affects other taxpayers or business in general. Not all of the provisions of the legislation or proposed legislation need affect the taxpayer's business; one provision will suffice. Examples of legislation or proposed legislation which meet the direct interest test are those which would increase or decrease the taxes applicable to the trade or business, increase or decrease the operating costs or earnings of the trade or business, or increase or decrease the administrative burdens connected with the trade or business.

NEW LAW EXPLAINED

Deductions for local lobbying expenses repealed.—The deduction for lobbying for local legislation is repealed for amounts paid or incurred after December 21, 2017 (Code Sec. 162(e)(2), as stricken by the Tax Cuts and Jobs Act (P.L. 115-97)). In addition to the elimination of the deduction for local lobbying expenses, the deduction for lobbying for Indian tribal government is also repealed, as an Indian tribal government is treated in the same manner as a local council or similar governing body (Code Sec. 162(e)(7), as stricken by the 2017 Tax Cuts Act).

> **Practical Analysis:** William D. Elliott, Partner at Elliott, Thomason & Gibson, LLP in Dallas, Texas, comments that lobbying expenses for local councils or similar governing bodies, including Indian tribes, is repealed, effective for amounts paid or incurred after date of enactment of the Act. This is an immediate effective date, instead of starting 2018.

▶ **Effective date.** The amendments made by this section apply to amounts paid or incurred on or after December 22, 2017, the date of the enactment (Act Sec. 13308(c) of the Tax Cuts and Jobs Act (P.L. 115-97)).

Law source: Law at ¶5295 and ¶6175. Committee Report at ¶10,490.

— Act Sec. 13308(a) of the Tax Cuts and Jobs Act (P.L. 115-97), striking Code Sec. 162(e)(2) and (7), and redesignating (e)(3), (e)(4), (e)(5), (e)(6), and (e)(8) as Code Sec. 162(e)(2), Code Sec. 162(e)(3), (e)(4), (e)(5), and (e)(6), respectively;

— Act Sec. 13308(b), amending Code Sec. 6033(e)(1)(B)(ii);

— Act Sec. 13308(c), providing the effective date.

¶560 Deduction for Living Expenses Incurred by Congressional Members

SUMMARY OF NEW LAW

The special provision allowing Members of Congress a deduction of up to $3,000 per year of living expenses incurred while on official business in the District of Columbia is repealed.

BACKGROUND

The tax home of a member of the United States Congress is the location of his home within the District from which he or she is elected. Thus, a legislator is allowed to deduct meals and lodging expenses incurred while on official business in the District of Columbia, up to a maximum amount of $3,000 per year (Code Sec. 162(a)). This deduction is in addition to deductible moving expenses.

NEW LAW EXPLAINED

Deduction for living expenses incurred by members of Congress repealed.— Members of Congress may no longer claim the deduction for up to $3,000 per year of living expenses incurred while on official business in the District of Columbia (Code Sec. 162(a), as amended by the Tax Cuts and Jobs Act (P.L. 115-97)).

▶ **Effective date.** The amendment made by this section applies to tax years beginning after December 22, 2017, the date of the enactment (Act Sec. 13311(b) of the Tax Cuts and Jobs Act (P.L. 115-97)).

Law source: Law at ¶5295.

— Act Sec. 13311(a) of the 2017 Tax Cuts Act (P.L. 115-97), amending Code Sec. 162(a);

— Act Sec. 13311(b), providing the effective date.

¶565 Deduction of FDIC Premiums

SUMMARY OF NEW LAW

The deduction for the applicable percentage of Federal Deposit Insurance Corporation (FDIC) premiums paid by banks and other financial institutions with consolidated assets of over $10 billion is limited after 2017. Banks and other financial institutions with more than $50 billion in assets may not deduct the applicable percentage of any FDIC premium paid.

BACKGROUND

In order for a bank and other lending institutions to maintain their status as insured depository institutions, it must make semi annual payments into the deposit insurance fund provided by the FDIC. These assessments are deductible as ordinary and necessary business expenses if the all events test has been satisfied (Rev. Rul. 80-230). For federal income tax purposes, banks are generally taxed as and treated as a C corporation (Reg. § 1.581-1).

NEW LAW EXPLAINED

Limitation of deductions of FDIC premiums.—The deduction of the applicable percentage of FDIC premiums for banks and other financial institutions with over $10 billion in consolidated assets is generally limited (Code Sec. 162(r), as added by the Tax Cuts and Jobs Act (P.L. 115-97)). Banks and other financial institutions with more than $50 billion in assets may not deduct the applicable percentage of any FDIC premium paid.

NEW LAW EXPLAINED

Applicable percentage. The applicable percentage is determined by subtracting $10 billion from the total amount of consolidated assets in a tax year, and the dividing that amount by $40 billion.

> **Example:** Bank X ended the tax year with $26 billion in consolidated assets. No deduction is allowed for 40 percent of FDIC premiums ($26 billion – $10 billion) / $40 billion.

> **Example:** Bank Y ended the tax year with $46 billion in consolidated assets. No deduction is allowed for 90 percent of FDIC premiums ($46 billion – $10 billion) / $40 billion.

Banks with $50 billion or more in consolidated assets may not deduct the entire FDIC premiums. Such institutions have an applicable percentage of 100 percent (Code Sec. 162(r)(3), as added by the 2017 Tax Cuts Act). This provision does not apply to banks and other financial institutions with $10 billion or less in consolidated assets at the end of the tax year (Code Sec. 162(r)(2), as added by the 2017 Tax Cuts Act).

FDIC premiums for this purpose refers to assessments imposed under section 7(b) of the Federal Deposit Insurance Act (12 U.S.C. sec. 1817(b)) (Code Sec. 162(r)(4), as added by the 2017 Tax Cuts Act). The term total consolidated assets in this provision has the same meaning as the term in section 165 of the Dodd-Frank Wall Street Reform and Consumer Protection Act (P.L. 111-203) (Code Sec. 162(r)(5), as added by the 2017 Tax Cuts Act).

Expanded affiliated groups. When determining the amount of consolidated assets held in a bank or financial institution, members of an expanded affiliated group are treated as a single taxpayer (Code Sec. 162(r)(6), as added by the 2017 Tax Cuts Act). An expanded affiliated group is defined under Code Sec. 1504(a), except that the phrase "more than 50 percent" is substituted for "at least 80 percent" in Code Sec. 1504(a)(2). Thus, under Code Sec. 162(r), an expanded affiliated group is one or more chains of includible corporations connected through stock ownership with a common parent that meets the following requirements:

- the common parent must directly own stock possessing more than 50 percent of the total voting power of at least one of the other includible corporations and having a value equal to at more than 50 percent of the total value of the stock of that corporation; and

- stock meeting the 50-percent test in each includible corporation other than the common parent must be owned directly by one or more of the other includible corporations.

Insurance companies and foreign corporations are exempt from the definition (Code Sec. 162(r)(6)(B)(i)(II), as added by the 2017 Tax Cuts Act). Partnerships or entities

NEW LAW EXPLAINED

other than corporations are considered members of an expanded affiliated group if such entity is controlled by a corporation in the group.

▶ **Effective date.** The amendments made by this section apply to tax years beginning after December 31, 2017 (Act Sec. 13531(b) of the Tax Cuts and Job Act (P.L. 115-97)).

Law source: Law at ¶5295. Committee Report at ¶10,740.

— Act Sec. 13531(a) of the 2017 Tax Cuts Act (P.L. 115-97), redesignating subsection Code Sec. 162(r) as subsection (s) and adding (r);

— Act Sec. 13531(b), providing the effective date.

ACCOUNTING FOR BUSINESSES

¶570 Cash Method of Accounting for Small Businesses, Including Exceptions for Inventories, UNICAP, and Small Construction Contracts

SUMMARY OF NEW LAW

The cash method of accounting and other simpler accounting methods have been made available to more taxpayers. Most taxpayers who meet a $25 million average annual gross receipts test will be able to use the cash method, will not be required to apply the inventory or uniform capitalization (UNICAP) rules, and will not be required to use the percentage of completion method for small construction contracts.

BACKGROUND

An accounting method includes both an overall system of accounting and the accounting treatment of any individual item. The accounting method used for tax purposes must clearly reflect income and must be consistently applied (Code Sec. 446(b)). Taxpayers can compute taxable income using the cash receipts and disbursements method or cash method, the accrual method, any other special method allowed under the income tax rules, such as a long-term contract method, or a hybrid method that combines any of the above methods (Code Sec. 446(c)).

Cash method of accounting. The cash method is the simplest of the overall accounting methods (Code Sec. 446(c)(1)). Under the cash method, taxpayers report income in the year in which it is received in the form of cash, property, or services with a determinable value. Cash-method taxpayers take deductions and credits in the year in which the expenses are actually paid, unless a special rule requires the expenses to be taken in a different year to clearly reflect income (Reg. § 1.446-1(c)(1)(i)).

Certain taxpayers cannot use the cash method for tax purposes and must adopt the accrual method. Under the general rule, entities that cannot use the cash method are:

BACKGROUND

(1) C corporations, (2) partnerships that have one or more C corporations as a partner or partners, (3) tax shelters, and (4) certain trusts subject to tax on unrelated business income (Code Sec. 448(a)). However, despite the general rule, C corporations and partnerships that have one or more C corporations as a partner or partners can use the cash method if they meet a $5 million gross receipts test, are farming businesses, or are qualified personal service corporations.

In addition, the cash method cannot be used by a taxpayer if the purchase, production, or sale of merchandise is an income-producing factor. In that case, the taxpayer must keep inventories and use the accrual method for the inventory items (Reg. § § 1.446-1(c)(2) and 1.471-1).

Large farming corporations. Large C corporations and partnerships with a C corporation partner that are engaged in the trade or business of farming are generally required to use the accrual method (Code Sec. 447(a)). Farming C corporations and farming partnerships with a C corporation partner that meet a $1 million gross receipts test and family farming C corporations that meet a $25 million gross receipts test are not required to use the accrual method and can use the cash method instead (Code Sec. 447(d)). Exceptions to the required use of the accrual method also apply for certain types of farming businesses.

A family farming C corporation that is required to change its method of accounting because it does not meet the $25 million gross receipts test must compute a Code Sec. 481 adjustment and include the amount in income over a period of 10 years, beginning with the year of the accounting method change (Code Sec. 447(f) and (i)). Prior to the Taxpayer Relief Act of 1997 (P.L. 105-34), a family farming corporation could avoid the 10-year recognition period by creating a suspense account that deferred recognition of the Code Sec. 481 adjustment indefinitely, pending the termination of the corporation or the happening of certain other events. For tax years ending after June 8, 1997, new suspense accounts could not be established, and existing suspense accounts were gradually being phased out over a period of 20 years (Code Sec. 447(i)(5)).

Businesses with inventory. Businesses must take inventories at the beginning and end of each tax year in which the production, purchase or sale of merchandise is an income-producing factor (Code Sec. 471(a); Reg. § 1.471-1). Although businesses with inventories generally must use the accrual method, certain small businesses do not need to account for inventories and can use the cash method. Small businesses qualify for this exception if they have average annual gross receipts of $1 million or less, or are engaged in certain trades or businesses and have average annual gross receipts of $10 million or less (Rev. Proc. 2001-10 and Rev. Proc. 2002-28).

UNICAP rules. Businesses that produce real or tangible personal property or acquire property for resale must use the uniform capitalization (UNICAP) rules and include the direct costs and a portion of the allocable indirect costs of producing or acquiring property in their inventory costs (Code Sec. 263A). However, businesses may qualify for an exception to the UNICAP rules for personal property purchased for resale if the business has average annual gross receipts of $10 million or less for the preceding three tax years (Code Sec. 263A(b)(2)). This exception does not apply to real property acquired for resale (Reg. § 1.263A-3(b)(1)).

¶570

BACKGROUND

Other exceptions to the required use of the UNICAP rules also apply, including exceptions for costs of raising, harvesting or growing trees, costs of producing animals or producing plants with a preproductive period of two years or less (unless the taxpayer is required to use the accrual method), and qualified creative expenses of freelance authors, photographers and artists (Code Sec. 263A(c)(5), (d)(1) and (h)).

Long-term construction contracts. Taxpayers generally must account for their long-term contracts using the percentage of completion method of accounting (Code Sec. 460(a)). Under the percentage of completion method, taxpayers recognize income from the contract as the contract is completed. The income for the year is equal to the percentage of the contract that was completed multiplied by the gross contract price. The percentage of the contract completed during the tax year is determined by comparing costs allocated to the contract and incurred before the end of the tax year with the estimated total contract costs (Code Sec. 460(b)).

The required use of the percentage of completion method and most of the cost allocation rules for long-term contracts do not apply to small construction contracts, home construction contracts, and residential construction contracts. A small construction contract is any contract for the construction or improvement of real property that: (1) is expected to be completed within the two-year period beginning on the commencement date of the contract, and (2) is performed by a taxpayer whose average annual gross receipts for the three tax years preceding the tax year in which the contract is entered into do not exceed $10 million (Code Sec. 460(e)(1)). In addition to the percentage of completion method, taxpayers can report income from small construction contracts under the completed contract method, the exempt-contract percentage of completion method, or any other permissible method (Reg. § 1.460-4(c)(1)).

Changes of accounting method. Taxpayers cannot change from an established ac-counting method to a different method unless they first obtain the IRS's consent for the change (Code Sec. 446(e)). The IRS has issued procedures that taxpayers must follow in order to receive the IRS's consent for an accounting method change (Rev. Proc. 2015-13). The IRS will grant automatic consent for certain changes in accounting method that are in the IRS's "List of Automatic Changes" (Rev. Proc. 2017-30). Code Sec. 481 adjustments are generally required in order to prevent duplication or omission of income items resulting from the accounting method change.

NEW LAW EXPLAINED

Single gross receipts test added for cash method, inventory, UNICAP, construc-tion contract rules.—A single $25 million gross receipts test has been put in place for determining whether certain taxpayers qualify as small taxpayers that can use the cash method of accounting, are not required to use inventories, are not required to apply the UNICAP rules, and are not required to use the percentage of completion method for a small construction contract (Act Sec. 13102 of the Tax Cuts and Jobs Act (P.L. 115-97)).

> **Comment:** The combined effect of the statutory changes is to replace a number of different gross receipts tests for determining what is a small taxpayer with a single gross receipts test with a $25 million threshold. In nearly all cases, the $25

NEW LAW EXPLAINED

million threshold is a significant increase from the prior thresholds which ranged from $1 million to $25 million. The changes not only increase the number of businesses that will qualify as a small taxpayer but also greatly simplify the gross receipts determinations.

Gross receipts test expanded. The exception to the general limit on the use of the cash method for small businesses is expanded for tax years beginning after December 31, 2017. Under the exception, a C corporation or a partnership with a C corporation partner that meets a gross receipts test can qualify to use the cash method of accounting (Code Sec. 448(b)(3), as amended by the 2017 Tax Cuts Act). A C corporation or a partnership with a C corporation partner meets the gross receipts test for a tax year if its average annual gross receipts for the three-tax-year period that ends with the tax year preceding such tax year do not exceed $25 million (Code Sec. 448(c)(1), as amended by the 2017 Tax Cuts Act). The average annual gross receipts amount of $25 million is adjusted for inflation for tax years beginning after December 31, 2018, using the Chained Consumer Price Index for All Urban Consumers (C-CPI-U) in the cost-of-living adjustment (see ¶125) (Code Sec. 448(c)(4), as added by the 2017 Tax Cuts Act).

> **Caution:** Tax shelters are not allowed to use the cash method even if they meet the gross receipts test (Code Sec. 448(a)(3)).

The steps for the gross receipts test are:

- determine gross receipts for each year in the three-tax-year period;
- compute the average annual gross receipts for the three-tax-year period; and
- determine if the average annual gross receipts for the three-tax-year period are $25 million or less (to be adjusted for inflation for tax years beginning after 2018).

> **Example:** A C corporation wants to determine if it can use the cash method under the expanded gross receipts test for the 2018 tax year. For the three tax years ending with the 2017 tax year, the corporation has gross receipts of $21 million, $26 million and $25 million (tax years 2015, 2016 and 2017, respectively). Its average annual gross receipts for the three-tax-year period are $24 million (($21 million + $26 million + $25 million) ÷ 3). The corporation meets the gross receipts test for 2018.

Comment: Many additional C corporations and partnerships with a corporate partner will be able to use the cash method under the $25 million gross receipts test since the prior test capped the amount of qualifying annual gross receipts at only $5 million.

Comment: The other exceptions to the general limitation on the use of the cash method continue to apply for qualified personal service corporations and taxpayers other than C corporations. Thus, qualified personal service corporations, partnerships without C corporation partners, S corporations, and other passthrough entities are allowed to use the cash method without regard to whether they meet the $25 million gross receipts test if the cash method clearly reflects

NEW LAW EXPLAINED

income and the entity is not a tax shelter (Conference Report on H.R. 1, Tax Cuts and Jobs Act (H. Rept. 115-466)).

A taxpayer making a change in accounting method under the Code Sec. 448 rules limiting the use of the cash method should treat the change as initiated by the taxpayer and made with the IRS's consent for purposes of any Code Sec. 481 adjustment (Code Sec. 448(d)(7), as amended by the 2017 Tax Cuts Act). The special Code Sec. 481 adjustment periods for Code Sec. 448 accounting method changes of up to four years and up to 10 years for a hospital have been eliminated for tax years beginning after December 31, 2017 (Code Sec. 448(d)(7), prior to amendment by the 2017 Tax Cuts Act).

> **Compliance Tip:** Taxpayers make a change of accounting method by filing Form 3115. The taxpayer should follow the IRS procedures for accounting method changes (Rev. Proc. 2015-13 and Rev. Proc. 2017-30).

Use of cash method by large farming corporations expanded. The exception to the required use of the accrual method by large farming C corporations and farming partnerships with a C corporation partner has been expanded. For tax years beginning after December 31, 2017, a farming C corporation or a farming partnership in which a C corporation is a partner can use the cash method if it meets the $25 million gross receipts test of Code Sec. 448(c) (discussed above) (Code Sec. 447(c), as amended by the 2017 Tax Cuts Act).

> **Comment:** Many additional farming corporations and farming partnerships with a corporate partner will be able to use the cash method under the $25 million gross receipts test since the prior test capped the amount of qualifying annual gross receipts at only $1 million.

> **Comment:** Since the test for *family* farming corporations was already set at average annual gross receipts of $25 million, the rules in Code Sec. 447 that applied to *family* farming corporations are no longer needed and have been removed (Code Sec. 447(d), (e), (h) and (i), prior to being stricken by the 2017 Tax Cuts Act). However, the rules under former Code Sec. 447(i) for establishing suspense accounts for Code Sec. 481 adjustments from accounting method changes will continue to apply to any suspense accounts established before the date of enactment (Act Sec. 13102(e)(2) of the 2017 Tax Cuts Act).

A farming corporation or farming partnership with a corporate partner making a change in accounting method under the Code Sec. 447 accounting method rules should treat the change as initiated by the taxpayer and made with the IRS's consent for purposes of any Code Sec. 481 adjustment (Code Sec. 447(d), as amended by the 2017 Tax Cuts Act).

Exception to required use of inventories expanded for small businesses. The exception to the required use of inventories for taxpayers that qualify as a small business has been expanded. For tax years beginning after December 31, 2017, a business is not required to use inventories if it meets the $25 million gross receipts test of Code Sec. 448(c) (discussed above) (Code Sec. 471(c)(1), as added by the 2017 Tax Cuts Act). Any taxpayer that is not a corporation or partnership should apply the gross receipts test as if each trade or business of the taxpayer were a corporation or a

NEW LAW EXPLAINED

partnership (Code Sec. 471(c)(3), as added by the 2017 Tax Cuts Act). Thus, in the case of a sole proprietorship, the $25 million gross receipts test is applied as if the sole proprietorship were a corporation or partnership (Conference Report on H.R. 1, Tax Cuts and Jobs Act (H. Rept. 115-466)).

> **Caution:** Tax shelters that are not allowed to use the cash method do not qualify as small businesses that can avoid using inventories (Code Sec. 448(a)(3); Code Sec. 471(c)(1), as added by the 2017 Tax Cuts Act).

A business that meets the $25 million gross receipts test can use a method of accounting for inventory that:

- treats inventory as non-incidental materials and supplies; or
- conforms to the business's financial accounting treatment of inventories (Code Sec. 471(c)(1)(B), as added by the 2017 Tax Cuts Act; Conference Report on H.R. 1, Tax Cuts and Jobs Act (H. Rept. 115-466)).

A business's financial accounting treatment of inventories is the method of accounting reflected in an applicable financial statement or, if the business does not have an applicable financial statement, in the business's books and records as prepared in accordance with its accounting procedures (Code Sec. 471(c)(1)(B), as added by the 2017 Tax Cuts Act). An "applicable financial statement" is defined in Code Sec. 451(b)(3) (see ¶580) (Code Sec. 471(c)(2), as added by the 2017 Tax Cuts Act).

A taxpayer making a change in accounting method under the exception to the required use of inventories for small businesses should treat the change as initiated by the taxpayer and made with the IRS's consent for purposes of any Code Sec. 481 adjustment (Code Sec. 471(c)(4), as added by the 2017 Tax Cuts Act).

Exception to required use of UNICAP rules expanded for small taxpayers. The exception to the UNICAP rules for small taxpayers that purchase personal property for resale has been expanded. For tax years beginning after December 31, 2017, a taxpayer is not required to apply the UNICAP rules for the tax year if it meets the $25 million gross receipts test of Code Sec. 448(c) (discussed above) (Code Sec. 263A(i)(1), as added by the 2017 Tax Cuts Act). The expanded exception to the UNICAP rules applies to any producer or reseller, other than a tax shelter, that meets the $25 million gross receipts test (Conference Report on H.R. 1, Tax Cuts and Jobs Act (H. Rept. 115-466)).

A taxpayer that is not a corporation or partnership should apply the gross receipts test as if each trade or business of the taxpayer were a corporation or a partnership (Code Sec. 263A(i)(2), as added by the 2017 Tax Cuts Act). Thus, in the case of a sole proprietorship, the $25 million gross receipts test is applied as if the sole proprietorship were a corporation or partnership (Conference Report on H.R. 1, Tax Cuts and Jobs Act (H. Rept. 115-466)).

> **Caution:** Tax shelters that are not allowed to use the cash method do not qualify as small businesses that can avoid the UNICAP rules (Code Sec. 448(a)(3); Code Sec. 263A(i)(1), as added by the 2017 Tax Cuts Act).

> **Comment:** The prior exception to the UNICAP rules only applied to small taxpayers that purchase personal property for resale while the expanded excep-

NEW LAW EXPLAINED

tion to the UNICAP rules applies to any *producer or reseller*, other than a tax shelter, that meets the $25 million gross receipts test (Conference Report on H.R. 1, Tax Cuts and Jobs Act (H. Rept. 115-466)). It also appears that the exception will apply to *real property* acquired for resale.

A taxpayer making a change in accounting method under the exception to the UNICAP rules for small businesses meeting the $25 million gross receipts test should treat the change as initiated by the taxpayer and made with the IRS's consent for purposes of any Code Sec. 481 adjustment (Code Sec. 263A(i)(3), as added by the 2017 Tax Cuts Act).

Small construction contract exception expanded. The small construction contract exception to the required use of the percentage of completion method for long-term contracts has been expanded. For contracts entered into after December 31, 2017, in tax years ending after such date, the exception applies to a construction contract entered into by a taxpayer:

- who estimates at the time the contract is entered into that the contract will be completed within the two-year period beginning on the contract commencement date; and

- who meets the $25 million gross receipts test of Code Sec. 448(c) (discussed above) for the tax year in which the contract is entered into (Code Sec. 460(e)(1)(B), as amended by the 2017 Tax Cuts Act).

A taxpayer that is not a corporation or partnership should apply the gross receipts test as if each trade or business of the taxpayer were a corporation or a partnership (Code Sec. 460(e)(2)(A), as added by the 2017 Tax Cuts Act). Thus, in the case of a sole proprietorship, the $25 million gross receipts test is applied as if the sole proprietorship were a corporation or partnership (Conference Report on H.R. 1, Tax Cuts and Jobs Act (H. Rept. 115-466)).

> **Caution:** The expanded exception for small contraction contracts cannot be applied by a tax shelter that is not allowed to use the cash method of accounting under Code Sec. 448(a)(3) (Code Sec. 460(e)(1)(B), as amended by the 2017 Tax Cuts Act).

If a taxpayer changes its method of accounting based on the small construction contract exception, then:

- the change is treated as initiated by the taxpayer and made with the IRS's consent; and

- the change is made on a cut-off basis for all similarly classified contracts entered into on or after the year of change (Code Sec. 460(e)(2)(B), as added by the 2017 Tax Cuts Act).

Practical Analysis: William D. Elliott, Partner at Elliott, Thomason & Gibson, LLP in Dallas, Texas, comments that the group of taxpayers that may use the cash method of accounting was expanded in several respects. A gross receipts test of $25 million annual gross receipts is added to permit cash method. The types of farming C

NEW LAW EXPLAINED

corporations was expanded to include the $25 million gross receipts test. Professional service corporations with C corporation partners or passthrough entities are entitled to the cash method, apart from the $25 million, if income is clearly reflected. Other liberalizations were enacted on inventory requirements and uniform capitalization rules for $25 million gross receipts taxpayers. Small construction contracts are made exempt from percentage-of-completion accounting method. The general effective date is 2018.

▶ **Effective date.** The amendments made by this section generally apply to tax years beginning after December 31, 2017 (Act Sec. 13102(e)(1) of the Tax Cuts and Jobs Act (P.L. 115-97)). The amendments made by this provision for small construction contracts apply to contracts entered into after December 31, 2017, in tax years ending after such date (Act Sec. 13102(e)(3) of the 2017 Tax Cuts Act).

Law source: Law at ¶5425, ¶5500, ¶5505, ¶5530, and ¶5550. Committee Report at ¶10,330.

— Act Sec. 13102(a)(1)-(4) of the Tax Cuts and Jobs Act (P.L. 115-97), amending Code Sec. 448(b)(3), (c), and (d)(7), and adding Code Sec. 448(c)(4);

— Act Sec. 13102(a)(5), amending Code Sec. 447(c) and (f), striking (d), (e), (h) and (i), and redesignating (f) and (g) as (d) and (e), respectively;

— Act Sec. 13102(b), amending (b)(2), redesignating Code Sec. 263A(i) as (j), and adding new Code Sec. 263A(i);

— Act Sec. 13102(c), redesignating Code Sec. 471(c) as (d) and adding new Code Sec. 471(c);

— Act Sec. 13102(d), amending Code Sec. 460(e)(1)(B), striking (e)(2) and (3), redesignating (e)(4), (5) and (6) as (e)(3), (4) and (5), respectively, and adding new Code Sec. 460(e)(2);

— Act Sec. 13102(e), providing the effective dates.

¶580 Accrual Method of Accounting for Deferral of Advance Payments and Income Based on Financial Accounting Treatment

SUMMARY OF NEW LAW

The income recognition rules for accrual-method taxpayers have been modified. First, amounts are generally included in income no later than when the amounts are included for financial accounting purposes. Second, accrual-method taxpayers can elect to defer including certain advance payments in income until the tax year after the tax year in which the payments were received, subject to limitations.

BACKGROUND

Taxpayers include gains, profits, and other income items in gross income in the tax year received, unless their accounting method requires the items to be accounted for

BACKGROUND

in a different year (Code Sec. 451(a)). Under the cash method, taxpayers report income in the year in which it is actually or constructively received in the form of cash, property, or services with a determinable value (Code Sec. 446(c)(1); Reg. § 1.446-1(c)(1)(i)).

Under the accrual method, taxpayers include items in income when all events have occurred that fix the taxpayer's right to receive the income and the amount can be determined with reasonable accuracy (Code Sec. 446(c)(2); Reg. § 1.446-1(c))(1)(ii)). This means that an item of income is included in gross income on the earliest of when payment is received, when the income amount is due, when the income is earned, or when title has passed. Thus, accrual-method taxpayers who are paid in advance for goods or services that they will provide in the future normally include the advance payments in income when received. Instead of reporting advance payments when they are received, accrual-method taxpayers can use one of two deferral methods to postpone reporting the advance payments to a later time. The methods apply to sales of goods and sales of services and certain goods.

Deferral of advance payments received for sales of goods. Under the deferral method for goods, accrual-method taxpayers can include advance payments for future sales of goods in income when the payments accrue (Reg. § 1.451-5). The method applies to advance payments from: (1) sales of goods held primarily for sale to customers in the ordinary course of the taxpayer's business, and (2) long-term contracts for building, installing, constructing, or manufacturing items uncompleted during the tax year. An accrual-method seller using the deferral method for goods can postpone including advance payments in income until the earlier of:

(1) the tax year in which the payments are properly accruable under the accounting method used for tax purposes; or

(2) the tax year in which the payments are included in gross receipts under the accounting method used for financial reports (Reg. § 1.451-5(b)).

Deferral of advance payments received for services and certain goods. Accrual-method taxpayers who receive advance payments for services to be performed in a later tax year normally include all of the payments in income in the year received. However, a taxpayer can choose to defer including qualifying advance payments in income. A taxpayer using the deferral method for services and certain goods must:

(1) include the advance payment in income in the tax year received to the extent the payment is recognized in revenue in the taxpayer's applicable financial statement or, if the taxpayer does not have an applicable financial statement, to the extent the payment is earned in that year; and

(2) include the remaining amount of the advance payment in income in the following tax year (Rev. Proc. 2004-34).

Under the deferral method, no advance payment can be deferred past the year following the year the payment is received. Thus, all of the advance payment must be included in income by the year following the year received regardless of whether all of the remaining services are provided in that year.

¶580

BACKGROUND

An advance payment for the deferral method for services and certain goods is a payment that: (1) is allowed to be included in gross income for tax purposes in the year it is received; and (2) in whole or in part, is earned in a later tax year or is recognized as revenue on the taxpayer's applicable financial statement in a later tax year (Rev. Proc. 2004-34).

An advance payment must be made for one of the following items:

(1) services;

(2) the sale of goods (for which the taxpayer does not use the deferral method for advance payments for sales of goods (Reg. § 1.451-5(b)(1)(ii)));

(3) the use of intellectual property;

(4) the occupancy or use of property, if the occupancy or use is ancillary to providing services to the property user;

(5) the sale, lease, or license of computer software;

(6) a guaranty or warranty contract related to one of the items listed above;

(7) subscriptions (other than prepaid subscriptions for which an election is made to include them in income over the years that the liability exists under Code Sec. 455);

(8) memberships in organizations (other than prepaid membership dues for which an election is made to include them in income over the years that the liability exists under Code Sec. 456);

(9) an eligible gift card sale; or

(10) any combination of the items listed above.

Advance payments do *not* include rents not listed above, insurance premiums whose recognition is governed by the insurance company rules, payments with respect to financial instruments, payments accounted for under the rules for service warranty contracts (Rev. Proc. 97-38), payments with respect to warranty and guaranty contracts under which a third party is the primary obligor, payments subject to the withholding rules for nonresident aliens or foreign corporations (Code Secs. 1441 and 1442), and payments of property transferred in connection with performance of services (Code Sec. 83).

A taxpayer's applicable financial statement is the first that it has of the following:

(1) a financial statement to be filed with the Securities and Exchange Commission (the 10-K or the Annual Statement to Shareholders);

(2) a certified audited financial statement accompanied by the report of an independent CPA that is used for credit purposes, reporting to shareholders, or any other substantial non-tax purpose; or

(3) another financial statement (other than a tax return) required to be provided to the federal or a state government or agency other than the IRS or SEC.

If the taxpayer does not have an applicable financial statement, the amount earned in the year of receipt must be included in taxable income in that year. The remainder of the advance payment is included in taxable income in the next tax year.

¶580

BACKGROUND

Original issue discount. Code Sec. 1271 is the first of a group of Code sections dealing with how to account for debt instruments with original issue discount (OID). A debt instrument has been issued at a discount if the instrument's stated redemption price at maturity is greater than its issue price. For most purposes, OID will be treated as interest. The holder of a debt instrument with OID will accrue and include the OID in income over the term of the instrument, regardless of when the stated interest, if any, is paid (Conference Report on H.R. 1, Tax Cuts and Jobs Act (H. Rept. 115-466)). Special rules also apply for determining the amount of OID for debt instruments that may be subject to prepayment and to pools of debt instruments where payments on the debt instruments may be accelerated by prepayments.

NEW LAW EXPLAINED

Special rules added on time for including amounts in income.—Two special rules have been added on the proper time for including amounts in income by accrual-method taxpayers. Under the first rule, amounts are generally included in income no later than when the amounts are included for financial accounting purposes (Code Sec. 451(b), as added by the Tax Cuts and Jobs Act (P.L. 115-97)). The second rule allows taxpayers to elect to defer including certain advance payments in income until the tax year after the tax year in which the payments were received, subject to limitations (Code Sec. 451(c), as added by the 2017 Tax Cuts Act). These income recognition rules generally apply to tax years beginning after December 31, 2017 (Act Sec. 13221(c) of the 2017 Tax Cuts Act). However, in the case of income from a debt instrument having original issue discount (OID), the rules apply to tax years beginning after December 31, 2018 (Act Sec. 13221(e)(1) of the 2017 Tax Cuts Act).

Amounts included in income based on financial accounting treatment. For an accrual-method taxpayer, the all-events test is met with respect to any item of gross income if all the events have occurred which fix the right to receive such income and the amount of such income can be determined with reasonable accuracy (Code Sec. 451(b)(1)(C), as added by the 2017 Tax Cuts Act). However, the all-events test with respect to any item of gross income or portion of such item cannot be treated as met any later than when the item of gross income or portion of such item is taken into account in revenue in the taxpayer's applicable financial statement or other financial statement specified by the IRS (Code Sec. 451(b)(1)(A), as added by the 2017 Tax Cuts Act).

Applicable financial statement. A taxpayer's applicable financial statement is:

(1) a financial statement that is certified as being prepared according to generally accepted accounting principles and is:

    (a) a 10-K or Annual Statement to Shareholders that is required to be filed with the U.S. Securities and Exchange Commission (SEC),

    (b) if there is no statement described in (a), an audited financial statement that is used for credit purposes, reporting to shareholders, partners, or other proprietors, or to beneficiaries, or any other substantial non-tax purpose, or

¶580

NEW LAW EXPLAINED

     (c) if there is no statement described in (a) or (b), a financial statement filed with any federal agency for purposes other than federal tax purposes;

  (2) if there is no statement described in (1), above, a financial statement that is made on the basis of international financial reporting standards and is filed with a foreign government agency that is equivalent to the SEC and which has reporting standards that are not less stringent than the SEC standards; or

  (3) if there is no statement described in (1) or (2), above, a financial statement filed with any other regulatory or governmental body specified by the IRS (Code Sec. 451(b)(3), as added by the 2017 Tax Cuts Act).

If the financial results of a taxpayer are reported on the applicable financial statement for a group of entities, the statement is treated as the applicable financial statement of the taxpayer (Code Sec. 451(b)(5), as added by the 2017 Tax Cuts Act).

Allocation of transaction price. In the case of a contract that contains multiple performance obligations, the allocation of the transaction price to each performance obligation is equal to the amount allocated to each performance obligation for purposes of including such item in revenue in the taxpayer's applicable financial statement (Code Sec. 451(b)(4), as added by the 2017 Tax Cuts Act).

Exceptions to financial statement rule. The rule for including amounts in income no later than they are included for financial accounting purposes does not apply to a taxpayer that does not have an applicable financial statement or other financial statement specified by the IRS. In addition, the rule does not apply to any item of gross income in connection with a mortgage servicing contract (Code Sec. 451(b)(1)(B), as added by the 2017 Tax Cuts Act). Income from mortgage servicing rights should continue to be recognized under the current rules where: (1) "normal" mortgage servicing rights are included in income upon the earlier of earned or received under the all-events test and not averaged over the life of the mortgage, and (2) "excess" mortgage servicing rights are treated as stripped coupons and subject to the original issue discount (OID) rules (Conference Report on H.R. 1, Tax Cuts and Jobs Act (H. Rept. 115-466)).

The rule for including amounts in income no later than they are included for financial accounting purposes also does not apply with respect to any item of gross income for which the taxpayer uses a special method of accounting provided under the income tax provisions of the Internal Revenue Code, other than the rules for bonds and debt instruments in Code Secs. 1271—1288 (Code Sec. 451(b)(2), as added by the 2017 Tax Cuts Act). Thus, accrual-method taxpayers apply the applicable financial statement rule before applying the special rules in Code Secs. 1271—1288, which cover the original issue discount (OID) rules and also rules on the treatment of market discount on bonds, discounts on short-term obligations, OID on tax-exempt bonds, and stripped bonds and stripped coupons (Conference Report on H.R. 1, Tax Cuts and Jobs Act (H. Rept. 115-466)).

Accrual-method taxpayers allowed to defer including advance payments in income. Generally, for tax years beginning after December 31, 2017, an accrual-method taxpayer who receives an advance payment during the tax year must either:

NEW LAW EXPLAINED

(1) include the advance payment in gross income for the tax year of receipt; or

(2) make an election to defer the inclusion of the advance payment in gross income with respect to the category of advance payments to which the advance payment belongs (Code Sec. 451(c)(1), as added by the 2017 Tax Cuts Act).

Under the deferral election, any portion of the advance payment that is required to be included in gross income under the financial statement rule described above would be included in gross income in the tax year in which it is received and the remaining portion of the advance payment would be included in gross income in the tax year following the tax year in which it is received (Code Sec. 451(c)(1)(B), as added by the 2017 Tax Cuts Act). An item of gross income is received by the taxpayer if it is actually or constructively received, or if it is due and payable to the taxpayer (Code Sec. 451(c)(4)(C), as added by the 2017 Tax Cuts Act).

> **Comment:** The new rule for deferring advance payments from income essentially codifies IRS guidance in Rev. Proc. 2004-34 on deferral of advance payments with some modifications.

Advance payment defined. An advance payment is any payment:

(1) the full inclusion of which in the taxpayer's gross income for the tax year of receipt is a permissible method of accounting without regard to this advance payment rule;

(2) any portion of which is included in revenue by the taxpayer in a 10-K or Annual Statement to Shareholders that is required to be filed with the U.S. Securities and Exchange Commission (SEC) or an audited financial statement that is used for credit purposes, reporting to shareholders, partners, or other proprietors, or to beneficiaries, or any other substantial non-tax purpose, for a subsequent tax year; and

(3) which is for goods, services, or such items as may be identified by the IRS (Code Sec. 451(c)(4)(A), as added by the 2017 Tax Cuts Act).

An advance payment does not include:

(1) rent;

(2) insurance premiums governed by subchapter L (Insurance Companies);

(3) payments with respect to financial instruments;

(4) payments with respect to warranty or guarantee contracts under which a third party is the primary obligor;

(5) payments subject to Code Sec. 871(a) or Code Sec. 881 (tax on certain amounts received from U.S sources by a nonresident alien or foreign corporation) or Code Sec. 1441 or Code Sec. 1442 (payments subject to the withholding rules for nonresident aliens or foreign corporations);

(6) payments to which Code Sec. 83 applies (property transferred in connection with the performance of services); and

(7) any other payment identified by the IRS for this purpose (Code Sec. 451(c)(4)(B), as added by the 2017 Tax Cuts Act).

NEW LAW EXPLAINED

For purposes of the advance payment rules, rules similar to the allocation of transaction price rules of Code Sec. 451(b)(4), above, apply (Code Sec. 451(c)(4)(D), as added by the 2017 Tax Cuts Act). Thus, if advance payments are received for a combination of services, goods, or other specified items, the taxpayer should allocate the transaction price according to the allocation made in the taxpayer's applicable financial statement (Conference Report on H.R. 1, Tax Cuts and Jobs Act (H. Rept. 115-466)).

Unless otherwise provided by the IRS, the deferral election for advance payments will not apply to advance payments received by a taxpayer during a tax year if the taxpayer ceases to exist during or with the close of such tax year (Code Sec. 451(c)(3), as added by the 2017 Tax Cuts Act). Thus, any deferred advance payment must be included in gross income if the taxpayer ceases to exist (Conference Report on H.R. 1, Tax Cuts and Jobs Act (H. Rept. 115-466)).

How to elect to defer inclusion of advance payments in income. The IRS is instructed to provide details on making the election to defer the inclusion of advance payments in income. This includes the time, form and manner, and the categories of advance payments. The election will be effective for the tax year with respect to which it is first made and for all subsequent tax years, unless the taxpayer obtains the IRS's consent to revoke the election (Code Sec. 451(c)(2), as added by the 2017 Tax Cuts Act).

Change of accounting method. The computation of taxable income under the deferral election for advance payments is treated as a method of accounting (Code Sec. 451(c)(2)(B), as added by the 2017 Tax Cuts Act). In the case of any qualified change of accounting method for the taxpayer's first tax year beginning after December 31, 2017, the change is treated as initiated by the taxpayer and made with the IRS's consent. A qualified change of accounting method is any change of accounting method that is required by the new income recognition rules or was prohibited and is now permitted under the new rules (Act Sec. 13221(d) of the 2017 Tax Cuts Act). For a qualified change of accounting method involving income from a debt instrument with original issue discount (OID), taxpayers should use a six-year period for taking into account any required Code Sec. 481 adjustments (Act Sec. 13221(e)(2) of the 2017 Tax Cuts Act).

▶ **Effective date.** The amendments made by this section generally apply to tax years beginning after December 31, 2017 (Act Sec. 13221(c) of the Tax Cuts and Jobs Act (P.L. 115-97)). In the case of income from a debt instrument having original issue discount (OID), the amendments made by this section apply to tax years beginning after December 31, 2018 (Act Sec. 13221(e)(1) of the 2017 Tax Cuts Act).

Law source: Law at ¶5510. Committee Report at ¶10,410.

— Act Sec. 13221(a) of the Tax Cuts and Jobs Act (P.L. 115-97), redesignating Code Sec. 451(b) through (i) as (c) through (j), respectively, and adding new (b);

— Act Sec. 13221(b), redesignating Code Sec. 451(c) through (j) (as redesignated by Act Sec. 13221(a)), as (d) through (k), respectively, and adding new (c);

— Act Sec. 13221(d).

— Act Sec. 13221(c) and (e)(1), providing the effective dates.

¶580

BUSINESS TAX CREDITS

¶585 Employer Credit for Paid Family and Medical Leave

SUMMARY OF NEW LAW

Eligible employers are entitled to claim a credit for paid family and medical leave equal to 12.5 percent of wages paid to qualifying employees during any period in which such employees are on leave under the Family and Medical Leave Act (FMLA) provided that the rate of payment is 50 percent of the wages normally paid to the employee. The credit is part of the general business credit and only available for wages paid in tax years beginning after December 31, 2017, and before January 1, 2020.

BACKGROUND

The Family and Medical Leave Act of 1993 (P.L. 103-3) requires an employer with 50 or more employees (within a 75 mile radius) to give eligible employees 12 weeks of unpaid leave for births, adoptions, and family illnesses. An employer is required to provide coverage for: (a) the birth of a child; (b) the placement of a child with the employee for adoption or foster care; (c) the employee to care for a seriously ill child, spouse or parent; and (d) an employee's own serious illness. An employer may require that a request for leave be supported by certification issued by the health care provider for the applicable party. Spouses who are employed by the same employer may be limited to an aggregate of 12 weeks if leave is sought for a birth, adoption, or to care for an ill parent.

In order to be eligible, an employee must have worked at least one year for the employer providing coverage. During that period, the employee must have worked at least 1,250 hours. Generally, an employer is entitled to 30 days' notice of an employee's intent to take leave if the leave is "foreseeable," such as for the birth or adoption of a child. However, the 30-day requirement is relaxed for unforeseen circumstances (e.g., a premature birth or a sudden change in medical condition).

An employer who provides health care coverage to employees is required to continue that coverage during the leave period. Health care coverage must be maintained at the level and under the conditions coverage would have been provided if the employee had continued being employed. If the employee fails to return to work at the end of 12 weeks for reasons other than the continued serious illness of the employee or another family member that necessitated the leave initially, the employer may recover the premium paid for maintenance of coverage during the leave period.

An employer is required to guarantee that employees will be allowed to return to the same, or an equivalent, job upon their return to work. Eligible employees retain all accrued benefits while on leave; however, they are not entitled to the accrual of any

BACKGROUND

seniority or employment benefits during the period of leave. An employer does not receive a tax credit for compensation paid to employees while on leave.

NEW LAW EXPLAINED

Employer credit for paid family and medical leave provided.—A tax credit is available for employers for paid leave provided under the Family and Medical Leave Act (FMLA) after 2017. An eligible employer is allowed the FMLA credit in an amount equal to the applicable percentage of the wages paid to qualifying employees during the period in which such employees are on leave (Code Sec. 45S(a)(1), as added by the Tax Cuts and Jobs Act (P.L. 115-97)). Applicable percentage means 12.5 percent increased (but not above 25 percent) by 0.25 percentage points for each percentage point by which the rate of payment exceeds 50 percent (Code Sec. 45S(a)(2), as added by the 2017 Tax Cuts Act).

> **Caution:** The FMLA credit is only available with respect to wages paid in tax years beginning in 2018. Wages incurred but unpaid in a tax year beginning in 2018 do not qualify for the credit (Act Sec. 13403(e) of the 2017 Tax Cuts Act). In addition, the credit terminates after 2019 and therefore may not be claimed to wages paid in tax years beginning after 2019 Code Sec. 45S(i), as added by the 2017 Tax Cuts Act).

The FMLA credit allowed with respect to any employee for any tax year shall not exceed an amount equal to the product of:

- the normal hourly wage rate of the employee for each hour (or fraction thereof) of actual services performed for the employer; and

- the number of hours (or fraction thereof for which the leave under FMLA is taken) (Code Sec. 45S(b)(1), as added by the 2017 Tax Cuts Act).

If an employee is not paid an hourly wage rate, the wages of such an employee should be prorated to an hourly wage rate in accordance with regulations established by the IRS (Code Sec. 45S(b)(2), as added by the 2017 Tax Cuts Act). The maximum amount of leave subject to the credit for any employee for any tax year may not exceed 12 weeks (Code Sec. 45S(b)(3), as added by the 2017 Tax Cuts Act).

Eligible employer. An eligible employer for purposes of the FMLA credit is an employer that has a written policy in place that meets the following requirements:

- The policy provides: (a) in the case of a qualifying employee who is not a part-time employee, not less than 2 weeks of annual paid FMLA leave, and (b) in the case of a qualifying employee who is a part-time employee, annual paid FMLA leave that is not less than an amount which bears the same ratio to the amount of annual paid FML that is provided to a qualified employee who is not part-time as (i) the number of hours the employee is expected to work during any week, over (ii) the number of hours an equivalent qualifying employee who is not part-time is expected to work during the week.

¶585

NEW LAW EXPLAINED

- The policy requires that the rate of payment under the program is not less than 50 percent of the wages normally paid to the employee for services performed for the employer (Code Sec. 45S(c)(1), as added by the 2017 Tax Cuts Act).

An "added employer" is not treated as an eligible employer unless the employer provides FMLA leave that conforms with a written policy that ensures that the employer (i) will not interfere with, restrain, or deny the exercise of or the attempt to exercise, any right provided under the policy, and (ii) will not discharge or in any other manner discriminate against any individual for opposing any practice prohibited by the policy (Code Sec. 45S(c)(2)(A), as added by the 2017 Tax Cuts Act). An "added employee" is defined as a qualifying employee who is not covered by Title I of the FMLA (P.L. 103-3) (Code Sec. 45S(c)(2)(B)(i), as added by the 2017 Tax Cuts Act). An "added employer" is defined to mean an eligible employer whether or not covered by Title I of the FMLA, who offers paid family and medical leave to added employees (Code Sec. 45S(c)(2)(B)(ii), as added by the 2017 Tax Cuts Act).

Entities that are treated as a single employer under Code Secs. 52(a) and (b) are treated as a single taxpayer for purposes of the FMLA credit (Code Sec. 45S(c)(3), as added by the 2017 Tax Cuts Act). In addition, any leave that is paid by a state or local government or is required by state or local law is not considered in determining the amount of paid FMLA leave that is provided by the employer (Code Sec. 45S(c)(4), as added by the 2017 Tax Cuts Act). Failure to provide paid family and medical leave by an employer will not subject an employer to any penalty, liability, or other consequence, except that the employer is not eligible to take the FMLA credit (Code Sec. 45S(c)(5), as added by the 2017 Tax Cuts Act).

Qualifying employee. A qualifying employee for purpose of the FMLA credit is any employee, which is defined in section 3(e) of the Fair Labor Standard Act of 1938, who has been employed by the employer for at least one year. In addition, the employee must have received in the preceding year compensation not in excess of an amount equal to 60 percent of the amount applicable for a highly-compensated employee under the nondiscrimination requirements rules for qualified retirement plans (Code Sec. 45S(d), as added by the 2017 Tax Cuts Act).

> **Comment:** The nondiscrimination requirements for qualified retirement plans provide that an employee is generally considered highly compensated if he or she: (1) was a five-percent owner at any time during the current or preceding year, or (2) had compensation from the employer for the preceding year in excess of $120,000 for 2018 (Code Sec. 414(q)(1)(B)(i); Notice 2017-64). Thus, a qualifying employee for purposes of the FMLA credit must not have received more than $72,000 in compensation in 2018 (60 percent × $120,000).

FMLA leave. Family and medical leave is defined as leave for any one or more purposes described in Sections 102(a)(1)(A)-(E) or (3) of the FMLA, whether that leave is provided under the Act or due to an employer's policy (Code Sec. 45S(e)(1), as added by the 2017 Tax Cuts Act). An eligible employee is entitled to FMLA leave under the following circumstances:

- the birth of a child of the employee and in order to care for such child;
- the placement of a child for adoption or foster care;

NEW LAW EXPLAINED

- a serious health condition of a spouse, child, or parent requiring the employee to care for such person;
- the employee's serious health condition that makes the employee unable to perform the functions of the employee's position;
- any "qualifying exigency" arising out of the fact that the employee's spouse, child, or parent is a military member on covered active duty or call to covered active duty status; or
- to care for a covered service member with a serious injury or illness.

If the employer provides paid leave as vacation leave, personal leave, or medical or sick leave (other than leave specifically for one or more of the purposes referred to above), that paid leave is not considered FMLA leave (Code Sec. 45S(e)(2), as added by the 2017 Tax Cuts Act).

IRS determinations. Determinations as to whether an employer or employee meets the requirements to be an "eligible employer" or "qualifying employee" for the FMLA credit are made by the IRS (Code Sec. 45S(f), as added by the 2017 Tax Cuts Act).

Wages. The term wages for purposes of the FMLA credit has the same meaning as that given in Code Sec. 3306(b), which is generally all remuneration paid for employment, including the cash value of all remuneration, including benefits, paid in any medium other than cash. Wages do not include any amount taken into account for purposes of determining any other business related tax credit (Code Sec. 45S(g), as added by the 2017 Tax Cuts Act).

Election to not claim credit. An employer may elect not to claim the FMLA credit (Code Sec. 45S(h)(1), as added by the 2017 Tax Cuts Act). The election can be made at any time before the expiration of the three-year period beginning on the last day for filing the tax return for the year of the election (without regard to extensions) (Code Sec. 45S(h)(2), as added by the 2017 Tax Cuts Act). The election is made in the manner prescribed by regulations as issued by the Secretary (Code Sec. 45S(h)(2), as added by the 2017 Tax Cuts Act).

The FMLA credit is treated as a component of the general business credit (Code Sec. 38(b), as amended by the 2017 Tax Cuts Act). The credit is allowed as a credit against the alternative minimum tax (AMT) (Code Sec. 38(c)(4)(B), as amended by the 2017 Tax Cuts Act).

▶ **Effective date.** The amendments made by this section apply to wages paid in tax years beginning after December 31, 2017 (Act Secs. 13403(e) of the Tax Cuts and Jobs Act (P.L. 115-97)).

Law source: Law at ¶5055, ¶5080, ¶5440, and ¶6255. Committee Report at ¶10,570.

— Act Sec. 13403(a) of the Tax Cuts and Jobs Act (P.L. 115-97), adding Code Sec. 45S;

— Act Sec. 13403(b), adding Code Sec. 38(b)(37);

— Act Sec. 13403(c), redesignating clauses Code Sec. 38(c)(4)(ix), (x), and (xi) as Code Sec. 38(c)(4)(x), (xi), and (xii) and adding Code Sec. 38(c)(4)(ix);

— Act Sec. 13403(d), amending Code Sec. 280C(a) and Code Sec. 6501(m);

— Act Sec. 13403(e), providing the effective date.

¶585

¶590 Rehabilitation Credit

SUMMARY OF NEW LAW

The 20 percent credit for qualified rehabilitation expenditures with respect to certified historic structures is now claimed ratably over a five-year period. In addition, the 10 percent credit for qualified rehabilitation expenditures with respect to non-historic structures first placed in service before 1936 is eliminated.

BACKGROUND

A rehabilitation credit is available to a taxpayer to encourage the preservation and rehabilitation of older and historic buildings. The credit is equal to the sum of:

- 10 percent of qualified rehabilitation expenditures (QREs) of the taxpayer for qualified rehabilitated buildings that are not certified historic structures; and

- 20 percent of the QREs of the taxpayer for certified historic structures (Code Sec. 47(a)).

Generally, the credit is claimed in the tax year in which the qualified rehabilitated building is placed in service (Code Sec. 47(b)). However, a taxpayer may elect to claim an advance credit for progress expenditures on certain rehabilitated buildings before the property is actually placed in service (Code Sec. 47(d)).

A "qualified rehabilitated building" is a building and its structural components for which depreciation is allowable and that has been substantially rehabilitated and placed in service before the beginning of the rehabilitation. A building is treated as substantially rehabilitated only if the QREs during a 24-month period (60 months for projects completed in phases) selected by the taxpayer and ending within the tax year for which the credit is claimed exceed the greater of the adjusted basis of the building (and its structural components) or $5,000. If the building is not a certified historic structure, it must have been placed in service before 1936. It also must satisfy a wall retention test, under which 50 percent or more of the existing external walls must be kept in place as external walls, 75 percent or more of the existing external walls must be kept in place as external or internal walls, and 75 percent or more of the existing internal structural framework must be kept in place (Code Sec. 47(c)(1)).

A "certified historic structure" is any building (and its structural components) that is (1) listed in the National Register of Historic Places, or (2) located in a registered historic district and certified by the Secretary of the Interior as being of historic significance (Code Sec. 47(c)(3)(A)). Only "certified rehabilitations" on certified historic structures or buildings in a registered historic district qualify for the credit. However, certification is not required to claim the credit for expenditures on buildings in registered historic districts if:

— the building is not a certified historic structure;

— the Secretary of the Interior has certified to the IRS that the building is not of historic significance to the district; and

BACKGROUND

— if certification that the building is not historically significant occurs after the rehabilitation begins, the taxpayer certifies to the IRS it was not aware of the certification requirement at the beginning of the rehabilitation (Code Sec. 47(c)(2)(B)(iv)).

NEW LAW EXPLAINED

Rehabilitation credit limited to certified historic structures; claimed ratably over five years.—The rehabilitation credit is limited to 20 percent of qualified rehabilitation expenditures (QREs) of the taxpayer for qualified rehabilitated buildings and is claimed ratably over a five-year period beginning in the tax year in which the rehabilitated building is placed in service (Code Sec. 47(a), as amended by the Tax Cuts and Jobs Act (P.L. 115-97)). The definition of a "qualified rehabilitated building" remains a building and its structural components for which depreciation is allowable and that has been substantially rehabilitated and placed in service before the beginning of the rehabilitation (Code Sec. 47(c)(1), as amended by the 2017 Tax Cuts Act). However, the building must be a certified historic structure, but any expenditure attributable to rehabilitation of the structure is not a QRE unless it is a certified rehabilitation (Code Sec. 47(c)(2)(B)(iv), as amended by the 2017 Tax Cuts Act). The 10 percent rehabilitation credit for QREs with respect to qualified rehabilitated buildings placed in service before 1936 that are not certified historic structures is eliminated.

> **Compliance Tip:** The rehabilitation credit is part of the investment credit that a taxpayer claims on Form 3468, Investment Credit.

> **State Tax Consequences:** States with historic building rehabilitation credits that incorporate federal law for purposes of determining eligibility and/or credit amounts will be affected by the changes to Code Sec. 47. For example, Maine allows a credit for QREs incurred for a certified historic structure in the state that is equal to the taxpayer's federal rehabilitation credit (limited to $100,000 annually per taxpayer). Therefore, any change in a taxpayer's federal rehabilitation credit resulting from the Code Sec. 47 amendments will also have a corresponding effect on the taxpayer's Maine credit. In addition, taxpayers in Wisconsin, which adopts the federal definitions of qualified rehabilitated buildings and qualified rehabilitation expenditures for its historic rehabilitation credit, may gain or lose eligibility for the state credit because of changes to Code Sec. 47.

▶ **Effective date.** The amendments made by this provision generally apply to amounts paid or incurred after December 31, 2017 (Act Sec. 13402(c)(1) of the Tax Cuts and Jobs Act (P.L. 115-97)). Under a transition rule, in case of qualified rehabilitation expenditures (for either a certified historic structure or a pre-1936 building), with respect to any building owned or leased by the taxpayer at all times after December 31, 2017, the 24-month period selected by the taxpayer, or the 60-month period selected by the taxpayer under the rule for phased rehabilitation, begins no later than the end of the 180-day period beginning on the date of the enactment, and the amendments made by the provision apply to such expenditures paid

NEW LAW EXPLAINED

or incurred after the end of the tax year in which such 24-month or 60-month period ends (Act Sec. 13402(c)(2) of the Tax Cuts Act).

Law source: Law at ¶5085 and ¶5260. Committee Report at ¶10,560.

— Act Sec. 13402(a) of the Tax Cuts and Jobs Act (P.L. 115-97), amending Code Sec. 47(a);

— Act Sec. 13402(b), amending Code Secs. 47(c)(1), (c)(2)(B), and 145(d)(4);

— Act Sec. 13402(c), providing the effective date.

¶595 Orphan Drug Credit

SUMMARY OF NEW LAW

The amount of the elective tax credit for qualified clinical testing expenses that are paid or incurred with respect to low or unprofitable drugs for rare diseases and conditions (i.e., the orphan drug credit) is reduced to 25 percent. In addition, taxpayers may elect a reduced credit in lieu of reducing otherwise allowable deductions.

BACKGROUND

A taxpayer that invests in the development of drugs to diagnose, treat, or prevent qualified rare diseases (i.e., those that affect fewer than 200,000 persons in the United States) and conditions can claim a nonrefundable tax credit equal to 50 percent of qualified clinical testing expenses incurred or paid during the development process under Sec. 526 of the Federal Food, Drug, and Cosmetic Act (Code Sec. 45C). The credit is part of the general business credit, and is subject to the limitations, as well as the carryback and carryforward rules, that apply to the general credit (Code Sec. 38(b)(12)).

Other tax credits and deductions claimed by a taxpayer claiming the orphan drug credit are restricted to prevent a double tax benefit for the same expenditure. For example, expenses used to claim the orphan drug tax credit cannot also be used to claim the research and development tax credit. Similarly, a taxpayer that is entitled to the credit may not also claim a deduction for the portion of the qualified clinical testing expenses that exceed the amount of allowable credit (Code Sec. 280C(b)). if the credit exceeds the amount of otherwise deductible clinical testing expenses, the excess may not be charged to the capital account.

NEW LAW EXPLAINED

Orphan drug credit amount reduced to 25 percent; election of reduced credit.— The amount of the orphan drug credit is reduced to 25 percent of qualified clinical testing expenses paid or incurred by a taxpayer for tax years beginning after December 31, 2017 (Code Sec. 45C(a), as amended by the Tax Cuts and Jobs Act (P.L. 115-97)). A

NEW LAW EXPLAINED

taxpayer also may elect a reduced credit amount in lieu of reducing otherwise allowable deductions. In the case of any tax year for which a reduced credit election is made, the amount of the credit will be the amount equal to the excess of: (1) the amount of credit otherwise determined without regard to the reduction, over (2) the product of the credit amount determined and the maximum income tax for a corporation. An election of reduced credit for any tax year must be made no later than the time for filing the taxpayer's return for the year (including extensions). Once made, the election is irrevocable.

> **Practical Analysis:** Charles R. Goulding, President, Energy Tax Savers and R&D Tax Savers in Syosset, New York, comments that the designation of Orphan Drug status came about with the passage of the Orphan Drug Act in January of 1983. The purpose of the enhanced credit is to encourage research related to cures for diseases with small populations that cannot justify the high costs of new drug discovery. Moreover, the compounds derived with Orphan Drug incentives can lead to new drugs applicable to broader populations. Since 1983, there has been a dramatic increase in drugs being designated as Orphan Drugs especially in the last few years. Hopefully, the decrease from a 50-percent credit to a 25-percent credit will not slow this growth trend.

▶ **Effective date.** The amendments made by this section apply to tax years beginning after December 31, 2017 (Act Sec. 13401(c) of the Tax Cuts and Jobs Act (P.L. 115-97).

Law source: Law at ¶5070 and ¶5440. Committee Report at ¶10,550.

— Act Sec. 13401(a) of the Tax Cuts and Jobs Act (P.L. 115-97), amending Code Sec. 45C(a);

— Act Sec. 13401(b), amending Code Sec. 280C(b);

— Act Sec. 13401(c), providing the effective date.

Compensation, Retirement, Education and Disability Benefits

6

COMPENSATION

COMPENSATION

¶605 Qualified Equity Grants

SUMMARY OF NEW LAW

Employees who are granted stock options are able to elect to defer recognition of income for up to five years. The election is not available to certain executives, highly compensated officers, and "one-percent owners" of the corporation. The corporation must maintain a written plan under which at least 80 percent of all employees providing services to the corporation are granted stock options with the same rights and privileges.

¶605

BACKGROUND

Specific income tax rules apply to property, including employer stock, that is transferred to an employee in connection with the performance of services (Code Sec. 83). These rules control the timing and the amount of the compensation that is recognized by the employee and deducted by the employer. Property includes real and personal property, other than money or an unfunded and unsecured promise to pay money in the future (Reg. § 1.83-3(e)).

If property is transferred in connection with the performance of services, the person who performed the services must include the excess of the fair market value of the property over any amount paid for the property in his or her gross income in the first tax year in which the property becomes substantially vested (Code Sec. 83(a)). Property is substantially vested if the rights of the person having the beneficial interest in the property are not subject to a substantial risk of forfeiture, or are freely transferable, whichever is applicable (Reg. § 1.83-3(b)). In general, an employee's right to stock or other property is subject to a substantial risk of forfeiture if the employee's right to full enjoyment of the property is subject to a condition, such as the future performance of substantial services. An employee's right to stock or other property is transferable if the employee can transfer an interest in the property to any person other than the transferor of the property (Code Sec 83(c)(1); Reg. § 1.83-3(c)).

> **Comment:** Under this rule, if the employee's right to the stock is substantially vested when the stock is transferred to the employee, the employee recognizes income in the tax year of the transfer, equal to the fair market value of the stock as of the transfer date (less any amount paid for the stock). If the employee's right to the stock is not substantially vested (i.e., is "nonvested") at the time of transfer, the employee does not recognize income attributable to the stock transfer until the tax year in which his or her right becomes substantially vested. In this case, the amount includible in the employee's income is the fair market value of the stock as of the date that the employee's right to the stock is substantially vested, less any amount paid for the stock.

A person who receives property (including employer stock) in connection with the performance of services can elect to have the excess of the fair market value of the restricted property over his or her cost included in gross income and taxed in the year the property is received, even though the property remains substantially nonvested (Code Sec. 83(b)). The election must be made no later than 30 days after the property is transferred (Reg. § 1.83-2(b)). If a proper and timely election under Code Sec. 83(b) is made, the amount of compensatory income is capped at the fair market value of the property as of the transfer date (less any amount paid for the property). Once made, the restricted property election cannot be revoked without IRS consent..

In the case of employer stock transferred to an employee, the employer is allowed a deduction (to the extent a deduction for a business expense is otherwise allowable) equal to the amount included in the employee's income as a result of transfer of the stock (Code Sec 83(h)). The employer deduction generally is permitted in the employer's tax year in which or with which ends the employee's tax year when the amount is included and properly reported in the employee's income (Reg. § 1.83-6).

¶605

BACKGROUND

The Code Sec. 83 rules—including the Code Sec. 83(b) election—are available for grants of "restricted stock" (nonvested stock), but do not generally apply to the grant of options on employer stock unless the option has a readily ascertainable fair market value (Code Sec. 83(e)(3); Reg. § 1.83-7).

Employment taxes and reporting. Unless an exception applies under the applicable rules, compensation provided to an employee constitutes wages subject to employment taxes: namely, the Federal Insurance Contributions Act (FICA) tax (i.e., Social Security tax), the Federal Unemployment Tax Act (FUTA) tax (i.e., unemployment tax), and income taxes required to be withheld from wages by employers. "Wages" generally means all remuneration for services performed by an employee for his or her employer, including the cash value of all remuneration (including benefits) paid in any medium other than cash (including employer stock) (see Code Sec. 3401).

An employer must furnish a statement of compensation information to each employee for a calendar year, including taxable compensation, FICA wages, and withheld income and FICA taxes (Code Sec. 6051). Information relating to certain nontaxable items must also be reported, such as certain retirement and health plan contributions. The employer makes the statement on Form W-2, Wage and Tax Statement, which the employer must furnish to the employee, and file with the Social Security Administration, by January 31 of the succeeding year.

Statutory options. Two types of statutory options apply with respect to employer stock: incentive stock options (ISOs) and options provided under an employee stock purchase plan (ESPP) (Code Secs. 421—424). Stock received by a statutory option is subject to special rules, rather than the rules for nonqualified options. No amount is includible in an employee's income on the grant, vesting, or exercise of a statutory option. In addition, generally no deduction is allowed to the employer regarding the option or the stock transferred to an employee.

Employment taxes do not apply to the grant or vesting of a statutory option, the transfer of stock pursuant to the option, or a disposition of the stock. However, certain special reporting requirements apply (Code Secs. 421(b), 3121(a)(22), and 3306(b)(19)).

Nonqualified deferred compensation. Compensation is generally includible in an employee's income when paid to the employee. However, in the case of a nonqualified deferred compensation plan, the amount of deferred compensation is first includible in income for the tax year when it is not subject to a substantial risk of forfeiture (unless the arrangement either is exempt from or meets the requirements of Code Sec. 409A) (Reg. § 1.409A-1(d)). This is so even if payment will not occur until a later year. In general, to meet the requirements of Code Sec. 409A, the time when nonqualified deferred compensation will be paid, and the amount paid must be specified at the time of deferral, with limits on further deferral after the time for payment. Various other requirements apply, including that payment can only occur on specific defined events.

Various exemptions from Code Sec. 409A apply, including transfers of property subject to Code Sec. 83. Nonqualified options may be structured so as not to be considered nonqualified deferred compensation (Reg. § 1.409A-1(b)(5)). A restricted stock unit (RSU) is an arrangement under which an employee has the right to receive

BACKGROUND

at a specified time in the future an amount determined by reference to the value of one or more shares of employer stock. An employee's right to receive the future amount may be subject to a condition, such as continued employment for a certain period or the attainment of certain performance goals. An arrangement providing RSUs is generally considered a nonqualified deferred compensation plan and is subject to the rules and limits of Code Sec. 409A. The employer deduction generally is allowed in the employer's tax year in which or with which ends the employee's tax year when the amount is included and properly reported in the employee's income (Code Sec. 404(a)(5)).

NEW LAW EXPLAINED

Treatment of qualified equity grants.—A qualified employee of a privately held company may elect to defer including in his or her gross income the amount of income attributable to qualified stock transferred to the employee by the employer (Code Sec. 83(i), as added by the Tax Cuts and Jobs Act (P.L. 115-97)). This election is an alternative to being taxed in the year in which the property vests under Code Sec. 83(a) or in the year it is received under Code Sec. 83(b). The election to defer income inclusion for qualified stock must be made no later than 30 days after the first date the employee's right to the stock is substantially vested or is transferable, whichever occurs earlier (Code Sec. 83(i)(4), as added by the 2017 Tax Cuts Act).

If a qualified employee elects to defer income inclusion, the employee must include the income in his or her gross income for the tax year that includes the earliest of:

* the first date the qualified stock becomes transferable, including transferable to the employer;

* the date the employee first becomes an excluded employee;

* the first date on which any stock of the employer becomes readily tradable on an established securities market;

* the date five years after the earlier of the first date the employee's right to the stock is transferable or is not subject to a substantial risk of forfeiture; or

* the date on which the employee revokes his or her inclusion deferral election (Code Sec. 83(i)(1), as added by the 2017 Tax Cuts Act).

The inclusion deferral election is made in a manner similar to that for a Code Sec. 83(b) election. The election is not allowed for income with respect to nonvested stock that is includible in gross income as a result of a Code Sec. 83(b) election (Code Sec. 83(i)(4)(B), as added by the 2017 Tax Cuts Act).

An employee may not make an inclusion deferral election for a year with respect to qualified stock if the corporation purchased any of its outstanding stock in the preceding calendar year, unless (1) at least 25 percent of the total dollar amount of the stock so purchased is stock with respect to which an inclusion deferral election is in effect ("deferral stock") and (2) the determination of which individuals from whom deferral stock is purchased is made on a reasonable basis (Code Sec. 83(i)(4)(B) and (C), as

¶605

NEW LAW EXPLAINED

added by the 2017 Tax Cuts Act). These two requirements are met if the corporation purchases all of its deferral stock (Code Sec. 83(i)(4)(C)(iii), as added by the 2017 Tax Cuts Act).

Stock that the corporation purchased from an individual is not treated as deferral stock (and the purchase is not treated as a purchase of deferral stock) if, immediately after the purchase, the individual holds any deferral stock for which a deferral election has been in effect for a longer period than the election regarding the purchased stock (Code Sec. 83(i)(4)(C)(ii), as added by the 2017 Tax Cuts Act).

Deferred income inclusion applies also for purposes of the employer's deduction of the amount of income attributable to the qualified stock. If an employee makes an inclusion deferral election, the employer's deduction is deferred until the employer's tax year in which or with which ends the tax year of the employee for which the amount is included in the employee's income as described above (Conference Report on H.R. 1, Tax Cuts and Jobs Act (H. Rept. 115-466); see Code Sec. 83(h)).

Qualified stock. Qualified stock is any stock in a corporation that is the employer of the qualified employee if (1) the stock is received in connection with the exercise of an option or in settlement of a restricted stock unit (RSU) and (2) the option or RSU was granted by the corporation in connection with the performance of services as an employee and during a calendar year in which such corporation was an eligible corporation (Code Sec. 83(i)(2)(A), as added by the 2017 Tax Cuts Act).

Qualified stock does not include any stock if, at the time the employee's right to the stock becomes substantially vested, the employee may sell the stock to, or otherwise receive cash in lieu of stock from, the corporation (Code Sec. 83(i)(2)(B), as added by the 2017 Tax Cuts Act). Qualified stock can only be such if it relates to stock received in connection with options or RSUs, and does not include stock received in connection with other forms of equity compensation, including stock appreciation rights or restricted stock (Conference Report on H.R. 1, Tax Cuts and Jobs Act (H. Rept. 115-466)).

A corporation is an eligible corporation for a calendar year if:

- no stock of the employer corporation (or any predecessor) is readily tradable on an established securities market during any preceding calendar year; and

- the corporation has a written plan under which, in the calendar year, not less than 80 percent of all employees who provide services to the corporation in the United States (or any U.S. possession) are granted stock options, or RSUs, with the same rights and privileges to receive qualified stock ("80-percent requirement") (Code Sec. 83(i)(2)(C), as added by the 2017 Tax Cuts Act).

  Comment: Under a transition rule, until the Treasury issues regulations or other implementing guidance, a corporation will be treated as being in compliance with the 80-percent requirement if it complies with a reasonable good-faith interpretation of the requirement (Act Sec. 13603(g) of the 2017 Tax Cuts Act).

In general, the determination of rights and privileges with respect to stock is determined in a manner similar to that under the Code Sec. 423(b)(5) employee stock purchase plan rules. Employees will not fail to be treated as having the same rights

NEW LAW EXPLAINED

and privileges to receive qualified stock solely because the number of shares available to all employees is not equal in amount, provided that the number of shares available to each employee is more than a *de minimis* amount. Further, rights and privileges with respect to the exercise of an option cannot be treated as the same as rights and privileges with respect to the settlement of an RSU (Code Sec. 83(i)(2)(C)(ii), as added by the 2017 Tax Cuts Act). The requirement that 80 percent of all applicable employees be granted stock options or RSUs with the same rights and privileges cannot be satisfied in a tax year by granting a combination of stock options and RSUs, and instead all such employees must either be granted stock options or be granted restricted stock units for that year (Conference Report on H.R. 1, Tax Cuts and Jobs Act (H. Rept. 115-466)).

All persons treated as a single employer under the Code Sec. 414(b) controlled group rules are treated as one corporation (Code Sec. 83(i)(5), as added by the 2017 Tax Cuts Act).

Qualified employees and excluded employees. A qualified employee is an individual who is not an "excluded employee," and who agrees, in the inclusion deferral election, to meet the requirements the IRS deems necessary to ensure that the employer corporation's income tax withholding requirements regarding the qualified stock are met (Code Sec. 83(i)(3)(A), as added by the 2017 Tax Cuts Act).

The deferral election is not available to "excluded employees" of the employer corporation. This is any employee:

(1) who is a one-percent owner of the corporation at any time during the calendar year, or was at any time during the 10 preceding calendar years;

(2) who is, or has been at any prior time, the chief executive officer or chief financial officer of the corporation, or an individual acting in either capacity;

(3) who is a family member of an individual described in (1) or (2); or

(4) who has been one of the four highest compensated officers of the corporation for the tax year or for any of the 10 preceding tax years (Code Sec. 83(i)(3)(B), as added by the 2017 Tax Cuts Act).

Notice, withholding, and reporting requirements. An election to defer income inclusion with respect to qualified stock must be made no later than 30 days after the first time the employee's right to the stock is substantially vested or is transferable, whichever occurs earlier (Code Sec. 83(i)(4), as added by the 2017 Tax Cuts Act).

Employers are required to provide notice to their employees that they are eligible for this election at the time (or a reasonable period before) the employee's right to the qualified stock is substantially vested (and income attributable to the stock would first be includible absent an inclusion deferral election) (Code Sec. 83(i)(6), as added by the 2017 Tax Cuts Act). The notice to the employee must:

- certify that the stock is qualified stock;

- notify the employee that he or she may be eligible to elect to defer income inclusion with respect to the stock; and

- notify the employee that, if he or she makes the election, the amount of income required to be included at the end of the deferral period will be

NEW LAW EXPLAINED

— based on the value of the stock at the time the employee's right to the stock first becomes substantially vested, notwithstanding that the stock's value may have declined during the deferral period (and even if the stock's value has declined below the employee's tax liability with respect to such stock), and

— subject to withholding as provided under the provision, as well as of the employee's required withholding responsibilities.

After December 31, 2017, an employer's failure to provide this notice can result in a fine of $100 for each failure, not to exceed $50,000 (Code Sec. 6652(p), as added by the 2017 Tax Cuts Act).

> **Comment:** Under a transition rule, until the Treasury issues regulations or other implementing guidance, a corporation will be treated as being in compliance with the employee notice requirement under Code Sec. 83(i)(6) if it complies with a reasonable good-faith interpretation of the requirement (Act Sec. 13603(g) of the 2017 Tax Cuts Act).

For withholding purposes, qualified stock with respect to which a Code Sec. 83(i) election is made, will be treated as wages received on the earliest date possible under Code Sec. 83(i)(1)(B) and in the amount included as income (Code Sec. 3401(i), as added by the 2017 Tax Cuts Act). For the tax year for which income subject to an inclusion deferral election is required to be included in income by the employee (as described above), the amount required to be included in income is treated as wages with respect to which the employer is required to withhold income tax at a rate not less than the highest income tax rate applicable to individual taxpayers (Code Sec. 3402(t), as added by the 2017 Tax Cuts Act).

Practical Analysis: Brigen Winters, Principal at Groom Law Group, Chartered in Washington, D.C., observes that under this Act Section a qualifying private company could offer its rank-and-file employees the opportunity to defer income tax inclusion on compensatory stock options or restricted stock units (RSUs) for up to five years. He also notes that the Conference Report language clarifies that to satisfy the requirement that 80 percent of all applicable employees be granted stock options or RSUs with the same rights and privileges, the company must grant either stock options or RSUs for the year and cannot grant a combination of stock options and RSUs. The requirement applies to both new hires and existing employees.

▶ **Effective date.** The amendments made by this section generally apply to stock attributable to options exercised, or restricted stock units settled, after December 31, 2017 (Act Sec. 13603(f)(1) of the Tax Cuts and Jobs Act (P.L. 115-97)). The penalty for the failure of an employer to provide notice of tax consequences to a qualified employee applies to failures after December 31, 2017 (Act Sec. 13603(f)(2) of the 2017 Tax Cuts Act).

Law source: Law at ¶5200, ¶5480, ¶5485, ¶5490, ¶6090, ¶6095, ¶6215, and ¶6275. Committee Report at ¶10,810.

— Act Sec. 13603(a) of the Tax Cuts and Jobs Act (P.L. 115-97), adding Code Sec. 83(i);

— Act Sec. 13603(b), adding Code Sec. 3401(i) and Code Sec. 3402(t);

¶605

NEW LAW EXPLAINED

— Act Sec. 13603(c), amending Code Sec. 422(b) and Code Sec. 423(b)(5), and adding Code Sec. 423(d) and Code Sec. 409A(d)(7);

— Act Sec. 13603(d), adding Code Sec. 6051(a)(16) and (17);

— Act Sec. 13603(e), adding Code Sec. 6652(p);

— Act Sec. 13603(g), providing a transition rule;

— Act Sec. 13603(f), providing the effective date.

¶610 Qualified Moving Expense Reimbursement

SUMMARY OF NEW LAW

The exclusion for qualified moving expense reimbursements is suspended for tax years 2018 through 2025.

BACKGROUND

Qualified moving expense reimbursements are excluded from an employee's gross income. Qualified moving expense reimbursements are amounts received (directly or indirectly) from an employer as payment for (or reimbursement of) expenses that would be deductible as moving expenses under Code Sec. 217 if directly paid or incurred by the employee (Code Sec. 132(g)).

Qualified moving expense reimbursements do not include amounts actually deducted by the individual in a prior year. Amounts excludable from gross income for income tax purposes as qualified moving expense reimbursements are also excluded from wages for employment tax purposes. Only reimbursements made under an accountable plan may be excluded from income. An accountable plan requires the employee to make an adequate accounting to the employer of the moving expenses and to return any excess reimbursements.

> **Comment:** Reimbursements that meet the definition of moving expenses, but are not made under an accountable plan are included in Box 1 of the employee's Form W-2. If the employee is claiming a moving expense deduction because he or she was not fully reimbursed, this amount must be carried to Form 3903, Moving Expenses, to reduce the otherwise allowable expenses.

NEW LAW EXPLAINED

Exclusion for qualified moving expenses reimbursement suspended.—The exclusion for qualified moving expense reimbursements is suspended for tax years 2018 through 2025 (Code Sec. 132(g), as amended by the Tax Cuts and Jobs Act (P.L. 115-97)). However, members of the U.S. Armed Forces on active duty who move pursuant to a military order and incident to a permanent change of station are still

NEW LAW EXPLAINED

permitted to exclude qualified moving expense reimbursements from their income (Code Sec. 132(g)(2), as amended by the 2017 Tax Cuts Act).

> **Practical Analysis:** Brian T. Whitlock, Adjunct Professor in the Gies College of Business at the University of Illinois at Urbana-Champaign, observes that this Act Section would require employers to report any payments or reimbursements made after December 31, 2017, and before January 1, 2026, of employee moving expenses as wages subject to income tax and employment tax withholding. See ¶260 for the companion provision that also removes the employee's ability to claim employee moving expenses as an adjustment to gross income for anyone other than members of the Armed Forces.

▶ **Effective date.** The amendment made by this section applies to tax years beginning after December 31, 2017 (Act Sec. 11048(b) of the Tax Cuts and Jobs Act (P.L. 115-97)).

Law source: Law at ¶5240. Committee Report at ¶10,230.

— Act Sec. 11048(a) of the Tax Cuts and Jobs Act (P.L. 115-97), amending Code Sec. 132(g);

— Act Sec. 11048(b) providing the effective date.

¶615 Qualified Bicycle Commuting Reimbursements

SUMMARY OF NEW LAW

After December 31, 2017, and before January 1, 2026, taxpayers are not permitted to exclude qualified bicycle commuting reimbursements from their income.

BACKGROUND

Employees are permitted to exclude up to $20 per month in qualified bicycle commuting reimbursements (Code Sec. 132(f)(1)(D)). A qualifying bicycle commuting month is any month during which the employee regularly uses the bicycle for a substantial portion of travel to a place of employment and during which the employee does not receive transportation in a commuter highway vehicle, a transit pass, or qualified parking from an employer.

Qualified reimbursements are any amount received from an employer during a 15-month period beginning with the first day of the calendar year as payment for reasonable expenses during that calendar year for the purchase of a bicycle and bicycle improvements, bicycle repair, and bicycle storage, provided that the employee uses the bicycle regularly for travel between the employee's residence and place of employment.

BACKGROUND

Amounts that are excludable from gross income for income tax purposes are also excluded from wages for employment tax purposes. Qualified bicycle commuting reimbursements cannot be funded by elective salary reduction contributions.

NEW LAW EXPLAINED

Exclusion for qualified bicycle commuting reimbursement suspended.—The exclusion from gross income and wages for qualified bicycle commuting reimbursements is suspended for tax years beginning after December 31, 2017, and before January 1, 2026 (Code Sec. 132(f)(8), as added by the Tax Cuts and Jobs Act (P.L. 115-97)).

Practical Analysis: Brian T. Whitlock, Adjunct Professor in the Gies College of Business at the University of Illinois at Urbana-Champaign, observes that this Act Section suspends the Code Sec. 132(f) exclusion from wages and requires employers to report any reimbursements for qualified bicycle commuting reimbursement made after December 31, 2017, and before January 1, 2026, as wages subject to income tax and employment tax withholding. Note: Act Sec. 13304 is the companion provision that also removes the employer's deduction for bicycle commuting as well as any other qualified transportation fringe provided under Code Sec. 132(f) unless necessary to ensure the safety of the employee. Presumably, reimbursing employees for late night transportation expenses would still be deductible under Code Sec. 274 because in large urban areas this transportation expense is necessary for the safety of the employee. See ¶807 for the companion provision that relates to the treatment by tax-exempt organizations of expenses related to disallowed fringe benefits.

▶ **Effective date.** The amendment made by this section applies to tax years beginning after December 31, 2017 (Act Sec. 11047(b)) of the Tax Cuts and Jobs Act (P.L. 115-97)).

Law source: Law at ¶5240. Committee Report at ¶10,220.

— Act Sec. 11047(a) of the Tax Cuts and Jobs Act (P.L. 115-97), adding Code Sec. 132(f)(8);

— Act Sec. 11047(b), providing the effective date.

RETIREMENT PLANS AND BENEFITS

¶620 Recharacterization of IRA Contributions

SUMMARY OF NEW LAW

The special rule that allows a contribution to one type of an IRA to be recharacterized as a contribution to the other type of IRA will no longer apply to a conversion contribution to a Roth IRA after 2017. Recharacterization is still permitted with respect to other contributions. For example, an individual may make a contribution

SUMMARY OF NEW LAW

for a year to a Roth IRA and, before the due date for the individual's income tax return for that year, recharacterize it as a contribution to a traditional IRA.

BACKGROUND

There are two basic types of individual retirement arrangements (IRAs): traditional IRAs, to which both deductible and nondeductible contributions may be made, and Roth IRAs, to which only nondeductible contributions may be made. The principal difference between these two types of IRAs is the timing of income tax inclusion.

Contributions to traditional IRAs and to Roth IRAs must be segregated into separate IRAs, meaning arrangements with separate trusts, accounts, or contracts, and separate IRA documents. Except in the case of a conversion or recharacterization, amounts cannot be transferred or rolled over between the two types of IRAs. A recharacterization election effectively reverses the contribution from one type of IRA to another (e.g., Roth to traditional or traditional to Roth). The contribution being recharacterized is treated as having been originally contributed to the second IRA on the same date and for the same tax year as that in which the contribution was made to the first IRA (Reg. § 1.408A-5).

If on or before the due date for any tax year, a taxpayer transfers in a trustee-to-trustee transfer any contribution to an IRA made during the tax year from that IRA to any other IRA, the contribution is treated as having been made to the transferee plan and not the transferor plan (Code Sec. 408A(d)(6)(A)). This rule is not available unless the amount transferred in a recharacterization is accompanied by any net income allocable to the contribution (Code Sec. 408A(d)(6)(B)(i)). Furthermore, it applies only to the extent no deduction was allowed with respect to the contribution to the transferor plan (Code Sec. 408A(d)(6)(B)(ii))

The election to recharacterize and the transfer of the assets must both take place on or before the due date (including extensions) of the tax return for the year for which the contribution was made for the first IRA. Once a recharacterization election has been made, it cannot be revoked. However, in some situations, the amount may be reconverted at a later date (Reg. § 1.408A-5).

NEW LAW EXPLAINED

Recharacterization of Roth IRA conversions are no longer permitted.—For tax years beginning after December 31, 2017, the special rule that allows a contribution to one type of IRA to be recharacterized as a contribution to the other type of IRA does not apply to a conversion contribution to a Roth IRA. Thus, recharacterization cannot be used to unwind a Roth IRA conversion (Code Sec. 408A(d)(6)(B)(iii), as amended by the Tax Cuts and Jobs Act (P.L. 115-97)).

> **Comment:** Earlier versions of the Tax Cuts and Jobs Act enacted by both the House and Senate eliminated recharacterization entirely. The provision was narrowed considerably in the reconciled version to target only conversions to Roth IRAs. Thus, for example, an individual may still make a contribution for a

NEW LAW EXPLAINED

year to a Roth IRA and, before the due date for the individual's income tax return for that year, recharacterize it as a contribution to a traditional IRA. In addition, an individual may still make a contribution to a traditional IRA and convert the traditional IRA to a Roth IRA, but the individual is precluded from later unwinding the conversion through a recharacterization.

Comment: The strategy behind recharacterizing a conversion hinged on changes in the market price of the IRA assets during the course of the year. The owner pays tax in a conversion based on the value of the assets on the conversion date, so the tax liability is locked in on that date. If the value of the assets goes up significantly, the conversion looks like a shrewd move because the tax bill would have been higher if the taxpayer had waited. If instead the value goes down (e.g., through a market correction or recession), the conversion looks like a foolish mistake because the tax bill is much higher than if the owner had waited until the asset prices fell. The option to recharacterize reduced the risk.

▶ **Effective date.** The amendments made by this section apply to tax years beginning after December 31, 2017 (Act Sec. 13611(b) of the Tax Cuts and Jobs Act (P.L. 115-97)).

Law source: Law at ¶5475. Committee Report at ¶10,830.

— Act Sec. 13611(a) of the Tax Cuts and Jobs Act (P.L. 115-97), amending Code Sec. 408A(d)(6);

— Act Sec. 13611(b), providing the effective date.

¶625 Rollovers of Plan Loan Offset Amounts

SUMMARY OF NEW LAW

For plan loan offset amounts that are treated as distributed after 2017, a participant whose plan terminates or who is severed from employment while having a plan loan outstanding will have until the due date for filing their tax return for that year to contribute the loan balance to an IRA in order to avoid the loan being taxed as a distribution.

BACKGROUND

Defined contribution plans are permitted, but not required, to allow plan loans. Loans are treated as distributions, unless the balance of all outstanding loans does not exceed the lesser of:

- $50,000, reduced by the excess, if any, of the participant's highest outstanding loan balance during the preceding one-year period ending on the day before the date of the new loan, over the outstanding balance on the date of the new loan; or

- the greater of $10,000 or half of the participant's vested accrued benefit under the plan (Code Sec. 72(p)(2)).

¶625

BACKGROUND

Only qualified employer plans can use this exception to distribution treatment, and for these purposes such plans include:

- qualified pension, profit-sharing, or stock bonus plans;

- qualified annuity plans;

- plans under which amounts are contributed for the purchase of employees' annuity contracts by employers that are charitable organizations or public schools; and

- government plans (Code Sec. 72(p)(4)).

If an employee fails to abide by the applicable rules, the loan is treated as a taxable distribution of the accrued benefit, and may be subject to the 10-percent penalty for early withdrawals (Code Sec. 72(p); Reg. § 1.72(p)-1, Q&A 11).

Loan distributions can also occur through a reduction (or offset) of the account balance. Typically, these distributions occur when the plan terminates or the employee terminates employment. If the employee does not repay the outstanding balance, it will be deducted from the account and is treated as a distribution. The offset loan balance must be included in the employee's gross income and may be subject to the 10-percent additional tax on early distributions. The distribution is reported on Form 1099-R (Reg. § 1.402(c)-2, Q&A 9).

An amount equal to the plan loan offset amount can be rolled over by the employee (or spousal distributee) to an eligible retirement plan within the 60-day period (Reg. § 1.402(c)-2, Q&A 9(a)).

NEW LAW EXPLAINED

Employees whose plans terminate or who are severed from employment have extra time to roll over plan loan offsets.—An employee can exclude from income a transfer of a qualified plan loan offset amount as long as it is made by the due date (including extensions) for filing the tax return for the tax year in which the amount is treated as distributed from a qualified employer plan (Code Sec. 402(c)(3)(C)(i), as added by the Tax Cuts and Jobs Act (P.L. 115-97)). A qualified plan loan offset amount is a plan loan offset amount that is distributed solely by reason of:

- the termination of the qualified employer plan, or

- a severance from employment (Code Sec. 402(c)(3)(C)(ii), as added by the 2017 Tax Cuts Act).

A "plan loan offset amount" is the amount by which the participant's accrued benefit under the plan is reduced in order to repay a loan from the plan (Code Sec. 402(c)(3)(C)(iii), as added by the 2017 Tax Cuts Act).

This treatment of plan loan offset amounts is available only if the loan qualifies under Code Sec. 72(p)(2) (Code Sec. 401(c)(3)(C)(iv), as added by the 2017 Tax Cuts Act) and only if the plan qualifies as a qualified employer plan under Code Sec. 72(p)(4) (Code Sec. 401(c)(3)(C)(v), as added by the 2017 Tax Cuts Act).

NEW LAW EXPLAINED

> **Practical Analysis:** Elizabeth Thomas Dold, Principal at Groom Law Group, Chartered in Washington, D.C., comments that unlike deemed distributions, loan offsets are treated as eligible rollover distributions. This permits participants to defer taxation on an outstanding loan balance, provided they have the funds available to transfer to an IRA or another tax qualified plan. This provision extends the rollover period from 60 days to the due date (including extensions) for filing the tax return for the year of the loan offset, provided that the offset was due to (1) plan termination or (2) failure to meet the repayment terms because of severance from employment. Triggering taxation of the outstanding loan balance upon plan termination (where the plan sponsor does not offer direct rollover of the loan note to another plan) or upon termination of employment (where the plan sponsor does not permit continued repayment by former employees) has historically been a rather harsh result. Therefore, this relief is welcomed, but it will require additional loan administration in short order with a January 1, 2018, effective date as the reason for the loan offset will need to be tracked, and loan policies/rollover notice (Code Sec. 402(f)) may need to be revised to reflect this special rule.

▶ **Effective date.** The amendment made by this section applies to plan loan offset amounts that are treated as distributed in tax years beginning after December 31, 2017 (Act Sec. 13613(c) of the Tax Cuts and Jobs Act (P.L. 115-97)).

Law source: Law at ¶5465. Committee Report at ¶10,850.

— Act Sec. 13613(a) and (b) of the Tax Cuts and Jobs Act (P.L. 115-97), amending Code Sec. 402(c)(3);

— Act Sec. 13613(c), providing the effective date.

¶630 Qualified 2016 Disaster Distributions from Retirement Plans

SUMMARY OF NEW LAW

The 10-percent additional tax under Code Sec. 72(t) is waived for any qualified 2016 disaster distribution. Eligible individuals who take such distributions can spread their taxable income over three years and have three years to repay the amount.

BACKGROUND

An individual who receives an early distribution from a retirement plan before turning age 59 ½ may be required to include at least part of the distribution as income. The taxable amount is generally subject to an additional 10-percent additional tax on that amount, unless the distribution falls under an exception (for example, if the distribution is used to pay for qualifying medical expenses) (Code Sec. 72(t)).

BACKGROUND

In March and August of 2016, storms and flooding occurred in the Mississippi River Delta affecting residents in Louisiana, Mississippi, and Texas. Major disaster areas were declared under the Robert T. Stafford Disaster Relief and Emergency Assistance Act for both of these sets of storms. The IRS issued hardship distribution relief for victims of the August storms (Announcement 2016-30).

NEW LAW EXPLAINED

Qualified 2016 disaster distributions provide relief.—Congress has provided relief for victims in the 2016 disasters area. The 10-percent additional tax under Code Sec. 72(t) is waived for any qualified 2016 disaster distribution. Eligible individuals who take such distributions can spread their taxable income over three years and have three years to repay the amount. A 2016 disaster area includes any area with respect to which a major disaster has been declared by the President under Section 401 of the Robert T. Stafford Disaster Relief and Emergency Assistance Act during calendar-year 2016 (Act Sec. 11028(a) of the Tax Cuts and Jobs Act (P.L. 115-97)).

The 10-percent additional tax under Code Sec. 72(t) is waived for any qualified 2016 disaster distribution (Act Sec. 11028(b)(1)(A) of the 2017 Tax Cuts Act). The aggregate dollar amount is limited to the excess (if any) of—

- $100,000, over

- the aggregate amounts treated as qualified 2016 disaster distributions received by such individual for all prior tax years (Act Sec. 11028(b)(1)(B)(i) of the 2017 Tax Cuts Act).

If an individual's total distributions from all plans exceed this amount, a plan will not lose its tax-exempt status merely because it treats such distribution as a qualified 2016 disaster distribution, provided that the aggregate amount of such distributions from all plans maintained by the employer (and any member of any controlled group that includes the employer) do not exceed the $100,000 limit (Act Sec. 11028(b)(1)(B)(ii) of the 2017 Tax Cuts Act). A controlled group for these purposes means any group treated as a single employer under Code Sec. 414(b), (c),(m), or (o) (Act Sec. 11028(b)(1)(B)(iii) of the 2017 Tax Cuts Act).

Qualified 2016 distribution. A qualified 2016 disaster distribution is any distribution from an eligible retirement plan made on or after January 1, 2016, and before January 1, 2018, to an individual whose principal place of abode at any time during calendar-year 2016 was located in a 2016 disaster area and who has sustained an economic loss by reason of the events giving rise to the Presidential declaration applicable to such area (Act Sec. 11028(b)(1)(D)(i) of the 2017 Tax Cuts Act). Eligible retirement plans include individual retirement accounts (Code Sec. 408(a)) or annuities (Code Sec. 408(b)), qualified plans (Code Sec. 401), annuity plans (Code Sec. 403(a)), eligible deferred compensation Code Sec. 457(b) plans, and tax-sheltered annuity plans (Code Sec. 403(b)) (Act Sec. 11028(b)(1)(D)(ii) of the 2017 Tax Cuts Act).

Qualified 2016 disaster distributions are exempt from trustee-to-trustee transfer and withholding rules (Code Sec. 401(a)(31), 402(f) and 3405) (Act Sec. 11028(b)(1)(F)(i)

NEW LAW EXPLAINED

of the 2017 Tax Cuts Act) and they are treated as meeting plan distribution requirements of Code Sec. 401(k)(2)(B)(i), Code Sec. 403(b)(7)(A)(ii), Code Sec. 403(b)(11), and Code Sec. 457(d)(1)(A) (Act Sec. 11028(b)(1)(F)(ii) of the 2017 Tax Cuts Act).

The amount distributed may be repaid over three years. Any individual who receives a qualified 2016 disaster distribution may, at any time during the three-year period beginning on the day after the date on which such distribution was received, make one or more contributions in an aggregate amount not to exceed the amount of such distribution to an eligible retirement plan of which such individual is a beneficiary and to which a rollover contribution of such distribution could be made under Code Sec. 402(c), Code Sec. 403(a)(4), Code Sec. 403(b)(8), Code Sec. 408(d)(3), or Code Sec. 457(e)(16), as applicable (Act Sec. 11028(b)(1)(C)(i) of the 2017 Tax Cuts Act).

Repayments are treated as rollover contributions. If a contribution is made with respect to a qualified 2016 disaster distribution from an eligible retirement plan other than an individual retirement plan, then the taxpayer will, to the extent of the amount of the contribution, be treated as having received the qualified 2016 disaster distribution in an eligible rollover distribution (Code Sec. 402(c)(4)), and as having transferred the amount to the eligible retirement plan in a direct trustee-to-trustee transfer within 60 days of the distribution (Act Sec. 11028(b)(1)(C)(ii) of the 2017 Tax Cuts Act). If a contribution is made with respect to a qualified 2016 disaster distribution from an individual retirement plan (Code Sec. 7701(a)(37)), then, to the extent of the amount of the contribution, the qualified 2016 disaster distribution is treated as a rollover contribution under Code Sec. 408(d)(3), and as having been transferred to the eligible retirement plan in a direct trustee-to-trustee transfer within 60 days of the distribution (Act Sec. 11028(b)(1)(C)(iii) of the 2017 Tax Cuts Act).

Plan amendment relief is to be provided (Act Sec. 11028(b)(2)(B)(ii) of the 2017 Tax Cuts Act).

Practical Analysis: Elizabeth Thomas Dold, Principal at Groom Law Group, Chartered in Washington, D.C., comments that additional disaster relief is always welcome, but it comes with some additional plan administration (e.g., reporting and withholding) and plan amendment requirements if the plan sponsor elects to offer it. Instead of following the existing parameters of Code Sec. 1400Q (like Hurricanes Katrina, Rita, Wilma, and more recently Hurricanes Harvey, Irma and Maria), this Act Section provides similar, but not as broad of relief (e.g., no loan relief here) for plan and IRA distribution in 2016 and 2017 for the various severe storms and flooding during 2016. It offers favorable tax treatment for distributions up to $100,000, and an ability to roll these funds back into a tax-favored arrangement within three years (but an amended participant return will also need to be filed to claim a refund of any taxes paid) to restore retirement funds. Therefore, for plan sponsors in regions with impacted participants, this provision is worth considering to assist your employees.

▶ **Effective date.** No specific effective date is provided by the Act. The provision is, therefore, considered effective on December 22, 2017, the date of enactment.

¶630

NEW LAW EXPLAINED

Law source: Law at ¶7015. Committee Report at ¶10,130.

— Act Sec. 11028(a) and (b) of the Tax Cuts and Jobs Act (P.L. 115-97).

¶635 Length-of-Service Award Exclusion for Bona Fide Public Safety Volunteers

SUMMARY OF NEW LAW

The dollar limit on the length-of-service award exclusion for bona fide public safety volunteers is doubled from $3,000 to $6,000, effective for tax years beginning after December 31, 2017.

BACKGROUND

Under Code Sec. 457, employees of a state or local government or a tax-exempt organization are not currently taxed on compensation deferred under an eligible deferred compensation plan. An eligible plan must meet participation, deferral, payout, trust, and other requirements. There are a number of plans to which the Code Sec. 457 rules do not apply (Code Sec. 457(e)(11)).

Plans that pay length-of-service awards to bona fide safety volunteers or to their beneficiaries on account of firefighting and prevention services, emergency medical services, or ambulance services performed by the volunteers are not subject to the Code Sec. 457 requirements for unfunded deferred compensation plans with respect to awards accrued after 1996 (Code Sec. 457(e)(11)(A)(ii) and (C); Reg. § 1.457-2(k)). A bona fide volunteer is an individual who does not receive any compensation for performing the qualified services other than (1) reimbursements or reasonable allowances for expenses incurred in performing the services or (2) benefits and nominal fees for performing the services that are reasonable and customarily paid by tax-exempt and governmental employers for such services (Code Sec. 457(e)(11)(B)(i)). A length-of-service award plan will not qualify for this treatment if the total amount of awards accrued for any year of service of any volunteer exceeds $3,000 (Code Sec. 457(e)(11)(B)(ii)).

NEW LAW EXPLAINED

$3,000 accrued benefit limit for bona fide public safety volunteers increased to $6,000.—The maximum deferral amount for length-of-service award exclusion is increased from $3,000 to $6,000, with inflation adjustments for years beginning after December 31, 2017 (Code Sec. 457(e)(11)(B), as amended by the Tax Cuts and Jobs Act (P.L. 115-97)).

NEW LAW EXPLAINED

In the case of a defined benefits plan paying solely length-of-service awards to bona fide volunteers on account of qualified services performed by such volunteers, the $6,000 limitation applies to the actuarial present value of the aggregate amount of length-of-service awards accruing with respect to any year of service. The actuarial present value with respect to any year is calculated using reasonable actuarial assumptions and methods, assuming payment will be made under the most valuable form of payment under the plan with payment commencing at the later of the earliest age at which unreduced benefits are payable under the plan or the participant's age at the time of the calculation (Code Sec. 457(e)(11)(B)(iv), as amended by the 2017 Tax Cuts Act).

> **Practical Analysis:** Elizabeth Thomas Dold, Principal at Groom Law Group, Chartered in Washington, D.C., comments that length-of-service programs for public safety volunteers were well overdue for a cost-of-living adjustment. The programs have historically been limited to $3,000 in annual accruals (plus earnings thereon), so the increase to $6,000 (plus a cost-of-living adjustment going forward) is fitting beginning in 2018. Plan sponsors should review their programs and consider plan amendments (and participant communications) to reflect the increased accruals and for defined benefit arrangements to follow the actuarial adjustment parameters therein and check with the plan's actuary to ensure compliance. Providing meaningful benefits for our indispensable public safety volunteers is indeed a worthy endeavor.

▶ **Effective date.** The amendments made by this section apply to tax years beginning after December 31, 2017 (Act Sec. 13612(d) of the Tax Cuts and Jobs Act (P.L. 115-97)).

Law source: Law at ¶5525. Committee Report at ¶10,840.

— Act Sec. 13612(a), (b), and (c) of the Tax Cuts and Jobs Act (P.L. 115-97), amending Code Sec. 457(e)(11);

— Act Sec. 13612(d), providing the effective date.

EDUCATION AND DISABILITY BENEFITS

¶640 Distributions from Qualified Tuition Programs

SUMMARY OF NEW LAW

Code Sec. 529 qualified tuition plans are modified to allow the plans to distribute no more than $10,000 in tuition expenses incurred during the tax year for designated beneficiaries enrolled at a public, private, or religious elementary or secondary school.

¶640

BACKGROUND

A qualified tuition program (commonly referred to as a QTP, qualified tuition plan, or 529 plan) is exempt from all federal income tax, except the tax on the unrelated business income of a charitable organization. There are two basic types of QTPs: prepaid tuition programs and college savings programs. Distributions can be made for qualified higher education expenses, which are defined as:

* the tuition, fees, books, supplies, and equipment required for the enrollment or attendance of a designated beneficiary at an eligible educational institution;

* the expenses incurred for special needs services for a special needs beneficiary in connection with enrollment or attendance at an eligible educational institution;

* the expenses for the purchase of computer or peripheral equipment, computer software, or Internet access and related services, if such equipment, software, or services are to be used primarily by the beneficiary during any of the years the beneficiary is enrolled at an eligible educational institution; and

* room and board incurred by a designated beneficiary who is enrolled at least half time at an eligible educational institution (Code Sec. 529(e)(3)(A)-(B)).

NEW LAW EXPLAINED

Distributions from qualified tuition programs allowed for elementary and secondary tuition.—Qualified tuition plans are modified to allow for distributions to be made for elementary and secondary tuition. The reference to qualified higher education expenses is expanded to include tuition in connection with attendance or enrollment at an elementary or secondary school (Code Sec. 529(c)(7), as added by the Tax Cuts and Jobs Act (P.L. 115-97)). Distributions for elementary or secondary tuition are limited to no more than $10,000 incurred during the tax year in connection with the enrollment or attendance of the designated beneficiary (Code Sec. 529(e)(3)(A), as added by the 2017 Tax Cuts Act). The limitation applies on a per-student, not per-account basis. As a result, if an individual is a designated beneficiary of multiple accounts, a maximum of $10,000 in distributions will be free of income tax, regardless of whether the funds are distributed from multiple accounts. Any distribution in excess of $10,000 would be subject to tax under the rules of Code Sec. 529 (Conference Report on H.R. 1, the Tax Cuts and Jobs Act (H.R. Rept. 115-466)).

▶ **Effective date.** The amendments made by this section apply to distributions made after December 31, 2017 (Act Sec. 11032(b) of the Tax Cuts and Jobs Act (P.L. 115-97)).

Law source: Law at ¶5580. Committee Report at ¶10,150.

— Act Sec. 11032(a)(1) of the Tax Cuts and Jobs Act of 2017 (P.L. 115-97), adding Code Sec. 529(c)(7);

— Act Sec. 11032(a)(2), amending Code Sec. 529(e)(3)(A);

— Act Sec. 11032(b), providing the effective date.

¶640

¶645 Contributions and Rollovers to ABLE Accounts

SUMMARY OF NEW LAW

Individuals are allowed to roll over amounts from qualified tuition plans (also known as Code Sec. 529 plans) to an ABLE account if the ABLE account is owned by the same designated beneficiary of the 529 plan or a member of the designated beneficiary's family before January 1, 2026. Under certain circumstances, the contribution limitation to ABLE accounts is increased for contributions made by the designated beneficiary before January 1, 2026.

BACKGROUND

Achieving a Better Life Experience (ABLE) programs can be established by a state, or agency or instrumentality of a state, to encourage individuals and families in saving funds to assist a disabled individual in paying qualified disability expenses through a tax-favored savings account (Code Sec. 529A(b)(1)). The structure and tax treatment of an ABLE account under the program are similar to qualified tuition programs under Code Sec. 529. Contributions to an ABLE account may only be made in cash in the form of a check, money order, credit card, electronic transfer, or similar method. Except for rollover contributions, the aggregate annual contributions to a single ABLE account cannot exceed the inflation-adjusted annual gift tax exclusion amount ($14,000 in 2017 and $15,000 in 2018 (Code Sec. 529A(b)(2); Rev. Proc. 2016-55; Rev. Proc. 2017-58).

A rollover distribution from one ABLE account to another, whether in the same ABLE program or a different ABLE program, that meets certain conditions is not includible in the distributee's gross income. In order to be excluded from income, the distribution must be paid into another ABLE account in a qualified ABLE program not later than the 60th day after the date of payment or distribution (Code Sec 529A(c)(1)(C)(i)).

To encourage low- and middle-income taxpayers to establish or maintain private savings accounts to ensure adequate savings for retirement, a nonrefundable credit for contributions or deferrals to retirement savings plans was established (Code Sec. 25B). As a nonrefundable personal credit, the qualified retirement savings contribution credit, commonly referred as the saver's credit, may not exceed income tax liability.

NEW LAW EXPLAINED

Contribution amount to ABLE accounts increased and rollovers from qualified tuition plans allowed.—The contribution limit to an ABLE account is temporarily increased in certain circumstances. While the general contribution limit remains the same (i.e., equal to annual gift-tax exclusion), it is increased with regard to contributions made by the designated beneficiary before January 1, 2026 (Code Sec. 529A(b)(2)(B), as amended by the Tax Cuts and Jobs Act (P.L. 115-97)). Specifically,

¶645

NEW LAW EXPLAINED

after the general limitation on contributions is reached, the designated beneficiary of the ABLE account may make additional contributions up to the lesser of: (1) his or her compensation includible in gross income for the tax year; or (2) the federal poverty line for a one-person household. The designated beneficiary, or a person acting on behalf of the designated beneficiary, is required to keep adequate records for purposes of ensuring, and is responsible for ensuring, that the additional contribution amount does not exceed this amount Code Sec. 529A(b)(2)(B)(ii) (Code Sec. 529A(b)(2), as amended by the 2017 Tax Cuts Act).

> **Caution:** The inflation-adjusted annual gift tax exclusion is $15,000 for 2018 based on the Rev. Proc. 2017-58 using the average CPI rate to compute the adjustment. However, the limit is adjusted annually for inflation for tax years beginning after December 31, 2017, using the Chained Consumer Price Index for All Urban Consumers (C-CPI-U) in the cost-of-living adjustment (see ¶125) (Code Sec. 2502(b)(2)(B), as added by the 2017 Tax Cuts Act). The change in methodology for making inflation adjustments using chained-CPI may result in smaller adjustments after 2017. As a result, the IRS may issue a revised inflation adjustment for the annual gift tax exclusion for 2018 using chained CPI.

For purposes of the increased contribution amount, the "designated beneficiary" is an employee, including a self-employed individual or owner-employee, for whom no contribution was made for the tax year to: (1) a defined contribution plan (including a 401(k) plan); (2) a 403(b) tax-sheltered annuity plan; and (3) an eligible 457(b) deferred compensation plan (Code Sec. 529A(b)(7)(A), as added by the 2017 Tax Cuts Act). In addition, "poverty line" has the same meaning that is given to the term by Section 673 of the Community Services Block Grant Act (P.L. 105-285) (Code Sec. 529A(b)(7)(B), as added by the 2017 Tax Cuts Act).

> **Comment:** "Poverty line" is defined in Section 673 of the Community Services Block Grant Act as the official poverty line set forth by the Office of Management and Budget based on the most recent census data. Annual adjustments are made to the poverty line by multiplying the official poverty line by the percentage change in the Consumer Price Index for All Urban Consumers.

The retirement savings contribution credit can be claimed by a designated beneficiary of an ABLE account for contributions made to the designated beneficiary's ABLE account before January 1, 2026 (Code Sec. 25B(d)(1)(D), as added by the 2017 Tax Cuts Act).

Rollovers to ABLE accounts. Amounts from qualified tuition plans (also known as section 529 accounts) can be rolled over to an ABLE account without penalty, if the ABLE account is owned by the designated beneficiary of that 529 account or a member of the designated beneficiary's family before January 1, 2026 (Code Sec. 529(c)(3)(C)(i)(III), as added by the 2017 Tax Cuts Act). Any rolled-over amounts count towards the overall limitation on amounts that can be contributed to an ABLE account within a tax year (flush language of Code Sec. 529(c)(3)(C)(i)(III), as added by the 2017 Tax Cuts Act). As provided in Code Sec. 529(c)(3)(A), an amount rolled over that is in excess of the limitation will be included in the beneficiary's gross income under the annuity rules of Code Sec. 72, unless excludable under another Code section.

¶645

NEW LAW EXPLAINED

Practical Analysis: Brian T. Whitlock, Adjunct Professor in the Gies College of Business at the University of Illinois at Urbana-Champaign notes that Section 11025 of the Act would permit amounts previously held in Code Sec. 529 educational savings accounts to be rolled over to Code Sec. 529A ABLE accounts established for individuals who became blind or disabled prior to having attained age 26. Such a rollover is ill advised. The rolled-over funds under this section would be counted as part of the overall limitation on amounts that can be contributed to an ABLE account within a tax year. Amounts in excess of the limitation would be includible in the income of the disabled person. This limit on tax-free rollovers is far too small to be meaningful. Where funds are held in a 529 educational savings account for the benefit of the disabled person, the family would be better served to change the beneficiary on the 529 account to another member of the family rather than roll over these assets into an 529A ABLE account that will revert to the state upon the death of the disabled person.

ABLE accounts fail to offer any meaningful benefit, and the 2017 Tax Cuts Act does nothing to change that result. Congress still has failed to expand the usage of Section 529A accounts to all disabled veterans regardless of age.

The only time when ABLE accounts make sense is to hold an account that was previously irrevocably held in the name of the disabled person or where the disabled person holds a small job and needs an account to hold their net earnings. Act Sec. 11024 gives the disabled person a savers credit (Code Sec. 25B) for funds that they personally add to their own ABLE account. For low-income taxpayers (*i.e.*, with income under $18,500), the credit could be as much as $1,000 on a contribution of $2,000 or more. The amount of the savers credit decreases as the income of the disabled person increases. The $15,000 annual limitation referred to above would be increased temporarily by the lesser of the federal poverty line for a one-person household (roughly $12,000) or the disabled person's total compensation for the tax year. It is unclear whether the rollover of Code Sec. 529 educational savings account assets to a Code Sec. 529A ABLE account would qualify for the savers credit, since the rollover provision is limited to $15,000 annual limit.

ABLE accounts are not an effective tool for families wishing to contribute funds for the benefit of a disabled person. Funds gifted by family members to ABLE accounts will revert to the state upon the death of the disabled person. Families wishing to gift funds to be held for the benefit of disabled family members would be better served by creating a private Supplemental Needs Trust. Even though the funds invested inside of a Supplemental Needs Trust are subject to income tax, the trust will not impact the disabled person's ability to receive Medicaid benefits, Social Security Disability Insurance benefits or SSI. The funds held inside of a Supplemental Needs Trust at the death of the disabled beneficiary may pass to other family members and they do not revert to the state.

▶ **Effective date.** The amendments made by these sections apply to tax years beginning after December 22, 2017, the date of enactment of this Act (Act Secs. 11024(c) and 11025(b) of the Tax Cuts and Jobs Act (P.L. 115-97)).

¶645

NEW LAW EXPLAINED

Law source: Law at ¶5035, ¶5580, and ¶5585. Committee Report at ¶10,090 and ¶10,100.

— Act Sec. 11024(a) of the Tax Cuts and Job Act (P.L. 115-97) amending Code Sec. 529A(b)(2) and adding Code Sec. 529A(b)(7);

— Act Sec. 11024(b), amending Code Sec. 25B(d)(1);

— Act Sec. 11025(a), amending Code Sec. 529(c)(3)(C)(i);

— Act Secs. 11024(c) and 11025(b), providing the effective date.

International Tax Provisions

7

TAXATION OF FOREIGN INCOME

FOREIGN TAX CREDIT

CFCs AND SUBPART F INCOME

BASE EROSION PREVENTION

TAXATION OF FOREIGN INCOME

¶705 Participation Exemption Deduction for Foreign-Source Portion of Dividends

SUMMARY OF NEW LAW

Effective generally for distributions after December 31, 2017, a 100-percent participation exemption deduction is allowed for the foreign-source portion of dividends received from specified 10-percent owned foreign corporations by U.S. corporate shareholders, subject to a one-year holding period (a participation dividends-received deduction (DRD)). No foreign tax credit or deduction is allowed for any taxes paid or accrued with respect to a dividend that qualifies for the deduction. The participation DRD is not available for hybrid dividends received from CFCs.

BACKGROUND

A U.S. person is subject to U.S. tax on its worldwide income. Generally, a U.S. person is currently taxed on directly earned foreign income (such as income earned directly from the conduct of a foreign business). However, a U.S. person that earns foreign-source income indirectly as a shareholder in a foreign corporation generally is not subject to U.S. tax until the foreign income is distributed to the U.S. person as a dividend.

> **Comment:** The United States is one of the few industrialized countries with a worldwide system of taxation and has the highest statutory corporate tax rates among countries that are members of the Organisation for Economic Co-operation and Development (OECD). The worldwide system of taxation and the high tax rates provide incentives for U.S. companies to keep foreign earnings offshore because such earnings are not taxed until repatriated to the United States.

Certain anti-deferral rules may currently tax a U.S. person on certain categories of passive or highly mobile foreign-source income, regardless of whether the income has been distributed to the U.S. person.

Subpart F and CFC rules. The main category of anti-deferral rules are the subpart F rules (Code Secs. 951—965). Under the subpart F rules, U.S. shareholders of a controlled foreign corporation (CFC) are currently taxed on their pro rata shares of

BACKGROUND

the CFC's subpart F income without regard to whether the income is distributed to the shareholders (Code Sec. 951(a)). A CFC generally is any foreign corporation in which U.S. shareholders own more than 50 percent of the corporation's stock (measured by vote or value) (Code Sec. 957). For this purpose, a U.S. shareholder is a U.S. person who owns at least 10 percent of the voting stock of the foreign corporation (Code Sec. 951(b)).

With certain exceptions, subpart F income generally includes passive income and other income that is readily movable from one taxing jurisdiction to another (Code Sec. 952). A U.S. shareholder of a CFC may exclude from its income actual distributions of the CFC's earnings and profits that were previously included in the shareholder's income under subpart F (Code Sec. 959).

PFIC regime. Another set of anti-deferral rules are the passive foreign investment company (PFIC) rules (Code Secs. 1291-1298). A PFIC is generally any foreign corporation if 75 percent or more of its gross income for the tax year consists of passive income, or 50 percent or more of its assets consists of assets that produce, or are held for the production of, passive income (Code Sec. 1297). Different sets of income inclusion rules apply to U.S. persons that are shareholders in a PFIC, regardless of their percentage ownership in the company.

Generally, a shareholder of a PFIC can make an election to treat the PFIC as a qualified electing fund (QEF) and depending on when the election is effective, the company may be either a "pedigreed" or an "unpedigreed" QEF with respect to that shareholder. When a PFIC carries the unpedigreed QEF designation, the shareholder is taxed under both Code Secs. 1291 and 1293. If the unpedigreed QEF is also a CFC for the tax year of the QEF election, the shareholder may make a deemed dividend election to limit taxation to one set of rules. In this case, the shareholder is treated as receiving a dividend on the qualification date, which is the first day of the PFIC's first tax year as a QEF, and the deemed dividend is taxed under Code Sec. 1291 as an excess distribution (Code Sec. 1291(d)(2)(B)).

Foreign tax credit. To prevent double taxation of foreign-source income, a foreign tax credit is generally available to offset, in whole or in part, the U.S. tax owed on foreign-source income, regardless of whether the income is earned directly by the U.S. taxpayer, repatriated as an actual dividend, or included in the taxpayer's income under one of the anti-deferral regimes (Code Secs. 901 and 960). The credit is allowed for any income, war profits, and excess profits taxes paid or accrued during the tax year to a foreign country or U.S. possession. The foreign tax credit cannot be used to offset U.S. tax on U.S.-source income, so it is generally limited to a taxpayer's U.S. tax liability on its foreign source taxable income (Code Sec. 904).

Holding period requirement. A corporation may claim a dividends-received deduction under Code Secs. 243 and 245 for certain dividends received with respect to stock that has been held for 46 days during the 91-day period beginning 45 days before the ex-dividend date. For preferred stock, the stock must be held for 91 days during the 181-day period beginning 90 days before the date on which the stock becomes ex-dividend. The holding period is reduced for any period during which the taxpayer's risk of loss with respect to the stock is diminished. No dividends-received deduction is allowed to the extent that the taxpayer is under an obligation (pursuant to a short

BACKGROUND

sale or otherwise) to make related payments with respect to positions in substantially similar or related property (Code Sec. 246(c)).

Extraordinary dividends. A corporate shareholder that receives an "extraordinary dividend" must reduce the basis of the stock with respect to which the dividend was received by the non-taxed portion of the dividend. There is an exception if the corporation has held the stock for more than two years before the earliest date on which either the amount or the payment of the dividend is declared, agreed to, or announced. The non-taxed portion of the extraordinary dividend is the excess, if any, of the amount of the dividend over the taxable portion of such dividend. The taxable portion of the dividend is the amount of the dividend includible in income, reduced by any allowable deduction with respect to the dividend under Code Secs. 243 and 245 (Code Sec. 1059).

NEW LAW EXPLAINED

100-percent participation exemption deduction allowed for foreign-source portion of dividends.—A 100-percent deduction is allowed for the foreign-source portion of dividends received from a specified 10-percent owned foreign corporation by a domestic corporation that is a U.S. shareholder of the foreign corporation (a participation dividends-received deduction (DRD)) (Code Sec. 245A(a), as added by the Tax Cuts and Jobs Act (P.L. 115-97)).

> **Comment:** The new law generally establishes a participation exemption (territorial) system for the taxation of foreign income that replaces the prior-law system of taxing U.S. corporations on the foreign earnings of their foreign subsidiaries when the earnings are distributed. The exemption, which is provided in the form of a participation DRD, is intended to encourage U.S. companies to repatriate their accumulated foreign earnings and invest them in the United States.

> **Caution:** Dividends from foreign companies that are less than 10 percent owned by domestic corporations are not eligible for the participation DRD and will continue to be treated the same as under prior law (i.e., such dividends generally will be taxed when distributed, subject to any applicable anti-deferral rules). Also, dividends received by non-corporate U.S. shareholders are not eligible for the participation DRD.

> **Comment:** According to the Conference Committee Report, it is intended that the term "dividend received" be interpreted broadly, consistently with the meaning of "amount received as dividends" and "dividends received" used in Code Sec. 243 and 245, respectively. Thus, for example, gain included in gross income as a dividend under Code Sec. 1248(a) or 964(e) would constitute a dividend for which the participation DRD may be available. Regulations or other guidance issued pursuant to the regulatory authority granted under Code Sec. 245A(g) (discussed below) may clarify the intended broad scope of the term "dividend received." For example, if a domestic corporation indirectly owns stock of a foreign corporation through a partnership and the domestic corporation would qualify for the participation DRD with respect to dividends from the foreign corporation if the domestic corporation owned the stock directly, the

NEW LAW EXPLAINED

domestic corporation would be allowed a participation DRD with respect to its distributive share of the partnership's dividend from the foreign corporation (Conference Report on H.R. 1, Tax Cuts and Jobs Act (H. Rept. 115-466)).

A specified 10-percent owned foreign corporation is any foreign corporation (other than a PFIC that is not also a CFC) with respect to which any domestic corporation is a U.S. shareholder (Code Sec. 245A(b), as added by the 2017 Tax Cuts Act).

> **Comment:** The subpart F definitions of a U.S. shareholder and CFC are expanded so that they are used for purposes of Title 26 (including the participation DRD), and not just the subpart F provisions (Code Secs. 951(b) and 957(a), as amended by the 2017 Tax Cuts Act). The U.S. shareholder definition is further expanded so that a U.S. shareholder includes a U.S. person that owns at least 10 percent of the total combined voting power of all classes of stock entitled to vote or at least 10 percent of the total value of all classes of stock of the foreign corporation (Act Sec. 14214(a) of the 2017 Tax Cuts Act, amending Code Sec. 951(b); see ¶745).

> **Comment:** Taxation of income earned by PFICs remains subject to the anti-deferral PFIC regime and dividends received from non-CFC PFICs are ineligible for the participation DRD.

> **Comment:** A domestic corporation includes a CFC treated as a domestic corporation for purposes of computing its taxable income (Reg. §1.952-2(b)(1)). Therefore, a CFC receiving a dividend from a 10-percent owned foreign corporation that constitutes subpart F income may be eligible for the DRD with respect to that income. In addition, the participation DRD is available only to C corporations that are not RICs or REITs (Conference Report on H.R. 1, Tax Cuts and Jobs Act (H. Rept. 115-466)).

Foreign-source portion of a dividend. The foreign-source portion of any dividend from a specified 10-percent owned foreign corporation is the amount that bears the same ratio to the dividend as (1) the undistributed foreign earnings of the specified 10-percent owned foreign corporation, bears to (2) the total undistributed earnings of that corporation (Code Sec. 245A(c)(1), as added by the 2017 Tax Cuts Act).

Undistributed earnings are the earnings and profits of a specified 10-percent owned foreign corporation (computed in accordance with Code Secs. 964(a) and 986) as of the close of the tax year of the specified 10-percent owned foreign corporation in which the dividend is distributed that are not reduced by dividends distributed during that tax year (Code Sec. 245A(c)(2), as added by the 2017 Tax Cuts Act).

> **Comment:** Under Code Sec. 959(d), a distribution of previously taxed income does not constitute a dividend, even if it reduces earnings and profits.

Undistributed foreign earnings of a specified 10-percent owned foreign corporation are the portion of the undistributed earnings of that corporation that is not attributable to (1) the corporation's income that is effectively connected with the conduct of a trade or business within the United States, and subject to tax under Chapter 1 of the Code, or (2) any dividend received (directly or through a wholly owned foreign corporation) from an 80-percent owned (by vote or value) domestic corporation (Code Sec. 245A(c)(3), as added by the 2017 Tax Cuts Act).

¶705

NEW LAW EXPLAINED

Foreign tax credit disallowance. No foreign tax credit or deduction is allowed for any taxes paid or accrued (or treated as paid or accrued) with respect to a dividend that qualifies for the participation DRD (Code Sec. 245A(d), as added by the 2017 Tax Cuts Act).

For purposes of computing the Code Sec. 904(a) foreign tax credit limitation, a domestic corporation that is a U.S. shareholder of a specified 10-percent owned foreign corporation must compute its foreign-source taxable income (and entire taxable income) by disregarding (1) the foreign-source portion of any dividend received from that foreign corporation for which a participation DRD is allowed, and (2) any deductions properly allocable or apportioned to that foreign source portion or the stock with respect to which it is paid. For this purpose, any term that is used in this rule and in Code Sec. 245A has the meaning used in Code Sec. 245A (Code Sec. 904(b)(5), as added by the 2017 Tax Cuts Act).

Hybrid dividends. The participation DRD is not available for any dividend received by a U.S. shareholder from a CFC if the dividend is a hybrid dividend (Code Sec. 245A(e)(1), as added by the 2017 Tax Cuts Act).

A hybrid dividend is an amount received from a CFC for which a participation DRD would otherwise be allowed and for which the CFC received a deduction (or other tax benefit) with respect to any income, war profits, or excess profits taxes imposed by any foreign country or U.S. possession (Code Sec. 245A(e)(4), as added by the 2017 Tax Cuts Act).

If a CFC with respect to which a domestic corporation is a U.S. shareholder receives a hybrid dividend from any other CFC with respect to which the domestic corporation is also a U.S. shareholder, then:

(1) the hybrid dividend is treated as subpart F income of the recipient CFC for the tax year of the CFC in which the dividend was received, and

(2) the U.S. shareholder must include an amount equal to the shareholder's pro rata share of such subpart F income in gross income (Code Sec. 245A(e)(2), as added by the 2017 Tax Cuts Act).

No foreign tax credit or deduction is allowed for any taxes paid or accrued (or treated as paid or accrued) with respect to any hybrid dividend received by a U.S. shareholder or included in the U.S. shareholder's income under the rules, discussed above (Code Sec. 245A(e)(3), as added by the 2017 Tax Cuts Act).

Special rule for purging distributions of PFICs. Any amount that is treated as a dividend pursuant to the deemed dividend election under Code Sec. 1291(d)(2)(B) is not treated as a dividend for purposes of the participation DRD (Code Sec. 245A(f), as added by the 2017 Tax Cuts Act).

Regulatory authority. The Secretary of the Treasury is authorized to issue regulations or other guidance that is necessary or appropriate to carry out these provisions, including regulations for the treatment of U.S. shareholders owning stock of a specified 10-percent owned foreign corporation through a partnership (Code Sec. 245A(g), as added by the 2017 Tax Cuts Act).

¶705

NEW LAW EXPLAINED

One-year holding period requirement. A domestic corporation is not permitted a participation DRD for any dividend on any share of stock that is held by the domestic corporation for 365 days or less during the 731-day period beginning on the date that is 365 days before the date on which the share becomes ex-dividend with respect to the dividend (Code Sec. 246(c)(5)(A), as added by the 2017 Tax Cuts Act).

> **Comment:** The special holding period rule for preference dividends in Code Sec. 246(c)(2) does not apply in this case.

The holding period requirement is treated as met only if the foreign corporation is a specified 10-percent owned foreign corporation and the taxpayer is a U.S. shareholder with respect to that specified 10-percent owned foreign corporation at *all* times during the required period (Code Sec. 246(c)(5)(B), as added by the 2017 Tax Cuts Act).

> **Comment:** Under Code Sec. 246, the participation DRD is not permitted for any dividend on any share of stock to the extent the domestic corporation that owns the share is under an obligation (under a short sale or otherwise) to make related payments with respect to positions in substantially similar or related property. In addition, the required holding periods must be reduced for any period during which the domestic corporation has diminished its risk of loss in respect of stock on which a dividend is paid.

Application of other rules. The participation DRD does not apply to dividends received from Code Sec. 501 tax-exempt organizations and farmers' cooperative associations exempt from tax under Code Sec. 521 (Code Sec. 246(a)(1), as amended by the 2017 Tax Cuts Act).

In addition, the participation DRD reduces the amount of the dividend includible in gross income for purposes of computing the nontaxed portion of an extraordinary dividend (Code Sec. 1059(b)(2)(B), as amended by the 2017 Tax Cuts Act).

Practical Analysis: Robert Misey, Chair of the International Department for Reinhart Boerner Van Deuren in Chicago and Milwaukee, comments that the participation exemption for foreign-source dividends puts U.S. companies on equal footing with their competitors incorporated in our trading partner countries. U.S. C corporations—and only U.S. C corporations—will be able to avoid the draconian deemed paid foreign tax credit regime, whereby a U.S. C corporation had to pay residual U.S. tax to the extent that the U.S. tax rate exceeded the foreign subsidiary's tax rate. Because the participation exemption eliminates double taxation, no foreign tax credits will be allowed.

With only C corporations being entitled to the participation exemption, we anticipate many other types of U.S. owners of foreign subsidiaries to contribute their foreign subsidiaries to U.S. C corporations. Accordingly, no U.S. corporate tax will be due and the U.S. individual will receive distributions, with the benefit of deferral, from the U.S. C corporation as a qualified dividend.

▶ **Effective date.** The amendments made by this section apply to distributions made (and for purposes of determining a taxpayer's foreign tax credit limitation under Code Sec. 904,

NEW LAW EXPLAINED

deductions with respect to tax years ending) after December 31, 2017 (Act Sec. 14101(f) of the Tax Cuts and Jobs Act (P.L. 115-97)).

Law source: Law at ¶5400, ¶5405, ¶5820, ¶5860, ¶5890, and ¶5955. Committee Report at ¶11,000, ¶11,010, ¶11,020, ¶11,030, and ¶11,040.

— Act Sec. 14101(a) of the Tax Cuts and Jobs Act (P.L. 115-97), adding Code Sec. 245A;

— Act Sec. 14101(b), amending Code Sec. 246(c);

— Act Sec. 14101(c), amending Code Sec. 246(a)(1) and Code Sec. 1059(b)(2)(B);

— Act Sec. 14101(d), adding Code Sec. 904(b)(5);

— Act Sec. 14101(e)(1), amending Code Sec. 951(b);

— Act Sec. 14101(e)(2), amending Code Sec. 957(a);

— Act Sec. 14101(f), providing the effective date.

¶707 Sales or Transfers Involving Specified 10-Percent Owned Foreign Corporations

SUMMARY OF NEW LAW

Amounts received by a domestic corporation upon the sale or exchange of stock in a foreign corporation held for at least one year that are treated as Section 1248 dividends are also treated as dividends for purposes of the participation dividends-received deduction (DRD). In addition, solely for purposes of determining a loss, a domestic corporation's basis in the stock of a specified 10-percent owned foreign corporation is reduced by the amount of the participation DRD allowable to the domestic corporation for dividends received with respect to that stock, effective for distributions made after December 31, 2017. In the case of a sale by a CFC of a lower-tier CFC, the foreign-source portion of the amount treated as a dividend under Code Sec. 964(e)(1) is treated as subpart F income. A U.S shareholder of the selling CFC includes in income a pro rata share of that amount and is allowed a participation DRD. Also, a loss recapture rule requires a domestic corporation that transfers, after December 31, 2017, substantially all of the assets of a foreign branch to a specified 10-percent owned foreign corporation in which it is a U.S. shareholder after the transfer to include in income the amount of transferred losses, subject to certain limitations. Finally, the active trade or business exception to the Code Sec. 367(a) outbound transfer rules is repealed, effective for transfers after December 31, 2017.

BACKGROUND

Generally, a U.S. person that earns foreign-source income indirectly as a shareholder in a foreign corporation is not subject to U.S. tax until the foreign income is distributed to the U.S. person as a dividend. Certain anti-deferral rules may currently

¶707

BACKGROUND

tax a U.S. person on certain categories of passive or highly mobile foreign-source income, regardless of whether the income has been distributed to the U.S. person.

The main category of anti-deferral rules are the subpart F rules (Code Secs. 951-965). Under the subpart F rules, U.S. shareholders of a controlled foreign corporation (CFC) are currently taxed on their pro rata shares of the CFC's subpart F income without regard to whether the income is distributed to the shareholders (Code Sec. 951(a)). A CFC generally is any foreign corporation in which U.S. shareholders own more than 50 percent of the corporation's stock (measured by vote or value) (Code Sec. 957). For this purpose, a U.S. shareholder is a U.S. person that owns at least 10 percent of the voting stock of the foreign corporation (Code Sec. 951(b)).

With certain exceptions, subpart F income generally includes passive income and other income that is readily movable from one taxing jurisdiction to another (Code Sec. 952). A U.S. shareholder of a CFC may exclude from its income actual distributions of the CFC's earnings and profits that were previously included in the shareholder's income under subpart F (Code Sec. 959).

In general, a 10-percent U.S. shareholder of a CFC increases its basis in the CFC stock with the amount of the CFC's earnings that are included in the shareholder's income under subpart F. Similarly, a 10-percent U.S. shareholder generally reduces its basis in the CFC stock in an amount equal to any distributions received from the CFC that are excluded from the shareholder's income as previously taxed under subpart F (Code Sec. 961).

Gain on a U.S. person's disposition of CFC stock that would otherwise be treated as capital gain, is included in the taxpayer's gross income as dividend income to the extent of the CFC's earnings and profits (E&P) attributable to the stock while the taxpayer held the shares. For this treatment to apply, the foreign corporation must be a CFC at any time during the five-year period ending on the date of the disposition, and the U.S. person must own 10 percent or more of the total combined voting power of the foreign corporation at any time during that five-year period. Any income previously taxed as subpart F income is not included in determining the CFC's E&P attributable to the stock sold, unless the income was distributed before the disposition. Any gain in excess of the CFC's E&P is treated as capital gain. In determining the gain from the disposition of the CFC stock, a shareholder's basis in the stock is increased by the CFC's subpart F income and decreased by any distribution (Code Sec. 1248).

Gain on the sale or exchange of stock in a foreign corporation by a CFC is included in the CFC's gross income as a dividend to the same extent that it would have been included under Code Sec. 1248(a) if the CFC were a U.S. person. A CFC is treated as having sold or exchanged stock if it is treated as having gain from the sale or exchange of the stock under the income tax provisions of the Code (Code Sec. 964(e)).

Active trade or business exception for Code Sec. 367 outbound transfers. Generally, if a U.S. person transfers property to a foreign corporation in connection with a corporate organization, reorganization, and liquidation, the foreign corporation is not treated as a corporation and the otherwise tax-free transfer is treated as a taxable exchange (Code Sec. 367(a)). There are a number of exceptions to the general gain recognition rule on the outbound transfers of property, including a transfer of

BACKGROUND

property to be used in an active trade or business outside of the United States (the active trade or business exception).

For the active trade or business exception to apply (i) the property must be eligible property (e.g., tangible property, financial assets, stock in trade, accounts receivables, etc.), (ii) the property must be transferred for use by the foreign corporation in the active conduct of a trade or business outside of the United States, and (iii) the U.S. transferor must comply with the reporting requirements of Code Sec. 6038B (Code Sec. 367(a)(3); Reg. § 1.367(a)-2(a)). In addition, four factual determinations must be made to determine whether the transferred property qualifies for the active trade or business exception (Reg. § 1.367(a)-2(d)(1)).

The active conduct of a trade or business exception does not apply in the case where a U.S. person transfers assets of a foreign branch with previously deducted losses to a foreign corporation. The U.S. person is required to recognize gain on the transfer equal to the sum of the previously deducted ordinary and capital losses of the branch (Code Sec. 367(a)(3)(C); Temp. Reg. § 1.367(a)-6T).

NEW LAW EXPLAINED

Special rules provided for sales or transfers involving specified 10-percent owned foreign corporations.—Sale of stock by U.S. persons. If a domestic corporation sells or exchanges stock in a foreign corporation held for one year or more, any amount received by the domestic corporation that is treated as a dividend under Code Sec. 1248 is treated as a dividend for purposes of the 100-percent participation exemption deduction for the foreign-source portion of dividends under Code Sec. 245A (the participation dividends-received deduction (DRD)) (Code Sec. 1248(j), as added by the Tax Cuts and Jobs Act (P.L. 115-97)).

> **Comment:** This rule allows gain on the disposition of the foreign corporation stock to be reduced or eliminated as a result of the recharacterization of the gain as a dividend for which a 100-percent participation DRD is allowed.

> **Comment:** The new law generally establishes a participation exemption (territorial) system for the taxation of foreign income that replaces the prior-law system of taxing U.S. corporations on the foreign earnings of their foreign subsidiaries when the earnings are distributed. The exemption, which is provided in the form of a participation DRD, is intended to encourage U.S. companies to repatriate their accumulated foreign earnings and invest them in the United States. See ¶ 705 for a discussion of the participation DRD.

Reduction in the basis of certain foreign stock. If a domestic corporation receives a dividend from a specified 10-percent owned foreign corporation in any tax year, solely for the purpose of determining a loss on the disposition of the stock of that foreign corporation in that tax year or any subsequent tax year, the domestic corporation's basis in that stock is reduced (but not below zero) by the amount of the participation DRD allowable to the domestic corporation with respect to that stock. The basis in the specified 10-percent owned foreign corporation stock is not reduced under this rule to the extent the basis was reduced under Code Sec. 1059 by reason of

¶707

NEW LAW EXPLAINED

a dividend for which the participation DRD was allowable (Code Sec. 961(d), as added by the 2017 Tax Cuts Act).

> **Compliance Tip:** Thus, the reduction in basis is for the portion of the dividend received from the foreign corporation that was exempt from tax by reason of the participation DRD in any tax year of the domestic corporation.

> **Comment:** The reduction in basis addresses the concern that taxpayers may obtain inappropriate double benefit that would otherwise be created as a result of the participation DRD. In particular, a distribution from a foreign corporation that is eligible for a participation DRD would reduce the value of the foreign corporation, thus reducing any built-in gain or increasing any built-in loss in the shareholder's stock of the foreign corporation. While reducing gain in this way is consistent with the application of Code Sec. 1248 to recharacterize such gain as a dividend for which a participation DRD is allowed (see above), increasing any loss in the stock will create an inappropriate double U.S. tax benefit - first, a tax-free distribution from the foreign corporation and second, a tax loss on the disposition of the foreign corporation's stock.

A specified 10-percent owned foreign corporation is any foreign corporation (other than a passive foreign investment company (PFIC) that is not also a CFC) with respect to which any domestic corporation is a U.S. shareholder (Code Sec. 245A(b), as added by the 2017 Tax Cuts Act; see ¶705).

> **Comment:** The subpart F definitions of a U.S. shareholder and CFC are expanded so that they are used for purposes of Title 26 (including the participation DRD), and not just the subpart F provisions (Act Sec. 14101(e)(1) and (2) of the 2017 Tax Cuts Act, amending Code Secs. 951(b) and 957(a), respectively; see ¶705). The U.S. shareholder definition is further expanded so that a U.S. shareholder includes a U.S. person that owns at least 10 percent of the total combined voting power of all classes of stock entitled to vote or at least 10 percent of the total value of all classes of stock of the foreign corporation (Act Sec. 14214(a) of the 2017 Tax Cuts Act, amending Code Sec. 951(b); see ¶745).

Sale by a CFC of a lower-tier CFC. If for any tax year of a CFC beginning after December 31, 2017, an amount is treated as a dividend under Code Sec. 964(e)(1) because of a sale or exchange by the CFC of stock in another foreign corporation held for one year or more, then:

(1) the foreign-source portion of the dividend is treated as subpart F income of the selling CFC for that tax year for purposes of the subpart F income inclusion rules;

(2) a U.S. shareholder with respect to the selling CFC includes in income for the tax year of the shareholder with or within which the tax year of the CFC ends, an amount equal to the shareholder's pro rata share of the amount treated as subpart F income under item (1), above; and

(3) a participation DRD is allowable to the U.S. shareholder with respect to the included subpart F income under item (2), above, in the same manner as if the subpart F income were a dividend received by the shareholder from the selling CFC (Code Sec. 964(e)(4)(A), as added by the 2017 Tax Cuts Act).

¶707

NEW LAW EXPLAINED

> **Practice Note:** The foreign-source portion of any amount treated as a dividend under this rule is determined in the same manner as the foreign-source portion of a dividend eligible for the participation DRD (see ¶705) (Code Sec. 964(e)(4)(C), as added by the 2017 Tax Cuts Act).

If a CFC sells or exchanges stock in another foreign corporation in a tax year of the selling CFC beginning after December 31, 2017, stock basis adjustment rules similar to the rules of Code Sec. 961(d) apply (Code Sec. 964(e)(4)(B), as added by the 2017 Tax Cuts Act).

Treatment of foreign branch losses transferred to specified 10-percent owned foreign corporations. If a domestic corporation transfers substantially all of the assets of a foreign branch (within the meaning of Code Sec. 367(a)(3)(C), as in effect before December 22, 2017, the date of the enactment of the 2017 Tax Cuts Act) to a specified 10-percent owned foreign corporation with respect to which it is a U.S. shareholder after the transfer, the domestic corporation includes in income, for the tax year of the transfer, an amount equal to the transferred loss amount, subject to certain limitations (Code Sec. 91(a), as added by the 2017 Tax Cuts Act).

The transferred loss amount, with respect to any transfer of substantially all of the assets of a foreign branch, is the excess (if any) of:

(1) the losses incurred by the foreign branch after December 31, 2017, and before the transfer, for which a deduction was allowed to the domestic corporation, over

(2) the sum of (i) any taxable income earned by the foreign branch in tax years after the tax year in which the loss is incurred and through the close of the tax year of the transfer, and (ii) gain recognized by reason of a Code Sec. 904(f)(3) overall foreign loss recapture arising out of disposition of assets on account of the underlying transfer (Code Sec. 91(b), as added by the 2017 Tax Cuts Act).

> **Comment:** According to the Conference Committee Report, this loss recapture rule addresses the concern that taxpayers may wish to arbitrarily apply the participation exemption system to foreign subsidiaries but not foreign branches. Specifically, a taxpayer may deduct losses from a foreign branch operation against U.S. taxable income and then incorporate that branch once it becomes profitable. Even though there are other loss recapture rules, such as Code Sec. 367(a)(3)(C), these rules generally rely on the worldwide system of taxation to recapture losses in excess of built-in gains by taxing future earnings when the earnings are repatriated to the United States. Instead of only recapturing such losses upon later repatriation of earnings, the new law intends to recapture the U.S. tax benefits of these losses immediately upon the incorporation of a foreign branch that has generated losses. This way, the repatriation of foreign earnings will not carry negative tax consequences, thus discouraging repatriation, which is one of the reasons to transition to a participation exemption system of taxation (Conference Report on H.R. 1, Tax Cuts and Jobs Act (H. Rept. 115-466)).

The transferred loss amount is reduced (but not below zero) by the amount of gain recognized by the taxpayer (other than gain recognized by reason of an overall foreign loss recapture) on account of the transfer (Code Sec. 91(c), as added by the 2017 Tax Cuts Act).

¶707

NEW LAW EXPLAINED

Amounts included in gross income under the above foreign branch loss recapture rules are treated as derived from sources within the United States (Code Sec. 91(d), as added by the 2017 Tax Cuts Act).

Consistent with regulations or other guidance as the Secretary of the Treasury may prescribe, proper adjustments are made in the adjusted basis of the taxpayer's stock in the specified 10-percent owned foreign corporation to which the transfer is made, and in the transferee's adjusted basis in the property transferred, to reflect amounts included in gross income under the foreign branch loss recapture rules, discussed above (Code Sec. 91(e), as added by the 2017 Tax Cuts Act).

Under a transition rule, the amount of gain taken into account under Code Sec. 91(c) is reduced by the amount of gain that would be recognized under Code Sec. 367(a)(3)(C) (determined without regard to the repeal of the Code Sec. 367(a)(3) active trade or business requirement by the 2017 Tax Cuts Act, discussed below) with respect to losses incurred before January 1, 2018 (Act Sec. 14102(d)(4) of the 2017 Tax Cuts Act).

Repeal of the active trade or business exception under Code Sec. 367. The active trade or business exception to the Code Sec. 367(a) rule requiring recognition of gain on the outbound transfer of property by a U.S. transferor to a foreign corporation is repealed (Act Sec. 14102(e)(1) of the 2017 Tax Cuts Act, striking Code Sec. 367(a)(3)).

> **Comment:** As a result of the repeal, transfers of property used in the active conduct of a trade or business from a U.S. corporation to a foreign corporation in an otherwise tax-free transaction will be treated as taxable exchanges since the foreign corporation will not be considered a corporation.

▶ **Effective date.** The amendments made by this section relating to sales or exchanges of foreign corporation stock by a domestic corporation and sales or exchanges of a lower-tier CFC stock by a CFC apply to sales or exchanges after December 31, 2017 (Act Secs. 14102(a)(2) and (c)(2) of Tax Cuts and Jobs Act (P.L. 115-97)). The amendment relating to the reduction of basis in stock of a specified 10-percent owned foreign corporation for purposes of determining loss applies to distributions made after December 31, 2017 (Act Sec. 14102(b)(2) of the 2017 Tax Cuts Act). The amendments relating to the transfer of loss amounts from foreign branches to certain foreign corporations and to the repeal of the active trade or business exception under Code Sec. 367 apply to transfers after December 31, 2017 (Act Secs. 14102(d)(3) and (e)(3) of the 2017 Tax Cuts Act). No specific effective dates are provided for the other provisions; therefore, such provisions are considered effective on December 22, 2017, the date of enactment.

Law source: Law at ¶5210, ¶5450, ¶5915, ¶5925, and ¶5985. Committee Report at ¶11,000, ¶11,010, ¶11,020, ¶11,030, and ¶11,050.

— Act Sec. 14102(a)(1) of the Tax Cuts and Jobs Act (P.L. 115-97), redesignating Code Sec. 1248(j) as Code Sec. 1248(k) and adding Code Sec. 1248(j);

— Act Sec. 14102(b)(1), adding Code Sec. 961(d);

— Act Sec. 14102(c)(1), adding Code Sec. 964(e)(4);

— Act Sec. 14102(d)(1), adding Code Sec. 91;

— Act Sec. 14102(d)(4);

— Act Sec. 14102(e)(1) and (2), amending Code Sec. 367(a);

— Act Sec. 14102(a)(2), (b)(2), (c)(2), (d)(3) and (e)(3), providing the effective date.

¶707

¶710 Treatment of Deferred Foreign Income Upon Transition to Participation Exemption System of Taxation

SUMMARY OF NEW LAW

A transition tax is generally imposed on accumulated foreign earnings, without requiring an actual distribution, upon the transition to the new participation exemption system. Under the transition rule, for the last tax year beginning before January 1, 2018, any U.S. shareholder of any CFC or other foreign corporation (other than a PFIC that is not a CFC) that is at least 10-percent owned by a domestic corporation must include in income its pro rata share of the accumulated post-1986 foreign earnings of the corporation as of November 2, 2017, or December 31, 2017, whichever amount is greater (mandatory inclusion). A portion of the mandatory income inclusion is deductible. The deduction amount depends upon whether the deferred earnings are held in cash or other assets. The deduction results in a reduced rate of tax of 15.5 percent for the included deferred foreign income held in liquid form and eight percent for the remaining deferred foreign income. A corresponding portion of the foreign tax credit is disallowed. The transition tax can be paid in installments over an eight-year period. Special rules are provided for U.S. shareholders that are S corporations or REITs, or that become expatriated entities after December 22, 2017.

BACKGROUND

A U.S. person is subject to U.S. tax on its worldwide income. Generally, a U.S. person is currently taxed on any directly earned foreign income (such as income earned directly from the conduct of a foreign business). However, a U.S. person that earns foreign-source income indirectly as a shareholder in a foreign corporation generally is not subject to U.S. tax until the foreign income is distributed to the U.S. person as a dividend.

> **Comment:** The United States is one of the few industrialized countries with a worldwide system of taxation and has the highest statutory corporate tax rates among OECD member countries. The worldwide system of taxation and the high tax rates provide incentives for U.S. companies to keep foreign earnings offshore because such earnings are not taxed until repatriated to the United States. As a result, many U.S. companies have accumulated significant untaxed and undistributed foreign earnings.

Certain anti-deferral rules may currently tax a U.S. person on certain categories of passive or highly mobile foreign-source income, regardless of whether the income has been distributed to the U.S. person.

Subpart F and CFC rules. The main category of anti-deferral rules are the subpart F rules (Code Secs. 951-965). Under the subpart F rules, U.S. shareholders of a controlled foreign corporation (CFC) are currently taxed on their pro rata shares of the CFC's subpart F income without regard to whether the income is distributed to the

BACKGROUND

shareholders (Code Sec. 951(a)). A CFC generally is any foreign corporation in which U.S. shareholders own more than 50 percent of the corporation's stock (measured by vote or value) (Code Sec. 957). For this purpose, a U.S. shareholder is a U.S. person who owns at least 10 percent of the voting stock of the foreign corporation (Code Sec. 951(b)).

With certain exceptions, subpart F income generally includes passive income and other income that is readily movable from one taxing jurisdiction to another (Code Sec. 952). A U.S. shareholder of a CFC may exclude from its income actual distributions of the CFC's earnings and profits that were previously included in the shareholder's income under subpart F (Code Sec. 959).

The subpart F amount included in the gross income of any U.S. shareholder for any tax year and attributable to a qualified activity is reduced by the amount of the shareholder's pro rata share of any qualified deficit. The term "qualified deficit" means any deficit in earnings and profits of the CFC for any prior tax year that began after December 31, 1986, and for which the CFC was a CFC, but only to the extent the deficit (i) is attributable to the same qualified activity as the activity giving rise to the income being offset, and (ii) has not previously been taken into account (Code Sec. 952(c)(1)(B)).

PFIC regime. Another set of anti-deferral rules are the passive foreign investment company (PFIC) rules (Code Secs. 1291-1298). A PFIC is generally any foreign corporation if 75 percent or more of its gross income for the tax year consists of passive income, or 50 percent or more of its assets consists of assets that produce, or are held for the production of, passive income (Code Sec. 1297). Different sets of income inclusion rules apply to U.S. persons that are shareholders in a PFIC, regardless of their percentage ownership in the company.

Foreign tax credit. To prevent double taxation of foreign-source income, a foreign tax credit is generally available to offset, in whole or in part, the U.S. tax owed on foreign-source income, regardless of whether the income is earned directly by the U.S. taxpayer, repatriated as an actual dividend, or included in the taxpayer's income under one of the anti-deferral regimes (Code Secs. 901 and 960). The credit is allowed for any income, war profits and excess profits taxes paid or accrued during the tax year to a foreign country or U.S. possession. The foreign tax credit cannot be used to offset U.S. tax on U.S.-source income, so it is generally limited to a taxpayer's U.S. tax liability on its foreign source taxable income (Code Sec. 904).

Temporary dividends-received deduction for repatriated foreign earnings. The American Jobs Creation Act of 2004 (P.L. 108-357) added Code Sec. 965 to provide a temporary 85-percent dividends-received deduction (DRD) for certain cash dividends received by U.S. corporate shareholders from CFCs during one tax year for which an election under Code Sec. 965 was in effect. The deduction provided temporary relief and was intended to reduce the U.S. tax on repatriated dividends, and thus, encourage U.S. companies to repatriate their accumulated foreign earnings and invest them in the United States. At the taxpayer's election, the deduction was available for dividends received either during the taxpayer's first tax year beginning

BACKGROUND

on or after October 22, 2004, or during the taxpayer's last tax year beginning before such date.

The temporary deduction was subject to a number of general limitations. It applied only to cash repatriations generally in excess of the taxpayer's average repatriation level calculated for a three-year base period preceding the year of the deduction. The amount of dividends eligible for the deduction was generally limited to the amount of earnings shown as permanently invested outside the United States on the taxpayer's recent audited financial statements. In addition, to qualify for the deduction, dividends were required to be invested in the United States according to a domestic reinvestment plan approved by the taxpayer's senior management and board of directors.

No foreign tax credit or deduction was allowed for foreign taxes attributable to the deductible portion of any dividend. For this purpose, the taxpayer was permitted to specifically identify which dividends were treated as carrying the deduction and which dividends were not. Deductions were also disallowed for expenses that were directly allocable to the deductible portion of any dividend.

Expatriated entities. Generally, in a corporate inversion transaction (1) a U.S. corporation or partnership (the expatriated entity) becomes a subsidiary of a foreign corporation (a surrogate foreign corporation) or otherwise transfers substantially all of its properties to it, (2) the former shareholders or partners of the expatriated entity hold 60 percent or more (by vote or value) of the stock of the surrogate foreign corporation after the transaction, and (3) the surrogate foreign corporation's expanded affiliated group (EAG) does not conduct substantial business activities in the foreign corporation's country of incorporation (Code Sec. 7874(a)(2)). In this case, a corporate inversion "tax" is imposed on the inversion gain of expatriated entities during the 10-year period after the inversion. If after the inversion transaction, former shareholders or partners of the expatriated entity hold 80 percent or more (by vote or value) of the stock of the surrogate foreign corporation after the transaction, the surrogate foreign corporation is treated as a domestic corporation for U.S. tax purposes (Code Sec. 7874(b)).

Real Estate Investment Trusts. To qualify as a real estate investment trust (REIT), an entity must meet certain income requirements. A REIT is restricted to earning certain types of generally passive income. Among other requirements, at least 75 percent of the gross income of a REIT in each tax year must consist of real estate-related income (Code Sec. 856). In addition, a REIT is required to distribute at least 90 percent of REIT income (other than net capital gain) annually (Code Sec. 857). Unlike a regular subchapter C corporation, a REIT is able to deduct the portion of its income that is distributed to its shareholders as a dividend or qualifying liquidating distribution each year. The distributed income of the REIT is not taxed at the entity level, but at the investor level.

NEW LAW EXPLAINED

Transition tax imposed on accumulated foreign earnings upon transition to participation exemption system.—A transition tax is imposed on accumulated

NEW LAW EXPLAINED

post-1986 foreign earnings determined as of a certain measurement date, without requiring an actual distribution, upon the transition to the new participation exemption system. The transition rule requires mandatory inclusion of such deferred foreign income as subpart F income by U.S. shareholders of deferred foreign income corporations. The included amount is taxed at a reduced rate that depends on whether the deferred earnings are held in cash or other assets (Code Sec. 965, as amended by the Tax Cuts and Jobs Act (P.L. 115-97)).

> **Comment:** In transitioning to the new participation exemption (territorial) system of taxation, many U.S. corporations with undistributed accumulated foreign earnings will be eligible for the 100-percent participation exemption deduction for foreign-source dividends under new Code Sec. 245A (a participation dividends-received deduction (DRD)). To avoid a potential windfall for such corporations, and to ensure that all distributions from foreign corporations are treated in the same manner under the participation exemption system, a transition rule is provided under which accumulated foreign earnings are taxed as if they had been distributed under prior law, but at a reduced rate of tax. Generally, the new participation exemption system for taxation of foreign income replaces the prior-law system of taxing U.S. corporations on the foreign earnings of their foreign subsidiaries when the earnings are distributed. The exemption is provided in the form of a participation DRD, which is intended to encourage U.S. companies to repatriate their accumulated foreign earnings and invest them in the United States. See ¶705 for a discussion of the participation DRD.

Subpart F income inclusion of deferred foreign income. As mentioned above, the mechanism for the mandatory inclusion of accumulated foreign earnings is subpart F. In particular, for the last tax year beginning before January 1, 2018, the subpart F income of a deferred foreign income corporation (as otherwise determined for that tax year under Code Sec. 952) is increased by the greater of (i) the accumulated post-1986 deferred foreign income of the corporation determined as of November 2, 2017, or (ii) the accumulated post-1986 deferred foreign income of the corporation determined as of December 31, 2017 (Code Sec. 965(a), as amended by the 2017 Tax Cuts Act).

> **Comment:** Foreign corporations no longer in existence and for which there is no tax year beginning or ending in 2017 are not within the scope of this transition rule.

For this purpose, a deferred foreign income corporation with respect to any U.S. shareholder is any specified foreign corporation of the U.S. shareholder that has accumulated post-1986 deferred foreign income as of November 2, 2017, or December 31, 2017, greater than zero (Code Sec. 965(d)(1), as amended by the 2017 Tax Cuts Act).

A specified foreign corporation is (1) a CFC, or (2) any foreign corporation in which a domestic corporation is a U.S. shareholder, other than a PFIC that is not a CFC. For purposes of the Code Sec. 951 subpart F inclusion rules and the Code Sec. 961 rules requiring adjustments to the basis of the CFC stock, a foreign corporation described in item (2), above, is treated as a CFC solely for purposes of taking into account the subpart F income of the corporation under the transition rule and determining the

NEW LAW EXPLAINED

U.S. shareholder pro rata share of that income (Code Sec. 965(e), as amended by the 2017 Tax Cuts Act).

> **Comment:** A non-CFC foreign corporation must have at least one U.S. shareholder that is a domestic corporation in order for the foreign corporation to be a specified foreign corporation. In addition, unlike the participation DRD that is available only to domestic corporations that are U.S. shareholders under subpart F, the transition rule applies to all U.S. shareholders of a specified foreign corporation. The subpart F definitions of a U.S. shareholder and CFC are expanded so that they are used for purposes of Title 26, and not just the subpart F provisions (Act Sec. 14101(e)(1) and (2) of the 2017 Tax Cuts Act, amending Code Secs. 951(b) and 957(a); see ¶705). The U.S. shareholder definition is further expanded so that a U.S. shareholder includes a U.S. person that owns at least 10 percent of the total combined voting power of all classes of stock entitled to vote or at least 10 percent of the total value of all classes of stock of the foreign corporation (Act Sec. 14214(a) of the 2017 Tax Cuts Act, amending Code Sec. 951(b); see ¶745).

> **Comment:** For purposes of taking into account its subpart F income under the transition rule, a noncontrolled 10/50 corporation is treated as a CFC (Conference Report on H.R. 1, Tax Cuts and Jobs Act (H. Rept. 115-466)).

The accumulated post-1986 deferred foreign income includes the post-1986 earnings and profits that (i) are not attributable to income that is effectively connected with the conduct of a trade or business in the United States and subject to tax under Chapter 1 of the Code, or (ii) if distributed, in the case of a CFC, would be excluded from the gross income of a U.S. shareholder as previously taxed income under Code Sec. 959 (Code Sec. 965(d)(2), as amended by the 2017 Tax Cuts Act).

To the extent provided in regulations or other guidance, the accumulated post-1986 deferred foreign income of a CFC that has non-U.S. shareholders is appropriately reduced by amounts which would be described in item (ii), above (i.e., amounts excluded from the U.S. shareholder's income as previously taxed earnings) if such shareholders were U.S. shareholders.

Post-1986 earnings and profits include the earnings and profits of the foreign corporation accumulated in tax years beginning after December 31, 1986, and determined (i) as of November 2, 2017, or December 31, 2017, whichever measurement date applies to the foreign corporation, and (ii) without decrease for dividends distributed during the last tax year beginning before January 1, 2018, other than dividends distributed to another specified foreign corporation. Post-1986 earnings and profits are computed under the rules of Code Secs. 964(a) and 986 for determining earnings and profits of a CFC, but only taking into account periods when the foreign corporation was a specified foreign corporation (Code Sec. 965(d)(3), as amended by the 2017 Tax Cuts Act).

> **Practice Note:** Therefore, post-1986 earnings and profits that are subject to the transition tax do not include earnings and profits that were accumulated by a foreign corporation prior to attaining its status as a specified foreign corporation. However, post-1986 earnings and profits are taken into account even if arising

¶710

NEW LAW EXPLAINED

from periods during which the U.S. shareholder did not own stock of the foreign corporation.

Reduction of amounts included in the U.S. shareholder's income. Consistent with the general operation of subpart F, each U.S. shareholder of a deferred foreign income corporation must include in income its pro rata share of the foreign corporation's subpart F income attributable to its accumulated post-1986 deferred foreign income. In the case where the taxpayer is a U.S. shareholder of at least one deferred foreign income corporation and at least one E&P deficit foreign corporation, the mandatory inclusion amount of the U.S. shareholder that otherwise would be taken into account as the U.S. shareholder's pro rata share of the subpart F income of each deferred foreign income corporation is reduced by the amount of the U.S. shareholder's aggregate foreign earnings and profits (E&P) deficit that is allocated to that deferred foreign income corporation (Code Sec. 965(b)(1), as amended by the 2017 Tax Cuts Act).

> **Comment:** In other words, the mandatory inclusion amount under the transition rule is reduced by the portion of the aggregate foreign E&P deficit allocated to the U.S. shareholder by reason of the shareholder's interest in one or more E&P deficit foreign corporations.

> **Practice Note:** For purposes of the mandatory inclusion rule, the determination of the U.S. shareholder's pro rata share of any amount with respect to any specified foreign corporation is determined under the subpart F inclusion rules by treating that amount in the same manner as subpart F income, and by treating the specified foreign corporation as a CFC. The portion of the U.S. shareholder's mandatory inclusion amount that is equal to the deduction allowed under Code Sec. 965(c) (discussed further below) is treated tax-exempt income for purposes of Code Sec. 705(a)(1)(B) (which requires an increase in a partner's basis in a partnership by the partner's distributive share of the partnership's tax-exempt income) and Code Sec. 1367(a)(1)(A) (which requires an increase in an S shareholder's basis in stock for tax-exempt income). However, that amount is not treated as tax-exempt income for purposes of determining whether an adjustment is made to an accumulated adjustment account under Code Sec. 1368(e)(1)(A) (Code Sec. 965(f), as amended by the 2017 Tax Cuts Act).

The U.S. shareholder allocates the aggregate foreign E&P deficit among the deferred foreign income corporations in which the shareholder is a U.S. shareholder. The aggregate foreign E&P deficit is allocable to a specified foreign corporation in the same ratio as (i) the U.S. shareholder's pro rata share of post-1986 deferred income in that corporation bears to (ii) the aggregate of the U.S. shareholder's pro rata share of accumulated post-1986 deferred foreign income from all deferred income companies of the shareholder (Code Sec. 965(b)(2), as amended by the 2017 Tax Cuts Act).

The aggregate foreign E&P deficit is the lesser of (i) the aggregate of the U.S. shareholder's pro rata shares of the specified E&P deficits of the E&P deficit foreign corporations of the shareholder, or (ii) the aggregate of the U.S. shareholder's pro rata share of the accumulated post-1986 deferred foreign income of all deferred foreign income corporations (Code Sec. 965(b)(3)(A)(i), as added by the 2017 Tax Cuts Act). If the amount described in (ii), above, is less than the amount described in (i), above,

NEW LAW EXPLAINED

then the shareholder must designate (in the form and manner determined by the Secretary of the Treasury):

(1) the amount of the specified E&P deficit that is to be taken into account for each E&P deficit corporation with respect to the taxpayer; and

(2) in the case of an E&P deficit corporation that has a qualified deficit (as defined in Code Sec. 952), the portion (if any) of the deficit taken into account under item (1), above, that is attributable to a qualified deficit, including the qualified activities to which such portion is attributable (Code Sec. 965(b)(3)(A)(ii), as added by the 2017 Tax Cuts Act).

An E&P deficit foreign corporation is any specified foreign corporation with respect to which the taxpayer is a U.S. shareholder, if as of November 2, 2017 (i) the specified foreign corporation has a deficit in post-1986 earnings and profits, (ii) the corporation was a specified foreign corporation, and (iii) the taxpayer was a U.S. shareholder of the corporation. The specified E&P deficit with respect to any E&P deficit foreign corporation is the amount of the deficit in its post-1986 earnings and profits, described in the previous sentence (Code Sec. 965(b)(3)(B), as amended by the 2017 Tax Cuts Act).

> **Comment:** Accordingly, the deficits of a foreign subsidiary that accumulated prior to its acquisition by the U.S. shareholder may be taken into account in determining the aggregate foreign E&P deficit of the U.S. shareholder.

> **Comment:** According to the Conference Committee Report, the deficits (including hovering deficits described in Reg. § 1.367(b)-17(d)(2)) of a foreign subsidiary that accumulated while it was a specified foreign corporation may be taken into account in determining the aggregate foreign E&P deficit of a U.S. shareholder. Therefore, the amount of post-1986 earnings and profits of a specified foreign corporation is the amount of positive earnings and profits accumulated as of the measurement date reduced by any deficit in earnings and profits of the specified foreign corporation as of the measurement date, without regard to the foreign tax credit limitation category of the earnings or deficit.

> For example, if a foreign corporation organized after December 31, 1986, has $100 of accumulated earnings and profits as of November 2, 2017, and December 31, 2017 (determined without reduction for dividends distributed during the tax year and after any increase for qualified deficits), which consist of $120 general limitation earnings and profits and a $20 passive limitation deficit, the foreign corporation's post-1986 earnings and profits would be $100, even if the $20 passive limitation deficit was a hovering deficit. Foreign income taxes related to the hovering deficit, however, would not generally be deemed paid by the U.S. shareholder recognizing an incremental income inclusion. However, it is expected that the Secretary may issue guidance to provide that, solely for purposes of calculating the amount of foreign income taxes deemed paid by the U.S. shareholder with respect to a mandatory inclusion, a hovering deficit may be absorbed by current year earnings and profits and the foreign income taxes related to the hovering deficit may be added to the specified foreign corporation's post-1986 foreign income taxes in that separate category on a pro rata basis

¶710

NEW LAW EXPLAINED

in the year of inclusion (Conference Report on H.R. 1, Tax Cuts and Jobs Act (H. Rept. 115-466)).

Treatment of earnings and profits in future years. For purposes of excluding previously taxed earnings from the U.S. shareholder's income in any tax year beginning with the last tax year beginning before January 1, 2018, an amount equal to the reduction for the U.S. shareholder's aggregate foreign E&P deficit allocated to the deferred foreign income corporation is treated as an amount included in the U.S. shareholder's gross income under the subpart F inclusion rules (Code Sec. 965(b)(4)(B), as amended by the 2017 Tax Cuts Act).

> **Comment:** Accordingly, the reduced earnings and profits are treated as previously taxed income when distributed.

In addition, the U.S. shareholder's pro rata share of the earnings and profits of any specified E&P deficit foreign corporation is increased by the amount of the corporation's specified E&P deficit taken into account in computing the mandatory inclusion. For purposes of determining subpart F income, this increase is attributable to the same activity to which the deficit taken into account was attributable (Code Sec. 965(b)(4)(A), as amended by the 2017 Tax Cuts Act).

Intragroup netting among U.S. shareholders in an affiliated group. The transition rule permits intragroup netting among U.S. shareholders in an affiliated group in which there is at least one U.S. shareholder with a net E&P surplus (i.e., the shareholder's mandatory inclusion amount is greater than zero) and another with a net E&P deficit (i.e., the aggregate foreign E&P deficit of the shareholder exceeds the shareholder's mandatory inclusion amount). The net E&P surplus shareholder may reduce its net surplus by the shareholder's applicable share of the group's aggregate unused E&P deficit, based on the group ownership percentage of the members (Code Sec. 965(b)(5), as amended by the 2017 Tax Cuts Act).

> **Comment:** Accordingly, deferred earnings of a U.S. shareholder are reduced by the shareholder's share of deficits as of November 2, 2017, from a specified foreign corporation that is not a deferred foreign income corporation, including the pro rata share of deficits of another U.S. shareholder in a different U.S. ownership chain within the same U.S. affiliated group.

The applicable share with respect to any E&P net surplus shareholder in the group is the amount that bears the same proportion to the group's aggregate unused E&P deficit as (i) the product of the shareholder's group ownership percentage, multiplied by the mandatory inclusion amount that would otherwise be taken into account by the shareholder, bears to (ii) the aggregate amount in item (i) determined with respect to all E&P net surplus shareholders in the group (Code Sec. 965(b)(5)(E), as amended by the 2017 Tax Cuts Act).

The group's aggregate unused E&P deficit is the lesser of the sum of the net E&P deficit of each E&P net deficit shareholder in the group (or a percentage of that amount based on the group ownership percentage of each shareholder), or the amount determined in item (ii), above (Code Sec. 965(b)(5)(D), as amended by the 2017 Tax Cuts Act).

NEW LAW EXPLAINED

The group ownership percentage with respect to a U.S. shareholder in the group is the percentage of the value of the U.S. shareholder stock that is held by other includible corporations in the group. However, the group ownership percentage of the common parent of the affiliated group is 100 percent (Code Sec. 965(b)(5)(F), as amended by the 2017 Tax Cuts Act).

> **Example:** A U.S. corporation has two domestic subsidiaries, X and Y, each of which it owns 100 percent and 80 percent, respectively. If X has a $1,000 net E&P surplus, and Y has $1,000 net E&P deficit, X is an E&P net surplus shareholder, and Y is an E&P net deficit shareholder. The net E&P surplus of X is reduced by the net E&P deficit of Y to the extent of the group's ownership percentage in Y, which is 80 percent. The remaining net E&P deficit of Y is unused. If the U.S. shareholder Z is also a wholly owned subsidiary of the same U.S. parent as X and Y, the group ownership percentage of Y is unchanged, and the surpluses of X and Z are reduced ratably by 800 of the net E&P deficit of Y.

> **Comment:** The Conference Committee Report states that it is expect that the Secretary of the Treasury will exercise his authority under the consolidated return provisions to appropriately limit the netting across chains of ownership within a group of related parties in the application of the mandatory inclusion rules. However, nothing in these rules is intended to be interpreted as limiting the Secretary's authority to use such regulatory authority to prescribe regulations on proper application of the mandatory inclusion rules on a consolidated basis for affiliated groups filing a consolidated return (Conference Report on H.R. 1, Tax Cuts and Jobs Act (H. Rept. 115-466)).

Deduction from mandatory inclusion. A U.S. shareholder of a specified foreign corporation is allowed a deduction of a portion of the increased subpart F income attributable to the mandatory inclusion of deferred foreign income. The amount of the deduction is the sum of (i) the 15.5-percent rate equivalent percentage of the inclusion amount that is the shareholder's aggregate foreign cash position, and (ii) the eight percent rate equivalent percentage of the portion of the inclusion amount that exceeds the shareholder's aggregate foreign cash position (Code Sec. 965(c)(1), as added by the 2017 Tax Cuts Act).

> **Comment:** The calculation is based on the highest rate of tax applicable to corporations in the tax year of inclusion, even if the U.S. shareholder is an individual.

The eight-percent rate equivalent percentage (or the 15.5-percent rate equivalent percentage) with respect to any U.S. shareholder for any tax year is the percentage that would result in the amount to which that percentage applies being subject to an eight-percent rate of tax (or a 15.5-percent rate of tax, respectively) determined by only taking into account a deduction equal to the percentage of that amount and the highest rate of tax under Code Sec. 11 for the tax year. In the case of any tax year of a U.S. shareholder to which Code Sec. 15 applies, the highest rate of tax under Code Sec. 11 before the effective date of the change in rates and the highest rate of tax under that section after the effective date of that change is each taken into account

NEW LAW EXPLAINED

under this rule in the same proportions as the portion of the year that is before and after that effective date, respectively (Code Sec. 965(c)(2), as added by the 2017 Tax Cuts Act).

> **Comment:** The use of rate equivalent percentages is intended to ensure that the rates of tax imposed on the deferred foreign income is similar for all U.S. shareholders, regardless of the year of the mandatory inclusion. By stating the permitted deduction in the form of a tax rate equivalent percentage, the transition rule ensures that the accumulated post-1986 deferred foreign income is subject to either an eight-percent or 15.5-percent rate of tax, depending on the underlying assets as of the measurement date, without regard to the corporate tax rate that may be in effect at the time of the inclusion. For example, fiscal-year corporate taxpayers may report the increased subpart F income in a tax year for which a reduced corporate tax rate would otherwise apply (on a prorated basis under Code Sec. 15), but the allowable deduction would be reduced so that the rate of U.S. tax on the income inclusion would be eight or 15.5 percent.

Aggregate foreign cash position. With respect to any U.S. shareholder, the aggregate foreign cash position is the greater of:

(1) the aggregate of the U.S. shareholder's pro rata share of the cash position of each specified foreign corporation of the U.S. shareholder determined as of the close of the last tax year of the specified foreign corporation that begins before January 1, 2018; or

(2) one half of the sum of:

    (a) the aggregate described in item (1), above, determined as of the close of the last tax year of each specified foreign corporation that ends before November 2, 2017, plus

    (b) the aggregate described in item (1), above, determined as of the close of the tax year of each specified foreign corporation that precedes the tax year referred to in item (a), above (Code Sec. 965(c)(3)(A), as amended by the 2017 Tax Cuts Act).

> **Comment:** In other words, the aggregate foreign cash position is the greater of the aggregate cash position as of the last day of the last tax year beginning before January 1, 2018, and the average aggregate cash position as of the last day of each of the last two years ending before the date of introduction (November 2, 2017).

The cash position of any specified foreign corporation is the sum of:

(1) cash held by the foreign corporation;

(2) the net accounts receivable of the foreign corporation (the excess (if any) of the corporation's accounts receivable over its accounts payable, determined under Code Sec. 461), plus

(3) the fair market value of the following assets held by the corporation:

    (a) Actively traded personal property for which there is an established financial market.

NEW LAW EXPLAINED

(b) Commercial paper, certificates of deposit, the securities of the Federal government and of any State or foreign government.

(c) Any foreign currency.

(d) Any obligation with a term of less than one year.

(e) Any asset that the Secretary identifies as being economically equivalent to the assets described above (Code Sec. 965(c)(3)(B) and (C), as amended by the 2017 Tax Cuts Act).

To avoid double counting, cash assets described in items (2), (3)(a) and (3)(d), above, are not taken into account in determining the aggregate foreign cash position to the extent that the U.S. shareholder demonstrates to the satisfaction of the Secretary that the amount is taken into account by the shareholder with respect to another specified foreign corporation (Code Sec. 965(c)(2)(D), as added by the 2017 Tax Cuts Act).

> **Comment:** Thus, cash holdings of a specified foreign corporation in the form of publicly traded stock may be excluded to the extent that a U.S. shareholder can demonstrate that the value of the stock was taken into account as cash or cash equivalent by another specified foreign corporation of the U.S. shareholder.

Cash positions of certain noncorporate entities. A noncorporate entity is treated as a specified foreign corporation of a U.S. shareholder for purposes of determining the shareholder's aggregate foreign cash position if (i) any interest in the entity is held by a specified foreign corporation of the U.S. shareholder (determined after application of this rule), and (ii) the entity would be a specified foreign corporation of the shareholder if the entity were a foreign corporation (Code Sec. 965(c)(2)(E), as added by the 2017 Tax Cuts Act).

> **Comment:** As stated in the Conference Committee Report, the cash position of a U.S. shareholder does not generally include the cash attributable to a direct ownership interest in a partnership, but cash positions of certain noncorporate foreign entities owned by a specified foreign corporation are taken into account if such entities would be specified foreign corporations if the entity were a foreign corporation. For example, if a U.S. shareholder owns a five-percent interest in a partnership, the balance of which is held by specified foreign corporations of the U.S. shareholder, the partnership is treated as a specified foreign corporation with respect to the U.S. shareholder, and the cash or cash equivalents held by the partnership are includible in the aggregate cash position of the U.S. shareholder on a look-through basis. It is expected that the Secretary will provide guidance for taking into account only the specified foreign corporation's share of the partnership's cash position, and not the five-percent interest directly owned by the U.S. shareholder (Conference Report on H.R. 1, Tax Cuts and Jobs Act (H. Rept. 115-466)).

Anti-abuse rule. The Secretary is authorized to disregard transactions that are determined to have the principal purpose of reducing the aggregate foreign cash position (Code Sec. 965(c)(2)(F), as added by the 2017 Tax Cuts Act).

Disallowance of foreign tax credit and deduction for taxes. No foreign tax credit or deduction is allowed for a portion (referred to as an applicable percentage) of any foreign income taxes paid or accrued (or deemed paid or accrued) with respect to any

NEW LAW EXPLAINED

mandatory inclusion amount for which a deduction is allowed under the above rules (Code Sec. 965(g)(1) and (3), as added by the 2017 Tax Cuts Act).

The disallowed portion of the foreign tax credit is 55.7 percent of foreign taxes paid attributable to the portion of the inclusion amount attributable to the U.S. shareholder's aggregate foreign cash position, plus 77.1 percent of foreign taxes paid attributable to the remaining portion of the mandatory inclusion amount (Code Sec. 965(g)(2), as added by the 2017 Tax Cuts Act).

> **Comment:** Other foreign tax credits used by a taxpayer against tax liability resulting from the deemed inclusion apply in full.

> **Comment:** As a result of this foreign tax credit disallowance rule, the foreign tax credit is limited to the taxable portion of the mandatory inclusion amount.

A special rule coordinates the disallowance of foreign tax credits, described above, with the Code Sec. 78 requirement that a domestic corporate shareholder is deemed to receive a dividend in an amount equal to foreign taxes it is deemed to have paid and for which it claimed a credit. Under the coordination rule, the foreign taxes treated as paid or accrued by a domestic corporation as a result of the mandatory inclusion are limited to those taxes in proportion to the taxable portion of the mandatory inclusion. The gross-up amount equals the total foreign income taxes multiplied by a fraction, the numerator of which is the taxable portion of the increased subpart F income inclusion under the transition rule and the denominator of which is the total increase in subpart F income under the transition rule (Code Sec. 965(g)(4), as added by the 2017 Tax Cuts Act).

Installment payments. A U.S. shareholder of a deferred foreign income corporation may elect to pay the net tax liability resulting from the mandatory inclusion of deferred foreign income in eight installments. If installment payment is elected, the payments for each of the first five years equals eight percent of the net tax liability. The amount of the sixth installment is 15 percent of the net tax liability, increasing to 20 percent for the seventh installment and 25 percent for the eighth installment (Code Sec. 965(h)(1), as added by the 2017 Tax Cuts Act).

The first installment must be paid on the due date (determined without regard to extensions) of the tax return for the last tax year that begins before January 1, 2018 (the tax year of the mandatory inclusion). Succeeding installments must be paid annually no later than the due dates (without extensions) for the income tax return of each succeeding tax year (Code Sec. 965(h)(2), as added by the 2017 Tax Cuts Act).

> **Comment:** Thus, a U.S. shareholder can elect to pay the transition tax arising from the mandatory inclusion over a period of eight years.

Making the election. An election to pay the net tax liability from the mandatory inclusion in installments must be made by the due date of the tax return for the last tax year that begins before January 1, 2018 (the tax year in which the pre-effective-date undistributed earnings are included in income under the transition rule). The Treasury Secretary has authority to prescribe the manner of making the election (Code Sec. 965(h)(5), as added by the 2017 Tax Cuts Act).

Net tax liability. The net tax liability that may be paid in installments is the excess of (i) the U.S. shareholder's net income tax for the tax year in which an amount is included

NEW LAW EXPLAINED

in income under the mandatory inclusion rules, over (ii) the taxpayer's net income tax for that year determined without regard to the mandatory inclusion and any income or deduction properly attributable to a dividend received by the U.S. shareholder from any deferred foreign income corporation. The net income tax is the regular tax liability reduced by the general business credit (Code Sec. 965(h)(6), as added by the 2017 Tax Cuts Act).

Acceleration rule. If (1) there is an addition to tax for failure to pay timely any required installment of the transition tax, (2) there is a liquidation or sale of substantially all of the U.S. shareholder's assets (including in a bankruptcy case), (3) the U.S. shareholder ceases business, or (4) another similar circumstance arises, the unpaid portion of all remaining installments is due on the date of the event (or, in a bankruptcy proceeding or similar case, the day before the petition is filed). This acceleration rule does not apply to the sale of substantially all the assets of the U.S. shareholder to a buyer if the buyer enters into an agreement with the Secretary under which the buyer is liable for the remaining installments due in the same manner as if the buyer were the U.S. shareholder (Code Sec. 965(h)(3), as added by the 2017 Tax Cuts Act).

Proration of deficiency to installments. If an election is made to pay the net tax liability from the mandatory inclusion in installments and a deficiency is later determined with respect to that net tax liability, the additional tax due is prorated among the installment payments. The portions of the deficiency prorated to an installment that was due before the deficiency was assessed must be paid upon notice and demand. The portion prorated to any remaining installment is payable with the timely payment of that installment payment. However, these rules do not apply if the deficiency is attributable to negligence, intentional disregard of rules or regulations, or fraud with intent to evade tax (Code Sec. 965(h)(4), as added by the 2017 Tax Cuts Act).

> **Comment:** If the deficiency is attributable to negligence, intentional disregard of rules or regulations, or fraud with intent to evade tax, the entire deficiency is payable upon notice and demand.

> **Comment:** The timely payment of an installment does not incur interest. If a deficiency is determined that is attributable to an understatement of the net tax liability due under the transition rule, the deficiency is payable with underpayment interest for the period beginning on the date on which the net tax liability would have been due, without regard to an election to pay in installments, and ending with the payment of the deficiency. Furthermore, any amount of deficiency prorated to a remaining installment also bears interest on the deficiency, but not on the original installment amount (Conference Report on H.R. 1, Tax Cuts and Jobs Act (H. Rept. 115-466)).

Special rules for S corporations. A special rule permits deferral of the transition net tax liability for shareholders of a U.S. shareholder that is an S corporation. Under this rule, any shareholder of the S corporation may elect to defer the payment of his portion of the net tax liability resulting from the mandatory inclusion until the shareholder's tax year in which a triggering event occurs. The deferred transition tax is assessed as an addition to tax on the shareholder's return for the tax year of the triggering event (Code Sec. 965(i)(1), as added by the 2017 Tax Cuts Act).

¶710

NEW LAW EXPLAINED

For purposes of this rule, the shareholder's net tax liability is the net tax liability that would be determined under the transition rule if the only subpart F income taken into account by the shareholder under the mandatory inclusion were allocations from the S corporation (Code Sec. 965(i)(3), as added by the 2017 Tax Cuts Act).

The S corporation shareholder must make the election to defer the transition tax not later than the due date for the shareholder's return for the tax year that includes the close of the S corporation's last tax year that begins before January 1, 2018, in which the mandatory inclusion is made. The election is made in the manner provided by the Secretary (Code Sec. 965(i)(8), as added by the 2017 Tax Cuts Act).

Triggering events. The following three types of events may trigger an end to deferral of the net tax liability of an S corporation shareholder:

(1) The corporation ceases to be an S corporation (determined as of the first day of the first tax year that the corporation is not an S corporation).

(2) A liquidation, a sale of substantially all of the S corporation's assets (including in a bankruptcy or similar case), a termination of the S corporation, a cessation of its business, or a similar event.

(3) A transfer of shares of stock in the S corporation by the electing taxpayer, whether by sale, death or otherwise, unless the transferee of the stock agrees with the Secretary to be liable for net tax liability in the same manner as the transferor (Code Sec. 965(i)(2), as added by the 2017 Tax Cuts Act).

Partial transfers of the S corporation stock trigger the end of deferral only with respect to the portion of tax properly allocable to the portion of stock sold.

Election to pay deferred liability in installments. After a triggering event occurs, an S corporation shareholder that has elected to defer the net tax liability may elect to pay the net tax liability in eight installments, subject to rules similar to those generally applicable absent deferral. However, if the triggering event is a liquidation, sale of substantially all corporate assets, termination of the S corporation or end of its business, or similar event, the installment payment election can be made only with the consent of the Secretary. The installment election must be made by the due date of the return for the tax year in which the triggering event occurs, and the first installment payment is required by that due date, determined without regard to extensions of time to file (Code Sec. 965(i)(4), as added by the 2017 Tax Cuts Act).

Joint and several liability; extension of limitation on collection. If a shareholder of an S corporation has elected deferral and a triggering event occurs, the S corporation and the electing shareholder are jointly and severally liable for any net tax liability and related interest or penalties (Code Sec. 965(i)(5), as added by the 2017 Tax Cuts Act). The period within which the IRS may collect a deferred liability does not begin before the date of the triggering event (Code Sec. 965(i)(6), as added by the 2017 Tax Cuts Act).

Annual reporting of net tax liability. If an election to defer payment of the net tax liability is in effect for an S corporation shareholder, the shareholder must report the amount of the deferred net tax liability on its return for the tax year for which the election is made and on each subsequent tax year return until the deferred amount has been fully assessed on the returns. Failure to include that information with each

NEW LAW EXPLAINED

income tax return during the period that the election is in effect will result in a penalty equal to five-percent of the amount that should have been reported. For this purpose, a deferred net tax liability is the amount of the net tax liability the payment of which has been deferred under these rules and which has not been assessed on a return of tax for any prior tax year (Code Sec. 965(i)(7), as added by the 2017 Tax Cuts Act).

Reporting by S corporations. An S corporation that is a U.S. shareholder of a specified foreign corporation is required to report on its income tax return the amount includible in gross income under the mandatory inclusion rules, as well as the amount of deduction from mandatory inclusion that would be allowable under the transition rule. In addition, the corporation must furnish a copy of that information to its shareholders. The information provided to shareholders also must include a statement of the shareholder's pro rata share of these amounts (Code Sec. 965(j), as added by the 2017 Tax Cuts Act).

Limitations on assessment extended. Under an exception to the otherwise generally applicable limitations period for assessment of tax, the period for the assessment of the transition net tax liability arising from the mandatory inclusion does not expire prior to six years from the date on which the tax return initially reflecting the mandatory inclusion was filed (Code Sec. 965(k), as added by the 2017 Tax Cuts Act).

Recapture for expatriated entities. A special recapture rule applies if a U.S. shareholder is allowed a deduction from mandatory inclusion under the transition rule and first becomes an expatriated entity at any time during the 10-year period beginning on December 22, 2017, with respect to a surrogate foreign corporation that first becomes a surrogate foreign corporation during that period (i.e., post-enactment). In this case, the tax imposed by Chapter 1 of the Code is increased for the first tax year in which the taxpayer becomes an expatriated entity by an amount equal to 35 percent of the amount of the allowed deduction from mandatory inclusion. In addition, no tax credits are allowed against the additional tax due as a result of the recapture rule (Code Sec. 965(l)(1), as added by the 2017 Tax Cuts Act).

> **Comment:** Although the amount due is computed by reference to the year in which the deemed subpart F income was originally reported, the additional tax arises and is assessed for the tax year in which the U.S. shareholder becomes an expatriated entity.

For purposes of this rule, an expatriated entity is a domestic corporation or partnership acquired in an inversion transaction and the surrogate foreign corporation is the foreign corporation acquiring the expatriated entity in the inversion transaction (Code Sec. 7874(a)(2)). However, an entity is not treated as an expatriated entity, and is not within the scope of this recapture rule, if the surrogate foreign corporation is treated as a domestic corporation under Code Sec. 7874(b) because former shareholders or partners of the acquired entity hold 80 percent or more (by vote or value) of the stock of the surrogate foreign corporation after the transaction (Code Sec. 965(l)(2) and (3), as added by the 2017 Tax Cuts Act).

Special rules for U.S. shareholders that are REITs. Special rules are provided if a U.S. shareholder is a REIT in order to reduce the burden of compliance with the transition rule by REITs. First, if a real estate investment trust (REIT) is a U.S.

NEW LAW EXPLAINED

shareholder in one or more deferred foreign income corporations, any amount required to be included as mandatory subpart F inclusion is not taken into account as gross income of the REIT for purposes of determining the qualified REIT's income in applying the Code Sec. 856(c)(2) and (3) income tests to any tax year for which the amount is taken into account under the subpart F inclusion (Code Sec. 965(m)(1)(A), as added by the 2017 Tax Cuts Act).

In addition, although a REIT generally must take into account the mandatory inclusion in determining its taxable income under Code Sec. 857(b), the REIT is allowed to make an election to defer the mandatory inclusion and take it into income over the period of eight years as follows:

(1) Eight percent of the amount in the case of each of the tax years in the five-tax year period beginning with the tax year in which the amount would otherwise be included.

(2) 15 percent of the amount in the case of the first tax year following that period.

(3) 20 percent of the amount in the case of the second tax year following that period.

(4) 25 percent of the amount in the case of the third tax year following that period (Code Sec. 965(m)(1)(B), as added by the 2017 Tax Cuts Act).

> **Comment:** A REIT is required to distribute at least 90 percent of the REIT income (other than net capital gain) annually under Code Sec. 857. A required inclusion under the transition rule may trigger a requirement that the REIT distribute an amount equal to 90 percent of that inclusion despite the fact that it did not receive distribution from the deferred foreign income corporation. To avoid the requirement that any distribution requirement be satisfied in one year, an election to defer the mandatory inclusion is permitted.

The election for deferred inclusion must be made not later than the due date for the first tax year in the five-tax year period in the manner provided by the Secretary (Code Sec. 965(m)(2)(A), as added by the 2017 Tax Cuts Act).

Special rules apply if the deferral election is in effect. Thus, in each of those years, the REIT may claim a partial deduction from mandatory inclusion under Code Sec. 965(c)(1) in the applicable percentages in proportion to the amount included in each of the eight years. The REIT also cannot elect to use the installment payment for any tax year from the eight-year period, discussed above (Code Sec. 965(m)(2)(B)(i), as added by the 2017 Tax Cuts Act).

In addition, if there is a liquidation or sale of substantially all the assets of the REIT (including in a bankruptcy or similar case), a cessation of business by the REIT, or any similar circumstance, any portion of the required inclusion not yet taken into income is accelerated and required to be included as gross income as of the day before the event and the unpaid portion of any tax liability with respect to such inclusion will be due on the date of the event (or in the case of a bankruptcy or similar case, the day before the petition is filed) (Code Sec. 965(m)(2)(B)(ii), as added by the 2017 Tax Cuts Act).

Election not to apply the NOL deduction. A U.S. shareholder of a deferred foreign income corporation can make an election for the last tax year beginning before

NEW LAW EXPLAINED

January 1, 2018 (the tax year of the mandatory subpart F inclusion) not to take into account the mandatory inclusion and certain other amounts (described below) in determining (i) the net operating loss (NOL) deduction under Code Sec. 172 for that tax year, or (ii) the amount of taxable income for that tax year which may be reduced by NOL carryovers or carrybacks to that tax year (Code Sec. 965(n)(1), as added by the 2017 Tax Cuts Act).

The amount not taken into account includes the mandatory inclusion and, in the case of a domestic corporation that chooses to have the benefits of subpart A of part III of subchapter N for the tax year, the taxes deemed to be paid by the corporation under the deemed-paid credit rules of Code Sec. 960(a) and (b) for the tax year with respect to the mandatory inclusion that are treated as dividends under Code Sec. 78 (Code Sec. 965(n)(2), as added by the 2017 Tax Cuts Act).

The election is made not later than the due date (including extensions) for filing the return for the tax year in the manner prescribed by the Secretary (Code Sec. 965(n)(3), as added by the 2017 Tax Cuts Act).

Regulations. The Secretary is authorized to issue regulations or other guidance as may be necessary or appropriate to carry out the mandatory inclusion provisions or to prevent the avoidance of the purposes of these rules, including through a reduction in earnings and profits through changes in entity classification, changes in accounting methods, or otherwise (Code Sec. 965(o), as added by the 2017 Tax Cuts Act).

> **Comment:** According to the Conference Committee Report, in order to avoid double-counting and double non-counting of earnings, the Secretary may provide guidance to adjust the amount of post-1986 earnings and profits of a specified foreign corporation to ensure that a single item of a specified foreign corporation is taken into account only once in determining the income of a U.S. shareholder subject to mandatory inclusion. Such an adjustment may be necessary, for example, when there is a deductible payment (e.g., interest or royalties) from one specified foreign corporation to another specified foreign corporation between measurement dates.
>
> In addition, taxpayers may engage in tax strategies designed to reduce the amount of post-1986 earnings and profits in order to decrease the amount of the mandatory inclusion. Such tax strategies may include a change in entity classification, accounting method, and tax year, or intragroup transactions such as distributions or liquidations. It is expected that the Secretary will prescribe rules to adjust the amount of post-1986 earnings and profits in such cases in order to prevent the avoidance of the purposes of the transition rule (Conference Report on H.R. 1, Tax Cuts and Jobs Act (H. Rept. 115-466)).

▶ **Effective date.** No specific effective date is provided. The amendment is, therefore, considered effective on December 22, 2017, the date of enactment.

Law source: Law at ¶5930. Committee Report at ¶11,000, ¶11,010, ¶11,020, ¶11,030, and ¶11,060.

— Act Sec. 14103(a) of the Tax Cuts and Jobs Act (P.L. 115-97), amending Code Sec. 965.

¶710

FOREIGN TAX CREDIT

¶715 Recapture of Overall Domestic Losses

SUMMARY OF NEW LAW

A taxpayer may elect to recapture pre-2018 unused overall domestic losses (ODLs) by recharacterizing up to 100 percent of the taxpayer's U.S. source taxable income as foreign source taxable income, from 2018 through 2027.

BACKGROUND

U.S. taxpayers are taxed on their worldwide income, but are allowed a foreign tax credit for foreign income taxes paid or accrued, in order to prevent the double taxation of foreign source income (Code Sec. 901). The foreign tax credit limitation provides that when the foreign income tax is higher than U.S. income tax, the foreign tax credit is limited to the U.S. tax that would be due on foreign income (Code Sec. 904). The purpose of the limitation is to protect the U.S. tax base and to prevent the reduction of U.S. tax on U.S. source income. The limitation is determined by multiplying a taxpayer's total U.S. tax liability (before the foreign tax credit) for the tax year by the ratio of the taxpayer's foreign source taxable income to worldwide taxable income (Code Sec. 904(a)).

The foreign tax credit limitation requires that the foreign tax credit limitation be calculated separately for certain categories of income or "baskets". There are generally two foreign separate limitation categories or baskets-a "passive category income" basket and a "general category income" basket (Reg. § 1.904-4). Foreign source taxable income for each category is gross income for the category, less expenses, losses and other deductions (referred to as deductions). The allocation and apportionment of deductions for purposes of determining the foreign tax credit limitation generally requires that the expense is first allocated to a specific class of income, and then apportioned, between the statutory groupings (i.e., foreign general and passive limitation income) and the residual grouping (i.e., U.S. source income) (Reg. § 1.861-8). The foreign tax credit limitation can be increased by increasing the portion of worldwide taxable income that is foreign source taxable income. Minimizing the expenses that are allocated or apportioned to foreign source income will increase foreign source taxable income.

Foreign and domestic losses can impact the foreign tax credit limitation. To the extent that the allocation and apportionment of the deductions results in a loss in a separate limitation income category, the loss is first used to reduce income in the other separate limitation income categories and then to reduce income of a different source. When this occurs, the loss recapture rules come in to play. For example, if an overall foreign loss (OFL) reduces U.S. source income or an overall domestic loss (ODL) reduces foreign source income, the loss is recaptured by recharacterizing a portion of the foreign source income or U.S. source income that is subsequently earned, as U.S. source income or foreign source income, respectively (Code Sec. 904(f) and (g)).

BACKGROUND

A domestic loss is the amount by which the U.S. source income is exceeded by the sum of properly allocated and apportioned deductions to that gross income, taking into account net operating carryforwards (Code Sec. 904(g)(2)(B); Reg. § 1.904(g)-2(c)(2)). An ODL is a loss that offsets or reduces foreign source taxable income, in a qualifying tax year, or any qualifying preceding year by reason of a loss carryback. A qualified tax year is a year in which the taxpayer elects the foreign tax credit. If there is a domestic loss in a year in which taxes are deducted, it may only be used in a preceding year in which the foreign tax credit is claimed (Code Sec. 904(g)(2); Reg. § 1.904(g)-1(c)).

A domestic loss that does not exceed the separate limitation income (SLI) is allocated and reduces the SLI amounts on a proportionate basis. SLI is the foreign source taxable income for each separate limitation income category. A separate limitation loss (SLL) for each category is the amount by which the foreign source gross income in the category is exceeded by the sum of the deductions are properly allocated and apportion to the category. SLLs are allocated proportionately among the separate categories that have SLI. The allocation of the domestic loss occurs after the allocation of the SLLs to SLI amounts (Reg. § 1.904(g)-3(e)).

ODL accounts are established for each separate category in which the SLI is offset by domestic loss. The balance in the accounts are ODLs, subject to recapture in a given year. If a domestic loss is carried back or carried forward as part of a net operating loss that reduces foreign source taxable income, the ODL is treated as sustained in the later of the year in which the domestic loss was incurred or the year to which the loss was carried. (Reg. §§ 1.904(f)-7(b)(1) and 1.904(g)-1(b)).

ODLs are recaptured by treating a portion of a taxpayer's U.S. source taxable income as foreign source taxable income (Reg. § 1.904(g)-2). If the taxpayer has ODL accounts attributable to more than one separate category, the recharacterized income is allocated among the categories on a pro rata basis. The amount of U.S. source taxable income subject to recapture is the lesser of the aggregate balance in the ODL accounts, to the extent not recaptured in prior years, or 50 percent of the taxpayer's U.S. taxable income for the year. The taxpayer who elects the foreign tax credit will have foreign source taxable income increased by the amount of the recapture, for purposes of the foreign tax credit limitation, increasing the amount of the foreign tax credit for the year. Once an amount is recaptured, the account is reduced by the amount of the recapture and recapture occurs each year until the account balance is zero.

> **Example:** In Year 1, the taxpayer has a domestic loss of $200 that it allocates proportionately to $1,000 of foreign source taxable income, $600 of foreign source taxable income or 60% in the general category ($120) and to $400 foreign source taxable income or 40% in the passive category ($80). The taxpayer has a $120 ODL account in the general category and a $80 ODL account in the passive category. In Year 2, U.S. taxable income is $100. The taxpayer may recapture $50, the lesser of 50% of the U.S. taxable income of $100 or the $200 aggregate balance in the ODL accounts. The $50 of U.S. taxable income is recharacterized

¶715

BACKGROUND

proportionately, 60% or $30 to general category income and 40% or $20 to passive category income. The ODL accounts are reduced to $90 in the general category ODL account and $60 in the passive category ODL account.

NEW LAW EXPLAINED

Recapture of ODLs accelerated.—A taxpayer who claims the foreign tax credit and has an overall domestic loss (ODL) may elect to recapture the ODL by recharacterizing up to 100 percent of U.S. source taxable income earned in subsequent years as foreign source taxable income. The amount that is recharacterized each year is limited to the lesser of the aggregate amount in the ODL account or up to 100 percent of the taxpayer's U.S. source taxable income for the year (Code Sec. 904(g)(5)(A), as added by the Tax Cuts and Jobs Act (P.L. 115-97)).

The increased recapture amount applies to the pre-2018 unused ODL, meaning a loss that arises in a qualified tax year beginning before January 1, 2018, and that has not been used for any tax year before that date (Code Sec. 904(g)(5)(B), as added by the 2017 Tax Cuts Act). A qualified tax year is a year for which the taxpayer elects the foreign tax credit (Code Sec. 904(g)(2)(C)). The pre-2018 unused ODL must be taken into account for tax years of the taxpayer beginning after December 31, 2017, and before January 1, 2028 (Code Sec. 904(g)(5)(C), as added by the Tax Cuts Act).

▶ **Effective date.** The amendments made by this section apply to tax years beginning after December 31, 2017 (Act Sec. 14304(b) of the Tax Cuts and Jobs Act (P.L. 115-97)).

Law source: Law at ¶5820. Committee Report at ¶11,000, ¶11,010, ¶11,020, ¶11,030, and ¶11,200.

— Act Sec. 14304(a) of the Tax Cuts and Jobs Act (P.L. 115-97), adding Code Sec. 904(g)(5);

— Act Sec. 14304(b), providing the effective date.

¶720 Deemed-Paid Foreign Tax Credit

SUMMARY OF NEW LAW

The Code Sec. 902 deemed-paid foreign tax credit is repealed and the Code Sec. 960 deemed-paid foreign tax credit is modified so that it is determined on a current year basis.

BACKGROUND

A foreign tax credit is allowed to a domestic corporation that owns at least 10 percent of the voting stock in a foreign corporation from which it receives a dividend (Code

BACKGROUND

Sec. 902). The credit is determined by reference to the portion of the foreign corporation's post-1986 foreign income taxes that the dividend received by the foreign corporation bears to the foreign corporation's post-1986 undistributed earnings. The credit is referred to as the "deemed-paid" or "indirect" credit (Code Sec. 902(a)).

The deemed-paid credit is allowed for foreign income taxes of the first-tier foreign corporation and lower-tier foreign corporations (second- through sixth-tier corporations). The lower-tier foreign corporation must be in a chain of corporations that includes the first-tier corporation. Each corporation in the chain must own at least 10 percent of the voting stock of the lower-tier corporation and the domestic shareholder must own at least five percent of the voting stock of the foreign corporation indirectly in the chain. A foreign corporation below the third-level must be a controlled foreign corporation (CFC) and the domestic corporation must be a U.S. shareholder (Code Sec. 902(b)).

A domestic corporation that has a subpart F inclusion under Code Sec. 951(a) can obtain an indirect or deemed-paid foreign tax credit for foreign income taxes paid or deemed paid by the foreign corporation. The principles of Code Sec. 902 are used to determine the portion of the CFC's post-1986 foreign taxes that are deemed-paid by the shareholder in connection with the subpart F inclusion (Code Sec. 960). The Code Sec. 960 credit is limited with respect to taxes deemed paid on amounts included in a domestic corporate U.S. shareholder's gross income under Code Sec. 956. Under Code Sec. 956, U.S. shareholders are taxed under subpart F on their pro rata share of the CFC's investment in U.S. property (the "Code Sec. 956 amount"). Under the limitation, the credit may not exceed the amount of taxes that would be deemed paid if the corporation had made an actual distribution of cash through a chain of ownership to the U.S. shareholder (Code Sec. 960(c)).

A change in a taxpayer's foreign tax liability may affect the taxpayer's foreign tax credit, including the deemed-paid credits under Code Sec. 902 and Code Sec. 960. If a taxpayer does not pay accrued taxes within two years of the close of the tax year to which the taxes relate, there is a foreign tax redetermination that affects the taxpayer's foreign tax credit because no credit is allowed for accrued taxes not paid before that date. Taxes subsequently paid are taken into account in the year to which the taxes relate (Code Sec. 905(c)(2)(B)). In the case of the deemed-paid credit, regulations provide that, in lieu of a redetermination, adjustments to the foreign corporation's pools of post-1986 undistributed earnings and post-1986 foreign income taxes are made. Accrued taxes that are subsequently paid after the two year period are taken into account in the pools for the year of payment (Code Sec. 905(c)(2)(B)(i)(I); Temp. Reg. § 1.905-3T(d)(2)).

A domestic corporation must include foreign taxes deemed paid in gross income under Code Sec. 78 (referred to as the "Code Sec. 78 gross-up").

Under a matching rule, taxpayers are prevented from claiming the foreign tax credit for foreign taxes that are paid or accrued, before the tax year in which the related income is taken into account (referred to as a foreign tax credit splitting event). Special rules apply to foreign taxes paid or accrued by Code Sec. 902 corporations (Code Sec. 909(b)).

¶720

BACKGROUND

A passive foreign investment company (PFIC) is a foreign corporation that meets either an income or asset test (Code Sec. 1297(a)). Under these tests, 75 percent or more of the corporation's gross income must be passive income or 50 percent or more of its average percentage of assets must produce passive income. A U.S. shareholder of a PFIC can make a qualified electing fund (QEF) election to include in gross income currently its pro rata share of the PFIC's ordinary earnings and net capital gain (Code Sec. 1293(a)). A domestic corporate shareholder of a PFIC that owns at least 10 percent of the QEF's voting stock can claim a Code Sec. 960 deemed-paid credit for foreign income taxes paid by the QEF. The credit is computed in the same manner as if there were a current inclusion under subpart F (Code Sec. 1293(f)(1)). If the shareholder is later entitled to exclude a distribution as earnings that were previously taxed, the rules of Code Sec. 959 apply and there is generally no foreign tax credits available for the later distribution (Code Sec. 1293(f)(2)). The amounts included in income are generally treated as income in the passive basket for purposes of the foreign tax credit limitation (Code Sec. 904(d)(2)(B)(ii)). If the PFIC is a Code Sec. 902 noncontrolled foreign corporation, the inclusion is treated as a dividend from the corporation and is subject to the look-through rule. Dividends paid by a Code Sec. 902 noncontrolled foreign corporation (a so-called "10/50" corporation) are subject to a look-through rule when calculating the foreign tax credit limitation for the dividends paid (Code Sec. 904(d)(4); Reg. § 1.904-5(c)(4)(iii)). If the PFIC is a CFC and the U.S. shareholder is a domestic corporation owning at least 10 percent of the voting stock, the look-through rules for CFCs apply (Code Sec. 904(d)(3)(H)).

NEW LAW EXPLAINED

Code Sec. 902 deemed-paid credit repealed.—The Code Sec. 902 deemed-paid foreign tax credit is repealed. The credit was allowed for income tax paid with respect to dividends received by a domestic corporation that owned 10 percent or more of the voting stock of a foreign corporation. The deemed-paid credit is repealed as a result of the implementation of the participation exemption system (Code Sec. 902, stricken by the Tax Cuts and Jobs Act (P.L. 115-97)).

Under the participation exemption system, a specified 10-percent owned foreign corporation (i.e., a foreign corporation with domestic corporate shareholders that own 10 percent or more of the foreign corporation's stock by vote or value) is provided a 100-percent deduction for the foreign-source portion of the dividends received from the foreign corporation (Code Sec. 245A, as added by the 2017 Tax Cuts Act). This deduction is referred to as the "participation DRD". No foreign tax credit or deduction is allowed for any foreign taxes paid or accrued with respect to the deductible portion of the dividend (see ¶ 705).

> **Comment:** The House Committee Report states that to continue to provide a Code Sec. 902 deemed-paid credit in light of the participation DRD would provide a double tax benefit, by allowing the dividend exemption and then reducing U.S. tax with a credit for taxes paid on the foreign source income (House Committee Report for Tax Cuts and Jobs Act (P.L. 115-97) (H. R. Rep. No. 115-409)).

NEW LAW EXPLAINED

Code Sec. 960 deemed-paid credit for subpart F inclusions. The Code Sec. 960 deemed-paid foreign tax credit for subpart F inclusions is retained, but modified as a result of the repeal of Code Sec. 902. The deemed-paid credit for subpart F inclusions is no longer computed under the principles of Code Sec. 902. Rather, the credit is determined on a current year basis. If income is included in the gross income of a domestic corporation that is a U.S. shareholder of a controlled foreign corporation (CFC), the deemed-paid credit is the amount of the foreign corporation's foreign income taxes properly attributable to the subpart F income inclusion (Code Sec. 960(a), as added by the 2017 Tax Cuts Act).

> **Comment:** The provision changes the method for computing the deemed-paid taxes, which required the domestic corporation to multiply the foreign subsidiary's post-1986 foreign income tax payments by the ratio of: (1) the Code Sec. 951(a)(1) inclusion, to (2) the foreign subsidiary's post-1986 undistributed earnings pool. The provision eliminates the need for tracking cumulative tax pools.

The look-through rule that applied for purposes of determining the foreign tax credit limitation for dividends received from a Code Sec. 902 noncontrolled foreign corporation now applies to dividends received from a noncontrolled 10-percent owned foreign corporation. A noncontrolled 10-percent owned foreign corporation is a specified foreign corporation, defined in Code Sec. 245A(b). The term also includes a passive foreign investment company, defined in Code Sec. 1297(a), with respect to which the taxpayer meets the stock ownership requirements of Code Sec. 902(a) or (b), as in effect before repeal by the 2017 Tax Cuts Act. A CFC will not be treated as a noncontrolled 10-percent owned foreign corporation with respect to any distribution out of its earnings and profits for periods during which it was a CFC (Code Sec. 904(d)(2)(E)(i) and (d)(4), as amended by the 2017 Tax Cuts Act).

> **Comment:** The limitation on the Code Sec. 960 deemed-paid credit with respect to Code Sec. 956 inclusions of domestic corporate shareholders in Code Sec. 960(c) was eliminated (Act Sec. 14301(b)(1), striking Code Sec. 960(c)). Note that provisions in the House-passed bill would have made the Code Sec. 956 amount zero with respect to a domestic corporation, while the Senate-passed bill excepted domestic corporations from Code Sec. 956. Code Sec. 956 was not modified in the final version of the 2017 Tax Cuts Act.

Code Sec. 960 deemed-paid credit and distributions from previously taxed earnings and profits. The amount of foreign taxes deemed paid upon a distribution of previously taxed income is also no longer determined under the principles of Code Sec. 902. If a domestic corporation that is a U.S. shareholder receives a distribution from a CFC, any part of which is excluded from gross income as previously taxed income under Code Sec. 959(a), the domestic corporation is deemed to pay the foreign corporation's foreign income taxes as: (1) are properly attributable to the previously taxed income, and (2) that were not deemed paid by the domestic corporation under Code Sec. 960, for the tax year or any prior tax year (Code Sec. 960(b)(1), as added by the 2017 Tax Cuts Act).

If a CFC receives a distribution from another CFC, any portion of which was excluded from gross income of the CFC because the amounts were attributable to previously taxed income under Code Sec. 959(b), the CFC receiving the distribution

NEW LAW EXPLAINED

will be deemed to have paid so much of the other CFC's taxes as: (1) are attributable to such portion, and (2) have not been deemed to have been paid by a domestic corporation under Code Sec. 960, for the tax year or any prior tax year (Code Sec. 960(b)(2), as added by the 2017 Tax Cuts Act).

Adjustments to the Code Sec. 960 deemed-paid credit. Accrued foreign income taxes that were not paid within two years from the close of the tax year to which they relate and so reduce the foreign tax credit, but that are subsequently paid, are taken into account for the tax year to which the taxes relate. The same rule applies for both taxes deemed paid under Code Sec. 960 and foreign income taxes directly paid (Code Sec. 905(c)(2)(B)(i), as amended by the 2017 Tax Cuts Act).

> **Comment:** Temp. Reg. § 1.905-3T(d)(2), which requires adjustments to the earnings and tax pools, in lieu of a foreign tax redetermination, is inconsistent with the determination of the Code Sec. 960 deemed-paid credit on a current basis.

Other provisions related to the Code Sec. 960 deemed-paid credit. For purposes of the Code Sec. 960 deemed-paid credit, the term foreign income taxes means income, war profits, or excess profits taxes paid or accrued to any foreign country or possession of the United States (Code Sec. 960(e), as added by the 2017 Tax Cuts Act).

The IRS may provide regulations or other guidance necessary to carry out the provisions of Code Sec. 960 (Code Sec. 960(f), as added by the 2017 Tax Cuts Act). According to the House Committee Report, this could include providing regulations with rules similar to those in Reg. § 1.904-6(a) for allocating taxes to specific foreign tax credit baskets. Under these rules, taxes are not attributable to an item of subpart F income if the base upon which the tax was imposed does not include the item of subpart F income. For example, if foreign law exempts from tax certain income from its tax base, no deemed credit can result from the subpart F inclusion. Tax that is not imposed on subpart F income is not attributable to subpart F income (House Committee Report for Tax Cuts and Jobs Act (P.L. 115-97) (H. R. Rep. No. 115-409)).

A domestic corporation that owns or is treated as owning under the attribution of ownership rules of Code Sec. 1298(a), the stock of a qualified electing fund (QEF) can claim the Code Sec. 960 deemed-paid credit for the inclusion of income of the QEF. The domestic corporation must meet the stock ownership requirements in Code Sec. 902(a) and (b), prior to repeal by the 2017 Tax Cuts Act (Code Sec. 1293(f)(3), as added by the 2017 Tax Cuts Act).

Code Sec. 78 gross-up. The Code Sec. 78 gross-up for foreign taxes deemed paid under Code Sec. 902, no longer applies, as a result of the repeal of Code Sec. 902. The gross-up applies to taxes deemed paid under Code Sec. 960(a) and (b). The Code Sec. 78 gross-up also applies to foreign income taxes deemed paid with respect to amounts of global intangible low-taxed income (GILTI) included in the gross income of a domestic corporation under Code Sec. 951A (see ¶735). A domestic corporation's deemed-paid credit for GILTI is 80 percent of the product of the corporation's inclusion percentage and the aggregate tested foreign income taxes paid or accrued, with respect to tested income, by each CFC with respect to which the domestic corporation is a U.S. shareholder. The Code Sec. 78 gross-up, however, takes into account 100 percent of the product of the inclusion percentage and aggregate tested foreign taxes. The Code Sec. 78 gross-up applies for all purposes, except for the

NEW LAW EXPLAINED

deductions for dividends received under Code Sec. 245 and Code Sec. 245A. The amounts are treated as a dividend received by a domestic corporation from a foreign corporation (Code Sec. 78, as amended by the 2017 Tax Cuts Act and Code Sec. 960(d), as added by the 2017 Tax Cuts Act).

Code Sec. 909 matching rule. The special matching rule that applied to Code Sec. 902 corporations is replaced with a rule that applies to specified 10-percent owned foreign corporations. Under the rule, if there is a foreign tax credit splitting event, a foreign income tax paid or accrued by a specified 10-percent owned foreign corporation will not be taken into account, for purposes of Code Sec. 960 or determining earnings and profits under Code Sec. 964(a), before the tax year in which the related income is taken into account by the corporation or a domestic corporation which is a U.S. shareholder of the corporation (Code Sec. 909(b), as amended by the 2017 Tax Cuts Act). A specified 10-percent owned foreign corporation is any corporation with respect to which a domestic corporation is a U.S. shareholder. The definition is modified for this purpose to include passive foreign investment companies, as defined under Code Sec. 1297, that are not CFCs (Code Sec. 245A(b), as added by the 2017 Tax Cuts Act) (see ¶705). A U.S. shareholder is a U.S. person who owns, either directly, indirectly, or constructively: (1) 10 percent or more of the total combined voting power of all classes of stock of the foreign corporation, or (2) 10 percent or more of the total value of shares of all classes of stock of the foreign corporation (see ¶745) (Code Sec. 951(b), as amended by the 2017 Tax Cuts Act).

Foreign tax credit limitation look-through rule. The look-through rule that applied for purposes of determining the foreign tax credit limitation for dividends received from a Code Sec. 902 noncontrolled foreign corporation now applies to dividends received from a noncontrolled 10-percent owned foreign corporation. A noncontrolled 10-percent owned foreign corporation is a specified 10-percent owned foreign corporation, defined in Code Sec. 245A(b) (see ¶705). The term also refers to a passive foreign investment company, defined in Code Sec. 1297(a), with respect to which the taxpayer meets the stock ownership requirements of Code Sec. 902(a) or (b), as in effect before repeal by the 2017 Tax Cuts Act. A CFC will not be treated as a noncontrolled 10-percent owned foreign corporation with respect to any distribution out of its earnings and profits for periods during which it was a CFC (Code Sec. 904(d)(2)(E)(i) and (d)(4), as amended by the 2017 Tax Cuts Act).

Dividends received deduction. The U.S. source portion of a dividend received from a 10-percent foreign corporation that may be deducted under Code Sec. 245 is the amount of the dividend multiplied by the ratio of post-1986 undistributed U.S. earnings to the post-1986 undistributed earnings. Post-1986 undistributed earnings were defined by reference to Code Sec. 902(c)(1). The definition of post-1986 undistributed earnings from Code Sec. 902(c)(1) is now included in Code Sec. 245 (Code Sec. 245(a)(4), as amended by the 2017 Tax Cuts Act).

▶   **Effective date.** The amendments made by this section apply to tax years of foreign corporations beginning after December 31, 2017, and to tax years of U.S. shareholders in which or with which such tax years of foreign corporations end (Act Sec. 14301(d) of the Tax Cuts and Jobs Act (P.L. 115-97)).

¶720

NEW LAW EXPLAINED

Law source: Law at ¶5195, ¶5395, ¶5590, ¶5600, ¶5700, ¶5790, ¶5810, ¶5815, ¶5820, ¶5825, ¶5830, ¶5835, ¶5840, ¶5845, ¶5895, ¶5905, ¶5910, ¶5995, ¶6000, and ¶6180. Committee Report at ¶11,000, ¶11,010, ¶11,020, ¶11,030, and ¶11,170.

— Act Sec. 14301(a) of the Tax Cuts and Jobs Act (P.L. 115-97), striking Code Sec. 902;

— Act Sec. 14301(b) amending Code Sec. 960, as amended by Act Sec. 14201 of the 2017 Tax Cuts Act;

— Act Sec. 14301(c), amending Code Secs. 78, 245(a)(4), 245(a)(10)(C), 535(b)(1), 545(b)(1), 814(f)(1), 865(h)(1)(B), 901(a), 901(e)(2), 901(f), 901(j)(1)(A), 901(j)(1)(B),901(k)(2),901(k)(6), 901(m)(1)(B), 904(d)(2)(E), 904(d)(4), 904(d)(6)(A), 904(h)(10)(A), 904(k), 905(c)(1), 905(c)(2)(B)(i), 906(a), 906(b), 907(b)(2)(B), 907(c)(3)(A), 907(c)(5), 907(f)(2)(B)(i), 908(a); 909(b), 909(d)(5); 958(a)(1), 959(d), 959(e), 1291(g)(2)(A), 6038(c)(1)(B), 6038(c)(4), and adding Code Sec. 1293(f);

— Act Sec. 14301(d), providing the effective date.

¶725 Foreign Tax Credit Limitation Baskets

SUMMARY OF NEW LAW

A new foreign tax credit limitation basket is added for foreign branch income.

BACKGROUND

U.S. taxpayers are taxed on their worldwide income, but are allowed a foreign tax credit for foreign income taxes paid or accrued, in order to prevent the double taxation of foreign source income (Code Sec. 901). The foreign tax credit limitation provides that when foreign income tax is higher than U.S. income tax, the foreign tax credit is limited to the U.S. tax that would be due on the foreign income (Code Sec. 904). The purpose of the limitation is to protect the U.S. tax base and to prevent the reduction of U.S. tax on U.S. source income. The limitation is determined by multiplying a taxpayer's total U.S. tax liability (before the foreign tax credit) for the tax year by the ratio of the taxpayer's foreign source taxable income to worldwide taxable income (Code Sec. 904(a)). If foreign taxes exceed the U.S. tax that would be due, the excess foreign taxes cannot be credited. Excess credits, however may be carried back one year and forward 10 years (Code Sec. 904(c)).

The foreign tax credit is determined on an overall basis, meaning that income and credits from all countries are combined. Determining the foreign tax credit on an overall basis can result in cross-crediting, which allows excess credits for taxes paid in high foreign tax countries to offset credits paid in lower foreign tax countries. The foreign tax credit limitation requires that the foreign tax credit limitation be calculated separately for certain categories of income or "baskets" to limit cross-crediting. There are generally two foreign limitation categories or baskets-a "passive category income" basket and a "general category income" basket (Reg. § 1.904-4). The separate

BACKGROUND

foreign tax credit limitations prevent the averaging of high foreign income taxes on income such as active business with low-taxed income such as that in the passive category. Cross-crediting is permitted with respect to the separate income categories-the overall combined tax rate on the basket may not be higher than the U.S. tax rate.

Taxpayers must determine their foreign tax credit carrybacks and carryforward separately for each category of income (Code Sec. 904(d)(1)). The carryback or carryforward can be claimed to the extent of the excess limit in the category (i.e., the amount by which the limit is more than the qualified taxes paid or accrued for that category).

Passive income is generally any type of income that would qualify as subpart F income foreign personal holding company income under Code Sec. 954(c) if the recipient was a controlled foreign corporation (CFC) (e.g., dividends, interest, rents, royalties, and annuities). Specified passive category income includes dividends from a domestic international sales corporation (DISC) or former DISC and distributions from a former foreign sales corporation (FSC) (Code Sec. 904(d)(2)(v); Reg. § 1.904-4(b)(3)). General category income includes income other than passive category income (Code Sec. 904(d)(2)(A)(ii)). Income that would otherwise be treated as passive category income is treated as general category income if it is earned by a qualifying financial services entity (Code Sec. 904(d)(2)(C), (D)). Additionally, high-taxed income (i.e., income that is subject to foreign tax at rates exceeding the rates in Code Sec. 1 and Code Sec. 11) is treated as general category income (Code Sec. 904(d)(2)(F)).

NEW LAW EXPLAINED

Foreign tax credit limitation basket added.—A new separate foreign tax credit limitation basket is added for foreign branch income (Code Sec. 904(d)(1)(B), as added by the Tax Cuts and Jobs Act (P.L. 115-97)). Foreign branch income means the business profits of a U.S. person that are attributable to one or more qualified business units (QBUs) in one or more foreign countries. A QBU is defined as any separate and clearly identified unit of a trade or business of a taxpayer that maintains separate books and records (Code Sec. 989(b)). The rules for determining the amount of business profits attributable to a QBU will be set forth in regulations (Code Sec. 904(d)(2)(J)(i), as added by the 2017 Tax Cuts Act).

> **Comment:** The income of a foreign branch is subject to U.S. tax and a foreign tax credit may be claimed. If the foreign branch is located in a high-tax country, absent the new foreign tax credit limitation basket, those taxes could offset taxes paid in low-tax countries in the general category basket. The addition of the new basket also means that carrybacks and carryforwards of excess foreign tax credits in the foreign branch company basket will be allowed only to the extent of the excess limitation in the basket.

The additional foreign tax credit limitation basket does not apply to income of the foreign branch that is passive category income (Code Sec. 904(d)(2)(J)(ii)). Passive category income includes passive income and specified passive income (Code Sec.

NEW LAW EXPLAINED

904(d)(2)(A)(i);Reg. §1.904-4(b)(1)). Passive income is generally any type of income that would qualify as subpart F income foreign personal holding company income under Code Sec. 954(c) if the recipient was a controlled foreign corporation (CFC) (e.g., dividends, interest, rents, royalties, and annuities). Specified passive category income includes dividends from a domestic international sales corporation (DISC) or former DISC and distributions from a former foreign sales corporation (FSC) (Code Sec. 904(d)(2)(v); Reg. §1.904-4(b)(3)).

> **Comment:** Passive category income is typically low-taxed income that would not be subject to cross-crediting.

> A new separate foreign tax credit limitation basket was also added for global intangible low-taxed income (see ¶735).

▶ **Effective date.** The amendments made by this section apply tax years beginning after December 31, 2017 (Act Sec. 14302(c) of the Tax Cuts and Jobs Act (P.L. 115-97)).

Law source: Law at ¶5820. Committee Report at ¶11,000, ¶11,010, ¶11,020, ¶11,030, and ¶11,180.

— Act Sec. 14302(a), of the Tax Cuts and Jobs Act (P.L. 115-97), amending Code Sec. 904(d)(1), as amended by Act Sec. 14201, by redesignating Code Sec. 904(d)(1)(B) and (C), as (C) and (D), respectively, and adding newCode Sec. 904(d)(1)(B);

— Act Sec. 14302(b)(1), adding Code Sec. 904(d)(2)(J);

— Act Sec. 14302(b)(2), amending Code Sec. 904(d)(2)(J), as amended by Act Sec. 14201.

— Act Sec. 14302(c), providing the effective date.

¶730 Source of Income Rules for Cross-Border Inventory Sales

SUMMARY OF NEW LAW

Income from cross-border sales of inventory is sourced on the basis of the production activities.

BACKGROUND

Income from the sale of inventory property that is produced by the taxpayer (in whole or in part) in the United States and sold outside of the United States (or vice versa) is sourced in part to the United States (U.S. source income) and in part outside of the United State (foreign source income). (Code Sec. 863(b)(2)). Income from the sales of inventory is first allocated between production activities and sales activities, using one of the following three methods: (1) 50-50 method (50 percent of the inventory sales income is sourced to the location of production and 50 percent of the inventory sales income is sourced to the location of sales), (2) independent factory price (IFP) method (taxpayer may establish an IFP to determine income from produc-

BACKGROUND

tion), and (3) books and records method (with IRS permission, taxpayer may use books of account to make the allocation) (Reg. § 1.863-3(b)).

After the allocation is made, the source of the gross income attributable to the production activity is determined based on the location of the production assets. Where production assets are located both in the United States and a foreign country, income is apportioned using a property fraction that takes into account the production assets at their adjusted tax basis (Reg. § 1.863-3(c)(1)).

 The source of the gross income attributable to the sales activity is the place of sale, which is generally where the title passes (title passage rule) (Reg. § § 1.863-3(c)(2) and 1.861-7(c)). Under a special rule, property that is produced in the United States, but destined for a U.S. market, may be U.S.-source income even if title passes in a foreign country. The rule is intended to prevent taxpayers from producing goods in the United States, passing title to the goods in a foreign country and then selling the goods to U.S. customers. For the rule to apply, the property must be wholly produced in the United States, and must be for use, consumption or disposition within the United States (T.D. 8687; Reg. § 1.863-3(c)(2)).

NEW LAW EXPLAINED

Cross-border inventory sales sourced based on production activities.—Gains, profits, and income from the sale or exchange of inventory property that is produced in whole or in part within the United States and sold outside of the United States (or vice versa) is allocated and apportioned between U.S. and foreign sources solely on the basis of the production activities with respect to the property (Code Sec. 863(b), as amended by the Tax Cuts and Jobs Act (P.L. 115-97)). Under the rule, if income is produced entirely in the United States, it is U.S. source income and income produced entirely in a foreign country is foreign source income. Inventory produced in both the United States and a foreign country is mixed-source income.

> **Comment:** Cross-border inventory sales will now be sourced without regard to the title passage rule. The title passage rule is seen as a means by which taxpayers can manipulate the source of income rules.

The current regulations, which provide rules for sourcing income attributable to production activity, should continue to apply with respect to determining where production activities are located and allocating and apportioning mixed-source income. The regulations provide rules for sourcing income attributable to production activity. Under the regulations, production activity means activity that creates, fabricates, manufactures, extracts, processes, cures or ages inventory. With some exceptions, the only production activities that are taken into account are those carried on by the taxpayer. The income attributable to production activities is sourced according to the location of the production assets, where the production activity is solely in the United States (Reg. § 1.863-3(c)(1)(i)(A)). Production assets include only tangible and intangible assets that are directly used by the taxpayer to produce inventory. Production assets do not include assets that are not directly used to

NEW LAW EXPLAINED

produce inventory, such as accounts receivable, marketing intangibles and customer lists (Reg. § 1.863-3(c)(1)(i)(B)).

If there is production both inside and outside of the United States, the regulations provide that the source of the income is determined by multiplying the income attributable to the production activities by the ratio of the average adjusted basis of the production assets located outside of the United States to the total adjusted basis of all production assets. The remaining income is U.S. source income (Reg. § 1.863-3(c)(1)(ii)).

> **Practical Analysis:** Robert Misey, Chair of the International Department for Reinhart Boerner Van Deuren in Chicago and Milwaukee, observes that a change in the rules for sourcing income for manufacturers will result in double taxation. Previously, the income on U.S.-manufactured goods sold abroad had been sourced under the "50-50" rule, whereby half was U.S.-source through the U.S. location of the manufacturing assets and half was foreign-source due to the sales activity of passing title abroad. The policy behind the 50-50 rule was that both the manufacturing and sales activity contributed to the production of the income. As a result of this Act Section, all U.S.-manufactured inventory sold abroad will be characterized as U.S.-source income. The end result is that none of the income will be foreign-source and no foreign tax credits will be available to U.S. manufacturers that sell their products abroad. Accordingly, the income will be taxed twice—once by a foreign country and again by the United States.

▶   **Effective date.** The amendment made by this section applies to tax years beginning after December 31, 2017 (Act Sec. 14303(b) of the Tax Cuts and Jobs Act (P.L. 115-97)).

Law source: Law at ¶5780. Committee Report at ¶11,000, ¶11,010, ¶11,020, ¶11,030, and ¶11,190.

— Act Sec. 14303(a) of the Tax Cuts and Jobs Act (P.L. 115-97), amending Code Sec. 863(b);

— Act Sec. 14303(b), providing the effective date.

CFCs AND SUBPART F INCOME

¶735   Foreign High Return Amounts of U.S. Shareholders of Controlled Foreign Corporations (CFCs)

SUMMARY OF NEW LAW

A current year inclusion of global intangible low-taxed income (GILTI) by a person who is a U.S. shareholder of a controlled foreign corporation (CFC) is required. Domestic corporations are provided with reduced rates of U.S. tax on their foreign-derived intangible income (FDII) and global intangible low-taxed income (GILTI).

BACKGROUND

In general, foreign income earned by a foreign subsidiary of a U.S. corporation is not subject to U.S. tax until it has been distributed to its U.S. parent in the form of a dividend. These dividends less credits obtained for foreign income taxes paid are regarded as taxable income of the U.S. corporation. The primary exception to the deferral of U.S. tax is the subpart F rules (Code Secs. 951-965).

A U.S. parent corporation is typically subject to current U.S. tax on subpart F income earned by its foreign subsidiaries and earnings invested by the subsidiaries in U.S. property, minus any foreign income taxes paid on that income. The U.S. corporation's taxable income is taxed at rates of 15 to 35 percent. This applies irrespective of whether the corporation's income is from tangible or intangible property.

For the subpart F rules to apply, the corporation must be a controlled foreign corporation (CFC), with substantial U.S. shareholders, meaning generally, those who own 10 percent or more of the voting stock of the foreign corporation (Code Sec. 951). However, the amount included in gross income under subpart F for any given year is limited to the current earnings and profits. The amount of the subpart F inclusions are reduced, in certain circumstances, by deficits in earnings and profits (Code Sec. 952(c)). This treatment differs from the normal rules for domestic corporations which treat any distribution for the year as a dividend to the extent of current earnings and profits, regardless of offsetting deficits in prior years.

A U.S. corporation owning at least 10 percent of the voting stock of a foreign corporation from which it receives dividends is treated as if it had paid a share of the foreign taxes paid by the foreign corporation in the year in which that corporation's earnings and profits become subject to U.S. tax as dividend income of the U.S. corporation. This is called the deemed-paid or indirect foreign tax credit (Code Sec. 902; Reg. § 1.78-1(a)). A U.S. corporation also gets a deemed credit with respect to amounts included in gross income that are attributable to deemed inclusions of a CFC's earnings and profits (Code Sec. 960).

A 10 percent-or-more U.S. shareholder of a CFC must report as a dividend the shareholder's pro rata share of the corporation's earnings and profits accumulated in tax years (beginning after 1962) in which the stock was held. The report must also be made upon disposition of the U.S. shareholder's stock, and the dividend cannot be greater than the gain on disposition (Code Sec. 1248). The earnings and profits of the foreign corporation function as a limitation on the amount treated as a dividend.

NEW LAW EXPLAINED

Global intangible low-taxed income and foreign-derived intangible income.—A person who is a U.S. shareholder of any controlled foreign corporation (CFC) is required to include its global intangible low-taxed income (GILTI) in gross income for the tax year in a manner generally similar to that for Subpart F inclusions (Code Sec. 951A(a), (f), as added by the Tax Cuts and Jobs Act (P.L. 115-97)). Specifically, GILTI that is included in gross income is treated in the same manner as amounts included under Code Sec. 951(a)(1)(A) when applying:

NEW LAW EXPLAINED

(1) Code Sec. 168(h)(2)(B) (exception from ACRS for certain property subject to U.S. tax that is used by a foreign person or entity)

(2) Code Sec. 535(b)(10) (adjustments to taxable income for CFCs)

(3) Code Sec. 851(b) (limitations on definition of a regulated investment company)

(4) Code Sec. 904(h)(1) (source rules for U.S. owned foreign corporations for purposes of the limitation on the foreign tax credit)

(5) Code Sec. 959 (exclusion from gross income of previously taxed earnings and profits)

(6) Code Sec. 961 (adjustments to the basis of stock held in a CFC by a U.S. shareholder)

(7) Code Sec. 962 (election by individuals to be taxed at corporate rates)

(8) Code Sec. 993(a)(1)(E) (dividends with respect to the stock of a related foreign export corporation are qualified export receipts)

(9) Code Sec. 996(f)(1) (allocation rules for DISC income)

(10) Code Sec. 1248(b)(1) (limitation on the tax applicable to individuals on the pro rata share of taxes paid by a foreign corporation)

(11) Code Sec. 1248(d)(1) (exclusion from earnings and profits of a foreign corporation)

(12) Code Sec. 6501(e)(1)(C) (substantial omission of constructive dividends)

(13) Code Sec. 6654(d)(2)(D) (treatment of Subpart F and possession credit income for the purposes of a failure by an individual to pay estimated income tax)

(14) Code Sec. 6655(e)(4) (treatment of Subpart F and possession credit income for the purposes of a failure by a corporation to pay estimated income tax) (Code Sec. 961A(f)(1)(A), as added by the 2017 Tax Cuts Act).

The Treasury may issue rules and other guidance to assist in coordinating the GILTI inclusion with provisions that require the determination of subpart F income at the CFC level (Code Sec. 961A(f)(1)(B), as added by the 2017 Tax Cuts Act).

GILTI defined. The term "global intangible low-taxed income" is defined as the excess (if any) of: (1) the U.S. shareholder's net CFC tested income for that tax year, over (2) the U.S. shareholder's net deemed tangible income return for that tax year (Code Sec. 951A(b)(1), as added by the 2017 Tax Cuts Act).

Net deemed tangible income return. The term "net deemed tangible income return" means with respect to any U.S. shareholder for the tax year, the excess (if any) of: (1) 10 percent of the aggregate of its pro rata share of the qualified business asset investment (QBAI) of each CFC in which it is a U.S. shareholder, over (2) the amount of interest expense taken into account in determining its net CFC tested income for the tax year to the extent that the interest expense exceeds the interest income properly allocable to the interest expense that is taken into account in determining its net CFC tested income (Code Sec. 951A(b)(2), as added by the 2017 Tax Cuts Act).

NEW LAW EXPLAINED

The formula for calculating GILTI is: GILTI = Net CFC Tested Income – [(10% × QBAI) – Interest Expense]. As noted in the Conference Agreement, if the amount of interest expense exceeds 10% × QBAI, then the quantity in brackets in the formula equals zero in the determination of GILTI (Conference Report on H.R. 1, Tax Cuts and Jobs Act (H. Rept. 115-466)).

Net CFC tested income and loss. A CFC's tested income for any tax year is the gross income of the corporation in excess of the properly allocated deductions, without regard to the following:

(1) effectively connected income of the CFC, defined in Code Sec. 952(b);

(2) gross income taken into account in determining subpart F income;

(3) gross income excluded from foreign base company income and insurance income as high-taxed income under Code Sec. 954(b)(4);

(4) dividends received from related persons, defined in Code Sec. 954(d)(3); and

(5) foreign oil and gas extraction income, as defined in Code Sec. 907(c)(1) (Code Sec. 951A(c)(2)(A), as added by the 2017 Tax Cuts Act).

A CFC's tested loss for any tax year is the excess of the properly allocated deductions over the CFC's tested income (Code Sec. 951A(c)(2)(B), as added by the 2017 Tax Cuts Act).

The term "net CFC tested income" means with respect to a U.S. shareholder for any tax year of the shareholder, the excess (if any) of (1) the aggregate of the shareholder's pro rata share of the tested income of each CFC with respect to which the shareholder is a U.S. shareholder for the tax year of the U.S. shareholder, over (2) the aggregate of the shareholder's pro rata share of the tested loss of each CFC with respect to which the shareholder is a U.S. shareholder for the tax year of the U.S. shareholder. The amounts are determined for each tax year of the CFC which ends in or with such tax year of the U.S. shareholder (Code Sec. 951A(c)(1), as added by the 2017 Tax Cuts Act).

> **Comment:** The definition of a U.S. shareholder was expanded by the 2017 Tax Cuts Act to include a U.S. person that owns at least 10 percent of the total value of all classes of stock of the foreign corporation, in addition to a U.S. person that owns at least 10 percent of the voting stock of the foreign corporation. The definition applies for purposes of Title 26 and not just subpart F (Code Sec. 951(b) and Code Sec. 957(a), as amended by the 2017 Tax Cuts Act).

Qualified business asset investment (QBAI). The term "qualified business asset investment" is defined by reference to specific tangible property used in a trade or business that is depreciable under Code Sec. 167. Specified tangible property is property used in the production of tested income, unless the rule for dual use property applies. Specifically, QBAI is the CFC's average aggregate adjusted bases as of the close of each quarter of the tax year in the property (Code Sec. 951A(d)(1), as added by the 2017 Tax Cuts Act). Dual use property—property used both in the production of tested income and income that is not tested—is treated as specified tangible property in the same proportion that the CFC's tested income produced with

NEW LAW EXPLAINED

respect to the property bears to the total gross income produced with respect to the property (Code Sec. 951A(d)(2)(B), as added by the 2017 Tax Cuts Act).

The adjusted basis of the property is determined using the alternative depreciation system under Code Sec. 168(g) and allocating depreciation deductions for the property ratably to each day during the period in the tax year to which the depreciation relates (Code Sec. 951A(d)(3), as added by the 2017 Tax Cuts Act).

Further, if a CFC holds an interest in a partnership at the end of the CFC's tax year, the CFC takes into account its distributive share of the aggregate of the partnership's adjusted basis in tangible property held by the partnership if the property is used in the trade or business of the partnership, is of a type to which a deduction is allowed under Code Sec. 167, and is used in the production of tested income. The CFC's distributive share of the adjusted basis of any property is the CFC's distributive share of income with respect to the property (Code Sec. 951A(d)(3)[sic], as added by the 2017 Tax Cuts Act; Conference Report on H.R. 1, Tax Cuts and Jobs Act (H. Rept. 115-466)).

Pro rata share. A shareholder's pro rata share for purposes of determining GILTI and net CFC tested income is determined under the rules of Code Sec. 951(a)(2) with respect to subpart F income. The pro rata shares are taken into account in the tax year of the U.S. shareholder in which or with which the tax year of the CFC ends (Code Sec. 951A(e)(1), as added by the 2017 Tax Cuts Act). A person is treated as a U.S. shareholder of a CFC only if the person owns, within the meaning of Code Sec. 958(a) (direct or indirect ownership) stock in the foreign corporation on the last day of the tax year of the foreign corporation on which the foreign corporation is a CFC (Code Sec. 951A(e)(2), as added by the 2017 Tax Cuts Act). A foreign corporation is treated as a CFC for any tax year if the foreign corporation is a CFC at any time during the tax year (Code Sec. 951A(e)(3), as added by the 2017 Tax Cuts Act).

Foreign tax credit. Foreign tax credits are allowed for foreign income taxes paid on GILTI included in the gross income of a domestic corporation. The foreign income taxes paid are restricted to 80 percent of the domestic corporation's inclusion percentage multiplied by the aggregate tested foreign income taxes paid or accrued by CFCs. The inclusion percentage is the ratio (which is expressed as a percentage) of the corporation's GILTI divided by the aggregate amounts of the shareholder's pro rata share of the tested income of each CFC where the shareholder is a U.S. shareholder for their tax year (Code Sec. 951A(d)(2), as added by the 2017 Tax Cuts Act).

Under the provision, these are considered deemed-paid credits for taxes properly attributed to tested income and a separate foreign tax credit basket is created for GILTI (see ¶725). No carryforward or carryback of excess taxes paid or accrued is permitted (Code Sec. 960(d), as added by the 2017 Tax Cuts Act).

Deduction for FDII and GILTI. Domestic corporations are provided with reduced rates of U.S. tax on foreign-derived intangible income (FDII) and global intangible low-taxed income (GILTI). For tax years beginning after December 31, 2017, and before January 1, 2026, a deduction is generally allowed in an amount equal to the sum of: (1) 37.5 percent of its FDII, plus (2) 50 percent of its GILTI, if any, and the amount treated as a dividend received by the corporation and attributable to its GILTI (Code Sec. 250(a)(1), as added by the 2017 Tax Cuts Act). For tax years

NEW LAW EXPLAINED

beginning after December 31, 2025, the deduction for FDII is 21.875 percent and 37.5 percent for GILTI (Code Sec. 250(a)(3), as added by the 2017 Tax Cuts Act). The amount of the deduction is limited based on taxable income. If the sum of a domestic corporation's FDII and GILTI amounts exceeds its taxable income, then the amount of the FDII and GILTI deduction is similarly reduced by an amount determined by the excess (Code Sec. 250(b)(2), as added by the 2017 Tax Cuts Act).

FDII defined. A domestic corporation's foreign-derived intangible income (FDII) is the portion of its intangible income, determined according to a codified formula, that is derived from serving foreign markets. This means income derived in connection with property that is sold by the taxpayer to any person who is not a U.S. person and that such property is for foreign use, consumption or disposition that is not within the United States (Code Sec. 250(b), as added by the 2017 Tax Cuts Act).

A domestic corporation's FDII is generally its deemed intangible income multiplied by the percentage of its deduction-eligible income that is foreign derived: FDII = Deemed Intangible Income × Foreign-Derived Deduction Eligible Income over Deduction Eligible Income. Deduction eligible income means the excess of the gross income of the domestic corporation over deductions (including taxes) properly allocated to gross income (Code Sec. 250(b)(3), as added by the 2017 Tax Cuts Act). This is determined without taking into account certain exceptions to deduction eligible income. These exceptions include:

- Subpart F income of the corporation determined under Code Sec. 951;
- GILTI of the corporation;
- Financial services income of the corporation;
- Dividends received from a CFC with respect to which the corporation is a U.S. shareholder;
- Domestic oil and gas extraction income of the corporation; and
- Foreign branch income of the corporation.

Deemed intangible income is the excess of the deduction eligible income over the deemed tangible income return of the corporation (Code Sec. 250(b)(2), as added by the 2017 Tax Cuts Act).

Foreign-derived deduction eligible income means deduction eligible income derived in connection with: (1) property sold by the taxpayer to any person who is not a U.S. person if the taxpayer satisfies the IRS that the property was for foreign use, and (2) services provided by the taxpayer if the taxpayer satisfies the IRS that the services are provided to any person or with respect to any property not located in the United States (Code Sec. 250(b)(4), as added by the 2017 Tax Cuts Act).

Special rules apply for purposes of determining foreign use, including rules for related parties (Code Sec. 250(b)(5), as added by the 2017 Tax Cuts Act). Foreign use is any use, disposition or consumption that does not occur within the U.S. Property that is provided to domestic intermediaries (not related parties), where the property is subject to further manufacture or modification in the U.S. is not treated as sold for foreign use even if it is subsequently used for foreign use (Code Sec. 250(b)(5)(B)(i), as added by the 2017 Tax Cuts Act). Services that are provided to another person (not a

¶735

NEW LAW EXPLAINED

related party) located in the U.S. are not treated as services for foreign use even if the person receiving the services uses the services in providing services for foreign use (Code Sec. 250(b)(5)(B)(ii), as added by the 2017 Tax Cuts Act).

If property is sold to a related party who is not a U.S. person, that sale will not be treated as a sale for foreign use unless:

(1) the property is ultimately sold (or used by the related party in connection with property that is sold or services provided) to another unrelated party who is not a U.S. person and

(2) the taxpayer establishes that the property is for foreign use (Code Sec. 250(b)(5)(C), as added by the 2017 Tax Cuts Act).

For service that are provided to related parties that are not located in the U.S., those services will be treated as provided for foreign use unless the taxpayer establishes that the service is not substantially similar to services provided by the related party to persons located in the U.S. (Code Sec. 250(b)(5)(C)(ii), as added by the 2017 Tax Cuts Act). Related parties are any member of an affiliated group, as defined in Code Sec. 1504(a), where corporations are connected through the ownership of a common parent, except for purposes of this provision that ownership is defining by owning 50 percent of the vote or value of the stock, of one or more of the corporations included in the affiliated group (Code Sec. 250(b)(5)(D), as added by the 2017 Tax Cuts Act). Any persons is treated as a member of the affiliated group (except for corporation) if they are controlled by members of the group or if they control a member of the group. Control is determined under Code Sec. 954(d)(3).

The Treasury may issue regulations or other guidance as necessary (Code Sec. 250(c), as added by the 2017 Tax Cuts Act).

> **Comment:** According to clarifications and modifications provided in the Conference Agreement, the deduction for FDII and GILTI is only available to C corporations that are not RICs or REITs. Further, the deduction for GILTI applies to the amount treated as a dividend received by a domestic corporation under Code Sec. 78 that is attributable to the corporation's GILTI amount under new Code Sec. 951A (Conference Report on H.R. 1, Tax Cuts and Jobs Act (H. Rept. 115-466)).

Practical Analysis: Stewart R. Lipeles, Partner at Baker & McKenzie LLP in Palo Alto, California, and Ethan S. Kroll, Associate at Baker & McKenzie LLP in Palo Alto, California, observe that this section of the Act effectively repeals deferral for multinational enterprises with low tax offshore structures, regardless of the degree of substance that the enterprises' offshore operations reflect. Specifically, Act Sec. 14201 introduces a new category of subpart F income, "global intangible low-taxed income," or "GILTI." Act Sec. 14201 is effective for tax years of CFCs beginning after December 31, 2017, and for United States shareholder tax years with which, or within which, the CFC years end.

A United States shareholder's GILTI for the shareholder's tax year equals the amount (if any) by which the shareholder's "net CFC tested income" for the year

NEW LAW EXPLAINED

exceeds the shareholder's "net deemed tangible income return" for the year. To determine its "net CFC tested income," a United States shareholder first calculates the "tested income" of each of its CFCs. Each CFC's tested income is the CFC's gross income, computed without taking into account the CFC's effectively connected income, subpart F income, income with respect to which the CFC elects the high tax exception to subpart F, related party dividends, insurance income, and foreign oil and gas extraction income, less any allocable deductions. If the allocable deductions exceed the CFC's gross income, the CFC has a "tested loss." The United States shareholder's "net CFC tested income" is the amount by which the aggregate "tested income" of all of its CFCs exceeds the aggregate "tested loss" of all its CFCs. If the United States shareholder does not wholly own the CFCs, the amount of the shareholder's "net CFC tested income" is determined taking into account only the shareholder's proportionate interest in the "tested income" and "tested loss" of the CFCs.

The United States shareholder's "net deemed tangible income return" is the aggregate of the amount by which 10 percent of each CFC's "qualified business asset investment," or "QBAI," exceeds the amount of the CFC's excess interest expense, if any, that the CFC's "tested income" calculation reflects. A CFC's QBAI for a tax year is the CFC's aggregate adjusted basis in depreciable tangible property used (i) in the CFC's trade or business and (ii) for the production of "tested income," as determined by averaging the property's basis on the four quarter ends of the year. As with "net CFC tested income," a shareholder's "net deemed tangible income return" takes into account only the shareholder's proportionate interest in the QBAI of the CFCs.

The United States shareholder subtracts its "net deemed tangible income return" from its "net CFC tested income" to arrive at the shareholder's gross GILTI. Under Act Sec. 14202, the shareholder is entitled to deduct 50 percent of this amount to arrive at its net GILTI. Under the new 21 percent corporate income tax rate, the shareholder's GILTI is therefore subject to an effective U.S. tax rate of 10.5 percent. For tax years beginning in 2026, the deduction decreases to 37.5 percent, resulting in an effective rate of 13.125 percent.

The United States shareholder may credit 80 percent of its foreign taxes that are "properly attributable" to the "tested income" of its CFCs against the U.S. tax on its GILTI. If the United States shareholder's GILTI amount is subject to an effective tax rate of at least 13.125 percent, 80 percent of which would be 10.5 percent, the United States shareholder presumably will not incur incremental U.S. tax in respect of its GILTI inclusion, at least until 2026. Act Sec. 14201 also establishes a separate foreign tax credit "basket" for GILTI taxes and thereby eliminates the opportunity to cross-credit GILTI taxes against U.S. tax on other foreign source income. In addition, Act Sec. 14201 amends Code Sec. 904(c) to eliminate the ability to carry forward or carry back GILTI taxes.

Act Sec. 14201 raises a number of policy and planning concerns. First, Act Sec. 14201 encourages taxpayers to increase investments in tangible property offshore. This result runs contrary to Congress's apparent objective of discouraging the offshoring of high value jobs and investment. Specifically, the more a CFC increases its U.S. tax basis in tangible property, the smaller the United States shareholder's

NEW LAW EXPLAINED

potential GILTI inclusion will be. As the Act did not eliminate Code Sec. 956, taxpayers are much more likely to have CFCs increase QBAI by investing offshore, and not in the United States, with a view to avoiding a 21 percent income inclusion on U.S. investments in tangible property under Code Sec. 956(c)(1)(A). Congress was apparently aware of this incentive. Act Sec. 14201 contains a directive instructing Treasury to issue "regulations or other guidance" as appropriate to prevent the avoidance of the purposes of the QBAI provision, including guidance that addresses transitory transactions involving property or transactions in which avoidance of the purposes of the relevant rules is "a factor." Regulations that Treasury issues under Act Sec. 14201 therefore may limit the ability of taxpayers to increase their QBAI amounts with a view to reducing their GILTI inclusions.

Second, GILTI's onerous foreign tax credit rules may result in taxpayers losing the benefit of taxes that are attributable to GILTI in some cases. Specifically, if a taxpayer does not have sufficient foreign source income in a given year, any taxes attributable to GILTI for that year may be lost because Act Sec. 14201 appears to prevent the taxpayer from carrying GILTI taxes forward or back. This result seems unwarranted, as one objective of Act Sec. 14201 is to impose a manner of minimum tax on U.S. multinationals. U.S. multinationals that in fact pay tax offshore should be entitled to the benefit of those taxes, even if that benefit accrues for U.S. tax purposes in a different year.

Third, as noted above, Act Sec. 14201 does not distinguish between passive and active returns. A U.S. multinational may derive low tax returns by using thousands of employees who substantially contribute to the manufacture of property the enterprise sells. Under the traditional subpart F framework, which the bill leaves largely intact, the presence of such activities is generally sufficient to exempt the enterprise from current U.S. tax on its low tax returns. Yet, under Act Sec. 14201, the enterprise's offshore operations are treated the same as those of a shell company that derives interest and royalties on passive investments. Act Sec. 14201 therefore signifies a sharp departure from historic U.S. international tax practice, as it effectively treats all low taxed offshore income as "bad," regardless of the economic substance behind this income.

Practical Analysis: Stewart R. Lipeles, Partner at Baker & McKenzie LLP in Palo Alto, California, and Ethan S. Kroll, Associate at Baker & McKenzie LLP in Palo Alto, California, comment that this Act Section introduces a welcome incentive for some companies to locate intangible property in the United States by offering an attractive 13.125 percent tax rate on certain returns. Specifically, Act Sec. 14202 allows a U.S. corporation to deduct 37.5 percent of its "foreign-derived intangible income" for the year, resulting in an effective tax rate of 13.125 percent on this income. The deduction decreases to 21.875 percent for tax years beginning in 2026, resulting in an effective tax rate of 16.406 percent. Section 14202 applies to tax years beginning after December 31, 2017.

The mechanism for determining a U.S. corporation's "foreign-derived intangible income" is relatively complex. The corporation determines its "foreign-derived intan-

NEW LAW EXPLAINED

gible income" by multiplying its "deemed intangible income" times the ratio of the corporation's "foreign-derived deduction eligible income" to its "deduction eligible income."

First, the corporation determines its "deemed intangible income." The corporation's "deemed intangible income" is the amount by which the corporation's "deduction eligible income" exceeds the corporation's "deemed tangible income return." The corporation's "deduction eligible income" is the corporation's gross income, without taking into account its subpart F income, "global intangible low-taxed income" or "GILTI" under new Code Sec. 951A (Act Sec. 14201), financial services income, dividends from CFCs, domestic oil and gas extraction income, or foreign branch income, less any allocable deductions. The corporation's "deemed tangible income return" is 10 percent of the corporation's "qualified business asset investment" or "QBAI," as defined in new Code Sec. 951A(d), *i.e.*, the GILTI provision. Thus, roughly speaking, the corporation's "deemed tangible income return" is 10 percent of the corporation's aggregate adjusted basis in depreciable tangible property used (i) in the corporation's trade or business and (ii) for the production of "deduction eligible income," as determined by averaging the property's basis on the four quarter ends of the year. The objective of this calculation is to carve out from the taxpayer's gross income a routine return that is not eligible for the preferential tax rate under Act Sec. 14202.

Next, the corporation determines its "foreign-derived deduction eligible income." "Foreign-derived deduction eligible income" refers to "deduction eligible income" that the corporation derives in connection with (i) property that the corporation sells, leases, licenses, exchanges, or otherwise disposes of (a) to a non-U.S. person, (b) for use, consumption, or disposition outside the United States, or (ii) services that the taxpayer provides to any person, or with respect to property, that is not located in the United States. Sales, etc., of property to unrelated parties for further manufacture or modification in the United States do not generate "foreign-derived deduction eligible income" even if there is a subsequent foreign use. The result is the same for services that a corporation provides to unrelated parties in the United States.

Transactions involving sales, *etc.*, of property to foreign affiliates generate "foreign-derived deduction eligible income" only if a related party ultimately sells the property to an unrelated, non-US person, or a related party uses the property in connection with property that is sold, or the provision of services, to an unrelated, non-US person. Providing services to an affiliate outside the United States only generates "foreign-derived deduction eligible income" if the service recipient does not provide "substantially similar" services to persons located in the United States.

At a high level, the calculations described above are ostensibly intended to provide a U.S. corporation with a preferential tax rate on the portion of its non-routine returns resulting from U.S. activities that relates to transactions with the non-U.S. market.

We make a few observations on Act Sec. 14202 below. First, the section's reference to "foreign-derived intangible income" is somewhat misleading. Although foreign returns on intangible property that U.S. corporations use to make products, provide services, or outlicense can benefit from this provision, the application of the provision does not turn on the presence or absence of intangible property. Any U.S. corporation that engages in transactions involving property or services with non-U.S. per-

NEW LAW EXPLAINED

sons located outside the United States can potentially earn "foreign-derived intangible income."

Second, the rules for related party transactions appear to allow for some round-tripping of goods. Specifically, these rules appear to permit a U.S. corporation to recognize "foreign-derived deduction eligible income" in the following fact pattern. A U.S. corporation licenses IP to a foreign affiliate, and the foreign affiliate uses the IP to make components. The affiliate then sells the components to the U.S. corporation, and the U.S. corporation incorporates the components in products. The U.S. corporation then sells the finished products back to the foreign affiliate, which sells the finished products to non-U.S. third parties. In this fact pattern, the U.S. corporation could recognize "foreign-derived deduction eligible income" twice—once on the IP license, and a second time on the sale of finished products. This result would be appropriate, as it would acknowledge the fact that successful multinational enterprises design, make, and sell products using interconnected global supply chains. Moreover, the U.S. corporation could have achieved the same tax result without round-tripping by structuring the foreign affiliate as a contract manufacturer with a cost plus return, as in that case the U.S. corporation could recognize roughly the same amount of "foreign-derived deduction eligible income."

Third, the definition of "deemed intangible income" may have the unintended effect of discouraging U.S. corporations from making capital investments in the United States. Under this definition, the greater a U.S. corporation's QBAI is, the smaller the pool of the U.S. corporation's income that can potentially benefit from Act Sec. 14202 becomes. Taken together with the benefit to taxpayers of increasing QBAI at the CFC level for purposes of Act Sec. 14201, *i.e.*, new Code Sec. 951A, taxpayers have a strong incentive to make capital investments offshore rather than in the United States. The immediate expensing rules in Act Sec. 13201 may mitigate this concern in part for the time being, however.

Fourth, the shelf life of Act Sec. 14202 may be limited, as the lower rate for "foreign-derived intangible income" could possibly constitute a prohibited export subsidy. The European Union previously challenged similar export incentives, such as the Foreign Sales Corporation and Extraterritorial Income regimes, and could also challenge Act Sec. 14202. Taxpayers that are considering entering into transactions to maximize the benefit of Act Sec. 14202, including by locating intangible property in the United States, may want to consider the longevity of this regime.

▶ **Effective date.** The GILTI provisions apply to tax years of foreign corporations beginning after December 31, 2017, and to tax years of U.S. shareholders in which or with which such tax years of foreign corporations end (Act Sec. 14201(d) of the Tax Cuts and Jobs Act (P.L. 115-97)). The deduction for foreign-derived intangible income and GILTI provisions apply to tax years beginning after December 31, 2017 (Act Sec. 14202(c) of the 2017 Tax Cuts Act).

Law source: Law at ¶5325, ¶5405, ¶5420, ¶5545, ¶5820, ¶5865, and ¶5910. Committee Report at ¶11,000, ¶11,010, ¶11,020, ¶11,030, ¶11,070, and ¶11,080.

— Act Sec. 14201(a) of the Tax Cuts and Jobs Act (P.L. 115-97), adding new Code Sec. 951A;

— Act Sec. 14201(b), adding new Code Sec. 960(d), redesignating Code Sec. 904(d)(1)(A) and (B) as (B) and (C), respectively, and adding new (A), and amending Code Sec. 904(c) and (d)(2)(A)(ii);

NEW LAW EXPLAINED

— Act Sec. 14202(a), adding new Code Sec. 250;

— Act Sec. 14202(b), amending Code Secs. 172(d), 246(b)(1), and 469(i)(3)(F)(iii);

— Act Sec. 14201(d) and Act Sec. 14202(c), providing the effective dates.

¶737 Foreign Base Company Oil Related Income

SUMMARY OF NEW LAW

Foreign base company oil related income is eliminated as a category of foreign base company income and so is no longer subpart F income.

BACKGROUND

Under the subpart F rules, certain income earned by a foreign corporation that is a controlled foreign corporation (CFC) may be currently taxed to U.S. shareholders, even though the earnings are not distributed to the shareholder (Code Secs. 951-965). In general, a CFC is any foreign corporation with respect to which U.S. shareholders own more than 50 percent of the total combined voting power of all classes of stock entitled to vote or the total value of the stock of the corporation (Code Sec. 957). The foreign corporation must be a CFC for an uninterrupted period of 30 days or more during the tax year (Code Sec. 951(a)). A U.S. shareholder is any U.S. person who owns 10 percent or more of the total combined voting power of all classes of stock of the foreign corporation (Code Sec. 951(b)).

Subpart F income is one of the categories of income currently taxed (Code Sec. 951(a)(1)(A)). One of the main categories of subpart F income is foreign base company income (Code Sec. 952). Foreign base company income is made up of several subcategories of income, one of which is foreign base company oil related income (Code Sec. 954(g)).

Foreign base company oil related income is foreign oil related income (FORI) or taxable income derived outside of the United States and its possessions from:

(1) the processing of minerals extracted from oil and gas wells into their primary products;

(2) the transportation of the minerals or primary products;

(3) the distribution or sale of the minerals or primary products;

(4) the disposition of assets used by the taxpayer in its trade or business, described above; or

(5) the performance of any related service (Code Sec. 907(c)(2)).

NEW LAW EXPLAINED

Foreign oil related income also includes dividends and interest from a foreign corporation for which taxes are deemed paid under Code Sec. 902 or Code Sec. 960 and a

NEW LAW EXPLAINED

taxpayer's distributable share of partnership income, to the extent the amounts are attributable to FORI (Code Sec. 907(c)(3)).

Foreign base company oil related income does not include oil related income of a CFC from sources within a foreign country where the oil or gas was extracted (extraction exception) or within the foreign country where the oil or gas is used or consumed (or is loaded in the foreign country on a vessel or aircraft as fuel for the vessel or aircraft) (use or consumption exception) (Code Sec. 954(g)(1)). Foreign base company oil related income does not include any income of a foreign corporation that is not a large oil producer (i.e., produces 1,000 barrels a day or more) (Code Sec. 954(g)(2)).

Foreign base company oil related income eliminated from foreign base company income.—Foreign oil related income is eliminated as a category of foreign base company income. Thus, U.S. shareholders of controlled foreign corporations (CFCs) are no longer required to include this type of income in gross income as subpart F income (Code Sec. 954(a), as amended by the Tax Cuts and Jobs Act (P.L. 115-97)). Foreign base company oil related income was defined as income of a foreign corporation and large oil producer (i.e., producer of 1,000 barrels a day or more) that is foreign oil related income (FORI), defined in Code Sec. 907(c)(2) and (c)(3). Foreign base company oil related income did not include oil related income of a CFC from sources within a foreign country where the oil or gas was extracted (extraction exception) or within the foreign country where the oil or gas is used or consumed (or is loaded in the foreign country on a vessel or aircraft as fuel for the vessel or aircraft) (use or consumption exception) (Code Sec. 954(g), prior to being stricken by the 2017 Tax Cuts Act).

> **Comment:** According to the House Committee Report, the foreign base company oil related income rules were not necessary in the context of the other international tax reforms. Moving to the participation exemption system could put U.S. oil and gas companies at a competitive disadvantage because of the loss of the Code Sec. 902 credit (see ¶705). Additionally, separate anti-base erosion rules under the bill (see ¶750 et seq.) make the separate anti-base erosion rules for oil and gas operations unnecessary (House Committee Report for the Tax Cuts and Jobs Act (P.L. 115-97) (H. R. Rep. No. 115-409)).

▶ **Effective date.** The amendments made by this section apply to tax years of foreign corporations beginning after December 31, 2017, and to tax years of U.S. shareholders with or within which such tax years of foreign corporations end (Act Sec. 14211(c) of the Tax Cuts and Jobs Act (P.L. 115-97)).

Law source: Law at ¶5870 and ¶5880. Committee Report at ¶11,000, ¶11,010, ¶11,020, ¶11,030, and ¶11,090.

— Act Sec. 14211(a) of the Tax Cuts and Jobs Act (P.L. 115-97), amending Code Sec. 954(a)(2) and (3), and striking Code Sec. 954(a)(5);

— Act Sec. 14211(b), amending Code Sec. 952(c)(1)(B)(iii) and Code Sec. 954(b)(4) and (5), and striking Code Sec. 954(b)(6) and (g); and

— Act Sec. 14211(c), providing the effective date.

¶737

¶741 Subpart F Inclusions for Withdrawal of Qualified Investments

SUMMARY OF NEW LAW

The subpart F inclusion for a CFC's previously excluded subpart F income withdrawn from foreign base company shipping operations is repealed. Also repealed is the subpart F inclusion for amounts withdrawn from qualified investment in less developed countries and decreases in export trade assets.

BACKGROUND

Prior to 1987, the subpart F rules partially favored shipping income. Code Sec. 954(b)(2), prior to repeal by the Tax Reform Act of 1986 (P.L. 99-514), provided a deferral from tax for foreign base company shipping income that was reinvested in foreign base company shipping operations. The exclusion applied only with respect to "qualified investments". After the repeal of the provision, taxpayers could not exclude foreign base company shipping income by making qualified investments. However, while total excluded income could not be increased, previously excluded income was not subject to tax until income was withdrawn from foreign base company shipping operations. A U.S. shareholder of a controlled foreign corporation (CFC) must include in its gross income its pro rata share of amounts of the corporation's subpart F income previously excluded that are withdrawn from foreign base company shipping operations (Code Sec. 951(a)(1)(A)(iii)). The amount of previously excluded subpart F income withdrawn from qualified investments in foreign base company shipping operations is generally equal to the decrease in investments in foreign base company shipping operations for the tax year (Code Sec. 955). The foreign base company income category for foreign base company shipping income was eliminated after December 31, 2004, by the American Jobs Creation Act of 2004 (P.L. 108-357). Parallel rules applied to qualified investments in less developed countries for the years 1962 through 1975 (i.e., generally stock and long-term debt obligations of less developed country corporations) (Code Secs. 955, as in effect prior to the Tax Reduction Act of 1975 (P.L. 94-12), and 951(a)(1)(A)(ii); Reg. §1.955-1).

An export trade corporation is a CFC that sells abroad products that it produces, manufactures, grows or extracts abroad. These corporations are allowed to reduce foreign base company income by the portion of their income that is export trade income (i.e., income derived from export trade activities). The provision was partially repealed in that any corporation that qualified as an export trade corporation for any year beginning before November 1, 1971, can continue to be treated as a export trade corporation if it does not fail to qualify as an export trade corporation for three consecutive tax years (Code Secs. 970, 971). If export trade income is deferred, it must be included in a U.S. shareholder's gross income under Code Sec. 951(a)(1)(A)(ii) if there is a decrease in export trade assets (Code Sec. 970(b)).

NEW LAW EXPLAINED

Subpart F inclusions for withdrawal of qualified investments repealed.—The provision repeals Code Sec. 955, which provides rules for determining a U.S. shareholder's pro rata share of the controlled foreign corporation's previously excluded subpart F income withdrawn from qualified investment in foreign base shipping operations (Act Sec. 14212(a) of the Tax Cuts and Jobs Act (P.L. 115-97), striking Code Sec. 955). The U.S. shareholder's corresponding subpart F inclusion for the decrease in investment in foreign base company shipping operations is repealed. Also repealed are the provisions requiring a subpart F inclusion for: (1) a U.S. shareholder's pro rata share of the corporation's previously excluded subpart F income withdrawn from investment in less developed countries, and (2) a decrease in export trade assets, with respect to deferred export trade income (Code Sec. 951(a)(1)(A), as amended by the 2017 Tax Cuts Act and Act Sec. 14213(b)(5), striking Code Sec. 970(b)).

> **Comment:** The House Committee Report states that because foreign base company shipping income is no longer taxed under subpart F, a corresponding decrease in the CFC's investment should not result in an income inclusion for a U.S. shareholder of the CFC (House Committee Report for the Tax Cuts and Jobs Act (P.L. 115-97) (H. R. Rep. No. 115-409)).

▶ **Effective date.** The amendments made by this section apply to tax years of foreign corporations beginning after December 31, 2017, and to tax years of U.S. shareholders in which or with which such tax years of foreign corporations end (Act Sec. 14212(c) of the Tax Cuts and Jobs Act (P.L. 115-97)).

Law source: Law at ¶5755, ¶5860, ¶5870, ¶5875, ¶5885, ¶5925, and ¶5935. Committee Report at ¶11,000, ¶11,010, ¶11,020, ¶11,030, and ¶11,100.

— Act Sec. 14212(a) of the Tax Cuts and Jobs Act (P.L. 115-97), striking Code Sec. 955;

— Act Sec. 14212(b), amending Code Secs. 951(a)(1)(A), 851(b), 952(c)(1)(B)(i), 953(c)(1)(C), 953(d)(4)(B)(iv)(II), and 964(b), and striking Code Secs. 951(a)(3) and 970(b);

— Act Sec. 14212(c), providing the effective date.

¶743 CFC Stock Attribution Rules

SUMMARY OF NEW LAW

Stock ownership may be attributed downward from a foreign person to a related U.S. person for purposes of determining whether a U.S. person is a U.S. shareholder of a corporation, such that the foreign corporation is a CFC.

BACKGROUND

Direct, indirect and constructive ownership is used to determine whether a U.S. person is a U.S. shareholder with respect to a foreign corporation, such that the

BACKGROUND

foreign corporation is a controlled foreign corporation (CFC), and for other provisions of subpart F (Code Sec. 958). Only the direct and indirect ownership rules, however, are used to determine the percentage of stock owned by a U.S. shareholders in computing the amount of the subpart F inclusion. Under the indirect stock ownership rules, stock that is owned directly by a foreign entity, such as a foreign corporation, foreign partnership or foreign estate, is considered to be owned indirectly by the shareholders, partners or beneficiaries, in proportion to their ownership in the entity. Attribution stops with the first U.S. person in the chain of ownership (Code Sec. 958(a)).

Constructive ownership takes into account stock actually owned by related persons. The rules of constructive ownership in Code Sec. 318(a) apply, with certain modifications (Code Sec. 958(b)).

The general constructive ownership rules provide rules for attributing stock ownership to an entity ("to attribution" rules of Code Sec. 318(a)(3)). Under these rules, stock owned, by or for, a partner or beneficiary of an estate is treated as owned by the partnership or estate (Code Sec. 318(a)(3)(A)). Stock owned, directly or indirectly, by or for a beneficiary of a trust is treated as owned by the trust, with special rules for contingent interest and grantor trusts (Code Sec. 318(a)(3)(B)). A corporation is considered as owning all of the stock owned directly or indirectly, by or for any person holding 50 percent or more in value of the corporation's stock, directly or indirectly (Code Sec. 318(a)(3)(C)). These rules are modified so that they cannot be applied to treat a U.S. person as owning stock owned by a person who is not a U.S. person (Code Sec. 958(b)(4); Reg. § 1.958-2(d)(2)).

NEW LAW EXPLAINED

> **Example:** Foreign Corporation A owns 100 percent of one class of stock of Domestic Corporation B and 100 percent of one class of stock of another Foreign Corporation C. Under the modified rule, Domestic Corporation B is not considered as owning the stock owned by its sole shareholder Foreign Corporation A, in Foreign Corporation C (Reg. § 1.958-2(g), Example 4).

CFC constructive stock ownership attribution rule modified.—The modified constructive ownership rule of Code Sec. 958(b)(4), which precludes the attribution rules of Code Sec. 318(a)(3) from applying when stock of a foreign person would be treated as owned by a U.S. person, is eliminated. Elimination of this provision allows for the downward attribution of stock ownership from a foreign person to a related U.S. person (Code Sec. 958(b), as amended by the Tax Cuts and Jobs Act (P.L. 115-97)).

> **Example:** Foreign Corporation A owns 100 percent of one class of stock of Domestic Corporation B and 100 percent of one class of stock of another Foreign Corporation C. Under the constructive ownership rule, Domestic Corporation B

NEW LAW EXPLAINED

is considered as owning the stock owned by its sole shareholder Foreign Corporation A, in Foreign Corporation C.

Comment: According to the Conference Committee Report, the reason for modifying the constructive stock ownership rule is to prevent the avoidance of the subpart F rules by turning off the constructive stock ownership rules that would otherwise treat a U.S. person as owning the stock of a foreign person. This type of avoidance transaction converts former CFCs to non-CFCs despite continuous ownership by U.S. shareholders (Conference Report on H.R. 1, Tax Cuts and Jobs Act (H. Rept. 115-466)). The subpart F inclusion amount continues to be determined based on direct or indirect ownership of the CFC, without application of the new downward attribution rule.

▶ **Effective date.** The amendments made by this section apply to: (1) the last tax year of foreign corporations beginning in January 1, 2018, and each subsequent tax year of such foreign corporations, and (2) tax years of U.S. shareholders in which or with which such tax years of foreign corporations end (Act Sec. 14213(b) of the Tax Cuts and Jobs Act (P.L. 115-97)).

Law source: Law at ¶5985. Committee Report at ¶11,000, ¶11,010, ¶11,020, ¶11,030, and ¶11,110.

— Act Sec. 14213(a) of the Tax Cuts and Jobs Act (P.L. 115-97), amending Code Sec. 958(b) and striking Code Sec. 958(b)(4);

— Act Sec. 14213(b), providing the effective date.

¶745 Definition of U.S. Shareholder

SUMMARY OF NEW LAW

The definition of a U.S. shareholder is expanded to include a shareholder who owns 10 percent or more of a foreign corporation's stock by value. The definition of a U.S. shareholder now applies for purposes of Title 26.

BACKGROUND

Under the subpart F rules, certain income earned by a foreign corporation that is a controlled foreign corporation (CFC) may be currently taxed to U.S. shareholders, even though the earnings are not distributed (Code Secs. 951-965). In general, a CFC is any foreign corporation with respect to which U.S. shareholders own more than 50 percent of the total combined voting power of all classes of stock entitled to vote or the total value of the stock of the corporation (Code Sec. 957). The foreign corporation must be a CFC for an uninterrupted period of 30 days or more during the tax year (Code Sec. 951(a)). A U.S. shareholder is any U.S. person who owns directly, indi-

BACKGROUND

rectly, or constructively, 10 percent or more of the total combined voting power of all classes of stock of the foreign corporation (Code Sec. 951(b)).

NEW LAW EXPLAINED

Definition of U.S. shareholder expanded.—The definition of a U.S. shareholder is expanded to include a U.S. shareholder who owns 10 percent or more of the foreign corporation's stock by value. A U.S. shareholder is defined as any U.S. person who owns directly, indirectly, or constructively: (1) 10 percent or more of the total combined voting power of all classes of stock of the foreign corporation, or (2) 10 percent or more of the total value of shares of all classes of stock of the foreign corporation (Code Sec. 951(b), as amended by the Tax Cuts and Jobs Act (P.L. 115-97)). The definition of a U.S. shareholder also applies for purposes of Title 26, and not just the subpart F provisions (Act Sec. 14101(e)(1) of the 2017 Tax Cuts Act, amending Code Sec. 951(b)).

> **Comment:** Expanding the definition of a U.S. shareholder also expands the number of shareholders who will be subject to the subpart F rules. The definition of a U.S. shareholder now corresponds to the definition of a CFC in Code Sec. 957(a), which looks to vote or value.

See ¶747 for a discussion of the elimination of the 30-day required period of CFC status.

▶ **Effective date.** The amendment made by this section applies to tax years of foreign corporations beginning after December 31, 2017, and to tax years of U.S. shareholders with or within which such tax years of foreign corporations end (Act Sec. 14214(b) of the Tax Cuts and Jobs Act (P.L. 115-97)).

Law source: Law at ¶5860. Committee Report at ¶11,000, ¶11,010, ¶11,020, ¶11,030, and ¶11,120.

— Act Sec. 14214(a) of the Tax Cuts and Jobs Act (P.L. 115-97), amending Code Sec. 951(b);

— Act Sec. 14214(b), providing the effective date.

¶747 Required Period of CFC Status

SUMMARY OF NEW LAW

The requirement that a foreign corporation must be a CFC for an uninterrupted period of 30 days or more before a U.S. shareholder is required to include amounts in gross income under subpart F is eliminated.

BACKGROUND

If a foreign corporation is a controlled foreign corporation (CFC) for an uninterrupted period of at least 30 days during the tax year, U.S. shareholders of the CFC are subject

BACKGROUND

to current taxation on the CFC's subpart F income, certain amounts of subpart F income withdrawn from investment and amounts determined under Code Sec. 956. In general, a CFC is any foreign corporation with respect to which U.S. shareholders own more than 50 percent of the total combined voting power of all classes of the stock entitled to vote or the total value of the stock of the corporation at any time during the tax year of the foreign corporation (Code Sec. 957). A U.S. shareholder is any U.S. person who owns directly, indirectly, or constructively, 10 percent or more of the total combined voting power of all classes of stock of the foreign corporation (Code Sec. 951(b)).

NEW LAW EXPLAINED

Required period of CFC status eliminated.—In determining whether a U.S. shareholder is required to include amounts in income under subpart F, the required period that the controlled foreign corporation (CFC) must be controlled by U.S. shareholders is eliminated (Code Sec. 951(a)(1), as amended by the Tax Cuts and Jobs Act (P.L. 115-97)). The foreign corporation is no longer required to be a CFC for an uninterrupted period of 30 days or more during the tax year. Instead, if the foreign corporation is a CFC at any time during the tax year, U.S. shareholders must include amounts in income under subpart F.

> **Comment:** The provision now corresponds to the definition of a CFC in Code Sec. 957, which only requires that the stock ownership requirements be met on any day during the tax year. The House Committee Report states that the original purpose of the provision to facilitate tax administration is no longer necessary in light of technology that tracks owner and corporate tax attributes on a daily basis. It also states that the rule presents opportunities for taxpayers to structure transactions to avoid tax (House Committee Report for the Tax Cuts and Jobs Act (P.L. 115-97) (H. Rept. 115-409)).

See ¶745 for a discussion of the expanded definition of a U.S. shareholder.

▶ **Effective date.** The amendment made by this section applies to tax years of foreign corporations beginning after December 31, 2017, and to tax years of U.S. shareholders with or within which such tax years of foreign corporations end (Act Sec. 14215(b) of the Tax Cuts and Jobs Act (P.L. 115-97)).

Law source: Law at ¶5860. Committee Report at ¶11,000, ¶11,010, ¶11,020, ¶11,030, and ¶11,130.

— Act Sec. 14215(a) of the Tax Cuts and Jobs Act (P.L. 115-97), amending Code Sec. 951(a)(1);

— Act Sec. 14215(b), providing the effective date.

BASE EROSION PREVENTION

¶750 Base Erosion and Anti-Abuse Tax

SUMMARY OF NEW LAW

Applicable taxpayers are required to pay tax equal to the base erosion minimum tax amount for the tax year. The base erosion minimum tax amount is generally derived by comparing 10 percent (five percent for tax years beginning in calendar year 2018) of the taxpayer's modified taxable income (determined by disregarding certain deductions with respect to base erosion payments made to foreign related persons) to the taxpayer's regular tax liability (reduced for certain credit amounts). For tax years beginning after December 31, 2025, the 10-percent rate is increased to 12.5 percent and the taxpayer's regular tax liability is reduced by the aggregate amount of allowable credits. Applicable taxpayers include corporations (except RICs, REITs, or S corporations) with average annual gross receipts of at least $500 million over the past three tax years and a base erosion percentage of three percent (determined by dividing the aggregate deductions with respect to base erosion payments by the aggregate amount of allowed deductions with some exceptions). An 11-percent rate and two percent base erosion percentage apply to taxpayers that are members of an affiliated group that includes a bank or registered securities dealer. In addition, new reporting requirements will require the collection of information regarding a tax-payer's base erosion payments, and the applicable penalty for failure to report is increased.

BACKGROUND

Foreign corporations are subject to tax in the United States on their U.S.-source income. There are two systems in place to tax this income. Regular tax rates apply to income that is effectively connected with a U.S. trade or business (effectively con-nected income or "ECI"), and a 30-percent tax rate applies to non-effectively con-nected income (fixed or determinable annual or periodical gains, profits and income or "FDAP income") (Code Secs. 864 and 871). FDAP income is subject to withholding at the source and the 30-percent tax rate may be reduced by an applicable income tax treaty (Code Secs. 871 and 881). ECI is subject to similar rules that apply to the business income of U.S. persons. Deductions are available to reduce the amount of ECI that is subject to tax in the United States (Reg. §1.874-1). As a result, foreign owned U.S. subsidiaries are able to reduce their U.S. tax liability through deductible payments of interest, royalties, management fees and reinsurance to related foreign parties (Code Secs. 871 and 881). These payments are thought to erode the U.S. tax base if they are subject to reduced or zero rates of tax withholding in the United States.

A domestic corporation that is 25-percent foreign owned must provide certain required information to the IRS on Form 5472, Information Return of a 25% Foreign-Owned U.S. Corporation or a Foreign Corporation Engaged in a U.S. Trade or

BACKGROUND

Business (Code Sec. 6038A). A corporation required to file Form 5472 must also maintain records (or cause another party to maintain records) necessary to determine the correct treatment of transactions with related parties (Code Sec. 6038A(a)). A corporation is 25-percent foreign owned if 25 percent or more of the total voting power or value of its stock is owned by at least one foreign person at any time during the tax year (Code Sec. 6038A(c)(1)). A related party is: (1) any 25-percent foreign shareholder of the domestic "reporting corporation," (2) any person related (within the meaning of Code Sec. 267(b) and Code Sec. 707(b)(1)) to the reporting corporation or to a 25-percent foreign shareholder of the reporting corporation, or (3) any other person related to the reporting corporation within the meaning of Code Sec. 482 (Code Sec. 6038A(c)(2)). In addition, any foreign related party must agree to authorize the domestic reporting corporation to act as its agent for purposes of an IRS examination of books and records or for the service and enforcement of a summons with respect to any transaction that it has with the reporting corporation (Code Sec. 6038A(e)(1)). If the related party does not make the requisite agency authorization or substantially comply with a summons for records or testimony, a noncompliance penalty may apply.

NEW LAW EXPLAINED

Tax imposed on base erosion payments of taxpayers with substantial gross receipts.—Applicable taxpayers are required to pay, for any tax year, a tax equal to the base erosion minimum tax amount for the year. The tax is paid in addition to any other income taxes imposed under Subtitle A of the Code (Code Sec. 59A(a), as added by the Tax Cuts and Jobs Act (P.L. 115-97)).

The base erosion minimum tax amount for any tax year is the excess, if any, of:

(1) 10 percent (five percent for tax years beginning in calendar year 2018) of the modified taxable income of the taxpayer for the tax year, over

(2) the regular tax liability for the tax year reduced (but not below zero) by the excess, if any, of:

   (a) the credits allowed against regular tax liability under Chapter 1 of the Code, over

   (b) the sum of (i) the credit allowed under Code Sec. 38 (the general business credit) that is allocable to the research credit determined under Code Sec. 41(a), plus (ii) the portion of the applicable Code Sec. 38 credits that do not exceed 80 percent of the lesser of the amount of those credits or the base erosion minimum tax amount (Code Sec. 59A(b)(1), as added by the 2017 Tax Cuts Act).

For tax years beginning after December 31, 2025, for purposes of determining the base erosion minimum tax amount, the 10-percent rate is increased to 12.5 percent of the taxpayer's modified taxable income and the regular tax liability is reduced (but not below zero) by the aggregate amount of allowable credits, rather than the excess described in item (2), above, (Code Sec. 59A(b)(2), as added by the 2017 Tax Cuts Act).

¶750

NEW LAW EXPLAINED

Applicable taxpayers that are members of an affiliated group that includes a bank or registered securities dealer under section 15(a) of the Securities Exchange Act of 1934 are subject to an additional increase of one percentage point in the tax rates, discussed above (i.e., 11 percent for tax years beginning on or before December 31, 2025, and 13.5 percent for tax years beginning after December 31, 2025) (Code Sec. 59A(b)(3), as added by the 2017 Tax Cuts Act).

For purposes of the above computation, the applicable Code Sec. 38 credits are the credits allowed under Code Sec. 38 for the tax year that are properly allocable to:

(1) the low-income housing credit under Code Sec. 42(a);

(2) the renewable electricity production credit under Code Sec. 45(a);

(3) the investment credit under Code Sec. 46, but only to the extent it is properly allocable to the Code Sec. 48 energy credit (Code Sec. 59A(b)(4), as added by the 2017 Tax Cuts Act).

An applicable taxpayer's modified taxable income is determined by computing the taxpayer's taxable income under Chapter 1 for the tax year without regard to (i) any base erosion tax benefit with respect to any base erosion payment, or (ii) the base erosion percentage of any net operating loss deduction allowed under Code Sec. 172 for the tax year (Code Sec. 59A(c)(1), as added by the 2017 Tax Cuts Act).

Base erosion payment. A base erosion payment is any amount paid or accrued by a taxpayer to a foreign person that is a related party of the taxpayer and with respect to which a deduction is allowable under Chapter 1 of the Code (Code Sec. 59A(d)(1), as added by the 2017 Tax Cuts Act). These payments include any amount paid or accrued by the taxpayer to the related party in connection with the acquisition by the taxpayer from the related party of property of a character subject to the allowance of depreciation (or amortization in lieu of depreciation) (Code Sec. 59A(d)(2), as added by the 2017 Tax Cuts Act). A base erosion payment also includes any premium or other consideration paid or accrued by the taxpayer to a foreign person that is a related party of the taxpayer for any reinsurance payments taken into account under Code Secs. 803(a)(1)(B) or 832(b)(4)(A) (Code Sec. 59A(d)(3), as added by the 2017 Tax Cuts Act).

> **Comment:** Base erosion payments generally do not include any amount that constitutes reductions in gross receipts including payments for costs of goods sold (COGS). However, an exception applies for certain payments to expatriated entities, described below.

Base erosion payments include any amount that results in a reduction of gross receipts of the taxpayer that is paid or accrued by the taxpayer with respect to: (1) a surrogate foreign corporation that is a related party of the taxpayer, but only if such corporation first became a surrogate foreign corporation after November 9, 2017, or (2) a foreign person that is a member of the surrogate foreign corporation's expanded affiliated group (EAG) (Code Sec. 59A(d)(4), as added by the 2017 Tax Cuts Act).

> **Practice Note:** For this purpose, a surrogate foreign corporation is a foreign corporation that: (1) acquires (after March 4, 2003) substantially all of the properties held by a U.S. corporation, or substantially all of the properties

NEW LAW EXPLAINED

constituting a trade or business of a domestic partnership, (2) after the acquisition, the U.S. corporation's former shareholders or the domestic partnership's former partners, own at least 60 percent of the stock (by vote or value) of the foreign acquiring corporation, and (3) the surrogate foreign corporation's EAG does not have substantial business activities in the country where that corporation is organized or created compared to the total business activities of the EAG (Code Sec. 7874(a)(2)(B)). A surrogate foreign corporation does not include a foreign corporation treated as a domestic corporation under Code Sec. 7874(b) (where the former shareholders of the U.S. corporation or the former partners of the domestic partnership hold 80 percent or more (by vote or value) of the stock of the foreign acquiring corporation after the transaction). The EAG includes the foreign acquiring corporation and all companies connected to it by a chain of greater than 50-percent ownership (Code Sec. 7874(c)(1)).

A base erosion payment does not include any amount paid or accrued by a taxpayer for services, if such services meet the requirements for eligibility for use of the services cost method described in Reg. §1.482-9, determined without regard to the requirement that the services not contribute significantly to fundamental risks of business success or failure, and if the payments for services have no markup component (Code Sec. 59A(d)(5), as added by the 2017 Tax Cuts Act).

Exception for certain payments in the ordinary course of trade or business. There is an exception provided for some types of payments made in the ordinary course of a trade or business. Under this exception, qualified derivative payments are generally not treated as base erosion payments (Code Sec. 59A(h)(1), as added by the 2017 Tax Cuts Act).

A qualified derivative payment is any payment made by a taxpayer pursuant to a derivative where the taxpayer:

(1) recognizes gain or loss as if the derivative were sold for its fair market value (FMV) on the last business day of the tax year (and at additional times that are required by Title 26 or the taxpayer's method of accounting),

(2) treats any gain or loss recognized as ordinary, and

(3) treats the character of all items of income, deduction, gain or loss regarding a payment pursuant to the derivative as ordinary (Code Sec. 59A(h)(2)(A), as added by the 2017 Tax Cuts Act).

Payments are not treated as qualified derivative payments unless the taxpayer includes in the information required to be reported under Code Sec. 6038B(b)(2), information that is necessary to identify which payments are to be treated as qualified derivative payments and such other information as the Secretary of the Treasury determines necessary (Code Sec. 59A(h)(2)(B), as added by the 2017 Tax Cuts Act).

The rule for qualified derivative payments does not apply if the payment would be treated as a base erosion payment if it was not made pursuant to a derivative (including royalty, interest or service payments), or where a contract has derivative and nonderivative component and the payment is allocable to the nonderivative component (Code Sec. 59A(h)(3), as added by the 2017 Tax Cuts Act).

¶750

NEW LAW EXPLAINED

For these purposes, a derivative is any contract (including any option, forward contract, futures contract, short position, swap, or similar contract) whose value, or any payment or other transfer with respect to said contract, is (directly or indirectly) determined by reference to one or more of the following:

(1) any share of stock of a corporation,

(2) any evidence of indebtedness,

(3) any commodity which is actively traded,

(4) any currency,

(5) any rate, price, amount, index, formula, or algorithm (Code Sec. 59A(h)(4)(A), as added by the 2017 Tax Cuts Act).

However, a derivative does not include any item described in items (1) through (5), above.

Except as otherwise provided by the Secretary, American depository receipts (and similar instruments), with respect to shares of stock in foreign corporations, are treated as shares of stock in such foreign corporations for purposes of Part VII, Subchapter A of Chapter 1 (Code Sec. 59A(h)(4)(B), as added by the 2017 Tax Cuts Act).

In addition, a derivative does not include any insurance, annuity, or endowment contract issued by an insurance company (to which subchapter L applies) or issued by any foreign corporation where subchapter L would apply if such foreign corporation were a domestic corporation (Code Sec. 59A(h)(4)(C), as added by the 2017 Tax Cuts Act).

Base erosion tax benefit. A base erosion tax benefit includes:

(1) any deduction allowed under Chapter 1 for the tax year with respect to any base erosion payment;

(2) for base erosion payments made to purchase property subject to depreciation (or amortization in lieu of depreciation), any deduction allowed in Chapter 1 for depreciation (or amortization in lieu of depreciation) for the tax year with respect to the property acquired with the payment;

(3) in the case of reinsurance payments, any reduction under Code Sec. 803(a)(1)(B) in the gross amounts of premiums or other consideration on insurance, annuity contracts or indemnity insurance, and any deduction under Code Sec. 832(b)(4)(A) from the amount of gross premiums written on insurance contracts during the tax year for the premiums paid for reinsurance; and

(4) in the case of a payment with respect to a surrogate foreign corporation or a foreign member of that corporation's expanded affiliated group, any reduction in gross receipts with respect to that payment in computing the taxpayer's gross income for the tax year (Code Sec. 59A(c)(2)(A), as added by the 2017 Tax Cuts Act).

The base erosion tax benefit attributable to any base erosion payment on which tax is imposed by Code Secs. 871 and 881, and with respect to which tax has been deducted and withheld under Code Secs. 1441 and 1442, is not taken into account in computing

NEW LAW EXPLAINED

modified taxable income or the base erosion percentage. However, the amount not taken into account in computing modified taxable income is reduced under rules similar to the rules under Code Sec. 163(j)(5)(B), as in effect before December 22, 2017, the date of the enactment of the 2017 Tax Cuts Act (which determines whether interest is treated as tax-exempt to the extent of a treaty reduction) (Code Sec. 59A(c)(2)(B), as added by the 2017 Tax Cuts Act).

For purposes of determining an applicable taxpayer's modified taxable income, in the case of a taxpayer to which Code Sec. 163(j) applies for the tax year, the reduction in the amount of interest for which a deduction is allowed by reason of that provision is treated as allocable first to interest paid or accrued to persons who are not related parties with respect to the taxpayer and then to related parties (Code Sec. 59A(c)(3), as added by the 2017 Tax Cuts Act).

Base erosion percentage. The base erosion percentage is the percentage, for any tax year, that is determined by dividing:

(1) the aggregate amount of base erosion tax benefits of the taxpayer for the tax year, by

(2) the aggregate amount of the deductions allowable to the taxpayer for the tax year, taking into account the base erosion tax benefits and disregarding: (i) any deduction allowed under Code Secs. 172, 245A or 250 for the tax year, (ii) any deduction for amounts paid or accrued for services to which the exception for the services cost method (described in Reg. § 1.482-9) applies, and (iii) any deduction for qualified derivative payments that are not treated as a base erosion payment (Code Sec. 59A(c)(4), as added by the 2017 Tax Cuts Act).

Applicable taxpayer. The base erosion tax applies to applicable taxpayers. Applicable taxpayers include corporations, other than a regulated investment company (RIC), a real estate investment trust (REIT), or an S corporation, that have average annual gross receipts of at least $500 million over the past three tax years and a base erosion percentage of three percent or higher for the tax year (two percent for taxpayers that are members of an affiliated group that includes a bank or registered securities dealer) (Code Sec. 59A(e)(1), as added by the 2017 Tax Cuts Act).

In the case of a foreign person (that is, any person who is not a U.S. person) the gross receipts of which are taken into account for purposes of this provision, the gross receipts test described above generally only takes into account gross receipts that are taken into account in determining ECI. This rule does not apply to the gross receipts of any U.S. person that are aggregated with the gross receipts of a foreign person under the aggregation rules, discussed below. In determining gross receipts, rules similar to the rules of Code Sec. 448(c)(3)(B), (C), and (D) apply (Code Sec. 59A(e)(2), and (f), as added by the 2017 Tax Cuts Act).

Under the aggregation rules, persons treated as a single employer under Code Sec. 52(a) are treated as one person for purposes of determining the average annual gross receipts and the base erosion percentage, except that the exception for foreign corporations under Code Sec. 1563(b)(2)(C) is disregarded (Code Sec. 59A(e)(3), as added by the 2017 Tax Cuts Act).

NEW LAW EXPLAINED

> **Comment:** Accordingly, if a foreign person's gross receipts are aggregated with a U.S. person's gross receipts, the gross receipts of the U.S. person that are aggregated with the foreign person's gross receipts are not limited to the gross receipts taken into account in determining ECI.

Related party. For purposes of the base erosion tax rules, a related party is: (i) any 25-percent owner (of the vote or value) of the taxpayer, (ii) any person who is related to the taxpayer, or to any 25-percent owner (of the vote or value) of the taxpayer, within the meaning of Code Secs. 267(b) or 707(b)(1), and (iii) any other person related to the taxpayer within the meaning of Code Sec. 482 (Code Sec. 59A(g)(1), as added by the 2017 Tax Cuts Act).

A 25-percent owner with respect to any corporation is any person who owns at least 25 percent of: (i) the total voting power of all classes of stock of a corporation entitled to vote, or (ii) the total value of all classes of stock of the corporation (Code Sec. 59A(g)(2), as added by the 2017 Tax Cuts Act).

For purposes of determining a related party, the Code Sec. 318 constructive stock ownership rules apply to these related party rules except that "10-percent" is substituted for "50-percent" in Code Sec. 318(a)(2)(C), and Code Sec. 318(a)(3)(A), (B) and (C) do not apply to cause a U.S. person to own stock owned by a person who is not a U.S. person (Code Sec. 59A(g)(3), as added by the 2017 Tax Cuts Act).

Regulatory authority. The Secretary of the Treasury is authorized to prescribe such regulations or other guidance as may be necessary or appropriate to carry out this provision, including regulations providing for such adjustments to the application of this provision necessary to prevent avoidance of the provision, including through: (1) the use of unrelated persons, conduit transactions, or other intermediaries, or (2) transactions or arrangements designed in whole or in part: (a) to characterize payments otherwise subject to this provision as payments not subject to this provision, or (b) to substitute payments not subject to this provision for payments otherwise subject to this provision. The regulations or other guidance may also include regulations for the application of the related party rules, including rules to prevent the avoidance of the exceptions to the application of Code Sec. 318 (Code Sec. 59A(i), as added by the 2017 Tax Cuts Act).

Reporting requirements and penalties. The Secretary of the Treasury is authorized to prescribe additional reporting requirements under Code Sec. 6038A relating to: (i) the name, principal place of business, and country or countries in which organized or resident, of each person that is a related party to the reporting corporation, and that had any transaction with the reporting corporation during its tax year, (ii) the manner of relation between the reporting corporation and each person referred to in (i), and (iii) the transactions between the reporting corporation and each related foreign person (Code Sec. 6038A(b)(1), as amended by the 2017 Tax Cuts Act).

Additional information is required regarding base erosion payments. Specifically, for purposes of information reporting under Code Secs. 6038A and 6038C, if the reporting corporation or the foreign corporation to which Code Sec. 6038C applies is an applicable taxpayer, the information that is required includes: (i) information that the Secretary determines necessary to determine the base erosion minimum tax amount, base erosion payments, and base erosion tax benefits of the taxpayer for purposes of

NEW LAW EXPLAINED

Code Sec. 59A for the tax year, and (ii) such other information as the Secretary of the Treasury determines is necessary. For these purposes, any term used in this provision and Code Sec. 59A has the meaning as when used in Code Sec. 59A (Code Sec. 6038A(b)(2), as amended by the 2017 Tax Cuts Act).

The $10,000 penalties for failure to furnish information or maintain records provided in Code Sec. 6038A(d)(1) and (2) are both increased to $25,000 (Code Sec. 6038A(d)(1) and (2), as amended by the 2017 Tax Cuts Act).

Other changes. The base erosion and anti-abuse tax of Code Sec. 59A is excluded from regular tax liability for purposes of the limitation on nonrefundable personal credits (Code Sec. 26(b)(2)(B), as added by the 2017 Tax Cuts Act). The new law also clarifies that a foreign corporation engaged in a trade or business within the United States during the tax year is subject to tax under Code Secs. 11 and 59A on its taxable income that is effectively connected with the conduct of a U.S. trade or business (Code Sec. 882(a)(1), as amended by the 2017 Tax Cuts Act). In addition, for purposes of the rules allowing a corporation to apply for a quick refund of an overpayment of estimated tax and the rules for estimated tax payments by corporations, income tax liability also includes the Code Sec. 59A base erosion tax (Code Sec. 6425(c)(1)(A) and Code Sec. 6655(g)(1)(A), (e)(2)(A) and (e)(2)(B), as amended by the 2017 Tax Cuts Act).

Practical Analysis: Stewart R. Lipeles, Partner at Baker & McKenzie LLP in Palo Alto, California, and Ethan S. Kroll, Associate at Baker & McKenzie LLP in Palo Alto, California, comment that this provision is a draconian measure that appears designed to penalize taxpayers that locate high value activities, assets, and/or operations outside the United States by denying them some or all of the benefit of deductions for outbound payments. Specifically, Act Section 14401 introduces a "base erosion and anti-abuse tax" or "BEAT" into the Code. The BEAT functions as a manner of alternative minimum tax by requiring taxpayers to which it applies to pay the greater of their regular tax liability or 10 percent of their "modified taxable income." For tax years beginning in 2018, the 10 percent rate is reduced to 5 percent, but this rate climbs to 12.5 percent for tax years starting in 2026. To be subject to the BEAT, a taxpayer must be a corporation, with average annual gross receipts of $500,000,000 for the prior three years, and with deductions attributable to outbound payments exceeding a specified percentage of the taxpayer's overall deductions. Section 14401 applies to "base erosion payments" paid or accrued in tax years beginning after December 31, 2017.

For purposes of Act Section 14401, a U.S. corporation generally computes its "modified taxable income" by adding back to taxable income (i) any "base erosion tax benefit with respect to any base erosion payment"—generally speaking, any deduction for a payment to a foreign related person, including for an amount attributable to amortization / depreciation on property that the corporation acquired from a foreign related person, and (ii) a percentage of the corporation's Code Sec. 172 net operating loss carryforwards. For U.S. corporations that inverted after November 9, 2017, the add back includes payments for inventory, including the cost of goods sold.

NEW LAW EXPLAINED

Act Sec. 14401 exempts from the BEAT payments at cost for services that qualify for the services cost method under Reg. § 1.482-9, "without regard to the requirement that the services not contribute significantly to fundamental risks of business success or failure." Outbound payments at cost for services that constitute the core business of a corporation may therefore fall outside the scope of the BEAT. Act Sec. 14401 does not eliminate the requirement that the services constitute either "specified covered services" that fall on an IRS "white list" or services for which the median comparable markup on total services costs is less than or equal to seven percent. Accordingly, an outbound payment for a high value service with a median comparable mark up of eight percent ostensibly would be fully subject to the BEAT, whereas an outbound payment at cost for a similar service with a median comparable mark up of seven percent would not. The cost plus seven percent ceiling makes no sense in light of the clear congressional intent to exclude payments for high value services from the BEAT, if they are in fact charged out to the U.S. corporation at cost (despite being high value), and suggests an oversight on the part of the drafters. Put another way, the exception described above suggests that the drafters of the BEAT did not intend the BEAT to apply to payments for services at cost. Thus, a U.S. corporation that compensates a foreign affiliate at cost arguably should be entitled to the benefit of the exception described above regardless of the median comparable markup on the services.

Act Sec. 14401 raises serious concerns. First and foremost, nothing in Act Sec. 14401 excludes amounts that constitute subpart F income in the hands of a CFC, including under new Code Sec. 951A (Act Sec. 14201), from the scope of the BEAT. If these amounts are subject to U.S. tax by virtue of being added back to a United States shareholder's "modified taxable income," the same amount will effectively be taxed twice in the United States.

Second, Act Sec. 14401 discriminates against services businesses in favor of distributors and manufacturers, at least outside the inverted company context, because outbound payments for inventory are fully excluded from the BEAT, whereas outbound payments for services are within the scope of the BEAT unless they qualify for the exception described above. There is no policy basis for distinguishing between a U.S. corporation that relies on services that foreign affiliates provide as inputs for the services that the U.S. corporation sells to its customers and a U.S. corporation that relies on manufacturing that foreign affiliates perform, or engage others to perform, in respect of products that the U.S. corporation sells to its customers. To resolve this distinction, the BEAT should extend the exception for inventory property to services, as payments for services are the economic equivalent of payments for inventory for services businesses.

Third, the BEAT may have the unintended consequence of encouraging corporations to shift more activities away from the United States. By having customers and suppliers enter into contracts directly with foreign affiliates, and by converting the U.S. parent into a service provider receiving inbound payments, a group could largely eliminate outbound payments from the United States that are potentially subject to the BEAT. Such a restructuring could well involve the migration of high level functions outside the United States, as the group begins to operate the core business offshore.

¶750

NEW LAW EXPLAINED

▶ **Effective date.** The amendments made by this section apply to base erosion payments (as defined in Code Sec. 59A(d), as added by the Tax Cuts and Jobs Act of 2017 (P.L. 115-97)) paid or accrued in tax years beginning after December 31, 2017 (Act Sec. 14401(e) of the 2017 Tax Cuts Act).

Law source: Law at ¶5040, ¶5155, ¶5800, ¶6185, ¶6245, and ¶6280. Committee Report at ¶11,000, ¶11,010, ¶11,020, ¶11,030, and ¶11,210.

— Act Sec. 14401(a) of the Tax Cuts and Jobs Act (P.L. 115-97), adding new Code Sec. 59A;

— Act Sec. 14401(b), amending Code Sec. 6038A(b), (d)(1) and (d)(2);

— Act Sec. 14401(c), adding Code Sec. 26(b)(2)(B);

— Act Sec. 14401(d), amending Code Secs. 882(a)(1), 6425(c)(1)(A), 6655(g)(1)(A), and 6655(e)(2)(A) and (B);

— Act Sec. 14401(e), providing the effective date.

¶755 Limits on Income Shifting Through Intangible Property Transfers

SUMMARY OF NEW LAW

The Code Sec. 936(h)(3)(B) definition of intangible property is modified to include goodwill, going concern value, and workforce in place as well as any other item the value of which is not attributable to tangible property or services of any individual. The Secretary of the Treasury is authorized to require the use of certain valuation methods in determining the value of intangible property in the context of Code Sec. 367(d) transfers and Code Sec. 482 intercompany pricing allocations.

BACKGROUND

Under the definition of intangible property in Code Sec. 936(h)(3)(B), intangible property includes the following:

(1) patent, invention, formula, process, design, pattern, or know-how;

(2) copyright or literary, musical, or artistic composition;

(3) trademark, trade name, or brand name;

(4) franchise, license, or contract;

(5) method, program, system, procedure, campaign, survey, study, forecast, estimate, customer list, or technical data; and

(6) any similar item.

Each of the above items must have substantial value independent of the services of any individual (Code Sec. 936(h)(3)(B)).

BACKGROUND

The above statutory definition of intangible property is used for purposes of the Code Sec. 367(d) rules for transfers of intangibles and the transfer pricing rules under Code Sec. 482. Generally, Code Sec. 367(d) requires income recognition by U.S. transferors on outbound transfers of intangibles described in Code Sec. 936(h)(3)(B), if the transfer occurs in a Code Sec. 351 or 361 exchange. For such transfers, the U.S. transferor is generally treated as having sold the intangible property in exchange for annual payments that are contingent upon the productivity or use of the property. The U.S. transferor must annually include in gross income, over the useful life of the property, an amount that is commensurate with the income attributable to the intangible and that represents an appropriate arms-length charge for the use of the property. The appropriate charge is determined under the transfer pricing rules of Code Sec. 482.

Code Sec. 482 authorizes the IRS to allocate income, deductions, and other tax items among related taxpayers in order to prevent the evasion of tax or to more clearly reflect income. Code Sec. 482 permits reallocation in any common control situation, including between two U.S. entities. However, Code Sec. 482 is largely employed in the international tax area where there is incentive for multinational operations to use transfer pricing to take advantage of different tax systems and effective tax rates. Generally, the transfer pricing price is subject to reallocation by the IRS if an arm's-length pricing standard is not maintained (Code Sec. 482).

> **Comment:** The statutory definition of intangible property has proved problematic especially in the transfer pricing context. Intangible assets and the income attributable to them are considered highly mobile. Countries are becoming increasingly aware of the need to improve their regulation as one means of retaining the tax base, preventing base erosion shifting of income across national borders and deterring tax evasion.

Even though both Code Sec. 367(d) and Code Sec. 482 rely on the statutory definition of intangible property in Code Sec. 936(h)(3)(B), this definition is regarded as unclear. Recurring definitional and methodological issues with respect to transfers of intangibles under these provisions have arisen in recent Tax Court cases (*Veritas Software Corp. v. Commissioner*, Dec. 58,016, 133 T.C. 297, (nonacq., Action on Decision Memorandum, AOD-2010-5; *Amazon v. Commissioner*, Dec. 60,857, 148 T.C. No. 8 (2017)).

Further, conventional valuation methodologies, which have been highly effective in reflecting an arm's-length price with respect to transfers of certain assets, have been less so with respect to the transfer of intangibles. This is particularly the case with Code Sec. 367(d) transfers of multiple intangible properties in one or more related transactions in the context of outbound restructurings of U.S. operations and of intercompany pricing allocations.

NEW LAW EXPLAINED

Intangible property definition modified and allowable valuation methods clarified.—The scope of the statutory definition of intangible property is revised to include goodwill, going concern value, and workforce in place as well as a residual category that

¶755

NEW LAW EXPLAINED

includes any other item the value or potential value of which is not attributable to tangible property or services of any individual. In addition, the requirement that each specific type of intangible property have substantial value independent of the services of any individual is removed so that the source or amount of value is no longer relevant in determining whether that property is within the scope of the definition (Code Sec. 936(h)(3)(B), as amended by the Tax Cuts and Jobs Act (P.L. 115-97)).

In addition, the new law clarifies the authority of the Secretary of the Treasury to specify the method to be used to determine the value of intangible property in the context of both Code Sec. 367(d) transfers as part of outbound restructurings of U.S. operations and Code Sec. 482 intercompany pricing allocations. Specifically, the Secretary will require: (i) the valuation of transfers of intangible property, including intangible property transferred with other property or services, on an aggregate basis, or (ii) the valuation of such a transfer on the basis of the realistic alternatives to such a transfer, if the Secretary determines that such basis is the most reliable means of valuation of such transfers (Code Sec. 367(d)(2)(D), as added by the 2017 Tax Cuts Act; Code Sec. 482, as amended by the 2017 Tax Cuts Act). In the Code Sec. 367(d)(2) context, the use of these valuation methods is required for purposes of determining if the annual amounts taken into account are commensurate with the income attributable to the intangible.

> **Comment:** Accordingly, the use of the aggregate basis valuation method is required in the case of transfers of multiple intangible properties in one or more related transactions if the Secretary determines that an aggregate basis achieves a more reliable result than an asset-by-asset approach. This is consistent with the position that the additional value resulting from the interrelation of intangible assets can be properly attributed to the underlying intangible assets in the aggregate, if doing so produces a more reliable result. This approach is also consistent with the cost-sharing regulations in Reg. § 1.482-7(g)(2)(iv).

> **Comment:** The provision codifies the realistic alternative principle, which is based on the concept that a taxpayer would only enter into a transaction if none of its realistic alternatives were economically preferable to the transaction undertaken.

▶ **Effective date.** The amendments made by this section apply to transfers in tax years beginning after December 31, 2017. Nothing in the amendment to the Code Sec. 936(h)(3)(B) definition of intangible property will be construed to create any inference with respect to the application of Code Sec. 936(h)(3) or the authority of the Secretary of the Treasury to provide regulations for such application, with respect to tax years beginning before January 1, 2018 (Act Sec. 14221(c) of the Tax Cuts and Jobs Act (P.L. 115-97)).

Law source: Law at ¶5450, ¶5560, and ¶5855. Committee Report at ¶11,000, ¶11,010, ¶11,020, ¶11,030, and ¶11,140.

— Act Sec.14221(a) of the Tax Cuts and Jobs Act (P.L. 115-97), amending Code Sec. 936(h)(3)(B);

— Act Sec. 14221(b), adding Code Sec. 367(d)(2)(D) and amending Code Sec. 482;

— Act Sec. 14221(c), providing the effective date.

¶760 Related Party Payments Involving Hybrid Entities or Hybrid Transactions

SUMMARY OF NEW LAW

A deduction is not allowed for any disqualified related party amount paid or accrued in a hybrid transaction or by, or to, a hybrid entity.

BACKGROUND

The choice of entity type has a significant impact on the legal and tax treatment of a business. In general, a business may elect to be taxed as a partnership, corporation, or disregarded entity (Reg. § 301.7701-3(a)). Of these three types of entities, the corporation pays tax on taxable income at the entity level, whereas liability for income tax is the responsibility of the owner(s) of a disregarded entity and partnership. Because the tax attributes of these entities flow through to the owners, the entities are known as pass-through entities or fiscally transparent entities. When an entity has not made a tax election (i.e., "check-the-box" election), a default tax classification is provided (Reg. § 301.7701-3(b)). Typically corporations are not fiscally transparent entities. Limited liability companies and miscellaneous foreign entities may or may not be fiscally transparent, and should be reviewed on a entity by entity case.

Under Reg. § 1.894-1(d)(3)(ii) and (iii), an entity that is "fiscally transparent" for U.S. tax purposes, but not fiscally transparent for foreign tax purposes is considered to be a hybrid entity. Generally, to be fiscally transparent, an entity's current year profits must be currently taxable to the entity owners. An entity is treated as a reverse hybrid entity when it is fiscally transparent for foreign tax purposes, but not fiscally transparent for U.S. tax purposes. Where entities are treated the same for both foreign and U.S. tax purposes they are not considered to be hybrids.

> **Example:** Company A is taxed as a partnership in the United States, but is taxed as a corporation in Foreign Country. For U.S. tax purposes, Company A is a hybrid entity that pays its own tax in Foreign Country, whereas income and deductions pass through to the owners in the United States.

The use of hybrid transactions and entities can create potential tax mismatches and exploit gaps in the domestic tax laws of multiple jurisdictions. These gaps and mismatches may result in a variety of tax advantages for cross-border arrangements and activity, such as:

- double nontaxation of income;
- multiple deductions for a single expense;
- deductions in one jurisdiction without corresponding taxable income in another jurisdiction;
- long-term deferral of income; and

¶760

BACKGROUND

- imported mismatches allowing for offset of includible income in the payee's jurisdiction.

As part of its Base Erosion and Profit Shifting (BEPS) framework, the multinational intergovernmental Organisation for Economic Cooperation and Development (OECD), has focused on combatting hybrid mismatch arrangements. Specifically, Action: 2 - Neutralising the Effects of Hybrid Mismatch Arrangements, issued by the OECD provides a set of recommendations designed to eliminate advantageous hybrid tax planning opportunities and deter companies from their use (OECD Publishing, OECD/G20 Base Erosion and Profit Shifting Project — Neutralising the Effects of Hybrid Mismatch Arrangements (Action 2), September 16, 2014).

NEW LAW EXPLAINED

Deduction for disqualified related party payments involving hybrid transactions or hybrid entities denied.—A deduction is disallowed for a disqualified related party amount paid or accrued pursuant to a hybrid transaction. A deduction is also disallowed for a disqualified related party amount paid or accrued by, or to, a hybrid entity (Code Sec. 267A(a), as added by the Tax Cuts and Jobs Act (P.L. 115-97)).

Any interest or royalty paid or accrued to a related party is a "disqualified related party amount" to the extent that under the tax law of the country where the related party is a resident for tax purposes or is subject to tax:

- the amount is not included in the income of the related party, or
- the related party is allowed a deduction for the amount (Code Sec. 267A(b)(1), as added the 2017 Tax Cuts Act).

A disqualified related party amount does not include any payment that is included in the gross income of a U.S. shareholder under subpart F and Code Sec. 951(a).

A "related party" means a related person as defined under Code Sec. 954(d)(3), except that the person is related to the payor rather than a controlled foreign corporation (CFC) (Code Sec. 267A(b)(2), as added by the 2017 Tax Cuts Act). Thus, a related person includes any individual, corporation, partnership, trust, or estate, that directly or indirectly, controls or is controlled by the payor (or is controlled by the same person that controls the payor). Control is ownership of more than 50 percent (by vote or value) of the corporation's stock or more than a 50 percent (by value) of the beneficial interests in a partnership, trust or estate.

> **Example:** Foreign Corporation owns two U.S. subsidiaries, a C corporation and an LLC. The LLC is treated as a partnership for U.S. tax purposes and a corporation for foreign tax purposes. Interest is paid by the C corporation to the LLC. The interest payment flows through LLC to the Foreign Corporation as a dividend and is excluded from tax under foreign country tax. The payment of the interest may not be deducted by the C corporation because the payment is a

NEW LAW EXPLAINED

> disqualified related party amount. Interest is paid to the Foreign Corporation, which controls the payor C corporation and so is a related party. The amount is not included in the income of the Foreign Corporation under the tax laws of the Foreign Corporation.

Hybrid transaction. A hybrid transaction means any transaction, series of transactions, agreement, or instrument, if one or more payments are treated as interest or royalties for federal income tax purposes, but are not treated as such for purposes of the tax law of the foreign country where the recipient of the payment is resident for tax purposes or is subject to tax (Code Sec. 267A(c), as added by the 2017 Tax Cuts Act).

Hybrid entity. A hybrid entity means any entity that is either:

(1) treated as fiscally transparent for federal income tax purposes, but not under the tax law of the foreign country where the entity is resident for tax purposes or is subject to tax, or

(2) treated as fiscally transparent under the tax law of the foreign country where the entity is resident for tax purposes or is subject to tax, but not for federal income tax purposes (Code Sec. 267A(d), as added by the 2017 Tax Cuts Act).

Regulations. The Secretary is authorized under Code Sec. 267A to issue regulations or other guidance as necessary and appropriate to carry out this provision, including regulations or other guidance providing rules for:

(1) denying deductions for conduit arrangements involving a hybrid transaction or hybrid entity;

(2) the application of this provision to foreign branches or domestic entities;

(3) applying this provision to certain structured transactions;

(4) denying all or a portion of a deduction claimed for an interest or a royalty payment that, as a result of the hybrid transaction or entity, is included in the recipient's income under a preferential tax regime of the country of residence of the recipient and has the effect of reducing the country's generally applicable statutory tax rate by at least 25 percent;

(5) denying all of a deduction claimed for an interest or a royalty payment if the amount is subject to a participation exemption system or other system providing for the exclusion or deduction of a substantial portion of the amount;

(6) rules for determining the tax residence of a foreign entity if the foreign entity is otherwise considered a resident of more than one country or of no country;

(7) exceptions to the general rule set forth in the provision; and

(8) requirements for record keeping and information in addition to any requirements imposed by Code Sec. 6038A (Code Sec. 276A(e), as added by the 2017 Tax Cuts Act).

▶ **Effective date.** The amendment made by this section applies to tax years beginning after December 31, 2017 (Act Sec. 14222(c) of the Tax Cuts and Jobs Act (P.L. 115-97)).

¶760

NEW LAW EXPLAINED

Law source: Law at ¶5430. Committee Report at ¶11,000, ¶11,010, ¶11,020, ¶11,030, and ¶11,150.

— Act Sec. 14222(a) of the Tax Cuts and Jobs Act (P.L. 115-97), adding new Code Sec. 267A;

— Act Sec. 14222(b);

— Act Sec. 14222(c), providing the effective date.

¶765 Surrogate Foreign Corporation Dividends

SUMMARY OF NEW LAW

Dividends received from surrogate foreign corporations are not eligible for lower tax rate treatment as qualified dividend income.

BACKGROUND

Reduced tax rates on dividends are intended to encourage certain types of equity investments. Accordingly, dividends paid by certain qualified foreign corporations to an individual shareholder are treated as qualified dividend income and are taxed at long-term capital gains rates (Code Sec. 1(h)(11)(C)).

> **Comment:** The tax rate for long-term capital gains is: 0 percent for taxpayers in the 10 or 15 percent brackets; 15 percent for taxpayers in the 25, 28, 33 or 35 percent brackets; and 20 percent for taxpayers in the 39.6 percent bracket (Code Sec. 1(h)).

A qualified foreign corporation is a corporation that is incorporated in a possession of the United States or a corporation that is eligible for benefits of a comprehensive income tax treaty with the United States that includes an exchange of information program (Code Sec. 1(h)(11)(C)(i)). Foreign corporations may also be treated as qualified foreign corporations if they pay dividends on stock that is readily tradable in an established U.S. securities market (Code Sec. 1(h)(11)(C)(ii)). If a foreign corporation is a passive foreign investment company (PFIC), as defined in Code Sec. 1297, during the year the dividend was paid or during the preceding tax year, then the corporation is not considered to be a qualified foreign corporation (Code Sec. 1(h)(11)C)(iii)).

NEW LAW EXPLAINED

Dividends from surrogate foreign corporations excluded from reduced rate.— Surrogate foreign corporations that are not treated as domestic corporations under Code Sec. 7874(b) are excluded from the meaning of qualified foreign corporation (Code Sec. 1(h)(11)(C)(iii), as amended by the Tax Cuts and Jobs Act (P.L. 115-97)). Generally, a surrogate foreign corporation is a foreign corporation that: (1) acquires

NEW LAW EXPLAINED

(after March 4, 2003) substantially all of the properties held by a U.S. corporation, (2) after the acquisition, the U.S. corporation's former shareholders own at least 60 percent of the stock (by vote or value) of the foreign acquiring corporation, and (3) the expanded affiliated group does not have substantial business activities in the country where the entity is organized or created compared to the total business activities of the expanded affiliated group (Code Sec. 7874(a)(2)(B)). Therefore, dividends paid after December 22, 2017, by surrogate foreign corporations that are not treated as domestic corporations under Code Sec. 7874(b), do not qualify as qualified dividend income under Code Sec. 1(h)(11)(B)(i) (Code Sec. 1(h)(11)(C)(iii), as amended by the 2017 Tax Cuts Act). As such, dividends paid to shareholders after December 22, 2017, by surrogate foreign corporations that are not treated as domestic corporations under Code Sec. 7874(b) are ineligible for the reduced tax rate applicable to qualified dividends.

> **Comment:** The Senate Budget Committee's explanation of the tax reform bill states that while reduced tax rates on dividends are meant to encourage equity investments, the Committee does not believe that investments in surrogate foreign corporations fits within this parameter (JCX-56R-17)

▶ **Effective date.** The amendments made by this section apply to dividends paid after December 22, 2017, the date of enactment (Act Sec. 14223(b) of the Tax Cuts and Jobs Act of 2017 (P.L. 115-97)).

Law source: Law at ¶5005. Committee Report at ¶11,000, ¶11,010, ¶11,020, ¶11,030, and ¶11,160.

— Act Sec. 14223(a) of the Tax Cuts and Jobs Act (P.L. 115-97)), amending Code Sec. 1(h)(11)(C)(iii) and adding (h)(11)(C)(iii)(II);

— Act Sec. 14223(b), providing the effective date.

¶770 Stock Compensation Excise Tax on Insiders in Expatriated Corporations

SUMMARY OF NEW LAW

The excise tax rate on stock compensation received by insiders in an expatriated corporation increases from 15 percent to 20 percent.

BACKGROUND

An excise tax is imposed on and payable by an individual who is a disqualified individual with respect to any expatriated corporation (Code Sec. 4985). The excise tax applies only if any of the expatriated corporation's shareholders recognize gains on any stock in the corporation by reason of the corporate inversion transaction that caused the expatriation.

BACKGROUND

Disqualified individuals generally include individuals who are officers, directors, and 10-percent-or-greater owners (including both private and publicly held corporations) with respect to the corporation during the 12-month period beginning on the date that precedes the expatriation by six months.

An inversion is a transaction in which, pursuant to a plan or a series of related transactions:

— a U.S. corporation or partnership becomes a subsidiary of a foreign-incorporated entity or otherwise transfers substantially all of its properties to such an entity after March 4, 2003;

— the former shareholders of the U.S. corporation hold (by reason of holding stock in the U.S. corporation) 60 percent or more (by vote or value) of the stock of the foreign incorporated entity after the transaction; and

— the foreign incorporated entity, considered together with all companies connected to it by a chain of greater than 50-percent ownership (i.e., the "expanded affiliated group") does not conduct substantial business activities in the entity's country of incorporation compared to the total worldwide business activities of the expanded affiliated group (Code Sec. 7874(a)(2)(B)).

NEW LAW EXPLAINED

The excise tax does not apply to a stock option which is exercised on the expatriation date or during the six-month period before that date and to the stock acquired in such exercise, if income is recognized under the usual restricted property transfer compensation rules of Code Sec. 83 on or before the expatriation date (Code Sec. 4985(d)(1)). Also, the excise tax does not apply to any other specified stock compensation which is exercised, sold, exchanged, distributed, cashed-out, or otherwise paid during such period in a transaction in which income, gain, or loss is recognized in full (Code Sec. 4985(d)(2)).

Excise tax on stock compensation of insiders in expatriated corporations increased.—The excise tax rate on stock compensation received by insiders in an expatriated corporation is increased from 15 percent to 20 percent, effective on the date of enactment for corporations that first become expatriated after that date. (Code Sec. 4985(a)(1), as amended by the Tax Cuts and Jobs Act (P.L. 115-97); Code Sec. 1(h)(1)(D)).

> **Practical Analysis:** Brigen Winters, Principal at Groom Law Group, Chartered in Washington, D.C., observes that the increased 20-percent excise tax would apply to stock options and other stock-based compensation held directly or indirectly (e.g., through a partnership or trust) by certain officers, directors and 10-percent owners upon certain transactions that result in an expatriated corporation. Additionally, the imposition of the excise tax would have no impact on the subsequent tax treatment of the stock compensation (e.g., the individual would not have basis in the stock

NEW LAW EXPLAINED

compensation upon the exercise of the option or receipt of other stock compensation).

▶   **Effective date.** The amendment made by this section applies to corporations first becoming expatriated corporations after December 22, 2017, the date of enactment of this Act (Act Sec. 13604(b) of the Tax Cuts and Jobs Act (P.L. 115-97)).

Law source: Law at ¶6130. Committee Report at ¶10,820.

— Act Sec. 13604(a) of the Tax Cuts and Jobs Act (P.L. 115-97), amending Code Sec. 4985(a)(1);

— Act Sec. 13604(b), providing the effective date.

OTHER INTERNATIONAL REFORMS

¶775 Insurance Business Exception to the Passive Foreign Investment Company Rules

SUMMARY OF NEW LAW

The rule for determining what is not considered passive income for a passive foreign investment company (PFIC) has been modified. The test for nonpassive income that is based on whether a corporation is predominantly engaged in an insurance business has been replaced with a test based on the amount of the corporation's insurance liabilities.

BACKGROUND

The passive foreign investment company (PFIC) rules apply to U.S. shareholders of foreign corporations that derive a significant amount of their income from investments in passive assets (Code Secs. 1291 and 1297). The PFIC rules attempt to eliminate the tax deferral that PFIC shareholders could otherwise receive because a foreign corporation is generally exempt from U.S. tax on foreign source income and its U.S. shareholders are generally not taxed until they dispose of their stock or receive a distribution (Senate Finance Committee Report and Conference Committee Report, Tax Reform Act of 1986 (P.L. 99-514)). The benefit of the tax deferral is eliminated by requiring a U.S. shareholder of a PFIC to pay a special tax plus an interest charge on gain recognized from the disposition or pledge of stock in the PFIC or upon the receipt of an excess distribution from the PFIC (Code Sec. 1291(a)).

When determining whether a foreign corporation is a PFIC under the income and asset tests (Code Sec. 1291(a)), passive income is income that would be considered foreign personal holding company income as defined in Code Sec. 954(c). However, passive income does not include any income that is: (1) derived in the active conduct

BACKGROUND

of a banking business by certain foreign corporations; (2) derived in the active conduct of an insurance business by a corporation that is predominantly engaged in an insurance business that would be subject to tax under subchapter L (Insurance Companies) if it were a domestic corporation; (3) interest, a dividend, rent, or a royalty that is received or accrued from a related person to the extent such amount is allocable to income of such related person that is not passive income; or (4) export trade income of an export trade corporation (ETC) under Code Sec. 971 (Code Sec. 1297(b)(2)).

NEW LAW EXPLAINED

Insurance business exception to PFIC rules modified.—The insurance business exception to the definition of passive income for the passive foreign investment company (PFIC) rules is modified for tax years beginning after December 31, 2017 (Code Sec. 1297(b)(2)(B), as amended by the Tax Cuts and Jobs Act (P.L. 115-97)). The test based on whether a corporation is predominantly engaged in an insurance business is replaced with a test based on the amount of the corporation's insurance liabilities (Code Sec. 1297(f)(1), as added by the 2017 Tax Cuts Act; Conference Report on H.R. 1, Tax Cuts and Jobs Act (H. Rept. 115-466)).

Except as provided in regulations, the term "passive income" does not include any income derived in the active conduct of an insurance business by a qualifying insurance corporation (Code Sec. 1297(b)(2)(B), as amended by the 2017 Tax Cuts Act). With respect to any tax year, a "qualifying insurance corporation" is a foreign corporation that:

(1) would be subject to tax under subchapter L of the Internal Revenue Code if the corporation were a domestic corporation; and

(2) has applicable insurance liabilities that are more than 25 percent of its total assets, determined on the basis of the insurance liabilities and total assets reported on the corporation's applicable financial statement for the last year ending with or within the tax year (Code Sec. 1297(f)(1), as added by the 2017 Tax Cuts Act).

A foreign corporation that fails to qualify as an insurance corporation because it does not have applicable insurance liabilities that are more than 25 percent of its total assets can apply an alternative facts and circumstances test (see "Alternative facts and circumstances test", below).

Insurance liabilities, financial statement, insurance regulatory body defined. For purposes of the insurance business test, the "applicable insurance liabilities" of any life insurance or property and casualty insurance business are its:

(1) loss and loss adjustment expenses; and

(2) reserves, other than deficiency, contingency, or unearned premium reserves, for both life and health insurance risks and life and health insurance claims with respect to contracts providing coverage for mortality or morbidity risks (Code Sec. 1297(f)(3), as added by the 2017 Tax Cuts Act).

NEW LAW EXPLAINED

The amount of any applicable insurance liability cannot exceed the lesser of such amount: (1) as reported to the applicable insurance regulatory body in the applicable financial statement (or, if less, the amount required by applicable law or regulation), or (2) as determined under regulations (Code Sec. 1297(f)(3)(B), as added by the 2017 Tax Cuts Act).

> **Comment:** In determining an insurance company's applicable insurance liabilities, its reserves include loss reserves for property and casualty, life, and health insurance contracts and annuity contracts. However, unearned premium reserves with respect to any type of risk are not treated as applicable insurance liabilities (Conference Report on H.R. 1, Tax Cuts and Jobs Act (H. Rept. 115-466)).

A corporation's "applicable financial statement" is a statement for financial reporting purposes that:

- is made on the basis of generally accepted accounting principles;
- is made on the basis of international financial reporting standards, if there is no statement that is made on the basis of generally accepted accounting principles; or
- unless otherwise provided in regulations, is the annual statement that must be filed with the applicable insurance regulatory body, if there is no statement that is made on the basis of generally accepted accounting principles or international financial reporting standards (Code Sec. 1297(f)(4)(A), as added by the 2017 Tax Cuts Act).

An "applicable insurance regulatory body" is the entity established by law to license, authorize or regulate an insurance business and to which the business files its applicable financial statement (Code Sec. 1297(f)(4)(B), as added by the 2017 Tax Cuts Act).

Alternative facts and circumstances test. If a corporation fails to qualify as a qualified insurance corporation solely because the percentage of its applicable insurance liabilities is 25 percent or less of its total assets, a U.S. person that owns stock in the corporation can elect to apply an alternative facts and circumstances test. Under the alternative facts and circumstances test, the U.S. person can elect to treat the stock as stock of a qualifying insurance corporation if:

(1) the percentage of the corporation's applicable insurance liabilities is at least 10 percent of its total assets; and

(2) based on the applicable facts and circumstances, the corporation is predominantly engaged in an insurance business and its failure to meet the more-than-25-percent threshold is due solely to run-off related or rating-related circumstances involving such insurance business (Code Sec. 1297(f)(2), as added by the 2017 Tax Cuts Act).

The applicable facts and circumstances for (2), above, would be determined under regulations to be provided by the IRS. Some of the facts and circumstances that tend to show that a corporation may not be predominantly engaged in an insurance business include a small number of insured risks with low likelihood but large potential costs; workers focused to a greater degree on investment activities than

NEW LAW EXPLAINED

underwriting activities; and low loss exposure (Conference Report on H.R. 1, Tax Cuts and Jobs Act (H. Rept. 115-466)).

A company is in "runoff" if it is not taking on new insurance business (and consequently has little or no premium income), and is using its remaining assets to pay off claims with respect to pre-existing insurance risks on its books (Conference Report on H.R. 1, Tax Cuts and Jobs Act (H. Rept. 115-466)).

▶ **Effective date.** The amendments made by this section apply to tax years beginning after December 31, 2017 (Act Sec. 14501(c) of the Tax Cuts and Jobs Act (P.L. 115-97)).

Law source: Law at ¶6005. Committee Report at ¶11,000, ¶11,010, ¶11,020, ¶11,030, and ¶11,220.

— Act Sec. 14501(a) of the Tax Cuts and Jobs Act (P.L. 115-97), amending Code Sec. 1297(b)(2)(B);

— Act Sec. 14501(b), adding new Code Sec. 1297(f);

— Act Sec. 14501(c), providing the effective date.

¶780 Interest Expense Allocation and Apportionment

SUMMARY OF NEW LAW

The fair market value method for allocating and apportioning interest expense may no longer be used.

BACKGROUND

U.S. taxpayers are taxed on their worldwide income, but are allowed a foreign tax credit for foreign income taxes paid or accrued, in order to prevent the double taxation of foreign source income (Code Sec. 901). The foreign tax credit limitation provides that when foreign income tax is higher than U.S. income tax, the foreign tax credit is limited to the U.S. tax that would be due on the foreign income (Code Sec. 904). The purpose of the limitation is to protect the U.S. tax base and to prevent the reduction of U.S. tax on U.S. source income. The limitation is determined by multiplying a taxpayer's total U.S. tax liability (before the foreign tax credit) for the tax year by the ratio of the taxpayer's foreign source taxable income to worldwide taxable income (Code Sec. 904(a)).

The foreign tax credit limitation requires that the foreign tax credit limitation be calculated separately for certain categories of income or "baskets". There are generally two foreign separate limitation categories or baskets—a "passive category income" basket and a "general category income" basket (Reg. §1.904-4). Foreign source taxable income for each category is gross income for the category, less expenses, losses and other deductions. The allocation and apportionment of deductions for purposes of determining the foreign tax credit limitation generally requires that the expense is first allocated to a specific class of income, and then apportioned between

BACKGROUND

the statutory groupings (i.e., foreign source general and passive limitation income) and the residual grouping (i.e., U.S. source income) (Reg. § 1.861-8). The foreign tax credit limitation can be increased by maximizing the portion of worldwide taxable income that is foreign source taxable income. Minimizing the amount of interest expense that is allocated and apportioned to foreign source income is one way to increase foreign source taxable income. The term interest expense refers to amounts deductible under Code Sec. 163.

The method for allocating and apportioning interest expense to U.S. or foreign source income recognizes that money is a fungible asset and, accordingly, interest expense is attributable to all activities and property without regard to the specific reason for incurring debt. Deductions for interest expense are considered related to all income-producing activities and assets of the taxpayer and are allocated to all gross income that the assets of the taxpayer generate (Code Sec. 864(e)(2); Temp. Reg. § 1.861-9T(a)).

Allocation and apportionment of interest expense must be made on the basis of the assets and not gross income. Under the asset method, taxpayers apportion interest expense to the various statutory groupings based on the average total value of the assets within the grouping for the tax year, according to the asset valuation rules and asset characterization rules of Temp. Reg. §§ 1.861-9T(g) and 1.861-12T. Taxpayers may choose to value their assets on the basis of either the tax book value (TBV) (i.e., adjusted basis), the alternative tax book value method or the fair market value method (Temp. Reg. § 1.861-9T(g)(1)(ii) and (h); Reg. § 1.861-9(i)).

NEW LAW EXPLAINED

Fair market value method of interest expense allocation and apportionment eliminated.—Taxpayers may no longer use the fair market value method to allocate and apportion interest expense. All allocations and apportionments of interest expense must be determined using the adjusted basis of the assets. The use of gross income to allocate and apportion interest expense continues to be disallowed (Code Sec. 864(e)(2), as amended by the Tax Cuts and Jobs Act (P.L. 115-97)).

> **Comment:** Use of the fair market value method required that certain documentation and information requirements be met (Rev. Proc. 2003-37). Use of this method was also more likely to result in disputes with the IRS. Electing the fair market value method, however, could result in an increase in foreign source taxable income, and therefore, foreign tax credit limitation, particularly if U.S. based assets have higher appreciated values than foreign assets. Use of the adjusted tax basis method, requires that assets located outside of the United States be depreciated using the alternative depreciation system (ADS) under Code Sec. 168(g). This method results in slower depreciation than that allowed under the Modified Accelerated Recovery System (MACRS), the method used for assets located in the United States. As a result, more interest expense is allocated to foreign source income, which can reduce foreign source taxable income and the taxpayer's foreign tax credit limitation. An election to use the alternative tax book value method under Reg. § 1.861-9(i) allows a taxpayer to

NEW LAW EXPLAINED

use the straight-line method, conventions and recovery periods for tangible property.

▶ **Effective date.** The amendment made by this section applies to tax years beginning after December 31, 2017 (Act Sec. 14502(b) of the Tax Cuts and Jobs Act (P.L. 115-97)).

Law source: Law at ¶5785. Committee Report at ¶11,000, ¶11,010, ¶11,020, ¶11,030, and ¶11,230.

— Act Sec. 14502(a) of the Tax Cuts and Jobs Act (P.L. 115-97), amending Code Sec. 864(e)(2);

— Act Sec. 14502(b), providing the effective date.

¶780

Exempt Organizations, Excise Taxes, Bonds, and Other Provisions

8

TAX-EXEMPT ORGANIZATIONS

¶805   Unrelated Business Taxable Income Separately Computed for Each Trade or Business Activity

SUMMARY OF NEW LAW

Exempt organizations with more than one unrelated business will be required to calculate unrelated business taxable income separately for each unrelated trade or business.

BACKGROUND

The income of an exempt organization is subject to the tax on unrelated business income imposed by Code Sec. 511 only if the income is from a trade or business that is regularly carried on by the organization and the trade or business is not substantially related—aside from the need of the organization for funds or the use it makes of the profits—to the organization's exercise or performance of the purposes or functions on which its exemption is based.

The unrelated business taxable income of an organization regularly carrying on two or more unrelated businesses is the aggregate of its gross income from all unrelated businesses, less the aggregate of the deductions allowed with respect to all such unrelated businesses (Reg. § 1.512(a)-1). As a result, an organization may use a deduction from one unrelated trade or business to offset income from another, thereby reducing total unrelated business taxable income.

The net operating loss deduction is allowed in determining unrelated business taxable income, but must reflect only taxable "business" income (Code Sec. 512(b)(6)). A net operating loss is allowable in a year where unrelated business income occurs. Losses can be carried back two years and forward 20 years (Code Sec. 172(b)(1)(A)). Years during which there is no unrelated business income do not count toward expiration of the carryforward period (Reg. § 1.512(b)-1(e)).

NEW LAW EXPLAINED

Unrelated business taxable income must be separately calculated for each unrelated business.—A special rule has been added for exempt organizations that have unrelated business taxable income from operating more than one unrelated business. For all purposes, including the calculating of any net operating loss deduction, the unrelated business taxable income of each trade or business will be determined separately and without regard to Code Sec. 512(b)(12), which generally permits a specific deduction of $1,000 (Code Sec. 512(a)(6)(A), as added by the Tax Cuts and Jobs Act (P.L. 115-97)).

The unrelated business taxable income of the exempt organization having more than one unrelated trade or business will be the sum of the unrelated business taxable

NEW LAW EXPLAINED

income of those unrelated businesses, less the specific deduction permitted by Code Sec. 512(b)(12) (Code Sec. 512(a)(6)(B), as added by the 2017 Tax Cuts Act). However, the unrelated business taxable income of any particular trade or business cannot be less than zero (Code Sec. 512(a)(6)(C), as added by the 2017 Tax Cuts Act).

The effects of the new rule are to prevent a deduction from one unrelated trade or business from offsetting income from another unrelated business in the same tax year, and to prevent the specific $1,000 deduction from being claimed more than once in a tax year regardless of how many unrelated businesses an exempt organization may have (Conference Report on H.R. 1, Tax Cuts and Jobs Act (H. Rept. 115-466). It does not, however, prevent the carryover of unused deductions to subsequent tax years if they were previously permitted and so long as they are utilized by the same unrelated business that generated such deduction.

A transition rule provides that net operating losses arising in tax years beginning before January 1, 2018, that are carried over to tax years beginning on or after January 1, 2018, are not subject to the rule requiring unrelated business taxable income to be computed separately for each trade or business for purposes of determining the amount of the NOL. The NOL will reduce unrelated business taxable income of the organization computed as the sum of the unrelated business taxable income from each of its trades or businesses, less the specific deduction of $1,000 (Act Sec. 13702(b)(2) of the 2017 Tax Cuts Act).

Practical Analysis: Brian T. Whitlock, Adjunct Professor in the Gies College of Business at the University of Illinois at Urbana-Champaign observes that Act Section 13702 will require exempt organizations to compute Unrelated Trade or Business Income (UBTI) for each trade or business activity separately. In addition, the Act Section will prohibit tax exempt organizations from offsetting the Net Operating Losses (NOL) of one trade or business activity against the UBTI generated in a second separate trade or business activity. Although the rule is effective for tax years beginning after December 31, 2017, NOLs may be carried for and need not be segregated and applied against income from the same activity.

Furthermore, Act Section 13703 will require exempt organizations to increase UBTI by amounts expended by the organization for expenses disallowed under Code Sec. 274 for any qualified transportation fringe benefits, qualified parking, or on-premises athletic facilities provided to employees. This Act Section was intended to mirror Sections 11047, 11048, and 13304 of the Act related to the disallowance of similar expenses for taxable business; however, none of these Act Sections related to taxable businesses affected the exclusion under Code Sec. 132(j)(4)(B) related to on-premises athletic facilities. This may need to be addressed in a technical correction.

▶ **Effective date.** The amendment made by this section generally applies to tax years beginning after December 31, 2017 (Act Sec. 13702(b)(1) of the Tax Cuts and Jobs Act (P.L. 115-97)). However, if any net operating loss (NOL) arising in a tax year beginning before January 1, 2018, is carried over to any succeeding tax year, then Code Sec.

¶805

NEW LAW EXPLAINED

512(a)(6)(A) will not apply to the NOL and the unrelated business taxable income of the exempt organization (after application of Code Sec. 512(a)(6)(B)) will be reduced by the amount of the NOL (Act Sec. 13702(b)(2) of the 2017 Tax Cuts Act).

Law source: Law at ¶5565. Committee Report at ¶10,870.

— Act Sec. 13702(a) of the Tax Cuts and Jobs Act (P.L. 115-97), adding Code Sec. 512(a)(6);

— Act Sec. 13702(b), providing the effective date.

¶807 Unrelated Business Taxable Income Increased by Certain Fringe Benefit Expenses

SUMMARY OF NEW LAW

Unrelated business taxable income will be increased by the nondeductible amount of certain fringe benefit expenses paid or incurred by an exempt organization after December 31, 2017.

BACKGROUND

The income of an exempt organization is subject to the tax on unrelated business income if two conditions are present: (1) the income must be from a trade or business regularly carried on by the organization, and (2) the trade or business must not be substantially related—aside from the need of the organization for funds or the use it makes of the profits—to the organization's exercise or performance of the purposes or functions on which its exemption is based (Code Secs. 511 and 512).

Unrelated business taxable income (UBTI), which is subject to the tax under Code Sec. 511, is the gross income derived by any organization from any unrelated trade or business regularly carried on by it, less the regular deductions allowed for income tax purposes which are directly connected with the carrying on of such trade or business (Code Sec. 512(a)).

Ordinary and necessary business expenses are generally tax deductible, while expenses incurred for personal reasons or pleasure are not deductible (Code Secs. 162 and 262). This distinction can be difficult to make when expenses have both personal and business components, such as entertainment, gift and travel expenses incurred to promote business. Code Sec. 274 addresses this problem by imposing additional limits on expenses that are otherwise deductible under other Internal Revenue Code provisions.

Fringe benefits are a form of compensation and, as such, must be included in income and are subject to withholding unless explicitly excluded under the Internal Revenue Code. Eight basic types of fringe benefits are excluded from an employee's gross income, including a no-additional-cost service, a qualified employee discount, a working condition fringe, a de minimis fringe, a qualified transportation fringe, a

BACKGROUND

qualified moving expense reimbursement, qualified retirement planning services, and qualified military base realignment and closure fringe benefit payments (Code Sec. 132). Special rules also exclude eating and athletic facilities, and the use of certain demonstrator automobiles.

NEW LAW EXPLAINED

Disallowed fringe benefits treated as additions to unrelated income.—The unrelated business taxable income (UBTI) of an exempt organization will be increased by the nondeductible amount of certain fringe benefit expenses incurred by the organization in that tax year, effective for amounts paid or incurred after December 31, 2017 (Code Sec. 512(a)(7), as added by the Tax Cuts and Jobs Act (P.L. 115-97)). These fringe benefits are expenses for which a deduction is not available due to Code Sec. 274, and specifically include:

- any qualified transportation fringe, as defined in Code Sec. 132(f);

- any parking facility used in connection with qualified parking, as defined in Code Sec. 132(f)(5)(C); and

- any on-premises athletic facility, as defined in Code Sec. 132(j)(4)(B).

To the extent the amount paid or incurred is directly connected with an unrelated trade or business that is regularly carried on by the organization, such amounts will *not* increase an organization's UBTI (Code Sec. 512(a)(7), as added by the 2017 Tax Cuts Act). Thus, the increases to UBTI for disallowed fringe benefits are for expenses paid or incurred by the organization that are not associated with any unrelated business of the organization.

> **Comment:** The increase in UBTI for certain fringe benefits is an *addition to* UBTI, rather than a change in the normal calculation of UBTI.

Regulations and other guidance. The IRS is directed to issue regulations or other guidance that may be necessary or appropriate to carry out the purposes of the rule on fringe benefit expenses, such as guidance on the appropriate allocation of depreciation and other costs of facilities used for parking or for on-premises athletic facilities (Code Sec. 512(a)(7), as added by the 2017 Tax Cuts Act).

▶ **Effective date.** The amendment made by this section applies to amounts paid or incurred after December 31, 2017 (Act Sec. 13703(b) of the Tax Cuts and Jobs Act (P.L. 115-97)).

Law source: Law at ¶5565. Committee Report at ¶10,880.

— Act Sec. 13703(a) of the Tax Cuts and Jobs Act (P.L. 115-97), adding Code Sec. 512(a)(7);

— Act Sec. 13703(b), providing the effective date.

¶807

¶810 Excise Tax on Excess Tax-Exempt Organization Executive Compensation

SUMMARY OF NEW LAW

A new excise tax has been established, payable by exempt organizations on remuneration in excess of $1 million and any excess parachute payments made to certain highly-compensated current and former employees in the tax year.

BACKGROUND

Generally, for-profit employers are allowed a deduction for reasonable compensation expenses under Code Sec. 162(a). In some cases, however, compensation in excess of specific levels is not deductible. A publicly held corporation cannot deduct compensation to a covered employee to the extent the compensation exceeds $1 million per tax year (Code Sec. 162(m)). The $1 million threshold is reduced (but not below zero) by excess parachute payments that are not deductible under the golden parachute provisions of Code Sec. 280G. These deduction limits generally do not affect tax-exempt organizations.

A payment in the nature of compensation made to or for the benefit of a disqualified individual is a parachute payment if:

- it is contingent on a change in the ownership or effective control of the corporation or the ownership of a substantial portion of the assets of a corporation, and its present value equals or exceeds 300 percent of the individual's average annual compensation for the last five years (a "change-in-control parachute payment"), or

- it is made under an agreement that violates securities laws (a "securities violation parachute payment").

Certain amounts are not considered parachute payments, including payments under a qualified retirement plan, a simplified employee pension plan, or a simple retirement account.

For this purpose, disqualified individuals (also called "covered employees") are employees, independent contractors, and other persons who perform personal services for a corporation *and* who are officers, shareholders or highly compensated individuals are subject to the golden parachute provisions. Disqualified individuals also include personal service corporations and similar entities (Code Sec. 280G(c)).

Negative tax consequences are imposed only on excess parachute payments. An excess parachute payment is the portion of any parachute payment that exceeds the base amount, which is the recipient's average annual compensation over the five years before the change in ownership, reduced, in the case of a change-in-control parachute payment, by the excess of the amount of the payment determined to be reasonable compensation for services performed before the date of the change over average compensation. The excess amount is determined separately for each parachute payment received.

¶810

NEW LAW EXPLAINED

Excise tax applies to remuneration of highly-compensated exempt organization executives.—A tax-exempt organization will be liable within a tax year for a 21 percent excise tax (equal to the maximum corporate tax rate on income) on the sum of:

- "remuneration" paid to a "covered employee" in excess of $1 million (not including any excess parachute payment) by an "applicable tax-exempt organization", and

- any excess parachute payments paid to a covered employee by that tax-exempt organization (Code Sec. 4960, as added by the Tax Cuts and Jobs Act of 2017 (P.L. 115-97)).

It should be noted that an exempt organization can be liable for this tax even when a covered employee's remuneration is less than $1 million if there is an excess parachute payment.

For purposes of this excise tax, there is a new definition for parachute payments that is limited to the payment of compensation to a covered employee when such payment is contingent on:

- the employee's separation from employment with the tax-exempt employer, and

- the aggregate present value of the compensation payments being equal or in excess of an amount equal to three times the base amount (Code Sec. 4960(c)(5)(B), as added by the 2017 Tax Cuts Act).

The base amount is determined under Code Sec. 280G(b)(3). However, certain payments are excluded from calculating the aggregate present value, including:

- payments under qualified plans, as described in Code Sec. 280G(b)(6));

- payments made to or under a tax-deferred annuity contract as described in Code Sec. 403(b), or the deferred compensation plan of a government employer as described in Code Sec. 457(b);

- payments to a doctor, nurse, or veterinarian for the performance of medical or veterinarian professional services; and

- payments to an individual who is not a highly compensated employee as defined in Code Sec. 414(q) (Code Sec. 4960(c)(5)(C), as added by the 2017 Tax Cuts Act).

In addition, compensation will be considered to be paid when no substantial risk of forfeiture (as defined in Code Sec. 457(f)(3)(B)) exists (Code Sec. 4960(a), as added by the 2017 Tax Cuts Act). Therefore, such compensation may be considered paid when fully vested even if not yet actually paid.

An "applicable tax-exempt organization" is one that is exempt from taxation under Code Sec. 501(a), a farmers' cooperative under Code Sec. 521(b)(1), a political organization described in Code Sec. 527(e)(1), or an organization that has income excluded from taxation under Code Sec. 115(1) (Code Sec. 4960(c)(1), as added by the 2017 Tax Cuts Act).

For purposes of this provision, a "covered employee" includes any current or former employee of the applicable tax-exempt organization who is one of the five highest

NEW LAW EXPLAINED

compensated employees for the current tax year, or a covered employee of the organization (or any predecessor organization) for any preceding tax year that began after December 31, 2016 (Code Sec. 4960(c)(2), as added by the 2017 Tax Cuts Act).

"Remuneration" generally means wages, as defined in Code Sec. 3401(a). Remuneration, for purposes of this section, specifically includes amounts required to be included in income by Code Sec. 457(f), but does not include:

- any designated Roth contribution under Code Sec. 402A(c); or
- any remuneration paid to a licensed medical professional (doctor, nurse, or veterinarian) for the performance of medical or veterinary services (Code Sec. 4960(c)(3), as added by the 2017 Tax Cuts Act).

The remuneration of a covered employee includes not only compensation paid by an applicable tax-exempt organization in a tax year, but also any compensation paid to that employee for employment by any related organization of the applicable tax-exempt organization in that same tax year. Related organizations include any person or government agency that, during the tax year:

- controls, or is controlled by, the organization;
- is controlled by one or more persons that control the organization;
- is a supported organization, as defined in Code Sec. 509(f)(3), of the organization;
- is a supporting organization, as defined in Code Sec. 509(a)(3), of the organization; or
- establishes, maintains, or makes contributions to an applicable tax-exempt organization that is a voluntary employees' beneficiary association (VEBA), as defined in Code Sec. 501(c)(9) (Code Sec. 4960(c)(4), as added by the 2017 Tax Cuts Act).

Any remuneration that is not deductible due to the $1 million limit on deductible compensation under Code Sec. 162(m) is not included in determining the total remuneration of a covered employee (Code Sec. 4960(c)(6), as added by the 2017 Tax Cuts Act). When remuneration from more than one employer is included in determining the tax imposed by Code Sec. 4960(a), each employer will be liable for its respective percentage of the total tax debt according to the percentage of income it paid into the employee's aggregate remuneration from all employers (Code Sec. 4960(c)(4), as added by the 2017 Tax Cuts Act).

Practical Analysis: Brigen Winters, Principal at Groom Law Group, Chartered in Washington, D.C., observes that compensation is treated as paid when there is no substantial risk of forfeiture as defined in Code Sec. 457(f)(3)(B), and compensation includes amounts required to be included in gross income under Code Sec. 457(f). This means that the excise tax could apply to, for example, pension plan amounts that have become vested under the Code Sec. 457(f)(3)(B) definition of substantial risk of forfeiture even though the participant has not yet received those amounts.

▶ **Effective date.** The amendment made by this section applies to tax years beginning after December 31, 2017 (Act Sec. 13602(c) of the Tax Cuts and Jobs Act of 2017 (P.L. 115-97)).

¶810

NEW LAW EXPLAINED

Law source: Law at ¶6115. Committee Report at ¶10,800.

— Act Sec. 13602(a) of the Tax Cuts and Jobs Act of 2017 (P.L. 115-97), adding Code Sec. 4960;

— Act Sec. 13602(c), providing the effective date.

¶815 Excise Tax Based on Investment Income of Private Colleges and Universities

SUMMARY OF NEW LAW

A new Code section imposes a 1.4 percent excise tax on the net investment income of certain private colleges and universities.

BACKGROUND

Private foundations (other than exempt operating foundations) are generally subject to a two-percent excise tax on their net investment income under Code Sec. 4940(a). Net investment income is gross investment income and net capital gain, less expenses paid or incurred in earning the gross investment income. Tax-exempt interest on governmental obligations and related expenses are excluded. Gross investment income means the gross amount of income from interest, dividends, rents, and royalties received by a private foundation from all sources, unless the income is taxable as unrelated business income under Code Sec. 511.

The two-percent excise tax is reduced to one percent on the net investment income of a private foundation if the amount of the qualifying charitable distributions made by the foundation during the tax year equals or exceeds the average historic level of its charitable distributions, determined by calculating the sum of: (1) an amount equal to the foundation's assets for the tax year multiplied by the average percentage payout for the base period, *plus* (2) one percent of the foundation's net investment income for the year (Code Sec. 4940(e)). In addition, the foundation must not have been subject to the excise tax under Code Sec. 4942 for failure to make minimum qualifying distributions during the "base period"—five tax years preceding the current tax year.

Private colleges and universities are generally considered 501(c)(3) educational organizations and thus public charities rather than private foundations. They are therefore not subject to the private foundation excise tax on net investment income.

NEW LAW EXPLAINED

Net investment income of private colleges and universities taxed.—A new Internal Revenue Code section imposes a 1.4 percent tax on the net investment income of certain private colleges and universities in each tax year beginning after December 31,

NEW LAW EXPLAINED

2017 (Code Sec. 4968 as added by the Tax Cuts and Jobs Act of 2017 (P.L. 115-97)). For this purpose, net investment income is defined by reference to Code Sec. 4940(c) which defines it for purposes of the excise tax applicable to private foundations.

The tax is imposed on "applicable educational institutions," defined as eligible educational institutions (as described in Code Sec. 25A(f)(2)) that:

- have at least 500 students during the preceding tax year, of which more than 50 percent are located in the United States,
- are private educational institutions and not state colleges and universities described in Code Sec. 511(a)(2)(B), and
- have assets with an aggregate fair market value of at least $500,000 per student (not including assets used directly in carrying out the institution's exempt purpose) as measured at the end of the preceding tax year.

For these purposes, the number of students of an institution is based on the daily average number of full-time students attending the institution, with part-time students being taken into account on a full-time student equivalent basis.

The assets and net investment income of any related organization are treated as assets and net investment income of the applicable educational institution. Related organizations include any organization that:

- controls, or is controlled by, an applicable education institution;
- is controlled by one or more persons who also control that educational institution; or
- is either a supported organization (as defined in Code Sec. 509(f)(3)) or a organization described in Code Sec. 509(a)(3) in regards to the educational institution during the tax year.

> **Practical Analysis:** Brian T. Whitlock, Adjunct Professor in the Gies College of Business at the University of Illinois at Urbana-Champaign, observes that this Act Section will impose an excise tax of 1.4 percent on the investment income earned by private colleges and universities as well as their supporting organizations similar to private foundations. Private colleges and universities were previously treated as public charities and not subject to an excise tax on net investment income. This type of excise tax is commonly referred to as the "audit tax", since it is at a relatively low rate. In recent years, a number of private universities have been publicly criticized for accumulating significant assets inside of endowment funds and only granting a limited amount of academic scholarships.

▶ **Effective date.** The amendment made by this section applies to tax years beginning after December 31, 2017 (Act Sec. 13701(c) of the Tax Cuts and Jobs Act of 2017 (P.L. 115-97)).

Law source: Law at ¶6120. Committee Report at ¶10,860.

— Act Sec. 13701(a) of the Tax Cut and Jobs Act of 2017 (P.L. 115-97), adding Code Sec. 4968;

— Act Sec. 13701(c), providing the effective date.

¶815

EXCISE TAXES ON ALCOHOL & TRANSPORTATION

¶820 Aircraft Management Services

SUMMARY OF NEW LAW

Payments made by aircraft owners for aircraft management services related to maintenance and support of, or flights on, the owner's aircraft are not subject to the excise tax imposed on the taxable transportation of persons or property by air.

BACKGROUND

An excise tax is imposed on amounts paid for the taxable transportation of persons by air (Code Sec. 4261). This tax consists of two parts: a 7.5 percent tax applied to the amount paid and a flat dollar amount for each domestic flight segment (Code Sec. 4261(a) and (b)). A separate 6.25 percent excise tax is imposed on amounts paid for the taxable transportation of property by air (Code Sec. 4271). These air transportation excise taxes are paid by the person making the payment (Code Sec. 4261(d); Code Sec. 4271(b)). Exemptions are allowed for certain transactions, such as air transportation for providing emergency medical services or skydiving (Code Sec. 4261(g); Code Sec. 4261(h)).

NEW LAW EXPLAINED

Payments for aircraft management services excluded from air transportation excise taxes.—Amounts paid by an aircraft owner to a provider of aircraft management services related to maintenance and support of the owner's aircraft or flights on the owner's aircraft are not subject to the excise tax on the air transportation of passengers under Code Sec. 4261 or the excise tax on the air transportation of property under Code Sec. 4271 (Code Sec. 4261(e)(5)(A), as added by the Tax Cuts and Jobs Act (P.L. 115-97)).

Exempt aircraft management services include (Code Sec. 4261(e)(5)(B), as added by the 2017 Tax Cuts Act):

- assisting an aircraft owner with administrative and support services, such as scheduling, flight planning, and weather forecasting;
- obtaining insurance;
- maintenance, storage, and fueling of aircraft;
- hiring, training, and provision of pilots and crew;
- establishing and complying with safety standards; and
- other services necessary to support flights operated by an aircraft owner.

An aircraft lessee is treated as an aircraft owner for exemption purposes unless the aircraft is leased under a disqualified lease. A "disqualified lease" is a lease from a

NEW LAW EXPLAINED

person providing aircraft management services with respect to the aircraft (or from a related person to the person providing the services) if the lease is for a term of 31 days or less (Code Sec. 4261(e)(5)(C), as added by the 2017 Tax Cuts Act).

The exclusion for aircraft management services applies on a pro rata basis if only a portion of the payment is attributable to aircraft management services related to the aircraft owner's aircraft (Code Sec. 4261(e)(5)(D), as added by the 2017 Tax Cuts Act). Excise tax must be collected on that portion paid attributable to flights on aircraft not owned by the aircraft owner.

▶ **Effective date.** The amendment made by this section apply to amounts paid after December 22, 2017, the date of enactment of the Act (Act Sec. 13822(b) of the Tax Cuts and Jobs Act (P.L. 115-97)).

Law source: Law at ¶6110. Committee Report at ¶10,980.

— Act Sec. 13822(a) of the Tax Cuts and Jobs Act (P.L. 115-97), adding Code Sec. 4261(e)(5);

— Act Sec. 13822(b), providing the effective date.

¶825 Production Period for Beer, Wine and Distilled Spirits

SUMMARY OF NEW LAW

The aging period for beer, wine, and distilled spirits is excluded from the production period for purposes of the UNICAP interest capitalization rules for interest paid or accrued during the 2018 and 2019 calendar years. Accordingly, producers of beer, wine and distilled spirits are able to deduct interest expenses attributable to a shorter production period for two years.

BACKGROUND

The uniform capitalization (UNICAP) rules require certain direct and indirect costs allocable to real or tangible personal property produced by the taxpayer to be included in either inventory or capitalized into the basis of such property, as applicable (Code Sec. 263A). For real or personal property acquired by the taxpayer for resale, Code Sec. 263A generally requires certain direct and indirect costs allocable to such property to be included in inventory.

In the case of interest expense, the UNICAP rules apply only to interest paid or incurred during the property's production period and that is allocable to property produced by the taxpayer or acquired for resale which:

• is either real property or property with a class life of at least 20 years;

• has an estimated production period exceeding two years; or

BACKGROUND

- has an estimated production period exceeding one year and a cost exceeding $1,000,000.

The term "production period" when used with respect to any property is the period beginning on the date on which production of the property begins, and ending on the date on which the property is ready to be placed in service or held for sale (Code Sec. 263A(f)(4)(B)). In the case of property that is customarily aged before it is sold (e.g., wine, tobacco, and whiskey), the production period includes the aging period (Reg. § 1.263A-12(d)(1)). This is because the property is not ready to be sold until the aging process is complete.

NEW LAW EXPLAINED

Aging period excluded from production period for beer, wine and distilled spirits.—The aging period for beer, wine, and distilled spirits (other than spirits that are unfit for use for beverage purposes) are excluded from the production period for purposes of the UNICAP interest capitalization rules Code Sec. 263A(f)(4) as added by the Tax Cuts and Jobs Act (P.L. 115-97)). Thus, producers of beer, wine and distilled spirits are able to deduct interest expenses (subject to any other applicable limitation) attributable to a shorter production period.

> **Caution:** The provision only applies in calendar years 2018 and 2019. See effective and expiration dates below.

Practical Analysis: Charles R. Goulding, President, Energy Tax Savers and R&D Tax Savers in Syosset, New York, comments that under existing tax law, beer, wine and distilled spirits have to capitalize interest from the start of production through the entire aging period. This new ability to exclude the aging period from capitalization is a major benefit for the spirits industry and particularly distilled spirits where aging often means higher quality. For example, Bourbon is often aged for five to 10 years and Scotch for 10–20 years. The new exclusion will not mean as much for wine and beer because most wine isn't meant to age and most wine aging ends before two years. Most beers are also better consumed when fresh.

▶ **Effective date.** The provision applies to interest costs paid or accrued in calendar years beginning after December 31, 2017 (Act Sec. 13801(c), of the Tax Cuts and Jobs Act (P.L. 115-97)).

Expiration date. The provision does not apply to interest costs paid or accrued after December 31, 2019 (Code Sec. 263A(f)(4)(B), as added by the Tax Cuts and Jobs Act

Law source: Law at ¶5425. Committee Report at ¶10,890.

— Act Sec. 13801(a) of the Tax Cuts and Jobs Act (P.L. 115-97), redesignating Code Sec. 263A(f)(4) as (5), and adding new Code Sec. 263A(f)(4);

— Act Sec. 13801(b), amending Code Sec. 263A(f)(5);

— Act Sec. 13801(c), providing the effective date.

¶830 Beer Excise Tax Rate Reduced

SUMMARY OF NEW LAW

The excise tax on beer is lowered to $16 per barrel on the first six million barrels brewed by the brewer or imported by the importer during a calendar year. Beer brewed or imported in excess of the six million barrel limit continues to be taxed at $18 per barrel. In the case of small brewers, such brewers would be taxed at a rate of $3.50 per barrel on the first 60,000 barrels domestically produced during a calendar year, and $16 per barrel on any further barrels produced. The provision applies to beer removed after December 31, 2017 and before January 1, 2020.

BACKGROUND

Federal excise taxes are imposed at different rates on distilled spirits, beer, and wine and are imposed on these products when produced or imported. The tax on beer brewed or produced, and removed from a U.S. brewery for consumption or sale, or imported into the United States, is imposed on every barrel, and proportionately on the fractional parts of a barrel (Code Sec. 5051(a)(1)). The rate of tax on beer is $18 per barrel, with a barrel containing 31 gallons.

Small brewers are subject to a reduced tax rate of $7 per barrel on the first 60,000 barrels of beer domestically produced and removed each year (Code Sec. 5051(a)(2)). Small brewers are defined as brewers producing fewer than two million barrels of beer during a calendar year.

The term "beer" generally means beer, ale, porter, stout, and other similar fermented beverages (including saké or similar products) of any name or description containing one-half of 1 percent or more of alcohol by volume, brewed or produced from malt, wholly or in part, or from any malt substitute (Code Sec. 5052(a)).

When beer is produced, the excise tax is not payable until the beer is removed from the brewery for consumption or sale. Generally, beer may be transferred between commonly owned breweries without payment of tax; however, tax liability follows these products. Imported bulk beer may be released from customs custody without payment of tax and transferred in bond to a brewery. Beer may be exported without payment of tax and may be withdrawn tax-free from the production facility for certain authorized uses, including industrial uses and non-beverage uses.

NEW LAW EXPLAINED

The excise tax rate on beer is reduced.—The rate of tax on beer is lowered to $16 per barrel on the first six million barrels brewed by the brewer or imported by the importer during the calendar year (Code Sec. 5051(a)(1), as amended by the Tax Cuts and Jobs Act of 2017 (P.L. 115-97)). Beer brewed or imported in excess of the six million barrel limit continues to be taxed at $18 per barrel. Small brewers are taxed at a different rate: $3.50 per barrel on the first 60,000 barrels domestically produced, and $16 per barrel on any further barrels produced (Code Sec. 5051(a)(2)(A), as amended by

NEW LAW EXPLAINED

the 2017 Tax Cuts Act). In the case of a controlled group of brewers, both the six million barrel limitation, and the two million barrel limitation to qualify as a small brewer, are applied and apportioned at the level of the controlled group (Code Sec. 5051(a)(5)(A), as added by the Tax Cuts Act.

> **Caution:** The reductions only apply to beer removed after December 31, 2017 and before January 1, 2020.

For barrels of beer that have been brewed or produced outside of the United States and imported into the United States, the reduced tax rate may be assigned by the brewer to any importer of such barrels pursuant to certain regulatory requirements (Code Sec. 5051(a)(4), as added by the 2017 Tax Cuts Act). These requirements will include:

- a limitation to ensure that the number of barrels of beer for which the reduced tax rate has been assigned by a brewer to any importer does not exceed the number of barrels produced by that brewer during the calendar year which were imported into the United States by the importer;

- procedures that allow a brewer and an importer to elect whether to receive the reduced tax rate;

- requirements that the brewer provide any information that is needed to assign the reduced tax rate; and

- procedures that allow the eligibility of the brewer and the importer for the reduced tax rate to be revoked if the brewer provided erroneous or fraudulent information which was material in qualifying for the reduced rate.

Any importer making an election to receive the reduced tax rate shall be deemed to be a member of the controlled group of the brewer (Code Sec. 5051(a)(4)(C); Code Sec. 5051(a)(5)(B), as added by the 2017 Tax Cuts Act). Foreign corporations may be members of the controlled group (Conference Report on H.R. 1, Tax Cuts and Jobs Act (H. Rept. 115-466)).

Under rules to be issued, two or more entities (whether or not under common control) that produce beer marketed under a similar brand, license, franchise, or other arrangement are treated as a single taxpayer for purposes of the beer excise tax (Code Sec. 5051(a)(5)(C), as added by the 2017 Tax Cuts Act).

Practical Analysis: Charles R. Goulding, President, Energy Tax Savers and R&D Tax Savers in Syosset, New York, comments that under Act Secs. 13802 and 13803, numerous Federal taxes for both small and large brewers are reduced. Federal excise taxes are lowered for both small and large brewers, and taxes are removed for the transfer of beer between bonded facilities. Reducing beer taxes is a popular provision as virtually every Congressional district has a craft brewer at some size level.

¶830

NEW LAW EXPLAINED

Federal excise taxes are reduced as follows:

- Small Brewers. 50-percent excise tax reduction ($7 to $3.50 per barrel) on first 60,000 barrels produced domestically and any production over 60,000 taxed at $16 per barrel.
- Large Brewers. 11.1-percent excise tax reduction ($18 to $16 per barrel) on first 6 million barrels produced or imported and any production over 6 million taxed at $18 per barrel.

For purposes of the Act, small brewers are defined as those producing less than 2 million barrels annually and large brewers are defined as those producing more than 2 million barrels annually.

Brewers can now also transfer beer from one brewery to another bonded facility without the payment of tax and may be mingled with beer at the receiving facility under certain conditions. Both of these provisions are set to expire at the end of 2019.

Of the more than 5,000 brewers in the United States, over 90 percent are considered small (craft) brewers, with the amount of craft breweries more than doubling since 2012. The U.S. beer industry has become highly competitive, with brewers of all sizes dedicating extensive resources to attracting and retaining customers.

According to the Beer Institute, more than 40 percent of the retail cost of beer goes toward taxes. With these changes, brewers (both large and small) should expect a significant reduction in operating taxes and improve the industry average margin of eight percent. Small craft brewers stand to see the biggest gain, as their Federal excise tax is cut in half on their first 60,000 barrels produced (a savings of $210,000 on this quantity).

Transfer Rules and Removal Without Tax. Previously, brewers had to have shared ownership in order to transfer the excise tax payable related to beer production which is payable when removed for the brewery. Now for the first time independent brewers may transfer the payment liability provided the transferor has no retained interest and the transferee assumes the payment liability. With the large increases in the number of breweries and resultant inter brewery transfers this relaxation is really about administrative convenience. The actual cash flow impact on the U.S. treasury should be minimal since beer must generally be fresh and presumably will be removed from the transferee brewery quickly. See ¶835.

▶ **Effective date.** The amendments made by this section apply to beer removed after December 31, 2017 (Act Sec. 13802(e), of the Tax Cuts and Jobs Act (P.L. 115-97)).

Expiration date. The provision expires for beer removed after December 31, 2019 (Code Sec. 5051(a)(1)(C) and (2)(A), as amended by the Tax Cuts and Jobs Act (P.L. 115-97)).

Law source: Law at ¶6150. Committee Report at ¶10,900.

— Act Sec. 13802(a) of the Tax Cuts and Jobs Act (P.L. 115-97), amending Code Sec. 5051(a)(1);

— Act Sec. 13802(b), amending Code Sec. 5051(a)(2)(A);

— Act Sec. 13802(c), adding Code Sec. 5051(a)(4) ;

— Act Sec. 13802(d), adding Code Sec. 5051(a)(5);

— Act Sec. 13802(e), providing the effective date.

¶830

¶835 Transfer of Beer Between Bonded Facilities

SUMMARY OF NEW LAW

Beer may be removed from one bonded brewery to another bonded brewery without payment of tax if the transfer is between independent proprietors and the transferee accepts responsibility for the tax.

BACKGROUND

Beer may be removed tax-free from one brewery to another brewery belonging to the same brewer, and may be mingled with the beer of the receiving brewery. If breweries are owned by separate corporations, and if one corporation owns the controlling interest in the other corporation, or if the controlling interest in each corporation is owned by the same person or persons, the breweries are considered to be owned by the same brewer (Code Sec. 5414).

NEW LAW EXPLAINED

Requirements relaxed for transfer of beer between bonded facilities.—The Code Sec. 5414 shared ownership requirement is relaxed. Specifically, a brewer may transfer beer from one bonded brewery to another without incurring tax, provided that:

- the breweries are owned by the same person;

- one brewery owns a controlling interest in the other or the same person or persons have a controlling interest in both breweries; or

- the proprietors of the transferring and receiving premises are independent of each other, and the transferor has divested itself of all interest in the transferred beer, and the transferee has accepted responsibility for payment of the tax (Code Sec. 5414, as amended by the Tax Cuts and Jobs Act (P.L. 115-97)).

> **Comment:** Previously, beer could only be transferred free of tax between breweries if both breweries are owned by the same brewer. The new law allows transfers between independent proprietors if the transferee accepts responsibility for the tax. The provision for independent proprietors, however, is temporary. In tax quarters beginning after 2019 the prior law rules of Code Sec. 5414 which applied only to breweries owned by the same brewer will be reinstated. See effective and expiration dates below.

For purposes of transferring the tax liability (last item above), relief from liability is effective from the time the beer is removed from the transferor's bonded premises, or from the time the transferor divests itself of all interest in the transferred beer, whichever is later.

▶ **Effective date.** The amendments made by this section apply to any calendar quarters beginning after December 31, 2017 (Act Sec. 13803(c) of the Tax Cuts and Jobs Act (P.L. 115-97)).

NEW LAW EXPLAINED

Expiration date. The provision expires for calendar quarters beginning after December 31, 2019.

Law source: Law at ¶6160 and ¶6165. Committee Report at ¶10,910.

— Act Sec. 13803(a) of the Tax Cuts and Jobs Act (P.L. 115-97), amending Code Sec. 5414;

— Act Sec. 13803(b), amending Code Sec. 5412;

— Act Sec. 13803(c), providing the effective date.

¶840 Wine Excise Tax Credit Expanded

SUMMARY OF NEW LAW

For wine removed after December 31, 2017 and before January 1, 2020, the credit against the wine excise tax for small domestic producers is made available to all wine producers and importers regardless of the number of gallons of wine produced. Foreign producers, however, must elect to assign the credit to importers.

BACKGROUND

Excise taxes are imposed at different rates on wine, depending on the wine's alcohol content and carbonation levels. A "still wine" is a non-sparkling wine. Generally, bulk and bottled wine may be transferred in bond between bonded premises; however, tax liability follows these products. Bulk natural wine may be released from customs custody without payment of tax and transferred in bond to a winery. Wine may be exported without payment of tax and may be withdrawn without payment of tax or free of tax from the production facility for certain authorized uses, including industrial uses and non-beverage uses.

The tax on wines, including imitation, substandard or artificial wine, and compounds sold as wine, containing not more than 24 percent alcohol by volume, produced in, in bond in, or imported into, the United States is determined as of the time of removal for consumption or sale. Wines containing more than 24 percent alcohol by volume are classed and taxed as distilled spirits. Still wines can not contain in excess of 0.392 gram of carbon dioxide per hundred milliliters of wine unless the Secretary authorizes tolerances to the limitation (Code Sec. 5041(a)).

The current tax rate tiers on wine are as follows:

- still wines not more than 14 percent alcohol: $1.07 per wine gallon
- still wines more than 14 percent, but not more than 21 percent, alcohol: $1.57 per wine gallon
- still wines more than 21 percent, but not more than 24 percent, alcohol: $3.15 per wine gallon
- still wines more than 24 percent alcohol: $13.50 per proof gallon (taxed as distilled spirits)

BACKGROUND

- champagne and other sparkling wines: $3.40 per wine gallon
- artificially carbonated wines: $3.30 per wine gallon

Wineries that are small domestic producers (having aggregate annual production not exceeding 250,000 gallons) receive a credit against the wine excise tax equal to 90 cents per gallon on the first 100,000 gallons of wine domestically produced and removed during a calendar year (Code Sec. 5041(c)). A "wine gallon" means a United States gallon of liquid measure equivalent to the volume of 231 cubic inches (Code Sec. 5041(d)). The credit is reduced (but not below zero) by one percent for each 1,000 gallons produced in excess of 150,000 gallons; the credit does not apply to sparkling wines. In the case of a controlled group, the 250,000 gallon limitation for wineries is applied to the controlled group, and the 100,000 gallons eligible for the credit are apportioned among the wineries who are component members of the group. The term "controlled group" is defined in Code Sec. 1563(a), except that the phrase "more than 50 percent" is substituted for the phrase "at least 80 percent" in each place it appears in Code Sec. 1563(a).

NEW LAW EXPLAINED

Wine excise tax credit temporarily extended to all producers and importers.— For wine removed after December 31, 2017 and before January 1, 2020, the credit against the wine excise tax for small domestic producers is modified by removing the 250,000 wine gallon domestic production limitation. This makes the credit available for all wine producers and importers (Code Sec. 5041(c), as amended by the Tax Cuts and Jobs Act (P.L. 115-97)). Sparkling wine producers and importers are now also eligible for the credit. With respect to wine produced in, or imported into, the United States during a calendar year, the credit amount is:

- on the first 30,000 wine gallons of wine, $1 per wine gallon;
- on the next 100,000 wine gallons of wine (after the first 30,000 gallons), 90¢ per wine gallon;
- on the next 620,000 wine gallons of wine (after the first 130,000 gallons), 53.5¢ per wine gallon.

With respect to hard cider, the credit amount is:

- on the first 30,000 wine gallons of hard cider, 6.2¢ per wine gallon;
- on the next 100,000 wine gallons of hard cider (after the first 30,000 gallons), 5.6¢ per wine gallon;
- on the next 620,000 wine gallons of hard cider (after the first 130,000 gallons), 3.3¢ per wine gallon.

> **Comment:** Note that the 2017 Tax Cuts Act increases the wine alcohol content level of the first two excise tax tiers from 14 percent alcohol to 16 percent alcohol for still wines removed after 2017 and before 2020 (Code Sec. 5041(b)(1) and (2), as amended by the 2017 Tax Cuts Act). See ¶845.

¶840

NEW LAW EXPLAINED

For wine gallons of wine that have been produced outside of the United States and imported into the United States, the tax credit is only available if it is assigned by the "foreign producer" to an electing importer of those wine gallons under regulatory requirements to be established (Code Sec. 5041(c)(8)(A), as added and amended by the 2017 Tax Cuts Act). These requirement include:

- a limitation to ensure that the number of wine gallons of wine for which the tax credit has been assigned by a foreign producer: (i) to any importer does not exceed the number of wine gallons of wine produced by the foreign producer, during the calendar year, that were imported into the United States by the importer; and (ii) to all importers does not exceed the 750,000 wine gallons of wine to which the tax credit applies;

- procedures that allow the election of a foreign producer to assign, and an importer to receive, the tax credit;

- requirements that the foreign producer provide any information determined to be necessary and appropriate for purposes of assigning the tax credit; and

- procedures that allow the eligibility of the foreign producer and the importer for the tax credit to be revoked if the foreign producer provides erroneous or fraudulent information that is deemed to be material for qualifying for the reduced tax rate (Code Sec. 5041(c)(9), as added by the 2017 Tax Cuts Act).

Any importer making an election to receive the reduced tax rate will deemed to be a member of the controlled group of the winemaker, within the meaning of Code Sec. 1563(a), except that the phrase "more than 50 percent" is substituted for the phrase "at least 80 percent" in each place it appears in Code Sec. 1563(a). Members of the controlled group may include foreign corporations (Code Sec. 5041(c)(9)(C), as added by the 2017 Tax Cuts Act; Conference Report on H.R. 1, Tax Cuts and Jobs Act (H. Rept. 115-466)).

▶ **Effective date.** The amendments made by this section apply to wine removed after December 31, 2017 (Act Sec. 13804(d), of the Tax Cuts and Jobs Act (P.L. 115-97)).

Expiration date. The provision expires for wine removed after December 31, 2019 (Code Sec. 5041(c)(8)(A), as added by the Tax Cuts and Jobs Act (P.L. 115-97)).

Law source: Law at ¶6145. Committee Report at ¶10,920.

— Act Sec. 13804(a) of the Tax Cuts and Jobs Act of 2017 (P.L. 115-97), amending Code Sec. 5041(c);

— Act Sec. 13804(b), amending Code Sec. 5041(c)(4);

— Act Sec. 13804(c), amending Code Sec. 5041(c);

— Act Sec. 13804(d), providing the effective date.

¶840

¶845 Alcohol Content Level of Wine Adjusted

SUMMARY OF NEW LAW

Alcohol-by-volume levels of the first two tiers of the excise tax on wine are modified by changing 14 percent to 16 percent, effective for wine removed after 2017 and before 2020..

BACKGROUND

Excise taxes are imposed at different rates on wine, depending on the wine's alcohol content and carbonation levels.

The current tax rate tiers on wine per Code Sec. 5041 are as follows:

- still wines not more than 14 percent alcohol: $1.07 per wine gallon
- still wines more than 14 percent, but not more than 21 percent, alcohol: $1.57 per wine gallon
- still wines more than 21 percent, but not more than 24 percent, alcohol: $3.15 per wine gallon
- still wines more than 24 percent alcohol: $13.50 per proof gallon (taxed as distilled spirits)
- champagne and other sparkling wines: $3.40 per wine gallon
- artificially carbonated wines: $3.30 per wine gallon

NEW LAW EXPLAINED

Alcohol content level of wine adjusted for application of excise taxes.—Alcohol-by-volume levels of the first two tiers of the excise tax on wine are modified by changing 14 percent to 16 percent, effective for wine removed after December 31, 2017 and before January 1, 2020. Therefore, a wine producer or importer may produce or import "still wine" (nonsparkling) that has an alcohol-by-volume level of up to 16 percent, and remain subject to the lowest rate of $1.07 per wine gallon (Code Sec. 5041(b) as amended by the Tax Cuts and Jobs Act (P.L. 115-97)).

▶ **Effective date.** The amendment made by this section applies to wine removed after December 31, 2017 (Act Sec. 13805(b), of the Tax Cuts and Jobs Act (P.L. 115-97)).

Expiration date. The provision does not apply to wine removed after December 31, 2019 (Code Sec. 5041(b), as amended by the Tax Cuts and Jobs Act (P.L. 115-97)).

Law source: Law at ¶6145. Committee Report at ¶10,930.

— Act Sec. 13805(a) of the Tax Cuts and Jobs Act (P.L. 115-97), amending Code Sec. 5041(b);

— Act Sec. 13805(b), providing the effective date.

¶850 Taxation of Mead and Certain Low-Alcohol by Volume Wines

SUMMARY OF NEW LAW

Mead and certain low-alcohol by volume wines are taxed at the lowest rate applicable to "still wine"—$1.07 per wine gallon of wine, effective for wine removed after December 31, 2017 and before January 1, 2020.

BACKGROUND

Excise taxes are imposed at different rates on wine, depending on the wine's alcohol content and carbonation levels. The current tax rate tiers on wine per Code Sec. 5041 are as follows:

- still wines not more than 14 percent alcohol: $1.07 per wine gallon
- still wines more than 14 percent, but not more than 21 percent, alcohol: $1.57 per wine gallon
- still wines more than 21 percent, but not more than 24 percent, alcohol: $3.15 per wine gallon
- still wines more than 24 percent alcohol: $13.50 per proof gallon (taxed as distilled spirits)
- champagne and other sparkling wines: $3.40 per wine gallon
- artificially carbonated wines: $3.30 per wine gallon

"Still wines" include those wines containing not more than 0.392 gram of carbon dioxide per hundred milliliters of wine (Code Sec. 5041(a)).

NEW LAW EXPLAINED

Mead and certain low-alcohol by volume wines taxed as still wines.—Mead and certain low-alcohol by volume wines are taxed at the lowest rate applicable to "still wine" of $1.07 per wine gallon for wine removed in 2018 and 2019 (Code Sec. 5041(h), as added by the Tax Cuts and Jobs Act (P.L. 115-97)).

> **Comment:** Note that the 2017 Tax Cuts Act increases the wine alcohol content level of the first two excise tax tiers from 14 percent alcohol to 16 percent alcohol for still wines. See ¶845.

"Mead" is defined as a wine that contains not more than 0.64 grams of carbon dioxide per hundred milliliters of wine, which is derived solely from honey and water, contains no fruit product or fruit flavoring, and contains less than 8.5 percent alcohol-by-volume (Code Sec. 5041(h)(2)(A), as added by the 2017 Tax Cuts Act). Sparkling wines eligible to be taxed at the lowest rate as "low alcohol by volume wine" are those wines that contain not more than 0.64 grams of carbon dioxide per hundred milliliters of wine, which are derived primarily from grapes or grape juice concentrate and water, which contain no fruit product or fruit flavoring other than

NEW LAW EXPLAINED

grape, and which contain less than 8.5 percent alcohol by volume (Code Sec. 5041(h)(2)(B), as added by the 2017 Tax Cuts Act).

▶ **Effective date.** The amendment made by this section applies to wine removed after December 31, 2017 (Act Sec. 13806(b) of the Tax Cuts and Jobs Act (P.L. 115-97)).

Expiration date. The provision does not apply to wine removed after December 31, 2019 (Code Sec. 5041(h)(3), as added by the Tax Cuts and Jobs Act (P.L. 115-97)).

Law source: Law at ¶6145. Committee Report at ¶10,940.

— Act Sec. 13806(a) of the Tax Cuts and Jobs Act (P.L. 115-97), amending Code Sec. 5041;

— Act Sec. 13806(b), providing the effective date.

¶855 Distilled Spirits Excise Tax Rate Reduced

SUMMARY OF NEW LAW

A tiered tax rate is created for distilled spirits removed in 2018 and 2019.

BACKGROUND

An excise tax is imposed on all distilled spirits produced in, or imported into, the United States (Code Sec. 5001). The tax liability legally comes into existence the moment the alcohol is produced or imported but payment of the tax is not required until a subsequent withdrawal or removal from the distillery, or, in the case of an imported product, from customs custody or bond (Code Sec. 5006).

Generally, bulk distilled spirits may be transferred in bond between bonded premises, but tax liability follows these products. Imported bulk distilled spirits may be released from customs custody without payment of tax and transferred in bond to a distillery. Distilled spirits may be exported without payment of tax and may be withdrawn without payment of tax or tax-free from the production facility for certain authorized uses, including industrial uses and non-beverage uses.

Distilled spirits are taxed at a rate of $13.50 per proof gallon. A "proof gallon" is a U.S. liquid gallon of proof spirits, or the alcoholic equivalent. Generally a proof gallon is a U.S. liquid gallon consisting of 50 percent alcohol. A proportionate tax is paid on all fractional parts of a proof gallon. Credits are allowed for wine content and flavors content of distilled spirits. "Wine content" means alcohol derived from wine, and "flavors content" means alcohol derived from flavors of a type for which drawback is allowable under Code Sec. 5114 (Code Sec. 5010).

NEW LAW EXPLAINED

Distilled spirits excise tax rate reduced.—A tiered tax rate for distilled spirits is created for distilled spirits removed in 2018 and 2019 (Code Sec. 5001(c)(1), as added by the Tax Cuts and Jobs Act (P.L. 115-97)). The tiers are as follows:

NEW LAW EXPLAINED

- $2.70 per proof gallon on the first 100,000 proof gallons of distilled spirits;

- $13.34 for all proof gallons on the next 22,130,000 (after the first 100,000 proof gallons); and

- $13.50 for amounts over 22,230,000 proof gallons.

Rules prevent a controlled group or a group under common control where one or more persons is not a corporation from receiving the lower rates on more than the applicable number of proof gallons of distilled spirits. Two or more entities (whether under common control or not) that produce distilled spirits marketed under a similar brand, franchise, license, or other arrangement are also treated as a single taxpayer for this purpose (Code Sec. 5001(c)(2), as added by the 2017 Tax Cuts Act). Importers of distilled spirits are also eligible for the lower rates (Code Sec. 5001(c)(3), as added by the 2017 Tax Cuts Act).

▶ **Effective date.** The amendments made by this section apply to distilled spirits removed after December 31, 2017 (Act Sec. 13807(d), of the Tax Cuts and Jobs Act (P.L. 115-97)).

Expiration date. The provision does not apply to distilled spirits removed after December 31, 2019 (Code Sec. 5001(c)(4), as added by the Tax Cuts and Jobs Act (P.L. 115-97)).

Law source: Law at ¶6140 and ¶6335. Committee Report at ¶10,950.

— Act Sec. 13807(a) of the Tax Cuts and Jobs Act (P.L. 115-97), redesignating Code Sec. 5001(c) as (d) and adding new Code Sec. 5001(c);

— Act Sec. 13807(b), amending Code Sec. 7652(f)(2);

— Act Sec. 13807(c), amending new Code Sec. 5001(c);

— Act Sec. 13807(d), providing the effective date.

¶860 Transfer of Bulk Distilled Spirits

SUMMARY OF NEW LAW

Distillers are allowed to transfer distilled spirits in bond in containers other than bulk containers without payment of tax for spirits transferred after 2017 and before 2020.

BACKGROUND

An excise tax is imposed on all distilled spirits produced in, or imported into, the United States (Code Sec. 5001). The tax liability comes into existence the moment the alcohol is produced or imported, but payment of the tax is not required until a subsequent withdrawal or removal from the distillery, or, in the case of an imported product, from customs custody or bond.

¶860

BACKGROUND

Generally, bulk distilled spirits may be transferred in bond between bonded premises without payment of tax. Tax liability follows these products (Code Sec. 5212). Bulk distilled spirits are spirits in a container having a capacity in excess of 1 gallon (Code Sec. 5002(a)(9)). Imported bulk distilled spirits may be released from customs custody without payment of tax and transferred in bond to a distillery. Distilled spirits may be exported without payment of tax and may be withdrawn without payment of tax or tax-free from the production facility for certain authorized uses, including industrial uses and non-beverage uses.

NEW LAW EXPLAINED

Transfer of distilled spirits in non-bulk containers allowed.—Distillers are allowed to transfer spirits in bond without payment of tax in approved containers other than bulk containers during 2018 and 2019 (Code Sec. 5212, as amended by the Tax Cuts and Jobs Act (P.L. 115-97)).

▶   **Effective date.** The amendment made by this section applies to distilled spirits transferred in bond after December 31, 2017 (Act Sec. 13808(b) of the Tax Cuts and Jobs Act (P.L. 115-97)).

   Expiration date. The provision does not apply to distilled spirits transferred in bond after December 31, 2019 (Code Sec. 5212, as amended by the Tax Cuts and Jobs Act (P.L. 115-97)).

Law source: Law at ¶6155. Committee Report at ¶10,960.

— Act Sec. 13808(a) of the Tax Cuts and Jobs Act (P.L. 115-97), amending Code Sec. 5212;

— Act Sec. 13808(b), providing the effective date.

BONDS

¶870 Advance Refunding Bonds

SUMMARY OF NEW LAW

Interest paid on advance refunding bonds issued after 2017 is not excludable from gross income as interest paid on state and local government bonds.

BACKGROUND

Interest received on exempt state and local bonds is generally excludable from income (Code Sec. 103). There are two types of exempt state and local bonds: governmental bonds that finance governmental facilities, and qualified private activity bonds in which a state or local government acts as a conduit to provide financing to private business or individuals (Code Secs. 103 and 141).

BACKGROUND

The exclusion may also apply to interest on bonds that are issued to retire an outstanding exempt bond (refunding bonds). There are two types of refunding bonds. A current refunding bond must be redeemed within 90 days of issuance of the refunding bonds. An advance refunding bond is issued more than 90 days before the redemption of the refunded bond. Interest on advance refunding bonds may be exempt only when several requirements are satisfied; for instance, most exempt bonds may be advance refunded only once, exempt advance refunding bonds generally must be called at the earliest redemption date, and the only private activity bonds that may be advance refunded with interest-exempt bonds are qualified 501(c)(3) bonds (Code Sec, 149(d)).

NEW LAW EXPLAINED

Exclusion eliminated for interest on advance refunding bonds.—Interest paid on advance refunding bonds issued after December 31, 2017, is not excludable from gross income (Code Sec. 149(d), as amended by the Tax Cuts and Jobs Act (P.L. 115-97)).

▶ **Effective date.** The amendments apply to advance refunding bonds issued after December 31, 2017 (Act Sec. 13532(c) of the Tax Cuts and Jobs Act (P.L. 115-97)).

Law source: Law at ¶5275 and ¶5280. Committee Report at ¶10,750.

— Act Sec. 13532(a) of the Tax Cuts and Jobs Act (P.L. 115-97), amending Code Sec. 149(d)(1);

— Act Sec. 13532(b), amending Code Secs. 148(f)(4)(C) and 149(d);

— Act Sec. 13532(c), providing the effective date.

¶875 Tax Credit Bonds

SUMMARY OF NEW LAW

New tax credit bonds cannot be issued after December 31, 2017.

BACKGROUND

State and local governments and other entities may issue various kinds of tax credit bonds to finance specific types of projects. Each kind of tax credit bond has its own set of rules regarding volume cap and allocation. The authority to issue some types of tax credit bonds has expired, and the volume cap to issue some of these bonds has been fully used.

A tax credit bond produces a tax credit for a taxpayer who holds the bond on the credit allowance date (Code Sec. 54A). Qualified tax credit bonds include:

• Qualified forestry conservation bonds which governments, local governments, and charitable organizations exempt from tax under Code Sec. 501(c)(3) may be author-

BACKGROUND

ized by the IRS to issue, the proceeds of which must be used to acquire certain land adjacent to U.S. Forest Service Land with restrictions to ensure conservation (Code Sec. 54B);

- Clean renewable energy bonds (Code Sec. 54) and new clean renewable energy bonds (Code Sec. 54C) which public power providers, cooperative electric companies, governmental bodies, clean renewable energy bond lenders, and certain not-for-profit electric utilities may issue, the proceeds of which must be used as capital expenditures incurred for qualified renewable energy facilities;

- Qualified energy conservation bonds which state governments and local governments may issue, the proceeds of which must be used for qualified conservation purposes (Code Sec. 54D);

- Qualified zone academy bonds which certain state and local governments are authorized to issue, the proceeds of which must be used to improve public schools (Code Sec. 54E for bonds issued on or after October 3, 2008, and Code Sec. 1397E for prior bonds);

- Qualified school construction bonds which state and local governments may issue if the proceeds are used to build, rehabilitate, or repair public schools or to purchase land on which to build a school (Code Sec. 54F), and

- Build America bonds which pay interest to the bondholders and also provide a tax credit (Code Sec. 54AA).

During 2009 and 2010, an issuer could elect to issue certain tax credit bonds as "direct-pay bonds." Instead of a credit to the holder, the federal government pays the issuer a percentage of the interest on the bonds. Tax credit bonds for which an issuer could make a direct-pay election include new clean renewable energy bonds, qualified energy conservation bonds, and qualified school construction bonds (Code Sec. 6431).

NEW LAW EXPLAINED

New tax credit bonds cannot be issued after 2017.—Tax credit bond provisions are repealed and new tax credit bonds cannot be issued after December 31, 2017 (Code Secs. 54, 54A, 54B, Code Sec. 54C, 54D, 54E, 54F, 54AA and 6431, stricken by the Tax Cut and Jobs Act of 2017 (P.L. 115-97)).

   Comment: Holders and issuers will continue receiving tax credits and payments for tax credit bonds already issued (House Committee Report for the Tax Cuts and Jobs Act of 2017 (P.L. 115-97) (H.R. Rep. No. 115-409)).

▶ **Effective date.** The amendments made by this section apply to bonds issued after December 31, 2017 (Act Sec. 13404(d) of the Tax Cut and Jobs Act of 2017 (P.L. 115-97)).

Law source: Law at ¶5095, ¶5100, ¶5105, ¶5110, ¶5115, ¶5120, ¶5125, ¶5130, ¶6035, ¶6220, ¶6240, and ¶6250. Committee Reports at ¶10,580, ¶11,000, ¶11,010, ¶11,020, and ¶11,030.

— Act Sec. 13404(a) and (b) of the Tax Cut and Jobs Act of 2017 (P.L. 115-97), striking Code Secs. 54, 54A, 54B, 54C, 54D, 54E, 54F, 54AA and 6431;

NEW LAW EXPLAINED

— Act Sec. 13404(c), providing conforming amendments to Code Secs. 54, 1397E, 6211, and 6401;

— Act Sec. 13404(d), providing the effective date.

TAX PRACTICE AND PROCEDURE

¶880 Time Limits to File Suit and Return Property for Wrongful Levies

SUMMARY OF NEW LAW

The time limit that the IRS has to return monetary proceeds from a wrongfully levied sale of property has been extended to two years from the date of levy. Additionally, the time limit for a taxpayer to bring a civil action for wrongful levy has been extended to two years from the date of the notice of seizure.

BACKGROUND

If a taxpayer fails to pay an assessed tax after notice and demand for payment, the IRS may seek collection of the taxes, including interest and penalties, by levy against all the taxpayer's property (real, personal, tangible, and intangible), including after-acquired property and rights to property (Code Sec. 6321; Reg. § 301.6321-1). Whether the taxpayer owns or has an interest in property is determined under the appropriate state law. Although a tax lien attaches to all of the debtor's property, some property is exempt from levy. Once a tax lien arises, it continues until the tax liability is paid or the lien becomes unenforceable due to a lapse of time (Code Sec. 6322).

A wrongful levy civil suit may be brought in district court by a person other than the taxpayer who owes the taxes, for the return of property believed to be wrongfully levied. This is generally done when the person making the request believes that the levy is wrongful because the property belongs to them, or that they have a security interest with priority over the IRS. The suit must be filed before the expiration of nine months from the date of the notice of seizure or notice of levy is delivered (Code Sec. 6532(c)).

> **Comment:** The IRC distinguishes between a "wrongful levy" and an "erroneous levy." A levy is considered "wrongful" when the IRS improperly attaches a levy to property belonging to a third-party in which the taxpayer has no rights. A levy is considered "erroneous" when the IRS attempts to levy the taxpayer's property (rather than a third-party's property), but violates an administrative procedure or law in the process.

> **Comment:** The nine-month period of time in which to initiate a wrongful levy suit has been held to be a jurisdictional prerequisite and cannot be equitably tolled (*Becton Dickinson and Co. v. Wolckenhauer*, CA-3, 2000-2 USTC ¶ 50,542, 215

BACKGROUND

F3d 340, cert. denied, 531 US 1071). However, one court has held that the statute of limitations should not be enforced when it deprives the taxpayer of due process (*Carter v. United States*, CA-6, 110 FAppx 591, aff'g W.D. Tenn., 2002-2 USTC ¶ 50,493, 216 FSupp 2d 700).

Once it is determined that property has been wrongfully levied, the IRS may return:

- the specific property that was wrongfully levied;

- if money was levied, then the exact amount of money levied; or

- if the property was sold, an amount not exceeding the greater of (1) the proceeds from the sale of the property; or (2) the fair market value of the property immediately before the levy (Code Sec. 6343(b)).

The return of the money or property by the IRS must occur within nine months from the date of levy (Code Sec. 6343(b)).

NEW LAW EXPLAINED

Time Limits for Wrongful Levy Civil Suits and the Return of Property Increased.—The time period for bringing a civil action in district court for wrongfully levied property is extended to two years from the date of levy (Code Sec. 6532(c), as amended by the Tax Cuts and Jobs Act (P.L. 115-97)). Additionally, the time period that the IRS has to return monetary proceeds from the sale of wrongfully levied property is also extended to two years (Code Sec. 6343(b), as amended by the 2017 Tax Cuts Act).

> **Practical Analysis:** William D. Elliott, Partner at Elliott, Thomason & Gibson, LLP in Dallas, Texas, comments that this Act Section extends from nine months to two years the period for filing suit for wrongful levy and for return of sale proceeds from sale of property that has been wrongfully levied upon is a welcome change. Those harmed by a wrongful levy have more time for seeking a remedy.

▶ **Effective date.** The amendments made by this section apply to levies made after December 22, 2017, the date of enactment, and levies made on or before December 22, 2017, if the nine-month period has not expired under Code Secs. 6343(b) (without regard to this section) as of such date (Act Sec. 11071(c) of the Tax Cuts and Jobs Act (P.L. 115-97)).

Law source: Law at ¶6235 and ¶6260. Committee Reports at ¶10,280, ¶11,000, ¶11,010, ¶11,020, and ¶11,030.

— Act Sec. 11071(a) of the Tax Cuts and Jobs Act (P.L. 115-97), amending Code Sec. 6343(b);

— Act Sec. 11071(b), amending Code Sec. 6532(c);

— Act Sec. 11071(c), providing the effective date.

¶880

Taxation of Insurance Companies

¶905 Net Operating Losses for Life Insurance Companies

SUMMARY OF NEW LAW

The operations loss deduction (OLD) for life insurance companies is repealed for losses arising in tax years beginning after December 31, 2017. Instead, life insurance companies are allowed a net operating loss (NOL) deduction.

BACKGROUND

Unlike corporations and other types of insurance companies, life insurance companies cannot claim an NOL deduction under Code Sec. 172. Instead, life insurance companies may claim an operations loss deduction (OLD) (Code Secs. 805(a)(5) and 810). The OLD for a tax year is the total of the operations loss carryovers and carrybacks to that year. The loss from operations for any tax year is the excess of life insurance deductions over life insurance gross income. The OLD cannot exceed a life

BACKGROUND

insurance company's taxable income (LICTI) for the tax year, after applying the company's dividends-received deduction.

Generally, the loss from operations may be carried back three tax years and carried forward 15 years, beginning with the earliest year to which it can be carried. If the company is a new life insurance company for the loss year, the loss may be carried forward 18 years. The company may elect to waive the entire carryback period for a loss. This election must be made by the original or extended due date of the company's return for the tax year of the loss and is permanent.

In determining the limitation on the aggregate amount of a life insurance company's dividends-received deductions under Code Sec. 246, the limit on the aggregate amount of deductions for dividends received from a domestic corporation under Code Sec. 243(a)(1) and for dividends received from a foreign corporation under Code Sec. 245 is based on the applicable percentage of the life insurance company's taxable income computed without regard to the OLD (Code Sec. 805(a)(4)(B)(ii)).

The 10 percent of taxable income limit on a life insurance company's charitable contribution deduction under Code Sec. 170 is determined without regard to the company's operations loss carryback to the tax year (Code Sec. 805(b)(2)(A)(iv)).

Special loss carryforward rules apply if there is a change in a life insurance company's form of organization or nature of its insurance business. The insurance company may carry forward any unused operating loss generated before the change in organization or business (Code Sec. 844). However, the operating loss carryforward cannot be more than the NOLs that would have been generated if the company had been taxed as a nonlife insurance company.

NEW LAW EXPLAINED

Example: In 2016, Pinnacle Corporation is a life insurance company. In the same year, Pinnacle Corporation suffers an operations loss of $150,000. In the following year, 2017, Pinnacle Corporation is a property and casualty insurance company. If Pinnacle had been a property and casualty insurance company in 2016, its NOL would have been $100,000. Pinnacle is eligible to carry over the operations loss to 2017, but only to the extent of $100,000.

Generally, the acquiring corporation in certain tax-free subsidiary liquidations or reorganizations takes limited carryovers of the acquired corporation's tax benefits, privileges, elective rights, and obligations (Code Sec. 381(a)). The manner in which an operation loss carryback or carryover of an acquired life insurance company is handled by an acquiring corporation is governed by the OLD rules (Code Sec. 381(d)).

In the case of a controlled foreign life insurance corporation, "Subpart F income" includes insurance income that is determined without regard to the operations loss deduction (Code Secs. 952(a)(1) and 953(b)(1)(B)).

¶905

NEW LAW EXPLAINED

Special rules limit the tax on the recovery of a foreign expropriation loss by a life insurance company and other corporations to the benefit previously received in deducting the loss (Code Sec. 1351). Foreign expropriation losses are losses sustained by reason of expropriation, intervention, seizure, or similar taking of property by a foreign government. If this provision applies, special adjustments must be made to NOLs, and in the case of a life insurance company, operations losses (Code Sec. 1351(i)(3)).

Operations loss deduction eliminated; NOL deduction allowed.—The operations loss deduction (OLD) for life insurance companies is repealed for losses arising in tax years beginning after December 31, 2017 (Act Secs. 13511(b)(1) and (b)(5) of the Tax Cuts and Jobs Act (P.L. 115-97), striking Code Secs. 810 and 805(a)(5), respectively). Instead, life insurance companies are allowed a net operating loss (NOL) deduction under Code Sec. 172 and are, therefore, subject to the same NOL rules as other corporations and insurance companies (see ¶ 515) (Code Sec. 805(b), as amended by the 2017 Tax Cuts Act). There are numerous references to the OLD of a life insurance company throughout the Code. The new law removes these references and in most cases replaces them with a reference to the NOL deduction.

> **Caution Note:** The repeal of the OLD rules puts the operating losses of life insurance companies on equal footing with other corporations. Thus, the NOL of a life insurance company may not be carried back and may be carried forward indefinitely. Nonlife insurance companies, however, are allowed to carry an NOL back two years and forward 20 years (Code Sec. 172(b)(1)(C), as added by the 2017 Tax Cuts Act). See ¶515 for a detailed discussion of changes made to NOLs.

Taxable income limitation on dividends-received deductions. In determining the limitation on the aggregate amount of a life insurance company's dividends-received deductions under Code Sec. 246, the limit on the aggregate amount of deductions for dividends received from a domestic corporation under Code Sec. 243(a)(1) and for dividends received from a foreign corporation under Code Sec. 245 is based on the applicable percentage of the life insurance company's taxable income computed without regard to the NOL deduction (Code Sec. 805(a)(4)(B)(ii), as amended by the 2017 Tax Cuts Act).

Charitable deduction limitation. The 10 percent of taxable income limit on a life insurance company's charitable contribution deduction is determined without regard to the company's NOL deduction (Code Sec. 805(b)(2)(A)(iv), as amended by the 2017 Tax Cuts Act).

Transition between life insurance status and nonlife insurance status. The rule which allowed a life insurance company that becomes a nonlife insurance company to deduct operations losses from a prior life insurance year as an NOL in a later nonlife insurance year is repealed (Act Sec. 13511(b)(2)(A) of the 2017 Tax Cuts Act, striking Code Sec. 844). The repealed rule also allowed a nonlife insurance company that becomes a life insurance company to deduct the amount of an NOL carryover from a prior nonlife insurance company year as an operations loss in a later life insurance year.

¶905

NEW LAW EXPLAINED

> **Comment:** This rule is no longer necessary since life insurance companies and nonlife insurance companies will both deduct NOLs going forward.

Acquiring corporation's treatment of acquired life insurance corporation's operations losses. The rule that referred to the OLD rules for determining the manner in which an operation loss carryback or carryover of an acquired life insurance company is handled by an acquiring corporation in certain tax-free acquisitive transactions is repealed (Act Sec. 13511(b)(3) of the 2017 Tax Cuts Act, striking Code Sec. 381(d)).

Subpart F income calculation. In determining the Subpart F income of a controlled foreign life insurance corporation, insurance income is determined without regard to the NOL deduction (Code Sec. 953(b)(1)(B), as amended by the 2017 Tax Cuts Act).

Recoveries of foreign expropriation losses. For purposes of the special rules regarding treatment of recoveries of foreign expropriation loss by life insurance companies and other corporations, the requirement for special adjustments to a life insurance company's operations losses is removed to reflect the repeal of the OLD (Code Sec. 1351(i)(3), as amended by the 2017 Tax Cuts Act).

▶ **Effective date.** The amendments made by this section apply to losses arising in tax years beginning after December 31, 2017 (Act Sec. 13511(c) of the Tax Cuts and Jobs Act of 2017 (P.L. 115-97)).

Law source: Law at ¶5665, ¶5685, ¶5715, ¶5735, ¶5875, ¶6010. Committee Report at ¶10,630.

— Act Sec. 13511(a) of the Tax Cuts and Jobs Act (P.L. 115-97), amending Code Sec. 805(b);

— Act Sec. 13511(b), amending Code Secs. 805(a)(4)(B)(ii), 805(b)(2)(A)(iv), 831(b)(3), 953(b)(1)(B), and 1351(i)(3), and striking Code Secs. 381(d), 805(a)(5), 810 and 844;

— Act Sec. 13511(c), providing the effective date.

¶910 Small Life Insurance Company Deduction

SUMMARY OF NEW LAW

The small life insurance company deduction is repealed for tax years beginning after 2017.

BACKGROUND

Life insurance companies may deduct 60 percent of their first $3 million of life insurance-related income (a small life insurance company deduction). The deduction is phased out for companies with income between $3 million and $15 million. The deduction is not available to life insurance companies with assets of at least $500 million (Code Sec. 806).

Transfer of installment obligations to controlled insurance companies. When an installment obligation is disposed of, gain or loss results except in a few types of tax-

BACKGROUND

free exchanges. Nonrecognition of gain treatment is generally denied for otherwise tax-free transfers of installment obligations to life insurance companies. Specifically, the transfer or deemed transfer of an installment obligation to a controlled life insurance company, or to a partnership with a controlled life insurance company as a partner, is subject to the rules requiring taxation on the disposition of installment obligations (Code Sec. 453B(e)(1)). However, the income reportable on the transfer or deemed transfer of the installment obligation is eligible for nonrecognition if the controlled life insurance company elects to determine its life insurance company taxable income using the installment method to report the income received on the obligation. Also, the controlled life insurance company must treat the installment income as income attributable to a noninsurance business (as defined in Code Sec. 806(b)(3) for purposes of the small life insurance company deduction) (Code Sec. 453B(e)(2)).

If a life insurance company was a corporation in the preceding tax year but not a controlled life insurance company, the corporation is treated as having transferred all installment obligations to a controlled life insurance company on the last day of the preceding tax year. Also, when a controlled life insurance company becomes a partner, the partnership is treated as having transferred its installment obligations to a controlled life insurance company on the last day of its preceding tax year (Code Sec. 453B(e)(1)).

NEW LAW EXPLAINED

Small life insurance company deduction repealed.—The small life insurance company deduction is repealed, effective for tax years beginning after December 31, 2017 (Act Sec. 13512(a) of the Tax Cuts and Jobs Act (P.L. 115-97), striking Code Sec. 806).

Other changes. For purposes of the rules regarding transfers of installment obligations to controlled insurance companies, noninsurance business is no longer defined by reference to the repealed small life insurance company deduction (Code Sec. 453B(e)(2)(B), as amended by the 2017 Tax Cuts Act).

Instead, noninsurance business is defined as any activity that is not an insurance business. For this purpose, any activity that is not an insurance business is treated as an insurance business if (i) it is of a type traditionally carried on by life insurance companies for investment purposes, but only if the carrying on of such activity (other than in the case of real estate) does not constitute the active conduct of a trade or business, or (ii) it involves the performance of administrative services in connection with plans providing life insurance, pension, or accident and health benefits (Code Sec. 453B(e)(3), as added by the 2017 Tax Cuts Act).

This definition also applies for purposes of certain special rules concerning life insurance companies in applying the at-risk limitation rules (Code Sec. 465(c)(7)(D)(v)(II), as amended by the 2017 Tax Cuts Act). The new law also removes references to the repealed small life insurance company deduction rules from other provisions.

▶ **Effective date.** The amendments made by this section apply to tax years beginning after December 31, 2017 (Act Sec. 13512(c) of the Tax Cuts and Jobs Act (P.L. 115-97)).

NEW LAW EXPLAINED

Law source: Law at ¶5520, ¶5540, ¶5655, ¶5660, ¶5665, ¶5670, ¶5730, and ¶5875. Committee Report at ¶10,640.

— Act Sec. 13512(a) of the Tax Cuts and Jobs Act (P.L. 115-97), striking Code Sec. 806;

— Act Sec. 13512(b), amending Code Secs. 453B(e), 465(c)(7)(D)(v)(II), 804, 805(a)(4)(B), 805(b)(2)(A), 842(c), and 953(b)(1), and striking Code Sec. 801(a)(2)(C);

— Act Sec. 13512(c), providing the effective date.

¶915 Computation of Life Insurance Company Reserves

SUMMARY OF NEW LAW

For tax years beginning after 2017, life insurance reserves for a contract are determined as the greater of the net surrender value or 92.81-percent of the statutory reserve. For existing contracts, the difference in reserve amounts under the old and new methods is taken into account as a deduction or income over an eight-year period. Income or loss resulting from a change in the basis for determining life insurance reserves is treated as adjustments attributable to a change in the method of accounting.

BACKGROUND

Life insurance companies include any net decrease in reserves in income and deduct any net increase in reserves (Code Sec. 807(a) and (b)). Six items that are either reserves or similar to reserves must be taken into account in determining whether reserves have had a net increase or a net decrease. Among other items, amounts that are discounted at an appropriate rate of interest and that are necessary to satisfy obligations arising under insurance or annuity contracts that did not involve life, accident, or health contingencies when the discount was computed, are taken into account. For this purpose, the appropriate rate of interest for any obligation is the highest of the following rates as of the time the obligation first did not involve life, accident, or health contingencies: (i) the applicable federal interest rate under Code Sec. 807(d)(2)(B)(i), (ii) the prevailing state assumed interest rate under Code Sec. 807(d)(2)(B)(ii), or (iii) the rate of interest assumed by the company in determining the guaranteed benefit (Code Sec. 807(c)).

For purposes of determining life insurance company taxable income, the life insurance reserves for any contract are the greater of either: (1) the net surrender value of the contract, or (2) a reserve amount determined by using a set formula (Code Sec. 807(d)). However, in no event can the amount of the reserves exceed the amount that would be taken into account with respect to the contract in determining statutory reserves (Code Sec. 807(d)(1)).

BACKGROUND

The "net surrender value" is the cash surrender value reduced by any surrender penalty, but any market value adjustment required on surrender is not taken into account (Code Sec. 807(e)).

Under the second alternative, the "reserve amount" for any contract is determined by using: (1) the tax reserve method applicable to the contract, (2) the greater of the applicable federal interest rate or the prevailing state assumed interest rate, and (3) the prevailing commissioners' standard tables for mortality or morbidity (Code Sec. 807(d)(2)).

Generally, the tax reserve method is the applicable National Association of Insurance Commissioners (NAIC) method in effect at the time the contract is issued (Code Sec. 807(d)(3)).

In general, Code Sec. 481 adjustments that are required as a result of an accounting method change are taken into account over four tax years for a positive adjustment and in the year of change for a negative adjustment (Code Sec. 446(e); Rev. Proc. 2015-13, 2015-5 I.R.B. 419). For a life insurance company that changes its method of computing reserves, income or loss resulting from the change is taken into account over a 10-year period (Code Sec. 807(f)).

Life insurance contract definition. For purposes of the Code, a life insurance contract is defined as any contract that qualifies as a life insurance contract under applicable state or foreign law and meets either: (1) the cash value accumulation test, or (2) the guideline premium or cash value corridor test (Code Sec. 7702(a)). A contract meets the guideline premium limitation requirement if the sum of the premiums paid under the contract does not at any time exceed the greater of: (1) the guideline single premium, or (2) the sum of the guideline level premiums to such date (Code Sec. 7702(c)(2)).

The guideline single premium for any contract is the premium required to fund future benefits under the contract (Code Sec. 7702(c)(3)(A)). The computation of the guideline single premium must take into account: (1) the mortality charge specified in the contract or such charges used in determining the statutory reserves for the contract if none is specified therein, (2) any other charges specified in the contract (either for expenses or supplemental benefits), and (3) interest at the greater of a six-percent annual effective rate or the rate or rates guaranteed on the issuance of the contract (Code Sec. 7702(c)(3)(B)).

Discounted unpaid losses. Before a deduction for loss reserves can be claimed, unpaid losses must be discounted in order to account for the time value of money (Code Sec. 846(a)). The deduction is basically limited to the amount of discounted unpaid losses. In the case of unpaid losses relating to disability insurance, other than credit disability insurance, the rules that apply to the treatment of noncancellable accident and health insurance contracts apply, with the following adjustments: (1) the company may use its own experience relating to mortality and morbidity, (2) the prevailing state-assumed interest rate to be used is the rate in effect for the year in which the loss occurred rather than the year in which the contract was issued, and (3) the rule limiting the amount of discounted losses to more than the aggregate amount of unpaid losses as reflected on the company's NAIC (National Association of Insurance Commissioners) annual statement applies (Code Sec. 846(f)(6)).

NEW LAW EXPLAINED

Computation of life insurance tax reserves revised.—For tax years beginning after December 31, 2017, life insurance reserves for any contract are generally determined as the greater of: (1) the net surrender value of the contract, or (2) 92.81-percent of the reserve computed under the tax reserve method prescribed by the National Association of Insurance Commissioners (NAIC) that covers the contract as of the date the reserve is determined (Code Sec. 807(d)(1)(A) and (d)(2), as added by the Tax Cuts and Jobs Act (P.L. 115-97), and Code Sec. 807(d)(3), as amended by the 2017 Tax Cuts Act).

For a variable contract, the amount of life insurance reserves for a contract equals the sum of: (1) the greater of the net surrender value of the contract, or the portion of the reserve that is separately accounted for under Code Sec. 817, plus (2) 92.81-percent of the excess of the reserve determined using the tax reserve method over the amount in (1) (Code Sec. 807(d)(1)(B), as added by the 2017 Tax Cuts Act).

A statutory cap applies, providing that the amount of the reserves cannot exceed the amount that would be taken into account with respect to the contract in determining statutory reserves (Code Sec. 807(d)(1)(C), as added by the 2017 Tax Cuts Act). In addition, in determining any reserve under Subchapter L (Insurance Companies), no amount or item can be taken into account more than once (Code Sec. 807(d)(1)(D), as added by the 2017 Tax Cuts Act).

For purposes of determining amounts that are discounted at an appropriate rate of interest and that are necessary to satisfy obligations arising under insurance or annuity contracts that did not involve life, accident, or health contingencies when the discount was computed, the appropriate rate of interest is the highest rate or rates permitted to be used to discount the obligations by the National Association of Insurance Commissioners as of the date the reserve is determined (Code Sec. 807(c), as amended by the 2017 Tax Cuts Act).

The rule providing that, in the case of a group contract, the date on which such contract is issued is the date as of which the master plan is issued (or, with respect to a benefit guaranteed to a participant after such date, the date as of which such benefit is guaranteed) is eliminated. Also eliminated is the provision for the treatment of substandard risks (Act Sec. 13517(a)(3)(A) of the 2017 Tax Cuts Act, striking Code Sec. 807(e)(2) and (5)).

In addition, the amount of the life insurance reserve for any qualified supplemental benefit is computed separately as though such benefit were under a separate contract. Supplemental benefits are any (i) guaranteed insurability, (ii) accidental death or disability benefit, (iii) convertibility, (iv) disability waiver benefit, or (v) other benefit prescribed by regulations, which is supplemental to a contract for which there is a reserve described in Code Sec. 807(c). Qualified supplemental benefit means any supplemental benefit if (i) there is a separately identified premium or charge for such benefit, and (ii) any net surrender value under the contract attributable to any other benefit is not available to fund such benefit (Code Sec. 807(e)(2), as redesignated and amended by the 2017 Tax Cuts Act).

¶915

NEW LAW EXPLAINED

The Secretary will require reporting (at the time and in the manner as the Secretary will prescribe) with respect to the opening balance and closing balance of reserves and also the method of computing reserves for purposes of determining income (Code Sec. 807(e)(6), as added by the 2017 Tax Cuts Act).

Life insurance contract definition. For purposes of the life insurance contract definition, the first item taken into account in computing the guideline single premium is reasonable mortality charges which meet the requirements prescribed in regulations to be promulgated by the Secretary or that do not exceed the mortality charges specified in the prevailing commissioners' standard tables (Code Sec. 7702(c)(3)(B)(i), as amended by the 2017 Tax Cuts Act).

For this purpose, prevailing commissioners' standard tables are the most recent commissioners' standard tables prescribed by the National Association of Insurance Commissioners which are permitted to be used in computing reserves for that type of contract under the insurance laws of at least 26 States when the contract was issued. If the prevailing commissioners' standard tables as of the beginning of any calendar year (the year of change) are different from the prevailing commissioners' standard tables as of the beginning of the preceding calendar year, the issuer may use the prevailing commissioners' standard tables as of the beginning of the preceding calendar year with respect to any contract issued after the change and before the close of the three-year period beginning on the first day of the year of change (Code Sec. 7702(f), as added by the 2017 Tax Cuts Act).

Prevailing state assumed interest rate. For purposes of Subchapter L, a prevailing state assumed interest rate is, with respect to any contract, the highest assumed interest rate permitted to be used in computing life insurance reserves for insurance contracts or annuity contracts (as the case may be) under the insurance laws of at least 26 states. For purposes of the preceding sentence, the effect of nonforfeiture laws of a state on interest rates for reserves is not taken into account. The prevailing state assumed interest rate with respect to any contract is determined as of the beginning of the calendar year in which the contract was issued (Code Sec. 808(g), as added by the 2017 Tax Cuts Act).

Other changes. To determine the amount of interest payments on a contract that has to be included in a life insurance company's reserves for the contract, interest to be paid or credited under an interest rate that is the interest rate in effect under Code Sec. 808(g), and that is guaranteed beyond the end of the tax year for which the reserves are being computed, has to be included in the reserves as if the higher interest rate were guaranteed only until the end of the tax year (Code Sec. 811(d), as amended by the 2017 Tax Cuts Act).

In the case of unpaid losses relating to disability insurance, other than credit disability insurance, the rules that apply to the treatment of noncancellable accident and health insurance contracts apply and the company may use its own experience relating to mortality and morbidity, except that the rule limiting the amount of discounted losses to more than the aggregate amount of unpaid losses as reflected on the company's NAIC

NEW LAW EXPLAINED

(National Association of Insurance Commissioners) annual statement applies (Code Sec. 846(f)(6), as amended by the 2017 Tax Cuts Act).

For purposes of determining foreign base company income, the special rules for income derived in the active conduct of insurance business, and in particular, the rules for determining the reserve amount are modified to clarify that the highest assumed interest rate permitted to be used in determining foreign statement reserves will apply (Code Sec. 954(i)(5)(B), as amended by the 2017 Tax Cuts Act).

Change in method of computing reserves treated as change in accounting method.—The special 10-year spread provision for a life insurance company that changes its method of computing reserves is eliminated. Instead, for a life insurance company that changes its method of computing reserves, income or loss resulting from the change is taken into account under Code Sec. 481 (i.e., with a one-year or four-year adjustment period), as an adjustment attributable to a change in the method of accounting. The change is treated as initiated by the taxpayer and made with the IRS's consent (Code Sec. 807(f)(1), as amended by the 2017 Tax Cuts Act).

▶ **Effective date.** The amendments made by this section apply to tax years beginning after December 31, 2017 (Act Secs. 13513(b) and 13517(c)(1) of the Tax Cuts and Jobs Act of 2017 (P.L. 115-97)).

Transition rule. For the first tax year beginning after December 31, 2017, the reserve with respect to any contract, determined under Code Sec. 807(d), at the end of the preceding tax year is determined as if the amendments made by Act Sec. 13517 of the 2017 Tax Cuts Act had applied to the reserve in the preceding tax year (Act Sec. 13517(c)(2) of the 2017 Tax Cuts Act).

Transition relief. If (i) the reserve determined under Code Sec. 807(d) (after the application of the preceding sentence) with respect to any contract as of the close of the year preceding the first tax year beginning after December 31, 2017, differs from (ii) the reserve that would have been determined with respect to that contract as of the close of that tax year under Code Sec. 807(d), determined without regard to the application of the first sentence, then the difference between the amount of the reserve described in (i) and the amount of the reserve described in (ii) is taken into account under the method provided in this transitional relief. Under this method, if the amount determined under (i) exceeds the amount determined under (ii), 1/18 of the excess is taken into account, for each of the eight succeeding tax years, as a deduction under Code Sec. 805(a)(2) or Code Sec. 832(c)(4), as applicable. If the amount determined under (ii) exceeds the amount determined under (i), 1/8 of the excess is included in gross income, for each of the eight succeeding tax years, under Code Sec. 803(a)(2) or Code Sec. 832(b)(1)(C), as applicable (Act S 13517(c)(3) of the 2017 Tax Cuts Act).

Law source: Law at ¶5675, ¶5680, ¶5690, ¶5740, ¶5750, ¶5880, and ¶6345. Committee Reports at ¶10,650 and ¶10,690.

— Act Sec. 13513(a) of the Tax Cuts and Jobs Act (P.L. 115-97), amending Code Sec. 807(f)(1);

— Act Sec. 13517(a), amending Code Secs. 807(c), 807(d), 807(e), and 7702(c)(3)(B), and adding Code Sec. 7702(f)(10);

¶915

NEW LAW EXPLAINED

— Act Sec. 13517(b), adding Code Sec. 808(g) and amending Code Secs. 811(d)(1), 846(f)(6)(A), 848(e)(1)(B)(iii), and 954(i)(5)(B);

— Act Secs. 13513(b) and 13517(c), providing the effective date.

¶920 Life Insurance Proration Rules for Determining Dividends Received Deduction

SUMMARY OF NEW LAW

For purposes of the life insurance company proration rules for reducing dividends received deductions and reserve deductions with respect to untaxed income, a company's share is 70 percent and a policyholder's share is 30 percent.

BACKGROUND

When calculating a life insurance company's taxable income, the company is subject to proration rules. The proration rules require a life insurance company to reduce its deductions, including dividends received deductions and reserve deductions with respect to untaxed income, in order to account for the portion of dividends and tax-exempt interest used to fund tax-deductible reserves for obligations to policyholders.

Specifically, under the proration rules, the net increase and net decrease in reserves are computed by reducing the ending balance of the reserve items by the policyholders' share of tax-exempt interest (Code Secs. 807(a)(2)(B) and (b)(1)(B)). Similarly, under the proration rules, a life insurance company is allowed a dividends received deduction for intercorporate dividends from non-affiliates only in proportion to the company's share of such dividends, but not for the policyholders' share (Code Secs. 805(a)(4) and 812).

The term "company's share" means the percentage that is obtained by dividing the company's share of net investment income by the net investment income for the tax year (Code Sec. 812(a)(1)). It is generally defined as: (i) the policy interest, for the tax year, plus (ii) the gross investment income's proportionate share of policyholder dividends for the tax year (Code Sec. 812(b)(1)).

Net investment income is defined as 90 percent of gross investment income, or 95 percent of gross investment income in the case of assets held in segregated asset accounts under variable contracts (Code Sec. 812(c)).

The policyholders' share of investment income is the excess of 100 percent of an item over the percentage determined under the formula contained within the definition of the company's share (Code Sec. 812(a)(2)).

NEW LAW EXPLAINED

Life insurance proration rules for reducing deductions modified.—For purposes of the life insurance company proration rules for reducing deductions, including divi-

NEW LAW EXPLAINED

dends received deductions and reserve deductions with respect to untaxed income, the company's share is 70 percent and the policyholder's share is 30 percent (Code Sec. 812, as amended by the Tax Cuts and Jobs Act of 2017 (P.L. 115-97)).

▶ **Effective date.** The amendments made by this section apply to tax years beginning after December 31, 2017 (Act Sec. 13518(c) of the Tax Cuts and Jobs Act of 2017 (P.L. 115-97)).

Law source: Law at ¶5695 and ¶5710. Committee Report at ¶10,700.

— Act Sec. 13518(a) of the Tax Cuts and Jobs Act of 2017 (P.L. 115-97), amending Code Sec. 812;

— Act Sec. 13518(b), amending Code Sec. 817A(e)(2);

— Act Sec. 13518(c), providing the effective date.

¶925 Proration Rule for Property and Casualty Insurance Companies

SUMMARY OF NEW LAW

For tax years beginning after 2017, the proration rule for reduction of losses incurred by property and casualty insurance companies is modified to replace the 15 percent reduction with a reduction equal to 5.25 percent divided by the top corporate income tax rate.

BACKGROUND

Property and casualty insurance companies are generally taxed each year on their taxable income at the same rate as corporations (Code Sec. 831). The taxable income of a property and casualty insurance company is determined as gross income less deductions. Gross income includes income from investment income, underwriting income, as well as gains and other income items. Deductions include, among other items, certain losses incurred during the tax year on insurance contracts (Code Sec. 832).

Under a proration rule, a property and casualty insurance company must reduce the amount of losses incurred by 15 percent of:

- tax-exempt interest received during the year;

- the deductible portion of dividends received during the year (with special rules for dividends from affiliates); and

- the increase for the tax year in policy cash values of life insurance policies and annuity and endowment contracts the company owns (Code Sec. 832(b)(5)(B)).

NEW LAW EXPLAINED

Proration rule for reduction of losses modified.—Effective for tax years beginning after 2017, the proration rule for reduction of losses incurred by property and casualty insurance companies is modified to replace the 15 percent reduction with a reduction equal to 5.25 percent divided by the highest corporate income tax rate under Code Sec. 11(b) (Code Sec. 832(b)(5)(B), as amended by the Tax Cuts and Jobs Act (P.L. 115-97)).

> **Comment:** The top corporate tax rate is 21 percent for tax years beginning after 2017, so the percentage reduction is 25 percent under the modified proration rule. See ¶305 for a discussion of the new corporate income tax rate.

▶ **Effective date.** The amendments made by this section apply to tax years beginning after December 31, 2017 (Act Sec. 13515(b) of the Tax Cuts and Jobs Act (P.L. 115-97)).

Law source: Law at ¶5720. Committee Report at ¶10,670.

— Act Sec. 13515(a) of the Tax Cuts and Jobs Act (P.L. 115-97), amending Code Sec. 832(b)(5)(B);

— Act Sec. 13515(b), providing the effective date.

¶930 Discounting Rules for Property and Casualty Insurance Companies

SUMMARY OF NEW LAW

The rate of interest used to discount unpaid losses is changed to a rate based on the corporate bond yield curve using a 60-month period. In addition, the period for determining loss payment patterns is extended for certain lines of business. Lastly, the election to use a taxpayer's own historical loss payment pattern for all lines of business is repealed and all taxpayers will now use an aggregate industry-experience based loss payment pattern.

BACKGROUND

When calculating "underwriting income," property and casualty insurance companies are allowed a deduction for losses incurred during the tax year on insurance contracts (Code Sec. 832(b)(5) and (c)(4)). The deduction is basically limited to the amount of discounted unpaid losses. The unpaid losses must be discounted in order to account for the time value of money. The amount of discounted unpaid losses at the end of any tax year is the sum of the present value of the unpaid losses in each line of business, in each accident year (Code Sec. 846(a)(1)). The amount is determined by using:

(1) the gross amount to be subjected to discounting (the undiscounted unpaid losses),

BACKGROUND

(2) the pattern of payment of claims, including the duration in years over which the claims will be paid (see below), and

(3) the rate of interest to be assumed in calculating the discounted reserve (Code Sec. 846(a)(2)).

The IRS develops a loss payment pattern for each line of business for each determination year. The pattern is derived from the historical loss payment pattern that is applicable to the line of business and applies to accident years ending with, or within, the determination year and each of the four succeeding years (Code Sec. 846(d)). The loss payment pattern for any line of business is based on the assumption that all losses are paid during the accident year, and the following three years, or in certain cases during the accident year and the 10 calendar years following the accident. There are also special rules for certain long-tail, international and reinsurance lines of business.

A company may also elect to apply the general loss discounting rules by reference to its own most recent historical loss payment pattern (Code Sec. 846(e)). If the election is made, the company should use its most recent experience as reported on its NAIC (National Association of Insurance Commissioners) annual statement. For each of the five years in the determination period, the company's most recent experience is to be used. The interest rate used to discount losses is the annual rate determined by the Secretary of the Treasury equal to the average of the applicable federal mid-term rates.

NEW LAW EXPLAINED

Discounting rules modified.—Interest rate used to discount unpaid losses. For tax years beginning after December 31, 2017, the interest rate used to discount unpaid losses is the annual rate determined by the Secretary of the Treasury based on the corporate bond yield curve as defined in Code Sec. 430(h)(2)(D)(i), but determined using a 60-month period instead of a 24-month period (Code Sec. 846(c)(2), as amended by the Tax Cuts and Jobs Act (P.L. 115-97).

> **Comment:** The "corporate bond yield curve" reflects the average of monthly yields on investment grade corporate bonds that are in the top three rating levels.

Computational rules for loss payment patterns. For tax years beginning after December 31, 2017, the period for determining certain loss payment patterns is extended and the additional five-year period for long-tail lines of business, and special rules for international and reinsurance lines of business are removed. There are two loss payment patterns—a 10-year loss payment pattern that applies to auto liability, other liability, medical malpractice, workers' compensation and multiple peril lines of business and a general three-year loss payment pattern that applies to all other lines of business (Code Sec. 846(d)(3), as amended by the 2017 Tax Cuts Act).

Under the three-year loss pattern, losses paid after the first year following the accident year are treated as paid equally in the second and third year following the accident year (Code Sec. 846(d)(3)(B)(i), as amended by the 2017 Tax Cuts Act).

¶930

NEW LAW EXPLAINED

There is a 14-year extension available to 10-year lines of business. The amount of the losses that were previously paid in the 10th year following an accident year, are treated as paid in the 10th year and each subsequent year in an amount equal to the average of the amounts paid in the seventh, eighth and ninth years (or, if lesser, the portion of the unpaid losses not taken into account). To the extent these unpaid losses have not been treated as paid before the 24th year after the accident year, they are treated as paid in that 24th year (Code Sec. 846(d)(3)(B)(ii), as amended by the 2017 Tax Cuts Act).

Repeal of historical payment pattern election. The election permitting a taxpayer to use its own historical loss payment pattern for all its lines of business is repealed. All taxpayers will now use an aggregate industry-experience based loss payment pattern (Act Sec. 13523(c) of the 2017 Tax Cuts Act, striking Code Sec. 846(e)).

Transitional rule. For the first tax year beginning after December 31, 2017, (i) the unpaid losses and expenses unpaid (as defined in Code Sec. 832(b)(5)(B) and (b)(6)) at the end of the preceding tax year, and (ii) the unpaid losses as defined in Code Secs. 807(c)(2) and 805(a)(1) at the end of the preceding tax year, will be determined as if the above amendments to Code Sec. 846 had applied to the unpaid losses and expenses unpaid in the preceding tax year. In addition, such unpaid losses and expenses unpaid will be determined by using the interest rate and loss payment pattern applicable to accident years ending with calendar year 2018, and any adjustment will be taken into account ratably in the first tax year beginning after December 31, 2017, and the seven succeeding tax years. For subsequent ax years, the amendments to Code Sec. 846 will be applied with respect to such unpaid losses and expenses unpaid by using the interest rate and loss payment patterns applicable to accident years ending with calendar year 2018 (Act Sec. 13523(e) of the 2017 Tax Cuts Act).

▶ **Effective date.** The amendments made by this section apply to tax years beginning after December 31, 2017 (Act Sec. 13523(d) of the Tax Cuts and Jobs Act (P.L. 115-97)).

Law source: Law at ¶5740. Committee Report at ¶10,730.

— Act Sec. 13523(a) of the Tax Cuts and Jobs Act (P.L. 115-97), amending Code Sec. 846(c)(2);

— Act Sec. 13523(b), amending Code Sec. 846(d)(3);

— Act Sec. 13523(c), amending Code Sec. 846;

— Act Sec. 13523(d), providing the effective date;

— Act Sec. 13523(e).

¶935 Capitalization of Certain Policy Acquisition Expenses of Insurance Companies

SUMMARY OF NEW LAW

The required time period for capitalization and amortization of specified policy acquisition expenses for insurance companies is increased from a 120-month period to a 180-month period. In addition, the percentage of net premiums used for determining general deductions treated as specified premium costs for a tax year after 2017 are increased to: (i) 2.09 percent for annuity contracts; (ii) 2.45 percent for group life insurance contracts; and (iii) 9.2 percent for all other specified insurance contracts.

BACKGROUND

A portion of the policy acquisition expenses that life insurance, casualty and property insurance companies may claim (referred to as "specified policy acquisition expenses") must be capitalized and amortized over a 120-month period beginning with the first month in the second half of the tax year (Code Sec. 848(a)). A special rule provides for a 60-month amortization of the first $5 million of specified policy acquisition expenses, with a phase-out. The phase-out reduces the amount amortized over 60 months by the excess of the insurance company's specified policy acquisition expenses for the taxable year over $10 million (Code Sec. 848(b)).

The specified policy acquisition expenses are equal to a portion of the insurance company's general deductions for a tax year. The amount of general deductions treated as specified policy acquisition expenses is equal to the sum of the applicable percentages of an insurance company's net premiums for the year from the three following classes of insurance contracts (Code Sec. 848(c)): (i) 1.75 percent for annuity contracts; (ii) 2.05 percent for group life insurance contracts; and (iii) 7.7 percent for all other specified insurance contracts.

NEW LAW EXPLAINED

Amortization period for specified policy acquisition expenses extended; applicable percentages of net premiums increased. —The amortization period for specified policy acquisition expenses is extended from a 120-month period to a 180-month period beginning with the first month in the second half of the tax year (Code Sec. 848(a)(2), as amended by the Tax Cuts and Jobs Act (P.L. 115-97)).

> **Comment:** The special rule providing for 60-month amortization of the first $5 million of specified policy acquisition expenses, with a phase out, is not changed (Code Sec. 848(b)).

The percentages of net premiums used to determine the amount of general deductions that are treated as specified policy acquisition costs are increased as follows:

- from 1.75 percent to 2.09 percent for annuity contracts;
- from 2.05 percent to 2.45 percent for group life insurance contracts; and

NEW LAW EXPLAINED

- from 7.7 percent to 9.2 percent for all other specified insurance contracts (Code Sec. 848(c), as amended by the 2017 Tax Cuts Act).

▶ **Effective date.** The amendments made by this section apply to net premiums for tax years beginning after December 31, 2017 (Act Sec. 13519(c)(1)) of the Tax Cuts and Jobs Act (P.L. 115-97)). Specified policy acquisition expenses first required to be capitalized in a tax year beginning before January 1, 2018, will continue to be allowed as a deduction ratably over the 120-month period beginning with the first month in the second half of such tax year (Act Sec. 13519(c)(2)) of the 2017 Tax Cuts Act).

Law source: Law at ¶5750. Committee Report at ¶10,710.

— Act Sec. 13519(a)(1) of the Tax Cuts and Jobs Act of 2017 (P.L. 115-97), amending Code Sec. 848(a)(2);

— Act Sec. 13519(a)(2)–(4), amending Code Sec. 848(c);

— Act Sec. 13519(b), amending Code Sec. 848(b)(1);

— Act Sec. 13519(c), providing the effective date.

¶940 Pre-1984 Policyholder Surplus Accounts

SUMMARY OF NEW LAW

Life insurance companies with pre-1984 operating income held in policyholder surplus accounts may no longer defer tax on this income until it is distributed to shareholders. For each of the eight tax years beginning after December 31, 2017, 1/8th of the remaining balance in a pre-1984 policyholder surplus account is treated as distributed and must be added to the life insurance company's taxable income for the year. The life insurance company's taxable income may not be less than zero.

BACKGROUND

Since the enactment of the Deficit Reduction Act of 1984 (P.L. 98-369), stock life insurance companies have not been allowed to add deferred income to policyholder surplus accounts. Amounts that previously were deferred into these accounts are generally subject to tax at the corporate rate when the amounts are treated as distributed to shareholders or subtracted from the policyholder surplus accounts (Code Sec. 815).

From 1959 through 1983, a life insurance company was subject to a three-phase taxable income computation.

- A company was taxed on the lesser of its gain from operations or its taxable investment income (Phase I) and, if gain from operations exceeded its taxable investment income, 50 percent of the excess (Phase II).

- The federal income tax on the other 50 percent of the gain from operations was deferred and was accounted for as part of a policyholder's surplus account. It was

BACKGROUND

generally taxed only when distributed to stockholders or upon corporate dissolution (Phase III).

To determine whether amounts had been distributed, a company maintained a shareholders surplus account, which generally included the company's previously taxed income that would be available for distribution to shareholders. Distributions to shareholders were treated as being, first, out of the shareholders surplus account, then out of the policyholders surplus account, and, finally, out of other accounts.

This three-phase tax system was eliminated by the Deficit Reduction Act, but life insurance companies continued to be permitted to defer the pre-1984 operating income held in their policyholder surplus accounts until the income was treated as distributed to policyholders or there was a corporate dissolution.

> **Comment:** The income tax on distributions to shareholders from policyholder surplus accounts was suspended during tax years beginning after December 31, 2004, and before January 1, 2007. In those years, distribution were treated as first made out of the policyholders surplus account, then out of the shareholders surplus accounts and then out of other accounts.

NEW LAW EXPLAINED

Special rules for distributions to shareholders from pre-1984 policy holders surplus accounts repealed.—The special rules for distributions to shareholders from pre-1984 policy holders surplus accounts are repealed, applicable to tax years beginning after December 31, 2017 (Act Sec. 13514(a) of the Tax Cuts and Jobs Act (P.L. 115-97), striking Code Sec. 815).

A stock life insurance company that has a balance (determined as of the close of the company's last tax year beginning before January 1, 2018) in an existing policyholder surplus account (as defined in Code Sec. 815 prior to its repeal) must include the balance in income over eight years. The tax imposed by Code Sec. 801 for the first eight tax years beginning after December 31, 2017, is e amount that would be imposed for that year on the sum of:

- life insurance taxable income for the year (within the meaning of Code Sec. 801, but not less than zero); plus
- 1/8th of the policyholder surplus account balance (Act Sec. 13514(d) of the 2017 Tax Cuts Act).

> **Comment:** Because taxable income for the tax year cannot be less than zero, life insurance company losses are not allowed to offset the amount of the policyholders surplus account balance subject to tax.

▶ **Effective date.** The amendments made by this section apply to tax years beginning after December 31, 2017 (Act Sec. 13514(c) of the Tax Cuts and Jobs Act (P.L. 115-97)).

Law source: Law at ¶5655 and ¶5705. Committee Report at ¶10,660.

— Act Sec. 13514(a) of the Tax Cuts and Jobs Act (P.L. 115-97), striking Code Sec. 815;

— Act Sec. 13514(b), striking Code Sec. 801(c);

NEW LAW EXPLAINED

— Act Sec. 13514(c), providing the effective date;

— Act Sec. 13514(d).

¶945 Reporting of Certain Life Insurance Contract Transactions

SUMMARY OF NEW LAW

Reporting requirements are imposed on persons acquiring life insurance contracts in reportable policy sales and on persons making payments of reportable death benefits. Issuers of life insurance contracts must also report the seller's basis in such contracts. In addition, the exceptions to the transfer for value rules do not apply to transfers of life insurance contracts that are reportable policy sales. Lastly, the method of determining the tax basis in a life insurance contract is clarified.

BACKGROUND

Amounts received under a life insurance contract paid by reason of the death of the insured are excluded from the recipient's income (Code Sec. 101(a)).

Under the transfer for value rules, if a life insurance contract is sold or otherwise transferred for valuable consideration, the amount paid by reason of the death of the insured that is excludable generally is limited (Code Sec. 101(a)(2)). Under the limitation, the excludable amount may not exceed the sum of (1) the actual value of the consideration, and (2) the premiums or other amounts subsequently paid by the transferee of the contract. So, for example, if a person buys a life insurance contract, and the consideration paid combined with subsequent premium payments on the contract are less than the amount of the death benefit the person later receives under the contract, then the difference is includable in the buyer's income.

There are two exceptions to the transfer for value rules. First, the rules do not apply in the case of a transfer if the contract or interest therein has a basis for determining gain or loss in the hands of a transferee determined in whole or in part by reference to such basis of such contract or interest therein in the hands of the transferor (Code Sec. 101(a)(2)(A)). Second, they do not apply if the transfer is to the insured, to a partner of the insured, to a partnership in which the insured is a partner, or to a corporation in which the insured is a shareholder or officer (Code Sec. 101(a)(2)(B)).

In Rev. Rul. 2009-14, the IRS ruled that a portion of the death benefit received by a buyer of a life insurance contract on the death of the insured is includable as ordinary income. The portion is the excess of the death benefit over the consideration and other amounts (e.g., premiums) paid for the contract. Upon sale of the contract by the purchaser of the contract, the gain is long-term capital gain, and in determining the gain, the basis of the contract is not reduced by the cost of insurance.

NEW LAW EXPLAINED

Reporting requirements provided for certain life insurance contract transactions.—New reporting requirements apply for acquisitions of life insurance contacts in reportable policy sales occurring after December 31, 2017, and for the payment of reportable death benefits after December 31, 2017 (Code Sec. 6050Y, as added by the Tax Cuts and Jobs Act (P.L. 115-97)).

For transfers after December 31, 2017, the exceptions to the transfer for value rules (Code Sec. 101(a)(2)(A) and (B)) do not apply to a transfer of a life insurance contract, or any interest in such a contract, that is a reportable policy sale (Code Sec. 101(a)(3)(A), as added by the 2017 Tax Cuts Act).

> **Comment:** Thus, some portion of the death benefit ultimately payable under such a contract may be includable in income (Conference Report on H.R. 1, Tax Cuts and Jobs Act (H. Rept. 115-466).

A "reportable policy sale" means the acquisition of an interest in a life insurance contract, directly or indirectly, if the acquirer has no substantial family, business, or financial relationship with the insured apart from the acquirer's interest in the life insurance contract. An indirect acquisition for these purposes would include acquisition of an interest in a partnership, trust, or other entity that holds an interest in the life insurance contract (Code Secs. 101(a)(3)(B) and 6050Y(d)(2), as added by the 2017 Tax Cuts Act).

In addition, the method of determining the tax basis in a life insurance contract is clarified (Code Sec. 1016(a)(1), as amended by the 2017 Tax Cuts Act).

Reporting by persons acquiring life insurance contracts. Any person who acquires a life insurance contract or any interest in a life insurance contract in a reportable policy sale during a tax year must make a return for the tax year (at the time and in the manner as the Secretary of the Treasury shall prescribe) setting forth:

- the name, address, and TIN of the person,
- the name, address, and TIN of each recipient of payment in the reportable policy sale,
- the date of the sale,
- the name of the issuer of the life insurance contract sold and the policy number of the contract, and
- the amount of each payment (Code Sec. 6050Y(a)(1), as added by the 2017 Tax Cuts Act).

Anyone required to make the return must furnish to each person named in the return a written statement showing:

- the name, address, and phone number of the information contact of the person required to make the return, and
- the information required to be shown on the return with respect to such person (except that in the case of an issuer of a life insurance contract, the statement is not required to include the amount of each payment) (Code Sec. 6050Y(a)(2), as added by the 2017 Tax Cuts Act).

¶945

NEW LAW EXPLAINED

For purposes of the reporting rules, a "payment" means the amount of cash and the fair market value of any consideration transferred in any reportable policy sale (Code Sec. 6050Y(d)(1), as added by the 2017 Tax Cuts Act). An "issuer" is any life insurance company that bears the risk with respect to a life insurance contract on the date of any required return or statement (Code Sec. 6050Y(d)(3), as added by the 2017 Tax Cuts Act).

Reporting by issuers of the seller's basis in life insurance contracts. Upon receipt of the written statement required under Code Sec. 6050Y(a)(2), or upon notice of a transfer of a life insurance contract to a foreign person, each issuer of a life insurance contract must make a return (at the time and in the manner as the Secretary shall prescribe) setting forth:

- the name, address, and TIN of the seller who transfers any interest in the contract in the sale,
- the investment in the contract (defined in Code Sec. 72(e)(6)) with respect to the seller, and
- the policy number of the contract (Code Sec. 6050Y(b)(1), as added by the 2017 Tax Cuts Act).

Every person required to make a return reporting the seller's basis must furnish to each person whose name is required to be set forth in the return a written statement showing:

- the name, address, and phone number of the information contact of the person required to make the return, and
- the information required to be shown on the return with respect to each seller whose name is required to be set forth in the return (Code Sec. 6050Y(b)(2), as added by the 2017 Tax Cuts Act).

In determining the basis of a life insurance or annuity contract, no adjustment is made for mortality, expense, or other reasonable charges incurred under the contract (Code Sec. 1016(a)(1), as amended by the 2017 Tax Cuts Act).

> **Caution:** This clarification to the method of determining the tax basis in a life insurance or annuity contract applies retroactively to transactions entered into after August 25, 2009 (Act Sec. 13521(b) of the 2017 Tax Cuts Act).

> **Comment:** This change reverses the position of the IRS in Rev. Rul. 2009-13 that on sale of a cash value life insurance contract, the insured's (seller's) basis is reduced by the cost of insurance for mortality, expense, or other reasonable charges incurred under an annuity or life insurance contract.

Reporting by persons making payments of reportable death benefits. Every person who makes a payment of reportable death benefits during any tax year must make a return for the tax year (at the time and in the manner as the Secretary shall prescribe) setting forth:

- the name, address, and TIN of the person making the payment,
- the name, address, and TIN of each recipient of the payment,
- the date of each payment,

NEW LAW EXPLAINED

- the gross amount of each payment, and
- the person's estimate of the investment in the contract (as defined in Code Sec. 72(e)(6)) with respect to the buyer) (Code Sec. 6050Y(c)(1), as added by the 2017 Tax Cuts Act).

Every person required to make a return reporting the payment of death benefits must furnish to each person named in the return a written statement showing:

- the name, address, and phone number of the information contact of the person required to make the return, and
- the information required to be shown on the return with respect to each recipient of payment whose name is required to be set forth in the return (Code Sec. 6050Y(c)(2), as added by the 2017 Tax Cuts Act).

A "reportable death benefit" is any amount paid by reason of the death of the insured under a life insurance contract that has been transferred in a reportable policy sale (Code Sec. 6050Y(d)(4), as added by the 2017 Tax Cuts Act).

Other changes. The rules under Code Sec. 6047 regarding information returns required to be filed by trustees and insurance companies with respect to plans covering self-employed individuals do not apply to any information that is required to be reported under Code Sec. 6050Y (Code Sec. 6047(g), as added by the 2017 Tax Cuts Act). Conforming changes reflecting the new reporting requirements are also made to the special rules under Code Sec. 6724 regarding information return penalties (Code Sec. 6724(d), as amended by the 2017 Tax Cuts Act).

▶ **Effective date.** The reporting provisions apply to reportable policy sales after December 31, 2017, and reportable death benefits paid after December 31, 2017 (Act Sec. 13520(d) of the Tax Cuts and Jobs Act (P.L. 115-97)). The tax basis clarification provision applies to transactions entered into after August 25, 2009 (Act Sec. 13521(b) of the 2017 Tax Cuts Act). The provision regarding the exception to the transfer for value rules applies to transfers after December 31, 2017 (Act Sec. 13522(c) of the 2017 Tax Cuts Act).

Law source: Law at ¶5215, ¶5940, ¶6200, ¶6210, and ¶6315. Committee Report at ¶10,720.

— Act Sec. 13520(a) of the Tax Cuts and Jobs Act (P.L. 115-97), adding Code Sec. 6050Y;

— Act Sec. 13520(c), amending Code Secs. 6047 and 6724(d);

— Act Sec. 13521(a), amending Code Sec. 1016(a)(1);

— Act Secs. 13522(a) and (b), amending Code Sec. 101(a);

— Act Secs. 13520(d), 13521(b), and 13522(c), providing the effective date.

¶950 Special Estimated Tax Payments for Insurance Companies

SUMMARY OF NEW LAW

The special estimated tax payment rules for insurance companies required to discount unpaid losses are repealed for tax years beginning after 2017.

¶950

BACKGROUND

Insurance companies that are required to discount unpaid losses are allowed to claim an additional deduction up to the excess of: (a) the undiscounted unpaid losses, over (b) related discounted unpaid losses. The deduction must be reduced by any amount that was claimed in a preceding year (Code Sec. 847(1)).

The additional deduction may be claimed only if estimated tax payments covering the amount of the tax benefit generated by the deduction have been made (Code Sec. 847(2)), and a company has established a special loss discount account to which it contributes an amount covering the deduction (Code Sec. 847(3)). Unused special estimated tax payments may be used as a regular estimated tax payment (under Code Sec. 6655) in the 16th year after the year for which a special estimated tax payment was made (Code Sec. 847(2)).

Special estimated tax payments may not be equated with a company's regular estimated tax payments under Code Sec. 6655. That is, they are not a component of regular estimated tax liability. Penalties or interest imposed on an underpayment of regular estimated tax liability do not apply to special estimated taxes. Also, the additional loss deduction is not a factor in the computation of regular estimated taxes. However, companies that overpay regular estimated taxes may use the over-payment to meet a special estimated tax payment liability.

As losses are paid, a corresponding subtraction must be made from the special loss discount account and included in a company's gross income (Code Sec. 847(5)). The balance of the special loss account of a company that liquidates or otherwise termi-nates its insurance business must be included in its income if the company does not transfer its assets to another corporation that may carry over the company's tax items. Companies that have not been subject to taxation in any tax year must include the preceding year's balance in gross income. Special estimated tax payments may be applied against any additional tax liability that arises out of an income inclusion, and unused payments are voided (Code Sec. 847(6)).

The earnings and profits of an insurance company are not to be reduced by the additional deduction for unreversed discount or increased by inclusions required due to reductions to the special loss discount account (Code Sec. 847(9)).

NEW LAW EXPLAINED

Special estimated tax payment rules for insurance companies repealed.—For tax years beginning after December 31, 2017, the special estimated tax payment rules for insurance companies required to discount unpaid losses are repealed (Act Sec. 13516(a) of the Tax Cuts and Jobs Act (P.L. 115-97), striking Code Sec. 847). Therefore, the election to apply Code Sec. 847, the additional deduction, the special loss discount account, the special estimated tax payment, and the refundable amount rules are all eliminated.

> **Comment:** The entire balance of an existing account is included in income of the taxpayer for the first tax year beginning after 2017, and the entire amount of existing special estimated tax payments are applied against the amount of additional tax attributable to this inclusion. Any special estimated tax payments

NEW LAW EXPLAINED

in excess of this amount are treated as estimated tax payments under Code Sec. 6655 (Conference Report on H.R. 1, Tax Cuts and Jobs Act (H. Rept. 115-466)).

▶ **Effective date.** The amendments made by this section apply to tax years beginning after December 31, 2017 (Act Sec. 13516(b) of the Tax Cuts and Jobs Act (P.L. 115-97)).

Law source: Law at ¶5745. Committee Report at ¶10,680.

— Act Sec. 13516(a) of the Tax Cuts and Jobs Act (P.L. 115-97), striking Code Sec. 847;

— Act Sec. 13516(b), providing the effective date.

Code Sections Added, Amended Or Repealed

[¶ 5001]

INTRODUCTION.

The Internal Revenue Code provisions amended by and Act to provide for reconciliation pursuant to titles II and V of the concurrent resolution on the budget for fiscal year 2018 [Tax Cuts and Jobs Act] (P.L. 115-97) are shown in the following paragraphs. Deleted Code material or the text of the Code Section prior to amendment appears in the amendment notes following each amended Code provision. *Any changed or added material is set out in italics.*

[¶ 5005] CODE SEC. 1. TAX IMPOSED.

* * *

(f) Phaseout of Marriage Penalty in 15-Percent Bracket; Adjustments in Tax Tables so that Inflation Will Not Result in Tax Increases.—

* * *

(2) Method of prescribing tables.—The table which under paragraph (1) is to apply in lieu of the table contained in subsection (a), (b), (c), (d), or (e), as the case may be, with respect to taxable years beginning in any calendar year shall be prescribed—

(A) except as provided in paragraph (8), by increasing the minimum and maximum dollar amounts for each bracket for which a tax is imposed under such table by the cost-of-living adjustment for such calendar year, determined—

(i) except as provided in clause (ii), by substituting "1992" for "2016" in paragraph (3)(A)(ii), and

(ii) in the case of adjustments to the dollar amounts at which the 36 percent rate bracket begins or at which the 39.6 percent rate bracket begins, by substituting "1993" for "2016" in paragraph (3)(A)(ii),

* * *

(3) Cost-of-living adjustment.—For purposes of this subsection—

(A) In general.—The cost-of-living adjustment for any calendar year is the percentage (if any) by which—

(i) the C-CPI-U for the preceding calendar year, exceeds

(ii) the CPI for calendar year 2016, multiplied by the amount determined under subparagraph (B).

(B) Amount determined.—The amount determined under this clause is the amount obtained by dividing—

(i) the C-CPI-U for calendar year 2016, by

(ii) the CPI for calendar year 2016.

(C) Special rule for adjustments with a base year after 2016.—For purposes of any provision of this title which provides for the substitution of a year after 2016 for "2016" in subparagraph (A)(ii), subparagraph (A) shall be applied by substituting "the C-CPI-U for calendar year 2016" for "the CPI for calendar year 2016" and all that follows in clause (ii) thereof.

* * *

(6) *C-CPI-U.—For purposes of this subsection—*

(A) IN GENERAL.—*The term "C-CPI-U" means the Chained Consumer Price Index for All Urban Consumers (as published by the Bureau of Labor Statistics of the Department of Labor). The values of the Chained Consumer Price Index for All Urban Consumers taken into account for purposes of determining the cost-of-living adjustment for any calendar year under this subsection shall be the latest values so published as of the date on which such Bureau publishes the initial value of the Chained Consumer Price Index for All Urban Consumers for the month of August for the preceding calendar year.*

(B) DETERMINATION FOR CALENDAR YEAR.—*The C-CPI-U for any calendar year is the average of the C-CPI-U as of the close of the 12-month period ending on August 31 of such calendar year.*

(7) ROUNDING.—

(A) IN GENERAL.—If any increase determined under paragraph (2)(A), section 63(c)(4), section 68(b)(2) or section 151(d)(4) is not a multiple of $50, such increase shall be rounded to the next lowest multiple of $50.

(B) TABLE FOR MARRIED INDIVIDUALS FILING SEPARATELY.—In the case of a married individual filing a separate return, subparagraph (A) (other than with respect to sections 63(c)(4) and 151(d)(4)(A)) shall be applied by substituting "$25" for "$50" each place it appears.

* * *

[CCH Explanation at ¶ 125. Committee Reports at ¶ 10,020.]

Amendments

• **2017, Tax Cuts and Jobs Act (P.L. 115-97)**

P.L. 115-97, § 11002(a):

Amended Code Sec. 1(f) by striking paragraph (3) and by inserting after paragraph (2) a new paragraph (3). **Effective** for tax years beginning after 12-31-2017. Prior to being stricken, Code Sec. 1(f)(3) read as follows:

(3) COST-OF-LIVING ADJUSTMENT.—For purposes of paragraph (2), the cost-of-living adjustment for any calendar year is the percentage (if any) by which—

(A) the CPI for the preceding calendar year, exceeds

(B) the CPI for calendar year 1992.

P.L. 115-97, § 11002(b):

Amended Code Sec. 1(f) by striking paragraph (7), by redesignating paragraph (6) as paragraph (7), and by inserting after paragraph (5) a new paragraph (6). **Effective**

for tax years beginning after 12-31-2017. Prior to being stricken, Code Sec. 1(f)(7) read as follows:

(7) SPECIAL RULE FOR CERTAIN BRACKETS.—In prescribing tables under paragraph (1) which apply to taxable years beginning in a calendar year after 1994, the cost-of-living adjustment used in making adjustments to the dollar amounts at which the 36 percent rate bracket begins or at which the 39.6 percent rate bracket begins shall be determined under paragraph (3) by substituting "1993" for "1992".

P.L. 115-97, § 11002(c)(1):

Amended Code Sec. 1(f)(2)(A). **Effective** for tax years beginning after 12-31-2017. Prior to amendment, Code Sec. 1(f)(2)(A) read as follows:

(A) except as provided in paragraph (8), by increasing the minimum and maximum dollar amounts for each rate bracket for which a tax is imposed under such table by the cost-of-living adjustment for such calendar year,

(h) MAXIMUM CAPITAL GAINS RATE.—

* * *

(11) DIVIDENDS TAXED AS NET CAPITAL GAIN.—

* * *

(C) QUALIFIED FOREIGN CORPORATIONS.—

* * *

(iii) EXCLUSION OF DIVIDENDS OF CERTAIN FOREIGN CORPORATIONS.—*Such term shall not include—*

(I) *any foreign corporation* which for the taxable year of the corporation in which the dividend was paid, or the preceding taxable year, is a passive foreign investment company (as defined in section 1297), *and*

(II) *any corporation which first becomes a surrogate foreign corporation (as defined in section 7874(a)(2)(B)) after the date of the enactment of this subclause, other than a foreign corporation which is treated as a domestic corporation under section 7874(b).*

* * *

[CCH Explanation at ¶ 765. Committee Reports at ¶ 11,160.]

Amendments

• **2017, Tax Cuts and Jobs Act (P.L. 115-97)**

P.L. 115-97, § 14223(a)(1)-(3):

Amended Code Sec. 1(h)(11)(C)(iii) by striking "shall not include any foreign corporation" and inserting "shall not include—

"(I) any foreign corporation",

by striking the period at the end and inserting ", and", and by adding at the end new subclause (II). **Effective** for dividends received after 12-22-2017.

(i) RATE REDUCTIONS AFTER 2000.—

(1) 10-PERCENT RATE BRACKET.—

* * *

(C) INFLATION ADJUSTMENT.—In prescribing the tables under subsection (f) which apply with respect to taxable years beginning in calendar years after 2003—

(i) the cost-of-living adjustment shall be determined under subsection (f)(3) by substituting "2002" for "2016" in subparagraph (A)(ii) thereof, and

(ii) the adjustments under clause (i) shall not apply to the amount referred to in subparagraph (B)(iii).

If any amount after adjustment under the preceding sentence is not a multiple of $50, such amount shall be rounded to the next lowest multiple of $50.

* * *

(3) MODIFICATIONS TO INCOME TAX BRACKETS FOR HIGH-INCOME TAXPAYERS.—

* * *

(C) INFLATION ADJUSTMENT.—For purposes of this paragraph, with respect to taxable years beginning in calendar years after 2013, each of the dollar amounts under clauses (i), (ii), and (iii) of subparagraph (B) shall be adjusted in the same manner as under paragraph (1)(C)(i), except that *subsection (f)(3)(A)(ii) shall be applied by substituting "2012" for "2016".*

* * *

[CCH Explanation at ¶ 125. Committee Reports at ¶ 10,020.]

Amendments

• **2017, Tax Cuts and Jobs Act (P.L. 115-97)**

P.L. 115-97, § 11002(c)(2)(A)-(B):

Amended Code Sec. 1(i) by striking "for '1992' in subparagraph (B)" in paragraph (1)(C) and inserting "for '2016' in

subparagraph (A)(ii)", and by striking "subsection (f)(3)(B) shall be applied by substituting '2012' for '1992'" in paragraph (3)(C) and inserting "subsection (f)(3)(A)(ii) shall be applied by substituting '2012' for '2016'". **Effective** for tax years beginning after 12-31-2017.

(j) MODIFICATIONS FOR TAXABLE YEARS 2018 THROUGH 2025.—

(1) IN GENERAL.—In the case of a taxable year beginning after December 31, 2017, and before January 1, 2026—

(A) subsection (i) shall not apply, and

(B) this section (other than subsection (i)) shall be applied as provided in paragraphs (2) through (6).

(2) RATE TABLES.—

(A) MARRIED INDIVIDUALS FILING JOINT RETURNS AND SURVIVING SPOUSES.—The following table shall be applied in lieu of the table contained in subsection (a):

If taxable income is:	The tax is:
Not over $19,050	10% of taxable income.
Over $19,050 but not over $77,400	$1,905, plus 12% of the excess over $19,050.

If taxable income is:	The tax is:
Over $77,400 but not over $165,000	$8,907, plus 22% of the excess over $77,400.
Over $165,000 but not over $315,000	$28,179, plus 24% of the excess over $165,000.
Over $315,000 but not over $400,000	$64,179, plus 32% of the excess over $315,000.
Over $400,000 but not over $600,000	$91,379, plus 35% of the excess over $400,000.
Over $600,000	$161,379 plus 37% of the excess over $600,000.

(B) HEADS OF HOUSEHOLDS.—*The following table shall be applied in lieu of the table contained in subsection (b):*

If taxable income is:	The tax is:
Not over $13,600	10% of taxable income.
Over $13,600 but not over $51,800	$1,360, plus 12% of the excess over $13,600.
Over $51,800 but not over $82,500	$5,944, plus 22% of the excess over $51,800.
Over $82,500 but not over $157,500	$12,698, plus 24% of the excess over $82,500.
Over $157,500 but not over $200,000	$30,698, plus 32% of the excess over $157,500.
Over $200,000 but not over $500,000	$44,298, plus 35% of the excess over $200,000.
Over $500,000	$149,298, plus 37% of the excess over $500,000.

(C) UNMARRIED INDIVIDUALS OTHER THAN SURVIVING SPOUSES AND HEADS OF HOUSEHOLDS.—*The following table shall be applied in lieu of the table contained in subsection (c):*

If taxable income is:	The tax is:
Not over $9,525	10% of taxable income.
Over $9,525 but not over $38,700	$952.50, plus 12% of the excess over $9,525.
Over $38,700 but not over $82,500	$4,453.50, plus 22% of the excess over $38,700.
Over $82,500 but not over $157,500	$14,089.50, plus 24% of the excess over $82,500.
Over $157,500 but not over $200,000	$32,089.50, plus 32% of the excess over $157,500.
Over $200,000 but not over $500,000	$45,689.50, plus 35% of the excess over $200,000.
Over $500,000	$150,689.50, plus 37% of the excess over $500,000.

(D) MARRIED INDIVIDUALS FILING SEPARATE RETURNS.—*The following table shall be applied in lieu of the table contained in subsection (d):*

If taxable income is:	The tax is:
Not over $9,525	10% of taxable income.
Over $9,525 but not over $38,700	$952.50, plus 12% of the excess over $9,525.
Over $38,700 but not over $82,500	$4,453.50, plus 22% of the excess over $38,700.
Over $82,500 but not over $157,500	$14,089.50, plus 24% of the excess over $82,500.
Over $157,500 but not over $200,000	$32,089.50, plus 32% of the excess over $157,500.
Over $200,000 but not over $300,000	$45,689.50, plus 35% of the excess over $200,000.
Over $300,000	$80,689.50, plus 37% of the excess over $300,000.

(E) ESTATES AND TRUSTS.—*The following table shall be applied in lieu of the table contained in subsection (e):*

If taxable income is:	The tax is:
Not over $2,550	10% of taxable income.
Over $2,550 but not over $9,150	$255, plus 24% of the excess over $2,550.
Over $9,150 but not over $12,500	$1,839, plus 35% of the excess over $9,150.
Over $12,500	$3,011.50, plus 37% of the excess over $12,500.

(F) REFERENCES TO RATE TABLES.—*Any reference in this title to a rate of tax under subsection (c) shall be treated as a reference to the corresponding rate bracket under subparagraph (C) of this paragraph, except that the reference in section 3402(q)(1) to the third lowest rate of tax applicable* under subsection (c) shall be treated as a reference to the fourth lowest rate of tax under subparagraph (C).

(3) ADJUSTMENTS.—

(A) NO ADJUSTMENT IN 2018.—The tables contained in paragraph (2) shall apply without adjustment for taxable years beginning after December 31, 2017, and before January 1, 2019.

(B) SUBSEQUENT YEARS.—For taxable years beginning after December 31, 2018, the Secretary shall prescribe tables which shall apply in lieu of the tables contained in paragraph (2) in the same manner as under paragraphs (1) and (2) of subsection (f) (applied without regard to clauses (i) and (ii) of subsection (f)(2)(A)), except that in prescribing such tables—

(i) subsection (f)(3) shall be applied by substituting "calendar year 2017" for "calendar year 2016" in subparagraph (A)(ii) thereof,

(ii) subsection (f)(7)(B) shall apply to any unmarried individual other than a surviving spouse or head of household, and

(iii) subsection (f)(8) shall not apply.

(4) SPECIAL RULES FOR CERTAIN CHILDREN WITH UNEARNED INCOME.—

(A) IN GENERAL.—In the case of a child to whom subsection (g) applies for the taxable year, the rules of subparagraphs (B) and (C) shall apply in lieu of the rule under subsection (g)(1).

(B) MODIFICATIONS TO APPLICABLE RATE BRACKETS.—In determining the amount of tax imposed by this section for the taxable year on a child described in subparagraph (A), the income tax table otherwise applicable under this subsection to the child shall be applied with the following modifications:

(i) 24-PERCENT BRACKET.—The maximum taxable income which is taxed at a rate below 24 percent shall not be more than the sum of—

(I) the earned taxable income of such child, plus

(II) the minimum taxable income for the 24-percent bracket in the table under paragraph (2)(E) (as adjusted under paragraph (3)) for the taxable year.

(ii) 35-PERCENT BRACKET.—The maximum taxable income which is taxed at a rate below 35 percent shall not be more than the sum of—

(I) the earned taxable income of such child, plus

(II) the minimum taxable income for the 35-percent bracket in the table under paragraph (2)(E) (as adjusted under paragraph (3)) for the taxable year.

(iii) 37-PERCENT BRACKET.—The maximum taxable income which is taxed at a rate below 37 percent shall not be more than the sum of—

(I) the earned taxable income of such child, plus

(II) the minimum taxable income for the 37-percent bracket in the table under paragraph (2)(E) (as adjusted under paragraph (3)) for the taxable year.

(C) COORDINATION WITH CAPITAL GAINS RATES.—For purposes of applying section 1(h) (after the modifications under paragraph (5)(A))—

(i) the maximum zero rate amount shall not be more than the sum of—

(I) the earned taxable income of such child, plus

(II) the amount in effect under paragraph (5)(B)(i)(IV) for the taxable year, and

(ii) the maximum 15-percent rate amount shall not be more than the sum of—

(I) the earned taxable income of such child, plus

(II) the amount in effect under paragraph (5)(B)(ii)(IV) for the taxable year.

(D) EARNED TAXABLE INCOME.—For purposes of this paragraph, the term "earned taxable income" means, with respect to any child for any taxable year, the taxable income of such child *reduced (but not below zero) by the net unearned income (as defined in subsection (g)(4)) of such child.*

(5) APPLICATION OF CURRENT INCOME TAX BRACKETS TO CAPITAL GAINS BRACKETS.—

(A) IN GENERAL.—*Section 1(h)(1) shall be applied—*

(i) *by substituting "below the maximum zero rate amount" for "which would (without regard to this paragraph) be taxed at a rate below 25 percent" in subparagraph (B)(i), and*

(ii) *by substituting "below the maximum 15-percent rate amount" for "which would (without regard to this paragraph) be taxed at a rate below 39.6 percent" in subparagraph (C)(ii)(I).*

(B) MAXIMUM AMOUNTS DEFINED.—*For purposes of applying section 1(h) with the modifications described in subparagraph (A)—*

(i) MAXIMUM ZERO RATE AMOUNT.—*The maximum zero rate amount shall be—*

(I) *in the case of a joint return or surviving spouse, $77,200,*

(II) *in the case of an individual who is a head of household (as defined in section 2(b)), $51,700,*

(III) *in the case of any other individual (other than an estate or trust), an amount equal to ½ of the amount in effect for the taxable year under subclause (I), and*

(IV) *in the case of an estate or trust, $2,600.*

(ii) MAXIMUM 15-PERCENT RATE AMOUNT.—*The maximum 15-percent rate amount shall be—*

(I) *in the case of a joint return or surviving spouse, $479,000 (½ such amount in the case of a married individual filing a separate return),*

(II) *in the case of an individual who is the head of a household (as defined in section 2(b)), $452,400,*

(III) *in the case of any other individual (other than an estate or trust), $425,800, and*

(IV) *in the case of an estate or trust, $12,700.*

(C) INFLATION ADJUSTMENT.—*In the case of any taxable year beginning after 2018, each of the dollar amounts in clauses (i) and (ii) of subparagraph (B) shall be increased by an amount equal to—*

(i) *such dollar amount, multiplied by*

(ii) *the cost-of-living adjustment determined under subsection (f)(3) for the calendar year in which the taxable year begins, determined by substituting "calendar year 2017" for "calendar year 2016" in subparagraph (A)(ii) thereof.*

If any increase under this subparagraph is not a multiple of $50, such increase shall be rounded to the next lowest multiple of $50.

(6) SECTION 15 NOT TO APPLY.—*Section 15 shall not apply to any change in a rate of tax by reason of this subsection.*

[CCH Explanation at ¶ 105. Committee Reports at ¶ 10,010.]
Amendments
• 2017, Tax Cuts and Jobs Act (P.L. 115-97)

P.L. 115-97, § 11001(a):

Amended Code Sec. 1 by adding at the end a new subsection (j). **Effective** for tax years beginning after 12-31-2017.

[¶ 5010]   CODE SEC. 11.   TAX IMPOSED.

* * *

(b) AMOUNT OF TAX.—*The amount of the tax imposed by subsection (a) shall be 21 percent of taxable income.*

* * *

[CCH Explanation at ¶ 305. Committee Reports at ¶ 10,310.]

Amendments

• **2017, Tax Cuts and Jobs Act (P.L. 115-97)**

P.L. 115-97, § 13001(a):

Amended Code Sec. 11(b). **Effective** for tax years beginning after 12-31-2017. For a special rule, see Act Sec. 13001(d), below. Prior to amendment, Code Sec. 11(b) read as follows:

(b) AMOUNT OF TAX.—

(1) IN GENERAL.—The amount of the tax imposed by subsection (a) shall be the sum of—

(A) 15 percent of so much of the taxable income as does not exceed $50,000,

(B) 25 percent of so much of the taxable income as exceeds $50,000 but does not exceed $75,000,

(C) 34 percent of so much of the taxable income as exceeds $75,000 but does not exceed $10,000,000, and

(D) 35 percent of so much of the taxable income as exceeds $10,000,000.

In the case of a corporation which has taxable income in excess of $100,000 for any taxable year, the amount of tax determined under the preceding sentence for such taxable year shall be increased by the lesser of (i) 5 percent of such excess, or (ii) $11,750. In the case of a corporation which has taxable income in excess of $15,000,000, the amount of the tax determined under the foregoing provisions of this paragraph shall be increased by an additional amount equal to the lesser of (i) 3 percent of such excess, or (ii) $100,000.

(2) CERTAIN PERSONAL SERVICE CORPORATIONS NOT ELIGIBLE FOR GRADUATED RATES.—Notwithstanding paragraph (1), the amount of the tax imposed by subsection (a) on the taxable income of a qualified personal service corporation (as defined in section 448(d)(2)) shall be equal to 35 percent of the taxable income.

P.L. 115-97, § 13001(d), provides:

(d) NORMALIZATION REQUIREMENTS.—

(1) IN GENERAL.—A normalization method of accounting shall not be treated as being used with respect to any public utility property for purposes of section 167 or 168 of the Internal Revenue Code of 1986 if the taxpayer, in computing its cost of service for ratemaking purposes and reflecting operating results in its regulated books of account, reduces the excess tax reserve more rapidly or to a greater extent than such reserve would be reduced under the average rate assumption method.

(2) ALTERNATIVE METHOD FOR CERTAIN TAX-PAYERS.—If, as of the first day of the taxable year that includes the date of enactment of this Act—

(A) the taxpayer was required by a regulatory agency to compute depreciation for public utility property on the basis of an average life or composite rate method, and

(B) the taxpayer's books and underlying records did not contain the vintage account data necessary to apply the average rate assumption method,

the taxpayer will be treated as using a normalization method of accounting if, with respect to such jurisdiction, the taxpayer uses the alternative method for public utility property that is subject to the regulatory authority of that jurisdiction.

(3) DEFINITIONS.—For purposes of this subsection—

(A) EXCESS TAX RESERVE.—The term "excess tax reserve" means the excess of—

(i) the reserve for deferred taxes (as described in section 168(i)(9)(A)(ii) of the Internal Revenue Code of 1986) as of the day before the corporate rate reductions provided in the amendments made by this section take effect, over

(ii) the amount which would be the balance in such reserve if the amount of such reserve were determined by assuming that the corporate rate reductions provided in this Act were in effect for all prior periods.

(B) AVERAGE RATE ASSUMPTION METHOD.—The average rate assumption method is the method under which the excess in the reserve for deferred taxes is reduced over the remaining lives of the property as used in its regulated books of account which gave rise to the reserve for deferred taxes. Under such method, during the time period in which the timing differences for the property reverse, the amount of the adjustment to the reserve for the deferred taxes is calculated by multiplying—

(i) the ratio of the aggregate deferred taxes for the property to the aggregate timing differences for the property as of the beginning of the period in question, by

(ii) the amount of the timing differences which reverse during such period.

(C) ALTERNATIVE METHOD.—The "alternative method" is the method in which the taxpayer—

(i) computes the excess tax reserve on all public utility property included in the plant account on the basis of the weighted average life or composite rate used to compute depreciation for regulatory purposes, and

(ii) reduces the excess tax reserve ratably over the remaining regulatory life of the property.

(4) TAX INCREASED FOR NORMALIZATION VIOLATION.—If, for any taxable year ending after the date of the enactment of this Act, the taxpayer does not use a normalization method of accounting for the corporate rate reductions provided in the amendments made by this section—

(A) the taxpayer's tax for the taxable year shall be increased by the amount by which it reduces its excess tax reserve more rapidly than permitted under a normalization method of accounting, and

(B) such taxpayer shall not be treated as using a normalization method of accounting for purposes of subsections (f)(2) and (i)(9)(C) of section 168 of the Internal Revenue Code of 1986.

(d) FOREIGN CORPORATIONS.—In the case of a foreign corporation, *the tax imposed by subsection (a)* shall apply only as provided by section 882.

[CCH Explanation at ¶310. Committee Reports at ¶10,300.]

Amendments

• 2017, Tax Cuts and Jobs Act (P.L. 115-97)

P.L. 115-97, §12001(b)(11):

Amended Code Sec. 11(d) by striking "the taxes imposed by subsection (a) and section 55" and inserting "the tax

imposed by subsection (a)". **Effective** for tax years beginning after 12-31-2017.

[¶5015] CODE SEC. 12. CROSS REFERENCES RELATING TO TAX ON CORPORATIONS.

* * *

(4) For rate of withholding in case of foreign corporations, see section 1442.

* * *

(6) *[Stricken.]*

(7) *[Stricken.]*

* * *

[CCH Explanation at ¶305 and ¶310. Committee Reports at ¶10,300 and ¶10,310.]

Amendments

• 2017, Tax Cuts and Jobs Act (P.L. 115-97)

P.L. 115-97, §12001(b)(12):

Amended Code Sec. 12 by striking paragraph (7). **Effective** for tax years beginning after 12-31-2017. Prior to being stricken, Code Sec. 12(7) read as follows:

(7) For alternative minimum tax, see section 55.

P.L. 115-97, §13001(b)(2)(B):

Amended Code Sec. 12 by striking paragraphs (4) and (6), and by redesignating paragraph (5) as paragraph (4). **Effec-**

tive for tax years beginning after 12-31-2017. Prior to being stricken, Code Sec. 12(4) and (6) read as follows:

(4) For alternative tax in case of capital gains, see section 1201(a).

* * *

(6) For limitation on benefits of graduated rate schedule provided in section 11(b), see section 1551.

[¶5020] CODE SEC. 23. ADOPTION EXPENSES.

* * *

(h) ADJUSTMENTS FOR INFLATION.—In the case of a taxable year beginning after December 31, 2002, each of the dollar amounts in subsection (a)(3) and paragraphs (1) and (2)(A)(i) of subsection (b) shall be increased by an amount equal to—

(1) such dollar amount, multiplied by

(2) the cost-of-living adjustment determined under section 1(f)(3) for the calendar year in which the taxable year begins, determined by substituting "calendar year 2001" *for "calendar year 2016" in subparagraph (A)(ii)* thereof.

If any amount as increased under the preceding sentence is not a multiple of $10, such amount shall be rounded to the nearest multiple of $10.

* * *

[CCH Explanation at ¶125. Committee Reports at ¶10,020.]

Amendments

• 2017, Tax Cuts and Jobs Act (P.L. 115-97)

P.L. 115-97, §11002(d)(1)(A):

Amended Code Sec. 23(h)(2) by striking "for 'calendar year 1992' in subparagraph (B)" and inserting "for 'calendar

year 2016' in subparagraph (A)(ii)". **Effective** for tax years beginning after 12-31-2017.

[¶5025] CODE SEC. 24. CHILD TAX CREDIT.

* * *

(h) SPECIAL RULES FOR TAXABLE YEARS 2018 THROUGH 2025.—

(1) IN GENERAL.—In the case of a taxable year beginning after December 31, 2017, and before January 1, 2026, this section shall be applied as provided in paragraphs (2) through (7).

(2) CREDIT AMOUNT.—Subsection (a) shall be applied by substituting "$2,000" for "$1,000".

(3) LIMITATION.—In lieu of the amount determined under subsection (b)(2), the threshold amount shall be $400,000 in the case of a joint return ($200,000 in any other case).

(4) PARTIAL CREDIT ALLOWED FOR CERTAIN OTHER DEPENDENTS.—

(A) IN GENERAL.—The credit determined under subsection (a) (after the application of paragraph (2)) shall be increased by $500 for each dependent of the taxpayer (as defined in section 152) other than a qualifying child described in subsection (c).

(B) EXCEPTION FOR CERTAIN NONCITIZENS.—Subparagraph (A) shall not apply with respect to any individual who would not be a dependent if subparagraph (A) of section 152(b)(3) were applied without regard to all that follows "resident of the United States".

(C) CERTAIN QUALIFYING CHILDREN.—In the case of any qualifying child with respect to whom a credit is not allowed under this section by reason of paragraph (7), such child shall be treated as a dependent to whom subparagraph (A) applies.

(5) MAXIMUM AMOUNT OF REFUNDABLE CREDIT.—

(A) IN GENERAL.—The amount determined under subsection (d)(1)(A) with respect to any qualifying child shall not exceed $1,400, and such subsection shall be applied without regard to paragraph (4) of this subsection.

(B) ADJUSTMENT FOR INFLATION.—In the case of a taxable year beginning after 2018, the $1,400 amount in subparagraph (A) shall be increased by an amount equal to—

(i) such dollar amount, multiplied by

(ii) the cost-of-living adjustment determined under section 1(f)(3) for the calendar year in which the taxable year begins, determined by substituting "2017" for "2016" in subparagraph (A)(ii) thereof.

If any increase under this clause is not a multiple of $100, such increase shall be rounded to the next lowest multiple of $100.

(6) EARNED INCOME THRESHOLD FOR REFUNDABLE CREDIT.—Subsection (d)(1)(B)(i) shall be applied by substituting "$2,500" for "$3,000".

(7) SOCIAL SECURITY NUMBER REQUIRED.—No credit shall be allowed under this section to a taxpayer with respect to any qualifying child unless the taxpayer includes the social security number of such child on the return of tax for the taxable year. For purposes of the preceding sentence, the term "social security number" means a social security number issued to an individual by the Social Security Administration, but only if the social security number is issued—

(A) to a citizen of the United States or pursuant to subclause (I) (or that portion of subclause (III) that relates to subclause (I)) of section 205(c)(2)(B)(i) of the Social Security Act, and

(B) before the due date for such return.

[CCH Explanation at ¶280. Committee Reports at ¶10,070.]

Amendments

• **2017, Tax Cuts and Jobs Act (P.L. 115-97)**

P.L. 115-97, §11022(a):

Amended Code Sec. 24 by adding at the end a new subsection (h). **Effective** for tax years beginning after 12-31-2017.

[¶ 5030] CODE SEC. 25A. HOPE AND LIFETIME LEARNING CREDITS.

* * *

(h) INFLATION ADJUSTMENTS.—

(1) DOLLAR LIMITATION ON AMOUNT OF CREDIT.—

(A) IN GENERAL.—In the case of a taxable year beginning after 2001, each of the $1,000 amounts under subsection (b)(1) shall be increased by an amount equal to—

(i) such dollar amount, multiplied by

(ii) the cost-of-living adjustment determined under section 1(f)(3) for the calendar year in which the taxable year begins, determined by substituting "calendar year 2000" *for "calendar year 2016" in subparagraph (A)(ii) thereof.*

* * *

(2) INCOME LIMITS.—

(A) IN GENERAL.—In the case of a taxable year beginning after 2001, the $40,000 and $80,000 amounts in subsection (d)(2) shall each be increased by an amount equal to—

(i) such dollar amount, multiplied by

(ii) the cost-of-living adjustment determined under section 1(f)(3) for the calendar year in which the taxable year begins, determined by substituting "calendar year 2000" *for "calendar year 2016" in subparagraph (A)(ii) thereof.*

* * *

[CCH Explanation at ¶ 125. Committee Reports at ¶ 10,020.]

Amendments

• **2017, Tax Cuts and Jobs Act (P.L. 115-97)**

P.L. 115-97, § 11002(d)(1)(B):

Amended Code Sec. 25A(h)(1)(A)(ii) and (2)(A)(ii) by striking "for 'calendar year 1992' in subparagraph (B)" and inserting "for 'calendar year 2016' in subparagraph (A)(ii)". **Effective** for tax years beginning after 12-31-2017.

[¶ 5035] CODE SEC. 25B. ELECTIVE DEFERRALS AND IRA CONTRIBUTIONS BY CERTAIN INDIVIDUALS.

* * *

(b) APPLICABLE PERCENTAGE.—For purposes of this section—

* * *

(3) INFLATION ADJUSTMENT.—In the case of any taxable year beginning in a calendar year after 2006, each of the dollar amount[s]in paragraph (1) shall be increased by an amount equal to—

(A) such dollar amount, multiplied by

(B) the cost-of-living adjustment determined under section 1(f)(3) for the calendar year in which the taxable year begins, determined by substituting "calendar year 2005" *for "calendar year 2016" in subparagraph (A)(ii) thereof.*

Any increase determined under the preceding sentence shall be rounded to the nearest multiple of $500.

* * *

[CCH Explanation at ¶ 125. Committee Reports at ¶ 10,020.]

Amendments

• **2017, Tax Cuts and Jobs Act (P.L. 115-97)**

P.L. 115-97, § 11002(d)(1)(C):

Amended Code Sec. 25B(b)(3)(B) by striking "for 'calendar year 1992' in subparagraph (B)" and inserting "for 'cal- endar year 2016' in subparagraph (A)(ii)". **Effective** for tax years beginning after 12-31-2017.

(d) Qualified Retirement Savings Contributions.—For purposes of this section—

(1) In general.—The term "qualified retirement savings contributions" means, with respect to any taxable year, the sum of—

(A) the amount of the qualified retirement contributions (as defined in section 219(e)) made by the eligible individual,

(B) the amount of—

(i) any elective deferrals (as defined in section 402(g)(3)) of such individual, and

(ii) any elective deferral of compensation by such individual under an eligible deferred compensation plan (as defined in section 457(b)) of an eligible employer described in section 457(e)(1)(A),

(C) the amount of voluntary employee contributions by such individual to any qualified retirement plan (as defined in section 4974(c)), *and*

(D) the amount of contributions made before January 1, 2026, by such individual to the ABLE account (within the meaning of section 529A) of which such individual is the designated beneficiary.

* * *

[CCH Explanation at ¶645. Committee Reports at ¶10,090.]

Amendments

• **2017, Tax Cuts and Jobs Act (P.L. 115-97)**

P.L. 115-97, §11024(b):

Amended Code Sec. 25B(d)(1) by striking "and" at the end of subparagraph (B)(ii), by striking the period at the end of subparagraph (C) and inserting ", and", and by inserting at the end a new subparapgraph (D). **Effective** for tax years beginning after 12-22-2017.

[¶5040] CODE SEC. 26. LIMITATION BASED ON TAX LIABILITY; DEFINITION OF TAX LIABILITY.

* * *

(b) Regular Tax Liability.—For purposes of this part—

* * *

(2) Exception for certain taxes.—For purposes of paragraph (1), any tax imposed by any of the following provisions shall not be treated as tax imposed by this chapter:

* * *

(B) section 59A (relating to base erosion and anti-abuse tax),

* * *

[CCH Explanation at ¶750. Committee Reports at ¶11,210.]

Amendments

• **2017, Tax Cuts and Jobs Act (P.L. 115-97)**

P.L. 115-97, §14401(c):

Amended Code Sec. 26(b)(2) by inserting after subparagraph (A) a new subparagraph (B). **Effective** for base erosion payments (as defined in Code Sec. 59A(d), as added by Act. Sec. 14401) paid or accrued in tax years beginning after 12-31-2017.

[¶5045] CODE SEC. 32. EARNED INCOME.

* * *

(b) Percentages and Amounts.—For purposes of subsection (a)—

* * *

(2) Amounts.—

* * *

(B) JOINT RETURNS.—

* * *

(ii) INFLATION ADJUSTMENT.—In the case of any taxable year beginning after 2015, the $5,000 amount in clause (i) shall be increased by an amount equal to—

(I) such dollar amount, multiplied by

(II) the cost of living adjustment determined under section 1(f)(3) for the calendar year in which the taxable year begins determined by substituting "calendar year 2008" *for "calendar year 2016" in subparagraph (A)(ii)* thereof.

* * *

[CCH Explanation at ¶ 125. Committee Reports at ¶ 10,020.]

Amendments
• **2017, Tax Cuts and Jobs Act (P.L. 115-97)**

'calendar year 2016' in subparagraph (A)(ii)". **Effective** for tax years beginning after 12-31-2017.

P.L. 115-97, § 11002(d)(1)(D):

Amended Code Sec. 32(b)(2)(B)(ii)(II) by striking "for 'calendar year 1992' in subparagraph (B)" and inserting "for

(j) INFLATION ADJUSTMENTS.—

(1) IN GENERAL.—In the case of any taxable year beginning after 1996, each of the dollar amounts in subsections (b)(2) and (i)(1) shall be increased by an amount equal to—

(A) such dollar amount, multiplied by

(B) the cost-of-living adjustment determined under section 1(f)(3) for the calendar year in which the taxable year begins, determined—

(i) in the case of amounts in subsections (b)(2)(A) and (i)(1), by substituting "calendar year 1995" *for "calendar year 2016" in subparagraph (A)(ii)* thereof, and

(ii) in the case of the $3,000 amount in subsection (b)(2)(B)(iii), by substituting "calendar year 2007" *for "calendar year 2016" in subparagraph (A)(ii)* of such section 1.

* * *

[CCH Explanation at ¶ 125. Committee Reports at ¶ 10,020.]

Amendments
• **2017, Tax Cuts and Jobs Act (P.L. 115-97)**

'calendar year 2016' in subparagraph (A)(ii)". **Effective** for tax years beginning after 12-31-2017.

P.L. 115-97, § 11002(d)(1)(D):

Amended Code Sec. 32(j)(1)(B)(i)-(ii) by striking "for 'calendar year 1992' in subparagraph (B)" and inserting "for

[¶ 5050] CODE SEC. 36B. REFUNDABLE CREDIT FOR COVERAGE UNDER A QUALIFIED HEALTH PLAN.

* * *

(f) RECONCILIATION OF CREDIT AND ADVANCE CREDIT.—

* * *

(2) EXCESS ADVANCE PAYMENTS.—

* * *

(ii) INDEXING OF AMOUNT.—In the case of any calendar year beginning after 2014, each of the dollar amounts in the table contained under clause (i) shall be increased by an amount equal to—

(I) such dollar amount, multiplied by

(II) the cost-of-living adjustment determined under section 1(f)(3) for the calendar year, determined by substituting "calendar year 2013" *for "calendar year 2016" in subparagraph (A)(ii)* thereof.

If the amount of any increase under clause (i) is not a multiple of $50, such increase shall be rounded to the next lowest multiple of $50.

* * *

[CCH Explanation at ¶ 125. Committee Reports at ¶ 10,020.]

Amendments

• **2017, Tax Cuts and Jobs Act (P.L. 115-97)**

P.L. 115-97, § 11002(d)(1)(E):

Amended Code Sec. 36B(f)(2)(B)(ii)(II) by striking "for 'calendar year 1992' in subparagraph (B)" and inserting "for 'calendar year 2016' in subparagraph (A)(ii)". **Effective** for tax years beginning after 12-31-2017.

[¶ 5055] CODE SEC. 38. GENERAL BUSINESS CREDIT.

* * *

(b) CURRENT YEAR BUSINESS CREDIT.—For purposes of this subpart, the amount of the current year business credit is the sum of the following credits determined for the taxable year:

* * *

(35) the portion of the new qualified plug-in electric drive motor vehicle credit to which section 30D(c)(1) applies,

(36) the small employer health insurance credit determined under section 45R, *plus*

(37) *in the case of an eligible employer (as defined in section 45S(c)), the paid family and medical leave credit determined under section 45S(a).*

* * *

[CCH Explanation at ¶ 585. Committee Reports at ¶ 10,570.]

Amendments

• **2017, Tax Cuts and Jobs Act (P.L. 115-97)**

P.L. 115-97, § 13403(b):

Amended Code Sec. 38(b) by striking "plus" at the end of paragraph (35), by striking the period at the end of para-graph (36) and inserting ", plus", and by adding at the end a new paragraph (37). **Effective** for wages paid in tax years beginning after 12-31-2017.

(c) LIMITATION BASED ON AMOUNT OF TAX.—

* * *

(4) SPECIAL RULES FOR SPECIFIED CREDITS.—

* * *

(B) SPECIFIED CREDITS.—For purposes of this subsection, the term "specified credits" means—

* * *

(ix) the credit determined under section 45S,

(x) the credit determined under section 46 to the extent that such credit is attributa-ble to the energy credit determined under section 48,

(xi) the credit determined under section 46 to the extent that such credit is attribu-table to the rehabilitation credit under section 47, but only with respect to qualified rehabilitation expenditures properly taken into account for periods after December 31, 2007, and

(xii) the credit determined under section 51.

* * *

(6) SPECIAL RULES.—

* * *

(E) CORPORATIONS.—*In the case of a corporation, this subsection shall be applied by treating the corporation as having a tentative minimum tax of zero.*

* * *

[CCH Explanation at ¶310 and ¶585. Committee Reports at ¶10,300 and ¶10,570.]

Amendments

• **2017, Tax Cuts and Jobs Act (P.L. 115-97)**

P.L. 115-97, §12001(b)(1):

Amended Code Sec. 38(c)(6) by adding at the end a new subparagraph (E). **Effective** for tax years beginning after 12-31-2017.

P.L. 115-97, §13403(c):

Amended Code Sec. 38(c)(4)(B) by redesignating clauses (ix) through (xi) as clauses (x) through (xii), respectively, and by inserting after clause (viii) a new clause (ix). **Effective** for wages paid in tax years beginning after 12-31-2017.

[¶5060] CODE SEC. 41. CREDIT FOR INCREASING RESEARCH ACTIVITIES.

* * *

(d) QUALIFIED RESEARCH DEFINED.—For purposes of this section—

(1) IN GENERAL.—The term "qualified research" means research—

≫→ *Caution: Code Sec. 41(d)(1)(A), below, as amended by P.L. 115-97, applies to amounts paid or incurred in tax years beginning after December 31, 2021.*

(A) with respect to which expenditures may be treated as *specified research or experimental expenditures under section 174,*

* * *

[CCH Explanation at ¶525. Committee Reports at ¶10,390.]

Amendments

• **2017, Tax Cuts and Jobs Act (P.L. 115-97)**

P.L. 115-97, §13206(d)(1):

Amended Code Sec. 41(d)(1)(A) by striking "expenses under section 174" and inserting "specified research or ex

perimental expenditures under section 174". **Effective** for amounts paid or incurred in tax years beginning after 12-31-2021.

(e) CREDIT ALLOWABLE WITH RESPECT TO CERTAIN PAYMENTS TO QUALIFIED ORGANIZATIONS FOR BASIC RESEARCH.—For purposes of this section—

* * *

(5) MAINTENANCE-OF-EFFORT AMOUNT.—For purposes of this subsection—

* * *

(C) COST-OF-LIVING ADJUSTMENT DEFINED.—

(i) IN GENERAL.—The cost-of-living adjustment for any calendar year is the cost-of-living adjustment for such calendar year determined under section 1(f)(3), by substituting "calendar year 1987" *for "calendar year 2016" in subparagraph (A)(ii)* thereof [of Code Sec. 1(f)(3)].

(ii) SPECIAL RULE WHERE BASE PERIOD ENDS IN A CALENDAR YEAR OTHER THAN 1983 OR 1984.—If the base period of any taxpayer does not end in 1983 or 1984, section 1(f)(3)(A)(ii) shall, for purposes of this paragraph, be applied by substituting the calendar year in which such base period ends for *2016.* Such substitution shall be in lieu of the substitution under clause (i).

* * *

[CCH Explanation at ¶ 125. Committee Reports at ¶ 10,020.]

Amendments

• **2017, Tax Cuts and Jobs Act (P.L. 115-97)**

P.L. 115-97, § 11002(d)(1)(F):

Amended Code Sec. 41(e)(5)(C)(i) by striking "for 'calendar year 1992' in subparagraph (B)" and inserting "for 'calendar year 2016' in subparagraph (A)(ii)". **Effective** for tax years beginning after 12-31-2017.

P.L. 115-97, § 11002(d)(2)(A)-(B):

Amended Code Sec. 41(e)(5)(C)(ii) by striking "1(f)(3)(B)" and inserting "1(f)(3)(A)(ii)", and by striking "1992" and inserting "2016". **Effective** for tax years beginning after 12-31-2017.

[¶ 5065] CODE SEC. 42. LOW-INCOME HOUSING CREDIT.

* * *

(e) REHABILITATION EXPENDITURES TREATED AS SEPARATE NEW BUILDING.—

* * *

(3) MINIMUM EXPENDITURES TO QUALIFY.—

* * *

(D) INFLATION ADJUSTMENT.—In the case of any expenditures which are treated under paragraph (4) as placed in service during any calendar year after 2009, the $6,000 amount in subparagraph (A)(ii)(II) shall be increased by an amount equal to—

(i) such dollar amount, multiplied by

(ii) the cost-of-living adjustment determined under section 1(f)(3) for such calendar year by substituting "calendar year 2008" *for "calendar year 2016" in subparagraph (A)(ii)* thereof.

Any increase under the preceding sentence which is not a multiple of $100 shall be rounded to the nearest multiple of $100.

* * *

[CCH Explanation at ¶ 125. Committee Reports at ¶ 10,020.]

Amendments

• **2017, Tax Cuts and Jobs Act (P.L. 115-97)**

P.L. 115-97, § 11002(d)(1)(G):

Amended Code Sec. 42(e)(3)(D)(ii) by striking "for 'calendar year 1992' in subparagraph (B)" and inserting "for 'calendar year 2016' in subparagraph (A)(ii)". **Effective** for tax years beginning after 12-31-2017.

(h) LIMITATION ON AGGREGATE CREDIT ALLOWABLE WITH RESPECT TO PROJECTS LOCATED IN A STATE.—

* * *

(3) HOUSING CREDIT DOLLAR AMOUNT FOR AGENCIES.—

* * *

(H) COST-OF-LIVING ADJUSTMENT.—

(i) IN GENERAL.—In the case of a calendar year after 2002, the $2,000,000 and $1.75 amounts in subparagraph (C) shall each be increased by an amount equal to—

(I) such dollar amount, multiplied by

(II) the cost-of-living adjustment determined under section 1(f)(3) for such calendar year by substituting "calendar year 2001" *for "calendar year 2016" in subparagraph (A)(ii)* thereof.

* * *

(6) BUILDINGS ELIGIBLE FOR CREDIT ONLY IF MINIMUM LONG-TERM COMMITMENT TO LOW-INCOME HOUSING.—

* * *

(G) ADJUSTED INVESTOR EQUITY.—

(i) IN GENERAL.—For purposes of subparagraph (E), the term "adjusted investor equity" means, with respect to any calendar year, the aggregate amount of cash taxpayers invested with respect to the project increased by the amount equal to—

(I) such amount, multiplied by

(II) the cost-of-living adjustment for such calendar year, determined under section 1(f)(3) by substituting the base calendar year *for "calendar year 2016" in subparagraph (A)(ii) thereof.*

An amount shall be taken into account as an investment in the project only to the extent there was an obligation to invest such amount as of the beginning of the credit period and to the extent such amount is reflected in the adjusted basis of the project.

(ii) COST-OF-LIVING INCREASES IN EXCESS OF 5 PERCENT NOT TAKEN INTO ACCOUNT.—Under regulations prescribed by the Secretary, *if the C-CPI-U for any calendar year (as defined in section 1(f)(6)) exceeds the C-CPI-U for the preceding calendar year by more than 5 percent, the C-CPI-U for the base calendar year shall be increased such that such excess shall never be taken into account under clause (i). In the case of a base calendar year before 2017, the C-CPI-U for such year shall be determined by multiplying the CPI for such year by the amount determined under section 1(f)(3)(B).*

* * *

[CCH Explanation at ¶ 125. Committee Reports at ¶ 10,020.]

Amendments

• 2017, Tax Cuts and Jobs Act (P.L. 115-97)

P.L. 115-97, § 11002(d)(1)(G):

Amended Code Sec. 42(h)(3)(H)(i)(II) by striking "for 'calendar year 1992' in subparagraph (B)" and inserting "for 'calendar year 2016' in subparagraph (A)(ii)". **Effective** for tax years beginning after 12-31-2017.

P.L. 115-97, § 11002(d)(3)(A)-(B):

Amended Code Sec. 42(h)(6)(G) by striking "for 'calendar year 1987'" in clause (i)(II) and inserting "for 'calendar year 2016' in subparagraph (A)(ii) thereof", and by striking "if the CPI for any calendar year" and all that follows in clause (ii) and inserting "if the C-CPI-U for any calendar year (as

defined in section 1(f)(6)) exceeds the C-CPI-U for the preceding calendar year by more than 5 percent, the C-CPI-U for the base calendar year shall be increased such that such excess shall never be taken into account under clause (i). In the case of a base calendar year before 2017, the C-CPI-U for such year shall be determined by multiplying the CPI for such year by the amount determined under section 1(f)(3)(B).". **Effective** for tax years beginning after 12-31-2017. Prior to being stricken, "if the CPI for any calendar year" and all that follows in clause (ii) read as follows:

if the CPI for any calendar year (as defined in section 1(f)(4)) exceeds the CPI for the preceding calendar year by more than 5 percent, the CPI for the base calendar year shall be increased such that such excess shall never be taken into account under clause (i).

[¶ 5070] CODE SEC. 45C. CLINICAL TESTING EXPENSES FOR CERTAIN DRUGS FOR RARE DISEASES OR CONDITIONS.

(a) GENERAL RULE.—For purposes of section 38, the credit determined under this section for the taxable year is an amount equal to *25 percent* of the qualified clinical testing expenses for the taxable year.

* * *

[CCH Explanation at ¶ 595. Committee Reports at ¶ 10,550.]

Amendments

• 2017, Tax Cuts and Jobs Act (P.L. 115-97)

P.L. 115-97, § 13401(a):

Amended Code Sec. 45C(a) by striking "50 percent" and inserting "25 percent". **Effective** for tax years beginning after 12-31-2017.

[¶ 5075] CODE SEC. 45R. EMPLOYEE HEALTH INSURANCE EXPENSES OF SMALL EMPLOYERS.

* * *

(d) ELIGIBLE SMALL EMPLOYER.—For purposes of this section—

* * *

(3) AVERAGE ANNUAL WAGES.—

* * *

(B) DOLLAR AMOUNT.—For purposes of paragraph (1)(B) and subsection (c)(2)—

* * *

(ii) SUBSEQUENT YEARS.—In the case of a taxable year beginning in a calendar year after 2013, the dollar amount in effect under this paragraph shall be equal to $25,000, multiplied by the cost-of-living adjustment under section 1(f)(3) for the calendar year, determined by substituting "calendar year 2012" *for "calendar year 2016" in subparagraph (A)(ii)* thereof.

* * *

[CCH Explanation at ¶ 125. Committee Reports at ¶ 10,020.]

Amendments

• **2017, Tax Cuts and Jobs Act (P.L. 115-97)**

P.L. 115-97, § 11002(d)(1)(H):

Amended Code Sec. 45R(d)(3)(B)(ii) by striking "for 'calendar year 1992' in subparagraph (B)" and inserting "for

'calendar year 2016' in subparagraph (A)(ii)". **Effective** for tax years beginning after 12-31-2017.

[¶ 5080] *CODE SEC. 45S. EMPLOYER CREDIT FOR PAID FAMILY AND MEDICAL LEAVE.*

(a) ESTABLISHMENT OF CREDIT.—

(1) IN GENERAL.—For purposes of section 38, in the case of an eligible employer, the paid family and medical leave credit is an amount equal to the applicable percentage of the amount of wages paid to qualifying employees during any period in which such employees are on family and medical leave.

(2) APPLICABLE PERCENTAGE.—For purposes of paragraph (1), the term "applicable percentage" means 12.5 percent increased (but not above 25 percent) by 0.25 percentage points for each percentage point by which the rate of payment (as described under subsection (c)(1)(B)) exceeds 50 percent.

(b) LIMITATION.—

(1) IN GENERAL.—The credit allowed under subsection (a) with respect to any employee for any taxable year shall not exceed an amount equal to the product of the normal hourly wage rate of such employee for each hour (or fraction thereof) of actual services performed for the employer and the number of hours (or fraction thereof) for which family and medical leave is taken.

(2) NON-HOURLY WAGE RATE.—For purposes of paragraph (1), in the case of any employee who is not paid on an hourly wage rate, the wages of such employee shall be prorated to an hourly wage rate under regulations established by the Secretary.

(3) MAXIMUM AMOUNT OF LEAVE SUBJECT TO CREDIT.—The amount of family and medical leave that may be taken into account with respect to any employee under subsection (a) for any taxable year shall not exceed 12 weeks.

(c) ELIGIBLE EMPLOYER.—For purposes of this section—

(1) IN GENERAL.—The term "eligible employer" means any employer who has in place a written policy that meets the following requirements:

(A) The policy provides—

(i) in the case of a qualifying employee who is not a part-time employee (as defined in section 4980E(d)(4)(B)), not less than 2 weeks of annual paid family and medical leave, and

(ii) in the case of a qualifying employee who is a part-time employee, an amount of annual paid family and medical leave that is not less than an amount which bears the same ratio to the

amount of annual paid family and medical leave that is provided to a qualifying employee described in clause (i) as—

(I) the number of hours the employee is expected to work during any week, bears to

(II) the number of hours an equivalent qualifying employee described in clause (i) is expected to work during the week.

(B) The policy requires that the rate of payment under the program is not less than 50 percent of the wages normally paid to such employee for services performed for the employer.

(2) SPECIAL RULE FOR CERTAIN EMPLOYERS.—

(A) IN GENERAL.—An added employer shall not be treated as an eligible employer unless such employer provides paid family and medical leave in compliance with a written policy which ensures that the employer—

(i) will not interfere with, restrain, or deny the exercise of or the attempt to exercise, any right provided under the policy, and

(ii) will not discharge or in any other manner discriminate against any individual for opposing any practice prohibited by the policy.

(B) ADDED EMPLOYER; ADDED EMPLOYEE.—For purposes of this paragraph—

(i) ADDED EMPLOYEE.—The term "added employee" means a qualifying employee who is not covered by title I of the Family and Medical Leave Act of 1993, as amended.

(ii) ADDED EMPLOYER.—The term "added employer" means an eligible employer (determined without regard to this paragraph), whether or not covered by that title I, who offers paid family and medical leave to added employees.

(3) AGGREGATION RULE.—All persons which are treated as a single employer under subsections (a) and (b) of section 52 shall be treated as a single taxpayer.

(4) TREATMENT OF BENEFITS MANDATED OR PAID FOR BY STATE OR LOCAL GOVERNMENTS.—For purposes of this section, any leave which is paid by a State or local government or required by State or local law shall not be taken into account in determining the amount of paid family and medical leave provided by the employer.

(5) NO INFERENCE.—Nothing in this subsection shall be construed as subjecting an employer to any penalty, liability, or other consequence (other than ineligibility for the credit allowed by reason of subsection (a) or recapturing the benefit of such credit) for failure to comply with the requirements of this subsection.

(d) QUALIFYING EMPLOYEES.—For purposes of this section, the term "qualifying employee" means any employee (as defined in section 3(e) of the Fair Labor Standards Act of 1938, as amended) who—

(1) has been employed by the employer for 1 year or more, and

(2) for the preceding year, had compensation not in excess of an amount equal to 60 percent of the amount applicable for such year under clause (i) of section 414(q)(1)(B).

(e) FAMILY AND MEDICAL LEAVE.—

(1) IN GENERAL.—Except as provided in paragraph (2), for purposes of this section, the term "family and medical leave" means leave for any 1 or more of the purposes described under subparagraph (A), (B), (C), (D), or (E) of paragraph (1), or paragraph (3), of section 102(a) of the Family and Medical Leave Act of 1993, as amended, whether the leave is provided under that Act or by a policy of the employer.

(2) EXCLUSION.—If an employer provides paid leave as vacation leave, personal leave, or medical or sick leave (other than leave specifically for 1 or more of the purposes referred to in paragraph (1)), that paid leave shall not be considered to be family and medical leave under paragraph (1).

(3) DEFINITIONS.—In this subsection, the terms "vacation leave", "personal leave", and "medical or sick leave" mean those 3 types of leave, within the meaning of section 102(d)(2) of that Act.

(f) Determinations Made by Secretary of Treasury.—For purposes of this section, any determination as to whether an employer or an employee satisfies the applicable requirements for an eligible employer (as described in subsection (c)) or qualifying employee (as described in subsection (d)), respectively, shall be made by the Secretary based on such information, to be provided by the employer, as the Secretary determines to be necessary or appropriate.

(g) Wages.—For purposes of this section, the term "wages" has the meaning given such term by subsection (b) of section 3306 (determined without regard to any dollar limitation contained in such section). Such term shall not include any amount taken into account for purposes of determining any other credit allowed under this subpart.

(h) Election to Have Credit Not Apply.—

(1) In General.—A taxpayer may elect to have this section not apply for any taxable year.

(2) Other Rules.—Rules similar to the rules of paragraphs (2) and (3) of section 51(j) shall apply for purposes of this subsection.

(i) Termination.—This section shall not apply to wages paid in taxable years beginning after December 31, 2019.

[CCH Explanation at ¶ 585. Committee Reports at ¶ 10,570.]

Amendments

• **2017, Tax Cuts and Jobs Act (P.L. 115-97)**

P.L. 115-97, § 13403(a)(1):

Amended subpart D of part IV of subchapter A of chapter 1 by adding at the end a new Code Sec. 45S. **Effective** for wages paid in tax years beginning after 12-31-2017.

[¶ 5085] CODE SEC. 47. REHABILITATION CREDIT.

(a) General Rule.—

(1) In General.—For purposes of section 46, for any taxable year during the 5-year period beginning in the taxable year in which a qualified rehabilitated building is placed in service, the rehabilitation credit for such year is an amount equal to the ratable share for such year.

(2) Ratable Share.—For purposes of paragraph (1), the ratable share for any taxable year during the period described in such paragraph is the amount equal to 20 percent of the qualified rehabilitation expenditures with respect to the qualified rehabilitated building, as allocated ratably to each year during such period.

* * *

[CCH Explanation at ¶ 590. Committee Reports at ¶ 10,560.]

Amendments

• **2017, Tax Cuts and Jobs Act (P.L. 115-97)**

P.L. 115-97, § 13402(a):

Amended Code Sec. 47(a). **Effective** generally for amounts paid or incurred after 12-31-2017. For a transition rule, see Act Sec. 13402(c)(2), below. Prior to amendment, Code Sec. 47(a) read as follows:

(a) General Rule.—For purposes of section 46, the rehabilitation credit for any taxable year is the sum of—

(1) 10 percent of the qualified rehabilitation expenditures with respect to any qualified rehabilitated building other than a certified historic structure, and

(2) 20 percent of the qualified rehabilitation expenditures with respect to any certified historic structure.

P.L. 115-97, § 13402(c)(2), provides:

(2) Transition Rule.—In the case of qualified rehabilitation expenditures with respect to any building—

(A) owned or leased by the taxpayer during the entirety of the period after December 31, 2017, and

(B) with respect to which the 24-month period selected by the taxpayer under clause (i) of section 47(c)(1)(B) of the Internal Revenue Code (as amended by subsection (b)), or the 60-month period applicable under clause (ii) of such section, begins not later than 180 days after the date of the enactment of this Act, the amendments made by this section shall apply to such expenditures paid or incurred after the end of the taxable year in which the 24-month period, or the 60-month period, referred to in subparagraph (B) ends.

(c) Definitions.—For purposes of this section—

(1) Qualified Rehabilitated Building.—

(A) In General.—The term "qualified rehabilitated building" means any building (and its structural components) if—

* * *

(iii) such building is a certified historic structure, and

* * *

(B) Substantially Rehabilitated Defined.—

(i) In General.—For purposes of subparagraph (A)(i), a building shall be treated as having been substantially rehabilitated only if the qualified rehabilitation expenditures during the 24-month period selected by the taxpayer (at the time and in the manner prescribed by regulation) and ending with or within the taxable year exceed the greater of—

(I) the adjusted basis of such building (and its structural components), or

(II) $5,000.

The adjusted basis of the building (and its structural components) shall be determined as of the beginning of the 1st day of such 24-month period, or of the holding period of the building, whichever is later. For purposes of the preceding sentence, the determination of the beginning of the holding period shall be made without regard to any reconstruction by the taxpayer in connection with the rehabilitation.

(ii) Special Rule For Phased Rehabilitation.—In the case of any rehabilitation which may reasonably be expected to be completed in phases set forth in architectural plans and specifications completed before the rehabilitation begins, clause (i) shall be applied by substituting "60-month period" for "24-month period".

(iii) Lessees.—The Secretary shall prescribe by regulation rules for applying this subparagraph to lessees.

(C) Reconstruction.—Rehabilitation includes reconstruction.

(2) Qualified Rehabilitation Expenditure Defined.—

* * *

(B) Certain Expenditures Not Included.—The term "qualified rehabilitation expenditure" does not include—

* * *

(iv) Certified Historic Structure.—Any expenditure attributable to the rehabilitation of a qualified rehabilitated building unless the rehabilitation is a certified rehabilitation (within the meaning of subparagraph (C)).

* * *

[CCH Explanation at ¶ 590. Committee Reports at ¶ 10,560.]

Amendments

• **2017, Tax Cuts and Jobs Act (P.L. 115-97)**

P.L. 115-97, § 13402(b)(1)(A)(i)-(iii):

Amended Code Sec. 47(c)(1) by amending subparagraph (A)(iii), by striking subparagraph (B), and by redesignating subparagraphs (C) and (D) as subparagraphs (B) and (C), respectively. **Effective** generally for amounts paid or incurred after 12-31-2017. For a transition rule, see Act Sec. 13402(c)(2), below. Prior to amendment, Code Sec. 47(c)(1)(A)(iii) and (B) read as follows:

(iii) in the case of any building other than a certified historic structure, in the rehabilitation process—

(I) 50 percent or more of the existing external walls of such building are retained in place as external walls,

(II) 75 percent or more of the existing external walls of such building are retained in place as internal or external walls, and

(III) 75 percent or more of the existing internal structural framework of such building is retained in place, and

(B) Building Must Be First Placed In Service Before 1936.— In the case of a building other than a certified historic structure, a building shall not be a qualified rehabilitated building unless the building was first placed in service before 1936.

P.L. 115-97, § 13402(b)(1)(B):

Amended Code Sec. 47(c)(2)(B)(iv). **Effective** generally for amounts paid or incurred after 12-31-2017. For a transition rule, see Act Sec. 13402(c)(2), below. Prior to amendment, Code Sec. 47(c)(2)(B)(iv) read as follows:

(iv) CERTIFIED HISTORIC STRUCTURE, ETC.—Any expenditure attributable to the rehabilitation of a certified historic structure or a building in a registered historic district, unless the rehabilitation is a certified rehabilitation (within the meaning of subparagraph (C)). The preceding sentence shall not apply to a building in a registered historic district if—

(I) such building was not a certified historic structure,

(II) the Secretary of the Interior certified to the Secretary that such building is not of historic significance to the district, and

(III) if the certification referred to in subclause (II) occurs after the beginning of the rehabilitation of such building, the

taxpayer certifies to the Secretary that, at the beginning of such rehabilitation, he in good faith was not aware of the requirements of subclause (II).

P.L. 115-97, § 13402(c)(2), provides:

(2) TRANSITION RULE.—In the case of qualified rehabilitation expenditures with respect to any building—

(A) owned or leased by the taxpayer during the entirety of the period after December 31, 2017, and

(B) with respect to which the 24-month period selected by the taxpayer under clause (i) of section 47(c)(1)(B) of the Internal Revenue Code (as amended by subsection (b)), or the 60-month period applicable under clause (ii) of such section, begins not later than 180 days after the date of the enactment of this Act, the amendments made by this section shall apply to such expenditures paid or incurred after the end of the taxable year in which the 24-month period, or the 60-month period, referred to in subparagraph (B) ends.

[¶ 5090] CODE SEC. 53. CREDIT FOR PRIOR YEAR MINIMUM TAX LIABILITY.

* * *

(d) DEFINITIONS.—For purposes of this section—

* * *

(2) TENTATIVE MINIMUM TAX.—The term "tentative minimum tax" has the meaning given to such term by section 55(b), *except that in the case of a corporation, the tentative minimum tax shall be treated as zero.*

(3) AMT TERM REFERENCES.—*In the case of a corporation, any references in this subsection to section 55, 56, or 57 shall be treated as a reference to such section as in effect before the amendments made by Tax Cuts and Jobs Act.*

[CCH Explanation at ¶ 310. Committee Reports at ¶ 10,300.]

Amendments

• **2017, Tax Cuts and Jobs Act (P.L. 115-97)**

P.L. 115-97, § 12001(b)(2):

Amended Code Sec. 53(d)(2) by inserting ", except that in the case of a corporation, the tentative minimum tax shall be treated as zero" before the period at the end. **Effective** for tax years beginning after 12-31-2017.

P.L. 115-97, § 12002(b):

Amended Code Sec. 53(d) by adding at the end a new paragraph (3). **Effective** for tax years beginning after 12-31-2017.

(e) PORTION OF CREDIT TREATED AS REFUNDABLE.—

(1) IN GENERAL.—*In the case of any taxable year of a corporation beginning in 2018, 2019, 2020, or 2021, the limitation under subsection (c) shall be increased by the AMT refundable credit amount for such year.*

(2) AMT REFUNDABLE CREDIT AMOUNT.—*For purposes of paragraph (1), the AMT refundable credit amount is an amount equal to 50 percent (100 percent in the case of a taxable year beginning in 2021) of the excess (if any) of—*

(A) *the minimum tax credit determined under subsection (b) for the taxable year, over*

(B) *the minimum tax credit allowed under subsection (a) for such year (before the application of this subsection for such year).*

(3) CREDIT REFUNDABLE.—*For purposes of this title (other than this section), the credit allowed by reason of this subsection shall be treated as a credit allowed under subpart C (and not this subpart).*

(4) SHORT TAXABLE YEARS.—*In the case of any taxable year of less than 365 days, the AMT refundable credit amount determined under paragraph (2) with respect to such taxable year shall be the amount which bears the same ratio to such amount determined without regard to this paragraph as the number of days in such taxable year bears to 365.*

[CCH Explanation at ¶ 310. Committee Reports at ¶ 10,300.]

• 2017, Tax Cuts and Jobs Act (P.L. 115-97)

P.L. 115-97, § 12002(a):

Amended Code Sec. 53 by adding at the end a new subsection (e). **Effective** for tax years beginning after 12-31-2017.

[¶ 5095] CODE SEC. 54. CREDITS TO HOLDERS OF CLEAN RENEWABLE ENERGY BONDS. [*Stricken.*]

[CCH Explanation at ¶ 875. Committee Reports at ¶ 10,580.]

Amendments

• 2017, Tax Cuts and Jobs Act (P.L. 115-97)

P.L. 115-97, § 13404(a):

Amended part IV of subchapter A of chapter 1 by striking subpart H (Code Sec. 54). **Effective** for bonds issued after 12-31-2017. Prior to being stricken, Code Sec. 54 read as follows:

SEC. 54. CREDIT TO HOLDERS OF CLEAN RENEWABLE ENERGY BONDS.

(a) ALLOWANCE OF CREDIT.—If a taxpayer holds a clean renewable energy bond on one or more credit allowance dates of the bond occurring during any taxable year, there shall be allowed as a credit against the tax imposed by this chapter for the taxable year an amount equal to the sum of the credits determined under subsection (b) with respect to such dates.

(b) AMOUNT OF CREDIT.—

(1) IN GENERAL.—The amount of the credit determined under this subsection with respect to any credit allowance date for a clean renewable energy bond is 25 percent of the annual credit determined with respect to such bond.

(2) ANNUAL CREDIT.—The annual credit determined with respect to any clean renewable energy bond is the product of—

(A) the credit rate determined by the Secretary under paragraph (3) for the day on which such bond was sold, multiplied by

(B) the outstanding face amount of the bond.

(3) DETERMINATION.—For purposes of paragraph (2), with respect to any clean renewable energy bond, the Secretary shall determine daily or cause to be determined daily a credit rate which shall apply to the first day on which there is a binding, written contract for the sale or exchange of the bond. The credit rate for any day is the credit rate which the Secretary or the Secretary's designee estimates will permit the issuance of clean renewable energy bonds with a specified maturity or redemption date without discount and without interest cost to the qualified issuer.

(4) CREDIT ALLOWANCE DATE.—For purposes of this section, the term "credit allowance date" means—

(A) March 15,

(B) June 15,

(C) September 15, and

(D) December 15.

Such term also includes the last day on which the bond is outstanding.

(5) SPECIAL RULE FOR ISSUANCE AND REDEMPTION.—In the case of a bond which is issued during the 3-month period ending on a credit allowance date, the amount of the credit determined under this subsection with respect to such credit allowance date shall be a ratable portion of the credit otherwise determined based on the portion of the 3-month period

during which the bond is outstanding. A similar rule shall apply when the bond is redeemed or matures.

(c) LIMITATION BASED ON AMOUNT OF TAX.—The credit allowed under subsection (a) for any taxable year shall not exceed the excess of—

(1) the sum of the regular tax liability (as defined in section 26(b)) plus the tax imposed by section 55, over

(2) the sum of the credits allowable under this part (other than subparts C, I, and J, section 1400N(l), and this section).

(d) CLEAN RENEWABLE ENERGY BOND.—For purposes of this section—

(1) IN GENERAL.—The term "clean renewable energy bond" means any bond issued as part of an issue if—

(A) the bond is issued by a qualified issuer pursuant to an allocation by the Secretary to such issuer of a portion of the national clean renewable energy bond limitation under subsection (f)(2),

(B) 95 percent or more of the proceeds of such issue are to be used for capital expenditures incurred by qualified borrowers for one or more qualified projects,

(C) the qualified issuer designates such bond for purposes of this section and the bond is in registered form, and

(D) the issue meets the requirements of subsection (h).

(2) QUALIFIED PROJECT; SPECIAL USE RULES.—

(A) IN GENERAL.—The term "qualified project" means any qualified facility (as determined under section 45(d) without regard to paragraph (10) and to any placed in service date) owned by a qualified borrower.

(B) REFINANCING RULES.—For purposes of paragraph (1)(B), a qualified project may be refinanced with proceeds of a clean renewable energy bond only if the indebtedness being refinanced (including any obligation directly or indirectly refinanced by such indebtedness) was originally incurred by a qualified borrower after the date of the enactment of this section.

(C) REIMBURSEMENT.—For purposes of paragraph (1)(B), a clean renewable energy bond may be issued to reimburse a qualified borrower for amounts paid after the date of the enactment of this section with respect to a qualified project, but only if—

(i) prior to the payment of the original expenditure, the qualified borrower declared its intent to reimburse such expenditure with the proceeds of a clean renewable energy bond,

(ii) not later than 60 days after payment of the original expenditure, the qualified issuer adopts an official intent to reimburse the original expenditure with such proceeds, and

(iii) the reimbursement is made not later than 18 months after the date the original expenditure is paid.

(D) TREATMENT OF CHANGES IN USE.—For purposes of paragraph (1)(B), the proceeds of an issue shall not be treated as used for a qualified project to the extent that a qualified borrower or qualified issuer takes any action within its control which causes such proceeds not to be used for a qualified project. The Secretary shall prescribe regulations specifying remedial actions that may be taken (including conditions to taking such remedial actions) to prevent an action described in the preceding sentence from causing a bond to fail to be a clean renewable energy bond.

(e) MATURITY LIMITATIONS.—

(1) DURATION OF TERM.—A bond shall not be treated as a clean renewable energy bond if the maturity of such bond exceeds the maximum term determined by the Secretary under paragraph (2) with respect to such bond.

(2) MAXIMUM TERM.—During each calendar month, the Secretary shall determine the maximum term permitted under this paragraph for bonds issued during the following calendar month. Such maximum term shall be the term which the Secretary estimates will result in the present value of the obligation to repay the principal on the bond being equal to 50 percent of the face amount of such bond. Such present value shall be determined without regard to the requirements of subsection (l)(6) and using as a discount rate the average annual interest rate of tax-exempt obligations having a term of 10 years or more which are issued during the month. If the term as so determined is not a multiple of a whole year, such term shall be rounded to the next highest whole year.

(f) LIMITATION ON AMOUNT OF BONDS DESIGNATED.—

(1) NATIONAL LIMITATION.—There is a national clean renewable energy bond limitation of $1,200,000,000.

(2) ALLOCATION BY SECRETARY.—The Secretary shall allocate the amount described in paragraph (1) among qualified projects in such manner as the Secretary determines appropriate, except that the Secretary may not allocate more than $750,000,000 of the national clean renewable energy bond limitation to finance qualified projects of qualified borrowers which are governmental bodies.

(g) CREDIT INCLUDED IN GROSS INCOME.—Gross income includes the amount of the credit allowed to the taxpayer under this section (determined without regard to subsection (c)) and the amount so included shall be treated as interest income.

(h) SPECIAL RULES RELATING TO EXPENDITURES.—

(1) IN GENERAL.—An issue shall be treated as meeting the requirements of this subsection if, as of the date of issuance, the qualified issuer reasonably expects—

(A) at least 95 percent of the proceeds of such issue are to be spent for one or more qualified projects within the 5-year period beginning on the date of issuance of the clean energy bond,

(B) a binding commitment with a third party to spend at least 10 percent of the proceeds of such issue will be incurred within the 6-month period beginning on the date of issuance of the clean energy bond or, in the case of a clean energy bond the proceeds of which are to be loaned to two or more qualified borrowers, such binding commitment will be incurred within the 6-month period beginning on the date of the loan of such proceeds to a qualified borrower, and

(C) such projects will be completed with due diligence and the proceeds of such issue will be spent with due diligence.

(2) EXTENSION OF PERIOD.—Upon submission of a request prior to the expiration of the period described in paragraph (1)(A), the Secretary may extend such period if the qualified issuer establishes that the failure to satisfy the 5-year requirement is due to reasonable cause and the related projects will continue to proceed with due diligence.

(3) FAILURE TO SPEND REQUIRED AMOUNT OF BOND PROCEEDS WITHIN 5 YEARS.—To the extent that less than 95 percent of the proceeds of such issue are expended by the close of the 5-year period beginning on the date of issuance (or if an extension has been obtained under paragraph (2), by the close of the extended period), the qualified issuer shall redeem all of the nonqualified bonds within 90 days after the end of such period. For purposes of this paragraph, the amount of the nonqualified bonds required to be redeemed shall be determined in the same manner as under section 142.

(i) SPECIAL RULES RELATING TO ARBITRAGE.—A bond which is part of an issue shall not be treated as a clean renewable energy bond unless, with respect to the issue of which the bond is a part, the qualified issuer satisfies the arbitrage requirements of section 148 with respect to proceeds of the issue.

(j) COOPERATIVE ELECTRIC COMPANY; QUALIFIED ENERGY TAX CREDIT BOND LENDER; GOVERNMENTAL BODY; QUALIFIED BORROWER.—For purposes of this section—

(1) COOPERATIVE ELECTRIC COMPANY.—The term "cooperative electric company" means a mutual or cooperative electric company described in section 501(c)(12) or section 1381(a)(2)(C), or a not-for-profit electric utility which has received a loan or loan guarantee under the Rural Electrification Act.

(2) CLEAN RENEWABLE ENERGY BOND LENDER.—The term "clean renewable energy bond lender" means a lender which is a cooperative which is owned by, or has outstanding loans to, 100 or more cooperative electric companies and is in existence on February 1, 2002, and shall include any affiliated entity which is controlled by such lender.

(3) GOVERNMENTAL BODY.—The term "governmental body" means any State, territory, possession of the United States, the District of Columbia, Indian tribal government, and any political subdivision thereof.

(4) QUALIFIED ISSUER.—The term "qualified issuer" means—

(A) a clean renewable energy bond lender,

(B) a cooperative electric company, or

(C) a governmental body.

(5) QUALIFIED BORROWER.—The term "qualified borrower" means—

(A) a mutual or cooperative electric company described in section 501(c)(12) or 1381(a)(2)(C), or

(B) a governmental body.

(k) SPECIAL RULES RELATING TO POOL BONDS.—No portion of a pooled financing bond may be allocable to any loan unless the borrower has entered into a written loan commitment for such portion prior to the issue date of such issue.

(l) OTHER DEFINITIONS AND SPECIAL RULES.—For purposes of this section—

(1) BOND.—The term "bond" includes any obligation.

(2) POOLED FINANCING BOND.—The term "pooled financing bond" shall have the meaning given such term by section 149(f)(6)(A).

(3) PARTNERSHIP; S CORPORATION; AND OTHER PASS-THRU ENTITIES.—

(A) IN GENERAL.—Under regulations prescribed by the Secretary, in the case of a partnership, trust, S corporation, or other pass-thru entity, rules similar to the rules of section 41(g) shall apply with respect to the credit allowable under subsection (a).

(B) NO BASIS ADJUSTMENT.—In the case of a bond held by a partnership or an S corporation, rules similar to the rules under section 1397E(l) (as in effect before its repeal by the Tax Cuts and Jobs Act) shall apply.

(4) RATABLE PRINCIPAL AMORTIZATION REQUIRED.—A bond shall not be treated as a clean renewable energy bond unless it is part of an issue which provides for an equal amount of

principal to be paid by the qualified issuer during each calendar year that the issue is outstanding.

(5) REPORTING.—Issuers of clean renewable energy bonds shall submit reports similar to the reports required under section 149(e).

Amendments

• 2017, Tax Cuts and Jobs Act (P.L. 115-97)

P.L. 115-97, §13404(c)(2):

Amended Code Sec. 54(l)(3)(B) by inserting "(as in effect before its repeal by the Tax Cuts and Jobs Act)" after "sec-

tion 1397E(I)" [sic]. **Effective** for bonds issued after 12-31-2017.

(m) TERMINATION.—This section shall not apply with respect to any bond issued after December 31, 2009.

[¶5100] CODE SEC. 54A. CREDIT TO HOLDERS OF QUALIFIED TAX CREDIT BONDS. [*Stricken.*]

[CCH Explanation at ¶875. Committee Reports at ¶10,580.]

Amendments

• 2017, Tax Cuts and Jobs Act (P.L. 115-97)

P.L. 115-97, §13404(a):

Amended part IV of subchapter A of chapter 1 by striking subpart I (Code Secs. 54A-54F). **Effective** for bonds issued after 12-31-2017. Prior to being stricken, Code Sec. 54A read as follows:

SEC. 54A. CREDIT TO HOLDERS OF QUALIFIED TAX CREDIT BONDS.

(a) ALLOWANCE OF CREDIT.—If a taxpayer holds a qualified tax credit bond on one or more credit allowance dates of the bond during any taxable year, there shall be allowed as a credit against the tax imposed by this chapter for the taxable year an amount equal to the sum of the credits determined under subsection (b) with respect to such dates.

(b) AMOUNT OF CREDIT.—

(1) IN GENERAL.—The amount of the credit determined under this subsection with respect to any credit allowance date for a qualified tax credit bond is 25 percent of the annual credit determined with respect to such bond.

(2) ANNUAL CREDIT.—The annual credit determined with respect to any qualified tax credit bond is the product of—

(A) the applicable credit rate, multiplied by

(B) the outstanding face amount of the bond.

(3) APPLICABLE CREDIT RATE.—For purposes of paragraph (2), the applicable credit rate is the rate which the Secretary estimates will permit the issuance of qualified tax credit bonds with a specified maturity or redemption date without discount and without interest cost to the qualified issuer. The applicable credit rate with respect to any qualified tax credit bond shall be determined as of the first day on which there is a binding, written contract for the sale or exchange of the bond.

(4) SPECIAL RULE FOR ISSUANCE AND REDEMPTION.—In the case of a bond which is issued during the 3-month period ending on a credit allowance date, the amount of the credit determined under this subsection with respect to such credit allowance date shall be a ratable portion of the credit otherwise determined based on the portion of the 3-month period during which the bond is outstanding. A similar rule shall apply when the bond is redeemed or matures.

(c) LIMITATION BASED ON AMOUNT OF TAX.—

(1) IN GENERAL.—The credit allowed under subsection (a) for any taxable year shall not exceed the excess of—

(A) the sum of the regular tax liability (as defined in section 26(b)) plus the tax imposed by section 55, over

(B) the sum of the credits allowable under this part (other than subparts C and J and this subpart).

(2) CARRYOVER OF UNUSED CREDIT.—If the credit allowable under subsection (a) exceeds the limitation imposed by paragraph (1) for such taxable year, such excess shall be carried to the succeeding taxable year and added to the credit allowable under subsection (a) for such taxable year (determined before the application of paragraph (1) for such succeeding taxable year).

(d) QUALIFIED TAX CREDIT BOND.—For purposes of this section—

(1) QUALIFIED TAX CREDIT BOND.—The term "qualified tax credit bond" means—

(A) a qualified forestry conservation bond,

(B) a new clean renewable energy bond,

(C) a qualified energy conservation bond,

(D) a qualified zone academy bond, or

(E) a qualified school construction bond,

which is part of an issue that meets requirements of paragraphs (2), (3), (4), (5), and (6).

(2) SPECIAL RULES RELATING TO EXPENDITURES.—

(A) IN GENERAL.—An issue shall be treated as meeting the requirements of this paragraph if, as of the date of issuance, the issuer reasonably expects—

(i) 100 percent of the available project proceeds to be spent for 1 or more qualified purposes within the 3-year period beginning on such date of issuance, and

(ii) a binding commitment with a third party to spend at least 10 percent of such available project proceeds will be incurred within the 6-month period beginning on such date of issuance.

(B) FAILURE TO SPEND REQUIRED AMOUNT OF BOND PROCEEDS WITHIN 3 YEARS.—

(i) IN GENERAL.—To the extent that less than 100 percent of the available project proceeds of the issue are expended by the close of the expenditure period for 1 or more qualified purposes, the issuer shall redeem all of the nonqualified bonds within 90 days after the end of such period. For purposes of this paragraph, the amount of the nonqualified bonds required to be redeemed shall be determined in the same manner as under section 142.

(ii) EXPENDITURE PERIOD.—For purposes of this subpart, the term "expenditure period" means, with respect to any issue, the 3-year period beginning on the date of issuance. Such term shall include any extension of such period under clause (iii).

(iii) EXTENSION OF PERIOD.—Upon submission of a request prior to the expiration of the expenditure period (determined without regard to any extension under this clause), the Secretary may extend such period if the issuer establishes that the failure to expend the proceeds within the original expenditure period is due to reasonable cause and the expenditures for qualified purposes will continue to proceed with due diligence.

(C) QUALIFIED PURPOSE.—For purposes of this paragraph, the term "qualified purpose" means—

(i) in the case of a qualified forestry conservation bond, a purpose specified in section 54B(e),

(ii) in the case of a new clean renewable energy bond, a purpose specified in section 54C(a)(1),

(iii) in the case of a qualified energy conservation bond, a purpose specified in section 54D(a)(1),

(iv) in the case of a qualified zone academy bond, a purpose specified in section 54E(a)(1), and

(v) in the case of a qualified school construction bond, a purpose specified in section 54F(a)(1).

(D) REIMBURSEMENT.—For purposes of this subtitle, available project proceeds of an issue shall be treated as spent for a qualified purpose if such proceeds are used to reimburse the issuer for amounts paid for a qualified purpose after the date that the Secretary makes an allocation of bond limitation with respect to such issue, but only if—

(i) prior to the payment of the original expenditure, the issuer declared its intent to reimburse such expenditure with the proceeds of a qualified tax credit bond,

(ii) not later than 60 days after payment of the original expenditure, the issuer adopts an official intent to reimburse the original expenditure with such proceeds, and

(iii) the reimbursement is made not later than 18 months after the date the original expenditure is paid.

(3) REPORTING.—An issue shall be treated as meeting the requirements of this paragraph if the issuer of qualified tax credit bonds submits reports similar to the reports required under section 149(e).

(4) SPECIAL RULES RELATING TO ARBITRAGE.—

(A) IN GENERAL.—An issue shall be treated as meeting the requirements of this paragraph if the issuer satisfies the requirements of section 148 with respect to the proceeds of the issue.

(B) SPECIAL RULE FOR INVESTMENTS DURING EXPENDITURE PERIOD.—An issue shall not be treated as failing to meet the requirements of subparagraph (A) by reason of any investment of available project proceeds during the expenditure period.

(C) SPECIAL RULE FOR RESERVE FUNDS.—An issue shall not be treated as failing to meet the requirements of subparagraph (A) by reason of any fund which is expected to be used to repay such issue if—

(i) such fund is funded at a rate not more rapid than equal annual installments,

(ii) such fund is funded in a manner reasonably expected to result in an amount not greater than an amount necessary to repay the issue, and

(iii) the yield on such fund is not greater than the discount rate determined under paragraph (5)(B) with respect to the issue.

(5) MATURITY LIMITATION.—

(A) IN GENERAL.—An issue shall be treated as meeting the requirements of this paragraph if the maturity of any bond which is part of such issue does not exceed the maximum term determined by the Secretary under subparagraph (B).

(B) MAXIMUM TERM.—During each calendar month, the Secretary shall determine the maximum term permitted under this paragraph for bonds issued during the following calendar month. Such maximum term shall be the term which the Secretary estimates will result in the present value of the obligation to repay the principal on the bond being equal to 50 percent of the face amount of such bond. Such

present value shall be determined using as a discount rate the average annual interest rate of tax-exempt obligations having a term of 10 years or more which are issued during the month. If the term as so determined is not a multiple of a whole year, such term shall be rounded to the next highest whole year.

(6) PROHIBITION ON FINANCIAL CONFLICTS OF INTEREST.—An issue shall be treated as meeting the requirements of this paragraph if the issuer certifies that—

(A) applicable State and local law requirements governing conflicts of interest are satisfied with respect to such issue, and

(B) if the Secretary prescribes additional conflicts of interest rules governing the appropriate Members of Congress, Federal, State, and local officials, and their spouses, such additional rules are satisfied with respect to such issue.

(e) OTHER DEFINITIONS.—For purposes of this subchapter—

(1) CREDIT ALLOWANCE DATE.—The term "credit allowance date" means—

(A) March 15,

(B) June 15,

(C) September 15, and

(D) December 15.

Such term includes the last day on which the bond is outstanding.

(2) BOND.—The term "bond" includes any obligation.

(3) STATE.—The term "State" includes the District of Columbia and any possession of the United States.

(4) AVAILABLE PROJECT PROCEEDS.—The term "available project proceeds" means—

(A) the excess of—

(i) the proceeds from the sale of an issue, over

(ii) the issuance costs financed by the issue (to the extent that such costs do not exceed 2 percent of such proceeds), and

(B) the proceeds from any investment of the excess described in subparagraph (A).

(f) CREDIT TREATED AS INTEREST.—For purposes of this subtitle, the credit determined under subsection (a) shall be treated as interest which is includible in gross income.

(g) S CORPORATIONS AND PARTNERSHIPS.—In the case of a tax credit bond held by an S corporation or partnership, the allocation of the credit allowed by this section to the shareholders of such corporation or partners of such partnership shall be treated as a distribution.

(h) BONDS HELD BY REAL ESTATE INVESTMENT TRUSTS.—If any qualified tax credit bond is held by a real estate investment trust, the credit determined under subsection (a) shall be allowed to beneficiaries of such trust (and any gross income included under subsection (f) with respect to such credit shall be distributed to such beneficiaries) under procedures prescribed by the Secretary.

(i) CREDITS MAY BE STRIPPED.—Under regulations prescribed by the Secretary—

(1) IN GENERAL.—There may be a separation (including at issuance) of the ownership of a qualified tax credit bond and the entitlement to the credit under this section with respect to such bond. In case of any such separation, the credit under this section shall be allowed to the person who on the credit allowance date holds the instrument evidencing the entitlement to the credit and not to the holder of the bond.

(2) CERTAIN RULES TO APPLY.—In the case of a separation described in paragraph (1), the rules of section 1286 shall apply to the qualified tax credit bond as if it were a stripped bond and to the credit under this section as if it were a stripped coupon.

[¶ 5105] CODE SEC. 54B. QUALIFIED FORESTRY CONSERVATION BONDS.
[*Stricken.*]

[CCH Explanation at ¶ 875. Committee Reports at ¶ 10,580.]

Amendments
• **2017, Tax Cuts and Jobs Act (P.L. 115-97)**

P.L. 115-97, § 13404(a):

Amended part IV of subchapter A of chapter 1 by striking subpart I (Code Secs. 54A-54F). **Effective** for bonds issued after 12-31-2017. Prior to being stricken, Code Sec. 54B read as follows:

SEC. 54B. QUALIFIED FORESTRY CONSERVATION BONDS.

(a) QUALIFIED FORESTRY CONSERVATION BOND.—For purposes of this subchapter, the term "qualified forestry conservation bond" means any bond issued as part of an issue if—

(1) 100 percent of the available project proceeds of such issue are to be used for one or more qualified forestry conservation purposes,

(2) the bond is issued by a qualified issuer, and

(3) the issuer designates such bond for purposes of this section.

(b) LIMITATION ON AMOUNT OF BONDS DESIGNATED.—The maximum aggregate face amount of bonds which may be designated under subsection (a) by any issuer shall not exceed the limitation amount allocated to such issuer under subsection (d).

(c) NATIONAL LIMITATION ON AMOUNT OF BONDS DESIGNATED.—There is a national qualified forestry conservation bond limitation of $500,000,000.

(d) ALLOCATIONS.—

(1) IN GENERAL.—The Secretary shall make allocations of the amount of the national qualified forestry conservation bond limitation described in subsection (c) among qualified forestry conservation purposes in such manner as the Secretary determines appropriate so as to ensure that all of such limitation is allocated before the date which is 24 months after the date of the enactment of this section.

(2) SOLICITATION OF APPLICATIONS.—The Secretary shall solicit applications for allocations of the national qualified forestry conservation bond limitation described in subsection (c) not later than 90 days after the date of the enactment of this section.

(e) QUALIFIED FORESTRY CONSERVATION PURPOSE.—For purposes of this section, the term "qualified forestry conservation purpose" means the acquisition by a State or any political subdivision or instrumentality thereof or a 501(c)(3) organization (as defined in section 150(a)(4)) from an unrelated person of forest and forest land that meets the following qualifications:

(1) Some portion of the land acquired must be adjacent to United States Forest Service Land.

(2) At least half of the land acquired must be transferred to the United States Forest Service at no net cost to the United States and not more than half of the land acquired may either remain with or be conveyed to a State.

(3) All of the land must be subject to a native fish habitat conservation plan approved by the United States Fish and Wildlife Service.

(4) The amount of acreage acquired must be at least 40,000 acres.

(f) QUALIFIED ISSUER.—For purposes of this section, the term "qualified issuer" means a State or any political subdivision or instrumentality thereof or a 501(c)(3) organization (as defined in section 150(a)(4)).

(g) SPECIAL ARBITRAGE RULE.—In the case of any qualified forestry conservation bond issued as part of an issue, section 54A(d)(4)(C) shall be applied to such issue without regard to clause (i).

(h) ELECTION TO TREAT 50 PERCENT OF BOND ALLOCATION AS PAYMENT OF TAX.—

(1) IN GENERAL.—If—

(A) a qualified issuer receives an allocation of any portion of the national qualified forestry conservation bond limitation described in subsection (c), and

(B) the qualified issuer elects the application of this subsection with respect to such allocation,

then the qualified issuer (without regard to whether the issuer is subject to tax under this chapter) shall be treated as having made a payment against the tax imposed by this chapter, for the taxable year preceding the taxable year in which the allocation is received, in an amount equal to 50 percent of the amount of such allocation.

(2) TREATMENT OF DEEMED PAYMENT.—

(A) IN GENERAL.—Notwithstanding any other provision of this title, the Secretary shall not use the payment of tax described in paragraph (1) as an offset or credit against any tax liability of the qualified issuer but shall refund such payment to such issuer.

(B) NO INTEREST.—Except as provided in paragraph (3)(A), the payment described in paragraph (1) shall not be taken into account in determining any amount of interest under this title.

(3) REQUIREMENT FOR, AND EFFECT OF, ELECTION.—

(A) REQUIREMENT.—No election under this subsection shall take effect unless the qualified issuer certifies to the Secretary that any payment of tax refunded to the issuer under this subsection will be used exclusively for 1 or more qualified forestry conservation purposes. If the qualified issuer fails to use any portion of such payment for such purpose, the issuer shall be liable to the United States in an amount equal to such portion, plus interest at the overpayment rate under section 6621 for the period from the date such portion was refunded to the date such amount is paid. Any such amount shall be assessed and collected in the same manner as tax imposed by this chapter, except that subchapter B of chapter 63 (relating to deficiency procedures) shall not apply in respect of such assessment or collection.

(B) EFFECT OF ELECTION ON ALLOCATION.—If a qualified issuer makes the election under this subsection with respect to any allocation—

(i) the issuer may issue no bonds pursuant to the allocation, and

(ii) the Secretary may not reallocate such allocation for any other purpose.

[¶ 5110] CODE SEC. 54C. NEW CLEAN RENEWABLE ENERGY BONDS. *[Stricken.]*

[CCH Explanation at ¶ 875. Committee Reports at ¶ 10,580.]

Amendments

• 2017, Tax Cuts and Jobs Act (P.L. 115-97)

P.L. 115-97, § 13404(a):

Amended part IV of subchapter A of chapter 1 by striking subpart I (Code Secs. 54A-54F). **Effective** for bonds issued after 12-31-2017. Prior to being stricken, Code Sec. 54C read as follows:

SEC. 54C. NEW CLEAN RENEWABLE ENERGY BONDS.

(a) NEW CLEAN RENEWABLE ENERGY BOND.—For purposes of this subpart, the term "new clean renewable energy bond" means any bond issued as part of an issue if—

(1) 100 percent of the available project proceeds of such issue are to be used for capital expenditures incurred by governmental bodies, public power providers, or cooperative electric companies for one or more qualified renewable energy facilities,

(2) the bond is issued by a qualified issuer, and

(3) the issuer designates such bond for purposes of this section.

(b) REDUCED CREDIT AMOUNT.—The annual credit determined under section 54A(b) with respect to any new clean renewable energy bond shall be 70 percent of the amount so determined without regard to this subsection.

(c) LIMITATION ON AMOUNT OF BONDS DESIGNATED.—

(1) IN GENERAL.—The maximum aggregate face amount of bonds which may be designated under subsection (a) by any issuer shall not exceed the limitation amount allocated under this subsection to such issuer.

(2) NATIONAL LIMITATION ON AMOUNT OF BONDS DESIGNATED.—There is a national new clean renewable energy bond limitation of $800,000,000 which shall be allocated by the Secretary as provided in paragraph (3), except that—

(A) not more than 33^{1}/$_{3}$ percent thereof may be allocated to qualified projects of public power providers,

(B) not more than 33^{1}/$_{3}$ percent thereof may be allocated to qualified projects of governmental bodies, and

(C) not more than 33^{1}/$_{3}$ percent thereof may be allocated to qualified projects of cooperative electric companies.

(3) METHOD OF ALLOCATION.—

(A) ALLOCATION AMONG PUBLIC POWER PROVIDERS.—After the Secretary determines the qualified projects of public power providers which are appropriate for receiving an allocation of the national new clean renewable energy bond limitation, the Secretary shall, to the maximum extent practicable, make allocations among such projects in such manner that the amount allocated to each such project bears the same ratio to the cost of such project as the limitation under paragraph (2)(A) bears to the cost of all such projects.

(B) ALLOCATION AMONG GOVERNMENTAL BODIES AND COOPERATIVE ELECTRIC COMPANIES.—The Secretary shall make allocations of the amount of the national new clean renewable energy bond limitation described in paragraphs (2)(B) and (2)(C) among qualified projects of governmental bodies and cooperative electric companies, respectively, in such manner as the Secretary determines appropriate.

(4) ADDITIONAL LIMITATION.—The national new clean renewable energy bond limitation shall be increased by $1,600,000,000. Such increase shall be allocated by the Secretary consistent with the rules of paragraphs (2) and (3).

(d) DEFINITIONS.—For purposes of this section—

(1) QUALIFIED RENEWABLE ENERGY FACILITY.—The term "qualified renewable energy facility" means a qualified facility (as determined under section 45(d) without regard to paragraphs (8) and (10) thereof and to any placed in service date) owned by a public power provider, a governmental body, or a cooperative electric company.

(2) PUBLIC POWER PROVIDER.—The term "public power provider" means a State utility with a service obligation, as such terms are defined in section 217 of the Federal Power Act (as in effect on the date of the enactment of this paragraph).

(3) GOVERNMENTAL BODY.—The term "governmental body" means any State or Indian tribal government, or any political subdivision thereof.

(4) COOPERATIVE ELECTRIC COMPANY.—The term "cooperative electric company" means a mutual or cooperative electric company described in section 501(c)(12) or section 1381(a)(2)(C).

(5) CLEAN RENEWABLE ENERGY BOND LENDER.—The term "clean renewable energy bond lender" means a lender which is a cooperative which is owned by, or has outstanding loans to, 100 or more cooperative electric companies and is in existence on February 1, 2002, and shall include any affiliated entity which is controlled by such lender.

(6) QUALIFIED ISSUER.—The term "qualified issuer" means a public power provider, a cooperative electric company, a governmental body, a clean renewable energy bond lender, or a not-for-profit electric utility which has received a loan or loan guarantee under the Rural Electrification Act.

[¶ 5115] CODE SEC. 54D. QUALIFIED ENERGY CONSERVATION BONDS. *[Stricken.]*

[CCH Explanation at ¶ 875. Committee Reports at ¶ 10,580.]

Amendments

• 2017, Tax Cuts and Jobs Act (P.L. 115-97)

P.L. 115-97, § 13404(a):

Amended part IV of subchapter A of chapter 1 by striking subpart I (Code Secs. 54A-54F). **Effective** for bonds issued after 12-31-2017. Prior to being stricken, Code Sec. 54D read as follows:

SEC. 54D. QUALIFIED ENERGY CONSERVATION BONDS.

(a) QUALIFIED ENERGY CONSERVATION BOND.—For purposes of this subchapter, the term "qualified energy conservation bond" means any bond issued as part of an issue if—

(1) 100 percent of the available project proceeds of such issue are to be used for one or more qualified conservation purposes,

(2) the bond is issued by a State or local government, and

(3) the issuer designates such bond for purposes of this section.

(b) REDUCED CREDIT AMOUNT.—The annual credit determined under section 54A(b) with respect to any qualified energy conservation bond shall be 70 percent of the amount so determined without regard to this subsection.

(c) LIMITATION ON AMOUNT OF BONDS DESIGNATED.—The maximum aggregate face amount of bonds which may be designated under subsection (a) by any issuer shall not exceed the limitation amount allocated to such issuer under subsection (e).

(d) NATIONAL LIMITATION ON AMOUNT OF BONDS DESIGNATED.—There is a national qualified energy conservation bond limitation of $3,200,000,000.

(e) ALLOCATIONS.—

(1) IN GENERAL.—The limitation applicable under subsection (d) shall be allocated by the Secretary among the States in proportion to the population of the States.

(2) ALLOCATIONS TO LARGEST LOCAL GOVERNMENTS.—

(A) IN GENERAL.—In the case of any State in which there is a large local government, each such local government shall be allocated a portion of such State's allocation which bears the same ratio to the State's allocation (determined without regard to this subparagraph) as the population of such large local government bears to the population of such State.

(B) ALLOCATION OF UNUSED LIMITATION TO STATE.—The amount allocated under this subsection to a large local government may be reallocated by such local government to the State in which such local government is located.

(C) LARGE LOCAL GOVERNMENT.—For purposes of this section, the term "large local government" means any municipality or county if such municipality or county has a population of 100,000 or more.

(3) ALLOCATION TO ISSUERS; RESTRICTION ON PRIVATE ACTIVITY BONDS.—Any allocation under this subsection to a State or large local government shall be allocated by such State or large local government to issuers within the State in a manner that results in not less than 70 percent of the allocation to such State or large local government being used to designate bonds which are not private activity bonds.

(4) SPECIAL RULES FOR BONDS TO IMPLEMENT GREEN COMMUNITY PROGRAMS.—In the case of any bond issued for the purpose of providing loans, grants, or other repayment mechanisms for capital expenditures to implement green community programs, such bond shall not be treated as a private activity bond for purposes of paragraph (3).

(f) QUALIFIED CONSERVATION PURPOSE.—For purposes of this section—

(1) IN GENERAL.—The term "qualified conservation purpose" means any of the following:

(A) Capital expenditures incurred for purposes of—

(i) reducing energy consumption in publicly-owned buildings by at least 20 percent,

(ii) implementing green community programs (including the use of loans, grants, or other repayment mechanisms to implement such programs),

(iii) rural development involving the production of electricity from renewable energy resources, or

(iv) any qualified facility (as determined under section 45(d) without regard to paragraphs (8) and (10) thereof and without regard to any placed in service date).

(B) Expenditures with respect to research facilities, and research grants, to support research in—

(i) development of cellulosic ethanol or other nonfossil fuels,

(ii) technologies for the capture and sequestration of carbon dioxide produced through the use of fossil fuels,

(iii) increasing the efficiency of existing technologies for producing nonfossil fuels,

(iv) automobile battery technologies and other technologies to reduce fossil fuel consumption in transportation, or

(v) technologies to reduce energy use in buildings.

(C) Mass commuting facilities and related facilities that reduce the consumption of energy, including expenditures to reduce pollution from vehicles used for mass commuting.

(D) Demonstration projects designed to promote the commercialization of—

(i) green building technology,

(ii) conversion of agricultural waste for use in the production of fuel or otherwise,

(iii) advanced battery manufacturing technologies,

(iv) technologies to reduce peak use of electricity, or

(v) technologies for the capture and sequestration of carbon dioxide emitted from combusting fossil fuels in order to produce electricity.

(E) Public education campaigns to promote energy efficiency.

(2) SPECIAL RULES FOR PRIVATE ACTIVITY BONDS.—For purposes of this section, in the case of any private activity bond, the term "qualified conservation purposes" shall not include any expenditure which is not a capital expenditure.

(g) POPULATION.—

(1) IN GENERAL.—The population of any State or local government shall be determined for purposes of this section as provided in section 146(j) for the calendar year which includes the date of the enactment of this section.

(2) SPECIAL RULE FOR COUNTIES.—In determining the population of any county for purposes of this section, any population of such county which is taken into account in determining the population of any municipality which is a large local government shall not be taken into account in determining the population of such county.

(h) APPLICATION TO INDIAN TRIBAL GOVERNMENTS.—An Indian tribal government shall be treated for purposes of this section in the same manner as a large local government, except that—

(1) an Indian tribal government shall be treated for purposes of subsection (e) as located within a State to the extent of so much of the population of such government as resides within such State, and

(2) any bond issued by an Indian tribal government shall be treated as a qualified energy conservation bond only if issued as part of an issue the available project proceeds of which are used for purposes for which such Indian tribal government could issue bonds to which section 103(a) applies.

[¶5120] CODE SEC. 54E. QUALIFIED ZONE ACADEMY BONDS. [*Stricken.*]

[CCH Explanation at ¶875. Committee Reports at ¶10,580.]

Amendments

• 2017, Tax Cuts and Jobs Act (P.L. 115-97)

P.L. 115-97, §13404(a):

Amended part IV of subchapter A of chapter 1 by striking subpart I (Code Secs. 54A-54F). **Effective** for bonds issued after 12-31-2017. Prior to being stricken, Code Sec. 54E read as follows:

SEC. 54E. QUALIFIED ZONE ACADEMY BONDS.

(a) QUALIFIED ZONE ACADEMY BONDS.—For purposes of this subchapter, the term "qualified zone academy bond" means any bond issued as part of an issue if—

(1) 100 percent of the available project proceeds of such issue are to be used for a qualified purpose with respect to a qualified zone academy established by an eligible local education agency,

(2) the bond is issued by a State or local government within the jurisdiction of which such academy is located, and

(3) the issuer—

(A) designates such bond for purposes of this section,

(B) certifies that it has written assurances that the private business contribution requirement of subsection (b) will be met with respect to such academy, and

(C) certifies that it has the written approval of the eligible local education agency for such bond issuance.

(b) PRIVATE BUSINESS CONTRIBUTION REQUIREMENT.—For purposes of subsection (a), the private business contribution requirement of this subsection is met with respect to any issue if the eligible local education agency that established the qualified zone academy has written commitments from private entities to make qualified contributions having a present value (as of the date of issuance of the issue) of not less than 10 percent of the proceeds of the issue.

(c) LIMITATION ON AMOUNT OF BONDS DESIGNATED.—

(1) NATIONAL LIMITATION.—There is a national zone academy bond limitation for each calendar year. Such limitation is $400,000,000 for 2008, $1,400,000,000 for 2009 and 2010, and $400,000,000 for 2011, 2012, 2013, 2014, 2015, and 2016 and, except as provided in paragraph (4), zero thereafter.

(2) ALLOCATION OF LIMITATION.—The national zone academy bond limitation for a calendar year shall be allocated by the Secretary among the States on the basis of their respective populations of individuals below the poverty line (as defined by the Office of Management and Budget). The limitation amount allocated to a State under the preceding sentence shall be allocated by the State education agency to qualified zone academies within such State.

(3) DESIGNATION SUBJECT TO LIMITATION AMOUNT.—The maximum aggregate face amount of bonds issued during any calendar year which may be designated under subsection (a) with respect to any qualified zone academy shall not exceed the limitation amount allocated to such academy under paragraph (2) for such calendar year.

(4) CARRYOVER OF UNUSED LIMITATION.—

(A) IN GENERAL.—If for any calendar year—

(i) the limitation amount for any State, exceeds

(ii) the amount of bonds issued during such year which are designated under subsection (a) with respect to qualified zone academies within such State,

the limitation amount for such State for the following calendar year shall be increased by the amount of such excess.

(B) LIMITATION ON CARRYOVER.—Any carryforward of a limitation amount may be carried only to the first 2 years following the unused limitation year. For purposes of the preceding sentence, a limitation amount shall be treated as used on a first-in first-out basis.

(C) COORDINATION WITH SECTION 1397E.—Any carryover determined under section 1397E(e)(4) (relating to carryover of unused limitation) with respect to any State to calendar year 2008 or 2009 shall be treated for purposes of this section as a carryover with respect to such State for such calendar year under subparagraph (A), and the limitation of subparagraph (B) shall apply to such carryover taking into account the calendar years to which such carryover relates.

(d) DEFINITIONS.—For purposes of this section—

(1) QUALIFIED ZONE ACADEMY.—The term "qualified zone academy" means any public school (or academic program within a public school) which is established by and operated under the supervision of an eligible local education agency to provide education or training below the postsecondary level if—

(A) such public school or program (as the case may be) is designed in cooperation with business to enhance the academic curriculum, increase graduation and employment rates, and better prepare students for the rigors of college and the increasingly complex workforce,

(B) students in such public school or program (as the case may be) will be subject to the same academic standards and assessments as other students educated by the eligible local education agency,

(C) the comprehensive education plan of such public school or program is approved by the eligible local education agency, and

(D)(i) such public school is located in an empowerment zone or enterprise community (including any such zone or community designated after the date of the enactment of this section), or

(ii) there is a reasonable expectation (as of the date of issuance of the bonds) that at least 35 percent of the students attending such school or participating in such program (as the case may be) will be eligible for free or reduced-cost lunches under the school lunch program established under the National School Lunch Act.

(2) ELIGIBLE LOCAL EDUCATION AGENCY.—For purposes of this section, the term "eligible local education agency" means any local educational agency as defined in section 8101 of the Elementary and Secondary Education Act of 1965.

(3) QUALIFIED PURPOSE.—The term "qualified purpose" means, with respect to any qualified zone academy—

(A) rehabilitating or repairing the public school facility in which the academy is established,

(B) providing equipment for use at such academy,

(C) developing course materials for education to be provided at such academy, and

(D) training teachers and other school personnel in such academy.

(4) QUALIFIED CONTRIBUTIONS.—The term "qualified contribution" means any contribution (of a type and quality acceptable to the eligible local education agency) of—

(A) equipment for use in the qualified zone academy (including state-of-the-art technology and vocational equipment),

(B) technical assistance in developing curriculum or in training teachers in order to promote appropriate market driven technology in the classroom,

(C) services of employees as volunteer mentors,

(D) internships, field trips, or other educational opportunities outside the academy for students, or

(E) any other property or service specified by the eligible local education agency.

[¶ 5125] CODE SEC. 54F. QUALIFIED SCHOOL CONSTRUCTION BONDS. [*Stricken.*]

[CCH Explanation at ¶ 875. Committee Reports at ¶ 10,580.]

Amendments

• 2017, Tax Cuts and Jobs Act (P.L. 115-97)

P.L. 115-97, §13404(a):

Amended part IV of subchapter A of chapter 1 by striking subpart I (Code Secs. 54A-54F). **Effective** for bonds issued after 12-31-2017. Prior to being stricken, Code Sec. 54F read as follows:

SEC. 54F. QUALIFIED SCHOOL CONSTRUCTION BONDS.

(a) QUALIFIED SCHOOL CONSTRUCTION BOND.—For purposes of this subchapter, the term "qualified school construction bond" means any bond issued as part of an issue if—

(1) 100 percent of the available project proceeds of such issue are to be used for the construction, rehabilitation, or repair of a public school facility or for the acquisition of land on which such a facility is to be constructed with part of the proceeds of such issue,

(2) the bond is issued by a State or local government within the jurisdiction of which such school is located, and

(3) the issuer designates such bond for purposes of this section.

(b) LIMITATION ON AMOUNT OF BONDS DESIGNATED.—The maximum aggregate face amount of bonds issued during any calendar year which may be designated under subsection (a) by any issuer shall not exceed the limitation amount allocated under subsection (d) for such calendar year to such issuer.

(c) NATIONAL LIMITATION ON AMOUNT OF BONDS DESIGNATED.—There is a national qualified school construction bond limitation for each calendar year. Such limitation is—

(1) $11,000,000,000 for 2009,

(2) $11,000,000,000 for 2010, and

(3) except as provided in subsection (e), zero after 2010.

(d) ALLOCATION OF LIMITATION.—

(1) ALLOCATION AMONG STATES.—Except as provided in paragraph (2)(C), the limitation applicable under subsection (c) for any calendar year shall be allocated by the Secretary among the States in proportion to the respective amounts each such State is eligible to receive under section 1124 of the Elementary and Secondary Education Act of 1965 (20 U.S.C. 6333) for the most recent fiscal year ending before such calendar year. The limitation amount allocated to a State under the preceding sentence shall be allocated by the State education agency (or such other agency as is authorized under State law to make such allocation) to issuers within such State.

(2) 40 PERCENT OF LIMITATION ALLOCATED AMONG LARGEST SCHOOL DISTRICTS.—

(A) IN GENERAL.—40 percent of the limitation applicable under subsection (c) for any calendar year shall be allocated under subparagraph (B) by the Secretary among local educational agencies which are large local educational agencies for such year.

(B) ALLOCATION FORMULA.—The amount to be allocated under subparagraph (A) for any calendar year shall be allocated among large local educational agencies in proportion to the respective amounts each such agency received under section 1124 of the Elementary and Secondary Education Act of 1965 (20 U.S.C. 6333) for the most recent fiscal year ending before such calendar year.

(C) REDUCTION IN STATE ALLOCATION.—The allocation to any State under paragraph (1) shall be reduced by the aggregate amount of the allocations under this paragraph to large local educational agencies within such State.

(D) ALLOCATION OF UNUSED LIMITATION TO STATE.—The amount allocated under this paragraph to a large local educational agency for any calendar year may be reallocated by such agency to the State in which such agency is located for such calendar year. Any amount reallocated to a State under the preceding sentence may be allocated as provided in paragraph (1).

(E) LARGE LOCAL EDUCATIONAL AGENCY.—For purposes of this paragraph, the term "large local educational agency" means, with respect to a calendar year, any local educational agency if such agency is—

(i) among the 100 local educational agencies with the largest numbers of children aged 5 through 17 from families living below the poverty level, as determined by the Secretary using the most recent data available from the Department of Commerce that are satisfactory to the Secretary, or

(ii) 1 of not more than 25 local educational agencies (other than those described in clause (i)) that the Secretary of Education determines (based on the most recent data available satisfactory to the Secretary) are in particular need of assistance, based on a low level of resources for school construction, a high level of enrollment growth, or such other factors as the Secretary deems appropriate.

(3) ALLOCATIONS TO CERTAIN POSSESSIONS.—The amount to be allocated under paragraph (1) to any possession of the United States other than Puerto Rico shall be the amount which would have been allocated if all allocations under paragraph (1) were made on the basis of respective populations of individuals below the poverty line (as defined by the Office of Management and Budget). In making other allocations, the amount to be allocated under paragraph (1) shall be reduced by the aggregate amount allocated under this paragraph to possessions of the United States.

(4) ALLOCATIONS FOR INDIAN SCHOOLS.—In addition to the amounts otherwise allocated under this subsection, $200,000,000 for calendar year 2009, and $200,000,000 for calendar year 2010, shall be allocated by the Secretary of the Interior for purposes of the construction, rehabilitation, and repair of schools funded by the Bureau of Indian Affairs. In the case of amounts allocated under the preceding sentence, Indian tribal governments (as defined in section 7701(a)(40)) shall be treated as qualified issuers for purposes of this subchapter.

(e) CARRYOVER OF UNUSED LIMITATION.—If for any calendar year—

(1) the amount allocated under subsection (d) to any State, exceeds

(2) the amount of bonds issued during such year which are designated under subsection (a) pursuant to such allocation,

the limitation amount under such subsection for such State for the following calendar year shall be increased by the amount of such excess. A similar rule shall apply to the amounts allocated under paragraphs (2) and (4) of subsection (d).

[¶ 5130] CODE SEC. 54AA. BUILD AMERICA BONDS. *[Stricken.]*

[CCH Explanation at ¶ 875. Committee Reports at ¶ 10,580.]

Amendments

• **2017, Tax Cuts and Jobs Act (P.L. 115-97)**

P.L. 115-97, § 13404(a):

Amended part IV of subchapter A of chapter 1 by striking subpart J (Code Sec. 54AA). **Effective** for bonds issued after 12-31-2017. Prior to being stricken, Code Sec. 54AA read as follows:

SEC. 54AA. BUILD AMERICA BONDS.

(a) IN GENERAL.—If a taxpayer holds a build America bond on one or more interest payment dates of the bond during any taxable year, there shall be allowed as a credit against the tax imposed by this chapter for the taxable year an amount equal to the sum of the credits determined under subsection (b) with respect to such dates.

(b) AMOUNT OF CREDIT.—The amount of the credit determined under this subsection with respect to any interest payment date for a build America bond is 35 percent of the amount of interest payable by the issuer with respect to such date.

(c) LIMITATION BASED ON AMOUNT OF TAX.—

(1) IN GENERAL.—The credit allowed under subsection (a) for any taxable year shall not exceed the excess of—

(A) the sum of the regular tax liability (as defined in section 26(b)) plus the tax imposed by section 55, over

(B) the sum of the credits allowable under this part (other than subpart C and this subpart).

(2) CARRYOVER OF UNUSED CREDIT.—If the credit allowable under subsection (a) exceeds the limitation imposed by paragraph (1) for such taxable year, such excess shall be carried to the succeeding taxable year and added to the credit allowable under subsection (a) for such taxable year (determined before the application of paragraph (1) for such succeeding taxable year).

(d) BUILD AMERICA BOND.—

(1) IN GENERAL.—For purposes of this section, the term "build America bond" means any obligation (other than a private activity bond) if—

(A) the interest on such obligation would (but for this section) be excludable from gross income under section 103,

(B) such obligation is issued before January 1, 2011, and

(C) the issuer makes an irrevocable election to have this section apply.

(2) APPLICABLE RULES.—For purposes of applying paragraph (1)—

(A) for purposes of section 149(b), a build America bond shall not be treated as federally guaranteed by reason of the credit allowed under subsection (a) or section 6431,

(B) for purposes of section 148, the yield on a build America bond shall be determined without regard to the credit allowed under subsection (a), and

(C) a bond shall not be treated as a build America bond if the issue price has more than a de minimis amount (determined under rules similar to the rules of section 1273(a)(3)) of premium over the stated principal amount of the bond.

(e) INTEREST PAYMENT DATE.—For purposes of this section, the term "interest payment date" means any date on which the holder of record of the build America bond is entitled to a payment of interest under such bond.

(f) SPECIAL RULES.—

(1) INTEREST ON BUILD AMERICA BONDS INCLUDIBLE IN GROSS INCOME FOR FEDERAL INCOME TAX PURPOSES.—For purposes of this title, interest on any build America bond shall be includible in gross income.

(2) APPLICATION OF CERTAIN RULES.—Rules similar to the rules of subsections (f), (g), (h), and (i) of section 54A shall apply for purposes of the credit allowed under subsection (a).

(g) SPECIAL RULE FOR QUALIFIED BONDS ISSUED BEFORE 2011.—In the case of a qualified bond issued before January 1, 2011—

(1) ISSUER ALLOWED REFUNDABLE CREDIT.—In lieu of any credit allowed under this section with respect to such bond, the issuer of such bond shall be allowed a credit as provided in section 6431.

(2) QUALIFIED BOND.—For purposes of this subsection, the term "qualified bond" means any build America bond issued as part of an issue if—

(A) 100 percent of the excess of—

(i) the available project proceeds (as defined in section 54A) of such issue, over

(ii) the amounts in a reasonably required reserve (within the meaning of section 150(a)(3)) with respect to such issue,

are to be used for capital expenditures, and

(B) the issuer makes an irrevocable election to have this subsection apply.

(h) REGULATIONS.—The Secretary may prescribe such regulations and other guidance as may be necessary or appropriate to carry out this section and section 6431.

[¶ 5135] CODE SEC. 55. ALTERNATIVE MINIMUM TAX IMPOSED.

(a) GENERAL RULE.—*In the case of a taxpayer other than a corporation, there* is hereby imposed (in addition to any other tax imposed by this subtitle) a tax equal to the excess (if any) of—

(1) the tentative minimum tax for the taxable year, over

(2) the regular tax for the taxable year.

[CCH Explanation at ¶ 310. Committee Reports at ¶ 10,300.]

Amendments

• 2017, Tax Cuts and Jobs Act (P.L. 115-97)

P.L. 115-97, § 12001(a):

Amended Code Sec. 55(a) by striking "There" and inserting "In the case of a taxpayer other than a corporation, there". **Effective** for tax years beginning after 12-31-2017.

(b) TENTATIVE MINIMUM TAX.—For purposes of this part—

(1) *AMOUNT OF TENTATIVE TAX.*—

(A) *IN GENERAL.*—*The tentative minimum tax for the taxable year is the sum of*—

(i) *26 percent of so much of the taxable excess as does not exceed $175,000, plus*

(ii) *28 percent of so much of the taxable excess as exceeds $175,000.*

The amount determined under the preceding sentence shall be reduced by the alternative minimum tax foreign tax credit for the taxable year.

(B) *TAXABLE EXCESS.*—*For purposes of this subsection, the term "taxable excess" means so much of the alternative minimum taxable income for the taxable year as exceeds the exemption amount.*

(C) *MARRIED INDIVIDUAL FILING SEPARATE RETURN.*—*In the case of a married individual filing a separate return, subparagraph (A) shall be applied by substituting 50 percent of the dollar amount otherwise applicable under clause (i) and clause (ii) thereof. For purposes of the preceding sentence, marital status shall be determined under section 7703.*

* * *

(3) MAXIMUM RATE OF TAX ON NET CAPITAL GAIN OF NONCORPORATE TAXPAYERS.—The amount determined under the first sentence of *paragraph (1)(A)* shall not exceed the sum of—

(A) the amount determined under such first sentence computed at the rates and in the same manner as if this paragraph had not been enacted on the taxable excess reduced by the lesser of—

(i) the net capital gain; or

(ii) the sum of—

(I) the adjusted net capital gain, plus

(II) the unrecaptured section 1250 gain, plus

(B) 0 percent of so much of the adjusted net capital gain (or, if less, taxable excess) as does not exceed an amount equal to the excess described in section 1(h)(1)(B), plus

(C) 15 percent of the lesser of—

(i) so much of the adjusted net capital gain (or, if less, taxable excess) as exceeds the amount on which tax is determined under subparagraph (B), or

(ii) the excess described in section 1(h)(1)(C)(ii), plus

(D) 20 percent of the adjusted net capital gain (or, if less, taxable excess) in excess of the sum of the amounts on which tax is determined under subparagraphs (B) and (C), plus

(E) 25 percent of the amount of taxable excess in excess of the sum of the amounts on which tax is determined under the preceding subparagraphs of this paragraph.

Terms used in this paragraph which are also used in section 1(h) shall have the respective meanings given such terms by section 1(h) but computed with the adjustments under this part.

[CCH Explanation at ¶310. Committee Reports at ¶10,300.]

Amendments

• **2017, Tax Cuts and Jobs Act (P.L. 115-97)**

P.L. 115-97, §12001(b)(3)(A):

Amended Code Sec. 55(b)(1). **Effective** for tax years beginning after 12-31-2017. Prior to amendment, Code Sec. 55(b)(1) read as follows:

(1) AMOUNT OF TENTATIVE TAX.—

(A) NONCORPORATE TAXPAYERS.—

(i) IN GENERAL.—In the case of a taxpayer other than a corporation, the tentative minimum tax for the taxable year is the sum of—

(I) 26 percent of so much of the taxable excess as does not exceed $175,000, plus

(II) 28 percent of so much of the taxable excess as exceeds $175,000.

The amount determined under the preceding sentence shall be reduced by the alternative minimum tax foreign tax credit for the taxable year.

(ii) TAXABLE EXCESS.—For purposes of this subsection, the term "taxable excess" means so much of the alternative

minimum taxable income for the taxable year as exceeds the exemption amount.

(iii) MARRIED INDIVIDUAL FILING SEPARATE RETURN.—In the case of a married individual filing a separate return, clause (i) shall be applied by substituting 50 percent of the dollar amount otherwise applicable under subclause (I) and subclause (II) thereof. For purposes of the preceding sentence, marital status shall be determined under section 7703.

(B) CORPORATIONS.—In the case of a corporation, the tentative minimum tax for the taxable year is—

(i) 20 percent of so much of the alternative minimum taxable income for the taxable year as exceeds the exemption amount, reduced by

(ii) the alternative minimum tax foreign tax credit for the taxable year.

P.L. 115-97, §12001(b)(3)(B):

Amended Code Sec. 55(b)(3) by striking "paragraph (1)(A)(i)" and inserting "paragraph (1)(A)". **Effective** for tax years beginning after 12-31-2017.

(c) REGULAR TAX.—

(1) IN GENERAL.—For purposes of this section, the term "regular tax" means the regular tax liability for the taxable year (as defined in section 26(b)) reduced by the foreign tax credit allowable under section 27(a). Such term shall not include any increase in tax under section 45(e)(11)(C), 49(b) or 50(a) or subsection (j) or (k) of section 42.

* * *

[CCH Explanation at ¶310. Committee Reports at ¶10,300.]

Amendments

• **2017, Tax Cuts and Jobs Act (P.L. 115-97)**

P.L. 115-97, §12001(b)(4):

Amended Code Sec. 55(c)(1) by striking ", the section 936 credit allowable under section 27(b), and the Puerto Rico

economic activity credit under section 30A" before the period at the end of the first sentence. **Effective** for tax years beginning after 12-31-2017.

(d) EXEMPTION AMOUNT.—For purposes of this section—

* * *

(2) PHASE-OUT OF EXEMPTION AMOUNT.—The exemption amount of any taxpayers shall be reduced (but not below zero) by an amount equal to 25 percent of the amount by which the alternative minimum taxable income of the taxpayer exceeds—

(A) $150,000 in the case of a taxpayer described in paragraph (1)(A),

(B) $112,500 in the case of a taxpayer described in paragraph (1)(B), *and*

(C) 50 percent of the dollar amount applicable under subparagraph (A) in the case of a taxpayer described in subparagraph (C) or (D) of paragraph (1).

In the case of a taxpayer described in paragraph (1)(C), alternative minimum taxable income shall be increased by the lesser of (i) 25 percent of the excess of alternative minimum taxable income (determined without regard to this sentence) over the minimum amount of such income (as so determined) for which the exemption amount under paragraph (1)(C) is zero, or (ii) such exemption amount (determined without regard to this paragraph).

(3) INFLATION ADJUSTMENT.—

(A) IN GENERAL.—In the case of any taxable year beginning in a calendar year after 2012, the amounts described in subparagraph (B) shall each be increased by an amount equal to—

(i) such dollar amount, multiplied by

(ii) the cost-of-living adjustment determined under section 1(f)(3) for the calendar year in which the taxable year begins, determined by substituting "calendar year 2011" for *"calendar year 2016" in subparagraph (A)(ii) thereof.*

(B) AMOUNTS DESCRIBED.—The amounts described in this subparagraph are—

(i) each of the dollar amounts contained in subsection *(b)(1)(A),*

(ii) each of the dollar amounts contained in subparagraphs (A), (B), and (D) of paragraph (1), and

(iii) each of the dollar amounts in subparagraphs (A) and (B) of *paragraph (2).*

(C) ROUNDING.—Any increased amount determined under subparagraph (A) shall be rounded to the nearest multiple of $100.

(4) SPECIAL RULE FOR TAXABLE YEARS BEGINNING AFTER 2017 AND BEFORE 2026.—

(A) IN GENERAL.—In the case of any taxable year beginning after December 31, 2017, and before January 1, 2026—

(i) paragraph (1) shall be applied—

(I) by substituting "$109,400" for "$78,750" in subparagraph (A), and

(II) by substituting "$70,300" for "$50,600" in subparagraph (B), and

(ii) paragraph (2) shall be applied—

(I) by substituting "$1,000,000" for "$150,000" in subparagraph (A),

(II) by substituting "50 percent of the dollar amount applicable under subparagraph (A)" for "$112,500" in subparagraph (B), and

(III) in the case of a taxpayer described in paragraph (1)(D), without regard to the substitution under subclause (I).

(B) INFLATION ADJUSTMENT.—

(i) IN GENERAL.—In the case of any taxable year beginning in a calendar year after 2018, the amounts described in clause (ii) shall each be increased by an amount equal to—

(I) such dollar amount, multiplied by

(II) the cost-of-living adjustment determined under section 1(f)(3) for the calendar year in which the taxable year begins, determined by substituting "calendar year 2017" for "calendar year 2016" in subparagraph (A)(ii) thereof.

(ii) AMOUNTS DESCRIBED.—The amounts described in this clause are the $109,400 amount in subparagraph (A)(i)(I), the $70,300 amount in subparagraph (A)(i)(II), and the $1,000,000 amount in subparagraph (A)(ii)(I).

(iii) ROUNDING.—Any increased amount determined under clause (i) shall be rounded to the nearest multiple of $100.

(iv) COORDINATION WITH CURRENT ADJUSTMENTS.—In the case of any taxable year to which subparagraph (A) applies, no adjustment shall be made under paragraph (3) to any of the numbers which are substituted under subparagraph (A) and adjusted under this subparagraph.

[CCH Explanations at ¶110, ¶125, and ¶310. Committee Reports at ¶10,020 and ¶10,300.]

Amendments

• **2017, Tax Cuts and Jobs Act (P.L. 115-97)**

P.L. 115-97, §11002(d)(1)(I):

Amended Code Sec. 55(d)(4)(A)(ii) by striking "for 'calendar year 1992' in subparagraph (B)" and inserting "for 'calendar year 2016' in subparagraph (A)(ii)". **Effective** for tax years beginning after 12-31-2017.

P.L. 115-97, §12001(b)(5)(A):

Amended Code Sec. 55(d), as amended by Act Sec. 11002, by striking paragraph (2) and redesignating paragraphs (3) and (4) as paragraphs (2) and (3), respectively. **Effective** for tax years beginning after 12-31-2017. Prior to being stricken, Code Sec. 55(d)(2) read as follows:

(2) CORPORATIONS.—In the case of a corporation, the term "exemption amount" means $40,000.

P.L. 115-97, § 12001(b)(5)(B)-(C):

Amended Code Sec. 55(d), as amended by Act Sec. 11002, in paragraph (2) (as redesignated by Act Sec. 12001(b)(5)(A)), by inserting "and" at the end of subparagraph (B), by striking ", and" at the end of subparagraph (C) and inserting a period, and by striking subparagraph (D), and in subparagraph (3) (as redesignated by Act Sec. 12001(b)(5)(A)), by striking "(b)(1)(A)(i)" in subparagraph (B)(i) and inserting "(b)(1)(A)", and by striking "paragraph

(e) [*Stricken.*]

(3)" in subparagraph (B)(iii) and inserting "paragraph (2)". **Effective** for tax years beginning after 12-31-2017. Prior to being stricken, Code Sec. 55(d)(2)(D) and read as follows:

(D) $150,000 in the case of a taxpayer described in paragraph (2).

P.L. 115-97, § 12003(a):

Amended Code Sec. 55(d), as amended by the preceding provisions of this Act, by adding at the end a new paragraph (4). **Effective** for tax years beginning after 12-31-2017.

[CCH Explanation at ¶ 310. Committee Reports at ¶ 10,300.]

Amendments

• **2017, Tax Cuts and Jobs Act (P.L. 115-97)**

P.L. 115-97, § 12001(b)(6):

Amended Code Sec. 55 by striking subsection (e). **Effective** for tax years beginning after 12-31-2017. Prior to being stricken, Code Sec. 55(e) read as follows:

(e) EXEMPTION FOR SMALL CORPORATIONS.—

(1) IN GENERAL.—

(A) $7,500,000 GROSS RECEIPTS TEST.—The tentative minimum tax of a corporation shall be zero for any taxable year if the corporation's average annual gross receipts for all 3-taxable-year periods ending before such taxable year does not exceed $7,500,000. For purposes of the preceding sentence, only taxable years beginning after December 31, 1993, shall be taken into account.

(B) $5,000,000 GROSS RECEIPTS TEST FOR FIRST 3-YEAR PERIOD.—Subparagraph (A) shall be applied by substituting "$5,000,000" for "$7,500,000" for the first 3-taxable-year period (or portion thereof) of the corporation which is taken into account under subparagraph (A).

(C) FIRST TAXABLE YEAR CORPORATION IN EXISTENCE.—If such taxable year is the first taxable year that such corporation is in existence, the tentative minimum tax of such corporation for such year shall be zero.

(D) SPECIAL RULES.—For purposes of this paragraph, the rules of paragraphs (2) and (3) of section 448(c) shall apply.

(2) PROSPECTIVE APPLICATION OF MINIMUM TAX IF SMALL CORPORATION CEASES TO BE SMALL.—In the case of a corporation whose tentative minimum tax is zero for any prior taxable year by reason of paragraph (1), the application of this part for taxable years beginning with the first taxable year such corporation ceases to be described in paragraph (1) shall be determined with the following modifications:

(A) Section 56(a)(1) (relating to depreciation) and section 56(a)(5) (relating to pollution control facilities) shall apply only to property placed in service on or after the change date.

(B) Section 56(a)(2) (relating to mining exploration and development costs) shall apply only to costs paid or incurred on or after the change date.

(C) Section 56(a)(3) (relating to treatment of long-term contracts) shall apply only to contracts entered into on or after the change date.

(D) Section 56(a)(4) (relating to alternative net operating loss deduction) shall apply in the same manner as if, in section 56(d)(2), the change date were substituted for "January 1, 1987" and the day before the change date were substituted for "December 31, 1986" each place it appears.

(E) Section 56(g)(2)(B) (relating to limitation on allowance of negative adjustments based on adjusted current earnings) shall apply only to prior taxable years beginning on or after the change date.

(F) Section 56(g)(4)(A) (relating to adjustment for depreciation to adjusted current earnings) shall not apply.

(G) Subparagraphs (D) and (F) of section 56(g)(4) (relating to other earnings and profits adjustments and depletion) shall apply in the same manner as if the day before the change date were substituted for "December 31, 1989" each place it appears therein.

(3) EXCEPTION.—The modifications in paragraph (2) shall not apply to—

(A) any item acquired by the corporation in a transaction to which section 381 applies, and

(B) any property the basis of which in the hands of the corporation is determined by reference to the basis of the property in the hands of the transferor, if such item or property was subject to any provision referred to in paragraph (2) while held by the transferor.

(4) CHANGE DATE.—For purposes of paragraph (2), the change date is the first day of the first taxable year for which the taxpayer ceases to be described in paragraph (1).

(5) LIMITATION ON USE OF CREDIT FOR PRIOR YEAR MINIMUM TAX LIABILITY.—In the case of a taxpayer whose tentative minimum tax for any taxable year is zero by reason of paragraph (1), section 53(c) shall be applied for such year by reducing the amount otherwise taken into account under section 53(c)(1) by 25 percent of so much of such amount as exceeds $25,000. Rules similar to the rules of section 38(c)(6)(B) shall apply for purposes of the preceding sentence.

[¶ 5140] CODE SEC. 56. ADJUSTMENTS IN COMPUTING ALTERNATIVE MINIMUM TAXABLE INCOME.

* * *

(b) ADJUSTMENTS APPLICABLE TO INDIVIDUALS.—In determining the amount of the alternative minimum taxable income of any taxpayer (other than a corporation), the following treatment shall apply (in lieu of the treatment applicable for purposes of computing the regular tax):

(1) Limitation on Deductions.—

* * *

(B) Medical Expenses.—In determining the amount allowable as a deduction under section 213, subsection (a) of section 213 shall be applied without regard to subsection (f) of such section. *This subparagraph shall not apply to taxable years beginning after December 31, 2016, and ending before January 1, 2019.*

* * *

(2) Circulation and Research and Experimental Expenditures.—

* * *

(C) Exception for certain research and experimental expenditures.—If the taxpayer materially participates (within the meaning of section 469(h)) in an activity, this paragraph shall not apply to any amount allowable as deduction under section 174(a) for expenditures paid or incurred in connection with such activity.

* * *

[CCH Explanation at ¶ 225 and ¶ 310. Committee Reports at ¶ 10,120 and ¶ 10,300.]

Amendments

• 2017, Tax Cuts and Jobs Act (P.L. 115-97)

P.L. 115-97, § 11027(b):

Amended Code Sec. 56(b)(1)(B) by adding at the end a new sentence. **Effective** for tax years beginning after 12-31-2016.

P.L. 115-97, § 12001(b)(7):

Amended Code Sec. 56(b)(2) by striking subparagraph (C) and by redesignating subparagraph (D) as subparagraph

(C). **Effective** for tax years beginning after 12-31-2017. Prior to being stricken, Code Sec. 56(b)(2)(C) read as follows:

(C) Special rule for personal holding companies.—In the case of circulation expenditures described in section 173, the adjustments provided in this paragraph shall apply also to a personal holding company (as defined in section 542).

(c) *[Stricken.]*

* * *

[CCH Explanation at ¶ 310. Committee Reports at ¶ 10,300.]

Amendments

• 2017, Tax Cuts and Jobs Act (P.L. 115-97)

P.L. 115-97, § 12001(b)(8)(A):

Amended Code Sec. 56 by striking subsection (c). **Effective** for tax years beginning after 12-31-2017. Prior to being stricken, Code Sec. 56(c) read as follows:

(c) Adjustments Applicable to Corporations.—In determining the amount of the alternative minimum taxable income of a corporation, the following treatment shall apply:

(1) Adjustment for adjusted current earnings.—Alternative minimum taxable income shall be adjusted as provided in subsection (g).

(2) Merchant marine capital construction funds.—In the case of a capital construction fund established under chapter 535 of title 46, United States Code—

(A) subparagraphs (A), (B), and (C) of section 7518(c)(1) (and the corresponding provisions of such chapter 535) shall not apply to—

(i) any amount deposited in such fund after after December 31, 1986, or

(ii) any earnings (including gains and losses) after December 31, 1986, on amounts in such fund, and

(B) no reduction in basis shall be made under section 7518(f) (or the corresponding provisions of such chapter 535) with respect to the withdrawal from the fund of any amount to which subparagraph (A) applies.

For purposes of this paragraph, any withdrawal of deposits or earnings from the fund shall be treated as allocable first to deposits made before (and earnings received or accrued before) January 1, 1987.

(3) Special deduction for certain organizations not allowed.—The deduction determined under section 833(b) shall not be allowed.

(g) *[Stricken.]*

[CCH Explanation at ¶310. Committee Reports at ¶10,300.]

Amendments

• 2017, Tax Cuts and Jobs Act (P.L. 115-97)

P.L. 115-97, §12001(b)(8)(A):

Amended Code Sec. 56 by striking subsection (g). **Effective** for tax years beginning after 12-31-2017. Prior to being stricken, Code Sec. 56(g) read as follows:

(g) ADJUSTMENTS BASED ON ADJUSTED CURRENT EARNINGS.—

(1) IN GENERAL.—The alternative minimum taxable income of any corporation for any taxable year shall be increased by 75 percent of the excess (if any) of—

(A) the adjusted current earnings of the corporation, over

(B) the alternative minimum taxable income (determined without regard to this subsection and the alternative tax net operating loss deduction).

(2) ALLOWANCE OF NEGATIVE ADJUSTMENTS.—

(A) IN GENERAL.—The alternative minimum taxable income for any corporation of any taxable year shall be reduced by 75 percent of the excess (if any) of—

(i) the amount referred to in subparagraph (B) of paragraph (1), over

(ii) the amount referred to in subparagraph (A) of paragraph (1).

(B) LIMITATION.—The reduction under subparagraph (A) for any taxable year shall not exceed the excess (if any) of—

(i) the aggregate increases in alternative minimum taxable income under paragraph (1) for prior taxable years, over

(ii) the aggregate reductions under subparagraph (A) of this paragraph for prior taxable years.

(3) ADJUSTED CURRENT EARNINGS.—For purposes of this subsection, the term "adjusted current earnings" means the alternative minimum taxable income for the taxable year—

(A) determined with the adjustments provided in paragraph (4), and

(B) determined without regard to this subsection and the alternative tax net operating loss deduction.

(4) ADJUSTMENTS.—In determining adjusted current earnings, the following adjustments shall apply:

(A) DEPRECIATION.—

(i) PROPERTY PLACED IN SERVICE AFTER 1989.—The depreciation deduction with respect to any property placed in service in a taxable year beginning after 1989 shall be determined under the alternative system of section 168(g). The preceding sentence shall not apply to any property placed in service after December 31, 1993, and the depreciation deduction with respect to such property shall be determined under the rules of subsection (a)(1)(A).

(ii) PROPERTY TO WHICH NEW ACRS SYSTEM APPLIES.—In the case of any property to which the amendments made by section 201 of the Tax Reform Act of 1986 apply and which is placed in service in a taxable year beginning before 1990, the depreciation deduction shall be determined—

(I) by taking into account the adjusted basis of such property (as determined for purposes of computing alternative minimum taxable income) as of the close of the last taxable year beginning before January 1, 1990, and

(II) by using the straight-line method over the remainder of the recovery period applicable to such property under the alternative system of section 168(g).

(iii) PROPERTY TO WHICH ORIGINAL ACRS SYSTEM APPLIES.—In the case of any property to which section 168 (as in effect on the day before the date of the enactment of the Tax Reform Act of 1986 and without regard to subsection (d)(1)(A)(ii) thereof) applies and which is placed in service in a taxable year beginning before 1990, the depreciation deduction shall be determined—

(I) by taking into account the adjusted basis of such property (as determined for purposes of computing the regular tax) as of the close of the last taxable year beginning before January 1, 1990, and

(II) by using the straight line method over the remainder of the recovery period which would apply to such property under the alternative system of section 168(g).

(iv) PROPERTY PLACED IN SERVICE BEFORE 1981.—In the case of any property not described in clause (i), (ii), or (iii), the amount allowable as depreciation or amortization with respect to such property shall be determined in the same manner as for purposes of computing taxable income.

(v) SPECIAL RULE FOR CERTAIN PROPERTY.—In the case of any property described in paragraph (1), (2), (3), or (4) of section 168(f), the amount of depreciation allowable for purposes of the regular tax shall be treated as the amount allowable under the alternative system of section 168(g).

(B) INCLUSION OF ITEMS INCLUDED FOR PURPOSES OF COMPUTING EARNINGS AND PROFITS.—

(i) IN GENERAL.—In the case of any amount which is excluded from gross income for purposes of computing alternative minimum taxable income but is taken into account in determining the amount of earnings and profits—

(I) such amount shall be included in income in the same manner as if such amount were includible in gross income for purposes of computing alternative minimum taxable income, and

(II) the amount of such income shall be reduced by any deduction which would have been allowable in computing alternative minimum taxable income if such amount were includible in gross income.

The preceding sentence shall not apply in the case of any amount excluded from gross income under section 108 (or the corresponding provisions of prior law) or under section 139A or 1357. In the case of any insurance company taxable under section 831(b), this clause shall not apply to any amount not described in section 834(b).

(ii) INCLUSION OF BUILDUP IN LIFE INSURANCE CONTRACTS.—In the case of any life insurance contract—

(I) the income on such contract (as determined under section 7702(g)) for any taxable year shall be treated as includible in gross income for such year, and

(II) there shall be allowed as a deduction that portion of any premium which is attributable to insurance coverage.

(iii) TAX EXEMPT INTEREST ON CERTAIN HOUSING BONDS.—Clause (i) shall not apply in the case of any interest on a bond to which section 57(a)(5)(C)(iii) applies.

(iv) TAX EXEMPT INTEREST ON BONDS ISSUED IN 2009 AND 2010.—

(I) IN GENERAL.—Clause (i) shall not apply in the case of any interest on a bond issued after December 31, 2008, and before January 1, 2011.

(II) TREATMENT OF REFUNDING BONDS.—For purposes of subclause (I), a refunding bond (whether a current or advance refunding) shall be treated as issued on the date of the issuance of the refunded bond (or in the case of a series of refundings, the original bond).

(III) EXCEPTION FOR CERTAIN REFUNDING BONDS.—Subclause (II) shall not apply to any refunding bond which is issued to refund any bond which was issued after December 31, 2003, and before January 1, 2009.

(C) DISALLOWANCE OF ITEMS NOT DEDUCTIBLE IN COMPUTING EARNINGS AND PROFITS.—

(i) IN GENERAL.—A deduction shall not be allowed for any item if such item would not be deductible for any taxable year for purposes of computing earnings and profits.

(ii) SPECIAL RULE FOR CERTAIN DIVIDENDS.—

(I) IN GENERAL.—Clause (i) shall not apply to any deduction allowable under section 243 or 245 for any dividend which is a 100-percent dividend or which is received from a 20-percent owned corporation (as defined in section 243(c)(2)), but only to the extent such dividend is attributable to income of the paying corporation which is subject to tax under this chapter (determined after the application of sections 30A, 936 (including subsections (a)(4), (i), and (j) thereof) and 921 (as in effect before its repeal by the FSC Repeal and Extraterritorial Income Exclusion Act of 2000)).

(II) 100-PERCENT DIVIDEND.—For purposes of subclause (I), the term "100 percent dividend" means any dividend if the percentage used for purposes of determining the amount allowable as a deduction under section 243 or 245 with respect to such dividend is 100 percent.

(iii) TREATMENT OF TAXES ON DIVIDENDS FROM 936 CORPORATIONS.—

(I) IN GENERAL.—For purposes of determining the alternative minimum foreign tax credit, 75 percent of any withholding or income tax paid to a possession of the United States with respect to dividends received from a corporation eligible for the credit provided by section 936 shall be treated as a tax paid to a foreign country by the corporation receiving the dividend.

(II) LIMITATION.—If the aggregate amount of the dividends referred to in subclause (I) for any taxable year exceeds the excess referred to in paragraph (1), the amount treated as tax paid to a foreign country under subclause (I) shall not exceed the amount which would be so treated without regard to this subclause multiplied by a fraction the numerator of which is the excess referred to in paragraph (1) and the denominator of which is the aggregate amount of such dividends.

(III) TREATMENT OF TAXES IMPOSED ON 936 CORPORATION.—For purposes of this clause, taxes paid by any corporation eligible for the credit provided by section 936 to a possession of the United States shall be treated as a withholding tax paid with respect to any dividend paid by such corporation to the extent such taxes would be treated as paid by the corporation receiving the dividend under rules similar to the rules of section 902 (and the amount of any such dividend shall be increased by the amount so treated).

(IV) SEPARATE APPLICATION OF FOREIGN TAX CREDIT LIMITATIONS.—In determining the alternative minimum foreign tax credit, section 904(d) shall be applied as if dividends from a corporation eligible for the credit provided by section 936 were a separate category of income referred to in a subparagraph of section 904(d)(1).

(V) COORDINATION WITH LIMITATION ON 936 CREDIT.—Any reference in this clause to a dividend received from a corporation eligible for the credit provided by section 936 shall be treated as a reference to the portion of any such dividend for which the dividends received deduction is disallowed under clause (i) after the application of clause (ii)(I).

(VI) APPLICATION TO SECTION 30A CORPORATIONS.—References in this clause to section 936 shall be treated as including references to section 30A.

(iv) SPECIAL RULE FOR CERTAIN DIVIDENDS RECEIVED BY CERTAIN COOPERATIVES.—In the case of an organization to which part I of subchapter T (relating to tax treatment of cooperatives) applies which is engaged in the marketing of agricultural or horticultural products, clause (i) shall not apply to any amount allowable as a deduction under section 245(c).

(v) DEDUCTION FOR DOMESTIC PRODUCTION.—Clause (i) shall not apply to any amount allowable as a deduction under section 199.

(vi) SPECIAL RULE FOR CERTAIN DISTRIBUTIONS FROM CONTROLLED FOREIGN CORPORATIONS.—Clause (i) shall not apply to any deduction allowable under section 965.

(D) CERTAIN OTHER EARNINGS AND PROFITS ADJUSTMENTS.—

(i) INTANGIBLE DRILLING COSTS.—The adjustments provided in section 312(n)(2)(A) shall apply in the case of amounts paid or incurred in taxable years beginning after December 31, 1989. In the case of a taxpayer other than an integrated oil company (as defined in section 291(b)(4)), in the case of any oil or gas well, this clause shall not apply in the case of amounts paid or incurred in taxable years beginning after December 31, 1992.

(ii) CERTAIN AMORTIZATION PROVISIONS NOT TO APPLY.—Sections 173 and 248 shall not apply to expenditures paid or incurred in taxable years beginning after December 31, 1989.

(iii) LIFO INVENTORY ADJUSTMENTS.—The adjustments provided in section 312(n)(4) shall apply, but only with respect to taxable years beginning after December 31, 1989.

(iv) INSTALLMENT SALES.—In the case of any installment sale in a taxable year beginning after December 31, 1989, adjusted current earnings shall be computed as if the corporation did not use the installment method. The preceding sentence shall not apply to the applicable percentage (as determined under section 453A) of the gain from any installment sale with respect to which section 453A(a)(1) applies.

(E) DISALLOWANCE OF LOSS ON EXCHANGE OF DEBT POOLS.—No loss shall be recognized on the exchange of any pool of debt obligations for another pool of debt obligations having substantially the same effective interest rates and maturities.

(F) DEPLETION.—

(i) IN GENERAL.—The allowance for depletion with respect to any property placed in service in a taxable year beginning after December 31, 1989, shall be cost depletion determined under section 611.

(ii) EXCEPTION FOR INDEPENDENT OIL AND GAS PRODUCERS AND ROYALTY OWNERS.—Clause (i) (and subparagraph (C)(i)) shall not apply to any deduction for depletion computed in accordance with section 613A(c).

(G) TREATMENT OF CERTAIN OWNERSHIP CHANGES.—If—

(i) there is an ownership change (within the meaning of section 382) in a taxable year beginning after 1989 with respect to any corporation, and

(ii) there is a net unrealized built-in loss (within the meaning of section 382(h)) with respect to such corporation,

then the adjusted basis of each asset of such corporation (immediately after the ownership change) shall be its proportionate share (determined on the basis of respective fair market values) of the fair market value of the assets of such corporation (determined under section 382(h)) immediately before the ownership change.

(H) ADJUSTED BASIS.—The adjusted basis of any property with respect to which an adjustment under this paragraph applies shall be determined by applying the treatment prescribed in this paragraph.

(I) TREATMENT OF CHARITABLE CONTRIBUTIONS.—Notwithstanding subparagraphs (B) and (C), no adjustment related to the earnings and profits effects of any charitable contribution shall be made in computing adjusted current earnings.

(5) OTHER DEFINITIONS.—For purposes of paragraph (4)—

(A) EARNINGS AND PROFITS.—The term "earnings and profits" means earnings and profits computed for purposes of subchapter C.

¶5140   Code Sec. 56(g)

(B) TREATMENT OF ALTERNATIVE MINIMUM TAXABLE INCOME.— The treatment of any item for purposes of computing alternative minimum taxable income shall be determined without regard to this subsection.

(6) EXCEPTION FOR CERTAIN CORPORATIONS.—This subsection shall not apply to any S corporation, regulated investment company, real estate investment trust, or REMIC.

[¶5145] CODE SEC. 58. DENIAL OF CERTAIN LOSSES.

(a) DENIAL OF FARM LOSS.—

* * *

(3) DETERMINATION OF LOSS.—In determining the amount of the loss from any tax shelter farm activity, the adjustments of sections 56 and 57 shall apply.

* * *

[CCH Explanation at ¶310. Committee Reports at ¶10,300.]

Amendments

• **2017, Tax Cuts and Jobs Act (P.L. 115-97)**

P.L. 115-97, §12001(b)(9):

Amended Code Sec. 58(a) by striking paragraph (3) and redesignating paragraph (4) as paragraph (3). **Effective** for

tax years beginning after 12-31-2017. Prior to being stricken, Code Sec. 58(a)(3) read as follows:

(3) APPLICATION TO PERSONAL SERVICE CORPORATIONS.—For purposes of paragraph (1), a personal service corporation (within the meaning of section 469(j)(2)) shall be treated as a taxpayer other than a corporation.

[¶5150] CODE SEC. 59. OTHER DEFINITIONS AND SPECIAL RULES.

(a) ALTERNATIVE MINIMUM TAX FOREIGN TAX CREDIT.—For purposes of this part—

(1) IN GENERAL.—The alternative minimum tax foreign tax credit for any taxable year shall be the credit which would be determined under section 27(a) for such taxable year if—

* * *

(C) the determination of whether any income is high-taxed income for purposes of section 904(d)(2) were made on the basis of the applicable rate specified in *section 55(b)(1) in lieu of the highest rate of tax specified in section 1.*

(2) PRE-CREDIT TENTATIVE MINIMUM TAX.—For purposes of this subsection, the term "pre-credit tentative minimum tax" *means the amount determined under the first sentence of section 55(b)(1)(A).*

* * *

[CCH Explanation at ¶310. Committee Reports at ¶10,300.]

Amendments

• **2017, Tax Cuts and Jobs Act (P.L. 115-97)**

P.L. 115-97, §12001(b)(3)(C)(i)-(ii):

Amended Code Sec. 59(a) by striking "subparagraph (A)(i) or (B)(i) of section 55(b)(1) (whichever applies) in lieu of the highest rate of tax specified in section 1 or 11 (whichever applies)" in paragraph (1)(C) and inserting "section 55(b)(1) in lieu of the highest rate of tax specified in section 1", and by striking "means" and all that follows in paragraph (2) and inserting "means the amount determined

under the first sentence of section 55(b)(1)(A).". **Effective** for tax years beginning after 12-31-2017. Prior to being stricken, "means" and all that follows in Code Sec. 59(a)(2) read as follows:

means—

(A) in the case of a taxpayer other than a corporation, the amount determined under the first sentence of section 55(b)(1)(A)(i), or

(B) in the case of a corporation, the amount determined under section 55(b)(1)(B)(i).

(b) *[Stricken.]*

* * *

[CCH Explanation at ¶310. Committee Reports at ¶10,300.]

Amendments

• **2017, Tax Cuts and Jobs Act (P.L. 115-97)**

P.L. 115-97, §12001(b)(10):

Amended Code Sec. 59 by striking subsection (b). **Effective** for tax years beginning after 12-31-2017. Prior to being stricken, Code Sec. 59(b) read as follows:

(b) MINIMUM TAX NOT TO APPLY TO INCOME ELIGIBLE FOR CREDITS UNDER SECTION 30A OR 936.—In the case of any corporation for which a credit is allowable for the taxable year under section 30A or 936, alternative minimum taxable income shall not include any income with respect to which a credit is determined under section 30A or 936.

(f) *[Stricken.]*

* * *

[CCH Explanation at ¶ 310. Committee Reports at ¶ 10,300.]

Amendments

• **2017, Tax Cuts and Jobs Act (P.L. 115-97)**

P.L. 115-97, § 12001(b)(10):

Amended Code Sec. 59 by striking subsection (f). **Effective** for tax years beginning after 12-31-2017. Prior to being stricken, Code Sec. 59(f) read as follows:

(f) COORDINATION WITH SECTION 291.—Except as otherwise provided in this part, section 291 (relating to cutback of corporate preferences) shall apply before the application of this part.

(j) TREATMENT OF UNEARNED INCOME OF MINOR CHILDREN.—

* * *

(2) INFLATION ADJUSTMENT.—In the case of any taxable year beginning in a calendar year after 1998, the dollar amount in paragraph (1)(B) shall be increased by an amount equal to the product of—

(A) such dollar amount, and

(B) the cost-of-living adjustment determined under section 1(f)(3) for the calendar year in which the taxable year begins, determined by substituting "1997" *for "2016" in subparagraph (A)(ii) thereof.*

If any increase determined under the preceding sentence is not a multiple of $50, such increase shall be rounded to the nearest multiple of $50.

[CCH Explanation at ¶ 125. Committee Reports at ¶ 10,020.]

Amendments

• **2017, Tax Cuts and Jobs Act (P.L. 115-97)**

P.L. 115-97, § 11002(d)(4):

Amended Code Sec. 59(j)(2)(B) by striking "for '1992' in subparagraph (B)" and inserting "for '2016' in subparagraph (A)(ii)". **Effective** for tax years beginning after 12-31-2017.

[¶ 5155] *CODE SEC. 59A. TAX ON BASE EROSION PAYMENTS OF TAXPAYERS WITH SUBSTANTIAL GROSS RECEIPTS.*

(a) IMPOSITION OF TAX.—*There is hereby imposed on each applicable taxpayer for any taxable year a tax equal to the base erosion minimum tax amount for the taxable year. Such tax shall be in addition to any other tax imposed by this subtitle.*

(b) BASE EROSION MINIMUM TAX AMOUNT.—*For purposes of this section—*

(1) IN GENERAL.—*Except as provided in paragraphs (2) and (3), the term "base erosion minimum tax amount" means, with respect to any applicable taxpayer for any taxable year, the excess (if any) of—*

(A) *an amount equal to 10 percent (5 percent in the case of taxable years beginning in calendar year 2018) of the modified taxable income of such taxpayer for the taxable year, over*

(B) *an amount equal to the regular tax liability (as defined in section 26(b)) of the taxpayer for the taxable year, reduced (but not below zero) by the excess (if any) of—*

(i) *the credits allowed under this chapter against such regular tax liability, over*

(ii) *the sum of—*

(I) *the credit allowed under section 38 for the taxable year which is properly allocable to the research credit determined under section 41(a), plus*

(II) *the portion of the applicable section 38 credits not in excess of 80 percent of the lesser of the amount of such credits or the base erosion minimum tax amount (determined without regard to this subclause).*

(2) MODIFICATIONS FOR TAXABLE YEARS BEGINNING AFTER 2025.—*In the case of any taxable year beginning after December 31, 2025, paragraph (1) shall be applied—*

(A) by substituting "12.5 percent" for "10 percent" in subparagraph (A) thereof, and

(B) by reducing (but not below zero) the regular tax liability (as defined in section 26(b)) for purposes of subparagraph (B) thereof by the aggregate amount of the credits allowed under this chapter against such regular tax liability rather than the excess described in such subparagraph.

(3) INCREASED RATE FOR CERTAIN BANKS AND SECURITIES DEALERS.—

(A) IN GENERAL.—In the case of a taxpayer described in subparagraph (B) who is an applicable taxpayer for any taxable year, the percentage otherwise in effect under paragraphs (1)(A) and (2)(A) shall each be increased by one percentage point.

(B) TAXPAYER DESCRIBED.—A taxpayer is described in this subparagraph if such taxpayer is a member of an affiliated group (as defined in section 1504(a)(1)) which includes—

(i) a bank (as defined in section 581), or

(ii) a registered securities dealer under section 15(a) of the Securities Exchange Act of 1934.

(4) APPLICABLE SECTION 38 CREDITS.—For purposes of paragraph (1)(B)(ii)(II), the term "applicable section 38 credits" means the credit allowed under section 38 for the taxable year which is properly allocable to—

(A) the low-income housing credit determined under section 42(a),

(B) the renewable electricity production credit determined under section 45(a), and

(C) the investment credit determined under section 46, but only to the extent properly allocable to the energy credit determined under section 48.

(c) MODIFIED TAXABLE INCOME.—For purposes of this section—

(1) IN GENERAL.—The term "modified taxable income" means the taxable income of the taxpayer computed under this chapter for the taxable year, determined without regard to—

(A) any base erosion tax benefit with respect to any base erosion payment, or

(B) the base erosion percentage of any net operating loss deduction allowed under section 172 for the taxable year.

(2) BASE EROSION TAX BENEFIT.—

(A) IN GENERAL.—The term "base erosion tax benefit" means—

(i) any deduction described in subsection (d)(1) which is allowed under this chapter for the taxable year with respect to any base erosion payment,

(ii) in the case of a base erosion payment described in subsection (d)(2), any deduction allowed under this chapter for the taxable year for depreciation (or amortization in lieu of depreciation) with respect to the property acquired with such payment,

(iii) in the case of a base erosion payment described in subsection (d)(3)—

(I) any reduction under section 803(a)(1)(B) in the gross amount of premiums and other consideration on insurance and annuity contracts for premiums and other consideration arising out of indemnity insurance, and

(II) any deduction under section 832(b)(4)(A) from the amount of gross premiums written on insurance contracts during the taxable year for premiums paid for reinsurance, and

(iv) in the case of a base erosion payment described in subsection (d)(4), any reduction in gross receipts with respect to such payment in computing gross income of the taxpayer for the taxable year for purposes of this chapter.

(B) TAX BENEFITS DISREGARDED IF TAX WITHHELD ON BASE EROSION PAYMENT.—

(i) IN GENERAL.—Except as provided in clause (ii), any base erosion tax benefit attributable to any base erosion payment—

(I) on which tax is imposed by section 871 or 881, and

(II) *with respect to which tax has been deducted and withheld under section 1441 or 1442,*

shall not be taken into account in computing modified taxable income under paragraph (1)(A) or the base erosion percentage under paragraph (4).

(ii) EXCEPTION.—*The amount not taken into account in computing modified taxable income by reason of clause (i) shall be reduced under rules similar to the rules under section 163(j)(5)(B) (as in effect before the date of the enactment of the Tax Cuts and Jobs Act).*

(3) SPECIAL RULES FOR DETERMINING INTEREST FOR WHICH DEDUCTION ALLOWED.—*For purposes of applying paragraph (1), in the case of a taxpayer to which section 163(j) applies for the taxable year, the reduction in the amount of interest for which a deduction is allowed by reason of such subsection shall be treated as allocable first to interest paid or accrued to persons who are not related parties with respect to the taxpayer and then to such related parties.*

(4) BASE EROSION PERCENTAGE.—*For purposes of paragraph (1)(B)—*

(A) IN GENERAL.—*The term "base erosion percentage" means, for any taxable year, the percentage determined by dividing—*

(i) *the aggregate amount of base erosion tax benefits of the taxpayer for the taxable year, by*

(ii) *the sum of—*

(I) *the aggregate amount of the deductions (including deductions described in clauses (i) and (ii) of paragraph (2)(A)) allowable to the taxpayer under this chapter for the taxable year, plus*

(II) *the base erosion tax benefits described in clauses (iii) and (iv) of paragraph (2)(A) allowable to the taxpayer for the taxable year.*

(B) CERTAIN ITEMS NOT TAKEN INTO ACCOUNT.—*The amount under subparagraph (A)(ii) shall be determined by not taking into account—*

(i) *any deduction allowed under section 172, 245A, or 250 for the taxable year,*

(ii) *any deduction for amounts paid or accrued for services to which the exception under subsection (d)(5) applies, and*

(iii) *any deduction for qualified derivative payments which are not treated as a base erosion payment by reason of subsection (h).*

(d) BASE EROSION PAYMENT.—*For purposes of this section—*

(1) IN GENERAL.—*The term "base erosion payment" means any amount paid or accrued by the taxpayer to a foreign person which is a related party of the taxpayer and with respect to which a deduction is allowable under this chapter.*

(2) PURCHASE OF DEPRECIABLE PROPERTY.—*Such term shall also include any amount paid or accrued by the taxpayer to a foreign person which is a related party of the taxpayer in connection with the acquisition by the taxpayer from such person of property of a character subject to the allowance for depreciation (or amortization in lieu of depreciation).*

(3) REINSURANCE PAYMENTS.—*Such term shall also include any premium or other consideration paid or accrued by the taxpayer to a foreign person which is a related party of the taxpayer for any reinsurance payments which are taken into account under sections 803(a)(1)(B) or 832(b)(4)(A).*

(4) CERTAIN PAYMENTS TO EXPATRIATED ENTITIES.—

(A) IN GENERAL.—*Such term shall also include any amount paid or accrued by the taxpayer with respect to a person described in subparagraph (B) which results in a reduction of the gross receipts of the taxpayer.*

(B) PERSON DESCRIBED.—*A person is described in this subparagraph if such person is a—*

(i) *surrogate foreign corporation which is a related party of the taxpayer, but only if such person first became a surrogate foreign corporation after November 9, 2017, or*

(ii) foreign person which is a member of the same expanded affiliated group as the surrogate foreign corporation.

(C) DEFINITIONS.—For purposes of this paragraph—

(i) SURROGATE FOREIGN CORPORATION.—The term "surrogate foreign corporation" has the meaning given such term by section 7874(a)(2)(B) but does not include a foreign corporation treated as a domestic corporation under section 7874(b).

(ii) EXPANDED AFFILIATED GROUP.—The term "expanded affiliated group" has the meaning given such term by section 7874(c)(1).

(5) EXCEPTION FOR CERTAIN AMOUNTS WITH RESPECT TO SERVICES.—Paragraph (1) shall not apply to any amount paid or accrued by a taxpayer for services if—

(A) such services are services which meet the requirements for eligibility for use of the services cost method under section 482 (determined without regard to the requirement that the services not contribute significantly to fundamental risks of business success or failure), and

(B) such amount constitutes the total services cost with no markup component.

(e) APPLICABLE TAXPAYER.—For purposes of this section—

(1) IN GENERAL.—The term "applicable taxpayer" means, with respect to any taxable year, a taxpayer—

(A) which is a corporation other than a regulated investment company, a real estate investment trust, or an S corporation,

(B) the average annual gross receipts of which for the 3-taxable-year period ending with the preceding taxable year are at least $500,000,000, and

(C) he base erosion percentage (as determined under subsection (c)(4)) of which for the taxable year is 3 percent (2 percent in the case of a taxpayer described in subsection (b)(3)(B)) or higher.

(2) GROSS RECEIPTS.—

(A) SPECIAL RULE FOR FOREIGN PERSONS.—In the case of a foreign person the gross receipts of which are taken into account for purposes of paragraph (1)(B), only gross receipts which are taken into account in determining income which is effectively connected with the conduct of a trade or business within the United States shall be taken into account. In the case of a taxpayer which is a foreign person, the preceding sentence shall not apply to the gross receipts of any United States person which are aggregated with the taxpayer's gross receipts by reason of paragraph (3).

(B) OTHER RULES MADE APPLICABLE.—Rules similar to the rules of subparagraphs (B), (C), and (D) of section 448(c)(3) shall apply in determining gross receipts for purposes of this section.

(3) AGGREGATION RULES.—All persons treated as a single employer under subsection (a) of section 52 shall be treated as 1 person for purposes of this subsection and subsection (c)(4), except that in applying section 1563 for purposes of section 52, the exception for foreign corporations under section 1563(b)(2)(C) shall be disregarded.

(f) FOREIGN PERSON.—For purposes of this section, the term "foreign person" has the meaning given such term by section 6038A(c)(3).

(g) RELATED PARTY.—For purposes of this section—

(1) IN GENERAL.—The term "related party" means, with respect to any applicable taxpayer—

(A) any 25-percent owner of the taxpayer,

(B) any person who is related (within the meaning of section 267(b) or 707(b)(1)) to the taxpayer or any 25-percent owner of the taxpayer, and

(C) any other person who is related (within the meaning of section 482) to the taxpayer.

(2) 25-PERCENT OWNER.—The term "25-percent owner" means, with respect to any corporation, any person who owns at least 25 percent of—

    (A) the total voting power of all classes of stock of a corporation entitled to vote, or

    (B) the total value of all classes of stock of such corporation.

  (3) SECTION 318 TO APPLY.—Section 318 shall apply for purposes of paragraphs (1) and (2), except that—

    (A) "10 percent" shall be substituted for "50 percent" in section 318(a)(2)(C), and

    (B) subparagraphs (A), (B), and (C) of section 318(a)(3) shall not be applied so as to consider a United States person as owning stock which is owned by a person who is not a United States person.

(h) EXCEPTION FOR CERTAIN PAYMENTS MADE IN THE ORDINARY COURSE OF TRADE OR BUSINESS.—For purposes of this section—

  (1) IN GENERAL.—Except as provided in paragraph (3), any qualified derivative payment shall not be treated as a base erosion payment.

  (2) QUALIFIED DERIVATIVE PAYMENT.—

    (A) IN GENERAL.—The term "qualified derivative payment" means any payment made by a taxpayer pursuant to a derivative with respect to which the taxpayer—

      (i) recognizes gain or loss as if such derivative were sold for its fair market value on the last business day of the taxable year (and such additional times as required by this title or the taxpayer's method of accounting),

      (ii) treats any gain or loss so recognized as ordinary, and

      (iii) treats the character of all items of income, deduction, gain, or loss with respect to a payment pursuant to the derivative as ordinary.

    (B) REPORTING REQUIREMENT.—No payments shall be treated as qualified derivative payments under subparagraph (A) for any taxable year unless the taxpayer includes in the information required to be reported under section 6038B(b)(2) with respect to such taxable year such information as is necessary to identify the payments to be so treated and such other information as the Secretary determines necessary to carry out the provisions of this subsection.

  (3) EXCEPTIONS FOR PAYMENTS OTHERWISE TREATED AS BASE EROSION PAYMENTS.—This subsection shall not apply to any qualified derivative payment if—

    (A) the payment would be treated as a base erosion payment if it were not made pursuant to a derivative, including any interest, royalty, or service payment, or

    (B) in the case of a contract which has derivative and nonderivative components, the payment is properly allocable to the nonderivative component.

  (4) DERIVATIVE DEFINED.—For purposes of this subsection—

    (A) IN GENERAL.—The term "derivative" means any contract (including any option, forward contract, futures contract, short position, swap, or similar contract) the value of which, or any payment or other transfer with respect to which, is (directly or indirectly) determined by reference to one or more of the following:

      (i) Any share of stock in a corporation.

      (ii) Any evidence of indebtedness.

      (iii) Any commodity which is actively traded.

      (iv) Any currency.

      (v) Any rate, price, amount, index, formula, or algorithm.

Such term shall not include any item described in clauses (i) through (v).

    (B) TREATMENT OF AMERICAN DEPOSITORY RECEIPTS AND SIMILAR INSTRUMENTS.—Except as otherwise provided by the Secretary, for purposes of this part, American depository receipts (and similar instruments) with respect to shares of stock in foreign corporations shall be treated as shares of stock in such foreign corporations.

(C) EXCEPTION FOR CERTAIN CONTRACTS.—Such term shall not include any insurance, annuity, or endowment contract issued by an insurance company to which subchapter L applies (or issued by any foreign corporation to which such subchapter would apply if such foreign corporation were a domestic corporation).

(i) REGULATIONS.—The Secretary shall prescribe such regulations or other guidance as may be necessary or appropriate to carry out the provisions of this section, including regulations—

(1) providing for such adjustments to the application of this section as are necessary to prevent the avoidance of the purposes of this section, including through—

(A) the use of unrelated persons, conduit transactions, or other intermediaries, or

(B) transactions or arrangements designed, in whole or in part—

(i) to characterize payments otherwise subject to this section as payments not subject to this section, or

(ii) to substitute payments not subject to this section for payments otherwise subject to this section and

(2) for the application of subsection (g), including rules to prevent the avoidance of the exceptions under subsection (g)(3).

[CCH Explanation at ¶750. Committee Reports at ¶11,210.]

Amendments

• 2017, Tax Cuts and Jobs Act (P.L. 115-97)

P.L. 115-97, §14401(a):

Amended subchapter A of chapter 1 by adding at the end a new part VII (Code Sec. 59A). **Effective** for base erosion payments (as defined in Code Sec. 59A(d), as added by Act. Sec. 14401) paid or accrued in tax years beginning after 12-31-2017.

[¶5160] CODE SEC. 61. GROSS INCOME DEFINED.

(a) GENERAL DEFINITION.—Except as otherwise provided in this subtitle, gross income means all income from whatever source derived, including (but not limited to) the following items:

* * *

⮕ *Caution: Caution: Code Sec. 61(a)(8), below, was stricken by P.L. 115-97, generally applicable to any divorce or separation instrument executed after December 31, 2018.*

(8) Alimony and separate maintenance payments;

⮕ *Caution: Caution: Former Code Sec. 61(a)(9)-(15) were redesignated by P.L. 115-97 as Code Sec. 61(a)(8)-(14), below, generally applicable to any divorce or separation instrument executed after December 31, 2018.*

(8) Annuities;

(9) Income from life insurance and endowment contracts;

(10) Pensions;

(11) Income from discharge of indebtedness;

(12) Distributive share of partnership gross income;

(13) Income in respect of a decedent; and

(14) Income from an interest in an estate or trust.

* * *

[CCH Explanation at ¶255. Committee Reports at ¶10,260.]

Amendments

• 2017, Tax Cuts and Jobs Act (P.L. 115-97)

P.L. 115-97, §11051(b)(1)(A):

Amended Code Sec. 61(a) by striking paragraph (8) and by redesignating paragraphs (9) through (15) as paragraphs (8) through (14), respectively. For the **effective** date, see Act

Sec. 11051(c)(1)-(2), below. Prior to being stricken, Code Sec. 61(a)(8) read as follows:

(8) Alimony and separate maintenance payments;

P.L. 115-97, §11051(c)(1)-(2), provides:

(c) EFFECTIVE DATE.—The amendments made by this section shall apply to—

(1) any divorce or separation instrument (as defined in section 71(b)(2) of the Internal Revenue Code of 1986 as in effect before the date of the enactment of this Act) executed after December 31, 2018, and

(2) any divorce or separation instrument (as so defined) executed on or before such date and modified after such date if the modification expressly provides that the amendments made by this section apply to such modification.

[¶ 5165] CODE SEC. 62. ADJUSTED GROSS INCOME DEFINED.

(a) GENERAL RULE.—For purposes of this subtitle, the term "adjusted gross income" means, in the case of an individual, gross income minus the following deductions:

* * *

⋙→ *Caution: Caution: Code Sec. 62(a)(10), below, was stricken by P.L. 115-97, generally applicable to any divorce or separation instrument executed after December 31, 2018.*

(10) ALIMONY.—The deduction allowed by section 215.

* * *

Nothing in this section shall permit the same item to be deducted more than once. *The deduction allowed by section 199A shall not be treated as a deduction described in any of the preceding paragraphs of this subsection.*

* * *

[CCH Explanation at ¶ 255 and ¶ 330. Committee Reports at ¶ 10,030 and ¶ 10,260.]

Amendments

• **2017, Tax Cuts and Jobs Act (P.L. 115-97)**

P.L. 115-97, § 11011(b)(1):

Amended Code Sec. 62(a) by adding at the end a new sentence. **Effective** for tax years beginning after 12-31-2017.

P.L. 115-97, § 11051(b)(2)(A):

Amended Code Sec. 62(a) by striking paragraph (10). For the **effective** date, see Act Sec. 11051(c), below. Prior to being stricken, Code Sec. 62(a)(10) read as follows:

(10) ALIMONY.—The deduction allowed by section 215.

P.L. 115-97, § 11051(c), provides:

(c) EFFECTIVE DATE.—The amendments made by this section shall apply to—

(1) any divorce or separation instrument (as defined in section 71(b)(2) of the Internal Revenue Code of 1986 as in effect before the date of the enactment of this Act) executed after December 31, 2018, and

(2) any divorce or separation instrument (as so defined) executed on or before such date and modified after such date if the modification expressly provides that the amendments made by this section apply to such modification.

(d) DEFINITION; SPECIAL RULES.—

* * *

(3) INFLATION ADJUSTMENT.—In the case of any taxable year beginning after 2015, the $250 amount in subsection (a)(2)(D) shall be increased by an amount equal to—

(A) such dollar amount, multiplied by

(B) the cost-of-living adjustment determined under section 1(f)(3) for the calendar year in which the taxable year begins, determined by substituting *"calendar year 2014" for "calendar year 2016" in subparagraph (A)(ii)* thereof.

Any increase determined under the preceding sentence shall be rounded to the nearest multiple of $50.

* * *

[CCH Explanation at ¶ 125. Committee Reports at ¶ 10,020.]

Amendments

• **2017, Tax Cuts and Jobs Act (P.L. 115-97)**

P.L. 115-97, § 11002(d)(1)(J):

Amended Code Sec. 62(d)(3)(B) by striking "for 'calendar year 1992' in subparagraph (B)" and inserting "for 'calendar

year 2016' in subparagraph (A)(ii)". **Effective** for tax years beginning after 12-31-2017.

[¶5170] CODE SEC. 63. TAXABLE INCOME DEFINED.

* * *

(b) INDIVIDUALS WHO DO NOT ITEMIZE THEIR DEDUCTIONS.—In the case of an individual who does not elect to itemize his deductions for the taxable year, for purposes of this subtitle, the term "taxable income" means adjusted gross income, minus—

(1) the standard deduction,

(2) the deduction for personal exemptions provided in section 151, *and*

(3) *the deduction provided in section 199A.*

[CCH Explanation at ¶330. Committee Reports at ¶10,030.]

Amendments

• **2017, Tax Cuts and Jobs Act (P.L. 115-97)**

P.L. 115-97, §11011(b)(2):

Amended Code Sec. 63(b) by striking "and" at the end of paragraph (1), by striking the period at the end of para-

graph (2) and inserting ", and", and by adding at the end a new paragraph (3). **Effective** for tax years beginning after 12-31-2017.

(c) STANDARD DEDUCTION.—For purposes of this subtitle—

* * *

(4) ADJUSTMENTS FOR INFLATION.—In the case of any taxable year beginning in a calendar year after 1988, each dollar amount contained in paragraph (2)(B), (2)(C), or (5) or subsection (f) shall be increased by an amount equal to—

(A) such dollar amount, multiplied by

(B) the cost-of-living adjustment determined under section 1(f)(3) for the calendar year in which the taxable year begins, by substituting *for "calendar year 2016" in subparagraph (A)(ii)* thereof—

(i) "calendar year 1987" in the case of the dollar amounts contained in paragraph (2)(B), (2)(C), or (5)(A) or subsection (f), and

(ii) "calendar year 1997" in the case of the dollar amount contained in paragraph (5)(B).

* * *

(7) SPECIAL RULES FOR TAXABLE YEARS 2018 THROUGH 2025.—*In the case of a taxable year beginning after December 31, 2017, and before January 1, 2026—*

(A) INCREASE IN STANDARD DEDUCTION.—*Paragraph (2) shall be applied—*

(i) *by substituting "$18,000" for "$4,400" in subparagraph (B), and*

(ii) *by substituting "$12,000" for "$3,000" in subparagraph (C).*

(B) ADJUSTMENT FOR INFLATION.—

(i) IN GENERAL.—*Paragraph (4) shall not apply to the dollar amounts contained in paragraphs (2)(B) and (2)(C).*

(ii) ADJUSTMENT OF INCREASED AMOUNTS.—*In the case of a taxable year beginning after 2018, the $18,000 and $12,000 amounts in subparagraph (A) shall each be increased by an amount equal to—*

(I) *such dollar amount, multiplied by*

(II) *the cost-of-living adjustment determined under section 1(f)(3) for the calendar year in which the taxable year begins, determined by substituting "2017" for "2016" in subparagraph (A)(ii) thereof.*

If any increase under this subparagraph is not a multiple of $50, such increase shall be rounded to the next lowest multiple of $50.

[CCH Explanation at ¶125 and ¶205. Committee Reports at ¶10,020 and ¶10,050.]

Amendments

• 2017, Tax Cuts and Jobs Act (P.L. 115-97)

P.L. 115-97, §11002(d)(1)(K):

Amended Code Sec. 63(c)(4)(B) by striking "for 'calendar year 1992' in subparagraph (B)" and inserting "for 'calendar year 2016' in subparagraph (A)(ii)". **Effective** for tax years beginning after 12-31-2017.

P.L. 115-97, §11021(a):

Amended Code Sec. 63(c) by adding at the end a new paragraph (7). **Effective** for tax years beginning after 12-31-2017.

(d) ITEMIZED DEDUCTIONS.—For purposes of this subtitle, the term "itemized deductions" means the deductions allowable under this chapter other than—

(1) the deductions allowable in arriving at adjusted gross income,

(2) the deduction for personal exemptions provided by section 151, *and*

(3) *the deduction provided in section 199A.*

* * *

[CCH Explanation at ¶330. Committee Reports at ¶10,030.]

Amendments

• 2017, Tax Cuts and Jobs Act (P.L. 115-97)

P.L. 115-97, §11011(b)(3):

Amended Code Sec. 63(d) by striking "and" at the end of paragraph (1), by striking the period at the end of para-

graph (2) and inserting ", and", and by adding at the end a new paragraph (3). **Effective** for tax years beginning after 12-31-2017.

[¶5175] CODE SEC. 67. 2-PERCENT FLOOR ON MISCELLANEOUS ITEMIZED DEDUCTIONS.

* * *

(g) SUSPENSION FOR TAXABLE YEARS 2018 THROUGH 2025.—Notwithstanding subsection (a), no miscella-neous itemized deduction shall be allowed for any taxable year beginning after December 31, 2017, and before January 1, 2026.

[CCH Explanation at ¶245. Committee Reports at ¶10,200.]

Amendments

• 2017, Tax Cuts and Jobs Act (P.L. 115-97)

P.L. 115-97, §11045(a):

Amended Code Sec. 67 by adding at the end a new subsection (g). **Effective** for tax years beginning after 12-31-2017.

[¶5180] CODE SEC. 68. OVERALL LIMITATION ON ITEMIZED DEDUCTIONS.

* * *

(b) APPLICABLE AMOUNT.—

* * *

(2) INFLATION ADJUSTMENT.—In the case of any taxable year beginning in calendar years after 2013, each of the dollar amounts under subparagraphs (A), (B), and (C) of paragraph (1) shall be shall be [sic] increased by an amount equal to—

(A) such dollar amount, multiplied by

(B) the cost-of-living adjustment determined under section 1(f)(3) for the calendar year in which the taxable year begins, except that section 1(f)(3)(A)(ii) shall be applied by substituting "2012" for "2016".

If any amount after adjustment under the preceding sentence is not a multiple of $50, such amount shall be rounded to the next lowest multiple of $50.

* * *

[CCH Explanation at ¶ 125. Committee Reports at ¶ 10,020.]

Amendments

• 2017, Tax Cuts and Jobs Act (P.L. 115-97)

P.L. 115-97, § 11002(d)(2)(A)-(B):

Amended Code Sec. 68(b)(2)(B) by striking "1(f)(3)(B)" and inserting "1(f)(3)(A)(ii)", and by striking "1992" and inserting "2016". **Effective** for tax years beginning after 12-31-2017.

(f) SECTION NOT TO APPLY.—*This section shall not apply to any taxable year beginning after December 31, 2017, and before January 1, 2026.*

[CCH Explanation at ¶ 250. Committee Reports at ¶ 10,210.]

Amendments

• 2017, Tax Cuts and Jobs Act (P.L. 115-97)

P.L. 115-97, § 11046(a):

Amended Code Sec. 68 by adding at the end a new subsection (f). **Effective** for tax years beginning after 12-31-2017.

»»→ *Caution: Caution: Code Sec. 71, below, was stricken by P.L. 115-97, generally applicable to any divorce or separation instrument executed after December 31, 2018.*

[¶ 5185] CODE SEC. 71. ALIMONY AND SEPARATE MAINTENANCE PAYMENTS. [*Stricken.*]

[CCH Explanation at ¶ 255. Committee Reports at ¶ 10,260.]

Amendments

• 2017, Tax Cuts and Jobs Act (P.L. 115-97)

P.L. 115-97, § 11051(b)(1)(B):

Amended part II of subchapter B of chapter 1 by striking Code Sec. 71. For the **effective** date, see Act Sec. 11051(c)(1)-(2), below.

P.L. 115-97, § 11051(c)(1)-(2), provides:

(c) EFFECTIVE DATE.—The amendments made by this section shall apply to—

(1) any divorce or separation instrument (as defined in section 71(b)(2) of the Internal Revenue Code of 1986 as in effect before the date of the enactment of this Act) executed after December 31, 2018, and

(2) any divorce or separation instrument (as so defined) executed on or before such date and modified after such date if the modification expressly provides that the amendments made by this section apply to such modification.

Prior to being stricken, Code Sec. 71 read as follows:

SEC. 71. ALIMONY AND SEPARATE MAINTENANCE PAYMENTS.

(a) GENERAL RULE.—Gross income includes amounts received as alimony or separate maintenance payments.

(b) ALIMONY OR SEPARATE MAINTENANCE PAYMENTS DEFINED.—For purposes of this section—

(1) IN GENERAL.—The term "alimony or separate maintenance payment" means any payment in cash if—

(A) such payment is received by (or on behalf of) a spouse under a divorce or separation instrument,

(B) the divorce or separation instrument does not designate such payment as a payment which is not includible in gross income under this section and not allowable as a deduction under section 215,

(C) in the case of an individual legally separated from his spouse under a decree of divorce or of separate maintenance, the payee spouse and the payor spouse are not members of the same household at the time such payment is made, and

(D) there is no liability to make any such payment for any period after the death of the payee spouse and there is no liability to make any payment (in cash or property) as a substitute for such payments after the death of the payee spouse.

(2) DIVORCE OR SEPARATION INSTRUMENT.—The term "divorce or separation instrument" means—

(A) a decree of divorce or separate maintenance or a written instrument incident to such a decree,

(B) a written separation agreement, or

(C) a decree (not described in subparagraph (A)) requiring a spouse to make payments for the support or maintenance of the other spouse.

(c) PAYMENTS TO SUPPORT CHILDREN.—

(1) IN GENERAL.—Subsection (a) shall not apply to that part of any payment which the terms of the divorce or separation instrument fix (in terms of an amount of money or a part of the payment) as a sum which is payable for the support of children of the payor spouse.

(2) TREATMENT OF CERTAIN REDUCTIONS RELATED TO CONTINGENCIES INVOLVING CHILD.—For purposes of paragraph (1), if any amount specified in the instrument will be reduced—

(A) on the happening of a contingency specified in the instrument relating to a child (such as attaining a specified age, marrying, dying, leaving school, or a similar contingency), or

(B) at a time which can clearly be associated with a contingency of a kind specified in subparagraph (A),

an amount equal to the amount of such reduction will be treated as an amount fixed as payable for the support of children of the payor spouse.

(3) SPECIAL RULE WHERE PAYMENT IS LESS THAN AMOUNT SPECIFIED IN INSTRUMENT.—For purposes of this subsection, if any payment is less than the amount specified in the instrument,

then so much of such payment as does not exceed the sum payable for support shall be considered a payment for such support.

(d) Spouse.—For purposes of this section, the term "spouse" includes a former spouse.

(e) Exception for Joint Returns.—This section and section 215 shall not apply if the spouses make a joint return with each other.

(f) Recomputation Where Excess Front-Loading of Alimony Payments.—

(1) In general.—If there are excess alimony payments—

(A) the payor spouse shall include the amount of such excess payments in gross income for the payor spouse's taxable year beginning in the 3rd post-separation year, and

(B) the payee spouse shall be allowed a deduction in computing adjusted gross income for the amount of such excess payments for the payee's taxable year beginning in the 3rd post-separation year.

(2) Excess alimony payments.—For purposes of this subsection, the term "excess alimony payments" mean the sum of—

(A) the excess payments for the 1st post-separation year, and

(B) the excess payments for the 2nd post-separation year.

(3) Excess payments for 1st post-separation year.—For purposes of this subsection, the amount of the excess payments for the 1st post-separation year is the excess (if any) of—

(A) the amount of the alimony or separate maintenance payments paid by the payor spouse during the 1st post-separation year, over

(B) the sum of—

(i) the average of—

(I) the alimony or separate maintenance payments paid by the payor spouse during the 2nd post-separation year, reduced by the excess payments for the 2nd post-separation year, and

(II) the alimony or separate maintenance payments paid by the payor spouse during the 3rd post-separation year, plus

(ii) $15,000.

(4) Excess payments for 2nd post-separation year.—For purposes of this subsection, the amount of the excess pay-

ments for the 2nd post-separation year is the excess (if any) of—

(A) the amount of the alimony or separate maintenance payments paid by the payor spouse during the 2nd post-separation year, over

(B) the sum of—

(i) the amount of the alimony or separate maintenance payments paid by the payor spouse during the 3rd post-separation year, plus

(ii) $15,000.

(5) Exceptions.—

(A) Where payment ceases by reason of death or remarriage.—Paragraph (1) shall not apply if—

(i) either spouse dies before the close of the 3rd post-separation year, or the payee spouse remarries before the close of the 3rd post-separation year, and

(ii) the alimony or separate maintenance payments cease by reason of such death or remarriage.

(B) Support payments.—For purposes of this subsection, the term "alimony or separate maintenance payment" shall not include any payment received under a decree described in subsection (b)(2)(C).

(C) Fluctuating payments not within control of payor spouse.—For purposes of this subsection, the term "alimony or separate maintenance payment" shall not include any payment to the extent it is made pursuant to a continuing liability (over a period of not less than 3 years) to pay a fixed portion or portions of the income from a business or property or from compensation for employment or self-employment.

(6) Post-separation years.—For purposes of this subsection, the term "1st post-separation years" means the 1st calendar year in which the payor spouse paid to the payee spouse alimony or separate maintenance payments to which this section applies. The 2nd and 3rd post-separation years shall be the 1st and 2nd succeeding calendar years, respectively.

(g) Cross References.—

(1) For deduction of alimony or separate maintenance payments, see section 215.

(2) For taxable status of income of an estate or trust in the case of divorce, etc., see section 682.

[¶5190] CODE SEC. 74. PRIZES AND AWARDS.

* * *

(d) Exception for Olympic and Paralympic Medals and Prizes.—

* * *

(2) Limitation based on adjusted gross income.—

* * *

(B) Coordination with other limitations.—For purposes of sections 86, 135, 137, 219, 221, 222, and 469, adjusted gross income shall be determined after the application of paragraph (1) and before the application of subparagraph (A).

[CCH Explanation at ¶ 530. Committee Reports at ¶ 10,460.]

Amendments

• 2017, Tax Cuts and Jobs Act (P.L. 115-97)

P.L. 115-97, § 13305(b)(1):

Amended Code Sec. 74(d)(2)(B) by striking "199," following "137,". **Effective** for tax years beginning after 12-31-2017.

[¶ 5195] CODE SEC. 78. *GROSS UP FOR DEEMED PAID FOREIGN TAX CREDIT.*

If a domestic corporation chooses to have the benefits of subpart A of part III of subchapter N (relating to foreign tax credit) for any taxable year, an amount equal to the taxes deemed to be paid by such corporation under subsections (a), (b), and (d) of section 960 (determined without regard to the phrase "80 percent of" in subsection (d)(1) thereof) for such taxable year shall be treated for purposes of this title (other than sections 245 and 245A) as a dividend received by such domestic corporation from the foreign corporation.

[CCH Explanation at ¶ 720. Committee Reports at ¶ 11,170.]

Amendments

• 2017, Tax Cuts and Jobs Act (P.L. 115-97)

P.L. 115-97, § 14301(c)(1):

Amended Code Sec. 78. **Effective** for tax years of foreign corporations beginning after 12-31-2017, and to tax years of United States shareholders in which or with which such tax years of foreign corporations end. Prior to amendment, Code Sec. 78 read as follows:

SEC. 78. DIVIDENDS RECEIVED FROM CERTAIN FOREIGN CORPORATIONS BY DOMESTIC CORPORATIONS CHOOSING FOREIGN TAX CREDIT.

If a domestic corporation chooses to have the benefits of subpart A of part III of subchapter N (relating to foreign tax credit) for any taxable year, an amount equal to the taxes deemed to be paid by such corporation under section 902(a) (relating to credit for corporate stockholder in foreign corporation) or under section 960(a)(1) (relating to taxes paid by foreign corporation) for such taxable year shall be treated for purposes of this title (other than section 245) as a dividend received by such domestic corporation from the foreign corporation.

[¶ 5200] CODE SEC. 83. PROPERTY TRANSFERRED IN CONNECTION WITH PERFORMANCE OF SERVICES.

* * *

(i) QUALIFIED EQUITY GRANTS.—

    (1) IN GENERAL.—For purposes of this subtitle—

        (A) TIMING OF INCLUSION.—If qualified stock is transferred to a qualified employee who makes an election with respect to such stock under this subsection, subsection (a) shall be applied by including the amount determined under such subsection with respect to such stock in income of the employee in the taxable year determined under subparagraph (B) in lieu of the taxable year described in subsection (a).

        (B) TAXABLE YEAR DETERMINED.—The taxable year determined under this subparagraph is the taxable year of the employee which includes the earliest of—

            (i) the first date such qualified stock becomes transferable (including, solely for purposes of this clause, becoming transferable to the employer),

            (ii) the date the employee first becomes an excluded employee,

            (iii) the first date on which any stock of the corporation which issued the qualified stock becomes readily tradable on an established securities market (as determined by the Secretary, but not including any market unless such market is recognized as an established securities market by the Secretary for purposes of a provision of this title other than this subsection),

            (iv) the date that is 5 years after the first date the rights of the employee in such stock are transferable or are not subject to a substantial risk of forfeiture, whichever occurs earlier, or

            (v) the date on which the employee revokes (at such time and in such manner as the Secretary provides) the election under this subsection with respect to such stock.

    (2) QUALIFIED STOCK.—

(A) IN GENERAL.—*For purposes of this subsection, the term "qualified stock" means, with respect to any qualified employee, any stock in a corporation which is the employer of such employee, if—*

(i) *such stock is received—*

(I) *in connection with the exercise of an option, or*

(II) *in settlement of a restricted stock unit, and*

(ii) *such option or restricted stock unit was granted by the corporation—*

(I) *in connection with the performance of services as an employee, and*

(II) *during a calendar year in which such corporation was an eligible corporation.*

(B) LIMITATION.—*The term "qualified stock" shall not include any stock if the employee may sell such stock to, or otherwise receive cash in lieu of stock from, the corporation at the time that the rights of the employee in such stock first become transferable or not subject to a substantial risk of forfeiture.*

(C) ELIGIBLE CORPORATION.—*For purposes of subparagraph (A)(ii)(II)—*

(i) IN GENERAL.—*The term "eligible corporation" means, with respect to any calendar year, any corporation if—*

(I) *no stock of such corporation (or any predecessor of such corporation) is readily tradable on an established securities market (as determined under paragraph (1)(B)(iii)) during any preceding calendar year, and*

(II) *such corporation has a written plan under which, in such calendar year, not less than 80 percent of all employees who provide services to such corporation in the United States (or any possession of the United States) are granted stock options, or are granted restricted stock units, with the same rights and privileges to receive qualified stock.*

(ii) SAME RIGHTS AND PRIVILEGES.—*For purposes of clause (i)(II)—*

(I) *except as provided in subclauses (II) and (III), the determination of rights and privileges with respect to stock shall be made in a similar manner as under section 423(b)(5),*

(II) *employees shall not fail to be treated as having the same rights and privileges to receive qualified stock solely because the number of shares available to all employees is not equal in amount, so long as the number of shares available to each employee is more than a de minimis amount, and*

(III) *rights and privileges with respect to the exercise of an option shall not be treated as the same as rights and privileges with respect to the settlement of a restricted stock unit.*

(iii) EMPLOYEE.—*For purposes of clause (i)(II), the term "employee" shall not include any employee described in section 4980E(d)(4) or any excluded employee.*

(iv) SPECIAL RULE FOR CALENDAR YEARS BEFORE 2018.—*In the case of any calendar year beginning before January 1, 2018, clause (i)(II) shall be applied without regard to whether the rights and privileges with respect to the qualified stock are the same.*

(3) QUALIFIED EMPLOYEE; EXCLUDED EMPLOYEE.—*For purposes of this subsection—*

(A) IN GENERAL.—*The term "qualified employee" means any individual who—*

(i) *is not an excluded employee, and*

(ii) *agrees in the election made under this subsection to meet such requirements as are determined by the Secretary to be necessary to ensure that the withholding requirements of the corporation under chapter 24 with respect to the qualified stock are met.*

(B) EXCLUDED EMPLOYEE.—*The term "excluded employee" means, with respect to any corporation, any individual—*

(i) *who is a 1-percent owner (within the meaning of section 416(i)(1)(B)(ii)) at any time during the calendar year or who was such a 1 percent owner at any time during the 10 preceding calendar years,*

(ii) who is or has been at any prior time—

(I) the chief executive officer of such corporation or an individual acting in such a capacity, or

(II) the chief financial officer of such corporation or an individual acting in such a capacity,

(iii) who bears a relationship described in section 318(a)(1) to any individual described in subclause (I) or (II) of clause (ii), or

(iv) who is one of the 4 highest compensated officers of such corporation for the taxable year, or was one of the 4 highest compensated officers of such corporation for any of the 10 preceding taxable years, determined with respect to each such taxable year on the basis of the shareholder disclosure rules for compensation under the Securities Exchange Act of 1934 (as if such rules applied to such corporation).

(4) ELECTION.—

(A) TIME FOR MAKING ELECTION.—An election with respect to qualified stock shall be made under this subsection no later than 30 days after the first date the rights of the employee in such stock are transferable or are not subject to a substantial risk of forfeiture, whichever occurs earlier, and shall be made in a manner similar to the manner in which an election is made under subsection (b).

(B) LIMITATIONS.—No election may be made under this section with respect to any qualified stock if—

(i) the qualified employee has made an election under subsection (b) with respect to such qualified stock,

(ii) any stock of the corporation which issued the qualified stock is readily tradable on an established securities market (as determined under paragraph (1)(B)(iii)) at any time before the election is made, or

(iii) such corporation purchased any of its outstanding stock in the calendar year preceding the calendar year which includes the first date the rights of the employee in such stock are transferable or are not subject to a substantial risk of forfeiture, unless—

(I) not less than 25 percent of the total dollar amount of the stock so purchased is deferral stock, and

(II) the determination of which individuals from whom deferral stock is purchased is made on a reasonable basis.

(C) DEFINITIONS AND SPECIAL RULES RELATED TO LIMITATION ON STOCK REDEMPTIONS.—

(i) DEFERRAL STOCK.—For purposes of this paragraph, the term "deferral stock" means stock with respect to which an election is in effect under this subsection.

(ii) DEFERRAL STOCK WITH RESPECT TO ANY INDIVIDUAL NOT TAKEN INTO ACCOUNT IF INDIVIDUAL HOLDS DEFERRAL STOCK WITH LONGER DEFERRAL PERIOD.—Stock purchased by a corporation from any individual shall not be treated as deferral stock for purposes of subparagraph (B)(iii) if such individual (immediately after such purchase) holds any deferral stock with respect to which an election has been in effect under this subsection for a longer period than the election with respect to the stock so purchased.

(iii) PURCHASE OF ALL OUTSTANDING DEFERRAL STOCK.—The requirements of subclauses (I) and (II) of subparagraph (B)(iii) shall be treated as met if the stock so purchased includes all of the corporation's outstanding deferral stock.

(iv) REPORTING.—Any corporation which has outstanding deferral stock as of the beginning of any calendar year and which purchases any of its outstanding stock during such calendar year shall include on its return of tax for the taxable year in which, or with which, such calendar year ends the total dollar amount of its outstanding stock so purchased during such calendar year and such other information as the Secretary requires for purposes of administering this paragraph.

(5) CONTROLLED GROUPS.—For purposes of this subsection, all persons treated as a single employer under section 414(b) shall be treated as 1 corporation.

(6) NOTICE REQUIREMENT.—Any corporation which transfers qualified stock to a qualified employee shall, at the time that (or a reasonable period before) an amount attributable to such stock would (but for this subsection) first be includible in the gross income of such employee—

(A) certify to such employee that such stock is qualified stock, and

(B) notify such employee—

(i) that the employee may be eligible to elect to defer income on such stock under this subsection, and

(ii) that, if the employee makes such an election—

(I) the amount of income recognized at the end of the deferral period will be based on the value of the stock at the time at which the rights of the employee in such stock first become transferable or not subject to substantial risk of forfeiture, notwithstanding whether the value of the stock has declined during the deferral period,

(II) the amount of such income recognized at the end of the deferral period will be subject to withholding under section 3401(i) at the rate determined under section 3402(t), and

(III) the responsibilities of the employee (as determined by the Secretary under paragraph (3)(A)(ii)) with respect to such withholding.

(7) RESTRICTED STOCK UNITS.—This section (other than this subsection), including any election under subsection (b), shall not apply to restricted stock units.

[CCH Explanation at ¶605. Committee Reports at ¶10,810.]

Amendments

• 2017, Tax Cuts and Jobs Act (P.L. 115-97)

P.L. 115-97, §13603(a):

Amended Code Sec. 83 by adding at the end a new subsection (i). **Effective** generally for stock attributable to options exercised, or restricted stock units settled, after 12-31-2017. For a transition rule, see Act Sec. 13603(g), below.

P.L. 115-97, §13603(g), provides:

(g) TRANSITION RULE.—Until such time as the Secretary (or the Secretary's delegate) issues regulations or other gui-

dance for purposes of implementing the requirements of paragraph (2)(C)(i)(II) of section 83(i) of the Internal Revenue Code of 1986 (as added by this section), or the requirements of paragraph (6) of such section, a corporation shall be treated as being in compliance with such requirements (respectively) if such corporation complies with a reasonable good faith interpretation of such requirements.

[¶5205] CODE SEC. 86. SOCIAL SECURITY AND TIER 1 RAILROAD RETIREMENT BENEFITS.

* * *

(b) TAXPAYERS TO WHOM SUBSECTION (a) APPLIES.—

* * *

(2) MODIFIED ADJUSTED GROSS INCOME.—For purposes of this subsection, the term "modified adjusted gross income" means adjusted gross income—

(A) determined without regard to this section and sections 135, 137, 221, 222, 911, 931, and 933, and

* * *

[CCH Explanation at ¶ 530. Committee Reports at ¶ 10,460.]

Amendments

• **2017, Tax Cuts and Jobs Act (P.L. 115-97)**

P.L. 115-97, § 13305(b)(1):

Amended Code Sec. 86(b)(2)(A) by striking "199," following "137,". **Effective** for tax years beginning after 12-31-2017.

[¶ 5210] *CODE SEC. 91. CERTAIN FOREIGN BRANCH LOSSES TRANSFERRED TO SPECIFIED 10-PERCENT OWNED FOREIGN CORPORATIONS.*

(a) IN GENERAL.—If a domestic corporation transfers substantially all of the assets of a foreign branch (within the meaning of section 367(a)(3)(C), as in effect before the date of the enactment of the Tax Cuts and Jobs Act) to a specified 10-percent owned foreign corporation (as defined in section 245A) with respect to which it is a United States shareholder after such transfer, such domestic corporation shall include in gross income for the taxable year which includes such transfer an amount equal to the transferred loss amount with respect to such transfer.

(b) TRANSFERRED LOSS AMOUNT.—For purposes of this section, the term "transferred loss amount" means, with respect to any transfer of substantially all of the assets of a foreign branch, the excess (if any) of—

(1) the sum of losses—

(A) which were incurred by the foreign branch after December 31, 2017, and before the transfer, and

(B) with respect to which a deduction was allowed to the taxpayer, over

(2) the sum of—

(A) any taxable income of such branch for a taxable year after the taxable year in which the loss was incurred and through the close of the taxable year of the transfer, and

(B) any amount which is recognized under section 904(f)(3) on account of the transfer.

(c) REDUCTION FOR RECOGNIZED GAINS.—The transferred loss amount shall be reduced (but not below zero) by the amount of gain recognized by the taxpayer on account of the transfer (other than amounts taken into account under subsection (b)(2)(B)).

(d) SOURCE OF INCOME.—Amounts included in gross income under this section shall be treated as derived from sources within the United States.

(e) BASIS ADJUSTMENTS.—Consistent with such regulations or other guidance as the Secretary shall prescribe, proper adjustments shall be made in the adjusted basis of the taxpayer's stock in the specified 10-percent owned foreign corporation to which the transfer is made, and in the transferee's adjusted basis in the property transferred, to reflect amounts included in gross income under this section.

[CCH Explanation at ¶ 707. Committee Reports at ¶ 11,050.]

Amendments

• **2017, Tax Cuts and Jobs Act (P.L. 115-97)**

P.L. 115-97, § 14102(d)(1):

Amended part II of subchapter B of chapter 1 by adding at the end a new Code Sec. 91. **Effective** for transfers after 12-31-2017. For a transition rule, see Act Sec. 14102(d)(4), below.

P.L. 115-97, § 14102(d)(4), provides:

(4) TRANSITION RULE.—The amount of gain taken into account under section 91(c) of the Internal Revenue Code of 1986, as added by this subsection, shall be reduced by the amount of gain which would be recognized under section 367(a)(3)(C) (determined without regard to the amendments made by subsection (e)) with respect to losses incurred before January 1, 2018.

[¶ 5215] CODE SEC. 101. CERTAIN DEATH BENEFITS.

(a) PROCEEDS OF LIFE INSURANCE CONTRACTS PAYABLE BY REASON OF DEATH.—

(1) GENERAL RULE.—Except as otherwise provided in *paragraphs (2) and (3)*, subsection (d), subsection (f), and subsection (j), gross income does not include amounts received (whether in a single sum or otherwise) under a life insurance contract, if such amounts are paid by reason of the death of the insured.

* * *

(3) EXCEPTION TO VALUABLE CONSIDERATION RULES FOR COMMERCIAL TRANSFERS.—

(A) IN GENERAL.—The second sentence of paragraph (2) shall not apply in the case of a transfer of a life insurance contract, or any interest therein, which is a reportable policy sale.

(B) REPORTABLE POLICY SALE.—For purposes of this paragraph, the term "reportable policy sale" means the acquisition of an interest in a life insurance contract, directly or indirectly, if the acquirer has no substantial family, business, or financial relationship with the insured apart from the acquirer's interest in such life insurance contract. For purposes of the preceding sentence, the term "indirectly" applies to the acquisition of an interest in a partnership, trust, or other entity that holds an interest in the life insurance contract.

* * *

[CCH Explanation at ¶ 945. Committee Reports at ¶ 10,720.]

Amendments

• **2017, Tax Cuts and Jobs Act (P.L. 115-97)**

P.L. 115-97, § 13522(a):

Amended Code Sec. 101(a) by inserting after paragraph (2) a new paragraph (3). **Effective** for transfers after 12-31-2017.

P.L. 115-97, § 13522(b):

Amended Code Sec. 101(a)(1) by striking "paragraph (2)" and inserting "paragraphs (2) and (3)". **Effective** for transfers after 12-31-2017.

[¶ 5220]   CODE SEC. 108.   INCOME FROM DISCHARGE OF INDEBTEDNESS.

* * *

(f) STUDENT LOANS.—

* * *

(5) DISCHARGES ON ACCOUNT OF DEATH OR DISABILITY.—

(A) IN GENERAL.—In the case of an individual, gross income does not include any amount which (but for this subsection) would be includible in gross income for such taxable year by reasons of the discharge (in whole or in part) of any loan described in subparagraph (B) after December 31, 2017, and before January 1, 2026, if such discharge was—

(i) pursuant to subsection (a) or (d) of section 437 of the Higher Education Act of 1965 or the parallel benefit under part D of title IV of such Act (relating to the repayment of loan liability),

(ii) pursuant to section 464(c)(1)(F) of such Act, or

(iii) otherwise discharged on account of the death or total and permanent disability of the student.

(B) LOANS DESCRIBED.—A loan is described in this subparagraph if such loan is—

(i) a student loan (as defined in paragraph (2)), or

(ii) a private education loan (as defined in section 140(7) of the Consumer Credit Protection Act (15 U.S.C. 1650(7))).

* * *

[CCH Explanation at ¶ 265. Committee Reports at ¶ 10,140.]
Amendments

• **2017, Tax Cuts and Jobs Act (P.L. 115-97)**

P.L. 115-97, § 11031(a):

Amended Code Sec. 108(f) by adding at the end a new paragraph (5). **Effective** for discharges of indebtedness after 12-31-2017.

[¶ 5225] CODE SEC. 118. CONTRIBUTIONS TO THE CAPITAL OF A CORPORATION.

* * *

(b) EXCEPTIONS.—For purposes of subsection (a), the term "contribution to the capital of the taxpayer" does not include—

(1) any contribution in aid of construction or any other contribution as a customer or potential customer, and

(2) any contribution by any governmental entity or civic group (other than a contribution made by a shareholder as such).

[CCH Explanation at ¶ 320. Committee Reports at ¶ 10,520.]

Amendments

• **2017, Tax Cuts and Jobs Act (P.L. 115-97)**

P.L. 115-97, § 13312(a)(1)-(3):

Amended Code Sec. 118 by striking subsections (b), (c), and (d), by redesignating subsection (e) as subsection (d), and by inserting after subsection (a) new subsections (b) and (c). **Effective** generally for contributions made after 12-22-2017. For an exception, see Act Sec. 13312(b)(2), below. Prior to being stricken, Code Sec. 118(b) read as follows:

(b) CONTRIBUTIONS IN AID OF CONSTRUCTION ETC.—For purposes of subsection (a), except as provided in subsection (c),

the term "contribution to the capital of the taxpayer" does not include any contribution in aid of construction or any other contribution as a customer or potential customer.

P.L. 115-97, § 13312(b)(2), provides:

(2) EXCEPTION.—The amendments made by this section shall not apply to any contribution, made after the date of enactment of this Act by a governmental entity, which is made pursuant to a master development plan that has been approved prior to such date by a governmental entity.

(c) REGULATIONS.—The Secretary shall issue such regulations or other guidance as may be necessary or appropriate to carry out this section, including regulations or other guidance for determining whether any contribution constitutes a contribution in aid of construction.

[CCH Explanation at ¶ 320. Committee Reports at ¶ 10,520.]

Amendments

• **2017, Tax Cuts and Jobs Act (P.L. 115-97)**

P.L. 115-97, § 13312(a)(1) and (3):

Amended Code Sec. 118 by striking subsection (c) and by inserting a new subsection (c). **Effective** generally for contributions made after 12-22-2017. For an exception, see Act Sec. 13312(b)(2), below. Prior to being stricken, Code Sec. 118(c) read as follows:

(c) SPECIAL RULES FOR WATER AND SEWERAGE DISPOSAL UTILITIES.—

(1) GENERAL RULE.—For purposes of this section, the term "contribution to the capital of the taxpayer" includes any amount of money or other property received from any person (whether or not a shareholder) by a regulated public utility which provides water or sewerage disposal services if—

(A) such amount is a contribution in aid of construction,

(B) in the case of contribution of property other than water or sewerage disposal facilities, such amount meets the requirements of the expenditure rule of paragraph (2), and

(C) such amount (or any property acquired or constructed with such amount) is not included in the taxpayer's rate base for ratemaking purposes.

(2) EXPENDITURE RULE.—An amount meets the requirements of this paragraph if—

(A) an amount equal to such amount is expended for the acquisition or construction of tangible property described in section 1231(b)—

(i) which is the property for which the contribution was made or is of the same type as such property, and

(ii) which is used predominantly in the trade or business of furnishing water or sewerage disposal services,

(B) the expenditure referred to in subparagraph (A) occurs before the end of the second taxable year after the year in which such amount was received, and

(C) accurate records are kept of the amounts contributed and expenditures made, the expenditures to which contributions are allocated, and the year in which the contributions and expenditures are received and made.

(3) DEFINITIONS.—For purposes of this subsection—

(A) CONTRIBUTION IN AID OF CONSTRUCTION.—The term "contribution in aid of construction" shall be defined by regulations prescribed by the Secretary, except that such term shall not include amounts paid as service charges for starting or stopping services.

(B) PREDOMINANTLY.—The term "predominantly" means 80 percent or more.

(C) REGULATED PUBLIC UTILITY.—The term "regulated public utility" has the meaning given such term by section 7701(a)(33), except that such term shall not include any utility which is not required to provide water or sewerage disposal services to members of the general public in its service area.

(4) DISALLOWANCE OF DEDUCTIONS AND CREDITS; ADJUSTED BASIS.—Notwithstanding any other provision of this subtitle, no deduction or credit shall be allowed for, or by reason of, any expenditure which constitutes a contribution in aid of construction to which this subsection applies. The adjusted basis of any property acquired with contributions in aid of construction to which this subsection applies shall be zero.

P.L. 115-97, § 13312(b)(2), provides:

(2) EXCEPTION. —The amendments made by this section shall not apply to any contribution, made after the date of enactment of this Act by a governmental entity, which is made pursuant to a master development plan that has been approved prior to such date by a governmental entity.

(d) [*Stricken.*]

[CCH Explanation at ¶ 320. Committee Reports at ¶ 10,520.]

Amendments

• **2017, Tax Cuts and Jobs Act (P.L. 115-97)**

P.L. 115-97, § 13312(a)(1):

Amended Code Sec. 118 by striking subsection (d). **Effective** generally for contributions made after 12-22-2017. For an exception, see Act Sec. 13312(b)(2), below. Prior to being stricken, Code Sec. 118(d) read as follows:

(d) STATUTE OF LIMITATIONS.—If the taxpayer for any taxable year treats an amount as a contribution to the capital of the taxpayer described in subsection (c), then—

(1) the statutory period for the assessment of any deficiency attributable to any part of such amount shall not expire before the expiration of 3 years from the date the Secretary is notified by the taxpayer (in such manner as the Secretary may prescribe) of—

(A) the amount of the expenditure referred to in subparagraph (A) of subsection (c)(2),

(B) the taxpayer's intention not to make the expenditures referred to in such subparagraph, or

(C) a failure to make such expenditure within the period described in subparagraph (B) of subsection (c)(2), and

(2) such deficiency may be assessed before the expiration of such 3-year period notwithstanding the provisions of any other law or rule of law which would otherwise prevent such assessment.

P.L. 115-97, § 13312(b)(2), provides:

(2) EXCEPTION.—The amendments made by this section shall not apply to any contribution, made after the date of enactment of this Act by a governmental entity, which is made pursuant to a master development plan that has been approved prior to such date by a governmental entity.

(*d*) CROSS REFERENCES.—

(1) For basis of property acquired by a corporation through a contribution to its capital, see section 362.

(2) For special rules in the case of contributions of indebtedness, see section 108(e)(6).

[CCH Explanation at ¶ 320. Committee Reports at ¶ 10,520.]

Amendments

• **2017, Tax Cuts and Jobs Act (P.L. 115-97)**

P.L. 115-97, § 13312(a)(1)-(2):

Amended Code Sec. 118 by striking subsection (d), and by redesignating subsection (e) as subsection (d). **Effective** generally for contributions made after 12-22-2017. For an exception, see Act Sec. 13312(b)(2), below.

P.L. 115-97, § 13312(b)(2), provides:

(2) EXCEPTION. — The amendments made by this section shall not apply to any contribution, made after the date of enactment of this Act by a governmental entity, which is made pursuant to a master development plan that has been approved prior to such date by a governmental entity.

[¶ 5230] CODE SEC. 121. EXCLUSION OF GAIN FROM SALE OF PRINCIPAL RESIDENCE.

* * *

(d) SPECIAL RULES.—

* * *

(3) PROPERTY OWNED BY SPOUSE OR FORMER SPOUSE.—For purposes of this section—

* * *

➤➤➤ *Caution: Code Sec. 121(d)(3)(B), below, as amended by P.L. 115-97, applies generally to any divorce or separation instrument executed after December 31, 2018.*

(B) PROPERTY USED BY FORMER SPOUSE PURSUANT TO DIVORCE DECREE, ETC.—Solely for purposes of this section, an individual shall be treated as using property as such individual's principal residence during any period of ownership while such individual's spouse or former spouse is granted use of the property under a divorce or separation instrument.

➤➤➤ *Caution: Code Sec.121(d)(3)(C), below, as added by P.L. 115-97, applies generally to any divorce or separation instrument executed after December 31, 2018.*

(C) DIVORCE OR SEPARATION INSTRUMENT.—For purposes of this paragraph, the term "divorce or separation instrument" means—

(i) a decree of divorce or separate maintenance or a written instrument incident to such a decree,

(ii) a written separation agreement, or

(iii) a decree (not described in clause (i)) requiring a spouse to make payments for the support or maintenance of the other spouse.

* * *

[CCH Explanation at ¶255. Committee Reports at ¶10,260.]
Amendments
• **2017, Tax Cuts and Jobs Act (P.L. 115-97)**

P.L. 115-97, §11051(b)(3)(A)(i)-(ii):

Amended Code Sec. 121(d)(3) by striking "(as defined in section 71(b)(2))" following "a divorce or separation instrument" in subparagraph (B), and by adding at the end a new subparagraph (C). For the **effective** date, see Act Sec. 11051(c)(1)-(2), below.

P.L. 115-97, §11051(c)(1)-(2), provides:

(c) EFFECTIVE DATE.—The amendments made by this section shall apply to—

(1) any divorce or separation instrument (as defined in section 71(b)(2) of the Internal Revenue Code of 1986 as in effect before the date of the enactment of this Act) executed after December 31, 2018, and

(2) any divorce or separation instrument (as so defined) executed on or before such date and modified after such date if the modification expressly provides that the amendments made by this section apply to such modification.

[¶5235] CODE SEC. 125. CAFETERIA PLANS.

* * *

(i) LIMITATION ON HEALTH FLEXIBLE SPENDING ARRANGEMENTS.—

* * *

(2) ADJUSTMENT FOR INFLATION.—In the case of any taxable year beginning after December 31, 2013, the dollar amount in paragraph (1) shall be increased by an amount equal to—

(A) such amount, multiplied by

(B) the cost-of-living adjustment determined under section 1(f)(3) for the calendar year in which such taxable year begins by substituting "calendar year 2012" *for "calendar year 2016" in subparagraph (A)(ii)* thereof.

If any increase determined under this paragraph is not a multiple of $50, such increase shall be rounded to the next lowest multiple of $50.

* * *

[CCH Explanation at ¶125. Committee Reports at ¶10,020.]
Amendments
• **2017, Tax Cuts and Jobs Act (P.L. 115-97)**

P.L. 115-97, §11002(d)(1)(L):

Amended Code Sec. 125(i)(2)(B) by striking "for 'calendar year 1992' in subparagraph (B)" and inserting "for 'calendar

year 2016' in subparagraph (A)(ii)". **Effective** for tax years beginning after 12-31-2017.

[¶5240] CODE SEC. 132. CERTAIN FRINGE BENEFITS.

* * *

(f) QUALIFIED TRANSPORTATION FRINGE.—

* * *

(6) INFLATION ADJUSTMENT.—

(A) IN GENERAL.—In the case of any taxable year beginning in a calendar year after 1999, the dollar amounts contained in subparagraphs (A) and (B) of paragraph (2) shall be increased by an amount equal to—

(i) such dollar amount, multiplied by

(ii) the cost-of-living adjustment determined under section 1(f)(3) for the calendar year in which the taxable year begins, by substituting "calendar year 1998" *for "calendar year 2016" in subparagraph (A)(ii)* thereof.

* * *

(8) SUSPENSION OF QUALIFIED BICYCLE COMMUTING REIMBURSEMENT EXCLUSION.—Paragraph (1)(D) shall not apply to any taxable year beginning after December 31, 2017, and before January 1, 2026.

[CCH Explanation at ¶125 and ¶615. Committee Reports at ¶10,020 and ¶10,220.]

Amendments

• **2017, Tax Cuts and Jobs Act (P.L. 115-97)**

P.L. 115-97, §11002(d)(5):

Amended Code Sec. 132(f)(6)(A)(ii) by striking "for 'calendar year 1992'" and inserting "for 'calendar year 2016' in subparagraph (A)(ii) thereof". **Effective** for tax years beginning after 12-31-2017.

P.L. 115-97, §11047(a):

Amended Code Sec. 132(f) by adding at the end a new paragraph (8). **Effective** for tax years beginning after 12-31-2017.

(g) QUALIFIED MOVING EXPENSE REIMBURSEMENT.—*For purposes of this section—*

(1) IN GENERAL.—The term "qualified moving expense reimbursement" means any amount received (directly or indirectly) by an individual from an employer as a payment for (or a reimbursement of) expenses which would be deductible as moving expenses under section 217 if directly paid or incurred by the individual. Such term shall not include any payment for (or reimbursement of) an expense actually deducted by the individual in a prior taxable year.

(2) SUSPENSION FOR TAXABLE YEARS 2018 THROUGH 2025.—Except in the case of a member of the Armed Forces of the United States on active duty who moves pursuant to a military order and incident to a permanent change of station, subsection (a)(6) shall not apply to any taxable year beginning after December 31, 2017, and before January 1, 2026.

* * *

[CCH Explanation at ¶610. Committee Reports at ¶10,230.]

Amendments

• **2017, Tax Cuts and Jobs Act (P.L. 115-97)**

P.L. 115-97, §11048(a)(1)-(2):

Amended Code Sec. 132(g) by striking "For purposes of this section, the term" and inserting "For purposes of this section—

"(1) IN GENERAL.—The term", and

by adding at the end a new paragraph (2). **Effective** for tax years beginning after 12-31-2017.

[¶5245] CODE SEC. 135. INCOME FROM UNITED STATES SAVINGS BONDS USED TO PAY HIGHER EDUCATION TUITION AND FEES.

* * *

(b) LIMITATIONS.—

* * *

(2) LIMITATION BASED ON MODIFIED ADJUSTED GROSS INCOME.—

* * *

(B) INFLATION ADJUSTMENT.—In the case of any taxable year beginning in a calendar year after 1990, the $40,000 and $60,000 amounts contained in subparagraph (A) shall be increased by an amount equal to—

(i) such dollar amount, multiplied by

(ii) the cost-of-living adjustment under section 1(f)(3) for the calendar year in which the taxable year begins, determined by substituting "calendar year 1989" *for "calendar year 2016" in subparagraph (A)(ii)* thereof.

* * *

[CCH Explanation at ¶ 125. Committee Reports at ¶ 10,020.]

Amendments

• 2017, Tax Cuts and Jobs Act (P.L. 115-97)

P.L. 115-97, § 11002(d)(1)(M):

Amended Code Sec. 135(b)(2)(B)(ii) by striking "for 'calendar year 1992' in subparagraph (B)" and inserting "for 'calendar year 2016' in subparagraph (A)(ii)". **Effective** for tax years beginning after 12-31-2017.

(c) DEFINITIONS.—For purposes of this section—

* * *

(4) MODIFIED ADJUSTED GROSS INCOME.—The term "modified adjusted gross income" means the adjusted gross income of the taxpayer for the taxable year determined—

(A) without regard to this section and sections 137, 221, 222, 911, 931, and 933, and

* * *

[CCH Explanation at ¶ 530. Committee Reports at ¶ 10,460.]

Amendments

• 2017, Tax Cuts and Jobs Act (P.L. 115-97)

P.L. 115-97, § 13305(b)(1):

Amended Code Sec. 135(c)(4)(A) by striking "199," following "sections 137,". **Effective** for tax years beginning after 12-31-2017.

[¶ 5250] CODE SEC. 137. ADOPTION ASSISTANCE PROGRAMS.

* * *

(b) LIMITATIONS.—

* * *

(3) DETERMINATION OF ADJUSTED GROSS INCOME.—For purposes of paragraph (2), adjusted gross income shall be determined—

(A) without regard to this section and sections 221, 222, 911, 931, and 933, and

* * *

[CCH Explanation at ¶ 530. Committee Reports at ¶ 10,460.]

Amendments

• 2017, Tax Cuts and Jobs Act (P.L. 115-97)

P.L. 115-97, § 13305(b)(1):

Amended Code Sec. 137(b)(3)(A) by striking "199," following "sections". **Effective** for tax years beginning after 12-31-2017.

(f) ADJUSTMENTS FOR INFLATION.—In the case of a taxable year beginning after December 31, 2002, each of the dollar amounts in subsection (a)(2) and paragraphs (1) and (2)(A) of subsection (b) shall be increased by an amount equal to—

(1) such dollar amount, multiplied by

(2) the cost-of-living adjustment determined under section 1(f)(3) for the calendar year in which the taxable year begins, determined by substituting "calendar year 2001" *for "calendar year 2016" in subparagraph (A)(ii)* thereof.

If any amount as increased under the preceding sentence is not a multiple of $10, such amount shall be rounded to the nearest multiple of $10.

[CCH Explanation at ¶125. Committee Reports at ¶10,020.]

Amendments

• **2017, Tax Cuts and Jobs Act (P.L. 115-97)**

P.L. 115-97, §11002(d)(1)(N):

Amended Code Sec. 137(f)(2) by striking "for 'calendar year 1992' in subparagraph (B)" and inserting "for 'calendar year 2016' in subparagraph (A)(ii)". **Effective** for tax years beginning after 12-31-2017.

[¶5255] CODE SEC. 139G. ASSIGNMENTS TO ALASKA NATIVE SETTLEMENT TRUSTS.

(a) IN GENERAL.—*In the case of a Native Corporation, gross income shall not include the value of any payments that would otherwise be made, or treated as being made, to such Native Corporation pursuant to, or as required by, any provision of the Alaska Native Claims Settlement Act (43 U.S.C. 1601 et seq.), including any payment that would otherwise be made to a Village Corporation pursuant to section 7(j) of the Alaska Native Claims Settlement Act (43 U.S.C. 1606(j)), provided that any such payments—*

(1) *are assigned in writing to a Settlement Trust, and*

(2) *were not received by such Native Corporation prior to the assignment described in paragraph (1).*

(b) INCLUSION IN GROSS INCOME.—*In the case of a Settlement Trust which has been assigned payments described in subsection (a), gross income shall include such payments when received by such Settlement Trust pursuant to the assignment and shall have the same character as if such payments were received by the Native Corporation.*

(c) AMOUNT AND SCOPE OF ASSIGNMENT.—*The amount and scope of any assignment under subsection (a) shall be described with reasonable particularity and may either be in a percentage of one or more such payments or in a fixed dollar amount.*

(d) DURATION OF ASSIGNMENT; REVOCABILITY.—*Any assignment under subsection (a) shall specify—*

(1) *a duration either in perpetuity or for a period of time, and*

(2) *whether such assignment is revocable.*

(e) PROHIBITION ON DEDUCTION.—*Notwithstanding section 247, no deduction shall be allowed to a Native Corporation for purposes of any amounts described in subsection (a).*

(f) DEFINITIONS.—*For purposes of this section, the terms "Native Corporation" and "Settlement Trust" have the same meaning given such terms under section 646(h).*

[CCH Explanation at ¶325. Committee Reports at ¶10,970.]

Amendments

• **2017, Tax Cuts and Jobs Act (P.L. 115-97)**

P.L. 115-97, §13821(a)(1):

Amended part III of subchapter B of chapter 1 by inserting before Code Sec. 140 a new Code Sec. 139G. **Effective** for tax years beginning after 12-31-2016.

[¶5260] CODE SEC. 145. QUALIFIED 501(c)(3) BOND.

* * *

(d) RESTRICTIONS ON BONDS USED TO PROVIDE RESIDENTIAL RENTAL HOUSING FOR FAMILY UNITS.—

* * *

(4) SUBSTANTIAL REHABILITATION.—

(A) IN GENERAL.—Except as provided in subparagraph (B), rules similar to the rules *of section 47(c)(1)(B)* shall apply in determining for purposes of paragraph (2)(C) whether property is substantially rehabilitated.

(B) Exception.—For purposes of subparagraph (A), clause (ii) *of section 47(c)(1)(B)* shall not apply, but the Secretary may extend the 24-month period in *section 47(c)(1)(B)(i)* where appropriate due to circumstances not within the control of the owner.

* * *

[CCH Explanation at ¶ 590. Committee Reports at ¶ 10,560.]

Amendments

• **2017, Tax Cuts and Jobs Act (P.L. 115-97)**

P.L. 115-97, § 13402(b)(2)(A)-(B):

Amended Code Sec. 145(d)(4) by striking "of section 47(c)(1)(C)" each place it appears and inserting "of section 47(c)(1)(B)", and by striking "section 47(c)(1)(C)(i)" and inserting "section 47(c)(1)(B)(i)". **Effective** generally for amounts paid or incurred after 12-31-2017. For a transition rule, see Act Sec. 13402(c)(2), below.

P.L. 115-97, § 13402(c)(2), provides:

(2) Transition Rule.—In the case of qualified rehabilitation expenditures with respect to any building—

(A) owned or leased by the taxpayer during the entirety of the period after December 31, 2017, and

(B) with respect to which the 24-month period selected by the taxpayer under clause (i) of section 47(c)(1)(B) of the Internal Revenue Code (as amended by subsection (b)), or the 60-month period applicable under clause (ii) of such section, begins not later than 180 days after the date of the enactment of this Act, the amendments made by this section shall apply to such expenditures paid or incurred after the end of the taxable year in which the 24-month period, or the 60-month period, referred to in subparagraph (B) ends.

[¶ 5265] CODE SEC. 146. VOLUME CAP.

* * *

(d) State Ceiling.—For purposes of this section.—

* * *

(2) Cost-of-Living Adjustment.—In the case of a calendar year after 2002, each of the dollar amounts contained in paragraph (1) shall be increased by an amount equal to—

(A) such dollar amount, multiplied by

(B) the cost-of-living adjustment determined under section 1(f)(3) for such calendar year by substituting *"calendar year 2001"* for *"calendar year 2016" in subparagraph (A)(ii)* thereof.

If any increase determined under the preceding sentence is not a multiple of $5 ($5,000 in the case of the dollar amount in paragraph (1)(B)), such increase shall be rounded to the nearest multiple thereof.

* * *

[CCH Explanation at ¶ 125. Committee Reports at ¶ 10,020.]

Amendments

• **2017, Tax Cuts and Jobs Act (P.L. 115-97)**

P.L. 115-97, § 11002(d)(1)(O):

Amended Code Sec. 146(d)(2)(B) by striking "for 'calendar year 1992' in subparagraph (B)" and inserting "for 'cal-

endar year 2016' in subparagraph (A)(ii)". **Effective** for tax years beginning after 12-31-2017.

[¶ 5270] CODE SEC. 147. OTHER REQUIREMENTS APPLICABLE TO CERTAIN PRIVATE ACTIVITY BONDS.

* * *

(c) Limitation on Use for Land Acquisition.—

* * *

(2) Exception for First-Time Farmers.—

* * *

(H) Adjustments for Inflation.—In the case of any calendar year after 2008, the dollar amount in subparagraph (A) shall be increased by an amount equal to—

(i) such dollar amount, multiplied by

    (ii) the cost-of-living adjustment determined under section 1(f)(3) for the calendar year, determined by substituting "calendar year 2007" *for "calendar year 2016" in subparagraph (A)(ii)* thereof.

If any amount as increased under the preceding sentence is not a multiple of $100, such amount shall be rounded to the nearest multiple of $100.

* * *

[CCH Explanation at ¶ 125. Committee Reports at ¶ 10,020.]

Amendments

• **2017, Tax Cuts and Jobs Act (P.L. 115-97)**

P.L. 115-97, § 11002(d)(1)(P):

Amended Code Sec. 147(c)(2)(H)(ii) by striking "for 'calendar year 1992' in subparagraph (B)" and inserting "for

'calendar year 2016' in subparagraph (A)(ii)". **Effective** for tax years beginning after 12-31-2017.

[¶ 5275] CODE SEC. 148. ARBITRAGE.

* * *

    (f) Required Rebate to the United States.—

* * *

        (4) Special rules for applying paragraph (2).—

* * *

          (C) Exception from rebate for certain proceeds to be used to finance construction expenditures.—

* * *

            (xiv) Elections.—Any election under this subparagraph (other than clauses (viii) and (ix)) shall be made on or before the date the bonds are issued; and, once made, shall be irrevocable.

            (xv) Time for payment of penalties.—Any penalty under this subparagraph shall be paid to the United States not later than 90 days after the period to which the penalty relates.

            (xvi) Treatment of bona fide debt service funds.—If the spending requirements of clause (ii) are met with respect to the available construction proceeds of a construction issue, then paragraph (2) shall not apply to earnings on a bona fide debt service fund for such issue.

* * *

[CCH Explanation at ¶ 870. Committee Reports at ¶ 10,750.]

Amendments

• **2017, Tax Cuts and Jobs Act (P.L. 115-97)**

P.L. 115-97, § 13532(b)(2):

Amended Code Sec. 148(f)(4)(C) by striking clause (xiv) and by redesignating clauses (xv) to (xvii) as clauses (xiv) to (xvi). **Effective** for advance refunding bonds issued after

12-31-2017. Prior to being stricken, Code Sec. 148(f)(4)(C)(xiv) read as follows:

    (xiv) Determination of initial temporary period.—For purposes of this subparagraph, the end of the initial temporary period shall be determined without regard to section 149(d)(3)(A)(iv).

[¶ 5280] CODE SEC. 149. BONDS MUST BE REGISTERED TO BE TAX EXEMPT; OTHER REQUIREMENTS.

* * *

    (d) Advance Refundings.—

        (1) In general.—Nothing in section 103(a) or in any other provision of law shall be construed to provide an exemption from Federal income tax for interest on any bond issued *to advance refund another bond.*

(2) ADVANCE REFUNDING.—For purposes of this part, a bond shall be treated as issued to advance refund another bond if it is issued more than 90 days before the redemption of the refunded bond.

(3) REGULATIONS.—The Secretary shall prescribe such regulations as may be necessary or appropriate to carry out the purposes of this subsection.

* * *

[CCH Explanation at ¶ 870. Committee Reports at ¶ 10,750.]

Amendments

• **2017, Tax Cuts and Jobs Act (P.L. 115-97)**

P.L. 115-97, § 13532(a):

Amended Code Sec. 149(d)(1) by striking "as part of an issue described in paragraph (2), (3), or (4)." and inserting "to advance refund another bond.". **Effective** for advance refunding bonds issued after 12-31-2017.

P.L. 115-97, § 13532(b)(1):

Amended Code Sec. 149(d) by striking paragraphs (2), (3), (4), and (6) and by redesignating paragraphs (5) and (7) as paragraphs (2) and (3). **Effective** for advance refunding bonds issued after 12-31-2017. Prior to being stricken, Code Sec. 149(d)(2), (3), (4), and (6) read as follows:

(2) CERTAIN PRIVATE ACTIVITY BONDS.—An issue is described in this paragraph if any bond (issued as part of such issue) is issued to advance refund a private activity bond (other than a qualified 501(c)(3) bond).

(3) OTHER BONDS.—

(A) IN GENERAL.—An issue is described in this paragraph if any bond (issued as part of such issue, hereinafter in this paragraph referred to as the "refunding bond," is issued to advance refund a bond unless—

(i) the refunding bond is only—

(I) the 1st advance refunding of the original bond if the original bond is issued after 1985, or

(II) the 1st or 2nd advance refunding of the original bond if the original bond was issued before 1986,

(ii) in the case of refunded bonds issued before 1986, the refunded bond is redeemed not later than the earliest date on which such bond may be redeemed at par or at a premium of 3 percent or less,

(iii) in the case of refunded bonds issued after 1985, the refunded bond is redeemed not later than the earliest date on which such bond may be redeemed,

(iv) the initial temporary period under section 148(c) ends—

(I) with respect to the proceeds of the refunding bond not later than 30 days after the date of issue of such bond, and

(II) with respect to the proceeds of the refunded bond on the date of issue of the refunding bond, and

(v) in the case of refunded bonds to which section 148(e) did not apply, on and after the date of issue of the refunding bond, the amount of proceeds of the refunded bond invested in higher yielding investments (as defined in section 148(b)) which are nonpurpose investments (as defined in section 148(f)(6)(A)) does not exceed—

(I) the amount so invested as part of a reasonably required reserve or replacement fund or during an allowable temporary period, and

(II) the amount which is equal to the lesser of 5 percent of the proceeds of the issue of which the refunded bond is a part or $100,000 (to the extent such amount is allocable to the refunded bond).

(B) SPECIAL RULES FOR REDEMPTIONS.—

(i) ISSUER MUST REDEEM ONLY IF DEBT SERVICE SAVINGS.—Clause (ii) and (iii) of subparagraph (A) shall apply only if the issuer may realize present value debt service savings (determined without regard to administrative expenses) in connection with the issue of which the refunding bond is a part.

(ii) REDEMPTIONS NOT REQUIRED BEFORE 90TH DAY.—For purposes of clauses (ii) and (iii) of subparagraph (A), the earliest date referred to in such clauses shall not be earlier than the 90th day after the date of issuance of the refunding bond.

(4) ABUSIVE TRANSACTIONS PROHIBITED.—An issue is described in this paragraph if any bond (issued as part of such issue) is issued to advance refund another bond and a device is employed in connection with the issuance of such issue to obtain a material financial advantage (based on arbitrage) apart from savings attributable to lower interest rates.

(6) SPECIAL RULES FOR PURPOSES OF PARAGRAPH (3).—For purposes of paragraph (3), bonds issued before the date of the enactment of this subsection shall be taken into account under subparagraph (A)(i) thereof except—

(A) a refunding which occurred before 1986 shall be treated as an advance refunding only if the refunding bond was issued more than 180 days before the redemption of the refunded bond, and

(B) a bond issued before 1986, shall be treated as advance refunded no more than once before March 15, 1986.

[¶ 5285] CODE SEC. 151. ALLOWANCE OF DEDUCTIONS FOR PERSONAL EXEMPTIONS.

* * *

(d) EXEMPTION AMOUNT.—For purposes of this section—

* * *

(4) INFLATION ADJUSTMENT.—*Except as provided in paragraph (5), in the case of* any taxable year beginning in a calendar year after 1989, the dollar amount contained in paragraph (1) shall be increased by an amount equal to—

(A) such dollar amount, multiplied by

(B) the cost-of-living adjustment determined under section 1(f)(3) for the calendar year in which the taxable year begins, by substituting *"calendar year 1988" for "calendar year 2016" in subparagraph (A)(ii) thereof.*

(5) SPECIAL RULES FOR TAXABLE YEARS 2018 THROUGH 2025.—In the case of a taxable year beginning after December 31, 2017, and before January 1, 2026—

(A) EXEMPTION AMOUNT.—The term "exemption amount" means zero.

(B) REFERENCES.—For purposes of any other provision of this title, the reduction of the exemption amount to zero under subparagraph (A) shall not be taken into account in determining whether a deduction is allowed or allowable, or whether a taxpayer is entitled to a deduction, under this section.

* * *

[CCH Explanation at ¶ 125 and ¶ 210. Committee Reports at ¶ 10,020 and ¶ 10,160.]

Amendments

• **2017, Tax Cuts and Jobs Act (P.L. 115-97)**

P.L. 115-97, § 11002(d)(1)(Q):

Amended Code Sec. 151(d)(4)(B) by striking "for 'calendar year 1992' in subparagraph (B)" and inserting "for 'calendar year 2016' in subparagraph (A)(ii)". **Effective** for tax years beginning after 12-31-2017.

P.L. 115-97, § 11041(a)(1)-(2):

Amended Code Sec. 151(d) by striking "In the case of" in paragraph (4) and inserting "Except as provided in para-graph (5), in the case of", and by adding at the end a new paragraph (5). **Effective** generally for tax years beginning after 12-31-2017. For special rule, see Act Sec. 11041(f)(2), below.

P.L. 115-97, § 11041(f)(2), provides:

(2) WAGE WITHHOLDING.—The Secretary of the Treasury may administer section 3402 for taxable years beginning before January 1, 2019, without regard to the amendments made by subsections (a) and (c).

[¶ 5290] CODE SEC. 152. DEPENDENT DEFINED.

* * *

(d) QUALIFYING RELATIVE.—For purposes of this section—

* * *

➤➤➤ *Caution: Code Sec. 152(d)(5), below, as amended by P.L. 115-97, applies generally to any divorce or separation instrument executed after December 31, 2018.*

(5) SPECIAL RULES FOR SUPPORT.—

(A) IN GENERAL.—For purposes of this subsection—

(i) payments to a spouse of alimony or separate maintenance payments shall not be treated as a payment by the payor spouse for the support of any dependent, and

(ii) in the case of the remarriage of a parent, support of a child received from the parent's spouse shall be treated as received from the parent.

(B) ALIMONY OR SEPARATE MAINTENANCE PAYMENT.—For purposes of subparagraph (A), the term "alimony or separate maintenance payment" means any payment in cash if—

(i) such payment is received by (or on behalf of) a spouse under a divorce or separation instrument (as defined in section 121(d)(3)(C)),

(ii) in the case of an individual legally separated from the individual's spouse under a decree of divorce or of separate maintenance, the payee spouse and the payor spouse are not members of the same household at the time such payment is made, and

(iii) there is no liability to make any such payment for any period after the death of the payee spouse and there is no liability to make any payment (in cash or property) as a substitute for such payments after the death of the payee spouse.

* * *

[CCH Explanation at ¶ 255. Committee Reports at ¶ 10,260.]

Amendments

• **2017, Tax Cuts and Jobs Act (P.L. 115-97)**

P.L. 115-97, § 11051(b)(3)(B):

Amended Code Sec. 152(d)(5). For the **effective** date, see Act Sec. 11051(c), below. Prior to amendment, Code Sec. 152(d)(5) read as follows:

(5) SPECIAL RULES FOR SUPPORT.—For purposes of this subsection—

(A) payments to a spouse which are includible in the gross income of such spouse under section 71 or 682 shall not be treated as a payment by the payor spouse for the support of any dependent, and

(B) in the case of the remarriage of a parent, support of a child received from the parent's spouse shall be treated as received from the parent.

P.L. 115-97, § 11051(c), provides:

(c) EFFECTIVE DATE.—The amendments made by this section shall apply to—

(1) any divorce or separation instrument (as defined in section 71(b)(2) of the Internal Revenue Code of 1986 as in effect before the date of the enactment of this Act) executed after December 31, 2018, and

(2) any divorce or separation instrument (as so defined) executed on or before such date and modified after such date if the modification expressly provides that the amendments made by this section apply to such modification.

[¶ 5295] CODE SEC. 162. TRADE OR BUSINESS EXPENSES.

(a) IN GENERAL.—There shall be allowed as a deduction all the ordinary and necessary expenses paid or incurred during the taxable year in carrying on any trade or business, including—

(1) a reasonable allowance for salaries or other compensation for personal services actually rendered;

(2) traveling expenses (including amounts expended for meals and lodging other than amounts which are lavish or extravagant under the circumstances) while away from home in the pursuit of a trade or business; and

(3) rentals or other payments required to be made as a condition to the continued use or possession, for purposes of the trade or business, of property to which the taxpayer has not taken or is not taking title or in which he has no equity.

For purposes of the preceding sentence, the place of residence of a Member of Congress (including any Delegate and Resident Commissioner) within the State, congressional district, or possession which he represents in Congress shall be considered his home, but amounts expended by such Members within each taxable year for living expenses shall not be deductible for income tax purposes. For purposes of paragraph (2), the taxpayer shall not be treated as being temporarily away from home during any period of employment if such period exceeds 1 year. The preceding sentence shall not apply to any Federal employee during any period for which such employee is certified by the Attorney General (or the designee thereof) as traveling on behalf of the United States in temporary duty status to investigate or prosecute, or provide support services for the investigation or prosecution of, a Federal crime.

* * *

[CCH Explanation at ¶ 560.]

Amendments

• **2017, Tax Cuts and Jobs Act (P.L. 115-97)**

P.L. 115-97, § 13311(a):

Amended Code Sec. 162(a) by striking "in excess of $3,000" following "deductible for income tax purposes" in

the matter following paragraph (3). **Effective** for tax years beginning after 12-22-2017.

(e) DENIAL OF DEDUCTION FOR CERTAIN LOBBYING AND POLITICAL EXPENDITURES.—

* * *

(2) APPLICATION TO DUES OF TAX-EXEMPT ORGANIZATIONS.—No deduction shall be allowed under subsection (a) for the portion of dues or other similar amounts paid by the taxpayer to an organization which is exempt from tax under this subtitle which the organization notifies the taxpayer under section 6033(e)(1)(A)(ii) is allocable to expenditures to which paragraph (1) applies.

(3) INFLUENCING LEGISLATION.—For purposes of this subsection—

(A) IN GENERAL.—The term "influencing legislation" means any attempt to influence any legislation through communication with any member or employee of a legislative body, or with any government official or employee who may participate in the formulation of legislation.

(B) LEGISLATION.—The term "legislation" has the meaning given such term by section 4911(e)(2).

(4) OTHER SPECIAL RULES.—

(A) EXCEPTION FOR CERTAIN TAXPAYERS.—In the case of any taxpayer engaged in the trade or business of conducting activities described in paragraph (1), paragraph (1) shall not apply to expenditures of the taxpayer in conducting such activities directly on behalf of another person (but shall apply to payments by such other person to the taxpayer for conducting such activities).

(B) DE MINIMIS EXCEPTION.—

(i) IN GENERAL.—Paragraph (1) shall not apply to any in-house expenditures for any taxable year if such expenditures do not exceed $2,000. In determining whether a taxpayer exceeds the $2,000 limit under this clause, there shall not be taken into account overhead costs otherwise allocable to activities described in paragraphs (1)(A) and (D).

(ii) IN-HOUSE EXPENDITURES.—For purposes of clause (i), the term "in-house expenditures" means expenditures described in paragraphs (1)(A) and (D) other than—

(I) payments by the taxpayer to a person engaged in the trade or business of conducting activities described in paragraph (1) for the conduct of such activities on behalf of the taxpayer, or

(II) dues or other similar amounts paid or incurred by the taxpayer which are allocable to activities described in paragraph (1).

(C) EXPENSES INCURRED IN CONNECTION WITH LOBBYING AND POLITICAL ACTIVITIES.—Any amount paid or incurred for research for, or preparation, planning, or coordination of, any activity described in paragraph (1) shall be treated as paid or incurred in connection with such activity.

(5) COVERED EXECUTIVE BRANCH OFFICIAL.—For purposes of this subsection, the term "covered executive branch official" means—

(A) the President,

(B) the Vice President,

(C) any officer or employee of the White House Office of the Executive Office of the President, and the 2 most senior level officers of each of the other agencies in such Executive Office, and

(D)(i) any individual serving in a position in level I of the Executive Schedule under section 5312 of title 5, United States Code, (ii) any other individual designated by the President as having Cabinet level status, and (iii) any immediate deputy of an individual described in clause (i) or (ii).

(6) CROSS REFERENCE.—

For reporting requirements and alternative taxes related to this subsection, see section 6033(e).

[CCH Explanation at ¶ 555. Committee Reports at ¶ 10,490.]

Amendments

• 2017, Tax Cuts and Jobs Act (P.L. 115-97)

P.L. 115-97, §13308(a):

Amended Code Sec. 162(e) by striking paragraphs (2) and (7) and by redesignating paragraphs (3), (4), (5), (6), and (8) as paragraphs (2), (3), (4), (5), and (6), respectively. **Effective**

for amounts paid or incurred on or after 12-22-2017. Prior to being stricken, Code Sec. 162(e)(2) and (7) read as follows:

(2) EXCEPTION FOR LOCAL LEGISLATION.—In the case of any legislation of any local council or similar governing body—

(A) paragraph (1)(A) shall not apply, and

(B) the deduction allowed by subsection (a) shall include all ordinary and necessary expenses (including, but not limited to, traveling expenses described in subsection (a)(2) and the cost of preparing testimony) paid or incurred during the taxable year in carrying on any trade or business—

(i) in direct connection with appearances before, submission of statements to, or sending communications to the committees, or individual members, of such council or body with respect to legislation or proposed legislation of direct interest to the taxpayer, or

(ii) in direct connection with communication of information between the taxpayer and an organization of which the taxpayer is a member with respect to any such legislation or proposed legislation which is of direct interest to the taxpayer and to such organization,

and that portion of the dues so paid or incurred with respect to any organization of which the taxpayer is a member which is attributable to the expenses of the activities described in clauses (i) and (ii) carried on by such organization.

* * *

(7) SPECIAL RULE FOR INDIAN TRIBAL GOVERNMENTS.—For purposes of this subsection, an Indian tribal government shall be treated in the same manner as a local council or similar governing body.

(f) FINES, PENALTIES, AND OTHER AMOUNTS.—

(1) IN GENERAL.—Except as provided in the following paragraphs of this subsection, no deduction otherwise allowable shall be allowed under this chapter for any amount paid or incurred (whether by suit, agreement, or otherwise) to, or at the direction of, a government or governmental entity in relation to the violation of any law or the investigation or inquiry by such government or entity into the potential violation of any law.

(2) EXCEPTION FOR AMOUNTS CONSTITUTING RESTITUTION OR PAID TO COME INTO COMPLIANCE WITH LAW.—

(A) IN GENERAL.—Paragraph (1) shall not apply to any amount that—

(i) the taxpayer establishes.—

(I) constitutes restitution (including remediation of property) for damage or harm which was or may be caused by the violation of any law or the potential violation of any law, or

(II) is paid to come into compliance with any law which was violated or otherwise involved in the investigation or inquiry described in paragraph (1),

(ii) is identified as restitution or as an amount paid to come into compliance with such law, as the case may be, in the court order or settlement agreement, and

(iii) in the case of any amount of restitution for failure to pay any tax imposed under this title in the same manner as if such amount were such tax, would have been allowed as a deduction under this chapter if it had been timely paid.

The identification under clause (ii) alone shall not be sufficient to make the establishment required under clause (i).

(B) LIMITATION.—Subparagraph (A) shall not apply to any amount paid or incurred as reimbursement to the government or entity for the costs of any investigation or litigation.

(3) EXCEPTION FOR AMOUNTS PAID OR INCURRED AS THE RESULT OF CERTAIN COURT ORDERS.—Paragraph (1) shall not apply to any amount paid or incurred by reason of any order of a court in a suit in which no government or governmental entity is a party.

(4) EXCEPTION FOR TAXES DUE.—Paragraph (1) shall not apply to any amount paid or incurred as taxes due.

(5) TREATMENT OF CERTAIN NONGOVERNMENTAL REGULATORY ENTITIES.—For purposes of this subsection, the following nongovernmental entities shall be treated as governmental entities:

(A) Any nongovernmental entity which exercises self-regulatory powers (including imposing sanctions) in connection with a qualified board or exchange (as defined in section 1256(g)(7)).

(B) To the extent provided in regulations, any nongovernmental entity which exercises self-regulatory powers (including imposing sanctions) as part of performing an essential governmental function.

* * *

[CCH Explanation at ¶ 545. Committee Reports at ¶ 10,470.]

<table>
<tr><td>

Amendments

• **2017, Tax Cuts and Jobs Act (P.L. 115-97)**

P.L. 115-97, § 13306(a)(1):

Amended Code Sec. 162(f). For the **effective** date, see Act Sec. 13306(a)(2), below. Prior to amendment, Code Sec. 162(f) read as follows:

(f) FINES AND PENALTIES.—No deduction shall be allowed under subsection (a) for any fine or similar penalty paid to a government for the violation of any law.

</td><td>

P.L. 115-97, § 13306(a)(2), provides:

(2) EFFECTIVE DATE.—The amendment made by this subsection shall apply to amounts paid or incurred on or after the date of the enactment of this Act, except that such amendments shall not apply to amounts paid or incurred under any binding order or agreement entered into before such date. Such exception shall not apply to an order or agreement requiring court approval unless the approval was obtained before such date.

</td></tr>
</table>

(m) CERTAIN EXCESSIVE EMPLOYEE REMUNERATION.—

* * *

(2) PUBLICLY HELD CORPORATION.—For purposes of this subsection, the term "publicly held corporation" means any corporation which is an issuer (as defined in section 3 of the Securities Exchange Act of 1934 (15 U.S.C. 78c))—

(A) the securities of which are required to be registered under section 12 of such Act (15 U.S.C. 78l), or

(B) that is required to file reports under section 15(d) of such Act (15 U.S.C. 78o(d)).

(3) COVERED EMPLOYEE.—For purposes of this subsection, the term "covered employee" means any employee of the taxpayer if—

(A) such employee is the principal executive officer or principal financial officer of the taxpayer at any time during the taxable year, or was an individual acting in such a capacity,

(B) the total compensation of such employee for the taxable year is required to be reported to shareholders under the Securities Exchange Act of 1934 by reason of such employee being among the 3 highest compensated officers for the taxable year *(other than any individual described in subparagraph (A))* , or

(C) was a covered employee of the taxpayer (or any predecessor) for any preceding taxable year beginning after December 31, 2016.

Such term shall include any employee who would be described in subparagraph (B) if the reporting described in such subparagraph were required as so described.

(4) APPLICABLE EMPLOYEE REMUNERATION.—For purposes of this subsection—

* * *

(B) EXCEPTION FOR EXISTING BINDING CONTRACTS.—The term "applicable employee remuneration" shall not include any remuneration payable under a written binding contract which was in effect on February 17, 1993, and which was not modified thereafter in any material respect before such remuneration is paid.

(C) REMUNERATION.—For purposes of this paragraph, the term "remuneration" includes any remuneration (including benefits) in any medium other than cash, but shall not include—

(i) any payment referred to in so much of section 3121(a)(5) as precedes subparagraph (E) thereof, and

(ii) any benefit provided to or on behalf of an employee if at the time such benefit is provided it is reasonable to believe that the employee will be able to exclude such benefit from gross income under this chapter.

For purposes of clause (i), section 3121(a)(5) shall be applied without regard to section 3121(v)(1).

(D) COORDINATION WITH DISALLOWED GOLDEN PARACHUTE PAYMENTS.—The dollar limitation contained in paragraph (1) shall be reduced (but not below zero) by the amount (if any) which would have been included in the applicable employee remuneration of the covered employee for the taxable year but for being disallowed under section 280G.

(E) COORDINATION WITH EXCISE TAX ON SPECIFIED STOCK COMPENSATION.—The dollar limitation contained in paragraph (1) with respect to any covered employee shall be reduced (but not below zero) by the amount of any payment (with respect to such employee) of the tax imposed by section 4985 directly or indirectly by the expatriated corporation (as defined in such section) or by any member of the expanded affiliated group (as defined in such section) which includes such corporation.

(F) SPECIAL RULE FOR REMUNERATION PAID TO BENEFICIARIES, ETC.—*Remuneration shall not fail to be applicable employee remuneration merely because it is includible in the income of, or paid to, a person other than the covered employee, including after the death of the covered employee.*

(5) SPECIAL RULE FOR APPLICATION TO EMPLOYERS PARTICIPATING IN THE TROUBLED ASSETS RELIEF PROGRAM.—

* * *

(E) EXECUTIVE REMUNERATION.—For purposes of this paragraph, the term "executive remuneration" means the applicable employee remuneration of the covered executive, as determined under paragraph (4) without regard to *subparagraph (B)* thereof. Such term shall not include any deferred deduction executive remuneration with respect to services performed in a prior applicable taxable year.

* * *

(G) COORDINATION.—Rules similar to the rules of subparagraphs *(D) and (E)* of paragraph (4) shall apply for purposes of this paragraph.

* * *

(6) SPECIAL RULE FOR APPLICATION TO CERTAIN HEALTH INSURANCE PROVIDERS.—

* * *

(D) APPLICABLE INDIVIDUAL REMUNERATION.—For purposes of this paragraph, the term "applicable individual remuneration" means, with respect to any applicable individual for any disqualified taxable year, the aggregate amount allowable as a deduction under this chapter for such taxable year (determined without regard to this subsection) for remuneration (as defined in paragraph (4) without regard to *subparagraph (B)* thereof) for services performed by such individual (whether or not during the taxable year). Such term shall not include any deferred deduction remuneration with respect to services performed during the disqualified taxable year.

* * *

(G) COORDINATION.—Rules similar to the rules of subparagraphs *(D) and (E)* of paragraph (4) shall apply for purposes of this paragraph.

* * *

[CCH Explanation at ¶ 540. Committee Reports at ¶ 10,790.]

Amendments

• **2017, Tax Cuts and Jobs Act (P.L. 115-97)**

P.L. 115-97, § 13601(a)(1):

Amended Code Sec. 162(m)(4) by striking subparagraphs (B) and (C) and by redesignating subparagraphs (D), (E), (F), and (G) as subparagraphs (B), (C), (D), and (E), respectively. **Effective** generally for tax years beginning after 12-31-2017. For an exception, see Act Sec. 13601(e)(2), below. Prior to being stricken, Code Sec. 162(m)(4)(B) and (C) read as follows:

(B) EXCEPTION FOR REMUNERATION PAYABLE ON COMMISSION BASIS.—The term "applicable employee remuneration" shall not include any remuneration payable on a commission basis solely on account of income generated directly by the individual performance of the individual to whom such remuneration is payable.

(C) OTHER PERFORMANCE-BASED COMPENSATION.—The term "applicable employee remuneration" shall not include any remuneration payable solely on account of the attainment of one or more performance goals, but only if—

(i) the performance goals are determined by a compensation committee of the board of directors of the taxpayer which is comprised solely of 2 or more outside directors,

(ii) the material terms under which the remuneration is to be paid, including the performance goals, are disclosed to shareholders and approved by a majority of the vote in a separate shareholder vote before the payment of such remuneration, and

(iii) before any payment of such remuneration, the compensation committee referred to in clause (i) certifies that the performance goals and any other material terms were in fact satisfied.

P.L. 115-97, § 13601(a)(2)(A):

Amended Code Sec. 162(m)(5)(E) and (6)(D) by striking "subparagraphs (B), (C), and (D)" and inserting "subparagraph (B)". **Effective** generally for tax years beginning after 12-31-2017. For an exception, see Act Sec. 13601(e)(2), below.

P.L. 115-97, § 13601(a)(2)(B):

Amended Code Sec. 162(m)(5)(G) and (6)(G) by striking "(F) and (G)" and inserting "(D) and (E)". **Effective** generally for tax years beginning after 12-31-2017. For an exception, see Act Sec. 13601(e)(2), below.

P.L. 115-97, § 13601(b)(1)-(3):

Amended Code Sec. 162(m)(3), in subparagraph (A), by striking "as of the close of the taxable year, such employee is the chief executive officer of the taxpayer or is" and inserting "such employee is the principal executive officer or principal financial officer of the taxpayer at any time during the taxable year, or was", in subparagraph (B) by striking "4" and inserting "3", and by striking "(other than the chief executive officer)" and inserting "(other than any individual described in subparagraph (A))", and by striking "or" at the end of subparagraph (A), by striking the period at the end of subparagraph (B) and inserting ", or", and by adding at the end a new subparagraph (C). **Effective** generally for tax years beginning after 12-31-2017. For an exception, see Act Sec. 13601(e)(2), below.

P.L. 115-97, § 13601(c)(1):

Amended Code Sec. 162(m)(2). **Effective** generally for tax years beginning after 12-31-2017. For an exception, see Act

Sec. 13601(e)(2), below. Prior to amendment, Code Sec. 162(m)(2) read as follows:

(2) PUBLICLY HELD CORPORATION.—For purposes of this subsection, the term "publicly held corporation" means any corporation issuing any class of common equity securities required to be registered under section 12 of the Securities Exchange Act of 1934.

P.L. 115-97, § 13601(c)(2):

Amended Code Sec. 162(m)(3), as amended by Act Sec. 13601(b), by adding at the end a new flush sentence. **Effective** generally for tax years beginning after 12-31-2017. For an exception, see Act Sec. 13601(e)(2), below.

P.L. 115-97, § 13601(d):

Amended Code Sec. 162(m)(4), as amended by Act Sec. 13601(a), by adding at the end a new subparagraph (F). **Effective** generally for tax years beginning after 12-31-2017. For an exception, see Act Sec. 13601(e)(2), below.

P.L. 115-97, § 13601(e)(2), provides:

(2) EXCEPTION FOR BINDING CONTRACTS.— The amendments made by this section shall not apply to remuneration which is provided pursuant to a written binding contract which was in effect on November 2, 2017, and which was not modified in any material respect on or after such date.

(o) TREATMENT OF CERTAIN EXPENSES OF RURAL MAIL CARRIERS.—

* * *

(3) DEFINITION OF QUALIFIED REIMBURSEMENTS.—For purposes of this subsection, the term "qualified reimbursements" means the amounts paid by the United States Postal Service to employees as an equipment maintenance allowance under the 1991 collective bargaining agreement between the United States Postal Service and the National Rural Letter Carriers' Association. Amounts paid as an equipment maintenance allowance by such Postal Service under later collective bargaining agreements that supersede the 1991 agreement shall be considered qualified reimbursements if such amounts do not exceed the amounts that would have been paid under the 1991 agreement, *adjusted by increasing any such amount under the 1991 agreement by an amount equal to—*

(A) *such amount, multiplied by*

(B) *the cost-of-living adjustment determined under section 1(f)(3) for the calendar year in which the taxable year begins, by substituting "calendar year 1990" for "calendar year 2016" in subparagraph (A)(ii) thereof.*

* * *

[CCH Explanation at ¶ 125. Committee Reports at ¶ 10,020.]

Amendments

• **2017, Tax Cuts and Jobs Act (P.L. 115-97)**

P.L. 115-97, § 11002(d)(6):

Amended Code Sec. 162(o)(3) by striking "adjusted for changes in the Consumer Price Index (as defined in section

1(f)(5)) since 1991" and inserting "adjusted by increasing any such amount under the 1991 agreement by an amount equal to—"and new subparagraphs (A) and (B). **Effective** for tax years beginning after 12-31-2017

(q) PAYMENTS RELATED TO SEXUAL HARASSMENT AND SEXUAL ABUSE.—*No deduction shall be allowed under this chapter for—*

(1) *any settlement or payment related to sexual harassment or sexual abuse if such settlement or payment is subject to a nondisclosure agreement, or*

(2) *attorney's fees related to such a settlement or payment.*

[CCH Explanation at ¶ 550. Committee Reports at ¶ 10,480.]

Amendments

• **2017, Tax Cuts and Jobs Act (P.L. 115-97)**

P.L. 115-97, § 13307(a):

Amended Code Sec. 162 by redesignating subsection (q) as subsection (r) and by inserting after subsection (p) a new

subsection (q). **Effective** for amounts paid or incurred on after 12-22-2017.

(r) DISALLOWANCE OF FDIC PREMIUMS PAID BY CERTAIN LARGE FINANCIAL INSTITUTIONS.—

(1) IN GENERAL.—No deduction shall be allowed for the applicable percentage of any FDIC premium paid or incurred by the taxpayer.

(2) EXCEPTION FOR SMALL INSTITUTIONS.—Paragraph (1) shall not apply to any taxpayer for any taxable year if the total consolidated assets of such taxpayer (determined as of the close of such taxable year) do not exceed $10,000,000,000.

(3) APPLICABLE PERCENTAGE.—For purposes of this subsection, the term "applicable percentage" means, with respect to any taxpayer for any taxable year, the ratio (expressed as a percentage but not greater than 100 percent) which—

(A) the excess of—

(i) the total consolidated assets of such taxpayer (determined as of the close of such taxable year), over

(ii) $10,000,000,000, bears to

(B) $40,000,000,000.

(4) FDIC PREMIUMS.—For purposes of this subsection, the term "FDIC premium" means any assessment imposed under section 7(b) of the Federal Deposit Insurance Act (12 U.S.C. 1817(b)).

(5) TOTAL CONSOLIDATED ASSETS.—For purposes of this subsection, the term "total consolidated assets" has the meaning given such term under section 165 of the Dodd-Frank Wall Street Reform and Consumer Protection Act (12 U.S.C. 5365).

(6) AGGREGATION RULE.—

(A) IN GENERAL.—Members of an expanded affiliated group shall be treated as a single taxpayer for purposes of applying this subsection.

(B) EXPANDED AFFILIATED GROUP.—

(i) IN GENERAL.—For purposes of this paragraph, the term "expanded affiliated group" means an affiliated group as defined in section 1504(a), determined—

(I) by substituting "more than 50 percent" for "at least 80 percent" each place it appears, and

(II) without regard to paragraphs (2) and (3) of section 1504(b).

(ii) CONTROL OF NON-CORPORATE ENTITIES.—A partnership or any other entity (other than a corporation) shall be treated as a member of an expanded affiliated group if such entity is controlled (within the meaning of section 954(d)(3)) by members of such group (including any entity treated as a member of such group by reason of this clause).

[CCH Explanation at ¶ 550 and ¶ 565. Committee Reports at ¶ 10,480 and ¶ 10,740.]

Amendments

• **2017, Tax Cuts and Jobs Act (P.L. 115-97)**

P.L. 115-97, § 13531(a):

Amended Code Sec. 162, as amended by Act Sec. 13307, by redesignating subsection (r) as subsection (s) and by

inserting after subsection (q) a new subsection (r). **Effective** for tax years beginning after 12-31-2017.

(s) CROSS REFERENCES.—

(1) For special rule relating to expenses in connection with subdividing real property for sale, see section 1237.

(2) For special rule relating to the treatment of payments by a transferee of a franchise, trademark, or trade name, see section 1253.

(3) For special rules relating to—

(A) funded welfare benefit plans, see section 419, and

(B) deferred compensation and other deferred benefits, see section 404.

[CCH Explanation at ¶ 565. Committee Reports at ¶ 10,740.]

Amendments

• **2017, Tax Cuts and Jobs Act (P.L. 115-97)**

P.L. 115-97, § 13307(a):

Amended Code Sec. 162 by redesignating subsection (q) as subsection (r). **Effective** for amounts paid or incurred after 12-22-2017.

P.L. 115-97, § 13531(a):

Amended Code Sec. 162, as amended by Act Sec. 13307, by redesignating subsection (r) as subsection (s). **Effective** for tax years beginning after 12-31-2017.

[¶ 5300] CODE SEC. 163. INTEREST.

* * *

(h) DISALLOWANCE OF DEDUCTION FOR PERSONAL INTEREST.—

* * *

(3) QUALIFIED RESIDENCE INTEREST.—For purposes of this subsection—

* * *

(F) SPECIAL RULES FOR TAXABLE YEARS 2018 THROUGH 2025.—

(i) IN GENERAL.—In the case of taxable years beginning after December 31, 2017, and before January 1, 2026—

(I) DISALLOWANCE OF HOME EQUITY INDEBTEDNESS INTEREST.—Subparagraph (A)(ii) shall not apply.

(II) LIMITATION ON ACQUISITION INDEBTEDNESS.—Subparagraph (B)(ii) shall be applied by substituting "$750,000 ($375,000[)]" for "$1,000,000 ($500,000[)]".

(III) TREATMENT OF INDEBTEDNESS INCURRED ON OR BEFORE DECEMBER 15, 2017.— Subclause (II) shall not apply to any indebtedness incurred on or before December 15, 2017, and, in applying such subclause to any indebtedness incurred after such date, the limitation under such subclause shall be reduced (but not below zero) by the amount of any indebtedness incurred on or before December 15, 2017, which is treated as acquisition indebtedness for purposes of this subsection for the taxable year.

(IV) BINDING CONTRACT EXCEPTION.—In the case of a taxpayer who enters into a written binding contract before December 15, 2017, to close on the purchase of a principal residence before January 1, 2018, and who purchases such residence before April 1, 2018, subclause (III) shall be applied by substituting "April 1, 2018" for "December 15, 2017".

(ii) TREATMENT OF LIMITATION IN TAXABLE YEARS AFTER DECEMBER 31, 2025.—In the case of taxable years beginning after December 31, 2025, the limitation under subparagraph (B)(ii) shall be applied to the aggregate amount of indebtedness of the taxpayer described in subparagraph (B)(i) without regard to the taxable year in which the indebtedness was incurred.

(iii) TREATMENT OF REFINANCINGS OF INDEBTEDNESS.—

(I) IN GENERAL.—In the case of any indebtedness which is incurred to refinance indebtedness, such refinanced indebtedness shall be treated for purposes of clause (i)(III) as incurred on the date that the original indebtedness was incurred to the extent the amount of

the indebtedness resulting from such refinancing does not exceed the amount of the refinanced indebtedness.

(II) LIMITATION ON PERIOD OF REFINANCING.—Subclause (I) shall not apply to any indebtedness after the expiration of the term of the original indebtedness or, if the principal of such original indebtedness is not amortized over its term, the expiration of the term of the 1st refinancing of such indebtedness (or if earlier, the date which is 30 years after the date of such 1st refinancing).

(iv) COORDINATION WITH EXCLUSION OF INCOME FROM DISCHARGE OF INDEBTEDNESS.—Section 108(h)(2) shall be applied without regard to this subparagraph.

* * *

[CCH Explanation at ¶ 220. Committee Reports at ¶ 10,180.]
Amendments
- **2017, Tax Cuts and Jobs Act (P.L. 115-97)**

P.L. 115-97, § 11043(a):

Amended Code Sec. 163(h)(3) by adding at the end a new subparagraph (F). **Effective** for tax years beginning after 12-31-2017.

(j) LIMITATION ON BUSINESS INTEREST.—

(1) IN GENERAL.—The amount allowed as a deduction under this chapter for any taxable year for business interest shall not exceed the sum of—

(A) the business interest income of such taxpayer for such taxable year,

(B) 30 percent of the adjusted taxable income of such taxpayer for such taxable year, plus

(C) the floor plan financing interest of such taxpayer for such taxable year.

The amount determined under subparagraph (B) shall not be less than zero.

(2) CARRYFORWARD OF DISALLOWED BUSINESS INTEREST.—The amount of any business interest not allowed as a deduction for any taxable year by reason of paragraph (1) shall be treated as business interest paid or accrued in the succeeding taxable year.

(3) EXEMPTION FOR CERTAIN SMALL BUSINESSES.—In the case of any taxpayer (other than a tax shelter prohibited from using the cash receipts and disbursements method of accounting under section 448(a)(3)) which meets the gross receipts test of section 448(c) for any taxable year, paragraph (1) shall not apply to such taxpayer for such taxable year. In the case of any taxpayer which is not a corporation or a partnership, the gross receipts test of section 448(c) shall be applied in the same manner as if such taxpayer were a corporation or partnership.

(4) APPLICATION TO PARTNERSHIPS, ETC.—

(A) IN GENERAL.—In the case of any partnership—

(i) this subsection shall be applied at the partnership level and any deduction for business interest shall be taken into account in determining the non-separately stated taxable income or loss of the partnership, and

(ii) the adjusted taxable income of each partner of such partnership—

(I) shall be determined without regard to such partner's distributive share of any items of income, gain, deduction, or loss of such partnership, and

(II) shall be increased by such partner's distributive share of such partnership's excess taxable income.

For purposes of clause (ii)(II), a partner's distributive share of partnership excess taxable income shall be determined in the same manner as the partner's distributive share of nonseparately stated taxable income or loss of the partnership.

(B) SPECIAL RULES FOR CARRYFORWARDS.—

*(i) I*N GENERAL.—*The amount of any business interest not allowed as a deduction to a partnership for any taxable year by reason of paragraph (1) for any taxable year—*

(I) shall not be treated under paragraph (2) as business interest paid or accrued by the partnership in the succeeding taxable year, and

(II) shall, subject to clause (ii), be treated as excess business interest which is allocated to each partner in the same manner as the non-separately stated taxable income or loss of the partnership.

*(ii) T*REATMENT OF EXCESS BUSINESS INTEREST ALLOCATED TO PARTNERS.—*If a partner is allocated any excess business interest from a partnership under clause (i) for any taxable year—*

(I) such excess business interest shall be treated as business interest paid or accrued by the partner in the next succeeding taxable year in which the partner is allocated excess taxable income from such partnership, but only to the extent of such excess taxable income, and

(II) any portion of such excess business interest remaining after the application of subclause (I) shall, subject to the limitations of subclause (I), be treated as business interest paid or accrued in succeeding taxable years.

For purposes of applying this paragraph, excess taxable income allocated to a partner from a partnership for any taxable year shall not be taken into account under paragraph (1)(A) with respect to any business interest other than excess business interest from the partnership until all such excess business interest for such taxable year and all preceding taxable years has been treated as paid or accrued under clause (ii).

*(iii) B*ASIS ADJUSTMENTS.—

*(I) I*N GENERAL.—*The adjusted basis of a partner in a partnership interest shall be reduced (but not below zero) by the amount of excess business interest allocated to the partner under clause (i)(II).*

*(II) S*PECIAL RULE FOR DISPOSITIONS.—*If a partner disposes of a partnership interest, the adjusted basis of the partner in the partnership interest shall be increased immediately before the disposition by the amount of the excess (if any) of the amount of the basis reduction under subclause (I) over the portion of any excess business interest allocated to the partner under clause (i)(II) which has previously been treated under clause (ii) as business interest paid or accrued by the partner. The preceding sentence shall also apply to transfers of the partnership interest (including by reason of death) in a transaction in which gain is not recognized in whole or in part. No deduction shall be allowed to the transferor or transferee under this chapter for any excess business interest resulting in a basis increase under this subclause.*

*(C) E*XCESS TAXABLE INCOME.—*The term "excess taxable income" means, with respect to any partnership, the amount which bears the same ratio to the partnership's adjusted taxable income as—*

(i) the excess (if any) of—

(I) the amount determined for the partnership under paragraph (1)(B), over

(II) the amount (if any) by which the business interest of the partnership, reduced by the floor plan financing interest, exceeds the business interest income of the partnership, bears to

(ii) the amount determined for the partnership under paragraph (1)(B).

*(D) A*PPLICATION TO S CORPORATIONS.—*Rules similar to the rules of subparagraphs (A) and (C) shall apply with respect to any S corporation and its shareholders.*

*(5) B*USINESS INTEREST.—*For purposes of this subsection, the term "business interest" means any interest paid or accrued on indebtedness properly allocable to a trade or business. Such term shall not include investment interest (within the meaning of subsection (d)).*

*(6) B*USINESS INTEREST INCOME.—*For purposes of this subsection, the term "business interest income" means the amount of interest includible in the gross income of the taxpayer for the taxable year which is*

properly allocable to a trade or business. Such term shall not include investment income (within the meaning of subsection (d)).

(7) TRADE OR BUSINESS.—For purposes of this subsection—

(A) IN GENERAL.—The term "trade or business" shall not include—

(i) the trade or business of performing services as an employee,

(ii) any electing real property trade or business,

(iii) any electing farming business, or

(iv) the trade or business of the furnishing or sale of—

(I) electrical energy, water, or sewage disposal services,

(II) gas or steam through a local distribution system, or

(III) transportation of gas or steam by pipeline,

if the rates for such furnishing or sale, as the case may be, have been established or approved by a State or political subdivision thereof, by any agency or instrumentality of the United States, by a public service or public utility commission or other similar body of any State or political subdivision thereof, or by the governing or ratemaking body of an electric cooperative.

(B) ELECTING REAL PROPERTY TRADE OR BUSINESS.—For purposes of this paragraph, the term "electing real property trade or business" means any trade or business which is described in section 469(c)(7)(C) and which makes an election under this subparagraph. Any such election shall be made at such time and in such manner as the Secretary shall prescribe, and, once made, shall be irrevocable.

(C) ELECTING FARMING BUSINESS.—For purposes of this paragraph, the term "electing farming business" means—

(i) a farming business (as defined in section 263A(e)(4)) which makes an election under this subparagraph, or

(ii) any trade or business of a specified agricultural or horticultural cooperative (as defined in section 199A(g)(2)) with respect to which the cooperative makes an election under this subparagraph.

Any such election shall be made at such time and in such manner as the Secretary shall prescribe, and, once made, shall be irrevocable.

(8) ADJUSTED TAXABLE INCOME.—For purposes of this subsection, the term "adjusted taxable income" means the taxable income of the taxpayer—

(A) computed without regard to—

(i) any item of income, gain, deduction, or loss which is not properly allocable to a trade or business,

(ii) any business interest or business interest income,

(iii) the amount of any net operating loss deduction under section 172,

(iv) the amount of any deduction allowed under section 199A, and

(v) in the case of taxable years beginning before January 1, 2022, any deduction allowable for depreciation, amortization, or depletion, and

(B) computed with such other adjustments as provided by the Secretary.

(9) FLOOR PLAN FINANCING INTEREST DEFINED.—For purposes of this subsection—

(A) IN GENERAL.—The term "floor plan financing interest" means interest paid or accrued on floor plan financing indebtedness.

(B) FLOOR PLAN FINANCING INDEBTEDNESS.—The term "floor plan financing indebtedness" means indebtedness—

(i) used to finance the acquisition of motor vehicles held for sale or lease, and

(ii) secured by the inventory so acquired.

(C) MOTOR VEHICLE.—The term "motor vehicle" means a motor vehicle that is any of the following:

(i) Any self-propelled vehicle designed for transporting persons or property on a public street, highway, or road.

(ii) A boat.

(iii) Farm machinery or equipment.

(10) CROSS REFERENCES.—

(A) For requirement that an electing real property trade or business use the alternative depreciation system, see section 168(g)(1)(F).

(B) For requirement that an electing farming business use the alternative depreciation system, see section 168(g)(1)(G).

* * *

[CCH Explanation at ¶ 510. Committee Reports at ¶ 10,420.]

Amendments

• **2017, Tax Cuts and Jobs Act (P.L. 115-97)**

P.L. 115-97, § 13301(a):

Amended Code Sec. 163(j). **Effective** for tax years beginning after 12-31-2017. Prior to amendment, Code Sec. 163(j) read as follows:

(j) LIMITATION ON DEDUCTION FOR INTEREST ON CERTAIN INDEBTEDNESS.—

(1) LIMITATION.—

(A) IN GENERAL.—If this subsection applies to any corporation for any taxable year, no deduction shall be allowed under this chapter for disqualified interest paid or accrued by such corporation during such taxable year. The amount disallowed under the preceding sentence shall not exceed the corporation's excess interest expense for the taxable year.

(B) DISALLOWED AMOUNT CARRIED TO SUCCEEDING TAXABLE YEAR.—Any amount disallowed under subparagraph (A) for any taxable year shall be treated as disqualified interest paid or accrued in the succeeding taxable year (and clause (ii) of paragraph (2)(A) shall not apply for purposes of applying this subsection to the amount so treated).

(2) CORPORATIONS TO WHICH SUBSECTION APPLIES.—

(A) IN GENERAL.—This subsection shall apply to any corporation for any taxable year if—

(i) such corporation has excess interest expense for such taxable year, and

(ii) the ratio of debt to equity of such corporation as of the close of such taxable year (or on any other day during the taxable year as the Secretary may by regulations prescribe) exceeds 1.5 to 1.

(B) EXCESS INTEREST EXPENSE.—

(i) IN GENERAL.—For purposes of this subsection, the term "excess interest expense" means the excess (if any) of—

(I) the corporation's net interest expense, over

(II) the sum of 50 percent of the adjusted taxable income of the corporation plus any excess limitation carryforward under clause (ii).

(ii) EXCESS LIMITATION CARRYFORWARD.—If a corporation has an excess limitation for any taxable year, the amount of such excess limitation shall be an excess limitation carryforward to the 1st succeeding taxable year and to the 2nd and 3rd succeeding taxable years to the extent not previously taken into account under this clause. The amount of such a carryforward taken into account for any such succeeding taxable year shall not exceed the excess interest expense for such succeeding taxable year (determined without regard to the carryforward from the taxable year of such excess limitation).

(iii) EXCESS LIMITATION.—For purposes of clause (ii), the term "excess limitation" means the excess (if any) of—

(I) 50 percent of the adjusted taxable income of the corporation, over

(II) the corporation's net interest expense.

(C) RATIO OF DEBT TO EQUITY.—For purposes of this paragraph, the term "ratio of debt to equity" means the ratio which the total indebtedness of the corporation bears to the sum of its money and all other assets reduced (but not below zero) by such total indebtedness. For purposes of the preceding sentence—

(i) the amount taken into account with respect to any asset shall be the adjusted basis thereof for purposes of determining gain,

(ii) the amount taken into account with respect to any indebtedness with original issue discount shall be its issue price plus the portion of the original issue discount previously accrued as determined under the rules of section 1272 (determined without regard to subsection (a)(7) or (b)(4) thereof), and

(iii) there shall be such other adjustments as the Secretary may by regulations prescribe.

(3) DISQUALIFIED INTEREST.—For purposes of this subsection, the term "disqualified interest" means—

(A) any interest paid or accrued by the taxpayer (directly or indirectly) to a related person if no tax is imposed by this subtitle with respect to such interest,

(B) any interest paid or accrued by the taxpayer with respect to any indebtedness to a person who is not a related person if—

(i) there is a disqualified guarantee of such indebtedness, and

(ii) no gross basis tax is imposed by this subtitle with respect to such interest, and

(C) any interest paid or accrued (directly or indirectly) by a taxable REIT subsidiary (as defined in section 856(l)) of a real estate investment trust to such trust.

(4) RELATED PERSON.—For purposes of this subsection—

(A) IN GENERAL.—Except as provided in subparagraph (B), the term "related person" means any person who is related (within the meaning of section 267(b) or 707(b)(1)) to the taxpayer.

(B) SPECIAL RULE FOR CERTAIN PARTNERSHIPS.—

(i) IN GENERAL.—Any interest paid or accrued to a partnership which (without regard to this subparagraph) is a related person shall not be treated as paid or accrued to a related person if less than 10 percent of the profits and capital interests in such partnership are held by persons with respect to whom no tax is imposed by this subtitle on such interest. The preceding sentence shall not apply to any interest allocable to any partner in such partnership who is a related person to the taxpayer.

(ii) SPECIAL RULE WHERE TREATY REDUCTION.—If any treaty between the United States and any foreign country reduces the rate of tax imposed by this subtitle on a partner's share of any interest paid or accrued to a partnership, such partner's interests in such partnership shall, for purposes of clause (i), be treated as held in part by a tax-exempt person and in part by a taxable person under rules similar to the rules of paragraph (5)(B).

(5) SPECIAL RULES FOR DETERMINING WHETHER INTEREST IS SUBJECT TO TAX.—

(A) TREATMENT OF PASS-THRU ENTITIES.—In the case of any interest paid or accrued to a partnership, the determination of whether any tax is imposed by this subtitle on such interest shall be made at the partner level. Rules similar to the rules of the preceding sentence shall apply in the case of any pass-thru entity other than a partnership and in the case of tiered partnerships and other entities.

(B) INTEREST TREATED AS TAX-EXEMPT TO EXTENT OF TREATY REDUCTION.—If any treaty between the United States and any foreign country reduces the rate of tax imposed by this subtitle on any interest paid or accrued by the taxpayer, such interest shall be treated as interest on which no tax is imposed by this subtitle to the extent of the same proportion of such interest as—

(i) the rate of tax imposed without regard to such treaty, reduced by the rate of tax imposed under the treaty, bears to

(ii) the rate of tax imposed without regard to the treaty.

(6) OTHER DEFINITIONS AND SPECIAL RULES.—For purposes of this subsection—

(A) ADJUSTED TAXABLE INCOME.—The term "adjusted taxable income" means the taxable income of the taxpayer—

(i) computed without regard to—

(I) any deduction allowable under this chapter for the net interest expense,

(II) the amount of any net operating loss deduction under section 172,

(III) any deduction allowable under section 199, and

(IV) any deduction allowable for depreciation, amortization, or depletion, and

(ii) computed with such other adjustments as the Secretary may by regulations prescribe.

(B) NET INTEREST EXPENSE.—The term "net interest expense" means the excess (if any) of—

(i) the interest paid or accrued by the taxpayer during the taxable year, over

(ii) the amount of interest includible in the gross income of such taxpayer for such taxable year.

The Secretary may by regulations provide for adjustments in determining the amount of net interest expense.

(C) TREATMENT OF AFFILIATED GROUP.—All members of the same affiliated group (within the meaning of section 1504(a)) shall be treated as 1 taxpayer.

(D) DISQUALIFIED GUARANTEE.—

(i) IN GENERAL.—Except as provided in clause (ii), the term "disqualified guarantee" means any guarantee by a related person which is—

(I) an organization exempt from taxation under this subtitle, or

(II) a foreign person.

(ii) EXCEPTIONS.—The term "disqualified guarantee" shall not include a guarantee—

(I) in any circumstances identified by the Secretary by regulation, where the interest on the indebtedness would have been subject to a net basis tax if the interest had been paid to the guarantor, or

(II) if the taxpayer owns a controlling interest in the guarantor.

For purposes of subclause (II), except as provided in regulations, the term "a controlling interest" means direct or indirect ownership of at least 80 percent of the total voting power and value of all classes of stock of a corporation, or 80 percent of the profit and capital interests in any other entity. For purposes of the preceding sentence, the rules of paragraphs (1) and (5) of section 267(c) shall apply; except that such rules shall also apply to interest in entities other than corporations.

(iii) GUARANTEE.—Except as provided in regulations, the term "guarantee" includes any arrangement under which a person (directly or indirectly through an entity or otherwise) assures, on a conditional or unconditional basis, the payment of another person's obligation under any indebtedness.

(E) GROSS BASIS AND NET BASIS TAXATION.—

(i) GROSS BASIS TAX.—The term "gross basis tax" means any tax imposed by this subtitle which is determined by reference to the gross amount of any item of income without any reduction for any deduction allowed by this subtitle.

(ii) NET BASIS TAX.—The term "net basis tax" means any tax imposed by this subtitle which is not a gross basis tax.

(7) COORDINATION WITH PASSIVE LOSS RULES, ETC.—This subsection shall be applied before sections 465 and 469.

(8) TREATMENT OF CORPORATE PARTNERS.—Except to the extent provided by regulations, in applying this subsection to a corporation which owns (directly or indirectly) an interest in a partnership—

(A) such corporation's distributive share of interest income paid or accrued to such partnership shall be treated as interest income paid or accrued to such corporation,

(B) such corporation's distributive share of interest paid or accrued by such partnership shall be treated as interest paid or accrued by such corporation, and

(C) such corporation's share of the liabilities of such partnership shall be treated as liabilities of such corporation.

(9) REGULATIONS.—The Secretary shall prescribe such regulations as may be appropriate to carry out the purposes of this subsection, including—

(A) such regulations as may be appropriate to prevent the avoidance of the purposes of this subsection,

(B) regulations providing such adjustments in the case of corporations which are members of an affiliated group as may be appropriate to carry out the purposes of this subsection,

(C) regulations for the coordination of this subsection with section 884, and

(D) regulations providing for the reallocation of shares of partnership indebtedness, or distributive shares of the partnership's interest income or interest expense.

[¶ 5305] CODE SEC. 164. TAXES.

* * *

(b) DEFINITIONS AND SPECIAL RULES.—For purposes of this section—

* * *

(6) LIMITATION ON INDIVIDUAL DEDUCTIONS FOR TAXABLE YEARS 2018 THROUGH 2025.—In the case of an individual and a taxable year beginning after December 31, 2017, and before January 1, 2026—

(A) foreign real property taxes shall not be taken into account under subsection (a)(1), and

(B) the aggregate amount of taxes taken into account under paragraphs (1), (2), and (3) of subsection (a) and paragraph (5) of this subsection for any taxable year shall not exceed $10,000 ($5,000 in the case of a married individual filing a separate return).

The preceding sentence shall not apply to any foreign taxes described in subsection (a)(3) or to any taxes described in paragraph (1) and (2) of subsection (a) which are paid or accrued in carrying on a trade or business or an activity described in section 212. For purposes of subparagraph (B), an amount paid in a taxable year beginning before January 1, 2018, with respect to a State or local income tax imposed for a taxable year beginning after December 31, 2017, shall be treated as paid on the last day of the taxable year for which such tax is so imposed.

* * *

[CCH Explanation at ¶ 215. Committee Reports at ¶ 10,170.]
Amendments
• **2017, Tax Cuts and Jobs Act (P.L. 115-97)**

P.L. 115-97, § 11042(a):

Amended Code Sec. 164(b) by adding at the end a new paragraph (6). **Effective** for tax years beginning after 12-31-2016.

[¶ 5310] CODE SEC. 165. LOSSES.

* * *

(d) WAGERING LOSSES.—Losses from wagering transactions shall be allowed only to the extent of the gains from such transactions. *For purposes of the preceding sentence, in the case of taxable years beginning after December 31, 2017, and before January 1, 2026, the term "losses from wagering transactions" includes any deduction otherwise allowable under this chapter incurred in carrying on any wagering transaction.*

* * *

[CCH Explanation at ¶ 240. Committee Reports at ¶ 10,250.]
Amendments
• **2017, Tax Cuts and Jobs Act (P.L. 115-97)**

P.L. 115-97, § 11050(a):

Amended Code Sec. 165(d) by adding at the end a new sentence. **Effective** for tax years beginning after 12-31-2017.

(h) TREATMENT OF CASUALTY GAINS AND LOSSES.—

* * *

(5) LIMITATION FOR TAXABLE YEARS 2018 THROUGH 2025.—

(A) IN GENERAL.—In the case of an individual, except as provided in subparagraph (B), any personal casualty loss which (but for this paragraph) would be deductible in a taxable year beginning after December 31, 2017, and before January 1, 2026, shall be allowed as a deduction under subsection (a) only to the extent it is attributable to a Federally declared disaster (as defined in subsection (i)(5)).

(B) EXCEPTION RELATED TO PERSONAL CASUALTY GAINS.—If a taxpayer has personal casualty gains for any taxable year to which subparagraph (A) applies—

(i) subparagraph (A) shall not apply to the portion of the personal casualty loss not attributable to a Federally declared disaster (as so defined) to the extent such loss does not exceed such gains, and

(ii) in applying paragraph (2) for purposes of subparagraph (A) to the portion of personal casualty loss which is so attributable to such a disaster, the amount of personal casualty gains taken into account under paragraph (2)(A) shall be reduced by the portion of such gains taken into account under clause (i).

* * *

[CCH Explanation at ¶ 235. Committee Reports at ¶ 10,190.]

Amendments

• **2017, Tax Cuts and Jobs Act (P.L. 115-97)**

P.L. 115-97, § 11044(a):

Amended Code Sec. 165(h) by adding at the end a new paragraph (5). **Effective** for losses incurred in tax years beginning after 12-31-2017.

[¶ 5315] CODE SEC. 168. ACCELERATED COST RECOVERY SYSTEM.

* * *

(b) APPLICABLE DEPRECIATION METHOD.—For purposes of this section—

* * *

(2) 150 PERCENT DECLINING BALANCE METHOD IN CERTAIN CASES.—Paragraph (1) shall be applied by substituting "150 percent" for "200 percent" in the case of—

(A) any 15-year or 20-year property not referred to in paragraph (3),

(B) any property (other than property described in paragraph (3)) which is a qualified smart electric meter or qualified smart electric grid system, or

(C) any property (other than property described in paragraph (3)) with respect to which the taxpayer elects under paragraph (5) to have the provisions of this paragraph apply.

(3) PROPERTY TO WHICH STRAIGHT LINE METHOD APPLIES.—The applicable depreciation method shall be the straight line method in the case of the following property:

* * *

(G) Qualified improvement property described in subsection (e)(6).

(H) [Stricken.]

(I) [Stricken.]

* * *

[CCH Explanation at ¶ 425 and ¶ 435. Committee Reports at ¶ 10,360 and ¶ 10,370.]

Amendments

• **2017, Tax Cuts and Jobs Act (P.L. 115-97)**

P.L. 115-97, § 13203(b):

Amended Code Sec. 168(b)(2) by striking subparagraph (B) and by redesignating subparagraphs (C) and (D) as subparagraphs (B) and (C), respectively. **Effective** for property placed in service after 12-31-2017, in tax years ending after such date. Prior to being stricken, Code Sec. 168(b)(2)(B) read as follows:

(B) any property used in a farming business (within the meaning of section 263A(e)(4)),

P.L. 115-97, § 13204(a)(2)(A)-(B):

Amended Code Sec. 168(b)(3) by striking subparagraphs (G), (H), and (I), and by inserting after subparagraph (F) a new subparagraph (G). **Effective** for property placed in service after 12-31-2017. Prior to being stricken, Code Sec. 168(b)(3)(G)-(I) read as follows:

(G) Qualified leasehold improvement property described in subsection (e)(6).

(H) Qualified restaurant property described in subsection (e)(7).

(I) Qualified retail improvement property described in subsection (e)(8).

(e) CLASSIFICATION OF PROPERTY.—For purposes of this section—

* * *

(3) CLASSIFICATION OF CERTAIN PROPERTY.—

* * *

(B) 5-YEAR PROPERTY.—The term "5-year property" includes—

* * *

(vii) any machinery or equipment (other than any grain bin, cotton ginning asset, fence, or other land improvement) which is used in a farming business (as defined in section 263A(e)(4)), the original use of which commences with the taxpayer *after December 31, 2017.*

* * *

(E) 15-YEAR PROPERTY.—The term "15-year property" includes—

* * *

(iv) initial clearing and grading land improvements with respect to gas utility property,

(v) any section 1245 property (as defined in section 1245(a)(3)) used in the transmission at 69 or more kilovolts of electricity for sale and the original use of which commences with the taxpayer after April 11, 2005, *and*

(vi) any natural gas distribution line the original use of which commences with the taxpayer after April 11, 2005, and which is placed in service before January 1, 2011.

* * *

(ix) [Stricken.]

* * *

(6) QUALIFIED IMPROVEMENT PROPERTY.—

(A) IN GENERAL.—The term "qualified improvement property" means any improvement to an interior portion of a building which is nonresidential real property if such improvement is placed in service after the date such building was first placed in service.

(B) CERTAIN IMPROVEMENTS NOT INCLUDED.—Such term shall not include any improvement for which the expenditure is attributable to—

(i) the enlargement of the building,

(ii) any elevator or escalator, or

(iii) the internal structural framework of the building.

(7) [Stricken.]

(8) [Stricken.]

* * *

[CCH Explanation at ¶425 and ¶435. Committee Reports at ¶10,360 and ¶10,370.]

Amendments

• 2017, Tax Cuts and Jobs Act (P.L. 115-97)

P.L. 115-97, §13203(a):

Amended Code Sec. 168(e)(3)(B)(vii) by striking "after December 31, 2008, and which is placed in service before January 1, 2010" and inserting "after December 31, 2017". **Effective** for property placed in service after 12-31-2017, in tax years ending after such date.

P.L. 115-97, §13204(a)(1)(A)(i)-(iv):

Amended Code Sec. 168(e)(3)(E) by striking clauses (iv), (v), and (ix), by inserting "and" at the end of clause (vii), by striking ", and" in clause (viii) and inserting a period, and

by redesignating clauses (vi), (vii), and (viii), as so amended, as clauses (iv), (v), and (vi), respectively. **Effective** for property placed in service after 12-31-2017. Prior to being stricken, Code Sec. 168(e)(3)(E)(iv), (v), and (ix) read as follows:

(iv) any qualified leasehold improvement property,

(v) any qualified restaurant property,

* * *

(ix) any qualified retail improvement property.

P.L. 115-97, §13204(a)(1)(B):

Amended Code Sec. 168(e) by striking paragraphs (6), (7), and (8). **Effective** for property placed in service after

12-31-2017. Prior to being stricken, Code Sec. 168(e)(6)-(8) read as follows:

(6) QUALIFIED LEASEHOLD IMPROVEMENT PROPERTY.—For purposes of this subsection—

(A) IN GENERAL.—The term "qualified leasehold improvement property" means any improvement to an interior portion of a building which is nonresidential real property if—

(i) such improvement is made under or pursuant to a lease (as defined in subsection (h)(7))—

(I) by the lessee (or any sublessee) of such portion, or

(II) by the lessor of such portion,

(ii) such portion is to be occupied exclusively by the lessee (or any sublessee) of such portion, and

(iii) such improvement is placed in service more than 3 years after the date the building was first placed in service.

(B) CERTAIN IMPROVEMENTS NOT INCLUDED.—Such term shall not include any improvement for which the expenditure is attributable to—

(i) the enlargement of the building,

(ii) any elevator or escalator,

(iii) any structural component benefitting a common area, or

(iv) the internal structural framework of the building.

(C) DEFINITIONS AND SPECIAL RULES.—For purposes of this paragraph—

(i) COMMITMENT TO LEASE TREATED AS LEASE.—A commitment to enter into a lease shall be treated as a lease, and the parties to such commitment shall be treated as lessor and lessee, respectively.

(ii) RELATED PERSONS.—A lease between related persons shall not be considered a lease. For purposes of the preceding sentence, the term "related persons" means—

(I) members of an affiliated group (as defined in section 1504), and

(II) persons having a relationship described in subsection (b) of section 267; except that, for purposes of this clause, the phrase "80 percent or more" shall be substituted for the phrase "more than 50 percent" each place it appears in such subsection.

(D) IMPROVEMENTS MADE BY LESSOR.—In the case of an improvement made by the person who was the lessor of such improvement when such improvement was placed in service, such improvement shall be qualified leasehold improvement property (if at all) only so long as such improvement is held by such person.

(E) EXCEPTION FOR CHANGES IN FORM OF BUSINESS.—Property shall not cease to be qualified leasehold improvement property under subparagraph (D) by reason of—

(i) death,

(ii) a transaction to which section 381(a) applies,

(iii) a mere change in the form of conducting the trade or business so long as the property is retained in such trade or business as qualified leasehold improvement property and the taxpayer retains a substantial interest in such trade or business,

(iv) the acquisition of such property in an exchange described in section 1031, 1033, or 1038 to the extent that the basis of such property includes an amount representing the adjusted basis of other property owned by the taxpayer or a related person, or

(v) the acquisition of such property by the taxpayer in a transaction described in section 332, 351, 361, 721, or 731 (or the acquisition of such property by the taxpayer from the transferee or acquiring corporation in a transaction described in such section), to the extent that the basis of the property in the hands of the taxpayer is determined by reference to its basis in the hands of the transferor or distributor.

(7) QUALIFIED RESTAURANT PROPERTY.—

(A) IN GENERAL.—The term "qualified restaurant property" means any section 1250 property which is—

(i) a building, or

(ii) an improvement to a building,

if more than 50 percent of the building's square footage is devoted to preparation of, and seating for on-premises consumption of, prepared meals.

(B) EXCLUSION FROM BONUS DEPRECIATION.—Property described in this paragraph which is not qualified improvement property shall not be considered qualified property for purposes of subsection (k).

(8) QUALIFIED RETAIL IMPROVEMENT PROPERTY.—

(A) IN GENERAL.—The term "qualified retail improvement property" means any improvement to an interior portion of a building which is nonresidential real property if—

(i) such portion is open to the general public and is used in the retail trade or business of selling tangible personal property to the general public, and

(ii) such improvement is placed in service more than 3 years after the date the building was first placed in service.

(B) IMPROVEMENTS MADE BY OWNER.—In the case of an improvement made by the owner of such improvement, such improvement shall be qualified retail improvement property (if at all) only so long as such improvement is held by such owner. Rules similar to the rules under paragraph (6)(B) shall apply for purposes of the preceding sentence.

(C) CERTAIN IMPROVEMENTS NOT INCLUDED.—Such term shall not include any improvement for which the expenditure is attributable to—

(i) the enlargement of the building,

(ii) any elevator or escalator,

(iii) any structural component benefitting a common area, or

(iv) the internal structural framework of the building.

P.L. 115-97, §13204(a)(4)(B)(i):

Amended Code Sec. 168(e), as amended by Act Sec. 13204(a)(1)(B), by adding at the end a new paragraph (6). **Effective** for property placed in service after 12-31-2017.

(g) ALTERNATIVE DEPRECIATION SYSTEM FOR CERTAIN PROPERTY.—

(1) IN GENERAL.—In the case of—

* * *

(D) any imported property covered by an Executive order under paragraph (6),

(E) any property to which an election under paragraph (7) applies,

(F) any property described in paragraph (8), and

(G) any property with a recovery period of 10 years or more which is held by an electing farming business (as defined in section 163(j)(7)(C)),

the depreciation deduction provided by section 167(a) shall be determined under the alternative depreciation system.

(2) ALTERNATIVE DEPRECIATION SYSTEM.—For purposes of paragraph (1), the alternative depreciation system is depreciation determined by using—

* * *

(C) a recovery period determined under the following table:

In the case of:	The recovery period shall be:
(i) Property not described in clause (ii) or (iii)	The class life.
(ii) Personal property with no class life	12 years.
(iii) Residential rental property	*30 years*
(iv) Nonresidential real property	*40 years*
(v) Any railroad grading or tunnel bore or water utility property	*50 years*

(3) SPECIAL RULES FOR DETERMINING CLASS LIFE.—

* * *

(B) SPECIAL RULE FOR CERTAIN PROPERTY ASSIGNED TO CLASSES.—For purposes of paragraph (2), in the case of property described in any of the following subparagraphs of subsection (e)(3), the class life shall be determined as follows:

If property is described in subparagraph:	The class life is:
(A)(iii)	4
(B)(ii)	5
(B)(iii)	9.5
(B)(vii)	10
(C)(i)	10
(C)(iii)	22
(C)(iv)	14
(D)(i)	15
(D)(ii)	20
(D)(v)	20
(E)(i)	24
(E)(ii)	24
(E)(iii)	20
(E)(iv)	20
(E)(v)	30
(E)(vi)	35
(F)	25

* * *

(8) ELECTING REAL PROPERTY TRADE OR BUSINESS.—The property described in this paragraph shall consist of any nonresidential real property, residential rental property, and qualified improvement property held by an electing real property trade or business (as defined in 163(j)(7)(B)).

* * *

[CCH Explanation at ¶ 425 and ¶ 435. Committee Reports at ¶ 10,370 and ¶ 10,380.]

Amendments

• **2017, Tax Cuts and Jobs Act (P.L. 115-97)**

P.L. 115-97, § 13204(a)(3)(A)(i)(I)-(III):

Amended Code Sec. 168(g) in paragraph (1) by striking "and" at the end of subparagraph (D), by inserting "and" at the end of subparagraph (E), and by inserting after subparagraph (E) a new subparagraph (F). **Effective** for tax years beginning after 12-31-2017.

P.L. 115-97, § 13204(a)(3)(A)(ii):

Amended Code Sec. 168(g) by adding at the end a new paragraph (8). **Effective** for tax years beginning after 12-31-2017.

P.L. 115-97, § 13204(a)(3)(B)(i)-(ii):

Amended the table contained in Code Sec. 168(g)(3)(B) by inserting after the item relating to subparagraph (D)(ii) a new item relating to subparagraph (D)(v), and by striking the item relating to subparagraph (E)(iv) and all that follows through the item relating to subparagraph (E)(ix) and inserting new items relating to subparagraphs (E)(iv)-(E)(vi). **Effective** for property placed in service after 12-31-2017. Prior to being stricken, the items relating to subparagraphs (E)(iv) through (E)(ix) in the table read as follows:

(E)(iv)	39
(E)(v)	39
(E)(vi)	20
(E)(vii)	30
(E)(viii)	35
(E)(ix)	39

P.L. 115-97, § 13204(a)(3)(C):

Amended the table contained in Code Sec. 168(g)(2)(C) by striking clauses (iii) and (iv) and inserting clauses (iii)-(v). **Effective** for property placed in service after 12-31-2017. Prior to being stricken, clauses (iii)-(iv) in the table read as follows:

(iii) Nonresidential real and residential rental property	40 years.
(iv) Any railroad grading or tunnel bore or water utility property	50 years.

P.L. 115-97, § 13205(a):

Amended Code Sec. 168(g)(1), as amended by Act Sec. 13204, by striking "and" at the end of subparagraph (E), by inserting "and" at the end of subparagraph (F), and by inserting after subparagraph (F) a new subparagraph (G). **Effective** for tax years beginning after 12-31-2017.

(i) DEFINITIONS AND SPECIAL RULES.—For purposes of this section—

* * *

(7) TREATMENT OF CERTAIN TRANSFEREES.—

(A) IN GENERAL.—In the case of any property transferred in a transaction described in subparagraph (B), the transferee shall be treated as the transferor for purposes of computing the depreciation deduction determined under this section with respect to so much of the basis in the hands of the transferee as does not exceed the adjusted basis in the hands of the transferor. In any case where this section as in effect before the amendments made by section 201 of the Tax Reform Act of 1986 applied to the property in the hands of the transferor, the reference in the preceding sentence to this section shall be treated as a reference to this section as so in effect.

(B) TRANSACTIONS COVERED.—The transactions described in this subparagraph are—

(i) any transaction described in section 332, 351, 361, 721, or 731, and

(ii) any transaction between members of the same affiliated group during any taxable year for which a consolidated return is made by such group.

(C) PROPERTY REACQUIRED BY THE TAXPAYER.—Under regulations, property which is disposed of and then reacquired by the taxpayer shall be treated for purposes of computing the deduction allowable under subsection (a) as if such property had not been disposed of.

* * *

[CCH Explanation at ¶ 355. Committee Reports at ¶ 10,620.]

Amendments

• **2017, Tax Cuts and Jobs Act (P.L. 115-97)**

P.L. 115-97, § 13001(d), provides:

(d) NORMALIZATION REQUIREMENTS.—

(1) IN GENERAL.—A normalization method of accounting shall not be treated as being used with respect to any public utility property for purposes of section 167 or 168 of the Internal Revenue Code of 1986 if the taxpayer, in computing its cost of service for ratemaking purposes and reflecting operating results in its regulated books of account, reduces the excess tax reserve more rapidly or to a greater extent than such reserve would be reduced under the average rate assumption method.

(2) ALTERNATIVE METHOD FOR CERTAIN TAX-PAYERS.—If, as of the first day of the taxable year that includes the date of enactment of this Act—

(A) the taxpayer was required by a regulatory agency to compute depreciation for public utility property on the basis of an average life or composite rate method, and

(B) the taxpayer's books and underlying records did not contain the vintage account data necessary to apply the average rate assumption method,

the taxpayer will be treated as using a normalization method of accounting if, with respect to such jurisdiction, the taxpayer uses the alternative method for public utility property that is subject to the regulatory authority of that jurisdiction.

(3) DEFINITIONS.—For purposes of this subsection—

(A) EXCESS TAX RESERVE.—The term "excess tax reserve" means the excess of—

(i) the reserve for deferred taxes (as described in section 168(i)(9)(A)(ii) of the Internal Revenue Code of 1986) as of the day before the corporate rate reductions provided in the amendments made by this section take effect, over

(ii) the amount which would be the balance in such reserve if the amount of such reserve were determined by assuming that the corporate rate reductions provided in this Act were in effect for all prior periods.

(B) AVERAGE RATE ASSUMPTION METHOD.—The average rate assumption method is the method under which the excess in the reserve for deferred taxes is reduced over the remaining lives of the property as used in its regulated books of account which gave rise to the reserve for deferred taxes. Under such method, during the time period in which the timing differences for the property reverse, the amount of the adjustment to the reserve for the deferred taxes is calculated by multiplying—

(i) the ratio of the aggregate deferred taxes for the property to the aggregate timing differences for the property as of the beginning of the period in question, by

(ii) the amount of the timing differences which reverse during such period.

(C) ALTERNATIVE METHOD.—The "alternative method" is the method in which the taxpayer—

(i) computes the excess tax reserve on all public utility property included in the plant account on the basis of the weighted average life or composite rate used to compute depreciation for regulatory purposes, and

(ii) reduces the excess tax reserve ratably over the remaining regulatory life of the property.

(4) TAX INCREASED FOR NORMALIZATION VIOLATION.—If, for any taxable year ending after the date of the enactment of this Act, the taxpayer does not use a normalization method of accounting for the corporate rate reductions provided in the amendments made by this section—

(A) the taxpayer's tax for the taxable year shall be increased by the amount by which it reduces its excess tax reserve more rapidly than permitted under a normalization method of accounting, and

(B) such taxpayer shall not be treated as using a normalization method of accounting for purposes of subsections (f)(2) and (i)(9)(C) of section 168 of the Internal Revenue Code of 1986.

P.L. 115-97, §13504(b)(1):

Amended Code Sec. 168(i)(7)(B) by striking the second sentence [the last sentence of Code Sec. 168(i)(7)]. **Effective** for partnership tax years beginning after 12-31-2017. Prior to being stricken, the second sentence of Code Sec. 168(i)(7)(B) [the last sentence of Code Sec. 168(i)(7)] read as follows:

Subparagraph (A) shall not apply in the case of a termination of a partnership under section 708(b)(1)(B).

(k) SPECIAL ALLOWANCE FOR CERTAIN PROPERTY.—

(1) ADDITIONAL ALLOWANCE.—In the case of any qualified property—

(A) the depreciation deduction provided by section 167(a) for the taxable year in which such property is placed in service shall include an allowance equal to *the applicable percentage* of the adjusted basis of the qualified property, and

(B) the adjusted basis of the qualified property shall be reduced by the amount of such deduction before computing the amount otherwise allowable as a depreciation deduction under this chapter for such taxable year and any subsequent taxable year.

(2) QUALIFIED PROPERTY.—For purposes of this subsection—

(A) IN GENERAL.—The term "qualified property" means property—

(i)(I) to which this section applies which has a recovery period of 20 years or less,

(II) which is computer software (as defined in section 167(f)(1)(B)) for which a deduction is allowable under section 167(a) without regard to this subsection,

(III) which is water utility property, *or*

(IV) *which is a qualified film or television production (as defined in subsection (d) of section 181) for which a deduction would have been allowable under section 181 without regard to subsections (a)(2) and (g) of such section or this subsection, or*

(V) *which is a qualified live theatrical production (as defined in subsection (e) of section 181) for which a deduction would have been allowable under section 181 without regard to subsections (a)(2) and (g) of such section or this subsection,*

(ii) *the original use of which begins with the taxpayer or the acquisition of which by the taxpayer meets the requirements of clause (ii) of subparagraph (E), and*

(iii) which is placed in service by the taxpayer before *January 1, 2027.*

(B) CERTAIN PROPERTY HAVING LONGER PRODUCTION PERIODS TREATED AS QUALIFIED PROPERTY.—

(i) IN GENERAL.—The term "qualified property" includes any property if such property—

(I) meets the requirements of clauses (i) and (ii) of subparagraph (A),

(II) is placed in service by the taxpayer before *January 1, 2028,*

(III) is acquired by the taxpayer (or acquired pursuant to a written contract entered into) before *January 1, 2027,*

(IV) has a recovery period of at least 10 years or is transportation property,

(V) is subject to section 263A, and

(VI) meets the requirements of clause (iii) of section 263A(f)(1)(B) (determined as if such clause also applies to property which has a long useful life (within the meaning of section 263A(f))).

(ii) ONLY PRE-*JANUARY 1, 2027* BASIS ELIGIBLE FOR ADDITIONAL ALLOWANCE.—In the case of property which is qualified property solely by reason of clause (i), paragraph (1) shall apply only to the extent of the adjusted basis thereof attributable to manufacture, construction, or production before *January 1, 2027.*

* * *

(E) SPECIAL RULES.—

(i) SELF-CONSTRUCTED PROPERTY.—In the case of a taxpayer manufacturing, constructing, or producing property for the taxpayer's own use, the requirements of subclause (III) of subparagraph (B)(i) shall be treated as met if the taxpayer begins manufacturing, constructing, or producing the property before *January 1, 2027.*

(ii) ACQUISITION REQUIREMENTS.—An acquisition of property meets the requirements of this clause if—

(I) such property was not used by the taxpayer at any time prior to such acquisition, and

(II) the acquisition of such property meets the requirements of paragraphs (2)(A), (2)(B), (2)(C), and (3) of section 179(d).

(iii) SYNDICATION.—For purposes of subparagraph (A)(ii), if—

(I) property is used by a lessor of such property and such use is the lessor's first use of such property,

(II) such property is sold by such lessor or any subsequent purchaser within 3 months after the date such property was originally placed in service (or, in the case of multiple units of property subject to the same lease, within 3 months after the date the final unit is placed in service, so long as the period between the time the first unit is placed in service and the time the last unit is placed in service does not exceed 12 months), and

(III) the user of such property after the last sale during such 3-month period remains the same as when such property was originally placed in service,

such property shall be treated as originally placed in service not earlier than the date of such last sale.

(F) COORDINATION WITH SECTION 280F.—For purposes of section 280F—

(i) AUTOMOBILES.—In the case of a passenger automobile (as defined in section 280F(d)(5)) which is qualified property, the Secretary shall increase the limitation under section 280F(a)(1)(A)(i) by $8,000.

(ii) LISTED PROPERTY.—The deduction allowable under paragraph (1) shall be taken into account in computing any recapture amount under section 280F(b)(2).

(iii) PHASE DOWN.—In the case of a passenger automobile *acquired by the taxpayer before September 28, 2017, and placed in service by the taxpayer after September 27, 2017,* clause (i) shall be applied by substituting for "$8,000"—

(I) in the case of an automobile placed in service during 2018, $6,400, and

(II) in the case of an automobile placed in service during 2019, $4,800.

* * *

(H) PRODUCTION PLACED IN SERVICE.—For purposes of subparagraph (A)—

(i) a qualified film or television production shall be considered to be placed in service at the time of initial release or broadcast, and

(ii) a qualified live theatrical production shall be considered to be placed in service at the time of the initial live staged performance.

(3) [Stricken.]

(4) [Stricken.]

(5) SPECIAL RULES FOR CERTAIN PLANTS BEARING FRUITS AND NUTS.—

(A) IN GENERAL.—In the case of any specified plant which is planted before *January 1, 2027,* or is grafted before such date to a plant that has already been planted, by the taxpayer in the ordinary course of the taxpayer's farming business (as defined in section 263A(e)(4)) during a taxable year for which the taxpayer has elected the application of this paragraph—

(i) a depreciation deduction equal to *the applicable percentage* of the adjusted basis of such specified plant shall be allowed under section 167(a) for the taxable year in which such specified plant is so planted or grafted, and

(ii) the adjusted basis of such specified plant shall be reduced by the amount of such deduction.

* * *

(F) [Stricken.]

(6) APPLICABLE PERCENTAGE.—For purposes of this subsection—

(A) IN GENERAL.—Except as otherwise provided in this paragraph, the term "applicable percentage" means—

(i) in the case of property placed in service after September 27, 2017, and before January 1, 2023, 100 percent,

(ii) in the case of property placed in service after December 31, 2022, and before January 1, 2024, 80 percent,

(iii) in the case of property placed in service after December 31, 2023, and before January 1, 2025, 60 percent,

(iv) in the case of property placed in service after December 31, 2024, and before January 1, 2026, 40 percent, and

(v) in the case of property placed in service after December 31, 2025, and before January 1, 2027, 20 percent.

(B) RULE FOR PROPERTY WITH LONGER PRODUCTION PERIODS.—In the case of property described in subparagraph (B) or (C) of paragraph (2), the term "applicable percentage" means—

(i) in the case of property placed in service after September 27, 2017, and before January 1, 2024, 100 percent,

(ii) in the case of property placed in service after December 31, 2023, and before January 1, 2025, 80 percent,

(iii) in the case of property placed in service after December 31, 2024, and before January 1, 2026, 60 percent,

(iv) in the case of property placed in service after December 31, 2025, and before January 1, 2027, 40 percent, and

(v) in the case of property placed in service after December 31, 2026, and before January 1, 2028, 20 percent.

(C) RULE FOR PLANTS BEARING FRUITS AND NUTS.—In the case of a specified plant described in paragraph (5), the term "applicable percentage" means—

(i) in the case of a plant which is planted or grafted after September 27, 2017, and before January 1, 2023, 100 percent,

(ii) in the case of a plant which is planted or grafted after December 31, 2022, and before January 1, 2024, 80 percent,

(iii) in the case of a plant which is planted or grafted after December 31, 2023, and before January 1, 2025, 60 percent,

(iv) in the case of a plant which is planted or grafted after December 31, 2024, and before January 1, 2026, 40 percent, and

(v) in the case of a plant which is planted or grafted after December 31, 2025, and before January 1, 2027, 20 percent.

* * *

(8) PHASE DOWN.—In the case of qualified property acquired by the taxpayer before September 28, 2017, and placed in service by the taxpayer after September 27, 2017, paragraph (6) shall be applied by substituting for each percentage therein—

(A) "50 percent" in the case of—

(i) property placed in service before January 1, 2018, and

(ii) property described in subparagraph (B) or (C) of paragraph (2) which is placed in service in 2018,

(B) "40 percent" in the case of—

(i) property placed in service in 2018 (other than property described in subparagraph (B) or (C) of paragraph (2)), and

(ii) property described in subparagraph (B) or (C) of paragraph (2) which is placed in service in 2019,

(C) "30 percent" in the case of—

(i) property placed in service in 2019 (other than property described in subparagraph (B) or (C) of paragraph (2)), and

(ii) property described in subparagraph (B) or (C) of paragraph (2) which is placed in service in 2020, and

(D) "0 percent" in the case of—

(i) property placed in service after 2019 (other than property described in subparagraph (B) or (C) of paragraph (2)), and

(ii) property described in subparagraph (B) or (C) of paragraph (2) which is placed in service after 2020.

(9) EXCEPTION FOR CERTAIN PROPERTY.—The term "qualified property" shall not include—

(A) any property which is primarily used in a trade or business described in clause (iv) of section 163(j)(7)(A), or

(B) any property used in a trade or business that has had floor plan financing indebtedness (as defined in paragraph (9) of section 163(j)), if the floor plan financing interest related to such indebtedness was taken into account under paragraph (1)(C) of such section.

(10) SPECIAL RULE FOR PROPERTY PLACED IN SERVICE DURING CERTAIN PERIODS.—

(A) IN GENERAL.—In the case of qualified property placed in service by the taxpayer during the first taxable year ending after September 27, 2017, if the taxpayer elects to have this paragraph apply for such taxable year, paragraphs (1)(A) and (5)(A)(i) shall be applied by substituting "50 percent" for "the applicable percentage".

(B) FORM OF ELECTION.—Any election under this paragraph shall be made at such time and in such form and manner as the Secretary may prescribe.

* * *

[CCH Explanation at ¶310, ¶410, and ¶425. Committee Reports at ¶10,300, ¶10,340, and ¶10,370.]

Amendments

- **2017, Tax Cuts and Jobs Act (P.L. 115-97)**

P.L. 115-97, §12001(b)(13):

Amended Code Sec. 168(k) by striking paragraph (4). **Effective** for tax years beginning after 12-31-2017. Prior to being stricken, Code Sec. 168(k)(4) read as follows:

(4) ELECTION TO ACCELERATE AMT CREDITS IN LIEU OF BONUS DEPRECIATION.—

(A) IN GENERAL.—If a corporation elects to have this paragraph apply for any taxable year—

(i) paragraphs (1) and (2)(F) shall not apply to any qualified property placed in service during such taxable year,

(ii) the applicable depreciation method used under this section with respect to such property shall be the straight line method, and

(iii) the limitation imposed by section 53(c) for such taxable year shall be increased by the bonus depreciation amount which is determined for such taxable year under subparagraph (B).

(B) BONUS DEPRECIATION AMOUNT.—For purposes of this paragraph—

(i) IN GENERAL.—The bonus depreciation amount for any taxable year is an amount equal to 20 percent of the excess (if any) of—

(I) the aggregate amount of depreciation which would be allowed under this section for qualified property placed in service by the taxpayer during such taxable year if paragraph (1) applied to all such property (and, in the case of any such property which is a passenger automobile (as defined in section 280F(d)(5)), if paragraph (2)(F) applied to such automobile), over

(II) the aggregate amount of depreciation which would be allowed under this section for qualified property placed in service by the taxpayer during such taxable year if paragraphs (1) and (2)(F) did not apply to any such property.

The aggregate amounts determined under subclauses (I) and (II) shall be determined without regard to any election made under subparagraph (A) or subsection (b)(2)(D), (b)(3)(D), or (g)(7).

(ii) LIMITATION.—The bonus depreciation amount for any taxable year shall not exceed the lesser of—

(I) 50 percent of the minimum tax credit under section 53(b) for the first taxable year ending after December 31, 2015, or

(II) the minimum tax credit under section 53(b) for such taxable year determined by taking into account only the adjusted net minimum tax for taxable years ending before January 1, 2016 (determined by treating credits as allowed on a first-in, first-out basis).

(iii) AGGREGATION RULE.—All corporations which are treated as a single employer under section 52(a) shall be treated—

(I) as 1 taxpayer for purposes of this paragraph, and

(II) as having elected the application of this paragraph if any such corporation so elects.

(C) CREDIT REFUNDABLE.—For purposes of section 6401(b), the aggregate increase in the credits allowable under part IV of subchapter A for any taxable year resulting from the application of this paragraph shall be treated as allowed under subpart C of such part (and not any other subpart).

(D) OTHER RULES.—

(i) ELECTION.—Any election under this paragraph may be revoked only with the consent of the Secretary.

(ii) PARTNERSHIPS WITH ELECTING PARTNERS.—In the case of a corporation which is a partner in a partnership and which makes an election under subparagraph (A) for the taxable year, for purposes of determining such corporation's distributive share of partnership items under section 702 for such taxable year—

(I) paragraphs (1) and (2)(F) shall not apply to any qualified property placed in service during such taxable year, and

(II) the applicable depreciation method used under this section with respect to such property shall be the straight line method.

(iii) CERTAIN PARTNERSHIPS.—In the case of a partnership in which more than 50 percent of the capital and profits interests are owned (directly or indirectly) at all times during the taxable year by 1 corporation (or by corporations treated as 1 taxpayer under subparagraph (B)(iii)), each partner shall compute its bonus depreciation amount under clause (i) of subparagraph (B) by taking into account its distributive share of the amounts determined by the partnership under subclauses (I) and (II) of such clause for the taxable year of the partnership ending with or within the taxable year of the partner.

P.L. 115-97, §13201(a)(1)(A)-(B):

Amended Code Sec. 168(k) by striking "50 percent" in paragraph (1)(A) and inserting "the applicable percentage", and by striking "50 percent" in paragraph (5)(A)(i) and inserting "the applicable percentage". For the **effective** date, see Act Sec. 13201(h)(1)-(2), below.

P.L. 115-97, §13201(a)(2):

Amended Code Sec. 168(k)(6). For the **effective** date, see Act Sec. 13201(h)(1)-(2), below. Prior to amendment, Code Sec. 168(k)(6) read as follows:

(6) PHASE DOWN.—In the case of qualified property placed in service by the taxpayer after December 31, 2017, paragraph (1)(A) shall be applied by substituting for "50 percent"—

(A) in the case of property placed in service in 2018 (or in the case of property placed in service in 2019 and described in paragraph (2)(B) or (C) (determined by substituting "2019" for "2020" in paragraphs (2)(B)(i)(III) and (ii) and paragraph (2)(E)(i)), "40 percent",

(B) in the case of property placed in service in 2019 (or in the case of property placed in service in 2020 and described in paragraph (2)(B) or (C), "30 percent".

P.L. 115-97, §13201(a)(3)(A):

Amended Code Sec. 168(k)(5) by striking subparagraph (F). For the **effective** date, see Act Sec. 13201(h)(1)-(2), below. Prior to being stricken, Code Sec. 168(k)(5)(F) read as follows:

(F) PHASE DOWN.—In the case of a specified plant which is planted after December 31, 2017 (or is grafted to a plant that has already been planted before such date), subparagraph (A)(i) shall be applied by substituting for "50 percent"—

(i) in the case of a plant which is planted (or so grafted) in 2018, "40 percent", and

(ii) in the case of a plant which is planted (or so grafted) during 2019, "30 percent".

P.L. 115-97, §13201(a)(3)(B):

Amended Code Sec. 168(k) by adding at the end a new paragraph (8). For the **effective** date, see Act Sec. 13201(h)(1)-(2), below.

P.L. 115-97, §13201(b)(1)(A)(i):

Amended Code Sec. 168(k)(2)(A)(iii), (B)(i)(III) and (ii), and (E)(i) by striking "January 1, 2020" each place it appears and inserting "January 1, 2027". For the **effective** date, see Act Sec. 13201(h)(1)-(2), below.

P.L. 115-97, §13201(b)(1)(A)(ii)(I)-(II):

Amended Code Sec. 168(k)(2)(B) by striking "January 1, 2021" in clause (i)(II) and inserting "January 1, 2028", and by striking "PRE-JANUARY 1, 2020" in the heading of clause (ii) and inserting "PRE-JANUARY 1, 2027". For the **effective** date, see Act Sec. 13201(h)(1)-(2), below.

P.L. 115-97, §13201(b)(1)(B):

Amended Code Sec. 168(k)(5)(A) by striking "January 1, 2020" and inserting "January 1, 2027". For the **effective** date, see Act Sec. 13201(h)(1)-(2), below.

P.L. 115-97, §13201(b)(2)(B):

Amended the heading of Code Sec. 168(k) by striking "ACQUIRED AFTER DECEMBER 31, 2007, AND BEFORE JANUARY 1, 2020" following "CERTAIN PROPERTY". For the **effective** date, see Act Sec. 13201(h)(1)-(2), below.

P.L. 115-97, §13201(c)(1):

Amended Code Sec. 168(k)(2)(A)(ii). For the **effective** date, see Act Sec. 13201(h)(1)-(2), below. Prior to amendment, Code Sec. 168(k)(2)(A)(ii) read as follows:

(ii) the original use of which commences with the taxpayer, and

P.L. 115-97, §13201(c)(2):

Amended Code Sec. 168(k)(2)(E)(ii). For the **effective** date, see Act Sec. 13201(h)(1)-(2), below. Prior to amendment, Code Sec. 168(k)(2)(E)(ii) read as follows:

(ii) SALE-LEASEBACKS.—For purposes of clause (iii) and subparagraph (A)(ii), if property is—

(I) originally placed in service by a person, and

(II) sold and leased back by such person within 3 months after the date such property was originally placed in service,

such property shall be treated as originally placed in service not earlier than the date on which such property is used under the leaseback referred to in subclause (II).

P.L. 115-97, §13201(c)(3):

Amended Code Sec. 168(k)(2)(E)(iii)(I). For the **effective** date, see Act Sec. 13201(h)(1)-(2), below. Prior to amendment, Code Sec. 168(k)(2)(E)(iii)(I) read as follows:

(I) property is originally placed in service by the lessor of such property,

P.L. 115-97, §13201(d):

Amended Code Sec. 168(k), as amended by Act Sec. 13201, by adding at the end a new paragraph (9). For the **effective** date, see Act Sec. 13201(h)(1)-(2), below.

P.L. 115-97, §13201(e):

Amended Code Sec. 168(k), as amended by Act Sec. 13201, by adding at the end a new paragraph (10). For the **effective** date, see Act Sec. 13201(h)(1)-(2), below.

P.L. 115-97, §13201(f):

Amended Code Sec. 168(k)(2)(F)(iii) by striking "placed in service by the taxpayer after December 31, 2017" and inserting "acquired by the taxpayer before September 28, 2017, and placed in service by the taxpayer after September 27, 2017". For the **effective** date, see Act Sec. 13201(h)(1)-(2), below.

P.L. 115-97, §13201(g)(1)(A)-(C):

Amended Code Sec. 168(k)(2)(A)(i), as amended by Act Sec. 13204, by striking "or" in subclause (II), by adding "or" after the comma in subclause (III), and by adding at the end new subclauses (IV) and (V). For the **effective** date, see Act Sec. 13201(h)(1)-(2), below.

P.L. 115-97, §13201(g)(2):

Amended Code Sec. 168(k)(2) by adding at the end a new subparagraph (H). For the **effective** date, see Act Sec. 13201(h)(1)-(2), below.

P.L. 115-97, §13201(h)(1)-(2), provides:

(h) EFFECTIVE DATE.—

(1) IN GENERAL.—Except as provided by paragraph (2), the amendments made by this section shall apply to property which—

(A) is acquired after September 27, 2017, and

(B) is placed in service after such date.

For purposes of the preceding sentence, property shall not be treated as acquired after the date on which a written binding contract is entered into for such acquisition.

(2) SPECIFIED PLANTS.—The amendments made by this section shall apply to specified plants planted or grafted after September 27, 2017.

P.L. 115-97, §13204(a)(4)(A)(i)-(iii):

Amended Code Sec. 168(k)(2)(A)(i) by inserting "or" after the comma in subclause (II), by striking "or" at the end of subclause (III), and by striking subclause (IV). **Effective** for property placed in service after 12-31-2017. Prior to being stricken, Code Sec. 168(k)(2)(A)(i)(IV) read as follows:

(IV) which is qualified improvement property,

P.L. 115-97, §13204(a)(4)(B)(ii):

Amended Code Sec. 168(k) by striking paragraph (3). **Effective** for property placed in service after 12-31-2017. Prior to being stricken, Code Sec. 168(k)(3) read as follows:

(3) QUALIFIED IMPROVEMENT PROPERTY.—For purposes of this subsection—

(A) IN GENERAL.—The term "qualified improvement property" means any improvement to an interior portion of a building which is nonresidential real property if such improvement is placed in service after the date such building was first placed in service.

(B) CERTAIN IMPROVEMENTS NOT INCLUDED.—Such term shall not include any improvement for which the expenditure is attributable to—

(i) the enlargement of the building,

(ii) any elevator or escalator, or

(iii) the internal structural framework of the building.

[¶ 5320] CODE SEC. 170. CHARITABLE, ETC., CONTRIBUTIONS AND GIFTS.

* * *

(b) PERCENTAGE LIMITATIONS.—

(1) INDIVIDUALS.—In the case of an individual, the deduction provided in subsection (a) shall be limited as provided in the succeeding subparagraphs.

* * *

(G) *INCREASED LIMITATION FOR CASH CONTRIBUTIONS.—*

(i) IN GENERAL.—In the case of any contribution of cash to an organization described in subparagraph (A), the total amount of such contributions which may be taken into account under subsection (a) for any taxable year beginning after December 31, 2017, and before January 1, 2026, shall not exceed 60 percent of the taxpayer's contribution base for such year.

(ii) CARRYOVER.—If the aggregate amount of contributions described in clause (i) exceeds the applicable limitation under clause (i) for any taxable year described in such clause, such excess shall be treated (in a manner consistent with the rules of subsection (d)(1)) as a charitable contribution to which clause (i) applies in each of the 5 succeeding years in order of time.

(iii) COORDINATION WITH SUBPARAGRAPHS (A) AND (B).—

(I) IN GENERAL.—Contributions taken into account under this subparagraph shall not be taken into account under subparagraph (A).

(II) LIMITATION REDUCTION.—For each taxable year described in clause (i), and each taxable year to which any contribution under this subparagraph is carried over under clause (ii), subparagraph (A) shall be applied by reducing (but not below zero) the contribution limitation allowed for the taxable year under such subparagraph by the aggregate contributions allowed under this subparagraph for such taxable year, and subparagraph (B) shall be applied by treating any reference to subparagraph (A) as a reference to both subparagraph (A) and this subparagraph.

(H) CONTRIBUTION BASE DEFINED.—For purposes of this section, the term "contribution base" means adjusted gross income (computed without regard to any net operating loss carryback to the taxable year under section 172).

(2) CORPORATIONS.—In the case of a corporation—

* * *

(D) TAXABLE INCOME.—For purposes of this paragraph, taxable income shall be computed without regard to—

* * *

(iv) any capital loss carryback to the taxable year under section 1212(a)(1)

(v) section 199A(g).

* * *

[CCH Explanation at ¶ 230, ¶ 330, and ¶ 530. Committee Reports at ¶ 10,030, ¶ 10,080, and ¶ 10,450.]

Amendments

• **2017, Tax Cuts and Jobs Act (P.L. 115-97)**

P.L. 115-97, § 11011(d)(5):

Amended Code Sec. 170(b)(2)(D) by striking "and" in clause (iv), by striking the period at the end of clause (v), and by adding at the end a new clause (vi). **Effective** for tax years beginning after 12-31-2017.

P.L. 115-97, § 11023(a):

Amended Code Sec. 170(b)(1) by redesignating subparagraph (G) as subparagraph (H) and by inserting after sub-paragraph (F) a new subparagraph (G). **Effective** for contributions in tax years beginning after 12-31-2017.

P.L. 115-97, § 13305(b)(2):

Amended Code Sec. 170(b)(2)(D), as amended by subtitle A, by striking clause (iv) and by redesignating clauses (v) and (vi) as clauses (iv) and (v). **Effective** for tax years beginning after 12-31-2017. Prior to being stricken, Code Sec. 170(b)(2)(D)(iv) read as follows:

(iv) section 199

(f) DISALLOWANCE OF DEDUCTION IN CERTAIN CASES AND SPECIAL RULES.—

* * *

(8) SUBSTANTIATION REQUIREMENT FOR CERTAIN CONTRIBUTIONS.—

* * *

(D) REGULATIONS.—The Secretary shall prescribe such regulations as may be necessary or appropriate to carry out the purposes of this paragraph, including regulations that may provide that some or all of the requirements of this paragraph do not apply in appropriate cases.

* * *

[CCH Explanation at ¶ 230. Committee Reports at ¶ 10,080.]

Amendments

• **2017, Tax Cuts and Jobs Act (P.L. 115-97)**

P.L. 115-97, § 13705(a):

Amended Code Sec. 170(f)(8) by striking subparagraph (D) and by redesignating subparagraph (E) as subparagraph (D). **Effective** for contributions made in tax years beginning after 12-31-2016. Prior to being stricken, Code Sec. 170(f)(8)(D) read as follows:

(D) SUBSTANTIATION NOT REQUIRED FOR CONTRIBUTIONS RE-PORTED BY THE DONEE ORGANIZATION.—Subparagraph (A) shall not apply to a contribution if the donee organization files a return, on such form and in accordance with such regulations as the Secretary may prescribe, which includes the information described in subparagraph (B) with respect to the contribution.

(l) TREATMENT OF CERTAIN AMOUNTS PAID TO OR FOR THE BENEFIT OF INSTITUTIONS OF HIGHER EDUCATION.—

(1) IN GENERAL.—*No deduction shall be allowed under this section for any amount described in paragraph (2).*

(2) AMOUNT DESCRIBED.—For purposes of paragraph (1), an amount is described in this paragraph if—

(A) the amount is paid by the taxpayer to or for the benefit of an educational organization—

(i) which is described in subsection (b)(1)(A)(ii), and

(ii) which is an institution of higher education (as defined in section 3304(f)), and

(B) the taxpayer receives (directly or indirectly) as a result of paying such amount the right to purchase tickets for seating at an athletic event in an athletic stadium of such institution.

If any portion of a payment is for the purchase of such tickets, such portion and the remaining portion (if any) of such payment shall be treated as separate amounts for purposes of this subsection.

* * *

[CCH Explanation at ¶ 230. Committee Reports at ¶ 10,080.]

Amendments

• **2017, Tax Cuts and Jobs Act (P.L. 115-97)**

P.L. 115-97, § 13704(a)(1)-(2):

Amended Code Sec. 170(l) by striking paragraph (1) and inserting a new paragraph (1), and in paragraph (2)(B), by

striking "such amount would be allowable as a deduction under this section but for the fact that" before "the taxpayer receives". **Effective** for contributions made in tax years beginning after 12-31-2017.

[¶ 5325] CODE SEC. 172. NET OPERATING LOSS DEDUCTION.

(a) DEDUCTION ALLOWED.—*There shall be allowed as a deduction for the taxable year an amount equal to the lesser of—*

(1) the aggregate of the net operating loss carryovers to such year, plus the net operating loss carrybacks to such year, or

(2) 80 percent of taxable income computed without regard to the deduction allowable under this section.

For purposes of this subtitle, the term "net operating loss deduction" means the deduction allowed by this subsection.

[CCH Explanation at ¶ 515. Committee Reports at ¶ 10,430.]

Amendments

• **2017, Tax Cuts and Jobs Act (P.L. 115-97)**

P.L. 115-97, § 13302(a)(1):

Amended Code Sec. 172(a). **Effective** for losses arising in tax years beginning after 12-31-2017. Prior to amendment, Code Sec. 172(a) read as follows:

(a) DEDUCTION ALLOWED.—There shall be allowed as a deduction for the taxable year an amount equal to the aggregate of (1) the net operating loss carryovers to such year, plus (2) the net operating loss carrybacks to such year. For purposes of this subtitle, the term "net operating loss deduction" means the deduction allowed by this subsection.

(b) NET OPERATING LOSS CARRYBACKS AND CARRYOVERS.—

(1) YEARS TO WHICH LOSS MAY BE CARRIED.—

(A) GENERAL RULE.—Except as otherwise provided in this paragraph, a net operating loss for any taxable year—

(i) *except as otherwise provided in this paragraph, shall not be a net operating loss carryback to any taxable year* preceding the taxable year of such loss, and

(ii) shall be a net operating loss carryover *to each taxable year* following the taxable year of the loss.

(B) FARMING LOSSES.—

(i) IN GENERAL.—In the case of any portion of a net operating loss for the taxable year which is a farming loss with respect to the taxpayer, such loss shall be a net operating loss carryback to each of the 2 taxable years preceding the taxable year of such loss.

(ii) FARMING LOSS.—For purposes of this section, the term "farming loss" means the lesser of—

(I) the amount which would be the net operating loss for the taxable year if only income and deductions attributable to farming businesses (as defined in section 263A(e)(4)) are taken into account, or

(II) the amount of the net operating loss for such taxable year.

(iii) COORDINATION WITH PARAGRAPH (2).—For purposes of applying paragraph (2), a farming loss for any taxable year shall be treated as a separate net operating loss for such taxable year to be taken into account after the remaining portion of the net operating loss for such taxable year.

(iv) ELECTION.—Any taxpayer entitled to a 2-year carryback under clause (i) from any loss year may elect not to have such clause apply to such loss year. Such election shall be made in such manner as prescribed by the Secretary and shall be made by the due date (including extensions of time) for filing the taxpayer's return for the taxable year of the net operating loss. Such election, once made for any taxable year, shall be irrevocable for such taxable year.

(C) INSURANCE COMPANIES.—In the case of an insurance company (as defined in section 816(a)) other than a life insurance company, the net operating loss for any taxable year—

(i) shall be a net operating loss carryback to each of the 2 taxable years preceding the taxable year of such loss, and

(ii) shall be a net operating loss carryover to each of the 20 taxable years following the taxable year of the loss.

(D) *[Stricken.]*

(E) *[Stricken.]*

(F) *[Stricken.]*

(2) AMOUNT OF CARRYBACKS AND CARRYOVERS.—The entire amount of the net operating loss for any taxable year (hereinafter in this section referred to as the "loss year") shall be carried to the earliest of the taxable years to which (by reason of paragraph (1)) such loss may be carried. The

portion of such loss which shall be carried to each of the other taxable years shall be the excess, if any, of the amount of such loss over the sum of the taxable income for each of the prior taxable years to which such loss may be carried. For purposes of the preceding sentence, the taxable income for any such prior taxable year *shall*—

(A) be computed with the modifications specified in subsection (d) other than paragraphs (1), (4), and (5) thereof, and by determining the amount of the net operating loss deduction without regard to the net operating loss for the loss year or for any taxable year thereafter,

(B) not be considered to be less than zero, and

(C) not exceed the amount determined under subsection (a)(2) for such prior taxable year.

* * *

[CCH Explanation at ¶ 515. Committee Reports at ¶ 10,430.]

Amendments

• 2017, Tax Cuts and Jobs Act (P.L. 115-97)

P.L. 115-97, § 13302(a)(2):

Amended Code Sec. 172(b)(2) by striking "shall be computed—"and all that follows and inserting "shall—"and new subparagraphs (A)-(C). **Effective** for losses arising in tax years beginning after 12-31-2017. Prior to being stricken, "shall be computed—"and all that follows in Code Sec. 172(b)(2) read as follows:

(2) AMOUNT OF CARRYBACKS AND CARRYOVERS.—The entire amount of the net operating loss for any taxable year (hereinafter in this section referred to as the "loss year") shall be carried to the earliest of the taxable years to which (by reason of paragraph (1)) such loss may be carried. The portion of such loss which shall be carried to each of the other taxable years shall be the excess, if any, of the amount of such loss over the sum of the taxable income for each of the prior taxable years to which such loss may be carried. For purposes of the preceding sentence, the taxable income for any such prior taxable year shall be computed—

(A) with the modifications specified in subsection (d) other than paragraphs (1), (4), and (5) thereof, and

(B) by determining the amount of the net operating loss deduction without regard to the net operating loss for the loss year or for any taxable year thereafter,

and the taxable income so computed shall not be considered to be less than zero.

P.L. 115-97, § 13302(b)(1)(A)-(B):

Amended Code Sec. 172(b)(1)(A) by striking "shall be a net operating loss carryback to each of the 2 taxable years" in clause (i) and inserting "except as otherwise provided in this paragraph, shall not be a net operating loss carryback to any taxable year", and by striking "to each of the 20 taxable years" in clause (ii) and inserting "to each taxable year". **Effective** for net operating losses arising in tax years ending after 12-31-2017.

P.L. 115-97, § 13302(b)(2):

Amended Code Sec. 172(b)(1) by striking subparagraphs (B) through (F). **Effective** for net operating losses arising in tax years ending after 12-31-2017. Prior to being stricken, Code Sec. 172(b)(1)(B)-(F) read as follows:

(B) SPECIAL RULES FOR REIT's.—

(i) IN GENERAL.—A net operating loss for a REIT year shall not be a net operating loss carryback to any taxable year preceding the taxable year of such loss.

(ii) SPECIAL RULE.—In the case of any net operating loss for a taxable year which is not a REIT year, such loss shall not be carried back to any taxable year which is a REIT year.

(iii) REIT YEAR.—For purposes of this subparagraph, the term "REIT year" means any taxable year for which the

provisions of part II of subchapter M (relating to real estate investment trusts) apply to the taxpayer.

(C) SPECIFIED LIABILITY LOSSES.—In the case of a taxpayer which has a specified liability loss (as defined in subsection (f)) for a taxable year, such specified liability loss shall be a net operating loss carryback to each of the 10 taxable years preceding the taxable year of such loss.

(D) EXCESS INTEREST LOSS.—

(i) IN GENERAL.—If—

(I) there is a corporate equity reduction transaction, and

(II) an applicable corporation has a corporate equity reduction interest loss for any loss limitation year,

then the corporate equity reduction interest loss shall be a net operating loss carryback and carryover to the taxable years described in subparagraph (A), except that such loss shall not be carried back to a taxable year preceding the taxable year in which the corporate equity reduction transaction occurs.

(ii) LOSS LIMITATION YEAR.—For purposes of clause (i) and subsection (g), the term "loss limitation year" means, with respect to any corporate equity reduction transaction, the taxable year in which such transaction occurs and each of the 2 succeeding taxable years.

(iii) APPLICABLE CORPORATION.—For purposes of clause (i), the term "applicable corporation" means—

(I) a C corporation which acquires stock, or the stock of which is acquired in a major stock acquisition,

(II) a C corporation making distributions with respect to, or redeeming, its stock in connection with an excess distribution, or

(III) a C corporation which is a successor of a corporation described in subclause (I) or (II).

(iv) OTHER DEFINITIONS.—

For definitions of terms used in this subparagraph, see subsection (h).

(E) RETENTION OF 3-YEAR CARRYBACK IN CERTAIN CASES.—

(i) IN GENERAL.—Subparagraph (A)(i) shall be applied by substituting "3 taxable years" for "2 taxable years" with respect to the portion of the net operating loss for the taxable year which is an eligible loss with respect to the taxpayer.

(ii) ELIGIBLE LOSS.—For purposes of clause (i), the term "eligible loss" means—

(I) in the case of an individual, losses of property arising from fire, storm, shipwreck, or other casualty, or from theft,

(II) in the case of a taxpayer which is a small business, net operating losses attributable to federally declared disasters (as defined by section 165(i)(5)), and

(III) in the case of a taxpayer engaged in the trade or business of farming (as defined in section 263A(e)(4)), net operating losses attributable to such federally declared disasters.

Such term shall not include any farming loss (as defined in subsection (h)).

(iii) SMALL BUSINESS.—For purposes of this subparagraph, the term "small business" means a corporation or partnership which meets the gross receipts test of section 448(c) for the taxable year in which the loss arose (or, in the case of a sole proprietorship, which would meet such test if such proprietorship were a corporation).

(iv) COORDINATION WITH PARAGRAPH (2).—For purposes of applying paragraph (2), an eligible loss for any taxable year shall be treated in a manner similar to the manner in which a specified liability loss is treated.

(F) FARMING LOSSES.—In the case of a taxpayer which has a farming loss (as defined in subsection (h)) for a taxable year, such farming loss shall be a net operating loss carryback to each of the 5 taxable years preceding the taxable year of such loss.

P.L. 115-97, § 13302(c)(1):

Amended Code Sec. 172(b)(1)(B), as amended by Act. Sec. 13302(b)(2), by adding at the end a new subparagraph (B). **Effective** for net operating losses arising in tax years ending after 12-31-2017.

P.L. 115-97, § 13302(d)(1):

Amended Code Sec. 172(b)(1), as amended by Act. Sec. 13302(b)(2) and (c)(1), by adding at the end a new subparagraph (C). **Effective** for net operating losses arising in tax years ending after 12-31-2017.

(d) MODIFICATIONS.—The modifications referred to in this section are as follows:

* * *

(6) MODIFICATIONS RELATED TO REAL ESTATE INVESTMENT TRUSTS.—In the case of any taxable year for which part II of subchapter M (relating to real estate investment trusts) applies to the taxpayer—

(A) the net operating loss for such taxable year shall be computed by taking into account the adjustments described in section 857(b)(2) (other than the deduction for dividends paid described in section 857(b)(2)(B));

(B) where such taxable year is a "prior taxable year" referred to in paragraph (2) of subsection (b), the term "taxable income" in such paragraph shall mean "real estate investment trust taxable income" (as defined in section 857(b)(2)); *and*

(C) *subsection (a)(2) shall be applied by substituting "real estate investment trust taxable income (as defined in section 857(b)(2) but without regard to the deduction for dividends paid (as defined in section 561))" for "taxable income".*

(7) *[Stricken.]*

(8) *QUALIFIED BUSINESS INCOME DEDUCTION.—The deduction under section 199A shall not be allowed.*

(9) *DEDUCTION FOR FOREIGN-DERIVED INTANGIBLE INCOME.—The deduction under section 250 shall not be allowed.*

* * *

[CCH Explanation at ¶ 330, ¶ 515, ¶ 530, and ¶ 735. Committee Reports at ¶ 10,030, ¶ 10,430, ¶ 10,460, and ¶ 11,080.]

Amendments

• **2017, Tax Cuts and Jobs Act (P.L. 115-97)**

P.L. 115-97, § 11011(d)(1):

Amended Code Sec. 172(d) by adding at the end a new paragraph (8). **Effective** for tax years beginning after 12-31-2017.

P.L. 115-97, § 13302(a)(3):

Amended Code Sec. 172(d)(6) by striking "and" at the end of subparagraph (A), by striking the period at the end of subparagraph (B) and inserting "; and", and by adding at the end a new subparagraph (C). **Effective** for losses arising in tax years beginning after 12-31-2017.

P.L. 115-97, § 13305(b)(3):

Amended Code Sec. 172(d) by striking paragraph (7). **Effective** for tax years beginning after 12-31-2017. Prior to being stricken, Code Sec. 172(d)(7) read as follows:

(7) MANUFACTURING DEDUCTION.—The deduction under section 199 shall not be allowed.

P.L. 115-97, § 14202(b)(1):

Amended Code Sec. 172(d), as amended by this Act, by adding at the end a new paragraph (9). **Effective** for tax years beginning after 12-31-2017.

(f) *[Stricken.]*

[CCH Explanation at ¶ 515. Committee Reports at ¶ 10,430.]

Amendments

• **2017, Tax Cuts and Jobs Act (P.L. 115-97)**

P.L. 115-97, § 13302(c)(2)(A):

Amended Code Sec. 172 by striking subsection (f). **Effective** for net operating losses arising in tax years ending after 12-31-2017. Prior to being stricken, Code Sec. 172(f) read as follows:

(f) RULES RELATING TO SPECIFIED LIABILITY LOSS.—For purposes of this section—

(1) IN GENERAL.—The term "specified liability loss" means the sum of the following amounts to the extent taken into account in computing the net operating loss for the taxable year:

(A) Any amount allowable as a deduction under section 162 or 165 which is attributable to—

(i) product liability, or

(ii) expenses incurred in the investigation or settlement of, or opposition to, claims against the taxpayer on account of product liability.

(B)(i) Any amount allowable as a deduction under this chapter (other than section 468(a)(1) or 468A(a)) which is in satisfaction of a liability under a Federal or State law requiring—

(I) the reclamation of land,

(II) the decommissioning of a nuclear power plant (or any unit thereof),

(III) the dismantlement of a drilling platform,

(IV) the remediation of environmental contamination, or

(V) a payment under any workers compensation act (within the meaning of section 461(h)(2)(C)(i)).

(ii) A liability shall be taken into account under this subparagraph only if—

(I) the act (or failure to act) giving rise to such liability occurs at least 3 years before the beginning of the taxable year, and

(II) the taxpayer used an accrual method of accounting throughout the period or periods during which such act (or failure to act) occurred.

(g) *[Stricken.]*

(2) LIMITATION.—The amount of the specified liability loss for any taxable year shall not exceed the amount of the net operating loss for such taxable year.

(3) SPECIAL RULE FOR NUCLEAR POWERPLANTS.—Except as provided in regulations prescribed by the Secretary, that portion of a specified liability loss which is attributable to amounts incurred in the decommissioning of a nuclear powerplant (or any unit thereof) may, for purposes of subsection (b)(1)(C), be carried back to each of the taxable years during the period—

(A) beginning with the taxable year in which such plant (or unit thereof) was placed in service, and

(B) ending with the taxable year preceding the loss year.

(4) PRODUCT LIABILITY.—The term "product liability" means—

(A) liability of the taxpayer for damages on account of physical injury or emotional harm to individuals, or damage to or loss of the use of property, on account of any defect in any product which is manufactured, leased, or sold by the taxpayer, but only if

(B) such injury, harm, or damage arises after the taxpayer has completed or terminated operations with respect to, and has relinquished possession of, such product.

(5) COORDINATION WITH SUBSECTION (b)(2).—For purposes of applying subsection (b)(2), a specified liability loss for any taxable year shall be treated as a separate net operating loss for such taxable year to be taken into account after the remaining portion of the net operating loss for such taxable year.

(6) ELECTION.—Any taxpayer entitled to a 10-year carryback under subsection (b)(1)(C) from any loss year may elect to have the carryback period with respect to such loss year determined without regard to subsection (b)(1)(C). Such election shall be made in such manner as may be prescribed by the Secretary and shall be made by the due date (including extensions of time) for filing the taxpayer's return for the taxable year of the net operating loss. Such election, once made for any taxable year, shall be irrevocable for that taxable year.

[CCH Explanation at ¶ 515. Committee Reports at ¶ 10,430.]

Amendments

• **2017, Tax Cuts and Jobs Act (P.L. 115-97)**

P.L. 115-97, § 13302(c)(2)(A):

Amended Code Sec. 172 by striking subsection (g). **Effective** for net operating losses arising in tax years ending after 12-31-2017. Prior to being stricken, Code Sec. 172(g) read as follows:

(g) CORPORATE EQUITY REDUCTION INTEREST LOSSES.—For purposes of this section—

(1) IN GENERAL.—The term "corporate equity reduction interest loss" means, with respect to any loss limitation year, the excess (if any) of—

(A) the net operating loss for such taxable year, over

(B) the net operating loss for such taxable year determined without regard to any allocable interest deductions otherwise taken into account in computing such loss.

(2) ALLOCABLE INTEREST DEDUCTIONS.—

(A) IN GENERAL.—The term "allocable interest deductions" means deductions allowed under this chapter for interest on the portion of any indebtedness allocable to a corporate equity reduction transaction.

(B) METHOD OF ALLOCATION.—Except as provided in regulations and subparagraph (E), indebtedness shall be allocated to a corporate equity reduction transaction in the manner prescribed under clause (ii) of section 263A(f)(2)(A) (without regard to clause (i) thereof).

(C) ALLOCABLE DEDUCTIONS NOT TO EXCEED INTEREST INCREASES.—Allocable interest deductions for any loss limitation year shall not exceed the excess (if any) of—

(i) the amount allowable as a deduction for interest paid or accrued by the taxpayer during the loss limitation year, over

(ii) the average of such amounts for the 3 taxable years preceding the taxable year in which the corporate equity reduction transaction occurred.

(D) DE MINIMIS RULE.—A taxpayer shall be treated as having no allocable interest deductions for any taxable year if the amount of such deductions (without regard to this subparagraph) is less than $1,000,000.

(E) SPECIAL RULE FOR CERTAIN UNFORESEEABLE EVENTS.—If an unforeseeable extraordinary adverse event occurs during a loss limitation year but after the corporate equity reduction transaction—

(i) indebtedness shall be allocated in the manner described in subparagraph (B) to unreimbursed costs paid or incurred in connection with such event before being allocated to the corporate equity reduction transaction, and

(ii) the amount determined under subparagraph (C)(i) shall be reduced by the amount of interest on indebtedness described in clause (i).

(3) CORPORATE EQUITY REDUCTION TRANSACTION.—

(A) IN GENERAL.—The term "corporate equity reduction transaction" means—

(i) a major stock acquisition, or

(ii) an excess distribution.

(B) MAJOR STOCK ACQUISITION.—

(i) IN GENERAL.—The term "major stock acquisition" means the acquisition by a corporation pursuant to a plan of such corporation (or any group of persons acting in concert with such corporation) of stock in another corporation representing 50 percent or more (by vote or value) of the stock in such other corporation.

(ii) EXCEPTION.—The term "major stock acquisition" does not include a qualified stock purchase (within the meaning of section 338) to which an election under section 338 applies.

(C) EXCESS DISTRIBUTION.—The term "excess distribution" means the excess (if any) of—

(i) the aggregate distributions (including redemptions) made during a taxable year by a corporation with respect to its stock, over

(ii) the greater of—

(I) 150 percent of the average of such distributions during the 3 taxable years immediately preceding such taxable year, or

(II) 10 percent of the fair market value of the stock of such corporation as of the beginning of such taxable year.

(D) RULES FOR APPLYING SUBPARAGRAPH (b).—For purposes of subparagraph (B)—

(i) PLANS TO ACQUIRE STOCK.—All plans referred to in subparagraph (B) by any corporation (or group of persons acting in concert with such corporation) with respect to another corporation shall be treated as 1 plan.

(ii) ACQUISITION DURING 24-MONTH PERIOD.—All acquisitions during any 24-month period shall be treated as pursuant to 1 plan.

(E) RULES FOR APPLYING SUBPARAGRAPH (c).—For purposes of subparagraph (C)—

(i) CERTAIN PREFERRED STOCK DISREGARDED.—Stock described in section 1504(a)(4), and distributions (including redemptions) with respect to such stock, shall be disregarded.

(ii) ISSUANCE OF STOCK.—The amounts determined under clauses (i) and (ii)(I) of subparagraph (C) shall be reduced by the aggregate amount of stock issued by the corporation during the applicable period in exchange for money or property other than stock in the corporation.

(4) OTHER RULES.—

(A) ORDERING RULE.—For purposes of paragraph (1), in determining the allocable interest deductions taken into account in computing the net operating loss for any taxable year, taxable income for such taxable year shall be treated as having been computed by taking allocable interest deductions into account after all other deductions.

(B) COORDINATION WITH SUBSECTION (b)(2).—For purposes of subsection (b)(2)—

(i) a corporate equity reduction interest loss shall be treated in a manner similar to the manner in which a specified liability loss is treated, and

(ii) in determining the net operating loss deduction for any prior taxable year referred to in the 3rd sentence of subsection (b)(2), the portion of any net operating loss which may not be carried to such taxable year under subsection (b)(1)(D) shall not be taken into account.

(C) MEMBERS OF AFFILIATED GROUPS.—Except as provided by regulations, all members of an affiliated group filing a consolidated return under section 1501 shall be treated as 1 taxpayer for purposes of this subsection and subsection (b)(1)(D).

(5) REGULATIONS.—The Secretary shall prescribe such regulations as may be necessary to carry out the purposes of this subsection, including regulations—

(A) for applying this subsection to successor corporations and in cases where a taxpayer becomes, or ceases to be, a member of an affiliated group filing a consolidated return under section 1501,

(B) to prevent the avoidance of this subsection through related parties, pass-through entities, and intermediaries, and

(C) for applying this subsection where more than 1 corporation is involved in a corporate equity reduction transaction.

(h) *[Stricken.]*

[CCH Explanation at ¶ 515. Committee Reports at ¶ 10,430.]

Amendments

• **2017, Tax Cuts and Jobs Act (P.L. 115-97)**

P.L. 115-97, § 13302(c)(2)(A):

Amended Code Sec. 172 by striking subsection (h). **Effective** for net operating losses arising in tax years ending after 12-31-2017. Prior to being stricken, Code Sec. 172(h) read as follows:

(h) RULES RELATING TO FARMING LOSSES.—For purposes of this section—

(1) IN GENERAL.—The term "farming loss" means the lesser of—

(A) the amount which would be the net operating loss for the taxable year if only income and deductions attributable to farming businesses (as defined in section 263A(e)(4)) are taken into account, or

(B) the amount of the net operating loss for such taxable year.

(2) COORDINATION WITH SUBSECTION (b)(2).—For purposes of applying subsection (b)(2), a farming loss for any taxable year shall be treated in a manner similar to the manner in which a specified liability loss is treated.

(3) ELECTION.—Any taxpayer entitled to a 5-year carryback under subsection (b)(1)(F) from any loss year may elect to have the carryback period with respect to such loss year determined without regard to subsection (b)(1)(F). Such election shall be made in such manner as may be prescribed by the Secretary and shall be made by the due date (including extensions of time) for filing the taxpayer's return for the taxable year of the net operating loss. Such election, once made for any taxable year, shall be irrevocable for such taxable year.

(f) SPECIAL RULE FOR INSURANCE COMPANIES.—In the case of an insurance company (as defined in section 816(a)) other than a life insurance company—

(1) the amount of the deduction allowed under subsection (a) shall be the aggregate of the net operating loss carryovers to such year, plus the net operating loss carrybacks to such year, and

(2) subparagraph (C) of subsection (b)(2) shall not apply.

[CCH Explanation at ¶ 515. Committee Reports at ¶ 10,430.]

Amendments

• **2017, Tax Cuts and Jobs Act (P.L. 115-97)**

P.L. 115-97, § 13302(d)(2):

Amended Code Sec. 172, as amended by Act. Sec. 13302(c)(2)(A), by redesignating subsection (f) as subsection (g) and inserting after subsection (e) a new subsection (f). **Effective** for losses arising in tax years beginning after 12-31-2017.

(g) CROSS REFERENCES.—

(1) For treatment of net operating loss carryovers in certain corporate acquisitions, see section 381.

(2) For special limitation on net operating loss carryovers in case of a corporate change of ownership, see section 382.

[CCH Explanation at ¶ 515. Committee Reports at ¶ 10,430.]

Amendments

• **2017, Tax Cuts and Jobs Act (P.L. 115-97)**

P.L. 115-97, § 13302(c)(2)(A):

Amended Code Sec. 172 by striking subsections (f), (g), and (h), and by redesignating subsection (i) as subsection (f). **Effective** for net operating losses arising in tax years ending after 12-31-2017.

P.L. 115-97, § 13302(d)(2):

Amended Code Sec. 172, as amended by Act Sec. 13302(c)(2)(A), by redesignating subsection (f) as subsection (g). **Effective** for losses arising in tax years beginning after 12-31-2017.

>>> → Caution: Code Sec. 174, below, as amended by P.L. 115-97, applies to amounts paid or incurred in tax years beginning after December 31, 2021.

[¶ 5330] CODE SEC. 174. *AMORTIZATION OF RESEARCH AND EXPERIMENTAL EXPENDITURES.*

(a) IN GENERAL.—In the case of a taxpayer's specified research or experimental expenditures for any taxable year—

(1) except as provided in paragraph (2), no deduction shall be allowed for such expenditures, and

(2) the taxpayer shall—

(A) charge such expenditures to capital account, and

(B) be allowed an amortization deduction of such expenditures ratably over the 5-year period (15-year period in the case of any specified research or experimental expenditures which are attributable to foreign research (within the meaning of section 41(d)(4)(F))) beginning with the midpoint of the taxable year in which such expenditures are paid or incurred.

(b) SPECIFIED RESEARCH OR EXPERIMENTAL EXPENDITURES.—For purposes of this section, the term "specified research or experimental expenditures" means, with respect to any taxable year, research or experimental expenditures which are paid or incurred by the taxpayer during such taxable year in connection with the taxpayer's trade or business.

(c) SPECIAL RULES.—

(1) LAND AND OTHER PROPERTY.—This section shall not apply to any expenditure for the acquisition or improvement of land, or for the acquisition or improvement of property to be used in connection with

the research or experimentation and of a character which is subject to the allowance under section 167 (relating to allowance for depreciation, etc.) or section 611 (relating to allowance for depletion); but for purposes of this section allowances under section 167, and allowances under section 611, shall be considered as expenditures.

(2) EXPLORATION EXPENDITURES.—This section shall not apply to any expenditure paid or incurred for the purpose of ascertaining the existence, location, extent, or quality of any deposit of ore or other mineral (including oil and gas).

(3) SOFTWARE DEVELOPMENT.—For purposes of this section, any amount paid or incurred in connection with the development of any software shall be treated as a research or experimental expenditure.

(d) TREATMENT UPON DISPOSITION, RETIREMENT, OR ABANDONMENT.—If any property with respect to which specified research or experimental expenditures are paid or incurred is disposed, retired, or abandoned during the period during which such expenditures are allowed as an amortization deduction under this section, no deduction shall be allowed with respect to such expenditures on account of such disposition, retirement, or abandonment and such amortization deduction shall continue with respect to such expenditures.

[CCH Explanation at ¶525. Committee Reports at ¶10,390.]

Amendments

• 2017, Tax Cuts and Jobs Act (P.L. 115-97)

P.L. 115-97, §13206(a):

Amended Code Sec. 174. **Effective** for amounts paid or incurred in tax years beginning after 12-31-2021. For a special rule, see Act Sec. 13206(b), below.

P.L. 115-97, §13206(b), provides:

(b) CHANGE IN METHOD OF ACCOUNTING.—The amendments made by subsection (a) shall be treated as a change in method of accounting for purposes of section 481 of the Internal Revenue Code of 1986 and—

(1) such change shall be treated as initiated by the taxpayer,

(2) such change shall be treated as made with the consent of the Secretary, and

(3) such change shall be applied only on a cut-off basis for any research or experimental expenditures paid or incurred in taxable years beginning after December 31, 2021, and no adjustments under section 481(a) shall be made.

Prior to amendment, Code Sec. 174 read as follows:

SEC. 174. RESEARCH AND EXPERIMENTAL EXPENDITURES.

(a) TREATMENT AS EXPENSES.—

(1) IN GENERAL.—A taxpayer may treat research or experimental expenditures which are paid or incurred by him during the taxable year in connection with his trade or business as expenses which are not chargeable to capital account. The expenditures so treated shall be allowed as a deduction.

(2) WHEN METHOD MAY BE ADOPTED.—

(A) WITHOUT CONSENT.—A taxpayer may, without the consent of the Secretary, adopt the method provided in this subsection for his first taxable year for which expenditures described in paragraph (1) are paid or incurred.

(B) WITH CONSENT.—A taxpayer may, with the consent of the Secretary, adopt at any time the method provided in this subsection.

(3) SCOPE.—The method adopted under this subsection shall apply to all expenditures described in paragraph (1). The method adopted shall be adhered to in computing taxable income for the taxable year and for all subsequent taxable years unless, with the approval of the Secretary, a change to a different method is authorized with respect to part or all of such expenditures.

(b) AMORTIZATION OF CERTAIN RESEARCH AND EXPERIMENTAL EXPENDITURES.—

(1) IN GENERAL.—At the election of the taxpayer, made in accordance with regulations prescribed by the Secretary, research or experimental expenditures which are—

(A) paid or incurred by the taxpayer in connection with his trade or business,

(B) not treated as expenses under subsection (a), and

(C) chargeable to capital account but not chargeable to property of a character which is subject to the allowance under section 167 (relating to allowance for depreciation, etc.) or section 611 (relating to allowance for depletion),

may be treated as deferred expenses. In computing taxable income, such deferred expenses shall be allowed as a deduction ratably over such period of not less than 60 months as may be selected by the taxpayer (beginning with the month in which the taxpayer first realizes benefits from such expenditures). Such deferred expenses are expenditures properly chargeable to capital account for purposes of section 1016(a)(1) (relating to adjustments to basis of property).

(2) TIME FOR AND SCOPE OF ELECTION.—The election provided by paragraph (1) may be made for any taxable year, but only if made not later than the time prescribed by law for filing the return for such taxable year (including extensions thereof). The method so elected, and the period selected by the taxpayer, shall be adhered to in computing taxable income for the taxable year for which the election is made and for all subsequent taxable years unless, with the approval of the Secretary, a change to a different method (or to a different period) is authorized with respect to part or all of such expenditures. The election shall not apply to any expenditure paid or incurred during any taxable year before the taxable year for which the taxpayer makes the election.

(c) LAND AND OTHER PROPERTY.—This section shall not apply to any expenditure for the acquisition or improvement of land, or for the acquisition or improvement of property to be used in connection with the research or experimentation and of a character which is subject to the allowance under section 167 (relating to allowance for depreciation, etc.) or section 611 (relating to allowance for depletion); but for purposes of this section allowances under section 167, and allowances under section 611, shall be considered as expenditures.

(d) EXPLORATION EXPENDITURES.—This section shall not apply to any expenditure paid or incurred for the purpose of ascertaining the existence, location, extent, or quality of any deposit of ore or other mineral (including oil and gas).

(e) ONLY REASONABLE RESEARCH EXPENDITURES ELIGIBLE.— This section shall apply to a research or experimental expenditure only to the extent that the amount thereof is reasonable under the circumstances.

(f) CROSS REFERENCES.—

(1) For adjustments to basis of property for amounts allowed as deductions as deferred expenses under subsection (b), see section 1016(a)(14).

(2) For election of 10-year amortization of expenditures allowable as a deduction under subsection (a), see section 59(e).

[¶5335] CODE SEC. 179. ELECTION TO EXPENSE CERTAIN DEPRECIABLE BUSINESS ASSETS.

* * *

(b) LIMITATIONS.—

(1) DOLLAR LIMITATION.—The aggregate cost which may be taken into account under subsection (a) for any taxable year shall not exceed $1,000,000.

(2) REDUCTION IN LIMITATION.—The limitation under paragraph (1) for any taxable year shall be reduced (but not below zero) by the amount by which the cost of section 179 property placed in service during such taxable year exceeds $2,500,000.

* * *

(6) INFLATION ADJUSTMENT.—

(A) IN GENERAL.—In the case of any taxable year beginning after *2018*, the dollar amounts in *paragraphs (1), (2), and (5)(A)* shall each be increased by an amount equal to—

(i) such dollar amount, multiplied by

(ii) the cost-of-living adjustment determined under section 1(f)(3) for the calendar year in which the taxable year begins, determined by substituting *calendar year 2017 for "calendar year 2016" in subparagraph (A)(ii)* thereof.

(B) ROUNDING.—The amount of any increase under subparagraph (A) shall be rounded to the nearest multiple of $10,000 (*$100 in the case of any increase in the amount under paragraph (5)(A)*).

* * *

[CCH Explanation at ¶125 and ¶405. Committee Reports at ¶10,020 and ¶10,320.]

Amendments

• **2017, Tax Cuts and Jobs Act (P.L. 115-97)**

P.L. 115-97, §11002(d)(1)(R):

Amended Code Sec. 179(b)(6)(A)(ii) by striking "for 'calendar year 1992' in subparagraph (B)" and inserting "for 'calendar year 2016' in subparagraph (A)(ii)". **Effective** for tax years beginning after 12-31-2017.

P.L. 115-97, §13101(a)(1):

Amended Code Sec. 179(b)(1) by striking "$500,000" and inserting "$1,000,000". **Effective** for property placed in service in tax years beginning after 12-31-2017.

P.L. 115-97, §13101(a)(2):

Amended Code Sec. 179(b)(2) by striking "$2,000,000" and inserting "$2,500,000". **Effective** for property placed in service in tax years beginning after 12-31-2017.

P.L. 115-97, §13101(a)(3)(A)(i)-(ii):

Amended Code Sec. 179(b)(6)(A), as amended by Act Sec. 11002(d), by striking "2015" and inserting "2018", and in clause (ii), by striking "calendar year 2014" and inserting "calendar year 2017". **Effective** for property placed in service in tax years beginning after 12-31-2017.

P.L. 115-97, §13101(a)(3)(B)(i)-(ii):

Amended Code Sec. 179(b)(6) by striking "paragraphs (1) and (2)" in subparagraph (A) and inserting "paragraphs (1), (2), and (5)(A)", and by inserting "($100 in the case of any increase in the amount under paragraph (5)(A))" after "$10,000" in subparagraph (B). **Effective** for property placed in service in tax years beginning after 12-31-2017.

(d) DEFINITIONS AND SPECIAL RULES.—

(1) SECTION 179 PROPERTY.—For purposes of this section, the term "section 179 property" means property—

(A) which is—

(i) tangible property (to which section 168 applies), or

      (ii) computer software (as defined in section 197(e)(3)(B)) which is described in section 197(e)(3)(A)(i) and to which section 167 applies,

    (B) which is—

      (i) section 1245 property (as defined in section 1245(a)(3)), or

      (ii) at the election of the taxpayer, qualified real property (as defined in subsection (f)), and

    (C) which is acquired by purchase for use in the active conduct of a trade or business.

Such term shall not include any property described in section 50(b) *(other than paragraph (2) thereof)*.

* * *

[CCH Explanation at ¶ 405. Committee Reports at ¶ 10,320.]

Amendments

• **2017, Tax Cuts and Jobs Act (P.L. 115-97)**

P.L. 115-97, § 13101(b)(1):

Amended Code Sec. 179(d)(1)(B). **Effective** for property placed in service in tax years beginning after 12-31-2017. Prior to amendment, Code Sec. 179(d)(1)(B) read as follows:

(B) which is section 1245 property (as defined in section 1245(a)(3)), and

P.L. 115-97, § 13101(c):

Amended the last sentence of Code Sec. 179(d)(1) by inserting "(other than paragraph (2) thereof)" after "section 50(b)". **Effective** for property placed in service in tax years beginning after 12-31-2017.

    (f) QUALIFIED REAL PROPERTY.—For purposes of this section, the term "qualified real property" means—

      (1) any qualified improvement property described in section 168(e)(6), and

      (2) any of the following improvements to nonresidential real property placed in service after the date such property was first placed in service:

        (A) Roofs.

        (B) Heating, ventilation, and air-conditioning property.

        (C) Fire protection and alarm systems.

        (D) Security systems.

[CCH Explanation at ¶ 405. Committee Reports at ¶ 10,320.]

Amendments

• **2017, Tax Cuts and Jobs Act (P.L. 115-97)**

P.L. 115-97, § 13101(b)(2):

Amended Code Sec. 179(f). **Effective** for property placed in service in tax years beginning after 12-31-2017. Prior to amendment, Code Sec. 179(f) read as follows:

(f) SPECIAL RULES FOR QUALIFIED REAL PROPERTY.—

(1) IN GENERAL.—If a taxpayer elects the application of this subsection for any taxable year, the term "section 179 property" shall include any qualified real property which is—

(A) of a character subject to an allowance for depreciation,

(B) acquired by purchase for use in the active conduct of a trade or business, and

(C) not described in the last sentence of subsection (d)(1).

(2) QUALIFIED REAL PROPERTY.—For purposes of this subsection, the term "qualified real property" means—

(A) qualified leasehold improvement property described in section 168(e)(6),

(B) qualified restaurant property described in section 168(e)(7), and

(C) qualified retail improvement property described in section 168(e)(8).

[¶ 5340] CODE SEC. 199. INCOME ATTRIBUTABLE TO DOMESTIC PRODUCTION ACTIVITIES. [*Stricken.*]

[CCH Explanation at ¶ 530. Committee Reports at ¶ 10,460.]

Amendments

• **2017, Tax Cuts and Jobs Act (P.L. 115-97)**

P.L. 115-97, § 13305(a):

Amended part VI of subchapter B of chapter 1, by striking Code Sec. 199. **Effective** for tax years beginning after 12-31-2017. Prior to being stricken, Code Sec. 199 read as follows:

SEC. 199. INCOME ATTRIBUTABLE TO DOMESTIC PRODUCTION ACTIVITIES.

(a) ALLOWANCE OF DEDUCTION.—There shall be allowed as a deduction an amount equal to 9 percent of the lesser of—

(1) the qualified production activities income of the taxpayer for the taxable year, or

(2) taxable income (determined without regard to this section) for the taxable year.

(b) DEDUCTION LIMITED TO WAGES PAID.—

(1) IN GENERAL.—The amount of the deduction allowable under subsection (a) for any taxable year shall not exceed 50 percent of the W-2 wages of the taxpayer for the taxable year.

(2) W-2 WAGES.—For purposes of this section—

(A) IN GENERAL.—The term "W-2 wages" means, with respect to any person for any taxable year of such person, the sum of the amounts described in paragraphs (3) and (8) of section 6051(a) paid by such person with respect to employment of employees by such person during the calendar year ending during such taxable year.

(B) LIMITATION TO WAGES ATTRIBUTABLE TO DOMESTIC PRODUCTION.—Such term shall not include any amount which is not properly allocable to domestic production gross receipts for purposes of subsection (c)(1).

(C) RETURN REQUIREMENT.—Such term shall not include any amount which is not properly included in a return filed with the Social Security Administration on or before the 60th day after the due date (including extensions) for such return.

(D) SPECIAL RULE FOR QUALIFIED FILM.—In the case of a qualified film, such term shall include compensation for services performed in the United States by actors, production personnel, directors, and producers.

(3) ACQUISITIONS, DISPOSITIONS, AND SHORT TAXABLE YEARS.—The Secretary shall provide for the application of this subsection in cases of a short taxable year or where the taxpayer acquires, or disposes of, the major portion of a trade or business or the major portion of a separate unit of a trade or business during the taxable year.

(c) QUALIFIED PRODUCTION ACTIVITIES INCOME.—For purposes of this section—

(1) IN GENERAL.—The term "qualified production activities income" for any taxable year means an amount equal to the excess (if any) of—

(A) the taxpayer's domestic production gross receipts for such taxable year, over

(B) the sum of—

(i) the cost of goods sold that are allocable to such receipts, and

(ii) other expenses, losses, or deductions (other than the deduction allowed under this section), which are properly allocable to such receipts.

(2) ALLOCATION METHOD.—The Secretary shall prescribe rules for the proper allocation of items described in paragraph (1) for purposes of determining qualified production activities income. Such rules shall provide for the proper allocation of items whether or not such items are directly allocable to domestic production gross receipts.

(3) SPECIAL RULES FOR DETERMINING COSTS.—

(A) IN GENERAL.—For purposes of determining costs under clause (i) of paragraph (1)(B), any item or service brought into the United States shall be treated as acquired by purchase, and its cost shall be treated as not less than its value immediately after it entered the United States. A similar rule shall apply in determining the adjusted basis of leased or rented property where the lease or rental gives rise to domestic production gross receipts.

(B) EXPORTS FOR FURTHER MANUFACTURE.—In the case of any property described in subparagraph (A) that had been exported by the taxpayer for further manufacture, the increase in cost or adjusted basis under subparagraph (A) shall not exceed the difference between the value of the property when exported and the value of the property when brought back into the United States after the further manufacture.

(C) TRANSPORTATION COSTS OF INDEPENDENT REFINERS.—

(i) IN GENERAL.—In the case of any taxpayer who is in the trade or business of refining crude oil and who is not a major integrated oil company (as defined in section 167(h)(5)(B), determined without regard to clause (iii) thereof) for the taxable year, in computing oil related qualified production activities income under subsection (d)(9)(B), the amount allocated to domestic production gross receipts under paragraph (1)(B) for costs related to the transportation of oil shall be 25 percent of the amount properly allocable under such paragraph (determined without regard to this subparagraph).

(ii) TERMINATION.—Clause (i) shall not apply to any taxable year beginning after December 31, 2021.

(4) DOMESTIC PRODUCTION GROSS RECEIPTS.—

(A) IN GENERAL.—The term "domestic production gross receipts" means the gross receipts of the taxpayer which are derived from—

(i) any lease, rental, license, sale, exchange, or other disposition of—

(I) qualifying production property which was manufactured, produced, grown, or extracted by the taxpayer in whole or in significant part within the United States,

(II) any qualified film produced by the taxpayer, or

(III) electricity, natural gas, or potable water produced by the taxpayer in the United States,

(ii) in the case of a taxpayer engaged in the active conduct of a construction trade or business, construction of real property performed in the United States by the taxpayer in the ordinary course of such trade or business, or

(iii) in the case of a taxpayer engaged in the active conduct of an engineering or architectural services trade or business, engineering or architectural services performed in the United States by the taxpayer in the ordinary course of such trade or business with respect to the construction of real property in the United States.

(B) EXCEPTIONS.—Such term shall not include gross receipts of the taxpayer which are derived from—

(i) the sale of food and beverages prepared by the taxpayer at a retail establishment,

(ii) the transmission or distribution of electricity, natural gas, or potable water, or

(iii) the lease, rental, license, sale, exchange, or other disposition of land.

(C) SPECIAL RULE FOR CERTAIN GOVERNMENT CONTRACTS.—Gross receipts derived from the manufacture or production of any property described in subparagraph (A)(i)(I) shall be treated as meeting the requirements of subparagraph (A)(i) if—

(i) such property is manufactured or produced by the taxpayer pursuant to a contract with the Federal Government, and

(ii) the Federal Acquisition Regulation requires that title or risk of loss with respect to such property be transferred to the Federal Government before the manufacture or production of such property is complete.

(D) PARTNERSHIPS OWNED BY EXPANDED AFFILIATED GROUPS.—For purposes of this paragraph, if all of the interests in the capital and profits of a partnership are owned by members of a single expanded affiliated group at all times during the taxable year of such partnership, the partnership and all members of such group shall be treated as a single taxpayer during such period.

(5) QUALIFYING PRODUCTION PROPERTY.—The term "qualifying production property" means—

(A) tangible personal property,

(B) any computer software, and

(C) any property described in section 168(f)(4).

(6) QUALIFIED FILM.—The term "qualified film" means any property described in section 168(f)(3) if not less than 50 percent of the total compensation relating to the production of such property is compensation for services performed in the United States by actors, production personnel, directors, and producers. Such term does not include property with respect to which records are required to be maintained under section 2257 of title 18, United States Code. A qualified film shall include any copyrights, trademarks, or other intangibles with respect to such film. The methods and means of distributing a qualified film shall not affect the availability of the deduction under this section.

(7) RELATED PERSONS.—

(A) IN GENERAL.—The term "domestic production gross receipts" shall not include any gross receipts of the taxpayer derived from property leased, licensed, or rented by the taxpayer for use by any related person.

(B) RELATED PERSON.—For purposes of subparagraph (A), a person shall be treated as related to another person if such persons are treated as a single employer under subsection (a) or (b) of section 52 or subsection (m) or (o) of section 414, except that determinations under subsections (a) and (b) of section 52 shall be made without regard to section 1563(b).

(d) DEFINITIONS AND SPECIAL RULES.—

(1) APPLICATION OF SECTION TO PASS-THRU ENTITIES.—

(A) PARTNERSHIPS AND S CORPORATIONS.—In the case of a partnership or S corporation—

(i) this section shall be applied at the partner or shareholder level,

(ii) each partner or shareholder shall take into account such person's allocable share of each item described in subparagraph (A) or (B) of subsection (c)(1) (determined without regard to whether the items described in such subparagraph (A) exceed the items described in such subparagraph (B)),

(iii) each partner or shareholder shall be treated for purposes of subsection (b) as having W-2 wages for the taxable year in an amount equal to such person's allocable share of the W-2 wages of the partnership or S corporation for the taxable year (as determined under regulations prescribed by the Secretary), and

(iv) in the case of each partner of a partnership, or shareholder of an S corporation, who owns (directly or indirectly) at least 20 percent of the capital interests in such partnership or of the stock of such S corporation—

(I) such partner or shareholder shall be treated as having engaged directly in any film produced by such partnership or S corporation, and

(II) such partnership or S corporation shall be treated as having engaged directly in any film produced by such partner or shareholder.

(B) TRUSTS AND ESTATES.—In the case of a trust or estate—

(i) the items referred to in subparagraph (A)(ii) (as determined therein) and the W-2 wages of the trust or estate for the taxable year, shall be apportioned between the beneficiaries and the fiduciary (and among the beneficiaries) under regulations prescribed by the Secretary, and

(ii) for purposes of paragraph (2), adjusted gross income of the trust or estate shall be determined as provided in section 67(e) with the adjustments described in such paragraph.

(C) REGULATIONS.—The Secretary may prescribe rules requiring or restricting the allocation of items and wages under this paragraph and may prescribe such reporting requirements as the Secretary determines appropriate.

(2) APPLICATION TO INDIVIDUALS.—In the case of an individual, subsections (a)(2) and (d)(9)(A)(iii) shall be applied by substituting "adjusted gross income" for "taxable income". For purposes of the preceding sentence, adjusted gross income shall be determined—

(A) after application of sections 86, 135, 137, 219, 221, 222, and 469, and

(B) without regard to this section.

(3) AGRICULTURAL AND HORTICULTURAL COOPERATIVES.—

(A) DEDUCTION ALLOWED TO PATRONS.—Any person who receives a qualified payment from a specified agricultural or horticultural cooperative shall be allowed for the taxable year in which such payment is received a deduction under subsection (a) equal to the portion of the deduction allowed under subsection (a) to such cooperative which is—

(i) allowed with respect to the portion of the qualified production activities income to which such payment is attributable, and

(ii) identified by such cooperative in a written notice mailed to such person during the payment period described in section 1382(d).

(B) COOPERATIVE DENIED DEDUCTION FOR PORTION OF QUALIFIED PAYMENTS.—The taxable income of a specified agricultural or horticultural cooperative shall not be reduced under section 1382 by reason of that portion of any qualified payment as does not exceed the deduction allowable under subparagraph (A) with respect to such payment.

(C) TAXABLE INCOME OF COOPERATIVES DETERMINED WITHOUT REGARD TO CERTAIN DEDUCTIONS.—For purposes of this section, the taxable income of a specified agricultural or horticultural cooperative shall be computed without regard to any deduction allowable under subsection (b) or (c) of section 1382 (relating to patronage dividends, per-unit retain allocations, and nonpatronage distributions).

(D) SPECIAL RULE FOR MARKETING COOPERATIVES.—For purposes of this section, a specified agricultural or horticultural cooperative described in subparagraph (F)(ii) shall be treated as having manufactured, produced, grown, or extracted in whole or significant part any qualifying production property marketed by the organization which its patrons have so manufactured, produced, grown, or extracted.

(E) QUALIFIED PAYMENT.—For purposes of this paragraph, the term "qualified payment" means, with respect to any person, any amount which—

(i) is described in paragraph (1) or (3) of section 1385(a),

(ii) is received by such person from a specified agricultural or horticultural cooperative, and

(iii) is attributable to qualified production activities income with respect to which a deduction is allowed to such cooperative under subsection (a).

(F) SPECIFIED AGRICULTURAL OR HORTICULTURAL COOPERATIVE.—For purposes of this paragraph, the term "specified agricultural or horticultural cooperative" means an organization to which part I of subchapter T applies which is engaged—

(i) in the manufacturing, production, growth, or extraction in whole or significant part of any agricultural or horticultural product, or

(ii) in the marketing of agricultural or horticultural products.

(4) SPECIAL RULE FOR AFFILIATED GROUPS.—

(A) IN GENERAL.—All members of an expanded affiliated group shall be treated as a single corporation for purposes of this section.

(B) EXPANDED AFFILIATED GROUP.—For purposes of this section, the term "expanded affiliated group" means an affiliated group as defined in section 1504(a), determined—

(i) by substituting "more than 50 percent" for "at least 80 percent" each place it appears, and

(ii) without regard to paragraphs (2) and (4) of section 1504(b).

(C) ALLOCATION OF DEDUCTION.—Except as provided in regulations, the deduction under subsection (a) shall be allocated among the members of the expanded affiliated group in proportion to each member's respective amount (if any) of qualified production activities income.

(5) TRADE OR BUSINESS REQUIREMENT.—This section shall be applied by only taking into account items which are attributable to the actual conduct of a trade or business.

(6) COORDINATION WITH MINIMUM TAX.—For purposes of determining alternative minimum taxable income under section 55—

(A) qualified production activities income shall be determined without regard to any adjustments under sections 56 through 59, and

(B) in the case of a corporation, subsection (a)(2) shall be applied by substituting "alternative minimum taxable income" for "taxable income".

(7) UNRELATED BUSINESS TAXABLE INCOME.—For purposes of determining the tax imposed by section 511, subsection (a)(1)(B) shall be applied by substituting "unrelated business taxable income" for "taxable income".

(8) TREATMENT OF ACTIVITIES IN PUERTO RICO.—

(A) IN GENERAL.—In the case of any taxpayer with gross receipts for any taxable year from sources within the Commonwealth of Puerto Rico, if all of such receipts are taxable under section 1 or 11 for such taxable year, then for purposes of determining the domestic production gross receipts of such taxpayer for such taxable year under subsection (c)(4), the term "United States" shall include the Commonwealth of Puerto Rico.

(B) SPECIAL RULE FOR APPLYING WAGE LIMITATION.—In the case of any taxpayer described in subparagraph (A), for purposes of applying the limitation under subsection (b) for any taxable year, the determination of W-2 wages of such taxpayer shall be made without regard to any exclusion under section 3401(a)(8) for remuneration paid for services performed in Puerto Rico.

(C) TERMINATION.—This paragraph shall apply only with respect to the first 11 taxable years of the taxpayer beginning after December 31, 2005, and before January 1, 2017.

(9) SPECIAL RULE FOR TAXPAYERS WITH OIL RELATED QUALIFIED PRODUCTION ACTIVITIES INCOME.—

(A) IN GENERAL.—If a taxpayer has oil related qualified production activities income for any taxable year beginning after 2009, the amount otherwise allowable as a deduction under subsection (a) shall be reduced by 3 percent of the least of—

(i) the oil related qualified production activities income of the taxpayer for the taxable year,

(ii) the qualified production activities income of the taxpayer for the taxable year, or

(iii) taxable income (determined without regard to this section).

(B) OIL RELATED QUALIFIED PRODUCTION ACTIVITIES INCOME.—For purposes of this paragraph, the term "oil related qualified production activities income" means for any taxable year the qualified production activities income which is attributable to the production, refining, processing, transportation, or distribution of oil, gas, or any primary product thereof during such taxable year.

(C) PRIMARY PRODUCT.—For purposes of this paragraph, the term "primary product'" has the same meaning as when used in section 927(a)(2)(C), as in effect before its repeal.

(10) REGULATIONS.—The Secretary shall prescribe such regulations as are necessary to carry out the purposes of this section, including regulations which prevent more than 1 taxpayer from being allowed a deduction under this section with respect to any activity described in subsection (c)(4)(A)(i).

[¶ 5345] CODE SEC. 199A. QUALIFIED BUSINESS INCOME.

(a) IN GENERAL.—In the case of a taxpayer other than a corporation, there shall be allowed as a deduction for any taxable year an amount equal to the sum of—

(1) the lesser of—

(A) the combined qualified business income amount of the taxpayer, or

(B) an amount equal to 20 percent of the excess (if any) of—

(i) the taxable income of the taxpayer for the taxable year, over

(ii) the sum of any net capital gain (as defined in section 1(h)), plus the aggregate amount of the qualified cooperative dividends, of the taxpayer for the taxable year, plus

(2) the lesser of—

(A) 20 percent of the aggregate amount of the qualified cooperative dividends of the taxpayer for the taxable year, or

(B) taxable income (reduced by the net capital gain (as so defined)) of the taxpayer for the taxable year.

The amount determined under the preceding sentence shall not exceed the taxable income (reduced by the net capital gain (as so defined)) of the taxpayer for the taxable year.

(b) COMBINED QUALIFIED BUSINESS INCOME AMOUNT.—For purposes of this section—

(1) IN GENERAL.—The term "combined qualified business income amount" means, with respect to any taxable year, an amount equal to—

(A) the sum of the amounts determined under paragraph (2) for each qualified trade or business carried on by the taxpayer, plus

(B) 20 percent of the aggregate amount of the qualified REIT dividends and qualified publicly traded partnership income of the taxpayer for the taxable year.

(2) DETERMINATION OF DEDUCTIBLE AMOUNT FOR EACH TRADE OR BUSINESS.—The amount determined under this paragraph with respect to any qualified trade or business is the lesser of—

(A) 20 percent of the taxpayer's qualified business income with respect to the qualified trade or business, or

(B) the greater of—

(i) 50 percent of the W–2 wages with respect to the qualified trade or business, or

(ii) the sum of 25 percent of the W–2 wages with respect to the qualified trade or business, plus 2.5 percent of the unadjusted basis immediately after acquisition of all qualified property.

(3) MODIFICATIONS TO LIMIT BASED ON TAXABLE INCOME.—

(A) EXCEPTION FROM LIMIT.—In the case of any taxpayer whose taxable income for the taxable year does not exceed the threshold amount, paragraph (2) shall be applied without regard to subparagraph (B).

(B) PHASE-IN OF LIMIT FOR CERTAIN TAXPAYERS.—

(i) IN GENERAL.—If—

(I) the taxable income of a taxpayer for any taxable year exceeds the threshold amount, but does not exceed the sum of the threshold amount plus $50,000 ($100,000 in the case of a joint return), and

(II) the amount determined under paragraph (2)(B) (determined without regard to this subparagraph) with respect to any qualified trade or business carried on by the taxpayer is less than the amount determined under paragraph (2)(A) with respect [to] such trade or business,

then paragraph (2) shall be applied with respect to such trade or business without regard to subparagraph (B) thereof and by reducing the amount determined under subparagraph (A) thereof by the amount determined under clause (ii).

(ii) AMOUNT OF REDUCTION.—The amount determined under this subparagraph is the amount which bears the same ratio to the excess amount as—

(I) the amount by which the taxpayer's taxable income for the taxable year exceeds the threshold amount, bears to

(II) $50,000 ($100,000 in the case of a joint return).

(iii) EXCESS AMOUNT.—For purposes of clause (ii), the excess amount is the excess of—

(I) the amount determined under paragraph (2)(A) (determined without regard to this paragraph), over

(II) the amount determined under paragraph (2)(B) (determined without regard to this paragraph).

(4) WAGES, ETC.—

(A) IN GENERAL.—The term "W–2 wages" means, with respect to any person for any taxable year of such person, the amounts described in paragraphs (3) and (8) of section 6051(a) paid by such person with respect to employment of employees by such person during the calendar year ending during such taxable year.

(B) LIMITATION TO WAGES ATTRIBUTABLE TO QUALIFIED BUSINESS INCOME.—Such term shall not include any amount which is not properly allocable to qualified business income for purposes of subsection (c)(1).

(C) RETURN REQUIREMENT.—*Such term shall not include any amount which is not properly included in a return filed with the Social Security Administration on or before the 60th day after the due date (including extensions) for such return.*

(5) ACQUISITIONS, DISPOSITIONS, AND SHORT TAXABLE YEARS.—*The Secretary shall provide for the application of this subsection in cases of a short taxable year or where the taxpayer acquires, or disposes of, the major portion of a trade or business or the major portion of a separate unit of a trade or business during the taxable year.*

(6) QUALIFIED PROPERTY.—*For purposes of this section:*

(A) IN GENERAL.—*The term "qualified property" means, with respect to any qualified trade or business for a taxable year, tangible property of a character subject to the allowance for depreciation under section 167—*

(i) *which is held by, and available for use in, the qualified trade or business at the close of the taxable year,*

(ii) *which is used at any point during the taxable year in the production of qualified business income, and*

(iii) *the depreciable period for which has not ended before the close of the taxable year.*

(B) DEPRECIABLE PERIOD.—*The term "depreciable period" means, with respect to qualified property of a taxpayer, the period beginning on the date the property was first placed in service by the taxpayer and ending on the later of—*

(i) *the date that is 10 years after such date, or*

(ii) *the last day of the last full year in the applicable recovery period that would apply to the property under section 168 (determined without regard to subsection (g) thereof).*

(c) QUALIFIED BUSINESS INCOME.—*For purposes of this section—*

(1) IN GENERAL.—*The term "qualified business income" means, for any taxable year, the net amount of qualified items of income, gain, deduction, and loss with respect to any qualified trade or business of the taxpayer. Such term shall not include any qualified REIT dividends, qualified cooperative dividends, or qualified publicly traded partnership income.*

(2) CARRYOVER OF LOSSES.—*If the net amount of qualified income, gain, deduction, and loss with respect to qualified trades or businesses of the taxpayer for any taxable year is less than zero, such amount shall be treated as a loss from a qualified trade or business in the succeeding taxable year.*

(3) QUALIFIED ITEMS OF INCOME, GAIN, DEDUCTION, AND LOSS.—*For purposes of this subsection—*

(A) IN GENERAL.—*The term "qualified items of income, gain, deduction, and loss" means items of income, gain, deduction, and loss to the extent such items are—*

(i) *effectively connected with the conduct of a trade or business within the United States (within the meaning of section 864(c), determined by substituting "qualified trade or business (within the meaning of section 199A)" for "nonresident alien individual or a foreign corporation" or for "a foreign corporation" each place it appears), and*

(ii) *included or allowed in determining taxable income for the taxable year.*

(B) EXCEPTIONS.—*The following investment items shall not be taken into account as a qualified item of income, gain, deduction, or loss:*

(i) *Any item of short-term capital gain, short-term capital loss, long-term capital gain, or long-term capital loss.*

(ii) *Any dividend, income equivalent to a dividend, or payment in lieu of dividends described in section 954(c)(1)(G).*

(iii) *Any interest income other than interest income which is properly allocable to a trade or business.*

(iv) *Any item of gain or loss described in subparagraph (C) or (D) of section 954(c)(1) (applied by substituting "qualified trade or business" for "controlled foreign corporation").*

(v) Any item of income, gain, deduction, or loss taken into account under section 954(c)(1)(F) (determined without regard to clause (ii) thereof and other than items attributable to notional principal contracts entered into in transactions qualifying under section 1221(a)(7)).

(vi) Any amount received from an annuity which is not received in connection with the trade or business.

(vii) Any item of deduction or loss properly allocable to an amount described in any of the preceding clauses.

(4) TREATMENT OF REASONABLE COMPENSATION AND GUARANTEED PAYMENTS.—Qualified business income shall not include—

(A) reasonable compensation paid to the taxpayer by any qualified trade or business of the taxpayer for services rendered with respect to the trade or business,

(B) any guaranteed payment described in section 707(c) paid to a partner for services rendered with respect to the trade or business, and

(C) to the extent provided in regulations, any payment described in section 707(a) to a partner for services rendered with respect to the trade or business.

(d) QUALIFIED TRADE OR BUSINESS.—For purposes of this section—

(1) IN GENERAL.—The term "qualified trade or business" means any trade or business other than—

(A) a specified service trade or business, or

(B) the trade or business of performing services as an employee.

(2) SPECIFIED SERVICE TRADE OR BUSINESS.—The term "specified service trade or business" means any trade or business—

(A) which is described in section 1202(e)(3)(A) (applied without regard to the words "engineering, architecture,") or which would be so described if the term "employees or owners" were substituted for "employees" therein, or

(B) which involves the performance of services that consist of investing and investment management, trading, or dealing in securities (as defined in section 475(c)(2)), partnership interests, or commodities (as defined in section 475(e)(2)).

(3) EXCEPTION FOR SPECIFIED SERVICE BUSINESSES BASED ON TAXPAYER'S INCOME.—

(A) IN GENERAL.—If, for any taxable year, the taxable income of any taxpayer is less than the sum of the threshold amount plus $50,000 ($100,000 in the case of a joint return), then—

(i) any specified service trade or business of the taxpayer shall not fail to be treated as a qualified trade or business due to paragraph (1)(A), but

(ii) only the applicable percentage of qualified items of income, gain, deduction, or loss, and the W–2 wages and the unadjusted basis immediately after acquisition of qualified property, of the taxpayer allocable to such specified service trade or business shall be taken into account in computing the qualified business income, W–2 wages, and the unadjusted basis immediately after acquisition of qualified property of the taxpayer for the taxable year for purposes of applying this section.

(B) APPLICABLE PERCENTAGE.—For purposes of subparagraph (A), the term "applicable percentage" means, with respect to any taxable year, 100 percent reduced (not below zero) by the percentage equal to the ratio of—

(i) the taxable income of the taxpayer for the taxable year in excess of the threshold amount, bears to

(ii) $50,000 ($100,000 in the case of a joint return).

(e) OTHER DEFINITIONS.—For purposes of this section—

(1) TAXABLE INCOME.—Taxable income shall be computed without regard to the deduction allowable under this section.

(2) THRESHOLD AMOUNT.—

(A) IN GENERAL.—The term "threshold amount" means $157,500 (200 percent of such amount in the case of a joint return).

(B) INFLATION ADJUSTMENT.—In the case of any taxable year beginning after 2018, the dollar amount in subparagraph (A) shall be increased by an amount equal to—

(i) such dollar amount, multiplied by

(ii) the cost-of-living adjustment determined under section 1(f)(3) for the calendar year in which the taxable year begins, determined by substituting "calendar year 2017" for "calendar year 2016" in subparagraph (A)(ii) thereof.

The amount of any increase under the preceding sentence shall be rounded as provided in section 1(f)(7).

(3) QUALIFIED REIT DIVIDEND.—The term "qualified REIT dividend" means any dividend from a real estate investment trust received during the taxable year which—

(A) is not a capital gain dividend, as defined in section 857(b)(3), and

(B) is not qualified dividend income, as defined in section 1(h)(11).

(4) QUALIFIED COOPERATIVE DIVIDEND.—The term "qualified cooperative dividend" means any patronage dividend (as defined in section 1388(a)), any per-unit retain allocation (as defined in section 1388(f)), and any qualified written notice of allocation (as defined in section 1388(c)), or any similar amount received from an organization described in subparagraph (B)(ii), which—

(A) is includible in gross income, and

(B) is received from—

(i) an organization or corporation described in section 501(c)(12) or 1381(a), or

(ii) an organization which is governed under this title by the rules applicable to cooperatives under this title before the enactment of subchapter T.

(5) QUALIFIED PUBLICLY TRADED PARTNERSHIP INCOME.—The term "qualified publicly traded partnership income" means, with respect to any qualified trade or business of a taxpayer, the sum of—

(A) the net amount of such taxpayer's allocable share of each qualified item of income, gain, deduction, and loss (as defined in subsection (c)(3) and determined after the application of subsection (c)(4)) from a publicly traded partnership (as defined in section 7704(a)) which is not treated as a corporation under section 7704(c), plus

(B) any gain recognized by such taxpayer upon disposition of its interest in such partnership to the extent such gain is treated as an amount realized from the sale or exchange of property other than a capital asset under section 751(a).

(f) SPECIAL RULES.—

(1) APPLICATION TO PARTNERSHIPS AND S CORPORATIONS.—

(A) IN GENERAL.—In the case of a partnership or S corporation—

(i) this section shall be applied at the partner or shareholder level,

(ii) each partner or shareholder shall take into account such person's allocable share of each qualified item of income, gain, deduction, and loss, and

(iii) each partner or shareholder shall be treated for purposes of subsection (b) as having W–2 wages and unadjusted basis immediately after acquisition of qualified property for the taxable year in an amount equal to such person's allocable share of the W–2 wages and the unadjusted basis immediately after acquisition of qualified property of the partnership or S corporation for the taxable year (as determined under regulations prescribed by the Secretary).

For purposes of clause (iii), a partner's or shareholder's allocable share of W–2 wages shall be determined in the same manner as the partner's or shareholder's allocable share of wage expenses. For purposes of such clause, partner's or shareholder's allocable share of the unadjusted basis immediately after acquisition of qualified property shall be determined in the same manner as the partner's or shareholder's allocable share of depreciation. For purposes of this subparagraph, in the case of an S corporation, an allocable share shall be the shareholder's pro rata share of an item.

(B) APPLICATION TO TRUSTS AND ESTATES.—Rules similar to the rules under section 199(d)(1)(B)(i) (as in effect on December 1, 2017) for the apportionment of W–2 wages shall apply to the apportionment of W–2 wages and the apportionment of unadjusted basis immediately after acquisition of qualified property under this section.

(C) TREATMENT OF TRADES OR BUSINESS IN PUERTO RICO.—

(i) IN GENERAL.—In the case of any taxpayer with qualified business income from sources within the commonwealth of Puerto Rico, if all such income is taxable under section 1 for such taxable year, then for purposes of determining the qualified business income of such taxpayer for such taxable year, the term "United States" shall include the Commonwealth of Puerto Rico.

(ii) SPECIAL RULE FOR APPLYING LIMIT.—In the case of any taxpayer described in clause (i), the determination of W–2 wages of such taxpayer with respect to any qualified trade or business conducted in Puerto Rico shall be made without regard to any exclusion under section 3401(a)(8) for remuneration paid for services in Puerto Rico.

(2) COORDINATION WITH MINIMUM TAX.—For purposes of determining alternative minimum taxable income under section 55, qualified business income shall be determined without regard to any adjustments under sections 56 through 59.

(3) DEDUCTION LIMITED TO INCOME TAXES.—The deduction under subsection (a) shall only be allowed for purposes of this chapter.

(4) REGULATIONS.—The Secretary shall prescribe such regulations as are necessary to carry out the purposes of this section, including regulations—

(A) for requiring or restricting the allocation of items and wages under this section and such reporting requirements as the Secretary determines appropriate, and

(B) for the application of this section in the case of tiered entities.

(g) DEDUCTION ALLOWED TO SPECIFIED AGRICULTURAL OR HORTICULTURAL COOPERATIVES.—

(1) IN GENERAL.—In the case of any taxable year of a specified agricultural or horticultural cooperative beginning after December 31, 2017, there shall be allowed a deduction in an amount equal to the lesser of—

(A) 20 percent of the excess (if any) of—

(i) the gross income of a specified agricultural or horticultural cooperative, over

(ii) the qualified cooperative dividends (as defined in subsection (e)(4)) paid during the taxable year for the taxable year, or

(B) the greater of—

(i) 50 percent of the W–2 wages of the cooperative with respect to its trade or business, or

(ii) the sum of 25 percent of the W–2 wages of the cooperative with respect to its trade or business, plus 2.5 percent of the unadjusted basis immediately after acquisition of all qualified property of the cooperative.

(2) LIMITATION.—The amount determined under paragraph (1) shall not exceed the taxable income of the specified agricultural or horticultural for the taxable year.

(3) SPECIFIED AGRICULTURAL OR HORTICULTURAL COOPERATIVE.—For purposes of this subsection, the term "specified agricultural or horticultural cooperative" means an organization to which part I of subchapter T applies which is engaged in—

(A) the manufacturing, production, growth, or extraction in whole or significant part of any agricultural or horticultural product,

(B) the marketing of agricultural or horticultural products which its patrons have so manufactured, produced, grown, or extracted, or

(C) the provision of supplies, equipment, or services to farmers or to organizations described in subparagraph (A) or (B).

(h) ANTI-ABUSE RULES.—The Secretary shall—

(1) apply rules similar to the rules under section 179(d)(2) in order to prevent the manipulation of the depreciable period of qualified property using transactions between related parties, and

(2) prescribe rules for determining the unadjusted basis immediately after acquisition of qualified property acquired in like-kind exchanges or involuntary conversions.

(i) TERMINATION.—This section shall not apply to taxable years beginning after December 31, 2025.

[CCH Explanation at ¶330. Committee Reports at ¶10,030.]
Amendments
• **2017, Tax Cuts and Jobs Act (P.L. 115-97)**

P.L. 115-97, §11011(a):

Amended part VI of subchapter B of chapter 1 by adding at the end a new Code Sec. 199A. **Effective** for tax years beginning after 12-31-2017.

[¶5350] CODE SEC. 213. MEDICAL, DENTAL, ETC., EXPENSES.

* * *

(d) DEFINITIONS.—For purposes of this section—

* * *

(10) ELIGIBLE LONG-TERM CARE PREMIUMS.—

* * *

(B) INDEXING.—

* * *

(ii) MEDICAL CARE COST ADJUSTMENT.—For purposes of clause (i), the medical care cost adjustment for any calendar year is the percentage (if any) by which—

(I) the medical care component of the C-CPI-U (as defined in section 1(f)(6)) for August of the preceding calendar year, exceeds

(II) such component of the CPI (as defined in section 1(f)(4)) for August of 1996, multiplied by the amount determined under section 1(f)(3)(B).

The Secretary shall, in consultation with the Secretary of Health and Human Services, prescribe an adjustment which the Secretary determines is more appropriate for purposes of this paragraph than the adjustment described in the preceding sentence, and the adjustment so prescribed shall apply in lieu of the adjustment described in the preceding sentence.

* * *

[CCH Explanation at ¶125. Committee Reports at ¶10,020.]
Amendments
• **2017, Tax Cuts and Jobs Act (P.L. 115-97)**

P.L. 115-97, §11002(d)(7):

Amended so much of Code Sec. 213(d)(10)(B)(ii) as precedes the last sentence. **Effective** for tax years beginning after 12-31-2017. Prior to amendment, so much of Code Sec. 213(d)(10)(B)(ii) as precedes the last sentence read as follows:

(ii) MEDICAL CARE COST ADJUSTMENT.—For purposes of clause (i), the medical care cost adjustment for any calendar year is the percentage (if any) by which—

(I) the medical care component of the Consumer Price Index (as defined in section 1(f)(5)) for August of the preceding calendar year, exceeds

(II) such component for August of 1996.

(f) SPECIAL RULES FOR 2013 THROUGH 2018.—In the case of any taxable year—

(1) beginning after December 31, 2012, and ending before January 1, 2017, in the case of a taxpayer if such taxpayer or such taxpayer's spouse has attained age 65 before the close of such taxable year, and

(2) beginning after December 31, 2016, and ending before January 1, 2019, in the case of any taxpayer,

subsection (a) shall be applied with respect to a taxpayer by substituting "7.5 percent" for "10 percent".

[CCH Explanation at ¶ 225. Committee Reports at ¶ 10,120.]

Amendments

• **2017, Tax Cuts and Jobs Act (P.L. 115-97)**

P.L. 115-97, § 11027(a):

Amended Code Sec. 213(f). **Effective** for tax years beginning after 12-31-2016. Prior to amendment, Code Sec. 213(f) read as follows:

(f) SPECIAL RULE FOR 2013, 2014, 2015, AND 2016.—In the case of any taxable year beginning after December 31, 2012, and ending before January 1, 2017, subsection (a) shall be applied with respect to a taxpayer by substituting "7.5 percent" for "10 percent" if such taxpayer or such taxpayer's spouse has attained age 65 before the close of such taxable year.

>>>→ *Caution: Code Sec. 215, below, was stricken by P.L. 115-97, generally applicable to any divorce or separation instrument executed after December 31, 2018.*

[¶ 5355] CODE SEC. 215. ALIMONY, ETC., PAYMENTS. [*Stricken.*]

[CCH Explanation at ¶ 255. Committee Reports at ¶ 10,260.]

Amendments

• **2017, Tax Cuts and Jobs Act (P.L. 115-97)**

P.L. 115-97, § 11051(a):

Amended part VII of subchapter B by striking Code Sec. 215. For the **effective** date, see Act Sec. 11051(c), below.

P.L. 115-97, § 11051(c), provides:

(c) EFFECTIVE DATE.—The amendments made by this section shall apply to—

(1) any divorce or separation instrument (as defined in section 71(b)(2) of the Internal Revenue Code of 1986 as in effect before the date of the enactment of this Act) executed after December 31, 2018, and

(2) any divorce or separation instrument (as so defined) executed on or before such date and modified after such date if the modification expressly provides that the amendments made by this section apply to such modification.

Prior to being stricken, Code Sec. 215 read as follows:

SEC. 215. ALIMONY, ETC., PAYMENTS.

(a) GENERAL RULE.—In the case of an individual, there shall be allowed as a deduction an amount equal to the alimony or separate maintenance payments paid during such individual's taxable year.

(b) ALIMONY OR SEPARATE MAINTENANCE PAYMENTS DEFINED.—For purposes of this section, the term "alimony or separate maintenance payment" means any alimony or separate maintenance payment (as defined in section 71(b)) which is includible in the gross income of the recipient under section 71.

(c) REQUIREMENT OF IDENTIFICATION NUMBER.—The Secretary may prescribe regulations under which—

(1) any individual receiving alimony or separate maintenance payments is required to furnish such individual's taxpayer identification number to the individual making such payments, and

(2) the individual making such payments is required to include such taxpayer identification number on such individual's return for the taxable year in which such payments are made.

(d) COORDINATION WITH SECTION 682.—No deduction shall be allowed under this section with respect to any payment if, by reason of section 682 (relating to income of alimony trusts), the amount thereof is not includible in such individual's gross income.

[¶ 5360] CODE SEC. 217. MOVING EXPENSES.

* * *

(k) SUSPENSION OF DEDUCTION FOR TAXABLE YEARS 2018 THROUGH 2025.—Except in the case of an individual to whom subsection (g) applies, this section shall not apply to any taxable year beginning after December 31, 2017, and before January 1, 2026.

[CCH Explanation at ¶ 260. Committee Reports at ¶ 10,240.]

Amendments

• **2017, Tax Cuts and Jobs Act (P.L. 115-97)**

P.L. 115-97, § 11049(a):

Amended Code Sec. 217 by adding at the end a new subsection (k). **Effective** for tax years beginning after 12-31-2017.

[¶ 5365] CODE SEC. 219. RETIREMENT SAVINGS.

* * *

(b) MAXIMUM AMOUNT OF DEDUCTION.—

* * *

(5) DEDUCTIBLE AMOUNT.—For purposes of paragraph (1)(A)—

* * *

(C) COST-OF-LIVING ADJUSTMENT.—

(i) IN GENERAL.—In the case of any taxable year beginning in a calendar year after 2008, the $5,000 amount under subparagraph (A) shall be increased by an amount equal to—

(I) such dollar amount, multiplied by

(II) the cost-of-living adjustment determined under section 1(f)(3) for the calendar year in which the taxable year begins, determined by substituting "calendar year 2007" for "calendar year 2016" in subparagraph (A)(ii) thereof.

* * *

[CCH Explanation at ¶ 125. Committee Reports at ¶ 10,020.]

Amendments

• **2017, Tax Cuts and Jobs Act (P.L. 115-97)**

P.L. 115-97, § 11002(d)(1)(S):

Amended Code Sec. 219(b)(5)(C)(i)(II) by striking "for 'calendar year 1992' in subparagraph (B)" and inserting "for

'calendar year 2016' in subparagraph (A)(ii)". **Effective** for tax years beginning after 12-31-2017.

(f) OTHER DEFINITIONS AND SPECIAL RULES.—

»»→ *Caution: Code Sec. 219(f)(1), below, as amended by P.L. 115-97, applies generally to any divorce or separation instrument executed after December 31, 2018.*

(1) COMPENSATION.—For purposes of this section, the term "compensation" includes earned income (as defined in section 401(c)(2)). The term "compensation" does not include any amount received as a pension or annuity and does not include any amount received as deferred compensation. For purposes of this paragraph, section 401(c)(2) shall be applied as if the term trade or business for purposes of section 1402 included service described in subsection (c)(6). The term compensation includes any differential wage payment (as defined in section 3401(h)(2)).

* * *

[CCH Explanation at ¶ 255. Committee Reports at ¶ 10,260.]

Amendments

• **2017, Tax Cuts and Jobs Act (P.L. 115-97)**

P.L. 115-97, § 11051(b)(3)(C):

Amended Code Sec. 219(f)(1) by striking the third sentence. For the **effective** date, see Act Sec. 11051(c)(1)-(2), below. Prior to being stricken, the third sentence of Code Sec. 219(f)(1) read as follows:

The term "compensation" shall include any amount includible in the individual's gross income under section 71 with respect to a divorce or separation instrument described in subparagraph (A) of section 71(b)(2).

P.L. 115-97, § 11051(c)(1)-(2), provides:

(c) EFFECTIVE DATE.—The amendments made by this section shall apply to—

(1) any divorce or separation instrument (as defined in section 71(b)(2) of the Internal Revenue Code of 1986 as in effect before the date of the enactment of this Act) executed after December 31, 2018, and

(2) any divorce or separation instrument (as so defined) executed on or before such date and modified after such date if the modification expressly provides that the amendments made by this section apply to such modification.

(g) LIMITATION ON DEDUCTION FOR ACTIVE PARTICIPANTS IN CERTAIN PENSION PLANS.—

* * *

(3) ADJUSTED GROSS INCOME; APPLICABLE DOLLAR AMOUNT.—For purposes of this subsection—

(A) ADJUSTED GROSS INCOME.—Adjusted gross income of any taxpayer shall be determined—

(i) after application of sections 86 and 469, and

(ii) without regard to sections 135, 137, 221, 222, and 911 or the deduction allowable under this section.

* * *

(8) INFLATION ADJUSTMENT.—In the case of any taxable year beginning in a calendar year after 2006, each of the dollar amounts in paragraphs (3)(B)(i), (3)(B)(ii), and (7)(A) shall each be increased by an amount equal to—

(A) such dollar amount, multiplied by

(B) the cost-of-living adjustment determined under section 1(f)(3) for the calendar year in which the taxable year begins, determined by substituting "calendar year 2005" *for "calendar year 2016" in subparagraph (A)(ii)* thereof.

Any increase determined under the preceding sentence shall be rounded to the nearest multiple of $1,000.

[CCH Explanation at ¶125 and ¶530. Committee Reports at ¶10,020 and ¶10,460.]

Amendments

• **2017, Tax Cuts and Jobs Act (P.L. 115-97)**

P.L. 115-97, §11002(d)(1)(S):

Amended Code Sec. 219(g)(8)(B) by striking "for 'calendar year 1992' in subparagraph (B)" and inserting "for 'calendar year 2016' in subparagraph (A)(ii)". **Effective** for tax years beginning after 12-31-2017.

P.L. 115-97, §13305(b)(1):

Amended Code Sec. 219(g)(3)(A)(ii) by striking "199," following "137,". **Effective** for tax years beginning after 12-31-2017.

[¶5370] CODE SEC. 220. ARCHER MSAs.

* * *

(f) TAX TREATMENT OF DISTRIBUTIONS.—

* * *

(7) TRANSFER OF ACCOUNT INCIDENT TO DIVORCE.—The transfer of an individual's interest in an Archer MSA to an individual's spouse or former spouse under a divorce or separation instrument described in *clause (i) of section 121(d)(3)(C)* shall not be considered a taxable transfer made by such individual notwithstanding any other provision of this subtitle, and such interest shall, after such transfer, be treated as an Archer MSA with respect to which such spouse is the account holder.

* * *

[CCH Explanation at ¶255. Committee Reports at ¶10,260.]

Amendments

• **2017, Tax Cuts and Jobs Act (P.L. 115-97)**

P.L. 115-97, §11051(b)(3)(D):

Amended Code Sec. 220(f)(7) by striking "subparagraph (A) of section 71(b)(2)" and inserting "clause (i) of section 121(d)(3)(C)". For the **effective** date, see Act Sec. 11051(c)(1)-(2), below.

P.L. 115-97, §11051(c)(1)-(2), provides:

(c) EFFECTIVE DATE.—The amendments made by this section shall apply to—

(1) any divorce or separation instrument (as defined in section 71(b)(2) of the Internal Revenue Code of 1986 as in effect before the date of the enactment of this Act) executed after December 31, 2018, and

(2) any divorce or separation instrument (as so defined) executed on or before such date and modified after such date if the modification expressly provides that the amendments made by this section apply to such modification.

(g) COST-OF-LIVING ADJUSTMENT.—In the case of any taxable year beginning in a calendar year after 1998, each dollar amount in subsection (c)(2) shall be increased by an amount equal to—

(1) such dollar amount, multiplied by

(2) the cost-of-living adjustment determined under section 1(f)(3) for the calendar year in which such taxable year begins by substituting "calendar year 1997" *for "calendar year 2016" in subparagraph (A)(ii)* thereof.

If any increase under the preceding sentence is not a multiple of $50, such increase shall be rounded to the nearest multiple of $50.

* * *

[CCH Explanation at ¶125. Committee Reports at ¶10,020.]

Amendments

• **2017, Tax Cuts and Jobs Act (P.L. 115-97)**

P.L. 115-97, §11002(d)(1)(T):

Amended Code Sec. 220(g)(2) by striking "for 'calendar year 1992' in subparagraph (B)" and inserting "for 'calendar

year 2016' in subparagraph (A)(ii)". **Effective** for tax years beginning after 12-31-2017.

[¶5375] CODE SEC. 221. INTEREST ON EDUCATION LOANS.

* * *

(b) MAXIMUM DEDUCTION.—

* * *

(2) LIMITATION BASED ON MODIFIED ADJUSTED GROSS INCOME.—

* * *

(C) MODIFIED ADJUSTED GROSS INCOME.—The term "modified adjusted gross income" means adjusted gross income determined—

(i) without regard to this section and sections 222, 911, 931, and 933, and

(ii) after application of sections 86, 135, 137, 219, and 469.

* * *

[CCH Explanation at ¶530. Committee Reports at ¶10,460.]

Amendments

• **2017, Tax Cuts and Jobs Act (P.L. 115-97)**

P.L. 115-97, §13305(b)(1):

Amended Code Sec. 221(b)(2)(C) by striking "199," following "this section and sections". **Effective** for tax years beginning after 12-31-2017.

(f) INFLATION ADJUSTMENTS.—

(1) IN GENERAL.—In the case of a taxable year beginning after 2002, the $50,000 and $100,000 amounts in subsection (b)(2) shall each be increased by an amount equal to—

(A) such dollar amount, multiplied by

(B) the cost-of-living adjustment determined under section 1(f)(3) for the calendar year in which the taxable year begins, determined by substituting "calendar year 2001" *for "calendar year 2016" in subparagraph (A)(ii)* thereof.

(2) ROUNDING.—If any amount as adjusted under paragraph (1) is not a multiple of $5,000, such amount shall be rounded to the next lowest multiple of $5,000.

[CCH Explanation at ¶125. Committee Reports at ¶10,020.]

Amendments

• **2017, Tax Cuts and Jobs Act (P.L. 115-97)**

P.L. 115-97, §11002(d)(1)(U):

Amended Code Sec. 221(f)(1)(B) by striking "for 'calendar year 1992' in subparagraph (B)" and inserting "for 'calendar

year 2016' in subparagraph (A)(ii)". **Effective** for tax years beginning after 12-31-2017.

[¶ 5380] CODE SEC. 222. QUALIFIED TUITION AND RELATED EXPENSES.

* * *

(b) DOLLAR LIMITATIONS.—

* * *

(2) APPLICABLE DOLLAR LIMIT.—

* * *

(C) ADJUSTED GROSS INCOME.—For purposes of this paragraph, adjusted gross income shall be determined—

(i) without regard to this section and sections 911, 931, and 933, and

(ii) after application of sections 86, 135, 137, 219, 221, and 469.

* * *

[CCH Explanation at ¶ 530. Committee Reports at ¶ 10,460.]
Amendments
• **2017, Tax Cuts and Jobs Act (P.L. 115-97)**

P.L. 115-97, § 13305(b)(1):

Amended Code Sec. 222(b)(2)(C) by striking "199," following "this section and sections". **Effective** for tax years beginning after 12-31-2017.

[¶ 5385] CODE SEC. 223. HEALTH SAVINGS ACCOUNTS.

* * *

(f) TAX TREATMENT OF DISTRIBUTIONS.—

* * *

(7) TRANSFER OF ACCOUNT INCIDENT TO DIVORCE.—The transfer of an individual's interest in a health savings account to an individual's spouse or former spouse under a divorce or separation instrument described in *clause (i) of section 121(d)(3)(C)* shall not be considered a taxable transfer made by such individual notwithstanding any other provision of this subtitle, and such interest shall, after such transfer, be treated as a health savings account with respect to which such spouse is the account beneficiary.

* * *

[CCH Explanation at ¶ 255. Committee Reports at ¶ 10,260.]
Amendments
• **2017, Tax Cuts and Jobs Act (P.L. 115-97)**

P.L. 115-97, § 11051(b)(3)(E):

Amended Code Sec. 223(f)(7) by striking "subparagraph (A) of section 71(b)(2)" and inserting "clause (i) of section 121(d)(3)(C)". For the **effective** date, see Act Sec. 11051(c)(1)-(2), below.

P.L. 115-97, § 11051(c)(1)-(2), provides:

(c) EFFECTIVE DATE.—The amendments made by this section shall apply to—

(1) any divorce or separation instrument (as defined in section 71(b)(2) of the Internal Revenue Code of 1986 as in effect before the date of the enactment of this Act) executed after December 31, 2018, and

(2) any divorce or separation instrument (as so defined) executed on or before such date and modified after such date if the modification expressly provides that the amendments made by this section apply to such modification.

(g) COST-OF-LIVING ADJUSTMENT.—

(1) IN GENERAL.—Each dollar amount in subsections (b)(2) and (c)(2)(A) shall be increased by an amount equal to—

(A) such dollar amount, multiplied by

(B) the cost-of-living adjustment determined under section 1(f)(3) for the calendar year in which such taxable year begins determined by substituting *for "calendar year 2016" in subparagraph (A)(ii)* thereof—

(i) except as provided in clause (ii), "calendar year 1997", and

(ii) in the case of each dollar amount in subsection (c)(2)(A), "calendar year 2003".

In the case of adjustments made for any taxable year beginning after 2007, section 1(f)(4) shall be applied for purposes of this paragraph by substituting "March 31" for "August 31", and the Secretary shall publish the adjusted amounts under subsections (b)(2) and (c)(2)(A) for taxable years beginning in any calendar year no later than June 1 of the preceding calendar year.

(2) ROUNDING.—If any increase under paragraph (1) is not a multiple of $50, such increase shall be rounded to the nearest multiple of $50.

* * *

[CCH Explanation at ¶ 125. Committee Reports at ¶ 10,020.]

Amendments

• **2017, Tax Cuts and Jobs Act (P.L. 115-97)**

P.L. 115-97, § 11002(d)(1)(V):

Amended Code Sec. 223(g)(1)(B) by striking "for 'calendar year 1992' in subparagraph (B)" and inserting "for 'calendar

year 2016' in subparagraph (A)(ii)". **Effective** for tax years beginning after 12-31-2017.

[¶ 5390] CODE SEC. 243. DIVIDENDS RECEIVED BY CORPORATIONS.

(a) GENERAL RULE.—In the case of a corporation, there shall be allowed as a deduction an amount equal to the following percentages of the amount received as dividends from a domestic corporation which is subject to taxation under this chapter:

(1) *50 percent*, in the case of dividends other than dividends described in paragraph (2) or (3);

(2) 100 percent, in the case of dividends received by a small business investment company operating under the Small Business Investment Act of 1958 (15 U.S.C. 661 and following); and

(3) 100 percent, in the case of qualifying dividends (as defined in subsection (b)(1)).

* * *

[CCH Explanation at ¶ 315. Committee Reports at ¶ 10,310.]

Amendments

• **2017, Tax Cuts and Jobs Act (P.L. 115-97)**

P.L. 115-97, § 13002(a)(1):

Amended Code Sec. 243(a)(1) by striking "70 percent" and inserting "50 percent". **Effective** for tax years beginning after 12-31-2017.

(c) INCREASED PERCENTAGE FOR DIVIDENDS FROM 20-PERCENT OWNED CORPORATIONS.—

(1) IN GENERAL.—In the case of any dividend received from a 20-percent owned corporation, subsection (a)(1) shall be applied by substituting *"65 percent"* for *"50 percent"*.

(2) 20-PERCENT OWNED CORPORATION.—For purposes of this section, the term "20-percent owned corporation" means any corporation if 20 percent or more of the stock of such corporation (by vote and value) is owned by the taxpayer. For purposes of the preceding sentence, stock described in section 1504(a)(4) shall not be taken into account.

* * *

[CCH Explanation at ¶ 315. Committee Reports at ¶ 10,310.]

Amendments

• **2017, Tax Cuts and Jobs Act (P.L. 115-97)**

P.L. 115-97, § 13002(a)(2)(A)-(B):

Amended Code Sec. 243(c)(1) by striking "80 percent" and inserting "65 percent", and by striking "70 percent" and inserting "50 percent". **Effective** for tax years beginning after 12-31-2017.

P.L. 115-97, § 13002(a)(3):

Amended the heading for Code Sec. 243(c) by striking "RETENTION OF 80-PERCENT DIVIDEND RECEIVED DEDUCTION" and inserting "INCREASED PERCENTAGE". **Effective** for tax years beginning after 12-31-2017.

[¶ 5395] CODE SEC. 245. DIVIDENDS RECEIVED FROM CERTAIN FOREIGN CORPORATIONS.

(a) Dividends From 10-Percent Owned Foreign Corporations.—

* * *

(4) Post-1986 undistributed earnings.—The term "post-1986 undistributed earnings" means the amount of the earnings and profits of the foreign corporation (computed in accordance with sections 964(a) and 986) accumulated in taxable years beginning after December 31, 1986—

(A) as of the close of the taxable year of the foreign corporation in which the dividend is distributed, and

(B) without diminution by reason of dividends distributed during such taxable year.

* * *

(10) Coordination with treaties.—If—

(A) any portion of a dividend received by a corporation from a qualified 10-percent-owned foreign corporation would be treated as from sources in the United States under paragraph (9),

(B) under a treaty obligation of the United States (applied without regard to this subsection), such portion would be treated as arising from sources outside the United States, and

(C) the taxpayer chooses the benefits of this paragraph,

this subsection shall not apply to such dividend (but subsections (a), (b), and (c) of section 904 and sections *907 and 960* shall be applied separately with respect to such portion of such dividend).

* * *

[CCH Explanation at ¶ 720. Committee Reports at ¶ 11,170.]

Amendments

• 2017, Tax Cuts and Jobs Act (P.L. 115-97)

P.L. 115-97, § 14301(c)(2):

Amended Code Sec. 245(a)(4). **Effective** for tax years of foreign corporations beginning after 12-31-2017, and to tax years of United States shareholders in which or with which such tax years of foreign corporations end. Prior to amendment, Code Sec. 245(a)(4) read as follows:

(4) Post-1986 undistributed earnings.—For purposes of this subsection, the term "post-1986 undistributed earnings" has the meaning given to such term by section 902(c)(1).

P.L. 115-97, § 14301(c)(3):

Amended Code Sec. 245(a)(10)(C) by striking "902, 907, and 960" and inserting "907 and 960". **Effective** for tax years of foreign corporations beginning after 12-31-2017, and to tax years of United States shareholders in which or with which such tax years of foreign corporations end.

(c) Certain Dividends Received From FSC.—

(1) In general.—In the case of a domestic corporation, there shall be allowed as a deduction an amount equal to—

(A) 100 percent of any dividend received from another corporation which is distributed out of earnings and profits attributable to foreign trade income for a period during which such other corporation was a FSC, and

(B) *50 percent (65 percent* in the case of dividends from a 20-percent owned corporation as defined in section 243(c)(2)) of any dividend received from another corporation which is distributed out of earnings and profits attributable to effectively connected income received or accrued by such other corporation while such other corporation was a FSC.

* * *

[CCH Explanation at ¶ 315. Committee Reports at ¶ 10,310.]

Amendments

• **2017, Tax Cuts and Jobs Act (P.L. 115-97)**

P.L. 115-97, § 13002(b)(1)-(2):

Amended Code Sec. 245(c)(1)(B) by striking "70 percent" and inserting "50 percent", and by striking "80 percent" and inserting "65 percent". **Effective** for tax years beginning after 12-31-2017.

[¶ 5400] *CODE SEC. 245A. DEDUCTION FOR FOREIGN SOURCE-PORTION OF DIVIDENDS RECEIVED BY DOMESTIC CORPORATIONS FROM SPECIFIED 10-PERCENT OWNED FOREIGN CORPORATIONS.*

(a) IN GENERAL.—*In the case of any dividend received from a specified 10-percent owned foreign corporation by a domestic corporation which is a United States shareholder with respect to such foreign corporation, there shall be allowed as a deduction an amount equal to the foreign-source portion of such dividend.*

(b) SPECIFIED 10-PERCENT OWNED FOREIGN CORPORATION.—*For purposes of this section—*

(1) IN GENERAL.—*The term "specified 10-percent owned foreign corporation" means any foreign corporation with respect to which any domestic corporation is a United States shareholder with respect to such corporation.*

(2) EXCLUSION OF PASSIVE FOREIGN INVESTMENT COMPANIES.—*Such term shall not include any corporation which is a passive foreign investment company (as defined in section 1297) with respect to the shareholder and which is not a controlled foreign corporation.*

(c) FOREIGN-SOURCE PORTION.—*For purposes of this section—*

(1) IN GENERAL.—*The foreign-source portion of any dividend from a specified 10-percent owned foreign corporation is an amount which bears the same ratio to such dividend as—*

(A) *the undistributed foreign earnings of the specified 10-percent owned foreign corporation, bears to*

(B) *the total undistributed earnings of such foreign corporation.*

(2) UNDISTRIBUTED EARNINGS.—*The term "undistributed earnings" means the amount of the earnings and profits of the specified 10-percent owned foreign corporation (computed in accordance with sections 964(a) and 986)—*

(A) *as of the close of the taxable year of the specified 10-percent owned foreign corporation in which the dividend is distributed, and*

(B) *without diminution by reason of dividends distributed during such taxable year.*

(3) UNDISTRIBUTED FOREIGN EARNINGS.—*The term "undistributed foreign earnings" means the portion of the undistributed earnings which is attributable to neither—*

(A) *income described in subparagraph (A) of section 245(a)(5), nor*

(B) *dividends described in subparagraph (B) of such section (determined without regard to section 245(a)(12)).*

(d) DISALLOWANCE OF FOREIGN TAX CREDIT, ETC.—

(1) IN GENERAL.—*No credit shall be allowed under section 901 for any taxes paid or accrued (or treated as paid or accrued) with respect to any dividend for which a deduction is allowed under this section.*

(2) DENIAL OF DEDUCTION.—*No deduction shall be allowed under this chapter for any tax for which credit is not allowable under section 901 by reason of paragraph (1) (determined by treating the taxpayer as having elected the benefits of subpart A of part III of subchapter N).*

(e) SPECIAL RULES FOR HYBRID DIVIDENDS.—

(1) IN GENERAL.—*Subsection (a) shall not apply to any dividend received by a United States shareholder from a controlled foreign corporation if the dividend is a hybrid dividend.*

(2) HYBRID DIVIDENDS OF TIERED CORPORATIONS.—*If a controlled foreign corporation with respect to which a domestic corporation is a United States shareholder receives a hybrid dividend from any other controlled foreign corporation with respect to which such domestic corporation is also a United States shareholder, then, notwithstanding any other provision of this title—*

(A) the hybrid dividend shall be treated for purposes of section 951(a)(1)(A) as subpart F income of the receiving controlled foreign corporation for the taxable year of the controlled foreign corporation in which the dividend was received, and

(B) the United States shareholder shall include in gross income an amount equal to the shareholder's pro rata share (determined in the same manner as under section 951(a)(2)) of the subpart F income described in subparagraph (A).

(3) DENIAL OF FOREIGN TAX CREDIT, ETC.—*The rules of subsection (d) shall apply to any hybrid dividend received by, or any amount included under paragraph (2) in the gross income of, a United States shareholder.*

(4) HYBRID DIVIDEND.—*The term "hybrid dividend" means an amount received from a controlled foreign corporation—*

(A) for which a deduction would be allowed under subsection (a) but for this subsection, and

(B) for which the controlled foreign corporation received a deduction (or other tax benefit) with respect to any income, war profits, or excess profits taxes imposed by any foreign country or possession of the United States.

(f) SPECIAL RULE FOR PURGING DISTRIBUTIONS OF PASSIVE FOREIGN INVESTMENT COMPANIES.—*Any amount which is treated as a dividend under section 1291(d)(2)(B) shall not be treated as a dividend for purposes of this section.*

(g) REGULATIONS.—*The Secretary shall prescribe such regulations or other guidance as may be necessary or appropriate to carry out the provisions of this section, including regulations for the treatment of United States shareholders owning stock of a specified 10 percent owned foreign corporation through a partnership.*

[CCH Explanation at ¶705. Committee Reports at ¶11,040.]

Amendments

• **2017, Tax Cuts and Jobs Act (P.L. 115-97)**

P.L. 115-97, §14101(a):

Amended part VIII of subchapter B of chapter 1 by inserting after Code Sec. 245 a new Code Sec. 245A. **Effective** for distributions made after 12-31-2017.

[¶5405] CODE SEC. 246. RULES APPLYING TO DEDUCTIONS FOR DIVIDENDS RECEIVED.

(a) DEDUCTION NOT ALLOWED FOR DIVIDENDS FROM CERTAIN CORPORATIONS.—

(1) IN GENERAL.—The deductions allowed by sections 243[,] *245, and 245A* shall not apply to any dividend from a corporation which, for the taxable year of the corporation in which the distribution is made, or for the next preceding taxable year of the corporation, is a corporation exempt from tax under section 501 (relating to certain charitable, etc., organizations) or section 521 (relating to farmers' cooperative associations).

* * *

[CCH Explanation at ¶ 705. Committee Reports at ¶ 11,040.]
Amendments
• 2017, Tax Cuts and Jobs Act (P.L. 115-97)
P.L. 115-97, § 14101(c)(1):
Amended Code Sec. 246(a)(1) by striking "and 245" and inserting "245, and 245A". **Effective** for distributions made after 12-31-2017.

(b) LIMITATION ON AGGREGATE AMOUNT OF DEDUCTIONS.—

(1) GENERAL RULE.—Except as provided in paragraph (2), the aggregate amount of the deductions allowed by section 243(a)(1), *subsection (a) and (b) of section 245, and section 250,* shall not exceed the percentage determined under paragraph (3) of the taxable income computed without regard to the deductions allowed by sections 172, *199A,* 243(a)(1), *subsection (a) and (b) of section 245, and section 250,* without regard to any adjustment under section 1059, and without regard to any capital loss carryback to the taxable year under section 1212(a)(1).

* * *

(3) SPECIAL RULES.—The provisions of paragraph (1) shall be applied—

(A) first separately with respect to dividends from 20-percent owned corporations (as defined in section 243(c)(2)) and the percentage determined under this paragraph shall be *65 percent*, and

(B) then separately with respect to dividends not from 20-percent owned corporations and the percentage determined under this paragraph shall be *50 percent* and the taxable income shall be reduced by the aggregate amount of dividends from 20-percent owned corporations (as so defined).

[CCH Explanation at ¶ 315, ¶ 330, ¶ 530, and ¶ 735. Committee Reports at ¶ 10,030, ¶ 10,310, ¶ 10,460, and ¶ 11,080.]
Amendments
• 2017, Tax Cuts and Jobs Act (P.L. 115-97)
P.L. 115-97, § 11011(d)(2):
Amended Code Sec. 246(b)(1) by inserting "199A," before "243(a)(1)". **Effective** for tax years beginning after 12-31-2017.

P.L. 115-97, § 13002(c)(1)-(2):
Amended Code Sec. 246(b)(3) by striking "80 percent" in subparagraph (A) and inserting "65 percent", and by striking "70 percent" in subparagraph (B) and inserting "50 percent". **Effective** for tax years beginning after 12-31-2017.

P.L. 115-97, § 13305(b)(1):
Amended Code Sec. 246(b)(1) by striking "199," following "sections 172,". **Effective** for tax years beginning after 12-31-2017.

P.L. 115-97, § 14202(b)(2)(A)-(B):
Amended Code Sec. 246(b)(1) by striking "and subsection (a) and (b) of section 245" the first place it appears and inserting ", subsection (a) and (b) of section 245, and section 250", [and] by striking "and subsection (a) and (b) of section 245" the second place it appears and inserting "subsection (a) and (b) of section 245, and 250". **Effective** for tax years beginning after 12-31-2017.

(c) EXCLUSION OF CERTAIN DIVIDENDS.—

(1) IN GENERAL.—No deduction shall be allowed under section 243[,] *245, or 245A,* in respect of any dividend on any share of stock—

(A) which is held by the taxpayer for 45 days or less during the 91-day period beginning on the date which is 45 days before the date on which such share becomes ex-dividend with respect to such dividend, or

(B) to the extent that the taxpayer is under an obligation (whether pursuant to a short sale or otherwise) to make related payments with respect to positions in substantially similar or related property.

* * *

(5) SPECIAL RULES FOR FOREIGN SOURCE PORTION OF DIVIDENDS RECEIVED FROM SPECIFIED 10-PERCENT OWNED FOREIGN CORPORATIONS.—

(A) 1-YEAR HOLDING PERIOD REQUIREMENT.—For purposes of section 245A—

(i) paragraph (1)(A) shall be applied—

(I) by substituting "365 days" for "45 days" each place it appears, and

(II) by substituting "731-day period" for "91-day period", and

(ii) paragraph (2) shall not apply.

(B) STATUS MUST BE MAINTAINED DURING HOLDING PERIOD.—For purposes of applying paragraph (1) with respect to section 245A, the taxpayer shall be treated as holding the stock referred to in paragraph (1) for any period only if—

(i) the specified 10-percent owned foreign corporation referred to in section 245A(a) is a specified 10-percent owned foreign corporation at all times during such period, and

(ii) the taxpayer is a United States shareholder with respect to such specified 10-percent owned foreign corporation at all times during such period.

* * *

[CCH Explanation at ¶705. Committee Reports at ¶11,040.]

Amendments

• **2017, Tax Cuts and Jobs Act (P.L. 115-97)**

P.L. 115-97, §14101(b)(1)-(2):

Amended Code Sec. 246(c) by striking "or 245" in paragraph (1) and inserting "245, or 245A", and by adding at the

end a new paragraph (5). **Effective** for distributions made after 12-31-2017.

[¶5410] CODE SEC. 246A. DIVIDENDS RECEIVED DEDUCTION REDUCED WHERE PORTFOLIO STOCK IS DEBT FINANCED.

(a) GENERAL RULE.—In the case of any dividend on debt-financed portfolio stock, there shall be substituted for the percentage which (but for this subsection) would be used in determining the amount of the deduction allowable under section 243 or 245(a) a percentage equal to the product of—

(1) *50 percent (65 percent* in the case of any dividend from a 20-percent owned corporation as defined in section 243(c)(2)), and

(2) 100 percent minus the average indebtedness percentage.

* * *

[CCH Explanation at ¶315. Committee Reports at ¶10,310.]

Amendments

• **2017, Tax Cuts and Jobs Act (P.L. 115-97)**

P.L. 115-97, §13002(d)(1)-(2):

Amended Code Sec. 246A(a)(1) by striking "70 percent" and inserting "50 percent", and by striking "80 percent" and

inserting "65 percent". **Effective** for tax years beginning after 12-31-2017.

[¶5415] CODE SEC. 247. CONTRIBUTIONS TO ALASKA NATIVE SETTLEMENT TRUSTS.

(a) IN GENERAL.—In the case of a Native Corporation, there shall be allowed a deduction for any contributions made by such Native Corporation to a Settlement Trust (regardless of whether an election under section 646 is in effect for such Settlement Trust) for which the Native Corporation has made an annual election under subsection (e).

(b) AMOUNT OF DEDUCTION.—The amount of the deduction under subsection (a) shall be equal to—

(1) in the case of a cash contribution (regardless of the method of payment, including currency, coins, money order, or check), the amount of such contribution, or

(2) in the case of a contribution not described in paragraph (1), the lesser of—

(A) the Native Corporation's adjusted basis in the property contributed, or

(B) the fair market value of the property contributed.

(c) LIMITATION AND CARRYOVER.—

(1) IN GENERAL.—Subject to paragraph (2), the deduction allowed under subsection (a) for any taxable year shall not exceed the taxable income (as determined without regard to such deduction) of the Native Corporation for the taxable year in which the contribution was made.

(2) CARRYOVER.—If the aggregate amount of contributions described in subsection (a) for any taxable year exceeds the limitation under paragraph (1), such excess shall be treated as a contribution described in subsection (a) in each of the 15 succeeding years in order of time.

(d) DEFINITIONS.—For purposes of this section, the terms "Native Corporation" and "Settlement Trust" have the same meaning given such terms under section 646(h).

(e) MANNER OF MAKING ELECTION.—

(1) IN GENERAL.—For each taxable year, a Native Corporation may elect to have this section apply for such taxable year on the income tax return or an amendment or supplement to the return of the Native Corporation, with such election to have effect solely for such taxable year.

(2) REVOCATION.—Any election made by a Native Corporation pursuant to this subsection may be revoked pursuant to a timely filed amendment or supplement to the income tax return of such Native Corporation.

(f) ADDITIONAL RULES.—

(1) EARNINGS AND PROFITS.—Notwithstanding section 646(d)(2), in the case of a Native Corporation which claims a deduction under this section for any taxable year, the earnings and profits of such Native Corporation for such taxable year shall be reduced by the amount of such deduction.

(2) GAIN OR LOSS.—No gain or loss shall be recognized by the Native Corporation with respect to a contribution of property for which a deduction is allowed under this section.

(3) INCOME.—Subject to subsection (g), a Settlement Trust shall include in income the amount of any deduction allowed under this section in the taxable year in which the Settlement Trust actually receives such contribution.

(4) PERIOD.—The holding period under section 1223 of the Settlement Trust shall include the period the property was held by the Native Corporation.

(5) BASIS.—The basis that a Settlement Trust has for which a deduction is allowed under this section shall be equal to the lesser of—

(A) the adjusted basis of the Native Corporation in such property immediately before such contribution, or

(B) the fair market value of the property immediately before such contribution.

(6) PROHIBITION.—No deduction shall be allowed under this section with respect to any contributions made to a Settlement Trust which are in violation of subsection (a)(2) or (c)(2) of section 39 of the Alaska Native Claims Settlement Act (43 U.S.C. 1629e).

(g) ELECTION BY SETTLEMENT TRUST TO DEFER INCOME RECOGNITION.—

(1) IN GENERAL.—In the case of a contribution which consists of property other than cash, a Settlement Trust may elect to defer recognition of any income related to such property until the sale or exchange of such property, in whole or in part, by the Settlement Trust.

(2) TREATMENT.—In the case of property described in paragraph (1), any income or gain realized on the sale or exchange of such property shall be treated as—

(A) for such amount of the income or gain as is equal to or less than the amount of income which would be included in income at the time of contribution under subsection (f)(3) but for the taxpayer's election under this subsection, ordinary income, and

(B) for any amounts of the income or gain which are in excess of the amount of income which would be included in income at the time of contribution under subsection (f)(3) but for the taxpayer's election under this subsection, having the same character as if this subsection did not apply.

Code Sec. 247(g)(2)(B) **¶5415**

(3) ELECTION.—

(A) IN GENERAL.—For each taxable year, a Settlement Trust may elect to apply this subsection for any property described in paragraph (1) which was contributed during such year. Any property to which the election applies shall be identified and described with reasonable particularity on the income tax return or an amendment or supplement to the return of the Settlement Trust, with such election to have effect solely for such taxable year.

(B) REVOCATION.—Any election made by a Settlement Trust pursuant to this subsection may be revoked pursuant to a timely filed amendment or supplement to the income tax return of such Settlement Trust.

(C) CERTAIN DISPOSITIONS.—

(i) IN GENERAL.—In the case of any property for which an election is in effect under this subsection and which is disposed of within the first taxable year subsequent to the taxable year in which such property was contributed to the Settlement Trust—

(I) this section shall be applied as if the election under this subsection had not been made,

(II) any income or gain which would have been included in the year of contribution under subsection (f)(3) but for the taxpayer's election under this subsection shall be included in income for the taxable year of such contribution, and

(III) the Settlement Trust shall pay any increase in tax resulting from such inclusion, including any applicable interest, and increased by 10 percent of the amount of such increase with interest.

(ii) ASSESSMENT.—Notwithstanding section 6501(a), any amount described in subclause (III) of clause (i) may be assessed, or a proceeding in court with respect to such amount may be initiated without assessment, within 4 years after the date on which the return making the election under this subsection for such property was filed.

[CCH Explanation at ¶ 325. Committee Reports at ¶ 10,970.]

Amendments

• 2017, Tax Cuts and Jobs Act (P.L. 115-97)

P.L. 115-97, § 13821(b)(1):

Amended part VIII of subchapter B of chapter 1 by inserting before Code Sec. 248 a new Code Sec. 247. **Effective** generally for tax years for which the period of limitation on refund or credit under Code Sec. 6511 has not expired. For a special rule, see Act Sec. 13821(b)(3)(B), below.

P.L. 115-97, § 13821(b)(3)(B), provides:

(B) ONE-YEAR WAIVER OF STATUTE OF LIMITATIONS.—If the period of limitation on a credit or refund resulting from the amendments made by paragraph (1) expires before the end of the 1-year period beginning on the date of the enactment of this Act, refund or credit of such overpayment (to the extent attributable to such amendments) may, nevertheless, be made or allowed if claim therefor is filed before the close of such 1-year period.

[¶ 5420] CODE SEC. 250. FOREIGN-DERIVED INTANGIBLE INCOME AND GLOBAL INTANGIBLE LOW-TAXED INCOME.

(a) ALLOWANCE OF DEDUCTION.—

(1) IN GENERAL.—In the case of a domestic corporation for any taxable year, there shall be allowed as a deduction an amount equal to the sum of—

(A) 37.5 percent of the foreign-derived intangible income of such domestic corporation for such taxable year, plus

(B) 50 percent of—

(i) the global intangible low-taxed income amount (if any) which is included in the gross income of such domestic corporation under section 951A for such taxable year, and

(ii) the amount treated as a dividend received by such corporation under section 78 which is attributable to the amount described in clause (i).

(2) LIMITATION BASED ON TAXABLE INCOME.—

(A) IN GENERAL.—If, for any taxable year—

(i) the sum of the foreign-derived intangible income and the global intangible low-taxed income amount otherwise taken into account by the domestic corporation under paragraph (1), exceeds

(ii) the taxable income of the domestic corporation (determined without regard to this section),

then the amount of the foreign-derived intangible income and the global intangible low-taxed income amount so taken into account shall be reduced as provided in subparagraph (B).

(B) REDUCTION.—For purposes of subparagraph (A)—

(i) foreign-derived intangible income shall be reduced by an amount which bears the same ratio to the excess described in subparagraph (A) as such foreign-derived intangible income bears to the sum described in subparagraph (A)(i), and

(ii) the global intangible low-taxed income amount shall be reduced by the remainder of such excess.

(3) REDUCTION IN DEDUCTION FOR TAXABLE YEARS AFTER 2025.—In the case of any taxable year beginning after December 31, 2025, paragraph (1) shall be applied by substituting—

(A) "21.875 percent" for "37.5 percent" in subparagraph (A), and

(B) "37.5 percent" for "50 percent" in subparagraph (B).

(b) FOREIGN-DERIVED INTANGIBLE INCOME.—For purposes of this section—

(1) IN GENERAL.—The foreign-derived intangible income of any domestic corporation is the amount which bears the same ratio to the deemed intangible income of such corporation as—

(A) the foreign-derived deduction eligible income of such corporation, bears to

(B) the deduction eligible income of such corporation.

(2) DEEMED INTANGIBLE INCOME.—For purposes of this subsection—

(A) IN GENERAL.—The term "deemed intangible income" means the excess (if any) of—

(i) the deduction eligible income of the domestic corporation, over

(ii) the deemed tangible income return of the corporation.

(B) DEEMED TANGIBLE INCOME RETURN.—The term "deemed tangible income return" means, with respect to any corporation, an amount equal to 10 percent of the corporation's qualified business asset investment (as defined in section 951A(d), determined by substituting "deduction eligible income" for "tested income" in paragraph (2) thereof and without regard to whether the corporation is a controlled foreign corporation).

(3) DEDUCTION ELIGIBLE INCOME.—

(A) IN GENERAL.—The term "deduction eligible income" means, with respect to any domestic corporation, the excess (if any) of—

(i) gross income of such corporation determined without regard to—

(I) any amount included in the gross income of such corporation under section 951(a)(1),

(II) the global intangible low-taxed income included in the gross income of such corporation under section 951A,

(III) any financial services income (as defined in section 904(d)(2)(D)) of such corporation,

(IV) any dividend received from a corporation which is a controlled foreign corporation of such domestic corporation,

(V) any domestic oil and gas extraction income of such corporation, and

(VI) any foreign branch income (as defined in section 904(d)(2)(J)), over

(ii) the deductions (including taxes) properly allocable to such gross income.

(B) DOMESTIC OIL AND GAS EXTRACTION INCOME.—*For purposes of subparagraph (A), the term "domestic oil and gas extraction income" means income described in section 907(c)(1), determined by substituting "within the United States" for "without the United States".*

(4) FOREIGN-DERIVED DEDUCTION ELIGIBLE INCOME.—*The term "foreign-derived deduction eligible income" means, with respect to any taxpayer for any taxable year, any deduction eligible income of such taxpayer which is derived in connection with—*

(A) *property—*

(i) *which is sold by the taxpayer to any person who is not a United States person, and*

(ii) *which the taxpayer establishes to the satisfaction of the Secretary is for a foreign use, or*

(B) *services provided by the taxpayer which the taxpayer establishes to the satisfaction of the Secretary are provided to any person, or with respect to property, not located within the United States.*

(5) RULES RELATING TO FOREIGN USE PROPERTY OR SERVICES.—*For purposes of this subsection—*

(A) FOREIGN USE.—*The term "foreign use" means any use, consumption, or disposition which is not within the United States.*

(B) PROPERTY OR SERVICES PROVIDED TO DOMESTIC INTERMEDIARIES.—

(i) PROPERTY.—*If a taxpayer sells property to another person (other than a related party) for further manufacture or other modification within the United States, such property shall not be treated as sold for a foreign use even if such other person subsequently uses such property for a foreign use.*

(ii) SERVICES.—*If a taxpayer provides services to another person (other than a related party) located within the United States, such services shall not be treated as described in paragraph (4)(B) even if such other person uses such services in providing services which are so described.*

(C) SPECIAL RULES WITH RESPECT TO RELATED PARTY TRANSACTIONS.—

(i) SALES TO RELATED PARTIES.—*If property is sold to a related party who is not a United States person, such sale shall not be treated as for a foreign use unless—*

(I) *such property is ultimately sold by a related party, or used by a related party in connection with property which is sold or the provision of services, to another person who is an unrelated party who is not a United States person, and*

(II) *the taxpayer establishes to the satisfaction of the Secretary that such property is for a foreign use.*

For purposes of this clause, a sale of property shall be treated as a sale of each of the components thereof.

(ii) SERVICE PROVIDED TO RELATED PARTIES.—*If a service is provided to a related party who is not located in the United States, such service shall not be treated described in subparagraph (A)(ii) unless the taxpayer established to the satisfaction of the Secretary that such service is not substantially similar to services provided by such related party to persons located within the United States.*

(D) RELATED PARTY.—*For purposes of this paragraph, the term "related party" means any member of an affiliated group as defined in section 1504(a), determined—*

(i) *by substituting "more than 50 percent" for "at least 80 percent" each place it appears, and*

(ii) *without regard to paragraphs (2) and (3) of section 1504(b).*

Any person (other than a corporation) shall be treated as a member of such group if such person is controlled by members of such group (including any entity treated as a member of such group by reason of this sentence) or controls any such member. For purposes of the preceding sentence, control shall be determined under the rules of section 954(d)(3).

(E) SOLD.—*For purposes of this subsection, the terms "sold", "sells", and "sale" shall include any lease, license, exchange, or other disposition.*

(c) REGULATIONS.—*The Secretary shall prescribe such regulations or other guidance as may be necessary or appropriate to carry out the provisions of this section.*

[CCH Explanation at ¶ 735. Committee Reports at ¶ 11,080.]

Amendments

• **2017, Tax Cuts and Jobs Act (P.L. 115-97)**

P.L. 115-97, § 14202(a):

Amended part VIII of subchapter B of chapter 1 by adding at the end a new Code Sec. 250. **Effective** for tax years beginning after 12-31-2017.

[¶ 5425] CODE SEC. 263A. CAPITALIZATION AND INCLUSION IN INVENTORY COSTS OF CERTAIN EXPENSES.

* * *

(b) PROPERTY TO WHICH SECTION APPLIES.—Except as otherwise provided in this section, this section shall apply to—

* * *

(2) PROPERTY ACQUIRED FOR RESALE.—*Real or personal property described in section 1221(a)(1) which is acquired by the taxpayer for resale.*

* * *

[CCH Explanation at ¶ 570. Committee Reports at ¶ 10,330.]

Amendments

• **2017, Tax Cuts and Jobs Act (P.L. 115-97)**

P.L. 115-97, § 13102(b)(2):

Amended Code Sec. 263A(b)(2). **Effective** for tax years beginning after 12-31-2017. Prior to amendment, Code Sec. 263A(b)(2) read as follows:

(2) PROPERTY ACQUIRED FOR RESALE.—

(A) IN GENERAL.—Real or personal property described in section 1221(a)(1) which is acquired by the taxpayer for resale.

(B) EXCEPTION FOR TAXPAYER WITH GROSS RECEIPTS OF $10,000,000 OR LESS.—Subparagraph (A) shall not apply to any personal property acquired during any taxable year by the taxpayer for resale if the average annual gross receipts of the taxpayer (or any predecessor) for the 3-taxable year period ending with the taxable year preceding such taxable year do not exceed $10,000,000.

(C) AGGREGATION RULES, ETC.—For purposes of subparagraph (B), rules similar to the rules of paragraphs (2) and (3) of section 448(c) shall apply.

(d) EXCEPTION FOR FARMING BUSINESSES.—

* * *

(2) TREATMENT OF CERTAIN PLANTS LOST BY REASON OF CASUALTY.—

* * *

(C) *SPECIAL TEMPORARY RULE FOR CITRUS PLANTS LOST BY REASON OF CASUALTY.—*

(i) IN GENERAL.—*In the case of the replanting of citrus plants, subparagraph (A) shall apply to amounts paid or incurred by a person (other than the taxpayer described in subparagraph (A)) if—*

(I) *the taxpayer described in subparagraph (A) has an equity interest of not less than 50 percent in the replanted citrus plants at all times during the taxable year in which such amounts were paid or incurred and such other person holds any part of the remaining equity interest, or*

(II) *such other person acquired the entirety of such taxpayer's equity interest in the land on which the lost or damaged citrus plants were located at the time of such loss or damage, and the replanting is on such land.*

(ii) TERMINATION.—Clause (i) shall not apply to any cost paid or incurred after the date which is 10 years after the date of the enactment of the Tax Cuts and Jobs Act.

* * *

[CCH Explanation at ¶ 440. Committee Reports at ¶ 10,400.]
Amendments
• **2017, Tax Cuts and Jobs Act (P.L. 115-97)**

P.L. 115-97, § 13207(a):

Amended Code Sec. 263A(d)(2) by adding at the end a new subparagraph (C). **Effective** for costs paid or incurred after 12-22-2017.

(f) SPECIAL RULES FOR ALLOCATION OF INTEREST TO PROPERTY PRODUCED BY THE TAXPAYER.—

* * *

(4) EXEMPTION FOR AGING PROCESS OF BEER, WINE, AND DISTILLED SPIRITS.—

(A) IN GENERAL.—For purposes of this subsection, the production period shall not include the aging period for—

(i) beer (as defined in section 5052(a)),

(ii) wine (as described in section 5041(a)), or

(iii) distilled spirits (as defined in section 5002(a)(8)), except such spirits that are unfit for use for beverage purposes.

(B) TERMINATION.—This paragraph shall not apply to interest costs paid or accrued after December 31, 2019.

(5) DEFINITIONS.—For purposes of this subsection—

(A) LONG USEFUL LIFE.—Property has a long useful life if such property is—

(i) real property, or

(ii) property with a class life of 20 years or more (as determined under section 168).

(B) PRODUCTION PERIOD.—The term "production period" means, when used with respect to any property, the period—

(i) beginning on the date on which production of the property begins, and

(ii) *except as provided in paragraph (4),* ending on the date on which the property is ready to be placed in service or is ready to be held for sale.

(C) PRODUCTION EXPENDITURES.—The term "production expenditures" means the costs (whether or not incurred during the production period) required to be capitalized under subsection (a) with respect to the property.

* * *

[CCH Explanation at ¶ 825. Committee Reports at ¶ 10,890.]
Amendments
• **2017, Tax Cuts and Jobs Act (P.L. 115-97)**

P.L. 115-97, § 13801(a)(1)-(2):

Amended Code Sec. 263A(f) by redesignating paragraph (4) as paragraph (5), and by inserting after paragraph (3) a new paragraph (4). **Effective** for interest costs paid or accrued in calendar years beginning after 12-31-2017.

P.L. 115-97, § 13801(b):

Amended Code Sec. 263A(f)(5)(B)(ii), as redesignated by Act Sec. 13801, by inserting "except as provided in paragraph (4)," before "ending on the date". **Effective** for interest costs paid or accrued in calendar years beginning after 12-31-2017.

(i) EXEMPTION FOR CERTAIN SMALL BUSINESSES.—

(1) IN GENERAL.—In the case of any taxpayer (other than a tax shelter prohibited from using the cash receipts and disbursements method of accounting under section 448(a)(3)) which meets the gross receipts

test of section 448(c) for any taxable year, this section shall not apply with respect to such taxpayer for such taxable year.

(2) APPLICATION OF GROSS RECEIPTS TEST TO INDIVIDUALS, ETC.—In the case of any taxpayer which is not a corporation or a partnership, the gross receipts test of section 448(c) shall be applied in the same manner as if each trade or business of such taxpayer were a corporation or partnership.

(3) COORDINATION WITH SECTION 481.—Any change in method of accounting made pursuant to this subsection shall be treated for purposes of section 481 as initiated by the taxpayer and made with the consent of the Secretary.

[CCH Explanation at ¶570. Committee Reports at ¶10,330.]

Amendments

• 2017, Tax Cuts and Jobs Act (P.L. 115-97)

P.L. 115-97, §13102(b)(1):

Amended Code Sec. 263A by redesignating subsection (i) as subsection (j) and by inserting after subsection (h) a new

subsection (i). **Effective** for tax years beginning after 12-31-2017.

(j) REGULATIONS.—The Secretary shall prescribe such regulations as may be necessary or appropriate to carry out the purposes of this section, including—

(1) regulations to prevent the use of related parties, pass-thru entities, or intermediaries to avoid the application of this section, and

(2) regulations providing for simplified procedures for the application of this section in the case of property described in subsection (b)(2).

[CCH Explanation at ¶570. Committee Reports at ¶10,330.]

Amendments

• 2017, Tax Cuts and Jobs Act (P.L. 115-97)

P.L. 115-97, §13102(b)(1):

Amended Code Sec. 263A by redesignating subsection (i) as subsection (j). **Effective** for tax years beginning after 12-31-2017.

[¶5430] CODE SEC. 267A. CERTAIN RELATED PARTY AMOUNTS PAID OR ACCRUED IN HYBRID TRANSACTIONS OR WITH HYBRID ENTITIES.

(a) IN GENERAL.—No deduction shall be allowed under this chapter for any disqualified related party amount paid or accrued pursuant to a hybrid transaction or by, or to, a hybrid entity.

(b) DISQUALIFIED RELATED PARTY AMOUNT.—For purposes of this section—

(1) DISQUALIFIED RELATED PARTY AMOUNT.—The term "disqualified related party amount" means any interest or royalty paid or accrued to a related party to the extent that—

(A) such amount is not included in the income of such related party under the tax law of the country of which such related party is a resident for tax purposes or is subject to tax, or

(B) such related party is allowed a deduction with respect to such amount under the tax law of such country.

Such term shall not include any payment to the extent such payment is included in the gross income of a United States shareholder under section 951(a).

(2) RELATED PARTY.—The term "related party" means a related person as defined in section 954(d)(3), except that such section shall be applied with respect to the person making the payment described in paragraph (1) in lieu of the controlled foreign corporation otherwise referred to in such section.

(c) HYBRID TRANSACTION.—For purposes of this section, the term "hybrid transaction" means any transaction, series of transactions, agreement, or instrument one or more payments with respect to which are treated as interest or royalties for purposes of this chapter and which are not so treated for purposes [of] the tax law of the foreign country of which the recipient of such payment is resident for tax purposes or is subject to tax.

(d) HYBRID ENTITY.—For purposes of this section, the term "hybrid entity" means any entity which is either—

(1) treated as fiscally transparent for purposes of this chapter but not so treated for purposes of the tax law of the foreign country of which the entity is resident for tax purposes or is subject to tax, or

(2) treated as fiscally transparent for purposes of such tax law but not so treated for purposes of this chapter.

(e) REGULATIONS.—The Secretary shall issue such regulations or other guidance as may be necessary or appropriate to carry out the purposes of this section, including regulations or other guidance providing for—

(1) rules for treating certain conduit arrangements which involve a hybrid transaction or a hybrid entity as subject to subsection (a),

(2) rules for the application of this section to branches or domestic entities,

(3) rules for treating certain structured transactions as subject to subsection (a),

(4) rules for treating a tax preference as an exclusion from income for purposes of applying subsection (b)(1) if such tax preference has the effect of reducing the generally applicable statutory rate by 25 percent or more,

(5) rules for treating the entire amount of interest or royalty paid or accrued to a related party as a disqualified related party amount if such amount is subject to a participation exemption system or other system which provides for the exclusion or deduction of a substantial portion of such amount,

(6) rules for determining the tax residence of a foreign entity if the entity is otherwise considered a resident of more than one country or of no country,

(7) exceptions from subsection (a) with respect to—

(A) cases in which the disqualified related party amount is taxed under the laws of a foreign country other than the country of which the related party is a resident for tax purposes, and

(B) other cases which the Secretary determines do not present a risk of eroding the Federal tax base,

(8) requirements for record keeping and information reporting in addition to any requirements imposed by section 6038A.

[CCH Explanation at ¶ 760. Committee Reports at ¶ 11,150.]
Amendments
• **2017, Tax Cuts and Jobs Act (P.L. 115-97)**
P.L. 115-97, § 14222(a):
Amended part IX of subchapter B of chapter 1 by inserting after Code Sec. 267 a new Code Sec. 267A. **Effective** for tax years beginning after 12-31-2017.

[¶ 5435] CODE SEC. 274. DISALLOWANCE OF CERTAIN ENTERTAINMENT, ETC., EXPENSES.

(a) ENTERTAINMENT, AMUSEMENT, RECREATION, OR QUALIFIED TRANSPORTATION FRINGES.—

(1) IN GENERAL.—No deduction otherwise allowable under this chapter shall be allowed for any item—

(A) ACTIVITY.—With respect to an activity which is of a type generally considered to constitute entertainment, amusement, or recreation, or

(B) FACILITY.—With respect to a facility used in connection with an activity referred to in subparagraph (A).

(2) SPECIAL RULES.—For purposes of applying paragraph (1)—

(A) Dues or fees to any social, athletic, or sporting club or organization shall be treated as items with respect to facilities.

(B) An activity described in section 212 shall be treated as a trade or business.

(C) [*Stricken.*]

(3) DENIAL OF DEDUCTION FOR CLUB DUES.—Notwithstanding the preceding provisions of this subsection, no deduction shall be allowed under this chapter for amounts paid or incurred for membership in any club organized for business, pleasure, recreation, or other social purpose.

(4) QUALIFIED TRANSPORTATION FRINGES.—No deduction shall be allowed under this chapter for the expense of any qualified transportation fringe (as defined in section 132(f)) provided to an employee of the taxpayer.

* * *

[CCH Explanation at ¶ 535. Committee Reports at ¶ 10,450.]

Amendments

• 2017, Tax Cuts and Jobs Act (P.L. 115-97)

P.L. 115-97, § 13304(a)(1)(A)-(C):

Amended Code Sec. 274(a) by striking "unless" and all that follows through "trade or business," in paragraph (1)(A), by striking the flush sentence at the end of paragraph (1), and by striking paragraph (2)(C). **Effective** for amounts incurred or paid after 12-31-2017. Prior to amendment, Code Sec. 274(a)(1) and (2)(C) read as follows:

(1) IN GENERAL.—No deduction otherwise allowable under this chapter shall be allowed for any item—

(A) ACTIVITY.—With respect to an activity which is of a type generally considered to constitute entertainment, amusement, or recreation, unless the taxpayer establishes that the item was directly related to, or, in the case of an item directly preceding or following a substantial and bona fide business discussion (including business meetings at a convention or otherwise), that such item was associated with, the active conduct of the taxpayer's trade or business, or

(B) FACILITY.—With respect to a facility used in connection with an activity referred to in subparagraph (A).

In the case of an item described in subparagraph (A), the deduction shall in no event exceed the portion of such item which meets the requirements of subparagraph (A).

* * *

(C) In the case of a club, paragraph (1)(B) shall apply unless the taxpayer establishes that the facility was used primarily for the furtherance of the taxpayer's trade or business and that the item was directly related to the active conduct of such trade or business.

P.L. 115-97, § 13304(c)(1)(A)-(B):

Amended Code Sec. 274(a), as amended by Act. Sec. 13304(a), by striking "OR RECREATION" in the heading and inserting "RECREATION, OR QUALIFIED TRANSPORTATION FRINGES", and by adding at the end a new paragraph (4). **Effective** for amounts incurred or paid after 12-31-2017.

(d) SUBSTANTIATION REQUIRED.—No deduction or credit shall be allowed—

(1) under section 162 or 212 for any traveling expense (including meals and lodging while away from home),

(2) for any expense for gifts, or

(3) with respect to any listed property (as defined in section 280F(d)(4)),

unless the taxpayer substantiates by adequate records or by sufficient evidence corroborating the taxpayer's own statement (A) the amount of such expense or other item, (B) the time and place of the travel or the date and description of the gift, (C) the business purpose of the expense or other item, and *(D) the business relationship to the taxpayer of the person receiving the benefit.* The Secretary may by regulations provide that some or all of the requirements of the preceding sentence shall not apply in the case of an expense which does not exceed an amount prescribed pursuant to such regulations. This subsection shall not apply to any qualified nonpersonal use vehicle (as defined in subsection (i)).

* * *

[CCH Explanation at ¶ 535. Committee Reports at ¶ 10,450.]

Amendments

• 2017, Tax Cuts and Jobs Act (P.L. 115-97)

P.L. 115-97, § 13304(a)(2)(A)(i)-(ii):

Amended Code Sec. 274(d) by striking paragraph (2) and redesignating paragraphs (3) and (4) as paragraphs (2) and (3), respectively, and in the flush text following paragraph (3) (as so redesignated), by striking ", entertainment, amusement, recreation, or use of the facility or property," following "the time and place of the travel," in item (B), and by

striking "(D) the business relationship to the taxpayer of persons entertained, using the facility or property, or receiving the gift" and inserting "(D) the business relationship to the taxpayer of the person receiving the benefit". **Effective** for amounts incurred or paid after 12-31-2017. Prior to being stricken, Code Sec. 274(d)(2) read as follows:

(2) for any item with respect to an activity which is of a type generally considered to constitute entertainment, amusement, or recreation, or with respect to a facility used in connection with such an activity,

(j) EMPLOYEE ACHIEVEMENT AWARDS.—

* * *

    (3) DEFINITIONS.—For purposes of this subsection—

        (A) EMPLOYEE ACHIEVEMENT AWARD.—

            (i) *IN GENERAL.—The term* "employee achievement award" means an item of tangible personal property which is—

                (I) transferred by an employer to an employee for length of service achievement or safety achievement,

                (II) awarded as part of a meaningful presentation, and

                (III) awarded under conditions and circumstances that do not create a significant likelihood of the payment of disguised compensation.

            (ii) TANGIBLE PERSONAL PROPERTY.—For purposes of clause (i), the term "tangible personal property" shall not include—

                (I) cash, cash equivalents, gift cards, gift coupons, or gift certificates (other than arrangements conferring only the right to select and receive tangible personal property from a limited array of such items pre-selected or pre-approved by the employer), or

                (II) vacations, meals, lodging, tickets to theater or sporting events, stocks, bonds, other securities, and other similar items.

* * *

[CCH Explanation at ¶ 537. Committee Reports at ¶ 10,510.]

Amendments

• **2017, Tax Cuts and Jobs Act (P.L. 115-97)**

P.L. 115-97, § 13310(a)(1)-(3):

Amended Code Sec. 274(j)(3)(A) by striking "The term" and inserting

    (l) [*Stricken.*]

"(i) IN GENERAL.—The term",

by redesignating clauses (i), (ii), and (iii) as subclauses (I), (II), and (III), respectively, and conforming the margins accordingly, and by adding at the end a new clause (ii). **Effective** for amounts paid or incurred after 12-31-2017.

[CCH Explanation at ¶ 535. Committee Reports at ¶ 10,450.]

Amendments

• **2017, Tax Cuts and Jobs Act (P.L. 115-97)**

P.L. 115-97, § 13304(a)(2)(B):

Amended Code Sec. 274 by striking subsection (l). **Effective** for amounts incurred or paid after 12-31-2017. Prior to being stricken, Code Sec. 274(l) read as follows:

(l) ADDITIONAL LIMITATIONS ON ENTERTAINMENT TICKETS.—

(1) ENTERTAINMENT TICKETS.—

(A) IN GENERAL.—In determining the amount allowable as a deduction under this chapter for any ticket for any activity or facility described in subsection (d)(2), the amount taken into account shall not exceed the face value of such ticket.

(B) EXCEPTION FOR CERTAIN CHARITABLE SPORTS EVENTS.—Subparagraph (A) shall not apply to any ticket for any sports event—

(i) which is organized for the primary purpose of benefiting an organization which is described in section 501(c)(3) and exempt from tax under section 501(a),

(ii) all of the net proceeds of which are contributed to such organization, and

(iii) which utilizes volunteers for substantially all of the work performed in carrying out such event.

(2) SKYBOXES, ETC.—In the case of a skybox or other private luxury box leased for more than 1 event, the amount allowable as a deduction under this chapter with respect to such events shall not exceed the sum of the face value of non-luxury box seat tickets for the seats in such box covered by the lease. For purposes of the preceding sentence, 2 or more related leases shall be treated as 1 lease.

    (l) TRANSPORTATION AND COMMUTING BENEFITS.—

        (1) IN GENERAL.—No deduction shall be allowed under this chapter for any expense incurred for providing any transportation, or any payment or reimbursement, to an employee of the taxpayer in connection with travel between the employee's residence and place of employment, except as necessary for ensuring the safety of the employee.

        (2) EXCEPTION.—In the case of any qualified bicycle commuting reimbursement (as described in section 132(f)(5)(F)), this subsection shall not apply for any amounts paid or incurred after December 31, 2017, and before January 1, 2026.

* * *

[CCH Explanation at ¶535. Committee Reports at ¶10,450.]

Amendments

• **2017, Tax Cuts and Jobs Act (P.L. 115-97)**

P.L. 115-97, §13304(c)(2):

Amended Code Sec. 274 by inserting after subsection (k) a new subsection (l). **Effective** for amounts incurred or paid after 12-31-2017.

(n) ONLY 50 PERCENT OF MEAL EXPENSES ALLOWED AS DEDUCTION.—

(1) IN GENERAL.—*The amount allowable as a deduction under this chapter for any expense for food or beverages shall not exceed 50 percent of the amount of such expense which would (but for this paragraph) be allowable as a deduction under this chapter.*

(2) EXCEPTIONS.—Paragraph (1) shall not apply to any expense if—

(A) such expense is described in paragraph (2), (3), (4), (7), (8), or (9) of subsection (e);

(B) in the case of an employer who pays or reimburses moving expenses of an employee, such expenses are includible in the income of the employee under section 82, or

(C) such expense is for food or beverages—

(i) required by any Federal law to be provided to crew members of a commercial vessel,

(ii) provided to crew members of a commercial vessel—

(I) which is operating on the Great Lakes, the Saint Lawrence Seaway, or any inland waterway of the United States, and

(II) which is of a kind which would be required by Federal law to provide food and beverages to crew members if it were operated at sea,

(iii) provided on an oil or gas platform or drilling rig if the platform or rig is located offshore, or

(iv) provided on an oil or gas platform or drilling rig, or at a support camp which is in proximity and integral to such platform or rig, if the platform or rig is located in the United States north of 54 degrees north latitude.

Clauses (i) and (ii) *of subparagraph (C)* shall not apply to vessels primarily engaged in providing luxury water transportation (determined under the principles of subsection (m)). In the case of the employee, the exception of subparagraph (A) shall not apply to expenses described *in subparagraph (B).*

(3) SPECIAL RULE FOR INDIVIDUALS SUBJECT TO FEDERAL HOURS OF SERVICE.—In the case of any expenses for food or beverages consumed while away from home (within the meaning of section 162(a)(2)) by an individual during, or incident to, the period of duty subject to the hours of service limitations of the Department of Transportation, paragraph (1) shall be applied by substituting "80 percent" for "50 percent".

[CCH Explanation at ¶535. Committee Reports at ¶10,450.]

Amendments

• **2017, Tax Cuts and Jobs Act (P.L. 115-97)**

P.L. 115-97, §13304(a)(2)(C):

Amended Code Sec. 274(n) by striking "AND ENTERTAINMENT" following "50 PERCENT OF MEAL" in the heading. **Effective** for amounts incurred or paid after 12-31-2017.

P.L. 115-97, §13304(a)(2)(D):

Amended Code Sec. 274(n)(1). **Effective** for amounts incurred or paid after 12-31-2017. Prior to amendment, Code Sec. 274(n)(1) read as follows:

(1) IN GENERAL.—The amount allowable as a deduction under this chapter for—

(A) any expense for food or beverages, and

(B) any item with respect to an activity which is of a type generally considered to constitute entertainment, amusement, or recreation, or with respect to a facility used in connection with such activity,

shall not exceed 50 percent of the amount of such expense or item which would (but for this paragraph) be allowable as a deduction under this chapter.

P.L. 115-97, §13304(a)(2)(E)(i)-(iv):

Amended Code Sec. 274(n)(2) by striking "in the case of an expense for food or beverages," before "such expense is excludable" in subparagraph (B), by striking subparagraph (C) and redesignating subparagraphs (D) and (E) as subparagraphs (C) and (D), respectively, by striking "of subparagraph (E)" [in] the last sentence and inserting "of subparagraph (D)", and by striking "in subparagraph (D)" in the last [penultimate] sentence and inserting "in subparagraph (C)". **Effective** for amounts incurred or paid after 12-31-2017. Prior to being stricken, Code Sec. 274(n)(2)(C) read as follows:

(C) such expense is covered by a package involving a ticket described in subsection (l)(1)(B),

P.L. 115-97, § 13304(b)(1)-(4):

Amended Code Sec. 274(n)(2), as amended by Act Sec. 13304(a), by striking subparagraph (B), by redesignating subparagraphs (C) and (D) as subparagraphs (B) and (C), respectively, by striking "of subparagraph (D)" in the last [penultimate] sentence and inserting "of subparagraph (C)", and by striking "in subparagraph (C)" in the last sentence and inserting "in subparagraph (B)". **Effective** for amounts incurred or paid after 12-31-2017. Prior to being stricken, Code Sec. 274(n)(2)(B) read as follows:

(B) such expense is excludable from the gross income of the recipient under section 132 by reason of subsection (e) thereof (relating to de minimis fringes),

➤➤➤→ *Caution: Code Sec. 274(o), below, as added by P.L. 115-97, applies to amounts incurred or paid after December 31, 2025.*

(o) MEALS PROVIDED AT CONVENIENCE OF EMPLOYER.—*No deduction shall be allowed under this chapter for—*

(1) *any expense for the operation of a facility described in section 132(e)(2), and any expense for food or beverages, including under section 132(e)(1), associated with such facility, or*

(2) *any expense for meals described in section 119(a).*

[CCH Explanation at ¶ 535. Committee Reports at ¶ 10,450.]

Amendments

• **2017, Tax Cuts and Jobs Act (P.L. 115-97)**

P.L. 115-97, § 13304(d)(1)-(2):

Amended Code Sec. 274, as amended by Act. Sec. 13304(c), by redesignating subsection (o) as subsection (p), and by inserting after subsection (n) a new subsection (o). **Effective** for amounts incurred or paid after 12-31-2025.

➤➤➤→ *Caution: Former Code Sec. 274(o) was redesignated as Code Sec. 274(p), below, by P.L. 115-97, applicable to amounts incurred or paid after December 31, 2025.*

(p) REGULATORY AUTHORITY.—The Secretary shall prescribe such regulations as he may deem necessary to carry out the purposes of this section, including regulations prescribing whether subsection (a) or subsection (b) applies in cases where both such subsections would otherwise apply.

[CCH Explanation at ¶ 535. Committee Reports at ¶ 10,450.]

Amendments

• **2017, Tax Cuts and Jobs Act (P.L. 115-97)**

P.L. 115-97, § 13304(d)(1):

Amended Code Sec. 274, as amended by Act. Sec. 13304(c), by redesignating subsection (o) as subsection (p). **Effective** for amounts incurred or paid after 12-31-2025.

[¶ 5440] CODE SEC. 280C. CERTAIN EXPENSES FOR WHICH CREDITS ARE ALLOWABLE.

(a) RULE FOR EMPLOYMENT CREDITS.—No deduction shall be allowed for that portion of the wages or salaries paid or incurred for the taxable year which is equal to the sum of the credits determined for the taxable year under sections 45A(a), 45P(a), *45S(a),* 51(a), 1396(a), 1400P(b), and 1400R. In the case of a corporation which is a member of a controlled group of corporations (within the meaning of section 52(a)) or a trade or business which is treated as being under common control with other trades or businesses (within the meaning of section 52(b)), this subsection shall be applied under rules prescribed by the Secretary similar to the rules applicable under subsections (a) and (b) of section 52.

[CCH Explanation at ¶585. Committee Reports at ¶10,570.]

Amendments

• **2017, Tax Cuts and Jobs Act (P.L. 115-97)**

P.L. 115-97, §13403(d)(1):

Amended Code Sec. 280C(a) by inserting "45S(a)," after "45P(a),". **Effective** for wages paid in tax years beginning after 12-31-2017.

(b) CREDIT FOR QUALIFIED CLINICAL TESTING EXPENSES FOR CERTAIN DRUGS.—

* * *

(3) ELECTION OF REDUCED CREDIT.—

(A) IN GENERAL.—In the case of any taxable year for which an election is made under this paragraph—

(i) paragraphs (1) and (2) shall not apply, and

(ii) the amount of the credit under section 45C(a) shall be the amount determined under subparagraph (B).

(B) AMOUNT OF REDUCED CREDIT.—The amount of credit determined under this subparagraph for any taxable year shall be the amount equal to the excess of—

(i) the amount of credit determined under section 45C(a) without regard to this paragraph, over

(ii) the product of—

(I) the amount described in clause (i), and

(II) the maximum rate of tax under section 11(b).

(C) ELECTION.—An election under this paragraph for any taxable year shall be made not later than the time for filing the return of tax for such year (including extensions), shall be made on such return, and shall be made in such manner as the Secretary shall prescribe. Such an election, once made, shall be irrevocable.

*(4) CONTROLLED GROUPS.—*In the case of a corporation which is a member of a controlled group of corporations (within the meaning of section 41(f)(5)) or a trade or business which is treated as being under common control with other trades or business (within the meaning of section 41(f)(1)(B)), this subsection shall be applied under rules prescribed by the Secretary similar to the rules applicable under subparagraphs (A) and (B) of section 41(f)(1).

[CCH Explanation at ¶595. Committee Reports at ¶10,550.]

Amendments

• **2017, Tax Cuts and Jobs Act (P.L. 115-97)**

P.L. 115-97, §13401(b):

Amended Code Sec. 280C(b) by redesignating paragraph (3) as paragraph (4) and by inserting after paragraph (2) a new paragraph (3). **Effective** for tax years beginning after 12-31-2017.

(c) CREDIT FOR INCREASING RESEARCH ACTIVITIES.—

»»→ *Caution: Code Sec. 280C(c)(1), below, as added by P.L. 115-97, applies to amounts paid or incurred in tax years beginning after December 31, 2021.*

(1) IN GENERAL.—If—

(A) the amount of the credit determined for the taxable year under section 41(a)(1), exceeds

(B) the amount allowable as a deduction for such taxable year for qualified research expenses or basic research expenses,

the amount chargeable to capital account for the taxable year for such expenses shall be reduced by the amount of such excess.

≫⟶ *Caution: Former Code Sec. 280C(c)(3) was redesignated as Code Sec. 280C(c)(2), below, by P.L. 115-97, applicable to amounts paid or incurred in tax years beginning after December 31, 2021.*

(2) ELECTION OF REDUCED CREDIT.—

(A) IN GENERAL.—In the case of any taxable year for which an election is made under this paragraph—

≫⟶ *Caution: Caution: Code 280C(c)(2)(A)(i), below, as redesignated and amended by P.L. 115-97, applies to amounts paid or incurred in tax years beginning after December 31, 2021.*

(i) *paragraph (1)* shall not apply, and

(ii) the amount of the credit under section 41(a) shall be the amount determined under subparagraph (B).

(B) AMOUNT OF REDUCED CREDIT.—The amount of credit determined under this subparagraph for any taxable year shall be the amount equal to the excess of—

(i) the amount of credit determined under section 41(a) without regard to this paragraph, over

(ii) the product of—

(I) the amount described in clause (i), and

(II) the maximum rate of tax under *section 11(b)*.

(C) ELECTION.—An election under this paragraph for any taxable year shall be made not later than the time for filing the return of tax for such year (including extensions), shall be made on such return, and shall be made in such manner as the Secretary may prescribe. Such an election, once made, shall be irrevocable.

≫⟶ *Caution: Former Code Sec. 280C(c)(4) was redesignated as Code Sec. 280C(c)(3), below, by P.L. 115-97, applicable to amounts paid or incurred in tax years beginning after December 31, 2021.*

(3) CONTROLLED GROUPS.—Paragraph (3) of subsection (b) shall apply for purposes of this subsection.

* * *

[CCH Explanation at ¶ 305 and ¶ 525. Committee Reports at ¶ 10,310 and ¶ 10,390.]

Amendments

• **2017, Tax Cuts and Jobs Act (P.L. 115-97)**

P.L. 115-97, § 13001(b)(1)(A):

Amended Code Sec. 280C(c)(3)(B)(ii)(II) by striking "section 11(b)(1)" and inserting "section 11(b)". **Effective** for tax years beginning after 12-31-2017.

P.L. 115-97, § 13206(d)(2)(A)-(D):

Amended Code Sec. 280C(c) by striking paragraph (1) and inserting a new paragraph (1), by striking paragraph (2), by redesignating paragraphs (3) (as amended by this Act) and (4) as paragraphs (2) and (3), respectively, and in paragraph (2), as redesignated by Act Sec. 13206(d)(2)(C), by striking "paragraphs (1) and (2)" and inserting "paragraph (1)". **Effective** for amounts paid or incurred in tax years beginning after 12-31-2021. Prior to being stricken, Code Sec. 280C(c)(1)-(2) read as follows:

(1) IN GENERAL.—No deduction shall be allowed for that portion of the qualified research expenses (as defined in section 41(b)) or basic research expenses (as defined in section 41(e)(2)) otherwise allowable as a deduction for the taxable year which is equal to the amount of the credit determined for such taxable year under section 41(a).

(2) SIMILAR RULE WHERE TAXPAYER CAPITALIZES RATHER THAN DEDUCTS EXPENSES.—If—

(A) the amount of the credit determined for the taxable year under section 41(a)(1), exceeds

(B) the amount allowable as a deduction for such taxable year for qualified research expenses or basic research expenses (determined without regard to paragraph (1)),

the amount chargeable to capital account for the taxable year for such expenses shall be reduced by the amount of such excess.

[¶5445] CODE SEC. 280F. LIMITATION ON DEPRECIATION FOR LUXURY AUTOMOBILES; LIMITATION WHERE CERTAIN PROPERTY USED FOR PERSONAL PURPOSES.

(a) LIMITATION ON AMOUNT OF DEPRECIATION FOR LUXURY AUTOMOBILES.—

    (1) DEPRECIATION.—

        (A) LIMITATION.—The amount of the depreciation deduction for any taxable year for any passenger automobile shall not exceed—

            (i) *$10,000* for the 1st taxable year in the recovery period,

            (ii) *$16,000* for the 2nd taxable year in the recovery period,

            (iii) *$9,600* for the 3rd taxable year in the recovery period, and

            (iv) *$5,760* for each succeeding taxable year in the recovery period.

        (B) DISALLOWED DEDUCTIONS ALLOWED FOR YEARS AFTER RECOVERY PERIOD.—

* * *

        (ii) *$5,760* LIMITATION.—The amount treated as an expense under clause (i) for any taxable year shall not exceed *$5,760*.

* * *

[CCH Explanation at ¶415. Committee Reports at ¶10,350.]

Amendments

• **2017, Tax Cuts and Jobs Act (P.L. 115-97)**

P.L. 115-97, §13202(a)(1)(A)-(D):

  Amended Code Sec. 280F(a)(1)(A) by striking "$2,560" in clause (i) and inserting "$10,000", by striking "$4,100" in clause (ii) and inserting "$16,000", by striking "$2,450" in clause (iii) and inserting "$9,600", and by striking "$1,475" in clause (iv) and inserting "$5,760". **Effective** for property placed in service after 12-31-2017, in tax years ending after such date.

P.L. 115-97, §13202(a)(2)(A):

  Amended Code Sec. 280F(a)(1)(B)(ii) by striking "$1,475" in the text and heading and inserting "$5,760". **Effective** for property placed in service after 12-31-2017, in tax years ending after such date.

(d) DEFINITIONS AND SPECIAL RULES.—For purposes of this section—

* * *

    (4) LISTED PROPERTY.—

        (A) IN GENERAL.—Except as provided in subparagraph (B), the term "listed property" means—

            (i) any passenger automobile,

            (ii) any other property used as a means of transportation,

            (iii) any property of a type generally used for purposes of entertainment, recreation, or amusement, and

            (iv) any other property of a type specified by the Secretary by regulations.

        (B) EXCEPTION FOR PROPERTY USED IN BUSINESS OF TRANSPORTING PERSONS OR PROPERTY.— Except to the extent provided in regulations, clause (ii) of subparagraph (A) shall not apply to any property substantially all of the use of which is in a trade or business of providing to unrelated persons services consisting of the transportation of persons or property for compensation or hire.

* * *

    (7) AUTOMOBILE PRICE INFLATION ADJUSTMENT.—

        (A) IN GENERAL.—In the case of any passenger automobile placed in service after *2018*, subsection (a) shall be applied by increasing each dollar amount contained in such subsection by the automobile price inflation adjustment for the calendar year in which such automobile is placed in service. Any increase under the preceding sentence shall be rounded to the nearest multiple of $100 (or if the increase is a multiple of $50, such increase shall be increased to the next higher multiple of $100).

(B) *AUTOMOBILE PRICE INFLATION ADJUSTMENT.—For purposes of this paragraph—*

(i) *IN GENERAL.—The automobile price inflation adjustment for any calendar year is the percentage (if any) by which—*

(I) *the C-CPI-U automobile component for October of the preceding calendar year, exceeds*

(II) *the automobile component of the CPI (as defined in section 1(f)(4)) for October of 2017, multiplied by the amount determined under 1(f)(3)(B).*

(ii) *C-CPI-U AUTOMOBILE COMPONENT.—The term "C-CPI-U automobile component" means the automobile component of the Chained Consumer Price Index for All Urban Consumers (as described in section 1(f)(6)).*

* * *

[CCH Explanation at ¶ 125, ¶ 415, and ¶ 420. Committee Reports at ¶ 10,020 and ¶ 10,350.]

Amendments

• **2017, Tax Cuts and Jobs Act (P.L. 115-97)**

P.L. 115-97, § 11002(d)(8):

Amended Code Sec. 280F(d)(7)(B). **Effective** for tax years beginning after 12-31-2017. Prior to amendment, Code Sec. 280F(d)(7)(B) read as follows:

(B) AUTOMOBILE PRICE INFLATION ADJUSTMENT.—For purposes of this paragraph—

(i) IN GENERAL.—The automobile price inflation adjustment for any calendar year is the percentage (if any) by which—

(I) the CPI automobile component for October of the preceding calendar year, exceeds

(II) the CPI automobile component for October of 1987.

(ii) CPI AUTOMOBILE COMPONENT.—The term "CPI automobile component" means the automobile component of the Consumer Price Index for All Urban Consumers published by the Department of Labor.

P.L. 115-97, § 13202(a)(2)(B)(i)-(ii):

Amended Code Sec. 280F(d)(7) by striking "1988" in subparagraph (A) and inserting "2018", and by striking "1987" in subparagraph (B)(i)(II) and inserting "2017". **Effective** for property placed in service after 12-31-2017, in tax years ending after such date.

P.L. 115-97, § 13202(b)(1)(A)-(C):

Amended Code Sec. 280F(d)(4)(A) by inserting "and" at the end of clause (iii), by striking clause (iv), and by redesignating clause (v) as clause (iv). **Effective** for property placed in service after 12-31-2017, in tax years ending after such date. Prior to being stricken, Code Sec. 280F(d)(4)(A)(iv) read as follows:

(iv) any computer or peripheral equipment (as defined in section 168(i)(2)(B)), and

P.L. 115-97, § 13202(b)(2):

Amended Code Sec. 280F(d)(4) by striking subparagraph (B) and by redesignating subparagraph (C) as subparagraph (B). **Effective** for property placed in service after 12-31-2017, in tax years ending after such date. Prior to being stricken, Code Sec. 280F(d)(4)(B) read as follows:

(B) EXCEPTION FOR CERTAIN COMPUTERS.—The term "listed property" shall not include any computer or peripheral equipment (as so defined) used exclusively at a regular business establishment and owned or leased by the person operating such establishment. For purposes of the preceding sentence, any portion of a dwelling unit shall be treated as a regular business establishment if (and only if) the requirements of section 280A(c)(1) are met with respect to such portion.

[¶ 5450] CODE SEC. 367. FOREIGN CORPORATIONS.

(a) TRANSFERS OF PROPERTY FROM THE UNITED STATES.—

* * *

(3) SPECIAL RULE FOR TRANSFER OF PARTNERSHIP INTERESTS.—Except as provided in regulations prescribed by the Secretary, a transfer by a United States person of an interest in a partnership to a foreign corporation in an exchange described in paragraph (1) shall, for purposes of this subsection, be treated as a transfer to such corporation of such person's pro rata share of the assets of the partnership.

(4) PARAGRAPH (2) NOT TO APPLY TO CERTAIN SECTION 361 TRANSACTIONS.—Paragraph (2) shall not apply in the case of an exchange described in subsection (a) or (b) of section 361. Subject to such basis adjustments and such other conditions as shall be provided in regulations, the preceding sentence shall not apply if the transferor corporation is controlled (within the meaning of section 368(c)) by 5 or fewer domestic corporations. For purposes of the preceding sentence, all members of the same affiliated group (within the meaning of section 1504) shall be treated as 1 corporation.

(5) SECRETARY MAY EXEMPT CERTAIN TRANSACTIONS FROM APPLICATION OF THIS SUBSECTION.—Paragraph (1) shall not apply to the transfer of any property which the Secretary, in order to carry out the purposes of this subsection, designates by regulation.

* * *

[CCH Explanation at ¶707. Committee Reports at ¶11,050.]

Amendments

• **2017, Tax Cuts and Jobs Act (P.L. 115-97)**

P.L. 115-97, §14102(e)(1):

Amended Code Sec. 367(a) by striking paragraph (3) and redesignating paragraphs (4), (5), and (6) as paragraphs (3), (4), and (5), respectively. **Effective** for transfers after 12-31-2017. Prior to being stricken, Code Sec. 367(a)(3) read as follows:

(3) EXCEPTION FOR TRANSFERS OF CERTAIN PROPERTY USED IN THE ACTIVE CONDUCT OF A TRADE OR BUSINESS.—

(A) IN GENERAL.—Except as provided in regulations prescribed by the Secretary, paragraph (1) shall not apply to any property transferred to a foreign corporation for use by such foreign corporation in the active conduct of a trade or business outside of the United States.

(B) PARAGRAPH NOT TO APPLY TO CERTAIN PROPERTY.—Except as provided in regulations prescribed by the Secretary, subparagraph (A) shall not apply to any—

(i) property described in paragraph (1) or (3) of section 1221(a) (relating to inventory and copyrights, etc.),

(ii) installment obligations, accounts receivable, or similar property,

(iii) foreign currency or other property denominated in foreign currency,

(iv) intangible property (within the meaning of section 936(h)(3)(B)), or

(v) property with respect to which the transferor is a lessor at the time of the transfer, except that this clause shall not apply if the transferee was the lessee.

(d) SPECIAL RULES RELATING TO TRANSFERS OF INTANGIBLES.—

* * *

(2) TRANSFER OF INTANGIBLES TREATED AS TRANSFER PURSUANT TO SALE OF CONTINGENT PAYMENTS.—

* * *

(C) TRANSFER OF FOREIGN BRANCH WITH PREVIOUSLY DEDUCTED LOSSES.—Except as provided in regulations prescribed by the Secretary, subparagraph (A) shall not apply to gain realized on the transfer of the assets of a foreign branch of a United States person to a foreign corporation in an exchange described in paragraph (1) to the extent that—

(i) the sum of losses—

(I) which were incurred by the foreign branch before the transfer, and

(II) with respect to which a deduction was allowed to the taxpayer, exceeds

(ii) the sum of—

(I) any taxable income of such branch for a taxable year after the taxable year in which the loss was incurred and through the close of the taxable year of the transfer, and

(II) the amount which is recognized under section 904(f)(3) on account of the transfer.

Any gain recognized by reason of the preceding sentence shall be treated for purposes of this chapter as income from sources outside the United States having the same character as such losses had.

P.L. 115-97, §14102(e)(2)(A)-(B):

Amended Code Sec. 367(a)(4), as redesignated by Act Sec. 14102(e)(1), by striking "Paragraphs (2) and (3)" and inserting "Paragraph (2)", and by striking "PARAGRAPHS (2) AND (3)" in the heading and inserting "PARAGRAPH (2)". **Effective** for transfers after 12-31-2017.

(D) REGULATORY AUTHORITY.—For purposes of the last sentence of subparagraph (A), the Secretary shall require—

(i) the valuation of transfers of intangible property, including intangible property transferred with other property or services, on an aggregate basis, or

(ii) the valuation of such a transfer on the basis of the realistic alternatives to such a transfer,

if the Secretary determines that such basis is the most reliable means of valuation of such transfers.

* * *

[CCH Explanation at ¶755. Committee Reports at ¶11,140.]

Amendments

• **2017, Tax Cuts and Jobs Act (P.L. 115-97)**

P.L. 115-97, §14221(b)(1):

Amended Code Sec. 367(d)(2) by adding at the end a new subparagraph (D). **Effective** for transfers in tax years beginning after 12-31-2017.

[¶5455] CODE SEC. 381. CARRYOVERS IN CERTAIN CORPORATE ACQUISITIONS.

* * *

(c) ITEMS OF THE DISTRIBUTOR OR TRANSFEROR CORPORATION.—The items referred to in subsection (a) are:

* * *

(20) CARRYFORWARD OF DISALLOWED BUSINESS INTEREST.—The carryover of disallowed business interest described in section 163(j)(2) to taxable years ending after the date of distribution or transfer.

* * *

[CCH Explanation at ¶510. Committee Reports at ¶10,420.]
Amendments
• **2017, Tax Cuts and Jobs Act (P.L. 115-97)**

P.L. 115-97, § 13301(b)(1):

Amended Code Sec. 381(c) by inserting after paragraph (19) a new paragraph (20). **Effective** for tax years beginning after 12-31-2017.

(d) *[Stricken.]*

[CCH Explanation at ¶905. Committee Reports at ¶10,630.]
Amendments
• **2017, Tax Cuts and Jobs Act (P.L. 115-97)**

P.L. 115-97, § 13511(b)(3):

Amended Code Sec. 381 by striking subsection (d). **Effective** for losses arising in tax years beginning after 12-31-2017. Prior to being stricken, Code Sec. 381(d) read as follows:

(d) OPERATIONS LOSS CARRYBACKS AND CARRYOVERS OF LIFE INSURANCE COMPANIES.—

For application of this part to operations loss carrybacks and carryovers of life insurance companies, see section 810.

[¶5460] CODE SEC. 382. LIMITATION ON NET OPERATING LOSS CARRYFORWARDS AND CERTAIN BUILT-IN LOSSES FOLLOWING OWNERSHIP CHANGE.

* * *

(d) PRE-CHANGE LOSS AND POST-CHANGE YEAR.—For purposes of this section—

* * *

(3) APPLICATION TO CARRYFORWARD OF DISALLOWED INTEREST.—The term "pre-change loss" shall include any carryover of disallowed interest described in section 163(j)(2) under rules similar to the rules of paragraph (1).

* * *

[CCH Explanation at ¶510. Committee Reports at ¶10,420.]
Amendments
• **2017, Tax Cuts and Jobs Act (P.L. 115-97)**

P.L. 115-97, § 13301(b)(2):

Amended Code Sec. 382(d) by adding at the end a new paragraph (3). **Effective** for tax years beginning after 12-31-2017.

(k) DEFINITIONS AND SPECIAL RULES.—For purposes of this section—

(1) LOSS CORPORATION.—The term "loss corporation" means a corporation entitled to use a net operating loss carryover or having a net operating loss for the taxable year in which the ownership change occurs. *Such term shall include any corporation entitled to use a carryforward of*

disallowed interest described in section 381(c)(20). Except to the extent provided in regulations, such term includes any corporation with a net unrealized built-in loss.

* * *

[CCH Explanation at ¶ 510. Committee Reports at ¶ 10,420.]

Amendments

• **2017, Tax Cuts and Jobs Act (P.L. 115-97)**

P.L. 115-97, § 13301(b)(3):

Amended Code Sec. 382(k)(1) by inserting after the first sentence a new sentence. **Effective** for tax years beginning after 12-31-2017.

(l) CERTAIN ADDITIONAL OPERATING RULES.—For purposes of this section—

* * *

(3) OPERATING RULES RELATING TO OWNERSHIP OF STOCK.—

* * *

(B) STOCK ACQUIRED BY REASON OF DEATH, GIFT, DIVORCE, SEPARATION, ETC.—If—

* * *

(iii) stock is acquired by a person pursuant to any divorce or separation instrument (within the meaning of *section 121(d)(3)(C)*),

* * *

[CCH Explanation at ¶ 255. Committee Reports at ¶ 10,260.]

Amendments

• **2017, Tax Cuts and Jobs Act (P.L. 115-97)**

P.L. 115-97, § 11051(b)(3)(F):

Amended Code Sec. 382(l)(3)(B)(iii) by striking "section 71(b)(2)" and inserting "section 121(d)(3)(C)". For the **effective** date, see Act Sec. 11051(c)(1)-(2), below.

P.L. 115-97, § 11051(c)(1)-(2), provides:

(c) EFFECTIVE DATE.—The amendments made by this section shall apply to—

(1) any divorce or separation instrument (as defined in section 71(b)(2) of the Internal Revenue Code of 1986 as in effect before the date of the enactment of this Act) executed after December 31, 2018, and

(2) any divorce or separation instrument (as so defined) executed on or before such date and modified after such date if the modification expressly provides that the amendments made by this section apply to such modification.

[¶ 5465] CODE SEC. 402. TAXABILITY OF BENEFICIARY OF EMPLOYEES' TRUST.

* * *

(c) RULES APPLICABLE TO ROLLOVERS FROM EXEMPT TRUSTS.—

* * *

(3) *TIME LIMIT ON TRANSFERS.—*

(A) IN GENERAL.—Except as provided in *subparagraphs (B) and (C),* paragraph (1) shall not apply to any transfer of a distribution made after the 60th day following the day on which the distributee received the property distributed.

(B) HARDSHIP EXCEPTION.—The Secretary may waive the 60-day requirement under subparagraph (A) where the failure to waive such requirement would be against equity or good conscience, including casualty, disaster, or other events beyond the reasonable control of the individual subject to such requirement.

(C) *ROLLOVER OF CERTAIN PLAN LOAN OFFSET AMOUNTS.—*

(i) IN GENERAL.—*In the case of a qualified plan loan offset amount, paragraph (1) shall not apply to any transfer of such amount made after the due date (including extensions) for filing the return of tax for the taxable year in which such amount is treated as distributed from a qualified employer plan.*

(ii) QUALIFIED PLAN LOAN OFFSET AMOUNT.—*For purposes of this subparagraph, the term "qualified plan loan offset amount" means a plan loan offset amount which is treated as distributed from a qualified employer plan to a participant or beneficiary solely by reason of—*

(I) *the termination of the qualified employer plan, or*

(II) *the failure to meet the repayment terms of the loan from such plan because of the severance from employment of the participant.*

(iii) PLAN LOAN OFFSET AMOUNT.—*For purposes of clause (ii), the term "plan loan offset amount" means the amount by which the participant's accrued benefit under the plan is reduced in order to repay a loan from the plan.*

(iv) LIMITATION.—*This subparagraph shall not apply to any plan loan offset amount unless such plan loan offset amount relates to a loan to which section 72(p)(1) does not apply by reason of section 72(p)(2).*

(v) QUALIFIED EMPLOYER PLAN.—*For purposes of this subsection, the term "qualified employer plan" has the meaning given such term by section 72(p)(4).*

* * *

[CCH Explanation at ¶ 625. Committee Reports at ¶ 10,850.]

Amendments

• **2017, Tax Cuts and Jobs Act (P.L. 115-97)**

P.L. 115-97, § 13613(a):

Amended Code Sec. 402(c)(3) by adding at the end a new subparagraph (C). **Effective** for plan loan offset amounts which are treated as distributed in tax years beginning after 12-31-2017.

P.L. 115-97, § 13613(b)(1)-(2):

Amended Code Sec. 402(c)(3) by striking "TRANSFER MUST BE MADE WITHIN 60 DAYS OF RECEIPT" in the heading and inserting "TIME LIMIT ON TRANSFERS", and by striking "subparagraph (B)" in subparagraph (A) and inserting "subparagraphs (B) and (C)". **Effective** for plan loan offset amounts which are treated as distributed in tax years beginning after 12-31-2017.

[¶ 5470] CODE SEC. 408. INDIVIDUAL RETIREMENT ACCOUNTS.

* * *

(d) TAX TREATMENT OF DISTRIBUTIONS.—

* * *

(6) TRANSFER OF ACCOUNT INCIDENT TO DIVORCE.—The transfer of an individual's interest in an individual retirement account or an individual retirement annuity to his spouse or former spouse under a divorce or separation instrument described in *clause (i) of section 121(d)(3)(C)* is not to be considered a taxable transfer made by such individual notwithstanding any other provision of this subtitle, and such interest at the time of the transfer is to be treated as an individual retirement account of such spouse, and not of such individual. Thereafter such account or annuity for purposes of this subtitle is to be treated as maintained for the benefit of such spouse.

* * *

[CCH Explanation at ¶ 255. Committee Reports at ¶ 10,260.]

Amendments

• **2017, Tax Cuts and Jobs Act (P.L. 115-97)**

P.L. 115-97, § 11051(b)(3)(G):

Amended Code Sec. 408(d)(6) by striking "subparagraph (A) of section 71(b)(2)" and inserting "clause (i) of section 121(d)(3)(C)". For the **effective** date, see Act Sec. 11051(c)(1)-(2), below.

P.L. 115-97, § 11051(c)(1)-(2), provides:

(c) EFFECTIVE DATE.—The amendments made by this section shall apply to—

(1) any divorce or separation instrument (as defined in section 71(b)(2) of the Internal Revenue Code of 1986 as in effect before the date of the enactment of this Act) executed after December 31, 2018, and

(2) any divorce or separation instrument (as so defined) executed on or before such date and modified after such date if the modification expressly provides that the amendments made by this section apply to such modification.

[¶5475] CODE SEC. 408A. ROTH IRAS.

* * *

(c) TREATMENT OF CONTRIBUTIONS.—

* * *

(3) LIMITS BASED ON MODIFIED ADJUSTED GROSS INCOME.—

* * *

(D) INFLATION ADJUSTMENT.—In the case of any taxable year beginning in a calendar year after 2006, the dollar amounts in subclauses (I) and (II) of subparagraph (B)(ii) shall each be increased by an amount equal to—

(i) such dollar amount, multiplied by

(ii) the cost-of-living adjustment determined under section 1(f)(3) for the calendar year in which the taxable year begins, determined by substituting "calendar year 2005" *for "calendar year 2016" in subparagraph (A)(ii)* thereof.

Any increase determined under the preceding sentence shall be rounded to the nearest multiple of $1,000.

* * *

[CCH Explanation at ¶125. Committee Reports at ¶10,020.]
Amendments
• **2017, Tax Cuts and Jobs Act (P.L. 115-97)**

P.L. 115-97, §11002(d)(1)(W):
Amended Code Sec. 408A(c)(3)(D)(ii) by striking "for 'calendar year 1992' in subparagraph (B)" and inserting "for

'calendar year 2016' in subparagraph (A)(ii)". **Effective** for tax years beginning after 12-31-2017.

(d) DISTRIBUTION RULES.—For purposes of this title—

* * *

(6) TAXPAYER MAY MAKE ADJUSTMENTS BEFORE DUE DATE.—

* * *

(B) SPECIAL RULES.—

* * *

(iii) *CONVERSIONS.—Subparagraph (A) shall not apply in the case of a qualified rollover contribution to which subsection (d)(3) applies (including by reason of subparagraph (C) thereof).*

* * *

[CCH Explanation at ¶620. Committee Reports at ¶10,830.]
Amendments
• **2017, Tax Cuts and Jobs Act (P.L. 115-97)**

P.L. 115-97, §13611(a):
Amended Code Sec. 408A(d)(6)(B) by adding at the end a new clause (iii). **Effective** for tax years beginning after 12-31-2017.

[¶5480] CODE SEC. 409A. INCLUSION IN GROSS INCOME OF DEFERRED COMPENSATION UNDER NONQUALIFIED DEFERRED COMPENSATION PLANS.

* * *

(d) OTHER DEFINITIONS AND SPECIAL RULES.—For purposes of this section:

* * *

(7) *TREATMENT OF QUALIFIED STOCK.—An arrangement under which an employee may receive qualified stock (as defined in section 83(i)(2)) shall not be treated as a nonqualified deferred compensation*

plan with respect to such employee solely because of such employee's election, or ability to make an election, to defer recognition of income under section 83(i).

* * *

[CCH Explanation at ¶ 605. Committee Reports at ¶ 10,810.]

Amendments

• **2017, Tax Cuts and Jobs Act (P.L. 115-97)**

P.L. 115-97, § 13603(c)(2):

Amended Code Sec. 409A(d) by adding at the end a new paragraph (7). **Effective** generally for stock attributable to options exercised, or restricted stock units settled, after 12-31-2017. For a transition rule, see Act Sec. 13603(g), below.

P.L. 115-97, § 13603(g), provides:

(g) TRANSITION RULE.—Until such time as the Secretary (or the Secretary's delegate) issues regulations or other gui-dance for purposes of implementing the requirements of paragraph (2)(C)(i)(II) of section 83(i) of the Internal Revenue Code of 1986 (as added by this section), or the requirements of paragraph (6) of such section, a corporation shall be treated as being in compliance with such requirements (respectively) if such corporation complies with a reasonable good faith interpretation of such requirements.

[¶ 5485] CODE SEC. 422. INCENTIVE STOCK OPTIONS.

* * *

(b) INCENTIVE STOCK OPTION.—For purposes of this part, the term "incentive stock option" means an option granted to an individual for any reason connected with his employment by a corporation, if granted by the employer corporation or its parent or subsidiary corporation, to purchase stock of any of such corporations, but only if—

(1) the option is granted pursuant to a plan which includes the aggregate number of shares which may be issued under options and the employees (or class of employees) eligible to receive options, and which is approved by the stockholders of the granting corporation within 12 months before or after the date such plan is adopted;

(2) such option is granted within 10 years from the date such plan is adopted, or the date such plan is approved by the stockholders, whichever is earlier;

(3) such option by its terms is not exercisable after the expiration of 10 years from the date such option is granted;

(4) the option price is not less than the fair market value of the stock at the time such option is granted;

(5) such option by its terms is not transferable by such individual otherwise than by will or the laws of descent and distribution, and is exercisable, during his lifetime, only by him; and

(6) such individual, at the time the option is granted, does not own stock possessing more than 10 percent of the total combined voting power of all classes of stock of the employer corporation or of its parent or subsidiary corporation.

Such term shall not include any option if (as of the time the option is granted) the terms of such option provide that it will not be treated as an incentive stock option. *Such term shall not include any option if an election is made under section 83(i) with respect to the stock received in connection with the exercise of such option.*

* * *

[CCH Explanation at ¶ 605. Committee Reports at ¶ 10,810.]

Amendments

• **2017, Tax Cuts and Jobs Act (P.L. 115-97)**

P.L. 115-97, § 13603(c)(1)(A):

Amended Code Sec. 422(b) by adding at the end a new sentence. **Effective** generally for stock attributable to options exercised, or restricted stock units settled, after 12-31-2017. For a transition rule, see Act Sec. 13603(g), below.

P.L. 115-97, § 13603(g), provides:

(g) TRANSITION RULE.—Until such time as the Secretary (or the Secretary's delegate) issues regulations or other guidance for purposes of implementing the requirements of paragraph (2)(C)(i)(II) of section 83(i) of the Internal Revenue Code of 1986 (as added by this section), or the requirements of paragraph (6) of such section, a corporation shall be treated as being in compliance with such requirements (respectively) if such corporation complies with a reasonable good faith interpretation of such requirements.

[¶ 5490] CODE SEC. 423. EMPLOYEE STOCK PURCHASE PLANS.

* * *

(b) EMPLOYEE STOCK PURCHASE PLAN.—For purposes of this part, the term "employee stock purchase plan" means a plan which meets the following requirements:

* * *

(5) under the terms of the plan, all employees granted such options shall have the same rights and privileges, except that the amount of stock which may be purchased by any employee under such option may bear a uniform relationship to the total compensation, or the basic or regular rate of compensation, of employees, the plan may provide that no employee may purchase more than a maximum amount of stock fixed under the plan, *and the rules of section 83(i) shall apply in determining which employees have a right to make an election under such section;*

* * *

[CCH Explanation at ¶ 605. Committee Reports at ¶ 10,810.]

Amendments

• **2017, Tax Cuts and Jobs Act (P.L. 115-97)**

P.L. 115-97, § 13603(c)(1)(B)(i):

Amended Code Sec. 423(b)(5) by striking "and" before "the plan" and by inserting ", and the rules of section 83(i) shall apply in determining which employees have a right to make an election under such section" before the semicolon at the end. **Effective** generally for stock attributable to options exercised, or restricted stock units settled, after 12-31-2017. For a transition rule, see Act Sec. 13603(g), below.

P.L. 115-97, § 13603(g), provides:

(g) TRANSITION RULE.—Until such time as the Secretary (or the Secretary's delegate) issues regulations or other guidance for purposes of implementing the requirements of paragraph (2)(C)(i)(II) of section 83(i) of the Internal Revenue Code of 1986 (as added by this section), or the requirements of paragraph (6) of such section, a corporation shall be treated as being in compliance with such requirements (respectively) if such corporation complies with a reasonable good faith interpretation of such requirements.

(d) COORDINATION WITH QUALIFIED EQUITY GRANTS.—An option for which an election is made under section 83(i) with respect to the stock received in connection with its exercise shall not be considered as granted pursuant an employee stock purchase plan.

[CCH Explanation at ¶ 605. Committee Reports at ¶ 10,810.]

Amendments

• **2017, Tax Cuts and Jobs Act (P.L. 115-97)**

P.L. 115-97, § 13603(c)(1)(B)(ii):

Amended Code Sec. 423 by adding at the end a new subsection (d). **Effective** generally for stock attributable to options exercised, or restricted stock units settled, after 12-31-2017. For a transition rule, see Act Sec. 13603(g), below.

P.L. 115-97, § 13603(g), provides :

(g) TRANSITION RULE.—Until such time as the Secretary (or the Secretary's delegate) issues regulations or other gui-

dance for purposes of implementing the requirements of paragraph (2)(C)(i)(II) of section 83(i) of the Internal Revenue Code of 1986 (as added by this section), or the requirements of paragraph (6) of such section, a corporation shall be treated as being in compliance with such requirements (respectively) if such corporation complies with a reasonable good faith interpretation of such requirements.

[¶ 5495] CODE SEC. 430. MINIMUM FUNDING STANDARDS FOR SINGLE-EMPLOYER DEFINED BENEFIT PENSION PLANS.

* * *

(c) SHORTFALL AMORTIZATION CHARGE.—

* * *

(7) INCREASES IN ALTERNATE REQUIRED INSTALLMENTS IN CASES OF EXCESS COMPENSATION OR EXTRAORDINARY DIVIDENDS OR STOCK REDEMPTIONS.—

* * *

(D) EXCESS EMPLOYEE COMPENSATION.—For purposes of this paragraph—

* * *

(vii) INDEXING OF AMOUNT.—In the case of any calendar year beginning after 2010, the dollar amount under clause (i)(II) shall be increased by an amount equal to—

(I) such dollar amount, multiplied by

(II) the cost-of-living adjustment determined under section 1(f)(3) for the calendar year, determined by substituting "calendar year 2009" *for "calendar year 2016" in subparagraph (A)(ii)* thereof.

If the amount of any increase under clause (i) is not a multiple of $1,000, such increase shall be rounded to the next lowest multiple of $1,000.

* * *

[CCH Explanation at ¶ 125. Committee Reports at ¶ 10,020.]

Amendments

• **2017, Tax Cuts and Jobs Act (P.L. 115-97)**

P.L. 115-97, § 11002(d)(1)(X):

Amended Code Sec. 430(c)(7)(D)(vii)(II) by striking "for 'calendar year 1992' in subparagraph (B)" and inserting "for

'calendar year 2016' in subparagraph (A)(ii)". **Effective** for tax years beginning after 12-31-2017.

[¶ 5500] CODE SEC. 447. METHOD OF ACCOUNTING FOR CORPORATIONS ENGAGED IN FARMING.

* * *

(c) EXCEPTION FOR CERTAIN CORPORATIONS.—For purposes of subsection (a), a corporation shall be treated as not being a corporation *for any taxable year* if it is—

(1) an S corporation, or

(2) *a corporation which meets the gross receipts test of section 448(c) for such taxable year.*

[CCH Explanation at ¶ 570. Committee Reports at ¶ 10,330.]

Amendments

• **2017, Tax Cuts and Jobs Act (P.L. 115-97)**

P.L. 115-97, § 13102(a)(5)(A)(i)-(ii):

Amended Code Sec. 447(c) by inserting "for any taxable year" after "not being a corporation" in the matter preced-

ing paragraph (1), and by amending paragraph (2). **Effective** for tax years beginning after 12-31-2017. Prior to amendment, Code Sec. 447(c)(2) read as follows:

(2) a corporation the gross receipts of which meet the requirements of subsection (d).

(d) *[Stricken.]*

[CCH Explanation at ¶ 570. Committee Reports at ¶ 10,330.]

Amendments

• **2017, Tax Cuts and Jobs Act (P.L. 115-97)**

P.L. 115-97, § 13102(a)(5)(C)(i):

Amended Code Sec. 447 by striking subsection (d). **Effective** for tax years beginning after 12-31-2017. Prior to being stricken, Code Sec. 447(d) read as follows:

(d) GROSS RECEIPTS REQUIREMENTS.—

(1) IN GENERAL.— A corporation meets the requirements of this subsection if, for each prior taxable year beginning after December 31, 1975, such corporation (and any predecessor corporation) did not have gross receipts exceeding $1,000,000. For purposes of the preceding sentence, all corporations which are members of the same controlled group of corporations (within the meaning of section 1563(a)) shall be treated as 1 corporation.

(2) SPECIAL RULES FOR FAMILY CORPORATIONS.—

(A) IN GENERAL.—In the case of a family corporation, paragraph (1) shall be applied—

(i) by substituting "December 31, 1985," for "December 31, 1975,"; and

(ii) by substituting "$25,000,000" for "$1,000,000".

(B) GROSS RECEIPTS TEST.—

(i) CONTROLLED GROUPS.—Notwithstanding the last sentence of paragraph (1), in the case of a family corporation—

(I) except as provided by the Secretary, only the applicable percentage of gross receipts of any other member of any controlled group of corporations of which such corporation is a member shall be taken into account, and

(II) under regulations, gross receipts of such corporation or of another member of such group shall not be taken into account by such corporation more than once.

(ii) PASS-THRU ENTITIES.—For purposes of paragraph (1), if a family corporation holds directly or indirectly any interest in a partnership, estate, trust or other pass-thru entity, such corporation shall take into account its proportionate share of the gross receipts of such entity.

(iii) APPLICABLE PERCENTAGE.—For purposes of clause (i), the term "applicable percentage" means the percentage equal to a fraction—

(I) the numerator of which is the fair market value of the stock of another corporation held directly or indirectly as of the close of the taxable year by the family corporation, and

(II) the denominator of which is the fair market value of all stock of such corporation as of such time.

For purposes of this clause, the term "stock" does not include stock described in section 1563(c)(1).

(C) FAMILY CORPORATION.—For purposes of this section, the term "family corporation" means—

(e) *[Stricken.]*

(i) any corporation if at least 50 percent of the total combined voting power of all classes of stock entitled to vote, and at least 50 percent of all other classes of stock of the corporation, are owned by members of the same family, and

(ii) any corporation described in subsection (h).

[CCH Explanation at ¶ 570. Committee Reports at ¶ 10,330.]

Amendments
- **2017, Tax Cuts and Jobs Act (P.L. 115-97)**

P.L. 115-97, § 13102(a)(5)(C)(i):

Amended Code Sec. 447 by striking subsection (e). **Effective** for tax years beginning after 12-31-2017. Prior to being stricken, Code Sec. 447(e) read as follows:

(e) MEMBERS OF THE SAME FAMILY.—For purposes of subsection (d)—

(1) the members of the same family are an individual, such individual's brothers and sisters, the brothers and sisters of such individual's parents and grandparents, the ancestors and lineal descendants of any of the foregoing, a spouse of any of the foregoing, and the estate of any of the foregoing,

(2) stock owned, directly or indirectly, by or for a partnership or trust shall be treated as owned proportionately by its partners or beneficiaries, and

(3) if 50 percent or more in value of the stock in a corporation (hereinafter in this paragraph referred to as "first corporation") is owned, directly or through paragraph (2), by or for members of the same family, such members shall be considered as owning each class of stock in a second corporation (or a wholly owned subsidiary of such second corporation) owned, directly or indirectly, by or for the first corporation, in that proportion which the value of the stock in the first corporation which such members so own bears to the value of all the stock in the first corporation.

For purposes of paragraph (1), individuals related by the half blood or by legal adoption shall be treated as if they were related by the whole blood.

(d) COORDINATION WITH SECTION 481.—Any change in method of accounting made pursuant to this section shall be treated for purposes of section 481 as initiated by the taxpayer and made with the consent of the Secretary.

[CCH Explanation at ¶ 570. Committee Reports at ¶ 10,330.]

Amendments
- **2017, Tax Cuts and Jobs Act (P.L. 115-97)**

P.L. 115-97, § 13102(a)(5)(B):

Amended Code Sec. 447(f). **Effective** for tax years beginning after 12-31-2017. Prior to amendment, Code Sec. 447(f) read as follows:

(f) COORDINATION WITH SECTION 481.—In the case of any taxpayer required by this section to change its method of accounting for any taxable year—

(1) such change shall be treated as having been made with the consent of the Secretary,

(2) for purposes of section 481(a)(2), such change shall be treated as a change not initiated by the taxpayer, and

(3) under regulations prescribed by the Secretary, the net amount of adjustments required by section 481(a) to be taken into account by the taxpayer in computing taxable income shall be taken into account in each of the 10 taxable years (or the remaining taxable years where there is a stated future life of less than 10 taxable years) beginning with the year of change.

P.L. 115-97, § 13102(a)(5)(C)(i)-(ii):

Amended Code Sec. 447 by striking subsections (d), (e), (h), and (i), and by redesignating subsections (f) and (g) (as amended by Act Sec. 13102(a)(5)(B)), as subsections (d) and (e), respectively. [Note: Act Sec. 13102(a)(5)(B) amended Code Sec. 447(f).—CCH] **Effective** for tax years beginning after 12-31-2017.

(e) CERTAIN ANNUAL ACCRUAL ACCOUNTING METHODS.—

* * *

[CCH Explanation at ¶ 570. Committee Reports at ¶ 10,330.]
Amendments
- **2017, Tax Cuts and Jobs Act (P.L. 115-97)**

P.L. 115-97, § 13102(a)(5)(C)(i)-(ii):

Amended Code Sec. 447 by striking subsections (d), (e), (h), and (i), and by redesignating subsections (f) and (g) (as amended by Act Sec. 13102(a)(5)(B)), as subsections (d) and (e), respectively. [Note: Act Sec. 13102(a)(5)(B) did not amend Code Sec. 447(g).—CCH] **Effective** for tax years beginning after 12-31-2017.

(h) *[Stricken.]*

[CCH Explanation at ¶ 570. Committee Reports at ¶ 10,330.]

Amendments

• **2017, Tax Cuts and Jobs Act (P.L. 115-97)**

P.L. 115-97, § 13102(a)(5)(C)(i):

Amended Code Sec. 447 by striking subsection (h). **Effective** generally for tax years beginning after 12-31-2017. Prior to being stricken, Code Sec. 447(h) read as follows:

(h) EXCEPTION FOR CERTAIN CLOSELY HELD CORPORATIONS.—

(1) IN GENERAL.—A corporation is described in this subsection if, on October 4, 1976, and at all times thereafter—

(A) members of 2 families (within the meaning of subsection (e)(1)) have owned (directly or through the application of subsection (e)) at least 65 percent of the total combined voting power of all classes of stock of such corporation entitled to vote, and at least 65 percent of the total number of shares of all other classes of stock of such corporation; or

(B)(i) members of 3 families (within the meaning of subsection (e)(1)) have owned (directly or through the application of subsection (e)) at least 50 percent of the total combined voting power of all classes of stock of such corporation entitled to vote, and at least 50 percent of the total number of shares of all other classes of stock of such corporation; and

(ii) substantially all of the stock of such corporation which is not so owned (directly or through the application

of subsection (e)) by members of such 3 families is owned directly—

(I) by employees of the corporation or members of their families (within the meaning of section 267(c)(4)), or

(II) by a trust for the benefit of the employees of such corporation which is described in section 401(a) and which is exempt from taxation under section 501(a).

(2) STOCK HELD BY EMPLOYEES, ETC.—For purposes of this subsection, stock which—

(A) is owned directly by employees of the corporation or members of their families (within the meaning of section 267(c)(4)) or by a trust described in paragraph (1)(B)(ii)(II), and

(B) was acquired on or after October 4, 1976, from the corporation or from a member of a family which, on October 4, 1976, was described in subparagraph (A) or (B)(i) of paragraph (1),

shall be treated as owned by a member of a family which, on October 4, 1976, was described in subparagraph (A) or (B)(i) of paragraph (1).

(3) CORPORATION MUST BE ENGAGED IN FARMING.—This subsection shall apply only in the case of a corporation which was, on October 4, 1976, and at all times thereafter, engaged in the trade or business of farming.

(i) *[Stricken.]*

[CCH Explanation at ¶ 570. Committee Reports at ¶ 10,330.]

Amendments

• **2017, Tax Cuts and Jobs Act (P.L. 115-97)**

P.L. 115-97, § 13102(a)(5)(C)(i):

Amended Code Sec. 447 by striking subsection (i). **Effective** generally for tax years beginning after 12-31-2017. For a special rule, see Act Sec. 13102(e)(2), below. Prior to being stricken, Code Sec. 447(i) read as follows:

(i) SUSPENSE ACCOUNT FOR FAMILY CORPORATIONS.—

(1) IN GENERAL.—If any family corporation is required by this section to change its method of accounting for any taxable year (hereinafter in this subsection referred to as the "year of the change"), notwithstanding subsection (f), such corporation shall establish a suspense account under this subsection in lieu of taking into account adjustments under section 481(a) with respect to amounts included in the suspense account.

(2) INITIAL OPENING BALANCE.—The initial opening balance of the account described in paragraph (1) shall be the lesser of—

(A) the net adjustments which would have been required to be taken into account under section 481 but for this subsection, or

(B) the amount of such net adjustments determined as of the beginning of the taxable year preceding the year of change.

If the amount referred to in subparagraph (A) exceeds the amount referred to in subparagraph (B), notwithstanding paragraph (1), such excess shall be included in gross income in the year of the change.

(3) INCLUSION WHERE CORPORATION CEASES TO BE A FAMILY CORPORATION.—

(A) IN GENERAL.—If the corporation ceases to be a family corporation during any taxable year, the amount in the suspense account (after taking into account prior reductions) shall be included in gross income for such taxable year.

(B) SPECIAL RULE FOR CERTAIN TRANSFERS.—For purposes of subparagraph (A), any transfer in a corporation after December 15, 1987, shall be treated as a transfer to a person whose ownership could not qualify such corporation as a family corporation unless it is a transfer—

(i) to a member of the family of the transferor, or

(ii) in the case of a corporation described in subsection (h), to a member of a family which on December 15, 1987, held stock in such corporation which qualified the corporation under subsection (h).

(4) SUBCHAPTER C TRANSACTIONS.—The application of this subsection with respect to a taxpayer which is a party to any transaction with respect to which there is nonrecognition of gain or loss to any party by reason of subchapter C shall be determined under regulations prescribed by the Secretary.

(5) TERMINATION.—

(A) IN GENERAL.—No suspense account may be established under this subsection by any corporation required by this section to change its method of accounting for any taxable year ending after June 8, 1997.

(B) PHASEOUT OF EXISTING SUSPENSE ACCOUNTS.—

(i) IN GENERAL.—Each suspense account under this subsection shall be reduced (but not below zero) for each taxable year beginning after June 8, 1997, by an amount equal to the lesser of—

(I) the applicable portion of such account, or

(II) 50 percent of the taxable income of the corporation for the taxable year, or, if the corporation has no taxable income for such year, the amount of any net operating loss (as defined in section 172(c)) for such taxable year.

For purposes of the preceding sentence, the amount of taxable income and net operating loss shall be determined without regard to this paragraph.

(ii) COORDINATION WITH OTHER REDUCTIONS.—The amount of the applicable portion for any taxable year shall be reduced (but not below zero) by the amount of any reduction required for such taxable year under any other provision of this subsection.

(iv) INCLUSION IN INCOME.—Any reduction in a suspense account under this paragraph shall be included in gross income for the taxable year of the reduction.

(C) APPLICABLE PORTION.—For purposes of subparagraph (B), the term "applicable portion" means, for any taxable year, the amount which would ratably reduce the amount in the account (after taking into account prior reductions) to zero over the period consisting of such taxable year and the remaining taxable years in such first 20 taxable years.

(D) AMOUNTS AFTER 20TH YEAR.—Any amount in the account as of the close of the 20th year referred to in subpara-

graph (C) shall be treated as the applicable portion for each succeeding year thereafter to the extent not reduced under this paragraph for any prior taxable year after such 20th year.

P.L. 115-97, § 13102(e)(2), provides:

(2) PRESERVATION OF SUSPENSE ACCOUNT RULES WITH RESPECT TO ANY EXISTING SUSPENSE ACCOUNTS.—So much of the amendments made by subsection (a)(5)(C) as relate to section 447(i) of the Internal Revenue Code of 1986 shall not apply with respect to any suspense account established under such section before the date of the enactment of this Act.

[¶ 5505] CODE SEC. 448. LIMITATION ON USE OF CASH METHOD OF ACCOUNTING.

* * *

(b) EXCEPTIONS.—

* * *

(3) ENTITIES WHICH MEET GROSS RECEIPTS TEST.—Paragraphs (1) and (2) of subsection (a) shall not apply to any corporation or partnership for any taxable year if such entity (or any predecessor) meets the gross receipts test of subsection (c) for such taxable year.

[CCH Explanation at ¶ 570. Committee Reports at ¶ 10,330.]

Amendments

• **2017, Tax Cuts and Jobs Act (P.L. 115-97)**

P.L. 115-97, § 13102(a)(2):

Amended Code Sec. 448(b)(3). **Effective** for tax years beginning after 12-31-2017. Prior to amendment, Code Sec. 448(b)(3) read as follows:

(3) ENTITIES WITH GROSS RECEIPTS OF NOT MORE THAN $5,000,000.—Paragraphs (1) and (2) of subsection (a) shall not apply to any corporation or partnership for any taxable year if, for all prior taxable years beginning after December 31, 1985, such entity (or any predecessor) met the $5,000,000 gross receipts test of subsection (c).

(c) GROSS RECEIPTS TEST.—For purposes of this section—

(1) IN GENERAL.—A corporation or partnership meets the gross receipts test of this subsection for any taxable year if the average annual gross receipts of such entity for the 3-taxable-year period ending with the taxable year which precedes such taxable year does not exceed $25,000,000.

(2) AGGREGATION RULES.—All persons treated as a single employer under subsection (a) or (b) of section 52 or subsection (m) or (o) of section 414 shall be treated as one person for purposes of paragraph (1).

(3) SPECIAL RULES.—For purposes of this subsection—

(A) NOT IN EXISTENCE FOR ENTIRE 3-YEAR PERIOD.—If the entity was not in existence for the entire 3-year period referred to in paragraph (1), such paragraph shall be applied on the basis of the period during which such entity (or trade or business) was in existence.

(B) SHORT TAXABLE YEARS.—Gross receipts for any taxable year of less than 12 months shall be annualized by multiplying the gross receipts for the short period by 12 and dividing the result by the number of months in the short period.

(C) GROSS RECEIPTS.—Gross receipts for any taxable year shall be reduced by returns and allowances made during such year.

(D) TREATMENT OF PREDECESSORS.—Any reference in this subsection to an entity shall include a reference to any predecessor of such entity.

(4) ADJUSTMENT FOR INFLATION.—In the case of any taxable year beginning after December 31, 2018, the dollar amount in paragraph (1) shall be increased by an amount equal to—

(A) such dollar amount, multiplied by

(B) the cost-of-living adjustment determined under section 1(f)(3) for the calendar year in which the taxable year begins, by substituting "calendar year 2017" for "calendar year 2016" in subparagraph (A)(ii) thereof.

If any amount as increased under the preceding sentence is not a multiple of $1,000,000, such amount shall be rounded to the nearest multiple of $1,000,000.

[CCH Explanation at ¶ 570. Committee Reports at ¶ 10,330.]

Amendments

• **2017, Tax Cuts and Jobs Act (P.L. 115-97)**

P.L. 115-97, § 13102(a)(1):

Amended so much of Code Sec. 448(c) as precedes paragraph (2). **Effective** for tax years beginning after 12-31-2017. Prior to amendment, so much of Code Sec. 448(c) as precedes paragraph (2) read as follows:

(c) $5,000,000 GROSS RECEIPTS TEST.—For purposes of this section—

(1) IN GENERAL.—A corporation or partnership meets the $5,000,000 gross receipts test of this subsection for any prior taxable year if the average annual gross receipts of such entity for the 3-taxable-year period ending with such prior taxable year does not exceed $5,000,000.

P.L. 115-97, § 13102(a)(3):

Amended Code Sec. 448(c) by adding at the end a new paragraph (4). **Effective** for tax years beginning after 12-31-2017.

(d) DEFINITIONS AND SPECIAL RULES.—For purposes of this section—

* * *

(7) COORDINATION WITH SECTION 481.—Any change in method of accounting made pursuant to this section shall be treated for purposes of section 481 as initiated by the taxpayer and made with the consent of the Secretary.

* * *

[CCH Explanation at ¶ 570. Committee Reports at ¶ 10,330.]

Amendments

• **2017, Tax Cuts and Jobs Act (P.L. 115-97)**

P.L. 115-97, § 13102(a)(4):

Amended Code Sec. 448(d)(7). **Effective** for tax years beginning after 12-31-2017. Prior to amendment, Code Sec. 448(d)(7) read as follows:

(7) COORDINATION WITH SECTION 481.—In the case of any taxpayer required by this section to change its method of accounting for any taxable year—

(A) such change shall be treated as initiated by the taxpayer,

(B) such change shall be treated as made with the consent of the Secretary, and

(C) the period for taking into account the adjustments under section 481 by reason of such change—

(i) except as provided in clause (ii), shall not exceed 4 years, and

(ii) in the case of a hospital, shall be 10 years.

[¶ 5510] CODE SEC. 451. GENERAL RULE FOR TAXABLE YEAR OF INCLUSION.

* * *

(b) INCLUSION NOT LATER THAN FOR FINANCIAL ACCOUNTING PURPOSES.—

(1) INCOME TAKEN INTO ACCOUNT IN FINANCIAL STATEMENT.—

(A) IN GENERAL.—In the case of a taxpayer the taxable income of which is computed under an accrual method of accounting, the all events test with respect to any item of gross income (or portion thereof) shall not be treated as met any later than when such item (or portion thereof) is taken into account as revenue in—

(i) an applicable financial statement of the taxpayer, or

(ii) such other financial statement as the Secretary may specify for purposes of this subsection.

(B) EXCEPTION.—This paragraph shall not apply to—

(i) a taxpayer which does not have a financial statement described in clause (i) or (ii) of subparagraph (A) for a taxable year, or

(ii) any item of gross income in connection with a mortgage servicing contract.

(C) ALL EVENTS TEST.—*For purposes of this section, the all events test is met with respect to any item of gross income if all the events have occurred which fix the right to receive such income and the amount of such income can be determined with reasonable accuracy.*

(2) COORDINATION WITH SPECIAL METHODS OF ACCOUNTING.—*Paragraph (1) shall not apply with respect to any item of gross income for which the taxpayer uses a special method of accounting provided under any other provision of this chapter, other than any provision of part V of subchapter P (except as provided in clause (ii) of paragraph (1)(B)).*

(3) APPLICABLE FINANCIAL STATEMENT.—*For purposes of this subsection, the term "applicable financial statement" means—*

(A) *a financial statement which is certified as being prepared in accordance with generally accepted accounting principles and which is—*

(i) *a 10–K (or successor form), or annual statement to shareholders, required to be filed by the taxpayer with the United States Securities and Exchange Commission,*

(ii) *an audited financial statement of the taxpayer which is used for—*

(I) *credit purposes,*

(II) *reporting to shareholders, partners, or other proprietors, or to beneficiaries, or*

(III) *any other substantial nontax purpose,*

but only if there is no statement of the taxpayer described in clause (i), or

(iii) *filed by the taxpayer with any other Federal agency for purposes other than Federal tax purposes, but only if there is no statement of the taxpayer described in clause (i) or (ii),*

(B) *a financial statement which is made on the basis of international financial reporting standards and is filed by the taxpayer with an agency of a foreign government which is equivalent to the United States Securities and Exchange Commission and which has reporting standards not less stringent than the standards required by such Commission, but only if there is no statement of the taxpayer described in subparagraph (A), or*

(C) *a financial statement filed by the taxpayer with any other regulatory or governmental body specified by the Secretary, but only if there is no statement of the taxpayer described in subparagraph (A) or (B).*

(4) ALLOCATION OF TRANSACTION PRICE.—*For purposes of this subsection, in the case of a contract which contains multiple performance obligations, the allocation of the transaction price to each performance obligation shall be equal to the amount allocated to each performance obligation for purposes of including such item in revenue in the applicable financial statement of the taxpayer.*

(5) GROUP OF ENTITIES.—*For purposes of paragraph (1), if the financial results of a taxpayer are reported on the applicable financial statement (as defined in paragraph (3)) for a group of entities, such statement shall be treated as the applicable financial statement of the taxpayer.*

[CCH Explanation at ¶ 580. Committee Reports at ¶ 10,410.]

Amendments

• 2017, Tax Cuts and Jobs Act (P.L. 115-97)

P.L. 115-97, § 13221(a):

Amended Code Sec. 451 by redesignating subsections (b) through (i) as subsections (c) through (j), respectively, and by inserting after subsection (a) a new subsection (b). **Effective** for tax years beginning after 12-31-2017. For a special rule, see Act Sec. 13221(d)-(e), below.

P.L. 115-97, § 13221(d)-(e), provides:

(d) COORDINATION WITH SECTION 481.—

(1) IN GENERAL.—In the case of any qualified change in method of accounting for the taxpayer's first taxable year beginning after December 31, 2017—

(A) such change shall be treated as initiated by the taxpayer, and

(B) such change shall be treated as made with the consent of the Secretary of the Treasury.

(2) QUALIFIED CHANGE IN METHOD OF ACCOUNTING.—For purposes of this subsection, the term "qualified change in method of accounting" means any change in method of accounting which—

(A) is required by the amendments made by this section, or

(B) was prohibited under the Internal Revenue Code of 1986 prior to such amendments and is permitted under such Code after such amendments.

(e) SPECIAL RULES FOR ORIGINAL ISSUE DISCOUNT.—Notwithstanding subsection (c), in the case of income from a debt instrument having original issue discount—

(1) the amendments made by this section shall apply to taxable years beginning after December 31, 2018, and

(2) the period for taking into account any adjustments under section 481 by reason of a qualified change in method of accounting (as defined in subsection (d)) shall be 6 years.

(c) Treatment of Advance Payments.—

(1) In General.—A taxpayer which computes taxable income under the accrual method of accounting, and receives any advance payment during the taxable year, shall—

(A) except as provided in subparagraph (B), include such advance payment in gross income for such taxable year, or

(B) if the taxpayer elects the application of this subparagraph with respect to the category of advance payments to which such advance payment belongs, the taxpayer shall—

(i) to the extent that any portion of such advance payment is required under subsection (b) to be included in gross income in the taxable year in which such payment is received, so include such portion, and

(ii) include the remaining portion of such advance payment in gross income in the taxable year following the taxable year in which such payment is received.

(2) Election.—

(A) In General.—Except as otherwise provided in this paragraph, the election under paragraph (1)(B) shall be made at such time, in such form and manner, and with respect to such categories of advance payments, as the Secretary may provide.

(B) Period to which election applies.—An election under paragraph (1)(B) shall be effective for the taxable year with respect to which it is first made and for all subsequent taxable years, unless the taxpayer secures the consent of the Secretary to revoke such election. For purposes of this title, the computation of taxable income under an election made under paragraph (1)(B) shall be treated as a method of accounting.

(3) Taxpayers ceasing to exist.—Except as otherwise provided by the Secretary, the election under paragraph (1)(B) shall not apply with respect to advance payments received by the taxpayer during a taxable year if such taxpayer ceases to exist during (or with the close of) such taxable year.

(4) Advance payment.—For purposes of this subsection—

(A) In General.—The term "advance payment" means any payment—

(i) the full inclusion of which in the gross income of the taxpayer for the taxable year of receipt is a permissible method of accounting under this section (determined without regard to this subsection),

(ii) any portion of which is included in revenue by the taxpayer in a financial statement described in clause (i) or (ii) of subsection (b)(1)(A) for a subsequent taxable year, and

(iii) which is for goods, services, or such other items as may be identified by the Secretary for purposes of this clause.

(B) Exclusions.—Except as otherwise provided by the Secretary, such term shall not include—

(i) rent,

(ii) insurance premiums governed by subchapter L,

(iii) payments with respect to financial instruments,

(iv) payments with respect to warranty or guarantee contracts under which a third party is the primary obligor,

(v) payments subject to section 871(a), 881, 1441, or 1442,

(vi) payments in property to which section 83 applies, and

(vii) any other payment identified by the Secretary for purposes of this subparagraph.

(C) Receipt.—For purposes of this subsection, an item of gross income is received by the taxpayer if it is actually or constructively received, or if it is due and payable to the taxpayer.

(D) ALLOCATION OF TRANSACTION PRICE.—For purposes of this subsection, rules similar to subsection (b)(4) shall apply.

[CCH Explanation at ¶ 580. Committee Reports at ¶ 10,410.]

Amendments

• **2017, Tax Cuts and Jobs Act (P.L. 115-97)**

P.L. 115-97, § 13221(b):

Amended Code Sec. 451, as amended by Act Sec. 13221(a), by redesignating subsections (c) through (j) as subsections (d) through (k), respectively, and by inserting after subsection (b) a new subsection (c). **Effective** for tax years beginning after 12-31-2017. For a special rule, see Act Sec. 13221(d)-(e), below.

P.L. 115-97, § 13221(d)-(e), provides:

(d) COORDINATION WITH SECTION 481.—

(1) IN GENERAL.—In the case of any qualified change in method of accounting for the taxpayer's first taxable year beginning after December 31, 2017—

(A) such change shall be treated as initiated by the taxpayer, and

(B) such change shall be treated as made with the consent of the Secretary of the Treasury.

(2) QUALIFIED CHANGE IN METHOD OF ACCOUNTING.—For purposes of this subsection, the term "qualified change in method of accounting" means any change in method of accounting which—

(A) is required by the amendments made by this section, or

(B) was prohibited under the Internal Revenue Code of 1986 prior to such amendments and is permitted under such Code after such amendments.

(e) SPECIAL RULES FOR ORIGINAL ISSUE DISCOUNT.—Notwithstanding subsection (c), in the case of income from a debt instrument having original issue discount—

(1) the amendments made by this section shall apply to taxable years beginning after December 31, 2018, and

(2) the period for taking into account any adjustments under section 481 by reason of a qualified change in method of accounting (as defined in subsection (d)) shall be 6 years.

(d) SPECIAL RULE IN CASE OF DEATH.—In the case of the death of a taxpayer whose taxable income is computed under an accrual method of accounting, any amount accrued only by reason of the death of the taxpayer shall not be included in computing taxable income for the period in which falls the date of the taxpayer's death.

[CCH Explanation at ¶ 580. Committee Reports at ¶ 10,410.]

Amendments

• **2017, Tax Cuts and Jobs Act (P.L. 115-97)**

P.L. 115-97, § 13221(a):

Amended Code Sec. 451 by redesignating subsection (b) as subsection (c). **Effective** for tax years beginning after 12-31-2017.

P.L. 115-97, § 13221(b):

Amended Code Sec. 451, as amended by Act Sec. 13221(a), by redesignating subsection (c) as subsection (d). **Effective** for tax years beginning after 12-31-2017.

(e) SPECIAL RULE FOR EMPLOYEE TIPS.—For purposes of subsection (a), tips included in a written statement furnished an employer by an employee pursuant to section 6053(a) shall be deemed to be received at the time the written statement including such tips is furnished to the employer.

[CCH Explanation at ¶ 580. Committee Reports at ¶ 10,410.]

Amendments

• **2017, Tax Cuts and Jobs Act (P.L. 115-97)**

P.L. 115-97, § 13221(a):

Amended Code Sec. 451 by redesignating subsection (c) as subsection (d). **Effective** for tax years beginning after 12-31-2017.

P.L. 115-97, § 13221(b):

Amended Code Sec. 451, as amended by Act Sec. 13221(a), by redesignating subsection (d) as subsection (e). **Effective** for tax years beginning after 12-31-2017.

(f) SPECIAL RULE FOR CROP INSURANCE PROCEEDS OR DISASTER PAYMENTS.—In the case of insurance proceeds received as a result of destruction or damage to crops, a taxpayer reporting on the cash receipts and disbursements method of accounting may elect to include such proceeds in income for the taxable year following the taxable year of destruction or damage, if he establishes that, under his practice, income from such crops would have been reported in a following taxable year. For purposes of the preceding sentence, payments received under the Agricultural Act of 1949, as amended, or title II of the Disaster Assistance Act of 1988, as a result of (1) destruction or damage to crops caused by drought, flood, or any other natural disaster, or (2) the inability to plant crops because of such a natural disaster shall be treated as insurance proceeds received as a result of destruction or damage to crops. An election under this subsection for any taxable year shall be made at such time and in such manner as the Secretary prescribes.

[CCH Explanation at ¶ 580. Committee Reports at ¶ 10,410.]

Amendments

• **2017, Tax Cuts and Jobs Act (P.L. 115-97)**

P.L. 115-97, § 13221(a):

Amended Code Sec. 451 by redesignating subsection (d) as subsection (e). **Effective** for tax years beginning after 12-31-2017.

P.L. 115-97, § 13221(b):

Amended Code Sec. 451, as amended by Act Sec. 13221(a), by redesignating subsection (e) as subsection (f). **Effective** for tax years beginning after 12-31-2017.

(g) SPECIAL RULE FOR PROCEEDS FROM LIVESTOCK SOLD ON ACCOUNT OF DROUGHT, FLOOD, OR OTHER WEATHER-RELATED CONDITIONS.—

(1) IN GENERAL.—In the case of income derived from the sale or exchange of livestock in excess of the number the taxpayer would sell if he followed his usual business practices, a taxpayer reporting on the cash receipts and disbursements method of accounting may elect to include such income for the taxable year following the taxable year in which such sale or exchange occurs if he establishes that, under his usual business practices, the sale or exchange would not have occurred in the taxable year in which it occurred if it were not for drought, flood, or other weather-related conditions, and that such conditions had resulted in the area being designated as eligible for assistance by the Federal Government.

(2) LIMITATION.—Paragraph (1) shall apply only to a taxpayer whose principal trade or business is farming (within the meaning of section 6420(c)(3)).

(3) SPECIAL ELECTION RULES.—If section 1033(e)(2) applies to a sale or exchange of livestock described in paragraph (1), the election under paragraph (1) shall be deemed valid if made during the replacement period described in such section.

[CCH Explanation at ¶ 580. Committee Reports at ¶ 10,410.]

Amendments

• **2017, Tax Cuts and Jobs Act (P.L. 115-97)**

P.L. 115-97, § 13221(a):

Amended Code Sec. 451 by redesignating subsection (e) as subsection (f). **Effective** for tax years beginning after 12-31-2017.

P.L. 115-97, § 13221(b):

Amended Code Sec. 451, as amended by Act Sec. 13221(a), by redesignating subsection (f) as subsection (g). **Effective** for tax years beginning after 12-31-2017.

(h) SPECIAL RULE FOR UTILITY SERVICES.—

(1) IN GENERAL.— In the case of a taxpayer the taxable income of which is computed under an accrual method of accounting, any income attributable to the sale or furnishing of utility services to customers shall be included in gross income not later than the taxable year in which such services are provided to such customers.

(2) DEFINITION AND SPECIAL RULE.—For purposes of this subsection—

(A) UTILITY SERVICES.—The term "utility services" includes—

(i) the providing of electrical energy, water, or sewage disposal,

(ii) the furnishing of gas or steam through a local distribution system,

(iii) telephone or other communication services, and

(iv) the transporting of gas or steam by pipeline.

(B) YEAR IN WHICH SERVICES PROVIDED.—The taxable year in which services are treated as provided to customers shall not, in any manner, be determined by reference to—

(i) the period in which the customers' meters are read, or

(ii) the period in which the taxpayer bills (or may bill) the customers for such service.

[CCH Explanation at ¶ 580. Committee Reports at ¶ 10,410.]

Amendments

• **2017, Tax Cuts and Jobs Act (P.L. 115-97)**

P.L. 115-97, § 13221(a):

Amended Code Sec. 451 by redesignating subsection (f) as subsection (g). **Effective** for tax years beginning after 12-31-2017.

P.L. 115-97, § 13221(b):

Amended Code Sec. 451, as amended by Act Sec. 13221(a), by redesignating subsection (g) as subsection (h). **Effective** for tax years beginning after 12-31-2017.

(i) TREATMENT OF INTEREST ON FROZEN DEPOSITS IN CERTAIN FINANCIAL INSTITUTIONS.—

(1) IN GENERAL.—In the case of interest credited during any calendar year on a frozen deposit in a qualified financial institution, the amount of such interest includible in the gross income of a qualified individual shall not exceed the sum of—

(A) the net amount withdrawn by such individual from such deposit during such calendar year, and

(B) the amount of such deposit which is withdrawable as of the close of the taxable year (determined without regard to any penalty for premature withdrawals of a time deposit).

(2) INTEREST TESTED EACH YEAR.—Any interest not included in gross income by reason of paragraph (1) shall be treated as credited in the next calendar year.

(3) DEFERRAL OF INTEREST DEDUCTION.—No deduction shall be allowed to any qualified financial institution for interest not includible in gross income under paragraph (1) until such interest is includible in gross income.

(4) FROZEN DEPOSIT.—For purposes of this subsection, the term "frozen deposit" means any deposit if, as of the close of the calendar year, any portion of such deposit may not be withdrawn because of—

(A) the bankruptcy or insolvency of the qualified financial institution (or threat thereof), or

(B) any requirement imposed by the State in which such institution is located by reason of the bankruptcy or insolvency (or threat thereof) of 1 or more financial institutions in the State.

(5) OTHER DEFINITIONS.—For purposes of this subsection, the terms "qualified individual", "qualified financial institution", and "deposit" have the same respective meanings as when used in section 165(l).

[CCH Explanation at ¶ 580. Committee Reports at ¶ 10,410.]

Amendments

• **2017, Tax Cuts and Jobs Act (P.L. 115-97)**

P.L. 115-97, § 13221(a):

Amended Code Sec. 451 by redesignating subsection (g) as subsection (h). **Effective** for tax years beginning after 12-31-2017.

P.L. 115-97, § 13221(b):

Amended Code Sec. 451, as amended by Act Sec. 13221(a), by redesignating subsection (h) as subsection (i). **Effective** for tax years beginning after 12-31-2017.

(j) SPECIAL RULE FOR CASH OPTIONS FOR RECEIPT OF QUALIFIED PRIZES.—

(1) IN GENERAL.—For purposes of this title, in the case of an individual on the cash receipts and disbursements method of accounting, a qualified prize option shall be disregarded in determining the taxable year for which any portion of the qualified prize is properly includible in gross income of the taxpayer.

(2) QUALIFIED PRIZE OPTION; QUALIFIED PRIZE.—For purposes of this subsection—

(A) IN GENERAL.—The term "qualified prize option" means an option which—

(i) entitles an individual to receive a single cash payment in lieu of receiving a qualified prize (or remaining portion thereof), and

(ii) is exercisable not later than 60 days after such individual becomes entitled to the qualified prize.

(B) QUALIFIED PRIZE.—The term "qualified prize" means any prize or award which—

(i) is awarded as a part of a contest, lottery, jackpot, game, or other similar arrangement,

(ii) does not relate to any past services performed by the recipient and does not require the recipient to perform any substantial future service, and

(iii) is payable over a period of at least 10 years.

(3) PARTNERSHIP, ETC.—The Secretary shall provide for the application of this subsection in the case of a partnership or other pass-through entity consisting entirely of individuals described in paragraph (1).

[CCH Explanation at ¶ 580. Committee Reports at ¶ 10,410.]

Amendments

• 2017, Tax Cuts and Jobs Act (P.L. 115-97)

P.L. 115-97, § 13221(a):

Amended Code Sec. 451 by redesignating subsection (h) as subsection (i). **Effective** for tax years beginning after 12-31-2017.

P.L. 115-97, § 13221(b):

Amended Code Sec. 451, as amended by Act Sec. 13221(a), by redesignating subsection (i) as subsection (j). **Effective** for tax years beginning after 12-31-2017.

(k) SPECIAL RULE FOR SALES OR DISPOSITIONS TO IMPLEMENT FEDERAL ENERGY REGULATORY COMMISSION OR STATE ELECTRIC RESTRUCTURING POLICY.—

(1) IN GENERAL.—In the case of any qualifying electric transmission transaction for which the taxpayer elects the application of this section, qualified gain from such transaction shall be recognized—

(A) in the taxable year which includes the date of such transaction to the extent the amount realized from such transaction exceeds—

(i) the cost of exempt utility property which is purchased by the taxpayer during the 4-year period beginning on such date, reduced (but not below zero) by

(ii) any portion of such cost previously taken into account under this subsection, and

(B) ratably over the 8-taxable year period beginning with the taxable year which includes the date of such transaction, in the case of any such gain not recognized under subparagraph (A).

(2) QUALIFIED GAIN.—For purposes of this subsection, the term "qualified gain" means, with respect to any qualifying electric transmission transaction in any taxable year—

(A) any ordinary income derived from such transaction which would be required to be recognized under section 1245 or 1250 for such taxable year (determined without regard to this subsection), and

(B) any income derived from such transaction in excess of the amount described in subparagraph (A) which is required to be included in gross income for such taxable year (determined without regard to this subsection).

(3) QUALIFYING ELECTRIC TRANSMISSION TRANSACTION.—For purposes of this subsection, the term "qualifying electric transmission transaction" means any sale or other disposition before January 1, 2008 (before January 1, 2017, in the case of a qualified electric utility), of—

(A) property used in the trade or business of providing electric transmission services, or

(B) any stock or partnership interest in a corporation or partnership, as the case may be, whose principal trade or business consists of providing electric transmission services,

but only if such sale or disposition is to an independent transmission company.

(4) INDEPENDENT TRANSMISSION COMPANY.—For purposes of this subsection, the term "independent transmission company" means—

(A) an independent transmission provider approved by the Federal Energy Regulatory Commission,

(B) a person—

(i) who the Federal Energy Regulatory Commission determines in its authorization of the transaction under section 203 of the Federal Power Act (16 U.S.C. 824b) or by declaratory order is not a market participant within the meaning of such Commission's rules applicable to independent transmission providers, and

(ii) whose transmission facilities to which the election under this subsection applies are under the operational control of a Federal Energy Regulatory Commission-approved independent transmission provider before the close of the period specified in such authorization, but not later than the date which is 4 years after the close of the taxable year in which the transaction occurs, or

(C) in the case of facilities subject to the jurisdiction of the Public Utility Commission of Texas—

(i) a person which is approved by that Commission as consistent with Texas State law regarding an independent transmission provider, or

(ii) a political subdivision or affiliate thereof whose transmission facilities are under the operational control of a person described in clause (i).

(5) EXEMPT UTILITY PROPERTY.—For purposes of this subsection:

(A) IN GENERAL.—The term "exempt utility property" means property used in the trade or business of—

(i) generating, transmitting, distributing, or selling electricity, or

(ii) producing, transmitting, distributing, or selling natural gas.

(B) NONRECOGNITION OF GAIN BY REASON OF ACQUISITION OF STOCK.—Acquisition of control of a corporation shall be taken into account under this subsection with respect to a qualifying electric transmission transaction only if the principal trade or business of such corporation is a trade or business referred to in subparagraph (A).

(C) EXCEPTION FOR PROPERTY LOCATED OUTSIDE THE UNITED STATES.—The term "exempt utility property" shall not include any property which is located outside the United States.

(6) QUALIFIED ELECTRIC UTILITY.—For purposes of this subsection, the term "qualified electric utility" means a person that, as of the date of the qualifying electric transmission transaction, is vertically integrated, in that it is both—

(A) a transmitting utility (as defined in section 3(23) of the Federal Power Act (16 U.S.C. 796(23))) with respect to the transmission facilities to which the election under this subsection applies, and

(B) an electric utility (as defined in section 3(22) of the Federal Power Act (16 U.S.C. 796(22))).

(7) SPECIAL RULE FOR CONSOLIDATED GROUPS.—In the case of a corporation which is a member of an affiliated group filing a consolidated return, any exempt utility property purchased by another member of such group shall be treated as purchased by such corporation for purposes of applying paragraph (1)(A).

(8) TIME FOR ASSESSMENT OF DEFICIENCIES.—If the taxpayer has made the election under paragraph (1) and any gain is recognized by such taxpayer as provided in paragraph (1)(B), then—

(A) the statutory period for the assessment of any deficiency, for any taxable year in which any part of the gain on the transaction is realized, attributable to such gain shall not expire prior to the expiration of 3 years from the date the Secretary is notified by the taxpayer (in such manner as the Secretary may by regulations prescribe) of the purchase of exempt utility property or of an intention not to purchase such property, and

(B) such deficiency may be assessed before the expiration of such 3-year period notwithstanding any law or rule of law which would otherwise prevent such assessment.

(9) PURCHASE.—For purposes of this subsection, the taxpayer shall be considered to have purchased any property if the unadjusted basis of such property is its cost within the meaning of section 1012.

(10) ELECTION.—An election under paragraph (1) shall be made at such time and in such manner as the Secretary may require and, once made, shall be irrevocable.

(11) NONAPPLICATION OF INSTALLMENT SALES TREATMENT.—Section 453 shall not apply to any qualifying electric transmission transaction with respect to which an election to apply this subsection is made.

[CCH Explanation at ¶ 580. Committee Reports at ¶ 10,410.]
Amendments
• 2017, Tax Cuts and Jobs Act (P.L. 115-97)

P.L. 115-97, § 13221(a):

Amended Code Sec. 451 by redesignating subsection (i) as subsection (j). **Effective** for tax years beginning after 12-31-2017.

P.L. 115-97, § 13221(b):

Amended Code Sec. 451, as amended by Act Sec. 13221(a), by redesignating subsection (j) as subsection (k). **Effective** for tax years beginning after 12-31-2017.

[¶ 5515] CODE SEC. 453A. SPECIAL RULES FOR NONDEALERS.

* * *

(c) INTEREST ON DEFERRED TAX LIABILITY.—

* * *

(3) DEFERRED TAX LIABILITY.—For purposes of this section, the term "deferred tax liability" means, with respect to any taxable year, the product of—

(A) the amount of gain with respect to an obligation which has not been recognized as of the close of such taxable year, multiplied by

(B) the maximum rate of tax in effect under section 1 or 11, whichever is appropriate, for such taxable year.

For purposes of applying the preceding sentence with respect to so much of the gain which, when recognized, will be treated as long-term capital gain, the maximum rate on net capital gain under section 1(h) shall be taken into account.

* * *

[CCH Explanation at ¶ 305. Committee Reports at ¶ 10,310.]
Amendments
• 2017, Tax Cuts and Jobs Act (P.L. 115-97)

P.L. 115-97, § 13001(b)(2)(C):

Amended Code Sec. 453A(c)(3) by striking "or 1201 (whichever is appropriate)" following "under section 1(h)". **Effective** for tax years beginning after 12-31-2017.

[¶ 5520] CODE SEC. 453B. GAIN OR LOSS ON DISPOSITION OF INSTALLMENT OBLIGATIONS.

* * *

(e) LIFE INSURANCE COMPANIES.—

* * *

(2) SPECIAL RULE WHERE LIFE INSURANCE COMPANY ELECTS TO TREAT INCOME AS NOT RELATED TO INSURANCE BUSINESS.—Paragraph (1) shall not apply to any transfer or deemed transfer of an installment obligation if the life insurance company elects (at such time and in such manner as the Secretary may by regulations prescribe) to determine its life insurance company taxable income—

* * *

(B) as if such income were an item attributable to a noninsurance business.

(3) NONINSURANCE BUSINESS.—

(A) IN GENERAL.—*For purposes of this subsection, the term "noninsurance business" means any activity which is not an insurance business.*

(B) CERTAIN ACTIVITIES TREATED AS INSURANCE BUSINESSES.—*For purposes of subparagraph (A), any activity which is not an insurance business shall be treated as an insurance business if—*

(i) *it is of a type traditionally carried on by life insurance companies for investment purposes, but only if the carrying on of such activity (other than in the case of real estate) does not constitute the active conduct of a trade or business, or*

(ii) *it involves the performance of administrative services in connection with plans providing life insurance, pension, or accident and health benefits.*

[CCH Explanation at ¶910. Committee Reports at ¶10,640.]

Amendments

• **2017, Tax Cuts and Jobs Act (P.L. 115-97)**

P.L. 115-97, §13512(b)(1)(A)-(B):

Amended Code Sec. 453B(e) by striking "(as defined in section 806(b)(3))" following "attributable to a noninsurance business" in paragraph (2)(B), and by adding at the end a new paragraph (3). **Effective** for tax years beginning after 12-31-2017.

[¶5525] CODE SEC. 457. DEFERRED COMPENSATION PLANS OF STATE AND LOCAL GOVERNMENTS AND TAX-EXEMPT ORGANIZATIONS.

* * *

(e) OTHER DEFINITIONS AND SPECIAL RULES.—For purposes of this section—

* * *

(11) CERTAIN PLANS EXCLUDED.—

* * *

(B) SPECIAL RULES APPLICABLE TO LENGTH OF SERVICE AWARD PLANS.—

* * *

(ii) LIMITATION ON ACCRUALS.—A plan shall not be treated as described in subparagraph (A)(ii) if the aggregate amount of length of service awards accruing with respect to any year of service for any bona fide volunteer exceeds $6,000.

(iii) COST OF LIVING ADJUSTMENT.—*In the case of taxable years beginning after December 31, 2017, the Secretary shall adjust the $6,000 amount under clause (ii) at the same time and in the same manner as under section 415(d), except that the base period shall be the calendar quarter beginning July 1, 2016, and any increase under this paragraph that is not a multiple of $500 shall be rounded to the next lowest multiple of $500.*

(iv) SPECIAL RULE FOR APPLICATION OF LIMITATION ON ACCRUALS FOR CERTAIN PLANS.—*In the case of a plan described in subparagraph (A)(ii) which is a defined benefit plan (as defined in section 414(j)), the limitation under clause (ii) shall apply to the actuarial present value of the aggregate amount of length of service awards accruing with respect to any year of service. Such actuarial present value with respect to any year shall be calculated using reasonable actuarial assumptions and methods, assuming payment will be made under the most valuable form of payment under the plan with payment commencing at the later of the earliest age at which unreduced benefits are payable under the plan or the participant's age at the time of the calculation.*

* * *

[CCH Explanation at ¶ 635. Committee Reports at ¶ 10,840.]

Amendments

• **2017, Tax Cuts and Jobs Act (P.L. 115-97)**

P.L. 115-97, § 13612(a):

Amended Code Sec. 457(e)(11)(B)(ii) by striking "$3,000" and inserting "$6,000". **Effective** for tax years beginning after 12-31-2017.

P.L. 115-97, § 13612(b):

Amended Code Sec. 457(e)(11)(B) by adding at the end a new clause (iii). **Effective** for tax years beginning after 12-31-2017.

P.L. 115-97, § 13612(c):

Amended Code Sec. 457(e)(11)(B), as amended by Act Sec. 13612(b), by adding at the end a new clause (iv). **Effective** for tax years beginning after 12-31-2017.

[¶ 5530] CODE SEC. 460. SPECIAL RULES FOR LONG-TERM CONTRACTS.

* * *

(c) ALLOCATION OF COSTS TO CONTRACT.—

* * *

(6) SPECIAL RULE FOR ALLOCATION OF BONUS DEPRECIATION WITH RESPECT TO CERTAIN PROPERTY.—

* * *

(B) QUALIFIED PROPERTY.—For purposes of this paragraph, the term "qualified property" means property described in section 168(k)(2) which—

(i) has a recovery period of 7 years or less, and

(ii) is placed in service before *January 1, 2027 (January 1, 2028* in the case of property described in section 168(k)(2)(B)).

* * *

[CCH Explanation at ¶ 410. Committee Reports at ¶ 10,340.]

Amendments

• **2017, Tax Cuts and Jobs Act (P.L. 115-97)**

P.L. 115-97, § 13201(b)(2)(A):

Amended Code Sec. 460(c)(6)(B)(ii) by striking "January 1, 2020 (January 1, 2021" and inserting "January 1, 2027 (January 1, 2028". For the **effective** date, see Act Sec. 13201(h)(1)-(2), below.

P.L. 115-97, § 13201(h)(1)-(2), provides:

(h) EFFECTIVE DATE.—

(1) IN GENERAL.—Except as provided by paragraph (2), the amendments made by this section shall apply to property which—

(A) is acquired after September 27, 2017, and

(B) is placed in service after such date. For purposes of the preceding sentence, property shall not be treated as acquired after the date on which a written binding contract is entered into for such acquisition.

(2) SPECIFIED PLANTS.—The amendments made by this section shall apply to specified plants planted or grafted after September 27, 2017.

(e) EXCEPTION FOR CERTAIN CONSTRUCTION CONTRACTS.—

(1) IN GENERAL.—Subsections (a), (b), and (c)(1) and (2) shall not apply to—

* * *

(B) any other construction contract entered into by a taxpayer *(other than a tax shelter prohibited from using the cash receipts and disbursements method of accounting under section 448(a)(3))*—

(i) who estimates (at the time such contract is entered into) that such contract will be completed within the 2-year period beginning on the contract commencement date of such contract, and

(ii) who meets the gross receipts test of section 448(c) for the taxable year in which such contract is entered into.

* * *

(2) RULES RELATED TO GROSS RECEIPTS TEST.—

(A) APPLICATION OF GROSS RECEIPTS TEST TO INDIVIDUALS, ETC.—For purposes of paragraph (1)(B)(ii), in the case of any taxpayer which is not a corporation or a partnership, the gross receipts test of section 448(c) shall be applied in the same manner as if each trade or business of such taxpayer were a corporation or partnership.

(B) COORDINATION WITH SECTION 481.—Any change in method of accounting made pursuant to paragraph (1)(B)(ii) shall be treated as initiated by the taxpayer and made with the consent of the Secretary. Such change shall be effected on a cut-off basis for all similarly classified contracts entered into on or after the year of change.

(3) CONSTRUCTION CONTRACT.—For purposes of this subsection, the term "construction contract" means any contract for the building, construction, reconstruction, or rehabilitation of, or the installation of any integral component to, or improvements of, real property.

(4) SPECIAL RULE FOR RESIDENTIAL CONSTRUCTION CONTRACTS WHICH ARE NOT HOME CONSTRUCTION CONTRACTS.—In the case of any residential construction contract which is not a home construction contract, subsection (a) (as in effect on the day before the date of the enactment of the Revenue Reconciliation Act of 1989) shall apply except that such subsection shall be applied—

(A) by substituting "70 percent" for "90 percent" each place it appears, and

(B) by substituting "30 percent" for "10 percent".

(5) DEFINITIONS RELATING TO RESIDENTIAL CONSTRUCTION CONTRACTS.—For purposes of this subsection—

(A) HOME CONSTRUCTION CONTRACT.—The term "home construction contract" means any construction contract if 80 percent of the estimated total contract costs (as of the close of the taxable year in which the contract was entered into) are reasonably expected to be attributable to activities referred to in paragraph (4) with respect to—

(i) dwelling units (as defined in section 168(e)(2)(A)(ii)) contained in buildings containing 4 or fewer dwelling units (as so defined), and

(ii) improvements to real property directly related to such dwelling units and located on the site of such dwelling units.

For purposes of clause (i), each townhouse or rowhouse shall be treated as a separate building.

(B) RESIDENTIAL CONSTRUCTION CONTRACT.—The term "residential construction contract" means any contract which would be described in subparagraph (A) if clause (i) of such subparagraph reads as follows:

"(i) dwelling units (as defined in section 168(e)(2)(A)(ii)), and"

* * *

[CCH Explanation at ¶ 570. Committee Reports at ¶ 10,330.]

Amendments

• **2017, Tax Cuts and Jobs Act (P.L. 115-97)**

P.L. 115-97, § 13102(d)(1)(A)-(B):

Amended Code Sec. 460(e)(1)(B) by inserting "(other than a tax shelter prohibited from using the cash receipts and disbursements method of accounting under section 448(a)(3))" after "taxpayer" in the matter preceding clause (i), and by amending clause (ii). **Effective** for contracts entered into after 12-31-2017, in tax years ending after such date. Prior to amendment, Code Sec. 460(e)(1)(B)(ii) read as follows:

(ii) whose average annual gross receipts for the 3 taxable years preceding the taxable year in which such contract is entered into do not exceed $10,000,000.

P.L. 115-97, § 13102(d)(2):

Amended Code Sec. 460(e) by striking paragraphs (2) and (3), by redesignating paragraphs (4), (5), and (6) as paragraphs (3), (4), and (5), respectively, and by inserting after paragraph (1) a new paragraph (2). **Effective** for contracts entered into after 12-31-2017, in tax years ending after such date. Prior to being stricken, Code Sec. 460(e)(2)-(3) read as follows:

(2) Determination of taxpayer's gross receipts.—For purposes of paragraph (1), the gross receipts of—

(A) all trades or businesses (whether or not incorporated) which are under common control with the taxpayer (within the meaning of section 52(b)),

(B) all members of any controlled group of corporations of which the taxpayer is a member, and

(C) any predecessor of the taxpayer or a person described in subparagraph (A) or (B),

for the 3 taxable years of such persons preceding the taxable year in which the contract described in paragraph (1) is entered into shall be included in the gross receipts of the taxpayer for the period described in paragraph (1)(B). The Secretary shall prescribe regulations which provide attribu-tion rules that take into account, in addition to the persons and entities described in the preceding sentence, taxpayers who engage in construction contracts through partnerships, joint ventures, and corporations.

(3) Controlled group of corporations.—For purposes of this subsection, the term "controlled group of corporations" has the meaning given to such term by section 1563(a), except that—

(A) "more than 50 percent" shall be substituted for "at least 80 percent" each place it appears in section 1563(a)(1), and

(B) the determination shall be made without regard to subsections (a)(4) and (e)(3)(C) of section 1563.

[¶ 5535] CODE SEC. 461. GENERAL RULE FOR TAXABLE YEAR OF DEDUCTION.

* * *

(l) Limitation on Excess Business Losses of Noncorporate Taxpayers.—

(1) Limitation.—In the case of taxable year of a taxpayer other than a corporation beginning after December 31, 2017, and before January 1, 2026—

(A) subsection (j) (relating to limitation on excess farm losses of certain taxpayers) shall not apply, and

(B) any excess business loss of the taxpayer for the taxable year shall not be allowed.

(2) Disallowed loss carryover.—Any loss which is disallowed under paragraph (1) shall be treated as a net operating loss carryover to the following taxable year under section 172.

(3) Excess business loss.—For purposes of this subsection—

(A) In general.—The term "excess business loss" means the excess (if any) of—

(i) the aggregate deductions of the taxpayer for the taxable year which are attributable to trades or businesses of such taxpayer (determined without regard to whether or not such deductions are disallowed for such taxable year under paragraph (1)), over

(ii) the sum of—

(I) the aggregate gross income or gain of such taxpayer for the taxable year which is attributable to such trades or businesses, plus

(II) $250,000 (200 percent of such amount in the case of a joint return).

(B) Adjustment for inflation.—In the case of any taxable year beginning after December 31, 2018, the $250,000 amount in subparagraph (A)(ii)(II) shall be increased by an amount equal to—

(i) such dollar amount, multiplied by

(ii) the cost-of-living adjustment determined under section 1(f)(3) for the calendar year in which the taxable year begins, determined by substituting "2017" for "2016" in subparagraph (A)(ii) thereof.

If any amount as increased under the preceding sentence is not a multiple of $1,000, such amount shall be rounded to the nearest multiple of $1,000.

(4) Application of subsection in case of partnerships and S corporations.—In the case of a partnership or S corporation—

(A) this subsection shall be applied at the partner or shareholder level, and

(B) each partner's or shareholder's allocable share of the items of income, gain, deduction, or loss of the partnership or S corporation for any taxable year from trades or businesses attributable to the partnership or S corporation shall be taken into account by the partner or shareholder in applying this subsection to the taxable year of such partner or shareholder with or within which the taxable year of the partnership or S corporation ends.

For purposes of this paragraph, in the case of an S corporation, an allocable share shall be the shareholder's pro rata share of an item.

(5) ADDITIONAL REPORTING.—*The Secretary shall prescribe such additional reporting requirements as the Secretary determines necessary to carry out the purposes of this subsection.*

(6) COORDINATION WITH SECTION 469.—*This subsection shall be applied after the application of section 469.*

[CCH Explanation at ¶ 520. Committee Reports at ¶ 10,040.]
Amendments
• **2017, Tax Cuts and Jobs Act (P.L. 115-97)**
P.L. 115-97, § 11012(a):
Amended Code Sec. 461 by adding at the end a new subsection (l). **Effective** for tax years beginning after 12-31-2017.

[¶ 5540] CODE SEC. 465. DEDUCTIONS LIMITED TO AMOUNT AT RISK.

* * *

(c) ACTIVITIES TO WHICH SECTION APPLIES.—

* * *

(7) EXCLUSION OF ACTIVE BUSINESSES OF QUALIFIED C CORPORATIONS.—

* * *

(D) SPECIAL RULES FOR APPLICATION OF SUBPARAGRAPH (c).—

* * *

(v) SPECIAL RULE FOR LIFE INSURANCE COMPANIES.—

* * *

(II) INSURANCE BUSINESS.—For purposes of subclause (I), the term "insurance business" means any business which is not a noninsurance business (within the meaning of *section 453B(e)(3)*).

* * *

[CCH Explanation at ¶ 910. Committee Reports at ¶ 10,640.]
Amendments
• **2017, Tax Cuts and Jobs Act (P.L. 115-97)**
P.L. 115-97, § 13512(b)(2):
Amended Code Sec. 465(c)(7)(D)(v)(II) by striking "section 806(b)(3)" and inserting "section 453B(e)(3)". **Effective** for tax years beginning after 12-31-2017.

[¶ 5545] CODE SEC. 469. PASSIVE ACTIVITY LOSSES AND CREDITS LIMITED.

* * *

(i) $25,000 OFFSET FOR RENTAL REAL ESTATE ACTIVITIES.—

* * *

(3) PHASE-OUT OF EXEMPTION.—

* * *

(F) ADJUSTED GROSS INCOME.—For purposes of this paragraph, adjusted gross income shall be determined without regard to—

* * *

(iii) the amounts allowable as a deduction under sections 219, 221, *222, and 250* and

* * *

[CCH Explanation at ¶ 530 and ¶ 735. Committee Reports at ¶ 10,460 and ¶ 11,080.]

Amendments

• 2017, Tax Cuts and Jobs Act (P.L. 115-97)

P.L. 115-97, § 13305(b)(1):

Amended Code Sec. 469(i)(3)(F)(iii) by striking "199," following "under sections". **Effective** for tax years beginning after 12-31-2017.

P.L. 115-97, § 14202(b)(3):

Amended Code Sec. 469(i)(3)(F)(iii) by striking "and 222" and inserting "222, and 250". **Effective** for tax years beginning after 12-31-2017.

[¶ 5550] CODE SEC. 471. GENERAL RULE FOR INVENTORIES.

* * *

(c) *EXEMPTION FOR CERTAIN SMALL BUSINESSES.—*

(1) *IN GENERAL.—In the case of any taxpayer (other than a tax shelter prohibited from using the cash receipts and disbursements method of accounting under section 448(a)(3)) which meets the gross receipts test of section 448(c) for any taxable year—*

(A) *subsection (a) shall not apply with respect to such taxpayer for such taxable year, and*

(B) *the taxpayer's method of accounting for inventory for such taxable year shall not be treated as failing to clearly reflect income if such method either—*

(i) *treats inventory as non-incidental materials and supplies, or*

(ii) *conforms to such taxpayer's method of accounting reflected in an applicable financial statement of the taxpayer with respect to such taxable year or, if the taxpayer does not have any applicable financial statement with respect to such taxable year, the books and records of the taxpayer prepared in accordance with the taxpayer's accounting procedures.*

(2) *APPLICABLE FINANCIAL STATEMENT.—For purposes of this subsection, the term "applicable financial statement" has the meaning given the term in section 451(b)(3).*

(3) *APPLICATION OF GROSS RECEIPTS TEST TO INDIVIDUALS, ETC.—In the case of any taxpayer which is not a corporation or a partnership, the gross receipts test of section 448(c) shall be applied in the same manner as if each trade or business of such taxpayer were a corporation or partnership.*

(4) *COORDINATION WITH SECTION 481.—Any change in method of accounting made pursuant to this subsection shall be treated for purposes of section 481 as initiated by the taxpayer and made with the consent of the Secretary.*

[CCH Explanation at ¶ 570. Committee Reports at ¶ 10,330.]

Amendments

• 2017, Tax Cuts and Jobs Act (P.L. 115-97)

P.L. 115-97, § 13102(c):

Amended Code Sec. 471 by redesignating subsection (c) as subsection (d) and by inserting after subsection (b) a new

subsection (c). **Effective** for tax years beginning after 12-31-2017.

(d) *CROSS REFERENCE.—*

For rules relating to capitalization of direct and indirect costs of property, see section 263A.

[CCH Explanation at ¶ 570. Committee Reports at ¶ 10,330.]
Amendments
• 2017, Tax Cuts and Jobs Act (P.L. 115-97)

P.L. 115-97, § 13102(c):

Amended Code Sec. 471 by redesignating subsection (c) as subsection (d). **Effective** for tax years beginning after 12-31-2017.

[¶ 5555] CODE SEC. 481. ADJUSTMENTS REQUIRED BY CHANGES IN METHOD OF ACCOUNTING.

* * *

(d) ADJUSTMENTS ATTRIBUTABLE TO CONVERSION FROM S CORPORATION TO C CORPORATION.—

(1) IN GENERAL.—In the case of an eligible terminated S corporation, any adjustment required by subsection (a)(2) which is attributable to such corporation's revocation described in paragraph (2)(A)(ii) shall be taken into account ratably during the 6-taxable year period beginning with the year of change.

(2) ELIGIBLE TERMINATED S CORPORATION.—For purposes of this subsection, the term "eligible terminated S corporation" means any C corporation—

(A) which—

(i) was an S corporation on the day before the date of the enactment of the Tax Cuts and Jobs Act, and

(ii) during the 2-year period beginning on the date of such enactment makes a revocation of its election under section 1362(a), and

(B) the owners of the stock of which, determined on the date such revocation is made, are the same owners (and in identical proportions) as on the date of such enactment.

[CCH Explanation at ¶ 370. Committee Reports at ¶ 10,780.]
Amendments
• **2017, Tax Cuts and Jobs Act (P.L. 115-97)**

P.L. 115-97, § 13543(a):

Amended Code Sec. 481 by adding at the end a new subsection (d). **Effective** 12-22-2017.

[¶ 5560] CODE SEC. 482. ALLOCATION OF INCOME AND DEDUCTIONS AMONG TAXPAYERS.

In any case of two or more organizations, trades, or businesses (whether or not incorporated, whether or not organized in the United States, and whether or not affiliated) owned or controlled directly or indirectly by the same interests, the Secretary may distribute, apportion, or allocate gross income, deductions, credits, or allowances between or among such organizations, trades, or businesses, if he determines that such distribution, apportionment, or allocation is necessary in order to prevent evasion of taxes or clearly to reflect the income of any of such organizations, trades, or businesses. In the case of any transfer (or license) of intangible property (within the meaning of section 936(h)(3)(B)), the income with respect to such transfer or license shall be commensurate with the income attributable to the intangible. *For purposes of this section, the Secretary shall require the valuation of transfers of intangible property (including intangible property transferred with other property or services) on an aggregate basis or the valuation of such a transfer on the basis of the realistic alternatives to such a transfer, if the Secretary determines that such basis is the most reliable means of valuation of such transfers.*

[CCH Explanation at ¶ 755. Committee Reports at ¶ 11,140.]
Amendments
• **2017, Tax Cuts and Jobs Act (P.L. 115-97)**

P.L. 115-97, § 14221(b)(2):

Amended Code Sec. 482 by adding at the end a new sentence. **Effective** for transfers in tax years beginning after 12-31-2017.

[¶ 5565] CODE SEC. 512. UNRELATED BUSINESS TAXABLE INCOME.

(a) DEFINITION.—For purposes of this title—

* * *

(6) SPECIAL RULE FOR ORGANIZATION WITH MORE THAN 1 UNRELATED TRADE OR BUSINESS.—In the case of any organization with more than 1 unrelated trade or business—

(A) unrelated business taxable income, including for purposes of determining any net operating loss deduction, shall be computed separately with respect to each such trade or business and without regard to subsection (b)(12),

(B) the unrelated business taxable income of such organization shall be the sum of the unrelated business taxable income so computed with respect to each such trade or business, less a specific deduction under subsection (b)(12), and

(C) for purposes of subparagraph (B), unrelated business taxable income with respect to any such trade or business shall not be less than zero.

(7) INCREASE IN UNRELATED BUSINESS TAXABLE INCOME BY DISALLOWED FRINGE.—*Unrelated business taxable income of an organization shall be increased by any amount for which a deduction is not allowable under this chapter by reason of section 274 and which is paid or incurred by such organization for any qualified transportation fringe (as defined in section 132(f)), any parking facility used in connection with qualified parking (as defined in section 132(f)(5)(C)), or any on-premises athletic facility (as defined in section 132(j)(4)(B)). The preceding sentence shall not apply to the extent the amount paid or incurred is directly connected with an unrelated trade or business which is regularly carried on by the organization. The Secretary shall issue such regulations or other guidance as may be necessary or appropriate to carry out the purposes of this paragraph, including regulations or other guidance providing for the appropriate allocation of depreciation and other costs with respect to facilities used for parking or for on-premises athletic facilities.*

* * *

[CCH Explanation at ¶ 805 and ¶ 807. Committee Reports at ¶ 10,870 and ¶ 10,880.]

Amendments

• **2017, Tax Cuts and Jobs Act (P.L. 115-97)**

P.L. 115-97, § 13702(a):

Amended Code Sec. 512(a) by adding at the end a new paragraph (6). **Effective** generally for tax years beginning after 12-31-2017. For a special rule, see Act Sec. 13702(b)(2), below.

P.L. 115-97, § 13702(b)(2), provides:

(2) CARRYOVERS OF NET OPERATING LOSSES.—If any net operating loss arising in a taxable year beginning before January 1, 2018, is carried over to a taxable year beginning on or after such date—

(A) subparagraph (A) of section 512(a)(6) of the Internal Revenue Code of 1986, as added by this Act, shall not apply to such net operating loss, and

(B) the unrelated business taxable income of the organization, after the application of subparagraph (B) of such section, shall be reduced by the amount of such net operating loss.

P.L. 115-97, § 13703(a):

Amended Code Sec. 512(a), as amended by this Act, by adding at the end a new paragraph (7). **Effective** for amounts paid or incurred after 12-31-2017.

(d) TREATMENT OF DUES OF AGRICULTURAL OR HORTICULTURAL ORGANIZATIONS.—

* * *

(2) INDEXATION OF $100 AMOUNT.—In the case of any taxable year beginning in a calendar year after 1995, the $100 amount in paragraph (1) shall be increased by an amount equal to—

* * *

(B) the cost-of-living adjustment determined under section 1(f)(3) for the calendar year in which the taxable year begins, by substituting "calendar year 1994" *for "calendar year 2016" in subparagraph (A)(ii) thereof.*

* * *

[CCH Explanation at ¶ 125. Committee Reports at ¶ 10,020.]

Amendments

• **2017, Tax Cuts and Jobs Act (P.L. 115-97)**

P.L. 115-97, § 11002(d)(1)(Y):

Amended Code Sec. 512(d)(2)(B) by striking "for 'calendar year 1992' in subparagraph (B)" and inserting "for 'cal-

endar year 2016' in subparagraph (A)(ii)". **Effective** for tax years beginning after 12-31-2017.

[¶ 5570] CODE SEC. 513. UNRELATED TRADE OR BUSINESS.

* * *

(h) CERTAIN DISTRIBUTIONS OF LOW COST ARTICLES WITHOUT OBLIGATION TO PURCHASE AND EXCHANGES AND RENTALS OF MEMBER LISTS.—

* * *

(2) LOW COST ARTICLE DEFINED.—For purposes of this subsection—

* * *

(C) INDEXATION OF $5 AMOUNT.—In the case of any taxable year beginning in a calendar year after 1987, the $5 amount in subparagraph (A) shall be increased by an amount equal to—

* * *

(ii) the cost-of-living adjustment determined under section 1(f)(3) for the calendar year in which the taxable year begins by substituting "calendar year 1987" *for "calendar year 2016" in subparagraph (A)(ii)* thereof.

* * *

[CCH Explanation at ¶ 125. Committee Reports at ¶ 10,020.]

Amendments

• **2017, Tax Cuts and Jobs Act (P.L. 115-97)**

P.L. 115-97, § 11002(d)(1)(Z):

Amended Code Sec. 513(h)(2)(C)(ii) by striking "for 'calendar year 1992' in subparagraph (B)" and inserting "for

'calendar year 2016' in subparagraph (A)(ii)". **Effective** for tax years beginning after 12-31-2017.

[¶ 5575] CODE SEC. 527. POLITICAL ORGANIZATIONS.

* * *

(b) TAX IMPOSED.—A tax is hereby imposed for each taxable year on the political organization taxable income of every political organization. Such tax shall be computed by multiplying the political organization taxable income by the highest rate of tax specified in section 11(b).

* * *

[CCH Explanation at ¶ 305. Committee Reports at ¶ 10,310.]

Amendments

• **2017, Tax Cuts and Jobs Act (P.L. 115-97)**

P.L. 115-97, § 13001(b)(2)(D)(i)-(ii):

Amended Code Sec. 527(b) by striking paragraph (2), and by striking all that precedes "is hereby imposed" and inserting:

"(b) TAX IMPOSED.—A tax".

Effective for tax years beginning after 12-31-2017. Prior to amendment, Code Sec. 527(b) read as follows:

(b) TAX IMPOSED.—

(1) IN GENERAL.—A tax is hereby imposed for each taxable year on the political organization taxable income of every

political organization. Such tax shall be computed by multiplying the political organization taxable income by the highest rate of tax specified in section 11(b).

(2) ALTERNATIVE TAX IN CASE OF CAPITAL GAINS.—If for any taxable year any political organization has a net capital gain, then, in lieu of the tax imposed by paragraph (1), there is hereby imposed a tax (if such a tax is less than the tax imposed by paragraph (1)) which shall consist of the sum of—

(A) a partial tax, computed as provided by paragraph (1), on the political organization taxable income determined by reducing such income by the amount of such gain, and

(B) an amount determined as provided in section 1201(a) on such gain.

[¶ 5580] CODE SEC. 529. QUALIFIED TUITION PROGRAMS.

* * *

(c) TAX TREATMENT OF DESIGNATED BENEFICIARIES AND CONTRIBUTORS.—

* * *

(3) DISTRIBUTIONS.—

* * *

(C) CHANGE IN BENEFICIARIES OR PROGRAMS.—

(i) ROLLOVERS.—Subparagraph (A) shall not apply to that portion of any distribution which, within 60 days of such distribution, is transferred—

(I) to another qualified tuition program for the benefit of the designated beneficiary,

(II) to the credit of another designated beneficiary under a qualified tuition program who is a member of the family of the designated beneficiary with respect to which the distribution was made, *or*

(III) *before January 1, 2026, to an ABLE account (as defined in section 529A(e)(6)) of the designated beneficiary or a member of the family of the designated beneficiary.*

Subclause (III) shall not apply to so much of a distribution which, when added to all other contributions made to the ABLE account for the taxable year, exceeds the limitation under section 529A(b)(2)(B)(i).

* * *

(7) TREATMENT OF ELEMENTARY AND SECONDARY TUITION.—*Any reference in this subsection to the term "qualified higher education expense" shall include a reference to expenses for tuition in connection with enrollment or attendance at an elementary or secondary public, private, or religious school.*

* * *

[CCH Explanation at ¶ 640 and ¶ 645. Committee Reports at ¶ 10,100 and ¶ 10,150.]

Amendments

• **2017, Tax Cuts and Jobs Act (P.L. 115-97)**

P.L. 115-97, § 11025(a):

Amended Code Sec. 529(c)(3)(C)(i) by striking "or" at the end of subclause (I), by striking the period at the end of subclause (II) and inserting ", or", and by adding at the end

a new subclause (III) and a new flush sentence. **Effective** for distributions after 12-22-2017.

P.L. 115-97, § 11032(a)(1):

Amended Code Sec. 529(c) by adding at the end a new paragraph (7). **Effective** for distributions made after 12-31-2017.

(e) OTHER DEFINITIONS AND SPECIAL RULES.—For purposes of this section—

* * *

(3) QUALIFIED HIGHER EDUCATION EXPENSES.—

(A) IN GENERAL.—The term "qualified higher education expenses" means—

(i) tuition, fees, books, supplies, and equipment required for the enrollment or attendance of a designated beneficiary at an eligible educational institution;

(ii) expenses for special needs services in the case of a special needs beneficiary which are incurred in connection with such enrollment or attendance[; and]

(iii) expenses for the purchase of computer or peripheral equipment (as defined in section 168(i)(2)(B)), computer software (as defined in section 197(e)(3)(B)), or Internet access and related services, if such equipment, software, or services are to be used primarily by the beneficiary during any of the years the beneficiary is enrolled at an eligible educational institution.

Clause (iii) shall not include expenses for computer software designed for sports, games, or hobbies unless the software is predominantly educational in nature. *The amount of cash distributions from all qualified tuition programs described in subsection (b)(1)(A)(ii) with respect to a beneficiary during any taxable year shall, in the aggregate, include not more than $10,000 in expenses described in subsection (c)(7) incurred during the taxable year.*

* * *

[CCH Explanation at ¶ 640. Committee Reports at ¶ 10,150.]

Amendments

• **2017, Tax Cuts and Jobs Act (P.L. 115-97)**

P.L. 115-97, § 11032(a)(2):

Amended Code Sec. 529(e)(3)(A) by adding at the end a new sentence. **Effective** for distributions made after 12-31-2017.

¶ 5580   Code Sec. 529(c)(3)(C)(i)(II)

[¶ 5585] CODE SEC. 529A. QUALIFIED ABLE PROGRAMS.

* * *

(b) QUALIFIED ABLE PROGRAM.—For purposes of this section—

* * *

(2) CASH CONTRIBUTIONS.—A program shall not be treated as a qualified ABLE program unless it provides that no contribution will be accepted—

(A) unless it is in cash, or

(B) *except in the case of contributions under subsection (c)(1)(C), if such contribution to an ABLE account would result in aggregate contributions from all contributors to the ABLE account for the taxable year exceeding the sum of—*

(i) *the amount in effect under section 2503(b) for the calendar year in which the taxable year begins, plus*

(ii) *in the case of any contribution by a designated beneficiary described in paragraph (7) before January 1, 2026, the lesser of—*

(I) *compensation (as defined by section 219(f)(1)) includible in the designated beneficiary's gross income for the taxable year, or*

(II) *an amount equal to the poverty line for a one-person household, as determined for the calendar year preceding the calendar year in which the taxable year begins.*

For purposes of this paragraph, rules similar to the rules of section 408(d)(4) (determined without regard to subparagraph (B) thereof) shall apply. *A designated beneficiary (or a person acting on behalf of such beneficiary) shall maintain adequate records for purposes of ensuring, and shall be responsible for ensuring, that the requirements of subparagraph (B)(ii) are met.*

* * *

(7) *SPECIAL RULES RELATED TO CONTRIBUTION LIMIT.—For purposes of paragraph (2)(B)(ii)—*

(A) *DESIGNATED BENEFICIARY.—A designated beneficiary described in this paragraph is an employee (including an employee within the meaning of section 401(c)) with respect to whom—*

(i) *no contribution is made for the taxable year to a defined contribution plan (within the meaning of section 414(i)) with respect to which the requirements of section 401(a) or 403(a) are met,*

(ii) *no contribution is made for the taxable year to an annuity contract described in section 403(b), and*

(iii) *no contribution is made for the taxable year to an eligible deferred compensation plan described in section 457(b).*

(B) *POVERTY LINE.—The term "poverty line" has the meaning given such term by section 673 of the Community Services Block Grant Act (42 U.S.C. 9902).*

[CCH Explanation at ¶ 645. Committee Reports at ¶ 10,090.]

Amendments

• **2017, Tax Cuts and Jobs Act (P.L. 115-97)**

P.L. 115-97, § 11024(a)(1):

Amended Code Sec. 529A(b)(2)(B). **Effective** for tax years beginning after 12-22-2017. Prior to amendment, Code Sec. 529A(b)(2)(B) read as follows:

(B) except in the case of contributions under subsection (c)(1)(C), if such contribution to an ABLE account would result in aggregate contributions from all contributors to the ABLE account for the taxable year exceeding the amount in effect under section 2503(b) for the calendar year in which the taxable year begins.

P.L. 115-97, § 11024(a)(2):

Amended Code Sec. 529A(b)(2) by adding at the end a new sentence. **Effective** for tax years beginning after 12-22-2017.

P.L. 115-97, § 11024(a)(3):

Amended Code Sec. 529A(b) by adding at the end a new paragraph (7). **Effective** for tax years beginning after 12-22-2017.

[¶ 5590] CODE SEC. 535. ACCUMULATED TAXABLE INCOME.

* * *

(b) ADJUSTMENTS TO TAXABLE INCOME.—For purposes of subsection (a), taxable income shall be adjusted as follows:

(1) TAXES.—There shall be allowed as a deduction Federal income and excess profits taxes and income, war profits, and excess profits taxes of foreign countries and possessions of the United States (to the extent not allowable as a deduction under section 275(a)(4)), accrued during the taxable year or deemed to be paid by a domestic corporation under *section 960* for the taxable year, but not including the accumulated earnings tax imposed by section 531 or the personal holding company tax imposed by section 541.

* * *

[CCH Explanation at ¶ 720. Committee Reports at ¶ 11,170.]

Amendments

• **2017, Tax Cuts and Jobs Act (P.L. 115-97)**

P.L. 115-97, § 14301(c)(4):

Amended Code Sec. 535(b)(1) by striking "section 902(a) or 960(a)(1)" and inserting "section 960". **Effective** for tax years of foreign corporations beginning after 12-31-2017, and to tax years of United States shareholders in which or with which such tax years of foreign corporations end.

(c) ACCUMULATED EARNINGS CREDIT.—

* * *

(5) CROSS REFERENCE.—*For limitation on credit provided in paragraph (2) or (3) in the case of certain controlled corporations, see section 1561.*

[CCH Explanation at ¶ 305. Committee Reports at ¶ 10,310.]

Amendments

• **2017, Tax Cuts and Jobs Act (P.L. 115-97)**

P.L. 115-97, § 13001(b)(5)(B):

Amended Code Sec. 535(c)(5). **Effective** for tax years beginning after 12-31-2017. Prior to amendment, Code Sec. 535(c)(5) read as follows:

(5) CROSS REFERENCE.—

For denial of credit provided in paragraph (2) or (3) where multiple corporations are formed to avoid tax, see section 1551, and for limitation on such credit in the case of certain controlled corporations, see section 1561.

[¶ 5595] CODE SEC. 537. REASONABLE NEEDS OF THE BUSINESS.

* * *

(b) SPECIAL RULES.—For purposes of subsection (a)—

* * *

(4) PRODUCT LIABILITY LOSS RESERVES.—The accumulation of reasonable amounts for the payment of reasonably anticipated product liability losses (as defined in section 172(f)) *(as in effect before the date of enactment of the Tax Cuts and Jobs Act)*, as determined under regulations prescribed by the Secretary, shall be treated as accumulated for the reasonably anticipated needs of the business.

* * *

[CCH Explanation at ¶ 515. Committee Reports at ¶ 10,430.]

Amendments

• **2017, Tax Cuts and Jobs Act (P.L. 115-97)**

P.L. 115-97, § 13302(c)(2)(B):

Amended Code Sec. 537(b)(4) by inserting "(as in effect before the date of enactment of the Tax Cuts and Jobs Act)" after "as defined in section 172(f)". **Effective** for net operating losses arising in tax years ending after 12-31-2017.

[¶ 5600] CODE SEC. 545. UNDISTRIBUTED PERSONAL HOLDING COMPANY INCOME.

* * *

(b) ADJUSTMENTS TO TAXABLE INCOME.—For the purposes of subsection (a), the taxable income shall be adjusted as follows:

(1) TAXES.—There shall be allowed as a deduction Federal income and excess profits taxes and income, war profits and excess profits taxes of foreign countries and possessions of the United States (to the extent not allowable as a deduction under section 275(a)(4)), accrued during the taxable year or deemed to be paid by a domestic corporation under *section 960* for the taxable year, but not including the accumulated earnings tax imposed by section 531 or the personal holding company tax imposed by section 541.

* * *

[CCH Explanation at ¶720. Committee Reports at ¶11,170.]

Amendments

• **2017, Tax Cuts and Jobs Act (P.L. 115-97)**

P.L. 115-97, §14301(c)(4):

Amended Code Sec. 545(b)(1) by striking "section 902(a) or 960(a)(1)" and inserting "section 960". **Effective** for tax years of foreign corporations beginning after 12-31-2017, and to tax years of United States shareholders in which or with which such tax years of foreign corporations end.

[¶5605] CODE SEC. 594. ALTERNATIVE TAX FOR MUTUAL SAVINGS BANKS CONDUCTING LIFE INSURANCE BUSINESS.

(a) ALTERNATIVE TAX.—In the case of a mutual savings bank not having capital stock represented by shares, authorized under State law to engage in the business of issuing life insurance contracts, and which conducts a life insurance business in a separate department the accounts of which are maintained separately from the other accounts of the mutual savings bank, there shall be imposed in lieu of the *tax imposed by section 11*, a tax consisting of the sum of the partial taxes determined under paragraphs (1) and (2):

(1) A partial tax computed on the taxable income determined without regard to any items of gross income or deductions properly allocable to the business of the life insurance department, at the rates and in the manner as if this section had not been enacted; and

(2) A partial tax computed on the income of the life insurance department determined without regard to any items of gross income or deductions not properly allocable to such department, at the rates and in the manner provided in subchapter L (sec. 801 and following) with respect to life insurance companies.

[CCH Explanation at ¶305. Committee Reports at ¶10,310.]

Amendments

• **2017, Tax Cuts and Jobs Act (P.L. 115-97)**

P.L. 115-97, §13001(b)(2)(E):

Amended Code Sec. 594(a) by striking "taxes imposed by section 11 or [section] 1201(a)" and inserting "tax imposed by section 11". **Effective** for tax years beginning after 12-31-2017.

[¶5610] CODE SEC. 613. PERCENTAGE DEPLETION.

(a) GENERAL RULE.—In the case of the mines, wells, and other natural deposits listed in subsection (b), the allowance for depletion under section 611 shall be the percentage, specified in subsection (b), of the gross income from the property excluding from such gross income an amount equal to any rents or royalties paid or incurred by the taxpayer in respect of the property. Such allowance shall not exceed 50 percent (100 percent in the case of oil and gas properties) of the taxpayer's taxable income from the property (computed without allowances for depletion *and without the deduction under section 199A*). For purposes of the preceding sentence, the allowable deductions taken into account with respect to expenses of mining in computing the taxable income from the property shall be decreased by an amount equal to so much of any gain which (1) is treated under section 1245 (relating to gain from disposition of certain depreciable property) as ordinary income, and (2) is properly allocable to the property. In no case shall the allowance for depletion under section 611 be less than it would be if computed without reference to this section.

* * *

[CCH Explanation at ¶ 330 and ¶ 530. Committee Reports at ¶ 10,030 and ¶ 10,460.]

Amendments

• **2017, Tax Cuts and Jobs Act (P.L. 115-97)**

P.L. 115-97, § 11011(d)(3):

Amended Code Sec. 613(a) by inserting "and without the deduction under section 199A" after "and without the deduction under section 199". **Effective** for tax years beginning after 12-31-2017.

P.L. 115-97, § 13305(b)(4):

Amended Code Sec. 613(a), as amended by Act Sec. 11011, by striking "and without the deduction under section 199" following "(computed without allowances for depletion". **Effective** for tax years beginning after 12-31-2017.

[¶ 5615] CODE SEC. 613A. LIMITATIONS ON PERCENTAGE DEPLETION IN CASE OF OIL AND GAS WELLS.

* * *

(d) LIMITATIONS ON APPLICATION OF SUBSECTION (c).—

(1) LIMITATION BASED ON TAXABLE INCOME.—The deduction for the taxable year attributable to the application of subsection (c) shall not exceed 65 percent of the taxpayer's taxable income for the year computed without regard to—

(A) any depletion on production from an oil or gas property which is subject to the provisions of subsection (c),

(B) *any deduction allowable under section 199A,*

(C) any net operating loss carryback to the taxable year under section 172,

(D) *any capital loss carryback to the taxable year under section 1212, and*

(E) in the case of a trust, any distributions to its beneficiary, except in the case of any trust where any beneficiary of such trust is a member of the family (as defined in section 267(c)(4)) of a settlor who created inter vivos and testamentary trusts for members of the family and such settlor died within the last six days of the fifth month in 1970, and the law in the jurisdiction in which such trust was created requires all or a portion of the gross or net proceeds of any royalty or other interest in oil, gas, or other mineral representing any percentage depletion allowance to be allocated to the principal of the trust.

* * *

[CCH Explanation at ¶ 330 and ¶ 530. Committee Reports at ¶ 10,030 and ¶ 10,460.]

Amendments

• **2017, Tax Cuts and Jobs Act (P.L. 115-97)**

P.L. 115-97, § 11011(d)(4):

Amended Code Sec. 613A(d)(1) by redesignating subparagraphs (C), (D), and (E) as subparagraphs (D), (E), and (F), respectively, and by inserting after subparagraph (B) a new subparagraph (C). **Effective** for tax years beginning after 12-31-2017.

P.L. 115-97, § 13305(b)(5):

Amended Code Sec. 613A(d)(1), as amended by Act Sec. 11011, by striking subparagraph (B) and by redesignating subparagraphs (C), (D), (E) and (F) as subparagraphs (B), (C), (D) and (E). **Effective** for tax years beginning after 12-31-2017. Prior to being stricken, Code Sec. 613A(d)(1)(B) read as follows:

(B) any deduction allowable under section 199,

[¶ 5620] CODE SEC. 641. IMPOSITION OF TAX.

* * *

(c) SPECIAL RULES FOR TAXATION OF ELECTING SMALL BUSINESS TRUSTS.—

* * *

(2) MODIFICATIONS.—For purposes of paragraph (1), the modifications of this paragraph are the following:

* * *

(E)(i) *Section 642(c) shall not apply.*

(ii) For purposes of section 170(b)(1)(G), adjusted gross income shall be computed in the same manner as in the case of an individual, except that the deductions for costs which are paid or incurred in connection with the administration of the trust and which would not have been

incurred if the property were not held in such trust shall be treated as allowable in arriving at adjusted gross income.

* * *

[CCH Explanation at ¶365. Committee Reports at ¶10,770.]
Amendments
• **2017, Tax Cuts and Jobs Act (P.L. 115-97)**

P.L. 115-97, §13542(a):

Amended Code Sec. 641(c)(2) by inserting after subparagraph (D) a new subparagraph (E). **Effective** for tax years beginning after 12-31-2017.

[¶5625] CODE SEC. 642. SPECIAL RULES FOR CREDITS AND DEDUCTIONS.

* * *

(b) DEDUCTION FOR PERSONAL EXEMPTION.—

* * *

(2) TRUSTS.—

* * *

(C) DISABILITY TRUSTS.—

* * *

(iii) YEARS WHEN PERSONAL EXEMPTION AMOUNT IS ZERO.—

(I) IN GENERAL.—*In the case of any taxable year in which the exemption amount under section 151(d) is zero, clause (i) shall be applied by substituting "$4,150" for "the exemption amount under section 151(d)".*

(II) INFLATION ADJUSTMENT.—*In the case of any taxable year beginning in a calendar year after 2018, the $4,150 amount in subparagraph (A) shall be increased in the same manner as provided in section 6334(d)(4)(C).*

* * *

[CCH Explanation at ¶210. Committee Reports at ¶10,160.]
Amendments
• **2017, Tax Cuts and Jobs Act (P.L. 115-97)**

P.L. 115-97, §11041(b):

Amended Code Sec. 642(b)(2)(C) by adding at the end a new clause (iii). **Effective** for tax years beginning after 12-31-2017.

≫→ *Caution: Caution: Code Sec. 682, below, was stricken by P.L. 115-97, generally applicable to any divorce or separation instrument executed after December 31, 2018.*

[¶5630] CODE SEC. 682. INCOME OF AN ESTATE OR TRUST IN CASE OF DIVORCE, ETC. [*Stricken.*]

[CCH Explanation at ¶255. Committee Reports at ¶10,260.]
Amendments
• **2017, Tax Cuts and Jobs Act (P.L. 115-97)**

P.L. 115-97, §11051(b)(1)(C):

Amended subpart F of part I of subchapter J of chapter 1 by striking Code Sec. 682. For the **effective** date, see Act Sec. 11051(c)(1)-(2), below.

P.L. 115-97, §11051(c)(1)-(2), provides:

(c) EFFECTIVE DATE.—The amendments made by this section shall apply to—

(1) any divorce or separation instrument (as defined in section 71(b)(2) of the Internal Revenue Code of 1986 as in effect before the date of the enactment of this Act) executed after December 31, 2018, and

(2) any divorce or separation instrument (as so defined) executed on or before such date and modified after such

date if the modification expressly provides that the amendments made by this section apply to such modification.

Prior to being stricken, Code Sec. 682 read as follows:

SEC. 682. INCOME OF AN ESTATE OR TRUST IN CASE OF DIVORCE, ETC.

(a) INCLUSION IN GROSS INCOME OF WIFE.—There shall be included in the gross income of a wife who is divorced or legally separated under a decree of divorce or of separate maintenance (or who is separated from her husband under a written separation agreement) the amount of the income of any trust which such wife is entitled to receive and which, except for this section, would be includible in the gross income of her husband, and such amount shall not, despite any other provision of this subtitle, be includible in the gross income of such husband. This subsection shall not apply to that part of any such income of the trust which the terms of the decree, written separation agreement, or trust instrument fix, in terms of an amount of money or a portion of such income, as a sum which is payable for the support of minor children of such husband. In case such income is less than the amount specified in the decree, agreement, or instrument, for the purpose of applying the preceding sentence, such income, to the extent of such sum payable for such support, shall be considered a payment for such support.

(b) WIFE CONSIDERED A BENEFICIARY.—For purposes of computing the taxable income of the estate or trust and the taxable income of a wife to whom subsection (a) applies, such wife shall be considered as the beneficiary specified in this part.

(c) CROSS REFERENCE.—

For definitions of "husband" and "wife", as used in this section, see section 7701(a)(17).

[¶ 5635] CODE SEC. 691. RECIPIENTS OF INCOME IN RESPECT OF DECEDENTS.

* * *

(c) DEDUCTION FOR ESTATE TAX.—

* * *

(4) COORDINATION WITH CAPITAL GAIN PROVISIONS.—For purposes of sections 1(h), 1202, and 1211, the amount taken into account with respect to any item described in subsection (a)(1) shall be reduced (but not below zero) by the amount of the deduction allowable under paragraph (1) of this subsection with respect to such item.

* * *

[CCH Explanation at ¶ 305. Committee Reports at ¶ 10,310.]

Amendments

• **2017, Tax Cuts and Jobs Act (P.L. 115-97)**

P.L. 115-97, § 13001(b)(2)(F):

Amended Code Sec. 691(c)(4) by striking "1201," following "sections 1(h),". **Effective** for tax years beginning after 12-31-2017.

[¶ 5640] CODE SEC. 704. PARTNER'S DISTRIBUTIVE SHARE.

* * *

(d) LIMITATION ON ALLOWANCE OF LOSSES.—

(1) IN GENERAL.—A partner's distributive share of partnership loss (including capital loss) shall be allowed only to the extent of the adjusted basis of such partner's interest in the partnership at the end of the partnership year in which such loss occurred.

(2) CARRYOVER.—Any excess of such loss over such basis shall be allowed as a deduction at the end of the partnership year in which such excess is repaid to the partnership.

(3) SPECIAL RULES.—

(A) IN GENERAL.—In determining the amount of any loss under paragraph (1), there shall be taken into account the partner's distributive share of amounts described in paragraphs (4) and (6) of section 702(a).

(B) EXCEPTION.—In the case of a charitable contribution of property whose fair market value exceeds its adjusted basis, subparagraph (A) shall not apply to the extent of the partner's distributive share of such excess.

* * *

[CCH Explanation at ¶ 340. Committee Reports at ¶ 10,610.]

Amendments

• **2017, Tax Cuts and Jobs Act (P.L. 115-97)**

P.L. 115-97, § 13503(a)(1)-(3):

Amended Code Sec. 704(d) by striking "A partner's distributive share" and inserting

"(1) IN GENERAL.—A partner's distributive share",

by striking "Any excess of such loss" and inserting

"(2) CARRYOVER.—Any excess of such loss",

and by adding at the end a new paragraph (3). **Effective** for partnership tax years beginning after 12-31-2017.

[¶ 5645] CODE SEC. 708. CONTINUATION OF PARTNERSHIP.

* * *

(b) TERMINATION.—

(1) GENERAL RULE.—For purposes of subsection (a), a partnership shall be considered as terminated *only if no part of any business*, financial operation, or venture of the partnership continues to be carried on by any of its partners in a partnership.

* * *

[CCH Explanation at ¶ 355. Committee Reports at ¶ 10,620.]

Amendments

• **2017, Tax Cuts and Jobs Act (P.L. 115-97)**

P.L. 115-97, § 13504(a)(1)-(2):

Amended Code Sec. 708(b)(1) by striking ", or" at the end of subparagraph (A) and all that follows and inserting a period, and by striking "only if" and all that follows through "no part of any business" and inserting "only if no part of any business". **Effective** for partnership tax years beginning after 12-31-2017. Prior to amendment, Code Sec. 708(b)(1) read as follows:

(1) GENERAL RULE.—For purposes of subsection (a), a partnership shall be considered as terminated only if—

(A) no part of any business, financial operation, or venture of the partnership continues to be carried on by any of its partners in a partnership, or

(B) within a 12-month period there is a sale or exchange of 50 percent or more of the total interest in partnership capital and profits.

[¶ 5650] CODE SEC. 743. SPECIAL RULES WHERE SECTION 754 ELECTION OR SUBSTANTIAL BUILT-IN LOSS.

* * *

(d) SUBSTANTIAL BUILT-IN LOSS.—

(1) IN GENERAL.—For purposes of this section, a partnership has a substantial built-in loss with respect to a transfer of an interest in the partnership if—

(A) the partnership's adjusted basis in the partnership property exceeds by more than $250,000 the fair market value of such property, or

(B) the transferee partner would be allocated a loss of more than $250,000 if the partnership assets were sold for cash equal to their fair market value immediately after such transfer.

* * *

[CCH Explanation at ¶ 345. Committee Reports at ¶ 10,600.]

Amendments

• **2017, Tax Cuts and Jobs Act (P.L. 115-97)**

P.L. 115-97, § 13502(a):

Amended Code Sec. 743(d)(1). **Effective** for transfers of partnership interests after 12-31-2017. Prior to amendment, Code Sec. 743(d)(1) read as follows:

(1) IN GENERAL.—For purposes of this section, a partnership has a substantial built-in loss with respect to a transfer of an interest in a partnership if the partnership's adjusted basis in the partnership property exceeds by more than $250,000 the fair market value of such property.

(e) ALTERNATIVE RULES FOR ELECTING INVESTMENT PARTNERSHIPS.—

* * *

(4) CERTAIN BASIS REDUCTIONS TREATED AS LOSSES.—In the case of a transferee partner whose basis in property distributed by the partnership is reduced under section 732(a)(2), the amount of the loss recognized by the transferor on the transfer of the partnership interest which is taken into account under paragraph (2) shall be reduced by the amount of such basis reduction.

(5) ELECTING INVESTMENT PARTNERSHIP.—For purposes of this subsection, the term "electing investment partnership" means any partnership if—

(A) the partnership makes an election to have this subsection apply,

(B) the partnership would be an investment company under section 3(a)(1)(A) of the Investment Company Act of 1940 but for an exemption under paragraph (1) or (7) of section 3(c) of such Act,

(C) such partnership has never been engaged in a trade or business,

(D) substantially all of the assets of such partnership are held for investment,

(E) at least 95 percent of the assets contributed to such partnership consist of money,

(F) no assets contributed to such partnership had an adjusted basis in excess of fair market value at the time of contribution,

(G) all partnership interests of such partnership are issued by such partnership pursuant to a private offering before the date which is 24 months after the date of the first capital contribution to such partnership,

(H) the partnership agreement of such partnership has substantive restrictions on each partner's ability to cause a redemption of the partner's interest, and

(I) the partnership agreement of such partnership provides for a term that is not in excess of 15 years.

The election described in subparagraph (A), once made, shall be irrevocable except with the consent of the Secretary.

(6) REGULATIONS.—The Secretary shall prescribe such regulations as may be appropriate to carry out the purposes of this subsection, including regulations for applying this subsection to tiered partnerships.

* * *

[CCH Explanation at ¶ 355. Committee Reports at ¶ 10,620.]

Amendments

• 2017, Tax Cuts and Jobs Act (P.L. 115-97)

P.L. 115-97, § 13504(b)(2):

Amended Code Sec. 743(e) by striking paragraph (4) and redesignating paragraphs (5), (6), and (7) as paragraphs (4),

(5), and (6). **Effective** for partnership tax years beginning after 12-31-2017. Prior to being stricken, Code Sec. 743(e)(4) read as follows:

(4) EFFECT OF TERMINATION OF PARTNERSHIP.—This subsection shall be applied without regard to any termination of a partnership under section 708(b)(1)(B).

[¶ 5655] CODE SEC. 801. TAX IMPOSED.

(a) TAX IMPOSED.—*A tax* is hereby imposed for each taxable year on the life insurance company taxable income of every life insurance company. Such tax shall consist of a tax computed as provided in section 11 as though the life insurance company taxable income were the taxable income referred to in section 11.

* * *

[CCH Explanation at ¶ 305 and ¶ 910. Committee Reports at ¶ 10,310 and ¶ 10,640.]

Amendments

• 2017, Tax Cuts and Job Act (P.L. 115-97)

P.L. 115-97, § 13001(b)(2)(G)(i)-(ii):

Amended Code Sec. 801(a) by striking paragraph (2), and by striking all that precedes "is hereby imposed" and inserting:

"(a) TAX IMPOSED.—A tax".

Effective for tax years beginning after 12-31-2017. Prior to amendment, Code Sec. 801(a) read as follows:

(a) TAX IMPOSED.—

(1) IN GENERAL.—A tax is hereby imposed for each taxable year on the life insurance company taxable income of every life insurance company. Such tax shall consist of a tax

computed as provided in section 11 as though the life insurance company taxable income were the taxable income referred to in section 11.

(2) ALTERNATIVE TAX IN CASE OF CAPITAL GAINS.—

(A) IN GENERAL.—If a life insurance company has a net capital gain for the taxable year, then (in lieu of the tax imposed by paragraph (1)), there is hereby imposed a tax (if such tax is less than the tax imposed by paragraph (1)).

(B) AMOUNT OF TAX.—The amount of the tax imposed by this paragraph shall be the sum of—

(i) a partial tax, computed as provided by paragraph (1), on the life insurance company taxable income reduced by the amount of the net capital gain, and

(ii) an amount determined as provided in section 1201(a) on such net capital gain.

(C) NET CAPITAL GAIN NOT TAKEN INTO ACCOUNT IN DETERMINING SMALL LIFE INSURANCE COMPANY DEDUCTION.—For purposes of subparagraph (B)(i), the amount allowable as a deduction under paragraph (2) of section 804 shall be determined by reducing the tentative LICTI by the amount of the net capital gain (determined without regard to items attributable to noninsurance businesses).

(c) [*Stricken.*]

[CCH Explanation at ¶ 940. Committee Reports at ¶ 10,660.]

Amendments

• 2017, Tax Cuts and Job Act (P.L. 115-97)

P.L. 115-97, § 13514(b):

Amended Code Sec. 801 by striking subsection (c). **Effective** for tax years beginning after 12-31-2017. For a special rule, see Act Sec. 13514(d), below. Prior to being stricken, Code Sec. 801(c) read as follows:

(c) TAXATION OF DISTRIBUTIONS FROM PRE-1984 POLICYHOLDERS SURPLUS ACCOUNT.—

For provision taxing distributions to shareholders from pre-1984 policyholders surplus account, see section 815.

P.L. 115-97, § 13514(d), provides:

(d) PHASED INCLUSION OF REMAINING BALANCE OF POLICYHOLDERS SURPLUS ACCOUNTS.—In the case of any stock life insurance company which has a balance (determined as of the close of such company's last taxable year beginning before January 1, 2018) in an existing policyholders surplus account (as defined in section 815 of the Internal Revenue Code of 1986, as in effect before its repeal), the tax imposed by section 801 of such Code for the first 8 taxable years beginning after December 31, 2017, shall be the amount which would be imposed by such section for such year on the sum of—

(1) life insurance company taxable income for such year (within the meaning of such section 801 but not less than zero), plus

(2) ⅛ of such balance.

P.L. 115-97, § 13512(b)(3):

Amended Code Sec. 801(a)(2) by striking subparagraph (C). **Effective** for tax years beginning after 12-31-2017. [Note: Code Sec. 801(a)(2)(C) was stricken by Act Sec. 13001(b)(2)(G)(i); therefore, this amendment cannot be made.—CCH]

[¶ 5660] CODE SEC. 804. LIFE INSURANCE DEDUCTIONS.

For purposes of this part, the term "life insurance deductions" *means the general deductions provided in section 805.*

[CCH Explanation at ¶ 910. Committee Reports at ¶ 10,640.]

Amendments

• 2017, Tax Cuts and Jobs Act (P.L. 115-97)

P.L. 115-97, § 13512(b)(4):

Amended Code Sec. 804 by striking "means—"and all that follows and inserting "means the general deductions provided in section 805.". **Effective** for tax years beginning after 12-31-2017. Prior to being stricken, "means—"and all that follows in Code Sec. 804 read as follows:

means—

(1) the general deductions provided in section 805, and

(2) the small life insurance company deduction (if any) determined under section 806(a).

[¶ 5665] CODE SEC. 805. GENERAL DEDUCTIONS.

(a) GENERAL RULE.—For purposes of this part, there shall be allowed the following deductions:

* * *

(4) DIVIDENDS RECEIVED BY COMPANY.—

* * *

(B) APPLICATION OF SECTION 246(b).—In applying section 246(b) (relating to limitation on aggregate amount of deductions for dividends received) for purposes of subparagraph (A), the limit on the aggregate amount of the deductions allowed by sections 243(a)(1) and 245 shall be the percentage determined under section 246(b)(3) of the life insurance company taxable income (and such limitation shall be applied as provided in section 246(b)(3)), computed without regard to—

(i) the deduction allowed under section 172,

(ii) the deductions allowed by sections 243(a)(1) and 245, and

(iii) any capital loss carryback to the taxable year under section 1212(a)(1),

but such limit shall not apply for any taxable year for which there is a loss from operations.

* * *

(5) [*Stricken.*]

* * *

[CCH Explanation at ¶905 and ¶910. Committee Reports at ¶10,630 and ¶10,640.]

Amendments
• 2017, Tax Cuts and Jobs Act (P.L. 115-97)

P.L. 115-97, §13511(b)(4):

Amended Code Sec. 805(a)(4)(B)(ii). **Effective** for losses arising in tax years beginning after 12-31-2017. Prior to amendment, Code Sec. 805(a)(4)(B)(ii) read as follows:

(ii) the operations loss deduction provided by section 810,

P.L. 115-97, §13511(b)(5):

Amended Code Sec. 805(a) by striking paragraph (5). **Effective** for losses arising in tax years beginning after

12-31-2017. Prior to be stricken, Code Sec. 805(a)(5) read as follows:

(5) OPERATIONS LOSS DEDUCTION.—The operations loss deduction (determined under section 810).

P.L. 115-97, §13512(b)(5):

Amended Code Sec. 805(a)(4)(B), as amended by this Act, by striking clause (i) and by redesignating clauses (ii), (iii), and (iv) as clauses (i), (ii), and (iii), respectively. **Effective** for tax years beginning after 12-31-2017. Prior to being stricken, Code Sec. 805(a)(4)(B)(i) read as follows:

(i) the small life insurance company deduction,

(b) MODIFICATIONS.—The modifications referred to in subsection (a)(8) are as follows:

* * *

(2) CHARITABLE, ETC., CONTRIBUTIONS AND GIFTS.—In applying section 170—

(A) the limit on the total deductions under such section provided by section 170(b)(2) shall be 10 percent of the life insurance company taxable income computed without regard to—

(i) the deduction provided by section 170,

(ii) the deductions provided by paragraphs (3) and (4) of subsection (a),

(iii) *any net operating loss carryback to the taxable year under section 172, and*

(iv) any capital loss carryback to the taxable year under section 1212(a)(1), and

* * *

(4) DIVIDENDS RECEIVED DEDUCTION.—Except as provided in subsection (a)(4), the deductions for dividends received provided by sections 243 and 245 shall not be allowed.

[CCH Explanation at ¶905 and ¶910. Committee Reports at ¶10,630 and ¶10,640.]

Amendments
• 2017, Tax Cuts and Jobs Act (P.L. 115-97)

P.L. 115-97, §13511(a):

Amended Code Sec. 805(b) by striking paragraph (4) and by redesignating paragraph (5) as paragraph (4). **Effective** for losses arising in tax years beginning after 12-31-2017. Prior to being stricken, Code Sec. 805(b)(4) read as follows:

(4) NET OPERATING LOSS DEDUCTION.—Except as provided by section 844, the deduction for net operating losses provided in section 172 shall not be allowed.

P.L. 115-97, §13511(b)(6):

Amended Code Sec. 805(b)(2)(A)(iv). **Effective** for losses arising in tax years beginning after 12-31-2017. Prior to amendment, Code Sec. 805(b)(2)(A)(iv) read as follows:

(iv) any operations loss carryback to the taxable year under section 810, and

P.L. 115-97, §13512(b)(6):

Amended Code Sec. 805(b)(2)(A), as amended by this Act, by striking clause (iii) and by redesignating clauses (iv) and (v) as clauses (iii) and (iv), respectively. **Effective** for tax years beginning after 12-31-2017. Prior to being stricken, Code Sec. 805(b)(2)(A)(iii) read as follows:

(iii) the small life insurance company deduction,

[¶ 5670] CODE SEC. 806. SMALL LIFE INSURANCE COMPANY DEDUCTION. [*Stricken.*]

[CCH Explanation at ¶ 910. Committee Reports at ¶ 10,640.]

Amendments

• **2017, Tax Cuts and Jobs Act (P.L. 115-97)**

P.L. 115-97, § 13512(a):

Amended part I of subchapter L of chapter 1 by striking Code Sec. 806. **Effective** for tax years beginning after 12-31-2017. Prior to being stricken, Code Sec. 806 read as follows:

SEC. 806. SMALL LIFE INSURANCE COMPANY DEDUCTION.

(a) SMALL LIFE INSURANCE COMPANY DEDUCTION.—

(1) IN GENERAL.—For purposes of section 804, the small life insurance company deduction for any taxable year is 60 percent of so much of the tentative LICTI for such taxable year as does not exceed $3,000,000.

(2) PHASEOUT BETWEEN $3,000,000 AND $15,000,000.—The amount of the small life insurance company deduction determined under paragraph (1) for any taxable year shall be reduced (but not below zero) by 15 percent of so much of the tentative LICTI for such taxable year as exceeds $3,000,000.

(3) SMALL LIFE INSURANCE COMPANY DEDUCTION NOT ALLOWABLE TO COMPANY WITH ASSETS OF $500,000,000 OR MORE.—

(A) IN GENERAL.—The small life insurance company deduction shall not be allowed for any taxable year to any life insurance company which, at the close of such taxable year, has assets equal to or greater than $500,000,000.

(B) ASSETS.—For purposes of this paragraph, the term "assets" means all assets of the company.

(C) VALUATION OF ASSETS.—For purposes of this paragraph, the amount attributable to—

(i) real property and stock shall be the fair market value thereof, and

(ii) any other asset shall be the adjusted basis of such asset for purposes of determining gain on sale or other disposition.

(D) SPECIAL RULE FOR INTERESTS IN PARTNERSHIPS AND TRUSTS.—For purposes of this paragraph—

(i) an interest in a partnership or trust shall not be treated as an asset of the company, but

(ii) the company shall be treated as actually owning its proportionate share of the assets held by the partnership or trust (as the case may be).

(b) TENTATIVE LICTI.—For purposes of this part—

(1) IN GENERAL.—The term "tentative LICTI" means life insurance company taxable income determined without regard to the small life insurance company deduction.

(2) EXCLUSION OF ITEMS ATTRIBUTABLE TO NONINSURANCE BUSINESSES.—The amount of the tentative LICTI for any taxable year shall be determined without regard to all items attributable to noninsurance businesses.

(3) NONINSURANCE BUSINESS.—

(A) IN GENERAL.—The term "noninsurance business" means any activity which is not an insurance business.

(B) CERTAIN ACTIVITIES TREATED AS INSURANCE BUSINESSES.—For purposes of subparagraph (A), any activity which is not an insurance business shall be treated as an insurance business if—

(i) it is of a type traditionally carried on by life insurance companies for investment purposes, but only if the carrying on of such activity (other than in the case of real estate) does not constitute the active conduct of a trade or business, or

(ii) it involves the performance of administrative services in connection with plans providing life insurance, pension, or accident and health benefits.

(C) LIMITATION ON AMOUNT OF LOSS FROM NONINSURANCE BUSINESS WHICH MAY OFFSET INCOME FROM INSURANCE BUSINESS.—In computing the life insurance company taxable income of any life insurance company, any loss from a noninsurance business shall be limited under the principles of section 1503(c).

(c) SPECIAL RULE FOR CONTROLLED GROUPS.—

(1) SMALL LIFE INSURANCE COMPANY DEDUCTION DETERMINED ON CONTROLLED GROUP BASIS.— For purposes of subsection (a)—

(A) all life insurance companies which are members of the same controlled group shall be treated as 1 life insurance company, and

(B) any small life insurance company deduction determined with respect to such group shall be allocated among the life insurance companies which are members of such group in proportion to their respective tentative LICTI's.

(2) NONLIFE INSURANCE MEMBERS INCLUDED FOR ASSET TEST.—For purposes of subsection (a)(3), all members of the same controlled group (whether or not life insurance companies) shall be treated as 1 company.

(3) CONTROLLED GROUP.—For purposes of this subsection, the term "controlled group" means any controlled group of corporations (as defined in section 1563(a)); except that subsections (a)(4) and (b)(2)(D) of section 1563 shall not apply.

(4) ADJUSTMENTS TO PREVENT EXCESS DETRIMENT OR BENEFIT.—Under regulations prescribed by the Secretary, proper adjustments shall be made in the application of this subsection to prevent any excess detriment or benefit (whether from year-to-year or otherwise) arising from the application of this subsection.

[¶ 5675] CODE SEC. 807. RULES FOR CERTAIN RESERVES.

* * *

(c) ITEMS TAKEN INTO ACCOUNT.—The items referred to in subsections (a) and (b) are as follows:

(1) The life insurance reserves (as defined in section 816(b)).

(2) The unearned premiums and unpaid losses included in total reserves under section 816(c)(2).

(3) The amounts (discounted at the appropriate rate of interest) necessary to satisfy the obligations under insurance and annuity contracts, but only if such obligations do not involve (at

the time with respect to which the computation is made under this paragraph) life, accident, or health contingencies.

(4) Dividend accumulations, and other amounts, held at interest in connection with insurance and annuity contracts.

(5) Premiums received in advance, and liabilities for premium deposit funds.

(6) Reasonable special contingency reserves under contracts of group term life insurance or group accident and health insurance which are established and maintained for the provision of insurance on retired lives, for premium stabilization, or for a combination thereof.

For purposes of paragraph (3), the appropriate rate of interest is the highest rate or rates permitted to be used to discount the obligations by the National Association of Insurance Commissioners as of the date the reserve is determined. In no case shall the amount determined under paragraph (3) for any contract be less than the net surrender value of such contract. For purposes of paragraph (2) and section 805(a)(1), the amount of the unpaid losses (other than losses on life insurance contracts) shall be the amount of the discounted unpaid losses as defined in section 846.

[CCH Explanation at ¶ 915. Committee Reports at ¶ 10,690.]

Amendments

• **2017, Tax Cuts and Jobs Act (P.L. 115-97)**

P.L. 115-97, § 13517(a)(1):

Amended the second sentence of Code Sec. 807(c). **Effective** generally for tax years beginning after 12-31-2017. For a transition rule, see Act Sec. 13517(c)(2)-(3), below. Prior to amendment, the second sentence of Code Sec. 807(c) read as follows:

For purposes of paragraph (3), the appropriate rate of interest for any obligation is whichever of the following rates is the highest as of the time such obligation first did not involve life, accident, or health contingencies: the applicable Federal interest rate under subsection (d)(2)(B)(i), the prevailing State assumed interest rate under subsection (d)(2)(B)(ii), or the rate of interest assumed by the company in determining the guaranteed benefit.

P.L. 115-97, § 13517(c)(2)-(3), provides:

(2) Transition Rule.—For the first taxable year beginning after December 31, 2017, the reserve with respect to any contract (as determined under section 807(d) of the Internal Revenue Code of 1986) at the end of the preceding taxable year shall be determined as if the amendments made by this section had applied to such reserve in such preceding taxable year.

(3) Transition Relief.—

(A) In General.—If—

(i) the reserve determined under section 807(d) of the Internal Revenue Code of 1986 (determined after application of paragraph (2)) with respect to any contract as of the close of the year preceding the first taxable year beginning after December 31, 2017, differs from

(ii) the reserve which would have been determined with respect to such contract as of the close of such taxable year under such section determined without regard to paragraph (2),

then the difference between the amount of the reserve described in clause (i) and the amount of the reserve described in clause (ii) shall be taken into account under the method provided in subparagraph (B).

(B) Method.—The method provided in this subparagraph is as follows:

(i) If the amount determined under subparagraph (A)(i) exceeds the amount determined under subparagraph (A)(ii), 1/8 of such excess shall be taken into account, for each of the 8 succeeding taxable years, as a deduction under section 805(a)(2) or 832(c)(4) of such Code, as applicable.

(ii) If the amount determined under subparagraph (A)(ii) exceeds the amount determined under subparagraph (A)(i), 1/8 of such excess shall be included in gross income, for each of the 8 succeeding taxable years, under section 803(a)(2) or 832(b)(1)(C) of such Code, as applicable.

(d) Method of Computing Reserves for Purposes of Determining Income.—

(1) Determination of Reserve.—

(A) In General.—*For purposes of this part (other than section 816), the amount of the life insurance reserves for any contract (other than a contract to which subparagraph (B) applies) shall be the greater of*—

(i) *the net surrender value of such contract, or*

(ii) *92.81 percent of the reserve determined under paragraph (2).*

(B) Variable Contracts.—*For purposes of this part (other than section 816), the amount of the life insurance reserves for a variable contract shall be equal to the sum of*—

(i) *the greater of*—

(I) *the net surrender value of such contract, or*

(II) *the portion of the reserve that is separately accounted for under section 817, plus*

(ii) *92.81 percent of the excess (if any) of the reserve determined under paragraph (2) over the amount in clause (i).*

(C) STATUTORY CAP.—*In no event shall the reserves determined under subparagraphs (A) or (B) for any contract as of any time exceed the amount which would be taken into account with respect to such contract as of such time in determining statutory reserves (as defined in paragraph (4)).*

(D) NO DOUBLE COUNTING.—*In no event shall any amount or item be taken into account more than once in determining any reserve under this subchapter.*

(2) AMOUNT OF RESERVE.—*The amount of the reserve determined under this paragraph with respect to any contract shall be determined by using the tax reserve method applicable to such contract.*

(3) TAX RESERVE METHOD.—For purposes of this subsection—

(A) IN GENERAL.—The term "tax reserve method" means—

* * *

(iii) NONCANCELLABLE ACCIDENT AND HEALTH INSURANCE CONTRACTS.—In the case of any noncancellable accident and health insurance contract, *the reserve method prescribed by the National Association of Insurance Commissioners which covers such contract as of the date the reserve is determined.*

(iv) OTHER CONTRACTS.—In the case of any contract not described in clause (i), (ii), or (iii)—

(I) the reserve method prescribed by the National Association of Insurance Commissioners which covers such contract *(as of the date the reserve is determined)*, or

(II) if no reserve method has been prescribed by the National Association of Insurance Commissioners which covers such contract, a reserve method which is consistent with the reserve method required under clause (i), (ii), or (iii) or under subclause (I) of this clause *as of the date the reserve is determined for* such contract (whichever is most appropriate).

(B) DEFINITION OF CRVM AND CARVM.—For purposes of this paragraph—

(i) CRVM.—The term "CRVM" means the Commissioners' Reserve Valuation Method prescribed by the National Association of Insurance Commissioners which is *applicable to the contract and in effect as of the date the reserve is determined.*

(ii) CARVM.—The term "CARVM" means the Commissioners' Annuities Reserve Valuation Method prescribed by the National Association of Insurance Commissioners which is *applicable to the contract and in effect as of the date the reserve is determined.*

* * *

(4) STATUTORY RESERVES.—The term "statutory reserves" means the aggregate amount set forth in the annual statement with respect to items described in section 807(c). Such term shall not include any reserve attributable to a deferred and uncollected premium if the establishment of such reserve is not permitted under section 811(c).

[CCH Explanation at ¶ 915. Committee Reports at ¶ 10,690.]

Amendments

• **2017, Tax Cuts and Jobs Act (P.L. 115-97)**

P.L. 115-97, § 13517(a)(2)(A)-(H):

Amended Code Sec. 807(d) by striking paragraphs (1), (2), (4), and (5), by redesignating paragraph (6) as paragraph (4), by inserting before paragraph (3) new paragraphs (1) and (2), by striking "(other than a qualified long-term care insurance contract, as defined in section 7702B(b)), a 2-year full preliminary term method" in paragraph (3)(A)(iii) and inserting ", the reserve method prescribed by the National Association of Insurance Commissioners which covers such contract as of the date the reserve is determined", by striking "(as of the date of issuance)" in paragraph (3)(A)(iv)(I) and inserting "(as of the date the reserve is determined)", by striking "as of the date of the issuance of" in paragraph

(3)(A)(iv)(II) and inserting "as of the date the reserve is determined for", by striking "in effect on the date of the issuance of the contract" in paragraph (3)(B)(i) and inserting "applicable to the contract and in effect as of the date the reserve is determined", and by striking "in effect on the date of the issuance of the contract" in paragraph (3)(B)(ii) and inserting "applicable to the contract and in effect as of the date the reserve is determined". **Effective** generally for tax years beginning after 12-31-2017. For a transition rule, see Act Sec. 13517(c)(2)-(3), below. Prior to being stricken, Code Sec. 807(d)(1), (2), (4), and (5) read as follows:

(1) IN GENERAL.—For purposes of this part (other than section 816), the amount of the life insurance reserves for any contract shall be the greater of—

(A) the net surrender value of such contract, or

(B) the reserve determined under paragraph (2).

In no event shall the reserve determined under the preceding sentence for any contract as of any time exceed the amount which would be taken into account with respect to such contract as of such time in determining statutory reserves (as defined in paragraph (6)).

(2) AMOUNT OF RESERVE.—The amount of the reserve determined under this paragraph with respect to any contract shall be determined by using—

(A) the tax reserve method applicable to such contract,

(B) the greater of—

(i) the applicable Federal interest rate, or

(ii) the prevailing State assumed interest rate, and

(C) the prevailing commissioners' standard tables for mortality and morbidity adjusted as appropriate to reflect the risks (such as substandard risks) incurred under the contract which are not otherwise taken into account.

* * *

(4) APPLICABLE FEDERAL INTEREST RATE; PREVAILING STATE ASSUMED INTEREST RATE.—For purposes of this subsection—

(A) APPLICABLE FEDERAL INTEREST RATE.—

(i) IN GENERAL.—Except as provided in clause (ii), the term "applicable Federal interest rate" means the annual rate determined by the Secretary under section 846(c)(2) for the calendar year in which the contract was issued.

(ii) ELECTION TO RECOMPUTE FEDERAL INTEREST RATE EVERY 5 YEARS.—

(I) IN GENERAL.—In computing the amount of the reserve with respect to any contract to which an election under this clause applies for periods during any recomputation period, the applicable Federal interest rate shall be the annual rate determined by the Secretary under section 846(c)(2) for the 1st year of such period. No change in the applicable Federal interest rate shall be made under the preceding sentence unless such change would equal or exceed ½ of 1 percentage point.

(II) RECOMPUTATION PERIOD.—For purposes of subclause (I), the term "recomputation period" means, with respect to any contract, the 5 calendar year period beginning with the 5th calendar year beginning after the calendar year in which the contract was issued (and each subsequent 5 calendar year period).

(III) ELECTION.—An election under this clause shall apply to all contracts issued during the calendar year for which the election was made or during any subsequent calendar year unless such election is revoked with the consent of the Secretary.

(IV) SPREAD NOT AVAILABLE.—Subsection (f) shall not apply to any adjustment required under this clause.

(B) PREVAILING STATE ASSUMED INTEREST RATE.—

(i) IN GENERAL.—The "prevailing State assumed interest rate" means, with respect to any contract, the highest assumed interest rate permitted to be used in computing life insurance reserves for insurance contracts or annuity contracts (as the case may be) under the insurance laws of at least 26 States. For purposes of the preceding sentence, the effect of nonforfeiture laws of a State on interest rates for reserves shall not be taken into account.

(ii) WHEN RATE DETERMINED.—The prevailing State assumed interest rate with respect to any contract shall be determined as of the beginning of the calendar year in which the contract was issued.

(5) PREVAILING COMMISSIONERS' STANDARD TABLES.—For purposes of this subsection—

(A) IN GENERAL.—The term "prevailing commissioners' standard tables" means, with respect to any contract, the most recent commissioners' standard tables prescribed by the National Association of Insurance Commissioners which are permitted to be used in computing reserves for that type of contract under the insurance laws of at least 26 States when the contract was issued.

(B) INSURER MAY USE OLD TABLES FOR 3 YEARS WHEN TABLES CHANGE.—If the prevailing commissioners' standard tables as of the beginning of any calendar year (hereinafter in this subparagraph referred to as the "year of change") is different from the prevailing commissioners' standard tables as of the beginning of the preceding calendar year, the issuer may use the prevailing commissioners' standard tables as of the beginning of the preceding calendar year with respect to any contract issued after the change and before the close of the 3-year period beginning on the first day of the year of change.

(C) SPECIAL RULE FOR CONTRACTS FOR WHICH THERE ARE NO COMMISSIONERS' STANDARD TABLES.—If there are no commissioners' standard tables applicable to any contract when it is issued, the mortality and morbidity tables used for purposes of paragraph (2)(C) shall be determined under regulations prescribed by the Secretary. When the Secretary by regulation changes the table applicable to a type of contract, the new table shall be treated (for purposes of subparagraph (B) and for purposes of determining the issue dates of contracts for which it shall be used) as if it were a new prevailing commissioner's standard table adopted by the twenty-sixth State as of a date (no earlier than the date the regulation is issued) specified by the Secretary.

(D) SPECIAL RULE FOR CONTRACTS ISSUED BEFORE 1948.—If—

(i) a contract was issued before 1948, and

(ii) there were no commissioners' standard tables applicable to such contract when it was issued,

the mortality and morbidity tables used in computing statutory reserves for such contracts shall be used for purposes of paragraph (2)(C).

(E) SPECIAL RULE WHERE MORE THAN 1 TABLE OR OPTION APPLICABLE.—If, with respect to any category of risks, there are 2 or more tables (or options under 1 or more tables) which meet the requirements of subparagraph (A) (or, where applicable, subparagraph (B) or (C)), the table (and option thereunder) which generally yields the lowest reserves shall be used for purposes of paragraph (2)(C).

P.L. 115-97, § 13517(c)(2)-(3), provides:

(2) TRANSITION RULE.—For the first taxable year beginning after December 31, 2017, the reserve with respect to any contract (as determined under section 807(d) of the Internal Revenue Code of 1986) at the end of the preceding taxable year shall be determined as if the amendments made by this section had applied to such reserve in such preceding taxable year.

(3) TRANSITION RELIEF.—

(A) IN GENERAL.—If—

(i) the reserve determined under section 807(d) of the Internal Revenue Code of 1986 (determined after application of paragraph (2)) with respect to any contract as of the close of the year preceding the first taxable year beginning after December 31, 2017, differs from

(ii) the reserve which would have been determined with respect to such contract as of the close of such taxable year under such section determined without regard to paragraph (2),

then the difference between the amount of the reserve described in clause (i) and the amount of the reserve described in clause (ii) shall be taken into account under the method provided in subparagraph (B).

(B) METHOD.—The method provided in this subparagraph is as follows:

(i) If the amount determined under subparagraph (A)(i) exceeds the amount determined under subparagraph (A)(ii), 1/8 of such excess shall be taken into account, for each of the 8 succeeding taxable years, as a deduction under section 805(a)(2) or 832(c)(4) of such Code, as applicable.

(ii) If the amount determined under subparagraph (A)(ii) exceeds the amount determined under subparagraph (A)(i), 1/8 of such excess shall be included in gross income, for each of the 8 succeeding taxable years, under section 803(a)(2) or 832(b)(1)(C) of such Code, as applicable.

(e) SPECIAL RULES FOR COMPUTING RESERVES.—

* * *

(2) QUALIFIED SUPPLEMENTAL BENEFITS.—

(A) QUALIFIED SUPPLEMENTAL BENEFITS TREATED SEPARATELY.—For purposes of this part, the amount of the life insurance reserve for any qualified supplemental benefit shall be computed separately as though such benefit were under a separate contract.

(B) QUALIFIED SUPPLEMENTAL BENEFIT.—For purposes of this paragraph, the term "qualified supplemental benefit" means any supplemental benefit described in subparagraph (C) if—

(i) there is a separately identified premium or charge for such benefit, and

(ii) any net surrender value under the contract attributable to any other benefit is not available to fund such benefit.

(C) SUPPLEMENTAL BENEFITS.—For purposes of this paragraph, the supplemental benefits described in this subparagraph are any—

(i) guaranteed insurability,

(ii) accidental death or disability benefit,

(iii) convertibility,

(iv) disability waiver benefit, or

(v) other benefit prescribed by regulations,

which is supplemental to a contract for which there is a reserve described in subsection (c).

(3) CERTAIN CONTRACTS ISSUED BY FOREIGN BRANCHES OF DOMESTIC LIFE INSURANCE COMPANIES.—

(A) IN GENERAL.—In the case of any qualified foreign contract, the amount of the reserve shall be not less than the minimum reserve required by the laws, regulations, or administrative guidance of the regulatory authority of the foreign country referred to in subparagraph (B) (but not to exceed the net level reserves for such contract).

(B) QUALIFIED FOREIGN CONTRACT.—For purposes of subparagraph (A), the term "qualified foreign contract" means any contract issued by a foreign life insurance branch (which has its principal place of business in a foreign country) of a domestic life insurance company if—

(i) such contract is issued on the life or health of a resident of such country,

(ii) such domestic life insurance company was required by such foreign country (as of the time it began operations in such country) to operate in such country through a branch, and

(iii) such foreign country is not contiguous to the United States.

(4) SPECIAL RULES FOR CONTRACTS ISSUED BEFORE JANUARY 1, 1989, UNDER EXISTING PLANS OF INSURANCE, WITH TERM INSURANCE OR ANNUITY BENEFITS.—For purposes of this part—

(A) IN GENERAL.—In the case of a life insurance contract issued before January 1, 1989, under an existing plan of insurance, the life insurance reserve for any benefit to which this paragraph applies shall be computed separately under subsection (d)(1) from any other reserve under the contract.

(B) BENEFITS TO WHICH THIS PARAGRAPH APPLIES.—This paragraph applies to any term insurance or annuity benefit with respect to which the requirements of clauses (i) and (ii) of paragraph (3)(C) are met.

(C) EXISTING PLAN OF INSURANCE.—For purposes of this paragraph, the term "existing plan of insurance" means, with respect to any contract, any plan of insurance which was filed by the company using such contract in one or more States before January 1, 1984, and is on file in the appropriate State for such contract.

(5) SPECIAL RULES FOR TREATMENT OF CERTAIN NONLIFE RESERVES.—

(A) IN GENERAL.—The amount taken into account for purposes of subsections (a) and (b) as—

(i) the opening balance of the items referred to in subparagraph (C), and

(ii) the closing balance of such items,

shall be 80 percent of the amount which (without regard to this subparagraph) would have been taken into account as such opening or closing balance, as the case may be.

(B) DESCRIPTION OF ITEMS.—For purposes of this paragraph, the items referred to in this subparagraph are the items described in subsection (c) which consist of unearned premiums and premiums received in advance under insurance contracts not described in section 816(b)(1)(B).

(6) REPORTING RULES.—*The Secretary shall require reporting (at such time and in such manner as the Secretary shall prescribe) with respect to the opening balance and closing balance of reserves and with respect to the method of computing reserves for purposes of determining income.*

[CCH Explanation at ¶ 915. Committee Reports at ¶ 10,690.]

Amendments

• **2017, Tax Cuts and Jobs Act (P.L. 115-97)**

P.L. 115-97, § 13517(a)(3)(A)-(D):

Amended Code Sec. 807(e) by striking paragraphs (2) and (5), by redesignating paragraphs (3), (4), (6), and (7) as paragraphs (2), (3), (4), and (5), respectively, by amending paragraph (2) (as so redesignated), and by adding at the end a new paragraph (6). **Effective** generally for tax years beginning after 12-31-2017. For a transition rule, see Act Sec. 13517(c)(2)-(3), below. Prior to being stricken, Code Sec. 807(e)(2) and (5) read as follows:

(2) ISSUANCE DATE IN CASE OF GROUP CONTRACTS.—For purposes of this section, in the case of a group contract, the date on which such contract is issued shall be the date as of which the master plan is issued (or, with respect to a benefit guaranteed to a participant after such date, the date as of which such benefit is guaranteed).

* * *

(5) TREATMENT OF SUBSTANDARD RISKS.—

(A) SEPARATE COMPUTATION.—Except to the extent provided in regulations, the amount of the life insurance reserve for any qualified substandard risk shall be computed separately under subsection (d)(1) from any other reserve under the contract.

(B) QUALIFIED SUBSTANDARD RISK.—For purposes of subparagraph (A), the term "qualified substandard risk" means any substandard risk if—

(i) the insurance company maintains a separate reserve for such risk,

(ii) there is a separately identified premium or charge for such risk,

(iii) the amount of the net surrender value under the contract is not increased or decreased by reason of such risk, and

(iv) the net surrender value under the contract is not regularly used to pay premium charges for such risk.

(C) LIMITATION ON AMOUNT OF LIFE INSURANCE RESERVE.—The amount of the life insurance reserve determined for any qualified substandard risk shall in no event exceed the sum of the separately identified premiums charged for such risk plus interest less mortality charges for such risk.

(D) LIMITATION ON AMOUNT OF CONTRACTS TO WHICH PARAGRAPH APPLIES.—The aggregate amount of insurance in force under contracts to which this paragraph applies shall not exceed 10 percent of the insurance in force (other than term insurance) under life insurance contracts of the company.

P.L. 115-97, § 13517(c)(2)-(3), provides:

(2) TRANSITION RULE.—For the first taxable year beginning after December 31, 2017, the reserve with respect to any contract (as determined under section 807(d) of the Internal Revenue Code of 1986) at the end of the preceding taxable year shall be determined as if the amendments made by this section had applied to such reserve in such preceding taxable year.

(3) TRANSITION RELIEF.—

(A) IN GENERAL.—If—

(i) the reserve determined under section 807(d) of the Internal Revenue Code of 1986 (determined after application of paragraph (2)) with respect to any contract as of the close of the year preceding the first taxable year beginning after December 31, 2017, differs from

(ii) the reserve which would have been determined with respect to such contract as of the close of such taxable year under such section determined without regard to paragraph (2),

then the difference between the amount of the reserve described in clause (i) and the amount of the reserve described in clause (ii) shall be taken into account under the method provided in subparagraph (B).

(B) METHOD.—The method provided in this subparagraph is as follows:

(i) If the amount determined under subparagraph (A)(i) exceeds the amount determined under subparagraph (A)(ii), 1/8 of such excess shall be taken into account, for each of the 8 succeeding taxable years, as a deduction under section 805(a)(2) or 832(c)(4) of such Code, as applicable.

(ii) If the amount determined under subparagraph (A)(ii) exceeds the amount determined under subparagraph (A)(i), 1/8 of such excess shall be included in gross income, for each of the 8 succeeding taxable years, under section 803(a)(2) or 832(b)(1)(C) of such Code, as applicable.

(f) ADJUSTMENT FOR CHANGE IN COMPUTING RESERVES.—

(1) TREATMENT AS CHANGE IN METHOD OF ACCOUNTING.—If the basis for determining any item referred to in subsection (c) as of the close of any taxable year differs from the basis for such determination as of the close of the preceding taxable year, then so much of the difference between—

(A) the amount of the item at the close of the taxable year, computed on the new basis, and

(B) the amount of the item at the close of the taxable year, computed on the old basis,

as is attributable to contracts issued before the taxable year shall be taken into account under section 481 as adjustments attributable to a change in method of accounting initiated by the taxpayer and made with the consent of the Secretary.

* * *

[CCH Explanation at ¶ 915. Committee Reports at ¶ 10,690.]

Amendments

• **2017, Tax Cuts and Jobs Act (P.L. 115-97)**

P.L. 115-97, § 13513(a):

Amended Code Sec. 807(f)(1). **Effective** for tax years beginning after 12-31-2017. Prior to amendment, Code Sec. 807(f)(1) read as follows:

(1) 10-YEAR SPREAD.—

(A) IN GENERAL.—For purposes of this part, if the basis for determining any item referred to in subsection (c) as of the close of any taxable year differs from the basis for such determination as of the close of the preceding taxable year, then so much of the difference between—

(i) the amount of the item at the close of the taxable year, computed on the new basis, and

(ii) the amount of the item at the close of the taxable year, computed on the old basis,

as is attributable to contracts issued before the taxable year shall be taken into account under the method provided in subparagraph (B).

(B) METHOD.—The method provided in this subparagraph is as follows:

(i) if the amount determined under subparagraph (A)(i) exceeds the amount determined under subparagraph (A)(ii), 1/10 of such excess shall be taken into account, for each of the succeeding 10 taxable years, as a deduction under section 805(a)(2); or

(ii) if the amount determined under subparagraph (A)(ii) exceeds the amount determined under subparagraph (A)(i), 1/10 of such excess shall be included in gross income, for each of the 10 succeeding taxable years, under section 803(a)(2).

[¶ 5680] CODE SEC. 808. POLICYHOLDER DIVIDENDS DEDUCTION.

* * *

(g) PREVAILING STATE ASSUMED INTEREST RATE.—For purposes of this subchapter—

(1) IN GENERAL.—The term "prevailing State assumed interest rate" means, with respect to any contract, the highest assumed interest rate permitted to be used in computing life insurance reserves for insurance contracts or annuity contracts (as the case may be) under the insurance laws of at least 26 States. For purposes of the preceding sentence, the effect of nonforfeiture laws of a State on interest rates for reserves shall not be taken into account.

(2) WHEN RATE DETERMINED.—The prevailing State assumed interest rate with respect to any contract shall be determined as of the beginning of the calendar year in which the contract was issued.

[CCH Explanation at ¶ 915. Committee Reports at ¶ 10,690.]

Amendments

• **2017, Tax Cuts and Jobs Act (P.L. 115-97)**

P.L. 115-97, § 13517(b)(1):

Amended Code Sec. 808 by adding at the end a new subsection (g). **Effective** generally for tax years beginning after 12-31-2017. For a transition rule, see Act Sec. 13517(c)(2)-(3), below.

P.L. 115-97, § 13517(c)(2)-(3), provides:

(2) TRANSITION RULE.—For the first taxable year beginning after December 31, 2017, the reserve with respect to any contract (as determined under section 807(d) of the Internal

Revenue Code of 1986) at the end of the preceding taxable year shall be determined as if the amendments made by this section had applied to such reserve in such preceding taxable year.

(3) TRANSITION RELIEF.—

(A) IN GENERAL.—If—

(i) the reserve determined under section 807(d) of the Internal Revenue Code of 1986 (determined after application of paragraph (2)) with respect to any contract as of the close of the year preceding the first taxable year beginning after December 31, 2017, differs from

(ii) the reserve which would have been determined with respect to such contract as of the close of such taxable year under such section determined without regard to paragraph (2),

then the difference between the amount of the reserve described in clause (i) and the amount of the reserve described in clause (ii) shall be taken into account under the method provided in subparagraph (B).

(B) METHOD.—The method provided in this subparagraph is as follows:

(i) If the amount determined under subparagraph (A)(i) exceeds the amount determined under subparagraph (A)(ii), 1/8 of such excess shall be taken into account, for each of the 8 succeeding taxable years, as a deduction under section 805(a)(2) or 832(c)(4) of such Code, as applicable.

(ii) If the amount determined under subparagraph (A)(ii) exceeds the amount determined under subparagraph (A)(i), 1/8 of such excess shall be included in gross income, for each of the 8 succeeding taxable years, under section 803(a)(2) or 832(b)(1)(C) of such Code, as applicable.

[¶ 5685] CODE SEC. 810. OPERATIONS LOSS DEDUCTION. [*Stricken.*]

[CCH Explanation at ¶ 905. Committee Reports at ¶ 10,630.]

Amendments

• 2017, Tax Cuts and Jobs Act (P.L. 115-97)

P.L. 115-97, § 13511(b)(1):

Amended part I of subchapter L of chapter 1 by striking Code Sec. 810. **Effective** for losses arising in tax years beginning after 12-31-2017. Prior to being stricken, Code Sec. 810 read as follows:

SEC. 810. OPERATIONS LOSS DEDUCTION.

(a) DEDUCTION ALLOWED.—There shall be allowed as a deduction for the taxable year an amount equal to the aggregate of—

(1) the operations loss carryovers to such year, plus

(2) the operations loss carrybacks to such year.

For purposes of this part, the term "operations loss deduction" means the deduction allowed by this subsection.

(b) OPERATIONS LOSS CARRYBACKS AND CARRYOVERS.—

(1) YEARS TO WHICH LOSS MAY BE CARRIED.—The loss from operations for any taxable year (hereinafter in this section referred to as the "loss year") shall be—

(A) an operations loss carryback to each of the 3 taxable years preceding the loss year,

(B) an operations loss carryover to each of the 15 taxable years following the loss year, and

(C) if the life insurance company is a new company for the loss year, an operations loss carryover to each of the 3 taxable years following the 15 taxable years described in subparagraph (B).

(2) AMOUNT OF CARRYBACKS AND CARRYOVERS.—The entire amount of the loss from operations for any loss year shall be carried to the earliest of the taxable years to which (by reason of paragraph (1)) such loss may be carried. The portion of such loss which shall be carried to each of the other taxable years shall be the excess (if any) of the amount of such loss over the sum of the offsets (as defined in subsection (d)) for each of the prior taxable years to which such loss may be carried.

(3) ELECTION FOR OPERATIONS LOSS CARRYBACKS.—In the case of a loss from operations for any taxable year, the taxpayer may elect to relinquish the entire carryback period for such loss. Such election shall be made by the due date (including extensions of time) for filing the return for the taxable year of the loss from operations for which the election is to be in effect, and, once made for any taxable year, such election shall be irrevocable for that taxable year.

(4) CARRYBACK FOR 2008 OR 2009 LOSSES.—

(A) IN GENERAL.—In the case of an applicable loss from operations with respect to which the taxpayer has elected the application of this paragraph, paragraph (1)(A) shall be applied by substituting any whole number elected by the taxpayer which is more than 3 and less than 6 for "3".

(B) APPLICABLE LOSS FROM OPERATIONS.—For purposes of this paragraph, the term "applicable loss from operations" means the taxpayer's loss from operations for a taxable year ending after December 31, 2007, and beginning before January 1, 2010.

(C) ELECTION.—

(i) IN GENERAL.—Any election under this paragraph may be made only with respect to 1 taxable year.

(ii) PROCEDURE.—Any election under this paragraph shall be made in such manner as may be prescribed by the Secretary, and shall be made by the due date (including extension of time) for filing the return for the taxpayer's last taxable year beginning in 2009. Any such election, once made, shall be irrevocable.

(D) LIMITATION ON AMOUNT OF LOSS CARRYBACK TO 5TH PRECEDING TAXABLE YEAR.—

(i) IN GENERAL.—The amount of any loss from operations which may be carried back to the 5th taxable year preceding the taxable year of such loss under subparagraph (A) shall not exceed 50 percent of the taxpayer's taxable income (computed without regard to the loss from operations for the loss year or any taxable year thereafter) for such preceding taxable year.

(ii) CARRYBACKS AND CARRYOVERS TO OTHER TAXABLE YEARS.—Appropriate adjustments in the application of the second sentence of paragraph (2) shall be made to take into account the limitation of clause (i).

(c) COMPUTATION OF LOSS FROM OPERATIONS.—For purposes of this section—

(1) IN GENERAL.—The term "loss from operations" means the excess of the life insurance deductions for any taxable year over the life insurance gross income for such taxable year.

(2) MODIFICATIONS.—For purposes of paragraph (1)—

(A) the operations loss deduction shall not be allowed, and

(B) the deductions allowed by sections 243 (relating to dividends received by corporations), and 245 (relating to dividends received from certain foreign corporations) shall be computed without regard to section 246(b) as modified by section 805(a)(4).

(d) OFFSET DEFINED.—

(1) IN GENERAL.—For purposes of subsection (b)(2), the term "offset" means, with respect to any taxable year, an amount equal to that increase in the operations loss deduction for the taxable year which reduces the life insurance company taxable income (computed without regard to paragraphs (2) and (3) of section 804) for such year to zero.

(2) OPERATIONS LOSS DEDUCTION.—For purposes of paragraph (1), the operations loss deduction for any taxable year

shall be computed without regard to the loss from operations for the loss year or for any taxable year thereafter.

(e) NEW COMPANY DEFINED.—For purposes of this part, a life insurance company is a new company for any taxable year only if such taxable year begins not more than 5 years after the first day on which it (or any predecessor, if section 381(c)(22) applies) was authorized to do business as an insurance company.

(f) APPLICATION OF SUBTITLES A AND F IN RESPECT OF OPERATION LOSSES.—Except as provided in section 805(b)(5), subtitles A and F shall apply in respect of operation loss carrybacks, operation loss carryovers, and the operations loss deduction under this part, in the same manner and to the same extent as such subtitles apply in respect of net operating loss carrybacks, net operating loss carryovers, and the net operating loss deduction.

(g) TRANSITIONAL RULE.—For purposes of this section and section 812 (as in effect before the enactment of the Life Insurance Tax Act of 1984), this section shall be treated as a continuation of such section 812.

[¶ 5690] CODE SEC. 811. ACCOUNTING PROVISIONS.

* * *

(d) METHOD OF COMPUTING RESERVES ON CONTRACT WHERE INTEREST IS GUARANTEED BEYOND END OF TAXABLE YEAR.—For purposes of this part (other than section 816), amounts in the nature of interest to be paid or credited under any contract for any period which is computed at a rate which—

(1) exceeds *the interest rate in effect under section 808(g)* for the contract for such period, and

(2) is guaranteed beyond the end of the taxable year on which the reserves are being computed,

shall be taken into account in computing the reserves with respect to such contract as if such interest were guaranteed only up to the end of the taxable year.

* * *

[CCH Explanation at ¶ 915. Committee Reports at ¶ 10,690.]

Amendments

• **2017, Tax Cuts and Jobs Act (P.L. 115-97)**

P.L. 115-97, § 13517(b)(2):

Amended Code Sec. 811(d)(1) by striking "the greater of the prevailing State assumed interest rate or applicable Federal interest rate in effect under section 807" and inserting "the interest rate in effect under section 808(g)". **Effective** generally for tax years beginning after 12-31-2017. For a transition rule, see Act Sec. 13517(c)(2)-(3), below.

P.L. 115-97, § 13517(c)(2)-(3), provides:

(2) TRANSITION RULE.—For the first taxable year beginning after December 31, 2017, the reserve with respect to any contract (as determined under section 807(d) of the Internal Revenue Code of 1986) at the end of the preceding taxable year shall be determined as if the amendments made by this section had applied to such reserve in such preceding taxable year.

(3) TRANSITION RELIEF.—

(A) IN GENERAL.—If—

(i) the reserve determined under section 807(d) of the Internal Revenue Code of 1986 (determined after application of paragraph (2)) with respect to any contract as of the close of the year preceding the first taxable year beginning after December 31, 2017, differs from

(ii) the reserve which would have been determined with respect to such contract as of the close of such taxable year under such section determined without regard to paragraph (2),

then the difference between the amount of the reserve described in clause (i) and the amount of the reserve described in clause (ii) shall be taken into account under the method provided in subparagraph (B).

(B) METHOD.—The method provided in this subparagraph is as follows:

(i) If the amount determined under subparagraph (A)(i) exceeds the amount determined under subparagraph (A)(ii), 1/8 of such excess shall be taken into account, for each of the 8 succeeding taxable years, as a deduction under section 805(a)(2) or 832(c)(4) of such Code, as applicable.

(ii) If the amount determined under subparagraph (A)(ii) exceeds the amount determined under subparagraph (A)(i), 1/8 of such excess shall be included in gross income, for each of the 8 succeeding taxable years, under section 803(a)(2) or 832(b)(1)(C) of such Code, as applicable.

[¶ 5695] CODE SEC. 812. *DEFINITION OF COMPANY'S SHARE AND POLICYHOLDER'S SHARE.*

(a) COMPANY'S SHARE.—*For purposes of section 805(a)(4), the term "company's share" means, with respect to any taxable year beginning after December 31, 2017, 70 percent.*

(b) POLICYHOLDER'S SHARE.—*For purposes of section 807, the term "policyholder's share" means, with respect to any taxable year beginning after December 31, 2017, 30 percent.*

[CCH Explanation at ¶ 920. Committee Reports at ¶ 10,700.]

Amendments

• 2017, Tax Cuts and Jobs Act (P.L. 115-97)

P.L. 115-97, § 13518(a):

Amended Code Sec. 812. **Effective** for tax years beginning after 12-31-2017. Prior to amendment, Code Sec. 812 read as follows:

SEC. 812. DEFINITION OF COMPANY'S SHARE AND POLICYHOLDERS' SHARE.

(a) GENERAL RULE.—

(1) COMPANY'S SHARE.—For purposes of section 805(a)(4), the term "company's share" means, with respect to any taxable year, the percentage obtained by dividing—

(A) the company's share of the net investment income for the taxable year, by

(B) the net investment income for the taxable year.

(2) POLICYHOLDERS' SHARE.—For purposes of section 807, the term "policyholders' share" means, with respect to any taxable year, the excess of 100 percent over the percentage determined under paragraph (1).

(b) COMPANY'S SHARE OF NET INVESTMENT INCOME.—

(1) IN GENERAL.—For purposes of this section, the company's share of net investment income is the excess (if any) of—

(A) the net investment income for the taxable year, over

(B) the sum of—

(i) the policy interest, for the taxable year, plus

(ii) the gross investment income's proportionate share of policyholder dividends for the taxable year.

(2) POLICY INTEREST.—For purposes of this subsection, the term "policy interest" means—

(A) required interest (at the greater of the prevailing State assumed rate or the applicable Federal interest rate) on reserves under section 807(c) (other than paragraph (2) thereof),

(B) the deductible portion of excess interest,

(C) the deductible portion of any amount (whether or not a policyholder dividend), and not taken into account under subparagraph (A) or (B), credited to—

(i) a policyholder's fund under a pension plan contract for employees (other than retired employees), or

(ii) a deferred annuity contract before the annuity starting date, and

(D) interest on amounts left on deposit with the company.

In any case where neither the prevailing State assumed interest rate nor the applicable Federal rate is used, another appropriate rate shall be used for purposes of subparagraph (A).

(3) GROSS INVESTMENT INCOME'S PROPORTIONATE SHARE OF POLICYHOLDER DIVIDENDS.—For purposes of paragraph (1), the gross investment income's proportionate share of policyholder dividends is—

(A) the deduction for policyholders' dividends determined under section 808 for the taxable year, but not including—

(i) the deductible portion of excess interest,

(ii) the deductible portion of policyholder dividends on contracts referred to in clauses (i) and (ii) of paragraph (2)(C), and

(iii) the deductible portion of the premium and mortality charge adjustments with respect to contracts paying excess interest for such year,

multiplied by

(B) the fraction—

(i) the numerator of which is gross investment income for the taxable year (reduced by the policy interest for such year), and

(ii) the denominator of which is life insurance gross income reduced by the excess (if any) of the closing balance for the items described in section 807(c) over the opening balance for such items for the taxable year.

For purposes of subparagraph (B)(ii), life insurance gross income shall be determined by including tax-exempt interest and by applying section 807(a)(2)(B) as if it did not contain clause (i) thereof.

(c) NET INVESTMENT INCOME—For purposes of this section, the term "net investment income" means—

(1) except as provided in paragraph (2), 90 percent of gross investment income; or

(2) in the case of gross investment income attributable to assets held in segregated asset accounts under variable contracts, 95 percent of gross investment income.

(d) GROSS INVESTMENT INCOME.—For purposes of this section, the term "gross investment income" means the sum of the following:

(1) INTEREST, ETC.—The gross amount of income from—

(A) interest (including tax-exempt interest), dividends, rents, and royalties,

(B) the entering into of any lease, mortgage, or other instrument or agreement from which the life insurance company derives interest, rents, or royalties,

(C) the alteration or termination of any instrument or agreement described in subparagraph (B), and

(D) the increase for any taxable year in the policy cash values (within the meaning of section 805(a)(4)(F)) of life insurance policies and annuity and endowment contracts to which section 264(f) applies.

(2) SHORT-TERM CAPITAL GAIN.—The amount (if any) by which the net short-term capital gain exceeds the net long-term capital loss.

(3) TRADE OR BUSINESS INCOME.—The gross income from any trade or business (other than an insurance business) carried on by the life insurance company, or by a partnership of which the life insurance company is a partner. In computing gross income under this paragraph, there shall be excluded any item described in paragraph (1).

Except as provided in paragraph (2), in computing gross investment income under this subsection, there shall be excluded any gain from the sale or exchange of a capital asset, and any gain considered as gain from the sale or exchange of a capital asset.

(e) DIVIDENDS FROM CERTAIN SUBSIDIARIES NOT INCLUDED IN GROSS INVESTMENT INCOME.—

(1) IN GENERAL.—For purposes of this section, the term "gross investment income" shall not include any dividend received by the life insurance company which is a 100 percent dividend.

(2) 100 PERCENT DIVIDEND DEFINED.—

(A) IN GENERAL.—Except as provided in subparagraphs (B) and (C), the term "100 percent dividend" means any dividend if the percentage used for purposes of determining the deduction allowable under section 243 or 245(b) is 100 percent.

(B) CERTAIN DIVIDENDS OUT OF TAX-EXEMPT INTEREST, ETC.— The term "100 percent dividend" does not include any distribution by a corporation to the extent such distribution is out of tax-exempt interest or out of dividends which are not 100 percent dividends (determined with the application of this subparagraph).

(C) CERTAIN DIVIDENDS RECEIVED BY FOREIGN CORPORATIONS.— The term "100 percent dividends" does not include any dividend described in section 805(a)(4)(E) (relating to certain dividends in the case of foreign corporations).

(f) NO DOUBLE COUNTING.—Under regulations, proper adjustments shall be made in the application of this section to prevent an item from being counted more than once.

[¶5700] CODE SEC. 814. CONTIGUOUS COUNTRY BRANCHES OF DOMESTIC LIFE INSURANCE COMPANIES.

* * *

(f) OTHER RULES.—

(1) TREATMENT OF FOREIGN TAXES.—No income, war profits, or excess profits taxes paid or accrued to any foreign country or possession of the United States which is attributable to income excluded under subsection (a) shall be taken into account for purposes of subpart A of part III of subchapter N (relating to foreign tax credit) or allowable as a deduction.

* * *

[CCH Explanation at ¶720. Committee Reports at ¶11,170.]

Amendments

• **2017, Tax Cuts and Jobs Act (P.L. 115-97)**

P.L. 115-97, §14301(c)(5)(A):

Amended Code Sec. 814(f)(1) by striking subparagraph (B). **Effective** for tax years of foreign corporations beginning after 12-31-2017, and to tax years of United States shareholders in which or with which such tax years of foreign corporations end. Prior to being stricken, Code Sec. 814(f)(1)(B) read as follows:

(B) TREATMENT OF REPATRIATED AMOUNTS.—For purposes of sections 78 and 902, where any amount is added to the life insurance company taxable income of the domestic life insurance company by reason of subsection (e)(2), the contiguous country life insurance branch shall be treated as a foreign corporation. Any amount so added shall be treated as a dividend paid by a foreign corporation, and the taxes

paid to any foreign country or possession of the United States with respect to such amount shall be deemed to have been paid by such branch.

P.L. 115-97, §14301(c)(5)(B):

Amended Code Sec. 814(f)(1) by striking all that precedes "No income" and inserting:

"(1) TREATMENT OF FOREIGN TAXES.—".

Effective for tax years of foreign corporations beginning after 12-31-2017, and to tax years of United States shareholders in which or with which such tax years of foreign corporations end. Prior to being stricken, all that precedes "No income" in Code Sec. 814(f)(1) read as follows:

(1) TREATMENT OF FOREIGN TAXES.—

(A) IN GENERAL.—

[¶5705] CODE SEC. 815. DISTRIBUTIONS TO SHAREHOLDERS FROM PRE-1984 POLICYHOLDERS SURPLUS ACCOUNT. [*Stricken.*]

[CCH Explanation at ¶940. Committee Reports at ¶10,660.]

Amendments

• **2017, Tax Cuts and Jobs Act (P.L. 115-97)**

P.L. 115-97, §13514(a):

Amended subpart D of part I of subchapter L by striking Code Sec. 815. **Effective** for tax years beginning after 12-31-2017. For a special rule, see Act Sec. 13514(d), below. Prior to being stricken, Code Sec. 815 read as follows:

SEC. 815. DISTRIBUTIONS TO SHAREHOLDERS FROM PRE-1984 POLICYHOLDERS SURPLUS ACCOUNT.

(a) GENERAL RULE.—In the case of a stock life insurance company which has an existing policyholders surplus account, the tax imposed by section 801 for any taxable year shall be the amount which would be imposed by such section for such year on the sum of—

(1) life insurance company taxable income for such year (but not less than zero), plus

(2) the amount of direct and indirect distributions during such year to shareholders from such account.

For purposes of the preceding sentence, the term "indirect distribution" shall not include any bona fide loan with arms-length terms and conditions.

(b) ORDERING RULE.—For purposes of this section, any distribution to shareholders shall be treated as made—

(1) first out of the shareholders surplus account, to the extent thereof,

(2) then out of the policyholders surplus account, to the extent thereof, and

(3) finally, out of other accounts.

(c) SHAREHOLDERS SURPLUS ACCOUNT.—

(1) IN GENERAL.—Each stock life insurance company which has an existing policyholders surplus account shall continue its shareholders surplus account for purposes of this part.

(2) ADDITIONS TO ACCOUNT.—The amount added to the shareholders surplus account for any taxable year beginning after December 31, 1983, shall be the excess of—

(A) the sum of—

(i) the life insurance company's taxable income (but not below zero),

(ii) the small life insurance company deduction provided by section 806, and

(iii) the deductions for dividends received provided by sections 243 and 245 (as modified by section 805(a)(4)) and the amount of interest excluded from gross income under section 103, over

(B) the taxes imposed for the taxable year by section 801 (determined without regard to this section).

If for any taxable year a tax is imposed by section 55, under regulations proper adjustments shall be made for such year and all subsequent taxable years in the amounts taken into account under subparagraphs (A) and (B) of this paragraph and subparagraph (B) of subsection (d)(3).

(3) SUBTRACTIONS FROM ACCOUNT.—There shall be subtracted from the shareholders surplus account for any taxable year the amount which is treated under this section as distributed out of such account.

(d) POLICYHOLDERS SURPLUS ACCOUNT.—

(1) IN GENERAL.—Each stock life insurance company which has an existing policyholders surplus account shall continue such account.

(2) NO ADDITIONS TO ACCOUNT.—No amount shall be added to the policyholders surplus account for any taxable year beginning after December 31, 1983.

(3) SUBTRACTIONS FROM ACCOUNT.—There shall be subtracted from the policyholders surplus account for any taxable year an amount equal to the sum of—

(A) the amount which (without regard to subparagraph (B)) is treated under this section as distributed out of the policyholders surplus account, and

(B) the amount by which the tax imposed for the taxable year by section 801 is increased by reason of this section.

(e) EXISTING POLICYHOLDERS SURPLUS ACCOUNT.—For purposes of this section, the term "existing policyholders surplus account" means any policyholders surplus account which has a balance as of the close of December 31, 1983.

(f) OTHER RULES APPLICABLE TO POLICYHOLDERS SURPLUS ACCOUNT CONTINUED.—Except to the extent inconsistent with the provisions of this part, the provisions of subsections (d), (e), (f), and (g) of section 815 (and of sections 819(b), 6501(c)(6), 6501(k), 6511(d)(6), 6601(d)(3), and 6611(f)(4)) as in effect before the enactment of the Tax Reform Act of 1984 are hereby made applicable in respect of any policyholders surplus account for which there was a balance as of December 31, 1983.

(g) SPECIAL RULES APPLICABLE DURING 2005 AND 2006.—In the case of any taxable year of a stock life insurance company beginning after December 31, 2004, and before January 1, 2007—

(1) the amount under subsection (a)(2) for such taxable year shall be treated as zero, and

(2) notwithstanding subsection (b), in determining any subtractions from an account under subsections (c)(3) and (d)(3), any distribution to shareholders during such taxable year shall be treated as made first out of the policyholders surplus account, then out of the shareholders surplus account, and finally out of other accounts.

P.L. 115-97, § 13514(d), provides:

(d) PHASED INCLUSION OF REMAINING BALANCE OF POLICYHOLDERS SURPLUS ACCOUNTS.—In the case of any stock life insurance company which has a balance (determined as of the close of such company's last taxable year beginning before January 1, 2018) in an existing policyholders surplus account (as defined in section 815 of the Internal Revenue Code of 1986, as in effect before its repeal), the tax imposed by section 801 of such Code for the first 8 taxable years beginning after December 31, 2017, shall be the amount which would be imposed by such section for such year on the sum of—

(1) life insurance company taxable income for such year (within the meaning of such section 801 but not less than zero), plus

(2) $1/8$ of such balance.

[¶5710] CODE SEC. 817A. SPECIAL RULES FOR MODIFIED GUARANTEED CONTRACTS.

* * *

(e) REGULATIONS.—The Secretary may prescribe regulations—

* * *

(2) to determine the interest rates applicable under sections 807(c)(3) *and 807(d)(2)(B)* with respect to a modified guaranteed contract annually, in a manner appropriate for modified guaranteed contracts and, to the extent appropriate for such a contract, to modify or waive the applicability of section 811(d),

* * *

[CCH Explanation at ¶920. Committee Reports at ¶10,700.]
Amendments
• **2017, Tax Cuts and Jobs Act (P.L. 115-97)**

P.L. 115-97, § 13518(b):

Amended Code Sec. 817A(e)(2) by striking ", 807(d)(2)(B), and 812" and inserting "and 807(d)(2)(B)". **Effective** for tax years beginning after 12-31-2017.

[¶5715] CODE SEC. 831. TAX ON INSURANCE COMPANIES OTHER THAN LIFE INSURANCE COMPANIES.

* * *

(b) ALTERNATIVE TAX FOR CERTAIN SMALL COMPANIES.—

* * *

(2) COMPANIES TO WHICH THIS SUBSECTION APPLIES.—

* * *

(D) INFLATION ADJUSTMENT.—In the case of any taxable year beginning in a calendar year after 2015, the dollar amount set forth in subparagraph (A)(i) shall be increased by an amount equal to—

(i) such dollar amount, multiplied by

(ii) the cost-of-living adjustment determined under section 1(f)(3) for such calendar year by substituting "calendar year 2013" for "calendar year 2016" in subparagraph (A)(ii) thereof.

If the amount as adjusted under the preceding sentence is not a multiple of $50,000, such amount shall be rounded to the next lowest multiple of $50,000.

(3) LIMITATION ON USE OF NET OPERATING LOSSES.—For purposes of this part, a net operating loss (as defined in section 172) shall not be carried—

(A) to or from any taxable year for which the insurance company is not subject to the tax imposed by subsection (a), or

(B) to any taxable year if, between the taxable year from which such loss is being carried and such taxable year, there is an intervening taxable year for which the insurance company was not subject to the tax imposed by subsection (a).

* * *

[CCH Explanation at ¶125 and ¶905. Committee Reports at ¶10,020 and ¶10,630.]

Amendments

• **2017, Tax Cuts and Jobs Act (P.L. 115-97)**

P.L. 115-97, §11002(d)(1)(AA):

Amended Code Sec. 831(b)(2)(D)(ii) by striking "for 'calendar year 1992' in subparagraph (B)" and inserting "for 'calendar year 2016' in subparagraph (A)(ii)". **Effective** for tax years beginning after 12-31-2017.

P.L. 115-97, §13511(b)(2)(B):

Amended Code Sec. 831(b)(3) by striking "except as provided in section 844," following "For purposes of this part,". **Effective** for losses arising in tax years beginning after 12-31-2017.

(e) CROSS REFERENCES.—

(1) For taxation of foreign corporations carrying on an insurance business within the United States, see section 842.

(2) For exemption from tax for certain insurance companies other than life, see section 501(c)(15).

[CCH Explanation at ¶305. Committee Reports at ¶10,310.]

Amendments

• **2017, Tax Cuts and Jobs Act (P.L. 115-97)**

P.L. 115-97, §13001(b)(2)(H):

Amended Code Sec. 831(e) by striking paragraph (1) and by redesignating paragraphs (2) and (3) as paragraphs (1)

and (2), respectively. **Effective** for tax years beginning after 12-31-2017. Prior to amendment, Code Sec. 831(e)(1) read as follows:

(1) For alternative tax in case of capital gains, see section 1201(a).

[¶5720] CODE SEC. 832. INSURANCE COMPANY TAXABLE INCOME.

* * *

(b) DEFINITIONS.—In the case of an insurance company subject to the tax imposed by section 831—

* * *

(5) LOSSES INCURRED.—

(B) REDUCTION OF DEDUCTION.—The amount which would (but for this subparagraph) be taken into account under subparagraph (A) shall be reduced by an amount equal to *the applicable percentage* of the sum of—

(i) tax-exempt interest received or accrued during such taxable year,

(ii) the aggregate amount of deductions provided by sections 243 and 245 for—

(I) dividends (other than 100 percent dividends) received during the taxable year, and

(II) 100 percent dividends received during the taxable year to the extent attributable (directly or indirectly) to prorated amounts, and

(iii) the increase for the taxable year in policy cash values (within the meaning of section 805(a)(4)(F)) of life insurance policies and annuity and endowment contracts to which section 264(f) applies.

In the case of a 100 percent dividend paid by an insurance company, the portion attributable to prorated amounts shall be determined under subparagraph (E)(ii). *For purposes of this subparagraph, the applicable percentage is 5.25 percent divided by the highest rate in effect under section 11(b).*

* * *

[CCH Explanation at ¶ 925. Committee Reports at ¶ 10,670.]

Amendments

• **2017, Tax Cuts and Jobs Act (P.L. 115-97)**

P.L. 115-97, § 13515(a)(1)-(2):

Amended Code Sec. 832(b)(5)(B) by striking "15 percent" and inserting "the applicable percentage", and by inserting at the end a new sentence. **Effective** for tax years beginning after 12-31-2017.

(c) DEDUCTIONS ALLOWED.—In computing the taxable income of an insurance company subject to the tax imposed by section 831, there shall be allowed as deductions:

* * *

(5) capital losses to the extent provided in subchapter P (relating to capital gains and losses) plus losses from capital assets sold or exchanged in order to obtain funds to meet abnormal insurance losses and to provide for the payment of dividends and similar distributions to policyholders. Capital assets shall be considered as sold or exchanged in order to obtain funds to meet abnormal insurance losses and to provide for the payment of dividends and similar distributions to policyholders to the extent that the gross receipts from their sale or exchange are not greater than the excess, if any, for the taxable year of the sum of dividends and similar distributions paid to policyholders in their capacity as such, losses paid, and expenses paid over the sum of the items described in section 834(b) (other than paragraph (1)(D) thereof) and net premiums received. In the application of section 1212 for purposes of this section, the net capital loss for the taxable year shall be the amount by which losses for such year from sales or exchanges of capital assets exceeds the sum of the gains from such sales or exchanges and whichever of the following amounts is the lesser:

(A) the taxable income (computed without regard to gains or losses from sales or exchanges of capital assets, or

(B) losses from the sale or exchange of capital assets sold or exchanged to obtain funds to meet abnormal insurance losses and to provide for the payment of dividends and similar distributions to policyholders;

* * *

[CCH Explanation at ¶305. Committee Reports at ¶10,310.]

Amendments

• **2017, Tax Cuts and Jobs Act (P.L. 115-97)**

P.L. 115-97, §13001(b)(2)(I):

Amended Code Sec. 832(c)(5) by striking "sec. 1201 and following," following "in subchapter P ("). **Effective** for tax years beginning after 12-31-2017.

[¶5725] CODE SEC. 834. DETERMINATION OF TAXABLE INVESTMENT INCOME.

* * *

(b) GROSS INVESTMENT INCOME.—For purposes of subsection (a), the term "gross investment income" means the sum of the following:

(1) The gross amount of income during the taxable year from—

(A) interest, dividends, rents, and royalties,

(B) the entering into of any lease, mortgage, or other instrument or agreement from which the insurance company derives interest, rents, or royalties,

(C) the alteration or termination of any instrument or agreement described in subparagraph (B), and

(D) gains from sales or exchanges of capital assets to the extent provided in subchapter P (relating to capital gains and losses).

* * *

[CCH Explanation at ¶305. Committee Reports at ¶10,310.]

Amendments

• **2017, Tax Cuts and Jobs Act (P.L. 115-97)**

P.L. 115-97, §13001(b)(2)(I):

Amended Code Sec. 834(b)(1)(D) by striking "sec. 1201 and following," following "in subchapter P ("). **Effective** for tax years beginning after 12-31-2017.

[¶5730] CODE SEC. 842. FOREIGN COMPANIES CARRYING ON INSURANCE BUSINESS.

* * *

(c) SPECIAL RULES FOR PURPOSES OF SUBSECTION (b).—

(1) REDUCTION IN SECTION 881 TAXES.—

(A) IN GENERAL.—The tax under section 881 (determined without regard to this paragraph) shall be reduced (but not below zero) by an amount which bears the same ratio to such tax as—

(i) the amount of the increase in effectively connected income of the company resulting from subsection (b), bears to

(ii) the amount which would be subject to tax under section 881 if the amount taxable under such section were determined without regard to sections 103 and 894.

(B) LIMITATION ON REDUCTION.—The reduction under subparagraph (A) shall not exceed the increase in taxes under part I or II (as the case may be) by reason of the increase in effectively connected income of the company resulting from subsection (b).

(2) DATA USED IN DETERMINING DOMESTIC ASSET/LIABILITY PERCENTAGES AND DOMESTIC INVESTMENT YIELDS.—Each domestic asset/liability percentage, and each domestic investment yield, for any taxable year shall be based on such representative data with respect to domestic insurance companies for the second preceding taxable year as the Secretary considers appropriate.

* * *

[CCH Explanation at ¶910. Committee Reports at ¶10,640.]

Amendments

• 2017, Tax Cuts and Jobs Act (P.L. 115-97)

P.L. 115-97, §13512(b)(7):

Amended Code Sec. 842(c) by striking paragraph (1) and by redesignating paragraphs (2) and (3) as paragraphs (1) and (2), respectively. **Effective** for tax years beginning after

12-31-2017. Prior to being stricken, Code Sec. 842(c)(1) read as follows:

(1) COORDINATION WITH SMALL LIFE INSURANCE COMPANY DEDUCTION.—In the case of a foreign company taxable under part I, subsection (b) shall be applied before computing the small life insurance company deduction.

[¶5735] CODE SEC. 844. SPECIAL LOSS CARRYOVER RULES. [*Stricken.*]

[CCH Explanation at ¶905. Committee Reports at ¶10,630.]

Amendments

• 2017, Tax Cuts and Jobs Act (P.L. 115-97)

P.L. 115-97, §13511(b)(2)(A):

Amended part III of subchapter L of chapter 1 by striking Code Sec. 844. **Effective** for losses arising in tax years beginning after 12-31-2017. Prior to being stricken, Code Sec. 844 read as follows:

SEC. 844. SPECIAL LOSS CARRYOVER RULES.

(a) GENERAL RULE.—If an insurance company—

(1) is subject to the tax imposed by part I or II of this subchapter for the taxable year, and

(2) was subject to the tax imposed by a different part of this subchapter for a prior taxable year,

then any operations loss carryover under section 810 (or the corresponding provisions of prior law) or net operating loss

carryover under section 172 (as the case may be) arising in such prior taxable year shall be included in its operations loss deduction under section 810(a) or net operating loss deduction under section 832(c)(10), as the case may be.

(b) LIMITATION.—The amount included under section 810(a) or 832(c)(10) (as the case may be) by reason of the application of subsection (a) shall not exceed the amount that would have constituted the loss carryover under such section if for all relevant taxable years the company had been subject to the tax imposed by the part referred to in subsection (a)(1) rather than the part referred to in subsection (a)(2). For purposes of applying the preceding sentence, section 810(b)(1)(C) (relating to additional years to which losses may be carried by new life insurance companies) shall not apply.

(c) REGULATIONS.—The Secretary shall prescribe such regulations as may be necessary to carry out the purposes of this section.

[¶5740] CODE SEC. 846. DISCOUNTED UNPAID LOSSES DEFINED.

* * *

(c) RATE OF INTEREST.—

* * *

(2) DETERMINATION OF ANNUAL RATE.—The annual rate determined by the Secretary under this paragraph for any calendar year shall be a rate determined on the basis of the corporate bond yield curve (as defined in section 430(h)(2)(D)(i), determined by substituting "60-month period" for "24-month period" therein).

[CCH Explanation at ¶930. Committee Reports at ¶10,730.]

Amendments

• 2017, Tax Cuts and Jobs Act (P.L. 115-97)

P.L. 115-97, §13523(a):

Amended Code Sec. 846(c)(2). **Effective** for tax years beginning after 12-31-2017. For a transition rule, see Act Sec. 13523(e), below. Prior to amendment, Code Sec. 846(c)(2) read as follows:

(2) DETERMINATION OF ANNUAL RATE.—

(A) IN GENERAL.—The annual rate determined by the Secretary under this paragraph for any calendar year shall be a rate equal to the average of the applicable Federal mid-term rates (as defined in section 1274(d) but based on annual compounding) effective as of the beginning of each of the calendar months in the test period.

(B) TEST PERIOD.—For purposes of subparagraph (A), the test period is the most recent 60-calendar-month period ending before the beginning of the calendar year for which the determination is made; except that there shall be excluded from the test period any month beginning before August 1, 1986.

P.L. 115-97, §13523(e), provides:

(e) TRANSITIONAL RULE.—For the first taxable year beginning after December 31, 2017—

(1) the unpaid losses and the expenses unpaid (as defined in paragraphs (5)(B) and (6) of section 832(b) of the Internal Revenue Code of 1986) at the end of the preceding taxable year, and

(2) the unpaid losses as defined in sections 807(c)(2) and 805(a)(1) of such Code at the end of the preceding taxable year,

shall be determined as if the amendments made by this section had applied to such unpaid losses and expenses unpaid in the preceding taxable year and by using the interest rate and loss payment patterns applicable to accident years ending with calendar year 2018, and any adjustment shall be taken into account ratably in such first taxable year and the 7 succeeding taxable years. For subsequent taxable years, such amendments shall be applied with respect to such unpaid losses and expenses unpaid by using the interest rate and loss payment patterns applicable to accident years ending with calendar year 2018.

(d) LOSS PAYMENT PATTERN.—

* * *

(3) COMPUTATIONAL RULES.—For purposes of this subsection—

* * *

(B) TREATMENT OF CERTAIN LOSSES.—

(i) 3-YEAR LOSS PAYMENT PATTERN.—*In the case of any line of business not described in subparagraph (A)(ii), losses paid after the 1st year following the accident year shall be treated as paid equally in the 2nd and 3rd year following the accident year.*

(ii) 10-YEAR LOSS PAYMENT PATTERN.—

(I) IN GENERAL.—*The period taken into account under subparagraph (A)(ii) shall be extended to the extent required under subclause (II).*

(II) COMPUTATION OF EXTENSION.—*The amount of losses which would have been treated as paid in the 10th year after the accident year shall be treated as paid in such 10th year and each subsequent year in an amount equal to the amount of the average of the losses treated as paid in the 7th, 8th, and 9th years after the accident year (or, if lesser, the portion of the unpaid losses not theretofore taken into account). To the extent such unpaid losses have not been treated as paid before the 24th year after the accident year, they shall be treated as paid in such 24th year.*

* * *

[CCH Explanation at ¶930. Committee Reports at ¶10,730.]

Amendments

• **2017, Tax Cuts and Jobs Act (P.L. 115-97)**

P.L. 115-97, §13523(b):

Amended Code Sec. 846(d)(3) by striking subparagraphs (B) through (G) and inserting a new subparagraph (B). **Effective** for tax years beginning after 12-31-2017. For a transition rule, see Act Sec. 13523(e), below. Prior to being stricken, Code Sec. 846(d)(3)(B)-(G) read as follows:

(B) TREATMENT OF CERTAIN LOSSES.—Except as otherwise provided in this paragraph—

(i) in the case of any line of business not described in subparagraph (A)(ii), losses paid after the 1st year following the accident year shall be treated as paid equally in the 2nd and 3rd year following the accident year, and

(ii) in the case of a line of business described in subparagraph (A)(ii), losses paid after the close of the period applicable under subparagraph (A)(ii) shall be treated as paid in the last year of such period.

(C) SPECIAL RULE FOR CERTAIN LONG-TAIL LINES.—In the case of any long-tail line of business—

(i) the period taken into account under subparagraph (A)(ii) shall be extended (but not by more than 5 years) to the extent required under clause (ii), and

(ii) the amount of losses which would have been treated as paid in the 10th year after the accident year shall be treated as paid in such 10th year and each subsequent year in an amount equal to the amount of the losses treated as paid in the 9th year after the accident year (or, if lesser, the portion of the unpaid losses not theretofore taken into account).

Notwithstanding clause (ii), to the extent such unpaid losses have not been treated as paid before the last year of the extension, they shall be treated as paid in such last year.

(D) LONG-TAIL LINE OF BUSINESS.—For purposes of subparagraph (C), the term "long-tail line of business" means any line of business described in subparagraph (A)(ii) if the amount of losses which (without regard to subparagraph (C)) would be treated as paid in the 10th year after the accident year exceeds the losses treated as paid in the 9th year after the accident year.

(E) SPECIAL RULE FOR INTERNATIONAL AND REINSURANCE LINES OF BUSINESS.—Except as otherwise provided by regulations, any determination made under subsection (a) with respect to unpaid losses relating to the international or reinsurance lines of business shall be made using, in lieu of the loss payment pattern applicable to the respective lines of business, a pattern determined by the Secretary under paragraphs (1) and (2) based on the combined losses for all lines of business described in subparagraph (A)(ii).

(F) ADJUSTMENTS IF LOSS EXPERIENCE INFORMATION AVAILABLE FOR LONGER PERIODS.—The Secretary shall make appropriate adjustments in the application of this paragraph if annual statement data with respect to payment of losses is available for longer periods after the accident year than the periods assumed under the rules of this paragraph.

(G) SPECIAL RULE FOR 9TH YEAR IF NEGATIVE OR ZERO.—If the amount of the losses treated as paid in the 9th year after the accident year is zero or a negative amount, subparagraphs (C)(ii) and (D) shall be applied by substituting the average of the losses treated as paid in the 7th, 8th, and 9th years after the accident year for the losses treated as paid in the 9th year after the accident year.

P.L. 115-97, §13523(e), provides:

(e) TRANSITIONAL RULE.—For the first taxable year beginning after December 31, 2017—

(1) the unpaid losses and the expenses unpaid (as defined in paragraphs (5)(B) and (6) of section 832(b) of the Internal Revenue Code of 1986) at the end of the preceding taxable year, and

(2) the unpaid losses as defined in sections 807(c)(2) and 805(a)(1) of such Code at the end of the preceding taxable year,

shall be determined as if the amendments made by this section had applied to such unpaid losses and expenses unpaid in the preceding taxable year and by using the interest rate and loss payment patterns applicable to accident years ending with calendar year 2018, and any adjustment shall be taken into account ratably in such first taxable year and the 7 succeeding taxable years. For subsequent taxable years, such amendments shall be applied with respect to such unpaid losses and expenses unpaid by using the interest rate and loss payment patterns applicable to accident years ending with calendar year 2018.

(e) [*Stricken.*]

[CCH Explanation at ¶ 930. Committee Reports at ¶ 10,730.]

Amendments

- **2017, Tax Cuts and Jobs Act (P.L. 115-97)**

P.L. 115-97, § 13523(c):

Amended Code Sec. 846, as amended by this Act, by striking subsection (e). **Effective** for tax years beginning after 12-31-2017. For a transition rule, see Act Sec. 13523(e), below. Prior to being stricken, Code Sec. 846(e) read as follows:

(e) ELECTION TO USE COMPANY'S HISTORICAL PAYMENT PATTERN.—

(1) IN GENERAL.—The taxpayer may elect to apply subsection (a)(2)(C) with respect to all lines of business by using a loss payment pattern determined by reference to the taxpayer's loss payment pattern for the most recent calendar year for which an annual statement was filed before the beginning of the accident year. Any such determination shall be made with the application of the rules of paragraphs (2)(C) and (3) of subsection (d).

(2) ELECTION.—

(A) IN GENERAL.—An election under paragraph (1) shall be made separately with respect to each determination year under subsection (d).

(B) PERIOD FOR WHICH ELECTION IN EFFECT.—Unless revoked with the consent of the Secretary, an election under paragraph (1) with respect to any determination year shall apply to accident years ending with the determination year and to each of the 4 succeeding accident years.

(C) TIME FOR MAKING ELECTION.—An election under paragraph (1) with respect to any determination year shall be made on the taxpayer's return for the taxable year in which (or with which) the determination year ends.

(3) NO ELECTION FOR INTERNATIONAL OR REINSURANCE BUSINESS.—No election under this subsection shall apply to any international or reinsurance line of business.

(4) REGULATIONS.—The Secretary shall prescribe such regulations as may be necessary or appropriate to carry out the purposes of this subsection including—

(A) regulations providing that a taxpayer may not make an election under this subsection if such taxpayer does not have sufficient historical experience for the line of business to determine a loss payment pattern, and

(B) regulations to prevent the avoidance (through the use of separate corporations or otherwise) of the requirement of this subsection that an election under this subsection applies to all lines of business of the taxpayer.

P.L. 115-97, § 13523(e), provides:

(e) TRANSITIONAL RULE.—For the first taxable year beginning after December 31, 2017—

(1) the unpaid losses and the expenses unpaid (as defined in paragraphs (5)(B) and (6) of section 832(b) of the Internal Revenue Code of 1986) at the end of the preceding taxable year, and

(2) the unpaid losses as defined in sections 807(c)(2) and 805(a)(1) of such Code at the end of the preceding taxable year,

shall be determined as if the amendments made by this section had applied to such unpaid losses and expenses unpaid in the preceding taxable year and by using the interest rate and loss payment patterns applicable to accident years ending with calendar year 2018, and any adjustment shall be taken into account ratably in such first taxable year and the 7 succeeding taxable years. For subsequent taxable years, such amendments shall be applied with respect to such unpaid losses and expenses unpaid by using the interest rate and loss payment patterns applicable to accident years ending with calendar year 2018.

(e) OTHER DEFINITIONS AND SPECIAL RULES.—For purposes of this section—

* * *

(6) SPECIAL RULE FOR CERTAIN ACCIDENT AND HEALTH INSURANCE LINES OF BUSINESS.—Any determination under subsection (a) with respect to unpaid losses relating to accident and health insurance lines of businesses (other than credit disability insurance) shall be made—

(A) in the case of unpaid losses relating to disability income, by using the general rules prescribed under section 807(d) applicable to noncancellable accident and health insurance contracts and using a mortality or morbidity table reflecting the taxpayer's experience; *except that the limitation of subsection (a)(3) shall apply, and*

(B) in all other cases, by using an assumption (in lieu of a loss payment pattern) that unpaid losses are paid in the middle of the year following the accident year.

[CCH Explanation at ¶930. Committee Reports at ¶10,730.]

Amendments

• **2017, Tax Cuts and Jobs Act (P.L. 115-97)**

P.L. 115-97, §13517(b)(3):

Amended Code Sec. 846(f)(6)(A) by striking "except that" and all that follows and inserting "except that the limitation of subsection (a)(3) shall apply, and". **Effective** generally for tax years beginning after 12-31-2017. For a transition rule, see Act Sec. 13517(c)(2)-(3), below. Prior to being stricken, "except that" and all that follows in Code Sec. 846(f)(6)(A) read as follows:

except that—

(i) the prevailing State assumed interest rate shall be the rate in effect for the year in which the loss occurred rather than the year in which the contract was issued, and

(ii) the limitation of subsection (a)(3) shall apply in lieu of the limitation of the last sentence of section 807(d)(1), and

P.L. 115-97, §13517(c)(2)-(3), provides:

(2) TRANSITION RULE.—For the first taxable year beginning after December 31, 2017, the reserve with respect to any contract (as determined under section 807(d) of the Internal Revenue Code of 1986) at the end of the preceding taxable year shall be determined as if the amendments made by this section had applied to such reserve in such preceding taxable year.

(3) TRANSITION RELIEF.—

(A) IN GENERAL.—If—

(i) the reserve determined under section 807(d) of the Internal Revenue Code of 1986 (determined after applica-

tion of paragraph (2)) with respect to any contract as of the close of the year preceding the first taxable year beginning after December 31, 2017, differs from

(ii) the reserve which would have been determined with respect to such contract as of the close of such taxable year under such section determined without regard to paragraph (2),

then the difference between the amount of the reserve described in clause (i) and the amount of the reserve described in clause (ii) shall be taken into account under the method provided in subparagraph (B).

(B) METHOD.—The method provided in this subparagraph is as follows:

(i) If the amount determined under subparagraph (A)(i) exceeds the amount determined under subparagraph (A)(ii), 1/8 of such excess shall be taken into account, for each of the 8 succeeding taxable years, as a deduction under section 805(a)(2) or 832(c)(4) of such Code, as applicable.

(ii) If the amount determined under subparagraph (A)(ii) exceeds the amount determined under subparagraph (A)(i), 1/8 of such excess shall be included in gross income, for each of the 8 succeeding taxable years, under section 803(a)(2) or 832(b)(1)(C) of such Code, as applicable.

P.L. 115-97, §13523(c):

Amended Code Sec. 846, as amended by this Act, by striking subsection (e) and by redesignating subsection (f) as subsection (e). **Effective** for tax years beginning after 12-31-2017.

(f) REGULATIONS.—The Secretary shall prescribe such regulations as may be necessary or appropriate to carry out the purposes of this section, including—

(1) regulations providing proper treatment of allocated reinsurance, and

(2) regulations providing appropriate adjustments in the application of this section to a taxpayer having a taxable year which is not the calendar year.

[CCH Explanation at ¶915. Committee Reports at ¶10,690.]

Amendments

• **2017, Tax Cuts and Jobs Act (P.L. 115-97)**

P.L. 115-97, §13523(c):

Amended Code Sec. 846, as amended by this Act, by redesignating subsection (g) as subsection (f). **Effective** for tax years beginning after 12-31-2017.

[¶5745] CODE SEC. 847. SPECIAL ESTIMATED TAX PAYMENTS. *[Stricken.]*

[CCH Explanation at ¶310 and ¶950. Committee Reports at ¶10,300 and ¶10,680.]

Amendments

• **2017, Tax Cuts and Jobs Act (P.L. 115-97)**

P.L. 115-97, §12001(b)(8)(B):

Amended Code Sec. 847 by striking the last sentence of paragraph (9). **Effective** for tax years beginning after 12-31-2017. Prior to being stricken, the last sentence of Code Sec. 847(9) read as follows:

Nothing in the preceding sentence shall be construed to affect the application of section 56(g) (relating to adjustments based on adjusted current earnings).

P.L. 115-97, §13516(a):

Amended part III of subchapter L of chapter 1 by striking Code Sec. 847. **Effective** for tax years beginning after

12-31-2017. Prior to being stricken, Code Sec. 847 read as follows:

SEC. 847. SPECIAL ESTIMATED TAX PAYMENTS.

In the case of taxable years beginning after December 31, 1987, of an insurance company required to discount unpaid losses (as defined in section 846)—

(1) ADDITIONAL DEDUCTION.—There shall be allowed as a deduction for the taxable year, if special estimated tax payments are made as required by paragraph (2), an amount not to exceed the excess of—

(A) the amount of the undiscounted, unpaid losses (as defined in section 846(b)) attributable to losses incurred in taxable years beginning after December 31, 1986, over

(B) the amount of the related discounted, unpaid losses determined under section 846,

to the extent such amount was not deducted under this paragraph in a preceding taxable year. Section 6655 shall be applied to any taxable year without regard to the deduction allowed under the preceding sentence.

(2) SPECIAL ESTIMATED TAX PAYMENTS.—The deduction under paragraph (1) shall be allowed only to the extent that such deduction would result in a tax benefit for the taxable year for which such deduction is allowed or any carryback year and only to the extent that special estimated tax payments are made in an amount equal to the tax benefit attributable to such deduction on or before the due date (determined without regard to extensions) for filing the return for the taxable year for which the deduction is allowed. If a deduction would be allowed but for the fact that special estimated tax payments were not timely made, such deduction shall be allowed to the extent such payments are made within a reasonable time, as determined by the Secretary, if all interest and penalties, computed as if this sentence did not apply, are paid. If amounts are included in gross income under paragraph (5) or (6) for any taxable year and an additional tax is due for such year (or any other year) as a result of such inclusion, an amount of special estimated tax payments equal to such additional tax shall be applied against such additional tax. If, after any such payment is so applied, there is an adjustment reducing the amount of such additional tax, in lieu of any credit or refund for such reduction, a special estimated tax payment shall be treated as made in an amount equal to the amount otherwise allowable as a credit or refund. To the extent that a special estimated tax payment is not used to offset additional tax due for any of the first 15 taxable years beginning after the year for which the payment was made, such special estimated tax payment shall be treated as an estimated tax payment made under section 6655 for the 16th year after the year for which the payment was made.

(3) SPECIAL LOSS DISCOUNT ACCOUNT.—Each company which is allowed a deduction under paragraph (1) shall, for purposes of this part, establish and maintain a special loss discount account.

(4) ADDITIONS TO SPECIAL LOSS DISCOUNT ACCOUNT.—There shall be added to the special loss discount account for each taxable year an amount equal to the amount allowed as a deduction for the taxable year under paragraph (1).

(5) SUBTRACTIONS FROM SPECIAL LOSS DISCOUNT ACCOUNT AND INCLUSION IN GROSS INCOME.—After applying paragraph (4), there shall be subtracted for the taxable year from the special loss discount account and included in gross income:

(A) The excess (if any) of the amount in the special loss discount account with respect to losses incurred in each taxable year over the amount of the excess referred to in paragraph (1) with respect to losses incurred in that year, and

(B) Any amount improperly subtracted from the special loss discount account under subparagraph (A) to the extent special estimated tax payments were used with respect to such amount.

To the extent that any amount added to the special loss discount account is not subtracted from such account before the 15th year after the year for which the amount was so added, such amount shall be subtracted from such account for such 15th year and included in gross income for such 15th year.

(6) RULES IN THE CASE OF LIQUIDATION OR TERMINATION OF TAXPAYER'S INSURANCE BUSINESS.—

(A) IN GENERAL.—If a company liquidates or otherwise terminates its insurance business and does not transfer or distribute such business in an acquisition of assets referred to in section 381(a), the entire amount remaining in such special loss discount account shall be subtracted and included in gross income. Except in the case where a company transfers or distributes its insurance business in an acquisition of assets, referred to in section 381(a), if the company is not subject to the tax imposed by section 801 or section 831 for any taxable year, the entire amount in the account at the close of the preceding taxable year shall be subtracted from the account in such preceding taxable year and included in gross income.

(B) ELIMINATION OF BALANCE OF PAYMENTS.—In any case to which subparagraph (A) applies, any special estimated tax payment remaining after the credit attributable to the inclusion under subparagraph (A) shall be voided.

(7) MODIFICATION OF THE AMOUNT OF SPECIAL ESTIMATED TAX PAYMENTS IN THE EVENT OF SUBSEQUENT MARGINAL RATE REDUCTION OR INCREASE.—In the event of a reduction in any tax rate provided under section 11 for any tax year after the enactment of this section, the Secretary shall prescribe regulations providing for a reduction in the amount of any special estimated tax payments made for years before the effective date of such section 11 rate reductions. Such reduction in the amount of such payments shall reduce the amount of such payments to the amount that they would have been if the special deduction permitted under paragraph (1) had occurred during a year that the lower marginal rate under section 11 applied. Similar rules shall be applied in the event of a marginal rate increase.

(8) TAX BENEFIT DETERMINATION.—The tax benefit attributable to the deduction under paragraph (1) shall be determined under regulations prescribed by the Secretary, by taking into account tax benefits that would arise from the carryback of any net operating loss for the year, as well as current year tax benefits. Tax benefits for the current year and carryback years shall include those that would arise from the filing of a consolidated return with another insurance company required to determine discounted, unpaid losses under section 846 without regard to the limitations on consolidation contained in section 1503(c). The limitations on consolidation contained in section 1503(c) shall not apply to the deduction allowed under paragraph (1).

(9) EFFECT ON EARNINGS AND PROFITS.—In determining the earnings and profits—

(A) any special estimated tax payment made for any taxable year shall be treated as a payment of income tax imposed by this title for such taxable year, and

(B) any deduction or inclusion under this section shall not be taken into account.

(10) REGULATIONS.—The Secretary shall prescribe such regulations as may be necessary or appropriate to carry out the purposes of this section, including regulations—

(A) providing for the separate application of this section with respect to each accident year,

(B) such adjustments in the application of this section as may be necessary to take into account the tax imposed by section 55, and

(C) providing for the application of this section in cases where the deduction allowed under paragraph (1) for any taxable year is less than the excess referred to in paragraph (1) for such year.

[¶ 5750] CODE SEC. 848. CAPITALIZATION OF CERTAIN POLICY ACQUISITION EXPENSES.

(a) GENERAL RULE.—In the case of an insurance company—

(1) specified policy acquisition expenses for any taxable year shall be capitalized, and

(2) such expenses shall be allowed as a deduction ratably over the *180-month* period beginning with the first month in the second half of such taxable year.

[CCH Explanation at ¶ 935. Committee Reports at ¶ 10,710.]

Amendments

• **2017, Tax Cuts and Jobs Act (P.L. 115-97)**

P.L. 115-97, § 13519(a)(1):

Amended Code Sec. 848(a)(2) by striking "120-month" and inserting "180-month". **Effective** generally for net premiums for tax years beginning after 12-31-2017. For a transition rule, see Act Sec. 13519(c)(2), below.

P.L. 115-97, § 13519(c)(2), provides:

(2) TRANSITION RULE.—Specified policy acquisition expenses first required to be capitalized in a taxable year beginning before January 1, 2018, will continue to be allowed as a deduction ratably over the 120-month period beginning with the first month in the second half of such taxable year.

(b) 5-YEAR AMORTIZATION FOR FIRST $5,000,000 OF SPECIFIED POLICY ACQUISITION EXPENSES.—

(1) IN GENERAL.—Paragraph (2) of subsection (a) shall be applied with respect to so much of the specified policy acquisition expenses of an insurance company for any taxable year as does not exceed $5,000,000 by substituting "60-month" for "*180-month*".

* * *

[CCH Explanation at ¶ 935. Committee Reports at ¶ 10,710.]

Amendments

• **2017, Tax Cuts and Jobs Act (P.L. 115-97)**

P.L. 115-97, § 13519(b):

Amended Code Sec. 848(b)(1) by striking "120-month" and inserting "180-month". **Effective** generally for net premiums for tax years beginning after 12-31-2017. For a transition rule, see Act Sec. 13519(c)(2), below.

P.L. 115-97, § 13519(c)(2), provides:

(2) TRANSITION RULE.—Specified policy acquisition expenses first required to be capitalized in a taxable year beginning before January 1, 2018, will continue to be allowed as a deduction ratably over the 120-month period beginning with the first month in the second half of such taxable year.

(c) SPECIFIED POLICY ACQUISITION EXPENSES.—For purposes of this section—

(1) IN GENERAL.—The term "specified policy acquisition expenses" means, with respect to any taxable year, so much of the general deductions for such taxable year as does not exceed the sum of —

(A) *2.09 percent* of the net premiums for such taxable year on specified insurance contracts which are annuity contracts,

(B) 2.05 percent of the net premiums for such taxable year on specified insurance contracts which are group life insurance contracts, and

(C) 7.7 percent of the net premiums for such taxable year on specified insurance contracts not described in subparagraph (A) or (B).

* * *

[CCH Explanation at ¶ 935. Committee Reports at ¶ 10,710.]

Amendments

• **2017, Tax Cuts and Jobs Act (P.L. 115-97)**

P.L. 115-97, § 13519(a)(2):

Amended Code Sec. 848(c)(1) by striking "1.75 percent" and inserting "2.09 percent". **Effective** generally for net premiums for tax years beginning after 12-31-2017. For a transition rule, see Act Sec. 13519(c)(2), below.

P.L. 115-97, § 13519(a)(3):

Amended Code Sec. 848(c)(2) by striking "2.05 percent" and inserting "2.45 percent". [Code Sec. 848(c)(2) does not

contain the text "2.05 percent"; therefore, this amendment cannot be made.—CCH.] **Effective** generally for net premiums for tax years beginning after 12-31-2017. For a transition rule, see Act Sec. 13519(c)(2), below.

P.L. 115-97, § 13519(a)(4):

Amended Code Sec. 848(c)(3) by striking "7.7 percent" and inserting "9.2 percent". [Code Sec. 848(c)(3) does exist; therefore, this amendment cannot be made.—CCH.] **Effective** generally for net premiums for tax years beginning after 12-31-2017. For a transition rule, see Act Sec. 13519(c)(2), below.

P.L. 115-97, §13519(c)(2), provides:

(2) TRANSITION RULE.—Specified policy acquisition expenses first required to be capitalized in a taxable year beginning before January 1, 2018, will continue to be allowed as a deduction ratably over the 120-month period beginning with the first month in the second half of such taxable year.

(e) CLASSIFICATION OF CONTRACTS.—For purposes of this section—

(1) SPECIFIED INSURANCE CONTRACT.—

* * *

(B) EXCEPTIONS.—The term "specified insurance contract" shall not include—

* * *

(iii) any qualified foreign contract (as defined in section *807(e)(3)* without regard to paragraph (5) of this subsection),

* * *

[CCH Explanation at ¶915. Committee Reports at ¶10,690.]

Amendments

• 2017, Tax Cuts and Jobs Act (P.L. 115-97)

P.L. 115-97, §13517(b)(4):

Amended Code Sec. 848(e)(1)(B)(iii) by striking "807(e)(4)" and inserting "807(e)(3)". **Effective** generally for tax years beginning after 12-31-2017. For a transition rule, see Act Sec. 13517(c)(2)-(3), below.

P.L. 115-97, §13517(c)(2)-(3), provides:

(2) TRANSITION RULE.—For the first taxable year beginning after December 31, 2017, the reserve with respect to any contract (as determined under section 807(d) of the Internal Revenue Code of 1986) at the end of the preceding taxable year shall be determined as if the amendments made by this section had applied to such reserve in such preceding taxable year.

(3) TRANSITION RELIEF.—

(A) IN GENERAL.—If—

(i) the reserve determined under section 807(d) of the Internal Revenue Code of 1986 (determined after application of paragraph (2)) with respect to any contract as of the close of the year preceding the first taxable year beginning after December 31, 2017, differs from

(ii) the reserve which would have been determined with respect to such contract as of the close of such taxable year under such section determined without regard to paragraph (2),

then the difference between the amount of the reserve described in clause (i) and the amount of the reserve described in clause (ii) shall be taken into account under the method provided in subparagraph (B).

(B) METHOD.—The method provided in this subparagraph is as follows:

(i) If the amount determined under subparagraph (A)(i) exceeds the amount determined under subparagraph (A)(ii), 1/8 of such excess shall be taken into account, for each of the 8 succeeding taxable years, as a deduction under section 805(a)(2) or 832(c)(4) of such Code, as applicable.

(ii) If the amount determined under subparagraph (A)(ii) exceeds the amount determined under subparagraph (A)(i), 1/8 of such excess shall be included in gross income, for each of the 8 succeeding taxable years, under section 803(a)(2) or 832(b)(1)(C) of such Code, as applicable.

(i) *[Stricken.]*

[CCH Explanation at ¶310. Committee Reports at ¶10,300.]

Amendments

• 2017, Tax Cuts and Jobs Act (P.L. 115-97)

P.L. 115-97, §12001(b)(8)(C):

Amended Code Sec. 848 by striking subsection (i). **Effective** for tax years beginning after 12-31-2017. Prior to being stricken, Code Sec. 848(i) read as follows:

(i) TREATMENT OF QUALIFIED FOREIGN CONTRACTS UNDER ADJUSTED CURRENT EARNINGS PREFERENCE.—For purposes of determining adjusted current earnings under section 56(g), acquisition expenses with respect to contracts described in clause (iii) of subsection (e)(1)(B) shall be capitalized and amortized in accordance with the treatment generally required under generally accepted accounting principles as if this subsection applied to such contracts for all taxable years.

[¶5755] CODE SEC. 851. DEFINITION OF REGULATED INVESTMENT COMPANY.

* * *

(b) LIMITATIONS.—A corporation shall not be considered a regulated investment company for any taxable year unless—

* * *

(3) at the close of each quarter of the taxable year—

(A) at least 50 percent of the value of its total assets is represented by—

(i) cash and cash items (including receivables), Government securities and securities of other regulated investment companies, and

(ii) other securities for purposes of this calculation limited, except and to the extent provided in subsection (e), in respect of any one issuer to an amount not greater in value than 5 percent of the value of the total assets of the taxpayer and to not more than 10 percent of the outstanding voting securities of such issuer, and

(B) not more than 25 percent of the value of its total assets is invested in—

(i) the securities (other than Government securities or the securities of other regulated investment companies) of any one issuer,

(ii) the securities (other than the securities of other regulated investment companies) of two or more issuers which the taxpayer controls and which are determined, under regulations prescribed by the Secretary, to be engaged in the same or similar trades or businesses or related trades or businesses, or

(iii) the securities of one or more qualified publicly traded partnerships (as defined in subsection (h)).

For purposes of paragraph (2), there shall be treated as dividends amounts included in gross income under *section 951(a)(1)(A)* or 1293(a) for the taxable year to the extent that, under section 959(a)(1) or 1293(c) (as the case may be), there is a distribution out of the earnings and profits of the taxable year which are attributable to the amounts so included. For purposes of paragraph (2), the Secretary may by regulation exclude from qualifying income foreign currency gains which are not directly related to the company's principal business of investing in stock or securities (or options and futures with respect to stock or securities). For purposes of paragraph (2), amounts excludable from gross income under section 103(a) shall be treated as included in gross income. Income derived from a partnership (other than a qualified publicly traded partnership as defined in subsection (h)) or trust shall be treated as described in paragraph (2) only to the extent such income is attributable to items of income of the partnership or trust (as the case may be) which would be described in paragraph (2) if realized by the regulated investment company in the same manner as realized by the partnership or trust.

* * *

[CCH Explanation at ¶741. Committee Reports at ¶11,100.]

Amendments

• **2017, Tax Cuts and Jobs Act (P.L. 115-97)**

P.L. 115-97, §14212(b)(1)(B):

Amended Code Sec. 851(b) by striking "section 951(a)(1)(A)(i)" in the flush language at the end and inserting "section 951(a)(1)(A)". **Effective** for tax years of foreign corporations beginning after 12-31-2017, and to tax years of United States shareholders in which or with which such tax years of foreign corporations end.

[¶5760] CODE SEC. 852. TAXATION OF REGULATED INVESTMENT COMPANIES AND THEIR SHAREHOLDERS.

* * *

(b) METHOD OF TAXATION OF COMPANIES AND SHAREHOLDERS.—

(1) IMPOSITION OF TAX ON REGULATED INVESTMENT COMPANIES.—There is hereby imposed for each taxable year upon the investment company taxable income of every regulated investment company a tax computed as provided in section 11, as though the investment company taxable income were the taxable income referred to in section 11.

* * *

(3) CAPITAL GAINS.—

(A) IMPOSITION OF TAX.—There is hereby imposed for each taxable year in the case of every regulated investment company a tax, determined as provided in *section 11(b)*, on the excess, if any, of the net capital gain over the deduction for dividends paid (as defined in section 561) determined with reference to capital gain dividends only.

* * *

[CCH Explanation at ¶305. Committee Reports at ¶10,310.]

Amendments

• 2017, Tax Cuts and Jobs Act (P.L. 115-97)

P.L. 115-97, §13001(b)(2)(J):

Amended Code Sec. 852(b)(3)(A) by striking "section 1201(a)" and inserting "section 11(b)". **Effective** for tax years beginning after 12-31-2017.

P.L. 115-97, §13001(b)(4):

Amended Code Sec. 852(b)(1) by striking the last sentence. **Effective** for tax years beginning after 12-31-2017.

Prior to being stricken, the last sentence of Code Sec. 852(b)(1) read as follows:

In the case of a regulated investment company which is a personal holding company (as defined in section 542) or which fails to comply for the taxable year with regulations prescribed by the Secretary for the purpose of ascertaining the actual ownership of its stock, such tax shall be computed at the highest rate of tax specified in section 11(b).

[¶5765] CODE SEC. 857. TAXATION OF REAL ESTATE INVESTMENT TRUSTS AND THEIR BENEFICIARIES.

* * *

(b) METHOD OF TAXATION OF REAL ESTATE INVESTMENT TRUSTS AND HOLDERS OF SHARES OR CERTIFICATES OF BENEFICIAL INTEREST.—

* * *

(3) CAPITAL GAINS.—

»»→ *Caution: P.L. 98-369, §1001(b)(13), amended Code Sec. 857(b)(3)(B), prior to redesignation as Code Sec. 857(b)(3)(A) by P.L. 115-97, below, by striking "1 year" and inserting "6 months". This amendment applies to property acquired after June 22, 1984, and before January 1, 1988.*

(A) TREATMENT OF CAPITAL GAIN DIVIDENDS BY SHAREHOLDERS.—A capital gain dividend shall be treated by the shareholders or holders of beneficial interests as a gain from the sale or exchange of a capital asset held for more than 6 months [1 year].

(B) DEFINITION OF CAPITAL GAIN DIVIDEND.—For purposes of this part, a capital gain dividend is any dividend, or part thereof, which is designated by the real estate investment trust as a capital gain dividend in a written notice mailed to its shareholders or holders of beneficial interests at any time before the expiration of 30 days after the close of its taxable year (or mailed to its shareholders or holders of beneficial interests with its annual report for the taxable year); except that, if there is an increase in the excess described in subparagraph (A)(ii) of this paragraph for such year which results from a determination (as defined in section 860(e)), such designation may be made with respect to such increase at any time before the expiration of 120 days after the date of such determination. If the aggregate amount so designated with respect to a taxable year of the trust (including capital gain dividends paid after the close of the taxable year described in section 858) is greater than the net capital gain of the taxable year, the portion of each distribution which shall be a capital gain dividend shall be only that proportion of the amount so designated which such net capital gain bears to the aggregate amount so designated. For purposes of this subparagraph, the amount of the net capital gain for any taxable year which is not a calendar year shall be determined without regard to any net capital loss attributable to transactions after December 31 of such year, and any such [net] capital loss shall be treated as arising on the 1st day of the next taxable year. To the extent provided in regulations, the preceding sentence shall apply also for purposes of computing the taxable income of the real estate investment trust.

(C) TREATMENT BY SHAREHOLDERS OF UNDISTRIBUTED CAPITAL GAINS.—

(i) Every shareholder of a real estate investment trust at the close of the trust's taxable year shall include, in computing his long-term capital gains in his return for his taxable year in which the last day of the trust's taxable year falls, such amount as the trust shall designate in respect of such shares in a written notice mailed to its shareholders at any time prior to the expiration of 60 days after the close of its taxable year (or mailed to its shareholders or holders of beneficial interests with its annual report for the taxable year), but the amount so includible by any shareholder shall not exceed that part of the amount subjected to tax in *paragraph (1)* which he would have received if all of such amount had been distributed as capital gain dividends by the trust to the holders of such shares at the close of its taxable year.

(ii) For purposes of this title, every such shareholder shall be deemed to have paid, for his taxable year under clause (i), *the tax imposed by paragraph (1) on undistributed capital gain* on the amounts required by this subparagraph to be included in respect of such shares in computing his long-term capital gains for that year; and such shareholders shall be allowed credit or refund as the case may be, for the tax so deemed to have been paid by him.

(iii) The adjusted basis of such shares in the hands of the holder shall be increased with respect to the amounts required by this subparagraph to be included in computing his long-term capital gains, by the difference between the amount of such includible gains and the tax deemed paid by such shareholder in respect of such shares under clause (ii).

(iv) In the event of such designation, *the tax imposed by paragraph (1) on undistributed capital gain* shall be paid by the real estate investment trust within 30 days after the close of its taxable year.

(v) The earnings and profits of such real estate investment trust, and the earnings and profits of any such shareholder which is a corporation, shall be appropriately adjusted in accordance with regulations prescribed by the Secretary.

(vi) As used in this subparagraph, the terms "shares" and "shareholders" shall include beneficial interests and holders of beneficial interests, respectively.

(D) COORDINATION WITH NET OPERATING LOSS PROVISIONS.—For purposes of section 172, if a real estate investment trust pays capital gain dividends during any taxable year, the amount of the net capital gain for such taxable year (to the extent such gain does not exceed the amount of such capital gain dividends) shall be excluded in determining—

(i) the net operating loss for the taxable year, and

(ii) the amount of the net operating loss of any prior taxable year which may be carried through such taxable year under section 172(b)(2) to a succeeding taxable year.

(E) CERTAIN DISTRIBUTIONS.—In the case of a shareholder of a real estate investment trust to whom section 897 does not apply by reason of the second sentence of section 897(h)(1) or subparagraph (A)(ii) or (C) of section 897(k)(2), the amount which would be included in computing long-term capital gains for such shareholder under *subparagraph (A) or (C)* (without regard to this subparagraph)—

(i) shall not be included in computing such shareholder's long-term capital gains, and

(ii) shall be included in such shareholder's gross income as a dividend from the real estate investment trust.

(F) UNDISTRIBUTED CAPITAL GAIN.—*For purposes of this paragraph, the term "undistributed capital gain" means the excess of the net capital gain over the deduction for dividends paid (as defined in section 561) determined with reference to capital gain dividends only.*

* * *

[CCH Explanation at ¶ 305. Committee Reports at ¶ 10,310.]
Amendments

• **2017, Tax Cuts and Jobs Act (P.L. 115-97)**

P.L. 115-97, § 13001(b)(2)(K)(i)-(iv):

Amended Code Sec. 857(b)(3) by striking subparagraph (A) and redesignating subparagraphs (B)-(F) as subparagraphs (A)-(E), respectively, in subparagraph (C), as so redesignated, by striking "subparagraph (A)(ii)" in clause (i) thereof and inserting "paragraph (1)", by striking "the tax imposed by subparagraph (A)(ii)" in clauses (ii) and (iv) thereof and inserting "the tax imposed by paragraph (1) on undistributed capital gain", in subparagraph (E), as so

redesignated, by striking "subparagraph (B) or (D)" and inserting "subparagraph (A) or (C)", and by adding at the end a new subparagraph (F). **Effective** for tax years beginning after 12-31-2017. Prior to being stricken, Code Sec. 857(b)(3)(A) read as follows:

(A) ALTERNATIVE TAX IN CASE OF CAPITAL GAINS.—If for any taxable year a real estate investment trust has a net capital gain, then, in lieu of the tax imposed by subsection (b)(1), there is hereby imposed a tax (if such tax is less than the tax imposed by such subsection) which shall consist of the sum of—

(i) a tax, computed as provided in subsection (b)(1), on the real estate investment trust taxable income (determined by excluding such net capital gain and by computing the deduction for dividends paid without regard to capital gains dividends), and

(ii) a tax determined at the rates provided in section 1201(a) on the excess of the net capital gain over the deduction for dividends paid (as defined in section 561) determined with reference to capital gains dividends only.

[¶5770] CODE SEC. 860E. TREATMENT OF INCOME IN EXCESS OF DAILY ACCRUALS ON RESIDUAL INTERESTS.

* * *

(e) TAX ON TRANSFERS OF RESIDUAL INTERESTS TO CERTAIN ORGANIZATIONS, ETC.—

* * *

(2) AMOUNT OF TAX.—The amount of the tax imposed by paragraph (1) on any transfer of a residual interest shall be equal to the product of—

* * *

(B) the highest rate of tax specified in *section 11(b)*.

* * *

(6) TREATMENT OF PASS-THRU ENTITIES.—

(A) IMPOSITION OF TAX.—If, at any time during any taxable year of a pass-thru entity, a disqualified organization is the record holder of an interest in such entity, there is hereby imposed on such entity for such taxable year a tax equal to the product of—

(i) the amount of excess inclusions for such taxable year allocable to the interest held by such disqualified organization, multiplied by

(ii) the highest rate of tax specified in *section 11(b)*.

* * *

[CCH Explanation at ¶305. Committee Reports at ¶10,310.]
Amendments
• 2017, Tax Cuts and Jobs Act (P.L. 115-97)

P.L. 115-97, §13001(b)(1)(B):

Amended Code Sec. 860E(e)(2)(B) and (6)(A)(ii) by striking "section 11(b)(1)" and inserting "section 11(b)". **Effective** for tax years beginning after 12-31-2017.

[¶5775] CODE SEC. 861. INCOME FROM SOURCES WITHIN THE UNITED STATES.

(a) GROSS INCOME FROM SOURCES WITHIN UNITED STATES.—The following items of gross income shall be treated as income from sources within the United States:

* * *

(2) DIVIDENDS.—The amount received as dividends—

(A) from a domestic corporation other than a corporation which has an election in effect under section 936, or

(B) from a foreign corporation unless less than 25 percent of the gross income from all sources of such foreign corporation for the 3-year period ending with the close of its taxable year preceding the declaration of such dividends (or for such part of such period as the corporation has been in existence) was effectively connected (or treated as effectively connected other than income described in section 884(d)(2)) with the conduct of a trade or business within the United States; but only in an amount which bears the same ratio to such dividends as the gross income of the corporation for such period which was effectively connected (or treated as effectively connected other than income described in section 884(d)(2)) with the conduct of a trade or business within the United States bears to its gross income from all sources; but dividends (other than dividends for which a deduction is allowable under section 245(b)) from a foreign corporation shall, for purposes of subpart A of part III (relating to foreign tax credit), be treated as income from sources without the United States to the extent (and only to the extent) exceeding the amount which is *100/50th* of the amount of the deduction allowable under section 245 in respect of such dividends, or

(C) from a foreign corporation to the extent that such amount is required by section 243(e) (relating to certain dividends from foreign corporations) to be treated as dividends from a domestic corporation which is subject to taxation under this chapter, and to such extent subparagraph (B) shall not apply to such amount, or

(D) from a DISC or former DISC (as defined in section 992(a)) except to the extent attributable (as determined under regulations prescribed by the Secretary) to qualified export receipts described in section 993(a)(1) (other than interest and gains described in section 995(b)(1)).

In the case of any dividend from a 20-percent owned corporation (as defined in section 243(c)(2)), subparagraph (B) shall be applied by substituting "*100/65th*" for "*100/50th*".

* * *

[CCH Explanation at ¶ 315. Committee Reports at ¶ 10,310.]

<table>
<tr><td>

Amendments

• **2017, Tax Cuts and Jobs Act (P.L. 115-97)**

P.L. 115-97, § 13002(e)(1)-(2):

Amended Code Sec. 861(a)(2) by striking "100/70th" and inserting "100/50th" in subparagraph (B), and in the flush

</td><td>

sentence at the end by striking "100/80th" and inserting "100/65th", and by striking "100/70th" and inserting "100/50th". **Effective** for tax years beginning after 12-31-2017.

</td></tr>
</table>

[¶ 5780] CODE SEC. 863. SPECIAL RULES FOR DETERMINING SOURCE.

* * *

(b) INCOME PARTLY FROM WITHIN AND PARTLY FROM WITHOUT THE UNITED STATES.—In the case of gross income derived from sources partly within and partly without the United States, the taxable income may first be computed by deducting the expenses, losses, or other deductions apportioned or allocated thereto and a ratable part of any expenses, losses, or other deductions which cannot definitely be allocated to some item or class of gross income; and the portion of such taxable income attributable to sources within the United States may be determined by processes or formulas of general apportionment prescribed by the Secretary. Gains, profits, and income—

(1) from services rendered partly within and partly without the United States,

(2) from the sale or exchange of inventory property (within the meaning of section 865(i)(1)) produced (in whole or in part) by the taxpayer within and sold or exchanged without the United States, or produced (in whole or in part) by the taxpayer without and sold or exchanged within the United States, or

(3) derived from the purchase of inventory property (within the meaning of section 865(i)(1)) within a possession of the United States and its sale or exchange within the United States,

shall be treated as derived partly from sources within and partly from sources without the United States. *Gains, profits, and income from the sale or exchange of inventory property described in paragraph (2) shall be allocated and apportioned between sources within and without the United States solely on the basis of the production activities with respect to the property.*

* * *

[CCH Explanation at ¶ 730. Committee Reports at ¶ 11,190.]

Amendments

• **2017, Tax Cuts and Jobs Act (P.L. 115-97)**

P.L. 115-97, § 14303(a):

Amended Code Sec. 863(b) by adding at the end a new sentence. **Effective** for tax years beginning after 12-31-2017.

[¶ 5785] CODE SEC. 864. DEFINITIONS AND SPECIAL RULES.

* * *

(c) EFFECTIVELY CONNECTED INCOME, ETC.—

(1) GENERAL RULE.—For purposes of this title—

(A) In the case of a nonresident alien individual or a foreign corporation engaged in trade or business within the United States during the taxable year, the rules set forth in paragraphs (2), (3), (4), (6), *(7), and (8)* shall apply in determining the income, gain, or loss which shall be treated as effectively connected with the conduct of a trade or business within the United States.

(B) Except as provided in paragraph (6)[,] *(7), or (8)* or in section 871(d) or sections 882(d) and (e), in the case of a nonresident alien individual or a foreign corporation not engaged in trade or business within the United States during the taxable year, no income, gain, or loss shall be treated as effectively connected with the conduct of a trade or business within the United States.

* * *

(8) GAIN OR LOSS OF FOREIGN PERSONS FROM SALE OR EXCHANGE OF CERTAIN PARTNERSHIP INTERESTS.—

(A) IN GENERAL.—Notwithstanding any other provision of this subtitle, if a nonresident alien individual or foreign corporation owns, directly or indirectly, an interest in a partnership which is engaged in any trade or business within the United States, gain or loss on the sale or exchange of all (or any portion of) such interest shall be treated as effectively connected with the conduct of such trade or business to the extent such gain or loss does not exceed the amount determined under subparagraph (B).

(B) AMOUNT TREATED AS EFFECTIVELY CONNECTED.—The amount determined under this subparagraph with respect to any partnership interest sold or exchanged—

(i) in the case of any gain on the sale or exchange of the partnership interest, is—

(I) the portion of the partner's distributive share of the amount of gain which would have been effectively connected with the conduct of a trade or business within the United States if the partnership had sold all of its assets at their fair market value as of the date of the sale or exchange of such interest, or

(II) zero if no gain on such deemed sale would have been so effectively connected, and

(ii) in the case of any loss on the sale or exchange of the partnership interest, is—

(I) the portion of the partner's distributive share of the amount of loss on the deemed sale described in clause (i)(I) which would have been so effectively connected, or

(II) zero if no loss on such deemed sale would be [sic] have been so effectively connected.

For purposes of this subparagraph, a partner's distributive share of gain or loss on the deemed sale shall be determined in the same manner as such partner's distributive share of the non-separately stated taxable income or loss of such partnership.

(C) COORDINATION WITH UNITED STATES REAL PROPERTY INTERESTS.—If a partnership described in subparagraph (A) holds any United States real property interest (as defined in section 897(c)) at the time of the sale or exchange of the partnership interest, then the gain or loss treated as effectively connected income under subparagraph (A) shall be reduced by the amount so treated with respect to such United States real property interest under section 897.

(D) SALE OR EXCHANGE.—For purposes of this paragraph, the term "sale or exchange" means any sale, exchange, or other disposition.

(E) SECRETARIAL AUTHORITY.—The Secretary shall prescribe such regulations or other guidance as the Secretary determines appropriate for the application of this paragraph, including with respect to exchanges described in section 332, 351, 354, 355, 356, or 361.

[CCH Explanation at ¶ 350. Committee Reports at ¶ 10,590.]

Amendments

• 2017, Tax Cuts and Jobs Act (P.L. 115-97)

P.L. 115-97, § 13501(a)(1):

Amended Code Sec. 864(c) by adding at the end a new paragraph (8). **Effective** for sales, exchanges, and dispositions on or after 11-27-2017.

P.L. 115-97, § 13501(a)(2)(A)-(B):

Amended Code Sec. 864(c)(1) by striking "and (7)" in subparagraph (A), and inserting "(7), and (8)", and by striking "or (7)" in subparagraph (B), and inserting "(7), or (8)". **Effective** for sales, exchanges, and dispositions on or after 11-27-2017.

(e) RULES FOR ALLOCATING INTEREST, ETC.—For purposes of this subchapter—

* * *

(2) *GROSS INCOME AND FAIR MARKET VALUE METHODS MAY NOT BE USED FOR INTEREST.—All allocations and apportionments of interest expense shall be determined using the adjusted bases of assets rather than on the basis of the fair market value of the assets or gross income.*

* * *

[CCH Explanation at ¶ 780. Committee Reports at ¶ 11,230.]

Amendments

• 2017, Tax Cuts and Jobs Act (P.L. 115-97)

P.L. 115-97, § 14502(a):

Amended Code Sec. 864(e)(2). **Effective** for tax years beginning after 12-31-2017. Prior to amendment, Code Sec. 864(e)(2) read as follows:

(2) GROSS INCOME METHOD MAY NOT BE USED FOR INTEREST.—All allocations and apportionments of interest expense shall be made on the basis of assets rather than gross income.

[¶ 5790] CODE SEC. 865. SOURCE RULES FOR PERSONAL PROPERTY SALES.

* * *

(h) TREATMENT OF GAINS FROM SALE OF CERTAIN STOCK OR INTANGIBLES AND FROM CERTAIN LIQUIDATIONS.—

(1) IN GENERAL.—In the case of gain to which this subsection applies—

(A) such gain shall be sourced outside the United States, but

(B) subsections (a), (b), and (c) of section 904 and sections 907 and 960 shall be applied separately with respect to such gain.

* * *

[CCH Explanation at ¶ 720. Committee Reports at ¶ 11,170.]

Amendments

• 2017, Tax Cuts and Jobs Act (P.L. 115-97)

P.L. 115-97, § 14301(c)(6):

Amended Code Sec. 865(h)(1)(B) by striking "902, 907," and inserting "907". **Effective** for tax years of foreign corporations beginning after 12-31-2017, and to tax years of United States shareholders in which or with which such tax years of foreign corporations end.

[¶ 5795] CODE SEC. 877A. TAX RESPONSIBILITIES OF EXPATRIATION.

(a) GENERAL RULES.—For purposes of this subtitle—

* * *

(3) EXCLUSION FOR CERTAIN GAIN.—

* * *

(B) ADJUSTMENT FOR INFLATION.—

(i) IN GENERAL.—In the case of any taxable year beginning in a calendar year after 2008, the dollar amount in subparagraph (A) shall be increased by an amount equal to—

(I) such dollar amount, multiplied by

(II) the cost-of-living adjustment determined under section 1(f)(3) for the calendar year in which the taxable year begins, by substituting "calendar year 2007" *for "calendar year 2016" in subparagraph (A)(ii)* thereof.

* * *

[CCH Explanation at ¶125. Committee Reports at ¶10,020.]

Amendments

• **2017, Tax Cuts and Jobs Act (P.L. 115-97)**

P.L. 115-97, §11002(d)(1)(BB):

Amended Code Sec. 877A(a)(3)(B)(i)(II) by striking "for 'calendar year 1992' in subparagraph (B)" and inserting "for

'calendar year 2016' in subparagraph (A)(ii)". **Effective** for tax years beginning after 12-31-2017.

[¶5800] CODE SEC. 882. TAX ON INCOME OF FOREIGN CORPORATIONS CONNECTED WITH UNITED STATES BUSINESS.

(a) IMPOSITION OF TAX.—

(1) IN GENERAL.—A foreign corporation engaged in trade or business within the United States during the taxable year shall be taxable as provided in section 11 *or 59A*, on its taxable income which is effectively connected with the conduct of a trade or business within the United States.

* * *

[CCH Explanation at ¶305, ¶310, and ¶750. Committee Reports at ¶10,300, ¶10,310, and ¶11,210.]

Amendments

• **2017, Tax Cuts and Jobs Act (P.L. 115-97)**

P.L. 115-97, §12001(b)(14):

Amended Code Sec. 882(a)(1) by striking ", 55," following "section 11". **Effective** for tax years beginning after 12-31-2017.

P.L. 115-97, §13001(b)(2)(L):

Amended Code Sec. 882(a)(1), as amended by Act Sec. 12001, by striking "or 1201(a)" following "section 11". **Effec**tive for tax years beginning after 12-31-2017.

P.L. 115-97, §14401(d)(2):

Amended Code Sec. 882(a)(1), as amended by this Act, by inserting "or 59A," after "section 11,"[sic]. **Effective** for base erosion payments (as defined in Code Sec. 59A(d), as added by Act. Sec. 14401) paid or accrued in tax years beginning after 12-31-2017.

[¶5805] CODE SEC. 897. DISPOSITION OF INVESTMENT IN UNITED STATES REAL PROPERTY.

(a) GENERAL RULE.—

* * *

(2) MINIMUM TAX ON NONRESIDENT ALIEN INDIVIDUALS.—

(A) IN GENERAL.—In the case of any nonresident alien individual, the taxable excess for purposes of *section 55(b)(1)* shall not be less than the lesser of—

(i) the individual's alternative minimum taxable income (as defined in section 55(b)(2)) for the taxable year, or

(ii) the individual's net United States real property gain for the taxable year.

* * *